West's Law School Advisory Board

CASES AND COMMENTARY ON
INTERNATIONAL LAW
Second Edition

By

Mark W. Janis
William F. Starr Professor of Law
University of Connecticut
Sometime Reader in Law & Fellow of Exeter College
University of Oxford

John E. Noyes
Professor of Law & Director,
International Legal Studies Program
California Western School of Law

AMERICAN CASEBOOK SERIES®

**WEST
GROUP**

A THOMSON COMPANY

ST. PAUL, MINN., 2001

American Casebook Series, and the West Group symbol
are registered trademarks used herein under license.

COPYRIGHT © 1997 WEST PUBLISHING CO.
COPYRIGHT © 2001 By WEST GROUP
            610 Opperman Drive
            P.O. Box 64526
            St. Paul, MN 55164–0526
            1–800–328–9352

ISBN 0–314–24651–7

 TEXT IS PRINTED ON 10% POST CONSUMER RECYCLED PAPER

1st Reprint — 2002

To Janet, Matthew, Robert, Philip, and Edward
—*MWJ*

To Barbara, Sarah, and Ellen
—*JEN*

*

Preface to the Second Edition

A comprehensive and scientific knowledge of international law is highly necessary, not only to lawyers practicing in our commercial ports, but to every [one] who is animated by liberal views, and a generous ambition to assume stations of high public trust. It would be exceedingly to the discredit of any person who should be called to take a share in the councils of the nation, if [that person] should be found deficient in the great leading principles of this law; and I think I cannot be mistaken in considering the elementary learning of the law of nations, as not only an essential part of the education of an American lawyer, but as proper to be academically taught.—James Kent, 1 *Commentaries on American Law* 20 (2d ed. 1832).

The teaching of international law in the American law school goes back at least as far as the Columbia lectures of Chancellor James Kent (1763-1847) and the four volumes of his *Commentaries on American Law* (1826-1830), the first great U.S. legal treatise. Kent's *Commentaries* begin with 200 pages devoted to the law of nations. The tradition of an American casebook on international law also dates to the last century. In 1893, Freeman Snow's *Cases and Opinions on International Law* made its appearance, followed in 1906 by a greatly developed and very influential revision, *Cases on International Law* by James Brown Scott.

Our casebook builds on this by now long-standing tradition, but departs from some of its immediate predecessors by providing an intellectual consolidation of what may have become a too-great proliferation of topics, issues, and cases. Our ambition is simply to teach: to give law professors and law students the cases and commentary necessary to achieve a first-class professional education in the fundamentals of international law. No matter what international law specialty a student may go on to study or to practice—international corporate law, international environmental law, international litigation, international human rights, etc.—we mean to lay the foundation for that study and practice in the pages that follow.

We believe that the order of our chapters constitutes a sensible organization for most courses in international law. Chapter 1 introduces international law, looking briefly at the subject's history and presenting and discussing two sample, albeit well-known, cases to illuminate the nature of international legal rules and international legal process. Chapters 2 and 3 examine the sources of international law in greater depth, showing the student how lawyers, judges, and jurists draw international legal rules from a variety of sources, *e.g.*, treaties, custom, general principles, *jus cogens*, and equity. Chapters 4 and 5 return to international legal process, exploring the ways in which international law is applied first in municipal courts and second in international tribunals. We then turn to the relationship between international law and the actors in international relations: individuals and international human rights law in Chapter 6, states in Chapter 7, and international organizations, governmental and non-governmental, in Chapter 8. Finally, we address four topics of great practical importance in modern international law: the use of force in Chapter 9, common spaces and the environment in Chapter 10, the law of the sea in Chapter 11, and international conflict of laws in Chapter 12.

Many chapters deserve six hours of class, *i.e.*, about two weeks. So, even though this casebook is a great deal briefer than most, there is still about twenty weeks of material between the covers; in most courses some pruning will need be done. Ordinarily, we expect that teachers will choose to teach Chapters 1 through 5 in about seven or eight weeks and then choose from among Chapters 6 to 12 for an additional six or seven weeks. We have tried to make the later seven chapters free-standing so that any of them can be taught in any order after the first five chapters are completed.

For students who wish to go beyond the casebook, quite a number of textbooks are available, including Ian Brownlie, *Principles of Public International Law* (Oxford 5th ed. 1998), Mark W. Janis, *An Introduction to International Law* (Aspen 3d ed. 1999), and *Oppenheim's International Law* (Longman 9th ed. by Robert Jennings & Arthur Watts 1992). There are thousands of other books, articles, cases, and treaties cited below. However, footnotes and string citations from excerpted materials have ordinarily been omitted; when footnotes have been retained in the materials, the original's number has been used; brackets or three asterisks mark other omissions.

Chapters 1, 3, 4, 5, 6, and 12 have been the principal responsibility of Mark Janis and Chapters 2, 7, 8, 9, 10, and 11 the principal responsibility of John Noyes, but the two of us have used these materials over quite a number of years and, by now, have traded many ideas and much wording on most pages. We have also been fortunate in the assistance of others, and at the risk of inadvertently leaving out some names, let us mention those who have helped along the way: William Aceves, William Alford, David Bederman, Howard Berman, Rudolf Bernhardt, Phillip Blumberg, Anthony Bradley, John Bridge, Ian Brownlie, Thomas Buergenthal, Arthur Campbell, Michael Dessent, Richard Edwards, Richard Fink, Peter Fitzgerald, Maria Frankowska, James Friedberg, Richard Graving, Christine Gray, Richard Kay, David Kennedy, Chin Kim, Harold Koh, Robert Lutz, William Lynch, Hugh Macgill, Phyllis Marion, James Maxeiner, Diane May, Samuel Menefee, John Murphy, James Nafziger, Michael Reisman, John Ryan, Philippe Sands, Henry Schermers, Stephen Schwebel, Steven Smith, Louis Sohn, Henry Steiner, Kenneth Vandevelde, and Carol Weisbrod. Several students and librarians at California Western School of Law, the University of Connecticut School of Law, the University of Oxford, and the Roger Williams University School of Law also provided able research support: Daniel Bender, Elizabeth Bonner, Sanja Djajic, Todd Dressel, Stephanie Edwards, Darlene Glenn, Barbara Glennan, Anne Gregory, Brent Houston, Edward Johnson, Kathleen Kim, Esra Krause, Kenneth Naide, Loretta Nelms-Reyes, Jane Petitmermet,

Rachel Smith, Risto Vahimets, Tara Velez, Linda Weathers, Bobbi Ann Weaver, Katherine Young, and Teodora Ziamous. The technical assistance of Carol Dulawan, Elizabeth Johnson, Margaret Kent, Cheryl Meegan, Sandra Michalik, Sandra Moreau, Mary Ellen Norvell, Anita Simons, Sonia Smith, Donna Vella, and Joan Wood was indispensable.

MARK W. JANIS
Hartford

JOHN E. NOYES
San Diego

March 2001

*

Acknowledgments

Excerpts from the following books, articles, cases, and treaties appear with the kind permission of the copyright holders.

—, "3rd Interim Report of the Committee on the Formation of Customary (General) International Law," International Law Association, Report of the 67th Conference 623 (1996). © 1996 by the International Law Association.

—, "An Agenda for Peace: Preventive Diplomacy, Peacemaking and Peace-keeping," 31 January 1992, A/27/277-S/24111, 17 June 1992 (An Agenda for Peace 1995) (2d ed. 1995). © 1995 by the United Nations.

Alvarez, Jose E., "The Once and Future Security Council," 18 The Washington Quarterly, No. 2, at 3 (Spring 1995). © 1995 by the Center for Strategic and International Studies (CSIS) and the MIT. Reprinted with permission of the MIT Press Journals and Professor J. Alvarez.

American Law Institute, Foreign Relations Law of the United States § 1 (1988) p. 7. © 1988 by the American Law Institute. Reprinted with permission.

—, AM&S Europe Ltd v. EC Commission, 2 Common Market Law Reports 264 (1982). Reprinted with permission by Sweet & Maxwell.

Anand, R.P., "Transit Passage and Overflight in International Straits," 26 Indian Journal of International Law 81 (1986). © 1986 by Indian Journal of International Law.

—, The Antarctic Treaty, December 1, 1959, 12 U.S.T. 794, 402 U.N.T.S. 71, 19 International Legal Materials 860. Reproduced with permission from 19 ILM 860 (1980). © The American Society of International Law.

Beddard, Ralph, Human Rights and Europe 4 (1980). © Professor R. Beddard.

Bederman, David J., "Revivalist Canons and Treaty Interpretation," 41 UCLA L. REV. 953 (1994). © 1994 by UCLA Law Review. Reprinted with permission of UCLA Law Review, William S. Hein & Co., Inc. and Professor D. Bederman.

Bederman, David J., "The Souls of International Organizations: Legal Personality and the Lighthouse at Cape Spartel," 36 VA. J. INT'L L. 275, 367 (1996). © 1996 by Virginia Journal of International Law. Reprinted with permission of the Virginia Journal of International Law.

—, The Belilos Case, European Court of Human Rights, Series A, No. 132, 10 European Human Rights Reports 466 (1988). Reprinted with permission of Sweet & Maxwell.

Bodin, Jean, The Six Bookes of a Commonweale, 1606 English translation of Jean Bodin, Republique (1576) (Kenneth Douglas McRae ed., 1962). Reprinted with permission of Professor Kenneth D. McRae.

Buergenthal, Thomas, "The Normative and Institutional Evolution of International Human Rights Law," Human Rights Quarterly 19:4 (1997), 702-723. © The Johns Hopkins University Press. Reprinted with permission of The Johns Hopkins University Press.

—, The Caroline Dispute, 29 British and Foreign State Papers 1129; 30 British and Foreign State Papers 195. Crown copyright is reproduced with the permission of the Controller of Her Majesty's Stationery Office.

—, Cession of Alaska (1867), 134 Consolidated Treaty Series 331 (1969). © 1969 by Oceana Publications, Inc.

Caron, David D., "Protection of the Stratospheric Ozone Layer and the Structure of International Environmental Lawmaking," 14 HASTINGS INT'L & COMP. L. REV. 755 (1991). © 1991 by University of California, Hastings College of Law. Reprinted from Hastings International and Comparative Law Review.

—, Committee of Inquiry into Shipping, Report 551 (London: HMSO, Comnd. 4338, 1970). Crown copyright is reproduced with the permission of the Controller of Her Majesty's Stationery Office.

Dale, William, "Human Rights in the United Kingdom - International Standards," 25 INT'L & COMP. L.Q. 292 (1976). Reproduced with permission of Oxford University Press.

—, Damian Thomas v. Jamaica, U.N. Human Rights Committee Communication No. 800/1998, U.N. Doc. CCPR/65/D/800/1998, 7 International Human Rights Report, No. 2, 326 (2000). Reprinted with permission of the Human Rights Law Centre.

—, The Declaration of Principles Governing the Sea-Bed and the Ocean Floor, and the Subsoil Thereof, Beyond the Limits of National Jurisdiction, G.A. Res. 2749 (XXV), 25 U.N. GAOR Supp. (No. 28), 24, U.N. Doc. A/8028 (1970). © 1970 by the United Nations.

—, The Dogger Bank Case (Great Britain v. Russia), Report of February 26, 1905, The Hague Court Rep. © 1916 by the Carnegie Endowment for International Peace.

—, The Eastern Greenland Case, P.C.I.J., Series A/B, No. 53 (1933), 3 World Court Report. Reprinted with permission of Oceana Publications, Inc.

Ford, Richard T., "Law's Territory (A History of Jurisdiction)," 97 MICH. L. REV. 843 (1999). © 1999 by Michigan Law Review. Reproduced with permission from The Michigan Law Review Association and Professor R. Ford.

Forsyth, David P., "Who Guards the Guardians: Third Parties and the Law of Armed Conflict," 70 AM. J. INT'L L. 41-61 (1976). Reproduced with permission from 70 AJIL 41-61 (1976). © The American Society of International Law.

Franck, Thomas M., "Nation Against Nation: What Happened to the U.N. Dream and What the U.S. Can do About It." © 1985 by Thomas B. Franck. Used with permission of Oxford University Press, Inc.

Franck, Thomas M., and Faiza Patel, "UN Police Action in Lieu of War: 'The Old Order Changeth,'" 85 AM. J. INT'L L. 63 (1991). Reproduced with permission from 85 AJIL 63 (1991). © The American Society of International Law.

—, "Global Solution Must Be Found to Problems of Management, Conservation, Chairman Tells Straddling and Highly Migratory Fish Stocks Conference," Conference on Straddling and Highly Migratory Fish Stocks 58th Meeting (AM), SEA/1475, 27 Mar. 1995. © 1995 by the United Nations.

—, The Golder Case, European Court of Human Rights, Judgment of 21 February 1975, Series A, No. 18. Extracts from the judgments of the European Court of Human Rights are reproduced with the permission of the Registrar of the European Court of Human Rights.

Grotius, Hugo, The Freedom of the Seas. © 1916 by the Carnegie Endowment for International Peace.

Henkin, Louis, "The Use of Force: Law and U.S. Policy," Right v. Might: International Law and the Use of Force 37 (1989). Reprinted with permission of the Council on Foreign Relations.

Henkin, Louis, "Will the U.S. Supreme Court Fail International Law?," Newsletter of the American Society of International Law, Aug.-Sept. 1992, at 1-2. © The American Society of International Law.

Janis, Mark W., "Individuals as Subjects of International Law," 17 CORNELL INT'L L.J. 61 (1984). © by Cornell International Law Journal.

Janis, Mark W., An Introduction to International Law 1-4, 201-04, 329-30 (3d ed. 1999). © Mark Janis.

Janis, Mark W., "The Doctrine of Forum Non Conveniens and the Bhopal Case," XXXIV NILR 192 (1987). Reprinted with the kind permission of Kluwer Law International.

—, The Kellogg-Briand Pact (1928), Renunciation of War as an Instrument of National Policy, 94 L.N.T.S. 57 (1929). © 1929 by the League of Nations. Reproduced with permission of the United Nations.

Koskenniemi, Martti, "The Future of Statehood," 32 HARV. INT'L L.J. 397, 408 (1991). © (1991) by the President and Fellows of Harvard College and the Harvard International Law Journal.

Lebow, Richard Ned, "Accidents and Crises: The Dogger Bank Affair," 31 Naval War College Review, No. 1, at 66 (Summer 1978). Reprinted with permission of the Naval War College Press.

Leurdijk, Dick, "NATO's Decisionmaking Towards Air Strikes on Kosovo," International Peacekeeping, Nov.-Dec. 1999, at 193. © Kluwer

Law International. Reprinted with the kind permission of Kluwer Law International and Mr. Dick A. Leurdijk.

Locke, John, Two Treatises of Government (P. Laslett, ed.), Book II, Chapter IX, section 123. Reprinted with permission of Cambridge University Press.

Lowenfeld, Andreas, International Litigation and Arbitration 588 (1993). Reprinted with permission of the West Group.

—, I Maccabees 8. Scripture quotation found on pp. 167-168 from I Maccabees 8 is taken from Today's English Version Deutero-canonicals/Apocrypha. Copyright © 1979, 1992 American Bible Society. Used by permission.

Mann, F. A., "Contempt of Court in the House of Lords & the European Court of Human Rights," 95 Law Quarterly Review 348 (1979). Reprinted with permission of Sweet & Maxwell.

Mazzola, Maria A., Note, "Forum Non Conveniens and Foreign Plaintiffs: Addressing the Unanswered Questions of Reyno," 6 FORDHAM INT'L L.J. 577 (1983). Reprinted with permission of Fordham International Law Journal.

Morison, Samuel Eliot, Commager, Henry Steele and Leuchtenberg, William E., 1 The Growth of the American Republic 204 (7th ed. 1980). Reprinted with permission of Oxford University Press, Inc.

—, The Naulilaa Case, *Portugal v. Germany*, Special Arbitral Tribunal, Judgment of 31 July 1928, 2 United Nations Report of International Arbitral Awards 1012 (1949). © 1949 by the United Nations.

—, North Atlantic Treaty, April 4, 1949, 34 U.N.T.S. 244. © 1949 by the United Nations.

Noyes, John E. "The Functions of Compromissory Clause in U.S. Treaties," 34 VA. J. INT'L L. 831 (1994). © by Virginia Journal of International Law Association.

Noyes, John E., and Smith, Brian D., "State Responsibility and the Principle of Joint and Several Liability," 13 YALE J. INT'L L. 225, 266-7 (1988). © 1988 by Yale Journal of International Law.

O'Connell, D.P., 1 State Succession in Municipal Law and International Law 7 (1967). © 1967 by Cambridge University Press.

Oxman, Bernard H., "The Regime of Warships Under the United Nations Convention on the Law of the Sea," 24 VA. J. INT'L L. 809, 861-62 (1984). © 1984 by Virginia Journal of International Law.

—, Peace of Westphalia (1648), 1 Consolidated Treaty Series 198 (1969). © 1969 by Oceana Publications, Inc.

—, Rainbow Warrior *(New Zealand v. France)*, 82 Int'l L. Rep. 559 (1990). Reprinted with the kind permission of Mr. Michael F. Hoellering and Cambridge University Press.

—, Regina v. Keyn, Great Britain, Court for Crown Cases Reserved, 2 Law Reports (Exchequer Division) 63 (1876). Reprinted with permission of the Council of Law Reporting for England & Wales.

Reisman, W. Michael, "Criteria for the Lawful Use of Force in International Law," 10 YALE J. INT'L L. 279 (1985). © 1985 by Yale Journal of International Law.

—, Report of the International Committee of Jurists on the Legal Aspects of the Aaland Islands Question, League of Nations Official Journal, Special Supp. No. 3 (1920). © 1920 by the League of Nations.

—, Report of the Secretary General Pursuant to Security Council Resolution 1026, S/1995/1031, December 13, 1995, 35 International Legal Materials 237 (1996). Reproduced with permission from 35 ILM 237 (1996). © The American Society of International Law.

—, Restatement (Third) of the Foreign Relations Law of the United States § 301, Comment a (1987). © 1987 by the American Law Institute.

Riesenfeld, Stefan A., "Sovereign Immunity in Perspective," 19 VAND. J. TRANSNAT'L. L 1 (1986). Permission granted to reprint from the Vanderbilt Journal of Transnational Law, which is the copyright holder.

Roberts, Adam and Kingsbury, Benedict, "Introduction: the UN's Roles in International Society since 1945," United Nations, Divided World (2d rev. ed. 1996). © 1996 by Adam Roberts and Benedict Kingsbury. Reprinted with the kind permission of Professor Adam Roberts and Professor Benedict Kingsbury, and by permission of Oxford University Press.

Rostow, Eugene V., "Until What? Enforcement Action or Collective Self-defense?," 85 AM. J. INT'L L. 506 (1999). Reproduced with permission from 85 AJIL 506 (1999). © The American Society of International Law.

Sadat, Leila Nadya & Carden, Richard, "The New International Criminal Court: An Uneasy Revolution," 88 GEO. L.J. 381 (2000). Reprinted with permission of the publisher, Georgetown Law Journal © 2000.

—, Safer Ships, Cleaner Seas, Report of Lord Donaldson's Inquiry Into the Prevention of Pollution from Merchant Shipping, Cm. 2560 (1994). Crown copyright is reproduced with the permission of the Controller of Her Majesty's Stationery Office.

—, "SAIGA" M/V, (No. 2), Saint Vincent and the Grenadines v. Guinea, International Tribunal for the Law of the Sea (1999), New Directions in the Law of the Sea: Global Developments, Booklet 17.B(12) Released 2000-2. Issued August 2000, pp. 24-27. © 2000 by Oceana Publications, Inc.

Sands, Philippe J. "The Environment, Community and International Law," 30 HARV. INT'L L.J. 393 (1988). © 1988 by the President and Fellows of Harvard College.

Schiffrin, Natalia, "Jamaica Withdraws the Right of Individual Petition under the International Covenant on Civil and Political Rights," 92 AM. J. INT'L L. 563 (1998). Reproduced with permission from 92 AJIL 563 (1998). © The American Society of International Law.

—, Security Council Resolution 661, S/RES/661 (1990), August 6, 1990, 29 International Legal Materials 1565 (1990). Reproduced with permission from 29 ILM 1565 (1990). © The American Society of International Law.

—, Security Council Resolution 678, S/RES.678 (1990), November 28, 1990, 29 International Legal Materials 1565 (1990). Reproduced with permission from 29 ILM 1565 (1990). © The American Society of International Law.

—, The Shrimp-Turtle Case, United States-Import Prohibition of Certain Shrimp and Shrimp Products, World Trade Organization, Report of the Appellate Body, AB-1998-4 (1998), 38 International Legal Materials 121 (1999). Reproduced with permission from 38 ILM 121 (1999). © The American Society of International Law.

Simma, Bruno, "NATO, the UN and the Use of Force: Legal Aspects," 10 European Journal of International Law 1 (1999). Reprinted with permission of the European Journal of International Law.

—, The Soering Case, European Court of Human Rights, Judgment of 7 July 1989, Ser. A: Vol. 161. Extracts from the judgments of the European Court of Human Rights are reproduced with the permission of the Registrar of the European Court of Human Rights.

—, The Sunday Times Case, European Court of Human Rights, Judgment of 26 April 1979, Ser. A: Vol. 30. Extracts from the judgments of the European Court of Human Rights are reproduced with the permission of the Registrar of the European Court of Human Rights.

—, Supplement to An Agenda for Peace, Position Paper of the Secretary-General on the Occasion of the Fiftieth Anniversary of the United Nations A/50/60-S/1995/1, 3 January 1995, at 5 (2d ed. 1995). © 1995 by the United Nations.

—, Supplement to An Agenda for Peace, Position Paper of the Secretary-General on the Occasion of the Fiftieth Anniversary of the United Nations A/50/60-S/1995/1, 3 January 1995, at 5 (2d ed. 1995). © 1995 by the United Nations.

—, "The Texaco/Libya Arbitration, Award of 19 January 1977." 17 ILM 1-37 (1978). Reproduced with permission from 17 ILM 1-37 (1978). © The American Society of International Law.

—, "The Tinoco Arbitration." 18 AM. J. INT'L L. 147-74 (1924). Reproduced with permission from 18 AJIL 147-74 (1924). © The American Society of International Law.

—, The Trail Smelter Case, *United States v. Canada*, 1941, U.N. Rep. Int'l Arb. Awards 1905 (1949). © 1949 by the United Nations.

—, Treaty of Paris (1783), 48 Consolidated Treaty Series 487 (1969). ©
1969 by Oceana Publications, Inc.

—, Treaty on Principles Governing the Activities of States in the Exploration and Use of Outer Space, Including the Moon and Other Celestial Bodies, Jan. 27, 1967, 18 U.S.T. 2410, 610 U.N.T.S. 205, 6 International Legal Materials 386 (1967). Reproduced with permission
from 6 ILM 386 (1967). © The American Society of International
Law.

Vagts, Detlev V., "An Introduction to International Civil Practice," 17
VAND. J. TRANSNAT'L L. 1 (1984). Permission granted to reprint from
the Vanderbilt Journal of Transnational Law, which is the copyright
holder.

Verdross, Alfred von, "Forbidden Treaties in International Law," 31 AM.
J. INT'L L. 571-77 (1937). Reproduced with permission from 31 AJIL
571-77 (1937). © The American Society of International Law.

Watt, Donald Cameron, "First Steps in Enclosure of the Oceans: The Origins of Truman's Proclamation on the Resources of the Continental
Shelf, 28 September 1945," 3 Marine Policy 211, 212 (1979). © 1979,
reprinted with permission from Elsevier Science.

Wildhaber, Luzius, "Parliamentary Participation in Treaty-Making,
Report on Swiss Law," 67 CHI. KENT L. REV. 437 (1991). © 1991 by
Chicago-Kent Law Review.

Wilson, Julian, "US exports in anti-trust: the primacy of economic muscle
over international law," International Litigation News, July 1995, at
3, 4. Published by the International Bar Association. Reprinted with
permission of International Litigation News.

Wright, Quincy, "National Courts and Human Rights – The Fujii Case,"
45 AM. J. INT'L L. 62 (1951). Reproduced with permission from 45
AJIL 62 (1951). © The American Society of International Law.

*

Summary of Contents

Table of Contents

Appendix

Table of Treaties and Other Instruments

Treaties and other instruments appearing as principal readings are in bold type.
Treaties and other instruments cited or discussed in the text are roman type.
References are to pages.

Table of Cases

The principal cases are in bold type. Cases cited or discussed in the text are roman type. References are to pages. Cases cited in principal cases and within other quoted materials are not included.

CASES AND COMMENTARY ON
INTERNATIONAL LAW

Second Edition

*

Chapter 1

THE NATURE OF INTERNATIONAL LAW

International law is sometimes compared unfavorably with other kinds of law, especially the law of nation states. At first glance, international law seems to lack an effective legislature, a generally competent judiciary, and a powerful executive. Yet, whatever its theoretical ambiguities, international law has been practiced by lawyers for centuries. This chapter explains the nature of international law by introducing the history of the discipline and by exploring two sample international law cases. These two cases, *Golder* and *Filartiga*, begin to show how international law is in fact, in the real world, legislated, adjudicated, and enforced.

A. THE HISTORY OF INTERNATIONAL LAW

MARK W. JANIS, AN INTRODUCTION TO INTERNATIONAL LAW
1–4 (3d ed. 1999).

The roots of international law run deep in history. In early religious and secular writings, there are many evidences of what we now know as international law; there are, for example, the detailed peace treaties and alliances concluded between the Jews and the Romans, Syrians, and Spartans. The Romans knew of a *jus gentium*, a law of nations, which Gaius, in the second century, saw as a law "common to all men," a universal law that could be applied by Roman courts to foreigners when the specific law of their own nation was unknown and when Roman law was inapposite. In the seventeenth century, the Dutch jurist Hugo Grotius argued that the law of nations also established legal rules that bound the sovereign states of Europe, then just emerging from medieval society, in their relations with one another. Grotius' classic of 1625, *The Law of War and Peace*, is widely acknowledged, more than any other work, as founding the modern discipline of the law of nations, a subject that, in 1789, the English philosopher Jeremy Bentham renamed "international law." Nowadays, the terms *the law of nations* and *international law* are used interchangeably.

1

At least since the end of the Thirty Years War in 1648, world politics has principally involved the relations of more or less independent sovereign states. An important part of international law has consequently had to do with the establishment of a set of mutually agreed-upon rules respecting the nature of these states and their fundamental rights and obligations inter se. If there is a single international legal principle underlying the modern state system, it probably is the one neatly framed by Montesquieu in 1748 and offered to Napoleon in 1806 by Talleyrand: "that nations ought to do to one another in peace, the most good, and in war, the least evil possible."

International law is sometimes conceived to be divided into public and private parts, the first concerning the legal relations of states, the second involving the law governing the foreign transactions of individuals and corporations. However, the public-private division of international law can be misleading. Many of the laws and processes traditionally within the ambit of public international law actually concern private, not public, parties, while much of the domain of private international law covers the transactions of public entities. Nonetheless, the terms *public* and *private* international law are highly popular and, in a rough kind of way, do compartmentalize legal rules addressing two problem areas: public international law mostly concerns the political interactions of states; private international law relates to legal aspects of the international economy and conflicts and cooperation among national legal systems.

Few deny that the rules of international law actually influence state behavior. Even international law's most famous jurisprudential critic, John Austin, acknowledged in 1832 that international legal rules were effective. At the same time, however, he argued that, because there was no international sovereign to enforce it, international law could not be the same sort of positive law as that enacted by sovereign states for internal application:

> [T]he law obtaining between nations is not positive law: for every positive law is set by a given sovereign to a person or persons in a state of subjection to its author. As I have already intimated, the law obtaining between nations is law (improperly so called) set by general opinion. The duties which it imposes are enforced by moral sanctions: by fear on the part of nations, or by fear on the part of sovereigns, of provoking general hostility, and incurring its probable evils, in case they shall violate maxims generally received and respected.

Just a few years later, in 1836, the United States diplomat Henry Wheaton, in the first great Anglo–American treatise on international law, was already grappling with Austin's characterization of the rules governing international politics as being a form of mere "morality." Wheaton accepted Austin's view that international law's principal sanction was "the hazard of provoking the hostility of other communities," but contended that "[e]xperience shows that these motives, even in the worst times, do really afford a considerable security for the observance of justice between States, if they do not furnish the perfect sanction annexed by the lawgiver to the observance of the municipal code of any particular State." Unlike Austin, Wheaton found international law sufficiently law-like to justify calling it "law," a definitional outcome reached by generations of subsequent international lawyers.

Whether the international rules regulating interstate behavior are to be properly termed "legal" or "moral" is in truth a question that can only be answered after one has made more or less arbitrary definitions of what really constitutes "law" and "morality," a sometimes sterile exercise.[12] Suffice it to say at this early stage of our own discussion that there are a great many rules regulating international politics commonly referred to as "international law" and that these rules are usually, for one reason or another, observed in international practice. Moreover, there is no doubt that the norms of international law are frequently applied as rules of decision by law courts, domestic as well as international.

B. AN INTERNATIONAL LAW SAMPLER

The two cases that follow explore some of the different ways in which international law is actually made, applied, and enforced. The *Golder Case* illustrates an international legal rule made by a treaty, adjudicated by an international court, and enforced by a regional international legal system. The *Filartiga Case* shows a customary or perhaps fundamental international legal norm adjudicated by a municipal—*i.e.*, a domestic—court and enforced (or not) by the ordinary mechanisms of that domestic legal system. The Notes and Questions that follow introduce several of the central issues about the rules, processes, actors, and domains of international law, topics that occupy us throughout the book.

THE GOLDER CASE

European Court of Human Rights,
Judgment of 21 February 1975, Series A, No. 18, 1979 WL 68155

1.   The Golder case was referred to the Court by the Government of the United Kingdom of Great Britain and Northern Ireland (hereinafter called "the Government"). The case has its origin in an application against the United Kingdom lodged with the European Commission of Human Rights (hereinafter called "the Commission") under Article 25 of the Convention for the Protection of Human Rights and Fundamental Freedoms (hereinafter referred to as "the Convention"), by a United Kingdom citizen, Mr. Sidney Elmer Golder. * * *

9.   The facts of the case may be summarized as follows.

10.   In 1965, Mr. Sidney Elmer Golder, a United Kingdom citizen born in 1923, was convicted in the United Kingdom of robbery with

---

12.   "The only intelligent way to deal with a verbal question like that concerning the definition of the word 'law' is to give up thinking and arguing about it." Williams, "International Law and the Controversy Concerning the Word 'Law,'" 22 *British Yearbook of International Law* 146, 163 (1945).

violence and was sentenced to 15 years' imprisonment. In 1969, Golder was serving his sentence in Parkhurst Prison on the Isle of Wight.

11.   On the evening of 24 October 1969, a serious disturbance occurred in a recreation area of the prison where Golder happened to be.

On 25 October, a prison officer, Mr. Laird, who had taken part and been injured in quelling the disturbance, made a statement identifying his assailants, in the course of which he declared: "Frazer was screaming . . . and Frape, Noonan and another prisoner whom I know by sight, I think his name is Golder . . . were swinging vicious blows at me."

12.   On 26 October Golder, together with other prisoners suspected of having participated in the disturbance, was segregated from the main body of prisoners. On 28 and 30 October, Golder was interviewed by police officers. At the second of these interviews he was informed that it had been alleged that he had assaulted a prison officer; he was warned that "the facts would be reported in order that consideration could be given whether or not he would be prosecuted for assaulting a prison officer causing bodily harm."

13.   Golder wrote to his Member of Parliament on 25 October and 1 November, and to a Chief Constable on 4 November 1969, about the disturbance of 24 October and the ensuing hardships it had entailed for him; the prison governor stopped these letters since Golder had failed to raise the subject-matter thereof through the authorized channels beforehand.

14.   In a second statement, made on 5 November 1969, Laird qualified as follows what he had said earlier:

"When I mentioned the prisoner Golder, I said 'I think it was Golder,' who was present with Frazer, Frape and Noonan, when the three latter were attacking me.

"If it was Golder and I certainly remember seeing him in the immediate group who were screaming abuse and generally making a nuisance of themselves, I am not certain that he made an attack on me.

"Later when Noonan and Frape grabbed me, Frazer was also present but I cannot remember who the other inmate was, but there were several there one of whom stood out in particular but I cannot put a name to him."

On 7 November, another prison officer reported that:

" . . . during the riot of that night I spent the majority of the time in the T.V. room with the prisoners who were not participating in the disturbance.

"740007, Golder was in this room with me and to the best of my knowledge took no part in the riot.

"His presence with me can be borne out by officer . . . who observed us both from the outside."

Golder was returned to his ordinary cell the same day.

15. Meanwhile, the prison authorities had been considering the various statements, and on 10 November prepared a list of charges which might be preferred against prisoners, including Golder, for offenses against prison discipline. Entries relating thereto were made in Golder's prison record. No such charge was eventually preferred against him and the entries in his prison record were marked "charges not proceeded with." Those entries were expunged from the prison record in 1971 during the examination of the applicant's case by the Commission.

16. On 20 March 1970, Golder addressed a petition to the Secretary of State for the Home Department, that is, the Home Secretary. He requested a transfer to some other prison and added:

"I understand that a statement wrongly accusing me of participation in the events of 24th October last, made by Officer Laird, is lodged in my prison record. I suspect that it is this wrong statement that has recently prevented my being recommended by the local parole board for parole.

"I would respectfully request permission to consult a solicitor with a view to taking civil action for libel in respect of this statement.... Alternatively, I would request that an independent examination of my record be allowed by Mrs. G.M. Bishop who is a magistrate. I would accept her assurance that this statement is not part of my record and be willing to accept then that the libel against me has not materially harmed me except for the two weeks I spent in the separate cells and so civil action would not be then necessary, providing that an apology was given to me for the libel...."

17. In England the matter of contacts of convicted prisoners with persons outside their place of detention is governed by the Prison Act 1952, as amended, and subordinate legislation made under that Act.

Section 47, sub-section 1, of the Prison Act provides that "the Secretary of State may make rules for the regulation and management of prisoners ... and for the ... treatment ... discipline and control of persons required to be detained...."

The rules made by the Home Secretary in the exercise of this power are the Prison Rules 1964, which were laid before Parliament and have the status of a Statutory Instrument. The relevant provisions concerning communications between prisoners and persons outside prison are contained in Rules 33, 34 and 37 as follows:

"Letters and visits generally

Rule 33

(1) The Secretary of State may, with a view to securing discipline and good order or the prevention of crime or in the interests of any persons, impose restrictions, either generally or in a particular case, upon the communications to be permitted between a prisoner and other persons.

(2) Except as provided by statute or these Rules, a prisoner shall not be permitted to communicate with any outside person, or that person with him, without the leave of the Secretary of State.

. . .

Personal letters and visits

Rule 34

. . .

(8) A prisoner shall not be entitled under this Rule to communicate with any person in connection with any legal or other business, or with any person other than a relative or friend, except with the leave of the Secretary of State.

. . .

Legal advisers

Rule 37

(1) The legal adviser of a prisoner in any legal proceedings, civil or criminal, to which the prisoner is a party shall be afforded reasonable facilities for interviewing him in connection with those proceedings, and may do so out of hearing but in sight of an officer.

(2) A prisoner's legal adviser may, with the leave of the Secretary of State, interview the prisoner in connection with any other legal business in the sight and hearing of an officer.''

18.   On 6 April 1970, the Home Office directed the prison governor to notify Golder of the reply to his petition of 20 March as follows:

"The Secretary of State has fully considered your petition but is not prepared to grant your request for transfer, nor can he find grounds for taking any action in regard to the other matters raised in your petition."

19.   Before the Commission, Golder submitted two complaints relating respectively to the stopping of his letters (as mentioned above at paragraph 13) and to the refusal of the Home Secretary to permit him to consult a solicitor. On 30 March 1971, the Commission declared the first complaint inadmissible, as all domestic remedies had not been exhausted, but accepted the second for consideration of the merits under Articles 6 § 1 and 8 of the Convention.

20.   Golder was released from prison on parole on 12 July 1972.
* * *

23.   Paragraphs 73, 99 and 110 of the Commission's report indicate that the Commission consider unanimously that there was a violation of Article 6 § 1. The Government disagree with this opinion.

24.   Article 6 § 1 provides:

"In the determination of his civil rights and obligations or of any criminal charge against him, everyone is entitled to a fair and public hearing within a reasonable time by an independent and impartial tribunal established by law. Judgment shall be pronounced publicly but the press and public may be excluded from all or part of the trial in the interests of morals, public order or national security in a democratic society, where the interests of juveniles or the protection of the private life of the parties so require, or to the extent strictly necessary in the opinion of the court in special circumstances where publicity would prejudice the interests of justice." * * *

32. * * *

The Government have submitted that the expressions "fair and public hearing" and "within a reasonable time," the second sentence in paragraph 1 ("judgment," "trial"), and paragraph 3 of Article 6 clearly presuppose proceedings pending before a court.

While the right to a fair, public and expeditious judicial procedure can assuredly apply only to proceedings in being, it does not, however, necessarily follow that a right to the very institution of such proceedings is thereby excluded * * *. * * *

35. * * *

Were Article 6 § 1 to be understood as concerning exclusively the conduct of an action which had already been initiated before a court, a Contracting State could, without acting in breach of that text, do away with its courts, or take away their jurisdiction to determine certain classes of civil actions and entrust it to organs dependent on the Government. Such assumptions, indissociable from a danger of arbitrary power, would have serious consequences which are repugnant to the aforementioned principles and which the Court cannot overlook (Lawless judgment of 1 July 1961, Series A no. 3, p. 52, and Delcourt judgment of 17 January 1970, Series A no. 11, pp. 14–15).

It would be inconceivable, in the opinion of the Court, that Article 6 § 1 should describe in detail the procedural guarantees afforded to parties in a pending lawsuit and should not first protect that which alone makes it in fact possible to benefit from such guarantees, that is, access to a court. The fair, public and expeditious characteristics of judicial proceedings are of no value at all if there are no judicial proceedings.

36. Taking all the preceding considerations together, it follows that the right of access constitutes an element which is inherent in the right stated by Article 6 § 1. * * *

40. * * *

In these circumstances, Golder could justifiably wish to consult a solicitor with a view to instituting legal proceedings. It was not for the Home Secretary himself to appraise the prospects of the action contemplated; it was for an independent and impartial court to rule on any claim that might be brought. In declining to accord the leave which had been requested, the Home Secretary failed to respect, in the person of Golder, the right to go before a court as guaranteed by Article 6 § 1. * * *

41. In the opinion of the majority of the Commission (paragraph 123 of the report) "the same facts which constitute a violation of Article 6 § 1 constitute also a violation of Article 8." The Government disagree with this opinion.

42. Article 8 of the Convention reads as follows:

"1. Everyone has the right to respect for his private and family life, his home and his correspondence.

2. There shall be no interference by a public authority with the exercise of this right except such as is in accordance with the law and is necessary in a democratic society in the interests of national security, public safety or the economic well-being of the country, for the prevention of disorder or crime, for the protection of health or morals, or for the protection of the rights and freedoms of others."

43. The Home Secretary's refusal of the petition of 20 March 1970 had the direct and immediate effect of preventing Golder from contacting a solicitor by any means whatever, including that which in the ordinary way he would have used to begin with, correspondence. While there was certainly neither stopping nor censorship of any message, such as a letter, which Golder would have written to a solicitor—or vice-versa—and which would have been a piece of correspondence within the meaning of paragraph 1 of Article 8, it would be wrong to conclude therefrom, as do the Government, that this text is inapplicable. Impeding someone from even initiating correspondence constitutes the most far-reaching form of "interference" (paragraph 2 of Article 8) with the exercise of the "right to respect for correspondence"; it is inconceivable that that should fall outside the scope of Article 8 while mere supervision indisputably falls within it. In any event, if Golder had attempted to write a solicitor notwithstanding the Home Secretary's decision or without requesting the required permission, that correspondence would have been stopped and he could have invoked Article 8; one would arrive at a paradoxical and hardly equitable result, if it were considered that in complying with the requirements of the Prison Rules 1964 he lost the benefit of the protection of Article 8. * * *

FOR THESE REASONS, THE COURT

1. *Holds* by nine votes to three that there has been a breach of Article 6 § 1;

2. *Holds* unanimously that there has been a breach of Article 8; * * *.

Notes and Questions

1. *European Human Rights Law.* The European Court of Human Rights in Strasbourg, France, can be described as an "international court" in at least two ways. Constitutionally, the Court is established by an international agreement: the 1950 European Convention for the Protection of Human Rights and Fundamental Freedoms, 213 U.N.T.S. 221 (1953)(signed at Rome November 4, 1950; entered into force September 3,

1953). More about international adjudication in general is found in Chapter 5. Substantively, the rules the Court applies are international law: human rights norms made and protected by the same European Human Rights Convention. As of November 2000, some 41 European countries were parties to the European Human Rights Convention and subject to the European Human Rights Court's jurisdiction. The structure and substance of European human rights law are more fully explored in Chapter 6. Also see Mark W. Janis, Richard S. Kay & Anthony W. Bradley, *European Human Rights Law* (2d ed. 2000); Ralph Beddard, *Human Rights and Europe* (3d ed. 1993); P. van Dijk & G.J.H. van Hoof, *Theory and Practice of the European Convention on Human Rights Norms* (3d ed. 1998).

2. *The Nature of Treaties.* In *Golder*, the European Court of Human Rights applies two substantive rules drawn from the 1950 European Human Rights Convention: Article 6(1) protecting fair trial and Article 8 protecting private and family life, home, and correspondence. The ordinary theory explaining the legally binding effect of an international agreement is that a sovereign state may exercise its sovereignty not only by making domestic law but also by making international law. Hence, Articles 6(1) and 8 oblige the U.K. in international law because of the U.K.'s own consent. Chapter 2 more fully explores treaties.

In this way, the European Convention on Human Rights resembles an international contract among states, but the Convention may also be said to resemble an international statute in that it provides a generally applicable set of rules for all its member-states. This helps explain why states are considered to be not only the legislators of international law but also subjects of international law. We consider the nature of the sovereign state in Chapter 7.

3. *The Efficacy of International Law.* After *Golder,* Britain changed its prison rules to comply with the Court's decision. What "sanction" could have been applied against the U.K. if the government had failed to comply with the ruling? Why should a sovereign state like the United Kingdom voluntarily comply with an international court judgment like *Golder*? What would the U.K. lose if it were to be expelled from other European institutions for failure to comply with decisions of the European Court of Human Rights? Could the U.K. expect other states to comply with the Convention if it repudiated the Court's judgment? Would repudiation spoil the U.K.'s reputation and make it more difficult for the government to conclude treaties in the future?

The many European countries that are parties to the European Convention on Human Rights have their own domestic legal rules and processes protecting human rights. Why should they also enter into an international legal system establishing European rules about human rights and setting up European institutions to enforce those rules? How close are the European Court of Human Rights and European human rights law in form and substance to the U.S. Supreme Court and U.S. constitutional law, especially the Bill of Rights?

FILARTIGA v. PENA–IRALA

630 F.2d 876 (2d Cir.1980).

IRVING R. KAUFMAN, CIRCUIT JUDGE:

Upon ratification of the Constitution, the thirteen former colonies were fused into a single nation, one which, in its relations with foreign states, is bound both to observe and construe the accepted norms of international law, formerly known as the law of nations. Under the Articles of Confederation, the several states had interpreted and applied this body of doctrine as a part of their common law, but with the founding of the "more perfect Union" of 1789, the law of nations became preeminently a federal concern.

Implementing the constitutional mandate for national control over foreign relations, the First Congress established original district court jurisdiction over "all causes where an alien sues for a tort only [committed] in violation of the law of nations." Judiciary Act of 1789, ch. 20, § 9(b), 1 Stat. 73, 77 (1789), *codified at* 28 U.S.C. § 1350. Construing this rarely-invoked provision, we hold that deliberate torture perpetrated under color of official authority violates universally accepted norms of the international law of human rights, regardless of the nationality of the parties. Thus, whenever an alleged torturer is found and served with process by an alien within our borders, § 1350 provides federal jurisdiction. Accordingly, we reverse the judgment of the district court dismissing the complaint for want of federal jurisdiction.

I

The appellants, plaintiffs below, are citizens of the Republic of Paraguay. Dr. Joel Filartiga, a physician, describes himself as a long-standing opponent of the government of President Alfredo Stroessner, which has held power in Paraguay since 1954. His daughter, Dolly Filartiga, arrived in the United States in 1978 under a visitor's visa, and has since applied for permanent political asylum. The Filartigas brought this action in the Eastern District of New York against Americo Norberto Pena–Irala (Pena), also a citizen of Paraguay, for wrongfully causing the death of Dr. Filartiga's seventeen-year old son, Joelito. Because the district court dismissed the action for want of subject matter jurisdiction, we must accept as true the allegations contained in the Filartigas' complaint and affidavits for purposes of this appeal.

The appellants contend that on March 29, 1978, Joelito Filartiga was kidnapped and tortured to death by Pena, who was then Inspector General of Police in Asuncion, Paraguay. Later that day, the police brought Dolly Filartiga to Pena's home where she was confronted with the body of her brother, which evidenced marks of severe torture. As she fled, horrified, from the house, Pena followed after her shouting, "Here you have what you have been looking for so long and what you deserve.

Now shut up." The Filartigas claim that Joelito was tortured and killed in retaliation for his father's political activities and beliefs.

Shortly thereafter, Dr. Filartiga commenced a criminal action in the Paraguayan courts against Pena and the police for the murder of his son. As a result, Dr. Filartiga's attorney was arrested and brought to police headquarters where, shackled to a wall, Pena threatened him with death. This attorney, it is alleged, has since been disbarred without just cause.

During the course of the Paraguayan criminal proceeding, which is apparently still pending after four years, another man, Hugo Duarte, confessed to the murder. Duarte, who was a member of the Pena household, claimed that he had discovered his wife and Joelito *in flagrante delicto*, and that the crime was one of passion. The Filartigas have submitted a photograph of Joelito's corpse showing injuries they believe refute this claim. Dolly Filartiga, moreover, has stated that she will offer evidence of three independent autopsies demonstrating that her brother's death "was the result of professional methods of torture." Despite his confession, Duarte, we are told, has never been convicted or sentenced in connection with the crime.

In July of 1978, Pena sold his house in Paraguay and entered the United States under a visitor's visa. He was accompanied by Juana Bautista Fernandez Villalba, who had lived with him in Paraguay. The couple remained in the United States beyond the term of their visas, and were living in Brooklyn, New York, when Dolly Filartiga, who was then living in Washington, D.C., learned of their presence. Acting on information provided by Dolly the Immigration and Naturalization Service arrested Pena and his companion, both of whom were subsequently ordered deported on April 5, 1979 following a hearing. They had then resided in the United States for more than nine months.

Almost immediately, Dolly caused Pena to be served with a summons and civil complaint at the Brooklyn Navy Yard, where he was being held pending deportation. The complaint alleged that Pena had wrongfully caused Joelito's death by torture and sought compensatory and punitive damages of $10,000,000. The Filartigas also sought to enjoin Pena's deportation to ensure his availability for testimony at trial. The cause of action is stated as arising under "wrongful death statutes; the U.N. Charter, the Universal Declaration on Human Rights; the U.N. Declaration Against Torture; the American Declaration of the Rights and Duties of Man; and other pertinent declarations, documents and practices constituting the customary international law of human rights and the law of nations," as well as 28 U.S.C. § 1350, Article II, sec. 2 and the Supremacy Clause of the U.S. Constitution. Jurisdiction is claimed under the general federal question provision, 28 U.S.C. § 1331 and, principally on this appeal, under the Alien Tort Statute, 28 U.S.C. § 1350.

* * * The Filartigas submitted the affidavits of a number of distinguished international legal scholars, who stated unanimously that the law of nations prohibits absolutely the use of torture as alleged in the

complaint.[4] Pena, in support of his motion to dismiss on the ground of *forum non conveniens*, submitted the affidavit of his Paraguayan counsel, Jose Emilio Gorostiaga, who averred that Paraguayan law provides a full and adequate civil remedy for the wrong alleged. Dr. Filartiga has not commenced such an action, however, believing that further resort to the courts of his own country would be futile. * * *

The district court continued the stay of deportation for forty-eight hours while appellants applied for further stays. These applications were denied by a panel of this Court on May 22, 1979, and by the Supreme Court two days later. Shortly thereafter, Pena and his companion returned to Paraguay.

II

Appellants rest their principal argument in support of federal jurisdiction upon the Alien Tort Statute, 28 U.S.C. § 1350, which provides: "The district courts shall have original jurisdiction of any civil action by an alien for a tort only, committed in violation of the law of nations or a treaty of the United States." Since appellants do not contend that their action arises directly under a treaty of the United States, a threshold question on the jurisdictional issue is whether the conduct alleged violates the law of nations. In light of the universal condemnation of torture in numerous international agreements, and the renunciation of torture as an instrument of official policy by virtually all of the nations of the world (in principle if not in practice), we find that an act of torture committed by a state official against one held in detention violates established norms of the international law of human rights, and hence the law of nations.

The Supreme Court has enumerated the appropriate sources of international law. The law of nations "may be ascertained by consulting the works of jurists, writing professedly on public law; or by the general usage and practice of nations; or by judicial decisions recognizing and enforcing that law." *United States v. Smith*, 18 U.S. (5 Wheat.) 153, 160–61, 5 L.Ed. 57 (1820); *Lopes v. Reederei Richard Schroder*, 225 F.Supp. 292, 295 (E.D.Pa.1963). In *Smith*, a statute proscribing "the crime of piracy [on the high seas] as defined by the law of nations," 3 Stat. 510(a) (1819), was held sufficiently determinate in meaning to afford the basis

4. Richard Falk, the Albert G. Milbank Professor of International Law and Practice at Princeton University, and a former Vice President of the American Society of International Law, avers that, in his judgment, "it is now beyond reasonable doubt that torture of a person held in detention that results in severe harm or death is a violation of the law of nations." Thomas Franck, professor of international law at New York University and Director of the New York University Center for International Studies offers his opinion that torture has now been rejected by virtually all nations, although it was once commonly used to extract confessions. Richard Lillich, the Howard W. Smith Professor of Law at the University of Virginia School of Law, concludes, after a lengthy review of the authorities, that officially perpetrated torture is "a violation of international law (formerly called the law of nations)." Finally, Myres MacDougal, a former Sterling Professor of Law at the Yale Law School, and a past President of the American Society of International Law, states that torture is an offense against the law of nations, and that "it has long been recognized that such offenses vitally affect relations between states."

for a death sentence. The *Smith* Court discovered among the works of Lord Bacon, Grotius, Bochard and other commentators a genuine consensus that rendered the crime "sufficiently and constitutionally defined." *Smith, supra*, 18 U.S. (5 Wheat.) at 162, 5 L.Ed. 57.

The Paquete Habana, 175 U.S. 677, 20 S.Ct. 290, 44 L.Ed. 320 (1900), reaffirmed that

> where there is no treaty, and no controlling executive or legislative act or judicial decision, resort must be had to the customs and usages of civilized nations; and, as evidence of these, to the works of jurists and commentators, who by years of labor, research and experience, have made themselves peculiarly well acquainted with the subjects of which they treat. Such works are resorted to by judicial tribunals, not for the speculations of their authors concerning what the law ought to be, but for trustworthy evidence of what the law really is.

Id. at 700, 20 S.Ct. at 299. Modern international sources confirm the propriety of this approach. * * *

The United Nations Charter (a treaty of the United States, *see* 59 Stat. 1033 (1945)) makes it clear that in this modern age a state's treatment of its own citizens is a matter of international concern. It provides:

> With a view to the creation of conditions of stability and well-being which are necessary for peaceful and friendly relations among nations . . . the United Nations shall promote . . . universal respect for, and observance of, human rights and fundamental freedoms for all without distinctions as to race, sex, language or religion.

Id. Art. 55. And further:

> All members pledge themselves to take joint and separate action in cooperation with the Organization for the achievement of the purposes set forth in Article 55.

Id. Art. 56.

While this broad mandate has been held not to be wholly self-executing, *Hitai v. Immigration and Naturalization Service*, 343 F.2d 466, 468 (2d Cir.1965), this observation alone does not end our inquiry. For although there is no universal agreement as to the precise extent of the "human rights and fundamental freedoms" guaranteed to all by the Charter, there is at present no dissent from the view that the guaranties include, at a bare minimum, the right to be free from torture. This prohibition has become part of customary international law, as evidenced and defined by the Universal Declaration of Human Rights, General Assembly Resolution 217(III)(A) (Dec. 10, 1948) which states, in the plainest of terms, "no one shall be subjected to torture."[10] The General Assembly has declared that the Charter precepts embodied in this

10. Eighteen nations have incorporated the Universal Declaration into their own constitutions. 48 *Revue Internationale de Droit Penal* Nos. 3 & 4, at 211 (1977).

Universal Declaration "constitute basic principles of international law." G.A.Res. 2625 (XXV) (Oct. 24, 1970).

Particularly relevant is the Declaration on the Protection of All Persons from Being Subjected to Torture, General Assembly Resolution 3452, 30 U.N. GAOR Supp. (No. 34) 91, U.N.Doc. A/1034 (1975) * * *. The Declaration expressly prohibits any state from permitting the dastardly and totally inhuman act of torture. Torture, in turn, is defined as "any act by which severe pain and suffering, whether physical or mental, is intentionally inflicted by or at the instigation of a public official on a person for such purposes as . . . intimidating him or other persons." The Declaration goes on to provide that "[w]here it is proved that an act of torture or other cruel, inhuman or degrading treatment or punishment has been committed by or at the instigation of a public official, the victim shall be afforded redress and compensation, in accordance with national law." This Declaration, like the Declaration of Human Rights before it, was adopted without dissent by the General Assembly. Nayar, "Human Rights: The United Nations and United States Foreign Policy," 19 *Harv. Int'l L.J.* 813, 816 n.18 (1978).

These U.N. declarations are significant because they specify with great precision the obligations of member nations under the Charter. Since their adoption, "[m]embers can no longer contend that they do not know what human rights they promised in the Charter to promote." Sohn, "A Short History of United Nations Documents on Human Rights," in *"The United Nations and Human Rights," 18th Report of the Commission* (Commission to Study the Organization of Peace ed. 1968). Moreover, a U.N. Declaration is, according to one authoritative definition, "a formal and solemn instrument, suitable for rare occasions when principles of great and lasting importance are being enunciated." 34 U.N. ESCOR, Supp. (No. 8) 15, U.N. Doc. E/cn.4/1/610 (1962)(memorandum of Office of Legal Affairs, U.N. Secretariat). Accordingly, it has been observed that the Universal Declaration of Human Rights "no longer fits into the dichotomy of 'binding treaty' against 'nonbinding pronouncement,' but is rather an authoritative statement of the international community." *E. Schwelb, Human Rights and the International Community* 70 (1964). Thus, a Declaration creates an expectation of adherence, and "insofar as the expectation is gradually justified by State practice, a declaration may by custom become recognized as laying down rules binding upon the States." 34 U.N. ESCOR, *supra.* Indeed, several commentators have concluded that the Universal Declaration has become, *in toto*, a part of binding, customary international law. Nayar, *supra*, at 816–17; Waldock, "Human Rights in Contemporary International Law and the Significance of the European Convention," *Int'l & Comp. L.Q.*, Supp. Publ. No. 11 at 15 (1965).

Turning to the act of torture, we have little difficulty discerning its universal renunciation in the modern usage and practice of nations. *Smith, supra*, 18 U.S. (5 Wheat.) at 160–61, 5 L.Ed. 57. The international consensus surrounding torture has found expression in numerous international treaties and accords. *E.g., American Convention on Human*

Rights, Art. 5, OAS Treaty Series No. 36 at 1, OAS Off. Rec. OEA/Ser 4 v/II 23, doc. 21, rev. 2 (English ed., 1975)("No one shall be subjected to torture or to cruel, inhuman or degrading punishment or treatment"); International Covenant on Civil and Political Rights, U.N. General Assembly Res. 2200 (XXI)A, U.N. Doc. A/6316 (Dec. 16, 1966)(identical language); European Convention for the Protection of Human Rights and Fundamental Freedoms, Art. 3, Council of Europe, European Treaty Series No. 5 (1968), 213 U.N.T.S. 211 (*semble*). The substance of these international agreements is reflected in modern municipal—*i.e.* national—law as well. Although torture was once a routine concomitant of criminal interrogations in many nations, during the modern and hopefully more enlightened era it has been universally renounced. According to one survey, torture is prohibited, expressly or implicitly, by the constitutions of over fifty-five nations, including both the United States and Paraguay. Our State Department reports a general recognition of this principle:

> There now exists an international consensus that recognizes basic human rights and obligations owed by all governments to their citizens.... There is no doubt that these rights are often violated; but virtually all governments acknowledge their validity.

Department of State, *Country Reports on Human Rights for 1979*, published as Joint Comm. Print, House Comm. on Foreign Affairs, and Senate Comm. on Foreign Relations, 96th Cong. 2d Sess. (Feb. 4, 1980), Introduction at 1. We have been directed to no assertion by any contemporary state of a right to torture its own or another nation's citizens. Indeed, United States diplomatic contacts confirm the universal abhorrence with which torture is viewed:

> In exchanges between United States embassies and all foreign states with which the United States maintains relations, it has been the Department of State's general experience that no government has asserted a right to torture its own nationals. Where reports of torture elicit some credence, a state usually responds by denial or, less frequently, by asserting that the conduct was unauthorized or constituted rough treatment short of torture.[15]

Memorandum of the United States as *Amicus Curiae* at 16 n.34.

Having examined the sources from which customary international law is derived—the usage of nations, judicial opinions and the works of jurists[16]—we conclude that official torture is now prohibited by the law

---

15. The fact that the prohibition of torture is often honored in the breach does not diminish its binding effect as a norm of international law. As one commentator has put it, "The best evidence for the existence of international law is that every actual State recognizes that it does exist and that it is itself under an obligation to observe it. States often violate international law, just as individuals often violate municipal law; but no more than individuals do States defend their violations by claiming that they are above the law." J. Brierly, *The Outlook for International Law* 4–5 (Oxford 1944).

16. *See also Ireland v. United Kingdom*, Judgment of Jan. 18, 1978 (European Court of Human Rights), *summarized in* [1978] Yearbook, European Convention on Human Rights 602 (Council of Europe)(holding that of nations. The prohibition is clear and unambiguous, and admits of no distinction between treatment of aliens and citizens. Accordingly, we must conclude that the dictum in *Dreyfus v. Von Finck*, [534 F.2d 24, 31 (2d Cir.), *cert. denied,* 429 U.S. 835, 97 S.Ct. 102, 50 L.Ed.2d 101 (1976)], to the effect that "violations of international law do not occur when the aggrieved parties are nationals of the acting state," is clearly out of tune with the current usage and practice of international law. The treaties and accords cited above, as well as the express foreign policy of our own government, all make it clear that international law confers fundamental rights upon all people vis-a-vis their own governments. While the ultimate scope of those rights will be a subject for continuing refinement and elaboration, we hold that the right to be free from torture is now among them. * * *

IV * * *

In the twentieth century the international community has come to recognize the common danger posed by the flagrant disregard of basic human rights and particularly the right to be free of torture. Spurred first by the Great War, and then the Second, civilized nations have banded together to prescribe acceptable norms of international behavior. From the ashes of the Second World War arose the United Nations Organization, amid hopes that an era of peace and cooperation had at last begun. Though many of these aspirations have remained elusive goals, that circumstance cannot diminish the true progress that has been made. In the modern age, humanitarian and practical considerations have combined to lead the nations of the world to recognize that respect for fundamental human rights is in their individual and collective interest. Among the rights universally proclaimed by all nations, as we have noted, is the right to be free of physical torture. Indeed, for purposes of civil liability, the torturer has become—like the pirate and slave trader before him—*hostis humani generis*, an enemy of all mankind. Our holding today, giving effect to a jurisdictional provision enacted by our First Congress, is a small but important step in the fulfillment of the ageless dream to free all people from brutal violence.

Notes and Questions

1. *Individuals as Subjects of International Law. Filartiga* involved international human rights claims of Paraguayan citizens against an official of the government of Paraguay. *Golder* concerned an Englishman's international human rights claim against his own government. Why in principle and practice should either the Paraguayan or U.K. government be subject to international law rules or process with respect to complaints by their own citizens?

J.L. Brierly in his classic British introduction to international law defined the discipline "as the body of rules and principles of action which are

Britain's subjection of prisoners to sleep deprivation, hooding, exposure to hissing noise, reduced diet and standing against a wall for hours was "inhuman and degrading," but not "torture" within meaning of European Convention on Human Rights).

binding upon civilized states in their relations with one another." J.L. Brierly, *The Law of Nations* 1 (4th ed. 1949). How well does Brierly's definition describe the law the rules of which were actually applied in *Filartiga* and *Golder*? How might this definition be reformulated in the light of these two cases where individual rights in international law are in issue? More about individual rights under international law is in Chapter 6.

2. *States as Subjects of International Legal Process.* In *Golder*, the United Kingdom was subject to the jurisdiction of the European Court of Human Rights because it had signed and ratified an international convention formally and explicitly accepting the jurisdiction of the Court. Furthermore, in accordance with the terms of the treaty the U.K. government had itself submitted the dispute to the Court for judgment. In *Filartiga* why should Paraguayan government officials be subject to the jurisdiction of United States federal courts in New York? If it appeared unlikely that the government of Paraguay would permit the Filartigas to sue in Paraguayan courts, would it be likely that the Paraguayan courts would respect or enforce a U.S. judgment in favor of the Filartigas? More on conflict and cooperation among national legal systems is found in Chapter 12.

3. *Perspectives on Litigating International Human Rights Law.* Each of the participants in *Filartiga* had a particular perspective on the case. Why did the Filartigas bring the case in a U.S. court? Presumably their battle was more about political goals and public recognition of their cause than actually to win monetary damages. Roberts B. Owen, the Legal Adviser to the U.S. Department of State at the time of the case, viewed Dr. Filartiga as "one of the leading political opponents of the present [Paraguayan] regime." Roberts B. Owen, "Address at the Annual Dinner of the American Branch of the International Law Association, the Princeton Club, New York City, November 14, 1980," *Proceedings and Committee Reports of the American Branch of the International Law Association 1981–1982*, at 14. Owen also described how lawyers for the U.S. government were divided about what side to take in *Filartiga*, some feeling that there was "a consensus that customary international law now imposes upon every government an obligation to refrain from torture" and others concerned that "our courts and our government would gradually become self-appointed policemen for the world." *Id.* at 16. Finally, "after much soul-searching and debate," the U.S. government chose to file its *amicus* brief for the plaintiff's position, Owen agreeing "that it is a good thing for the U.S. courts to be available to provide remedies for persons aggrieved by violations of internationally protected rights." *Id.*

In some cases it may be possible for litigants like the Filartigas to win significant monetary damages to redress violations of international law. Professor Murphy has pointed out that in Alien Tort Claims Act litigation "the chances for a successful civil suit are substantially greater than those for a successful criminal prosecution." John F. Murphy, "Civil Liability for the Commission of International Crimes as an Alternative to Criminal Prosecution," 12 *Harvard Human Rights Journal* 1, 47 (1999).

Over and above his judgment, Judge Kaufman had strong views about the case. He authored an article on *Filartiga* in which he wrote that "the decision breaks new ground in the body of law governing torture." Irving R. Kaufman, "A Legal Remedy for International Torture?," *New York Times*

Magazine, Nov. 9, 1980, at 44. Several years later he chose *Filartiga* to conclude an article about his judicial career. Irving R. Kaufman, "The Anatomy of Decisionmaking," 53 *Fordham Law Review* 1, 20–22 (1984). The *Filartiga* judgment continues to evoke controversy. See the debate between Steven R. Schneebaum and Richard A. Hibey et al., the defense team for Ferdinand Marcos, in "At Issue: International Law: Should U.S. courts decide international human rights violations?," *ABA Journal*, Feb. 1990, at 34.

The lawyers who brought the *Filartiga* case also had a point-of-view. They later explained that they turned to the Alien Tort Claims Act, "a little-used 200–year old statute," in their search for a way to give lawyers "the opportunity to establish that officials who violate the rights of their own citizens could be brought to justice in U.S. courts." After *Filartiga* their goal "was to bring more cases, obtain more circuit court opinions in our favor and make the *Filartiga* principle unassailable." They plainly acknowledge that they are "political lawyers, [wanting] to use the *Filartiga* precedent to fight those who were violating human rights." Michael Ratner & Beth Stephens, "The Center for Constitutional Rights: Using Law and the *Filartiga* Principle in the Fight for Human Rights," in American Civil Liberties Union, *International Civil Liberties Report*, Dec. 1993, at 29. In general, for the relation between municipal courts and international law, see Chapter 4.

4. *The Nature of Customary International Law.* In theory, at least, customary international law is developed as a result of the actual practice of states. If the Paraguayan government and other governments do actually torture their own citizens, how can there be a rule of customary international law proscribing such practice? Is the court in *Filartiga* truly applying customary international law, or is it perhaps finding and applying rules drawn from some sort of fundamental international law, an international human rights law analogous to municipal constitutional guarantees of human rights?

Note the diverse evidences of international law employed by the *Filartiga* court in deciding that international law prohibits torture. Does the court give any one kind of evidence primacy over the others? Do some evidences seem more or less persuasive? Does the judgment demonstrate that Paraguay has consented to the rule prohibiting torture or only that the community of nations generally supports such a rule? Chapter 3 further explores customary international law and the various non-consensual sources of international law, such as *jus cogens.*

5. *The Efficacy of International Law.* Although one might assume that national courts, like the United States federal courts, are usually more efficacious than international courts, here the expectation is reversed. Though the decision of the international court in *Golder* was respected, the decisions of the national courts in *Filartiga* were not. On remand, the district court imposed a judgment for $10,385,364 against Pena–Irala in order "to reflect adherence to the world community's proscription of torture and to attempt to deter its practice," 577 F.Supp. 860, 867 (E.D.N.Y.1984), but these damages were never paid.

6. *The Organization of the Book.* The international rules and processes introduced in the international law sampler cases, *Golder* and *Filartiga*, are

explored in more depth below. Chapter 2 examines treaties. Chapter 3 turns to customary international law and other sources of international law such as general principles of law, natural law, *jus cogens*, and equity. Chapter 4 considers the role of national courts in applying international law. Chapter 5 discusses public international arbitration and the International Court of Justice. The later chapters in the book deal with a variety of the actors involved with and some of the substantive issues addressed by international law: Chapter 6 the protection of individuals (including European human rights law); Chapter 7 the rights, duties, and relations of sovereign states; Chapter 8 international organizations and especially the United Nations; Chapter 9 the use of force; Chapter 10 international regimes and common spaces, *i.e.*, Antarctica, outer space, and the environment; Chapter 11 the law of the sea; and Chapter 12 international conflict of laws.

Chapter 2

TREATIES

The primary focus of this Chapter is on treaties, with which international lawyers frequently work. Treaties are one of the major sources of international law; the notion of sources is introduced in Part A. Treaties number in the tens of thousands and address virtually every area of human endeavor. Part B of this Chapter reproduces several treaties, indicating something of their variety and raising questions about how and why they are made. Part C then addresses aspects of the law of treaties, a body of rules about the making, interpretation, and termination of treaties. The Vienna Convention on the Law of Treaties, which is often consulted on such rules, is reproduced in the Appendix of this book.

A. THE SOURCES OF INTERNATIONAL LAW

The term "sources" can be used in at least two ways when referring to the sources of international law. One way is to think of a *material source* of an international rule: the place one looks to actually read a rule of international law. So, for example, any given treaty may prescribe a specific legal obligation, *e.g.*, the United Nations Charter provides in Article 2(4) that "All Members shall refrain in their international relations from the threat or use of force against the territorial integrity or political independence of any State, or in any other manner inconsistent with the Purposes of the United Nations."

A second way to think about a source of international law is to think about a *formal source* of international law, that is, a fashion in which international lawyers, judges, and jurists agree that international law may be made. The notion of a formal source of international law is related to ideas in the philosophy of law about rules of recognition and validating norms. For any legal system to function effectively in practice, the participants in that system must agree on what counts as a legal rule and what does not. An ordinary starting point for international lawyers from most any part of the globe when thinking about the formal sources of international law is Article 38 of the Statute of the International Court of Justice.

STATUTE OF THE INTERNATIONAL COURT
OF JUSTICE, ARTICLE 38

June 26, 1945, 59 Stat. 1031, T.S. No. 993.

1. The Court, whose function is to decide in accordance with international law such disputes as are submitted to it, shall apply:

(a) international conventions, whether general or particular, establishing rules expressly recognized by the contesting States;

(b) international custom, as evidence of a general practice accepted as law;

(c) the general principles of law recognized by civilized nations;

(d) subject to the provisions of Article 59, judicial decisions and the teachings of the most highly qualified publicists of the various nations, as subsidiary means for the determination of rules of law.

2. This provision shall not prejudice the power of the Court to decide a case *ex aequo et bono*, if the parties agree thereto.

Notes and Questions

1. *Sources Not Listed in Article 38.* Article 38 of the ICJ Statute is often taken to be a listing of the sources of international law, but note the following reservations. First, Article 38 nowhere mentions "sources." Strictly speaking, Article 38 is an instruction only to the judges of the International Court; it does not by its terms apply to other international courts or lawyers. Second, in practice, judges on other tribunals (and even sometimes those on the ICJ itself) and other practicing international lawyers do use other sources of international law than those listed in Article 38, *e.g.*, natural law, equity, *jus cogens*, the resolutions of international organizations. These other sources of international law are considered alongside customary law and the general principles of law in Chapter 3.

2. *Judicial Decisions as Sources of International Law.* Article 38(1)(d) refers to Article 59, which reads: "The decision of the Court has no binding force except between the parties and in respect of that particular case." This language seems to be meant to limit any inference that the reference to "judicial decisions" allows judicial precedent itself to be a source of international law. Although judicial precedent is quite an ordinary source of law in common law legal systems like those in the United States and England, many civil law legal systems formally restrict the judicial role to merely applying the law. As we shall see in Chapter 3 and throughout the book, Article 59 has, however, not prevented the International Court from relying heavily on its own past decisions as a guide in finding customary international law.

3. Ex Aequo et Bono. Article 38(2) allows the Court to decide *ex aequo et bono*, by what is equal and good, if the parties agree, but there has never been such agreement. Neither the International Court of Justice nor its predecessor, the Permanent Court of International Justice, has ever played

an *ex aequo et bono* role in more than 75 years. Article 38(2) has, however, caused problems for the Court's use of equity, a topic also explored in Chapter 3.

4. *The Hierarchy of the Sources of International Law.* Are treaties the primary source of international law? Partly because "international conventions" are listed first in Article 38(1), the judges of the ICJ and other international lawyers have often given treaties pride of place among the sources of international law. There are other reasons too for thinking of treaties as primary among the rules of international law. Treaties ordinarily clearly show the legal rule because they are in written form. Moreover, treaties are subject to the explicit acceptance of states. Treaties therefore can often be clearer in their terms and more certain in their acceptance than other sorts of international law sources. Furthermore, since the 19th century treaties have been widely used by states. Many areas that used to be the province of customary international law, *e.g.*, the law of the sea and the law of treaties, have now been put into conventions. However, as we shall see here and in Chapter 3, treaties do not cover all topics in international law, nor do they include all states as parties. Sometimes treaties may even be trumped by other forms of international law, especially natural law or *jus cogens*, and they always need to be interpreted in practice by judges or commentators who will use other sources of international law in their interpretations.

B. A TREATY SAMPLER

The conclusion of treaties between nations is a natural feature of human society. For as long as there have been written records, there have been international compacts. The six sample agreements excerpted below span more than two thousand years. Among other things, they demonstrate the permanence of treaties as part of the human experience. They also introduce treaties as vehicles for (1) military and political alliances, (2) peace-making, (3) the creation of new states, (4) the exchange of territory, and (5) the control of international violence. Today, as before, treaties constitute the most frequent sort of international law made in practice. The treaties below give students an idea of the actual "feel" and nature of international agreements, rather than leaving them to read about treaties second hand in court cases.

THE TREATY BETWEEN THE JEWS AND THE ROMANS (CIRCA 160 B.C.)

1 Maccabees 8:1–29 (*Good News Bible with Deuterocanonicals/Apocrypha*).

Judas had heard about the Romans and their reputation as a military power. He knew that they welcomed all those who joined them as allies and that those who came to them could be sure of the friendship of Rome. People had told him about the wars the Romans had fought and their heroic acts among the Gauls, whom they had conquered and forced to pay taxes. He had been told what they had done in Spain when they captured the silver mines and the gold mines there. By careful planning and persistence, they had conquered the whole country, even though it was far from Rome. They had overcome the kings from distant lands who had fought against them; they had defeated them so badly that the survivors had to pay annual taxes. They had fought and conquered Philip and Perseus, kings of Macedonia, and all who had joined them against Rome. They had even defeated Antiochus the Great, king of Syria, who had attacked them with 120 elephants, cavalry, chariots, and a powerful army. They took him alive and forced him and his successors to pay heavy taxes, to give hostages, and to surrender India, Media, Lydia, and some of their best lands. They took these and gave them to King Eumenes.

When the Greeks made plans to attack and destroy them, the Romans learned of the plans and sent a general to fight against them. The Romans killed many of the Greeks, took their wives and children captive, plundered their possessions, occupied their land, tore down their fortresses, and made them slaves, as they are today. They also destroyed or made slaves of other kingdoms, the islands, and everyone who had ever fought against them. But they maintained their friendship with their allies and those who relied on them for protection. They conquered kings near and far, and everyone who heard of their reputation was afraid of them. They helped some men to become kings, while they deposed others; they had become a world power. In spite of all this, no Roman ever tried to advance his own position by wearing a crown or putting on royal robes. They created a senate, and each day 320 senators came together to deliberate about the affairs of the people and their well-being. Each year they entrusted to one man the responsibility of governing them and controlling their whole territory. Everyone obeyed this one man, and there was no envy or jealousy among them.

Judas chose Eupolemus, the son of John and grandson of Accos, and Jason son of Eleazar and sent them to Rome to make a treaty of friendship and alliance with the Romans. He did this to eliminate Syrian oppression, since the Jews clearly saw that they were being reduced to slavery. After a long and difficult journey, Eupolemus and Jason reached Rome and entered the Senate. They addressed the assembly in these terms: "Judas Maccabeus, his brothers, and the Jewish people have sent us here to make a mutual defense treaty with you, so that we may be officially recorded as your friends and allies."

The Romans accepted the proposal, and what follows is a copy of the letter which was engraved on bronze tablets and sent to Jerusalem to remain there as a record of the treaty:

> May things go well forever for the Romans and for the Jewish nation on land and sea! May they never have enemies, and may they never go to war! But if war is declared first against Rome or any of her allies anywhere, the Jewish nation will come to her aid with whole-hearted support, as the situation may require. And to those at war with her, the Jews shall not give or supply food, arms, money,

or ships, as was agreed in Rome. The Jews must carry out their obligations without receiving anything in return.

In the same way, if war is declared first against the Jewish nation, the Romans will come to their aid with hearty support, as the situation may require. And to their enemies there shall not be given or supplied food, arms, money, or ships, as was agreed in Rome. The Romans must carry out their obligations without deception.

These are the terms of the treaty that the Romans have made with the Jewish people.

Notes and Questions

1. *The Historical Permanence of Treaties.* The Treaty Between the Jews and the Romans we have from the Bible. Despite its antiquity, this treaty of peace and alliance has quite a modern ring to it and is not all that dissimilar in language or purpose from many treaties, like that of the North Atlantic Treaty Organization, in force today.

2. *Reciprocity and Good Faith.* The first part of the extract is more or less its legislative history. What does it tell us about the reasons why the Jews sought a treaty? What were the reasons the Romans consented? How was the treaty to be enforced? If the Romans had not had such a good record of respecting their treaty commitments, would the Jews have been as eager to enter into an alliance with them? Reciprocal good faith always seems to have been one of the key components in ensuring the obligatory force of treaties.

3. *In Written Form.* Why was it important that the Jewish–Roman treaty be in writing? Was it to make sure the terms were clear? Would it help ensure the continuing efficacy of the treaty after those who negotiated the agreement had passed from the scene? What could have been the disadvantages of an unwritten agreement?

4. *Religion and International Law.* The so-called "father" of international law, the Dutch jurist Hugo de Groot (or Grotius), relied heavily on the Bible for his evidences of the law of nations in his seminal treatise of 1625, *De Jure Belli Ac Pacis, The Law of War and Peace.* Grotius cited a great number of treaties that were made between the Jews and their neighbors as proof for the proposition that treaties with non-believers were permitted. His other principal evidences were drawn from the great Greek and Roman classical authors. See Mark W. Janis, "Religion and the Literature of International Law: Some Standard Texts," in *Religion and International Law* 121, 124 (Mark W. Janis & Carolyn Evans eds. 1999).

5. *The Inter-temporal Problem.* On the face of it, does the Treaty between the Jews and the Romans look to be part of "international law" as we now understand the concept? Would the Jews and the Romans have thought of the Treaty as creating "legal" obligations? How possible is it for people in one time or place to use terms and concepts common to peoples from other times and places? Questions like this are sometimes thought of as part of the "inter-temporal" problem of international law.

THE PEACE OF WESTPHALIA (1648)

1 Consolidated Treaty Series 198.

A Treaty of Peace between the Empire *and* Sweden, *concluded and sign'd at* Osnabrug *the* 24th *of* October, 1648. *The King of* France *was comprehended in this Treaty as an Ally of* Sweden.

Be it known to all and singular whom it does concern, or whom it may in any manner concern, That after the Differences and Troubles which began several years ago in the *Roman* Empire, had come to such a height, that not only all *Germany*, but likewise some neighbouring Kingdoms, especially *Sweden* and *France*, found themselves so involv'd in them, that from thence there arose a long and cruel War; * * *. At last it fell out by an Effect of the Divine Bounty, that both sides turn'd their Thoughts towards the means of making Peace, and that by a mutual Agreement made at *Hamburg* the 25th of *December* N.S. or the 15th O.S. 1641. between the Parties, the 11th N.S. or the 1st O.S. 1643. was by common Consent appointed for beginning the Assembly or Congress of Plenipotentiaries at *Osnabrug*, and at *Munster* in *Westphalia*.

* * * After having invok'd the Assistance of God, and reciprocally exchang'd the Originals of their respective full Powers, they transacted and agreed among themselves, to the Glory of God, and Safety of the Christian World (the Electors, Princes and States of the Sacred *Roman* Empire being present, approving and consenting) the Articles of Peace and Amity, whereof the Tenour follows.

The Re-establishment of Peace and Amity.

I. That there be a Christian, universal and perpetual Peace, and a true and sincere Friendship and Amity between his Sacred Imperial Majesty, the House of *Austria*, and all his Allies and Adherents, and the Heirs and Successors of each of them, chiefly the King of *Spain*, and the Electors, Princes and States of the Empire, of the one side; and her Sacred Royal Majesty, and the Kingdom of *Sweden*, her Allies and Adherents, and the Heirs and Successors of each of them, especially the most Christian King, the respective Electors, Princes and States of the Empire, of the other side; and that this Peace be observ'd and cultivated sincerely and seriously, so that each Party may procure the Benefit, Honour and Advantage of one another, and thereby the Fruits of this Peace and Amity may be seen to grow up and flourish anew, by a sure and reciprocal maintaining of a good and faithful Neighbourhood between the *Roman* Empire and the Kingdom of *Sweden* reciprocally.

An Amnesty From All Hostility.

II. That there be on both sides a perpetual Oblivion and Amnesty of all that has been done since the beginning of these Troubles, in what Place or in what Manner soever Hostilities may have been exercis'd by the one or the other Party; so that neither for any of those things, nor upon any other Account or Pretext whatsoever, any Act of Hostility or Enmity, Vexation or Hindrance shall be exercis'd or suffer'd, or caus'd to be exercis'd, either as to Persons, Conditions, Goods or Security, either by one's self or by others, in private, or openly, directly or indirectly, under form of Right or Law, or by open Deed, either within, or in any Place whatsoever without the Empire, notwithstanding all former Compacts to the contrary; but that all Injuries, Violences, Hostilities and Damages, and all Expences that either side has been oblig'd to be at, as well before as during the War, and all Libels by Words or Writing shall be entirely forgotten, without any regard to Persons or Things; so that whatever might be demanded or pretended by one against the other upon this account, shall be bury'd in perpetual Oblivion. * * *

POINT OF ECCLESIASTICAL GRIEVANCES, OR OF RELIGION.

V. Now whereas the Grievances of the one and the other Religion, which were debated amongst the Electors, Princes and States of the Empire, have been partly the Cause and Occasion of the present War, it has been agreed and transacted in the following manner.

1. * * * That there be an exact and reciprocal Equality amongst all the Electors, Princes and States of both Religions * * *. * * *

LIBERTY OF CONSCIENCE.

28. It has moreover been found good, that those of the Confession of *Augsburg* [Protestants], who are Subjects of the Catholicks, and the Catholick Subjects of the States of the Confession of *Augsburg*, who had not the public or private Exercise of their religion in any time of the year 1624 and who after the Publication of the Peace shall possess and embrace a Religion different from that of the Lord of the Territory, shall in consequence of the said Peace be patiently suffer'd and tolerated, without any Hindrance or Impediment to attend their Devotions in their Houses and in private, with all Liberty of Conscience, and without any Inquisition or Trouble, and even to assist in their Neighbourhood, as often as they have a mind, at the publick Exercise of their Religion, or send their children to foreign Schools of their Religion, or have them instructed in their Families by private Masters; provided the said Vassals and Subjects do their Duty in all other things, and hold themselves in due Obedience and Subjection, without giving occasion to any Disturbance or Commotion. In like manner Subjects, whether they be Catholicks, or of the Confession of *Augsburg*, shall not be despis'd any where upon account of their Religion, nor excluded from the Community of Merchants, Artizans or Companies, nor depriv'd of Successions, Legacies, Hospitals, Lazar–Houses, or Alms–Houses, and other Privileges or Rights, and far less of Church-yards, and the Honour of Burial; nor shall any more be exacted of them for the Expence of their Funerals, than the Dues usually paid for Burying–Places in Parish–Churches: so that in these and all other the like things they shall be treated in the same manner as Brethren and Sisters, with equal Justice and Protection. * * *

THE RE-ESTABLISHMENT OF THE ESTATES OF THE
EMPIRE TO THEIR ANCIENT RIGHTS.

VIII.   And in order to prevent for the future all Differences in the Political State, all and every the Electors, Princes, and States of the *Roman* Empire shall be so establish'd and confirm'd in their ancient Rights, Prerogatives, Liberties, Privileges, free Exercise of their Territorial Right, as well in Spirituals and Temporals, Seigneuries, Regalian Rights, and in the possession of all these things, by virtue of the present Transaction, that they may not be molested at any time in any manner, under any pretext whatsoever.

1.   That they enjoy without contradiction the Right of Suffrage in all Deliberations touching the Affairs of the Empire, especially in the manner of interpreting Laws, resolving upon a War, imposing Taxes, ordering Levies and quartering of Soldiers, building for the publick Use new Fortresses in the Lands of the States, and reinforcing old Garisons, making of Peace and Alliances, and treating of other such-like Affairs; so that none of those or the like things shall be done or receiv'd afterwards, without the Advice and Consent of a free Assembly of all the States of the Empire: That, above all, each of the Estates of the Empire shall freely and for ever enjoy the Right of making Alliances among themselves, or with Foreigners, for the Preservation and Security of every one of them: provided nevertheless that these Alliances be neither against the Emperor nor the Empire, nor the publick Peace, nor against this Transaction especially; and that they be made without prejudice in every respect to the Oath whereby every one of them is bound to the Emperor and the Empire.

Notes and Questions

1.   *The Peace of Westphalia.* This excerpt is from the Treaty of Osnabruck between Sweden and the Holy Roman Empire. The Peace of Westphalia also included a second agreement, the Treaty of Munster, between France and the Empire. The Peace of Westphalia brought to a close the bloody Thirty Years War. One of the central issues of the War was the right of princes and peoples to choose to be Catholic or Protestant. Besides the Treaty's general provisions respecting amity and amnesty, some of the clauses about religious liberty have been reproduced above.

The Peace of Westphalia is for many historians and lawyers the real beginning of the era of "modern international relations" and hence of "modern international law." Yet, the Peace itself was drafted by Europeans well familiar with international compacts, who probably had little idea that others would view their newly crafted Peace as an innovation. What makes the Peace of Westphalia so compelling as a "starting point"? Besides ending the Thirty Years War, the Peace of Westphalia in Article VIII "re-established" the "electors, princes, and states of the Roman Empire" to "their ancient Rights." Were these "ancient Rights," described as protecting the German states from any "molestation," a kind of state sovereignty that became the fundamental building block for modern international politics?

2. *Sovereignty and International Law.* Note how ironic it is that states had to agree in a treaty to limit their sovereignty in order to assure their sovereignty. The success of international law as a political and intellectual discipline over the past four centuries has had much to do with international law's utility in regulating and cementing a world political system based on more or less sovereign states.

It should be no surprise that the modern intellectual constructs of state sovereignty and international law both emerged at the same time as the Thirty Years War. A principal craftsman of the notion of the sovereign state was the English philosopher, Thomas Hobbes, who published his celebration of the sovereign state, *Leviathan*, in 1651. Hobbes argued that all humankind required "a Common Power, to keep them in awe, and to direct their actions to the Common Benefit." Meantime, Hugo Grotius fashioned a legal system in his *De Jure Belli Ac Pacis* (1625) that explained that no sovereign state was so powerful as not to need the advantages of laws based on natural law and positive consent. It is this powerful combination of Hobbes's sovereign state and Grotius's international law that have defined much of international relations for more than three centuries ever since. See Mark W. Janis, "Sovereignty and International Law: Hobbes and Grotius," in *Essays in Honour of Wang Tieya* 391 (Ronald St. John Macdonald ed. 1994).

THE TREATY OF PARIS (1783)

United States and Great Britain, 12 Bevans 8, 48 Consolidated Treaty Series 487.

Concluded at Paris September 3, 1783; ratified by Congress January 14, 1784; proclaimed January 14, 1784.

In the name of the Most Holy and Undivided Trinity.

It having pleased the Divine Providence to dispose the hearts of the Most Serene and Most Potent Prince George the Third, by the grace of God King of Great Britain, France, and Ireland, Defender of the Faith, Duke of Brunswick and Lunenburg, Arch–Treasurer and Prince Elector of the Holy Roman Empire, & c. and of the United States of America, to forget all past misunderstandings and differences that have unhappily interrupted the good correspondence and friendship which they mutually wish to restore; and to establish such a beneficial and satisfactory intercourse between the two countries, upon the ground of reciprocal advantages and mutual convenience, as may promote and secure to both perpetual peace and harmony; and having for this desirable end already laid the foundation of peace and reconciliation, by the provisional articles signed at Paris, on the 30th of November, 1782, by the Commissioners empowered on each part; which articles were agreed to be inserted in, and to constitute the treaty of peace proposed to be concluded between the Crown of Great Britain and the said United States, but which treaty was not to be concluded until terms of peace should be agreed upon between Great Britain and France, and His Britannick Majesty should be ready to conclude such treaty accordingly; and the treaty between Great Britain and France having since been concluded, His Britannick Majesty and the United States of America, in order to carry into effect the provisional articles above mentioned, according to the tenor thereof, have constituted and appointed, that is to say, his Britannick Majesty, on his part, David Hartley, Esq., Member of the Parliament of Great Britain: and the said United States, on their part, John Adams, Esq., late a Commissioner of the United States of America at the Court of Versailles, late Delegate in Congress from the State of Massachusets, and Chief Justice of the said State, and Minister Plenipotentiary of the said United States to their High Mightinesses the States General of the United Netherlands; Benjamin Franklin, Esq., late Delegate in Congress from the State of Pennsylvania, President of the Convention of the said State, and Minister Plenipotentiary from the United States of America at the Court of Versailles; John Jay, Esq., late President of Congress, and Chief Justice of the State of New York, and Minister Plenipotentiary from the said United States at the Court of Madrid; to be the Plenipotentiaries for the concluding and signing the present definitive treaty: who, after having reciprocally communicated their respective full powers, have agreed upon and confirmed the following articles:

Article I. His Britannick Majesty acknowledges the said United States, viz. New Hampshire, Massachusets Bay, Rhode Island and Providence Plantations, Connecticut, New York, New Jersey, Pennsylvania, Delaware, Maryland, Virginia, North Carolina, South Carolina, and Georgia, to be Free, Sovereign and Independent States; that he treats with them as such; and for himself, his heirs and successors, relinquishes all claims to the government, propriety, and territorial rights of the same, and every part thereof.

II. And that all disputes which might arise in future on the subject of the boundaries of the said United States may be prevented, it is hereby agreed and declared, that the following are, and shall be, their boundaries, viz. From the north-west angle of Nova Scotia, viz. that angle which is formed by a line drawn due north from the source of Saint Croix river to the Highlands, along the said Highlands which divide those rivers that empty themselves into the river St. Lawrence, from those which fall into the Atlantic ocean, to the north-westernmost head of Connecticut river; thence down along the middle of that river to the forty-fifth degree of north latitude; from thence, by a line due west on said latitude until it strikes the river Iroquois or Cataraquy; thence along the middle of said river into Lake Ontario; through the middle of said lake, until it strikes the communication by water between that lake and lake Erie; thence along the middle of said communication into lake Erie; through the middle of said lake until it arrives at the water communication between that lake and lake Huron; thence along the middle of said water communication into the lake Huron; thence through the middle of said lake to the water communication between that lake and lake Superior; thence through lake Superior, northward of the Isles Royal and Phelipeaux, to the Long Lake; thence through the middle of said Long Lake, and the water communication between it and the Lake of the Woods, to the said Lake of the Woods; thence through the said lake to the most north-western point thereof, and from thence

on a due west course to the river Mississippi; thence by a line to be
drawn along the middle of the said river Mississippi, until it shall
intersect the northernmost part of the thirty-first degree of north
latitude:—South, by a line to be drawn due east from the determination
of the line last mentioned, in the latitude of thirty-one degrees north of
the equator, to the middle of the river Apalachicola or Catahouche;
thence along the middle thereof to its junction with the Flint river;
thence strait to the head of St. Mary's river, and thence down along the
middle of St. Mary's River to the Atlantic ocean:—East, by a line to be
drawn along the middle of the river St. Croix, from its mouth in the bay
of Fundy, to its source; and from its source directly north to the
aforesaid Highlands, which divide the rivers that fall into the Atlantic
ocean from those which fall into the river St. Lawrence: comprehending
all islands within twenty leagues of any part of the shores of the United
States, and lying between lines to be drawn due east from the points
where the aforesaid boundaries between Nova Scotia on the one part,
and East Florida on the other, shall respectively touch the bay of Fundy,
and the Atlantic ocean; excepting such islands as now are, or heretofore
have been, within the limits of the said province of Nova Scotia.

III.   It is agreed, that the people of the United States shall continue
to enjoy, unmolested, the right to take fish of every kind of the grand
bank and on all the other banks of Newfoundland: also in the gulph of
Saint Lawrence, and at all other places in the sea where the inhabitants
of both countries used at any time heretofore to fish. And also that the
inhabitants of the United States shall have liberty to take fish of every
kind on such part of the coast of Newfoundland as British fishermen
shall use, (but not to dry or cure the same on that island) and also on the
coasts, bays, and creeks of all other of His Britannick Majesty's dominions in America; and that the American fishermen shall have liberty to
dry and cure fish in any of the unsettled bays, harbours, and creeks of
Nova Scotia, Magdalen Islands, and Labrador, so long as the same shall
remain unsettled; but so soon as the same, or either of them, shall be
settled, it shall not be lawful for the said fishermen to dry or cure fish at
such settlement without a previous agreement for that purpose with the
inhabitants, proprietors, or possessors of the ground.

IV.   It is agreed, that creditors on either side shall meet with no
lawful impediment to the recovery of the full value, in sterling money, of
all *bona fide* debts heretofore contracted.

V.   It is agreed, that the Congress shall earnestly recommend it to
the legislatures of the respective states, to provide for the restitution of
all estates, rights, and properties, which have been confiscated, belonging
to real British subjects: and also of the estates, rights, and properties, of
persons resident in districts in the possession of his Majesty's arms, and
who have not borne arms against the said United States: and that
persons of any other description shall have free liberty to go to any part
or parts of any of the Thirteen United States, and therein to remain
twelve months unmolested in their endeavours to obtain the restitution
of such of their estates, rights, and properties, as may have been

confiscated: and that Congress shall also earnestly recommend to the several states, a reconsideration and revision of all acts or laws regarding the premises, so as to render the said laws or acts perfectly consistent not only with justice and equity, but with that spirit of conciliation which, on the return of the blessings of peace, should universally prevail. And that Congress shall also earnestly recommend to the several states, that the estates, rights, and properties, of such last-mentioned persons shall be restored to them, they refunding to any persons who may be now in possession the *bona fide* price (where any has been given) which such persons may have paid on purchasing any of the said lands, rights, or properties, since the confiscation.

And it is agreed, that all persons who have any interest in confiscated lands, either by debts, marriage settlements or otherwise, shall meet with no lawful impediment in the prosecution of their just rights.

VI. That there shall be no future confiscations made, nor any prosecutions commenced against any person or persons, for or by reason of the part which he or they may have taken in the present war; and that no person shall, on that account, suffer any future loss or damage either in his person, liberty, or property; and that those who may be in confinement on such charges at the time of the ratification of the treaty in America, shall be immediately set at liberty, and the prosecutions so commenced be discontinued.

VII. There shall be a firm and perpetual peace between His Britannick Majesty and the said States, and between the subjects of the one and the citizens of the other, wherefore, all hostilities, both by sea and land, shall from henceforth cease: all prisoners on both sides shall be set at liberty, and his Britannick Majesty shall, with all convenient speed, and without causing any destruction, or carrying away any negroes, or other property of the American inhabitants, withdraw all his armies, garrisons, and fleets, from the said United States, and from every port, place, and harbour within the same; leaving in all fortifications the American artillery that may be therein: and shall also order and cause all archives, records, deeds, and papers, belonging to any of the said States, or their citizens, which in the course of the war may have fallen into the hands of his officers, to be forthwith restored and delivered to the proper states and persons to whom they belong.

VIII. The navigation of the river Mississippi, from its source to the ocean, shall for ever remain free and open to the subjects of Great Britain, and the citizens of the United States.

IX. In case it should so happen, that any place or territory belonging to Great Britain, or to the United States, should have been conquered by the arms of either from the other, before the arrival of the said provisional articles in America, it is agreed, that the same shall be restored without difficulty, and without requiring any compensation.

X. The solemn ratifications of the present treaty, expedited in good and due form, shall be exchanged between the contracting parties in the space of six months, or sooner if possible, to be computed from the day of the signature of the present treaty.

In witness whereof, we the under-signed, their Ministers Plenipotentiary, have, in their name, and in virtue of our full powers, signed with our hands the present definitive treaty, and caused the seals of our arms to be affixed thereto.

Done at Paris, this third day of September, in the year of our Lord one thousand seven hundred and eighty-three.

D. HARTLEY.

JOHN ADAMS.
B. FRANKLIN.
JOHN JAY.

Notes and Questions

1. *Recognition of the United States.* Did Article I of the 1783 Peace of Paris merely declare Britain's formal recognition of the sovereignty of the United States as it had been already objectively established in 1776 by the United States itself in the Declaration of Independence? Or did the Peace of Paris itself constitute the sovereignty of the United States as of January 14, 1784, when the Treaty came into force? These alternatives reflect the theoretical distinction in international law between the so-called "declaratory" and "constitutive" theories of recognition, a topic to which we return in Chapter 7.

U.S. Supreme Court Justice Chase wrote in 1795:

I have ever considered it as the established doctrine of the United States, that their independence originated from, and commenced with, the declaration of congress, on the 4th of July, 1776; and that no other period can be fixed on for its commencement; and that all laws made by the legislatures of the several states, after the declaration of independence, were the laws of sovereign and independent governments.

Ware v. Hylton, 3 U.S. (3 Dall.) 199, 224, 1 L.Ed. 568, 579 (1796).

2. *Effect of Treaties on Third Parties.* Does Article II delimiting the boundaries of the United States in 1783 legally bind any nation except the United States and the United Kingdom? What would be the effect at international law if France or Spain had protested the U.S.-U.K. territorial delimitation? See Articles 34–38 of the Vienna Convention on the Law of Treaties, reproduced in the Appendix, and the discussion of customary international law in Chapter 3.

3. *Maritime Issues.* Article III concerns fishing off the shores of the United States and Canada. Fishing disputes between the two countries have continued into the present day. In 1984, the International Court of Justice decided the *Gulf of Maine Case* and again divided fishing rights between the United States and Canada in the area. Definition of the Maritime Boundary in the Gulf of Maine Area, 1984 I.C.J. 246, 1984 WL 499.

4. *The Peace of Paris and the U.S. Constitution.* The inability or unwillingness of state courts to protect the rights of British subjects detailed in Articles IV, V, and VI, led Britain to remain in occupation of much of what was then the Northwest Territory (later the states of Illinois, Indiana, Michigan, Ohio, and Wisconsin). This in turn was one impetus to the calling of the Constitutional Convention in 1787, to the establishment of U.S. federal courts in 1789 under the new U.S. Constitution, and to the mention of treaties in the Constitution's supremacy clause. See Chapter 4.

On balance, the Peace of Paris was a diplomatic triumph for the new United States:

> This Peace of Paris certainly gives the lie to the epigram that "America never lost a war, or won a peace conference." Considering that the British still held New York, Charleston, Savannah, Detroit, and several other posts in the Northwest, that Washington's army was almost incapable of further effort, and that the British navy had recovered command of the sea, it is surprising what wide boundaries and favorable terms the United States obtained.

Samuel Eliot Morison, Henry Steele Commager & William E. Leuchtenberg, 1 *The Growth of the American Republic* 204 (7th ed. 1980).

THE CESSION OF ALASKA (1867)
11 Bevans 1216, 15 Stat. 539, Treaty Series 301,
134 Consolidated Treaty Series 331.

Convention signed at Washington March 30, 1867

Senate advice and consent to ratification April 9, 1867

Ratified by Russia May 3, 1867

Ratified by the President of the United States May 28, 1867

Ratifications exchanged at Washington June 20, 1867

Entered into force June 20, 1867

Proclaimed by the President of the United States June 20, 1867

The United States of America and His Majesty the Emperor of all the Russias, being desirous of strengthening, if possible, the good understanding which exists between them, have, for that purpose, appointed as their Plenipotentiaries: the President of the United States, William H. Seward, Secretary of State; and His Majesty the Emperor of all the Russias, the Privy Counsellor Edward de Stoeckl, his Envoy Extraordinary and Minister Plenipotentiary to the United States.

And the said Plenipotentiaries, having exchanged their full powers, which were found to be in due form, have agreed upon and signed the following articles:

Article I.

His Majesty the Emperor of all the Russias agrees to cede to the United States, by this convention, immediately upon the exchange of the ratifications thereof, all the territory and dominion now possessed by his said Majesty on the continent of America and in the adjacent islands, the same being contained within the geographical limits herein set forth, to wit: The eastern limit is the line of demarcation between the Russian and the British possessions in North America, as established by the convention between Russia and Great Britain, of February 28–16, 1825, and described in Articles III and IV of said convention, in the following terms:

"Commencing from the southernmost point of the island called Prince of Wales Island, which point lies in the parallel of 54 degrees 40 minutes north latitude, and between the 131st and the 133d degree of west longitude, (meridian of Greenwich,) the said line shall ascend to the north along the channel called Portland channel, as far as the point of the continent where it strikes the 56th degree of north latitude; from this last mentioned point, the line of demarcation shall follow the summit of the mountains situated parallel to the coast as far as the point of intersection of the 141st degree of west longitude, (the same meridian); and finally, from the said point of intersection, the said meridian line of the 141st degree, in its prolongation as far as the Frozen ocean.

"IV. With reference to the line of demarcation laid down in the preceding article, it is understood—

"1st. That the island called Prince of Wales Island shall belong wholly to Russia," (now, by this cession, to the United States.)

"2d. That whenever the summit of the mountains which extend in a direction parallel to the coast from the 56th degree of north latitude to the point of intersection of the 141st degree of west longitude shall prove to be at the distance of more than ten marine leagues from the ocean, the limit between the British possessions and the line of coast which is to belong to Russia as above mentioned (that is to say, the limit to the possessions ceded by this convention) shall be formed by a line parallel to the winding of the coast, and which shall never exceed the distance of ten marine leagues therefrom."

The western limit within which the territories and dominion conveyed, are contained, passes through a point in Behring's straits on the parallel of 65 degrees 30 minutes north latitude, at its intersection by the meridian which passes midway between the islands of Krusenstern, or Ignalook, and the island of Ratmanoff, or Noonarbook, and proceeds due north, without limitation, into the same Frozen ocean. The same western limit, beginning at the same initial point, proceeds thence in a course nearly southwest, through Behring's straits and Behring's sea, so as to pass midway between the northwest point of the island of St. Lawrence and the southeast point of Cape Choukotski, to the meridian of 172 west longitude; thence, from the intersection of that meridian, in a southwesterly direction, so as to pass midway between the island of Attou and the Copper island of the Kormandorski couplet or group, in the North Pacific ocean, to the meridian of 193 degrees west longitude, so as to include in the territory conveyed the whole of the Aleutian islands east of that meridian.

ARTICLE II.

In the cession of territory and dominion made by the preceding article, are included the right of property in all public lots and squares, vacant lands, and all public buildings, fortifications, barracks, and other edifices which are not private individual property. It is, however, understood and agreed, that the churches which have been built in the ceded territory by the Russian government, shall remain the property of such members of the Greek Oriental Church resident in the territory, as may choose to worship therein. Any government archives, papers, and documents relative to the territory and dominion aforesaid, which may be now existing there, will be left in the possession of the agent of the United States; but an authenticated copy of such of them as may be required, will be, at all times, given by the United States to the Russian government or to such Russian officers or subjects, as they may apply for.

ARTICLE III.

The inhabitants of the ceded territory, according to their choice, reserving their natural allegiance, may return to Russia within three years; but if they should prefer to remain in the ceded territory, they, with the exception of uncivilized native tribes, shall be admitted to the enjoyment of all the rights, advantages and immunities of citizens of the United States, and shall be maintained and protected in the free enjoyment of their liberty, property and religion. The uncivilized tribes will be subject to such laws and regulations as the United States, may from time to time, adopt in regard to aboriginal tribes of that country.

ARTICLE IV.

His Majesty, the Emperor of all the Russias shall appoint, with convenient despatch, an agent or agents for the purpose of formally delivering to a similar agent or agents appointed on behalf of the United States, the territory, dominion, property, dependencies and appurtenances which are ceded as above, and for doing any other act which may be necessary in regard thereto. But the cession, with the right of immediate possession, is nevertheless to be deemed complete and absolute on the exchange of ratifications, without waiting for such formal delivery.

ARTICLE V.

Immediately after the exchange of the ratifications of this convention, any fortifications or military posts which may be in the ceded territory, shall be delivered to the agent of the United States, and any Russian troops which may be in the Territory shall be withdrawn as soon as may be reasonably and conveniently practicable.

ARTICLE VI.

In consideration of the cession aforesaid, the United States agree to pay at the Treasury in Washington, within ten months after the exchange of the ratifications of this convention, to the diplomatic representative or other agent of his Majesty the Emperor of all the Russias, duly authorized to receive the same, seven million two hundred thousand dollars in gold. The cession of territory and dominion herein made is hereby declared to be free and unincumbered by any reservations, privileges, franchises, grants, or possessions, by any associated companies, whether corporate or incorporate, Russian or any other, or by any parties, except merely private individual property holders; and the cession hereby made, conveys all the rights, franchises, and privileges now belonging to Russia in the said territory or dominion, and appurtenances thereto.

ARTICLE VII.

When this Convention shall have been duly ratified by the President of the United States, by and with the advice and consent of the Senate, on the one part, and on the other by His Majesty the Emperor of all the Russias, the ratification shall be exchanged at Washington within three months from the date hereof, or sooner, if possible.

In faith whereof, the respective plenipotentiaries have signed this convention, and thereto affixed the seals of their arms.

Done at Washington, the thirtieth day of March in the year of our Lord one thousand eight hundred and sixty-seven.

WILLIAM H. SEWARD
EDOUARD DE STOECKL

THE KELLOGG–BRIAND PACT (1928)

Renunciation of War as an Instrument of National Policy, 2 Bevans
732, 46 Stat. 2343, Treaty Series 796, 94 L.N.T.S. 57.

Treaty signed at Paris August 27, 1928

Senate advice and consent to ratification January 15, 1929

Ratified by the President of the United States January 17, 1929

Ratifications deposited at Washington March 2–July 24, 1929

Entered into force July 24, 1929

Proclaimed by the President of the United States July 24, 1929

The President of the German Reich, the President of the United States of America, His Majesty the King of the Belgians, the President of the French Republic, His Majesty the King of Great Britain, Ireland and the British Dominions Beyond the Seas, Emperor of India, His Majesty the King of Italy, His Majesty the Emperor of Japan, the President of the Republic of Poland, the President of the Czechoslovak Republic,

Deeply sensible of their solemn duty to promote the welfare of mankind;

Persuaded that the time has come when a frank renunciation of war as an instrument of national policy should be made to the end that the peaceful and friendly relations now existing between their peoples may be perpetuated;

Convinced that all changes in their relations with one another should be sought only by pacific means and be the result of a peaceful and orderly process, and that any signatory Power which shall hereafter seek to promote its national interests by resort to war should be denied the benefits furnished by this Treaty;

Hopeful that, encouraged by their example, all the other nations of the world will join in this humane endeavor and by adhering to the present Treaty as soon as it comes into force bring their peoples within the scope of its beneficent provisions, thus uniting the civilized nations of the world in a common renunciation of war as an instrument of their national policy;

Have decided to conclude a Treaty and for that purpose have appointed * * * Plenipotentiaries * * * who, having communicated to one another their full powers found in good and due form have agreed upon the following articles:

ARTICLE I

The High Contracting Parties solemnly declare in the names of their respective peoples that they condemn recourse to war for the solution of international controversies, and renounce it as an instrument of national policy in their relations with one another.

ARTICLE II

The High Contracting Parties agree that the settlement or solution of all disputes or conflicts of whatever nature or of whatever origin they may be, which may arise among them, shall never be sought except by pacific means.

ARTICLE III

The present Treaty shall be ratified by the High Contracting Parties named in the Preamble in accordance with their respective constitutional requirements, and shall take effect as between them as soon as all their several instruments of ratification shall have been deposited at Washington.

This Treaty shall, when it has come into effect as prescribed in the preceding paragraph, remain open as long as may be necessary for adherence by all the other Powers of the world. Every instrument evidencing the adherence of a Power shall be deposited at Washington and the Treaty shall immediately upon such deposit become effective as between the Power thus adhering and the other Powers parties hereto.

It shall be the duty of the Government of the United States to furnish each Government named in the Preamble and every Government subsequently adhering to this Treaty with a certified copy of the Treaty and of every instrument of ratification or adherence. It shall also be the duty of the Government of the United States telegraphically to notify such Governments immediately upon the deposit with it of each instrument of ratification or adherence.

IN FAITH WHEREOF the respective Plenipotentiaries have signed this Treaty in the French and English languages both texts having equal force, and hereunto affix their seals.

DONE at Paris, the twenty-seventh day of August in the year one thousand nine hundred and twenty-eight.

[For Germany:]
Gustav Stresemann

[For the United States:]
Frank B. Kellogg

[For the United Kingdom:]
Cushendun

[For the Dominion of Canada:]
W. L. Mackenzie King

[For the Commonwealth of Australia:]
A. J. McLachlan

[For the Dominion of New Zealand:]
C. J. Parr

[For the Union of South Africa:]
J. S. Smit

[For the Irish Free State:]
Liam T. MacCosgair

[For Belgium:]
Paul Hymans

[For France:]
Ari Briand

[For India:]
Cushendun

[For Italy:]
G. Manzoni

[For Japan:]
Uchida

[For Poland:]
August Zaleski

[For Czechoslovakia:]
Dr. Eduard Benes

Notes and Questions

1. *The Efficacy of International Law.* The Cession of Alaska and the Kellogg–Briand Pact make a nice contrast when discussing the efficacy of international law. It is easy to see how the 1867 Cession of Alaska "worked"—Russia ceded the Alaska Territory to the United States and the United States paid the Tsar $7,200,000 in gold. After the conclusion of the treaty, Russian officials left Alaska, U.S. officials arrived, and money changed hands. It is much more difficult to see how the 1928 Kellogg–Briand Pact "worked." What good were "solemn" renunciations of war, especially in light of the developments in world politics in the 1930's and 1940's: the participation of Germany and the Soviet Union in the Spanish Civil War, the invasion of Ethiopia by Italy, the invasion of Manchuria by Japan, the invasion of Czechoslovakia by Germany, the invasion of Poland by Germany and the Soviet Union, the invasion of the Baltic States and Finland by the Soviet Union, the invasion of France, the Netherlands, Belgium, Denmark, Norway, and the Soviet Union by Germany, the German attack on the United Kingdom, the Japanese invasion of China, Malaya, Indonesia, and the Philippines, and the Japanese attack on the United States? If the Treaty of Cession of Alaska shows treaties at their most efficacious, does not the Kellogg–Briand Pact show them at their least efficacious?

2. *"Hard" and "Soft" International Law.* Are both the Cession of Alaska and the Kellogg-Briand Pact the same sort of "international law"?

Some international lawyers distinguish between "hard" and "soft" international law, a distinction with at least two meanings. First, the distinction may refer to the difference between rules of law meant to be followed and norms meant merely to set out preferred outcomes. Are these two treaties examples of this distinction? Second, the distinction between "hard" and "soft" law may refer to the difference between formal sources of law (such as treaties) and instruments that are not formally legal sources (such as mutual declarations of government leaders issued at the end of a diplomatic conference). Such declarations may contain "non-binding" statements of principle. Can soft law of this second type have any legal significance?

Is it fair to conclude that the Kellogg–Briand Pact was only aspirational? If so, was it wrong then to try and execute individuals for the violation of its principles as was done at the Nuremberg trial of Nazi war criminals? See Chapter 6.

3. *Bilateral and Multilateral Treaties.* It is conceptually possible for issues addressed in a multilateral treaty such as the Kellogg–Briand Pact to be dealt with in a series of bilateral agreements. The Kellogg–Briand Pact was initiated when the French Foreign Minister, Aristide Briand, encouraged by some influential U.S. citizens, proposed that the United States and France conclude a bilateral treaty banning war as an instrument of national policy. The United States responded by proposing a multilateral treaty, and negotiations, leading to the Kellogg–Briand Pact, resulted. See E.H. Carr, *International Relations Between the Two World Wars 1919–1939*, at 117–20 (1947). Why was the Kellogg–Briand Pact drawn up as a multilateral treaty? Would the conclusion of a series of bilateral agreements have been too cumbersome? Was the subject matter of the Kellogg–Briand Pact also particularly appropriate for multilateral treatment? Is it more likely that the rules established in a multilateral treaty will pass into customary international law? Use of multilateral treaties increased significantly in the twentieth century.

4. *Entry Into Force.* Article III of the Kellogg–Briand Pact provides that it enters into force when all the negotiating states have accepted the treaty and deposited their instruments of ratification with the "depositary" (in this case, the United States government). A multilateral treaty may contain provisions making the treaty's entry into force subject to a variety of conditions. For example, the 1982 United Nations Convention on the Law of the Sea entered into force in November 1994 in accordance with its Article 308, which provides that the Convention "shall enter into force 12 months after the date of deposit of the sixtieth instrument of ratification or accession." Twenty-five states with merchant fleets comprising not less than 50 per cent of the world's gross tonnage had to accept the 1974 International Convention for the Safety of Life at Sea before it could enter into force. What factors influence decisions concerning the number or characteristics of accepting states necessary for a treaty's entry into force? Why should treaty negotiators sometimes seek a delay between the final necessary acceptance of a treaty and the date on which it formally enters into force? Article 24 of the Vienna Convention on the Law of Treaties contains the generally accepted rule concerning the entry into force of a treaty that contains no provision on the matter.

CORDELL HULL, THE MEMOIRS OF CORDELL HULL
Vol. 1, at 831–843 (1948).

New decisions confronted us in the summer of 1940 as Great Britain's plight on the high seas grew acute. Contrasted with the period before we entered the First World War, it was perilous. A quarter of a century before, Britain had the assistance of the French and Italian fleets in the Atlantic and Mediterranean, and of the Japanese fleet in the Pacific. Now the French fleet lay immobile, German submarines operated out of French ports, the Italian Navy was an enemy and the Japanese Navy a potential enemy. Britain's shipping losses were rising dangerously. If she were to survive, it was necessary for her not only to purchase huge quantities of war supplies in this country, but also to get them safely to the United Kingdom.

British Ambassador Lord Lothian came in to see me on August 4, the day before my departure for White Sulphur Springs, and expressed his Government's "urgent desire" to purchase from us a number of older type destroyers. Britain, he said, needed them to bridge over what he described as her "present emergency situation." * * *

When Lothian came to my office on August 4 I could appreciate Britain's dangers as fully as he could depict them. He said Britain had lost five destroyers during the previous week alone. Destroyers, he pointed out, were vitally important in combating submarine activities and other enemy action in the English Channel where large warships could not be used to advantage.

He said he had already discussed the question with the President while I was at Havana, and now desired to lay the situation before me in the hope that something might be done within the next few weeks. * * *

I also pointed out the legal difficulties in the way of our selling the destroyers. The United States Code forbade the departure of vessels from American waters outfitted for cruising against a foreign nation with which we were at peace. Also, the National Defense Act, approved June 28, 1940, forbade the sale of naval equipment without the approval of the Chief of Naval Operations, and military equipment without the approval of the Chief of Staff of the Army. * * *

During my three weeks rest at White Sulphur Springs I had a private telephone line into my apartment there and received daily pouches from the State Department, hence closely followed and participated in the destroyers-bases negotiations in the hands of the President and Welles. A few hours after I returned to Washington on August 23, I went to the White House to attend a Cabinet meeting. * * *

In talking over the bases with the President, I found he had an amazing personal knowledge of almost all of them. He had either cruised, swum, or fished in those harbors. He knew how many feet deep and wide they were and how many ships they would take.

He also knew the penurious condition of the native populations of most of the islands, and consequently did not want to assume the burden of administering those populations. Therefore he had changed, during my absence from Washington, from his original idea of outright purchase of the bases to that of 99–year leases. I had originally favored outright cession, but was willing to agree to leases instead. * * *

That evening [August 24] I met Lothian at the White House * * *. * * *

Lothian argued * * * that, if the transaction were treated as a bargain, Mr. Churchill did not feel that he could give us, in return for fifty "oldish destroyers," the right to get whatever air and naval bases in Newfoundland, Bermuda, the Bahamas, Jamaica, St. Lucia, Trinidad, and British Guiana we might choose to ask for, "because the British Government might incur the charge of defaulting on its share of the bargain if it created difficulties about any particular thing the United States Government wanted."

"I think," he said, "Mr. Churchill feels that British public opinion would not support a bargain of this kind if it was presented as a contract and that it would in practice lead to the most dangerous controversies between the United States and Great Britain. * * *."

In general, Lothian argued to the President and me that there should not be cold commercial bargaining but a friendly interest between the two Governments. This would afford a basis for gifts back and forth which would be voluntary and apparently without definite understanding in advance.

After Lothian had finished his arguments, I said for the third time to the Ambassador, and for the first time to the President, that the latter had no authority whatever to make a gift of public property to any Government or individual. Mr. Roosevelt at once agreed with me. I said, and he agreed, that a different arrangement would be necessary to achieve our objectives.

The President thereupon left it to me to work out a solution with Lothian.

The following morning I called to my office Green H. Hackworth, Legal Adviser of the State Department, whose advice was always invaluable to me, and Judge Townsend of the Department of Justice, to try to find a way out. After some discussion, Hackworth suddenly suggested that there might be a compromise after all between Churchill's desire for reciprocal gifts and our own legal position that the President could not give away the destroyers but had to get something in return.

Since the British had not stated precisely what bases they intended to lease to us, why not divide them into two parcels? The first would comprise the bases in Newfoundland and Bermuda. These Britain could lease us as an outright gift. The second would comprise the bases around the Caribbean, strategically more valuable to us because of their nearness to the Panama Canal. These could be leased to us in consideration of the cession of the 50 destroyers.

I saw at once that here was the formula for which we had been looking.

We thereupon set to work to redraft the proposals. Leaving Hackworth and Townsend to complete the drafting, I telephoned the President, told him Hackworth had offered a solution, and asked if I could send Hackworth to outline it to him. That afternoon Hackworth and Townsend saw the President, who agreed to the compromise. * * *

Lothian having cabled to London the location of the bases the President had in mind, Churchill agreed and himself added the island of Antigua, in the Caribbean, which he said might be useful as a base for flying boats.

That steaming night of August 27, Lothian, Knox, and Stark all appeared at my apartment at about ten-thirty. For more than an hour we four went over the draft I had given Stark. Lothian at first had a few suggestions for revision, but eventually seemed quite satisfied and said he would send the note to his Government.

The negotiations now remained in abeyance for two days, until Lothian could hear from his Government. On August 29 I handed the Ambassador an informal memorandum from myself to argue further our idea that the destroyers and bases should not be dealt with as outright gifts. * * *

That night at seven o'clock Lord Lothian called at my apartment and left with me his Government's counterproposal. I called Admirals Stark and Woodson and also Green Hackworth to my apartment, and we went over it carefully. We found that Lothian's draft differed in only a few details from my proposal, and added the island of Antigua, which was quite agreeable to us. We made a few changes in the text, and I then telephoned Lothian, who came back to my apartment at ten-thirty. He agreed to our changes.

The following day, August 30, I telephoned the changes to the President at Hyde Park and received his approval.

We drafted at the State Department a message for the President to send to Congress along with the exchange of notes between Lothian and myself. I sent all three documents to the President at Hyde Park on August 31. It was understood that the notes should be signed and exchanged on Monday September 2. The President gave his approval to the three documents, making only a slight change in the message, and handed them to me when I met him at the Union Station in Washington Sunday afternoon September 1.

The President also handed me a letter from himself, which said: "I have carefully read the note from the British Ambassador and your reply thereto as Secretary of State of the United States.

"I give my full and cordial approval to both of these notes." He signed his full name.

Lord Lothian, who had spent the week end in Boston, returned to Washington Monday afternoon, and came to my apartment at seven o'clock that evening. There we signed and exchanged the notes confirming the destroyers-bases transactions.

Lothian also handed me his reply to an *aide-mémoire* I had previously given him requesting assurances concerning the disposition of the British fleet. My *aide-mémoire* had referred to the June 4 speech of the Prime Minister in which he said that if the waters surrounding the British Isles became untenable for British warships, the British fleet would in no event be surrendered or sunk but would be sent overseas for the defense of other parts of the Empire. It then asked "whether the foregoing statement represents the settled policy of the British Government."

Lothian stated in his reply: "His Majesty's Ambassador is instructed by the Prime Minister to inform Mr. Secretary Hull that this statement certainly does represent the settled policy of His Majesty's Government. Mr. Churchill must however observe that these hypothetical contingencies seem more likely to concern the German fleet or what is left of it than the British fleet."

The last sentence was Churchill's own addition. The Prime Minister now agreed to having the exchange of *aides-mémoire* published on condition that the main notes regarding the bases and destroyers should be made public first.

The following morning, September 3, I sent to the White House the President's message to Congress, which he had signed and handed to me; the destroyers-bases notes, and an opinion of Attorney General Robert H. Jackson declaring the transaction legal. All these were for communication to Congress. * * *

Thus were concluded within a week negotiations among the most momentous in our history. As the President said in his message to Congress: "This is the most important action in the reinforcement of our national defense that has been taken since the Louisiana Purchase. Then as now, considerations of safety from overseas attack were fundamental."

Mention of the Louisiana Purchase was not without significance because it, too, had been made without authorization from Congress and, though the reaction to the destroyers-bases exchange throughout the nation was, in general, wholeheartedly favorable, some opponents objected that Congress should have given its approval.

We based our stand, however, on the necessity for defense. "Preparation for defense," said the President's message, "is an inalienable prerogative of a sovereign state. Under present circumstances this exercise of sovereign right is essential to the maintenance of our peace and safety."

The President pointed out that the exchange was not inconsistent in any sense with our status of peace. He put the value of the new bases to the Western Hemisphere as "beyond calculation." They were essential, he said, to the protection of the Panama Canal, Central America, the northern portion of South America, the Antilles, Canada, Mexico, and our Eastern and Gulf seaboards.

In conformity with the thought I had expressed to Lord Lothian when he first broached the subject of bases and destroyers with me on August 4—namely, that any bases we obtained in this hemisphere must be for the benefit of all the American Republics—I sent instructions on September 6 to our diplomatic missions in those countries. I requested them to notify those Governments that we had acquired leases to British bases not only for our own defense but also for more effective cooperation with the other American Republics in the common defense of the hemisphere. "The resulting facilities at these bases," I added, "will, of course, be made available alike to all American Republics on the fullest cooperative basis for the common defense of the hemisphere and in entire harmony with the spirit of the pronouncements made and the understandings reached at the conferences of Lima, Panama, and Havana."

A few international lawyers might have argued that we had violated the Hague Convention of 1907 in that we, a neutral, had sold warships to a belligerent. However, that convention started off with the proposition that "belligerents are bound to respect the sovereign rights of neutral Powers." Neutrals like Poland, Norway, Denmark, The Netherlands, Luxemburg, and Belgium, could testify that the principles of the Hague Convention had not protected them. The convention laid down rights and duties of neutrals and belligerents alike, and the Axis dictators, who had wrecked the convention and alone would have a motive for questioning our transaction, were estopped, by every rule of reason and law, from raising the question. It would be absurd to contend that the convention, which represented a compromise between rights and duties of belligerents on the one hand and neutrals on the other, should bind only the neutrals.

The destroyers-bases transaction went into effect with great speed. The destroyers, reconditioned and stocked with food and munitions, were turned over to Britain at once. Experts of both Governments met and agreed on the exact sites of the eight bases we had acquired, extending along four thousand miles of Atlantic seaboard.

To judge from the many cables I received from our diplomatic missions abroad in the days that followed, the effect of the destroyers-bases deal went far beyond the physical fact that Britain now had 50 more destroyers and we had eight more bases. It was a demonstration to the world that this Government believed that Britain had a real chance to hold fast against all Hitler's might. It showed that we were willing to go beyond ordinary methods and to find new means to aid the major democracy fighting Nazism.

THE HULL–LOTHIAN AGREEMENT (1940)

54 Stat. 2405, 12 Bevans 551.

The British Ambassador (Lothian) to the U.S. Secretary of State (Hull):

BRITISH EMBASSY
WASHINGTON, D.C.,
September 2nd, 1940

SIR,

I have the honour under instructions from His Majesty's Principal Secretary of State for Foreign Affairs to inform you that in view of the friendly and sympathetic interest of His Majesty's Government in the United Kingdom in the national security of the United States and their desire to strengthen the ability of the United States to cooperate effectively with the other nations of the Americas in the defence of the Western Hemisphere, His Majesty's Government will secure the grant to the Government of the United States, freely and without consideration, of the lease for immediate establishment and use of naval and air bases and facilities for entrance thereto and the operation and protection thereof, on the Avalon Peninsula and on the southern coast of Newfoundland, and on the east coast and on the Great Bay of Bermuda.

Furthermore, in view of the above and in view of the desire of the United States to acquire additional air and naval bases in the Caribbean and in British Guiana, and without endeavouring to place a monetary or commercial value upon the many tangible and intangible rights and properties involved, His Majesty's Government will make available to the United States for immediate establishment and use naval and air bases and facilities for entrance thereto and the operation and protection thereof, on the eastern side of the Bahamas, the southern coast of Jamaica, the western coast of St. Lucia, the west coast of Trinidad in the Gulf of Paria, in the island of Antigua and in British Guiana within fifty miles of Georgetown, in exchange for naval and military equipment and material which the United States Government will transfer to His Majesty's Government.

All the bases and facilities referred to in the preceding paragraphs will be leased to the United States for a period of ninety-nine years, free from all rent and charges other than such compensation to be mutually agreed on to be paid by the United States in order to compensate the owners of private property for loss by expropriation or damage arising out of the establishment of the bases and facilities in question.

His Majesty's Government, in the leases to be agreed upon, will grant to the United States for the period of the leases all the rights, power, and authority within the bases leased, and within the limits of the territorial waters and air spaces adjacent to or in the vicinity of such bases, necessary to provide access to and defence of such bases, and appropriate provisions for their control.

Without prejudice to the above-mentioned rights of the United States authorities and their jurisdiction within the leased areas, the adjustment and reconciliation between the jurisdiction of the authorities of the United States within these areas and the jurisdiction of the authorities of the territories in which these areas are situated, shall be determined by common agreement.

The exact location and bounds of the aforesaid bases, the necessary seaward, coast and anti-aircraft defences, the location of sufficient military garrisons, stores and other necessary auxiliary facilities shall be determined by common agreement.

His Majesty's Government are prepared to designate immediately experts to meet with experts of the United States for these purposes. Should these experts be unable to agree in any particular situation, except in the case of Newfoundland and Bermuda, the matter shall be settled by the Secretary of State of the United States and His Majesty's Secretary of State for Foreign Affairs.

I have the honour to be, with the highest consideration, Sir,

Your most obedient, humble servant,

LOTHIAN

The U.S. Secretary of State (Hull) to the British Ambassador (Lothian):

DEPARTMENT OF STATE
WASHINGTON
September 2, 1940

EXCELLENCY:

I have received your note of September 2, 1940, of which the text is as follows:

[Here the text of the preceding letter is quoted verbatim.]

I am directed by the President to reply to your note as follows:

The Government of the United States appreciates the declarations and the generous action of His Majesty's Government as contained in your communication which are destined to enhance the national security of the United States and greatly to strengthen its ability to cooperate effectively with the other nations of the Americas in the defense of the Western Hemisphere. It therefore gladly accepts the proposals.

The Government of the United States will immediately designate experts to meet with experts designated by His Majesty's Government to determine upon the exact location of the naval and air bases mentioned in your communication under acknowledgment.

In consideration of the declarations above quoted, the Government of the United States will immediately transfer to His Majesty's Government fifty United States Navy destroyers generally referred to as the twelve hundred-ton type.

Accept, Excellency, the renewed assurances of my highest consideration.

CORDELL HULL

Notes and Questions

1. *Bilateral v. Multilateral Treaty Negotiations.* Contrast the intimate bilateral negotiations leading up to the Hull–Lothian Agreement with the enormous multilateral context of some modern treaty-drafting conferences. The 1982 United Nations Convention on the Law of the Sea, for example, was the result of more than fifteen years of multilateral negotiation, first during 1968–1973 in Committees of the United Nations and then during 1974–1982 in the Third United Nations Conference on the Law of the Sea (UNCLOS III). Altogether, thousands of diplomats from more than 150 states met hundreds of times. The negotiating agenda was complex, encompassing virtually every issue relating to use of and control over the oceans and ocean resources. States with common initial negotiating positions on one issue often found themselves at odds concerning other issues. Excellent studies of the UNCLOS III negotiations are found in: Edward L. Miles, *Global Ocean Politics: The Decision Process at the Third United Nations Conference on the Law of the Sea, 1973–1982* (1998); Clyde Sanger, *Ordering the Oceans: The Making of the Law of the Sea* (1987); and William Wertenbaker, "The Law of the Sea," *The New Yorker,* Aug. 1, 1983, at 38 (Part I), Aug. 8, 1983, at 56 (Part II). More on the law of the sea is found in Chapter 11.

2. *Treaties as International Contracts or International Statutes.* Can it be said that the domestic legal analogy to the Hull–Lothian negotiations is the drafting of a contract while the municipal analogy to the U.N. Law of the Sea Conference is the meeting of a legislative assembly? Does that make some treaties rather like contracts and others more like statutes?

3. *Terminology.* The Hull–Lothian Agreement took the form of an exchange of notes between the British and U.S. governments. International agreements in fact have various designations:

> Among the terms used are: treaty, convention, agreement, protocol, covenant, charter, statute, act, declaration, *concordat*, exchange of notes, agreed minute, memorandum of agreement, memorandum of understanding, and *modus vivendi*. Whatever their designation, all agreements have the same legal status, except as their provisions or the circumstances of their conclusion indicate otherwise.

Restatement (Third) of the Foreign Relations Law of the United States § 301, Comment a (1987).

4. *Domestic Interests in Treaty Negotiations.* Note that the drafting of the Hull–Lothian Agreement involved the U.S. State Department, including

Secretary of State Hull and Legal Adviser Hackworth, the Justice Department, and President Roosevelt. At the U.N. Law of the Sea Conference, the U.S. delegation often numbered more than a hundred persons. This permitted various U.S. "interests" to be represented, including the Departments of State, Defense, Interior, Commerce, and Justice. Altogether some 20 U.S. government agencies participated in the U.S. Inter-agency Task Force that "coordinated" U.S. law of the sea negotiations. As Ann Hollick, a long-time commentator on U.S. law of the sea politics, has written, the U.S. delegation "was usually the scene of more intense negotiations than was UNCLOS itself," leading to important problems in making and executing U.S. policy, to "discontent and suspicion" among delegates from other countries, and to impatience in Congress. Ann L. Hollick, *U.S. Foreign Policy and the Law of the Sea* 35 (1981). Ultimately, the Reagan administration repudiated the core positions of the Nixon, Ford, and Carter administrations and refused to sign, much less to promote the ratification of, the 1982 Law of the Sea Convention. See Chapter 11.

    5. *The Legality of Executive Agreements in U.S. Law.* The Hull–Lothian Agreement was an "international executive agreement" (of which more in Chapter 4), but was it legal at U.S. law? Did the Hull–Lothian Agreement violate federal law prohibiting the departure, much less the sale, of warships to a combatant when the U.S. was a neutral in a war? Did it violate the 1907 Hague Convention on Rights and Duties of Neutral Powers in Naval War, 36 Stat. 2415, 1 Bevans 723, a multilateral treaty accepted by the United States that prohibited the supply of warships by a neutral country to a belligerent? If so, can an executive agreement "undo" a treaty approved by the Senate? Could the President legally make the Hull–Lothian Agreement without a two-thirds vote of the Senate expressing its advice and consent in accordance with Article II, § 2 of the U.S. Constitution? On the last point, Attorney General Jackson opined to President Roosevelt on August 27, 1940:

>   The President's power over foreign relations while "delicate, plenary and exclusive" is not unlimited. Some negotiations involve commitments as to the future which would carry an obligation to exercise powers vested in the Congress. Such Presidential arrangements are customarily submitted for ratification by a two-thirds vote of the Senate before the future legislative power of the country is committed. However, the acquisitions which you are proposing to accept are without express or implied promises on the part of the United States to be performed in the future. * * * The Executive Agreement obtains an opportunity to establish naval and air bases for the protection of our coastline but it imposes no obligation upon the Congress to appropriate money to improve the opportunity. It is not necessary for the Senate to ratify an opportunity that entails no obligation.

5 G.H. Hackworth, *Digest of International Law* 405–06 (1943). Is Jackson's statement persuasive? Do you think Cordell Hull was effectively kept out of some of the negotiations because it was feared he had a legalistic attitude? Critical views of the Hull–Lothian Agreement are to be found in Robert Shogan, *Hard Bargain* (1995), and in Aaron Xavier Fellmeth, "A Divorce Waiting to Happen: Franklin Roosevelt and the Law of Neutrality, 1935–1941," 3 *Buffalo Journal of International Law* 413 (1996–1997).

6. *Dualism*. How do the problems of the "legality" of the Hull–Lothian Agreement differ at U.S. and international law? Even if the Hull–Lothian Agreement were illegal in U.S. law, that illegality would not prevent the U.S. from still being bound in international law to honor its treaty obligation to the U.K. The International Court has ruled: "It is a generally accepted principle of international law that in the relations between powers who are contracting parties to a treaty, the provisions of municipal law cannot prevail over those in a treaty." Greco–Bulgarian Communities Case, 1930 P.C.I.J., Ser. B, No. 17, at 32. The principle is reaffirmed in Article 27 of the Vienna Convention on the Law of Treaties. That there are separate spheres of municipal and international law is sometimes referred to as "dualism." See Chapter 4.

C. THE LAW OF TREATIES

This Part introduces a detailed and complex area of international law, the law of treaties. The law of treaties plays roughly the same role in international law as the law of contracts plays in municipal law: it establishes rules about the making and interpretation of agreements, their observation, modification, and termination. Throughout this Part, we see that courts, both international and municipal, may have to grapple with law of treaty issues.

THE BELILOS CASE

European Court of Human Rights, Series A, No. 132, 10 *European Human Rights Reports* 466 (1988), 1988 WL 623982.

THE FACTS

I. *The circumstances of the case*

9. Mrs. Marlène Belilos, who is a Swiss citizen, lives in Lausanne and was a student there at the material time.

1. *The Lausanne Police Board*

10. In a report of 16 April 1981 the Lausanne police laid an information against her for having contravened the municipality's General Police Regulations by having taken part in a demonstration in the streets of the city on 4 April for which permission had not been sought in advance. The march had been organised by the *Lausanne bouge* ("Lausanne on the move") movement, which on the preceding days had distributed leaflets calling on people to join the demonstration, and some 60 or 70 people had taken part; they were requesting that the municipality should provide an autonomous youth centre.

At a sitting held on 29 May, the municipal Police Board, in the applicant's absence, imposed on her a fine of 200 Sfr. * * *

12. [During two hearings, Belilos denied participating in the demonstration and challenged the Police Board's legitimacy.] [T]he Police Board noted that its jurisdiction could not be disputed and it concluded that it had "satisfied itself in the course of its inquiries that the

defendant [had] indeed participated in the demonstration on 4 April 1981." Having regard to the fact, on the one hand, that Mrs. Belilos had not played an active rôle but, on the other hand, that this was not a first offence, the Board reduced the fine to 120 Sfr; it also ordered her to pay costs of 22 Sfr.

[Belilos unsuccessfully appealed to the Criminal Cassation Division of the Vaud Cantonal Court.]

3. *The Federal Court*

14. The applicant lodged a public-law appeal against this decision with the Federal Court. In her submission, Switzerland's interpretative declaration in respect of the Convention [see paragraph 38 below] did not mean that an administrative authority such as the Police Board was empowered to determine the merits of a criminal charge. Such a jurisdiction was conceivable only if judicial review were ultimately available. This was not so in the present case, however, as the Criminal Cassation Division of the Vaud Cantonal Court and the Federal Court had limited powers, which did not normally allow them to review questions of fact (on which the Police Board's findings were final), for example by examining witnesses. Furthermore, under section 12 of the Vaud Municipal Decisions Act the municipality could delegate its powers to a senior police official, who was an agent of the executive; that being so, the Police Board was acting as judge in its own cause.

15. On 2 November 1982, the Federal Court (1st Public–Law Division) delivered a judgment dismissing the appeal on the following grounds:

"2. The guarantee of a fair trial provided for in Article 6(1) ECHR [European Convention on Human Rights] lays down *inter alia* that 'everyone is entitled to a fair ... hearing ... by an independent and impartial tribunal established by law....'

(a) The sole issue raised by the appellant's complaint is whether Article 6 ECHR precludes proceedings whereby the facts are established by a body such as the Police Board, which is not an independent tribunal. * * *

(b) The scope of Article 6(1) ECHR must be examined in the light of Switzerland's interpretative declaration, according to which: 'the Swiss Federal Council considers that the guarantee of fair trial in Article 6(1) of the Convention, ... is intended solely to ensure ultimate control by the judiciary over the acts or decisions of the public authorities....' * * * [T]he guarantee of a fair trial must be assessed having regard to the entire procedure.

3. * * * [J]udicial review of * * * municipal decisions [concerning minor criminal offenses] is effected by the Cassation Division of the Cantonal Court, which may determine both whether the correct procedure has been followed * * * and whether the law has been properly applied * * *. It does not therefore have full competence to re-examine the facts. However, that is not necessary under

Article 6(1) ECHR provided that appeal lies to a judicial authority which not only reviews the correctness of the procedure—including 'whether there are serious doubts as to the facts found'—but may also be called upon to consider complaints of 'incorrect application of the law' and of 'misuse of discretion in the application of the law.' The Cantonal Court therefore enjoys a much more extensive power of review than the Federal Court in a public-law appeal, where jurisdiction is restricted to ensuring that a decision is not arbitrary, * * *. Moreover, where the Cantonal Cassation Division quashes a decision because there are serious doubts as to the facts found, it may request the municipal authority, to which it remits the case, to carry out additional investigative measures. * * *."

[Belilos applied to the European Commission on Human Rights on March 24, 1983. On May 7, 1986, the Commission unanimously found that there had been a breach of Article 6(1), and the case then proceeded to the European Court of Human Rights.]

JUDGMENT

I. *The Government's preliminary objection*

38.   By way of a preliminary objection, the Government argued that Mrs. Belilos's application was incompatible with the international undertakings entered into by Switzerland under Article 6(1) of the Convention. It relied on the interpretative declaration made when the instrument of ratification was deposited [in November 1974], which is worded as follows:

"The Swiss Federal Council considers that the guarantee of fair trial in Article 6(1) of the Convention, in the determination of civil rights and obligations or any criminal charge against the person in question is intended solely to ensure ultimate control by the judiciary over the acts or decisions of the public authorities relating to such rights or obligations or the determination of such a charge."

In its submission, the [European] Commission [on Human Rights] should have declined to exercise jurisdiction as the application related to a right that was not recognised by the Confederation.

39.   The Court will examine the nature of the declaration in issue and then, if appropriate, its validity for the purposes of Article 64 of the Convention, which reads as follows:

"1. Any State may, when signing the Convention or when depositing its instrument of ratification, make a reservation in respect of any particular provision of the Convention to the extent that any law then in force in its territory is not in conformity with the provision. Reservations of a general character shall not be permitted under this Article.

2. Any reservation made under this Article shall contain a brief statement of the law concerned."

A. *The nature of the declaration* * * *

41. The Commission * * * reached the conclusion that the declaration was a mere interpretative declaration which did not have the effect of a reservation; it based its view both on the wording of the declaration and on the preparatory work. The latter showed that Switzerland's intention had been to deal with the situation arising as a result of the Court's judgment of 16 July 1971 in the RINGEISEN case, *i.e.* in respect of administrative proceedings relating to civil rights[.]† [Switzerland] did not, on the other hand, provide any indication of how the declaration might be applied as a reservation in the case of criminal proceedings. More generally, the Commission considered that if a State made both reservations and interpretative declarations at the same time, the latter could only exceptionally be equated with the former.

42. In the Government's submission, on the other hand, the declaration was a "qualified" interpretative declaration. It consequently was in the nature of a reservation within the meaning of Article 2(1)(d) of the Vienna Convention on the Law of Treaties of 23 May 1969, which provides:

> " 'Reservation' means a unilateral statement, however phrased or named, made by a State, when signing, ratifying, accepting, approving or acceding to a treaty, whereby it purports to exclude or to modify the legal effect of certain provisions of the treaty in their application to that State."

43. The first of the considerations relied on by the Government was the purpose of the declaration. It claimed that it was to preserve proceedings which, while coming within the "civil" or "criminal" ambit of Article 6(1), initially took place before administrative authorities, in such a way that the court or courts to which appeal lay did not—or did not fully—review the facts. The declaration thus reflected the wish to respect the cantons' distinctive features, recognised in the Federal Constitution, with regard to procedure and the administration of justice. At the same time, the declaration was a "reaction" to the RINGEISEN judgment previously cited. * * *

47. The government derived an additional argument from the fact that there had been no reaction from the Secretary General of the Council of Europe or from the States Parties to the Convention.

The Secretary General had made no comment when he notified the Council of Europe member States of the reservations and interpretative declarations contained in Switzerland's instrument of ratification. Yet, so the Government maintained, it was open to him as the depositary, who had important prerogatives, to ask for clarifications and to make observations on the instruments he received, as he had shown in the case of the declaration made under Article 25 by the Turkish Government on 28 January 1987. As far as the reservations and interpretative declarations of Switzerland were concerned, it had, when they were in

---

† In the Ringeisen Case, 1 Eur. Human Rights Rep. 455, the European Court of Human Rights ruled that Article 6(1) of the European Convention on Human Rights applied to any proceeding in which private rights and obligations were at issue.—Eds.

the process of formulation, made extensive enquiries of the Council of Europe's Legal Affairs Directorate so as to ensure that there was no objection from the Secretary General.

As to the States Parties, they did not deem it necessary to ask Switzerland for explanations regarding the declaration in question and had therefore considered it acceptable as a reservation under Article 64 or under general international law. The Swiss Government inferred that it could in good faith take the declaration as having been tacitly accepted for the purposes of Article 64.

The Court does not agree with that analysis. The silence of the depositary and the Contracting States does not deprive the Convention institutions of the power to make their own assessment.

48. * * * Like the Commission and the Government, the Court recognises that it is necessary to ascertain the original intention of those who drafted the declaration. In its view, the documents show that Switzerland * * * has always been concerned to avoid the consequences which a broad view of the right of access to the courts—a view taken in the RINGEISEN judgment—would have for the system of public administration and of justice in the cantons and consequently to put forward the declaration as qualifying Switzerland's consent to be bound by the Convention.

49. The question whether a declaration described as "interpretative" must be regarded as a "reservation" is a difficult one, particularly—in the instant case—because the Swiss Government has made both "reservations" and "interpretative declarations" in the same instrument of ratification. More generally, the Court recognises the great importance, rightly emphasised by the Government, of the legal rules applicable to reservations and interpretative declarations made by States Parties to the Convention. Only reservations are mentioned in the Convention, but several States have also (or only) made interpretative declarations, without always making a clear distinction between the two.

In order to establish the legal character of such a declaration, one must look behind the title given to it and seek to determine the substantive content. In the present case, it appears that Switzerland meant to remove certain categories of proceedings from the ambit of Article 6(1) and to secure itself against an interpretation of that Article which it considered to be too broad. However, the Court must see to it that the obligations arising under the Convention are not subject to restrictions which would not satisfy the requirements of Article 64 as regards reservations. Accordingly, it will examine the validity of the interpretative declaration in question, as in the case of a reservation, in the context of this provision.

B. *The validity of the declaration * * ***

   2. *Compliance with Article 64 of the Convention*

   51. The Court must * * * ascertain whether the relevant declaration by Switzerland satisfied the requirements of Article 64 of the Convention.

   (a) Article 64(1)

   52. [The applicant] maintained that the declaration sought to remove all civil and criminal cases from the judiciary and transfer them to the executive, in disregard of a principle that was vital to any democratic society, namely the separation of powers. As "ultimate control by the judiciary" was a pretence if it did not cover the facts, such a system, she claimed, had the effect of excluding the guarantee of a fair trial, which was a cardinal rule of the Convention. Switzerland's declaration accordingly did not satisfy the basic requirements of Article 64, which expressly prohibited reservations of a general character and prohibited by implication those which were incompatible with the Convention.

   53. The Government * * * asserted Switzerland's declaration was not of a general character.

   It argued, in the first place, that it referred expressly to a specific provision of the Convention, paragraph 1 of Article 6 * * *.

   In the second place, it argued that it was worded in a way that made it possible to determine its scope clearly and that was sufficiently precise for other States Parties and for the Convention institutions. The Federal Council's intention had been to limit the extent of the guarantee of a fair trial, in particular in cases in which an administrative authority determined a criminal charge. It had in good faith chosen the expression "ultimate control by the judiciary" to denote a review of the cassation type, initiated by means of an application for a declaration of nullity (*pourvoi en nullité*) and confined to questions of law, *i.e.* examination of the propriety of the public authority's decision from the point of view of its conformity with the law. It had thus faithfully paraphrased—and extended to the criminal aspect of Article 6—the argument put forward by Mr. Fawcett on behalf of the Commission minority in the RINGEISEN case. It was, moreover, the Government continued, wrong to criticise the declaration—some 15 years after it had been made—for being general and vague, on the basis primarily of the case law subsequently developed by the Convention institutions * * *. * * *

   At the hearing before the Court the Government mentioned a third point: compatibility with the object and purpose of the Convention. It considered such compatibility to be beyond doubt in the instant case, as the declaration related only to a particular aspect—not the substance—of the right to a fair trial. * * *

   55. The Court [concludes:] By "reservation of a general character" in Article 64 is meant in particular a reservation couched in terms that are too vague or broad for it to be possible to determine their exact meaning and scope. While the preparatory work and the Government's explanations clearly show what the respondent State's concern was at

the time of ratification, they cannot obscure the objective reality of the actual wording of the declaration. The words "ultimate control by the judiciary over the acts or decisions of the public authorities relating to [civil] rights or obligations or the determination of [a criminal] charge" do not make it possible for the scope of the undertaking by Switzerland to be ascertained exactly, in particular as to which categories of dispute are included and as to whether or not the "ultimate control by the judiciary" takes in the facts of the case. They can therefore be interpreted in different ways, whereas Article 64(1) requires precision and clarity. In short, they fall foul of the rule that reservations must not be of a general character.

[The Court also finds that Switzerland's reservation did not comply with Article 64(2) since it did not contain "a brief statement of the law concerned."]

C. *Conclusion*

60.   In short, the declaration in question does not satisfy two of the requirements of Article 64 of the Convention, with the result that it must be held to be invalid. At the same time, it is beyond doubt that Switzerland is, and regards itself as, bound by the Convention irrespective of the validity of the declaration. Moreover, the Swiss Government recognised the Court's competence to determine the latter issue, which they argued before it. The Government's preliminary objection must therefore be rejected.

II.   *Alleged violation of Article 6(1)*

61.   The applicant claimed to be the victim of a violation of Article 6(1) of the Convention, which reads:

> "In the determination of his civil rights and obligations or of any criminal charge against him, everyone is entitled to a fair and public hearing within a reasonable time by an independent and impartial tribunal established by law. Judgment shall be pronounced publicly but the press and public may be excluded from all or part of the trial in the interests of morals, public order or national security in a democratic society, where the interests of juveniles or the protection of the private life of the parties so require, or to the extent strictly necessary in the opinion of the court in special circumstances where publicity would prejudice the interests of justice."

In her view, the Lausanne Police Board was not an "independent and impartial tribunal;" furthermore, neither the Criminal Cassation Division of the Vaud Cantonal Court nor the Federal Court had provided sufficiently extensive "ultimate control by the judiciary," as they were unable to reconsider the findings of fact which had been made by a purely administrative body, the Police Board.

62. The Court notes that those appearing before it did not dispute the applicability of Article 6(1) in the instant case, apart from the effect of Switzerland's interpretative declaration.

[The Court concludes that Switzerland violated Article 6(1).]

CONCURRING OPINION OF JUDGE DE MEYER * * *

The object and purpose of the European Convention on Human Rights is not to create, but to recognise, rights which must be respected and protected even in the absence of any instrument of positive law.

It is difficult to see how reservations can be accepted in respect of provisions recognising rights of this kind. It may even be thought that such reservations, and the provisions permitting them, are * * * null and void unless they relate only to arrangements for implementation, without impairing the actual substance of the rights in question.

This is the only spirit in which Article 64 of the Convention should be interpreted and applied; at most, that Article may allow a State to give itself, as a purely temporary measure, "at the time of" the signature or ratification of the Convention, a brief space in which to bring into line any laws "then in force in its territory" which do not yet sufficiently respect and protect the fundamental rights recognised in the Convention.

Notes and Questions

1. *The Source of the Law of Treaties.* What is the source of legal rules governing reservations, treaty interpretation, treaty termination, and other matters related to treaties? Note that Switzerland invoked the Vienna Convention on the Law of Treaties, even though that country was not a party to the Vienna Convention at the time of the *Belilos Case.* (Switzerland acceded to the Vienna Convention in 1990.) The Vienna Convention was drafted by the International Law Commission (a body of legal experts representing the various states) and adopted and opened for signature in 1969 by a diplomatic conference. Prior to the Vienna Convention, no treaty codified the law of treaties. After the Vienna Convention entered into force in 1980, it became binding as treaty law for those states that accepted it—90 states as of September 2000. According to the International Court of Justice in the *Gabcíkovo–Nagymaros Case*, which is excerpted later in this Part, many Vienna Convention rules are regarded as customary international law. We explore customary international law in Chapter 3.

2. *Reservations, Understandings, and Declarations.* Was the *Belilos* Court persuasive when it concluded that the Swiss declaration concerning Article 6(1) was, in effect, really a reservation? The distinction between reservations and "mere interpretative declarations" is significant, because only reservations may formally limit the scope of a state's acceptance of a treaty. Nevertheless, declarations and understandings suggest how a state, in its diplomatic practice, is likely to interpret articles or words in a treaty. Will a state's declarations and understandings also limit how its municipal courts interpret a treaty? In the United States, the Senate has attached

understandings and declarations to its advice and consent to the ratification of some treaties, and the question whether such understandings and declarations impermissibly encroach on the U.S. judiciary's power to interpret treaties is a controversial one. In Chapter 4, we explore how authority concerning treaties is allocated among various branches of the U.S. federal government, and between the federal and state governments.

3. *Reservations and the Binding Effect of Treaties.* Should not the silence of other states parties to the European Convention on Human Rights in the face of Switzerland's reservation to Article 6(1) suffice to validate the reservation? See paragraph 47 of the Court's opinion, and compare Article 20(5) of the Vienna Convention on the Law of Treaties. And once the Court found the reservation invalid, what should be the consequences? The effect of the Court's decision was that Switzerland's reservation was severed from its acceptance of the Convention. But why should Switzerland be legally bound by the European Convention at all, when its consent was conditioned on the reservation? In this regard, how significant is it that Switzerland is not merely a party to the European Convention, but also a party to litigation before an international court? How significant is it that the Convention is a human rights treaty, aiming to create a common European guarantee of certain individual rights? That at the time of the decision the European Convention had been in effect and the European Court of Human Rights had been operating with a significant caseload for several years? The *Belilos Case* represented a change in the practice of the European Commission of Human Rights and the European Court, which had previously accepted states' reservations at face value. See Susan Marks, "Reservations Unhinged: The *Belilos* Case Before the European Court of Human Rights," 39 *International and Comparative Law Quarterly* 300, 300–01 (1990). Other cases and related notes concerning the European Convention on Human Rights are to be found in Chapter 1 (*Golder*) and Chapter 6 (*Sunday Times* and *Soering*).

4. *The Aftermath of the* Belilos Case. In Switzerland, the European Court's decision in the *Belilos Case* had legal and political consequences. First, the decision led the canton of Vaud to change its legislation, requiring cases like that of Marlène Belilos to be brought before an ordinary court rather than the Police Board. Second, the Swiss Council of States debated and defeated a proposal to denounce the European Convention provisionally and to reissue a valid reservation. Third, however, the Council did reformulate its declaration regarding Article 6(1) of the European Convention. The new declaration differs from the one found invalid in *Belilos* (see paragraph 38 of the opinion) in that it: (1) deletes the former declaration's references to criminal cases, retaining only the references to civil rights and obligations; (2) defines "ultimate control by the judiciary" to mean "a control by the judiciary limited to the application of the law, such as a cassation control;" and (3) enumerates 7 federal and 523 cantonal statutes that are to be exempted from the application of Article 6(1) of the Convention. Luzius Wildhaber, "Parliamentary Participation in Treaty–Making, Report on Swiss Law," 67 *Chicago-Kent Law Review* 437, 456–57 (1991). Would the European Court regard the reformulated declaration as sufficient to shield Switzerland from a violation of Article 6(1) if Swiss procedures in a civil case differed from those required under that Article?

The European Court of Human Rights, for its part, has reaffirmed the approach it took towards the effect of invalid reservations in the *Belilos Case.* In Loizidou v. Turkey, 20 Eur. Human Rights Rep. 99 (1995), the Court examined the legality of Turkish reservations purporting to limit Turkey's acceptances of the competence of the European Commission and European Court to hear individual cases. The Court, noting "the special character of the Convention as an instrument of European public order (*'ordre public'*) for the protection of individual human beings," *id.* ¶ 93, ruled that Turkey's reservations were illegal, severed the invalid reservations, and found that Turkey's acceptances were valid without limitation.

5. *Reservations Not Expressly Authorized by Treaty.* Article 64 of the European Convention on Human Rights addresses the permissibility of reservations to that Convention. Should reservations be allowed if a treaty is silent on the issue? Articles 2(1)(d) and 19–21 of the Vienna Convention on the Law of Treaties follow the International Court of Justice's decision in the Reservations to the Genocide Convention Case, 1951 I.C.J. 15, 1951 WL 3, and accept reservations that are compatible with a treaty's object and purpose. Could application of the Vienna Convention rules mean that states parties to the same treaty may be bound by different obligations? That a state accepting a treaty but attaching a reservation to it may be a treaty party with some states that have accepted that treaty, but not with others that have accepted the same treaty? What justifies rules permitting such a confused state of affairs?

In the *Reservations to the Genocide Convention Case,* the United Nations General Assembly had asked the International Court of Justice, which is the principal judicial organ of the United Nations, for its advice concerning the legal effect of reservations to the multilateral Convention on the Prevention and Punishment of the Crime of Genocide. (See Chapter 5 for discussion of the Court and its advisory jurisdiction.) The majority noted that the "Convention was manifestly adopted for a purely humanitarian and civilizing purpose," and continued:

> The object and purpose of the Genocide Convention imply that it was the intention of the General Assembly and of the States which adopted it that as many States as possible should participate. The complete exclusion from the Convention of one or more States would not only restrict the scope of its application, but would detract from the authority of the moral and humanitarian principles which are its basis. It is inconceivable that the contracting parties readily contemplated that an objection to a minor reservation should produce such a result. But even less could the contracting parties have intended to sacrifice the very object of the Convention in favour of a vain desire to secure as many participants as possible. The object and purpose of the Convention thus limit both the freedom of making reservations and that of objecting to them. It follows that it is the compatibility of a reservation with the object and purpose of the Convention that must furnish the criterion for the attitude of a State in making the reservation on accession as well as for the appraisal by a State in objecting to the reservation. Such is the rule of conduct which must guide every State in the appraisal which it must make, individually and from its own standpoint, of the admissibility of any reservation. * * *

* * * As no State can be bound by a reservation to which it has not consented, it necessarily follows that each State objecting to it will or will not, on the basis of its individual appraisal within the limits of the criterion of the object and purpose stated above, consider the reserving State to be a party to the Convention.

Id. at 23–24, 26. Contrast the views of Judges Guerrero, Sir Arnold McNair, Read, and Hsu Mo, who dissented in the case:

We believe that the integrity of the terms of the Convention is of greater importance than mere universality in its acceptance. * * *

It is an undeniable fact that the tendency of all international activities in recent times has been towards the promotion of the common welfare of the international community with a corresponding restriction of the sovereign power of individual States. So, when a common effort is made to promote a great humanitarian object, as in the case of the Genocide Convention, every interested State naturally expects every other interested State not to seek any individual advantage or convenience, but to carry out the measures resolved upon by common accord. Hence, each party must be given the right to judge the acceptability of a reservation and to decide whether or not to exclude the reserving State from the Convention, and we are not aware of any case in which this right has been abused. It is therefore not universality at any price that forms the first consideration. It is rather the acceptance of common obligations—keeping step with like-minded States—in order to attain a high objective for all humanity, that is of paramount importance. Such being the case, the conclusion is irresistible that it is necessary to apply to the Genocide Convention with even greater exactitude than ever the existing rule which requires the consent of all parties to any reservation to a multilateral convention. In the interests of the international community, it would be better to lose as a party to the Convention a State which insists in face of objections on a modification of the terms of the Convention, than to permit it to become a party against the wish of a State or States which have irrevocably and unconditionally accepted all the obligations of the Convention.

Id. at 31, 46–47.

The majority and dissenting opinions in the *Reservations to the Genocide Convention Case* reflect differing views about the contractual nature of treaties. The majority decision presumes that states have a great deal of discretion to bind themselves or not to the provisions of international agreements. The dissenting opinion takes, if you will, a more statutory approach towards treaties, paying rather more attention to the will of the international community. In a multilateral treaty with a significant moral mission, should community sentiment play a larger role than in a more transactional bilateral agreement, say the Cession of Alaska?

6. *Effects on Treaty Negotiations.* How do the rules in Articles 19–21 of the Vienna Convention on the Law of Treaties affect the conduct of multilateral treaty negotiations? Some multilateral treaties—for example, the 1982 U.N. Convention on the Law of the Sea, which addresses a wide range of oceans issues—expressly prohibit reservations. Why do some multilateral treaties permit reservations, while other treaties prohibit them?

EASTERN AIRLINES, INC. v. FLOYD

499 U.S. 530, 111 S.Ct. 1489, 113 L.Ed.2d 569 (1991).

JUSTICE MARSHALL delivered the opinion of the Court.

Article 17 of the Warsaw Convention[1] sets forth conditions under which an international air carrier can be held liable for injuries to passengers. This case presents the question whether Article 17 allows recovery for mental or psychic injuries unaccompanied by physical injury or physical manifestation of injury.

I

On May 5, 1983, an Eastern Airlines flight departed from Miami, bound for the Bahamas. Shortly after takeoff, one of the plane's three jet engines lost oil pressure. The flight crew shut down the failing engine and turned the plane around to return to Miami. Soon thereafter, the second and third engines failed due to loss of oil pressure. The plane began losing altitude rapidly, and the passengers were informed that the plane would be ditched in the Atlantic Ocean. Fortunately, after a period of descending flight without power, the crew managed to restart an engine and land the plane safely at Miami International Airport.

Respondents, a group of passengers on the flight, brought separate complaints against petitioner, Eastern Airlines, Inc. (Eastern), each claiming damages solely for mental distress arising out of the incident. The District Court entertained each complaint in a consolidated proceeding. Eastern conceded that the engine failure and subsequent preparations for ditching the plane amounted to an "accident" under Article 17 of the Convention but argued that Article 17 also makes physical injury a condition of liability. * * * The District Court concluded that mental anguish alone is not compensable under Article 17.

The Court of Appeals for the Eleventh Circuit reversed, holding that the phrase "lésion corporelle" in the authentic French text of Article 17 encompasses purely emotional distress. To support its conclusion, the court examined the French legal meaning of the term "lésion corporelle," the concurrent and subsequent history of the Convention, and cases interpreting Article 17. We granted certiorari [and] now hold that Article 17 does not allow recovery for purely mental injuries.

II

"When interpreting a treaty, we 'begin "with the text of the treaty and the context in which the written words are used."'" *Volkswagenwerk Aktiengesellschaft v. Schlunk*, 486 U.S. 694, 699 (1988), quoting *Société Nationale Industrielle Aérospatiale v. United States District Court*, 482 U.S. 522, 534 (1987), quoting *Air France v. Saks*, 470 U.S.

---

1. Convention for the Unification of Certain Rules Relating to International Transportation by Air, Oct. 12, 1929, 49 Stat. 3000, T.S. No. 876 (1934), note following 49 U.S.C. App. § 1502 (hereinafter Warsaw Convention or Convention).

392, 397 (1985). "Other general rules of construction may be brought to bear on difficult or ambiguous passages." *Volkswagenwerk, supra,* at 700. Moreover, " 'treaties are construed more liberally than private agreements, and to ascertain their meaning we may look beyond the written words to the history of the treaty, the negotiations, and the practical construction adopted by the parties.' " *Saks, supra,* at 396, quoting *Choctaw Nation of Indians v. United States,* 318 U.S. 423, 431–432 (1943). We proceed to apply these methods in turn.

A

Because the only authentic text of the Warsaw Convention is in French, the French text must guide our analysis. See *Saks, supra,* at 397–399. The text reads as follows:

> "Le transporteur est responsable du dommage survenu *en cas de mort, de blessure ou de toute autre lésion corporelle* subie par un voyageur lorsque l'accident qui a causé le dommage s'est produit à bord de l'aéronef ou au cours de toutes opérations d'embarquement et de débarquement." 49 Stat. 3005 (emphasis added).

The American translation of this text, employed by the Senate when it ratified the Convention in 1934, reads:

> "The carrier shall be liable for damage sustained *in the event of the death or wounding of a passenger or any other bodily injury* suffered by a passenger, if the accident which caused the damage so sustained took place on board the aircraft or in the course of any of the operations of embarking or disembarking." 49 Stat. 3018 (emphasis added).

Thus, under Article 17, an air carrier is liable for passenger injury only when three conditions are satisfied: (1) there has been an accident, in which (2) the passenger suffered "mort," "blessure," "ou ... toute autre lésion corporelle," and (3) the accident took place on board the aircraft or in the course of operations of embarking or disembarking. As petitioner concedes, the incident here took place on board the aircraft and was an "accident" for purposes of Article 17. Moreover, respondents concede that they suffered neither "mort" nor "blessure" from the mishap. Therefore, the narrow issue presented here is whether, under the proper interpretation of "lésion corporelle," condition (2) is satisfied when a passenger has suffered only a mental or psychic injury.

We must consider the "French legal meaning" of "lésion corporelle" for guidance as to the shared expectations of the parties to the Convention because the Convention was drafted in French by continental jurists. Perhaps the simplest method of determining the meaning of a phrase appearing in a foreign legal text would be to consult a bilingual dictionary. Such dictionaries suggest that a proper translation of "lésion corporelle" is "bodily injury." See, *e.g.,* J. Jéraute, Vocabulaire Français–Anglais et Anglais–Français de Termes et Locutions Juridiques 205 (1953) (translating "bodily harm" or "bodily injury" as "lésion ou blessure corporelle"); see also *id.,* at 95 (translating the term "lésion" as "injury, damage, prejudice, wrong"), *id.* at 41 (giving as one sense of "corporel" the English word "bodily"), 3 Grand Larousse de la Langue Française 1833 (1987) (defining "lésion" as a "[m]odification de la structure d'un tissu vivant sous l'influence d'une cause morbide"). These translations, if correct, clearly suggest that Article 17 does *not* permit recovery for purely psychic injuries. [However,] we recognize that dictionary definitions may be too general for purposes of treaty interpretation. Our concerns are partly allayed when, as here, the dictionary translation accords with the wording used in the "two main translations of the 1929 Convention in English" [*i.e.*, the U.S. and British translations]. We turn, then, to French legal materials to determine whether French jurists' contemporary understanding of the term "lésion corporelle" differed from its translated meaning.

In 1929, as in the present day, lawyers trained in French civil law would rely on the following principal sources of French law: (1) legislation, (2) judicial decisions, and (3) scholarly writing. See generally 1 M. Planiol & G. Ripert, Traité élémentaire de droit civil, pt. 1, Nos. 10, 122, 127 (12th ed. 1939) (Louisiana State Law Inst. trans. 1959); F. Geny, Methode d'Interpretation et Sources en Droit Prive Positif Nos. 45–50 (2d ed. 1954) (Louisiana State Law Inst. trans. 1963); R. David, French Law: Its Structure, Sources, and Methodology 154 (M. Kindred trans. 1972). Our review of these materials indicates neither that "lésion corporelle" was a widely used legal term in French law nor that the term specifically encompassed psychic injuries.

Turning first to legislation, we find no French legislative provisions in force in 1929 that contained the phrase "lésion corporelle." * * *

Turning next to cases, we likewise discover no French court decisions in or before 1929 that explain the phrase "lésion corporelle," nor do the parties direct us to any. * * *

Turning finally to French treatises and scholarly writing covering the period leading up to the Warsaw Convention, we find no materials (and the parties have brought none to our attention) indicating that "lésion corporelle" embraced psychic injury. Subsequent to the adoption of the Warsaw Convention, some scholars have argued that "lésion corporelle" as used in Article 17 should be interpreted to encompass such injury. See, *e.g.*, Mankiewicz[, The Liability Regime of the International Air Carrier] 146 [(1981) (hereinafter Mankiewicz)] (arguing that "in French law the expression *lésion corporelle* covers any 'personal' injury whatsoever"); G. Miller, Liability in International Air Transport 128 (1977) (hereinafter Miller) (arguing that "a liberal interpretation of [Article 17] would be more in line with the spirit of the Convention"). These scholars draw on the fact that, by 1929, France—unlike many other countries—permitted tort recovery for mental distress. However, this *general* proposition of French tort law does not demonstrate that the *specific* phrase chosen by the contracting parties—"lésion corporelle"—covers purely psychic injury.

We find it noteworthy, moreover, that scholars who read "lésion corporelle" as encompassing psychic injury do not base their argument on explanations of this term in French cases or French treatises or even in the French Civil Code; rather, they chiefly rely on the principle of French tort law that any damage can "give rise to reparation when it is real and has been verified." 2 Planiol & Ripert, *supra*, at pt. 1, No. 868. We do not dispute this principle of French law. However, * * * since our task is to "give the specific words of the treaty a meaning consistent with the shared expectations of the contracting parties," *Saks, supra*, at 399, we find it unlikely that those parties' apparent understanding of the term "lésion corporelle" as "bodily injury" would have been displaced by a meaning abstracted from the French law of damages. Particularly is this so when the cause of action for psychic injury that evidently was possible under French law in 1929 would not have been recognized in many other countries represented at the Warsaw Convention.

Nor is this conclusion altered by our examination of Article 17's structure. In the decision below, the Court of Appeals found that the Article's wording "suggests that the drafters did not intend to exclude any particular category of damages," because if they had intended "to refer only to injury caused by physical impact," they "would not have singled out and specifically referred to a particular case of physical impact such as *blessure* ('wounding')." This argument, which has much the same force as the surplusage canon of domestic statutory construction, is plausible. Yet one might draw a contrary inference from the same language. * * * [O]ne meaning of "lésion" is a change in the structure of an organ due to injury or disease. If "blessure" refers to injuries causing visible ruptures in the body (a common meaning of a "wounding"), "lésion corporelle" might well refer to a more general category of physical injuries that includes internal injuries caused, for example, by physical impact, smoke or exhaust inhalation, or oxygen deprivation. Admittedly, this inference still runs afoul of the Court of Appeals' surplusage argument. However, because none of the other sources of French legal meaning noted above support the Court of Appeals' construction, we are reluctant to give this argument dispositive weight. The same structural argument offered by the Court of Appeals was advanced by one of the German delegates to the Warsaw Convention. See *Palagonia v. Trans World Airlines*, 110 Misc. 2d 478, 483, 442 N.Y.S.2d 670, 673–674 (Sup. 1978) (quoting testimony of Otto Riese). Accordingly, the official German translation of "lésion corporelle" adopted by Austria, Germany, and Switzerland uses German terms whose closest English translation is apparently "infringement on the health." See Mankiewicz 146. We are reluctant, however, to place much weight on an English translation of a German translation of a French text, particularly when we have been unable to find (and the parties have not cited) any German, Austrian, or Swiss cases adhering to the broad interpretation of Article 17 that the German delegate evidently espoused. In sum, neither the Warsaw Convention itself nor any of the applicable French legal sources demonstrates that "lésion corporelle" should be translated other than as "bodily injury"—a narrow meaning excluding purely mental injuries. However, because a broader interpretation of "lésion corporelle" reaching purely mental injuries is plausible, and the term is both ambiguous and difficult, we turn to additional aids to construction.

B

Translating "lésion corporelle" as "bodily injury" is consistent, we think, with the negotiating history of the Convention. "The treaty that became the Warsaw Convention was first drafted at an international conference in Paris in 1925." *Air France v. Saks*, 47 U.S. at 401. See generally [1925 Paris] Conférence Internationale de Droit Privé Aérien (1936) (hereinafter Paris Conference). The final protocol of the Paris Conference contained an article specifying that: " 'The carrier is liable for accidents, losses, breakdowns, and delays. It is not liable if it can prove that it has taken reasonable measures designed to pre-empt damage....' " It appears that "this expansive provision, broadly holding carriers liable in the event of an accident, would almost certainly have permitted recovery for all types of injuries, including emotional distress." Sisk, Recovery for Emotional Distress Under the Warsaw Convention: The Elusive Search for the French Legal Meaning of *Lésion Corporelle*, 25 Texas Int'l L.J. 127, 142 (1990), citing Miller 124.

The Paris Conference appointed a committee of experts, the Comité International Technique d'Experts Juridiques Aeriens (CITEJA), to revise its final protocol for presentation to the Warsaw Conference. The CITEJA draft split the liability article of the Paris Conference's protocol into three provisions with one addressing damages for injury to passengers, the second addressing injury to goods, and the third addressing losses caused by delay. The CITEJA subsection on injury to passengers introduced the phrase "en cas de mort, de blessure ou de toute autre lésion corporelle." This language was retained in Article 17 ultimately adopted by the Warsaw Conference. Although there is no definitive evidence explaining why the CITEJA drafters chose this narrower language, we believe it is reasonable to infer that the Conference adopted the narrower language to limit the types of recoverable injuries.[9]

Our review of the documentary record for the Warsaw Conference confirms—and courts and commentators appear universally to agree—that there is no evidence that the drafters or signatories of the Warsaw

---

9. Courts and commentators, including the Court of Appeals, have cited the doctoral thesis of a French scholar, Yvonne Blanc–Dannery, as extrinsic evidence of the Warsaw parties' intent. According to Mankiewicz, the Blanc–Dannery thesis was written under the supervision of Georges Ripert. Georges Ripert was a leading French delegate at the Warsaw Convention and an expert of the French Government at the CITEJA proceedings. Mankiewicz translates a passage from the Blanc–Dannery thesis as follows: " 'The use of the expression *lésion* after the words "death" and "wounding" encompasses and contemplates cases of traumatism and nervous troubles, the consequences of which do not immediately become manifest in the organism but which can be related to the accident.' " * * * Even if Mankiewicz's translation is accurate, * * * Blanc–Dannery's asserted definition is not supported by evidence from the CITEJA or Warsaw proceedings. In the absence of such support we find the Blanc–Dannery thesis to have little or no value as evidence of the drafters' intent.

Convention specifically considered liability for psychic injury or the meaning of "lésion corporelle." Two explanations commonly are offered for why the subject of mental injuries never arose during the Convention proceedings: (1) many jurisdictions did not recognize recovery for mental injury at that time, or (2) the drafters simply could not contemplate a psychic injury unaccompanied by a physical injury. Indeed, the unavailability of compensation for purely psychic injury in many common and civil law countries at the time of the Warsaw Conference persuades us that the signatories had no specific intent to include such a remedy in the Convention. [The Court surveys the status of recovery for mental distress in France, the United Kingdom, U.S. jurisdictions, the Netherlands, Germany, Switzerland, and the Soviet Union.] Because such a remedy was unknown in many, if not most, jurisdictions in 1929, the drafters most likely would have felt compelled to make an unequivocal reference to purely mental injury if they had specifically intended to allow such recovery.

In this sense, we find it significant that, when the parties to a different international transport treaty wanted to make it clear that rail passengers could recover for purely psychic harms, the drafters made a specific modification to this effect. The liability provision of the Berne Convention on International Rail, drafted in 1952, originally conditioned liability on "la mort, les blessures et toute autre atteinte, à l'intégrité corporelle." International Convention Concerning the Carriage of Passengers and Luggage By Rail, Berne, Oct. 25, 1952, 242 U.N.T.S. 355, Article 28, p. 390. The drafters subsequently modified this provision to read "l'intégrité physique *ou mentale.*" See Additional Convention to the International Convention Concerning the Carriage of Passengers and Luggage by Rail (CIV) of Feb. 25, 1961, Relating to the Liability of the Railway for Death of and Personal Injury to Passengers, done Feb. 26, 1966, Art. 2, reprinted in Transport: International Transport Treaties V–52 (Kluwer Publishers) (Supp. 1–10, Jan. 1986) (emphasis added).

The narrower reading of "lésion corporelle" also is consistent with the primary purpose of the contracting parties to the Convention: limiting the liability of air carriers in order to foster the growth of the fledgling commercial aviation industry. Indeed, it was for this reason that the Warsaw delegates imposed a maximum recovery of $8,300 for an accident—a low amount even by 1929 standards. Whatever may be the current view among Convention signatories, in 1929 the parties were more concerned with protecting air carriers and fostering a new industry than providing full recovery to injured passengers, and we read "lésion corporelle" in a way that respects that legislative choice.

C

We also conclude that, on balance, the evidence of the post–1929 "conduct" and "interpretations of the signatories," supports the narrow translation of "lésion corporelle."

In the years following adoption of the Convention, some scholars questioned whether Article 17 extended to mental or emotional injury. See, *e.g.*, Beaumont, Need for Revision and Amplification of the Warsaw Convention, 16 J. Air L. & Com. 395, 402 (1949); R. Coquoz, Le Droit Privé International Aérien 122 (1938); Sullivan, The Codification of Air Carrier Liability by International Convention, 7 J. Air. L. 1, 19 (1936). In 1951, a committee composed of 20 Warsaw Convention signatories met in Madrid and adopted a proposal to substitute "affection corporelle" for "lésion corporelle" in Article 17. The French delegate to the committee proposed this substitution because, in his view, the word "lésion" was too narrow, in that it "presupposed a rupture in the tissue, or a dissolution of continuity" which might not cover an injury such as mental illness or lung congestion caused by a breakdown in the heating apparatus of the aircraft. The United States delegate opposed this change if it "implied the inclusion of mental injury or emotional disturbances or upsets which were not connected with or the result of bodily injury," but the committee adopted it nonetheless. Although the committee's proposed amendment was never subsequently implemented, its discussion and vote in Madrid suggest that, in the view of the 20 signatories on the committee, "lésion corporelle" in Article 17 had a distinctly physical scope.

In finding that the signatories' post–1929 conduct supports the broader interpretation of "lésion corporelle," the Court of Appeals relied on three international agreements: The Hague Protocol of 1955, The Montreal Agreement of 1966, and the Guatemala City Protocol of 1971. For each of these agreements, the Court of Appeals emphasized that English translations rendered "lésion corporelle" as "personal injury," instead of "bodily injury." In our view, none of these agreements support the broad interpretation of "lésion corporelle" reached by the Court of Appeals. * * *

We must also consult the opinions of our sister signatories in searching for the meaning of a "lésion corporelle." *See Saks*, 470 U.S., at 404. The only apparent judicial decision from a sister signatory addressing recovery for purely mental injuries under Article 17 is that of the Supreme Court of Israel. That court held that Article 17 does allow recovery for purely psychic injuries. See *Cie Air France* v. *Teichner*, 39 Revue Française de Droit Aérien, at 243, 23 Eur. Tr. L., at 102.

Teichner arose from the hijacking in 1976 of an Air France flight to Entebbe, Uganda. Passengers sought compensation for psychic injuries caused by the ordeal of the hijacking and detention at the Entebbe Airport. While acknowledging that the negotiating history of the Warsaw Convention was silent as to the availability of such compensation, the court determined that "desirable jurisprudential policy" ("la politique jurisprudentielle souhaitable") favored an expansive reading of Article 17 to reach purely psychic injuries. In reaching this conclusion, the court emphasized the post–1929 development of the aviation industry and the evolution of Anglo–American and Israeli law to allow recovery for psychic injury in certain circumstances. In addition, the court followed the view of Miller that this expansive construction was desirable to avoid an apparent conflict between the French and English versions of the Guatemala City Protocol.

Although we recognize the deference owed to the Israeli court's interpretation of Article 17, we are not persuaded by that court's reasoning. Even if we were to agree that allowing recovery for purely psychic injury is desirable as a policy goal, we cannot give effect to such policy without convincing evidence that the signatories' intent with respect to Article 17 would allow such recovery. As discussed, neither the language, negotiating history, nor postenactment interpretations of Article 17 clearly evidences such intent. Nor does the Guatemala City Protocol support the Israeli court's conclusion because nothing in the Protocol purports to amend Article 17 to reach mental injuries. Moreover, although the Protocol reflects a liberalization of attitudes toward passenger recovery in that it provides for strict liability, see Article IV, the fact that the Guatemala City Protocol is still not in effect after almost 20 years since it was drafted should caution *against* attaching significance to it.

Moreover, we believe our construction of Article 17 better accords with the Warsaw Convention's stated purpose of achieving uniformity of rules governing claims arising from international air transportation. * * * [T]he Montreal Agreement subjects international carriers to strict liability for Article 17 injuries sustained on flights connected with the United States. Recovery for mental distress traditionally has been subject to a high degree of proof, both in this country and others. We have no doubt that subjecting international air carriers to *strict* liability for purely mental distress would be controversial for most signatory countries. Our construction avoids this potential source of divergence.

III

We conclude that an air carrier cannot be held liable under Article 17 when an accident has not caused a passenger to suffer death, physical injury, or physical manifestation of injury. * * *

Eastern urges us to hold that the Warsaw Convention provides the exclusive cause of action for injuries sustained during international air transportation. The Court of Appeals did not address this question, and we did not grant certiorari to consider it. We therefore decline to reach it here.

The judgment of the Court of Appeals is reversed.

Notes and Questions

1. *The Warsaw Convention.* Issues arising under the 1929 Warsaw Convention and subsequent protocols have frequently been litigated in municipal courts. One general goal of the Convention was, as the *Floyd* Court stated, to "achiev[e] uniformity of rules governing claims arising from international air transportation," especially with respect to claims for per-

sonal injuries arising out of accidents, for damaged or lost baggage, and for damages caused by flight delays. Another goal was to balance the interests of passengers seeking recovery with airlines' interests in limiting their liability, which resulted in caps on damages. For background, see Andreas F. Lowenfeld & Allan I. Mendelsohn, "The United States and the Warsaw Convention," 80 *Harvard Law Review* 497 (1967).

2. *Lack of Uniformity in Treaty Interpretation.* Why might different municipal courts reach different results in similar cases involving the same treaty, and how significant are the risks that they will do so? First, different courts could use different methods of treaty interpretation, as the U.S. and Israeli Supreme Courts did in *Floyd* and *Teichner* when interpreting Article 17 of the Warsaw Convention. Second, a court might find that a treaty provision implicitly refers to its own municipal law. See Zicherman v. Korean Air Lines Co., Ltd., 516 U.S. 217, 116 S.Ct. 629, 133 L.Ed.2d 596 (1996) (concluding that the term *"dommage"* in the French text of Article 17 of the Warsaw Convention means "legally cognizable harm," but that "Article 17 leaves it to adjudicating courts to specify what harm is cognizable"). Third, a municipal court might not view the treaty rule as controlling, in light of competing rules of domestic law. In El Al Israel Airlines, Ltd. v. Tseng, 525 U.S. 155, 119 S.Ct. 662, 142 L.Ed.2d 576 (1999), the plaintiff argued that she had a cause of action under New York state law for assault and false imprisonment when she was searched for explosives at Kennedy Airport before boarding an international flight. The Supreme Court, answering the question left open at the end of *Floyd*, concluded that Article 17 of the Warsaw Convention provided the exclusive basis for liability, preempting state law claims. (More on the relationship between treaties and U.S. state law appears in Chapter 4.)

Are the risks of nonuniform interpretation unavoidable? Consider especially the possibility that different courts will use different treaty interpretation methods. How could this risk be minimized? Should an international tribunal have exclusive jurisdiction to hear Warsaw Convention cases, or to hear appeals or references from national courts? Should a municipal court more or less automatically defer to previous interpretations of a treaty article made by foreign courts? Can treaty negotiators themselves provide for more uniform interpretations by national courts? The drafters of the Warsaw Convention eliminated one possible source of ambiguity by providing that only the French text was "authentic."

3. *Treaty Interpretation and the Vienna Convention on the Law of Treaties.* The *Floyd* Court did not cite Articles 31–32 of the Vienna Convention on the Law of Treaties, which set out rules governing treaty interpretation. Did the Court nonetheless follow the approach of the Vienna Convention? Should it? Other U.S. courts and the U.S. State Department have invoked these rules. See Maria Frankowska, "The Vienna Convention on the Law of Treaties Before United States Courts," 28 *Virginia Journal of International Law* 287, 299, 326–52 (1988).

4. *The Textual Approach to Treaty Interpretation.* Some courts have considered the text of a treaty as essentially the first and last stop in treaty interpretation. In Ludecke v. Canadian Pacific Airlines, Ltd., 98 D.L.R.3d 52 (1979), the Canadian Supreme Court construed Article 3(2) of the Warsaw

Convention. The Article provides that "if the carrier accepts a passenger without a passenger ticket having been delivered," the carrier may not avail itself "of those provisions of this Convention which exclude or limit the liability." In *Ludecke*, the plaintiff sought damages, above the low Convention cap, resulting from the death of her husband, a passenger on board a Canadian Pacific flight that had crashed en route to Tokyo. The husband had been issued a ticket referring to Warsaw Convention limits on liability in 4–1/2 point type. Plaintiff cited U.S. cases providing that delivery of a ticket containing illegible statements "amounts to no delivery." The *Ludecke* court denied plaintiff recovery. Although the judge suggested that the Convention's limitations on carrier liability may have been "harsh and unreasonable," he concluded that the text of Article 3(2) was "plain and can admit of no misunderstanding. * * * It is clear that the carrier delivered a ticket and thus preserved its right to the limitation." *Id.* at 57–58. In Chan v. Korean Air Lines, 490 U.S. 122, 109 S.Ct. 1676, 104 L.Ed.2d 113 (1989), the U.S. Supreme Court cited *Ludecke* with approval, adopting a textual approach in interpreting Article 3 and rejecting recourse to the *travaux préparatiores* where "the result the text produces is not necessarily absurd." *Id.* at 134, 109 S.Ct. at 1683, 104 L.Ed.2d at 126.

5. *Comparing Statutory Interpretation and Treaty Interpretation.* Should treaty interpretation methodology differ from statutory interpretation? How do a treaty's *travaux préparatoires* differ from a statute's legislative history? See David J. Bederman, "Revivalist Canons and Treaty Interpretation," 41 *UCLA Law Review* 953 (1994). Professor Bederman has compared how ambiguities in U.S. statutes and treaties may be cured:

> Despite all the debate regarding the allocation of interpretative power between Congress and the courts over statutes, all agree that, provided a statute is at least constitutional, Congress always has the last word in construction. Congress can and does fix its drafting mistakes after being prompted by the courts. * * *

> With treaties, however, there is no convenient way to cure defects in construction. Treaties have dual status in both international and domestic law. An American court could adopt an interpretation at variance with our treaty partners, but that new construction would have no force on the international plane. In such a situation, the United States could well be in default of its international obligations. To reconcile the internal and international meanings of a treaty, the United States government would be forced to renegotiate the agreement. Because any process of negotiation is consensual, there is no guarantee that a reconciliation could occur.

Id. at 1023–24.

6. *Subsequent Practice and Treaty Modification.* Note the reliance in the *Floyd Case* on subsequent practice, a factor also referred to in Article 31(3)(b) of the Vienna Convention on the Law of Treaties. Whose practice should count: that of airlines? Of officials in government foreign affairs offices? Of administrative agencies? Of municipal courts? Should consistent practice of a few, or many, or all treaty parties be required to provide credible evidence of changes in treaty interpretation? Compare subsequent practice as a factor guiding treaty interpretation with a formal modification

of a treaty, which some parties to a multilateral treaty may make by agreement. See Article 41 of the Vienna Convention.

7. *Amendments.* How else can treaties change? States parties to treaties may amend them. An amendment is typically regarded as a new treaty, binding only on states that affirmatively accept it. See Articles 39–40 of the Vienna Convention. Because multilateral treaty negotiations are often time-consuming and cumbersome, however, states sometimes provide mechanisms for amending technical treaty provisions that vary the normal rules for amendments. For example, Article XII(1)(a) of the 1978 International Convention on Standards of Training, Certification and Watchkeeping of Seafarers, 1361 U.N.T.S. 2, provides the following procedures for amending the Convention's Annex: (1) an amendment is proposed by a state party and submitted to the International Maritime Organization; (2) the amendment is adopted by two-thirds of all the treaty parties voting in the I.M.O.'s Maritime Safety Committee, assuming at least one-third of those parties are present when the vote is taken; (3) the amendment is then "deemed accepted" at the end of two years after it has been communicated to the treaty parties (or at the end of a different period set at the time of its adoption in the Maritime Safety Committee), unless within the relevant period "either more than one third of Parties, or Parties the combined merchant fleets of which constitute not less than fifty per cent of the gross tonnage of the world's merchant shipping of ships of 100 gross register tons or more, notify the Secretary–General that they object to the amendment;" (4) absent special exemptions concerning entry into force, the amendment enters into force for all treaty parties, "except those which have objected to the amendment * * * and which have not withdrawn such objections," six months after it is deemed accepted. As of May 31, 2000, 134 states, representing 97.93 per cent of the world shipping tonnage, had accepted this Convention and its amendment procedures.

CASE CONCERNING THE GABCÍKOVO–NAGYMAROS PROJECT

Hungary/Slovakia, 1997 I.C.J. 3, 1997 WL 289957,
37 *International Legal Materials* 162 (1998).

[On September 16, 1977, Hungary and Czechoslovakia entered into a treaty providing for diversion of the Danube River, which formed the countries' common boundary for approximately 85 miles, and the building of various structures. Under the treaty, which was to be implemented through a Joint Contractual Plan, the Danube was to be diverted into a by-pass canal in Czechoslovak territory, by means of a dam to be built by both countries at Dunakiliti. Water released from a reservoir at Dunakiliti would then power a hydroelectric plant on the by-pass canal at Gabcíkovo, in Czechoslovak territory. A structure farther downstream at Nagymaros was to generate additional power and moderate the flow of waters released from Dunakiliti; if not moderated, this flow could adversely affect water management and navigation farther down the Danube. The planned construction is shown in Figure 2.1 below.

In May 1989, in response to public protest over environmental consequences of the Gabcíkovo–Nagymaros project, the government of Hungary suspended its work on the project for a few weeks. Some of the environmental concerns with this project, including effects on water quality, on plants and animals in the Danube basin, and on the availability of water in particular localities, had been recognized in 1977. In the 1980s, however, knowledge about the environment increased, and, as Soviet influence in Eastern Europe waned, people challenged the environmental policies of the governments there. Czechoslovakia became convinced that Hungary would abandon the project, and began to plan its own "provisional solution," known as Variant C. This plan called for a dam at Cunovo, on Czechoslovak territory, to divert the waters into the bypass canal (instead of the dam at Dunakiliti, which was a joint project), and made no provision for the joint works at Nagymaros. Variant C is illustrated in Figure 2.2 below.

Hungary unilaterally denounced the 1977 treaty on May 16, 1992. Czechoslovakia started to divert waters into the by-pass canal in October 1992, and the Gabcíkovo hydroelectric plant began operating in November 1992. In June 1993, following the break-up of Czechoslovakia into the separate states of Slovakia and the Czech Republic, Hungary and Slovakia agreed to submit several questions related to their dispute over the Gabcíkovo–Nagymaros project to the International Court of Justice.

The Court first decided that Hungary's suspension and later abandonment of the joint project were not justified by the defense of necessity, and therefore these wrongful acts were not legally excused. According to the Court, which relied on the definition of necessity in the International Law Commission's Draft Articles on State Responsibility, Hungary's environmental concerns did not amount to necessity because Hungary could show no grave and imminent peril. Second, the Court ruled that Czechoslovakia's implementation of Variant C was an internationally wrongful act. Slovakia's effort to justify Variant C as an "approximate application" of the 1977 treaty failed; since Variant C eschewed joint efforts and operated entirely within Slovak territory, Variant C did not operate "within the limits of the treaty in question." 1997 I.C.J. at 53. The excerpt below concerns the third question posed to the Court: Hungary's arguments that the 1977 treaty was terminated, pursuant to the law of treaties, when Hungary denounced it in May 1992.]

47. * * * [T]he law of treaties and the law of State responsibility * * * have a scope that is distinct. A determination of whether a convention is or is not in force, and whether it has or has not been properly suspended or denounced, is to be made pursuant to the law of treaties. On the other hand, an evaluation of the extent to which the suspension or denunciation of a convention, seen as incompatible with the law of treaties, involves the responsibility of the State which proceeded to it, is to be made under the law of State responsibility.

Figure 2.1. Illustration of the Gabcíkovo–Nagymaros project, as planned under the 1977 Hungary–Czechoslovak treaty (not to scale).

Figure 2.2. Illustration of "Variant C," as implemented by Czechoslovakia in 1992 (not to scale).

Thus the Vienna Convention of 1969 on the Law of Treaties confines itself to defining—in a limitative manner—the conditions in which a treaty may lawfully be denounced or suspended; while the effects of a denunciation or suspension seen as not meeting those conditions are, on the contrary, expressly excluded from the scope of the Convention by operation of Article 73. It is moreover well established that, when a State has committed an internationally wrongful act, its international responsibility is likely to be involved whatever the nature of the obligation it has failed to respect. * * *

89. By the terms of Article 2, paragraph 1(c), of the Special Agreement, the Court is asked, thirdly, to determine

"what are the legal effects of the notification, on 19 May 1992, of the termination of the Treaty by the Republic of Hungary." * * *

98. Th[is] question * * * deals with treaty law since the Court is asked to determine what the legal effects are of the notification of termination of the Treaty. The question is whether Hungary's notification of 19 May 1992 brought the 1977 Treaty to an end, or whether it did not meet the requirements of international law, with the consequence that it did not terminate the Treaty.

99. * * * The Vienna Convention is not directly applicable to the 1977 Treaty inasmuch as both States ratified that Convention only after the Treaty's conclusion. Consequently only those rules which are declaratory of customary law are applicable to the 1977 Treaty. * * * [T]his is the case, in many respects, with Articles 60 to 62 of the Vienna Convention, relating to termination or suspension of the operation of a treaty. On this, the Parties, too, were broadly in agreement.

100. The 1977 Treaty does not contain any provision regarding its termination. Nor is there any indication that the parties intended to admit the possibility of denunciation or withdrawal. On the contrary, the Treaty establishes a long-standing and durable regime of joint investment and joint operation. Consequently, the parties not having agreed otherwise, the Treaty could be terminated only on the limited grounds enumerated in the Vienna Convention.

101. The Court will now turn to the first ground advanced by Hungary, that of the state of necessity. In this respect, the Court will merely observe that, even if a state of necessity is found to exist, it is not a ground for the termination of a treaty. It may only be invoked to exonerate from its responsibility a State which has failed to implement a treaty. Even if found justified, it does not terminate a Treaty; the Treaty may be ineffective as long as the condition of necessity continues to exist; it may in fact be dormant, but—unless the parties by mutual agreement terminate the Treaty—it continues to exist. As soon as the

state of necessity ceases to exist, the duty to comply with treaty obligations revives.

102. Hungary also relied on the principle of the impossibility of performance as reflected in Article 61 of the Vienna Convention on the Law of Treaties. Hungary's interpretation of the wording of Article 61 is, however, not in conformity with the terms of that Article, nor with the intentions of the Diplomatic Conference which adopted the Convention. Article 61, paragraph 1, requires the "permanent disappearance or destruction of an object indispensable for the execution" of the treaty to justify the termination of a treaty on grounds of impossibility of performance. During the conference, a proposal was made to extend the scope of the article by including in it cases such as the impossibility to make certain payments because of serious financial difficulties. * * * [T]he participating States were not prepared to consider such situations to be a ground for terminating or suspending a treaty. * * *

103. Hungary contended that the essential object of the Treaty—an economic joint investment which was consistent with environmental protection and which was operated by the two contracting parties jointly—had permanently disappeared and that the Treaty had thus become impossible to perform. It is not necessary for the Court to determine whether the term "object" in Article 61 can also be understood to embrace a legal régime as in any event, even if that were the case, it would have to conclude that in this instance that régime had not definitively ceased to exist. The 1977 Treaty—and in particular its Articles 15, 19 and 20—actually made available to the parties the necessary means to proceed at any time, by negotiation, to the required readjustments between economic imperatives and ecological imperatives. The Court would add that, if the joint exploitation of the investment was no longer possible, this was originally because Hungary did not carry out most of the works for which it was responsible under the 1977 Treaty; Article 61, paragraph 2, of the Vienna Convention expressly provides that impossibility of performance may not be invoked for the termination of a treaty by a party to that treaty when it results from that party's own breach of an obligation flowing from that treaty.

104. Hungary further argued that it was entitled to invoke a number of events which, cumulatively, would have constituted a fundamental change of circumstances. In this respect it specified profound changes of a political nature, the Project's diminishing economic viability, the progress of environmental knowledge and the development of new norms and prescriptions of international environmental law * * *.

The Court recalls that, in the *Fisheries Jurisdiction* case, it stated that,

"Article 62 of the Vienna Convention on the Law of Treaties ... may in many respects be considered as a codification of existing customary law on the subject of the termination of a treaty relationship on account of change of circumstances." (*I.C.J. Reports 1973*, p. 63, para. 36)

The prevailing political situation was certainly relevant for the conclusion of the 1977 Treaty. But the Court will recall that the Treaty provided for a joint investment programme for the production of energy, the control of floods and the improvement of navigation on the Danube. In the Court's view, the prevalent political conditions were thus not so closely linked to the object and purpose of the Treaty that they constituted an essential basis of the consent of the parties and, in changing, radically altered the extent of the obligations still to be performed. The same holds good for the economic system in force at the time of the conclusion of the 1977 Treaty. Besides, even though the estimated profitability of the Project might have appeared less in 1992 than in 1977, it does not appear from the record before the Court that it was bound to diminish to such an extent that the treaty obligations of the parties would have been radically transformed as a result.

The Court does not consider that new developments in the state of environmental knowledge and of environmental law can be said to have been completely unforeseen. What is more, the formulation of Articles 15, 19 and 20, designed to accommodate change, made it possible for the parties to take account of such developments and to apply them when implementing those treaty provisions.

The changed circumstances advanced by Hungary are, in the Court's view, not of such a nature, either individually or collectively, that their effect would radically transform the extent of the obligations still to be performed in order to accomplish the Project. A fundamental change of circumstances must have been unforeseen; the existence of the circumstances at the time of the Treaty's conclusion must have constituted an essential basis of the consent of the parties to be bound by the Treaty. The negative and conditional wording of Article 62 of the Vienna Convention on the Law of Treaties is a clear indication moreover that the stability of treaty relations requires that the plea of fundamental change of circumstances be applied only in exceptional cases.

105. The Court will now examine Hungary's argument that it was entitled to terminate the 1977 Treaty on the ground that Czechoslovakia had violated * * * a number of other conventions and rules of general international law; and that the planning, construction and putting into operation of Variant C also amounted to a material breach of the 1977 Treaty.

106. As to that part of Hungary's argument which was based on other treaties and general rules of international law, the Court is of the view that it is only a material breach of the treaty itself, by a State party to that treaty, which entitles the other party to rely on it as a ground for terminating the treaty. The violation of other treaty rules or of rules of general international law may justify the taking of certain measures, including countermeasures, by the injured State, but it does not constitute a ground for termination under the law of treaties. * * *

108. Hungary's main argument for invoking a material breach of the Treaty was the construction and putting into operation of Variant C.

* * * Czechoslovakia violated the Treaty only when it diverted the waters of the Danube into the bypass canal in October 1992. * * *

In the Court's view, therefore, the notification of termination by Hungary on 19 May 1992 was premature. No breach of the Treaty by Czechoslovakia had yet taken place and consequently Hungary was not entitled to invoke any such breach of the Treaty as a ground for terminating it when it did.

109. In this regard, it should be noted that, according to Hungary's Declaration of 19 May 1992, the termination of the 1977 Treaty was to take effect as from 25 May 1992, that is only six days later. Both Parties agree that Articles 65 to 67 of the Vienna Convention on the Law of Treaties, if not codifying customary law, at least generally reflect customary international law and contain certain procedural principles which are based on an obligation to act in good faith. As the Court stated in its Advisory Opinion on the *Interpretation of the Agreement of 25 March 1951 between the WHO and Egypt* (in which case the Vienna Convention did not apply):

> "Precisely what periods of time may be involved in the observance of the duties to consult and negotiate, and what period of notice of termination should be given, are matters which necessarily vary according to the requirements of the particular case. In principle, therefore, it is for the parties in each case to determine the length of those periods by consultation and negotiation in good faith." (*I.C.J. Reports 1980*, p. 96, para. 49.)

The termination of the Treaty by Hungary was to take effect six days after its notification. On neither of these dates had Hungary suffered injury resulting from acts of Czechoslovakia. The Court must therefore confirm its conclusion that Hungary's termination of the Treaty was premature.

110. Nor can the Court overlook that Czechoslovakia committed the internationally wrongful act of putting into operation Variant C as a result of Hungary's own prior wrongful conduct. As was stated by the Permanent Court of International Justice:

> "It is, moreover, a principle generally accepted in the jurisprudence of international arbitration, as well as by municipal courts, that one Party cannot avail himself of the fact that the other has not fulfilled some obligation or has not had recourse to some means of redress, if the former Party has, by some illegal act, prevented the latter from fulfilling the obligation in question, or from having recourse to the tribunal which would have been open, to him." (*Factory at Chorzów, Jurisdiction, Judgment No. 8, 1927, P.C.I.J., Series A, No. 9*, p. 31.)

Hungary, by its own conduct, had prejudiced its right to terminate the Treaty; this would still have been the case even if Czechoslovakia, by the time of the purported termination, had violated a provision essential to the accomplishment of the object or purpose of the Treaty.

111. Finally, the Court will address Hungary's claim that it was entitled to terminate the 1977 Treaty because new requirements of international law for the protection of the environment precluded performance of the Treaty.

112. Neither of the Parties contended that new peremptory norms of environmental law had emerged since the conclusion of the 1977 Treaty, and the Court will consequently not be required to examine the scope of Article 64 of the Vienna Convention on the Law of Treaties. On the other hand, the Court wishes to point out that newly developed norms of environmental law are relevant for the implementation of the Treaty and that the parties could, by agreement, incorporate them through the application of Articles 15, 19 and 20 of the Treaty. These articles do not contain specific obligations of performance but require the parties, in carrying out their obligations to ensure that the quality of water in the Danube is not impaired and that nature is protected, to take new environmental norms into consideration when agreeing upon the means to be specified in the Joint Contractual Plan.

By inserting these evolving provisions in the Treaty, the parties recognized the potential necessity to adapt the Project. Consequently, the Treaty is not static, and is open to adapt to emerging norms of international law. By means of Articles 15 and 19, new environmental norms can be incorporated in the Joint Contractual Plan.

The responsibility to do this was a joint responsibility. The obligations contained in Articles 15, 19 and 20 are, by definition, general and have to be transformed into specific obligations of performance through a process of consultation and negotiation. Their implementation thus requires a mutual willingness to discuss in good faith actual and potential environmental risks. * * *

The awareness of the vulnerability of the environment and the recognition that environmental risks have to be assessed on a continuous basis have become much stronger in the years since the Treaty's conclusion. These new concerns have enhanced the relevance of Articles 15, 19 and 20. * * *

114. Finally, Hungary maintained that by their conduct both parties had repudiated the Treaty and that a bilateral treaty repudiated by both parties cannot survive. The Court is of the view, however, that although it has found that both Hungary and Czechoslovakia failed to comply with their obligations under the 1977 Treaty, this reciprocal wrongful conduct did not bring the Treaty to an end nor justify its termination. The Court would set a precedent with disturbing implications for treaty relations and the integrity of the rule *pacta sunt servanda* if it were to conclude that a treaty in force between States, which the parties have implemented in considerable measure and at great cost over a period of years, might be unilaterally set aside on grounds of reciprocal non-compliance. It would be otherwise, of course, if the parties decided to terminate the Treaty by mutual consent. But in this case, while Hungary purported to terminate the Treaty, Czechoslo-

vakia consistently resisted this act and declared it to be without legal effect.

115. In the light of the conclusions it has reached above, the Court, in reply to the question put to it in Article 2, paragraph 1(c), of the Special Agreement (see paragraph 89), finds that the notification of termination by Hungary of 19 May 1992 did not have the legal effect of terminating the 1977 Treaty and related instruments. * * *

155. For these reasons,

THE COURT,

(1) Having regard to Article 2, paragraph 1, of the Special Agreement, * * *

D. By eleven votes to four,

Finds that the notification, on 19 May 1992, of the termination of the Treaty of 16 September 1977 and related instruments by Hungary did not have the legal effect of terminating them; * * *

(2) Having regard to Article 2, paragraph 2, and Article 5 of the Special Agreement,

A. By twelve votes to three,

Finds that Slovakia, as successor to Czechoslovakia, became a party to the Treaty of 16 September 1977 as from 1 January 1993; * * *

B. By thirteen votes to two,

Finds that Hungary and Slovakia must negotiate in good faith in the light of the prevailing situation, and must take all necessary measures to ensure the achievement of the objectives of the Treaty of 16 September 1977, in accordance with such modalities as they may agree upon; * * *

C. By thirteen votes to two,

Finds that, unless the Parties otherwise agree, a joint operational régime must be established in accordance with the Treaty of 16 September 1977; * * *

D. By twelve votes to three,

Finds that unless the Parties otherwise agree, Hungary shall compensate Slovakia for the damage sustained by Czechoslovakia and by Slovakia on account of the suspension and abandonment by Hungary of works for which it was responsible; and Slovakia shall compensate Hungary for the damage it has sustained on account of the putting into operation of the "provisional solution" by Czechoslovakia and its maintenance in service by Slovakia; * * *

E. By thirteen votes to two,

Finds that the settlement of accounts for the construction and operation of the works must be effected in accordance with the relevant provisions of the Treaty of 16 September 1977 and related instruments, taking due account of such measures as will have been taken by the

Parties in application of points 2 B and 2 C of the present operative paragraph.

Notes and Questions

1. *The International Court of Justice.* The *Gabcíkovo–Nagymaros Case* is our first principal excerpt from a decision of the International Court of Justice. The ICJ, the successor to the Permanent International Court of Justice, was created as a part of the United Nations at the end of World War II. More on the ICJ appears in Chapter 5. For now, note how the Court obtained jurisdiction: by mutual consent of Hungary and Slovakia in a "special agreement"—a treaty—in which the parties asked the Court to rule on specific legal questions related to this particular dispute.

2. *The Law of State Responsibility and the Law of Treaties.* In paragraph 47 of its opinion, the Court drew a doctrinal distinction between the law of state responsibility and the law of treaties. If a state suspends or denounces a treaty when such action is not authorized under the law of treaties, its conduct will be unlawful, making the state responsible in international law. The law of state responsibility recognizes limited justifications to excuse an otherwise unlawful act; in this case, Hungary unsuccessfully argued "necessity" as a justification. Principles of state responsibility apply in a wide variety of situations; we address aspects of the law of state responsibility in several places in this book, and particularly in Chapters 6 and 10.

3. *Treaty Termination and Fundamental Change of Circumstances.* When can a valid treaty legally be terminated under the law of treaties? What grounds have parallels in domestic contract law? Among other arguments, the Court considered the claim of "fundamental change of circumstances" (also known as *rebus sic stantibus*). Why did this argument fail to justify Hungary's termination of the 1977 Treaty? There certainly were dramatic changes after the conclusion of the 1977 Treaty: (1) the fall of Communism in Eastern Europe and the associated abandonment of efforts to integrate socialist economies and navigation capabilities; (2) changed estimates of the economic profitability of the agreed works; (3) the emergence of Slovakia and the Czech Republic as entirely new states, successors to Czechoslovakia (more on state succession appears in Chapter 7); (4) increased knowledge about environmental hazards and risks; and (5) the emergence of environmentally active segments of the populations in the former Soviet bloc countries. What *would* constitute a "fundamental change of circumstances"? Is termination of a treaty for reasons of fundamentally changed circumstances just a special case of treaty interpretation, depending, as many have argued, on an implied treaty clause authorizing termination in such circumstances? Or is it better to view a rule relieving parties of their treaty obligations when a fundamental change of circumstances occurs as an objective rule of international law not derived from an implied clause? How can the doctrine of *rebus sic stantibus* be reconciled with the principle of *pacta sunt servanda, i.e.,* the rule that treaties are binding on the parties and must be performed in good faith (see Article 26 of the Vienna Convention)? Some positivist international lawyers criticized the notion of *rebus sic stantibus*, arguing that it undermined the role of treaties in

stabilizing interstate relations. See Hans Kelsen, *Principles of International Law* 498 (2d ed., Robert W. Tucker ed. 1966). Although Article 62 of the Vienna Convention on the Law of Treaties recognizes that a fundamental change of circumstances can justify terminating or suspending operation of a treaty, the Article certainly sets out stringent prerequisites for termination or suspension. The Vienna Convention also authorizes recourse to a third-party mechanism to settle disputes over the interpretation or application of Article 62. See Vienna Convention, Article 66 and Annex.

4. Jus Cogens. The *Gabcíkovo–Nagymaros* Court, in paragraph 112, noted the possibility that emergence of a new "peremptory norm" of international law may cause the termination of an existing treaty, citing Article 64 of the Vienna Convention on the Law of the Treaties. We explore such peremptory (*jus cogens*) norms in Chapter 3.

5. *Notice.* Why did the Court address the procedural requirements of Articles 65–67 of the Vienna Convention on the Law of Treaties? Was it necessary to address these requirements, in light of the Court's conclusion, in paragraph 110, that Hungary's own prior wrongful denunciation of the 1977 Treaty had prejudiced its right to invoke Czechoslovakia's implementation of Variant C as a material breach that would justify termination of the Treaty? Was the Court trying to signal that formalities in the law of treaties are important in the typical situation in which disputes over treaty implementation or termination will not be the subject of international adjudication? See Daniel Reichart–Facilides, "Down the Danube: The Vienna Convention on the Law of Treaties and the *Case Concerning the Gabcïkovo–Nagymaros Project*," 47 *International and Comparative Law Quarterly* 837, 848–49 (1998).

6. *Accommodating Changes in International Environmental Law.* How can parties to a treaty legally change how it operates, if, after the treaty has entered into force, the parties discover that carrying out the treaty will violate some new or evolving norm of international environmental law? Must the parties either, on the one hand, violate that norm, or, on the other, formally amend the treaty or replace it with a new treaty? Among other possibilities, note that treaties may incorporate mechanisms to allow adjustments that will accommodate new legal norms. See paragraph 112 of the Court's opinion. More on international environmental law appears in Chapter 10.

7. *Effect of the* Gabcíkovo–Nagymaros *Judgment.* One commentator has stated: "Judging from the reactions of the media in Hungary and Slovakia in the aftermath of the Court's Judgment, both countries welcomed the outcome of the case." Peter H.F. Bekker, "International Decision," 92 *American Journal of International Law* 273, 277 (1998). Why should this be? Why would the two states not have preferred the Court to have declared the 1977 Treaty at an end? After all, Hungary had suspended and denounced the 1977 Treaty, and Slovakia had supported Czechoslovakia's implementation of Variant C, which was inconsistent with the 1977 Treaty. What was likely to happen after the Court's decision? Note that Slovakia returned to the ICJ in September 1998, arguing that Hungary was unwilling to implement the Court's 1997 judgment and asking the Court "to determine the modalities for executing the Judgment." *ICJ Communiqué* No. 98/28 (1998).

THE EASTERN GREENLAND CASE

Denmark/Norway, 1933 P.C.I.J., Ser. A/B, No. 53, 3 *World Court Reports* 151 (Manley O. Hudson ed., reprinted 1969).

By an Application instituting proceedings, filed with the Registry of the Court on July 12th, 1931, in accordance with Article 40 of the Statute and Article 35 of the Rules of Court, the Royal Danish Government, relying on the optional clause of Article 36, paragraph 2, of the Statute, brought before the Permanent Court of International Justice a suit against the Royal Norwegian Government on the ground that the latter Government had, on July 10th, 1931, published a proclamation declaring that it had proceeded to occupy certain territories in Eastern Greenland, which, in the contention of the Danish Government, were subject to the sovereignty of the Crown of Denmark. The Application, after thus indicating the subject of the dispute, proceeds, subject to the subsequent presentation of any cases, counter-cases and any other documents or evidence, to formulate the claim by asking the Court for judgment to the effect that "the promulgation of the above-mentioned declaration of occupation and any steps taken in this respect by the Norwegian Government constitute a violation of the existing legal situation and are accordingly unlawful and invalid." * * *

At the beginning of the present century, opinion again began to be manifested in favour of the more effective occupation of the uncolonized areas in Greenland, in order that the risk of foreign settlement might be obviated.

During the Great War of 1914 to 1918, Denmark by treaty ceded to the United States of America her West Indian Islands—the Danish Antilles—and, during the negotiations for the conclusion of the treaty, broached to the American Secretary of State—at first in conversation and subsequently, on December 27th, 1915, by a written communication—the question of the extension of Danish activities throughout all Greenland. As the result, the United States signed on August 4th, 1916, the same day as the treaty for cession of the Antilles, a declaration to the effect that the United States would not object to the Danish Government extending their political and economic interests to the whole of Greenland.

On July 12th, 1919, the Danish Minister of Foreign Affairs instructed the Danish Minister at Christiania that a Committee had just been constituted at the Peace Conference "for the purpose of considering the claims that may be put forward by different countries to Spitzbergen," and that the Danish Government would be prepared to renew before this Committee the unofficial assurance already given (on April 2nd, 1919) to the Norwegian Government, according to which Denmark, having no special interests at stake in Spitzbergen, would raise no objection to Norway's claims upon that archipelago. In making this statement to the Norwegian Minister for Foreign Affairs, the Danish Minister was to point out "that the Danish Government had been anxious for some years past to obtain the recognition by all the interested Powers of Denmark's sovereignty over the whole of Greenland, and that she intended to place that question before the above-mentioned Committee;" and, further, that the Danish Government felt confident that the extension of its political and economic interests to the whole of Greenland "would not encounter any difficulties on the part of the Norwegian Government."

On July 14th, 1919, the Danish Minister saw M. Ihlen, the Norwegian Minister of Foreign Affairs, who merely replied on this occasion "that the question would be considered." The Norwegian Minister recorded his conversation with the Danish representative in a minute, the accuracy of which has not been disputed by the Danish Government. On July 22nd following, M. Ihlen made a statement to the Danish Minister to the effect "that the Norwegian Government would not make any difficulties in the settlement of this question" (i.e., the question raised on July 14th by the Danish Government). These are the words recorded in the minute by M. Ihlen himself. According to the report made by the Danish Minister to his own Government, M. Ihlen's words were that "the plans of the Royal [Danish] Government respecting Danish sovereignty over the whole of Greenland ... would meet with no difficulties on the part of Norway." It is this statement by the Norwegian Minister for Foreign Affairs which is described in this judgment as the "Ihlen declaration." * * *

This declaration by M. Ihlen has been relied on by Counsel for Denmark as a recognition of an existing Danish sovereignty in Greenland. The Court is unable to accept this point of view. A careful examination of the words used and of the circumstances in which they were used, as well as of the subsequent developments, shows that M. Ihlen cannot have meant to be giving then and there a definitive recognition of Danish sovereignty over Greenland, and shows also that he cannot have been understood by the Danish Government at the time as having done so. In the text of M. Ihlen's minute, submitted by the Norwegian Government, which has not been disputed by the Danish Government, the phrase used by M. Ihlen is couched in the future tense: *"ne fera pas de difficultés"*; he had been informed that it was at the Peace Conference that the Danish Government intended to bring up the question: and two years later—when assurances had been received from the Principal Allied Powers—the Danish Government made a further application to the Norwegian Government to obtain the recognition which they desired of Danish sovereignty over all Greenland.

Nevertheless, the point which must now be considered is whether the Ihlen declaration—even if not constituting a definitive recognition of Danish sovereignty—did not constitute an engagement obliging Norway to refrain from occupying any part of Greenland.

The Danish request and M. Ihlen's reply were recorded by him in a minute, worded as follows:

I. The Danish Minister informed me to-day that his Government has heard from Paris that the question of Spitzbergen will be examined by a Commission of four members (American, British, French, Italian). If the Danish Government is questioned by this Commission, it is prepared to reply that Denmark has no interests in Spitzbergen, and that it has no reason to oppose the wishes of Norway in regard to the settlement of this question.

Furthermore, the Danish Minister made the following statement:

The Danish Government has for some years past been anxious to obtain the recognition of all the interested Powers of Denmark's sovereignty over the whole of Greenland, and it proposes to place this question before the above-mentioned Committee at the same time. During the negotiations with the U.S.A. over the cession of the Danish West Indies, the Danish Government raised this question in so far as concerns recognition by the Government of the U.S.A., and it succeeded in inducing the latter to agree that, concurrently with the conclusion of a convention regarding the cession of the said islands, it would make a declaration to the effect that the Government of the U.S.A. would not object to the Danish Government extending their political and economic interests to the whole of Greenland.

The Danish Government is confident (he added) that the Norwegian Government will not make any difficulties in the settlement of this question.

I replied that the question would be examined.

14/7–19 Ih.

II. To-day I informed the Danish Minister that the Norwegian Government would not make any difficulties in the settlement of this question.

22/7–19 Ih.

The incident has, therefore, reference, first to the attitude to be observed by Denmark before the Committee of the Peace Conference at Paris in regard to Spitzbergen, this attitude being that Denmark would not "oppose the wishes of Norway in regard to the settlement of this question"; as is known, these wishes related to the sovereignty over Spitzbergen. Secondly, the request showed that "the Danish Government was confident that the Norwegian Government would not make any difficulty" in the settlement of the Greenland question; the aims that Denmark had in view in regard to the last-named island were to secure the "recognition by all the Powers concerned of Danish sovereignty over the whole of Greenland," and that there should be no opposition "to the Danish Government extending their political and economic interests to the whole of Greenland." It is clear from the relevant Danish documents which preceded the Danish Minister's *démarche* at Christiania on July 14th, 1919, that the Danish attitude in the Spitzbergen question and the Norwegian attitude in the Greenland question were regarded in Denmark as interdependent, and this interdependence appears to be reflected also in M. Ihlen's minute of the interview. Even if this interdependence—which, in view of the affirmative reply of the Norwegian Government, in whose name the Minister for Foreign Affairs was speaking, would have created a bilateral engagement—is not held to have been established, it can hardly be denied that what Denmark was asking of Norway ("not to make any difficulties in the settlement of the [Greenland] question") was equivalent to what she was indicating her readiness to concede in the Spitzbergen question (to refrain from opposing "the wishes of Norway in regard to the settlement of this question"). What Denmark desired to obtain from Norway was that the latter should do nothing to obstruct the Danish plans in regard to Greenland. The declaration which the Minister for Foreign Affairs gave on July 22nd, 1919, on behalf of the Norwegian Government, was definitely affirmative: "I told the Danish Minister to-day that the Norwegian Government would not make any difficulty in the settlement of this question."

The Court considers it beyond all dispute that a reply of this nature given by the Minister for Foreign Affairs on behalf of his Government in response to a request by the diplomatic representative of a foreign Power, in regard to a question falling within his province, is binding upon the country to which the Minister belongs. * * *

The Court readily understands that Norway should feel concern for the interests of the Norwegian hunters and fishermen on the East coast of Greenland; but it cannot forget, in this connection, that as early as December 1921, Denmark announced her willingness to do everything in her power to make arrangements to safeguard Norwegian subjects against any loss they might incur as a result of the Decree of May 10th, 1921 (letter from the Danish Minister at Christiania dated December 19th, 1921, to the Norwegian Minister for Foreign Affairs). The Convention of July 9th, 1924, was a confirmation of Denmark's friendly disposition in respect of these Norwegian hunting and fishing interests.

What the Court cannot regard as being in accordance with the undertaking of July 22nd, 1919, is the endeavour to replace an unconditional and definitive undertaking by one which was subject to reservations: and what it is even more difficult for the Court to admit is that, notwithstanding the undertaking of July 22nd, 1919, by which she promised to refrain from making difficulties in the settlement of the Greenland question, Norway should have stipulated that "Eastern Greenland must be Norwegian." This pretension was already apparent at the end of a letter of January 12th, 1923, from the Norwegian Minister at Copenhagen to the Danish Minister for Foreign Affairs; and it was enunciated very definitely on September 28th, 1923, in the minutes of the sixth meeting of the Conference which drew up the Convention of July 9th, 1924, and again in the Protocol signed on January 28th, 1924, referred to above.

The Court is unable to read into the words of the Ihlen declaration "in the settlement of this question" (i.e., the Greenland question) a condition which would render the promise to refrain from making any difficulties inoperative should a settlement not be reached. The promise was unconditional and definitive. It was so understood by the Norwegian Minister for Foreign Affairs when he told the Danish Minister at Christiania on November 7th, 1919, that "it was a pleasure to Norway to recognize Danish sovereignty over Greenland" (dispatch from the Danish Minister at Christiania to the Danish Minister for Foreign Affairs of November 8th, 1919). It was also in the same sense that the Danish Minister at Christiania had understood the Ihlen declaration, when he informed the Danish Minister for Foreign Affairs on July 22nd, 1919, that M. Ihlen had told him "that the plans of the Royal Government in regard to the sovereignty of Denmark over the whole of Greenland would not encounter any difficulties on the part of Norway."

It follows that, as a result of the undertaking involved in the Ihlen declaration of July 22nd, 1919, Norway is under an obligation to refrain from contesting Danish sovereignty over Greenland as a whole, and *a fortiori* to refrain from occupying a part of Greenland.

Notes and Questions

1. *Unwritten Treaties*. Did the Court decide that there was a "treaty" between Norway and Denmark trading Norwegian claims to Greenland for Danish claims to Spitzbergen? May a treaty be unwritten? How was the Ihlen Declaration enough to commit Norway in international law? Would a like assurance be binding in the domestic law of contract?

What does the case say to states and diplomats about the possible legal effects of their negotiating behavior? Here are some observations of Dean Rusk, U.S. Secretary of State in the Kennedy and Johnson administrations between 1961 and 1969, that show that the lesson of *Eastern Greenland* has not been entirely forgotten.

> One evening, after a highball or two, I suggested to [the Foreign Minister of Honduras] that we toss a coin for these islands [the Swan Islands in the Caribbean claimed by both Honduras and the U.S.]. Fortunately, he refused because the International Court of Justice seemed to say in the *Greenland* case that a government has a right to rely upon the statement of a Foreign Minister with respect to a territorial matter. If there is anything clear about our Constitution, it is that the Secretary of State cannot go around the world tossing coins for American territory.

Dean Rusk, "The Role and Problems of Arbitration with Respect to Political Disputes," in *Resolving Transnational Disputes Through International Arbitration* 15, 18 (Thomas E. Carbonneau ed. 1984).

2. *The Validity of Treaties Made in Violation of Municipal Constitutional Requirements*. Should it make any difference that Norwegian constitutional law required Parliamentary assent to the making of treaties? Should Denmark have been on notice about this Norwegian municipal rule? Should Denmark have reasonably expected that the Norwegian Foreign Minister (or the Danish Foreign Minister) would be able legally to bind the state with simply a verbal statement? Does Article 46 of the Vienna Convention on the

Law of Treaties satisfactorily treat the issue of compliance with municipal procedures for treaty-making?

3. *"Bargains" in International Relations.* Was there a "bargain" struck at the 1919 Paris Conference whereby Denmark traded its claims to Spitzbergen for Norway's claims to Greenland? Was there also a bargain made in 1916 between Denmark and the United States when Denmark ceded the Danish Antilles in the West Indies to the U.S.? The U.S. declared it "would not object to the Danish Government extending their political and economic interests to the whole of Greenland." Compared to Norway, would the United States be just as or more committed to respect Danish sovereignty over all of Greenland? After all, the U.S. declaration was made in writing, and Denmark legally ceded territories to which it had undisputed title.

Could the legal commitment found by the Court to have been made by Norway be something quite different from a treaty? Could it, for example, be seen as a consummated transaction, a bargain made by the two states, with the Court simply enforcing good faith respect for the status quo? Or might the Ihlen Declaration be looked upon as an act of state in customary international law, binding Norway because of the reasonable expectations of Denmark? Or was the Ihlen Declaration simply a unilateral promise enforceable at international law?

Chapter 3

CUSTOM AND THE NON–CONSENSUAL SOURCES OF INTERNATIONAL LAW

At first glance, one might think that treaties provide all that international law needs by way of rules. Nowadays, there are tens of thousands of international agreements, most all of which offer the distinct advantages of explicitly expressing international norms and the consent of sovereign states. However, other sorts of international law remain just as important as before. This is so for at least two reasons. First, all treaty provisions need to be interpreted and, if treaty interpretation is not to be pure discretion, some guidance from other forms of law is called for. Second, treaties never bind all states, and there need to be some rules of more general application. In the pages of this chapter that follow, we explore first custom, often conceived as constituting an implicit sort of international agreement, and then the non-consensual sources of international law, where the pretense that international law is always based on the consent of states is finally abandoned.

A. CUSTOMARY INTERNATIONAL LAW

Next to treaties, international lawyers work most often with customary international law. As you read through the materials in this Part, evaluate the role of decision-makers in determining rules of custom and consider whether custom is best viewed as a consensual source of international law.

THE PAQUETE HABANA

175 U.S. 677, 20 S.Ct. 290, 44 L.Ed. 320 (1900).

MR. JUSTICE GRAY delivered the opinion of the court.

These are two appeals from decrees of the District Court of the United States for the Southern District of Florida, condemning two fishing vessels and their cargoes as prize of war.

Each vessel was a fishing smack, running in and out of Havana, and regularly engaged in fishing on the coast of Cuba; sailed under the Spanish flag; was owned by a Spanish subject of Cuban birth, living in the city of Havana; was commanded by a subject of Spain, also residing in Havana; and her master and crew had no interest in the vessel, but were entitled to shares, amounting in all to two thirds, of her catch, the other third belonging to her owner. Her cargo consisted of fresh fish, caught by her crew from the sea, put on board as they were caught, and kept and sold alive. Until stopped by the blockading squadron, she had no knowledge of the existence of the war, or of any blockade. She had no arms or ammunition on board, and made no attempt to run the blockade after she knew of its existence, nor any resistance at the time of the capture. * * *

Both the fishing vessels were brought by their captors into Key West. A libel for the condemnation of each vessel and her cargo as prize of war was there filed on April 27, 1898; a claim was interposed by her master, on behalf of himself and the other members of the crew, and of her owner; evidence was taken, showing the facts above stated; and on May 30, 1898, a final decree of condemnation and sale was entered, "the court not being satisfied that as a matter of law, without ordinance, treaty or proclamation, fishing vessels of this class are exempt from seizure."

Each vessel was thereupon sold by auction; the Paquete Habana for the sum of $490; and the Lola for the sum of $800. There was no other evidence in the record of the value of either vessel or of her cargo. * * *

We are then brought to the consideration of the question whether, upon the facts appearing in these records, the fishing smacks were subject to capture by the armed vessels of the United States during the recent war with Spain.

By an ancient usage among civilized nations, beginning centuries ago, and gradually ripening into a rule of international law, coast fishing vessels, pursuing their vocation of catching and bringing in fresh fish, have been recognized as exempt, with their cargoes and crews, from capture as prize of war.

This doctrine, however, has been earnestly contested at the bar; and no complete collection of the instances illustrating it is to be found, so far as we are aware, in a single published work, although many are referred to and discussed by the writers on international law, notably in 2 Ortolan, Règles Internationales et Diplomatie de la Mer, (4th ed.) lib. 3, c. 2, pp. 51–56; in 4 Calvo, Droit International, (5th ed.) §§ 2367–2373; in De Boeck, Propriété Privée Ennemie sous Pavillon Ennemi, §§ 191–196; and in Hall, International Law, (4th ed.) § 148. It is therefore worth the while to trace the history of the rule, from the earliest accessible sources, through the increasing recognition of it, with occasional setbacks, to what we may now justly consider as its final establishment in our own country and generally throughout the civilized world.

The earliest acts of any government on the subject, mentioned in the books, either emanated from, or were approved by, a King of England.

In 1403 and 1406, Henry IV issued orders to his admirals and other officers, entitled "Concerning Safety for Fisherman—*De Securitate pro Piscatoribus.*" By an order of October 26, 1403, reciting that it was made pursuant to a treaty between himself and the King of France; and for the greater safety of the fishermen of either country, and so that they could be, and carry on their industry, the more safely on the sea, and deal with each other in peace; and that the French King had consented that English fishermen should be treated likewise; it was ordained that French fishermen might, during the then pending season for the herring fishery, safely fish for herrings and all other fish, from the harbor of Gravelines and the island of Thanet to the mouth of the Seine and the harbor of Hautoune. And by an order of October 5, 1406, he took into his safe conduct, and under his special protection, guardianship and defense, all and singular the fishermen of France, Flanders and Brittany, with their fishing vessels and boats, everywhere on the sea, through and within his dominions, jurisdictions and territories, in regard to their fishery, while sailing, coming and going, and, at their pleasure, freely and lawfully fishing, delaying or proceeding, and returning homeward with their catch of fish, without any molestation or hindrance whatever; and also their fish, nets, and other property and goods soever; and it was therefore ordered that such fishermen should not be interfered with, provided they should comport themselves well and properly, and should not, by color of these presents, do or attempt, or presume to do or attempt, anything that could prejudice the King, or his kingdom of England, or his subjects. 8 Rymer's Foedera, 336, 451.

The treaty made October 2, 1521, between the Emperor Charles V and Francis I of France, through their ambassadors, recited that a great and fierce war had arisen between them, because of which there had been, both by land and by sea, frequent depredations and incursions on either side, to the grave detriment and intolerable injury of the innocent subjects of each; and that a suitable time for the herring fishery was at hand, and, by reason of the sea being beset by the enemy, the fishermen did not dare to go out, whereby the subject of their industry, bestowed by heaven to allay the hunger of the poor, would wholly fail for the year, unless it were otherwise provided—*quo fit, ut piscaturae commoditas, ad pauperum levandam famem a coelesti numine concessa, cessare hoc anno omnino debeat, nisi aliter provideatur.* And it was therefore agreed that the subjects of each sovereign, fishing in the sea, or exercising the calling of fishermen, could and might, until the end of the next January, without incurring any attack, depredation, molestation, trouble or hindrance soever, safely and freely, everywhere in the sea, take herrings and every other kind of fish, the existing war by land and sea notwithstanding; and further that, during the time aforesaid, no subject of either sovereign should commit, or attempt or presume to commit, any depredation, force, violence, molestation or vexation, to or upon such fishermen, or their vessels, supplies, equipments, nets and fish, or other goods soever truly appertaining to fishing. * * *

The herring fishery was permitted, in time of war, by French and Dutch edicts in 1536. Bynkershoek Quæstiones Juris Publicæ, lib. 1, c. 3; 1 Emerigon des Assurances, c. 4, sect. 9; c. 12, sect. 19, § 8.

France, from remote times, set the example of alleviating the evils of war in favor of all coast fishermen. In the compilation entitled Us et Coutumes de la Mer, published by Cleirac in 1661, and in the third part thereof, containing "Maritime or Admiralty Jurisdiction—*la Jurisdiction de la Marine ou d'Admirauté*—as well in time of peace as in time of war," article 80 is as follows: "The admiral may in time of war accord fishing truces—*tresves pescheresses*—to the enemy and to his subjects; provided that the enemy will likewise accord them to Frenchmen." Cleirac, 544. Under this article, reference is made to articles 49 and 79 respectively of the French ordinances concerning the Admiralty in 1543 and 1584, of which it is but a reproduction. 4 Pardessus, Collection de Lois Maritimes, 319; 2 Ortolan, 51. And Cleirac adds, in a note, this quotation from Froissart's Chronicles: "Fishermen on the sea, whatever war there were in France and England, never did harm to one another; so they are friends, and help one another at need—*Pescheurs sur mer, quelque guerre qui soit en France et Angleterre, jamais ne se firent mal l'un à l'autre; ainçois sont amis, et s'aydent l'un à l'autre au besoin.*"

The same custom would seem to have prevailed in France until towards the end of the seventeenth century. For example, in 1675, Louis XIV and the States General of Holland, by mutual agreement, granted to Dutch and French fishermen the liberty, undisturbed by their vessels of war, of fishing along the coasts of France, Holland and England. D'Hauterive et De Cussy, Traités de Commerce, pt. 1, vol. 2, p. 278. But by the ordinances of 1681 and 1692 the practice was discontinued, because, Valin says, of the faithless conduct of the enemies of France, who, abusing the good faith with which she had always observed the treaties, habitually carried off her fishermen, while their own fished in safety. 2 Valin sur l'Ordonnance de la Marine, (1776) 689, 690; 2 Ortolan, 52; De Boeck, § 192.

The doctrine which exempts coast fishermen with their vessels and cargoes from capture as prize of war has been familiar to the United States from the time of the War of Independence.

On June 5, 1779, Louis XVI, our ally in that war, addressed a letter to his admiral, informing him that the wish he had always had of alleviating, as far as he could, the hardships of war, had directed his attention to that class of his subjects which devoted itself to the trade of fishing, and had no other means of livelihood; that he had thought that the example which he should give to his enemies, and which could have no other source than the sentiments of humanity which inspired him, would determine them to allow to fishermen the same facilities which he should consent to grant; and that he had therefore given orders to the commanders of all his ships not to disturb English fishermen, nor to arrest their vessels laden with fresh fish, even if not caught by those vessels; provided they had no offensive arms, and were not proved to have made any signals creating a suspicion of intelligence with the enemy; and the admiral was directed to communicate the King's intentions to all officers under his control. By a royal order in council of November 6, 1780, the former orders were confirmed; and the capture and ransom, by a French cruiser, of *The John and Sarah*, an English vessel, coming from Holland, laden with fresh fish, were pronounced to be illegal. 2 Code des Prises, (ed. 1784) 721, 901, 903.

Among the standing orders made by Sir James Marriott, Judge of the English High Court of Admiralty, was one of April 11, 1780, by which it was "ordered, that all causes of prize of fishing boats or vessels taken from the enemy may be consolidated in one monition, and one sentence or interlocutory, if under 50 tons burden, and not more than six in number." Marriott's Formulary, 4. But by the statements of his successor, and of both French and English writers, it appears that England, as well as France, during the American Revolutionary War, abstained from interfering with the coast fisheries. *The Young Jacob and Johanna*, 1 C. Rob. 20; 2 Ortolan, 53; Hall, § 148.

In the treaty of 1785 between the United States and Prussia, article 23, (which was proposed by the American Commissioners, John Adams, Benjamin Franklin and Thomas Jefferson, and is said to have been drawn up by Franklin,) provided that, if war should arise between the contracting parties, "all women and children, scholars of every faculty, cultivators of the earth, artisans, manufacturers and fishermen, unarmed and inhabiting unfortified towns, villages or places, and in general all others whose occupations are for the common subsistence and benefit of mankind, shall be allowed to continue their respective employments, and shall not be molested in their persons; nor shall their houses or goods be burnt or otherwise destroyed, nor their fields wasted, by the armed force of the enemy, into whose power, by the events of war, they may happen to fall; but if anything is necessary to be taken from them for the use of such armed force, the same shall be paid for at a reasonable price." 8 Stat. 96; 1 Kent Com. 91 note; Wheaton's History of the Law of Nations, 306, 308. Here was the clearest exemption from hostile molestation or seizure of the persons, occupations, houses and goods of unarmed fishermen inhabiting unfortified places. The article was repeated in the later treaties between the United States and Prussia of 1799 and 1828. 8 Stat. 174, 384. And Dana, in a note to his edition of Wheaton's International Law, says: "In many treaties and decrees, fishermen catching fish as an article of food are added to the class of persons whose occupation is not to be disturbed in war." Wheaton's International Law, (8th ed.) § 345, note 168. * * *

In the war with Mexico in 1846, the United States recognized the exemption of coast fishing boats from capture. In proof of this, counsel have referred to records of the Navy Department, which this court is clearly authorized to consult upon such a question. *Jones v. United States*, 137 U.S. 202; *Underhill v. Hernandez*, 168 U.S. 250, 253.

By those records it appears that Commodore Conner, commanding the Home Squadron blockading the east coast of Mexico, on May 14, 1846, wrote a letter from the ship Cumberland, off Brazos Santiago, near the southern point of Texas, to Mr. Bancroft, the Secretary of the Navy, enclosing a copy of the commodore's "instructions to the commanders of the vessels of the Home Squadron, showing the principles to be observed in the blockade of the Mexican ports," one of which was that "Mexican boats engaged in fishing on any part of the coast will be allowed to pursue their labors unmolested"; and that on June 10, 1846, those instructions were approved by the Navy Department * * *. * * *

International law is part of our law, and must be ascertained and administered by the courts of justice of appropriate jurisdiction, as often as questions of right depending upon it are duly presented for their determination. For this purpose, where there is no treaty, and no controlling executive or legislative act or judicial decision, resort must be had to the customs and usages of civilized nations; and, as evidence of these, to the works of jurists and commentators, who by years of labor, research and experience, have made themselves peculiarly well acquainted with the subjects of which they treat. Such works are resorted to by judicial tribunals, not for the speculations of their authors concerning what the law ought to be, but for trustworthy evidence of what the law really is. *Hilton v. Guyot*, 159 U.S. 113, 163, 164, 214, 215.

Wheaton places, among the principal sources of international law, "Text-writers of authority, showing what is the approved usage of nations, or the general opinion respecting their mutual conduct, with the definitions and modifications introduced by general consent." As to these he forcibly observes: "Without wishing to exaggerate the importance of these writers, or to substitute, in any case, their authority for the principles of reason, it may be affirmed that they are generally impartial in their judgment. They are witnesses of the sentiments and usages of civilized nations, and the weight of their testimony increases every time that their authority is invoked by statesmen, and every year that passes without the rules laid down in their works being impugned by the avowal of contrary principles." Wheaton's International Law, (8th ed.) § 15.

Chancellor Kent says: "In the absence of higher and more authoritative sanctions, the ordinances of foreign States, the opinions of eminent statesmen, and the writings of distinguished jurists, are regarded as of great consideration on questions not settled by conventional law. In cases where the principal jurists agree, the presumption will be very great in favor of the solidity of their maxims; and no civilized nation, that does not arrogantly set all ordinary law and justice at defiance, will venture to disregard the uniform sense of the established writers on international law." 1 Kent Com. 18.

It will be convenient, in the first place, to refer to some leading French treatises on international law, which deal with the question now before us, not as one of the law of France only, but as one determined by the general consent of civilized nations.

"Enemy ships," say Pistoye and Duverdy, in their Treatise on Maritime Prizes, published in 1855, "are good prize. Not all, however; for it results from the unanimous accord of the maritime powers that an exception should be made in favor of coast fishermen. Such fishermen are respected by the enemy, so long as they devote themselves exclusively to fishing." 1 Pistoye et Duverdy, tit. 6, c. 1, p. 314.

[The Court cites other jurists.]

This review of the precedents and authorities on the subject appears to us abundantly to demonstrate that at the present day, by the general consent of the civilized nations of the world, and independently of any express treaty or other public act, it is an established rule of international law, founded on considerations of humanity to a poor and industrious order of men, and of the mutual convenience of belligerent States, that coast fishing vessels, with their implements and supplies, cargoes and crews, unarmed, and honestly pursuing their peaceful calling of catching and bringing in fresh fish, are exempt from capture as prize of war.

The exemption, of course, does not apply to coast fishermen or their vessels, if employed for a warlike purpose, or in such a way as to give aid or information to the enemy; nor when military or naval operations create a necessity to which all private interests must give way.

Nor has the exemption been extended to ships or vessels employed on the high sea in taking whales or seals, or cod or other fish which are not brought fresh to market, but are salted or otherwise cured and made a regular article of commerce.

This rule of international law is one which prize courts, administering the law of nations are bound to take judicial notice of, and to give effect to, in the absence of any treaty or other public act of their own government in relation to the matter. * * *

To this subject, in more than one aspect, are singularly applicable the words uttered by Mr. Justice Strong, speaking for this court: "Undoubtedly, no single nation can change the law of the sea. That law is of universal obligation, and no statute of one or two nations can create obligations for the world. Like all the laws of nations, it rests upon the common consent of civilized communities. It is of force, not because it was prescribed by any superior power, but because it has been generally accepted as a rule of conduct. Whatever may have been its origin, whether in the usages of navigation, or in the ordinances of maritime States, or in both, it has become the law of the sea only by the concurrent sanction of those nations who may be said to constitute the commercial world. Many of the usages which prevail, and which have the force of law, doubtless originated in the positive prescriptions of some single State, which were at first of limited effect, but which, when generally accepted, became of universal obligation." "This is not giving to the statutes of any nation extra-territorial effect. It is not treating them as general maritime laws; but it is recognition of the historical fact that by common consent of mankind these rules have been acquiesced in as of general obligation. Of that fact, we think, we may take judicial note. Foreign municipal laws must indeed be proved as facts, but it is not so with the law of nations." *The Scotia,* 14 Wall. 170, 187, 188.

The position taken by the United States during the recent war with Spain was quite in accord with the rule of international law, now generally recognized by civilized nations, in regard to coast fishing vessels.

On April 21, 1898, the Secretary of the Navy gave instructions to Admiral Sampson, commanding the North Atlantic Squadron, to "immediately institute a blockade of the north coast of Cuba, extending from Cardenas on the east to Bahia Honda on the west." Bureau of Navigation Report of 1898, appx. 175. The blockade was immediately instituted accordingly. On April 22, the President issued a proclamation, declaring that the United States had instituted and would maintain that blockade, "in pursuance of the laws of the United States, and the law of nations applicable to such cases." 30 Stat. 1769. And by the act of Congress of April 25, 1898, c. 189, it was declared that the war between the United States and Spain existed on that day, and had existed since and including April 21. 30 Stat. 364.

On April 26, 1898, the President issued another proclamation, which, after reciting the existence of the war, as declared by Congress, contained this further recital: "It being desirable that such war should be conducted upon principles in harmony with the present views of nations and sanctioned by their recent practice." This recital was followed by specific declarations of certain rules for the conduct of the war by sea, making no mention of fishing vessels. 30 Stat. 1770. But the proclamation clearly manifests the general policy of the Government to conduct the war in accordance with the principles of international law sanctioned by the recent practice of nations.

On April 28, 1898, (after the capture of the two fishing vessels now in question,) Admiral Sampson telegraphed to the Secretary of the Navy as follows: "I find that a large number of fishing schooners are attempting to get into Havana from their fishing grounds near the Florida reefs and coasts. They are generally manned by excellent seamen, belonging to the maritime inscription of Spain, who have already served in the Spanish navy, and who are liable to further service. As these trained men are naval reserves, have a semi-military character, and would be most valuable to the Spaniards as artillerymen, either afloat or ashore, I recommend that they should be detained prisoners of war, and that I should be authorized to deliver them to the commanding officer of the army at Key West." To that communication the Secretary of the Navy, on April 30, 1898, guardedly answered: "Spanish fishing vessels attempting to violate blockade are subject, with crew, to capture, and any such vessel or crew considered likely to aid enemy may be detained." Bureau of Navigation Report of 1898, appx. 178. The Admiral's despatch assumed that he was not authorized, without express order, to arrest coast fishermen peaceably pursuing their calling; and the necessary implication and evident intent of the response of the Navy Department were that Spanish coast fishing vessels and their crews should not be interfered with, so long as they neither attempted to violate the blockade, nor were considered likely to aid the enemy.

The Paquete Habana, as the record shows, was a fishing sloop of 25 tons burden, sailing under the Spanish flag, running in and out of Havana, and regularly engaged in fishing on the coast of Cuba. Her crew consisted of but three men, including the master, and, according to a common usage in coast fisheries, had no interest in the vessel, but were entitled to two thirds of her catch; the other third belonging to her Spanish owner who, as well as the crew, resided in Havana. On her last voyage, she sailed from Havana along the coast of Cuba about 200 miles and fished for 25 days off the cape at the west end of the island within the territorial waters of Spain and was going back to Havana with her cargo of live fish, when she was captured by one of the blockading squadron on April 25, 1898. She had no arms or ammunition on board; she had no knowledge of the blockade or even of the war until she was stopped by a blockading vessel; she made no attempt to run the blockade and no resistance at the time of the capture; nor was there any evidence whatever of likelihood that she or her crew would aid the enemy.

In the case of the Lola, the only differences in the facts were that she was a schooner of 35 tons burden and had a crew of six men, including the master; that after leaving Havana and proceeding some 200 miles along the coast of Cuba, she went on about 100 miles farther to the coast of Yucatan, and there fished for eight days; and that, on her return, when near Bahia Honda on the coast of Cuba, she was captured with her cargo of live fish on April 27, 1898. These differences afford no ground for distinguishing the two cases.

Each vessel was of a moderate size, such as is not unusual in coast fishing smacks, and was regularly engaged in fishing on the coast of Cuba. The crew of each were few in number, had no interest in the vessel, and received, in return for their toil and enterprise, two thirds of her catch; the other third going to her owner by way of compensation for her use. Each vessel went out from Havana to her fishing ground and was captured when returning along the coast of Cuba. The cargo of each consisted of fresh fish caught by her crew from the sea and kept alive on board. Although one of the vessels extended her fishing trip across the Yucatan Channel and fished on the coast of Yucatan, we cannot doubt that each was engaged in the coast fishery and not in a commercial adventure within the rule of international law.

The two vessels and their cargoes were condemned by the District Court as prize of war; the vessels were sold under its decrees; and it does not appear what became of the fresh fish of which their cargoes consisted.

Upon the facts proved in either case, it is the duty of this court, sitting as the highest prize court of the United States, and administering the law of nations, to declare and adjudge that the capture was unlawful, and without probable cause; and it is therefore, in each case,

Ordered, that the decree of the District Court be reversed, and the proceeds of the sale of the vessel, together with the proceeds of any sale of her cargo, be restored to the claimant, with damages and costs.

Notes and Questions

1. The Paquete Habana. The 1900 judgment of the U.S. Supreme Court in *The Paquete Habana* is probably the best-known decision of a U.S. court finding and applying customary international law. The case is frequently cited with respect to at least three issues: (1) the manner of determining rules of customary international law; (2) the way in which customary international law is incorporated into the municipal law of the United States; and (3) the proper relationship between the U.S. courts and the executive branch in legal matters touching on international relations. At this point, we are especially interested in the first issue.

2. *Usages as Law.* Justice Gray opined that the rule providing for the exemption of coastal fishing vessels from capture as prizes of war began as "an ancient usage among civilized nations" and then "gradually ripened into a rule of international law." Regardless of what proof of the rule might be offered, why should such a transformative proposition be valid? Why should or how can the "usages" of states "ripen" into legal rules? Why should states or municipal courts give such "ripened usages" the force of law and apply them as rules of decision in cases before them? Are there any analogies in municipal law to the notion of usages ripening into obligatory rules of law?

3. *Evidences of Law.* Turning to his proof, what did Justice Gray employ as factual evidences "to trace the history of the rule"? Beginning with the first recitations, the orders of Henry IV in 1403 and 1406, in what sense are these evidences "international" usages? Is the next bit of proof, the 1521 treaty between Emperor Charles V and Francis I of France, any more "international"? Of all the evidences and usages shown, are some more persuasive as forms of proof than others?

4. *Contradictory Practice.* When can it be said that a usage "ripens" into a rule of customary international law? What about contradictory practice? For example, the 1675 agreement between Louis XIV and the States General of Holland had to be discontinued in 1681 and 1692 because the enemies of the French monarch "habitually carried off his fishermen, while their own fished in safety." Does such contradictory practice prevent the rule from ripening? Does one know if the rule has ripened by merely weighing the cited bits of practice? Or must the record of practice be overwhelmingly conclusive before the rule ripens?

5. Opinio Juris. Ordinarily in positivist theory, it is said that customary international law is based on state practice and *opinio juris*, the belief that states act in a certain way because legally bound to do so. Is there any proof of *opinio juris* in *Paquete Habana*? *Opinio juris* is vital if custom is to

be deemed the implicit agreement of states. If *opinio juris* is often a legal fiction, what is the real nature of customary international law? Does state practice without clear *opinio juris* still constitute a consensual source of international law?

In an interesting challenge to a positivist account of *Paquete Habana*, Professors Goldsmith and Posner have offered a rational choice theory of the case, viewing "the behaviors associated with the fishing exemption rule as some combination of coincidence of interest, coercion, and bilateral cooperation." Jack L. Goldsmith & Eric Posner, "Understanding the Resemblance between Modern and Traditional Customary International Law," 40 *Virginia Journal of International Law* 639, 660 (2000).

6. *Custom and Municipal Law.* Note briefly here the other two "lessons" of *Paquete Habana* mentioned in Note 1. First, the Supreme Court held that "international law is part of our law," an important proposition about the incorporation of customary international law into U.S. municipal law. Second, the Supreme Court noted that it was "the general policy of the Government to conduct the war in accordance with the principles of international law." Did this satisfactorily establish why the Supreme Court had the constitutional authority to trump an executive decision with customary international law? Had both the President and the Court agreed that the actions of the Executive ought in any case be subject to customary international law? See Jordan Paust, "*Paquete* and the President: Rediscovering the Brief for the United States," 34 *Virginia Journal of International Law* 981 (1994). We return to the incorporation of customary international law and to the balance of powers in foreign relations among the President, the Congress, and U.S. courts in Chapter 4.

THE ASYLUM CASE

Colombia v. Peru, 1950 I.C.J. 266, 1950 WL 10.

[Victor Raúl Haya de la Torre, the unsuccessful leader of a military rebellion in Peru in 1948, sought political asylum in the Colombian embassy in Lima. Peru, however, rejected Colombia's assertion of diplomatic asylum for Haya de la Torre and refused to give him safe-conduct to leave the country, insisting that he, instead, be given over to Peru for trial for military rebellion. The dispute was referred to the International Court of Justice, which first decided that Colombia had no treaty right to unilaterally declare Haya de la Torre entitled to the status of a political offender eligible for diplomatic asylum. The ICJ then turned to customary international law:]

The Colombian Government has finally invoked "American international law in general." In addition to the rules arising from agreements which have already been considered, it has relied on an alleged regional or local custom peculiar to Latin–American states.

The Party which relies on a custom of this kind must prove that this custom is established in such a manner that it has become binding on the other Party. The Colombian Government must prove that the rule invoked by it is in accordance with a constant and uniform usage practised by the States in question, and that this usage is the expression of a right appertaining to the State granting asylum and a duty incumbent on the territorial State. This follows from Article 38 of the Statute of the Court which refers to international custom as "evidence of a general practice accepted as law."

In support of its contention concerning the existence of such a custom, the Colombian government has referred to a large number of extradition treaties which, as already explained, can have no bearing on the question now under consideration. It has cited conventions and agreements which do not contain any provision concerning the alleged rule of unilateral and definitive qualification such as the Montevideo Convention of 1889 on international penal law, the Bolivarian Agreement of 1911 and the Havana Convention of 1928. It has invoked conventions which have not been ratified by Peru, such as the Montevideo Conventions of 1933 and 1939. The Convention of 1933, has, in fact, been ratified by not more than eleven States and the Convention of 1939 by two States only.

It is particularly the Montevideo Convention of 1933 which Counsel for the Colombian Government has also relied on in this connexion. It is contended that this Convention has merely codified principles which were already recognized by Latin–American custom, and that it is valid against Peru as a proof of customary law. The limited number of States which have ratified this Convention reveals the weakness of this argument, and furthermore, it is invalidated by the preamble which states that this Convention modifies the Havana Convention.

Finally, the Colombian Government has referred to a large number of particular cases in which diplomatic asylum was in fact granted and respected. But it has not shown that the alleged rule of unilateral and definitive qualification was invoked or—if in some cases it was in fact invoked—that it was, apart from conventional stipulations, exercised by the States granting asylum as a right appertaining to them and respected by the territorial States as a duty incumbent on them and not merely for reasons of political expediency. The facts brought to the knowledge of the Court disclose so much uncertainty and contradiction, so much fluctuation and discrepancy in the exercise of diplomatic asylum and in the official views expressed on various occasions, there has been so much inconsistency in the rapid succession of conventions on asylum, ratified by some States and rejected by others, and the practice has been so much influenced by considerations of political expediency in the various cases, that it is not possible to discern in all this any constant and uniform usage, accepted as law, with regard to the alleged rule of unilateral and definitive qualification of the offense.

The Court cannot therefore find that the Colombian Government has proved the existence of such a custom. But even it could be supposed that such a custom existed between certain Latin–American States only, it could not be invoked against Peru which, far from having by its attitude adhered to it, has, on the contrary, repudiated it by refraining from ratifying the Montevideo Conventions of 1933 and 1939, which were the first to include a rule concerning the qualification of the offence in matters of diplomatic asylum.

In the written Pleadings and during the oral proceedings, the Government of Colombia relied upon official communiqués published by the Peruvian Ministry of Foreign Affairs on October 13th and 26th, 1948, and the Government of Peru relied upon a Report of the Advisory Committee of the Ministry of Foreign Affairs of Colombia dated September 2nd, 1937; on the question of qualification, these documents state views which are contrary to those now maintained by these Governments. The Court, whose duty it is to apply international law in deciding the present case, cannot attach decisive importance to any of these documents.

For these reasons, the Court has arrived at the conclusion that Colombia, as the State granting asylum, is not competent to qualify the offence by a unilateral and definitive decision, binding on Peru.

Notes and Questions

1. *The* Asylum Case. At the time, the ICJ's judgment in the *Asylum Case* was attacked because it "unmistakably pronounced a death sentence upon the institution of asylum." Manuel R. Garcia–Mora, "The Colombian–Peruvian Asylum Case and the Doctrine of Human Rights," 37 *Virginia Law Review* 927, 965 (1951). This was too great an alarm; the political offender doctrine has remained alive and well. See L.C. Green, "The Right of Asylum in International Law," 3 *University of Malaya Law Review* 223 (1961). Indeed, many Latin American countries, albeit not Peru, responded to the *Asylum Case* by drafting the Caracas Convention on Diplomatic Asylum, specifically providing that "it shall rest with the state granting asylum to determine the nature of the offence or the motive for the nature of the offence or the motive for the prosecution." *Id*. at 238–39.

2. *Regional and Particular Custom*. The more lasting contribution of the *Asylum Case* has been its proposition, though not proved by the practice in this case, that there can be a regional or particular rule of customary international law. A more successful argument based on a non-universal customary rule was accepted by the Court in the Anglo–Norwegian Fisheries Case, 1951 I.C.J. 116, 139, 1951 WL 17, respecting Norway's assertion of a wider than ordinary exclusive fishing zone: "The notoriety of the facts, the general toleration of the international community, Great Britain's position in the North Sea, her own interest in the question, and her prolonged abstention would in any case warrant Norway's enforcement of her system against the United Kingdom." Might it have been sounder for the PCIJ in the *Eastern Greenland Case* in Chapter 2 to view the Ihlen Declaration as evidence of a particular custom rather than as a tacit treaty binding Norway and Denmark?

3. *The Persistent Objector*. Is a state bound by a rule of customary international law if it persistently objected to the rule from the time it is first asserted? What practical difficulties might attend an effort to maintain persistent objector status?

THE LOTUS CASE

France v. Turkey,
1927 P.C.I.J., Ser. A, No. 10.

By a special agreement signed at Geneva on October 12th, 1926, between the Governments of the French and Turkish Republics * * * the Court has to decide the following questions:

"(1) Has Turkey, contrary to Article 15 of the Convention of Lausanne of July 24th, 1923, respecting conditions of residence and business and jurisdiction, acted in conflict with the principles of international law—and if so, what principles—by instituting, following the collision which occurred on August 2nd, 1926, on the high seas between the French steamer Lotus and the Turkish steamer Boz–Kourt and upon the arrival of the French steamer at Constantinople—as well as against the captain of the Turkish steamship—joint criminal proceedings in pursuance of Turkish law against M. Demons, officer of the watch on board the Lotus at the time of the collision, in consequence of the loss of the Boz–Kourt having involved the death of eight Turkish sailors and passengers?

"(2) Should the reply be in the affirmative, what pecuniary reparation is due to M. Demons, provided, according to the principles of international law, reparation should be made in similar cases?" * * *

THE FACTS. * * *

On August 2nd, 1926, just before midnight, a collision occurred between the French mail steamer Lotus, proceeding to Constantinople, and the Turkish collier Boz–Kourt, between five and six nautical miles to the north of Cape Sigri (Mitylene). The Boz–Kourt, which was cut in two, sank and eight Turkish nationals who were on board perished. After having done everything possible to succour the shipwrecked persons, of whom ten were able to be saved, the Lotus continued on its course to Constantinople, where it arrived on August 3rd.

At the time of the collision, the officer of the watch on board the Lotus was Monsieur Demons, a French citizen, lieutenant in the merchant service and first officer of the ship, whilst the movements of the Boz–Kourt were directed by its captain, Hassan Bey, who was one of those saved from the wreck.

As early as August 3rd the Turkish police proceeded to hold an enquiry into the collision on board the Lotus; and on the following day, August 4th, the captain of the Lotus handed in his master's report at the French Consulate–General, transmitting a copy to the harbour master.

On August 5th, Lieutenant Demons was requested by the Turkish authorities to go ashore to give evidence. The examination, the length of which incidentally resulted in delaying the departure of the Lotus, led to the placing under arrest of Lieutenant Demons—without previous notice being given to the French Consul–General—and Hassan Bey, amongst others. This arrest, which has been characterized by the Turkish Agent as arrest pending trial (*arrestation préventive*), was effected in order to ensure that the criminal prosecution instituted against the two officers, on a charge of manslaughter, by the Public Prosecutor of Stamboul, on the complaint of the families of the victims of the collision, should follow its normal course.

The case was first heard by the Criminal Court of Stamboul on August 28th. On that occasion, Lieutenant Demons submitted that the Turkish Courts had no jurisdiction; the Court, however, overruled his objection. When the proceedings were resumed on September 11th, Lieutenant Demons demanded his release on bail: this request was complied with on September 13th, the bail being fixed at 6,000 Turkish pounds.

On September 15th, the Criminal Court delivered its judgment, the terms of which have not been communicated to the Court by the Parties. It is, however, common ground, that it sentenced Lieutenant Demons to 80 days' imprisonment and a fine of 22 pounds, Hassan Bey being sentenced to a slightly more severe penalty.

It is also common ground between the Parties that the Public Prosecutor of the Turkish Republic entered an appeal against this decision, which had the effect of suspending its execution until a decision upon the appeal had been given; that such decision has not yet been given; but that the special agreement of October 12th, 1926, did not have the effect of suspending "the criminal proceedings ... now in progress in Turkey."

The action of the Turkish judicial authorities with regard to Lieutenant Demons at once gave rise to many diplomatic representations and other steps on the part of the French Government or its representatives in Turkey, either protesting against the arrest of Lieutenant Demons or demanding his release, or with a view to obtaining the transfer of the case from the Turkish Courts to the French Courts.

As a result of these representations, the Government of the Turkish Republic declared on September 2nd, 1926, that "it would have no objection to the reference of the conflict of jurisdiction to the Court at The Hague."

The French Government having, on the 6th of the same month, given "its full consent to the proposed solution," the two Governments appointed their plenipotentiaries with a view to the drawing up of the special agreement to be submitted to the Court; this special agreement was signed at Geneva on October 12th, 1926, as stated above, and the ratifications were deposited on December 27th, 1926.

THE LAW.

I.

Before approaching the consideration of the principles of international law contrary to which Turkey is alleged to have acted—thereby infringing the terms of Article 15 of the Convention of Lausanne of July 24th, 1923, respecting conditions of residence and business and jurisdiction—, it is necessary to define, in the light of the written and oral proceedings, the position resulting from the special agreement. For, the Court having obtained cognizance of the present case by notification of a special agreement concluded between the Parties in the case, it is rather to the terms of this agreement than to the submissions of the Parties that the Court must have recourse in establishing the precise points which it has to decide. In this respect the following observations should be made:

1.—The collision which occurred on August 2nd, 1926, between the S.S. *Lotus*, flying the French flag, and the S.S. *Boz–Kourt*, flying the Turkish flag, took place on the high seas: the territorial jurisdiction of any State other than France and Turkey therefore does not enter into account.

2.—The violation, if any, of the principles of international law would have consisted in the taking of criminal proceedings against Lieutenant Demons. It is not therefore a question relating to any particular step in these proceedings—such as his being put to trial, his arrest, his detention pending trial or the judgment given by the Criminal Court of Stamboul—but of the very fact of the Turkish Courts exercising criminal jurisdiction. That is why the arguments put forward by the Parties in both phases of the proceedings relate exclusively to the question whether Turkey has or has not, according to the principles of international law, jurisdiction to prosecute in this case. * * *

Article 6 of the Turkish Penal Code, Law No. 765 of March 1st, 1926 (Official Gazette No. 320 of March 13th, 1926), runs as follows:

[*Translation.*]

"Any foreigner who, apart from the cases contemplated by Article 4, commits an offence abroad to the prejudice of Turkey or of a Turkish subject, for which offence Turkish law prescribes a penalty involving loss of freedom for a minimum period of not less than one year, shall be punished in accordance with the Turkish Penal Code provided that he is arrested in Turkey. The penalty shall however be reduced by one third and instead of the death penalty, 20 years of penal servitude shall be awarded.

"Nevertheless, in such cases, the prosecution will only be instituted at the request of the Minister of Justice or on the complaint of the injured Party.

"If the offence committed injures another foreigner, the guilty person shall be punished at the request of the Minister of Justice, in accordance with the provisions set out in the first paragraph of this article, provided however that:

"(1) the article in question is one for which Turkish law prescribes a penalty involving loss of freedom for a minimum period of three years;

"(2) there is no extradition treaty or that extradition has not been accepted either by the government of the locality where the guilty person has committed the offence or by the government of his own country."

Even if the Court must hold that the Turkish authorities had seen fit to base the prosecution of Lieutenant Demons upon the above-mentioned Article 6, the question submitted to the Court is not whether that article is compatible with the principles of international law; it is more general. The Court is asked to state whether or not the principles of international law prevent Turkey from instituting criminal proceedings against Lieutenant Demons under Turkish law. Neither the conformity of Article 6 in itself with the principles of international law nor the application of that article by the Turkish authorities constitutes the point at issue; it is the very fact of the institution of proceedings which is held by France to be contrary to those principles. * * *

II.

Having determined the position resulting from the terms of the special agreement, the Court must now ascertain which were the principles of international law that the prosecution of Lieutenant Demons could conceivably be said to contravene.

It is Article 15 of the Convention of Lausanne of July 24th, 1923, respecting conditions of residence and business and jurisdiction, which refers the contracting Parties to the principles of international law as regards the delimitation of their respective jurisdiction.

This clause is as follows:

"Subject to the provisions of Article 16, all questions of jurisdiction shall, as between Turkey and the other contracting Powers, be decided in accordance with the principles of international law."

The French Government maintains that the meaning of the expression "principles of international law" in this article should be sought in the light of the evolution of the Convention. Thus it states that during the preparatory work, the Turkish Government, by means of an amendment to the relevant article of a draft for the Convention, sought to extend its jurisdiction to crimes committed in the territory of a third State, provided that, under Turkish law, such crimes were within the jurisdiction of Turkish Courts. This amendment, in regard to which the representatives of France and Italy made reservations, was definitely rejected by the British representative; and the question having been subsequently referred to the Drafting Committee, the latter confined itself in its version of the draft to a declaration to the effect that questions of jurisdiction should be decided in accordance with the principles of international law. The French Government deduces from these facts that the prosecution of Demons is contrary to the intention which guided the preparation of the Convention of Lausanne.

The Court must recall in this connection what it has said in some of its preceding judgments and opinions, namely, that there is no occasion to have regard to preparatory work if the text of a convention is sufficiently clear in itself. Now the Court considers that the words "principles of international law," as ordinarily used, can only mean international law as it is applied between all nations belonging to the community of States. * * *

III.

The Court, having to consider whether there are any rules of international law which may have been violated by the prosecution in pursuance of Turkish law of Lieutenant Demons, is confronted in the first place by a question of principle which, in the written and oral arguments of the two Parties, has proved to be a fundamental one. The French Government contends that the Turkish Courts, in order to have jurisdiction, should be able to point to some title to jurisdiction recognized by international law in favour of Turkey. On the other hand, the Turkish Government takes the view that Article 15 allows Turkey jurisdiction whenever such jurisdiction does not come into conflict with a principle of international law.

The latter view seems to be in conformity with the special agreement itself, No. 1 of which asks the Court to say whether Turkey has acted contrary to the principles of international law and, if so, what principles. According to the special agreement, therefore, it is not a question of stating principles which would permit Turkey to take criminal proceedings, but of formulating the principles, if any, which might have been violated by such proceedings.

This way of stating the question is also dictated by the very nature and existing conditions of international law.

International law governs relations between independent States. The rules of law binding upon States therefore emanate from their own free will as expressed in conventions or by usages generally accepted as expressing principles of law and established in order to regulate the relations between these co-existing independent communities or with a view to the achievement of common aims. Restrictions upon the independence of States cannot therefore be presumed.

Now the first and foremost restriction imposed by international law upon a State is that—failing the existence of a permissive rule to the contrary—it may not exercise its power in any form in the territory of another State. In this sense jurisdiction is certainly territorial; it cannot be exercised by a State outside its territory except by virtue of a permissive rule derived from international custom or from a convention.

It does not, however, follow that international law prohibits a State from exercising jurisdiction in its own territory, in respect of any case which relates to acts which have taken place abroad, and in which it cannot rely on some permissive rule of international law. Such a view would only be tenable if international law contained a general prohibition to States to extend the application of their laws and the jurisdiction of their courts to persons, property and acts outside their territory, and if, as an exception to this general prohibition, it allowed States to do so in certain specific cases. But this is certainly not the case under international law as it stands at present. Far from laying down a general prohibition to the effect that States may not extend the application of their laws and the jurisdiction of their courts to persons, property and acts outside their territory, it leaves them in this respect a wide measure of discretion which is only limited in certain cases by prohibitive rules; as regards other cases, every State remains free to adopt the principles which it regards as best and most suitable. * * *

In these circumstances, all that can be required of a State is that it should not overstep the limits which international law places upon its jurisdiction; within these limits, its title to exercise jurisdiction rests in its sovereignty.

It follows from the foregoing that the contention of the French Government to the effect that Turkey must in each case be able to cite a rule of international law authorizing her to exercise jurisdiction, is opposed to the generally accepted international law to which Article 15 of the Convention of Lausanne refers. * * *

IV.

The Court will now proceed to ascertain whether general international law, to which Article 15 of the Convention of Lausanne refers, contains a rule prohibiting Turkey from prosecuting Lieutenant Demons.

For this purpose, it will in the first place examine the value of the arguments advanced by the French Government, without however omitting to take into account other possible aspects of the problem, which might show the existence of a restrictive rule applicable in this case.

The arguments advanced by the French Government, other than those considered above, are, in substance, the three following:

(1) International law does not allow a State to take proceedings with regard to offenses committed by foreigners abroad, simply by reason of the nationality of the victim; and such is the situation in the present case because the offence must be regarded as having been committed on board the French vessel.

(2) International law recognizes the exclusive jurisdiction of the State whose flag is flown as regards everything which occurs on board a ship on the high seas.

(3) Lastly, this principle is especially applicable in a collision case.

As regards the first argument, the Court feels obliged in the first place to recall that its examination is strictly confined to the specific situation in the present case, for it is only in regard to this situation that its decision is asked for.

As has already been observed, the characteristic features of the situation of fact are as follows: there has been a collision on the high seas between two vessels flying different flags, on one of which was one of the persons alleged to be guilty of the offence, whilst the victims were on board the other.

This being so, the Court does not think it necessary to consider the contention that a State cannot punish offences committed abroad by a foreigner simply by reason of the nationality of the victim. For this contention only relates to the case where the nationality of the victim is the only criterion on which the criminal jurisdiction of the State is based. Even if that argument were correct generally speaking—and in regard to this the Court reserves its opinion—it could only be used in the present case if international law forbade Turkey to take into consideration the fact that the offence produced its effects on the Turkish vessel and consequently in a place assimilated to Turkish territory in which the application of Turkish criminal law cannot be challenged, even in regard to offenses committed there by foreigners. But no such rule of international law exists. No argument has come to the knowledge of the Court from which it could be deduced that States recognize themselves to be under an obligation towards each other only to have regard to the place where the author of the offence happens to be at the time of the offence. On the contrary, it is certain that the courts of many countries, even of countries which have given their criminal legislation a strictly territorial character, interpret criminal law in the sense that offences, the authors of which at the moment of commission are in the territory of another State, are nevertheless to be regarded as having been committed in the national territory, if one of the constituent elements of the offence, and more especially its effects, have taken place there. French courts have, in regard to a variety of situations, given decisions sanctioning this way of interpreting the territorial principle. Again, the Court does not know of any cases in which governments have protested against the fact that the criminal law of some country contained a rule to this effect or that the courts of a country construed their criminal law in this sense. Consequently, once it is admitted that the effects of the offence were produced on the Turkish vessel, it becomes impossible to hold that there is a rule of international law which prohibits Turkey from prosecuting Lieutenant Demons because of the fact that the author of the offence was on board the French ship. * * *

The second argument put forward by the French Government is the principle that the State whose flag is flown has exclusive jurisdiction over everything which occurs on board a merchant ship on the high seas.

It is certainly true that—apart from certain special cases which are defined by international law—vessels on the high seas are subject to no authority except that of the State whose flag they fly. In virtue of the principle of the freedom of the seas, that is to say, the absence of any territorial sovereignty upon the high seas, no State may exercise any kind of jurisdiction over foreign vessels upon them. Thus, if a war vessel, happening to be at the spot where a collision occurs between a vessel flying its flag and a foreign vessel, were to send on board the latter an officer to make investigations or to take evidence, such an act would undoubtedly be contrary to international law.

But it by no means follows that a State can never in its own territory exercise jurisdiction over acts which have occurred on board a foreign ship on the high seas. A corollary of the principle of the freedom of the seas is that a ship on the high seas is assimilated to the territory of the State the flag of which it flies, for, just as in its own territory, that State exercises its authority upon it, and no other State may do so. All that can be said is that by virtue of the principle of the freedom of the seas, a ship is placed in the same position as national territory; but there is nothing to support the claim according to which the rights of the State under whose flag the vessel sails may go farther than the rights which it exercises within its territory properly so called. It follows that what occurs on board a vessel on the high seas must be regarded as if it occurred on the territory of the State whose flag the ship flies. If, therefore, a guilty act committed on the high seas produces its effects on a vessel flying another flag or in foreign territory, the same principles must be applied as if the territories of two different States were concerned, and the conclusion must therefore be drawn that there is no rule of international law prohibiting the State to which the ship on which the effects of the offence have taken place belongs, from regarding the offence as having been committed in its territory and prosecuting, accordingly, the delinquent.

This conclusion could only be overcome if it were shown that there was a rule of customary international law which, going further than the principle stated above, established the exclusive jurisdiction of the State whose flag was flown. The French Government has endeavored to prove the existence of such a rule, having recourse for this purpose to the teachings of publicists, to decisions of municipal and international tribunals, and especially to conventions which, whilst creating exceptions to the principle of the freedom of the seas by permitting the war and police vessels of a State to exercise a more or less extensive control over the merchant vessels of another State, reserve jurisdiction to the courts of the country whose flag is flown by the vessel proceeded against.

In the Court's opinion, the existence of such a rule has not been conclusively proved.

In the first place, as regards teachings of publicists, and apart from the question as to what their value may be from the point of view of establishing the existence of a rule of customary law, it is no doubt true that all or nearly all writers teach that ships on the high seas are subject exclusively to the jurisdiction of the State whose flag they fly. But the important point is the significance attached by them to this principle; now it does not appear that in general, writers bestow upon this principle a scope differing from or wider than that explained above and which is equivalent to saying that the jurisdiction of a State over vessels on the high seas is the same in extent as its jurisdiction in its own territory. On the other hand, there is no lack of writers who, upon a close study of the special question whether a State can prosecute for offences committed on board a foreign ship on the high seas, definitely come to the conclusion that such offences must be regarded as if they had been committed in the territory of the State whose flag the ship flies, and that consequently the general rules of each legal system in regard to offences committed abroad are applicable.

In regard to precedents, it should first be observed that, leaving aside the collision cases which will be alluded to later, none of them relates to offences affecting two ships flying the flags of two different countries, and that consequently they are not of much importance in the case before the Court. The case of the *Costa Rica Packet* is no exception, for the prauw on which the alleged depredations took place was adrift without flag or crew, and this circumstance certainly influenced, perhaps decisively, the conclusion arrived at by the arbitrator.

On the other hand, there is no lack of cases in which a State has claimed a right to prosecute for an offence, committed on board a foreign ship, which it regarded as punishable under its legislation. Thus Great Britain refused the request of the United States for the extradition of John Anderson, a British seaman who had committed homicide on board an American vessel, stating that she did not dispute the jurisdiction of the United States but that she was entitled to exercise hers concurrently. This case, to which others might be added, is relevant in spite of Anderson's British nationality, in order to show that the principle of the exclusive jurisdiction of the country whose flag the vessel flies is not universally accepted. * * *

Finally, as regards conventions expressly reserving jurisdiction exclusively to the State whose flag is flown, it is not absolutely certain that this stipulation is to be regarded as expressing a general principle of law rather than as corresponding to the extraordinary jurisdiction which these conventions confer on the state-owned ships of a particular country in respect of ships of another country on the high seas. Apart from that, it should be observed that these conventions relate to matters of a particular kind, closely connected with the policing of the seas, such as the slave trade, damage to submarine cables, fisheries, etc., and not to common-law offences. Above all it should be pointed out that the offences contemplated by the conventions in question only concern a single ship; it is impossible therefore to make any deduction from them in regard to matters which concern two ships and consequently the jurisdiction of two different States.

The Court therefore has arrived at the conclusion that the second argument put forward by the French Government does not, any more than the first, establish the existence of a rule of international law prohibiting Turkey from prosecuting Lieutenant Demons.

It only remains to examine the third argument advanced by the French Government and to ascertain whether a rule specially applying to collision cases has grown up, according to which criminal proceedings regarding such cases come exclusively within the jurisdiction of the State whose flag is flown.

In this connection, the Agent for the French Government has drawn the Court's attention to the fact that questions of jurisdiction in collision cases, which frequently arise before civil courts, are but rarely encountered in the practice of criminal courts. He deduces from this that, in practice, prosecutions only occur before the courts of the State whose flag is flown and that circumstance is proof of a tacit consent on the part of States and, consequently, shows what positive international law is in collision cases.

In the Court's opinion, this conclusion is not warranted. Even if the rarity of the judicial decisions to be found among the reported cases were sufficient to prove in point of fact the circumstance alleged by the Agent for the French Government, it would merely show that States had often, in practice, abstained from instituting criminal proceedings, and not that they recognized themselves as being obliged to do so; for only if such abstention were based on their being conscious of having a duty to abstain would it be possible to speak of an international custom. The alleged fact does not allow one to infer that States have been conscious of having such a duty; on the other hand, as will presently be seen, there are other circumstances calculated to show that the contrary is true.

So far as the Court is aware there are no decisions of international tribunals in this matter; but some decisions of municipal courts have been cited. Without pausing to consider the value to be attributed to the judgments of municipal courts in connection with the establishment of the existence of a rule of international law, it will suffice to observe that the decisions quoted sometimes support one view and sometimes the other. Whilst the French Government have been able to cite the *Ortigia–Oncle–Joseph* case before the Court of Aix and the *Franconia–Strathclyde* case before the British Court for Crown Cases Reserved, as being in favour of the exclusive jurisdiction of the state whose flag is flown, on the other hand the *Ortigia–Oncle–Joseph* case before the Italian Courts and the *Ekbatana–West–Hinder* case before the Belgian Courts have been cited in support of the opposing contention.

Lengthy discussions have taken place between the Parties as to the importance of each of these decisions as regards the details of which the Court confines itself to a reference to the Cases and Counter–Cases of the Parties. The Court does not think it necessary to stop to consider them. It will suffice to observe that, as municipal jurisprudence is thus divided, it is hardly possible to see in it an indication of the existence of the restrictive rule of international law which alone could serve as a basis for the contention of the French Government. * * *

The Court, having arrived at the conclusion that the arguments advanced by the French Government either are irrelevant to the issue or do not establish the existence of a principle of international law precluding Turkey from instituting the prosecution which was in fact brought against Lieutenant Demons, observes that in the fulfilment of its task of itself ascertaining what the international law is, it has not confined itself to a consideration of the arguments put forward, but has included in its researches all precedents, teachings and facts to which it had access and which might possibly have revealed the existence of one of the principles of international law contemplated in the special argument. The result of these researches has not been to establish the existence of any such principle. It must therefore be held that there is no principle of international law, within the meaning of Article 15 of the Convention of Lausanne of July 24th, 1923, which precludes the institution of the criminal proceedings under consideration. Consequently, Turkey, by instituting, in virtue of the discretion which international law leaves to every sovereign State, the criminal proceedings in question, has not, in the absence of such principles, acted in a manner contrary to the principles of international law within the meaning of the special agreement. * * *

FOR THESE REASONS,

The Court,

having heard both Parties,

gives by the President's casting vote—the votes being equally divided—, judgment to the effect

(1) that, following the collision which occurred on August 2nd, 1926, on the high seas between the French steamship *Lotus* and the Turkish steamship *Boz–Kourt*, and upon the arrival of the French ship at Stamboul, and in consequence of the loss of the *Boz–Kourt* having involved the death of eight Turkish nationals, Turkey, by instituting criminal proceedings in pursuance of Turkish law against Lieutenant Demons, officer of the watch on board the *Lotus* at the time of the collision, has not acted in conflict with the principles of international law, contrary to Article 15 of the Convention of Lausanne of July 24th, 1923, respecting conditions of residence and business and jurisdiction;

(2) that, consequently, there is no occasion to give judgment on the question of the pecuniary reparation which might have been due to Lieutenant Demons if Turkey, by prosecuting him as above stated, had acted in a manner contrary to the principles of international law.

Notes and Questions

1. *Positivism and International Law. Lotus* involved a narrow, albeit interesting, jurisdictional issue in international conflict of laws, but the PCIJ sought to teach a far broader lesson. The judgment in *Lotus* has become one of the most usually cited positivist opinions about the nature of international law, because it argued in part III that the "rules of law binding upon States therefore emanate from their own free will as expressed in conventions or by usages generally accepted as expressing principles of law." The ruling half of an evenly divided Court in *Lotus* maintained that all international legal rules are based on state consent: "Restrictions upon the independence of States cannot therefore be presumed." No room was given to general principles,

fundamental norms, natural law, or equity as sources of international law; state sovereignty was seen as the fundamental principle of international law from which all other international legal principles and rules are derived. Looking at other cases above, *e.g., Filartiga* and *Paquete Habana*, and below, *e.g., Texaco/Libya, AM & S, Smith,* and *North Sea Continental Shelf,* is the strict positivism of the *Lotus* judgment too restrictive?

2. *The Burden of Proof.* In the context of the case, the positivist presumption meant that the Court put the burden of proof on France rather than on Turkey. The Court ruled that France had to prove that there was a rule of customary international law restricting Turkish independence rather than making Turkey prove that its prosecution of Lieutenant Demons was sanctioned by international law. Given the uncertainty of the evidence of customary international law, was not this allocation of the burden of proof crucial to the outcome of the case? Would a less positivist position have enabled the Court to rely less heavily on the burden of proof as a way of deciding the case?

3. *Tacit Agreement and the Formation of Rules of Customary International Law.* In order to satisfy its burden of proof in *Lotus,* would France have had to establish that Turkey itself, in its international relations, affirmatively consented to a rule of international law that prohibited the prosecution of Lieutenant Demons in Turkish court? Or would it suffice, under a positivist conception of universal custom, to establish expressions of consent by some states, followed by the silence of other states? Is it possible to establish tacit consent?

Does a voluntarist account of customary international law accurately reflect how it develops? Consider the following view:

> * * * When one examines the emergence of such universally applicable customary rules and principles as those relating to diplomatic immunities, the prohibition of piracy and privateering, and sovereign rights over the continental shelf, it is impossible to show that every State positively consented to the emergence of the rule in question. Yet it is virtually unanimously accepted by the authorities that these rules have come to bind all States.

> The nature of the process by which these customary rules emerged seems to be more along the following lines. Some States actively created the practice, some by initiating it, some by imitating it, and others still, who were directly affected by the claims in question, by acquiescing in it. This initiation, imitation and acquiescence may plausibly be described in terms of consent. But others still, who were not directly affected, sat by and did nothing, and in due course found themselves bound by the emerging rule.

"3rd Interim Report of the Committee on the Formation of Customary (General) International Law," in *International Law Association, Report of the 67th Conference* 623, 630 (1996). Does "sitting by and doing nothing" signify acquiescence or tacit consent?

4. *Reversal of the Rule in* Lotus. As a matter of maritime law, many observers strongly disagreed with the *Lotus* decision, feeling that it exposed shipboard officers to double prosecution and could lead to unnecessary

delays in maritime traffic. In the 1958 Geneva Convention on the High Seas, Article 11(1) provides that in cases involving collisions on the high seas, only the flag state or the national state of the accused may prosecute the officer in a case of a collision on the high seas. The same anti-*Lotus* rule resurfaced in Article 97(1) of the 1982 U.N. Convention on the Law of the Sea. These treaty articles illustrate how a treaty may sometimes reverse a rule of customary international law. Should custom be able to reverse a treaty rule?

5. *Treaty Interpretation.* Note that in *Lotus* two treaties were involved as well as customary international law. The first treaty, the special agreement of October 12, 1926, provided authority for the Permanent Court of International Justice to hear the case and set the questions that the Court was to address. The second treaty was the 1923 Convention of Lausanne, Article 15 of which referred to "principles of international law." The PCIJ took that phrase to refer to customary international law. Was the Court's reluctance to examine the *travaux préparatoires* of Article 15 appropriate? Compare the approach toward treaty interpretation taken in the *Floyd Case* in Chapter 2, and see Articles 31–32 of the Vienna Convention on the Law of Treaties (see Appendix).

THE TEXACO/LIBYA ARBITRATION

Award of 19 January 1977, 17 *International Legal Materials* 1 (1978).

Acting in his capacity as Sole Arbitrator [Professor René-Jean Dupuy], pursuant to the appointment made on 18 December 1974 by the President of the International Court of Justice, of an arbitration between, on the one hand, the Government of the Libyan Arab Republic and, on the other, California Asiatic Oil Company and Texaco Overseas Petroleum Company,

The undersigned Sole Arbitrator has rendered the following award on the merits:

I. THE FACTS

1. The present arbitration arises out of 14 Deeds of Concession concluded between the competent Libyan Authorities (Petroleum Commission or Petroleum Ministry, depending on the date of the contracts) and the above-mentioned companies * * *. * * *

3. Among the provisions which are contained in the model contract annexed to the Petroleum Law of 1955 and reproduced in the contracts concluded by the concessionaire companies, Clause 16 is worth, at this time, special mention. * * *

The final version of Clause 16 * * * reads as follows:

> "The Government of Libya will take all steps necessary to ensure that the Company enjoys all the rights conferred by this Concession. The contractual rights expressly created by this concession shall not be altered except by mutual consent of the parties.
>
> This Concession shall throughout the period of its validity be construed in accordance with the Petroleum Law and the Regula-

tions in force on the date of execution of the agreement of amendment by which this paragraph (2) was incorporated into this concession agreement. Any amendment to or repeal of such Regulations shall not affect the contractual rights of the Company without its consent." * * *

7. Law No. 11 of 1974 (the Decree of Nationalization of 11 February 1974) nationalized the totality of the properties, rights, assets and interests of California Asiatic Oil Company and Texaco Overseas Petroleum Company arising out of the 14 Deeds of Concession held by those companies. The more important aspects of this second text may be summarized as follows:

—it was directed against only the plaintiff companies, to the exclusion of any other company or enterprise;

—the text provided for the nationalization of all the properties and interests, rights and assets of California Asiatic Oil Company and Texaco Overseas Petroleum Company;

—the provisions relating to possible compensation (Article 2) were nothing more than a repetition of those which were already contained in Law No. 66 of 1973 (Article 2);

—the transfer of all the properties, rights and assets to N.O.C. [the Libyan National Oil Company] was confirmed (Article 6);

—finally, Article 7 effected a fundamental change in Amoseas, a company governed by foreign law; it was changed into a non-profit company, the assets of which were completely owned by N.O.C. Amoseas lost its name and was renamed the "Om el Jawabi Company."

II. THE PROCEDURE

8. The Tribunal should now, on the one hand, recall and complete the indications already given in its Preliminary Award of 27 November 1975 relating to the arbitration procedure and, on the other, pronounce on the law applicable to the arbitration of which it has been seized.

A. *The Development of the Procedure:*

9.—by two separate letters, dated 2 September 1973, California Asiatic Oil Company and Texaco Overseas Petroleum Company notified the Government of the Libyan Arab Republic that, pursuant to Article 20(1) of the Law on Petroleum of 1955 and to Clause 28 of the Deeds of Concession, they intended to submit to arbitration the dispute between them and the Government and advised the Government that they had appointed as arbitrator a member of the New York Bar, Mr. Fowler Hamilton.

—during the time which was allowed it by Clause 28 of the Deeds of Concession (and which expired on 1 December 1973), the Government of the Libyan Arab Republic did not appoint its arbitrator and, by a circular letter of 8 December 1973, it declared that it rejected the request for arbitration;

—the Libyan Government's failure and refusal to appoint an arbitrator led the companies to use the provision of Clause 28 of the Deeds of Concession which allows the concessionaires to request that the President of the International Court of Justice appoint a Sole Arbitrator: this was the purpose of the joint letter which the two companies sent on 3 April 1974 to the President of the International Court of Justice * * *. * * *

III. THE MERITS

17. In their final submissions, those which were stated both at the close of their Memorial on the Merits and at the close of the oral hearings, the plaintiffs requested that the Arbitral Tribunal rule:

"A. Finding in favor of the Companies as follows:

(1) that the Deeds of Concession are binding on the Parties;

(2) that Libya, in adopting the Decrees of 1973 and 1974 and by its subsequent action pursuant thereto, breached its obligations under the Deeds of Concession;

(3) that Libya be held to perform the Deeds of Concession and fulfill their terms; and

(4) that Libya have 90 days after the award, being from the time of the declaration of the award or from the date fixed by the Sole Arbitrator, to inform the Arbitral Tribunal of the measures which it has taken in order to comply with and to execute the award." * * *

SECTION I: Concerning the Binding Nature of the Deeds of Concession
* * *

*B. How did the parties to these Deeds of Concession deal with the question of the applicable law? * * *

23. What was the law applicable to these contracts? It is this particular question that the parties intended to resolve in adopting Clause 28 of the Deeds of Concession in a form which must be recalled here:

"This concession shall be governed by and interpreted in accordance with the principles of the law of Libya common to the principles of international law and in the absence of such common principles then by and in accordance with the general principles of law, including such of those principles as may have been applied by international tribunals."

Thus, a complex system to determine the law applicable or the "choice of law" has been provided by the contracting parties involving a two-tier system:

—the principles of Libyan law were applicable to the extent that such principles were common to principles of international law;

—alternatively, in the absence of such conformity, reference was made to general principles of law. * * *

1. First question: Did the parties have the right to choose the law or the system of law which was to govern their contract? * * *

32.   For the time being, it will suffice to note that the evolution which has occurred in the old case law of the Permanent Court of International Justice is due to the fact that, while the old case law viewed the contract as something which could not come under international law because it could not be regarded as a treaty between States, under the new concept treaties are not the only type of agreements governed by such law. And it should be added that, although they are not to be confused with treaties, contracts between States and private persons can, under certain conditions, come within the ambit of a particular and new branch of international law: the international law of contracts. * * *

Section II: Did the Libyan Government, in adopting the nationalization measures of 1973 and 1974, breach its obligations under the contracts?

53.   The Tribunal must now rule on the point whether, in adopting nationalization measures in 1973 and 1974, the defendant Government has, or has not, breached its obligations arising from the contracts it executed. For this purpose, this Tribunal should examine the various reasons which could be envisaged in order to justify the defendant Government's behavior and which, if established, would constitute reasons for freeing or exonerating it from the obligation which it had assumed and from its related responsibilities.

Three types of reasons could be put forward in order to justify, or attempt to justify, the behavior of the defendant government:

—the first reason could be based on the nature of the contracts under dispute: if they were administrative contracts, they could give rise, under certain conditions, to amendments or even to abrogation on the part of the contracting State; in relation to concession contracts, the nationalization measures would then be analyzed as being decisions bringing about, at least implicitly, abrogation;

—the second reason could be based on the concept of sovereignty and on the very nature of measures of nationalization;

—the third reason, lastly, could be deduced from the present status of international law, and in particular from certain resolutions concerning natural resources and wealth as adopted, in the last few years, by the United Nations. * * *

> *C.   The present state of international law and the resolutions concerning natural resources and wealth adopted by the United Nations*

80.   This Tribunal has stated that it intends to rule on the basis of positive law, but now it is necessary to determine precisely the content of

positive law and to ascertain the place which resolutions by the General Assembly of the United Nations could occupy therein.

In its Preliminary Award of 27 November 1975, this Tribunal postponed the examination of the objection raised by the Libyan Government in its Memorandum of 26 July 1974 according to which:

"Nationalization is an act related to the sovereignty of the State. This fact has been recognized by the consecutive Resolutions of the United Nations on the sovereignty of States over their natural resources, the last being Resolution No. 3171 of the United Nations General Assembly adopted on December 13, 1973, as well as paragraph (4/E) of Resolution No. 3201 (S–VI) adopted on 1 May, 1974. The said Resolutions confirm that every State maintains complete right to exercise full sovereignty over its natural resources and recognize Nationalization as being a legitimate and internationally recognized method to ensure the sovereignty of the State upon such resources. Nationalization, being related to the sovereignty of the State, is not subject to foreign jurisdiction. Provisions of the International Law do not permit a dispute with a State to be referred to any Jurisdiction other than its national Jurisdiction. In affirmance of this principle, Resolutions of the General Assembly provide that any dispute related to Nationalization or its consequences should be settled in accordance with provisions of domestic law of the State."

81.   * * *

The practice of the United Nations, referred to in the Libyan Government's Memorandum, does not contradict in any way the status of international law as indicated above. This Tribunal wishes first to recall the relevant passages for this case of Resolution 1803 (XVII) entitled "Permanent Sovereignty over Natural Resources," as adopted by the General Assembly on 14 December 1962:

"3. In cases where authorization is granted, the capital imported and the earnings on that capital shall be governed by the terms thereof, by the national legislation in force, and by international law....

4. Nationalization, expropriation or requisitioning shall be based on grounds or reasons of public utility, security or the national interest which are recognized as overriding purely individual or private interests, both domestic and foreign. In such cases the owner shall be paid appropriate compensation, in accordance with the rules in force in the State taking such measures in the exercise of its sovereignty and in accordance with international law...."

82. The Memorandum of the Libyan Government which has just been quoted relies, however, on more recent Resolutions of the General Assembly (3171 and 3201 (S–VI), in particular) which, according to this Government would as a practical matter rule out any recourse to international law and would confer an exclusive and unlimited competence upon the legislation and courts of the host country.

Although not quoted in the Libyan Memorandum, since subsequent to the date of 26 July 1974, Resolution 3281 (XXIX), proclaimed under the title "Charter of Economic Rights and Duties of the States" and adopted by the General Assembly on 12 December 1974, should also be mentioned with the two Resolutions in support of the contention made by the Libyan Government. Two portions of such Resolutions are of particular interest in the present case:

—Resolution 3201 (S–VI) adopted by the General Assembly on 1 May 1974 under the title "Declaration on the Establishment of a New International Economic Order," Article 4, paragraph (e):

"Full permanent sovereignty of every State over its natural resources and all economic activities. In order to safeguard these resources, each State is entitled to exercise effective control over them and their exploitation with means suitable to its own situation, including the right to nationalization or transfer of ownership to its nationals, this right being an expression of the full permanent sovereignty of the State. No State may be subjected to economic, political or any other type of coercion to prevent the free and full exercise of this inalienable right."

—Article 2 of Resolution 3281 (XXIX):

"1. Every State has and shall freely exercise full permanent sovereignty, including possession, use and disposal, over all its wealth, natural resources and economic activities.

2.   Each State has the right . . .

c) To nationalize, expropriate or transfer ownership of foreign property, in which case appropriate compensation should be paid by the State adopting such measures, taking into account its relevant laws and regulations and all circumstances that the State considers pertinent. In any case where the question of compensation gives rise to a controversy, it shall be settled under the domestic law of the nationalizing State and by its tribunals, unless it is freely and mutually agreed by all States concerned that other peaceful means be sought on the basis of the sovereign equality of States and in accordance with the principal [sic] of free choice of means."

Substantial differences thus exist between Resolution 1803 (XVII) and the subsequent Resolutions as regards the role of international law in the exercise of permanent sovereignty over natural resources. This aspect of the matter is directly related to the instant case under consideration; this Tribunal is obligated to consider the legal validity of the above-mentioned Resolutions and the possible existence of a custom resulting therefrom.

83.   The general question of the legal validity of the Resolutions of the United Nations has been widely discussed by the writers. This Tribunal will recall first that, under Article 10 of the U.N. Charter, the General Assembly only issues "recommendations," which have long

appeared to be texts having no binding force and carrying no obligations for the Member States (see Sloan, "The Binding Force of a 'Recommendation' of the General Assembly of the United Nations," 25 Brit.Y.B. Int'l L. 1 *et seq.* (1948); Fitzmaurice, "The Law and Procedure of the International Court of Justice, 1951–4: Questions of Jurisdiction, Competence and Procedure," 34 Brit.Y.B. Int'l L. 1 *et seq.* (1958); Virally, "La Valeur Juridique des Recommendations des Organisations Internationales," 2 Annuaire Français de Droit International ("A.F.D.I.") 66 *et seq.* (1956); Vallat, "The Competence of the United Nations General Assembly," 97 R.C.A.D.I. 203 *et seq.* (1959); Galino, "Las Resoluciones de la Asemblea General de las Naciones Unidas y su Fuerza Legal," Revista Española de Derecho Internacional 96 *et seq.* (1958); Johnson, "The Effect of Resolutions of the General Assembly of the United Nations," 32 Brit.Y.B. Int'l L. 97 *et seq.* (1955)).

Refusal to recognize any legal validity of United Nations Resolutions must, however, be qualified according to the various texts enacted by the United Nations. These are very different and have varying legal value, but it is impossible to deny that the United Nations' activities have had a significant influence on the content of contemporary international law. In appraising the legal validity of the above-mentioned Resolutions, this Tribunal will take account of the criteria usually taken into consideration, *i.e.*, the examination of voting conditions and the analysis of the provisions concerned.

84.   (1) With respect to the first point, Resolution 1803 (XVII) of 14 December 1962 was passed by the General Assembly by 87 votes to 2, with 12 abstentions. It is particularly important to note that the majority voted for this text, including many States of the Third World, but also several Western developed countries with market economies, including the most important one, the United States. The principles stated in this Resolution were therefore assented to by a great many States representing not only all geographical areas but also all economic systems.

From this point of view, this Tribunal notes that the affirmative vote of several developed countries with a market economy was made possible in particular by the inclusion in the Resolution of two references to international law, and one passage relating to the importance of international cooperation for economic development. According to the representative of Tunisia:

> "... the result of the debate on this question was that the balance of the original draft resolution was improved—a balance between, on the one hand, the unequivocal affirmation of the inalienable right of States to exercise sovereignty over their natural resources and, on the other hand, the reconciliation or adaptation of this sovereignty to international law, equity and the principles of international cooperation." (17 U.N. GAOR 1122, U.N. Doc. A/PV.1193 (1962).)

The reference to international law, in particular in the field of nationalization, was therefore an essential factor in the support given by several Western countries to Resolution 1803 (XVII).

85.   On the contrary, it appears to this Tribunal that the conditions under which Resolutions 3171 (XXVII), 3201 (S–VI) and 3281 (XXIX) (Charter of the Economic Rights and Duties of States) were notably different:

—Resolution 3171 (XXVII) was adopted by a recorded vote of 108 votes to 1, with 16 abstentions, but this Tribunal notes that a separate vote was requested with respect to the paragraph in the operative part mentioned in the Libyan Government's Memorandum whereby the General Assembly stated that the application of the principle according to which nationalizations effected by States as the expression of their sovereignty implied that it is within the right of each State to determine the amount of possible compensation and the means of their payment, and that any dispute which might arise should be settled in conformity with the national law of each State instituting measures of this kind. As a consequence of a roll-call, this paragraph was adopted by 86 votes to 11 (Federal Republic of Germany, Belgium, Spain, United States, France, Israel, Italy, Japan, The Netherlands, Portugal, United Kingdom), with 28 abstentions (South Africa, Australia, Austria, Barbados, Canada, Ivory Coast, Denmark, Finland, Ghana, Greece, Haiti, India, Indonesia, Ireland, Luxembourg, Malawi, Malaysia, Nepal, Nicaragua, Norway, New Zealand, Philippines, Rwanda, Singapore, Sri Lanka, Sweden, Thailand, Turkey).

This specific paragraph concerning nationalizations, disregarding the role of international law, not only was not consented to by the most important Western countries, but caused a number of the developing countries to abstain.

—Resolution 3201 (S–VI) was adopted without a vote by the General Assembly, but the statements made by 38 delegates showed clearly and explicitly what was the position of each main group of countries. The Tribunal should therefore note that the most important Western countries were opposed to abandoning the compromise solution contained in Resolution 1803 (XVII).

—The conditions under which Resolution 3281 (XXIX), proclaiming the Charter of Economic Rights and Duties of States, was adopted also show unambiguously that there was no general consensus of the States with respect to the most important provisions and in particular those concerning nationalization. Having been the subject matter of a roll-call vote, the Charter was adopted by 118 votes to 6, with 10 abstentions. The analysis of votes on specific sections of the Charter is most significant insofar as the present case is concerned. From this point of view, paragraph 2(c) of Article 2 of the Charter, which limits consideration of the characteristics of compensation to the State and does not refer to international law, was voted by 104 to 16, with 6 abstentions, all of the industrialized countries with market economies having abstained or having voted against it.

86.   * * * As this Tribunal has already indicated, the legal value of the resolutions which are relevant to the present case can be determined

on the basis of circumstances under which they were adopted and by analysis of the principles which they state:

—With respect to the first point, the absence of any binding force of the resolutions of the General Assembly of the United Nations implies that such resolutions must be accepted by the members of the United Nations in order to be legally binding. In this respect, the Tribunal notes that only Resolution 1803 (XVII) of 14 December 1962 was supported by a majority of Member States representing all of the various groups. By contrast, the other Resolutions mentioned above, and in particular those referred to in the Libyan Memorandum, were supported by a majority of States but not by any of the developed countries with market economies which carry on the largest part of international trade.

87.   (2) With respect to the second point, to wit the appraisal of the legal value on the basis of the principles stated, it appears essential to this Tribunal to distinguish between those provisions stating the existence of a right on which the generality of the States has expressed agreement and those provisions introducing new principles which were rejected by certain representative groups of States and having nothing more than a *de lege ferenda* value only in the eyes of the States which have adopted them; as far as the others are concerned, the rejection of these same principles implies that they consider them as being *contra legem*. With respect to the former, which proclaim rules recognized by the community of nations, they do not create a custom but confirm one by formulating it and specifying its scope, thereby making it possible to determine whether or not one is confronted with a legal rule. As has been noted by Ambassador Castañeda, "[such resolutions] do not create the law; they have a declaratory nature of noting what does exist" (129 R.C.A.D.I. 204 (1970), at 315).

On the basis of the circumstances of adoption mentioned above and by expressing an *opinio juris communis*, Resolution 1803 (XVII) seems to this Tribunal to reflect the state of customary law existing in this field. Indeed, on the occasion of the vote on a resolution finding the existence of a customary rule, the States concerned clearly express their views. The consensus by a majority of States belonging to the various representative groups indicates without the slightest doubt universal recognition of the rules therein incorporated, *i.e.*, with respect to nationalization and compensation of the use of the rules in force in the nationalizing State, but all this in conformity with international law.

88.   While Resolution 1803 (XVII) appears to a large extent as the expression of a real general will, this is not at all the case with respect to the other Resolutions mentioned above, which has been demonstrated previously by analysis of the circumstances of adoption. In particular, as regards the Charter of Economic Rights and Duties of States, several factors contribute to denying legal value to those provisions of the document which are of interest in the instant case.

—In the first place, Article 2 of this Charter must be analyzed as a political rather than as a legal declaration concerned with the ideological strategy of development and, as such, supported only by non-industrialized States.

—In the second place, this Tribunal notes that in the draft submitted by the Group of 77 to the Second Commission, the General Assembly was invited to adopt the Charter "as a first measure of codification and progressive development" within the field of the international law of development. However, because of the opposition of several States, this description was deleted from the text submitted to the vote of the Assembly. * * *

89. Such an attitude is further reinforced by an examination of the general practice of relations between States with respect to investments. This practice is in conformity, not with the provisions of Article 2(c) of the above-mentioned Charter conferring exclusive jurisdiction on domestic legislation and courts, but with the exception stated at the end of this paragraph. Thus a great many investment agreements entered into between industrial States or their nationals, on the one hand, and developing countries, on the other, state, in an objective way, the standards of compensation and further provide, in case of dispute regarding the level of such compensation, the possibility of resorting to an international tribunal. In this respect, it is particularly significant in the eyes of this Tribunal that no fewer than 65 States, as of 31 October 1974, had ratified the Convention on the Settlement of Investment Disputes between States and Nationals of other States, dated March 18, 1965. * * *

SECTION V. Operative part:

FOR THESE REASONS,

The undersigned Sole Arbitrator

1. pronounces and decides that the Deeds of Concession in dispute are binding upon the parties;

2. pronounces and decides that the Libyan Government, the defendant, in adopting measures of nationalization in 1973 and 1974, breached its obligations arising from the said Deeds of Concession;

3. pronounces and decides that the Libyan Government, the defendant, is legally bound to perform these contracts and to give them full effect * * *.

Notes and Questions

1. *"Mixed" International Arbitrations.* One of the advantages of international arbitration is that it can be tailor-made to fit specific cases. Here the Deeds of Concession between the U.S. oil companies and the Libyan government provided that an aggrieved party could request the President of the International Court of Justice to appoint a sole arbitrator if the other party refused to make an appointment to a three-judge panel. Appointment by the President of the International Court did not, of course, make this an ICJ proceeding. Here, because both private and public parties were involved,

the procedure was a "mixed" form of international arbitration. Why would the parties drafting the Deeds of Concession have chosen international arbitration to settle their disputes? Why would Libya renege on its promise to arbitrate?

2. *Individuals and International Law*. The excerpts from the case focus on the question of the legal effect of United Nations General Assembly resolutions and only touch on a variety of other interesting issues in international law raised by the opinion. Paragraph 23 recited the choice-of-law provision in Clause 28 of the Deeds of Concession, which referred to Libyan law, international law, and the general principles of law. In his opinion, the Arbitrator, Professor Dupuy, reviewed and rejected the positivist doctrine of the 19th and early 20th centuries that held that international law could only bind states. Neither the classical law of nations of the 17th and 18th centuries nor the modern international law of the later 20th century have held such a restrictive view. Both permit individuals, including private corporations, as well as states to be subjects of international law. The Arbitrator found that under modern international law, contracts may be "delocalized" from municipal law and "internationalized." Paragraph 32 summed up this analysis. More on individuals as subjects of international law is to be found in Chapter 6.

3. *The Role of U.N. General Assembly Resolutions in Making Customary International Law*. The large part of the *Texaco/Libya Case* excerpted above concerns Libya's contention that international law permitted the Government to nationalize foreign investments without reference to any standards of foreign or international law. The Libyan argument rested on the foundations of the 1973 and 1974 U.N. General Assembly resolutions proclaiming a New International Economic Order (NIEO). The legal question for the Arbitrator was whether these NIEO resolutions had any legal force, especially in the light of U.N. General Assembly Resolution 1803 (XVII) of 1962, which recited that in the case of nationalization "the owner shall be paid appropriate compensation, in accordance with the rules in force in the State taking such measures in the exercise of its sovereignty, and in accordance with international law." The NIEO resolutions seemed to leave such compensation questions simply to the law of the nationalizing state. As the Arbitrator wrote, there were "substantial differences" between the rules in the 1962 and NIEO resolutions. The Arbitrator felt obliged "to consider the legal validity of the above-mentioned Resolutions and the possible existence of a custom resulting therefrom." Though U.N. General Assembly resolutions are formally only "recommendations," the Arbitrator needed to explore whether they could nonetheless pass into customary international law. What theory justifies treating some General Assembly resolutions as customary international law? What is the state practice? The *opinio juris*? As a matter of law-finding, what are the advantages and disadvantages of resolutions *vis-à-vis* other possible forms of customary international law? Since Article 10 of the U.N. Charter deems General Assembly resolutions "recommendations," did it violate the spirit as well as the letter of the Charter to give resolutions, by any logic, the force of law? Contrarily, given the absence of any general international legislative organ, was there good reason to try to "elevate" the status of General Assembly resolutions?

4. *Evaluating General Assembly Resolutions*. In looking at General Assembly voting, was the Arbitrator right in disregarding majority voting and relying instead on consensus? Was the Arbitrator right in putting great weight on the fact that the 1962 Resolution was "assented to by a great many states representing not only all geographical areas but also all economic systems"? Even if only such a consensus could elevate a resolution from a recommendation to a custom, did not the voting for the NIEO resolutions at least demonstrate that most states no longer supported the 1962 rule? Was it possible that the General Assembly actions in 1973–1974 destroyed the old customary rule but failed to establish a new rule? Would this have left a *Lotus*-like gap in international law?

In looking to the votes of states on General Assembly resolutions, should the votes of some states be given proportionately greater weight? This could be based on population, economic or political power, or their contributions to the U.N. budget.

5. *The Efficacy of the Arbitral Award*. On September 25, 1977, Libya agreed to pay Texaco and Standard Oil of California $76 million in crude oil to compensate them for the nationalization of their subsidiaries. The agreement effectively terminated the international arbitral proceedings. "Libya to Compensate Two U.S. Companies," *New York Times*, Sept. 26, 1977, at 55. What were the inducements for Libya finally to compensate the American oil companies? What difference might the arbitral award have made? Would Libya be looking to reassure potential new foreign investors? Was there fear of diplomatic pressure? Was Libya afraid of recognition and enforcement actions brought on the basis of the arbitral judgment in third countries? The New York Convention on the Recognition and Enforcement of Foreign Arbitral Awards, June 10, 1958, 330 U.N.T.S. 38 (in force for 123 states as of June 2000), in fact does provide for the recognition and enforcement of many foreign arbitral awards, and is widely used in commercial cases. See A.J. van den Berg, *The New York Arbitration Convention of 1958* (1981). More on the New York Convention appears in Chapter 12.

B. GENERAL PRINCIPLES OF LAW

Sometimes neither treaties nor custom provide a rule to decide a case involving international law. Then the judge or other seeker may look outside the theoretically consensual sources to non-consensual sources. The first such source we examine is general principles of law.

THE AM & S CASE

Australian Mining & Smelting Europe Ltd. v. E.C. Commission,
European Court of Justice, [1982] 2 *Common Market Law Reports* 264.

Second Opinion of the Advocate General (Sir Gordon Slynn)

In February 1979, officials of the [European Community's] Commission required the applicants to make available documents which they wished to see in connection with an investigation being conducted pursuant to Article 14(1) of Council Regulation 17 of 6 February 1962. This was said to be an investigation of competitive conditions concerning the production and distribution of zinc metal and its alloys and zinc concentrates in order to verify that there is no infringement of Articles 85 and 86 of the EEC Treaty [relating to the European Community's competition law]. The applicants produced copies of most of the documents. Some, however, were not produced; so far as relevant, on the basis that they were covered by legal confidentiality, which entitled the applicants to withhold them. * * *

The parties were invited to state at the re-opened oral hearing their views on the law as to, and legal opinions relating to, the existence and extent of the protection granted in investigative proceedings instituted by public authorities for the purpose of detecting offenses of an economic nature, especially in the field of competition, to correspondence passing between

(a) two lawyers,

(b) an independent lawyer and his client,

(c) an undertaking and a lawyer in a permanent contractual relationship, or who is an employee of the undertaking,

(d) a legal adviser to, and an employee of, an undertaking or an employee of an associated undertaking,

(e) employees of an undertaking, or different but associated undertakings, where the correspondence mentions legal advice given by an independent lawyer or legal adviser serving one of the undertakings or other undertakings in the same group. * * *

The Commission's investigative powers for the purpose of carrying out the duties assigned to it by Article 89 of the EEC Treaty, and provisions adopted under Article 87 of the Treaty, are so far as relevant conferred by Article 14 of Regulation 17. It may "undertake all necessary investigations into undertakings and associations of undertakings" and, to that end, its authorised officials are empowered to examine books and business records, to take copies of them, and to ask for oral explanations. There is no reference to any exemption or protection which may be claimed on the basis of legal confidence. Is that silence conclusive that no such protection is capable of applying in any form and in any situation? In my view it is not. The essential enquiry is, first, whether there is a principle of Community law existing independently of the regulation, and, secondly, whether the regulation does on a proper construction restrict the application of that principle. The question is not whether a principle of Community law derogates from Article 14, but whether Article 14 excludes the application of a principle of Community law. * * *

That general principles which have not been expressly stated in the Treaty or in subordinate legislation may exist as part of Community law, the observance of which the Court is required to ensure, needs no emphasis. This was made clear in an article by Judge Pescatore to be found in *Les Cahiers de Droit Européen*. It does not seem to me that the principle is limited to "fundamental rights" which are more particularly dealt with in the article. It has a broader base. Such indeed appears to be accepted by both parties to this application. The Commission argue that there has to be a consensus among the laws of all the member–States, and that the Court cannot establish a principle which goes beyond that accepted by any one of the member–States.

It cited no specific authority for that proposition, nor indicated what is the necessary level or degree of consensus required to establish the existence of a general principle. The CCBE [Consultative Committee of the Bars and Law Societies of the European Community], whose views broadly on the point were adopted by the applicants, submits that the aim of Community law is to find the best solution in qualitative terms, having regard to the spirit, orientation and general tendency of the national laws. * * *

That national law may be looked at on a comparative basis as an aid to consideration of what is Community law is shown in many cases * * *. Such a course is followed not to import national laws as such into Community law, but to use it as a means of discovering an *unwritten* principle of Community law. The suggestions made at times in this case, implicitly if not explicitly, that the applicants were trying to force into an unreceptive mould a purely local rule of the common law seems to me unfair to the argument of the applicants, who were seeking, like the CCBE and the United Kingdom Government, to distil a principle which is part of Community law by reference to national laws and which, in its detailed application, required adaptation to Community procedures.

In looking at national laws it does not seem to me that it can be a pre-condition of the existence of a rule of Community law that the principle should be expressed identically, or should be applied in identical form, in all of the member–States. Unanimity, as to a subject which is relevant to a Community law problem, may well be a strong indication of the existence of a rule of Community law. Total unanimity of expression and application is not, however, necessary. It is at best unlikely, not least as the Community grows in size. It seems to me highly probable that there are differences in the various member–States in the application of the principles of *"la bonne administration de la justice,"* rejection of *"un deni de justice"* and in the *"principe de proportionalité."* Yet such differences do not prevent such principles from being part of Community law. * * *

The Court has been provided with extracts from legislation, case decisions and the opinions of academic authors and a welter of case references. Rather than set those out *in extenso* I propose to summarise what seems to me to be the relevant features for present purposes, fully conscious of the risks that a summary may oversimplify and is incomplete. I deal first with the general position as to the protection of legal confidence and then consider the position in relation to competition law.

In Belgium, it seems that confidential communications between lawyer and client are protected and cannot be seized or used as evidence. Although the basis of the rule may have been that information confided to the lawyer must be protected, it seems from the opinion of Monsieur l'Auditeur Huberlant and the decision of the Counseil d'Etat of 8 June 1961, that it also covers confidential advice given to the client. There exists also a more general principle which protects the privacy of correspondence—see Articles 10 and 22 of the Constitution.

In Denmark, the rule of the professional secret prevents lawyers from giving evidence of confidential information confided to them in their professional capacity and a lawyer can refuse to produce documents covered by professional secrecy. Communications between an accused person and his lawyer are protected in the hands of the accused under section 786 of the Code of Procedure. This rule seems to apply also in civil proceedings.

In Germany, confidential communications to a lawyer are protected in his hands, and breach of the professional confidentiality by a lawyer is a criminal offence. Thus such documents in the hands of the lawyer cannot be seized (section 97 of the Code of Criminal Procedure). Documents in the hands of the client can, it appears, be seized unless they come into existence after the commencement of criminal proceedings.

In France, breach of the rule of professional secrecy is a criminal offence, and although it seems that documents may be seized in some circumstances even in the hands of the lawyer, the importance of the rule is stressed in Lemaire *"Les règles de la profession de l'avocat"* which has been provided for the Court. This rule appears to be closely linked with the right to a fair trial (*les droits de la défense*).

The principle of the *"droits de la défense"* appears to cover confidential documents passing in both directions between lawyer and client and includes protection from seizure of legal advice given to the client before commencement of proceedings and found in his possession or in the possession of a person associated with him. There is also it seems a wider protection for confidential letters than exists under the common law systems. * * *

In Greece it seems that confidential communications in the hands of lawyers are protected in investigative proceedings instituted by judicial or administrative authorities. Documents in the hands of the client are covered by the general principle of privacy defined in Article 9 of the Constitution. The power to search the client's premises is circumscribed by sections 253 *et seq.* of the Code of Criminal Procedure.

In Ireland and the United Kingdom, although there may be differences in detail, broadly the law of the two member–States is the same and it is set out more fully in the opinion of Warner A. G. It should be repeated, however, that it covers both (a) communications between a person and his lawyer for the purpose of obtaining or giving legal advice whether or not in connexion with pending or contemplated legal proceedings and (b) communications between a person and his lawyer and other persons for the dominant purpose of preparing for pending or contemplated legal proceedings.

In Italy, as in most of the member–States, the law forbids lawyers from giving evidence of the information confided in them by their clients and entitles them to withhold documents covered by the doctrine of professional secrecy. On the other hand, it seems that, in the case of criminal investigations, documents held by a lawyer may be seized unless they have been entrusted to him for the preparation of his client's defence. Protection is wider in civil proceedings but it does not, in any case, appear to extend to documents in the hands of the client. It seems that, in the case of lawyers, professional secrecy is a reflection of the right to a fair trial guaranteed by Article 24 of the Constitution.

In Luxembourg, rules of professional secrecy and *'les droits de la défense,'* it would seem, protect legal confidences in the hands of the lawyer, and of the client after proceedings have begun, but little case law has been produced showing the application of these rules in practice.

Dutch law forbids the revelation of confidences by persons exercising a profession, such as lawyers. Coupled with this there is a right to refuse to give evidence on matters covered by professional secrecy. These matters include not only the information revealed by the client but also, in the case of lawyers, the legal advice they have given. Section 98 of the Code of Criminal Procedure provides that, when the premises of someone bound by professional secrecy are searched, the doctrine of professional secrecy must be observed and documents covered by it cannot be seized. There appears to be no authority holding or denying that legal correspondence found in the hands of the client is protected.

This summary is substantially, if not entirely, accepted by the Commission, the applicants and the body representing the Bars of all the member–States as being a fair and acceptable statement of the laws of the member–States.

It seems to me significant that they were able to reach agreement as to the existence of the principles which are set out in the document which they prepared to read to the Court.

From this it is plain, as indeed seems inevitable, that the position in all the member–States is not identical. It is to my mind equally plain that there exists in all the member–States a recognition that the public interest and the proper administration of justice demand as a general rule that a client should be able to speak freely, frankly and fully to his lawyer. * * * Whether it is described as the right of the client or the duty of the lawyer, this principle has nothing to do with the protection or privilege of the lawyer. It springs essentially from the basic need of a man in a civilised society to be able to turn to his lawyer for advice and help, and if proceedings begin, for representation; it springs no less from the advantages to a society which evolves complex law reaching into all the business affairs of persons, real and legal, that they should be able to know what they can do under the law, what is forbidden, where they must tread circumspectly, where they run risks. * * *

JUDGMENT

By application lodged at the Court Registry on 4 October 1979 Australian Mining & Smelting Europe Limited (hereinafter referred to as "AM & S Europe") which is based in the United Kingdom, instituted proceedings pursuant to the second paragraph of Article 173 of the EEC Treaty to have Article 1 (b) of an individual decision notified to it, namely Commission Decision 79/760/EEC of 6 July 1979 declared void. That provision required the applicant to produce for examination by officers of the Commission charged with carrying out an investigation of all the documents for which legal privilege was claimed, as listed in the appendix to AM & S Europe's letter of 26 March 1979 to the Commission.

The application is based on the submission that in all the member–States written communications between lawyer and client are protected by virtue of a principle common to all those States, although the scope of that protection and the means of securing it vary from one country to another. According to the applicant, it follows from that principle which, in its view, also applies "within possible limits" in Community law, that the Commission may not when undertaking an investigation pursuant to Article 14 (3) of Council Regulation 17 of 6 February 1962, claim production, at least in their entirety, of written communications between lawyer and client if the undertaking claims protection and takes "reasonable steps to satisfy the Commission that the protection is properly claimed" on the ground that the documents in question are in fact covered by legal privilege. * * *

The contested decision, based on the principle that it is for the Commission to determine whether a given document should be used or not, requires AM & S Europe to allow the Commission's authorised inspectors to examine the documents in question in their entirety. Claiming that those documents satisfy the conditions for legal protection as described above, the applicant has requested the Court to declare Article 1 (b) of the above-mentioned decision void, or, alternatively, to declare it void in so far as it requires the disclosures to the Commission's inspector of the whole of each of the documents for which the applicant claims protection on the grounds of legal confidence. * * *

(a) *The interpretation of Article 14 of Regulation 17*

The purpose of Council Regulation 17 which was adopted pursuant to the first subparagraph of Article 87 (1) of the Treaty, is, according to paragraph (2)(a) and (b) of that Article, "to ensure compliance with the prohibitions laid down in Article 85 (1) and in Article 86" of the Treaty and "to lay down detailed rules for the application of Article 85 (3)." The regulation is thus intended to ensure that the aim stated in Article 3 (f) of the Treaty is achieved. To that end it confers on the Commission wide powers of investigation and of obtaining information by providing in the eighth recital in its preamble that the Commission must be empowered, throughout the Common Market, to require such information to be supplied and to undertake such investigations "as are necessary" to bring to light infringements of Articles 85 and 86 of the Treaty.

In Articles 11 and 14 of the regulation, therefore, it is provided that the Commission may obtain "information" and undertake the "necessary" investigations, for the purpose of proceedings in respect of infringements of the rules governing competition. Article 14 (1) in particular empowers the Commission to require production of business records, that is to say, documents concerning the market activities of the undertaking, in particular as regards compliance with those rules. Written communications between lawyer and client fall, in so far as they have a bearing on such activities, within the category of documents referred to in Articles 11 and 14.

Furthermore, since the documents which the Commission may demand are, as Article 14 (1) confirms, those whose disclosure it considers 'necessary' in order that it may bring to light an infringement of the Treaty rules on competition, it is in principle for the Commission itself, and not the undertaking concerned or a third party, whether an expert or an arbitrator, to decide whether or not a document must be produced to it.

(b) *Applicability of the protection of confidentiality in Community law*

However, the above rules do not exclude the possibility of recognising, subject to certain conditions, that certain business records are of a confidential nature. Community law, which derives from not only the economic but also the legal interpenetration of the member–States, must take into account the principles and concepts common to the laws of those States concerning the observance of confidentiality, in particular, as regards certain communications between lawyer and client. That confidentiality serves the requirement, the importance of which is recognised in all of the member–States, that any person must be able, without constraint, to consult a lawyer whose profession entails the giving of independent legal advice to all those in need of it.

As far as the protection of written communications between lawyer and client is concerned, it is apparent from the legal systems of the member–States that, although the principle of such protection is generally recognised, its scope and the criteria for applying it vary, as has, indeed, been conceded both by the applicant and by the parties who have intervened in support of its conclusions.

Whilst in some of the member–States the protection against disclosure afforded to written communications between lawyer and client is based principally on a recognition of the very nature of the legal profession, inasmuch as it contributes towards the maintenance of the rule of law, in other member–States the same protection is justified by the more specific requirement (which, moreover, is also recognised in the first-mentioned States) that the rights of the defence must be respected.

Apart from these differences, however, there are to be found in the national laws of the member–States common criteria inasmuch as those laws protect, in similar circumstances, the confidentiality of written communications between lawyer and client provided that, on the one hand, such communications are made for the purposes and in the interests of the client's rights of defence and, on the other hand, they emanate from independent lawyers, that is to say, lawyers who are not bound to the client by relationship of employment.

Viewed in that context Regulation 17 must be interpreted as protecting, in its turn, the confidentiality of written communications between lawyer and client subject to those two conditions, and thus incorporating such elements of that protection as are common to the laws of the member–States. * * *

In view of all these factors it must therefore be concluded that although Regulation 17, and in particular Article 14 thereof, interpreted in the light of its wording, structure and aims, and having regard to the laws of the member–States, empowers the Commission to require, in course of an investigation within the meaning of that Article, production of the business documents the disclosure of which it considers necessary, including written communications between lawyer and client, for proceedings in respect of any infringements of Articles 85 and 86 of the Treaty, that power is, however, subject to a restriction imposed by the need to protect confidentiality, on the conditions defined above, and provided that the communications in question are exchanged between an independent lawyer, that is to say one who is not bound to his client by a relationship of employment, and his client. * * *

(d) *The confidential nature of the documents at issue*

It is apparent from the documents which the applicant lodged at the Court on 9 March 1981 that almost all the communications which they include were made or are connected with legal opinions which were given towards the end of 1972 and during the first half of 1973.

It appears that the communications in question were drawn up during the period preceding, and immediately following, the accession of the United Kingdom to the Community, and that they are principally concerned with how far it might be possible to avoid conflict between the applicant and the Community authorities on the applicant's position, in particular with regard to the Community provisions on competition. In spite of the time which elapsed between the said communications and the initiation of a procedure, those circumstances are sufficient to justify considering the communications as falling within the context of the rights of the defence and the lawyer's specific duties in that connection. They must therefore be protected from disclosure.

In view of that relationship and in the light of the foregoing considerations the written communications at issue must accordingly be considered, in so far as they emanate from an independent lawyer entitled to practise his profession in a member–State, as confidential and on that ground beyond the Commission's power of investigation under Article 14 of Regulation 17.

Notes and Questions

1. *EC Competition Law.* The European Community (now the European Union) has a comprehensive system of competition (antitrust) law and procedure. The EC Commission has the power to investigate and to prosecute possible monopolistic and anti-competitive economic activities. In *AM & S*, since the U.K. had just joined the Common Market, what kinds of questions about its on-going activities and EC competition law would a company like AM & S probably have asked its lawyers? How would the answers to these questions have helped the investigations of the Commission?

2. *The Advocate General.* The reading begins with the opinion of Sir Gordon Slynn, one of the EC's Advocates General. The Advocate General is a position unknown to the United States but is somewhat akin to an official *amicus* or friend of the court in U.S. practice. In European Court of Justice (ECJ) cases the opinions of the Advocates General ordinarily are published both because they amplify ECJ opinions and because they have some persuasive value of their own.

3. *Gaps in the Law.* EC competition law is, of course, a form of international law. It is constituted fundamentally by treaty rules like Articles 85–89 of the Treaty of Rome and partly by rules like Council Regulation 17 generated by delegated powers given to the institutions making up the EC, a regional international organization. The legal question in this case was what to do when there was a gap (a *lacuna*) in international law. Here neither the Rome Treaty nor the rules made by the EC institutions determined whether there was a right to lawyer-client confidentiality in EC law, and if there was such a right how it was defined. Should international courts like the ECJ be more or less reluctant than municipal courts to fill gaps when formal sources are silent? Should it make a difference that some municipal legal systems (often in the common law tradition) are more willing than others (often in the civil law tradition) to let courts fill gaps in law?

4. *General Principles of Law.* In *AM & S*, the European Court of Justice turned to general principles of law to fill a gap. Did the fact that municipal legal systems used certain similar rules make it plain that states had consented to establishing a rule in international law? What are other consensual arguments justifying the use of general principles to find or develop rules of international law? Non-consensual arguments? Was the Advocate General seeking to avoid the gap problem when he presumed that looking at national laws meant "not to import national laws as such into Community law," but to use the search "as a means of discovering an *unwritten* principle of Community law"? Was this "discovery" really just a justification for a form of judicial discretion and law-making?

Is judicial review itself by now a general principle of law? If so, does that mean that international courts should increasingly exercise a power of international law-making? See Erica de Wet, "Judicial Review as an Emerging General Principle of Law and Its Implications for the International Court of Justice," 47 *Netherlands International Law Review* 181 (2000).

5. *The ECJ Judgment.* The ECJ masks any judicial dissent with a single judgment that never discloses the individual votes or opinions of the panel. Did the judgment in *AM & S* show signs of being a compromise? Was it more or less well reasoned than the opinion of the Advocate General? Was it more or less formal, *i.e.*, apparently based on the words of the Treaty of Rome and Council Regulation No. 17? Did the judges adequately explain why communications with independent (out-of-house) counsel were to be protected by privilege but not those with in-house counsel?

6. *"Civilized Nations."* General principles of law are included among the sources of international that the International Court of Justice is permitted to apply. Article 38(1)(c) of the ICJ Statute authorizes the Court to use "the general principles of law recognized by civilized nations." When the clause was originally drafted for the Permanent Court of International Justice in 1920, the term "civilized nations" was meant to exclude most non–European nations; nowadays the term has been rejected by commentators and judges alike. See Gerrit W. Gong, *The Standard of "Civilization" in International Society* (1984).

7. *The Comparative Law Search.* Of course, *AM & S* was a case before the European Court of Justice, not the ICJ, and accordingly the ECJ needed only compare the domestic practices of the nine states then members of the European Community. The basic theory behind general principles of law is that some legal principles are so general or fundamental that they are to be found in all or nearly all legal systems. In *AM & S* the presumption was that if rules protecting lawyer-client communication could be found in every municipal legal system within the European Community, then such rules were to be presumed to be included within the body of EC law. In a case before the ICJ, should that Court be obliged to look to the municipal legal systems of all of its nearly 200 member states to discern a general principle?

8. *The Problem of In-house and Foreign Lawyers.* Notice that the search for common legal rules in *AM & S* was conducted on the assumption that only the minimum content of rules found in all relevant European municipal legal systems would be presumed to exist in EC law. This "lowest common denominator" approach thus excluded communications with certain kinds of lawyers. Most notably, the *AM & S* decision refused to protect the communications both of in-house counsel and of foreign lawyers not accredited by an EC member nation. For early hostile reactions, see Joseph P. Griffin, Book Review, 79 *American Journal of International Law* 834 (1985)(reviewing C.S. Kerse, *EEC Antitrust Procedure, Supplement 1984*). Nonetheless, the discriminatory distinction persists, not only in EC law, but in the municipal practice of seven of the fifteen EU member states: Austria, Belgium, France, Italy, Luxembourg, the Netherlands, and Sweden. See Mary Daly, "Cultural, Ethical, and Legal Challenges," 46 *Emory Law Journal* 1057, 1102–08 (1997). The on-going plight of in-house counsel under the *AM & S* rule is described in Maurits Dolmans, "Attorney–Client Privilege for In–House Counsel: A European Proposal," 4 *Columbia Journal of European Law* 125 (1998).

C. NATURAL LAW AND *JUS COGENS*

We have now explored the three principal formal sources of international law set forth in Article 38(1) of the Statute of the International Court of Justice; these are the rules that the Court "shall apply" as it decides "in accordance with international law such disputes as submitted to it": "(a) international conventions, whether general or particular, establishing rules expressly recognized by the contesting states [Treaties, Chapter 2]; (b) international custom, as evidence of a general practice accepted as law [Customary International Law, Chapter 3.A]; (c) the general principles of law recognized by civilized nations [General Principles of Law, Chapter 3.B]." Although the first two sources—Treaty and Custom—may be said by positivists to be more or less consensual among states, the third source—General Principles of Law—clearly involves, as we have seen, some judicial or doctrinal initiative beyond a search for inter-state agreement on rules. Indeed, the same may well be true even for most rules of customary international law.

Historically, one of the most important sources of the law of nations was natural law, but nowadays the function of this avowedly non-consensual source has been largely replaced by the notion of *jus cogens* or compelling norm. *Jus cogens* is sometimes dated from the work in the 1930's of the Austrian law professor, Alfred von Verdross. An excerpt from his work follows an example of earlier use of a natural law concept in the 1820 U.S. Supreme Court piracy judgment, *Smith*. The notes hark back to Chapter 1's *Filartiga Case* where natural law, *jus cogens*, customary international law, and general principles of law all seem to be blended. We then explore the related concept of obligations *erga omnes*, using the ICJ's unhappy 1966 decision in the *South West Africa Cases* as the focus for a comparison of *erga omnes* and *jus cogens*. A good question to keep in mind throughout this Part is what role should there be in modern international law for non-consensual norms?

UNITED STATES v. SMITH

18 U.S. (5 Wheat.) 153, 5 L.Ed. 57 (1820).

This was an indictment for piracy against the prisoner Thomas Smith, before the Circuit Court of Virginia, on the act of Congress, of the 3d of March, 1819, c.76.

The jury found a special verdict as follows: "We, of the jury, find, that the prisoner, Thomas Smith, in the month of March, 1819, and others, were part of the crew of a private armed vessel, called the Creollo, (commissioned by the government of Buenos Ayres, a colony then at war with Spain,) and lying in the port of Margaritta; that in the month of March, 1819, the said prisoner and others of the crew mutinied, confined their officer, left the vessel, and in the said port of Margaritta, seized by violence a vessel called the Irresistible, a private armed vessel, lying in that port, commissioned by the government of

Artigas, who was also at war with Spain; that the said prisoner and others, having so possessed themselves of the said vessel, the Irresistible, appointed their officers, proceeded to sea on a cruize, without any documents or commission whatever; and while on that cruize, in the month of April, 1819, on the high seas, committed the offence charged in the indictment, by the plunder and robbery of the Spanish vessel therein mentioned. If the plunder and robbery aforesaid be piracy under the act of the Congress of the United States, entitled, 'An act to protect the commerce of the United States, and punish the crime of piracy,' then we find the said prisoner guilty; if the plunder and robbery, above stated, be not piracy under the said act of Congress, then we find him, not guilty."

The Circuit Court divided on the question, whether this be piracy as defined by the law of nations, so as to be punishable under the act of Congress, of the 3d of March, 1819, and thereupon the question was certified to this Court for its decision.* * *

MR. JUSTICE STORY delivered the opinion of the court. The act of Congress upon which this indictment is founded provides, "that if any person or persons whatsoever, shall, upon the high seas, commit the crime of piracy, as defined by the law of nations, and such offender or offenders shall be brought into, or found in the United States, every such offender or offenders shall, upon conviction thereof, &c. be punished with death."

The first point made at the bar is, whether this enactment be a constitutional exercise of the authority delegated to Congress upon the subject of piracies. The constitution declares, that Congress shall have power "to define and punish piracies and felonies committed on the high seas, and offences against the law of nations." The argument which has been urged in behalf of the prisoner is, that Congress is bound to define, in terms, the offence of piracy, and is not at liberty to leave it to be ascertained by judicial interpretation. * * *

But supposing Congress were bound in all the cases included in the clause under consideration to define the offence, still there is nothing which restricts it to a mere logical enumeration in detail of all the facts constituting the offence. Congress may as well define by using a term of a known and determinate meaning, as by an express enumeration of all the particulars included in that term. That is certain which is by necessary reference made certain. When the act of 1790 declares, that any person who shall commit the crime of robbery, or murder, on the high seas, shall be deemed a pirate, the crime is not less clearly ascertained than it would be by using the definitions of these terms as they are found in our treatises of the common law. In fact, by such a reference, the definitions are necessarily included, as much as if they stood in the text of the act. In respect to murder, where "malice aforethought" is of the essence of the offence, even if the common law definition were quoted in express terms, we should still be driven to deny that the definition was perfect, since the meaning of "malice afore-thought" would remain to be gathered from the common law. There would then be no end to our difficulties, or our definitions, for each would involve some terms which might still require some new explanation. Such a construction of the constitution is, therefore, wholly inadmissible. To define piracies, in the sense of the constitution, is merely to enumerate the crimes which shall constitute piracy; and this may be done either by a reference to crimes having a technical name, and determinate extent, or by enumerating the acts in detail, upon which the punishment is inflicted.

It is next to be considered, whether the crime of piracy is defined by the law of nations with reasonable certainty. What the law of nations on this subject is, may be ascertained by consulting the works of jurists, writing professedly on public law; or by the general usage and practice of nations; or by judicial decisions recognising and enforcing that law. There is scarcely a writer on the law of nations, who does not allude to piracy as a crime of a settled and determinate nature; and whatever may be the diversity of definitions, in other respects, all writers concur, in holding, that robbery, or forcible depredations upon the sea, *animo furandi*, is piracy. The same doctrine is held by all the great writers on maritime law, in terms that admit of no reasonable doubt. The common law, too, recognises and punishes piracy as an offence, not against its own municipal code, but as an offence against the law of nations, (which is part of the common law,) as an offence against the universal law of society, a pirate being deemed an enemy of the human race. Indeed, until the statute of 28th of Henry VIII, ch. 15, piracy was punishable in England only in the admiralty as a civil law offence; and that statute, in changing the jurisdiction, has been universally admitted not to have changed the nature of the offence. Sir Charles Hedges, in his charge at the Admiralty sessions, in the case of Rex v. Dawson, (5 *State Trials*,) declared in emphatic terms, that "piracy is only a sea term for robbery, piracy being a robbery committed within the jurisdiction of the admiralty." Sir Leoline Jenkins, too, on a like occasion, declared that "a robbery, when committed upon the sea, is what we call a 'piracy;'" and he cited the civil law writers, in proof. And it is manifest from the language of Sir William Blackstone,[a] in his comments on piracy, that he considered the common law definition as distinguishable in no essential respect from that of the law of nations. So that, whether we advert to writers on the common law, or the maritime law, or the law of nations, we shall find that they universally treat of piracy as an offence against the law of nations, and that its true definition by that law is robbery

---

a. To show that piracy is defined by the law of nations, the following citations are believed to be sufficient: [Story fills almost eighteen subsequent pages with citations at length from, *inter alia*, Grotius, Bynkershoek, Azuni, Bacon, Martens, Rutherforth, Woodeson, Bulamaqui, Calvinus, Bouchard, Bonnemant, Valin, Straccha, Casaregis, Brown, Beames, Molloy, Marshall, Viner, Cowell, Comyn, Coke, Jenkins, Targa, Hawkins, Blackstone, Hedges, Holt, Ward, and Erskine. Pp. 163–180. He concludes:] The foregoing collection of doctrines, extracted from writers on the civil law, the law of nations, the maritime law, and the common law, in the most ample manner confirms the opinion of the Court in the case in the text; and it is with great diffidence submitted to the learned reader to aid his future researches in a path, which, fortunately for us, it has not been hitherto necessary to explore with minute accuracy.

upon the sea. And the general practice of all nations in punishing all persons, whether natives or foreigners, who have committed this offence against any persons whatsoever, with whom they are in amity, is a conclusive proof that the offence is supposed to depend, not upon the particular provisions of any municipal code, but upon the law of nations, both for its definition and punishment. We have, therefore, no hesitation in declaring, that piracy, by the law of nations, is robbery upon the sea, and that it is sufficiently and constitutionally defined by the fifth section of the act of 1819. * * *

It is to be certified to the Circuit Court, that upon the facts stated, the case is piracy, as defined by the law of nations, so as to be punishable under the act of Congress of the 3d of March, 1819.

Notes and Questions

1. *An Enemy of All Mankind.* Remember the next-to-last line of the *Filartiga* judgment in Chapter 1: "Indeed, for purposes of civil liability, the torturer has become—like the pirate and the slave trader before him—*hostis humani generis*, an enemy of all mankind." *Smith* was one of the two principal cases relied on by the *Filartiga* court to demonstrate that rules of the law of nations "may be ascertained by consulting the works of the jurists, writing professedly on public law; or by the general usage and practice of nations; or by judicial decisions recognizing and enforcing that law." The other was *Paquete Habana.* The similarities between *Filartiga* and *Smith* are great, even greater than between *Filartiga* and *Paquete Habana.* Most important, both *Smith* and *Filartiga* held that an individual could be found guilty of violating the law of nations. In *Paquete Habana* the guilty party was a state. Pirate, slave trader, torturer—all were viewed as acting so contrary to fundamental norms that their actions were seen to be universally proscribed and their persons subject to punishment by all courts.

2. *Custom? General Principle? Natural Law? Jus Cogens?* Another similarity between *Filartiga* and *Smith* is their mutual confusion about what the source of the rule is. In contrast, *Paquete Habana* and *AM & S* are clearer: *Paquete Habana* weighed evidences of state practice to find custom, and *AM & S* examined comparative municipal law rules to find a general principle. However, do there not seem to be traces of custom, general principles, natural law, and *jus cogens* in both *Filartiga* and *Smith*? *Smith* and *Filartiga* were both cited in Beanal v. Freeport–McMoran, Inc., 197 F.3d 161 (5th Cir.1999), where the court rejected an Indonesian citizen's claims that environmental degradation amounted to cultural genocide because it destroyed a tribe's cultural and social framework. The legal evidence presented described only an "amorphous right * * * devoid of discernable means to define or identify conduct that constitutes a violation of international law." *Id.* at 168. The *Beanal* court, like the courts in *Smith* and *Filartiga*, did not make it clear whether it was looking for a rule of customary international law, general principles of law, natural law, or *jus cogens*, but its language, like that of *Smith* and *Filartiga*, looked for some sort of universality: "it would be imprudent for a United States tribunal to declare an amorphous cause of action under international law that has failed

to garner universal acceptance." *Id.* Can it be said that *Smith, Filartiga*, and *Beanal* all looked to find some non-treaty international law rule general or universal enough to bind apparently non-consenting states? How well does this kind of search fit into the positivist insistence in *Lotus* that all rules of international law must be based on state consent?

3. *A Positivist Gloss on Piracy.* Positivists rejected the notion that international law provided a substantive definition of the crime of piracy. In 1932, a Harvard research project proposed a treaty premised on the view "that piracy is not a crime by the law of nations." Instead, piracy "is the basis of an extraordinary jurisdiction in every state to seize and to prosecute and punish persons, and to seize and dispose of property, for factual offenses which are committed outside the * * * ordinary jurisdiction of the prosecuting state and which do not involve attacks on its peculiar interests." Harvard Research Project, 26 *American Journal of International Law Supplement* 739, 760 (1932). According to this positivist view, piracy is "solely a municipal law crime, the only question of international law being the extent of a state's jurisdiction to apply its criminal law to an accused foreigner acting outside the territorial jurisdiction of the prescribing state." Alfred P. Rubin, *The Law of Piracy* 360 (2d ed. 1998).

4. *Piracy in U.S. Law.* The statute used to convict Thomas Smith remains in the U.S. Code, although the penalty for its violation has been reduced from death to life in prison. See 18 U.S.C. § 1651. Would this statute support a criminal conviction in U.S. court today? See John E. Noyes, "An Introduction to the International Law of Piracy," 21 *California Western International Law Journal* 105, 117–18 (1990). Other U.S. statutes contain additional provisions concerning piracy. See 18 U.S.C. §§ 1652–1661. For proposals to revise the U.S. municipal law of piracy, see Samuel Pyeatt Menefee, " 'Yo Heave Ho!': Updating America's Piracy Laws," 21 *California Western International Law Journal* 151 (1990).

ALFRED VON VERDROSS, "FORBIDDEN TREATIES IN INTERNATIONAL LAW"

31 *American Journal of International Law* 571 (1937).

I.   THE PRINCIPLE * * *

Our starting-point is the uncontested rule that, as a matter of principle, states are free to conclude treaties on any subject whatsoever. All we have to investigate, therefore, is whether this rule does or does not admit certain exceptions. The answer to this question depends on the preliminary question, whether general international law contains rules which have the character of *jus cogens*. For it is obvious that if general international law consists *exclusively* of noncompulsory norms, states are always free to agree on treaty norms which deviate from general international law, without by doing so, violating general international law. If, on the other hand, general international law does contain also norms which have the character of *jus cogens*, things are very different. For it is the quintessence of norms of this character that they prescribe a certain, positive or negative behavior unconditionally; norms of this character, therefore, cannot be derogated from by the will of the contracting parties.

The existence of such norms in general international law is particularly contested by those authors who base the whole international law on the agreement of the *wills* of the states; consequently, they know no other international law but treaty law. But they overlook the fact that each treaty presupposes a number of norms necessary for the very coming into existence of an international treaty. These are the norms determining which persons are endowed with the capacity to act in international law, what intrinsic and extrinsic conditions must be fulfilled that an international treaty may come into existence, what juridical consequences are attached to the conclusion of an international treaty. These principles concerning the conditions of the validity of treaties cannot be regarded as having been agreed upon by treaty; they must be regarded as valid independently of the will of the contracting parties. That is the reason why the *possibility* of norms of general international law, norms determining the limits of the freedom of the parties to conclude treaties, cannot be denied *a priori*.

But this reasoning does not decide the problem whether such compulsory norms concerning the contents of international treaties do exist in fact. A careful investigation, however, reveals the existence of such norms. Two groups of these norms can be distinguished. The first group consists of different, single, compulsory norms of customary international law. General international law requires states, for instance, not to disturb each other in the use of the high seas. An international treaty between two or among more states tending to exclude other states from the use of the high seas, would be in contradiction to a compulsory principle of general international law. International law authorizes states to occupy and to annex *terra nullius*. In consequence, an international treaty by which two states would bind themselves to prevent other states from making such acquisitions of territory would be violative of general international law. In the same way, a treaty binding the contracting parties to prevent third states from the exercise of other rights of sovereignty acknowledged by general international law, such as passage through the territorial waters of other states, would be in contradiction to international law.

But apart from these and other positive norms of general international law, there is a second group which constitutes *jus cogens*. This second group consists of the general principle prohibiting states from concluding treaties *contra bonos mores*. This prohibition, common to the juridical orders of all civilized states, is the consequence of the fact that every juridical order regulates the rational and moral coexistence of the members of a community. No juridical order can, therefore, admit treaties between juridical subjects, which are obviously in contradiction to the ethics of a certain community. * * *

II. The Different Kinds of International Treaties *Contra Bonos Mores*

The application in international law of the general principle, according to which treaties *contra bonos mores* are void, is not free from difficulties. These difficulties are the consequence of the fact that the ethics of the international community are much less developed than the ethics of national communities; further, the international community embraces different juridical systems, built upon different moral conceptions. But, on the other hand, these difficulties must not be overestimated. For, as we shall show, there are between the subjects of international law far-reaching agreements concerning many single values notwithstanding different basic conceptions.

In order to advance the solution of our problem, it is necessary to see what treaties are regarded as being *contra bonos mores* by the law of civilized nations. To this problem the decisions of the courts of civilized nations give an unequivocal answer. The analysis of these decisions shows that everywhere such treaties are regarded as being *contra bonos mores* which *restrict the liberty of one contracting party in an excessive or unworthy manner or which endanger its most important rights.*

This and similar formulas prove that the law of civilized states starts with the idea which demands the establishment of a juridical order guaranteeing the rational and moral coexistence of the members. It follows that all those norms of treaties which are incompatible with this goal of all positive law—a goal which is implicitly presupposed—must be regarded as void.

This general principle is not disproved by the fact that different states have different conceptions as to the position of the members of the community. There is, *e.g.*, a different conception as to the position of men toward the community under a democratic, fascist or socialistic régime. But everywhere treaties are regarded as immoral which force one contracting party into a situation which is in contradiction to the ethics of the community.

In order to know what international treaties are immoral, we must ask what are the moral tasks states have to accomplish in the international community. In doing so, we must restrict ourselves to find those principles which correspond to the universal ethics of the international community. We must, so to speak, try to find the *ethical minimum* recognized by all the states of the international community, and must leave aside those particular tasks of the state represented only by particular régimes.

Using the utmost prudence, we can say that the following tasks most certainly devolve upon a state recognized by the modern international community: *maintenance of law and order within the state, defense against external attacks, care for the bodily and spiritual welfare of citizens at home, protection of citizens abroad.* A treaty norm, therefore, which prevents a state from fulfilling one of these essential tasks must be regarded as immoral.

On this basis the following international treaties are immoral and, consequently, void:

1. An international treaty binding a state to reduce its police or its organization of courts in such a way that it is no longer able to protect at all or in an adequate manner, the life, the liberty, the honor or the property of men on its territory. Such a treaty would, however, also be violative of positive international law, if the state were prevented from protecting the above-named rights of *aliens*, because international law obliges states to protect aliens in ways common to civilized nations (principle of the international minimum standard).

2. An international treaty binding a state to reduce its army in such a way as to render it defenseless against external attacks. It is immoral to keep a state as a sovereign community and to forbid it at the same time to defend its existence.

The situation is different if a state is placed under the protectorate of another state, because in this case the defense of the protected state against external attacks is the duty of the protecting state. The same is true if the existence of a state is effectively guaranteed by one or more Powers, because in this case the defense is the duty of the guarantor. But it would be immoral to oblige a state to remain defenseless.

3. An international treaty binding a state to close its hospitals or schools, to extradite or sterilize its women, to kill its children, to close its factories, to leave its fields unploughed, or in other ways to expose its population to distress. * * *

III. The Determination of the Immorality of Treaties

As the conclusion of immoral treaties is forbidden by general international law, no valid obligation can come into existence concerning the immoral contents of a treaty. Therefore, every arbitration tribunal or the Permanent Court, to which a conflict is submitted in which such a treaty is involved, is under a duty to take judicial notice that such treaties are void, even if there be no demand by a party to this effect. This principle follows from the consideration that all organs of international law have to apply international law. They cannot, therefore, order a state to do something forbidden by international law. The statement that the contents of a treaty are immoral has, therefore, no constitutive, but simply a declaratory character; it states that no obligation with such contents has ever come into existence.

In consequence, a formal voidance of immoral contents of treaties is not necessary. The burdened state has the right simply to refuse the fulfillment of such an obligation. If the other party contests the immorality and if agreement cannot be reached by diplomatic means, the conflict has to be submitted to an arbitral or judicial procedure, as it is certainly a legal dispute.

If, however, there is no obligation of this kind between the parties, and if they do not agree to submit the dispute in question to an arbitral or judicial procedure *ad hoc*, the Council of the League of Nations has jurisdiction, provided that both the parties to the dispute are members of the League. If this is not the case, two solutions are possible: either one state submits to the refusal of the other contracting party to fulfill the treaty, or it resorts to self-help in order to enforce its alleged right. In this case another immoral treaty may be made, which again would be void in international law. For never can the immoral contents of a treaty really become law no matter how often it may borrow the external form of the law.

IV. PROPOSALS

In consequence of the above deductions, this writer ventures to propose * * *:

A treaty norm is void if it is either in violation of a compulsory norm of general international law or *contra bonos mores*.

A treaty norm is *contra bonos mores* if a state is prevented by an international treaty from fulfilling the universally recognized tasks of a civilized state.

Such tasks are: the maintenance of the public order, the defense of the state against external attacks, the care for the bodily and spiritual welfare of its citizens at home and the protection of nationals abroad.

If the immorality of a treaty norm is contested, the dispute has to be submitted to the decision of an arbitration tribunal or of the Permanent Court of International Justice.

Notes and Questions

1. *The Challenge to Legal Positivism.* This 1937 article by Vienna's Professor Alfred von Verdross has been singled out as an important step in the development of Article 53 of the Vienna Convention on the Law of the Treaties concerning peremptory norms of international law. E. Jimenez de Arechaga, *El Derecho Internacional Contemporaneo* 79 (1980). Verdross's article was an affirmative answer to the question of whether there may ever be rules of international law not made by state consent. As such, it challenged the notions of legal positivists who read moral and natural law out of municipal and international law, a formalistic position that became increasingly uncomfortable as totalitarian parties captured the machineries of state power in 20th-century Europe. To what extent do beliefs in legal positivism and that states alone are legitimate sources of legal rules depend on an unrealistic expectation that governments will always act responsibly?

2. *Kinds of* Jus Cogens. Verdross's first category of compulsory norms contains rules drawn from "general international law" that constrain treaty-making. How certain must a rule of general international law be before it can trump a contrary treaty rule? How many states must agree in a treaty before a first category compulsory norm can be upset? Compare the formulation in Articles 53 and 66(a) of the Vienna Convention on the Law of Treaties, which are in the Appendix. Two of Verdross's three examples of the first category concern the purported illegality of treaty restraints on uses of the oceans. How true are such assertions today, after recent developments in the law of the sea? See Chapter 11.

Verdross's second category of compulsory norms contains *jus cogens* rules prohibiting treaties *contra bonos mores*, a category he justified as stemming from the general principles of law recognized by civilized nations. Such norms trump both conventional and customary law. Does it make sense to treat such norms as general principles *à la* 38(1)(c) of the ICJ Statute? Why not simply accept them as a form of natural or fundamental law? If they are not viewed as natural or fundamental law, how are they different from natural law?

3. *An "Ethical Minimum" to the Law.* Verdross granted that the ethics of democratic, fascist, and socialist regimes are different, but he argued that there is at least an "ethical minimum" to them all. Given the record of World War II, should a *jus cogens* norm need meet even such an "ethical minimum"?

4. *Individuals and* Jus Cogens. Are Verdross's four sorts of immoral treaties too oriented to the protection of weak states and too little directed to the protection of even weaker individuals? Should there be (are there) such fundamental norms of international law protecting individuals? What should they be? How can they be justified as "real" international law?

THE SOUTH WEST AFRICA CASES

Ethiopia v. South Africa; Liberia v. South Africa, 1966 I.C.J. 6, 325, 1966 WL 2.

1. In the present proceedings the two applicant States, the Empire of Ethiopia and the Republic of Liberia (whose cases are identical and will for present purposes be treated as one case), acting in the capacity of States which were members of the former League of Nations, put forward various allegations of contraventions of the League of Nations Mandate for South West Africa, said to have been committed by the respondent State, the Republic of South Africa, as the administering authority.

2. * * * The Court, by its Judgment of 21 December 1962, * * * found that it had "jurisdiction to adjudicate upon the merits of the dispute."

3. In the course of the proceedings on the merits, the Parties put forward various contentions on such matters as whether the Mandate for South West Africa was still in force,—and if so, whether the Mandatory's obligation under Article 6 of the Mandate to furnish annual reports to the Council of the former League of Nations concerning its administration of the mandated territory had become transformed by one means or another into an obligation to furnish such reports to the General Assembly of the United Nations, or had, on the other hand, lapsed entirely;—whether there had been any contravention by the Respondent of the second paragraph of Article 2 of the Mandate which required the Mandatory to "promote to the utmost the material and moral well-being and the social progress of the inhabitants of the territory,"—whether there had been any contravention of Article 4 of the Mandate, prohibiting (except for police and local defence purposes) the "military training of the natives," and forbidding the establishment of military or naval

bases, or the erection of fortifications in the territory. The Applicants also alleged that the Respondent had contravened paragraph 1 of Article 7 of the Mandate (which provides that the Mandate can only be modified with the consent of the Council of the League of Nations) by attempting to modify the Mandate without the consent of the General Assembly of the United Nations which, so it was contended, had replaced the Council of the League for this and other purposes. * * *

4. * * * In this connection, there was one matter that appertained to the merits of the case but which had an antecedent character, namely the question of the Applicants' standing in the present phase of the proceedings,—not, that is to say, of their standing before the Court itself, which was the subject of the Court's decision in 1962, but the question, as a matter of the merits of the case, of their legal right or interest regarding the subject-matter of their claim, as set out in their final submission. * * *

10. The mandates system, as is well known, was formally instituted by Article 22 of the Covenant of the League of Nations. As there indicated, there were to be three categories of mandates, designated as "A", "B" and "C" mandates respectively, the Mandate for South West Africa being one of the "C" category. The differences between these categories lay in the nature and geographical situation of the territories concerned, the state of development of their peoples, and the powers accordingly to be vested in the administering authority, or mandatory, for each territory placed under mandate. But although it was by Article 22 of the League Covenant that the system as such was established, the precise terms of each mandate, covering the rights and obligations of the mandatory, of the League and its organs, and of the individual members of the League, in relation to each mandated territory, were set out in separate instruments of mandate which, with one exception * * * took the form of resolutions of the Council of the League.

11. These instruments, whatever the differences between certain of their terms, had various features in common as regards their structure. For present purposes, their substantive provisions may be regarded as falling into two categories. On the one hand, and of course as the principal element of each instrument, there were the articles defining the mandatory's powers, and its obligations in respect of the inhabitants of the territory and towards the League and its organs. These provisions, relating to the carrying out of the mandates as mandates, will hereinafter be referred to as "conduct of the mandate," or simply "conduct" provisions. On the other hand, there were articles conferring in different degrees, according to the particular mandate or category of mandate, certain rights relative to the mandated territory, directly upon the members of the League as individual States, or in favour of their nationals. Many of these rights were of the same kind as are to be found in certain provisions of ordinary treaties of commerce, establishment and navigation concluded between States. Rights of this kind will hereinafter be referred to as "special interests" rights, embodied in the "special interests" provisions of the mandates. * * * "C" mandates * * * were

confined to provisions for freedom for missionaries ("nationals of any State Member of the League of Nations") to "enter into, travel and reside in the territory for the purpose of prosecuting their calling"—(Mandate for South West Africa, Article 5). In the present case, the dispute between the Parties relates exclusively to the former of these two categories of provisions, and not to the latter. * * *

13. In addition to the classes of provisions so far noticed, every instrument of mandate contained a jurisdictional clause which * * * provided for a reference of disputes to the Permanent Court of International Justice and, so the Court found in the first phase of the case, as already mentioned, this reference was now, by virtue of Article 37 of the Court's Statute, to be construed as a reference to the present Court.

14. * * * [T]he question is whether the various mandatories had any direct obligation towards the other members of the League individually, as regards the carrying out of the "conduct" provisions of the mandates. * * *

33. * * * [E]ven as members of the League when that organization still existed, the Applicants did not, in their individual capacity as States, possess any separate self-contained right which they could assert, independently of, or additionally to, the right of the League, in the pursuit of its collective, institutional activity, to require the due performance of the Mandate in discharge of the "sacred trust." This right was vested exclusively in the League, and was exercised through its competent organs. Each member of the League could share in its collective, institutional exercise by the League, through their participation in the work of its organs, and to the extent that these organs themselves were empowered under the mandates system to act. By their right to activate these organs (of which they made full use), they could procure consideration of mandates questions as of other matters within the sphere of action of the League. But no right was reserved to them, individually as States, and independently of their participation in the institutional activities of the League, as component parts of it, to claim in their own name,—still less as agents authorized to represent the League,—the right to invigilate the sacred trust,—to set themselves up as separate custodians of the various mandates. This was the role of the League organs. * * *

49. The Court must now turn to certain questions of a wider character. Throughout this case it has been suggested, directly or indirectly, that humanitarian considerations are sufficient in themselves to generate legal rights and obligations, and that the Court can and should proceed accordingly. The Court does not think so. It is a court of law, and can take account of moral principles only in so far as these are given a sufficient expression in legal form. Law exists, it is said, to serve a social need; but precisely for that reason it can do so only through and within the limits of its own discipline. Otherwise, it is not a legal service that would be rendered. * * *

51. * * * [T]he Court must examine what is perhaps the most important contention of a general character that has been advanced in

connection with this aspect of the case, namely the contention by which it is sought to derive a legal right or interest in the conduct of the mandate from the simple existence, or principle, of the "sacred trust." The sacred trust, it is said, is a "sacred trust of civilization." Hence all civilized nations have an interest in seeing that it is carried out. An interest, no doubt;—but in order that this interest may take on a specifically legal character, the sacred trust itself must be or become something more than a moral or humanitarian ideal. In order to generate legal rights and obligations, it must be given juridical expression and be clothed in legal form. One such form might be the United Nations trusteeship system,—another, as contained in Chapter XI of the Charter concerning non-self-governing territories, which makes express reference to "a sacred trust." In each case the legal rights and obligations are those, and only those, provided for by the relevant texts, whatever these may be. * * *

99. In the light of these various considerations, the Court finds that the Applicants cannot be considered to have established any legal right or interest appertaining to them in the subject-matter of the present claims, and that, accordingly, the Court must decline to give effect to them.

100. For these reasons,

THE COURT

by the President's casting vote—the votes being equally divided,

decides to reject the claims of the Empire of Ethiopia and the Republic of Liberia. * * *

DISSENTING OPINION OF JUDGE JESSUP

Having very great respect for the Court, it is for me a matter of profound regret to find it necessary to record the fact that I consider the Judgment which the Court has just rendered by the casting vote of the President in the *South West Africa* case, completely unfounded in law. In my opinion, the Court is not legally justified in stopping at the threshold of the case, avoiding a decision on the fundamental question whether the policy and practice of apartheid in the mandated territory of South West Africa is compatible with the discharge of the "sacred trust" confided to the Republic of South Africa as Mandatory. * * *

The Court now * * * *on a theory not advanced by the Respondent in its final submissions of 5 November 1965,* decides that the claim must be rejected on the ground that the Applicants have no legal right or interest.

The Applicants have not asked for an award of damages or for any other material amend for the own individual benefit. They have in effect and in part, asked for a declaratory judgment interpreting certain provisions of the Mandate for South West Africa. The Court having decided in 1962 that they had standing *(locus standi)* to bring the action, they are now entitled to a declaratory judgment without any further showing of interest. * * *

My separate opinion in 1962 also called attention to the fact that in more recent times, the same general appreciation of a right to turn to the International Court of Justice for interpretation, application or fulfillment of a treaty having a broad humanitarian interest, is recognized in—

> "the Genocide Convention, which came into force on 12 January 1951 on the deposit of the twentieth ratification. [It] provides in Article IX:
>
>> 'Disputes between the Contracting Parties relating to the interpretation, application or fulfilment of the present Convention, including those relating to the responsibility of a State for genocide or for any of the other acts enumerated in article III, shall be submitted to the International Court of Justice at the request of any of the parties to the dispute.'
>
> As this Court said of the Genocide Convention: 'In such a convention the contracting States do not have any interests of their own; they merely have, one and all, a common interest, namely the accomplishment of those high purposes which are the *raison d'être* of the convention. Consequently, in a convention of this type one cannot speak of individual advantages or disadvantages to States, or of the maintenance of a perfect contractual balance between rights and duties. The high ideals which inspired the Convention provide, by virtue of the common will of the parties, the foundation and measure of all its provisions.' (*I.C.J. Reports 1951*, at p. 23)" * * *

The standing of Applicants in the present cases rests squarely on the right recognized in paragraph 2 of Article 7 of the Mandate for South West Africa, which is a right appertaining to many States. But it must also be recognized that Applicants as African States, do in addition have a special interest in the present and future of the mandated territory of South West Africa and its inhabitants. This special interest is perhaps even greater than that of some maritime State in the right of passage through the Kiel Canal. "Geographical contiguity" is recognized in paragraph 6 of Article 22 of the Covenant of the League as one of the bases for the allocation of the "C" mandates. It is trite to refer to the shrinkage of territorial space by modern means of transportation and communication, but in a very real sense all African States south of the Sahara are contiguous to each other, and their interrelated interests—geographical and other—cannot be denied. * * *

The Judgment of the Court rests upon the assertion that even though—as the Court decided in 1962—the Applicants had *locus standi* to institute the actions in this case, this does not mean that they have the legal interest which would entitle them to a judgment on the merits. No authority is produced in support of this assertion which suggests a procedure of utter futility. Why should any State institute any proceeding if it lacked standing to have judgment rendered in its favour if it succeeded in establishing its legal or factual contentions on the merits? Why would the Court tolerate a situation in which the parties would be put to great trouble and expense to explore all the details of the merits and only thereafter be told that the Court would pay no heed to all their arguments and evidence because the case was dismissed on a preliminary ground which precluded any investigation of the merits? * * *

Notes and Questions

1. *Standing to Litigate.* Judge Philip Jessup, whom the United States had nominated to the ICJ, argued that the Court refused to decide the merits of Ethiopia's and Liberia's claim on grounds—lack of standing—that were decided in their favor in 1962. Was the Court in 1966 reluctant to find that Ethiopia and Liberia had standing because it feared that South Africa would not respect an adverse ruling on the merits? Professor Perez has suggested that "[i]t might have been disastrous for the Court to reach the merits yet see its decision ignored by the major powers who alone were capable of compelling South Africa's compliance through Security Council action." Antonio F. Perez, "The Passive Virtues and the World Court: Pro-Dialogic Abstention by the International Court of Justice," 18 *Michigan Journal of International Law* 399, 413 (1997). Does the ICJ gain or lose legitimacy when it fails to decide a case because of fears its decision will not be enforced? On concerns about the efficacy of the ICJ, see Chapter 5.

2. Jus Cogens *and Obligations* Erga Omnes. Compare the reluctance of the Court to permit Ethiopia and Liberia to protect a "sacred trust" in Southwest Africa with Professor Verdross's insistence on the role of *jus cogens* in international law. The ICJ has moved closer to the positions advanced by Professor Verdross and Judge Jessup. In 1970, in paragraphs 33 and 34 of the *Barcelona Traction Case*, reproduced in Chapter 6, the Court recognized the concept of "obligations *erga omnes*"—"the obligations of a State toward the international community as a whole." The Court cited, as examples, the international legal proscriptions against interstate aggression, genocide, slavery, and racial discrimination. Does this mean that the ICJ would now allow a state to pursue a judicial action in the common interest with regard to such issues? What would be the implications for the Court if it did so? Note that the content of obligations *erga omnes* has been debated. The International Law Commission, for example, endorsed both the concept and the list in *Barcelona Traction*. U.N. GAOR, 31st Sess., Supp. No. 10, at 170, U.N. Doc. A/31/10 (1976), art. 19(3), *reprinted in* 2 *Yearbook of the International Law Commission* 73, U.N. Doc. A/CN.4/Ser.A/1976/Add.1 (1976). The Commission added obligations based on the prohibition of colonial domination by force and obligations essential to preserve the human environment, such as those prohibiting massive pollution of the seas or the atmosphere. How close are the concepts of *jus cogens* and obligations *erga omnes*? Are they both forms of natural law? Is every *jus cogens* norm an obligation *erga omnes*? Is the reverse true?

3. *Defining* Jus Cogens. How do we know what is and is not a *jus cogens* norm? The ICJ has held that the principles underlying the Genocide Convention are peremptory (*i.e., jus cogens*) norms. Reservations to the Convention on Genocide Case, 1951 I.C.J. 15, 1951 WL 3, excerpted in

Chapter 2. In the *Military and Paramilitary Activities In and Against Nicaragua Case*, the Court cited authorities indicating that Article 2(4) of the U.N. Charter condemning the use of force had moved from treaty rule to a norm of *jus cogens*. 1986 I.C.J. 14, 1986 WL 522 (Merits), especially paragraph 190. We explore Article 2(4) and the *Nicaragua Case* in Chapter 9. Are human rights norms more likely to be *jus cogens* than other kinds of international rules? See Frank J. Garcia, "The Global Market and Human Rights: Trading Away the Human Rights Principle," 25 *Brooklyn Journal of International Law* 51 (1999).

4. *The Mandates System.* The League of Nations mandates system and the United Nations trusteeship system were international efforts to provide for the administration of former colonies and non-self-governing territories. Administered territories eventually became independent states—South West Africa is the present-day Namibia—through a process in which the international law principle of self-determination played a role. We consider self-determination in Chapter 7.

D. EQUITY

Although equity is not explicitly mentioned as a source of law in Article 38(1) of the Statute of the International Court of Justice, international lawyers and tribunals—including the ICJ itself—sometimes apply equity. With respect to the materials in this section, consider what authority there is for the use of equity, the content of the equitable principles that are found, and the relationship between equity and other sources of international law.

THE CAYUGA INDIANS CASE

American and British Claims Arbitration, *Nielsen Reports* 203, 307 (1926).

This is a claim of Great Britain, on behalf of the Cayuga Indians in Canada, against the United States by virtue of certain treaties between the State of New York and the Cayuga Nation in 1789, 1790, and 1795, and the Treaty of 1814 between the United States and Great Britain, known as the Treaty of Ghent.

At the time of the American Revolution, the Cayugas, a tribe of the Six Nations or Iroquois, occupied that part of Central New York lying about Cayuga Lake. During the Revolution, the Cayugas took the side of Great Britain, and as a result their territory was invaded and laid waste by Continental troops. Thereupon the greater part of the tribe removed to Buffalo Creek, and after 1784 a considerable portion removed thence to the Grand River in Canada. By 1790 the majority of the tribe were probably in Canada. In 1789 the State of New York entered into a treaty with the Cayugas who remained at Cayuga Lake, recognized as the Cayuga Nation, whereby the latter ceded the lands formerly occupied by the Tribe to New York and the latter covenanted to pay an annuity of $500 to the nation. In this treaty a reservation at Cayuga Lake was provided for. As there was much dissatisfaction with this treaty on the part of the Indians, who asserted that they were not properly represented, it was confirmed by a subsequent treaty in 1790 and finally by one in 1795, executed by the principal chiefs and warriors both from Buffalo Creek and from the Grand River. By the terms of the latter treaty, in which, as we hold, the covenants of the prior treaties were merged, the State covenanted, among other things, with the "Cayuga Nation" to pay to the said "Cayuga Nation" 1800 dollars a year forever thereafter, at Canandaigua, in Ontario County, the money to be paid to "the Agent of Indian Affairs under the United States for the time being, residing within this State" and, if there was no such agent, then to a person to be appointed by the Governor. Such agent or person appointed by the Governor was to pay the money to the "Cayuga Nation," taking the receipt of the nation and also a receipt on the counterpart of the treaty, left in the possession of the Indians, according to a prescribed form. By this treaty the reservation provided for in the Treaty of 1789 was sold to the State.

There are receipts upon the counterpart of the Treaty of 1795 down to and including 1809, and these receipts and the receipt for 1810, retained by New York, show that the only persons who can be identified among those to whom the money was paid, and the only persons who can be shown to have held prominent positions in the tribe, were then living in Canada. In 1811 an entire change appears. From that time a new set of names, of quite different character, appear on the receipts retained by New York. From that time there are no receipts upon the counterpart. Since that time, it is conceded, no part of the moneys paid under the treaty has come in any way to the Cayugas in Canada, but the whole has been paid to Cayugas in the United States, and since 1829 in accordance with treaties in which the Canadian Cayugas had no part or in accordance with legislation of New York. The claim is: (1) That the Cayugas in Canada, who assert that they have kept up their tribal organization and undoubtedly have included in their number the principal personages of the tribe according to its original organization, are the "Cayuga Nation," covenantees in the Treaty of 1795, and that as such they, or Great Britain on their behalf, should receive the whole amount of the annuity from 1810 to the present. In this connection it is argued that the covenant could only be discharged by payment to those in possession of the counterpart of the treaty and indorsement of a receipt thereon, as in the treaty prescribed. (2) In the alternative, that the Canadian Cayugas, as a part of the posterity of the original nation, and numerically the greater part, have a proportion of the annuity for the future and a proportion of the payments since 1810, to be ascertained by reference to the relative numbers in the United States and in Canada for the time being.

As the occasion of the change that took place in and after 1811 was the division of the tribe at the time of the War of 1812, those in the United States and those in Canada taking the part of the United States and of Great Britain, respectively, Great Britain invokes Article IX of the Treaty of Ghent, by which the United States agreed to restore to the Indians with whom that Government had been a war "all the possessions, rights, and privileges which they may have enjoyed or been entitled to" in 1811 before the war. * * *

It can not be doubted that until the Cayugas permanently divided, all the sachems and warriors, wherever they lived, whether at Cayuga Lake, Buffalo Creek, or the Grand River in Canada, were regarded as entitled to and did share in the money paid on the annuity. Indeed it is reasonably certain that the larger number and the more important of those who signed the Treaty of 1795 were then, or were soon thereafter, permanently established in Canada. It is clear that the greater number and more important of those who signed the annuity receipts from the date of the treaty until 1810 were Canadian Cayugas. We find the person through whom, by the terms of the treaty, the money was to be paid, writing to the Governor of New York in 1797 that the Canadian Cayugas had not received their fair proportion in a previous payment and proposing to make the sum up to them at the next payment. Everything indicates that down to the division the money was regarded as payable to and was paid to and divided among the Cayugas as a people. The claim of the Canadian Cayugas, who are in fact the greater part of that people, is founded in the elementary principle of justice that requires us to look at the substance and not stick in the bark of the legal form.

But there are special circumstances making the equitable claim of the Canadian Cayugas especially strong.

In the first place, the Cayuga Nation had no international status. As has been said, it existed as a legal unit only by New York law. It was a *de facto* unit, but *de jure* was only what Great Britain chose to recognize as to the Cayugas who moved to Canada and what New York recognized as to the Cayugas in New York or in their relations with New York. As to the annuities, therefore, the Cayugas were a unit of New York law, so far as New York law chose to make them one. When the tribe divided, this anomalous and hard situation gave rise to obvious claims according to universally recognized principles of justice.

In the second place, we must bear in mind the dependent legal position of the individual Cayugas. Legally they could do nothing except under the guardianship of some sovereign. They could not determine what should be the nation, nor even whether there should be a nation legally. New York continued to deal with the New York Cayugas as a "nation." Great Britain dealt with the Canadian Cayugas as individuals. The very language of the treaty was in this sense imposed on them. What to them was a covenant with the people of the tribe and its posterity had to be put into legal terms of a covenant with a legal unit that might and did come to be but a fraction of the whole. American Courts have agreed from the beginning in pronouncing the position of the Indians an anomalous one. Miller J., in *United States v. Kagama*, 118 U.S. 375, 381. When a situation legally so anomalous is presented, recourse must be had to generally recognized principles of justice and fair dealing in order to determine the rights of the individuals involved. The same considerations of equity that have repeatedly been invoked by the courts where strict regard to the legal personality of a corporation would lead to inequitable results or to results contrary to legal policy, may be invoked here. In such cases courts have not hesitated to look behind the legal person and consider the human individuals who were the real beneficiaries. Those considerations are even more cogent where we are dealing with Indians in a state of pupilage toward the sovereign with whom they were treating.

There is the more warrant for so doing under the terms of the treaty by virtue of which we are sitting. It provides that decision shall be made in accordance with principles of international law and of equity. Merignhac considers that an arbitral tribunal is justified in reaching a decision on universally recognized principles of justice where the terms of submission are silent as to the grounds of decision and even where the grounds of decision are expressed to be the "principles of international law." He considers, however, that the appropriate formula is that "international law is to be applied with equity." *Traité théorique et pratique de l'arbitrage international*, § 303. It is significant that the present treaty uses the phrase "principles of international law and equity." When used in a general arbitration treaty, this can only mean to provide for the possibility of anomalous cases such as the present.

An examination of the provisions of arbitration treaties shows a recognition that something more than the strict law must be used in the grounds of decision of arbitral tribunals in certain cases; that there are cases in which—like the courts of the land—these tribunals must find the grounds of decision, must find the right and the law, in general considerations of justice, equity, and right dealing guided by legal analogies and by the spirit and received principles of international law.
* * *

* * * Our conclusion on this branch of the cause is that, according to general and universally recognized principles of justice and the analogy of the way in which English and American courts, on proper occasions, look behind what in such cases they call "the corporate fiction" in the interests of justice or of the policy of the law (Daimler Company, Ltd. *v.* Continental Tyre and Rubber Company, Ltd. [1916] 2 A.C. 307, 315–316, 338 ff.; 1 Cook (Corporations, 8 ed. § 2)), on the division of the Cayuga Nation the Cayuga Indians permanently settled in Canada became entitled to their proportionate share of the annuity and that such share ought to have been paid to them from 1810 to the present time.

Notes and Questions

1. *The Definition of the "Cayuga Nation."* In the *Cayuga Indians Case* how was the "Cayuga Nation" defined? Were there different definitions of it made in U.S. law, in British law, and in international law? Were the agreements of 1789, 1790, and 1795 between the United States and the Cayuga Nation governed by U.S. or international law? What about the 1814 Treaty of Ghent between the United States and Great Britain?

2. *Individual and Group Rights in International Law.* Notice how the arbitral panel looked behind the "legal person" of the Cayuga Nation so it could protect "human individuals who were the real beneficiaries" of the treaties. How much deference should international law show to other "legal persons"? Was the peculiarity here that the Cayuga Nation was a "nation" but not a "state," and thus unable to vindicate its own international legal rights? Questions about the relationship of individuals to international law and their international legal rights and obligations vis-à-vis their own and other states are raised in Chapter 6, and questions about the group rights of "peoples" are addressed in Chapter 7.

3. *The Varieties of Equity.* The treaty providing for the resolution of the *Cayuga Indians* dispute explicitly called for the application of "the principles of international law and of equity." Therefore, the arbitral tribunal was not concerned that its use of equity necessarily be within the rules of international law, *i.e.*, that it be equity *intra legem*. The tribunal had a warrant to apply equity at least in place of the law, *i.e.*, equity *praeter legem*, and perhaps even against the law, *i.e.*, equity *contra legem*. Did the *Cayuga Indians* tribunal really venture beyond equity *intra legem*? Can it really be said that the tribunal moved to fill gaps in international law or to reverse international law?

The arbitral tribunal was persuaded that "as a matter of justice" the Canadian Cayugas had a good claim against the United States: "The claim of the Canadian Cayugas, who are in fact the greater part of that people, is founded in the elementary principle of justice that requires us to look at the substance and not stick in the bark of the legal form." Should international law be more or less able than municipal law "to look at the substance" of disputes and "not stick in the bark of the legal form"? On the one hand, formal agreements among sovereign states may deserve special respect. On the other hand, without municipal-type legislative organs, international law may become especially rigid.

THE MEUSE CASE

Judge Hudson's Opinion,
1937 P.C.I.J., Ser. A/B, No. 70, at 73.

The Netherlands Government has asked the Court to say that the alimentation of certain canals by the Neerhaeren Lock with water taken from the Meuse elsewhere than at Maestricht is contrary to the Treaty of 1863, and to order that Belgium should discontinue that alimentation. On the other hand, the Belgian Government has asked the Court to say that the alimentation of these canals has not become contrary to the Treaty of 1863 by reason of the fact that lock-water discharged by the *bona fide* operation for the passage of boats of the Neerhaeren Lock, which cannot be treated more unfavourably than the Bosscheveld Lock, is confused with water of the Meuse taken by the *prise d'eau* at Maestricht. In its submissions the Belgian Government does not ask the Court to say that the operation of the Bosscheveld Lock results in an alimentation of the canals which constitutes a violation of the Treaty; but the Belgian Agent contends that if the Court should decide that the functioning of the Belgian lock at Neerhaeren is in opposition to the Treaty of 1863, it ought to admit *a fortiori* that the functioning of the Netherlands lock of Bosscheveld is not more regular (*n'est pas non plus régulier*). A further submission of the Belgian Government, offered alternatively (*trés subsidiairement*), asks the Court to say that by the construction of works contrary to the provisions of the Treaty the Netherlands has lost the right to invoke the Treaty against Belgium.

On this presentation of the case, the Court must consider the functioning of the Bosscheveld Lock in connection with that of the Neerhaeren Lock. The first question is, therefore, whether the two locks are to be placed on the same footing. * * *

It must be concluded that, in law as well as in fact, the Bosscheveld Lock and the Neerhaeren Lock are in the same position. The latter cannot be treated more unfavourably than the former. If the discharge of lock-water into the Zuid–Willemsvaart by one of these locks is in accordance with the Treaty, it is equally so with respect to the other lock; if such discharge is a violation of the Treaty as to one lock, it is a violation also as to the other lock.

The question arises, therefore, whether in this case the Court must pronounce upon the legality or the illegality of the alimentation which results from the operation of either the Neerhaeren Lock or the Bosscheveld Lock. If the operation of both locks were thought to be in conformity with the Treaty of 1863, the submissions of the Netherlands Government as to the Neerhaeren Lock would of course be rejected. It remains to be considered whether that result would be reached if the operation of both locks were thought to be in violation of the Treaty of 1863.

There can be no question here as to the good faith of either Party. Each Party has proceeded on its own view of the Treaty of 1863. Each has taken action which has led to the same result, in fact and in law. If the Court were called upon to give judgment on the action of both of the Parties, it could do so with due regard to the equal positions of the Parties; but here it is asked by one Party to condemn the action taken by the other. Aside from the fact that the moving Party is the one whose action preceded that of the other, that the Bosscheveld Lock was put into service in 1931 and the Neerhaeren Lock only in 1934, is this a case in which affirmative relief should be given by the Court? Or should it be said, in the terms of the alternative Belgian submission, that the Netherlands has in some measure *perdu le droit d'invoquer* the Treaty against Belgium?

What are widely known as principles of equity have long been considered to constitute a part of international law, and as such they have often been applied by international tribunals. Mérignhac, *Traité théorique et pratique de l'Arbitrage international* (1895), p. 295; Ralston, *Law and Procedure of International Tribunals* (new ed., 1926), pp. 53–57. A sharp division between law and equity, such as prevails in the administration of justice in some States, should find no place in international jurisprudence; even in some national legal systems, there has been a strong tendency towards the fusion of law and equity. Some international tribunals are expressly directed by the *compromis* which control them to apply "law and equity." See the Cayuga Indians Case, Nielsen's Report of the United States–British Claims Arbitration (1926), p. 307. Of such a provision, a special tribunal of the Permanent Court of Arbitration said in 1922 that "the majority of international lawyers seem to agree that these words are to be understood to mean general principles of justice as distinguished from any particular systems of jurisprudence." Proceedings of the United States–Norwegian Tribunal (1922), p. 141. Numerous arbitration treaties have been concluded in recent years which apply to differences "which are justiciable in their nature by reason of being susceptible of decision by the application of the principles of law or equity." Whether the reference in an arbitration treaty is to the application of "law and equity" or to justiciability dependent on the possibility of applying "law or equity," it would seem to envisage equity as a part of law.

The Court has not been expressly authorized by its Statute to apply equity as distinguished from law. Nor, indeed, does the Statute expressly direct its application of international law, though as has been said on several occasions the Court is "a tribunal of international law." Series A, No. 7, p. 19; Series A, Nos. 20/21, p. 124. Article 38 of the Statute expressly directs the application of "general principles of law recognized by civilized nations," and in more than one nation principles of equity have an established place in the legal system. The Court's recognition of equity as a part of international law is in no way restricted by the special power conferred upon it "to decide a case *ex aequo et bono*, if the parties agree thereto." * * *

It would seem to be an important principle of equity that where two parties have assumed an identical or a reciprocal obligation, one party which is engaged in a continuing non-performance of that obligation should not be permitted to take advantage of a similar non-performance of that obligation by the other party. The principle finds expression in the so-called maxims of equity which exercised great influence in the creative period of the development of the Anglo–American law. Some of these maxims are, "Equality is equity"; "He who seeks equity must do equity." It is in line with such maxims that "a court of equity refuses relief to a plaintiff whose conduct in regard to the subject-matter of the litigation has been improper." 13 Halsbury's *Laws of England* (2nd ed., 1934), p. 87. A very similar principle was received into Roman Law. The obligations of a vendor and a vendee being concurrent, "neither could compel the other to perform unless he had done, or tendered, his own part." Buckland, *Text Book of Roman Law* (2nd ed., 1932), p. 493. The *exceptio non adimpleti contractus* required a claimant to prove that he had performed or offered to perform his obligation. Girard, *Droit romain* (8th ed., 1929), p. 567; Saleilles, in 6 *Annales de Droit commercial*, (1892), p. 287, and 7 *id.* (1893), pp. 24, 97 and 175. This conception was the basis of Articles 320 and 322 of the German Civil Code, and even where a code is silent on the point Planiol states the general principle that "dans tout rapport synallagmatique, chacune des deux parties ne peut exiger la prestation qui lui est due que si elle-offre elle-même d'exécuter son obligation." Planiol, *Droit civil*, Vol. 2 (6th ed., 1912), p. 320. * * *

One result of applying the principle will be that even if the Court should be of the opinion that the Belgian action with regard to the functioning of the Neerhaeren Lock is contrary to the Treaty of 1863, it should nevertheless refuse in this case to order Belgium to discontinue that action. In equity, the Netherlands is not in a position to have such relief decreed to her. Belgium cannot be ordered to discontinue the operation of the Neerhaeren Lock when the Netherlands is left free to continue the operation of the Bosscheveld Lock.

Notes and Questions

1. *Justifying Hudson's Recourse to Equity.* Unlike the arbitrators in the *Cayuga Indians Case*, Judge Hudson in the *Meuse Case* had no explicit charge from the states involved to apply equity as well as law to the dispute. How then did Hudson justify his use of equity? If the principles of equity are part of international law, does any kind of equity exist outside international law? Given Hudson's reasoning, was an "international law and equity" authorization *à la Cayuga Indians* simply redundant?

2. *Searching for General Principles.* Hudson noted that equity could be a type of "general principle" which the Court is authorized to apply under Article 38(1)(c) of its Statute. How thorough a search of municipal law did Judge Hudson make in search of his general principle? How did it compare to Advocate General Slynn's search of municipal law in the *AM & S Case*? Was Hudson's search meant to be universal? If so, did it succeed?

3. *The Effect of Applying Equity.* What was the effect of Judge Hudson's application of equity to the facts of the *Meuse Case*? What were the parties supposed to do if they accepted Hudson's decision?

4. Ex Aequo et Bono. By Article 38(2) of its Statute, the International Court of Justice may decide a case *ex aequo et bono,* but only if the states party to the dispute specifically authorize it to do so. The Court has never been so authorized. What in practice would be the difference between applying equitable principles pursuant to Article 38(1)(c) and deciding *ex aequo et bono* pursuant to Article 38(2)?

THE NORTH SEA CONTINENTAL SHELF CASES

Federal Republic of Germany v. Denmark; Federal Republic of Germany v. Netherlands, 1969 I.C.J. 3, 1969 WL 1.

By a letter of 16 February 1967, received in the Registry on 20 February 1967, the Minister for Foreign Affairs of the Netherlands transmitted to the Registrar:

(*a*) an original copy, signed at Bonn on 2 February 1967 for the Governments of Denmark and the Federal Republic of Germany, of a Special Agreement for the submission to the Court of a difference between those two States concerning the delimitation, as between them, of the continental shelf in the North Sea;

(*b*) an original copy, signed at Bonn on 2 February 1967 for the Governments of the Federal Republic of Germany and the Netherlands, of a Special Agreement for the submission to the Court of a difference between those two States concerning the delimitation, as between them, of the continental shelf in the North Sea;

(*c*) an original copy, signed at Bonn on 2 February 1967 for the three Governments aforementioned, of a Protocol relating to certain procedural questions arising from the above-mentioned Special Agreements.

Articles 1 to 3 of the Special Agreement between the Governments of Denmark and the Federal Republic of Germany [and another between the Governments of the Netherlands and the Federal Republic of Germany are] as follows:

"Article 1

(1) The International Court of Justice is requested to decide the following question:

What principles and rules of international law are applicable to the delimitation as between the Parties of the areas of the continental shelf in the North Sea which appertain to each of them beyond the partial boundary determined by the above-mentioned Convention of 9 June 1965?

(2) The Governments of the Kingdom of Denmark and of the Federal Republic of Germany [and of the Netherlands] shall delimit the continental shelf in the North Sea as between their countries by agreement in pursuance of the decision requested from the International Court of Justice. * * *." * * *

3. As described in Article 4 of the North Sea Policing of Fisheries Convention of 6 May 1882, the North Sea, which lies between continental Europe and Great Britain in the east-west direction, is roughly oval in shape and stretches from the straits of Dover northwards to a parallel drawn between a point immediately north of the Shetland Islands and the mouth of the Sogne Fiord in Norway, about 75 kilometres above Bergen, beyond which is the North Atlantic Ocean. In the extreme northwest, it is bounded by a line connecting the Orkney and Shetland island groups; while on its north-eastern side, the line separating it from the entrances to the Baltic Sea lies between Hanstholm at the northwest point of Denmark, and Lindesnes at the southern tip of Norway. Eastward of this line the Skagerrak begins. Thus, the North Sea has to some extent the general look of an enclosed sea without actually being one. Round its shores are situated, on its eastern side and starting from the north, Norway, Denmark, the Federal Republic of Germany, the Netherlands, Belgium and France; while the whole western side is taken up by Great Britain, together with the island groups of the Orkneys and

Shetlands. From this it will be seen that the continental shelf of the Federal Republic is situated between those of Denmark and the Netherlands.

4. The waters of the North Sea are shallow, and the whole seabed consists of continental shelf at a depth of less than 200 metres, except for the formation known as the Norwegian Trough, a belt of water 200–650 metres deep, fringing the southern and south-western coasts of Norway to a width averaging about 80–100 kilometres. Much the greater part of this continental shelf has already been the subject of delimitation by a series of agreements concluded between the United Kingdom (which, as stated, lies along the whole western side of it) and certain of the States on the eastern side, namely Norway, Denmark and the Netherlands. These three delimitations were carried out by the drawing of what are known as "median lines" which, for immediate present purposes, may be described as boundaries drawn between the continental shelf areas of "opposite" States, dividing the intervening spaces equally between them. * * *

5. In addition to the partial boundary lines Federal Republic/Denmark and Federal Republic/Netherlands, which * * * were respectively established by the agreements of 9 June 1965 and 1 December 1964, and which are shown as lines A–B and C–D on Map 3 * * * another line has been drawn in this area, namely that represented by the line E–F on that map. This line, which divides areas respectively claimed (to the north of it) by Denmark, and (to the south of it) by the Netherlands, is the outcome of an agreement between those two countries dated 31 March 1966, reflecting the view taken by them as to what are the correct boundary lines between their respective continental shelf areas and that of the Federal Republic, beyond the partial boundaries A–B and C–D already drawn. These further and unagreed boundaries to seaward, are shown on Map 3 by means of the dotted lines B–E and D–E. They are the lines, the correctness of which in law the Court is in effect, though indirectly, called upon to determine. Also shown on Map 3 are the two pecked lines B–F and D–F, representing approximately the boundaries which the Federal Republic would have wished to obtain in the course of the negotiations that took place between the Federal Republic and the other two Parties prior to the submission of the matter to the Court. The nature of these negotiations must now be described.

6. Under the agreements of December 1964 and June 1965, already mentioned, the partial boundaries represented by the map lines A–B and C–D had, according to the information furnished to the Court by the Parties, been drawn mainly by application of the principle of equidistance, using that term as denoting the abstract concept of equidistance. A line so drawn, known as an "equidistance line," may be described as one which leaves to each of the parties concerned all those portions of the continental shelf that are nearer to a point on its own coast than they are to any point on the coast of the other party. An equidistance line may consist either of a "median" line between "opposite" States, or of a "lateral" line between "adjacent" States. In certain geographical

configurations of which the Parties furnished examples, a given equidistance line may partake in varying degree of the nature both of a median and of a lateral line. There exists nevertheless a distinction to be drawn between the two, which will be mentioned in its place.

7. The further negotiations between the Parties for the prolongation of the partial boundaries broke down mainly because Denmark and the Netherlands respectively wished this prolongation also to be effected on the basis of the equidistance principle,—and this would have resulted in the dotted lines B–E and D–E, shown on Map 3; whereas the Federal Republic considered that such an outcome would be inequitable because it would unduly curtail what the Republic believed should be its proper share of continental shelf area, on the basis of proportionality to the length of its North Sea coastline. It will be observed that neither of the lines in question, taken by itself, would produce this effect, but only both of them together—an element regarded by Denmark and the Netherlands as irrelevant to what they viewed as being two separate and self-contained delimitations, each of which should be carried out without reference to the other.

8. The reason for the result that would be produced by the two lines B–E and D–E, taken conjointly, is that in the case of a concave or recessing coast such as that of the Federal Republic on the North Sea, the effect of the use of the equidistance method is to pull the line of the boundary inwards, in the direction of the concavity. Consequently, where two such lines are drawn at different points on a concave coast, they will, if the curvature is pronounced, inevitably meet at a relatively short distance from the coast, thus causing the continental shelf area they enclose, to take the form approximately of a triangle with its apex to seaward and, as it was put on behalf of the Federal Republic, "cutting off" the coastal State from the further areas of the continental shelf outside of and beyond this triangle. The effect of concavity could of course equally be produced for a country with a straight coastline if the coasts of adjacent countries protruded immediately on either side of it. In contrast to this, the effect of coastal projections, or of convex or outwardly curving coasts such as are, to a moderate extent, those of Denmark and the Netherlands, is to cause boundary lines drawn on an equidistance basis to leave the coast on divergent courses, thus having a widening tendency on the area of continental shelf off that coast. These two distinct effects, which are shown in sketches I–III * * *, are directly attributable to the use of the equidistance method of delimiting continental shelf boundaries off recessing or projecting coasts. It goes without saying that on these types of coasts the equidistance method produces exactly similar effects in the delimitation of the lateral boundaries of the territorial sea of the States concerned. However, owing to the very close proximity of such waters to the coasts concerned, these effects are much less marked and may be very slight,—and there are other aspects involved, which will be considered in their place. It will suffice to mention here that, for instance, a deviation from a line drawn perpendicular to the general direction of the coast, of only 5 kilometres, at a

Map 3
(See paragraphs 5-9)

Sketches illustrating the geographical situations described in paragraph 8 of the Judgment

distance of about 5 kilometres from that coast, will grow into one of over 30 at a distance of over 100 kilometres.

9. After the negotiations, separately held between the Federal Republic and the other two Parties respectively, had in each case, for the reasons given in the two preceding paragraphs, failed to result in any agreement about the delimitation of the boundary extending beyond the partial one already agreed, tripartite talks between all the Parties took place in The Hague in February–March 1966, in Bonn in May and again in Copenhagen in August. These also proving fruitless, it was then decided to submit the matter to the Court. * * *

25. The Court now turns to the legal position regarding the equidistance method. The first question to be considered is whether the 1958 Geneva Convention on the Continental Shelf is binding for all the Parties in this case—that is to say whether, as contended by Denmark and the Netherlands, the use of this method is rendered obligatory for the present delimitations by virtue of the delimitations provision (Article 6) of that instrument, according to the conditions laid down in it. Clearly, if this is so, then the provisions of the Convention will prevail in the relations between the Parties, and would take precedence of any rules having a more general character, or derived from another source. On that basis the Court's reply to the question put to it in the Special Agreements would necessarily be to the effect that as between the Parties the relevant provisions of the Convention represented the applicable rules of law—that is to say constituted the law for the Parties—and its sole remaining task would be to interpret those provisions, in so far as their meaning was disputed or appeared to be uncertain, and to apply them to the particular circumstances involved.

26. The relevant provisions of Article 6 of the Geneva Convention, paragraph 2 of which Denmark and the Netherlands contend not only to be applicable as a conventional rule, but also to represent the accepted rule of general international law on the subject of continental shelf delimitation, as it exists independently of the Convention, read as follows:

"1. Where the same continental shelf is adjacent to the territories of two or more States whose coasts are opposite each other, the boundary of the continental shelf appertaining to such States shall be determined by agreement between them. In the absence of agreement, and unless another boundary line is justified by special circumstances, the boundary is the median line, every point of which is equidistant from the nearest point of the baselines from which the breadth of the territorial sea of each State is measured.

2. Where the same continental shelf is adjacent to the territories of two adjacent States, the boundary of the continental shelf shall be determined by agreement between them. In the absence of agreement, and unless another boundary line is justified by special circumstances, the boundary shall be determined by application of the principle of equidistance from the nearest points of the baselines from which the breadth of the territorial sea of each State is measured."

The Convention received 46 signatures and, up-to-date, there have been 39 ratifications or accessions. It came into force on 10 June 1964, having received the 22 ratifications or accessions required for that purpose (Article 11), and was therefore in force at the time when the various delimitations of continental shelf boundaries described earlier (paragraphs 1 and 5) took place between the Parties. But, under the formal provisions of the Convention, it is in force for any individual State only in so far as, having signed it within the time-limit provided for that purpose, that State has also subsequently ratified it; or, not having signed within that time-limit, has subsequently acceded to the Convention. Denmark and the Netherlands have both signed and ratified the Convention, and are parties to it, the former since 10 June 1964, the latter since 20 March 1966. The Federal Republic was one of the signatories of the Convention, but has never ratified it, and is consequently not a party.

27.   It is admitted on behalf of Denmark and the Netherlands that in these circumstances the Convention cannot, as such, be binding on the Federal Republic, in the sense of the Republic being contractually bound by it. But it is contended that the Convention, or the régime of the Convention, and in particular of Article 6, has become binding on the Federal Republic in another way,—namely because, by conduct, by public statements and proclamations, and in other ways, the Republic has unilaterally assumed the obligations of the Convention; or has manifested its acceptance of the conventional régime; or has recognized it as being generally applicable to the delimitation of continental shelf areas. * * *

28.   As regards these contentions, it is clear that only a very definite, very consistent course of conduct on the part of a State in the situation of the Federal Republic could justify the Court in upholding them; and, if this had existed—that is to say if there had been a real intention to manifest acceptance or recognition of the applicability of the conventional régime—then it must be asked why it was that the Federal Republic did not take the obvious step of giving expression to this readiness by simply ratifying the Convention. In principle, when a number of States, including the one whose conduct is invoked, and those invoking it, have drawn up a convention specifically providing for a particular method by which the intention to become bound by the régime of the convention is to be manifested—namely by the carrying out of certain prescribed formalities (ratification, accession), it is not lightly to be presumed that a State which has not carried out these formalities, though at all times fully able and entitled to do so, has nevertheless somehow become bound in another way. Indeed if it were a question not of obligation but of rights,—if, that is to say, a State which, though entitled to do so, had not ratified or acceded, attempted to claim rights under the convention, on the basis of a declared willingness to be bound by it, or of conduct evincing acceptance of the conventional régime, it would simply be told that, not having become a party to the convention it could not claim any rights under it until the professed willingness and acceptance had been manifested in the prescribed form.

29.   A further point, not in itself conclusive, but to be noted, is that if the Federal Republic had ratified the Geneva Convention, it could have entered—and could, if it ratified now, enter—a reservation to Article 6, by reason of the faculty to do so conferred by Article 12 of the Convention. This faculty would remain, whatever the previous conduct of the Federal Republic might have been—a fact which at least adds to the difficulties involved by the Danish–Netherlands contention.

30.   Having regard to these considerations of principle, it appears to the Court that only the existence of a situation of estoppel could suffice to lend substance to this contention,—that is to say if the Federal Republic were now precluded from denying the applicability of the

conventional régime, by reason of past conduct, declarations, etc., which not only clearly and consistently evinced acceptance of that régime, but also had caused Denmark or the Netherlands, in reliance on such conduct, detrimentally to change position or suffer some prejudice. Of this there is no evidence whatever in the present case. * * *

37. It is maintained by Denmark and the Netherlands that the Federal Republic, whatever its position may be in relation to the Geneva Convention, considered as such, is in any event bound to accept delimitation on an equidistance-special circumstances basis, because the use of this method is not in the nature of a merely conventional obligation, but is, or must now be regarded as involving, a rule that is part of the *corpus* of general international law;—and, like other rules of general or customary international law, is binding on the Federal Republic automatically and independently of any specific assent, direct or indirect, given by the latter. This contention has both a positive law and a more fundamentalist aspect. As a matter of positive law, it is based on the work done in this field by international legal bodies, on State practice and on the influence attributed to the Geneva Convention itself,—the claim being that these various factors have cumulatively evidenced or been creative of the *opinio juris sive necessitatis*, requisite for the formation of new rules of customary international law. In its fundamentalist aspect, the view put forward derives from what might be called the natural law of the continental shelf, in the sense that the equidistance principle is seen as a necessary expression in the field of delimitation of the accepted doctrine of the exclusive appurtenance of the continental shelf to the nearby coastal State, and therefore as having an *a priori* character of so to speak juristic inevitability.

[The Court first analyzes and rejects the *a priori* argument, concluding:]

55. In the light of this history, and of the record generally, it is clear that at no time was the notion of equidistance as an inherent necessity of continental shelf doctrine entertained. Quite a different outlook was indeed manifested from the start in current legal thinking. It was, and it really remained to the end, governed by two beliefs;— namely, first, that no one single method of delimitation was likely to prove satisfactory in all circumstances, and that delimitation should, therefore, be carried out by agreement (or by reference to arbitration); and secondly, that it should be effected on equitable principles. It was in pursuance of the first of these beliefs that in the draft that emerged as Article 6 of the Geneva Convention, the Commission gave priority to delimitation by agreement,—and in pursuance of the second that it introduced the exception in favour of "special circumstances." Yet the record shows that, even with these mitigations, doubts persisted, particularly as to whether the equidistance principle would in all cases prove equitable.

56. In these circumstances, it seems to the Court that the inherency contention as now put forward by Denmark and the Netherlands

inverts the true order of things in point of time and that, so far from an equidistance rule having been generated by an antecedent principle of proximity inherent in the whole concept of continental shelf appurtenance, the latter is rather a rationalization of the former—an *ex post facto* construct directed to providing a logical juristic basis for a method of delimitation propounded largely for different reasons, cartographical and other. Given also that * * * the theory cannot be said to be endowed with any quality of logical necessity either, the Court is unable to accept it. * * *

60. The conclusions so far reached leave open, and still to be considered, the question whether on some basis other than that of an *a priori* logical necessity, i.e., through positive law processes, the equidistance principle has come to be regarded as a rule of customary international law, so that it would be obligatory for the Federal Republic in that way, even though Article 6 of the Geneva Convention is not, as such, opposable to it. For this purpose it is necessary to examine the status of the principle as it stood when the Convention was drawn up, as it resulted from the effect of the Convention, and in the light of State practice subsequent to the Convention; but it should be clearly understood that in the pronouncements the Court makes on these matters it has in view solely the delimitation provisions (Article 6) of the Convention, not other parts of it, nor the Convention as such.

61. The first of these questions can conveniently be considered in the form suggested on behalf of Denmark and the Netherlands themselves in the course of the oral hearing, when it was stated that they had not in fact contended that the delimitation article (Article 6) of the Convention "embodied already received rules of customary law in the sense that the Convention was merely declaratory of existing rules." Their contention was, rather, that although prior to the Conference, continental shelf law was only in the formative stage, and State practice lacked uniformity, yet "the process of the definition and consolidation of the emerging customary law took place through the work of the International Law Commission, the reaction of governments to that work and the proceedings of the Geneva Conference"; and this emerging customary law became "crystallized in the adoption of the Continental Shelf Convention by the Conference."

62. Whatever validity this contention may have in respect of at least certain parts of the Convention, the Court cannot accept it as regards the delimitation provision (Article 6), the relevant parts of which were adopted almost unchanged from the draft of the International Law Commission that formed the basis of discussion at the Conference. The status of the rule in the Convention therefore depends mainly on the processes that led the Commission to propose it. These processes have already been reviewed in connection with the Danish–Netherlands contention of an *a priori* necessity for equidistance, and the Court considers this review sufficient for present purposes also, in order to show that the principle of equidistance, as it now figures in Article 6 of the Convention, was proposed by the Commission with considerable hesitation, somewhat

on an experimental basis, at most *de lege ferenda*, and not at all *de lege lata* or as an emerging rule of customary international law. This is clearly not the sort of foundation on which Article 6 of the Convention could be said to have reflected or crystallized such a rule.

63. The foregoing conclusion receives significant confirmation from the fact that Article 6 is one of those in respect of which, under the reservations article of the Convention (Article 12) reservations may be made by any State on signing, ratifying or acceding,—for, speaking generally, it is a characteristic of purely conventional rules and obligations that, in regard to them, some faculty of making unilateral reservations may, within certain limits, be admitted;—whereas this cannot be so in the case of general or customary law rules and obligations which, by their very nature, must have equal force for all members of the international community, and cannot therefore be the subject of any right of unilateral exclusion exercisable at will by any one of them in its own favour. Consequently, it is to be expected that when, for whatever reason, rules or obligations of this order are embodied, or are intended to be reflected in certain provisions of a convention, such provisions will figure amongst those in respect of which a right of unilateral reservation is not conferred, or is excluded. This expectation is, in principle, fulfilled by Article 12 of the Geneva Continental Shelf Convention, which permits reservations to be made to all the articles of the Convention "other than to Articles 1 to 3 inclusive"—these three Articles being the ones which, it is clear, were then regarded as reflecting, or as crystallizing, received or at least emergent rules of customary international law relative to the continental shelf, amongst them the question of the seaward extent of the shelf; the juridical character of the coastal State's entitlement; the nature of the rights exercisable; the kind of natural resources to which these relate; and the preservation intact of the legal status as high seas of the waters over the shelf, and the legal status of the superjacent air-space.

64. The normal inference would therefore be that any articles that do not figure among those excluded from the faculty of reservation under Article 12, were not regarded as declaratory of previously existing or emergent rules of law; and this is the inference the Court in fact draws in respect of Article 6 (delimitation), having regard also to the attitude of the International Law Commission to this provision, as already described in general terms. Naturally this would not of itself prevent this provision from eventually passing into the general *corpus* of customary international law by one of the processes considered in paragraphs 70–81 below. But that is not here the issue. What is now under consideration is whether it originally figured in the Convention as such a rule. * * *

69. In the light of these various considerations, the Court reaches the conclusion that the Geneva Convention did not embody or crystallize any pre-existing or emergent rule of customary law, according to which the delimitation of continental shelf areas between adjacent States must, unless the Parties otherwise agree, be carried out on a equidistance-special circumstances basis. A rule was of course embodied in Article 6 of

the Convention, but as a purely conventional rule. Whether it has since acquired a broader basis remains to be seen: *qua* conventional rule however, as has already been concluded, it is not opposable to the Federal Republic.

70.   The Court must now proceed to the last stage in the argument put forward on behalf of Denmark and the Netherlands. This is to the effect that even if there was at the date of the Geneva Convention no rule of customary international law in favour of the equidistance principle, and no such rule was crystallized in Article 6 of the Convention, nevertheless such a rule has come into being since the Convention, partly because of its own impact, partly on the basis of subsequent State practice,—and that this rule, being now a rule of customary international law binding on all States, including therefore the Federal Republic, should be declared applicable to the delimitation of the boundaries between the Parties' respective continental shelf areas in the North Sea.

71.   In so far as this contention is based on the view that Article 6 of the Convention has had the influence, and has produced the effect, described, it clearly involves treating that Article as a norm-creating provision which has constituted the foundation of, or has generated a rule which, while only conventional or contractual in its origin, has since passed into the general *corpus* of international law, and is now accepted as such by the *opinio juris*, so as to have become binding even for countries which have never, and do not, become parties to the Convention. There is no doubt that this process is a perfectly possible one and does from time to time occur: it constitutes indeed one of the recognized methods by which new rules of customary international law may be formed. At the same time this result is not lightly to be regarded as having been attained. * * *

75.   The Court must now consider whether State practice in the matter of continental shelf delimitation has, subsequent to the Geneva Convention, been of such a kind as to satisfy this requirement. Leaving aside cases which, for various reasons, the Court does not consider to be reliable guides as precedents, such as delimitations effected between the present Parties themselves, or not relating to international boundaries, some 15 cases have been cited in the course of the present proceedings, occurring mostly since the signature of the 1958 Geneva Convention, in which continental shelf boundaries have been delimited according to the equidistance principle—in the majority of the cases by agreement, in a few others unilaterally—or else the delimitation was foreshadowed but has not yet been carried out. Amongst these 15 are the four North Sea delimitations United Kingdom/Norway–Denmark–Netherlands, and Norway/Denmark already mentioned in paragraph 4 of this Judgment. But even if these various cases constituted more than a very small proportion of those potentially calling for delimitation in the world as a whole, the Court would not think it necessary to enumerate or evaluate them separately, since there are, *a priori*, several grounds which deprive them of weight as precedents in the present context.

76. To begin with, over half the States concerned, whether acting unilaterally or conjointly, were or shortly became parties to the Geneva Convention, and were therefore presumably, so far as they were concerned, acting actually or potentially in the application of the Convention. From their action no inference could legitimately be drawn as to the existence of a rule of customary international law in favour of the equidistance principle. As regards those States, on the other hand, which were not, and have not become parties to the Convention, the basis of their action can only be problematical and must remain entirely speculative. Clearly, they were not applying the Convention. But from that no inference could justifiably be drawn that they believed themselves to be applying a mandatory rule of customary international law. There is not a shred of evidence that they did and * * * there is no lack of other reasons for using the equidistance method, so that acting, or agreeing to act in a certain way, does not of itself demonstrate anything of a juridical nature. * * *

81. The Court accordingly concludes that if the Geneva Convention was not in its origins or inception declaratory of a mandatory rule of customary international law enjoining the use of the equidistance principle for the delimitation of continental shelf areas between adjacent States, neither has its subsequent effect been constitutive of such a rule; and that State practice up-to-date has equally been insufficient for the purpose. * * *

83. The legal situation therefore is that the Parties are under no obligation to apply either the 1958 Convention, which is not opposable to the Federal Republic, or the equidistance method as a mandatory rule of customary law, which it is not. But as between States faced with an issue concerning the lateral delimitation of adjacent continental shelves, there are still rules and principles of law to be applied; and in the present case it is not the fact either that rules are lacking, or that the situation is one for the unfettered appreciation of the Parties. Equally, it is not the case that if the equidistance principle is not a rule of law, there has to be as an alternative some other single equivalent rule.

84. As already indicated, the Court is not called upon itself to delimit the areas of continental shelf appertaining respectively to each Party, and in consequence is not bound to prescribe the methods to be employed for the purposes of such a delimitation. The Court has to indicate to the Parties the principles and rules of law in the light of which the methods for eventually effecting the delimitation will have to be chosen. The Court will discharge this task in such a way as to provide the Parties with the requisite directions, without substituting itself for them by means of a detailed indication of the methods to be followed and the factors to be taken into account for the purposes of a delimitation the carrying out of which the Parties have expressly reserved to themselves.

85. It emerges from the history of the development of the legal régime of the continental shelf, which has been reviewed earlier, that the

essential reason why the equidistance method is not to be regarded as a rule of law is that, if it were to be compulsorily applied in all situations, this would not be consonant with certain basic legal notions which, as has been observed in paragraphs 48 and 55, have from the beginning reflected the *opinio juris* in the matter of delimitation; those principles being that delimitation must be the object of agreement between the States concerned, and that such agreement must be arrived at in accordance with equitable principles. On a foundation of very general precepts of justice and good faith, actual rules of law are here involved which govern the delimitation of adjacent continental shelves—that is to say, rules binding upon State for all delimitations;—in short, it is not a question of applying equity simply as a matter of abstract justice, but of applying a rule of law which itself requires the application of equitable principles, in accordance with the ideas which have always underlain the development of the legal régime of the continental shelf in this field, namely:

(*a*) the parties are under an obligation to enter into negotiations with a view to arriving at an agreement, and not merely to go through a formal process of negotiation as a sort of prior condition for the automatic application of a certain method of delimitation in the absence of agreement; they are under an obligation so to conduct themselves that the negotiations are meaningful, which will not be the case when either of them insists upon its own position without contemplating any modification of it;

(*b*) the parties are under an obligation to act in such a way that, in the particular case, and taking all the circumstances into account, equitable principles are applied,—for this purpose the equidistance method can be used, but other methods exist and may be employed, alone or in combination, according to the areas involved;

(*c*) * * * the continental shelf of any State must be the natural prolongation of its land territory and must not encroach upon what is the natural prolongation of the territory of another State. * * *

88.   The Court comes next to the rule of equity. The legal basis of that rule in the particular case of the delimitation of the continental shelf as between adjoining States has already been stated. It must however be noted that the rule rests also on a broader basis. Whatever the legal reasoning of a court of justice, its decisions must by definition be just, and therefore in that sense equitable. Nevertheless, when mention is made of a court dispensing justice or declaring the law, what is meant is that the decision finds its objective justification in considerations lying not outside but within the rules, and in this field it is precisely a rule of law that calls for the application of equitable principles. There is consequently no question in this case of any decision *ex aequo et bono*, such as would only be possible under the conditions prescribed by Article 38, paragraph 2, of the Court's Statute. * * *

89.   It must next be observed that, in certain geographical circumstances which are quite frequently met with, the equidistance method,

despite its known advantages, leads unquestionably to inequity, in the following sense:

(a) The slightest irregularity in a coastline is automatically magnified by the equidistance line as regards the consequences for the delimitation of the continental shelf. Thus it has been seen in the case of concave or convex coastlines that if the equidistance method is employed, then the greater the irregularity and the further from the coastline the area to be delimited, the more unreasonable are the results produced. So great an exaggeration of the consequences of a natural geographical feature must be remedied or compensated for as far as possible, being of itself creative of inequity.

(b) In the case of the North Sea in particular, where there is no outer boundary to the continental shelf, it happens that the claims of several States converge, meet and intercross in localities where, despite their distance from the coast, the bed of the sea still unquestionably consists of continental shelf. A study of these convergences, as revealed by the maps, shows how inequitable would be the apparent simplification brought about by a delimitation which, ignoring such geographical circumstances, was based solely on the equidistance method. * * *

91. Equity does not necessarily imply equality. There can never be any question of completely refashioning nature, and equity does not require that a State without access to the sea should be allotted an area of continental shelf, any more than there could be a question of rendering the situation of a State with an extensive coastline similar to that of a State with a restricted coastline. Equality is to be reckoned within the same plane, and it is not such natural inequalities as these that equity could remedy. But in the present case there are three States whose North Sea coastlines are in fact comparable in length and which, therefore, have been given broadly equal treatment by nature except that the configuration of one of the coastlines would, if the equidistance method is used, deny to one of these States treatment equal or comparable to that given the other two. Here indeed is a case where, in a theoretical situation of equality within the same order, an inequity is created. What is unacceptable in this instance is that a State should enjoy continental shelf rights considerably different from those of its neighbours merely because in the one case the coastline is roughly convex in form and in the other it is markedly concave, although those coastlines are comparable in length. It is therefore not a question of totally refashioning geography whatever the facts of the situation but, given a geographical situation of quasi-equality as between a number of States, of abating the effects of an incidental special feature from which an unjustifiable difference of treatment could result. * * *

101. For these reasons,

THE COURT,

by eleven votes to six,

finds that, in each case,

(A) the use of the equidistance method of delimitation not being obligatory as between the Parties; and

(B) there being no other single method of delimitation the use of which is in all circumstances obligatory;

(C) the principles and rules of international law applicable to the delimitation as between the Parties of the areas of the continental shelf in the North Sea which appertain to each of them beyond the partial boundary determined by the agreements of 1 December 1964 and 9 June 1965, respectively, are as follows:

(1) delimitation is to be effected by agreement in accordance with equitable principles, and taking account of all the relevant circumstances, in such a way as to leave as much as possible to each Party all those parts of the continental shelf that constitute a natural prolongation of its land territory into and under the sea, without encroachment on the natural prolongation of the land territory of the other;

(2) if, in the application of the preceding sub-paragraph, the delimitation leaves to the Parties areas that overlap, these are to be divided between them in agreed proportions or, failing agreement, equally, unless they decide on a régime of joint jurisdiction, user, or exploitation for the zones of overlap or any part of them;

(D) in the course of the negotiations, the factors to be taken into account are to include:

(1) the general configuration of the coasts of the Parties, as well as the presence of any special or unusual features;

(2) so far as known or readily ascertainable, the physical and geological structure, and natural resources, of the continental shelf areas involved;

(3) the element of a reasonable degree of proportionality, which a delimitation carried out in accordance with equitable principles ought to bring about between the extent of the continental shelf areas appertaining to the coastal State and the length of its coast measured in the general direction of the coastline, account being taken for this purpose of the effects, actual or prospective, of any other continental shelf delimitations between adjacent States in the same region.

Notes and Questions

1. *A Hierarchy of Sources?* The *North Sea* judgment provides an excellent resume of the sources of international law, beginning with treaties, moving to custom, and finishing with general principles of law and equity. Did the ICJ's ordering of the sources reflect a necessary hierarchy of the sources of international law, *i.e.*, do treaties necessarily "trump" custom which in turn "trumps" general principles and equity? Note too the Court's

willingness to consider, in paragraphs 37 and 55, arguments based not on positive law, but on the "more fundamentalist" view that principles of general international law governing delimitation might be derived, as a matter of "juristic inevitability," from "the natural law of the continental shelf." Where would such general international law fit in a hierarchy of sources?

Pay special attention to the Court's detailed analysis of the ways in which customary international law might relate to Article 6(2) of the 1958 Continental Shelf Convention. The three-step process went: the Convention might (1) "embody" or codify the custom, (2) "crystallize" the custom, or (3) contribute to the subsequent development of the custom. Was the Court's rejection of possibility (3) as persuasive as its rejection of (1) and (2)? Looking at *North Sea*, Professor Schachter pointed out that a new treaty might not only itself contribute to the development of custom but might also generate complying practice that contributed to custom. Oscar Schachter, "Entangled Treaty and Custom," in *International Law at a Time of Perplexity* 717, 723–29 (Y. Dinstein ed. 1989).

2. *The Gap Problem.* What were the perils if the ICJ simply came up empty handed in its search for an applicable rule? Was the Court willing to rule that international law provides no guidance for Germany, Denmark, and the Netherlands? Would such a finding of a *lacuna* or gap have fulfilled the expectations of the three countries when they entrusted the dispute to the Court?

3. *The Recourse to Equity in* North Sea. Compare the source of equitable principles to the source of such principles in *Meuse. North Sea* showed no borrowing from municipal legal systems. Where then did the equitable rule come from? Did it really emerge from customary international law, as the Court seemed to suggest by its reference to *opinio juris* in paragraph 85? Did the Court cite sufficient evidence of state practice?

Note that the ICJ was asked to decide what "principles and rules of international law" were applicable to the delimitation of continental shelf between West Germany and Denmark, and between West Germany and the Netherlands. Could the parties have asked the Court to decide the case *ex aequo et bono* pursuant to Article 38(2) of the ICJ Statute? What extra power would the Court have had in *North Sea* if it had an *ex aequo et bono* authorization?

4. *Article 38(1)(d) of the ICJ Statute.* Once rendered, the *North Sea* judgment became part of the corpus of evidence of international law. Could other courts deciding continental shelf cases rely on *North Sea* as a subsidiary source of international law per Article 38(1)(d)? How would a subsequent delimitation case differ then from *North Sea*, especially if the countries affected by the judgment were to adopt it without protest? Can the ICJ's exercise of discretion be a doubtful exercise yet still provide a sound foundation for subsequent practice?

5. *The Content of Equitable Principles in* North Sea. What principles of equity did the Court use? If it would be inequitable to give comparable coastlines different allotments of continental shelf, why was it equitable to deprive land-locked countries of all continental shelf belonging to their

continent? Why was this a better kind of equity than one based on equidistance or on population, economic need, or use?

6. *The Need to Delimit the Continental Shelf.* Note the geographical elements of the problem as sketched in Map 3. Because of the indentation of the German shore, delimitation by the equidistance method bent the line along the route D–E–B. Germany preferred D–F–B. Why had it not been important to delimit the shelf prior to the 1960's? See Chapter 11 for further discussion of the continental shelf.

7. *The Parties' Choice of Tribunal.* Why did the three states choose to come to the Court? What did they expect the ICJ to contribute to the resolution of the dispute? Why could there have been any hope that the Court might help in ways that diplomatic negotiations had not?

8. *Different Meanings of Equity.* Note the use of equity in the Charter of Economic Rights and Duties of States considered by Professor Dupuy in the *Texaco/Libya Arbitration.* There are at least 12 references to equity in the Charter: "the development of international economic relations on a just and equitable basis," "a new system of international economic relations based on equity, sovereign equality, and interdependence of the interests of developed and developing countries," a "new international economic order, based on equity," "equitable benefits for all peace-loving states," "a just and equitable economic and social order," "more rational and equitable international economic relations," "mutual and equitable benefit" (twice), "remunerative and equitable prices," "equitable development of the world economy," "share equitably," and "stable, equitable and remunerative prices for primary products." What did these references to equity mean? Were the meanings all the same? Compare the use of "equity" in promoting the New International Economic Order with its use in international arbitral and judicial decisions like *Cayuga Indians, Meuse,* and *North Sea.*

9. *The Parties' Delimitation of the North Sea Continental Shelf.* The *North Sea* judgment left Germany, Denmark, and the Netherlands to agree on the delimitation of the continental shelf taking into account the Court's statement of applicable equitable principles; the Court itself was not asked to draw maritime boundaries for the parties, as was true in some later cases. See, *e.g.,* Maritime Delimitation in the Area between Greenland and Jan Mayen, 1993 I.C.J. 38, 1993 WL 285808. The parties eventually negotiated a division of the continental shelf. See Agreements Delimiting the Continental Shelf in the North Sea, Jan. 28, 1971, 10 I.L.M. 600 (1971).

Chapter 4

INTERNATIONAL LAW AND
MUNICIPAL LAW

In most instances, when international legal rules are applied in practice, they are applied by municipal courts. Decisions about whether international legal rules are available as domestic rules of decision, *i.e.*, about the "incorporation" of international law into domestic legal process, are ordinarily made by municipal legal systems. Those decisions are generally governed by the municipal legal system's own constitutional law.

In this chapter, we look only at the rules governing the incorporation of international law into U.S. law. Such rules about incorporation are easily grouped into those involving treaties and those concerning all other forms of international law, a category traditionally called, in England and America, "the law of nations."

A. TREATIES IN MUNICIPAL LAW

The most important U.S. constitutional law decision concerning the relationship of international law and U.S. municipal law is *Foster & Elam* where Chief Justice Marshall introduces the concept, though not the exact term, of "self-executing treaties." Besides noting how and why Chief Justice Marshall employs the concept of self-executing treaties, pay particular attention to why the litigants and the Court in *Foster & Elam* need to know whether the treaty provision in question can serve as a rule of decision.

FOSTER & ELAM v. NEILSON
27 U.S. (2 Pet.) 253, 7 L.Ed. 415 (1829).

Mr. Chief Justice Marshall delivered the opinion of the Court.

This suit was brought by the plaintiffs in error [Foster & Elam], in the court of the United States for the eastern district of Louisiana, to recover a tract of land lying in that district, about 30 miles east of the Mississippi, and in the possession of the defendant [Neilson]. The plaintiffs claimed under a grant for 40,000 arpents of land, made by the

Spanish governor, on the 2d of January 1804, to Jayme Joydra, and ratified by the king of Spain on the 29th of May 1804. The petition and order of survey are dated in September 1803, and the return of the survey itself was made on the 27 of October in the same year. The defendant excepted to the petition of the plaintiffs, alleging that it does not show a title on which they can recover; that the territory within which the land claimed is situated, had been ceded, before the grant, to France, and by France to the United States; and that the grant is void, being made by persons who had no authority to make it. The court sustained the exception, and dismissed the petition. The cause is brought before this court by writ of error.

The case presents this very intricate, and, at one time, very interesting question: To whom did the country between the Iberville and the Perdido rightfully belong, when the title now asserted by the plaintiffs was acquired? This question has been repeatedly discussed, with great talent and research, by the government of the United States and that of Spain. The United States have perseveringly and earnestly insisted, that by the treaty of St. Ildefonso, made on the 1st of October, in the year 1800, Spain ceded the disputed territory, as part of Louisiana, to France; and that France, by the treaty of Paris, signed on the 30th of April 1803, and ratified on the 21st of October, in the same year, ceded it to the United States. Spain has, with equal perseverance and earnestness, maintained, that her cession to France comprehended that territory only which was, at that time, denominated Louisiana, consisting of the island of New Orleans, and the country she received from France, west of the Mississippi.

[Marshall introduces and discusses the complicated and disputed negotiations among France, Spain, Great Britain, and the United States over the territory and then suggests that perhaps the Court need not actually answer the question about ownership.]

* * * A "treaty of amity, settlement and limits, between the United States of America and the king of Spain," was signed at Washington, on the 22d day of February 1819. By the second article, "his Catholic majesty cedes to the United States, in full property and sovereignty, all the territories which belong to him, situated to the eastward of the Mississippi, known by the name of East and West Florida." The eighth article stipulates, "that all the grants of land made before the 24th of January 1818, by his Catholic majesty, or by his lawful authorities, in the said territories ceded by his majesty to the United States, shall be ratified and confirmed to the persons in possession of the lands, to the same extent that the same grants would be valid, if the territories had remained under the dominion of his Catholic majesty." * * *

* * * [W]e think, the sound construction of the eighth article will not enable this court to apply its provisions to the present case. The words of the article are, that "all the grants of land, made before the 24 of January 1818, by his Catholic majesty, & c., shall be ratified and confirmed to the persons in possession of the lands, to the same extent

that the same grants would be valid, if the territories had remained under the dominion of his Catholic majesty." Do these words act directly on the grants, so as to give validity to those not otherwise valid? Or do they pledge the faith of the United States to pass acts which shall ratify and confirm them?

A treaty is, in its nature, a contract between two nations, not a legislative act. It does not generally effect, of itself, the object to be accomplished; especially, so far as its operation is infra-territorial; but is carried into execution by the sovereign power of the respective parties to the instrument.

In the United States, a different principle is established. Our constitution declares a treaty to be the law of the land. It is, consequently, to be regarded in courts of justice as equivalent to an act of the legislature, whenever it operates of itself, without the aid of any legislative provision. But when the terms of the stipulation import a contract—when either of the parties engages to perform a particular act, the treaty addresses itself to the political, not the judicial department; and the legislature must execute the contract before it can become a rule for the court.

The article under consideration does not declare that all the grants made by his Catholic majesty, before the 24th of January 1818, shall be valid, to the same extent as if the ceded territories had remained under his dominion. It does not say, that those grants are hereby confirmed. Had such been its language, it would have acted directly on the subject, and would have repealed those acts of congress which were repugnant to it; but its language is, that those grants shall be ratified and confirmed to the persons in possession, &c. By whom shall they be ratified and confirmed? This seems to be the language of contract; and if it is, the ratification and confirmation which are promised must be the act of the legislature. Until such act shall be passed, the court is not at liberty to disregard the existing laws on the subject. * * *

Notes and Questions

1. *The Application of International Law by Municipal Courts*. We now move from the legislative process of international law—how to find and make international legal rules—to the discipline's judicial and executive process—who applies the rules of international law and how such decisions are made effective. We begin with municipal courts. The great majority of international law cases that are settled by formal judicial process are decided by domestic not by international courts. For most lawyers practicing international law, domestic law courts are the usual fora foreseen in negotiations and employed in litigation. Here for reasons of space and audience we look only at the municipal practice of the United States. *American International Law Cases* publishes cases in which U.S. state and federal courts have used international law. The first 50 volumes of the third series of *American International Law Cases* contain over 2000 such cases, just from the years 1990–1993.

2. *The Self-executing Treaty Doctrine.* The overwhelming majority of U.S. court cases involving international law concern treaties; the most important is *Foster & Elam v. Neilson.* Not only did the case establish the proposition of the "self-executing" treaty in U.S. law, but it introduced the notion into international law generally, making *Foster & Elam* one of the most significant U.S. contributions to the discipline world-wide.

3. *Dualism and Monism.* Note that in *Foster & Elam* Marshall's approach to the nature of international law was fundamentally "dualistic," *i.e.*, he saw international law and municipal law not as parts of an integrated "monistic" legal system but each as a separate and discrete legal system. Accordingly, rules from one system must be specially incorporated into the other in order that they be applied there. Did Marshall justify this presumption? Did his justification depend either on the idea that treaties are contracts between nations or on the deference that Marshall accorded the sovereign power of states within their own territory?

4. *Treaties and the Supremacy Clause.* Although Chief Justice Marshall did not find the 1819 Treaty of Amity to be self-executing in *Foster & Elam,* he did establish the doctrine of self-executing treaties in U.S. law by relying on Article VI(2) of the Constitution, the Supremacy Clause:

> This Constitution, and the laws of the United States which shall be made in Pursuance thereof; and all Treaties made, or which shall be made, under the Authority of the United States, shall be the supreme law of the land; and the Judges in every State shall be bound thereby, any thing in the Constitution or Laws of any State to the contrary notwithstanding.

Note that the wording of the Supremacy Clause hints that the Founders' central concern was to bind the judges of the states to uphold the U.S. Constitution, federal laws, and U.S. treaties *vis-à-vis* state laws and constitutions. *Foster & Elam* involved, but avoided, a potential clash between federal law and a U.S. treaty. For discussion of various uses of the self-executing treaty doctrine in U.S. courts, see Carlos Manuel Vázquez, "The Four Doctrines of Self–Executing Treaties," 89 *American Journal of International Law* 695 (1995).

5. *The Self-executing Nature of the 1819 Treaty of Amity.* That Marshall's approach in *Foster & Elam* was formal, looking at the literal language of the 1819 Treaty of Amity, was confirmed in United States v. Percheman, 32 U.S. (7 Pet.) 51, 8 L.Ed. 604 (1833). In *Percheman,* when Marshall examined the Spanish-language version of the Treaty, he held that the selfsame Article 8 of the 1819 Treaty was in truth self-executing. However, unlike the land at issue in *Foster & Elam,* which was located "between the Iberville and the Perdido" rivers, the land that Percheman claimed under an 1815 Spanish grant was located east of the Perdido, in present-day Florida, territory unambiguously outside the area of the Louisiana Purchase.

6. *Self-executing and Non-self-executing Treaties.* As treaties have become more pervasive in international and municipal practice, the debate about when and when not to incorporate treaties directly has become ever more heated. Should a court presume that a treaty is or is not self-executing? For the historical background, see the recent exchange between Professors Yoo, Flaherty, and Vázquez: John C. Yoo, "Globalism and the

Constitution: Treaties, Non–Self–Execution and the Original Understanding," 99 *Columbia Law Review* 1955 (1999); Martin S. Flaherty, "History Right? Historical Scholarship, Original Understanding and Treaties as Supreme Law of the Land," 99 *Columbia Law Review* 2095 (1999); Carlos Manuel Vázquez, "Response: Laughing at Treaties," 99 *Columbia Law Review* 2154 (1999); John C. Yoo, "Rejoinder: Treaties and Public Lawmaking: A Textual and Structural Defense of Non–Self–Execution," 99 *Columbia Law Review* 2218 (1999).

ASAKURA v. CITY OF SEATTLE

265 U.S. 332, 44 S.Ct. 515, 68 L.Ed. 1041 (1924).

Mr. Justice Butler delivered the opinion of the Court.

Plaintiff in error is a subject of the Emperor of Japan, and, since 1904, has resided in Seattle, Washington. Since July, 1915, he has been engaged in business there as a pawnbroker. The city passed an ordinance, which took effect July 2, 1921, regulating the business of pawnbroker and repealing former ordinances on the same subject. It makes it unlawful for any person to engage in the business unless he shall have a license, and the ordinance provides "that no such license shall be granted unless the applicant be a citizen of the United States." Violations of the ordinance are punishable by fine or imprisonment or both. Plaintiff in error brought this suit in the Superior Court of King County, Washington, against the city, its Comptroller and its Chief of Police to restrain them from enforcing the ordinance against him. He attacked the ordinance on the ground that it violates the treaty between the United States and the Empire of Japan, proclaimed April 5, 1911, 37 Stat. 1504; violates the constitution of the State of Washington, and also the due process and equal protection clauses of the Fourteenth Amendment of the Constitution of the United States. He declared his willingness to comply with any valid ordinance related to the business of pawnbroker. It was shown that he had about $5,000 invested in his business, which would be broken up and destroyed by the enforcement of the ordinance. The Superior Court granted the relief prayed. On appeal, the Supreme Court of the State held the ordinance valid and reversed the decree. The case is here on writ of error under § 237 of the Judicial Code.

Does the ordinance violate the treaty? Plaintiff in error invokes and relies upon the following provisions: "The citizens or subjects of each of the High Contracting Parties shall have liberty to enter, travel and reside in the territories of the other to carry on trade, wholesale and retail, to own or lease and occupy houses, manufactories, warehouses and shops, to employ agents of their choice, to lease land for residential and commercial purposes, and generally to do anything incident to or necessary for trade upon the same terms as native citizens or subjects, submitting themselves to the laws and regulations there established.... The citizens or subjects of each ... shall receive, in the territories of the other, the most constant protection and security for their persons and property...."

A treaty made under the authority of the United States "shall be the supreme law of the land; and the judges in every State shall be bound thereby, any thing in the constitution or laws of any State to the contrary notwithstanding." Constitution, Art. VI, § 2.

The treaty-making power of the United States is not limited by any express provision of the Constitution, and, though it does not extend "so far as to authorize what the Constitution forbids," it does extend to all proper subjects of negotiation between our government and other nations. The treaty was made to strengthen friendly relations between the two nations. As to the things covered by it, the provision quoted establishes the rule of equality between Japanese subjects while in this country and native citizens. Treaties for the protection of citizens of one country residing in the territory of another are numerous, and make for good understanding between nations. The treaty is binding within the State of Washington. The rule of equality established by it cannot be rendered nugatory in any part of the United States by municipal ordinances or state laws. It stands on the same footing of supremacy as do the provisions of the Constitution and laws of the United States. It operates of itself without the aid of any legislation, state or national; and it will be applied and given authoritative effect by the courts.

The purpose of the ordinance complained of is to regulate, not to prohibit, the business of pawnbroker. But it makes it impossible for aliens to carry on the business. It need not be considered whether the State, if it sees fit, may forbid and destroy the business generally. Such a law would apply equally to aliens and citizens, and no question of conflict with the treaty would arise. The grievance here alleged is that plaintiff in error, in violation of the treaty, is denied equal opportunity. * * *

By definition contained in the ordinance, pawnbrokers are regarded as carrying on a "business." A feature of it is the lending of money upon the pledge or pawn of personal property which, in case of default, may be sold to pay the debt. While the amounts of the loans made in that business are relatively small and the character of property pledged as security is different, the transactions are similar to loans made by banks on collateral security. * * * We have found no state legislation abolishing or forbidding the business. Most, if not all, of the States provide for licensing pawnbrokers and authorize regulation by municipalities. While regulation has been found necessary in the public interest, the business is not on that account to be excluded from the trade and commerce referred to in the treaty. Many worthy occupations and lines of legitimate business are regulated by state and federal laws for the protection of the public against fraudulent and dishonest practices. There is nothing in the character of the business of pawnbroker which requires it to be excluded from the field covered by the above quoted provision, and it must be held that such business is "trade" within the meaning of the treaty. The ordinance violates the treaty. The question in the present case relates solely to Japanese subjects who have been admitted to this country. We do not pass upon the right of admission or the construction of the treaty in this respect, as that question is not before us and would require consideration of other matters with which it is not now necessary to deal. We need not consider other grounds upon which the ordinance is attacked.

Decree reversed.

Notes and Questions

1. *Treaties and State Law. Asakura* is an example of a state law being "trumped" by a U.S. treaty rule. The case cited *Foster & Elam* for the proposition that a treaty "operates of itself without the aid of any legislation, state or national; and it will be applied and given authoritative effect by the Courts." But did the *Asakura* Court analyze the problem of self-execution? Was it plain that the treaty norm applied in *Asakura* was self-executing by the test set out in *Foster & Elam*? What arguments might be made for and against it being self-executing?

2. *The* Asakura *Case and U.S.–Japanese Relations. Asakura* was decided at a time when U.S. politics were increasingly hostile to Japanese immigration to the United States. Despite opposition from Japan and from the U.S. State Department, the House and Senate overwhelmingly passed legislation in 1924 that barred Japanese nationals from settling in the United States. The anti–Japanese bill passed the House 326–71 and the Senate 62–6. The Japanese Ambassador warned that the bill "would seriously wound the proper susceptibilities of the Japanese nation" and could endanger "the otherwise happy and mutually advantageous relations existing between our two countries." "Immigration Bill Is Passed Intact, Barring Japanese," *New York Times*, Apr. 13, 1924, at 1; "Immigration Bill Passes the Senate by Vote of 62 to 6," *New York Times*, Apr. 19, 1924, at 1. U.S.–Japanese relations of course did not improve over the next few decades. Another case involving anti–Japanese acts, *Sei Fujii*, decided after the Second World War, follows.

SEI FUJII v. CALIFORNIA
38 Cal.2d 718, 242 P.2d 617 (1952).

GIBSON, CHIEF JUSTICE.

Plaintiff, an alien Japanese who is ineligible to citizenship under our naturalization laws, appeals from a judgment declaring that certain land purchased by him in 1948 had escheated to the state. There is no treaty between this country and Japan which confers upon plaintiff the right to own land, and the sole question presented on this appeal is the validity of the California alien land law.

UNITED NATIONS CHARTER

It is first contended that the land law has been invalidated and superseded by the provisions of the United Nations Charter pledging the member nations to promote the observance of human rights and fundamental freedoms without distinction as to race. Plaintiff relies on statements in the preamble and in articles 1, 55 and 56 of the Charter.

It is not disputed that the charter is a treaty, and our federal Constitution provides that treaties made under the authority of the United States are part of the supreme law of the land and that the judges in every state are bound thereby. U.S. Const., art. VI. A treaty, however, does not automatically supersede local laws which are inconsistent with it unless the treaty provisions are self-executing. In the words of Chief Justice Marshall: A treaty is "to be regarded in courts of justice as equivalent to an act of the Legislature, whenever it operates of itself, without the aid of any legislative provision. But when the terms of the stipulation import a contract—when either of the parties engages to perform a particular act, the treaty addresses itself to the political, not the judicial department; and the Legislature must execute the contract, before it can become a rule for the court." Foster v. Neilson, 1829, 2 Pet. (U.S.) 253, 314, 7 L.Ed. 415.

In determining whether a treaty is self-executing courts look to the intent of the signatory parties as manifested by the language of the instrument, and, if the instrument is uncertain, recourse may be had to the circumstances surrounding its execution. * * *

In order for a treaty provision to be operative without the aid of implementing legislation and to have the force and effect of a statute, it must appear that the framers of the treaty intended to prescribe a rule that, standing alone, would be enforceable in the courts. * * *

It is clear that the provisions of the preamble and of Article 1 of the charter which are claimed to be in conflict with the alien land law are not self-executing. They state general purposes and objectives of the United Nations Organization and do not purport to impose legal obligations on the individual member nations or to create rights in private persons. It is equally clear that none of the other provisions relied on by plaintiff is self-executing. Article 55 declares that the United Nations "shall promote: * * * universal respect for, and observance of, human rights and fundamental freedoms for all without distinction as to race, sex, language, or religion," and in Article 56, the member nations "pledge themselves to take joint and separate action in cooperation with the Organization for the achievement of the purposes set forth in Article 55." Although the member nations have obligated themselves to cooperate with the international organization in promoting respect for, and observance of, human rights, it is plain that it was contemplated that future legislative action by the several nations would be required to accomplish the declared objectives, and there is nothing to indicate that these provisions were intended to become rules of law for the courts of this county upon the ratification of the charter.

The language used in articles 55 and 56 is not the type customarily employed in treaties which have been held to be self-executing and to create rights and duties in individuals. For example, the treaty involved in Clark v. Allen, 331 U.S. 503, 507–508, 67 S.Ct. 1431, 1434, 91 L.Ed. 1633, relating to the rights of a national of one country to inherit real property located in another country, specifically provided that "such national shall be allowed a term of three years in which to sell the [property] ... and withdraw the proceeds ..." free from any discriminatory taxation. In Nielsen v. Johnson, 279 U.S. 47, 50, 49 S.Ct. 223, 73 L.Ed. 607, the provision treated as being self-executing was equally definite. There each of the signatory parties agreed that "no higher or other duties, charges, or taxes of any kind, shall be levied" by one country on removal of property therefrom by citizens of the other country "than are or shall be payable in each state, upon the same, when removed by a citizen or subject of such state respectively." In other instances treaty provisions were enforced without implementing legislation where they prescribed in detail the rules governing rights and obligations of individuals or specifically provided that citizens of one nation shall have the same rights while in the other country as are enjoyed by that country's own citizens. * * * *Asakura v. Seattle*, 265 U.S. 332, 340, 44 S.Ct. 515, 516, 68 L.Ed. 1041; * * *.

It is significant to note that when the framers of the charter intended to make certain provisions effective without the aid of implementing legislation they employed language which is clear and definite and manifests that intention. For example, Article 104 provides: "The Organization shall enjoy in the territory of each of its Members such legal capacity as may be necessary for the exercise of its functions and the fulfillment of its purposes." Article 105 provides: "1. The Organization shall enjoy in the territory of each of its Members such privileges and immunities as are necessary for the fulfillment of its purposes. 2. Representatives of the Members of the United Nations and officials of the Organization shall similarly enjoy such privileges and immunities as are necessary for the independent exercise of their functions in connection with the Organization." In Curran v. City of New York, 191 Misc. 229, 77 N.Y.S.2d 206, 212, these articles were treated as being self-executory.

The provisions in the charter pledging cooperation in promoting observance of fundamental freedoms lack the mandatory quality and definiteness which would indicate an intent to create justiciable rights in private persons immediately upon ratification. Instead, they are framed as a promise of future action by the member nations. Secretary of State Stettinius, Chairman of the United States delegation at the San Francisco Conference where the charter was drafted, stated in his report to President Truman that Article 56 "pledges the various countries to cooperate with the organization by joint and separate action in the achievement of the economic and social objectives of the organization without infringing upon their right to order their national affairs according to their own best ability, in their own way, and in accordance with their own political and economic institutions and processes." * * *

The humane and enlightened objectives of the United Nations Charter are, of course, entitled to respectful consideration by the courts and legislatures of every member nation, since that document expresses the universal desire of thinking men for peace and for equality of rights and opportunities. The charter represents a moral commitment of foremost importance, and we must not permit the spirit of our pledge to be compromised or disparaged in either our domestic or foreign affairs. We are satisfied, however, that the charter provisions relied on by plaintiff were not intended to supersede existing domestic legislation, and we cannot hold that they operate to invalidate the alien land law.

[The court concludes, however, that the California Alien Land Law is invalid, because it violates the 14th Amendment to the U.S. Constitution.]

Notes and Questions

1. *The California Alien Land Law.* The 1920 California Alien Land Law had originally aimed at preventing the ownership of land by Asian nationals. By 1952, however, it affected principally Japanese aliens, since by then nationals of the Philippines, China, and India could effectively seek U.S. naturalization. See Lawrence E. Davies, "California's Law on Land is Upset," *New York Times*, Apr. 18, 1952, at 7.

2. *The Self-executing Treaty Doctrine and the U.N. Charter.* Is it self-evident that the *Sei Fujii* court was correct in holding the U.N. Charter provisions at issue not to be self-executing? The District Court of Appeal of California had found the Charter provisions self-executing. See Sei Fujii v. State, 217 P.2d 481 (Cal.App.1950), *rehearing denied*, 218 P.2d 595 (Cal.App. 1950). When treaty provisions concerning individual rights conflict with state legislation, does a better case exist for finding the treaty to be self-executing than when a treaty conflicts with Congressional action? Quincy Wright noted that Article 56 of the U.N. Charter imposes obligations on the United States as a party, and that Charter provisions do not prevent U.S. courts from interpreting and enforcing the obligations. Quincy Wright, "National Courts and Human Rights—The Fujii Case," 45 *American Journal of International Law* 62 (1951). The critical question then became, in Wright's view, whether U.S. obligations under Article 56 were of a character that U.S. courts "can apply." "[C]ommon sense suggests that 'separate action in cooperation with the organization' implies, as a minimum, abstention from separate action, such as enforcement of racially discriminating land laws, which would oppose the purposes of the organization." *Id.* at 72. Wright concluded:

> National courts may not always give a sound interpretation to treaty obligations in respect to human rights, but they are more likely to be guided by general principles than are local legislatures. * * * There is no fundamental reason why the function of incorporating international law into municipal law should be regarded as a legislative rather than a judicial function.

Id. at 80–81. See also Richard Lillich, "Invoking International Human Rights Law in Domestic Courts," 54 *University of Cincinnati Law Review* 367 (1985).

Professor Lockwood surveyed the use of the United Nations Charter in state and federal courts from 1946 to 1955 and found that "the Charter played a significant role in helping American courts find the United States Constitution—to redefine the due process and equal protection clauses of the

14th Amendment and the due process clause of the Fifth Amendment to reflect antiracial discrimination norms central to the Charter." Bert B. Lockwood, Jr., "The United Nations Charter and United States Civil Rights Litigation: 1946–1955," 69 *Iowa Law Review* 901, 902 (1984). Lockwood examined *Sei Fujii* and the seminal U.S. Supreme Court civil rights cases, in which human rights provisions of the Charter were raised but not addressed by the Court, and concluded that the Charter was "an important influence on the judiciary, *sub silentio.*" *Id.* at 949. The United States, however, can do better. Professor Buergenthal concluded that the United States lags behind other Western democracies in implementing international treaties protecting human rights. Thomas Buergenthal, "Modern Constitutions and Human Rights Treaties," 36 *Columbia Journal of Transnational Law* 211 (1997).

3. *Applying the Self-executing Treaty Rule.* If the 1911 treaty analyzed in *Asakura* had been still in force in 1948, would it have conferred upon Sei Fujii the right to own land? Why was the *Sei Fujii* court more concerned than the *Asakura* court to analyze whether a treaty rule, in this case the U.N. Charter, was self-executing? Should a U.S. court presume that a treaty provision is or is not self-executing? Is the court under any special obligation to try to give effect to treaty purposes if the language of the treaty can be read both ways? Should the positions of other countries be taken into account in determining the incorporation of a treaty into U.S. municipal law?

4. *Treaties and State Law.* A federal treaty "trumps" state law only when the treaty provision is incorporated in U.S. law either because it is self-executing or because it has been implemented by congressional legislation. In *Missouri v. Holland* which follows, the Supreme Court did not need to address the self-executing treaty doctrine because Congress had passed a statute implementing the treaty at issue.

MISSOURI v. HOLLAND

252 U.S. 416, 40 S.Ct. 382, 64 L.Ed. 641 (1920).

Mr. Justice Holmes delivered the opinion of the court.

This is a bill in equity brought by the State of Missouri to prevent a game warden of the United States from attempting to enforce the Migratory Bird Treaty Act of July 3, 1918, c. 128, 40 Stat. 755, and the regulations made by the Secretary of Agriculture in pursuance of the same. The ground of the bill is that the statute is an unconstitutional interference with the rights reserved to the States by the Tenth Amendment, and that the acts of the defendant done and threatened under that authority invade the sovereign right of the State and contravene its will manifested in statutes. * * *

On December 8, 1916, a treaty between the United States and Great Britain was proclaimed by the President. It recited that many species of birds in their annual migrations traversed certain parts of the United States and of Canada, that they were of great value as a source of food and in destroying insects injurious to vegetation, but were in danger of extermination through lack of adequate protection. It therefore provided for specified close seasons and protection in other forms, and agreed that the two powers would take or propose to their law-making bodies the necessary measures for carrying the treaty out. The above mentioned Act of July 3, 1918, entitled an act to give effect to the convention, prohibited the killing, capturing or selling any of the migratory birds included in the terms of the treaty except as permitted by regulations compatible with those terms, to be made by the Secretary of Agriculture. Regulations were proclaimed on July 31, and October 25, 1918. It is unnecessary to go into any details, because, as we have said, the question raised is the general one whether the treaty and statute are void as an interference with the rights reserved to the States.

To answer this question it is not enough to refer to the Tenth Amendment, reserving the powers not delegated to the United States, because by Article II, § 2, the power to make treaties is delegated expressly, and by Article VI treaties made under the authority of the United States, along with the Constitution and laws of the United States made in pursuance thereof, are declared the supreme law of the land. If the treaty is valid there can be no dispute about the validity of the statute under Article I, § 8, as a necessary and proper means to execute the powers of the Government. The language of the Constitution as to the supremacy of treaties being general, the question before us is narrowed to an inquiry into the ground upon which the present supposed exception is placed.

It is said that a treaty cannot be valid if it infringes the Constitution, that there are limits, therefore, to the treaty-making power, and that one such limit is that what an act of Congress could not do unaided, in derogation of the powers reserved to the States, a treaty cannot do. An earlier act of Congress [of March 4, 1913] that attempted by itself and not in pursuance of a treaty to regulate the killing of migratory birds within the States had been held bad in the District Court. *United States v. Shauver*, 214 Fed. Rep. 154. *United States v. McCullagh*, 221 Fed. Rep. 288. Those decisions were supported by arguments that migratory birds were owned by the States in their sovereign capacity for the benefit of their people, and that under cases like *Geer v. Connecticut*, 161 U.S. 519, this control was one that Congress had no power to displace. The same argument is supposed to apply now with equal force.

Whether the two cases cited were decided rightly or not they cannot be accepted as a test of the treaty power. Acts of Congress are the supreme law of the land only when made in pursuance of the Constitution, while treaties are declared to be so when made under the authority of the United States. It is open to question whether the authority of the United States means more than the formal acts prescribed to make the convention. We do not mean to imply that there are no qualifications to the treaty-making power; but they must be ascertained in a different way. It is obvious that there may be matters of the sharpest exigency for the national well being that an act of Congress could not deal with but that a treaty followed by such an act could, and it is not lightly to be assumed that, in matters requiring national action, "a power which must belong to and somewhere reside in every civilized government'' is not to be found. What was said in that case with regard to the powers of the States applies with equal force to the powers of the nation in cases where the States individually are incompetent to act. We are not yet discussing the particular case before us but only are considering the validity of the test proposed. With regard to that we may add that when we are dealing with words that also are a constituent act, like the Constitution of the United States, we must realize that they have called into life a being the development of which could not have been foreseen completely by the most gifted of its begetters. It was enough for them to realize or to hope that they had created an organism; it has taken a century and has cost their successors much sweat and blood to prove that they created a nation. The case before us must be considered in the light of our whole experience and not merely in that of what was said 100 years ago. The treaty in question does not contravene any prohibitory words to be found in the Constitution. The only question is whether it is forbidden by some invisible radiation from the general terms of the Tenth Amendment. We must consider what this country has become in deciding what that Amendment has reserved.

The State as we have intimated founds its claim of exclusive authority upon an assertion of title to migratory birds, an assertion that is embodied in statute. No doubt it is true that as between a State and its inhabitants the State may regulate the killing and sale of such birds, but it does not follow that its authority is exclusive of paramount powers. To put the claim of the State upon title is to lean upon a slender reed. Wild birds are not in the possession of anyone; and possession is the beginning of ownership. The whole foundation of the State's rights is the presence within their jurisdiction of birds that yesterday had not arrived, tomorrow may be in another State and in a week a thousand miles away. If we are to be accurate we cannot put the case of the State upon higher ground than that the treaty deals with creatures that for the moment are within the state borders, that it must be carried out by officers of the United States within the same territory, and that but for the treaty the State would be free to regulate this subject itself.

As most of the laws of the United States are carried out within the States and as many of them deal with matters which in the silence of such laws the State might regulate, such general grounds are not enough to support Missouri's claim. Valid treaties of course "are as binding within the territorial limits of the States as they are elsewhere throughout the dominion of the United States." No doubt the great body of private relations usually fall within the control of the State, but a treaty may override its power. We do not have to invoke the later developments of constitutional law for this proposition; it was recognized as early as *Hopkirk v. Bell*, 3 Cranch, 454, with regard to statutes of limitation, and even earlier, as to confiscation, in *Ware v. Hylton*, 3 Dall. 199. It was assumed by Chief Justice Marshall with regard to the escheat of land to the State in *Chirac v. Chirac*, 2 Wheat. 259, 275. So as to a limited jurisdiction of foreign consuls within a State. *Wildenhus's Case*, 120 U.S.

1. Further illustration seems unnecessary, and it only remains to consider the application of established rules to the present case.

Here a national interest of very nearly the first magnitude is involved. It can be protected only by national action in concert with that of another power. The subject matter is only transitorily within the State and has no permanent habitat therein. But for the treaty and the statute there soon might be no birds for any powers to deal with. We see nothing in the Constitution that compels the Government to sit by while a food supply is cut off and the protectors of our forests and our crops are destroyed. It is not sufficient to rely upon the States. The reliance is vain, and were it otherwise, the question is whether the United States is forbidden to act. We are of opinion that the treaty and statute must be upheld.

Decree affirmed.

Notes and Questions

1. *Constitution-based Limitations to the Treaty-making Power.* Justice Holmes wrote that "we do not mean to imply that there are no qualifications to the treaty-making power; but they must be ascertained in a different way." How well did he explicate that way? Is the problem here that Missouri's alleged constitutional prohibition was via "some invisible radiation from the general terms of the Tenth Amendment"? Would a specific constitutional prohibition, *e.g.*, respecting rights to a jury trial in criminal cases, suffice as a qualification on or a limitation to the treaty-making power? In *Reid v. Covert*, 354 U.S. 1, 77 S.Ct. 1222, 1 L.Ed.2d 1148 (1957), which concerned rights to a jury trial under Article III and the Fifth and Sixth Amendments, the Supreme Court held that "no agreement with a foreign nation can confer power on the Congress, or on any other branch of Government, which is free from the restraints of the Constitution." *Id.* at 16, 77 S.Ct. at 1230, 1 L.Ed.2d at 1163.

Justice Holmes in *Missouri v. Holland* justified the Supreme Court's decision in part because "a national interest of very nearly the first magnitude is involved." The Treaty was commended in the press as "probably the most important movement for the protection of birds ever instituted in this country or the Dominion." "Safety for the Birds," *New York Times*, Dec. 5, 1916, at 10. Would Missouri's authority to regulate migratory birds have been greater if the national need had been less?

In *Missouri v. Holland*, questions about the scope of the treaty-making power were posed starkly because a federal statute regulating migratory birds, passed before the 1916 treaty was concluded, had been struck down. Did Holmes mean to say that the federal government could achieve ends by way of treaty-making when it cannot do so by simple legislation?

2. *The Historical Context.* Note Holmes's language about Americans' cost in "sweat and blood to prove that they created a nation." Holmes had fought and been wounded in the Civil War. Many of his classmates had been killed. Would the Court have been inclined before 1861 to so subordinate state to federal interests? Federalism has become a stronger current in the

United States in recent years. What pull it should have on the commitment of foreign affairs to the federal government has emerged as a newly controversial issue. See the Supreme Court's 2000 judgment and the notes about Massachusetts' Burma Law in *Crosby* below.

WHITNEY v. ROBERTSON

124 U.S. 190, 8 S.Ct. 456, 31 L.Ed. 386 (1888).

Mr. Justice Field delivered the opinion of the court.

The plaintiffs are merchants, doing business in the city of New York, and in August, 1882, they imported a large quantity of "centrifugal and molasses sugars," the produce and manufacture of the island of San Domingo. These goods were similar in kind to sugars produced in the Hawaiian Islands, which are admitted free of duty under the treaty with the king of those islands, and the act of Congress, passed to carry the treaty into effect. They were duly entered at the custom house at the port of New York, the plaintiffs claiming that by the treaty with the Republic of San Domingo the goods should be admitted on the same terms, that is, free of duty, as similar articles, the produce and manufacture of the Hawaiian Islands. The defendant, who was at the time collector of the port, refused to allow this claim, treated the goods as dutiable articles under the acts of Congress, and exacted duties on them to the amount of $21,936. The plaintiffs appealed from the collector's decision to the Secretary of the Treasury, by whom the appeal was denied. They then paid under protest the duties exacted, and brought the present action to recover the amount. * * *

The treaty with the king of the Hawaiian Islands [of January 30, 1875] provides for the importation into the United States, free of duty, of various articles, the produce and manufacture of those islands, in consideration, among other things, of like exemption from duty, on the importation into that country, of sundry specified articles which are the produce and manufacture of the United States. 19 Stat. 625. The language of the first two articles of the treaty, which recite the reciprocal engagements of the two countries, declares that they are made in consideration "of the rights and privileges" and "as an equivalent therefor," which one concedes to the other.

The plaintiffs rely for a like exemption of the sugars imported by them from San Domingo upon the 9th article of the treaty with the Dominican Republic [of February 8, 1867], which is as follows: "No higher or other duty shall be imposed on the importation into the United States of any article the growth, produce, or manufacture of the Dominican Republic, or of her fisheries; and no higher or other duty shall be imposed on the importation into the Dominican Republic of any article the growth, produce, or manufacture of the United States, or their fisheries, than are or shall be payable on the like articles the growth, produce, or manufacture of any other foreign country, or its fisheries." 15 Stat. 473, 478. * * *

But * * * there is [a] complete answer to the pretensions of the plaintiffs. The Act of Congress under which the duties were collected authorized their exaction. It is of general application, making no exceptions in favor of goods of any country. It was passed after the Treaty with the Dominican Republic; and if there be any conflict between the stipulations of the Treaty and the requirements of the law the latter must control. * * * By the Constitution a treaty is placed on the same footing, and made of like obligation, with an act of legislation. Both are declared by that instrument to be the supreme law of the land, and no superior efficacy is given to either over the other. When the two relate to the same subject, the courts will always endeavor to construe them so as to give effect to both, if that can be done without violating the language of either; but if the two are inconsistent, the one last in date will control the other, provided always the stipulation of the treaty on the subject is self-executing. If the country with which the treaty is made is dissatisfied with the action of the legislative department, it may present its complaint to the executive head of the government, and take such other measures as it may deem essential for the protection of its interests. The courts can afford no redress. Whether the complaining nation has just cause of complaint, or our country was justified in its legislation, are not matters for judicial cognizance.

Judgment affirmed.

Notes and Questions

1. *The Last-in-time Rule.* Though the Court in *Whitney* refused to enforce a U.S. treaty promising to provide most favored nation treatment to imports from San Domingo (present-day Dominican Republic), it made the general proposition that in case of a conflict between a federal statute and a treaty, "the one last in date will control," a proposition favorable to the status of international agreements. Does Article VI(2) of the Constitution, the Supremacy Clause, itself prescribe any rule as to the relationship between federal law and treaties? Is any other solution preferable to the last-in-time rule? How far should the courts go as they "always endeavor to construe" treaties and federal statutes "so as to give effect to both"?

2. *Dualism, Treaties, and the Role of Courts.* Note that the Supreme Court took a dualistic view of the relationship between international law and municipal law: "If the country with which the treaty is made is dissatisfied with the action of the legislative department, it may present its complaint to the executive head of the government, and take such other measures as it may deem essential for the protection of its interests." Dualism remains popular in the United States as a way to protect the U.S. democratic decision-making process, especially the domestic legislative process. See Jonathan Turley, "Dualistic Values in the Age of International Legisprudence," 44 *Hastings Law Journal* 185 (1993).

In Great Britain, where no treaty is considered self-executing, the courts have taken a comparable stand about the dualistic nature of international law and municipal law. For example, in *The Parlement Belge* the British court refused to incorporate a treaty provision that gave immunity to a

Belgian packet-boat conveying mails because the immunity had not been enacted into statutory form by the British Parliament. (1878–79) 4 P.D. 129. Responding to an objection that this broke faith with Belgium, the judge wrote: "I acknowledge the hardship, but the remedy, in my opinion, is not to be found in depriving the British subject without his consent, direct or implied, or his right of action against a wrong-doer, but by the agency of diplomacy, and proper measures of compensation arrangement, between the Governments of Great Britain and Belgium." *Id.* at 155. Where, then, in the *Whitney Case* should the government of San Domingo have gone to complain about the actions of the United States?

Many civil law jurisdictions take an opposite tack from the tradition in Great Britain and provide that treaties, and indeed international law in general, are supreme over municipal law in municipal courts, even if not incorporated by legislation. See Mark W. Janis, *An Introduction to International Law* 97–102 (3d ed. 1999).

UNITED STATES v. BELMONT

301 U.S. 324, 57 S.Ct. 758, 81 L.Ed. 1134 (1937).

MR. JUSTICE SUTHERLAND delivered the opinion of the Court.

This is an action at law brought by petitioner against respondents in a federal district court to recover a sum of money deposited by a Russian corporation (Petrograd Metal Works) with August Belmont, a private banker doing business in New York City under the name of August Belmont & Co. August Belmont died in 1924; and respondents are the duly-appointed executors of his will. A motion to dismiss the complaint for failure to state facts sufficient to constitute a cause of action was sustained by the district court, and its judgment was affirmed by the court below. The facts alleged, so far as necessary to be stated, follow.

The corporation had deposited with Belmont, prior to 1918, the sum of money which petitioner seeks to recover. In 1918, the Soviet Government duly enacted a decree by which it dissolved, terminated and liquidated the corporation (together with others), and nationalized and appropriated all of its property and assets of every kind and wherever situated, including the deposit account with Belmont. As a result, the deposit became the property of the Soviet Government, and so remained until November 16, 1933, at which time the Soviet Government released and assigned to petitioner all amounts due to that government from American nationals, including the deposit account of the corporation with Belmont. Respondents failed and refused to pay the amount upon demand duly made by petitioner.

The assignment was effected by an exchange of diplomatic correspondence between the Soviet Government and the United States. The purpose was to bring about a final settlement of the claims and counterclaims between the Soviet Government and the United States; and it was agreed that the Soviet Government would take no steps to enforce claims against American nationals; but all such claims were released and assigned to the United States, with the understanding that the Soviet

Government was to be duly notified of all amounts realized by the United States from such release and assignment. The assignment and requirement for notice are parts of the larger plan to bring about a settlement of the rival claims of the high contracting parties. The continuing and definite interest of the Soviet Government in the collection of assigned claims is evident; and the case, therefore, presents a question of public concern, the determination of which well might involve the good faith of the United States in the eyes of a foreign government. The court below held that the assignment thus effected embraced the claim here in question; and with that we agree.

That court, however, took the view that the situs of the bank deposit was within the State of New York; that in no sense could it be regarded as an intangible property right within Soviet territory; and that the nationalization decree, if enforced, would put into effect an act of confiscation. And it held that a judgment for the United States could not be had, because, in view of that result, it would be contrary to the controlling public policy of the State of New York. The further contention is made by respondents that the public policy of the United States would likewise be infringed by such a judgment. The two questions thus presented are the only ones necessary to be considered.

First. We do not pause to inquire whether in fact there was any policy of the State of New York to be infringed, since we are of opinion that no state policy can prevail against the international compact here involved. * * *

We take judicial notice of the fact that coincident with the assignment set forth in the complaint, the President recognized the Soviet Government, and normal diplomatic relations were established between that government and the Government of the United States, followed by an exchange of ambassadors. The effect of this was to validate, so far as this country is concerned, all acts of the Soviet Government here involved from the commencement of its existence. The recognition, establishment of diplomatic relations, the assignment, and agreements with respect thereto, were all parts of one transaction, resulting in an international compact between the two governments. That the negotiations, acceptance of the assignment and agreements and understandings in respect thereof were within the competence of the President may not be doubted. Governmental power over internal affairs is distributed between the national government and the several states. Governmental power over external affairs is not distributed, but is vested exclusively in the national government. And in respect of what was done here, the Executive had authority to speak as the sole organ of that government. The assignment and the agreements in connection therewith did not, as in the case of treaties, as that term is used in the treaty making clause of the Constitution (Art. II, § 2), require the advice and consent of the Senate.

A treaty signifies "a compact made between two or more independent nations with a view to the public welfare." *Altman & Co. v. United*

States, 224 U.S. 583, 600. But an international compact, as this was, is not always a treaty which requires the participation of the Senate. There are many such compacts, of which a protocol, a modus vivendi, a postal convention, and agreements like that now under consideration are illustrations. * * * [A]lthough this might not be a treaty requiring ratification by the Senate, it was a compact negotiated and proclaimed under the authority of the President, and as such was a "treaty" within the meaning of the Circuit Court of Appeals Act, the construction of which might be reviewed upon direct appeal to this court.

Plainly, the external powers of the United States are to be exercised without regard to state laws or policies. The supremacy of a treaty in this respect has been recognized from the beginning. Mr. Madison, in the Virginia Convention, said that if a treaty does not supersede existing state laws, as far as they contravene its operation, the treaty would be ineffective. "To counteract it by the supremacy of the state laws, would bring on the Union the just charge of national perfidy, and involve us in war." 3 Elliot's Debates 515. And see *Ware v. Hylton*, 3 Dall. 199, 236–237. And while this rule in respect of treaties is established by the express language of cl. 2, Art. VI, of the Constitution, the same rule would result in the case of all international compacts and agreements from the very fact that complete power over international affairs is in the national government and is not and cannot be subject to any curtailment of interference on the part of the several states. Compare *United States v. Curtiss–Wright Export Corp.*, 299 U.S. 304, 316, et seq. In respect of all international negotiations and compacts, and in respect of our foreign relations generally, state lines disappear. As to such purposes the State of New York does not exist. Within the field of its powers, whatever the United States rightfully undertakes, it necessarily has warrant to consummate. And when judicial authority is invoked in aid of such consummation, state constitutions, state laws, and state policies are irrelevant to the inquiry and decision. It is inconceivable that any of them can be interposed as an obstacle to the effective operation of a federal constitutional power. Cf. *Missouri v. Holland*, 252 U.S. 416; *Asakura v. Seattle*, 265 U.S. 332, 341.

Notes and Questions

1. *The Roosevelt–Litvinov Agreement.* The *Belmont Case* validated the Roosevelt–Litvinov agreement, a matter of some importance in U.S.–U.S.S.R. relations. At the time of the Supreme Court's decision there were some 15 similar law suits in the U.S. courts involving more than $8,000,000. The Petrograd/Metal Works deposit with August Belmont & Co. was itself only $25,438. "Pact with Soviet on Claims Upheld," *New York Times*, May 4, 1937, at 14. To gain U.S. recognition of the Soviet Union, Maxim Litvinov also pledged that the U.S.S.R. would not propagandize in the United States and that it would give religious freedom to U.S. citizens resident in the Soviet Union. The Soviet Union also gave up its claims against the United States for damage caused by U.S. troops during a 1918 intervention in

Siberia. The exchange of letters comprising the Roosevelt–Litvinov agreement appears at 28 *American Journal of International Law* 1 (Supp. 1934). For more on the case, see Stephen Millett, *The Constitutionality of Executive Agreements: An Analysis of United States v. Belmont* (1990).

2. *Executive Agreements and the Constitution.* Is it plain that the Constitution meant to give all international agreements supremacy over state laws or only those that had been favorably reviewed by the Senate? As a result of cases like *Belmont*, the term "treaty" really has two meanings in the U.S. Constitution. First, there is the "treaty" in Article II(2) that requires the "advice and consent" of the Senate. Second, there is the "treaty" in Article VI(2) that, along with the Constitution and U.S. law, is given supremacy. Should executive agreements benefit from *Whitney's* last-in-time rule? The U.S. Supreme Court has not ruled on this issue, but the Fourth Circuit has upheld a previously-enacted statute against an executive agreement about agriculture imports. United States v. Guy W. Capps, Inc., 204 F.2d 655 (4th Cir.1953), *aff'd on other grounds*, 348 U.S. 296, 75 S.Ct. 326, 99 L.Ed. 329 (1955).

UNITED STATES v. CURTISS–WRIGHT

299 U.S. 304, 57 S.Ct. 216, 81 L.Ed. 255 (1936).

Mr. Justice Sutherland delivered the opinion of the Court.

On January 27, 1936, an indictment was returned in the court below, the first count of which charges that appellees, beginning with the 29th day of May, 1934, conspired to sell in the United States certain arms of war, namely 15 machine guns, to Bolivia, a country then engaged in armed conflict in the Chaco, in violation of the Joint Resolution of Congress approved May 28, 1934, and the provisions of a proclamation issued on the same day by the President of the United States pursuant to authority conferred by § 1 of the resolution. In pursuance of the conspiracy, the commission of certain overt acts was alleged, details of which need not be stated. The Joint Resolution (c. 365, 48 Stat. 811) follows:

Resolved by the Senate and House of Representatives of the United States of America in Congress assembled, That if the President finds that the prohibition of the sale of arms and munitions of war in the United States to those countries now engaged in armed conflict in the Chaco may contribute to the reestablishment of peace between those countries, and if after consultation with the governments of other American Republics and with their cooperation, as well as that of such other governments as he may deem necessary, he makes proclamation to that effect, it shall be unlawful to sell, except under such limitations and exceptions as the President prescribes, any arms or munitions of war in any place in the United States to the countries now engaged in that armed conflict, or to any person, company, or association acting in the interest of either country, until otherwise ordered by the President or by Congress. * * *

First. It is contended that by the Joint Resolution, the going into effect and continued operation of the resolution was conditioned (a) upon the President's judgment as to its beneficial effect upon the reestablishment of peace between the countries engaged in armed conflict in the Chaco; (b) upon the making of a proclamation, which was left to his unfettered discretion, thus constituting an attempted substitution of the President's will for that of Congress; (c) upon the making of a proclamation putting an end to the operation of the resolution, which again was left to the President's unfettered discretion; and (d) further, that the extent of its operation in particular cases was subject to limitation and exception by the President, controlled by no standard. In each of these particulars, appellees urge that Congress abdicated its essential functions and delegated them to the Executive.

Whether, if the Joint Resolution had related solely to internal affairs it would be open to the challenge that it constituted an unlawful delegation of legislative power to the Executive, we find it unnecessary to determine. The whole aim of the resolution is to affect a situation entirely external to the United States, and falling within the category of foreign affairs. The determination which we are called to make, therefore, is whether the Joint Resolution, as applied to that situation, is vulnerable to attack under the rule that forbids a delegation of the lawmaking power. In other words, assuming (but not deciding) that the challenged delegation, if it were confined to internal affairs, would be invalid, may it nevertheless be sustained on the ground that its exclusive aim is to afford a remedy for a hurtful condition within foreign territory?

It will contribute to the elucidation of the question if we first consider the differences between the powers of the federal government in respect of foreign or external affairs and those in respect of domestic or internal affairs. That there are differences between them, and that these differences are fundamental, may not be doubted.

The two classes of powers are different, both in respect of their origin and their nature. The broad statement that the federal government can exercise no powers except those specifically enumerated in the Constitution, and such implied powers as are necessary and proper to carry into effect the enumerated powers, is categorically true only in respect of our internal affairs. In that field, the primary purpose of the Constitution was to carve from the general mass of legislative powers *then possessed by the states* such portions as it was thought desirable to vest in the federal government, leaving those not included in the enumeration still in the states. *Carter v. Carter Coal Co.*, 298 U.S. 238, 294. That this doctrine applies only to powers which the states had, is self evident. And since the states severally never possessed international powers, such powers could not have been carved from the mass of state powers but obviously were transmitted to the United States from some other source. During the colonial period, those powers were possessed exclusively by and were entirely under the control of the Crown. By the Declaration of Independence, "the Representatives of the United States of America" declared the United [not the several] Colonies to be free and independent states, and as such to have "full Power to levy War, conclude Peace, contract Alliances, establish Commerce and to do all other Acts and Things which Independent States may of right do."

As a result of the separation from Great Britain by the colonies acting as a unit, the powers of external sovereignty passed from the Crown not to the colonies severally, but to the colonies in their collective and corporate capacity as the United States of America. Even before the Declaration, the colonies were a unit in foreign affairs, acting through a common agency—namely the Continental Congress, composed of delegates from the 13 colonies. That agency exercised the powers of war and peace, raised an army, created a navy, and finally adopted the Declaration of Independence. Rulers come and go; governments end and forms of government change; but sovereignty survives. A political society cannot endure without a supreme will somewhere. Sovereignty is never held in suspense. When, therefore, the external sovereignty of Great Britain in respect of the colonies ceased, it immediately passed to the Union. That fact was given practical application almost at once. The treaty of peace, made on September 23, 1783, was concluded between his Brittanic Majesty and the "United States of America."

The Union existed before the Constitution, which was ordained and established among other things to form "a more perfect Union." Prior to that event, it is clear that the Union, declared by the Articles of Confederation to be "perpetual," was the sole possessor of external sovereignty and in the Union it remained without change save in so far as the Constitution in express terms qualified its exercise. The Framers' Convention was called and exerted its powers upon the irrefutable postulate that though the states were several their people in respect of foreign affairs were one. In that convention, the entire absence of state power to deal with those affairs was thus forcefully stated by Rufus King:

"The states were not 'sovereigns' in the sense contended for by some. They did not possess the peculiar features of sovereignty,—they could not make war, nor peace, nor alliances, nor treaties. Considering them as political beings, they were dumb, for they could not speak to any foreign sovereign whatever. They were deaf, for they could not hear any propositions from such sovereign. They had not even the organs or facilities of defence or offence, for they could not of themselves raise troops, or equip vessels, for war."

It results that the investment of the federal government with the powers of external sovereignty did not depend upon the affirmative grants of the Constitution. The powers to declare and wage war, to conclude peace, to make treaties, to maintain diplomatic relations with other sovereignties, if they had never been mentioned in the Constitution, would have vested in the federal government as necessary concomitants of nationality. Neither the Constitution nor the laws passed in pursuance of it have any force in foreign territory unless in respect of our own citizens; and operations of the nation in such territory must be governed by treaties, international understandings and compacts, and the principles of international law. As a member of the family of nations, the right and power of the United States in that field are equal to the right and power of the other members of the international family. Otherwise, the United States is not completely sovereign. The power to acquire territory by discovery and occupation, the power to expel undesirable aliens, the power to make such international agreements as do not constitute treaties in the constitutional sense, none of which is expressly affirmed by the Constitution, nevertheless exist as inherently inseparable from the conception of nationality. This the court recognized, and in each of the cases cited found the warrant for its conclusions not in the provisions of the Constitution, but in the law of nations.

In *Burnet v. Brooks*, 288 U.S. 378, 396, we said, "As a nation with all the attributes of sovereignty, the United States is vested with all the powers of government necessary to maintain an effective control of international relations."

Not only, as we have shown, is the federal power over external affairs in origin and essential character different from that over internal affairs, but participation in the exercise of the power is significantly limited. In this vast external realm, with its important, complicated, delicate and manifold problems, the President alone has the power to speak or listen as a representative of the nation. He *makes* treaties with the advice and consent of the Senate; but he alone negotiates. Into the field of negotiation the Senate cannot intrude; and Congress itself is powerless to invade it. As Marshall said in his great argument of March 7, 1800, in the House of Representatives: "The President is the sole organ of the nation in its external relations, and its sole representative with foreign nations." The Senate Committee on Foreign Relations at a very early day in our history (February 15, 1816), reported to the Senate, among other things, as follows:

"The President is the constitutional representative of the United States with regard to foreign nations. He manages our concerns with foreign nations and must necessarily be most competent to determine when, how, and upon what subjects negotiation may be urged with the greatest prospect of success. For his conduct he is responsible to the Constitution. The committee consider this responsibility the surest pledge for the faithful discharge of his duty. They think the interference of the Senate in the direction of foreign negotiations calculated to diminish that responsibility and thereby to impair the best security for the national safety. The nature of transactions with foreign nations, moreover, requires caution and unity of design, and their success frequently depends on secrecy and dispatch."

It is important to bear in mind that we are here dealing not alone with an authority vested in the President by an exertion of legislative power, but with such an authority plus the very delicate, plenary and exclusive power of the President as the sole organ of the federal government in the field of international relations—a power which does not require as a basis for its exercise an act of Congress, but which, of course, like every other governmental power, must be exercised in subordination to the applicable provisions of the Constitution. It is quite apparent that if, in the maintenance of our international relations, embarrassment—perhaps serious embarrassment—is to be avoided and success for our aims achieved, congressional legislation which is to be made effective through negotiation and inquiry within the international field must often accord to the President a degree of discretion and freedom from statutory restriction which would not be admissible were domestic affairs alone involved. Moreover, he, not Congress, has the better opportunity of knowing the conditions which prevail in foreign countries, and especially is this true in time of war. He has his confidential sources of information. He has his agents in the form of diplomatic, consular and other officials. Secrecy in respect of information gathered by them may be highly necessary, and the premature disclosure of it productive of harmful results. Indeed, so clearly is this true that the first President refused to accede to a request to lay before the House of Representatives the instructions, correspondence and documents relating to the negotiation of the Jay Treaty—a refusal the wisdom of which was recognized by the House itself and has never since been doubted. In his reply to the request, President Washington said:

"The nature of foreign negotiations requires caution, and their success must often depend on secrecy; and even when brought to a conclusion a full disclosure of all the measures, demands, or eventual concessions which may have been proposed or contemplated would be extremely impolitic; for this might have a pernicious influence on future negotiations, or produce immediate inconveniences, perhaps danger and mischief, in relation to other powers. The necessity of such caution and secrecy was one cogent reason for vesting the power of making treaties in the President, with the advice and consent of the Senate, the principle on which that body was formed confining it to a small number of members. To admit, then, a right in the House of Representatives to demand and to have as a matter of course all the papers respecting a negotiation with a foreign power would be to establish a dangerous precedent." * * *

In the light of the foregoing observations, it is evident that this court should not be in haste to apply a general rule which will have the effect of condemning legislation like that under review as constituting an unlawful delegation of legislative power. The principles which justify such legislation find overwhelming support in the unbroken legislative practice which has prevailed almost from the inception of the national government to the present day. * * *

Practically every volume of the United States Statutes contains one or more acts or joint resolutions of Congress authorizing action by the President in respect of subjects affecting foreign relations, which either leave the exercise of the power to his unrestricted judgment, or provide a standard far more general than that which has always been considered requisite with regard to domestic affairs. * * *

The uniform, long-continued and undisputed legislative practice just disclosed rests upon an admissible view of the Constitution which, even if the practice found far less support in principle than we think it does, we should not feel at liberty at this late day to disturb.

We deem it unnecessary to consider, *seriatim*, the several clauses which are said to evidence the unconstitutionality of the Joint Resolution as involving an unlawful delegation of legislative power. It is enough to summarize by saying that, both upon principle and in accordance with precedent, we conclude there is sufficient warrant for the broad discretion vested in the President to determine whether the enforcement of the statute will have a beneficial effect upon the reestablishment of peace in the affected countries; whether he shall make proclamation to bring the resolution into operation; whether and when the resolution shall cease to operate and to make proclamation accordingly; and to prescribe limitations and exceptions to which the enforcement of the resolution shall be subject.

Notes and Questions

1. *The Historical Context. Curtiss–Wright* was politically significant. When three companies and four individuals were indicted for running machine guns to Bolivia in its Chaco War against Paraguay, the indictment was front-page news. "Gun–Running Laid to Aircraft Heads," *New York Times*, Jan. 28, 1936, at 1. After a federal district judge held that the President had no power to outlaw shipments of arms to belligerent nations, the case went to the U.S. Supreme Court where in oral argument there was sharp questioning by judges well-experienced in foreign affairs, *e.g.*, by Chief Justice Hughes, who had been Secretary of State, and Justice Sutherland, who had been a member of the Senate Foreign Relations Committee. "Presidential Ban on Arms Held Void," *New York Times*, Mar. 26, 1936, at 15; "Embargo Argued in Supreme Court," *New York Times*, Nov. 20, 1936, at 10. The 7–1 opinion in *Curtiss–Wright* in favor of the President was again first-page news. "High Court Backs Neutrality Power Held by President," *New York Times*, Dec. 22, 1936, at 1. *Curtiss–Wright* was thought to be a significant contribution to President Roosevelt's attempts to keep all of the Americas out of the impending war in Europe. Delbert Clark, "Monroe Doctrine 'Expanded': American Republics' Joint Policy on Peace Removes Old 'Unilateral' Stigma," *New York Times*, Dec. 27, 1936, at E5.

2. *Executive Lawmaking.* In *Curtiss–Wright*, Justice Sutherland was at pains to distinguish executive lawmaking in the international realm from that sort of executive lawmaking that the Supreme Court had struck down in a series of judgments limiting the President's domestic power. See, for example, the Court's judgments in A.L.A. Schechter Poultry Corp. v. United States, 295 U.S. 495, 55 S.Ct. 837, 79 L.Ed. 1570 (1935), and Carter v. Carter Coal Co., 298 U.S. 238, 56 S.Ct. 855, 80 L.Ed. 1160 (1936). In a few months the Court would retreat even on the domestic front. See NLRB v. Jones & Laughlin Steel Corp., 301 U.S. 1, 57 S.Ct. 615, 81 L.Ed. 893 (1937).

3. *The Source of Foreign Affairs Powers.* Did the judgment in *Curtiss–Wright* mean that some federal powers in international affairs are extra-

constitutional? In *Missouri v. Holland*, Justice Holmes looked at the wording of Article VI(2) of the Constitution and noted that "Acts of Congress are the supreme law of the land only when made in pursuance of the Constitution, while treaties are declared to be so when made under the authority of the United States." Does the wording of the Supremacy Clause advance the notion that the federal government possesses powers in foreign affairs that go beyond the Constitution? Justice Sutherland wrote in *Curtiss–Wright*: "A political society cannot endure without a supreme will somewhere. Sovereignty is never held in suspense."

Note that, "[a]lthough the concept of executive plenary power over foreign relations found its fullest expression in *Curtiss-Wright*, Justice Sutherland's method of finding extra-constitutional authority for federal action over foreign affairs was entirely familiar to Supreme Court jurisprudence." Sarah H. Cleveland, "The Plenary Background of Curtiss–Wright," 70 *University of Colorado Law Review* 1127, 1135 (1999). Throughout the 19th century the Court had expanded the federal executive branch's extra-constitutional powers at the expense of both Congress and the states in a number of fields, including Indian affairs, immigration, and territories. *Id.* at 1136–54.

4. *The History of the Foreign Relations Powers*. Did foreign relations powers pass directly to the United States during the American Revolution? Justice Chase in *Ware v. Hylton* in 1795 was much nearer the event than the Court in *Curtiss–Wright* when he wrote:

> In June 1776, the convention of Virginia formally declared, that Virginia was a free, sovereign, and independent state; and on the 4th of July, 1776, following, the United States, in congress assembled, declared the 13 united colonies free and independent states; and that, as such, they had full power to levy war, conclude peace, & c. I consider this as a declaration, not that the united colonies jointly, in a collective capacity, were independent states, & c. but that each of them was a sovereign and independent state, that is, that each of them had a right to govern itself by its own authority and its own laws, without any control from any other power upon earth.

Ware v. Hylton, 3 U.S. (3 Dall.) 199, 224, 1 L.Ed. 568, 579 (1796). Later in his opinion Justice Chase proved willing to acknowledge that Congress had some necessary powers even before the ratification of the Articles of Confederation in 1781:

> The powers of congress [between 1774 and 1781] originated from necessity, and arose out of, and were only limited by events; or, in other words, they were revolutionary in their very nature. Their extent depended on the exigencies and necessities of public affairs. It was absolutely and indispensably necessary that congress should possess the power of conducting the war against Great Britain, and therefore, if not expressly given by all (as it was by some of the states), I do not hesitate to say, that congress did rightfully possess such power. The authority to make war, of necessity, implies the power to make peace; or the war must be perpetual. I entertain this general idea, that the several states retained all internal sovereignty; and that congress properly possessed the great rights of external sovereignty * * *.

Id. at 232, 1 L.Ed. at 582.

5. *The Balance of Foreign Relations Powers Among the Different Branches.* Note that even if one concludes that the federal government has special powers in the field of foreign relations, it is still unclear as to what the balance of foreign relations powers are among the Congress, the President, and the federal courts. Although Justice Sutherland's opinion in *Curtiss–Wright* was a strong endorsement of Presidential powers, the executive acts in question were based on a congressional resolution. The next case, *Dames & Moore*, explains more about setting a proper balance among the three branches of the federal government in matters concerning foreign affairs.

DAMES & MOORE v. REGAN

453 U.S. 654, 101 S.Ct. 2972, 69 L.Ed.2d 918 (1981).

Justice Rehnquist delivered the opinion of the Court.

The questions presented by this case touch fundamentally upon the manner in which our Republic is to be governed. Throughout the nearly two centuries of our Nation's existence under the Constitution, this subject has generated considerable debate. We have had the benefit of commentators such as John Jay, Alexander Hamilton, and James Madison writing in The Federalist Papers at the Nation's very inception, the benefit of astute foreign observers of our system such as Alexis de Tocqueville and James Bryce writing during the first century of the Nation's existence, and the benefit of many other treatises as well as more than 400 volumes of reports of decisions of this Court. As these writings reveal it is doubtless both futile and perhaps dangerous to find any epigrammatical explanation of how this country has been governed.
* * *

* * * We are confined to a resolution of the dispute presented to us. That dispute involves various Executive Orders and regulations by which the President nullified attachments and liens on Iranian assets in the United States, directed that these assets be transferred to Iran, and suspended claims against Iran that may be presented to an International Claims Tribunal. This action was taken in an effort to comply with an Executive Agreement between the United States and Iran. We granted certiorari before judgment in this case, and set an expedited briefing and argument schedule, because lower courts had reached conflicting conclusions on the validity of the President's actions and, as the Solicitor General informed us, unless the Government acted by July 19, 1981, Iran could consider the United States to be in breach of the Executive Agreement. * * *

* * * [T]he decisions of the Court in this area have been rare, episodic, and afford little precedential value for subsequent cases. The tensions present in any exercise of executive power under the tripartite system of Federal Government established by the Constitution have been reflected in opinions by Members of this Court more than once. The

Court stated in *United States* v. *Curtiss–Wright Export Corp.*, 299 U.S. 304, 319–320 (1936):

"[W]e are here dealing not alone with an authority vested in the President by an exertion of legislative power, but with such an authority plus the very delicate, plenary and exclusive power of the President as the sole organ of the federal government in the field of international relations—a power which does not require as a basis for its exercise an act of Congress, but which, of course, like every other governmental power, must be exercised in subordination to the applicable provisions of the Constitution."

And yet 16 years later, Justice Jackson in his concurring opinion in *Youngstown* [*Sheet & Tube Co.* v. *Sawyer*, 343 U.S. 579, 72 S.Ct. 863, 96 L.Ed. 1153 (1952)], which both parties agree brings together as much combination of analysis and common sense as there is in this area, focused not on the "plenary and exclusive power of the President" but rather responded to a claim of virtually unlimited powers for the Executive by noting:

"The example of such unlimited executive power that must have most impressed the forefathers was the prerogative exercised by George III, and the description of its evils in the Declaration of Independence leads me to doubt that they were creating their new Executive in his image."

As we now turn to the factual and legal issues in this case, we freely confess that we are obviously deciding only one more episode in the never-ending tension between the President exercising the executive authority in a world that presents each day some new challenge with which he must deal and the Constitution under which we all live and which no one disputes embodies some sort of system of checks and balances.

I

On November 4, 1979, the American Embassy in Tehran was seized and our diplomatic personnel were captured and held hostage. In response to that crisis, President Carter, acting pursuant to the International Emergency Economic Powers Act, 91 Stat. 1626, 50 U.S.C. §§ 1701–1706 (1976 ed., Supp. III) (hereinafter IEEPA), declared a national emergency on November 14, 1979, and blocked the removal or transfer of "all property and interests in property of the Government of Iran, its instrumentalities and controlled entities and the Central Bank of Iran which are or become subject to the jurisdiction of the United States...." Exec. Order No. 12170, 3 CFR 457 (1980), note following 50 U.S.C. § 1701 (1976 ed., Supp. III). President Carter authorized the Secretary of the Treasury to promulgate regulations carrying out the blocking order. On November 15, 1979, the Treasury Department's Office of Foreign Assets Control issued a regulation providing that "[u]nless licensed or authorized ... any attachment, judgment, decree, lien, execution, garnishment, or other judicial process is null and void with respect to any property in which on or since [November 14, 1979,] there existed an interest of Iran." 31 CFR § 535.203(e) (1980). The regulations also made clear that any licenses or authorizations granted could be "amended, modified, or revoked at any time." § 535.805.

On November 26, 1979, the President granted a general license authorizing certain judicial proceedings against Iran but which did not allow the "entry of any judgment or of any decree or order of similar or analogous effect...." § 535.504(a). On December 19, 1979, a clarifying regulation was issued stating that "the general authorization for judicial proceedings contained in § 535.504(a) includes pre-judgment attachment." § 535.418.

On December 19, 1979, petitioner Dames & Moore filed suit in the United States District Court for the Central District of California against the Government of Iran, the Atomic Energy Organization of Iran, and a number of Iranian banks. In its complaint, petitioner alleged that its wholly owned subsidiary, Dames & Moore International, S. R. L., was a party to a written contract with the Atomic Energy Organization, and that the subsidiary's entire interest in the contract had been assigned to petitioner. Under the contract, the subsidiary was to conduct site studies for a proposed nuclear power plant in Iran. As provided in the terms of the contract, the Atomic Energy Organization terminated the agreement for its own convenience on June 30, 1979. Petitioner contended, however, that it was owed $3,436,694.30 plus interest for services performed under the contract prior to the date of termination. The District Court issued orders of attachment directed against property of the defendants, and the property of certain Iranian banks was then attached to secure any judgment that might be entered against them.

On January 20, 1981, the Americans held hostage were released by Iran pursuant to an Agreement entered into the day before and embodied in two Declarations of the Democratic and Popular Republic of Algeria. The Agreement stated that "[i]t is the purpose of [the United States and Iran] ... to terminate all litigation as between the Government of each party and the nationals of the other, and to bring about the settlement and termination of all such claims through binding arbitration." In furtherance of this goal, the Agreement called for the establishment of an Iran–United States Claims Tribunal which would arbitrate any claims not settled within six months. Awards of the Claims Tribunal are to be "final and binding" and "enforceable ... in the courts of any nation in accordance with its laws." Under the Agreement, the United States is obligated

> "to terminate all legal proceedings in United States courts involving claims of United States persons and institutions against Iran and its state enterprises, to nullify all attachments and judgments obtained therein, to prohibit all further litigation based on such claims, and to bring about the termination of such claims through binding arbitration."

In addition, the United States must "act to bring about the transfer" by July 19, 1981, of all Iranian assets held in this country by American banks. One billion dollars of these assets will be deposited in a security account in the Bank of England, to the account of the Algerian Central Bank, and used to satisfy awards rendered against Iran by the Claims Tribunal.

On January 19, 1981, President Carter issued a series of Executive Orders implementing the terms of the agreement. Exec. Orders Nos. 12276–12285, 46 Fed. Reg. 7913–7932. These Orders revoked all licenses permitting the exercise of "any right, power, or privilege" with regard to Iranian funds, securities, or deposits; "nullified" all non–Iranian interests in such assets acquired subsequent to the blocking order of November 14, 1979; and required those banks holding Iranian assets to transfer them "to the Federal Reserve Bank of New York, to be held or transferred as directed by the Secretary of the Treasury." Exec. Order No. 12294, 46 Fed. Reg. 7919.

On February 24, 1981, President Reagan issued an Executive Order in which he "ratified" the January 19th Executive Orders. Exec. Order No. 12294, 46 Fed. Reg. 14111. Moreover, he "suspended" all "claims which may be presented to the ... Tribunal" and provided that such claims "shall have no legal effect in any action now pending in any court of the United States." The suspension of any particular claim terminates if the Claims Tribunal determines that it has no jurisdiction over that claim; claims are discharged for all purposes when the Claims Tribunal either awards some recovery and that amount is paid, or determines that no recovery is due.

Meanwhile, on January 27, 1981, petitioner moved for summary judgment in the District Court against the Government of Iran and the Atomic Energy Organization, but not against the Iranian banks. The District Court granted petitioner's motion and awarded petitioner the amount claimed under the contract plus interest. Thereafter, petitioner attempted to execute the judgment by obtaining writs of garnishment and execution in state court in the State of Washington, and a sheriff's sale of Iranian property in Washington was noticed to satisfy the judgment. However, by order of May 28, 1981, as amended by order of June 8, the District Court stayed execution of its judgment pending appeal by the Government of Iran and the Atomic Energy Organization. The District Court also ordered that all prejudgment attachments obtained against the Iranian defendants be vacated and that further proceedings against the bank defendants be stayed in light of the Executive Orders discussed above.

On April 28, 1981, petitioner filed this action in the District Court for declaratory and injunctive relief against the United States and the Secretary of the Treasury, seeking to prevent enforcement of the Executive Orders and Treasury Department regulations implementing the Agreement with Iran. * * *

II

The parties and the lower courts, confronted with the instant questions, have all agreed that much relevant analysis is contained in *Youngstown Sheet & Tube Co. v. Sawyer*, 343 U.S. 579 (1952). Justice Black's opinion for the Court in that case, involving the validity of President Truman's effort to seize the country's steel mills in the wake of a nationwide strike, recognized that "[t]he President's power, if any, to issue the order must stem either from an act of Congress or from the Constitution itself." Justice Jackson's concurring opinion elaborated in a general way the consequences of different types of interaction between the two democratic branches in assessing Presidential authority to act in any given case. When the President acts pursuant to an express or implied authorization for Congress, he exercises not only his powers but also those delegated by Congress. In such a case the executive action "would be supported by the strongest of presumptions and the widest latitude of judicial interpretation, and the burden of persuasion would rest heavily upon any who might attack it." When the President acts in the absence of congressional authorization he may enter "a zone of twilight in which he and Congress may have concurrent authority, or in which its distribution is uncertain." In such a case the analysis becomes more complicated, and the validity of the President's action, at least so far as separation-of-powers principles are concerned, hinges on a consideration of all the circumstances which might shed light on the views of the Legislative Branch toward such action, including "congressional inertia, indifference or quiescence." Finally, when the President acts in contravention of the will of Congress, "his power is at its lowest ebb," and the Court can sustain his actions "only by disabling the Congress from acting upon the subject." * * *

III

In nullifying post-November 14, 1979, attachments and directing those persons holding blocked Iranian funds and securities to transfer them to the Federal Reserve Bank of New York for ultimate transfer to Iran, President Carter cited five sources of express or inherent power. The Government, however, has principally relied on § 1702(a)(1) (1976 ed., Supp. III) [of the IEPPA], as authorization for these actions. Section 1702(a)(1) provides in part:

> "At the times and to the extent specified in section 1701 of this title, the President may, under such regulations as he may prescribe, by means of instructions, licenses, or otherwise—

> "(A) investigate, regulate, or prohibit—

> "(i) any transactions in foreign exchange,

> "(ii) transfers of credit or payments between, by, through, or to any banking institution, to the extent that such transfers or payments involve any interest of any foreign country or a national thereof,

"(iii) the importing or exporting of currency or securities, and

"(B) investigate, regulate, direct and compel, nullify, void, prevent or prohibit, any acquisition, holding, withholding, use, transfer, withdrawal, transportation, importation or exportation of, or dealing in, or exercising any right, power, or privilege with respect to, or transactions involving, any property in which any foreign country or a national thereof has any interest;

"by any person, or with respect to any property, subject to the jurisdiction of the United States." * * *

[Justice Rehnquist concludes that these provisions of the IEEPA explicitly authorized the President to nullify the attachments and transfer the assets.]

Because the President's action in nullifying the attachments and ordering the transfer of the assets was taken pursuant to specific congressional authorization, it is "supported by the strongest of presumptions and the widest latitude of judicial interpretation, and the burden of persuasion would rest heavily upon any who might attack it." *Youngstown,* 343 U.S., at 637 (Jackson, J., concurring). Under the circumstances of this case, we cannot say that petitioner has sustained that heavy burden. A contrary ruling would mean that the Federal Government as a whole lacked the power exercised by the President, and that we are not prepared to say.

IV

Although we have concluded that the IEEPA constitutes specific congressional authorization to the President to nullify the attachments and order the transfer of Iranian assets, there remains the question of the President's authority to suspend claims pending in American courts. Such claims have, of course, an existence apart from the attachments which accompanied them. In terminating these claims through Executive Order No. 12294, the President purported to act under authority of both the IEEPA and 22 U.S.C. § 1732, the so-called "Hostage Act." 48 Fed. Reg. 14111 (1981).

We conclude that although the IEEPA authorized the nullification of the attachments, it cannot be read to authorize the suspension of the claims. The claims of American citizens against Iran are not in themselves transactions involving Iranian property or efforts to exercise any rights with respect to such property. An *in personam* lawsuit, although it might eventually be reduced to judgment and that judgment might be executed upon, is an effort to establish liability and fix damages and does not focus on any particular property within the jurisdiction. The terms of the IEEPA therefore do not authorize the President to suspend claims in American courts.

[Similarly, the Hostage Act does not authorize the President to suspend the claims.]

Although we have declined to conclude that the IEEPA or the Hostage Act directly authorizes the President's suspension of claims for the reasons noted, we cannot ignore the general tenor of Congress' legislation in this area in trying to determine whether the President is acting alone or at least with the acceptance of Congress. As we have noted, Congress cannot anticipate and legislate with regard to every possible action the President may find it necessary to take or every possible situation in which he might act. * * *

Not infrequently in affairs between nations, outstanding claims by nationals of one country against the government of another country are "sources of friction" between the two sovereigns. *United States v. Pink,* 315 U.S. 203, 225 (1942). To resolve these difficulties, nations have often entered into agreements settling the claims of their respective nationals. As one treatise writer puts it, international agreements settling claims by nationals of one state against the government of another "are established international practice reflecting traditional international theory." L. Henkin, Foreign Affairs and the Constitution 262 (1972). Consistent with that principle, the United States has repeatedly exercised its sovereign authority to settle the claims of its nationals against foreign countries. Though those settlements have sometimes been made by treaty, there has also been a longstanding practice of settling such claims by executive agreement without the advice and consent of the Senate. Under such agreements, the President has agreed to renounce or extinguish claims of United States nations against foreign governments in return for lump-sum payments or the establishment of arbitration procedures. * * * It is clear that the practice of settling claims continues today. Since 1952, the President has entered into at least 10 binding settlements with foreign nations, including an $80 million settlement with the Peoples Republic of China.

Crucial to our decision today is the conclusion that Congress has implicitly approved the practice of claim settlement by executive agreement. This is best demonstrated by Congress' enactment of the International Claims Settlement Act of 1949, 64 Stat. 13, as amended, 22 U.S.C. § 1621 *et seq.* (1976 ed. and Supp. IV). * * * By creating a procedure to implement future settlement agreements, Congress placed its stamp of approval on such agreements. * * *

In addition to congressional acquiescence in the President's power to settle claims, prior cases of this Court have also recognized that the President does have some measure of power to enter into executive agreements without obtaining the advice and consent of the Senate. In *United States v. Pink,* 315 U.S. 203 (1942), for example, the Court upheld the validity of the Litvinov Assignment, which was part of an Executive Agreement whereby the Soviet Union assigned to the United States amounts owed to it by American nationals so that outstanding claims of other American nationals could be paid. The Court explained that the resolution of such claims was integrally connected with normalizing United States relations with a foreign state:

"Power to remove such obstacles to full recognition as settlement of claims of our nationals ... certainly is a modest implied power of the President.... No such obstacle can be placed in the way of rehabilitation of relations between this country and another nation, unless the historic conception of the powers and responsibilities ... is to be drastically revised."

Similarly, Judge Learned Hand recognized:

"The constitutional power of the President extends to the settlement of mutual claims between a foreign government and the United States, at least when it is an incident to the recognition of that government; and it would be unreasonable to circumscribe it to such controversies. The continued mutual amity between the nation and other powers again and again depends upon a satisfactory compromise of mutual claims; the necessary power to make such compromises has existed from the earliest times and been exercised by the foreign offices of all civilized nations." *Ozanic v. United States*, 188 F.2d 228, 231 (C.A.2 1951). * * *

In light of all of the foregoing—the inferences to be drawn from the character of the legislation Congress has enacted in the area, such as the IEEPA and the Hostage Act, and from the history of acquiescence in executive claims settlement—we conclude that the President was authorized to suspend pending claims pursuant to Executive Order No. 12294. As Justice Frankfurter pointed out in *Youngstown*, 343 U.S., at 610–611, "a systematic, unbroken, executive practice, long pursued to the knowledge of the Congress and never before questioned ... may be treated as a gloss on 'Executive Power' vested in the President by § 1 of Art. II." Past practice does not, by itself, create power, but "long-continued practice, known to and acquiesced in by Congress, would raise a presumption that the [action] had been [taken] in pursuance of its consent...." *United States v. Midwest Oil Co.*, 236 U.S. 459, 474 (1915). Such practice is present here and such a presumption is also appropriate. In light of the fact that Congress may be considered to have consented to the President's action in suspending claims, we cannot say that action exceeded the President's powers.

Notes and Questions

1. *The Hostages Crisis. Dames & Moore* grew out of the 1979–1981 hostages crisis. We look again at the U.S.–Iran conflict when we read the *Diplomatic and Consular Staff Case* in Chapter 5. Why did President Carter block all Iranian assets in the United States? Why did he initially permit private suits against Iran like that brought by Dames & Moore? Did the executive branch "use" private litigants to further the goals of American foreign policy? On President Carter's attempt to end the hostages crisis before he left office, see Jimmy Carter, *Keeping Faith: Memoirs of a President* 580–95 (1982). President Carter wrote that the "release of the American hostages had almost become an obsession with me." *Id.* at 594. For an account of the role of U.S. law firms in negotiating the assets-for-

hostages agreement, see James B. Stewart, *The Partners: Inside America's Most Powerful Law Firms* 19–52 (1983).

2. *The* Youngstown *Test.* The test articulated by Justice Jackson in Youngstown Sheet & Tube Co. v. Sawyer, 343 U.S. 579, 72 S.Ct. 863, 96 L.Ed. 1153 (1952), was used quite effectively by Justice Rehnquist in *Dames & Moore.* In *Youngstown*, the test was employed to invalidate President Truman's seizure of steel mills during the Korean War because the Presidential act conflicted with Congressional intent. However, in *Dames & Moore*, the test was used to validate the acts of Presidents Carter and Reagan to end the Iranian hostage crisis. The Presidential acts easier to validate were those nullifying attachments of Iranian property and transferring the assets to the Federal Reserve Bank. Here it seems that the President acted well within the specific authorization of Congress in the International Emergency Economic Powers Act. More difficult for the Court were the Presidential acts suspending U.S. litigation in favor of claims arbitration before an international tribunal in The Hague. How persuasive need evidence be that suspension of claims was an ordinary feature of U.S. international practice? The "10 binding settlements with foreign nations" noted by the Court can be distinguished from the suspension of claims in *Dames & Moore, e.g.,* because made pursuant to powers specifically delegated to the President in peace treaties or because they involved lump sum payments to the United States for distribution to claimants. See "Supreme Court, 1980 Term," 95 *Harvard Law Review* 91, 192–98 (1981). But even if there was sufficient relevant evidence that suspension of claims was customary, how did that custom make the suspension constitutional?

3. *The Continuing Relevance of* Curtiss–Wright. How did *Dames & Moore* treat the broad language of *Curtiss–Wright*? Did Justice Rehnquist mean to incorporate *Curtiss–Wright's* apparent endorsement of executive powers free from foundation in an act of Congress? Or did he mean to limit such powers with the three-tier analysis of *Youngstown*? If the role of the executive *vis-à-vis* the Congress in the realm of foreign affairs is left somewhat ambiguous after *Curtiss–Wright* and *Dames & Moore*, is that a desirable or undesirable state of affairs?

4. *The Status of Executive Agreements.* Although scholars have exhaustively explored the original intent of the drafters of the Constitution, it is far from agreed whether it was originally intended that executive agreements have much the same force in domestic law as treaties approved by the Senate. See Bruce Ackerman & David Golove, "Is NAFTA Constitutional?," 108 *Harvard Law Review* 799 (1995); Laurence H. Tribe, "Taking Text and Structure Seriously: Reflections on Free–Form Method in Constitutional Interpretation," 108 *Harvard Law Review* 1221 (1995); Michael D. Ramsey, "Executive Agreements and the (Non)Treaty Power," 77 *North Carolina Law Review* 134 (1998). In practice, executive agreements have proven to be enormously important. *Dames & Moore* justified and set controls on what is ever more a rising tide: between 1980 and 1992, some 4,510 new executive agreements were made against only 218 treaties that received the advice and consent of the Senate. Detlev F. Vagts, "International Agreements, the Senate and the Constitution," 36 *Columbia Journal of Transnational Law* 143, 145 (1997). It is hard to see how the U.S. could honor its international obligations in practice if every international agreement required Senate

approval. As Professor Vagts has observed, "[r]unning the likes of 6,500 agreements through the Senate for its advice and consent would be enormously disruptive and would likely prevent the conduct of almost all other business, unless some massive unanimous consent operation could be mounted." *Id.*

5. *The Constitution and U.S. International Legal Obligations.* If the Supreme Court had found that the executive branch could not lawfully terminate the legal suits against Iran in United States courts, would this have affected the international legal obligations of the United States? What would have been the practical effect? The possibility that the United States might not be able to honor its international legal commitment to Iran persuaded the Supreme Court to hold a rare special session to decide the case. Linda Greenhouse, "High Court Hears Iran Assets Case," *New York Times*, June 25, 1981, at D3.

6. *The* Breard *Case.* The Supreme Court was less concerned with the United States complying with its international legal obligations in Breard v. Greene, 523 U.S. 371, 118 S.Ct. 1352, 140 L.Ed.2d 529 (1998). In *Breard* a 6–3 majority of the Court refused to stay Virginia's execution of a Paraguayan citizen who had not been informed of his right to contact the Paraguayan consulate pursuant to the Vienna Convention on Consular Relations, Apr. 24, 1963, 21 U.S.T. 77, 596 U.N.T.S. 261. Moreover, a Paraguayan complaint against the United States was pending before the International Court of Justice. The Supreme Court majority held that "[e]ven were Breard's Vienna Convention claim properly raised and proved, it is extremely doubtful that the violation should result in the overturning of a final judgment of conviction without some showing that the violation had an effect on the trial." *Id.* at 377, 118 S.Ct. at 1355, 140 L.Ed.2d at 538. The three dissenting judges were ready to hear the issues raised by the case. As Justice Breyer argued, "the international aspects of the cases have provided us with the advantage of additional briefing even in the short time available. More time would likely mean additional briefing and argument, perhaps, for example, on the potential relevance of proceedings in an international forum." *Id.* at 381, 118 S.Ct. at 1357, 140 L.Ed.2d at 540–41.

Despite an order of the ICJ to delay, Virginia executed Breard. Virginia's Governor noted both the U.S. Supreme Court opinion and the conflicting advice of President Clinton's Secretary of State and Attorney General (Madeline Albright urged a stay; but Janet Reno argued that Virginia was not bound to listen to the International Court). "Statement by Governor Jim Gilmore concerning the Execution of Angel Breard," Commonwealth of Virginia Office of the Governor Press Release, Apr. 14, 1998. However, "[u]nder the international law of state responsibility, compliance with the internal laws of the Commonwealth of Virginia and of the federal laws of the United States cannot relieve the U.S. from international responsibility for an admitted violation of the Vienna Convention and a potential violation of the UN Charter." Peter H.F. Bekker & Keith Highet, "International Court of Justice Orders U.S. to Stay Execution of Paraguayan National in Virginia," *ASIL Flash Insight* (April 1998). Why would the United States be more concerned with honoring its international legal obligations to Iran in *Dames & Moore* than with honoring those to Paraguay in *Breard*?

7. *The* Madej Case. A majority of the Illinois Supreme Court cited *Breard, inter alia,* in ruling that Illinois' violation of the Vienna Convention in respect of a Polish national should not delay his execution. People v. Madej, 193 Ill.2d 395, 739 N.E.2d 423 (2000). In a vigorous dissent joined by Illinois' Chief Justice, Justice Heiple wrote:

> Defendant, a Polish citizen residing in the United States as a permanent resident alien, was, along with other offenses, tried and convicted of murder and sentenced to death. This court affirmed defendant's convictions and sentence on direct appeal. Subsequently, defendant filed a section 2–1401 petition for relief from judgment and a petition for a writ of *mandamus* based upon an alleged violation of his rights under the Vienna Convention on Consular Relations.

> The Vienna Convention is a binding international treaty to which the United States and the Republic of Poland are parties. Article 36 of the Vienna Convention required the State to inform defendant of his right to contact a Polish consular official at the time of his arrest. This was not done. Upon belatedly learning of the defendant's situation, however, the Polish government has now intervened on defendant's behalf.

> Although there is no dispute that the State violated the Vienna Convention by failing to provide defendant the required consular notification, the majority declines to provide defendant any relief for this violation. Because this case raises important issues of international relations and the rights of all persons, domestic and foreign, I respectfully dissent.

> The State suggests that a letter of apology to the Polish government would rectify this oversight. Whether this apology would be sent before or after defendant's execution was not specified.

> What is cavalierly dismissed here is that the consular notification requirement is meant to ensure that foreign nationals imprisoned abroad have adequate legal representation and that they should be tried in accordance with principles of justice generally recognized in the international community by allowing consular officials to consult with the defendant and with attorneys, court officials and prosecutors. It is important to note that this protection is designed for Americans abroad as well as for foreign nationals in the United States. In the instant case, however, the Polish Consul General was not even aware of defendant's situation until 1998, some 16 years after his conviction and sentence.

> The question arises, how can we expect protection under this treaty for American citizens abroad if we do not extend equal protection to foreign nationals residing in the United States? The answer is, we cannot. The decision reached in this case thus has implications reaching far beyond the execution of this defendant.

> For the breach of this international convention, defendant's convictions and sentence should be reversed and the cause remanded for a new trial in compliance with the solemn treaty obligations of the United States, which, under our constitution, are the supreme law of the land.

Id. at ___, 739 N.E.2d at 432.

UNITED STATES v. ALVAREZ–MACHAIN

504 U.S. 655, 112 S.Ct. 2188, 119 L.Ed.2d 441 (1992).

CHIEF JUSTICE REHNQUIST delivered the opinion of the Court.

The issue in this case is whether a criminal defendant, abducted to the United States from a nation with which it has an extradition treaty, thereby acquires a defense to the jurisdiction of this country's courts. We hold that he does not, and that he may be tried in federal district court for violations of the criminal law of the United States.

Respondent, Humberto Alvarez–Machain, is a citizen and resident of Mexico. He was indicted for participating in the kidnap and murder of United States Drug Enforcement Administration (DEA) special agent Enrique Camarena–Salazar and a Mexican pilot working with Camarena, Alfredo Zavala–Avelar. The DEA believes that respondent, a medical doctor, participated in the murder by prolonging Agent Camarena's life so that others could further torture and interrogate him. On April 2, 1990, respondent was forcibly kidnapped from his medical office in Guadalajara, Mexico, to be flown by private plane to El Paso, Texas, where he was arrested by DEA officials. The District Court concluded that DEA agents were responsible for respondent's abduction, although they were not personally involved in it. *United States v. Caro–Quintero*, 745 F.Supp. 599, 602–604, 609 (C.D.Cal.1990).[2]

Respondent moved to dismiss the indictment, claiming that his abduction constituted outrageous governmental conduct, and that the District Court lacked jurisdiction to try him because he was abducted in violation of the extradition treaty between the United States and Mexico. Extradition Treaty, May 4, 1978, [1979] United States–United Mexican States, 31 U.S.T. 5059, T.I.A.S. No. 9656 (Extradition Treaty or Treaty). The District Court rejected the outrageous governmental conduct claim, but held that it lacked jurisdiction to try respondent because his abduction violated the Extradition Treaty. The District Court discharged respondent and ordered that he be repatriated to Mexico.

The Court of Appeals affirmed the dismissal of the indictment and the repatriation of respondent * * *.

* * * We granted certiorari, and now reverse.

Although we have never before addressed the precise issue raised in the present case, we have previously considered proceedings in claimed violation of an extradition treaty and proceedings against a defendant brought before a court by means of a forcible abduction. We addressed the former issue in *United States v. Rauscher*, 119 U.S. 407 (1886); more precisely, the issue of whether the Webster–Ashburton Treaty of 1842, 8 Stat. 576, which governed extraditions between England and the United

---

2. Apparently, DEA officials had attempted to gain respondent's presence in the United States through informal negotiations with Mexican officials, but were un- successful. DEA officials then, through a contact in Mexico, offered to pay a reward and expenses in return for the delivery of respondent to the United States.

States, prohibited the prosecution of defendant Rauscher for a crime other than the crime for which he had been extradited. Whether this prohibition, known as the doctrine of specialty, was an intended part of the treaty had been disputed between the two nations for some time. Justice Miller delivered the opinion of the Court, which carefully examined the terms and history of the treaty; the practice of nations in regards to extradition treaties; the case law from the States; and the writings of commentators, and reached the following conclusion:

> "[A] person who has been brought within the jurisdiction of the court by *virtue of proceedings under an extradition treaty,* can only be tried for one of the offences described in that treaty, and for the offence with which he is charged in the proceedings for his extradition, until a reasonable time and opportunity have been given him, after his release or trial upon such charge, to return to the country from whose asylum he had been forcibly taken under those proceedings."

In addition, Justice Miller's opinion noted that any doubt as to this interpretation was put to rest by two federal statutes which imposed the doctrine of specialty upon extradition treaties to which the United States was a party. Unlike the case before us today, the defendant in *Rauscher* had been brought to the United States by way of an extradition treaty; there was no issue of a forcible abduction.

In *Ker v. Illinois*, 119 U.S. 436 (1886), also written by Justice Miller and decided the same day as *Rauscher,* we addressed the issue of a defendant brought before the court by way of a forcible abduction. Frederick Ker had been tried and convicted in an Illinois court for larceny; his presence before the court was procured by means of forcible abduction from Peru. A messenger was sent to Lima with the proper warrant to demand Ker by virtue of the extradition treaty between Peru and the United States. The messenger, however, disdained reliance on the treaty processes, and instead forcibly kidnapped Ker and brought him to the United States. We distinguished Ker's case from *Rauscher,* on the basis that Ker was not brought into the United States by virtue of the extradition treaty between the United States and Peru, and rejected Ker's argument that he had a right under the extradition treaty to be returned to this country only in accordance with its terms. We rejected Ker's due process argument more broadly, holding in line with "the highest authorities" that "such forcible abduction is no sufficient reason why the party should not answer when brought within the jurisdiction of the court which has the right to try him for such an offence, and presents no valid objection to his trial in such court." * * *

The only differences between *Ker* and the present case are that *Ker* was decided on the premise that there was no governmental involvement in the abduction; and Peru, from which Ker was abducted, did not object to his prosecution. Respondent finds these differences to be dispositive, * * * contending that they show that respondent's prosecution, like the prosecution of Rauscher, violates the implied terms of a valid extradition treaty. * * * Therefore, our first inquiry must be whether the abduction of respondent from Mexico violated the extradition treaty between the United States and Mexico. If we conclude that the Treaty does not prohibit respondent's abduction, the rule in *Ker* applies, and the court need not inquire as to how respondent came before it.

In construing a treaty, as in construing a statute, we first look to its terms to determine its meaning. *Air France v. Saks*, 470 U.S. 392, 397 (1985); *Valentine v. United States ex. rel. Neidecker*, 299 U.S. 5, 11 (1936). The Treaty says nothing about the obligations of the United States and Mexico to refrain from forcible abductions of people from the territory of the other nation, or the consequences under the Treaty if such an abduction occurs. Respondent submits that Article 22(1) of the Treaty which states that it "shall apply to offenses specified in Article 2 [including murder] committed before and after this Treaty enters into force," evidences an intent to make application of the Treaty mandatory for those offenses. However, the more natural conclusion is that Article 22 was included to ensure that the Treaty was applied to extraditions requested after the Treaty went into force, regardless of when the crime of extradition occurred.

More critical to respondent's argument is Article 9 of the Treaty which provides:

> "1. Neither Contracting Party shall be bound to deliver up its own nationals, but the executive authority of the requested Party shall, if not prevented by the laws of that Party, have the power to deliver them up if, in its discretion, it be deemed proper to do so.

> "2. If extradition is not granted pursuant to paragraph 1 of this Article, the requested Party shall submit the case to its competent authorities for the purpose of prosecution, provided that Party has jurisdiction over the offense."

According to respondent, Article 9 embodies the terms of the bargain which the United States struck: if the United States wishes to prosecute a Mexican national, it may request that individual's extradition. Upon a request from the United States, Mexico may either extradite the individual, or submit the case to the proper authorities for prosecution in Mexico. In this way, respondent reasons, each nation preserved its right to choose whether its nationals would be tried in its own courts or by the courts of the other nation. This preservation of rights would be frustrated if either nation were free to abduct nationals of the other nation for the purposes of prosecution. More broadly, respondent reasons, as did the Court of Appeals, that all the processes and restrictions on the obligation to extradite established by the Treaty would make no sense if either nation were free to resort to forcible kidnapping to gain the presence of an individual for prosecution in a manner not contemplated by the Treaty.

We do not read the Treaty in such a fashion. Article 9 does not purport to specify the only way in which one country may gain custody of a national of the other country for the purposes of prosecution. In the absence of an extradition treaty, nations are under no obligation to surrender those in their country to foreign authorities for prosecution. Extradition treaties exist so as to impose mutual obligations to surrender individuals in certain defined sets of circumstances, following established procedures. See 1 J. Moore, A Treatise on Extradition and Interstate Rendition, § 72 (1891). The Treaty thus provides a mechanism which would not otherwise exist, requiring, under certain circumstances, the United States and Mexico to extradite individuals to the other country, and establishing the procedures to be followed when the Treaty is invoked.

The history of negotiation and practice under the Treaty also fails to show that abductions outside of the Treaty constitute a violation of the Treaty. As the Solicitor General notes, the Mexican government was made aware, as early as 1906, of the *Ker* doctrine, and the United States position that it applied to forcible abductions made outside of the terms of the United States–Mexico Extradition Treaty. Nonetheless, the current version of the Treaty, signed in 1978, does not attempt to establish a rule that would in any way curtail the effect of *Ker*. Moreover, although language which would grant individuals exactly the right sought by respondent had been considered and drafted as early as 1935 by a prominent group of legal scholars sponsored by the faculty of Harvard Law School, no such clause appears in the current treaty.[13]

Thus, the language of the Treaty, in the context of its history, does not support the proposition that the Treaty prohibits abductions outside of its terms. The remaining question, therefore, is whether the Treaty should be interpreted so as to include an implied term prohibiting prosecution where the defendant's presence is obtained by means other than those established by the Treaty.

Respondent contends that the Treaty must be interpreted against the backdrop of customary international law, and that international abductions are "so clearly prohibited in international law" that there was no reason to include such a clause in the Treaty itself. The international censure of international abductions is further evidenced, according to respondent, by the United Nations Charter and the Charter of the Organization of American States. Respondent does not argue that these sources of international law provide an independent basis for the right respondent asserts not to be tried in the United States, but rather that they should inform the interpretation of the Treaty terms. * * *

Respondent and his *amici* may be correct that respondent's abduction was "shocking," and that it may be in violation of general interna-

---

13. In Article 16 of the Draft Convention on Jurisdiction with Respect to Crime, the Advisory Committee of the Research in International Law proposed:

"In exercising jurisdiction under this Convention, no State shall prosecute or punish any person who has been brought within its territory or a place subject to its authority by recourse to measures in violation of international law or international convention without first obtaining the consent of the State or States whose rights have been violated by such measures." Harvard Research in International Law, 29 Am. J. Int'l L. 442 (Supp. 1935).

tional law principles. Mexico has protested the abduction of respondent through diplomatic notes, and the decision of whether respondent should be returned to Mexico, as a matter outside of the Treaty, is a matter for the Executive Branch. We conclude, however, that respondent's abduction was not in violation of the Extradition Treaty between the United States and Mexico, and therefore the rule of *Ker v. Illinois* is fully applicable to this case. The fact of respondent's forcible abduction does not therefore prohibit his trial in a court in the United States for violations of the criminal laws of the United States.

The judgment of the Court of Appeals is therefore reversed, and the case is remanded for further proceedings consistent with this opinion.

So ordered.

JUSTICE STEVENS, with whom JUSTICE BLACKMUN and JUSTICE O'CONNOR join, dissenting.

The Court correctly observes that this case raises a question of first impression. The case is unique for several reasons. It does not involve an ordinary abduction by a private kidnaper, or bounty hunter, as in *Ker v. Illinois,* 119 U.S. 436 (1886); nor does it involve the apprehension of an American fugitive who committed a crime in one State and sought asylum in another, as in *Frisbie v. Collins,* 342 U.S. 519 (1952). Rather, it involves this country's abduction of another country's citizen; it also involves a violation of the territorial integrity of that other country, with which this country has signed an extradition treaty.

A Mexican citizen was kidnaped in Mexico and charged with a crime committed in Mexico; his offense allegedly violated both Mexican and American law. Mexico has formally demanded on at least two separate occasions[1] that he be returned to Mexico and has represented that he will be prosecuted and, if convicted, punished for his alleged offense.[2] It is clear that Mexico's demand must be honored if this official abduction violated the 1978 Extradition Treaty between the United States and Mexico. In my opinion, a fair reading of the treaty in light of our decision in *United States v. Rauscher,* 119 U.S. 407 (1886), and applicable principles of international law, leads inexorably to the conclusion that the District Court, *United States v. Caro–Quintero,* 745 F.Supp. 599

---

1. The abduction of respondent occurred on April 2, 1990. Mexico responded quickly and unequivocally. On April 18, 1990, Mexico requested an official report on the role of the United States in the abduction, and on May 16, 1990, and July 19, 1990, it sent diplomatic notes of protest from the Embassy of Mexico to the United States Department of State. See Brief for United Mexican States as *Amicus Curiae* (Mexican *Amicus*) 5–6; App. to Mexican *Amicus* 1a–24a. In the May 16th note, Mexico said that it believed that the abduction was "carried out with the knowledge of persons working for the U.S. government, in violation of the procedure established in

the extradition treaty in force between the two countries," and in the July 19th note, it requested the provisional arrest and extradition of the law enforcement agents allegedly involved in the abduction.

2. Mexico has already tried a number of members involved in the conspiracy that resulted in the murder of the DEA agent. For example, Rafael Caro–Quintero, a co-conspirator of Alvarez–Machain in this case, has already been imprisoned in Mexico on a 40–year sentence. See Brief for Lawyers Committee for Human Rights as *Amicus Curiae* 4.

(C.D.Cal.1990), and the Court of Appeals for the Ninth Circuit, 946 F.2d 1466 (1991) (*per curiam*), correctly construed that instrument.

I

The extradition treaty with Mexico is a comprehensive document containing 23 articles and an appendix listing the extraditable offenses covered by the agreement. The parties announced their purpose in the preamble: The two Governments desire "to cooperate more closely in the fight against crime and, to this end, to mutually render better assistance in matters of extradition." From the preamble, through the description of the parties' obligations with respect to offenses committed within as well as beyond the territory of a requesting party, the delineation of the procedures and evidentiary requirements for extradition, the special provisions for political offenses and capital punishment, and other details, the Treaty appears to have been designed to cover the entire subject of extradition. Thus, Article 22, entitled "Scope of Application" states that the "Treaty shall apply to offenses specified in Article 2 committed before and after this Treaty enters into force," and Article 2 directs that "[e]xtradition shall take place, subject to this Treaty, for willful acts which fall within any of [the extraditable offenses listed in] the clauses of the Appendix." Moreover, as noted by the Court, Article 9 expressly provides that neither Contracting Party is bound to deliver up its own nationals, although it may do so in its discretion, but if it does not do so, it "shall submit the case to its competent authorities for purposes of prosecution."

Petitioner's claim that the Treaty is not exclusive, but permits forcible governmental kidnaping, would transform these, and other, provisions into little more than verbiage. For example, provisions requiring "sufficient" evidence to grant extradition (Art. 3), withholding extradition for political or military offenses (Art. 5), withholding extradition when the person sought has already been tried (Art. 6), withholding extradition when the statute of limitations for the crime has lapsed (Art. 7), and granting the requested State discretion to refuse to extradite an individual who would face the death penalty in the requesting country (Art. 8), would serve little purpose if the requesting country could simply kidnap the person. As the Court of Appeals for the Ninth Circuit recognized in a related case, "[e]ach of these provisions would be utterly frustrated if a kidnapping were held to be a permissible course of governmental conduct." *United States v. Verdugo–Urquidez,* 939 F.2d 1341, 1349 (1991). In addition, all of these provisions "only make sense if they are understood as *requiring* each treaty signatory to comply with those procedures whenever it wishes to obtain jurisdiction over an individual who is located in another treaty nation."

It is true, as the Court notes, that there is no express promise by either party to refrain from forcible abductions in the territory of the other Nation. Relying on that omission, the Court, in effect, concludes that the Treaty merely creates an optional method of obtaining jurisdiction over alleged offenders, and that the parties silently reserved the right to resort to self help whenever they deem force more expeditious than legal process.[11] If the United States, for example, thought it more expedient to torture or simply to execute a person rather than to attempt extradition, these options would be equally available because they, too, were not explicitly prohibited by the Treaty.[12] That, however, is a highly improbable interpretation of a consensual agreement, which on its face appears to have been intended to set forth comprehensive and exclusive rules concerning the subject of extradition.[14] In my opinion, "the manifest scope and object of the treaty itself," *Rauscher,* 119 U.S., at 422, plainly imply a mutual undertaking to respect the territorial integrity of the other contracting party. That opinion is confirmed by a consideration of the "legal context" in which the Treaty was negotiated.[15] *Cannon v. University of Chicago,* 441 U.S. 677, 699 (1979).

II

In *Rauscher,* the Court construed an extradition treaty that was far less comprehensive than the 1978 Treaty with Mexico. The 1842 Treaty with Great Britain determined the boundary between the United States and Canada, provided for the suppression of the African slave trade, and also contained one paragraph authorizing the extradition of fugitives "in certain cases." In Article X, each Nation agreed to "deliver up to justice all persons" properly charged with any one of seven specific crimes, including murder. After Rauscher had been extradited for murder, he was charged with the lesser offense of inflicting cruel and unusual punishment on a member of the crew of a vessel on the high seas. Although the treaty did not purport to place any limit on the jurisdiction of the demanding State after acquiring custody of the fugitive, this Court held that he could not be tried for any offense other than murder. Thus, the treaty constituted the exclusive means by which the United States

11. To make the point more starkly, the Court has, in effect, written into Article 9 a new provision, which says: "Notwithstanding paragraphs 1 and 2 of this Article, either Contracting Party can, without the consent of the other, abduct nationals from the territory of one Party to be tried in the territory of the other."

12. It is ironic that the United States has attempted to justify its unilateral action based on the kidnaping, torture, and murder of a federal agent by authorizing the kidnaping of respondent, for which the American law enforcement agents who participated have now been charged by Mexico. This goes to my earlier point, that extradition treaties promote harmonious relations by providing for the orderly surrender of a person by one State to another, and without such treaties, resort to force often followed.

14. Mexico's understanding is that "[t]he extradition treaty governs comprehensively the delivery of all persons for trial in the requesting state 'for an offense committed outside the territory of the requesting Party.'" And Canada, with whom the United States also shares a large border and with whom the United States also has an extradition treaty, understands the treaty to be "the exclusive means for a requesting government to obtain . . . a removal" of a person from its territory, unless a Nation otherwise gives its consent.

15. The United States has offered no evidence from the negotiating record, ratification process, or later communications with Mexico to support the suggestion that a different understanding with Mexico was reached. See M. Bassiouni, International Extradition: United States Law and Practice Ch. 2, § 4.3, at p. 82 ("Negotiations, preparatory works, and diplomatic correspondence are an integral part of th[e] surrounding circumstances, and [are] often relied on by courts in ascertaining the intentions of the parties") (footnote omitted).

could obtain jurisdiction over a defendant within the territorial jurisdiction of Great Britain.

The Court noted that the Treaty included several specific provisions, such as the crimes for which one could be extradited, the process by which the extradition was to be carried out, and even the evidence that was to be produced, and concluded that "the fair purpose of the treaty is, that the person shall be delivered up to be tried for that offence and for no other." The Court reasoned that it did not make sense for the treaty to provide such specifics only to have the person "pas[s] into the hands of the country which charges him with the offence, free from all the positive requirements and just implications of the treaty under which the transfer of his person takes place." To interpret the treaty in a contrary way would mean that a country could request extradition of a person for one of the seven crimes covered by the treaty, and then try the person for another crime, such as a political crime, which was clearly not covered by the treaty; this result, the Court concluded, was clearly contrary to the intent of the parties and the purpose of the treaty.

Rejecting an argument that the sole purpose of Article X was to provide a procedure for the transfer of an individual from the jurisdiction of one sovereign to another, the Court stated:

"No such view of solemn public treaties between the great nations of the earth can be sustained by a tribunal called upon to give judicial construction to them.

"The opposite view has been attempted to be maintained in this country upon the ground that there is no express limitation in the treaty of the right of the country in which the offence was committed to try the person for the crime alone for which he was extradited, and that once being within the jurisdiction of that country, no matter by what contrivance or fraud or by what pretence of establishing a charge provided for by the extradition treaty he may have been brought within the jurisdiction, he is, when here, liable to be tried for any offence against the laws as though arrested here originally. This proposition of the absence of express restriction in the treaty of the right to try him for other offenses than that for which he was extradited, is met by the manifest scope and object of the treaty itself."

Thus, the Extradition Treaty, as understood in the context of cases that have addressed similar issues, suffices to protect the defendant from prosecution despite the absence of any express language in the Treaty itself purporting to limit this Nation's power to prosecute a defendant over whom it had lawfully acquired jurisdiction.

Although the Court's conclusion in *Rauscher* was supported by a number of judicial precedents, the holdings in these cases were not nearly as uniform as the consensus of international opinion that condemns one Nation's violation of the territorial integrity of a friendly neighbor.[20] It is shocking that a party to an extradition treaty might believe that it has secretly reserved the right to make seizures of citizens in the other party's territory.[21] Justice Story found it shocking enough that the United States would attempt to justify an American seizure of a foreign vessel in a Spanish port:

> "But, even supposing, for a moment, that our laws had required an entry of The Apollon, in her transit, does it follow that the power to arrest her was meant to be given, after she had passed into the exclusive territory of a foreign nation? We think not. *It would be monstrous* to suppose that our revenue officers were authorized to enter into foreign ports and territories, for the purpose of seizing vessels which had offended against our laws. It cannot be presumed that Congress would voluntarily justify such a clear violation of the laws of nations." *The Apollon,* 9 Wheat. 362, 370–371 (1824) (emphasis added).

The law of Nations, as understood by Justice Story in 1824, has not changed. Thus, a leading treatise explains:

> "A State must not perform acts of sovereignty in the territory of another State.

> "It is . . . a breach of International Law for a State to send its agents to the territory of another State to apprehend persons accused of having committed a crime. Apart from other satisfaction, the first duty of the offending State is to hand over the person in question to the State in whose territory he was apprehended." 1 Oppenheim's International Law 295, and n.1 (H. Lauterpacht 8th ed. 1955).

Commenting on the precise issue raised by this case, the chief reporter for the American Law Institute's Restatement of Foreign Relations used language reminiscent of Justice Story's characterization of an official seizure in a foreign jurisdiction as "monstrous":

> "When done without consent of the foreign government, abducting a person from a foreign country is a gross violation of international

---

20. This principle is embodied in Article 17 of the Charter of the Organization of American States, Apr. 30, 1948, 2 U.S.T. 2394, T.I.A.S. No. 2361, as amended by the Protocol of Buenos Aires, Feb. 27, 1967, 21 U.S.T. 607, T.I.A.S. No. 6847, as well as numerous provisions of the United Nations Charter, June 26, 1945, 59 Stat. 1031, T.S. No. 993 (to which both the United States and Mexico are signatories). See generally Mann, Reflections on the Prosecution of Persons Abducted in Breach of International Law, in International Law at a Time of Perplexity 407 (Y. Dinstein and M. Tabory eds. 1989).

21. When Abraham Sofaer, Legal Adviser of the State Department, was questioned at a congressional hearing, he resisted the notion that such seizures were acceptable: " 'Can you imagine us going into Paris and seizing some person we regard as a terrorist . . .? [H]ow would we feel if some foreign nation—let us take the United Kingdom—came over here and seized some terrorist suspect in New York City, or Boston, or Philadelphia, . . . because we refused through the normal channels of international, legal communications, to extradite that individual?' "Bill To Authorize Prosecution of Terrorists and Others Who Attack U.S. Government Employees and Citizens Abroad: Hearing before the Subcommittee on Security and Terrorism of the Senate Committee on the Judiciary, 99th Cong., 1st Sess., 63 (1985).

law and gross disrespect for a norm high in the opinion of mankind. It is a blatant violation of the territorial integrity of another state; it eviscerates the extradition system (established by a comprehensive network of treaties involving virtually all states)."

In the *Rauscher* case, the legal background that supported the decision to imply a covenant not to prosecute for an offense different from that for which extradition had been granted was far less clear than the rule against invading the territorial integrity of a treaty partner that supports Mexico's position in this case. If *Rauscher* was correctly decided—and I am convinced that it was—its rationale clearly dictates a comparable result in this case.

III

A critical flaw pervades the Court's entire opinion. It fails to differentiate between the conduct of private citizens, which does not violate any treaty obligation, and conduct expressly authorized by the Executive Branch of the Government, which unquestionably constitutes a flagrant violation of international law, and in my opinion, also constitutes a breach of our Treaty obligations. * * *

IV

As the Court observes at the outset of its opinion, there is reason to believe that respondent participated in an especially brutal murder of an American law enforcement agent. That fact, if true, may explain the Executive's intense interest in punishing respondent in our courts. Such an explanation, however, provides no justification for disregarding the Rule of Law that this Court has a duty to uphold.[33] That the Executive may wish to reinterpret the Treaty to allow for an action that the Treaty in no way authorizes should not influence this Court's interpretation. Indeed, the desire for revenge exerts "a kind of hydraulic pressure ... before which even well settled principles of law will bend," *Northern Securities Co. v. United States,* 193 U.S. 197, 401 (1904) (Holmes, J., dissenting), but it is precisely at such moments that we should remember and be guided by our duty "to render judgment evenly and dispassionately according to law, as each is given understanding to ascertain and apply it." *United States v. Mine Workers,* 330 U.S. 258, 342 (1947) (Rutledge, J., dissenting). The way that we perform that duty in a case of this kind sets an example that other tribunals in other countries are sure to emulate.

---

33. As Justice Brandeis so wisely urged: "In a government of laws, existence of the government will be imperilled if it fails to observe the law scrupulously. Our Government is the potent, the omnipresent teacher. For good or for ill, it teaches the whole people by its example. Crime is contagious. If the Government becomes a lawbreaker, it breeds contempt for law; it invites every man to become a law unto himself; it invites anarchy. To declare that in the administration of the criminal law the end justifies the means—to declare that the Government may commit crimes in order to secure the conviction of a private criminal—would bring terrible retribution. Against that pernicious doctrine this Court should resolutely set its face." *Olmstead v. United States,* 277 U.S. 438, 485 (1928) (Brandeis, J., dissenting).

The significance of this Court's precedents is illustrated by a recent decision of the Court of Appeal of the Republic of South Africa. Based largely on its understanding of the import of this Court's cases—including our decision in *Ker v. Illinois*—that court held that the prosecution of a defendant kidnaped by agents of South Africa in another country must be dismissed. *S v. Ebrahim*, S. Afr. L. Rep. (Apr.–June 1991).[36] The Court of Appeal of South Africa—indeed, I suspect most courts throughout the civilized world—will be deeply disturbed by the "monstrous" decision the Court announces today. For every Nation that has an interest in preserving the Rule of Law is affected, directly or indirectly, by a decision of this character. As Thomas Paine warned, an "avidity to punish is always dangerous to liberty" because it leads a nation "to stretch, to misinterpret, and to misapply even the best of laws." To counter that tendency, he reminds us:

> "He that would make his own liberty secure must guard even his enemy from oppression; for if he violates this duty he establishes a precedent that will reach to himself."

I respectfully dissent.

Notes and Questions

1. *The Aftermath of* Alvarez–Machain. Mexico declared its outrage with the *Alvarez–Machain* decision. Tim Golden, "After Court Ruling, Mexico Tells U.S. Drug Agents to Halt Activity," *New York Times*, June 16, 1992, at 19. Political leaders in the Caribbean, Latin America, Canada, Australia, and Europe also objected to the decision. See Jonathan A. Bush, "How Did We Get Here? Foreign Abduction After *Alvarez–Machain*," 45 *Stanford Law Review* 939, 941–42 & nn.11–15 (1993). The Supreme Court's judgment appeared all the more preposterous when the trial judge ultimately acquitted the Mexican doctor on the grounds that the U.S. government's evidence against him "had been based on 'hunches' and the 'wildest speculation' and had failed to support the charges that he had participated in the torture of the drug agent." Seth Mydans, "Judge Clears Mexican in Agent's Killing," *New York Times*, Dec. 15, 1992, at A20. President-elect Bill Clinton condemned *Alvarez–Machain*: "I think that in the absence of some evidence the [Mexican] government was actually taking a dive or trying to thwart us that the principle the Supreme Court articulated was way too broad." Frank J. Murray, "Clinton Hits Court's Kidnapping Decision," *The Washington Times*, Dec. 16, 1992, at A4. The *Washington Post* opined that "the U.S. government's performance was both embarrassing and badly misguided." "The Collapse of the Alvarez Case," *Washington Post*, Dec. 17, 1992, at A22. As President, Mr. Clinton promised Mexico that the United States government would not conduct any cross-border kidnapping. Steven A. Holmes, "U.S. Gives Mexico Abduction Pledge," *New York Times*, June 22, 1993, at A11. The *Alvarez–Machain* decision reportedly contributed directly to Mexi-

---

36. The South African court agreed with appellant that an "abduction represents a violation of the applicable rules of international law, that these rules are part of [South African] law, and that this violation of the law deprives the Court ... of its competence to hear [appellant's] case...."

co's rejection of U.S. assistance in combatting the illegal drug industry, and Mexico's drug arrests dropped to 9,728 in 1995, from 27,369 in 1992. Molly Moore & John Ward Anderson, "Drugs Flow as Policing is 'Mexicanized': Diminished U.S. Role Below Border Plays Into Traffickers' Hands," *Washington Post*, Sept. 8, 1996, at A1.

Following the dismissal of U.S. criminal charges against him, Dr. Alvarez–Machain filed a civil claim for damages against the U.S. government. Patrick J. McDonnell, "Doctor Kidnaped by DEA Files $20–million Claim," *Los Angeles Times*, July 10, 1993, at A21; Patrick J. McDonnell, "Scars of an Abduction," *Los Angeles Times*, Feb. 10, 1995, Metro, Pt. B, at 1. In 1996, the U.S. Court of Appeals for the Ninth Circuit ruled, *inter alia*, that Dr. Alvarez–Machain could pursue his tort claims, his claims alleging that U.S. officials violated his constitutional rights by conduct occurring in the United States, and his claims under the U.S. Torture Victim Protection Act. Alvarez–Machain v. United States, 96 F.3d 1246 (9th Cir.1996). In 1999, the U.S. District Court for the Central District of California ruled on various motions for summary judgment, and concluded that Dr. Alvarez–Machain could proceed to trial on claims of assault, battery, and intentional infliction of emotional distress arising from a U.S. agent's acts in Mexico, and on an additional claim of intentional infliction of emotional distress stemming from other alleged actions of U.S. agents in Texas. Alvarez–Machain v. United States, No. CV93–4072 (C.D.Cal.1999).

More than 20 others, however, were convicted in Mexico and the United States for participating in the DEA agent's murder; litigation concerning their trials still continues. "Man Denied New Trial in Agent's Death," *Washington Post*, Aug. 20, 1998, at A16; United States v. Zuno–Arce, 25 F.Supp.2d 1087 (C.D.Cal.1998), *aff'd*, 209 F.3d 1095 (9th Cir.2000).

2. Alvarez–Machain *and International Law*. International lawyers generally condemned the *Alvarez–Machain* judgment. Professor Louis Henkin, then President of the American Society of International Law, wrote:

> During its past term, the U.S. Supreme Court had one of its infrequent opportunities to take international law seriously and to assure that the Executive Branch takes international law seriously. The Supreme Court failed. The Attorney General was "gratified."

> * * * [T]he "victory" for the Department of Justice may prove to be pyrrhic. The judicial-executive distortion of standard extradition treaties is remediable, and our treaty partners will no doubt find their remedies. In reaction to general outrage, the United States will—at the least—have to disown that interpretation if it is to maintain its network of extradition treaties, as important to the United States as to any state in the world.

> The larger, longer question is whether the Government of the United States—all branches—is prepared to commit itself to taking international law seriously. * * *

> If the Attorney General continues to refuse to take international law seriously, if the Supreme Court refuses to compel the Department of Justice to take international law seriously, it is up to the President of the United States. * * *

If the President will not act, it will be up to Congress. The Constitution put international law in the special care of Congress when it gave to that branch the power to define offenses against the Law of Nations. * * *

Louis Henkin, "Will the U.S. Supreme Court Fail International Law?," *Newsletter of the American Society of International Law*, Aug.–Sept. 1992, at 1, 1–2. Should Congress have responded to *Alvarez–Machain* by making it a federal crime for any U.S. official to kidnap any person in violation of international law? Under Article I, § 8 of the U.S. Constitution (see Appendix), Congress has the power to "define and punish * * * Offences against the Law of Nations."

A few commentators have argued that the result in *Alvarez–Machain* could have been "saved" under international law by focusing not on the U.S.–Mexican extradition treaty and the legality of the kidnapping in Mexico, but on the legality under customary international law of trying in municipal court defendants whose presence before the court was obtained without extradition. "[T]he United States has an international obligation to foreign states not to invade their territory to obtain fugitives," and violation of that obligation may lead to the payment of reparations or even the extradition of the kidnappers to the foreign state. "But there is no obligation not to try the person." John M. Rogers, *International Law and United States Law* 177 (1999). As reflected in the text at footnote 36 of Justice Stevens's dissent, however, some authorities dispute the legality of the practice of trying fugitives abducted from abroad.

3. *The Reconciliation of Treaty and Municipal Acts.* Was *Alvarez–Machain* an example of stretching the possible interpretation of an international agreement so far to avoid conflict with a local law or act that the interpretation exceeds the limits of plausibility? Professor Bederman has criticized *Alvarez-Machain* as contributing to a "dismal picture of deference" of the Supreme Court to the executive branch's interpretation of treaties. David J. Bederman, "Deference or Deception: Treaty Rights as Political Questions," 70 *University of Colorado Law Review* 1439, 1469 (1999). Arguably, the Court's justification for its strained interpretation was to reconcile U.S. acts with U.S. international obligations. Would it be better to acknowledge that they conflict, and then choose to defer either to international law or to executive action, *e.g.*, on the grounds of judicial deference to the executive in matters of international relations?

4. *The PLO Case.* Another judgment that apparently "stretched" the interpretation of a treaty so as to avoid conflict with U.S. domestic law was United States v. Palestine Liberation Organization, 695 F.Supp. 1456 (S.D.N.Y.1988), where a U.S. district court judge ruled that the 1987 Anti–Terrorism Act would not be applied to close down the Palestine Liberation Organizations's (the "PLO") New York office because, as a Permanent Observer to the 1947 United Nations, the PLO was protected by the U.S.–U.N. Headquarters Agreement, June 26, 1947, 61 Stat. 3416, 11 U.N.T.S. 11. Rejecting the U.S. government's argument that the Anti–Terrorism Act trumped the Headquarters Agreement because of the later-in-time rule, the judge held that there was insufficient proof that Congress meant to override the treaty obligations of the United States.

The Reagan Administration was split in the aftermath of the *PLO Case*. A high Justice Department official told the *New York Times* that "[t]here is a unanimous belief in this department that the decision should be appealed," but the State Department's Legal Adviser, Abraham Sofaer, countered: "It was a grave mistake for Congress to attempt to close the P.L.O. office. It would violate the United Nations Headquarters Agreement." Clovis Maksoud, the representative of the Arab League in the United States, stated that an appeal "would erode the credibility of the United States in the Middle East." Robert Pear, "U.S. Officials Split Over Whether to Appeal Ruling on P.L.O.," *New York Times*, Aug. 28, 1988, § 1, at 5.

Finally, President Reagan himself had to resolve the dispute between Justice and State. He decided not to appeal the District Court's judgment. On August 29, 1988, the Justice Department issued the following statement: "It is the Administration's normal policy to appeal adverse District Court decisions of this kind. But it was decided, in light of foreign policy considerations, including the U.S. role as host to the United Nations organization, not to appeal in this instance." Robert Pear, "U.S. Will Allow P.L.O. to Maintain Its Office at U.N.," *New York Times*, Aug. 30, 1988, at A1.

Professor Rosalyn Higgins, now a judge on the International Court of Justice, called the *PLO Case* "a remarkable piece of judicial reasoning, at once admirably purpose-oriented but unpersuasive." Rosalyn Higgins, *Problems and Process: International Law and How We Use It* 215 (1994). Note that the court had to reconcile two competing principles of interpretation in applying international law. One was the rule in *Whitney* that in a conflict between a treaty and a statute "the one last in date will control the other." The other was also enunciated in *Whitney*, *i.e.*, "the courts will always endeavor to construe [a competing treaty and federal statute] so as to give effect to both." Is the fact that neither the President nor the Congress sought to disturb the district court's ruling dispositive of whether the judge got the legislative intent of the statute right? Or did the President and the Congress simply want to say one thing in the statute and do another in practice?

5. *The Political Question Doctrine*. U.S. courts sometimes invoke the "political question doctrine" to abstain from deciding sensitive foreign policy questions. According to Justice Powell, the doctrine involves a three-part inquiry: "(i) Does the issue involve resolution of questions committed by the text of the Constitution to a coordinate branch of Government? (ii) Would resolution of the question demand that a court move beyond areas of judicial expertise? (iii) Do prudential considerations counsel against judicial intervention?" Goldwater v. Carter, 444 U.S. 996, 998, 100 S.Ct. 533, 534, 62 L.Ed.2d 428, 428 (1979) (Powell, J., concurring). See also Baker v. Carr, 369 U.S. 186, 82 S.Ct. 691, 7 L.Ed.2d 663 (1962). In the *PLO Case* discussed in the preceding Note, the court, although acknowledging that "not all questions touching upon international relations are automatically political questions," nevertheless relied on the political question doctrine to conclude that it would not order the executive branch to arbitrate its dispute concerning the PLO mission. 695 F.Supp. at 1463. The International Court of Justice had ruled, in an advisory opinion, that arbitration of the dispute concerning the PLO mission was required under the U.S.-U.N. Headquarters Agreement. Applicability of the Obligation to Arbitrate Under Section 21 of the

United Nations Headquarters Agreement of 26 June 1947, 1988 I.C.J. 12. Why did the U.S. Supreme Court not rely on the political question doctrine in *Alvarez–Machain*?

CROSBY v. NATIONAL FOREIGN TRADE COUNCIL

530 U.S. 363, 120 S.Ct. 2288, 147 L.Ed.2d 352 (2000)

Justice Souter delivered the opinion of the Court.

The issue is whether the Burma law of the Commonwealth of Massachusetts, restricting the authority of its agencies to purchase goods or services from companies doing business with Burma, is invalid under the Supremacy Clause of the National Constitution owing to its threat of frustrating federal statutory objectives. We hold that it is.

I

In June 1996, Massachusetts adopted "An Act Regulating State Contracts with Companies Doing Business with or in Burma (Myanmar)." The statute generally bars state entities from buying goods or services from any person (defined to include a business organization) identified on a "restricted purchase list" of those doing business with Burma. Although the statute has no general provision for waiver or termination of its ban, it does exempt from boycott any entities present in Burma solely to report the news, or to provide international telecommunication goods or services, or medical supplies.

" 'Doing business with Burma' " is defined broadly to cover any person

"(a) having a principal place of business, place of corporation or its corporate headquarters in Burma (Myanmar) or having any operations, leases, franchises, majority-owned subsidiaries, distribution agreements, or any other similar agreements in Burma (Myanmar), or being the majority-owned subsidiary, licensee or franchise of such a person;

"(b) providing financial services to the government of Burma (Myanmar), including providing direct loans, underwriting government securities, providing any consulting advice or assistance, providing brokerage services, acting as a trustee or escrow agent, or otherwise acting as an agent pursuant to a contractual agreement;

"(c) promoting the importation or sale of gems, timber, oil, gas or other related products, commerce in which is largely controlled by the government of Burma (Myanmar), from Burma (Myanmar);

"(d) providing any goods or services to the government of Burma (Myanmar)."

There are three exceptions to the ban: (1) if the procurement is essential, and without the restricted bid, there would be no bids or insufficient competition; (2) if the procurement is of medical supplies;

and (3) if the procurement efforts elicit no "comparable low bid or offer" by a person not doing business with Burma, meaning an offer that is no more than 10 percent greater than the restricted bid. To enforce the ban, the Act requires petitioner Secretary of Administration and Finance to maintain a "restricted purchase list" of all firms "doing business with Burma."

In September 1996, three months after the Massachusetts law was enacted, Congress passed a statute imposing a set of mandatory and conditional sanctions on Burma. See Foreign Operations, Export Financing, and Related Programs, Appropriations Act, 1997, § 570, 110 Stat. 3009–166 to 3009–167. The federal Act has five basic parts, three substantive and two procedural.

First, it imposes three sanctions directly on Burma. It bans all aid to the Burmese Government except for humanitarian assistance, counter-narcotics efforts, and promotion of human rights and democracy. § 570(a)(1). The statute instructs United States representatives to international financial institutions to vote against loans or other assistance to or for Burma, § 570(a)(2), and it provides that no entry visa shall be issued to any Burmese government official unless required by treaty or to staff the Burmese mission to the United Nations, § 570(a)(3). These restrictions are to remain in effect "[u]ntil such time as the President determines and certifies to Congress that Burma has made measurable and substantial progress in improving human rights practices and implementing democratic government." § 570(a).

Second, the federal Act authorizes the President to impose further sanctions subject to certain conditions. He may prohibit "United States persons" from "new investment" in Burma, and shall do so if he determines and certifies to Congress that the Burmese Government has physically harmed, rearrested, or exiled Daw Aung San Suu Kyi (the opposition leader selected to receive the Nobel Peace Prize), or has committed "large-scale repression of or violence against the Democratic opposition." § 570(b). "New investment" is defined as entry into a contract that would favor the "economic development of resources located in Burma," or would provide ownership interests in or benefits from such development, § 570(f)(2), but the term specifically excludes (and thus excludes from any Presidential prohibition) "entry into, performance of, or financing of a contract to sell or purchase goods, services, or technology," *ibid.*

Third, the statute directs the President to work to develop "a comprehensive, multilateral strategy to bring democracy to and improve human rights practices and the quality of life in Burma." § 570(c). He is instructed to cooperate with members of the Association of Southeast Asian Nations (ASEAN) and with other countries having major trade and investment interests in Burma to devise such an approach, and to pursue the additional objective of fostering dialogue between the ruling State Law and Order Restoration Council (SLORC) and democratic opposition groups. *Ibid.*

As for the procedural provisions of the federal statute, the fourth section requires the President to report periodically to certain congressional committee chairmen on the progress toward democratization and better living conditions in Burma as well as on the development of the required strategy, § 570(d). And the fifth part of the federal Act authorizes the President "to waive, temporarily or permanently, any sanction [under the federal Act] ... if he determines and certifies to Congress that the application of such sanction would be contrary to the national security interests of the United States." § 570(e).

On May 20, 1997, the President issued the Burma Executive Order No. 13047, 3 CFR 202 (1997 Comp.). He certified for purposes of § 570(b) that the Government of Burma had "committed large-scale repression of the democratic opposition in Burma" and found that the Burmese Government's actions and policies constituted "an unusual and extraordinary threat to the national security and foreign policy of the United States," a threat characterized as a national emergency. The President then prohibited new investment in Burma "by United States persons," any approval or facilitation by a United States person of such new investment by foreign persons, and any transaction meant to evade or avoid the ban. The order generally incorporated the exceptions and exemptions addressed in the statute. Finally, the President delegated to the Secretary of State the tasks of working with ASEAN and other countries to develop a strategy for democracy, human rights, and the quality of life in Burma, and of making the required congressional reports.

II

Respondent National Foreign Trade Council (Council) is a nonprofit corporation representing companies engaged in foreign commerce; 34 of its members were on the Massachusetts restricted purchase list in 1998. Three withdrew from Burma after the passage of the state Act, and one member had its bid for a procurement contract increased by 10 percent under the provision of the state law allowing acceptance of a low bid from a listed bidder only if the next-to-lowest bid is more than 10 percent higher.

In April 1998, the Council filed suit in the United States District Court for the District of Massachusetts, seeking declaratory and injunctive relief against the petitioner state officials charged with administering and enforcing the state Act (whom we will refer to simply as the State). The Council argued that the state law unconstitutionally infringed on the federal foreign affairs power, violated the Foreign Commerce Clause, and was preempted by the federal Act. After detailed stipulations, briefing, and argument, the District Court permanently enjoined enforcement of the State Act, holding that it "unconstitutionally impinge[d] on the federal government's exclusive authority to regulate foreign affairs."

The United States Court of Appeals for the First Circuit affirmed on three independent grounds. It found the state Act unconstitutionally interfered with the foreign affairs power of the National Government under *Zschernig v. Miller*, 389 U.S. 429, 88 S.Ct. 664, 19 L.Ed.2d 683 (1968); violated the dormant Foreign Commerce Clause, U.S. Const. Art. I, § 8, cl. 3; and was preempted by the congressional Burma Act.

The State's petition for certiorari challenged the decision on all three grounds and asserted interests said to be shared by other state and local governments with similar measures.[5] Though opposing certiorari, the Council acknowledged the significance of the issues and the need to settle the constitutionality of such laws and regulations. We granted certiorari to resolve these important questions, and now affirm.

III

A fundamental principle of the Constitution is that Congress has the power to preempt state law. Art. VI, cl. 2; *Gibbons v. Ogden*, 9 Wheat. 1, 211, 6 L.Ed. 23 (1824); *Savage v. Jones*, 225 U.S. 501, 533, 32 S.Ct. 715, 56 L.Ed. 1182 (1912). Even without an express provision for preemption, we have found that state law must yield to a congressional Act in at least two circumstances. When Congress intends federal law to "occupy the field," state law in that area is preempted. And even if Congress has not occupied the field, state law is naturally preempted to the extent of any conflict with a federal statute. We will find preemption where it is impossible for a private party to comply with both state and federal law, and where "under the circumstances of [a] particular case, [the challenged state law] stands as an obstacle to the accomplishment and execution of the full purposes and objectives of Congress." What is a sufficient obstacle is a matter of judgment, to be informed by examining the federal statute as a whole and identifying the purpose and intended effects:

> "For when the question is whether a Federal act overrides a state law, the entire scheme of the statute must of course be considered and that which needs must be implied is of no less force than that which is expressed. If the purpose of the act cannot otherwise be accomplished—if its operation within its chosen field else must be frustrated and its provisions be refused their natural effect—the state law must yield to the regulation of Congress within the sphere of its delegated power."

Applying this standard, we see the state Burma law as an obstacle to the accomplishment of Congress's full objectives under the federal Act. We find that the state law undermines the intended purpose and "natural effect" of at least three provisions of the federal Act, that is, its delegation of effective discretion to the President to control economic sanctions against Burma, its limitation of sanctions solely to United States persons and new investment, and its directive to the President to

---

5. "At least nineteen municipal governments have enacted analogous laws restricting purchases from companies that do business in Burma."

proceed diplomatically in developing a comprehensive, multilateral strategy towards Burma.

A

First, Congress clearly intended the federal act to provide the President with flexible and effective authority over economic sanctions against Burma. Although Congress immediately put in place a set of initial sanctions (prohibiting bilateral aid, § 570(a)(1), support for international financial assistance, § 570(a)(2), and entry by Burmese officials into the United States, § 570(a)(3)), it authorized the President to terminate any and all of those measures upon determining and certifying that there had been progress in human rights and democracy in Burma. § 570(a). It invested the President with the further power to ban new investment by United States persons, dependent only on specific Presidential findings of repression in Burma. § 570(b). And, most significantly, Congress empowered the President "to waive, temporarily or permanently, any sanction [under the federal act] ... if he determines and certifies to Congress that the application of such sanction would be contrary to the national security interests of the United States." § 570(e).

This express investiture of the President with statutory authority to act for the United States in imposing sanctions with respect to the government of Burma, augmented by the flexibility to respond to change by suspending sanctions in the interest of national security, recalls Justice Jackson's observation in *Youngstown Sheet & Tube Co. v. Sawyer*, 343 U.S. 579, 635, 72 S.Ct. 863, 96 L.Ed. 1153 (1952): "When the President acts pursuant to an express or implied authorization of Congress, his authority is at its maximum, for it includes all that he possesses in his own right plus all that Congress can delegate." See also *id.*, at 635–636, n. 2, 72 S.Ct. 863 (noting that the President's power in the area of foreign relations is least restricted by Congress and citing *United States v. Curtiss–Wright Export Corp.*, 299 U.S. 304, 57 S.Ct. 216, 81 L.Ed. 255 (1936)). Within the sphere defined by Congress, then, the statute has placed the President in a position with as much discretion to exercise economic leverage against Burma, with an eye toward national security, as our law will admit. And it is just this plenitude of Executive authority that we think controls the issue of preemption here. The President has been given this authority not merely to make a political statement but to achieve a political result, and the fullness of his authority shows the importance in the congressional mind of reaching that result. It is simply implausible that Congress would have gone to such lengths to empower the President if it had been willing to compromise his effectiveness by deference to every provision of state statute or local ordinance that might, if enforced, blunt the consequences of discretionary action.

And that is just what the Massachusetts Burma law would do in imposing a different, state system of economic pressure against the Burmese political regime. * * * Quite simply, if the Massachusetts law is enforceable the President has less to offer and less economic and diplomatic leverage as a consequence. In *Dames & Moore v. Regan*, 453 U.S. 654, 101 S.Ct. 2972, 69 L.Ed.2d 918 (1981), we used the metaphor of the bargaining chip to describe the President's control of funds valuable to a hostile country; here, the state Act reduces the value of the chips created by the federal statute. It thus "stands as an obstacle to the accomplishment and execution of the full purposes and objectives of Congress."

B

Congress manifestly intended to limit economic pressure against the Burmese Government to a specific range. The federal Act confines its reach to United States persons, § 570(b), imposes limited immediate sanctions, § 570 (a), places only a conditional ban on a carefully defined area of "new investment," § 570(f)(2), and pointedly exempts contracts to sell or purchase goods, services, or technology, § 570(f)(2). These detailed provisions show that Congress's calibrated Burma policy is a deliberate effort "to steer a middle path," *Hines, supra,* at 73.

The State has set a different course, and its statute conflicts with federal law at a number of points by penalizing individuals and conduct that Congress has explicitly exempted or excluded from sanctions. While the state Act differs from the federal in relying entirely on indirect economic leverage through third parties with Burmese connections, it otherwise stands in clear contrast to the congressional scheme in the scope of subject matter addressed. It restricts all contracts between the State and companies doing business in Burma, except when purchasing medical supplies and other essentials (or when short of comparable bids). It is specific in targeting contracts to provide financial services, and general goods and services, to the Government of Burma, and thus prohibits contracts between the State and United States persons for goods, services, or technology, even though these transactions are explicitly exempted from the ambit of new investment prohibition when the President exercises his discretionary authority to impose sanctions under the federal Act. § 570(f)(2).

As with the subject of business meant to be affected, so with the class of companies doing it: the state Act's generality stands at odds with the federal discreteness. The Massachusetts law directly and indirectly imposes costs on all companies that do any business in Burma, save for those reporting news or providing international telecommunications goods or services, or medical supplies. It sanctions companies promoting the importation of natural resources controlled by the government of Burma, or having any operations or affiliates in Burma. The State Act thus penalizes companies with pre-existing affiliates or investments, all of which lie beyond the reach of the federal act's restrictions on "new investment" in Burmese economic development. §§ 570(b), 570(f)(2). The state Act, moreover, imposes restrictions on foreign companies as well as domestic, whereas the federal Act limits its reach to United States persons. * * *

C

Finally, the state Act is at odds with the President's intended authority to speak for the United States among the world's nations in developing a "comprehensive, multilateral strategy to bring democracy to and improve human rights practices and the quality of life in Burma." § 570(c). Congress called for Presidential cooperation with members of ASEAN and other countries in developing such a strategy, directed the President to encourage a dialogue between the government of Burma and the democratic opposition, and required him to report to the Congress on the progress of his diplomatic efforts, § 570(d). As with Congress's explicit delegation to the President of power over economic sanctions, Congress's express command to the President to take the initiative for the United States among the international community invested him with the maximum authority of the National Government, cf. *Youngstown Sheet & Tube Co.*, 343 U.S., at 635, 72 S.Ct. 863, in harmony with the President's own constitutional powers, U.S. Const., Art. II, § 2, cl. 2 ("[The President] shall have Power, by and with the Advice and Consent of the Senate, to make Treaties" and "shall appoint Ambassadors, other public Ministers and Consuls"); § 3 ("[The President] shall receive Ambassadors and other public Ministers"). This clear mandate and invocation of exclusively national power belies any suggestion that Congress intended the President's effective voice to be obscured by state or local action.

Again, the state Act undermines the President's capacity, in this instance for effective diplomacy. It is not merely that the differences between the state and federal Acts in scope and type of sanctions threaten to complicate discussions; they compromise the very capacity of the President to speak for the Nation with one voice in dealing with other governments. We need not get into any general consideration of limits of state action affecting foreign affairs to realize that the President's maximum power to persuade rests on his capacity to bargain for the benefits of access to the entire national economy without exception for enclaves fenced off willy-nilly by inconsistent political tactics. When such exceptions do qualify his capacity to present a coherent position on behalf of the national economy, he is weakened, of course, not only in dealing with the Burmese regime, but in working together with other nations in hopes of reaching common policy and "comprehensive" strategy. Cf. *Dames & Moore*, 453 U.S., at 673–674, 101 S.Ct. 2972.

While the threat to the President's power to speak and bargain effectively with other nations seems clear enough, the record is replete with evidence to answer any skeptics. First, in response to the passage of the state Act, a number of this country's allies and trading partners filed formal protests with the National Government, see 181 F.3d, at 47 (noting protests from Japan, the European Union (EU), and ASEAN), including an official *Note Verbale* from the EU to the Department of State protesting the state Act. EU officials have warned that the state Act "could have a damaging effect on bilateral EU–US relations." Hugo Paemen, Ambassador, European Union, Delegation of the European

Commission, to William F. Weld, Governor, State of Massachusetts, Jan. 23, 1997.

Second, the EU and Japan have gone a step further in lodging formal complaints against the United States in the World Trade Organization (WTO), claiming that the state Act violates certain provisions of the Agreement on Government Procurement, and the consequence has been to embroil the National Government for some time now in international dispute proceedings under the auspices of the WTO. In their brief before this Court, EU officials point to the WTO dispute as threatening relations with the United States, and note that the state Act has become the topic of "intensive discussions" with officials of the United States at the highest levels, those discussions including exchanges at the twice yearly EU–U.S. Summit.

Third, the Executive has consistently represented that the state Act has complicated its dealings with foreign sovereigns and proven an impediment to accomplishing objectives assigned it by Congress. Assistant Secretary of State Larson, for example, has directly addressed the mandate of the federal Burma law in saying that the imposition of unilateral state sanctions under the state Act "complicates efforts to build coalitions with our allies" to promote democracy and human rights in Burma. A. Larson, State and Local Sanctions: Remarks to the Council of State Governments 5 (Dec. 8, 1998). "[T]he EU's opposition to the Massachusetts law has meant that U.S. Government high level discussions with EU officials often have focused not on what to do about Burma, but on what to do about the Massachusetts Burma law." This point has been consistently echoed in the State Department:

> "While the [Massachusetts sanctions on Burma] were adopted in pursuit of a noble goal, the restoration of democracy in Burma, these measures also risk shifting the focus of the debate with our European Allies away from the best way to bring pressure against the State Law and Order Restoration Council (SLORC) to a potential WTO dispute over its consistency with our international obligations. Let me be clear. We are working with Massachusetts in the WTO dispute settlement process. But we must be honest in saying that the threatened WTO case risks diverting United States' and Europe's attention from focusing where it should be—on Burma."

This evidence in combination is more than sufficient to show that the state Act stands as an obstacle in addressing the congressional obligation to devise a comprehensive, multilateral strategy. * * *

In this case, repeated representations by the Executive Branch supported by formal diplomatic protests and concrete disputes are more than sufficient to demonstrate that the state Act stands in the way of Congress's diplomatic objectives. * * *

V

Because the state Act's provisions conflict with Congress's specific delegation to the President of flexible discretion, with limitation of sanctions to a limited scope of actions and actors, and with direction to develop a comprehensive, multilateral strategy under the federal Act, it is preempted, and its application is unconstitutional, under the Supremacy Clause.

The judgment of the Court of Appeals for the First Circuit is affirmed.

It is so ordered.

Notes and Questions

1. Crosby *and American Federalism.* The *Crosby* judgment was rendered in a period when concerns of federalism again were controversial in U.S. law. Some commentators have argued that nowadays it is more appropriate for states to take a larger role in international politics. See Joel P. Trachtman, "Nonactor States in U.S. Foreign Relations," 92 *American Society of International Law Proceedings* 350 (1998); Curtis A. Bradley, "The Treaty Power and American Federalism," 97 *Michigan Law Review* 390 (1998). Most, however, have supported the long-standing position that the United States should speak with one voice in foreign affairs. See Brannon P. Denning & Jack H. McCall, Jr., "The Constitutionality of State and Local 'Sanctions' Against Foreign Countries: Affairs of State, States' Affairs, or a Sorry State of Affairs?," 26 *Hastings Constitutional Law Quarterly* 307 (1999); Martin S. Flaherty, "Are We to be a Nation? Federal Power vs. 'States' Rights' in Foreign Affairs," 70 *University of Colorado Law Review* 1277 (1999). *Crosby* put a unanimous Supreme Court, as well as the district court judge and the three judges on the First Circuit, on the side of the traditionalists. Note the Court's references to, *inter alia, Curtiss–Wright* and *Dames & Moore.* Is there much left to the academic argument for more say for the states in regulating foreign trade? If *Crosby* had not struck down the Massachusetts Burma Law, would other nations, *e.g.,* the European Union and Japan, then have retaliated against Massachusetts by discouraging investment there and punishing Massachusetts companies? Would that have made the Massachusetts legislature change its stand?

2. Crosby *and* Alvarez–Machain. Compare *Crosby* and *Alvarez–Machain.* Why has the Supreme Court followed traditional case law and doctrine in *Crosby,* but not in *Alvarez–Machain?* Are the two judgments similar in that both are deferential to the power of the federal government's political branches, the President and Congress, in foreign affairs?

3. *The Grounds of the* Crosby *Judgment.* The Supreme Court in *Crosby* chose to base its holding on only one of the three grounds propounded by the First Circuit. In the words of Justice Souter, the Massachusetts Burma Law: "is invalid under the supremacy clause of the National Constitution owing to its threat of frustrating federal statutory objectives." Would the Supreme Court have invalidated the Massachusetts Burma Law without the federal Burma Act? Would either of the First Circuit's other two grounds—unconstitutional interference with the foreign affairs power of the federal government or violation of the dormant Foreign Commerce Clause—have been sufficient? Given the many federal laws relating to international trade, is

there much room left for state regulation regardless of any eventual Supreme Court judgment relating to the other two grounds of the First Circuit?

B. CUSTOMARY INTERNATIONAL LAW IN MUNICIPAL LAW

RESPUBLICA v. DE LONGCHAMPS

Court of Oyer and Terminer at Philadelphia,
1 U.S. (1 Dall.) 111, 1 L.Ed. 59 (1784).

CHARLES JULIAN DE LONGCHAMPS, commonly called the *Chevalier de Longchamps*, was indicted, that "he, on the 17th of May 1784, in the dwelling-house of his excellency the French minister plenipotentiary, in the presence of Francis Barbe Marbois, unlawfully and insolently did threaten and menace bodily harm and violence to the person of the said Francis Barbe Marbois, he being consul-general of France to the United States, consul for the state of Pennsylvania, Secretary of the French legation &c. resident in the house aforesaid, and under the protection of the law of nations and this commonwealth." And that "afterwards, to wit on the 19th of May, in the public street, &c., he, said Charles Julian de Longchamps, unlawfully, premeditatedly and violently, in and upon the person of the said Francis Barbe Marbois, under the protection of the laws of the nations, and in the peace of this commonwealth, then and there being, an assault did make, and him, the said Francis Barbe Marbois unlawfully and violently did strike and otherwise, &c., in violation of the laws of nations, against the peace and dignity of the United States and of the commonwealth of Pennsylvania."—To these charges, the defendant pleaded not guilty.

The evidence in support of the first count, was, that on the 17th of May, de Longchamps went to the house of the minister of France, and after some conversation with Monsieur Marbois, was heard to exclaim in a loud and menacing tone, "*Je vous deshonnerera, Policon, Coquin,*" addressing himself to that gentleman. That the noise being heard by the minister, he repaired to the room from which it issued, and that, in his presence, the defendant repeated the insult offered to Monsieur Marbois, in nearly the same terms.

In support of the second count, it appeared, that de Longchamps and Monsieur Marbois, having met in Market street, near the coffee-house, entered into a long conversation, in the course of which, the latter said, that he would complain to the civil authority, and the former replied, "you are a blackguard." The witnesses generally deposed, that de Longchamps struck the cane of Monsieur Marbois, before that gentleman used any violent gestures, or even appeared incensed; but that as soon as the stroke was given, Monsieur Marbois employed his stick with great severity, until the spectators interfered and separated the parties. One of the witnesses, indeed, said, that previously to engaging with their canes, he observed the two gentlemen, at the same instant, lay their hands on each others shoulders, in a manner so gentle, that he, who had heard it was customary among the French to part with mutual salutations, imagined a ceremony of that kind was about to take place, and was surprised to see de Longchamps step back, and strike the cane of Monsieur Marbois.

On the part of the defendant, evidence was produced of his having served with honour in the French armies, and his commission of sub-brigadier in the dragoons of Noailles, was read. It appeared, that the occasion of his calling on Monsieur Marbois, was to obtain authentications of these, and some other papers relative to his family, his rank in France, and his military promotions, in order to refute several publications, which had been made in the newspapers, injurious to his character and pretensions. The refusal of Monsieur Marbois to grant the authentications required, was the ground of de Longchamps' resentment, and the immediate cause of his menaces at the minister's house. * * *

McKean, Chief Justice.—This is a case of the first impression in the United States. It must be determined on the principles of the laws of nations, which form a part of the municipal law of Pennsylvania; and, if the offenses charged in the indictment have been committed, there can be no doubt, that those laws have been violated. The words used in the minister's house (which is to be considered as a foreign domicil, where the minister resides in full representation of his sovereign, and where the laws of the state do not extend), may be compared to the same words applied to the Judges in a court of justice, where they sit in representation of the majesty of the people of Pennsylvania. In that case, the offender would be immediately committed to jail, without the preliminary process of an indictment by a grand jury; and, in the case before us, if the offender is convicted, he may certainly be punished by fine and imprisonment.

In actions of slander, words were formerly construed in the mildest sense they would admit; but reason has superceded such forced interpretations, and words are now to be taken according to their ordinary import and meaning. Those expressed by the defendant are evidently of a tendency so opprobrious and violent, that they cannot fail to aggravate the outrage which has been committed.

As to the assault, this is, perhaps, one of that kind, in which the insult is more to be considered, than the actual damage; for, though no great bodily pain is suffered by a blow on the palm of the hand, or the skirt of the coat, yet these are clearly within the legal definition of assault and battery, and among gentlemen, too often, induce duelling, and terminate in murder. As, therefore, anything attached to the person, partakes of its inviolability; de Longchamps' striking Monsieur Marbois' cane, is a sufficient justification of that gentleman's subsequent conduct. * * *

Charles Julian de Longchamps: You have been indicted for unlawfully and violently threatening and menacing bodily harm and violence to the person of the Honorable Francis Barbe de Marbois, secretary to the legation from France, and consul-general of France to the United States of America, in the mansion-house of the minister plenipotentiary of France; and for an assault and battery committed upon the said secretary and consul, in a public street in the City of Philadelphia. To this Indictment you have pleaded, that you were not guilty, and for trial put yourself upon the country; an unbiased jury, upon a fair trial, and clear evidence, have found you guilty.

These offenses having been thus legally ascertained and fixed upon you, his Excellency the President, and the Honorable the Supreme Executive Council, attentive to the honor and interest of this state, were pleased to inform the judges of this court, as they had frequently done before, that the minister of France had earnestly repeated a demand, that you, having appeared in his house in the uniform of a French regiment, and having called yourself an officer in the troops of his Majesty, should be delivered up to him for these outrages, as a Frenchman to be sent to France; and wished us in this stage of your prosecution, to take into mature consideration, and in the most solemn manner to determine:—

1. Whether you could be legally delivered up by council, according to the claim made by the late minister of France?

2. If you could not be thus legally delivered up, whether your offenses in violation of the law of nations, being now ascertained and verified according to the laws of this commonwealth, you ought not to be imprisoned, until his most Christian Majesty shall declare, that the reparation is satisfactory?

3. If you can be imprisoned, whether any legal act can be done by council, for causing you to be so imprisoned?

To these questions we have given the following answers in writing:—* * *

"1. And as to the first question, we answer, That it is our opinion, that, in this case, Charles Julian de Longchamps cannot be legally delivered up by council, according to the claim made by the minister of France. Though, we think, cases may occur, where council could, *pro bono publico*, and to prevent atrocious offenders evading punishment, deliver them up to the justice of the country to which they belong, or where the offenses were committed.

"2. Punishments must be inflicted in the same county where the criminals were tried and convicted, unless the record of the attainder be removed into the supreme court, which may award execution in the county where it sits; they must be such as the laws expressly prescribe; or where no stated or fixed judgment is directed, according to the legal discretion of the court; but judgments must be certain and definite in all respects. Therefore, we conclude, that the defendant cannot be imprisoned, until his most Christian Majesty shall declare that the reparation is satisfactory.

"3. The answer to the last question is rendered unnecessary by the above answer to the second question."

The foregoing answers having been given, it only remains for the court to pronounce sentence upon you. This sentence must be governed by a due consideration of the enormity and dangerous tendency of the offenses you have committed, of the willfulness, deliberation, and malice, wherewith they were done, of the quality and degree of the offended and offender, the provocation given, and all other circumstances which may any way aggravate or extenuate the guilt.

The first crime in the indictment is an infraction of the law of nations. This law, in its full extent, is part of the law of this state, and is to be collected from the practice of different nations, and the authority of writers. The person of a public minister is sacred and inviolable. Whoever offers any violence to him, not only affronts the sovereign he represents, but also hurts the common safety and well-being of nations—he is guilty of a crime against the whole world.

All the reasons, which establish the independency and inviolability of the person of a minister, apply likewise to secure the immunities of his house. It is to be defended from all outrage; it is under a peculiar protection of the laws; to invade its freedom, is a crime against the state and all other nations.

The *comites* of a minister, or those of his train, partake also of his inviolability. The independency of a minister extends to all his household; these are so connected with him, that they enjoy his privileges and follow his fate. The secretary to the embassy has his commission from the sovereign himself; he is the most distinguished character in the suite of a public minister, and is in some instances considered as a kind of public minister himself. Is it not, then, an extraordinary insult, to use threats of bodily harm to his person, in the domicil of the minister plenipotentiary? If this is tolerated, his freedom of conduct is taken away, the business of his sovereign cannot be transacted, and his dignity and grandeur will be tarnished.

You then have been guilty of an atrocious violation of the law of nations; you have grossly insulted gentlemen, the peculiar objects of this law (gentlemen of amiable characters, and highly esteemed by the government of this state), in a most wanton and unprovoked manner: and it is now the interest as well as duty of the government, to animadvert upon your conduct with a becoming severity—such a severity as may tend to reform yourself, to deter others from the commission of the like crime, preserve the honor of the state, and maintain peace with our great and good ally, and the whole world. * * *

Upon the whole THE COURT, after a most attentive consideration of every circumstance in this case, do award, and direct me to pronounce the following sentence:—

That you pay a fine of 100 French crowns to the commonwealth; that you be imprisoned until the 4th day of July 1786, which will make a little more than two years imprisonment in the whole; that you then give good security to keep the peace, and be of good behaviour to all public ministers, secretaries to embassies, and consuls, as well as to all the liege people of Pennsylvania, for the space of seven years, by entering into a recognisance, yourself in a thousand pounds, and two securities in 500 pounds each: that you pay the costs of this prosecution, and remain committed until this sentence be complied with.

Notes and Questions

1. *The Law of Nations in Municipal Law.* The *de Longchamps Case* preceded the establishment of the federal judiciary. McKean, Chief Justice of Pennsylvania, recited Blackstone's familiar eighteenth-century formula of the English common law: "the law of nations * * * forms a part of the municipal law." The doctrine of the incorporation of the law of nations into the common law predated the Constitution and the Supremacy Clause of Article VI. What are we to make of the fact that the Supremacy Clause mentions treaties but not the law of nations? Was or is the law of nations the same as customary international law?

2. *The Political Context.* Would American sovereignty have been imperilled if the new United States had delivered up de Longchamps to be shipped off to France as was sought by the French Minister? Or if the United States had imprisoned de Longchamps for so long as the French King should dictate? Was it politically useful to rely on the law of nations in refusing the French requests? The Marbois-de Longchamps affair was a cause of concern among leading Americans, including Benjamin Franklin, George Washington, Thomas Jefferson, James Madison, John Adams, James Monroe, John Jay, Benjamin Harrison, and Charles Pinckney. See William R. Casto, "The Federal Courts' Protective Jurisdiction Over Torts Committed in Violation of the Law of Nations," 18 *Connecticut Law Review* 467, 492 n.143 (1986). A little over a week after de Longchamps assaulted Marbois, Thomas Jefferson wrote to James Madison to complain that Pennsylvania was "so indecisive" in taking steps with respect to the case: "They have not yet declared what they can or will do.... The affair is represented to Congress who will have the will but not the power to interpose. It will probably go next to France and bring on serious consequences." Letter of May 25, 1784, *quoted in id.* at 493 n.146. The *de Longchamps Case* provided ammunition for those favoring the creation of a federal judiciary under the U.S. Constitution with jurisdiction to hear cases involving foreign citizens.

3. *Crimes in Violation of the Law of Nations.* Was it fair to de Longchamps that he should be subjected to a fine of 100 French crowns and more than two years' imprisonment for an infraction of the law of nations, a law "collected from the practice of different nations, and the authority of writers"? How certain was that law? Should the law have been found in some specific statute of the United States or Pennsylvania? After United States v. Hudson & Goodwin, 11 U.S. (7 Cranch) 32, 3 L.Ed. 259 (1812), and United States v. Coolidge, 14 U.S. (1 Wheat.) 415, 4 L.Ed. 124 (1816), the doctrine of "common law crimes" lost favor. Defendants today are prosecuted in the United States only for violations of criminal statutes.

A criminal statute, however, may define a crime by explicitly incorporating the law of nations. For example, 18 U.S.C. § 1651 applies to anyone who, "on the high seas, commits the crime of piracy as defined by the law of nations, and is afterwards brought into or found in the United States." In United States v. Smith, 18 U.S. (5 Wheat.) 153, 5 L.Ed. 57 (1820), Justice Story found this statute sufficiently definite to support the conviction and execution of several men for the crime of piracy. See *Smith* in Chapter 3.

AMERADA HESS v. ARGENTINE REPUBLIC

830 F.2d 421 (2d Cir.1987), *reversed on other grounds,*
488 U.S. 428, 109 S.Ct. 683, 102 L.Ed.2d 818 (1989).

[The issue before the court was whether a federal district court could exercise subject matter jurisdiction over Argentina under the Alien Tort Statute, which establishes district court jurisdiction over "any civil action by an alien for a tort only, committed in violation of the law of nations or a treaty of the United States." See *Filartiga* in Chapter 1. Argentina argued that the U.S. Foreign Sovereign Immunities Act (FSIA) was the only statute that could be used to establish jurisdiction over a foreign government.]

FEINBERG, CHIEF JUDGE: * * *

I. BACKGROUND

Because the district court dismissed [the] complaint for lack of jurisdiction, we must accept appellants' allegations as true. In 1977, Amerada [Hess Shipping Corporation] entered a long-term time-charter agreement with United [Carriers, Inc.] for use of the oil tanker HERCULES. Amerada used HERCULES to carry oil from Alaska, around the southern tip of South America, to its refinery in the United States Virgin Islands. This route took HERCULES near the area in the South Atlantic where, in April 1982, an armed conflict began between Argentina and the United Kingdom that became known in this country as the Falklands War.

On May 25, 1982, HERCULES embarked from the Virgin Islands, without cargo but fully fueled, headed for Alaska. On June 3, in an effort to protect United States interest ships, the United States Maritime Administration telexed to both the United Kingdom and Argentina a list of United States flag vessels and United States interest Liberian tankers (like HERCULES) that would be traversing the South Atlantic, to ensure that these neutral vessels would not be attacked. The list included HERCULES.

By June 8, HERCULES was about 600 nautical miles off the Argentine coast and nearly 500 miles from the Falkland Islands, in international waters, well outside the "exclusion zones" declared by the warring parties. That afternoon, HERCULES was attacked without warning in three different strikes by Argentine aircraft using bombs and air-to-surface rockets.

Following these attacks, HERCULES, damaged but not destroyed, headed for safe refuge in the port of Rio de Janeiro, Brazil. Although HERCULES arrived safely in Brazil, her deck and hull had both suffered extensive damage, and a bomb that had penetrated her side remained undetonated in one of her tanks. Following an investigation by the Brazilian navy, United determined that it would be unreasonably hazardous to attempt removal of the undetonated bomb. Accordingly, on July 20, 1982, approximately 250 miles off the Brazilian coast, HERCU-LES was scuttled. United's loss on the sunken ship is claimed at $10,000,000 and Amerada's loss on the fuel that went down with the ship is claimed at $1,901,259.07.

Following a series of unsuccessful attempts to receive a hearing of their claims by the Argentine government or to retain Argentine attorneys to prosecute their claims in the courts of that country, appellants filed their suits in the district court. The district court found that a "foreign state is subject to jurisdiction in the courts of this nation if, and only if, an FSIA exception empowers the court to hear the case." Concluding that no FSIA exception covered these facts, the district court dismissed the suits for lack of jurisdiction. This consolidated appeal followed.

II. Violation of International Law

The facts alleged by appellants, if proven, would constitute a clear violation of international law. * * *

International treaties and conventions dating at least as far back as the last century recognize the right of a neutral ship to free passage on the high seas. Broad international recognition of the rights of neutrals can be found in paragraph 3 of The Declaration of Paris of 1856: "Neutral goods, with the exception of contraband of war, are not liable to capture under enemy's flag."

A more contemporary statement of the international concern and accord on this issue may be found in The Geneva Convention on the High Seas of 1958 (Convention on the High Seas), to which both Argentina and the United States were signatories. The Convention on the High Seas maps the general usage and practice of nations with regard to the rights of neutral ships in time of war. Article 22 of that treaty states that a warship encountering a foreign merchant vessel on the high seas may not board her without grounds for suspecting her of engaging in piracy, or the slave trade, or traveling under false colors. Even when there are grounds for such suspicion, the proper course is to investigate by sending an officer to inspect the ship's documents or even to board her, not to commence an attack. If such inspection fails to support the suspicions, the merchant vessel shall "be compensated for any loss or damage that may have been sustained." Article 23 of the Convention on the High Seas makes similar provisions for aircraft that have grounds to suspect a neutral vessel. Clearly, Argentina's alleged conduct in this case, bombing HERCULES and refusing compensation, violates the Convention on the High Seas. More recently, the Law of the Sea Convention of 1982 explicitly incorporated these provisions into its text. Argentina is a signatory to the Law of the Sea Convention and the United States has endorsed the relevant sections of it.

Other international accords adopted by the United States supporting a similar view of the rights of neutral ships include The London Naval Conference of 1909, the International Convention Concerning the Rights and Duties of Neutral Powers in Naval War (Hague Convention, 1907) and the Pan–American Convention Relating to Maritime Neutrality of 1928, to which Argentina was a signatory. No agreement has been called to our attention that would cast doubt on this line of authority.

As to "judicial decisions recognizing or enforcing" the rights of neutral ships on the high seas, federal courts have recognized in a variety of contexts that attacking a merchant ship without warning or seizing a neutral's goods on the high seas requires restitution. See, e.g., *Talbot v. Jansen,* 3 U.S. (3 Dall.) 133, 161, 1 L.Ed. 540 (1795); *The Lusitania,* 251 F.715, 732–36 (S.D.N.Y.1918) (dictum); cf. The I'm Alone (Canada v. United States), 3 U.N. Rep.Int.Arb.Awards 1609 (1933). Similarly, the academic literature on the rights of neutrals is of one voice with regard to a neutral's right of passage. See, e.g., Rappaport, "Freedom of the Seas," 2 Encyclopedia of Amer.For.Policy 387 (1978); Restatement of Foreign Relations Law of the United States (Revised) § 521 reporters' note 1, § 522 (Tent.Draft No. 6 1985).

In short, it is beyond controversy that attacking a neutral ship in international waters, without proper cause for suspicion or investigation, violates international law. Indeed, the relative paucity of cases regarding this customary rule of international law underscores the longstanding nature of this aspect of freedom of the high seas. Where the attacker has refused to compensate the neutral, such action is analogous to piracy, one of the earliest recognized violations of international law. See 4 W. Blackstone, Commentaries 68, 72. Argentina has cited no contrary authority.

[The court examines the Alien Tort Statute and the Foreign Sovereign Immunities Act, concluding that both statutes provide grounds for subject matter jurisdiction over Argentina.]

Notes and Questions

1. *The Foreign Sovereign Immunities Act and the Supreme Court's Reversal.* The Supreme Court overruled the decision of the Second Circuit in *Amerada Hess,* holding that the Foreign Sovereign Immunities Act of 1976 provides the sole basis for suing foreign government and that no exception in the FSIA gave Amerada Hess and United Carriers the right to sue Argentina in this case. 488 U.S. 428, 109 S.Ct. 683, 102 L.Ed.2d 818 (1989). The Supreme Court, however, did not need to rule and did not rule on the alleged violation of customary international law by Argentina. Accordingly, the Second Circuit's reasoning on the laws of neutral shipping was not reviewed by the high court. Excerpts from the Supreme Court's opinion appear in Chapter 12.

2. *A Proper Forum?* The Second Circuit seemed concerned that Amerada Hess and United Carriers have some forum to hear their claim. It was alleged that Argentine lawyers refused to bring the claim in Argentine courts for fear of reprisal and that the U.S. government for political reasons chose not to prosecute the claim diplomatically against Argentina, especially after the United States sided with the United Kingdom in the Falklands War. If U.S. courts, as well as Argentine courts and U.S. diplomacy, were closed to plaintiffs, where else could they pursue their action?

As a matter of policy, were U.S. courts the proper fora for this dispute? Plaintiffs here were Liberian subsidiaries of U.S. corporations. Should the U.S. have been more or less responsible for providing a forum for the claims if the plaintiffs had been themselves U.S. corporations? Did it matter in *de Longchamps* that neither plaintiff nor defendant was a U.S. citizen?

3. *The Roles of Customary International Law in U.S. Municipal Law.* The relationship between customary international law and U.S. municipal law was also explored in two cases already considered, Filartiga v. Pena–Irala, 630 F.2d 876 (2d Cir.1980) (in Chapter 1), and The Paquete Habana, 175 U.S. 677, 20 S.Ct. 290, 44 L.Ed. 320 (1900) (in Chapter 3). In *Filartiga*, as in the Second Circuit's opinion in *Amerada Hess*, the court looked to customary international law because it was construing a U.S. statute that expressly referred to the "law of nations." In *The Paquete Habana*, the Supreme Court derived the rule of decision directly from customary international law, even though no U.S. statute referred to it. It is *The Paquete Habana* where the famous quote, "International law is part of our law," appears. How should U.S. courts today use customary international law when no statute expressly requires its application? The doctrine that the law of nations or customary international law is part of the common law of the United States is discussed in Mark W. Janis, *An Introduction to International Law* 102–08 (3d ed. 1999), Louis Henkin, "International Law as Law in the United States," 82 *Michigan Law Review* 1555 (1984), and Harold G. Maier, "The Authoritative Sources of Customary International Law in the United States," 10 *Michigan Journal of International Law* 450 (1989). Assertions that the United States should no longer incorporate customary international law, see Curtis A. Bradley & Jack L. Goldsmith, "Customary International Law as Federal Common Law: A Critique of the Modern Position," 110 *Harvard Law Review* 815 (1997), have met stiff resistance on both historical and policy grounds. See Harold Hongju Koh, "Commentary: Is International Law Really State Law?," 111 *Harvard Law Review* 1824 (1998); Jordan J. Paust, "Customary International Law and Human Rights Treaties *Are* Law of the United States," 20 *Michigan Journal of International Law* 301 (1999).

U.S. courts have long maintained that they should seek to interpret U.S. statutes in ways consistent with the United States' international obligations. See Murray v. The Charming Betsy, 6 U.S. (2 Cranch) 64, 2 L.Ed. 208 (1804). Should the use of customary international law as an aid in construing a statute be as problematic for a U.S. judge as the use of customary international law as a rule of decision?

4. *Foreign Relations Law.* Rules affecting relations among states or among nationals of different states come under a variety of different names.

In English, "international law" is the most ordinary term, but "the law of nations," "transnational law," "universal law," "the common law of mankind," and "the law of the world public order" also appear. Yet another appellation is "foreign relations law," the term adopted by the American Law Institute.

The 1988 ALI *Restatement of the Foreign Relations Law of the United States* defines "foreign relations law" as:

(a) international law as it applies to the United States in its relations with other states; and

(b) domestic law that has substantial significance for the foreign relations of the United States or has other substantial international consequences.

The first part of the ALI definition treats international law in a more or less traditional sense, albeit limited to rules applicable to the United States. The second part has to do, *inter alia*, with the incorporation of treaties and customary international law into U.S. law, but it also concerns the separation of foreign relations power among the three branches of the federal government. Professors Franck and Glennon define "the law of foreign relations" as having for its subject "the conduct of United States foreign relations and the constitutional distribution of powers, prerogatives and rights within the nation." Thomas M. Franck & Michael J. Glennon, *Foreign Relations and National Security Law* v (2d ed. 1993).

Chapter 5

INTERNATIONAL
DISPUTE SETTLEMENT

The process of interpreting, applying, and enforcing international law involves not only municipal courts but occasionally various forms of international dispute settlement procedures. In this chapter, we introduce both public international arbitration and the one more or less universal international court, the International Court of Justice (ICJ), and its predecessors. Our story begins with the Permanent Court of Arbitration (PCA), established in 1899 in The Hague. The PCA was followed by the Permanent Court of International Justice (PCIJ) in 1921, and the ICJ in 1945. The ICJ and its predecessors have never had a heavy caseload: two, three, or four adjudicated cases a year have been typical. However, these decided cases have been a very influential source of international law in the 20th century.

While reading the cases excerpted below, keep in mind the question: when and why do states agree to submit disputes to international arbitration or adjudication? As infrequent as such submissions are, there is no doubt that governments sometimes do wish for their disagreements to be settled by international arbiters or judges. What makes an international dispute "court-friendly" or "court-unfriendly"? An intelligent answer to this question might help us determine not only what international disputes are likely to go to formal international dispute settlement procedures but also which international decisions once rendered will be respected by states in practice.

A. PUBLIC INTERNATIONAL ARBITRATION

RICHARD NED LEBOW, "ACCIDENTS AND CRISES: THE DOGGER BANK AFFAIR"
31 *Naval War College Review*, No. 1, at 66 (Summer 1978).

Russian expansion into Manchuria in the latter part of the 19th century brought her into conflict with Japan. Russian penetration of Korea, which directly challenged Japan's economic and political primacy in that country, brought the conflict to a head. St. Petersburg's intransigence made a mockery of negotiations and Japan broke relations with Russia on 8 February 1904.

That very morning Japanese torpedo boats and destroyers launched a daring surprise attack against the Russian Pacific Squadron in its moorings at Port Arthur. The attack was followed up the next day by a long-range naval bombardment of the Russian anchorage. When the smoke had cleared the Japanese Navy was supreme in the Far East. They inflicted a further defeat upon the Russians at Chemulpo in August. On land, the Japanese were equally successful. Their army moved into Manchuria and forced the Russians to retreat down the Liaotung Peninsula. By 14 May they had invested Port Arthur.

The relief of Port Arthur became Moscow's most urgent objective. General Kuropatkin, the Russian Commander–in–Chief, ordered the navy to ready its idle Baltic Fleet for service in the Pacific. Departure of the armada awaited completion of four new battleships, during which time the Baltic Fleet, considered to be the least seaworthy component of the navy, received special training. The deteriorating military situation in the Far East forced Admiral Rozhestvensky to cut his training exercises short and on 14 October 1904 the 42 ships of the hastily assembled Second Pacific Squadron departed the Baltic port of Libau for the 10,000 mile journey to Port Arthur.

As the fleet steamed through the Baltic it was warned to be on the lookout for Japanese torpedo boats disguised as trawlers which were planning an ambush somewhere between The Skaw and English Channel. This far-fetched notion had gained credence in St. Petersburg because of the reports of a Captain Hartling, sent to Copenhagen sometime earlier to organize a Russian counterintelligence network. Hartling's agents, anxious to justify their expense, had reported the existence of suspicious vessels in isolated Danish and Norwegian harbors. Rumors of a Japanese "suicide squadron" had also been picked up by the European press which speculated about the effect of Britain's assumed collusion with her Japanese ally upon Anglo–Russian relations.

According to all reports the prospect of a torpedo attack reduced Admiral Rozhestvensky, a man with no command experience, to a state of extreme anxiety. He doubled all watches, arranged to have searchlights sweep the surrounding sea at night and instructed guncrews to remain by their stations around the clock. The admiral ordered that "No vessel of any sort whatsoever must be allowed to get in amongst the fleet." Approaching merchantmen were warned away, often by a shot across their bows. Tension rose on the evening of 20 October, following receipt of a warning that unidentified torpedo boats had departed from secret bases in Norway. Later that night, *Navarin* reported sighting enemy reconnaissance balloons.

The expected attack failed to materialize and as morning broke the fleet steamed into the North Sea, ominously shrouded by fog. More alarming intelligence came in during the day warning of floating mines and trawlers with torpedo tubes preparing to attack the fleet. At dusk, the cruiser *Kamchatka*, which had become separated from the main body of the fleet, reported that it was under attack by eight torpedo boats and was returning fire. Ninety minutes later action stations were sounded abroad the flagship *Suvorov* in response to two flares sighted from the bridge. Shortly thereafter the order to engage the enemy was flashed down the line as searchlights revealed ships barely a half mile away. Battleships and cruisers opened fire and kept up an intensive barrage for 20 minutes until the admiral could discern only a few battered trawlers bobbing hopelessly in the water. The fleet steamed off concluding that the torpedo boats had fled from the scene.

The "enemy" engaged by Russian gunners was the Gamecock fleet of fishing boats which had left Hull for the Dogger Bank 2 days before and was then 200 miles northeast of the Spurn. They were identifiable as trawlers by their sails and red, white and green lights. These lights were probably the flares sighted on the bridge of *Suvorov*. When the firing began, one of the deckhands, illuminated by the searchlights, held up a plaice while his mate displayed a large haddock in the hope of signaling their peaceful intent. Their efforts were unsuccessful and when the barrage finally ceased one trawler had been sent to the bottom and five damaged. Two seamen were dead and six seriously wounded. Fortunately for the fishermen Russian gunnery had proven extremely inaccurate.

News of the incident reached London on Monday, 23 October. The next day the M.P. from Hull brought a deputation of fishermen to the Foreign Office where they produced shell splinters to substantiate their story. The Wednesday morning papers carried a more detailed account of the incident and public opinion was so incensed that the Russian Ambassador needed a police escort to leave his Embassy. Trafalgar Square was filled with protesters and the evening papers demanded strong action. The *Standard* raised the question that was on everybody's mind: was the "wretched Baltic fleet with its inefficient commanders, its drafts of raw landsmen, its blundering navigators and incompetent engineers" to be permitted to continue on its journey? The czarist regime was unpopular in England and as more details were released to the press public sentiment was adamant in favor of going after the Russian Fleet. Valentine Chirol, foreign editor of *The Times*, warned the foreign office that "the feeling in this country is such that no government can trifle with it."

The Balfour government, about to face an election, was particularly susceptible to popular pressure. However, the Cabinet did not act solely in response to public opinion. The majority were hostile to Russia and quite prepared to retaliate against her fleet. The Earl of Selbourne, First Lord of the Admiralty, was the most bellicose but Walter Long and Gerald Balfour, neither of whom normally displayed any interest in foreign affairs, also urged military action unless the Russians put into port and removed the officers responsible for the outrage. Admiral Fisher, who had recently been promoted to First Sea Lord, thought it a superb opportunity to destroy the Russian Fleet. It "is ours," he informed Selbourne, "whenever we like to take it." The King himself referred to the incident as "a most dastardly outrage" and urged a military response although he later moderated his position, fearing that war with Russia would only be in Germany's interest.

Lord Lansdowne, the Foreign Secretary, would have had support for any action against Russia he proposed. But he was an advocate of détente with Russia and was intent on resolving the incident peaceably. Lansdowne was nevertheless as outraged as his colleagues and thought Rozhestvensky's failure to stop and search for survivors particularly reprehensible. He was not convinced of the accidental nature of the incident, attributing it instead to the Russian propensity to "shoot first and ask questions later." In his opinion this trigger happy policy made a mockery of maritime law which Britain more than any other nation was dependent upon for her survival. Lansdowne believed that such incidents were likely to recur unless Russia was compelled to adhere to the established rules and customs that governed maritime behavior. Like other members of the Cabinet he also believed that Britain's reputation as a great power was at stake. * * *

* * * Unwilling to let the hostage fleet escape the prime minister and foreign secretary agreed that Russia must be sent an ultimatum demanding that Rozhestvensky call at the Spanish port of Vigo and put ashore the officers responsible for the incident along with witnesses. The Russians were also to give satisfaction that the investigation of the incident would be complete and impartial. * * *

The Royal Navy had already begun preparations for a showdown. Six battleships of the Home Fleet had been ordered to Gibraltar and the reserve fleet of six battleships was being readied for action. Cruisers were sent to shadow the Russian Fleet, Gibraltar was put on a war footing, and the powerful Mediterranean Fleet was hurriedly recalled from the Austrian and Italian ports it was visiting. By the evening of 26 October, 28 battleships, 44 cruisers and their supporting vessels stood poised off Gibraltar ready to intercept the Russian Fleet which in the graphic words of First Sea Lord Fisher had become the "ham of a strategic sandwich."

On 27 October, [Russian Foreign Minister] Lamsdorff called on Hardinge [the British Minister in St. Petersburg] to warn that "he considered the general purport [of the ultimatum] to be humiliating and unacceptable to a Great Power." Lansdowne and Balfour, in receipt of Hardinge's report that afternoon, were pessimistic about the chances for peace. Their hopes plummeted in response to a second cable from St. Petersburg containing Rozhestvensky's account of the incident. The Russian admiral claimed that his fleet had been set upon by two torpedo boats but that he had tried to avoid firing on the trawlers even though they were in apparent complicity with the torpedo boats. Lansdowne told the Russian Ambassador that the admiral's version "seemed to bristle with improbabilities" and did not alter the situation.

Lansdowne and [Russian Ambassador] Benckendorff conferred at length exploring possible ways out of the crisis. Paul Cambon, the French Ambassador, also participated in these talks. As the representative of France, Russia's ally, and the architect of the Anglo–French Entente, Cambon shared the trust of both sides. He acted as translator, as Benckendorff spoke Russian and French but Lansdowne knew only English, and attempted to bridge the gap between the two men created by their uncomplementary personalities. "Benckendorff is too vague, Lansdowne too reserved," he confided to his son, "and when I am not between them, they inhabit different planets."

The main impediment to a solution was the British demand for an inquiry in which British officers would participate. This was seen as humiliating by the Russians. Cambon nevertheless urged acceptance as did the French Foreign Minister in Paris. On the 27th, the three men agreed that an inquiry conducted by some august international body might be more palatable to the Czar as he had urged the creation of boards of arbitration at the Hague Conference. The suggestion, attributed by Benckendoff to Cambon, was cabled to Lamsdorff who cleverly presented it to the Czar as his own idea in order to secure the autocrat's approval.

No word had been received from St. Petersburg when it came time for Balfour to depart for Southampton on the morning of the 28th. The mood at the Foreign Office was gloomy and remained so until a cable arrived from Hardinge reporting that the Czar approved of an international court of inquiry. A second cable contained the welcome news that Rozhestvensky had received orders to send the ships involved in the attack on the fishing boats to Vigo, that the guilty parties, as determined by the international board of inquiry, would be punished by Russian courts and that measures would be implemented to prevent further incidents. In return Lamsdorff requested that Balfour give credit to Russia in his speech for having expressed its prompt regrets and offering to pay proper compensation.

Upon his arrival at Southampton Balfour was handed a telegram reporting the Russian capitulation. Much relieved, the Prime Minister deleted those parts of his speech which were the equivalent to a declaration of war and told the good news to the cheering crowd. The Royal Navy remained on a war footing until her cruisers had "escorted" Rozhestvensky's fleet half way down the coast of Africa.

THE DOGGER BANK CASE

Great Britain v. Russia, Report of February 26, 1905,
The Hague Court Reports 403 (James Brown Scott ed. 1916).

1. The commissioners [five admirals from Britain, Russia, the United States, France, and Austria], after a minute and prolonged examination of the whole of the facts brought to their knowledge in regard to the incident submitted to them for inquiry by the declaration of St. Petersburg of the 12th (25th) November, 1904, have proceeded to

make, in this report, an analysis of these facts in their logical sequence.* * *

9.   Toward 1 o'clock in the morning of 9th (22d) October, 1904, the night was rather dark, a slight, low fog partly clouding the air. The moon only showed intermittently between the clouds. A moderate wind blew from the southeast, raising a long swell, which gave the ships a roll of 5° on each side.

The course followed by the squadron toward the southwest would have taken the last two divisions, as the event proved, close past the usual fishing ground of the fleet of Hull trawlers, which was composed of some thirty of these small steamboats, and was spread over an area of several miles.

It appears from the concordant testimony of the British witnesses that all these boats carried their proper lights, and were trawling in accordance with their usual rules, under the direction of their "admiral," and in obedience to the signals given by the conventional rockets.

10.   Judging from the communications received by wireless telegraphy, the divisions which preceded that of Admiral Rojdestvensky across these waters had signaled nothing unusual.

It became known afterward, in particular, that Admiral Folkersam, having been led to pass round the fishing fleet on the north, threw his electric searchlight on the nearest trawlers at close quarters, and, having seen them to be harmless vessels, quietly continued his voyage.

11.   A short time afterwards the last division of the squadron, led by the *Souvoroff* flying Admiral Rojdestvensky's flag, arrived in its run close to the spot where the trawlers were fishing.

The direction in which this division was sailing led it nearly toward the main body of the fleet of trawlers, round which and to the south of which it would therefore be obliged to sail, when the attention of the officers of the watch on the bridges of the *Souvoroff* was attracted by a green rocket, which put them on their guard. This rocket, sent up by the "admiral" of the fishing fleet, indicated in reality, according to regulation, that the trawlers were to trawl on the starboard tack.

Almost immediately after this first alarm, and as shown by the evidence, the lookout men, who, from the bridges of the *Souvoroff*, were scanning the horizon with their night glasses, discovered "on the crest of the waves on the starboard bow, at an approximate distance of 18 to 20 cables," a vessel which aroused their suspicions because they saw no light, and because she appeared to be bearing down upon them.

When the suspicious-looking vessel was shown up by the searchlight, the lookout men thought they recognized a torpedo boat proceeding at great speed.

It was on account of these appearances that Admiral Rojdestvensky ordered fire to be opened on this unknown vessel.

The majority of the commissioners express the opinion, on this subject, that the responsibility for this action and the results of the fire to which the fishing fleet was exposed are to be attributed to Admiral Rojdestvensky.

12. Almost immediately after fire was opened to starboard, the *Souvoroff* caught sight of a little boat on her bow barring the way, and was obliged to turn sharply to the left to avoid running it down. This boat, however, on being lit up by the searchlight, was seen to be a trawler.

To prevent the fire of the ships being directed against this harmless vessel, the searchlight was immediately thrown up at an angle of 45°.

The admiral then made the signal to the squadron "not to fire on the trawlers."

But at the same time that the searchlight had lit up this fishing vessel, according to the evidence of witnesses, the lookout men on board the *Souvoroff* perceived to port another vessel, which appeared suspicious from the fact of its presenting the same features as were presented by the object of their fire to starboard.

Fire was immediately opened on this second object, and was, therefore, being kept up on both sides of the ship, the line of ships having resumed their original course by a correcting movement without changing speed.

13. According to the standing orders of the fleet, the Admiral indicated the objects against which the fire should be directed by throwing his searchlight upon them; but as each vessel swept the horizon in every direction with her own searchlights to avoid being taken by surprise, it was difficult to prevent confusion.

The fire, which lasted from ten to twelve minutes, caused great loss to the trawlers. Two men were killed and six others wounded; the *Crane* sank; the *Snipe*, the *Mino*, the *Moulmein*, the *Gull*, and the *Majestic* were more or less damaged.

On the other hand, the cruiser *Aurora* was hit by several shots.

The majority of the commissioners observe that they have not sufficiently precise details to determine what was the object fired on by the vessels; but the commissioners recognize unanimously that the vessels of the fishing fleet did not commit any hostile act; and, the majority of the commissioners being of opinion that there were no torpedo boats either among the trawlers nor anywhere near, the opening of the fire by Admiral Rojdestvensky was not justifiable.

The Russian commissioner, not considering himself justified in sharing this opinion, expresses the conviction that it was precisely the suspicious-looking vessels approaching the squadron with hostile intent which provoked the fire.

Notes and Questions

1. *Incentives to Arbitrate.* Looking at Lebow's account of the Dogger Bank Affair, what were the inducements for Britain to go to international arbitration? Why was Russia willing to accept an international inquiry into the activities of her Navy? Why did France seek to bring the two sides together? What role did public opinion in Britain play in building up war fever? In facilitating an arbitral solution to the conflict?

2. *The Composition of the Arbitral Panel.* Note that the arbitral panel in *Dogger Bank* was composed not of lawyers or judges but of naval officers. What would have been the advantages and disadvantages of employing admirals instead of jurists as arbitrators? Would it have been probably Britain or Russia that would have preferred admirals rather than international lawyers on the panel?

The fact that Britain and Russia could choose their arbitrators in *Dogger Bank* was and remains an ordinary feature of arbitration. Indeed, party choice of the tribunal is probably the most important general distinction between arbitration and adjudication as forms of dispute settlement, whether public (as in much of international law) or private (as in most commercial disputes). Sometimes, arbitrators are less bound than judges to apply strict rules of law to the case before them, but, other times, arbitrators are just as rule-minded as judges. Did the *Dogger Bank* arbitrators see their role as being appliers of strict rules of international law or more as being appliers of some sort of maritime or naval "common sense"?

3. *Compensation.* James Brown Scott, the editor of the *Reports* of the Permanent Court of Arbitration, noted that "Russia accepted the decision and paid damages to the extent of about $300,000." *Hague Court Reports* 403 (James Brown Scott ed. 1916). Were Russia's misgivings about permitting the arbitration justified? Would Russia have been better off to have simply paid damages at the outset? Or did the lapse of time and the decision of an arbitral panel make the payment of damages more palatable to the Russians?

Dogger Bank was the kind of dispute 19th-century international arbitration enthusiasts hoped would be settled by law rather than by war. As Merrills observed, "The *Dogger Bank* episode furnishes a striking example of the value of the international inquiry commission as an instrument of dispute settlement. Had the issue been investigated by two national inquiries, it is almost certain that * * * they would have exacerbated matters by coming to opposite conclusions." J.G. Merrills, *International Dispute Settlement* 47 (3d ed. 1998).

4. *The Permanent Court of Arbitration.* Founded by the 1899 Hague Peace Conference, the Permanent Court of Arbitration was the world's first permanent and universal court of arbitration. See Mark W. Janis, *An Introduction to International Law* 117–20 (3d ed. 1999). Did the availability of permanent international arbitral machinery at The Hague make it more likely that the parties would go to arbitration? What might be done to make it even more likely that states use a form of international arbitration in a time of crisis?

Although the Permanent Court of Arbitration still formally exists, it has been rarely used since the establishment of the International Court in 1921. The PCA continues to share the Peace Palace in The Hague with the ICJ. It is just a little mysterious why the PCA still exists, although there have been proposals from time to time for its revitalization. Perhaps it is the hope that some more good may yet come of it that keeps the PCA alive in form if not very much in function. The PCA does play a role in electing judges to the International Court of Justice. See Article 4 of the Court's Statute in the Appendix.

5. *Public and Private International Arbitration.* Despite the atrophy of the PCA after 1921, public international arbitration continues to flourish, albeit outside the halls of the Peace Palace. A good example of modern public international arbitration is the *Rainbow Warrior Case* below. Private or commercial international arbitration (between private litigants) and mixed international arbitration (between a state and a private litigant) are even more frequent nowadays. There are many hundreds of such cases a year. We have already seen an example of a mixed international arbitration, the *Texaco/Libya Case*, in Chapter 3, in the context of our discussion of the determination of customary international law. A private international arbitration is at issue in the *Scherk Case* in Chapter 12 below, where we discuss party choice in international conflict of laws.

Our second example of public international arbitration, the *Rainbow Warrior Case* below, contains an interesting discussion of state responsibility, a topic to which we return in Chapters 6 and 10. For now, ask, along with the Tribunal, what kind of satisfaction France ought to give New Zealand for France's breach of its treaty obligations?

THE RAINBOW WARRIOR CASE

New Zealand v. France,
France–New Zealand Arbitration Tribunal,
82 *International Law Reports* 500 (1990).

[In July 1985, French secret service agents affixed mines that sank the *Rainbow Warrior*, a ship belonging to the international nongovernmental organization, Greenpeace International, while the *Rainbow Warrior* was in harbor in New Zealand. A crew member on the vessel, Fernando Pereira, died as a result. Two of the French agents, Major Mafart and Captain Prieur, were arrested in New Zealand, pleaded guilty to criminal charges, and were each sentenced to ten years in jail. At the diplomatic level, France demanded the release of its agents; New Zealand sought compensation for the incident, and complained about French threats to disrupt trade between Europe and New Zealand should New Zealand not release Mafart and Prieur. France and New Zealand asked the Secretary–General of the United Nations to mediate the dispute; they agreed in advance to accept the Secretary–General's ruling. In 1986, the Secretary–General decided that France should pay $7 million to New Zealand and agree not to take certain steps that would injure New Zealand's trade with Europe. 74 Int'l L. Rep. 241. In addition, the ruling also contained provisions concerning the release of the two French agents. France and New Zealand implemented the ruling in a 1986 agreement, which required that Major Mafart and Captain Prieur be transferred to a French military base on Hao, an island in the Pacific, "for a period of not less than three years," and that they be "prohibited from leaving the island for any reason, except with the mutual consent of the two governments."

The 1990 arbitration excerpted below involves France's decision to evacuate Major Mafart and Captain Prieur from Hao to France before the three-year period had run. France sought New Zealand's consent to Major Mafart's transfer on December 11, 1987, for health-related reasons. New Zealand asked that its doctors examine Mafart, but France refused to permit a New Zealand military plane carrying New Zealand doctors to land in Hao. Mafart left Hao for France on December 14, 1987, without New Zealand's consent, and France allowed Mafart to remain in France after his treatment, despite New Zealand doctors' conclusions that he could be safely returned to Hao. Captain Prieur left Hao for France in May 1988 after France sought New Zealand's consent on the ground that she was pregnant. France agreed to an independent examination of Prieur in Hao by New Zealand doctors, but Prieur left the day before the doctors arrived, France claiming that Prieur's father was dying. Captain Prieur also never returned to Hao.

This 1990 arbitration was authorized under a provision of the 1986 France–New Zealand agreement providing for arbitration of disputes arising out of the prior accord. New Zealand invoked the provision. On February 14, 1989, the two states concluded a Supplemental Agreement designating three arbitrators (one appointed by each state and one appointed jointly by both states). The Supplemental Agreement also specified the procedures that the Tribunal was to follow, and stated that the Tribunal's decisions would be based on the 1986 agreement between France and New Zealand and on "applicable rules and principles of international law."]

75.   * * * [F]or the decision of the present case, both the customary Law of Treaties and the customary Law of State Responsibility are relevant and applicable. The customary Law of Treaties, as codified in the Vienna Convention proclaimed in Article 26, under the title "*Pacta sunt servanda*" that

"Every treaty in force is binding upon the parties to it and must be performed by them in good faith."

This fundamental provision is applicable to the determination whether there have been violations of that principle and in particular, whether material breaches of treaty obligations have been committed.

Moreover, certain specific provisions of customary law in the Vienna Convention are relevant in this case such as Article 60 which gives a precise definition of the concept of a material breach of a treaty, and Article 70, which deals with the legal consequences of the expiry of a treaty.

On the other hand, the legal consequences of a breach of a treaty, including the determination of the circumstances that may exclude wrongfulness (and render the breach only apparent) and the appropriate remedies for breach, are subjects that belong to the customary Law of State Responsibility.

The reason is that the general principles of International Law concerning State responsibility are equally applicable in the case of breach of treaty obligation, since in the international law field there is no distinction between contractual and tortious responsibility, so that any violation by a State of any obligation, of whatever origin, gives rise to State responsibility and consequently, to the duty of reparation. * * *

76.   Under the title "Circumstances Precluding Wrongfulness" the International Law Commission proposed in Articles 29 to 35 a set of rules which include three provisions on *force majeure* and fortuitous event (Article 31), distress (Article 32), and state of necessity (Article 33), which may be relevant to the decision on this case. * * *

77.   * * * New Zealand is right in asserting that the excuse of *force majeure* is not of relevance in this case because the test of its applicability is of absolute and material impossibility, and because a circumstance rendering performance more difficult or burdensome does not constitute a case of *force majeure*. Consequently, this excuse is of no relevance in the present case.

78.   Article 32 of the Articles drafted by the International Law Commission deals with another circumstance which may preclude wrongfulness in international law, namely, that of the "distress" of the author of the conduct which constitutes the act of State whose wrongfulness is in question. * * *

The question therefore is to determine whether the circumstances of distress in a case of extreme urgency involving elementary humanitarian considerations affecting the acting organs of the State may exclude wrongfulness in this case.

79.   In accordance with the previous legal considerations, three conditions would be required to justify the conduct followed by France in respect to Major Mafart and Captain Prieur:

1) the existence of very exceptional circumstances of extreme urgency involving medical or other considerations of an elementary nature, provided always that a prompt recognition of the existence of those exceptional circumstances is subsequently obtained from the other interested party or is clearly demonstrated.

2) The reestablishment of the original situation of compliance with the assignment in Hao as soon as the reasons of emergency invoked to justify the repatriation had disappeared.

3) The existence of a good faith effort to try to obtain the consent of New Zealand in terms of the 1986 Agreement.

THE CASE OF MAJOR MAFART

80. The New Zealand reaction to the French initiative for the removal of Major Mafart appears to have been conducted in conformity with the above considerations.

The decision to send urgently a medical doctor to Hao in order to verify the existence of the invoked ground of serious risk to life clearly implied that if the alleged conditions were confirmed, then the requested consent would be forthcoming.

Unfortunately, it proved impossible to proceed with that verification while Major Mafart was still on the island. * * * [N]one of the parties is to blame for the failure in carrying out the very difficult task of verifying *in situ* Major Mafart's health during that weekend.

81. * * * [H]aving accepted the offer to verify whether Major Mafart had required an urgent sanitary evacuation, subsequent consent to that measure would necessarily be implied unless there was an immediate and formal denial by New Zealand of the existence of the medical conditions which had determined Major Mafart's urgent removal, accompanied by a formal request by New Zealand authorities for his immediate return to Hao, or at least to Papeete. And this did not occur. * * *

88. * * * [T]he Tribunal:

by a majority declares that the French Republic did not breach its obligations to New Zealand by removing Major Mafart from the island of Hao on 13 December 1987;

declares that the French Republic committed a material and continuing breach of its obligations to New Zealand by failing to order the return of Major Mafart to the island of Hao as from 12 February 1988. * * *

THE CASE OF CAPTAIN PRIEUR

93. The facts * * * show that New Zealand would not oppose Captain Prieur's departure, if that became necessary because of special care which might be required by her pregnancy. They also indicated that France and New Zealand agreed that Captain Prieur would be examined by Dr. Brenner, a New Zealand physician, before returning to Paris. * * *

94. * * * [I]t appears that during the day of 5 May the French Government suddenly decided to present the New Zealand Government with the *fait accompli* of Captain Prieur's hasty return for a new reason, the health of Mrs. Prieur's father, who was seriously ill, hospitalized for cancer. Indisputably the health of Mrs. Prieur's father, who unfortunately would die on 16 May, and the concern for allowing Mrs. Prieur to visit her dying father constitute humanitarian reasons worthy of consideration by both Governments under the 1986 Agreement. But the events of 5 May (French date) prove that the French Republic did not make efforts in good faith to obtain New Zealand's consent. First of all, it must be

remembered that France and New Zealand agreed that Captain Prieur would be examined in Hao on 6 May, which would allow her to return to France immediately. For France, in this case, it was only a question of gaining 24 or 36 hours. Of course, the health of Mrs. Prieur's father, who had been hospitalized for several months, could serve as grounds for such acute and sudden urgency: but, in this case, New Zealand would have had to be informed very precisely and completely, and not be presented with a decision that had already been made. * * *

* * * New Zealand was really not asked for its approval, as compliance with France's obligations required even under extremely urgent circumstances: it was indeed demanded so firmly that it was bound to provoke a strong reaction from New Zealand.

101.   * * * [T]he Tribunal:

declares that the French Republic committed a material breach of its obligations to New Zealand by not endeavoring in good faith to obtain on 5 May 1988 New Zealand's consent to Captain Prieur's leaving the island of Hao;

declares that as a consequence the French Republic committed a material breach of its obligations by removing Captain Prieur from the island of Hao on 5 and 6 May 1988;

declares that the French Republic committed a material and continuing breach of its obligations to New Zealand by failing to order the return of Captain Prieur to the island of Hao. * * *

110.   In the present case the Tribunal must find that the infringement of the special regime designed by the Secretary–General to reconcile the conflicting views of the Parties has provoked indignation and public outrage in New Zealand and caused a new, additional nonmaterial damage. This damage is of a moral, political and legal nature, resulting from the affront to the dignity and prestige not only of New Zealand as such, but of its highest judicial and executive authorities as well.

111.   It follows from the foregoing findings that New Zealand is entitled to appropriate remedies. It claims certain declarations, to the effect that France has breached the First Agreement. But New Zealand seeks as well an order for the return of the agents. * * *

112.   For its part, the French Republic maintains that adequate reparation for moral or legal damage can only take the form of satisfaction, generally considered as the remedy *par excellence* in cases of nonmaterial damage. Invoking the decisions of the International Court of Justice, France maintains that whenever the damage suffered amounts to no more than a breach of the law, a declaration by the judge of this breach constitutes appropriate satisfaction. France points out, moreover, that, rather than *restitutio*, what New Zealand is demanding is the cessation of the denounced behaviour * * *. * * *

114.   * * * The recent jurisprudence of the International Court of Justice confirms that an offer for the cessation or discontinuance of

wrongful acts or omissions is only justified in case of continuing breaches of international obligations which are still in force at the time the judicial order is issued (*The United States Diplomatic and Consular Staff in Teheran Case*, I.C.J. Reports, 1979, p. 21, para. 38 to 41, and 1980, para. 95, No. 1; *The Case Concerning Military and Paramilitary Activities in and Against Nicaragua*, I.C.J. Reports, 1984, p. 187, and 1986, para. 292, p. 149). * * *

It would be * * * illogical to issue the order requested by New Zealand, which is really an order for the cessation or discontinuance of a certain French conduct, rather than a *restitutio*. The reason is that this conduct, namely to keep the two agents in Paris, is not longer unlawful, since the international obligation expired on 22 July 1989. Today, France is no longer obliged to return the two agents to Hao and submit them to the special regime. * * *

115. On the other hand, the French contention that satisfaction is the only appropriate remedy for non-material damage is also not justified in the circumstances of the present case.

The granting of a form of reparation other than satisfaction has been recognized and admitted in the relations between the parties by the Ruling of the Secretary–General of 9 July 1986, which has been accepted and implemented by both Parties to this case.

In the Memorandum presented to the Secretary–General, the New Zealand Government requested compensation for non-material damage, stating that it was "entitled to compensation for the violation of sovereignty and the affront and insult that involved."

The French Government opposed this claim, contending that the compensation "could concern only the material damage suffered by New Zealand, the moral damage being compensated by the offer of apologies."

But the Secretary–General did not make any distinction, ruling instead that the French Government "should pay the sum of U.S. dollars 7 million to the Government of New Zealand as *compensation for all the damage it has suffered.*" * * *

* * * [T]he compensation constituted a reparation not just for material damage—such as the cost of the police investigation—but for non-material damage as well, regardless of material injury and independent therefrom. * * *

119. New Zealand has not however requested the award of monetary compensation—even as a last resort should the Tribunal not make the declarations and orders for the return of the agents.

120. * * * [T]he Tribunal has decided not to make an order for monetary compensation. * * *

122. There is a long established practice of States and international Courts and Tribunals of using satisfaction as a remedy or form of reparation (in the wide sense) for the breach of an international obligation. This practice relates particularly to the case of moral or legal

damage done directly to the State, especially as opposed to the case of damage to persons involving international responsibilities. * * *

Satisfaction in this sense can take and has taken various forms. Arangio–Ruiz [in his 1989 report for the International Law Commission on state responsibility] mentions regrets, punishment of the responsible individuals, safeguards against repetition, the payment of symbolic or nominal damages or of compensation on a broader basis, and a decision of an international tribunal declaring the unlawfulness of the State's conduct.

123.   It is to the last of these forms of satisfaction for an international wrong that the Tribunal now turns. * * * The Tribunal accordingly decides to make four declarations of material breach of its obligations by France and further decides in compliance with Article 8 of the Agreement of 14 February 1989 to make public the text of its Award. For the foregoing reasons the Tribunal:

> declares that the condemnation of the French Republic for its breaches of its treaty obligations to New Zealand, made public by the decision of the Tribunal, constitutes in the circumstances appropriate satisfaction for the legal and moral damage caused to New Zealand. * * *

126.   Th[e] important relationship [between New Zealand and France], the nature of the decisions made by the Tribunal, and the earlier discussion of monetary compensation lead the Tribunal to make a recommendation. The recommendation, addressed to the two Governments, is intended to assist them in putting an end to the present unhappy affair. * * *

128.   The power of an arbitral tribunal to address recommendations to the parties to a dispute, in addition to the formal finding and obligatory decisions contained in the award, has been recognized in previous arbitral decisions. * * *

For the foregoing reasons the Tribunal:

> in light of the above decisions, recommends that the Governments of the French Republic and of New Zealand set up a fund to promote close and friendly relations between the citizens of the two countries, and that the Government of the French Republic make an initial contribution equivalent to US Dollars 2 million to that fund.

Notes and Questions

1.   *The Political Context.* France's sinking of the *Rainbow Warrior* was prompted by Greenpeace's protests against French atmospheric nuclear testing in the South Pacific. France's nuclear testing program had begun well before the *Rainbow Warrior* was sunk in July 1985. Indeed, New Zealand and Australia had challenged the legality of France's nuclear testing before the International Court of Justice in 1973. France refused to appear in the cases, but its public statements that its 1974 series of atmospheric

tests would be its last persuaded the Court to dismiss the cases. The Court concluded that "the objective of the Applicant has in effect been accomplished, inasmuch as the Court finds that France has undertaken the obligation to hold no further nuclear tests in the South Pacific." Nuclear Test Cases (New Zealand v. France), 1974 I.C.J. 457, 475, 1974 WL 4; Nuclear Tests Case (Australia v. France), 1974 I.C.J. 253, 270, 1974 WL 3. France subsequently withdrew its acceptance of the compulsory jurisdiction of the ICJ and resumed nuclear testing.

France conducted a nuclear test at Morurua atoll in the South Pacific just two months before the sinking of the *Rainbow Warrior*. Greenpeace was planning to sail the vessel to the French nuclear testing area in protest later in 1985. France admitted the attack. On September 22, 1985, the French Prime Minister confirmed that agents of the French secret service had acted on official orders and had sunk the vessel. French officials at the time expressed regret and indicated France's readiness to make reparations to New Zealand.

2. *Compensating the Victims of the Attack.* France paid 2.3 million French francs to the widow, children, and parents of Fernando Pereira, the crew member killed aboard the *Rainbow Warrior*. France also agreed to a separate arbitration with Greenpeace after negotiations with that organization failed to reach a settlement. On October 3, 1987, that arbitral tribunal ordered France to pay Greenpeace $8.1 million. Philip Shabecoff, "France Must Pay Greenpeace $8 Million in Sinking of Ship," *New York Times*, Oct. 3, 1987, at A2.

3. *The Decisions to Arbitrate.* What motivated New Zealand and France to agree to the 1986 arbitration? Why did the states believe that recourse to arbitration was more desirable than continuing diplomatic negotiations? Why did France and New Zealand ask the Secretary–General of the United Nations to rule on the scope of France's responsibility for the sinking? The agreement to submit the dispute to the Secretary–General asked for an "equitable and principled" ruling, and the two states agreed to abide by it. France and New Zealand in fact negotiated most of the provisions of the Secretary–General's ruling behind the scenes, and the Secretary–General endorsed them. As noted in paragraph 115 of the 1990 arbitration, the Secretary–General's 1986 ruling included compensation for non-material damage; compensation was one item the Secretary–General decided himself. See Lakshman Guruswamy, Geoffrey Palmer & Burns Weston, *International Environmental Law and World Order* 163 (1994).

Because of a provision in the 1986 bilateral agreement between France and New Zealand, New Zealand could institute the 1990 arbitration unilaterally. Had France and New Zealand not concluded the 1990 Supplemental Agreement designating the arbitrators, or had the two states had not agreed on the third member of the tribunal, the 1986 agreement authorized the Secretary–General of the United Nations to make the necessary appointments. What did New Zealand hope to gain by the 1990 arbitration?

4. *The Variety of Arbitral Functions.* How do the roles and functions of the tribunal in the 1990 *Rainbow Warrior* arbitration compare with the roles and functions of the tribunal in the *Dogger Bank* dispute?

5. *The Aftermath.* France complied almost immediately with the arbitral tribunal's recommendation to contribute $2 million to a fund to promote friendly relations. J. Scott Davidson, "The Rainbow Warrior Arbitration Concerning the Treatment of the French Agents Mafart and Prieur," 40 *International and Comparative Law Quarterly* 446, 456 (1991). Michael Rocard, the French Prime Minister, also visited New Zealand in May 1991 and formally apologized for the 1985 bombing. Nevertheless, tensions continued. France resumed its nuclear testing in the South Pacific, and New Zealand expressed outrage when, in July 1991, France awarded Alain Mafart a medal for distinguished service. Richard Long, "New Zealand Disgust as France Honours Bomber," *The Times (London)*, July 6, 1991, at 9. A new round of French nuclear testing in 1995 led New Zealand and other Pacific states to protest anew. New Zealand complained to the International Court that the testing was contrary to the *Nuclear Test Cases* described in Note 1. The Court disagreed, however, noting that those cases concerned atmospheric testing, whereas the more recent French testing was non-atmospheric. See Request for an Examination of the Situation in Accordance with Paragraph 63 of the Court's Judgment of 20 December 1974 in the Nuclear Tests (New Zealand v. France) Case, 1995 I.C.J. 288, 1995 WL 805134.

6. *Compromissory Clauses in Treaties.* The Case Concerning the Air Services Agreement of 27 March 1946, United States v. France, 54 Int'l L. Rep. 304 (1978), concerned the interpretation of the 1946 U.S.–France Air Services Agreement. The Agreement contained a clause, known as a compromissory clause, that authorized a panel of arbitrators to hear disputes concerning the interpretation or application of the Agreement, but arbitration was actually conducted pursuant to a separate *compromis*. The arbitral tribunal held, *inter alia*, that in some circumstances a state may take countermeasures even while an international arbitration is ongoing. See the discussion of countermeasures in Chapter 9.

A separate *compromis* to arbitrate has been employed in virtually every modern interstate arbitration, even when compromissory clauses—which are found in many different types of treaties—authorize the submission of disputes arising under treaties to arbitral tribunals. See Christine Gray & Benedict Kingsbury, "Inter–State Arbitration Since 1945: Overview and Evaluation," in *International Courts for the Twenty–First Century* 55, 61 (Mark W. Janis ed. 1992). Why should states conclude such separate *compromis* when there already are compromissory clauses? What functions do compromissory clauses serve, other than providing the basis for consent to arbitral proceedings?

* * * [C]ompromissory clauses may well serve different and even multiple functions, depending on the nature and subject matters of the treaties in which they are found. * * *

One potential function of compromissory clauses in U.S. treaties is in fact to promote binding third-party dispute resolution, as a way to help settle interstate disputes or to provide a forum in which details affecting ongoing relations may be worked out. * * *

The "dispute settlement" function * * * overlaps with the function of strengthening and reaffirming treaty rules. Under the [World Trade Organization system,] for example, the United States often may perceive

an advantage to the prompt resolution of issues in order to provide guidelines for future action, under which affected industries and states may plan their future conduct. The establishment of such guidelines may be the paramount achievement of a third-party proceeding. Furthermore, where compromissory clauses appear in a series of bilateral agreements that functionally substitute for a multilateral treaty regime, as is the case with bilateral investment treaties and air transport agreements, a tribunal decision can establish or affirm a norm that will be applied in many situations beyond the one involving the particular parties to the dispute. For these reasons, the United States may occasionally prefer to seek actual adjudication or arbitration of a dispute.
* * *

[In addition,] compromissory clauses may well help to create a sense that particular treaty norms are legitimate, and thereby promote a psychological willingness to abide by them relatively closely, even without any proceedings. * * * [W]hen states find close adherence to certain intended treaty standards to be particularly beneficial, they may employ a variety of mechanisms, including compromissory clauses, to promote attitudes of expected compliance on the part of treaty partners.

John E. Noyes, "The Functions of Compromissory Clauses in U.S. Treaties," 34 *Virginia Journal of International Law* 831, 898–900 (1994).

B. THE INTERNATIONAL COURT

The failure of diplomacy and the Permanent Court of Arbitration to solve the problems prompting the 1914 outbreak of the First World War inspired the 1919 Paris Peace Conference to create the Permanent Court of International Justice (PCIJ) as the judicial arm of the new League of Nations. When the League and the PCIJ in their turn failed to arrest the onset of the Second World War, the new peace-makers in 1944–1945 established both the United Nations and a new judicial institution, the International Court of Justice (ICJ). In form and even perhaps in function, there are few differences between the PCIJ (1921–1945) and the ICJ (1945 on); together they are commonly known as the "International Court" or the "World Court." Both have always been housed at The Hague in the Netherlands in the Peace Palace, also the home of the PCA, the tribunal to virtually all extents and purposes replaced by the International Court. See Mark W. Janis, *An Introduction to International Law* 122–25 (3d ed. 1999).

1. THE JURISDICTION OF THE INTERNATIONAL COURT

It is possible to understand better the kinds of disputes that can come before the International Court of Justice by carefully reading the exact delegations of jurisdiction made to the Court by its constituting treaty. There is a contentious jurisdiction based on Article 36 of the Court's Statute, which is an integral part of the United Nations Charter. The Court also has jurisdiction to render advisory opinions pursuant to Article 65 of its Statute and Article 96 of the U.N. Charter itself.

STATUTE OF THE INTERNATIONAL COURT OF JUSTICE, ARTICLES 36, 65

June 26, 1945, 59 Stat. 1031, T.S. No. 993.

Article 36

1. The jurisdiction of the Court comprises all cases which the parties refer to it and all matters specially provided for in the Charter of the United Nations or in treaties and conventions in force.

2. The states parties to the present Statute may at any time declare that they recognize as compulsory *ipso facto* and without special agreement, in relation to any other state accepting the same obligation, the jurisdiction of the Court in all legal disputes concerning:

    a.   the interpretation of a treaty;

    b.   any question of international law;

    c.   the existence of any fact which, if established, would constitute a breach of an international obligation;

    d.   the nature or extent of the reparation to be made for the breach of an international obligation.

3. The declarations referred to above may be made unconditionally or on condition of reciprocity on the part of several or certain states, or for a certain time.

4. Such declarations shall be deposited with the Secretary–General of the United Nations, who shall transmit copies thereof to the parties to the Statute and to the Registrar of the Court.

5. Declarations made under Article 36 of the Statute of the Permanent Court of International Justice and which are still in force shall be deemed, as between the parties to the present Statute, to be acceptances of the compulsory jurisdiction of the International Court of Justice for the period which they still have to run and in accordance with their terms.

6. In the event of a dispute as to whether the Court has jurisdiction, the matter shall be settled by the decision of the Court.

Article 65

1. The Court may give an advisory opinion on any legal question at the request of whatever body may be authorized by or in accordance with the Charter of the United Nations to make such a request.

2. Questions upon which the advisory opinion of the Court is asked shall be laid before the Court by means of a written request containing an exact statement of the question upon which an opinion is required, and accompanied by all documents likely to throw light upon the question.

CHARTER OF THE UNITED NATIONS, ARTICLE 96

June 26, 1945, 59 Stat. 1031, T.S. No. 993.

1. The General Assembly or the Security Council may request the International Court of Justice to give an advisory opinion on any legal question.

2. Other organs of the United Nations and specialized agencies, which may at any time be so authorized by the General Assembly, may also request advisory opinions of the Court on legal questions arising within the scope of their activities.

2. CONTENTIOUS CASES AT THE INTERNATIONAL COURT

As with our discussion of public international arbitration and the *Dogger Bank* and *Rainbow Warrior* cases above, here, as we explore the International Court, keep in mind some key questions. When and why do sovereign states agree to submit disputes to third-party legal settlement? When and why are governments willing to be bound by the decisions of international tribunals? Note in *Minquiers and Ecrehos* below, that France's and Britain's consent to the jurisdiction of the ICJ comes *after* the dispute had already arisen. Look carefully at their Special Agreement, a form of *compromis*, submitting their case to the Court.

THE MINQUIERS AND ECREHOS CASE

France v. United Kingdom, 1953 I.C.J. 47, 1953 WL 7.

By a letter dated December 5th, 1951, the British Ambassador to the Netherlands transmitted to the Registry on behalf of his Government a certified copy of a Special Agreement concluded between the Government of the United Kingdom of Great Britain and Northern Ireland and the Government of the French Republic, signed on December 29th, 1950, the instruments of ratification in respect of which were exchanged at Paris on September 24th, 1951. * * *

By Article I of the Special Agreement, signed on December 29th, 1950, the Court is requested

"to determine whether the sovereignty over the islets and rocks (in so far as they are capable of appropriation) of the Minquiers and Ecrehos groups respectively belongs to the United Kingdom or the French Republic."

Having thus been requested to decide whether these groups belong either to France or to the United Kingdom, the Court has to determine which of the Parties has produced the more convincing proof of title to one or the other of these groups, or to both of them. By the formulation of Article I the Parties have excluded the status of *res nullius* as well as that of *condominium*. * * *

By the Special Agreement the Court is requested to determine the sovereignty over the islets and rocks in so far as they are capable of appropriation. These words must be considered as relating to islets and rocks which are physically capable of appropriation. The Court is requested to decide in general to which Party sovereignty over each group as a whole belongs, without determining in detail the facts relating to the particular units of which the groups consist.

These groups lie between the British Channel Island of Jersey and the coast of France and consist each of two or three habitable islets, many smaller islets and a great number of rocks. The Ecrehos group lies north-east of Jersey, 3.9 sea-miles from that island, measured from the rock nearest thereto and permanently above water, and 6.6 sea-miles from the coast of France, measured in the same way. The Minquiers group lies south of Jersey, 9.8 sea-miles therefrom and 16.2 sea-miles from the French mainland, measured in the same way. This group lies 8 sea-miles from the Chausey Islands which belong to France.

Both Parties contend that they have respectively an ancient or original title to the Ecrehos and the Minquiers, and that their title has always been maintained and was never lost. The present case does not therefore present the characteristics of a dispute concerning the acquisition of sovereignty over *terra nullius*.

The United Kingdom Government derives the ancient title invoked by it from the conquest of England in 1066 by William Duke of Normandy. By this conquest England became united within the Duchy of Normandy, including the Channel Islands, and this union lasted until 1204 when King Philip Augustus of France drove the Anglo–Norman forces out of Continental Normandy. But his attempts to occupy also the Islands were not successful, except for brief periods when some of them were taken by French forces. On this ground the United Kingdom Government submits the view that all of the Channel Islands, including the Ecrehos and the Minquiers, remained, as before, united with England and that this situation of fact was placed on a legal basis by subsequent Treaties concluded between the English and French Kings.

The French Government does not dispute that the Islands of Jersey, Guernsey, Alderney, Sark, Herm and Jethou continued to be held by the King of England; but it denies that the Ecrehos and Minquiers groups were held by him after the dismemberment of the Duchy of Normandy in 1204. After that event, these two groups were, it is asserted, held by the King of France together with some other islands close to the continent, and reference is made to the same medieval Treaties as those which are invoked by the United Kingdom Government.

In such circumstances it must be examined whether these Treaties, invoked by both Parties, contain anything which might throw light upon the status of the Ecrehos and the Minquiers.

The Treaty of Lambeth of 1217, to which the Parties have referred, cannot be said to contain anything which might elucidate this question. The Treaty of Paris of 1259, which appears to be the principal Treaty on which the Parties rely, enumerates in Article 4 all the lands which the King of England should hold in fee of the King of France in Saintonge beyond the river Charente as well as Bordeaux, Bayonne and Gascony and "all the land which he holds on this side of the Sea of England in fee and in demesne and the islands, if any there be, which the king of England holds which are of the realm of france, and he shall hold of us as peer of france and duke of Aquitaine." These terms seem to refer to islands which the King of England held as Duke of Aquitaine, and not to the Channel Islands. But even assuming that these Islands were also included, the article refers in any case only to islands, if any there be, which are held by the English King. It does not say which islands were at that time held by him. [Similarly, the Court finds that neither the Treaty of Calcais of 1360 nor the Treaty of Tropes of 1420 refers specifically to the Minquiers and Ecrehos.]

There are, however, other documents which provide some indication as to the possession of the islets in dispute.

By a Charter of January 14th, 1200, King John of England granted to one of his Barons, Piers des Préaux, the Islands of Jersey, Guernsey and Alderney "to have and to hold of us by service of three knights' fees." Three years later, by a Charter of 1203, Piers des Préaux granted to the Abbey of Val–Richer "the island of Escrehou in entirety," stating that the King of England "gave me the islands" (*insulas mihi dedit*). This shows that he treated the Ecrehos as an integral part of the fief of the Islands which he had received from the King. In an Order from the English King of July 5th, 1258, the Sub–Warden of the Islands was ordered "to guard the islands of Gernere and Geresey, and the king's other islands in his keeping." In Letters Patent of the English King, dated June 28th, 1360, it was provided that the "keeper of the islands of Gernseye, Jerseye, Serk and Aurneye, and the other islands adjacent thereto" may have the keeping for a further period. The Truce of London of 1471 provided in Article 3 that the King of France would not make any hostile act against the Kingdom of England and other lands specially mentioned, including the Islands "of guernsey, Jersey and alderney [and] other territories, islands, lands and lordships, which are, or will be, held and possessed by the said lord King of England or by his subjects." A Papal Bull of January 20th, 1500, transferring the Channel Islands from the Diocese of Coutances to the Diocese of Winchester, mentioned "the islands of Jersey and Guernsey, Chausey, Alderney, Herm and Sark," while two commercial Treaties of 1606 and 1655 mentioned only Jersey and Guernsey.

[The Court reviews the political history of the Channel Islands and concludes:] What is of decisive importance, in the opinion of the Court, is not indirect presumptions deduced from events in the Middle Ages, but the evidence which relates directly to the possession of the Ecrehos and Minquiers groups.

[The Court turns first to the Ecrehos.]

It has already been mentioned that the Charter of 1200 of the English King, whereby he granted the fief of the Channel Islands to Piers des Préaux, and the Charter of 1203, whereby the latter in turn granted the Ecrehos to the Abbey of Val–Richer, show that the Ecrehos were treated by him as an integral part of his fief.

The grant of the Ecrehos was in frankalmoin. The French Government contends that such a grant had the effect of severing the feudal link between Piers des Préaux and the Abbey, so that the Ecrehos no longer formed a part of the fief of the Channel Islands. The view submitted by that Government is that the Ecrehos remained subject to the Duke of Normandy through the intermediary of the Abbey of Val–Richer, which was situated on the French mainland, and that, when the King of France succeeded to the rights of the Duke after the occupation of Continental Normandy in 1204, the Abbey "passed under his protection, as did the Ecrehos, whose overlord he became."

This contention renders it necessary to consider the Charter of 1203 more closely. It provided the following: * * *

".... Know ye all that I, having regard to the mercy of God, have granted and given and by my present charter have confirmed to God and to the church of St. Mary of Val–Richer and to the monks there serving God, for the salvation of the soul of John, illustrious king of England, who gave me the islands, and for the salvation of the souls of myself and of my father and mother and of all my ancestors, the island of Escrehou in entirety, for the building there of a church in honour of God and of the blessed Mary, so that the divine mysteries be daily celebrated there, to have and possess [it] and whatever in the same island they shall be able to increase and build, freely and quietly, fully and honourably, in free pure and perpetual alms. I have further granted to the aforesaid monks whatever by my men of Jersey, and of Guernsey, and of Alderney, having regard to charity, shall be reasonably given to them, saving my right."

It appears clearly from the *Grand Coutumier de Normandie* of the thirteenth century, chapters XXVIII and XXXII, that land held in frankalmoin was a tenure, and that such a grant in frankalmoin to an ecclesiastical institution did not have the effect of severing feudal ties. The text of the first part of Chapter XXXII is as follows:

[*Translation*]

"They are said to hold by alms who hold lands given in pure alms to God and his servants, wherein the donors retain nothing to themselves or their heirs save only the patronal domain; and they hold from them by alms only, as from patrons. None can make alms out of any land, save only that which is his own therein. Wherefore note that neither the duke, nor barons, nor anyone, ought to sustain any detriment if their men make alms of the lands which they hold of them; and their lords shall exercise their justice and levy their rights in the lands so put in alms, notwithstanding."

This text shows that the grantor retained the "patronal domain" (*dominium patronale*). According to this ancient Norman custom, Piers des Préaux did not by his grant drop out of the feudal chain as far as the Ecrehos was concerned. He continued to hold the Ecrehos as a part of his fief of the Channel Islands, with the Abbot of Val–Richer as his vassal and the King of England as his overlord, and the King continued to exercise his justice and levy his rights in the land so put in alms. By granting the Ecrehos in frankalmoin to the Abbey, Piers des Préaux did not, and could not, alienate the island from the fief of the Channel Islands; it remained a part of that fief.

This view is contested by the French Government on the ground that Piers des Préaux had not in the Charter reserved any feudal service and that he therefore had not created any feudal tenure. It seems that no such condition for the creation of a *"teneure par omosne,"* or frankalmoin, was required by the ancient Norman custom, as described in the *Coutumier*. But even assuming that a condition or reservation was required, the grant to the Abbey did contain such a condition or reservation. As is seen from the text of the Charter, the Abbey was to build a church in the Ecrehos "so that the divine mysteries be daily celebrated there," and when the grant was said to be given "for the salvation of the soul of John, illustrious king of England ... and for the salvation of the souls of myself and of my father and mother and all my ancestors," this could, in view of the custom at that time, only mean that a service of prayers was reserved in the Charter. That this must also have been the view of the Abbot himself and of his successors is seen from the records of certain *Quo Warranto* proceedings held in Jersey in 1309 before the King's itinerant Justices. The Assize Rolls show that a chapel had in fact been built in the Ecrehos, and that the Prior of that chapel, appearing before the Justices, gave evidence that he and his fellow monk, dwelling in the chapel throughout the whole year, "always celebrate for the lord the King and his progenitors." These records show that the Prior himself as well as the Justices called the grant a *tenura*.

Shortly after his grant of 1203 Piers de Préaux forfeited the fief of the Channel Islands, which thereupon reverted to the English King and were administered by Wardens appointed by that King, except for certain periods in the thirteenth and the beginning of the fourteenth century, when the Islands were again granted in fee. Up to 1309, there is no indication that any change had occurred as to the connection of the Ecrehos with the Channel Islands.

The object of the *Quo Warranto* proceedings of 1309 mentioned above was to enquire into the property and revenue of the English King. These proceedings, which were numerous, took the form of calling upon persons to justify their possession of property. The Abbot of Val–Richer was summoned before the King's Justices to answer regarding a mill and the *advocatio* of the Priory of the Ecrehos as well as a rent. * * * When therefore the Abbot of Val–Richer was summoned before the King's Justices in Jersey to answer for this *advocatio*, it must have been on the ground that the Ecrehos, to which the *advocatio* was attached, was within the domain of the English King. And when the Prior of the

Ecrehos appeared as the Abbot's attorney in answer to the summons, jurisdiction in respect of the Ecrehos was exercised by the Justices, who decided that "it is permitted to the said Prior to hold the *premissa* as he holds them as long as it shall please the lord the King."

[The Court reviews more of the history of the Priory and finds that later in the Middle Ages, the Priory "was abandoned and the chapel fell into ruins. The close relationship between the Ecrehos and Jersey ceased and for a considerable period thereafter the islets were only occasionally visited by Jerseymen for the purpose of fishing and collecting seaweed." From the sixteenth to the eighteenth century, the Ecrehos were more or less abandoned.]

From the beginning of the nineteenth century the connection between the Ecrehos and Jersey became closer again because of the growing importance of the oyster fishery in the waters surrounding the islets, and Jersey authorities took, during the subsequent period, action in many ways in respect of the islets. Of the manifold facts invoked by the United Kingdom Government, the Court attaches, in particular, probative value to the acts which relate to the exercise of jurisdiction and local administration and to legislation.

In 1826 criminal proceedings were instituted before the Royal Court in Jersey against a Jerseyman for having shot at a person on the Ecrehos. Similar judicial proceedings in Jersey in respect of criminal offences committed on the Ecrehos took place in 1881, 1883, 1891, 1913 and 1921. On the evidence produced the Court is satisfied that the Courts of Jersey, in criminal cases such as these, have no jurisdiction in the matter of a criminal offence committed outside the Bailiwick of Jersey, even though the offence be committed by a British subject resident in Jersey, and that Jersey authorities took action in these cases because the Ecrehos were considered to be within the Bailiwick. These facts show therefore that Jersey courts have exercised criminal jurisdiction in respect of the Ecrehos during nearly a hundred years.

Evidence produced shows that the law of Jersey has for centuries required the holding of an inquest on corpses found within the Bailiwick where it was not clear that death was due to natural causes. Such inquests on corpses found at the Ecrehos were held in 1859, 1917 and 1948 and are additional evidence of the exercise of jurisdiction in respect of these islets.

Since about 1820, and probably earlier, persons from Jersey have erected and maintained some habitable houses or huts on the islets of the Ecrehos, where they have stayed during the fishing season. Some of these houses or huts have, for the purpose of parochial rates, been included in the records of the Parish of St. Martin in Jersey, which have been kept since 1889, and they have been assessed for the levying of local taxes. Rating schedules for 1889 and 1950 were produced in evidence.

A register of fishing boats for the port of Jersey shows that the fishing boat belonging to a Jersey fisherman, who lived permanently on an islet of the Ecrehos for more than forty years, was entered in that register in 1872, the port or place of the boat being indicated as "Ecrehos Rocks," and that the licence of that boat was cancelled in 1882. According to a letter of June, 1876, from the Principal Customs Officer of Jersey, an official of that Island visited occasionally the Ecrehos for the purpose of endorsing the licence of that boat.

It is established that contracts of sale relating to real property on the Ecrehos islets have been passed before the competent authorities of Jersey and registered in the public registry of deeds of that island. Examples of such registration of contracts are produced for 1863, 1881, 1884 and some later years.

In 1884, a custom-house was established in the Ecrehos by Jersey customs authorities. The islets have been included by Jersey authorities within the scope of their census enumerations, and in 1901 an official enumerator visited the islets for the purpose of taking the census.

These various facts show that Jersey authorities have in several ways exercised ordinary local administration in respect of the Ecrehos during a long period of time.

By a British Treasury Warrant of 1875, constituting Jersey as a Port of the Channel Islands, the "Ecrehou Rocks" were included within the limits of that port. This legislative Act was a clear manifestation of British sovereignty over the Ecrehos at a time when a dispute as to such sovereignty had not yet arisen. The French Government protested in 1876 on the ground that this Act derogated from the Fishery Convention of 1839. But this protest could not deprive the Act of its character as a manifestation of sovereignty.

Of other facts which throw light upon the dispute, it should be mentioned that Jersey authorities have made periodical official visits to the Ecrehos since 1885, and that they have carried out various works and constructions there, such as a slipway in 1895, a signal post in 1910 and the placing of a mooring buoy in 1939.

The French Government, in addition to the alleged original feudal title considered above, has invoked the fact that the States of Jersey in 1646 prohibited the inhabitants of Jersey from fishing without special permission at the Ecrehos and the Chausey Islands, and that they restricted visits to the Ecrehos in 1692 because of the war between England and France. This shows, it is contended, that the Ecrehos were not considered as British territory. But the Court does not consider that this is the necessary or natural inference to be drawn from these facts.

In the course of the diplomatic exchanges between the two Governments in the beginning of the nineteenth century concerning fisheries off the coast of Cotentin, the French Ambassador in London addressed to the Foreign Office a Note, dated June 12th, 1820, attaching two charts sent from the French Ministry of Marine to the French Ministry of Foreign Affairs purporting to delimit the areas within which the fishermen of each country were entitled to exclusive rights of fishery. In these charts a blue line marking territorial waters was drawn along the coast of the French mainland and round the Chausey Islands, which were indicated as French, and a red line marking territorial waters was drawn round Jersey, Alderney, Sark and the Minquiers, which were indicated as British. No line of territorial waters was drawn round the Ecrehos group, one part of which was included in the red line for Jersey and consequently marked as belonging to Great Britain and the other part apparently treated as *res nullius*. When the French Government in 1876 protested against the British Treasury Warrant of 1875 and challenged British sovereignty over the Ecrehos, it did not itself claim sovereignty, but continued to treat the Ecrehos as *res nullius*. In a letter of March 26th, 1884, from the French Ministry of Foreign Affairs to the French Minister of Marine, it was stated that the British Government had not ceased to claim the Ecrehos as a dependency to the Channel Islands, and it was suggested that French fishermen should be prohibited access to the Ecrehos. It does not appear that any such measure was taken, and subsequently, in a Note to the Foreign Office of December 15th, 1886, the French Government claimed for the first time sovereignty over the Ecrehos "*à la lumière des nouvelles données historiques et géologiques.*"

The Court being now called upon to appraise the relative strength of the opposing claims to sovereignty over the Ecrehos in the light of the facts considered above, finds that the Ecrehos group in the beginning of the thirteenth century was considered and treated as an integral part of the fief of the Channel Islands which were held by the English King, and that the group continued to be under the dominion of that King, who in the beginning of the 14th century exercised jurisdiction in respect thereof. The Court further finds that British authorities during the greater part of the nineteenth century and in the twentieth century have exercised State functions in respect of the group. The French Government, on the other hand, has not produced evidence showing that it has any valid title to the group. In such circumstances it must be concluded that the sovereignty over the Ecrehos belongs to the United Kingdom.

[The Court examines the claims to the Minquiers in similar detail.]

The Court,

unanimously,

finds that the sovereignty over the islets and rocks of the Ecrehos and Minquiers groups, in so far as these islets and rocks are capable of appropriation, belongs to the United Kingdom.

Notes and Questions

1. *The Decision to Adjudicate.* What made the Minquiers and Ecrehos dispute susceptible to resolution by the International Court? What did the governments of the United Kingdom and France each gain and lose by suspending diplomatic negotiations while the Court heard the case? Would France or Britain believe it had the better claim? Does hope of success or fear of failure affect a state's attitude?

Why choose the International Court rather than an *ad hoc* panel of international arbitrators? In delimiting the continental shelf a quarter century later, the same two countries appointed an arbitral tribunal unrelated to the ICJ. See Arbitration between the United Kingdom of Great Britain and Northern Ireland and the French Republic on the Delimitation of the Continental Shelf, Decisions of the Court of Arbitration, June 30, 1977, Mar. 14, 1978, 18 I.L.M. 397 (1979).

2. *Territorial Dispute Settlement.* Territorial disputes seem a favorite kind of issue for international adjudication whether by the ICJ or by another sort of forum. For example, five-judge chambers of the ICJ, authorized under Article 26 of the Court's Statute, have been constituted to hear territorial delimitation cases between the Canada and United States, 1984 I.C.J. 246, 1984 WL 499, between Burkina Faso and Mali, 1985 I.C.J. 6, 1985 WL 136, and between El Salvador and Honduras, 1992 I.C.J. 351, 1992 WL 457492. Are territorial disputes especially amenable to legal argument and judicial settlement? We look at five-judge panels in the *ELSI case* below.

In *Minquiers and Ecrehos*, what kind of proof do the lawyers need to collect and argue? How does the Court weigh the evidence and apply legal rules to reach its judgment? Are territorial disputes good legal fodder because of the nature of their facts?

3. *Compliance With ICJ Decisions.* Why are states likely to comply with ICJ decisions like those in *Minquiers and Ecrehos*? Did both states mean to comply with any eventual judgment when they consented to the *compromis*? Note how France and the United Kingdom formulated the question the Court was authorized to decide. By minimizing the possibility that the Court would find the islets to be either *terra nullius* or subject to a joint condominium regime, the parties seemingly maximized the possibility that the Court would rule that only one or the other state had sovereignty over the islets. If either France or the U.K. ran a significant risk of losing the case in the ICJ, was this risk worth running because it would be easier politically for the government to give up the islets in a court case than in diplomatic negotiations? Does the ICJ sometimes serve a "scapegoat function"?

4. *The Norman Invasion.* On July 10, 1994, the Ecrehos were "invaded" by 150 French citizens from Normandy who sought to reopen the dispute about the ownership of the islets at a time when Jersey was seeking to extend its territorial waters from three to 12 miles. Despite assurances from the government of Jersey that traditional French fishing rights would not be impaired, the Norman party came to the Ecrehos to protest. They were restrained from tearing down the Union Jack, but Jersey authorities permitted them to hold a mass and to plant a Norman flag of two yellow lions rampant on a red ground beside a temporary altar. Marcus Binney & Michael Hornsby, "Jersey Police Outwit Norman Invasion," *The Times (London)*, July 11, 1994, at 5.

5. *"Consensual" Submissions.* Although in a formal sense all cases submitted to the ICJ are "consensual," sometimes consent is given after, sometimes before, the dispute arises. In *Minquiers and Ecrehos* consent was given *after* the dispute arose, and both France and Britain were agreeable at the time about going to court. Note how different "consent" is in the

Diplomatic and Counsular Staff Case below. Iran's consent was given prior to any dispute with the United States and, at the time of the case, Iran resisted the ICJ proceedings.

THE DIPLOMATIC AND CONSULAR STAFF CASE

United States v. Iran,
1980 I.C.J. 3, 1980 WL 368.

1. On 29 November 1979, the Legal Adviser of the Department of State of the United States of America handed to the Registrar an Application instituting proceedings against the Islamic Republic of Iran in respect of a dispute concerning the seizure and holding as hostages of members of the United States diplomatic and consular staff and certain other United States nationals. * * *

[The United States also applied for an interim order to protect the hostages. Iran refused to plead or argue before the International Court. In December 1979, the ICJ delivered an order instructing Iran to release the hostages immediately, 1979 I.C.J. 7, but Iran failed to comply. The case went forward on the merits.]

10. No pleadings were filed by the Government of Iran, which also was not represented at the oral proceedings, and no submissions were therefore presented on its behalf. The position of that Government was, however, defined in two communications addressed to the Court by the Minister for Foreign Affairs of Iran; the first of these was a letter dated 9 December 1979 and transmitted by telegram the same day [the text of which was set out in full in the Court's Order of 15 December 1979], the second was a letter transmitted by telex dated 16 March 1980 and received on 17 March 1980, the text of which followed closely that of the letter of 9 December 1979 and reads as follows:

[*Translation from French*]

"I have the honour to acknowledge receipt of the telegram concerning the meeting of the International Court of Justice to be held on 17 March 1980 at the request of the Government of the United States of America, and to set forth to you below, once again, the position of the Government of the Islamic Republic of Iran in that respect:

The Government of the Islamic Republic of Iran wishes to express its respect for the International Court of Justice, and for its distinguished Members, for what they have achieved in the quest for a just and equitable solution to legal conflicts between States, and respectfully draws the attention of the Court to the deep-rootedness and the essential character of the Islamic Revolution of Iran, a revolution of a whole oppressed nation against its oppressors and their masters, the examination of whose numerous repercussions is essentially and directly a matter within the national sovereignty of Iran.

The Government of the Islamic Republic of Iran considers that the Court cannot and should not take cognizance of the case which the Government of the United States of America has submitted to it, and in the most significant fashion, a case confined to what is called the question of the 'hostages of the American Embassy in Tehran.'

For this question only represents a marginal and secondary aspect of an overall problem, one such that it cannot be studied separately, and which involves, *inter alia*, more than 25 years of continual interference by the United States in the internal affairs of Iran, the shameless exploitation of our country, and numerous crimes perpetrated against the Iranian people, contrary to and in conflict with all international and humanitarian norms.

The problem involved in the conflict between Iran and the United States is thus not one of the interpretation and the application of the treaties upon which the American Application is based, but results from an overall situation containing much more fundamental and more complex elements. Consequently, the Court cannot examine the American Application divorced from its proper context, namely the whole political dossier of the relations between Iran and the United States over the last 25 years.

With regard to the request for provisional measures, as formulated by the United States, it in fact implies that the Court should have passed judgment on the actual substance of the case submitted to it, which the Court cannot do without breach of the norms governing its jurisdiction. Furthermore, since provisional measures are by definition intended to protect the interest of the parties, they cannot be unilateral, as they are in the request submitted by the American Government."

[Despite Iran's refusal to participate, the Court rules it has enough information to decide the case. The Court then examines the factual background respecting the seizure of the hostages.]

17. At approximately 10:30 a.m. on 4 November 1979, during the course of a demonstration of approximately 3,000 persons, the United States Embassy compound in Tehran was overrun by a strong armed group of several hundred people. The Iranian security personnel are reported to have simply disappeared from the scene; at all events it is established that they made no apparent effort to deter or prevent the demonstrators from seizing the Embassy's premises. The invading group (who subsequently described themselves as "Muslim Student Followers of the Imam's Policy," and who will hereafter be referred to as "the militants") gained access by force to the compound and to the ground floor of the Chancery building. Over two hours after the beginning of the attack, and after the militants had attempted to set fire to the Chancery building and to cut through the upstairs steel doors with a torch, they gained entry to the upper floor; one hour later they gained control of the main vault. The militants also seized the other buildings, including the various residences, on the Embassy compound. In the course of the

attack, all the diplomatic and consular personnel and other persons present in the premises were seized as hostages, and detained in the Embassy compound; subsequently other United States personnel and one United States private citizen seized elsewhere in Tehran were brought to the compound and added to the number of hostages.

18. During the three hours or more of the assault, repeated calls for help were made from the Embassy to the Iranian Foreign Ministry, and repeated efforts to secure help from the Iranian authorities were also made through direct discussions by the United States Chargé d'affaires, who was at the Foreign Ministry at the time, together with two other members of the mission. From there he made contact with the Prime Minister's Office and the Foreign Ministry officials. A request was also made to the Iranian Chargé d'affaires in Washington for assistance in putting an end to the seizure of the Embassy. Despite these repeated requests, no Iranian security forces were sent in time to provide relief and protection to the Embassy. In fact when Revolutionary Guards ultimately arrived on the scene, despatched by the Government "to prevent clashes," they considered that their task was merely to "protect the safety of both the hostages and the students," according to statements subsequently made by the Iranian Government's spokesman, and by the operations commander of the Guards. No attempt was made by the Iranian Government to clear the Embassy premises, to rescue the persons held hostage, or to persuade the militants to terminate their action against the Embassy. * * *

21. The premises of the United States Embassy in Tehran have remained in the hands of the militants; and the same appears to be the case with the Consulates at Tabriz and Shiraz. Of the total number of United States citizens seized and held as hostages, 13 were released on 18–20 November 1979, but the remainder have continued to be held up to the present time. The release of the 13 hostages was effected pursuant to a decree by the Ayatollah Khomeini addressed to the militants dated 17 November 1979, in which he called upon the militants to "hand over the blacks and the women, if it is proven they did not spy, to the Ministry of Foreign Affairs so that they may be immediately expelled from Iran."

22. The persons still held hostage in Iran include, according to the information furnished to the Court by the United States, at least 28 persons having the status, duly recognized by the Government of Iran, of "member of the diplomatic staff" within the meaning of the Vienna Convention on Diplomatic Relations of 1961; at least 20 persons having the status, similarly recognized, of "member of the administrative and technical staff" within the meaning of that Convention; and two other persons of United States nationality not possessing either diplomatic or consular status. Of the persons with the status of member of the diplomatic staff, four are members of the Consular Section of the Mission.

23. Allegations have been made by the Government of the United States of inhumane treatment of hostages; the militants and Iranian authorities have asserted that the hostages have been well treated, and have allowed special visits to the hostages by religious personalities and by representatives of the International Committee of the Red Cross. The specific allegations of ill-treatment have not however been refuted. Examples of such allegations, which are mentioned in some of the sworn declarations of hostages released in November 1979, are as follows: at the outset of the occupation of the Embassy some were paraded bound and blindfolded before hostile and chanting crowds; at least during the initial period of their captivity, hostages were kept bound, and frequently blindfolded, denied mail or any communication with their government or with each other, subjected to interrogation, threatened with weapons.

24. Those archives and documents of the United States Embassy which were not destroyed by the staff during the attack on 4 November have been ransacked by the militants. Documents purporting to come from this source have been disseminated by the militants and by the Government-controlled media. * * *

28. * * * On 25 November 1979, the Secretary–General of the United Nations addressed a letter to the President of the Security Council referring to the seizure of the United States Embassy in Tehran and the detention of its diplomatic personnel, and requesting an urgent meeting of the Security Council "in an effort to seek a peaceful solution to the problem." The Security Council met on 27 November and 4 December 1979; on the latter occasion, no representative of Iran was present, but the Council took note of a letter of 13 November 1979 from the Supervisor of the Iranian Foreign Ministry to the Secretary–General. The Security Council then adopted resolution 457 (1979), calling on Iran to release the personnel of the Embassy immediately, to provide them with protection and to allow them to leave the country. The resolution also called on the two Governments to take steps to resolve peacefully the remaining issues between them, and requested the Secretary–General to lend his good offices for the immediate implementation of the resolution, and to take all appropriate measures to that end. It further stated that the Council would "remain actively seized of the matter" and requested the Secretary–General to report to it urgently on any developments with regard to his efforts. * * *

33. It is to be regretted that the Iranian Government has not appeared before the Court in order to put forward its arguments on the questions of law and of fact which arise in the present case; and that, in consequence, the Court has not had the assistance it might have derived from such arguments or from any evidence adduced in support of them. Nevertheless, in accordance with its settled jurisprudence, the Court, in applying Article 53 of its Statute, must first take up, *proprio motu*, any preliminary question, whether of admissibility or of jurisdiction, that appears from the information before it to arise in the case and the decision of which might constitute a bar to any further examination of the merits of the Applicant's case. The Court will, therefore, first address

itself to the considerations put forward by the Iranian Government in its letters of 9 December 1979 and 16 March 1980, on the basis of which it maintains that the Court ought not to take cognizance of the present case.

34.   The Iranian Government in its letter of 9 December 1979 drew attention to what it referred to as the "deep rootedness and the essential character of the Islamic Revolution of Iran, a revolution of a whole oppressed nation against its oppressors and their masters." The examination of the "numerous repercussions" of the revolution, it added, is "a matter essentially and directly within the national sovereignty of Iran." However, as the Court pointed out in its Order of 15 December 1979,

> "a dispute which concerns diplomatic and consular premises and the detention of internationally protected persons, and involves the interpretation or application of multilateral conventions codifying the international law governing diplomatic and consular relations, is one which by its very nature falls within international jurisdiction."

36.   The Court * * * in its Order of 15 December 1979, made it clear that the seizure of the United States Embassy and Consulates and the detention of internationally protected persons as hostages cannot be considered as something "secondary" or "marginal," having regard to the importance of the legal principles involved. It also referred to a statement of the Secretary–General of the United Nations, and to Security Council resolution 457 (1979), as evidencing the importance attached by the international community as a whole to the observance of those principles in the present case as well as its concern at the dangerous level of tension between Iran and the United States. The Court, at the same time, pointed out that no provision of the Statute or Rules contemplates that the Court should decline to take cognizance of one aspect of a dispute merely because that dispute has other aspects, however important. It further underlined that, if the Iranian Government considered the alleged activities of the United States in Iran legally to have a close connection with the subject-matter of the United States' Application, it was open to that Government to present its own arguments regarding those activities to the Court either by way of defence in a Counter–Memorial or by way of a counter-claim.

37.   The Iranian Government, notwithstanding the terms of the Court's Order, did not file any pleadings and did not appear before the Court. By its own choice, therefore, it has forgone the opportunities offered to it under the Statute and Rules of Court to submit evidence and arguments in support of its contention in regard to the "overall problem." Even in its later letter of 16 March 1980, the Government of Iran confined itself to repeating what it had said in its letter of 9 December 1979, without offering any explanations in regard to the points to which the Court had drawn attention in its Order of 15 December 1979. It has provided no explanation of the reasons why it considers that the violations of diplomatic and consular law alleged in the United States' Application cannot be examined by the Court sepa-

rately from what it describes as the "overall problem" involving "more than 25 years of continual interference by the United States in the internal affairs of Iran." Nor has it made any attempt to explain, still less define, what connection, legal or factual, there may be between the "overall problem" of its general grievances against the United States and the particular events that gave rise to the United States' claims in the present case which, in its view, precludes the separate examination of those claims by the Court. This was the more necessary because legal disputes between sovereign States by their very nature are likely to occur in political contexts, and often form only one element in a wider and long-standing political dispute between the States concerned. Yet never has the view been put forward before that, because a legal dispute submitted to the Court is only one aspect of a political dispute, the Court should decline to resolve for the parties the legal questions at issue between them. Nor can any basis for such a view of the Court's functions or jurisdiction be found in the Charter or the Statute of the Court; if the Court were, contrary to its settled jurisprudence, to adopt such a view, it would impose a far-reaching and unwarranted restriction upon the role of the Court in the peaceful solution of international disputes.

38. It follows that the considerations and arguments put forward in the Iranian Government's letters of 9 December 1979 and 16 March 1980 do not, in the opinion of the Court, disclose any ground on which it should conclude that it cannot or ought not to take cognizance of the present case. * * *

45. Article 53 of the Statute requires the Court, before deciding in favour of an Applicant's claim, to satisfy itself that it has jurisdiction, in accordance with Articles 36 and 37, empowering it to do so. In the present case the principal claims of the United States relate essentially to alleged violations by Iran of its obligations to the United States under the Vienna Conventions of 1961 on Diplomatic Relations and of 1963 on Consular Relations. With regard to these claims the United States has invoked as the basis for the Court's jurisdiction Article I of the Optional Protocols concerning the Compulsory Settlement of Disputes which accompany these Conventions. The United Nations publication *Multilateral Treaties in respect of which the Secretary–General Performs Depository Functions* lists both Iran and the United States as parties to the Vienna Conventions of 1961 and 1963, as also to their accompanying Protocols concerning the Compulsory Settlement of Disputes, and in each case without any reservation to the instrument in question. The Vienna Conventions, which codify the law of diplomatic and consular relations, state principles and rules essential for the maintenance of peaceful relations between States and accepted throughout the world by nations of all creeds, cultures and political complexions. Moreover, the Iranian Government has not maintained in its communications to the Court that the two Vienna Conventions and Protocols are not in force as between Iran and the United States. Accordingly, as indicated in the Court's Order of 15 December 1979, the Optional Protocols manifestly provide a possible basis for the Court's jurisdiction, with respect to the

United States' claims under the Vienna Conventions of 1961 and 1963. It only remains, therefore, to consider whether the present dispute in fact falls within the scope of their provisions.

46. The terms of Article I, which are the same in the two Protocols, provide:

> "Disputes arising out of the interpretation or application of the Convention shall lie within the compulsory jurisdiction of the International Court of Justice and may accordingly be brought before the Court by an application made by any party to the dispute being a Party to the present Protocol."

The United States' claims here in question concern alleged violations by Iran of its obligations under several articles of the Vienna Conventions of 1961 and 1963 with respect to the privileges and immunities of the personnel, the inviolability of the premises and archives, and the provision of facilities for the performance of the functions of the United States Embassy and Consulates in Iran. In so far as its claims relate to two private individuals held hostage in the Embassy, the situation of these individuals falls under the provisions of the Vienna Convention of 1961 guaranteeing the inviolability of the premises of embassies, and of Article 5 of the 1963 Convention concerning the consular functions of assisting nationals and protecting and safeguarding their interests. By their very nature all these claims concern the interpretation or application of one or other of the two Vienna Conventions. * * *

50. However, the United States also presents claims in respect of alleged violations by Iran * * * of the Treaty of Amity, Economic Relations, and Consular Rights of 1955 between the United States and Iran, which entered into force on 16 June 1957. With regard to these claims the United States has invoked paragraph 2 of Article XXI of the Treaty as the basis for the Court's jurisdiction. The claims of the United States under this Treaty overlap in considerable measure with its claims under the two Vienna Conventions and more especially the Convention of 1963. * * *

54. No suggestion has been made by Iran that the 1955 Treaty was not in force on 4 November 1979 when the United States Embassy was overrun and its nationals taken hostage, or on 29 November when the United States submitted the dispute to the Court. The very purpose of a treaty of amity * * * is to promote friendly relations between the two countries concerned, and between their two peoples, more especially by mutual undertakings to ensure the protection and security of their nationals in each other's territory. It is precisely when difficulties arise that the treaty assumes its greatest importance, and the whole object of Article XXI, paragraph 2, of the 1955 Treaty was to establish the means for arriving at a friendly settlement of such difficulties by the Court or by other peaceful means. It would, therefore, be incompatible with the whole purpose of the 1955 Treaty if recourse to the Court under Article XXI, paragraph 2, were now to be found not to be open to the parties precisely at the moment when such recourse was most needed. Further-

more, although the machinery for the effective operation of the 1955 Treaty has, no doubt, now been impaired by reason of diplomatic relations between the two countries having been broken off by the United States, its provisions remain part of the corpus of law applicable between the United States and Iran. * * *

56. * * * The events which are the subject of the United States' claims fall into two phases which it will be convenient to examine separately.

57. The first of these phases covers the armed attack on the United States Embassy by militants on 4 November 1979, the overrunning of its premises, the seizure of its inmates as hostages, the appropriation of its property and archives and the conduct of the Iranian authorities in the face of those occurrences. The attack and the subsequent overrunning, bit by bit, of the whole Embassy premises, was an operation which continued over a period of some three hours without any body of police, any military unit or any Iranian official intervening to try to stop or impede it from being carried through to its completion. The result of the attack was considerable damage to the Embassy premises and property, the forcible opening and seizure of its archives, the confiscation of the archives and other documents found in the Embassy and, most grave of all, the seizure by force of its diplomatic and consular personnel as hostages, together with two United States nationals.

58. No suggestion has been made that the militants, when they executed their attack on the Embassy, had any form of official status as recognized "agents" or organs of the Iranian State. Their conduct in mounting the attack, overrunning the Embassy and seizing its inmates as hostages cannot, therefore, be regarded as imputable to that State on that basis. Their conduct might be considered as itself directly imputable to the Iranian State only if it were established that, in fact, on the occasion in question the militants acted on behalf of the State, having been charged by some competent organ of the Iranian State to carry out a specific operation. The information before the Court does not, however, suffice to establish with the requisite certainty the existence at that time of such a link between the militants and any competent organ of the State.

59. Previously, it is true, the religious leader of the country, the Ayatollah Khomeini, had made several public declarations inveighing against the United States as responsible for all his country's problems. In so doing, it would appear, the Ayatollah Khomeini was giving utterance to the general resentment felt by supporters of the revolution at the admission of the former Shah to the United States. The information before the Court also indicates that a spokesman for the militants, in explaining their action afterwards, did expressly refer to a message issued by the Ayatollah Khomeini, on 1 November 1979. In that message the Ayatollah Khomeini had declared that it was "up to the dear pupils, students and theological students to expand with all their might their attacks against the United States and Israel, so they may force the

United States to return the deposed and criminal shah, and to condemn this great plot'' (that is, a plot to stir up dissension between the main streams of Islamic thought). In the view of the Court, however, it would be going too far to interpret such general declarations of the Ayatollah Khomeini to the people or students of Iran as amounting to an authorization from the State to undertake the specific operation of invading and seizing the United States Embassy. To do so would, indeed, conflict with the assertions of the militants themselves who are reported to have claimed credit for having devised and carried out the plan to occupy the Embassy. Again, congratulations after the event, such as those reportedly telephoned to the militants by the Ayatollah Khomeini on the actual evening of the attack, and other subsequent statements of official approval, though highly significant in another context shortly to be considered, do not alter the initially independent and unofficial character of the militants' attack on the Embassy.

60.   The first phase, here under examination, of the events complained of also includes the attacks on the United States Consulates at Tabriz and Shiraz. Like the attack of the Embassy, they appear to have been executed by militants not having an official character, and successful because of lack of sufficient protection.

61.   The conclusion just reached by the Court, that the initiation of the attack on the United States Embassy on 4 November 1979, and of the attacks on the Consulates at Tabriz and Shiraz the following day, cannot be considered as in itself imputable to the Iranian State does not mean that Iran is, in consequence, free of any responsibility in regard to those attacks; for its own conduct was in conflict with its international obligations. By a number of provisions of the Vienna Conventions of 1961 and 1963, Iran was placed under the most categorical obligations, as a receiving State, to take appropriate steps to ensure the protection of the United States Embassy and Consulates, their staffs, their archives, their means of communication and the freedom of movement of the members of their staffs.

62.   Thus, after solemnly proclaiming the inviolability of the premises of a diplomatic mission, Article 22 of the 1961 Convention continues in paragraph 2:

> *"The receiving State is under a special duty to take all appropriate steps to protect the premises of the mission against any intrusion or damage and to prevent any disturbance of the peace of the mission or impairment of its dignity."* (Emphasis added.)

So, too, after proclaiming that the person of a diplomatic agent shall be inviolable, and that he shall not be liable to any form of arrest or detention, Article 29 provides:

> "The receiving State shall treat him with due respect and *shall take all appropriate steps to prevent any attack on his person, freedom or dignity."* (Emphasis added.)

The obligation of a receiving State to protect the inviolability of the archives and documents of a diplomatic mission is laid down in Article 24, which specifically provides that they are to be "inviolable at any time and wherever they may be." Under Article 25 it is required to "accord full facilities for the performance of the functions of the mission," under Article 26 to "ensure to all members of the mission freedom of movement and travel in its territory," and under Article 27 to "permit and protect free communication on the part of the mission for all official purposes." Analogous provisions are to be found in the 1963 Convention regarding the privileges and immunities and consular missions and their staffs. In the view of the Court, the obligations of the Iranian Government here in question are not merely contractual obligations established by the Vienna Conventions of 1961 and 1963, but also obligations under general international law.

63.   The facts * * * establish to the satisfaction of the Court that on 4 November 1979 the Iranian Government failed altogether to take any "appropriate steps" to protect the premises, staff and archives of the United States' mission against attack by the militants, and to take any steps either to prevent this attack or to stop it before it reached its completion. They also show that on 5 November 1979 the Iranian Government similarly failed to take appropriate steps for the protection of the United States Consulates at Tabriz and Shiraz. In addition they show, in the opinion of the Court, that the failure of the Iranian Government to take such steps was due to more than mere negligence or lack of appropriate means. * * *

67.   This inaction of the Iranian Government by itself constituted clear and serious violation of Iran's obligations to the United States under the provisions of Article 22, paragraph 2, and Articles 24, 25, 26, 27 and 29 of the 1961 Vienna Convention on Diplomatic Relations, and Articles 5 and 36 of the 1963 Vienna Convention on Consular Relations. Similarly, with respect to the attacks on the Consulates at Tabriz and Shiraz, the inaction of the Iranian authorities entailed clear and serious breaches of its obligations under the provisions of several further articles of the 1963 Convention on Consular Relations. So far as concerns the two private United States nationals seized as hostages by the invading militants, that inaction entailed, albeit incidentally, a breach of its obligations under Article II, paragraph 4, of the 1955 Treaty of Amity, Economic Relations, and Consular Rights which, in addition to the obligations of Iran existing under general international law, requires the parties to ensure "the most constant protection and security" to each other's nationals in their respective territories. * * *

69.   The second phase of the events which are the subject of the United States' claims comprises the whole series of facts which occurred following the completion of the occupation of the United States Embassy by the militants, and the seizure of the Consulates at Tabriz and Shiraz. The occupation having taken place and the diplomatic and consular personnel of the United States' mission having been taken hostage, the action required of the Iranian Government by the Vienna Conventions

and by general international law was manifest. Its plain duty was at once to make every effort, and to take every appropriate step, to bring these flagrant infringements of the inviolability of the premises, archives and diplomatic and consular staff of the United States Embassy to a speedy end, to restore the Consulates at Tabriz and Shiraz to United States control, and in general to re-establish the status quo and to offer reparation for the damage.

70.   No such step was, however, taken by the Iranian authorities. At a press conference on 5 November the Foreign Minister, Mr. Yazdi, conceded that "according to international regulations the Iranian Government is dutybound to safeguard the life and property of foreign nationals." But he made no mention of Iran's obligation to safeguard the inviolability of foreign embassies and diplomats; and he ended by announcing that the action of the students "enjoys the endorsement and support of the government, because America herself is responsible for this incident." As to the Prime Minister, Mr. Bazargan, he does not appear to have made any statement on the matter before resigning his office on 5 November. * * *

73.   The seal of official government approval was finally set on this situation by a decree issued on 17 November 1979 by the Ayatollah Khomeini. His decree began with the assertion that the American Embassy was "a centre of espionage and conspiracy" and that "those people who hatched plots against our Islamic movement in that place do not enjoy international diplomatic respect." He went on expressly to declare that the premises of the Embassy and the hostages would remain as they were until the United States had handed over the former Shah for trial and returned his property to Iran. This statement of policy the Ayatollah qualified only to the extent of requesting the militants holding the hostages to "hand over the blacks and the women, if it is proven that they did not spy, to the Ministry of Foreign Affairs so that they may be immediately expelled from Iran." As to the rest of the hostages, he made the Iranian Government's intentions all too clear:

> "The noble Iranian nation will not give permission for the release of the rest of them. Therefore, the rest of them will be under arrest until the American Government acts according to the wish of the nation." * * *

79.   The Court moreover cannot conclude its observations on the series of acts which it has found to be imputable to the Iranian State and to be patently inconsistent with its international obligations under the Vienna Conventions of 1961 and 1963 without mention also of another fact. This is that judicial authorities of the Islamic Republic of Iran and the Minister of Foreign Affairs have frequently voiced or associated themselves with, a threat first announced by the militants, of having some of the hostages submitted to trial before a court or some other body. These threats may at present merely be acts in contemplation. But the Court considers it necessary here and now to stress that, if the intention to submit the hostages to any form of criminal trial or

investigation were to be put into effect, that would constitute a grave breach by Iran of its obligations under Article 31, paragraph 1, of the 1961 Vienna Convention. This paragraph states in the most express terms: "A diplomatic agent shall enjoy immunity from the criminal jurisdiction of the receiving State." Again, if there were an attempt to compel the hostages to bear witness, a suggestion renewed at the time of the visit to Iran of the Secretary–General's Commission, Iran would without question be violating paragraph 2 of that same Article of the 1961 Vienna Convention which provides that: "A diplomatic agent is not obliged to give evidence as a witness."

80.   The facts of the present case, viewed in the light of the applicable rules of law, thus speak loudly and clearly of successive and still continuing breaches by Iran of its obligations to the United States under the Vienna Conventions of 1961 and 1963, as well as under the Treaty of 1955. * * *

90.   On the basis of the foregoing detailed examination of the merits of the case, the Court finds that Iran, by committing successive and continuing breaches of the obligations laid upon it by the Vienna Conventions of 1961 and 1963 on Diplomatic and Consular Relations, the Treaty of Amity, Economic Relations, and Consular Rights of 1955, and the applicable rules of general international law, has incurred responsibility towards the United States. As to the consequences of this finding, it clearly entails an obligation on the part of the Iranian State to make reparation for the injury thereby caused to the United States. Since however Iran's breaches of its obligations are still continuing, the form and amount of such reparation cannot be determined at the present date.

91.   At the same time the Court finds itself obliged to stress the cumulative effect of Iran's breaches of its obligations when taken together. A marked escalation of these breaches can be seen to have occurred in the transition from the failure on the part of the Iranian authorities to oppose the armed attack by the militants on 4 November 1979 and their seizure of the Embassy premises and staff, to the almost immediate endorsement by those authorities of the situation thus created, and then to their maintaining deliberately for many months the occupation of the Embassy and detention of its staff by a group of armed militants acting on behalf of the State for the purpose of forcing the United States to bow to certain demands. Wrongfully to deprive human beings of their freedom and to subject them to physical constraint in conditions of hardship is in itself manifestly incompatible with the principles of the Charter of the United Nations, as well as with the fundamental principles enunciated in the Universal Declaration of Human Rights. But what has above all to be emphasized is the extent and seriousness of the conflict between the conduct of the Iranian State and its obligations under the whole corpus of the international rules of which diplomatic and consular law is comprised, rules the fundamental character of which the Court must here again strongly affirm. In its Order of 15 December 1979, the Court made a point of stressing that the obligations laid on States by the two

Vienna Conventions are of cardinal importance for the maintenance of good relations between States in the interdependent world of today. "There is no more fundamental prerequisite for the conduct of relations between States," the Court there said, "than the inviolability of diplomatic envoys and embassies, so that throughout history nations of all creeds and cultures have observed reciprocal obligations for that purpose." The institution of diplomacy, the Court continued, has proved to be "an instrument essential for effective co-operation in the international community, and for enabling States, irrespective of their differing constitutional and social systems, to achieve mutual understanding and to resolve their differences by peaceful means."

92.   It is a matter of deep regret that the situation which occasioned those observations has not been rectified since they were made. Having regard to their importance the Court considers it essential to reiterate them in the present Judgment. The frequency with which at the present time the principles of international law governing diplomatic and consular relations are set at naught by individuals or groups of individuals is already deplorable. But this case is unique and of very particular gravity because here it is not only private individuals or groups of individuals that have disregarded and set at naught the inviolability of a foreign embassy, but the government of the receiving State itself. Therefore in recalling yet again the extreme importance of the principles of law which it is called upon to apply in the present case, the Court considers it to be its duty to draw the attention of the entire international community, of which Iran itself has been a member since time immemorial, to the irreparable harm that may be caused by events of the kind now before the Court. Such events cannot fail to undermine the edifice of law carefully constructed by mankind over a period of centuries, the maintenance of which is vital for the security and well-being of the complex international community of the present day, to which it is more essential than ever that the rules developed to ensure the ordered progress of relations between its members should be constantly and scrupulously respected.

93.   Before drawing the appropriate conclusions from its findings on the merits in this case, the Court considers that it cannot let pass without comment the incursion into the territory of Iran made by the United States military units on 24–25 April 1980 * * *. No doubt the United States Government may have had understandable preoccupations with respect to the well-being of its nationals held hostage in its Embassy for over five months. No doubt also the United States Government may have had understandable feelings of frustration at Iran's long-continued detention of the hostages, notwithstanding two resolutions of the Security Council as well as the Court's own Order of 15 December 1979 calling expressly for their immediate release. Nevertheless, in the circumstances of the present proceedings, the Court cannot fail to express its concern in regard to the United States' incursion into Iran. When, as previously recalled, this case had become ready for hearing on 19 February 1980, the United States Agent requested the Court, owing

to the delicate stage of certain negotiations, to defer setting a date for the hearings. Subsequently, on 11 March, the Agent informed the Court of the United States Government's anxiety to obtain an early judgment on the merits of the case. The hearings were accordingly held on 18, 19 and 20 March, and the Court was in course of preparing the present judgment adjudicating upon the claims of the United States against Iran when the operation of 24 April 1980 took place. The Court therefore feels bound to observe that an operation undertaken in those circumstances, from whatever motive, is of a kind calculated to undermine respect for the judicial process in international relations; and to recall that in * * * its Order of 15 December 1979 the Court had indicated that no action was to be taken by either party which might aggravate the tension between the two countries.

94.   At the same time, however, the Court must point out that neither the question of the legality of the operation of 24 April 1980, under the Charter of the United Nations and under general international law, nor any possible question of responsibility flowing from it, is before the Court. It must also point out that this question can have no bearing on the evaluation of the conduct of the Iranian Government over six months earlier, on 4 November 1979, which is the subject-matter of the United States' Application. It follows that the findings reached by the Court in this Judgment are not affected by that operation.

95.   For these reasons,

THE COURT,

1.   By thirteen votes to two,

Decides that the Islamic Republic of Iran, by the conduct which the Court has set out in this Judgment, has violated in several respects, and is still violating, obligations owed by it to the United States of America under international conventions in force between the two countries, as well as under long-established rules of general international law;

IN FAVOUR: *President* Sir Humphrey Waldock; *Vice-President* Elias; *Judges* Forster, Gros, Lachs, Nagendra Singh, Ruda, Mosler, Oda, Ago, El–Erian, Sette–Camara and Baxter.

AGAINST: *Judges* Morozov and Tarazi.

2.   By thirteen votes to two,

Decides that the violations of these obligations engage the responsibility of the Islamic Republic of Iran towards the United States of America under international law;

IN FAVOUR: *President* Sir Humphrey Waldock; *Vice-President* Elias; *Judges* Forster, Gros, Lachs, Nagendra Singh, Ruda, Mosler, Oda, Ago, El–Erian, Sette–Camara and Baxter.

AGAINST: *Judges* Morozov and Tarazi.

3.   Unanimously,

Decides that the Government of the Islamic Republic of Iran must immediately take all steps to redress the situation resulting from the events of 4 November 1979 and what followed from these events, and to that end:

(*a*) must immediately terminate the unlawful detention of the United States Chargé d'affaires and other diplomatic and consular staff and other United States nationals now held hostage in Iran, and must immediately release each and every one and entrust them to the protecting Power (Article 45 of the 1961 Vienna Convention on Diplomatic Relations);

(*b*) must ensure that all the said persons have the necessary means of leaving Iranian territory, including means of transport;

(*c*) must immediately place in the hands of the protecting Power the premises, property, archives and documents of the United States Embassy in Tehran and of its Consulates in Iran;

4.   Unanimously,

Decides that no member of the United States diplomatic or consular staff may be kept in Iran to be subjected to any form of judicial proceedings or to participate in them as a witness;

5.   By twelve votes to three,

Decides that the Government of the Islamic Republic of Iran is under an obligation to make reparation to the Government of the United States of America for the injury caused to the latter by the events of 4 November 1979 and what followed from these events;

IN FAVOUR: *President* Sir Humphrey Waldock; *Vice–President* Elias; *Judges* Forster, Gros, Nagendra Singh, Ruda, Mosler, Oda, Ago, El–Erian, Sette–Camara and Baxter.

AGAINST: *Judges* Lachs, Morozov and Tarazi.

6.   By fourteen votes to one,

Decides that the form and amount of such reparation, failing agreement between the Parties, shall be settled by the Court, and reserves for this purpose the subsequent procedure in the case.

IN FAVOUR: *President* Sir Humphrey Waldock; *Vice–President* Elias; *Judges* Forster, Gros, Lachs, Nagendra Singh, Ruda, Mosler, Tarazi, Oda, Ago, El–Erian, Sette–Camara and Baxter.

AGAINST: *Judge* Morozov.

Notes and Questions

1.   *The Decision to Litigate.* Why did the United States bring the *Diplomatic and Consular Staff Case* to the International Court? Was it likely that Iran would comply with an adverse judgment? Was the legal issue ever in much doubt? What could the United States gain if Iran disregarded the judgment? What could the U.S. lose?

2. *The Role of Public Opinion.* What exactly was the "public" that was being swayed by the Court proceedings in *Diplomatic and Consular Staff*? Was it U.S. public opinion that was being shown that something was being done to free the hostages? Was it public or governmental opinion in third states?

3. *Resolving the Hostages Crisis.* Efforts to resolve the hostages crisis proceeded through diplomatic channels, at the U.N. Security Council, before the ICJ, by a failed U.S. helicopter rescue mission, and by the freezing of Iranian assets in the United States and abroad. Ultimately, in January 1981, a U.S.–Iranian treaty, negotiated through the good offices of Algeria, resulted in the release of the U.S. hostages, the unfreezing of Iranian assets, and the establishment of the Iran–U.S. Claims Tribunal to decide disputes among Iran, the United States, and nationals of those countries. *Dames & Moore*, a U.S. case related to the creation of the Iran–U.S. Claims Tribunal and the unfreezing of Iranian assets, appears in Chapter 4. More on state responsibility is found in Chapters 6 and 10, and the succession of the international obligations of a state following a radical change in its government, such as had occurred in Iran, is discussed in Chapter 7.

4. *The ICJ as a Public Forum.* Should the Court be concerned if it is being used as a forum in which to appeal to and influence public opinion? Should the Court turn away cases where it seems likely that a state will refuse to appear and to comply with the orders of the Court? If the Court is used as a public forum, can it still serve a judicial role? Is it enough to say that, whatever the circumstances, the Court can usefully add the words of a new judgment to the corpus of international law doctrine?

5. *The Problem of the Non-appearing Respondent.* Why have Iceland, France, Turkey, Iran, and the United States refused to argue before the Court in cases in which the Court found that it had been vested with jurisdiction by mutual party consent to a form of compulsory jurisdiction? What is left of any sort of ICJ compulsory jurisdiction in the light of the recent pattern of non-appearing states? Has there been a "loss in respect for the ICJ when it acts like a court in name but not in deed"? Mark W. Janis, "Somber Reflections on the Compulsory Jurisdiction of the International Court," 81 *American Journal of International Law* 144, 146 (1987).

DECLARATION OF MALAWI RECOGNIZING THE COMPULSORY JURISDICTION OF THE ICJ

International Court of Justice, *Yearbook 1996–1997*, at 105.

On behalf of the Government of Malawi, I declare under Article 36, paragraph 2, of the Statute of the International Court of Justice that I recognize as compulsory *ipso facto* and without special agreement, in relation to any other State accepting the same obligation, on condition of reciprocity, the jurisdiction of the International Court of Justice in all legal disputes which may arise in respect of facts or situations subsequent to this declaration concerning:

(a) the interpretation of a treaty;

(b) any question of international law;

(c) the existence of any fact which, if established, would constitute a breach of an international obligation;

(d) the nature or extent of the reparation to be made for the breach of an international obligation:

Provided that this declaration shall not apply to—

(i) disputes with regard to matters which are essentially within the domestic jurisdiction of the Republic of Malawi as determined by the Government of Malawi;

(ii) disputes in regard to which the parties of the dispute have agreed or shall agree to have recourse to some other method of peaceful settlement; or

(iii) disputes concerning any question relating to or arising out of belligerent or military occupation.

The Government of Malawi also reserves the right at any time, by means of a notification addressed to the Secretary–General of the United Nations, to add to, amend, or withdraw any of the foregoing reservations or any that may hereafter be added. Such notification shall be effective on the date of their receipt by the Secretary–General of the United Nations.

Given under my hand in Zomba this 22nd day of November 1966.

> *(Signed)* H. Kamuzu Banda,
> President and
> Minister for External Affairs.

Notes and Questions

1. *The Utility of Compulsory Jurisdiction.* What is the utility of the ICJ's compulsory jurisdiction clause, Article 36(2) of the ICJ Statute, reproduced at page 261 above? Only about one-third of all states have joined Malawi in filing declarations with the Court accepting its compulsory jurisdiction. Some previously-consenting states, like the United States and France, have withdrawn their declarations. Are prior treaty submissions like that in the *Diplomatic and Consular Staff Case* also not useful? Would it be better if the ICJ relied solely on *ad hoc* submissions on the lines of *Minquiers and Ecrehos?*

2. *Attaching Conditions to 36(2) Declarations.* As Malawi's declaration illustrates, some states attach conditions to their 36(2) declarations. Concerns with reciprocity have led the Court to allow a respondent state to invoke the "reservations" attached to an applicant state's declaration to deprive the Court of jurisdiction, even if the respondent state's own 36(2) declaration would otherwise subject it to jurisdiction.

Note especially Malawi's self-judging domestic jurisdiction reservation. Should the Court accept such a reservation as valid at all? If the Court were to reject a self-judging domestic reservation, should the rest of the 36(2) declaration containing such a reservation be deemed valid or invalid? Should the Court subject invocations of such a reservation to a test of reasonableness? In Certain Norwegian Loans (France v. Norway), 1957 I.C.J. 9, 1957 WL 3, the Court allowed Norway to rely on a self-judging domestic reservation attached to France's then-in-effect 36(2) declaration.

3. ADVISORY OPINIONS AT THE INTERNATIONAL COURT

As we have seen, the ICJ has the authority pursuant to Article 96 of the U.N. Charter and Article 65 of its Statute to render advisory opinions. These are only given at the request of designated international organizations and, unlike judgments in the ICJ's contentious cases, are not legally binding. In practice, however, many advisory opinions have served functions rather similar to Court judgments. One such example is the *Western Saraha Case* below. Ask why Morocco sought to persuade the U.N. General Assembly to request an advisory opinion from the Court.

ADVISORY OPINION ON THE WESTERN SAHARA

1975 I.C.J. 12, 1975 WL 5.

1. The questions upon which the advisory opinion of the Court has been asked were laid before the Court by a letter dated 17 December 1974, filed in the Registry on 21 December 1974, addressed by the Secretary–General of the United Nations to the President of the Court. In his letter the Secretary–General informed the Court that, by resolution 3292 (XXIX) adopted on 13 December 1974, the General Assembly of the United Nations had decided to request the Court to give an advisory opinion at an early date on the questions set out in the resolution. The text of that resolution is as follows:

> *"The General Assembly,*
>
> *Recalling* its resolution 1514 (XV) of 14 December 1960 containing the Declaration on the Granting of Independence to Colonial Countries and Peoples,
>
> *Recalling also* its resolutions 2072 (XX) of 16 December 1965, 2229 (XXI) of 20 December 1966, 2354 (XXII) of 19 December 1967, 2428 (XXIII) of 18 December 1968, 2591 (XXIV) of 16 December 1969, 2711 (XXV) of 14 December 1970, 2983 (XXVII) of 14 December 1972 and 3162 (XXVIII) of 14 December 1973,
>
> *Reaffirming* the right of the population of the Spanish Sahara to self-determination in accordance with resolution 1514 (XV),
>
> *Considering* that the persistence of a colonial situation in Western Sahara jeopardizes stability and harmony in the north-west African region,
>
> *Taking into account* the statements made in the General Assembly on 30 September and 2 October 1974 by the Ministers of Foreign Affairs of the Kingdom of Morocco and of the Islamic Republic of Mauritania,

Taking note of the statements made in the Fourth Committee by the representatives of Morocco and Mauritania, in which the two countries acknowledged that they were both interested in the future of the Territory,

Having heard the statements by the representative of Algeria,

Having heard the statements by the representative of Spain,

Noting that during the discussion a legal controversy arose over the status of the said territory at the time of its colonization by Spain,

Considering, therefore, that it is highly desirable that the General Assembly, in order to continue the discussion of this question at its thirtieth session, should receive an advisory opinion on some important legal aspects of the problem,

Bearing in mind Article 96 of the Charter of the United Nations and Article 65 of the Statute of the International Court of Justice,

1.   *Decides* to request the International Court of Justice, without prejudice to the application of the principles embodied in General Assembly resolution 1514 (XV), to give an advisory opinion at an early date on the following questions:

I.   Was Western Sahara (Río de Oro and Sakiet El Hamra) at the time of colonization by Spain a territory belonging to no one (*terra nullius*)?

If the answer to the first question is in the negative,

II.   What were the legal ties between this territory and the Kingdom of Morocco and the Mauritanian entity?;

2.   *Calls upon* Spain, in its capacity as administering Power in particular, as well as Morocco and Mauritania, in their capacity as interested parties, to submit to the International Court of Justice all such information and documents as may be needed to clarify those questions;

3.   *Urges* the administering Power to postpone the referendum it contemplated holding in Western Sahara until the General Assembly decides on the policy to be followed in order to accelerate the decolonization process in the territory, in accordance with resolution 1514 (XV), in the best possible conditions, in the light of the advisory opinion to be given by the International Court of Justice"
* * * * * *

14.   Under Article 65, paragraph 1, of the Statute:

"The Court may give an advisory opinion on any legal question at the request of whatever body may be authorized by or in accordance with the Charter of the United Nations to make such a request."

The present request has been made pursuant to Article 96, paragraph 1, of the Charter of the United Nations, under which the General Assembly may seek the Court's advisory opinion on any legal question. * * *

16. It has been suggested that the questions posed by the General Assembly are not legal, but are either factual or are questions of a purely historical or academic character.

17. It is true that, in order to reply to the questions, the Court will have to determine certain facts, before being able to assess their legal significance.

However, a mixed question of law and fact is none the less a legal question within the meaning of Article 96, paragraph 1, of the Charter and Article 65, paragraph 1, of the Statute. As the Court observed in its Opinion concerning the *Legal Consequences for States of the Continued Presence of South Africa in Namibia (South West Africa) notwithstanding Security Council Resolution 276 (1970)*:

> "In the view of the Court, the contingency that there may be factual issues underlying the question posed does not alter its character as a 'legal question' as envisaged in Article 96 of the Charter. The reference in this provision to legal questions cannot be interpreted as opposing legal to factual issues. Normally, to enable a court to pronounce on legal questions, it must also be acquainted with, take into account and, if necessary, make findings as to the relevant factual issues." * * *

23. Article 65, paragraph 1, of the Statute, which establishes the power of the Court to give an advisory opinion, is permissive and, under it, that power is of a discretionary character. In exercising this discretion, the International Court of Justice, like the Permanent Court of International Justice, has always been guided by the principle that, as a judicial body, it is bound to remain faithful to the requirements of its judicial character even in giving advisory opinions. If the question is a legal one which the Court is undoubtedly competent to answer, it may none the less decline to do so. As this Court has said in previous Opinions, the permissive character of Article 65, paragraph 1, gives it the power to examine whether the circumstances of the case are of such a character as should lead it to decline to answer the request. It has also said that the reply of the Court, itself an organ of the United Nations, represents its participation in the activities of the Organization and, in principle, should not be refused. By lending its assistance in the solution of a problem confronting the General Assembly, the Court would discharge its functions as the principal judicial organ of the United Nations. The Court has further said that only "compelling reasons" should lead it to refuse to give a requested advisory opinion.

24. Spain has put forward a series of objections which in its view would render the giving of an opinion in the present case incompatible with the Court's judicial character. Certain of these are based on the consequences said to follow from the absence of Spain's consent to the adjudication of the questions referred to the Court. Another relates to

the alleged academic nature, irrelevance or lack of object of those questions. Spain has asked the Court to give priority to the examination of the latter. The Court will, however, deal with the objections founded on the lack of Spain's consent to adjudication of the questions, before turning to the objection which concerns the subject-matter of the questions themselves.

25. Spain has made a number of observations relating to the lack of its consent to the proceedings, which, it considers, should lead the Court to decline to give an opinion. These observations may be summarized as follows:

(a) In the present case the advisory jurisdiction is being used to circumvent the principle that jurisdiction to settle a dispute requires the consent of the parties.

(b) The questions, as formulated, raise issues concerning the attribution of territorial sovereignty over Western Sahara.

(c) The Court does not possess the necessary information concerning the relevant facts to enable it to pronounce judicially on the questions submitted to it.

26. The first of the above observations is based on the fact that on 23 September 1974 the Minister for Foreign Affairs of Morocco addressed a communication to the Minister of Foreign Affairs of Spain recalling the terms of a statement by which His Majesty King Hassan II had on 17 September 1974 proposed the joint submission to the International Court of Justice of an issue expressed in the following terms:

> "You, the Spanish Government, claim that the Sahara was *res nullius*. You claim that it was a territory or property left uninherited, you claim that no power and no administration had been established over the Sahara: Morocco claims the contrary. Let us request the arbitration of the International Court of Justice at The Hague.... It will state the law on the basis of the titles submitted...."

Spain has stated before the Court that it did not consent and does not consent now to the submission of this issue to the jurisdiction of the Court.

27. Spain considers that the subject of the dispute which Morocco invited it to submit jointly to the Court for decision in contentious proceedings, and the subject of the questions on which the advisory opinion is requested, are substantially identical; thus the advisory procedure is said to have been used as an alternative after the failure of an attempt to make use of the contentious jurisdiction with regard to the same question. Consequently, to give a reply would, according to Spain, be to allow the advisory procedure to be used as a means of bypassing the consent of a State, which constitutes the basis of the Court's jurisdiction. If the Court were to countenance such a use of its advisory jurisdiction, the outcome would be to obliterate the distinction between the two spheres of the Court's jurisdiction, and the fundamental princi-

ple of the independence of States would be affected, for States would find their disputes with other States being submitted to the Court, by this indirect means, without their consent; this might result in compulsory jurisdiction being achieved by majority vote in a political organ. Such circumvention of the well-established principle of consent for the exercise of international jurisdiction would constitute, according to this view, a compelling reason for declining to answer the request. * * *

29. It is clear that Spain has not consented to the adjudication of the questions formulated in resolution 3292 (XXIX). It did not agree to Morocco's proposal for the joint submission to the Court of the issue raised in the communication of 23 September 1974. Spain made no reply to the letter setting out the proposal, and this was properly understood by Morocco as signifying its rejection by Spain. As to the request for an advisory opinion, the records of the discussions in the Fourth Committee and in the plenary of the General Assembly confirm that Spain raised objections to the Court's being asked for an opinion on the basis of the two questions formulated in the present request. The Spanish delegation stated that it was prepared to join in the request only if the questions put were supplemented by another question establishing a satisfactory balance between the historical and legal exposition of the matter and the current situation viewed in the light of the Charter of the United Nations and the relevant General Assembly resolution on the decolonization of the territory. In view of Spain's persistent objections to the questions formulated in resolution 3292 (XXIX), the fact that it abstained and did not vote against the resolution cannot be interpreted as implying its consent to the adjudication of those questions by the Court. Moreover, its participation in the Court's proceedings cannot be understood as implying that it has consented to the adjudication of the questions posed in resolution 3292 (XXIX), for it has persistently maintained its objections throughout.

[The Court reviews cases where it declined to give an advisory opinion because of the opposition of an interested state.]

33. In certain circumstances, therefore, the lack of consent of an interested State may render the giving of an advisory opinion incompatible with the Court's judicial character. An instance of this would be when the circumstances disclose that to give a reply would have the effect of circumventing the principle that a State is not obliged to allow its disputes to be submitted to judicial settlement without its consent. If such a situation should arise, the powers of the Court under the discretion given to it by Article 65, paragraph 1, of the Statute, would afford sufficient legal means to ensure respect for the fundamental principle of consent to jurisdiction.

34. The situation existing in the present case is not, however, the one envisaged above. There is in this case a legal controversy, but one which arose during the proceedings of the General Assembly and in relation to matters with which it was dealing. It did not arise independently in bilateral relations. In a communication addressed on 10 No-

vember 1958 to the Secretary–General of the United Nations, the Spanish Government stated: "Spain possesses no non-self-governing territories, since the territories subject to its sovereignty in Africa are, in accordance with the legislation now in force, considered to be and classified as provinces of Spain." This gave rise to the "most explicit reservations" of the Government of Morocco, which, in a communication to the Secretary–General of 20 November 1958, stated that it "claim[ed] certain African territories at present under Spanish control as an integral part of Moroccan national territory." * * *

39. * * * The object of the General Assembly has not been to bring before the Court, by way of a request for advisory opinion, a dispute or legal controversy, in order that it may later, on the basis of the Court's opinion, exercise its powers and functions for the peaceful settlement of that dispute or controversy. The object of the request is an entirely different one: to obtain from the Court an opinion which the General Assembly deems of assistance to it for the proper exercise of its functions concerning the decolonization of the territory.

40. The General Assembly, as appears from paragraph 3 of resolution 3292 (XXIX), has asked the Court for an opinion so as to be in a position to decide "on the policy to be followed in order to accelerate the decolonization process in the territory . . . in the best possible conditions, in the light of the advisory opinion. . . ." The true object of the request is also stressed in the preamble of resolution 3292 (XXIX), where it is stated "that it is highly desirable that the General Assembly, in order to continue the discussion of this question at its thirtieth session, should receive an advisory opinion on some important legal aspects of the problem."

41. What the Court said in a similar context, in its Advisory Opinion on *Reservations to the Convention on the Prevention and Punishment of the Crime of Genocide*, applies also to the present case: "The object of this request for an Opinion is to guide the United Nations in respect of its own action." The legitimate interest of the General Assembly in obtaining an opinion from the Court in respect of its own future action cannot be affected or prejudiced by the fact that Morocco made a proposal, not accepted by Spain, to submit for adjudication by the Court a dispute raising issues related to those contained in the request. * * *

42. Furthermore, the origin and scope of the dispute, as above described, are important in appreciating, from the point of view of the exercise of the Court's discretion, the real significance in this case of the lack of Spain's consent. The issue between Morocco and Spain regarding Western Sahara is not one as to the legal status of the territory today, but one as to the rights of Morocco over it at the time of colonization. The settlement of this issue will not affect the rights of Spain today as the administering Power, but will assist the General Assembly in deciding on the policy to be followed in order to accelerate the decolonization process in the territory. It follows that the legal position of the State

which has refused its consent to the present proceedings is not "in any way compromised by the answers that the Court may give to the questions put to it." * * *

75.   Having established that it is seised of a request for advisory opinion which it is competent to entertain and that it should comply with that request, the Court will now examine the two questions which have been referred to it by General Assembly resolution 3292 (XXIX). These questions are so formulated that an answer to the second is called for only if the answer to the first is in the negative:

"I.   Was Western Sahara (Río de Oro and Sakiet El Hamra) at the time of colonization by Spain a territory belonging to no one (*terra nullius*)?

If the answer to the first question is in the negative,

II.   What were the legal ties between this territory and the Kingdom of Morocco and the Mauritanian entity?" * * *

79.   Turning to Question I, the Court observes that the request specifically locates the question in the context of "the time of colonization by Spain," and it therefore seems clear that the words "Was Western Sahara ... a territory belonging to no one (*terra nullius*)?" have to be interpreted by reference to the law in force at that period. The expression "*terra nullius*" was a legal term of art employed in connection with "occupation" as one of the accepted legal methods of acquiring sovereignty over territory. "Occupation" being legally an original means of peaceably acquiring sovereignty over territory otherwise than by cession or succession, it was a cardinal condition of a valid "occupation" that the territory should be terra nullius—a territory belonging to no-one—at the time of the act alleged to constitute the "occupation." In the view of the Court, therefore, a determination that Western Sahara was a "*terra nullius*" at the time of colonization by Spain would be possible only if it were established that at the time the territory belonged to no-one in the sense that it was then open to acquisition through the legal process of "occupation."

80.   Whatever differences of opinion there may have been among jurists, the State practice of the relevant period indicates that territories inhabited by tribes or peoples having a social and political organization were not regarded as *terrae nullius*. It shows that in the case of such territories the acquisition of sovereignty was not generally considered as effected unilaterally through "occupation" of *terra nullius* by original title but through agreements concluded with local rulers. On occasion, it is true, the word "occupation" was used in a non-technical sense denoting simply acquisition of sovereignty; but that did not signify that the acquisition of sovereignty through such agreements with authorities of the country was regarded as an "occupation" of a "*terra nullius*" in the proper sense of these terms. On the contrary, such agreements with local rulers, whether or not considered as an actual "cession" of the territory, were regarded as derivative roots of title, and not original titles obtained by occupation of *terrae nullius*.

81. In the present instance, the information furnished to the Court shows that at the time of colonization Western Sahara was inhabited by peoples which, if nomadic, were socially and politically organized in tribes and under chiefs competent to represent them. It also shows that, in colonizing Western Sahara, Spain did not proceed on the basis that it was establishing its sovereignty over *terrae nullius*. In its Royal Order of 26 December 1884, far from treating the case as one of occupation of *terra nullius*, Spain proclaimed that the King was taking the Río de Oro under his protection on the basis of agreements which had been entered into with the chiefs of the local tribes: the Order referred expressly to "the documents which the independent tribes of this part of the coast" had "signed with the representative of the Sociedad Española de Africanistas," and announced that the King had confirmed "the deeds of adherence" to Spain. Likewise, in negotiating with France concerning the limits of Spanish territory to the north of the Río de Oro, that is, in the Sakiet El Hamra area, Spain did not rely upon any claim to the acquisition of sovereignty over a *terra nullius*.

82. Before the Court, differing views were expressed concerning the nature and legal value of agreements between a State and local chiefs. But the Court is not asked by Question I to pronounce upon the legal character or the legality of the titles which led to Spain becoming the administering Power of Western Sahara. It is asked only to state whether Western Sahara (Río de Oro and Sakiet El Hamra) at the time of colonization by Spain was "a territory belonging to no one (*terra nullius*)." As to this question, the Court is satisfied that, for the reasons which it has given, its answer must be in the negative. Accordingly, the Court does not find it necessary first to pronounce upon the correctness or otherwise of Morocco's view that the territory was not *terra nullius* at the time because the local tribes, so it maintains, were then subject to the sovereignty of the Sultan of Morocco; nor upon Mauritania's corresponding proposition that the territory was not *terra nullius* because the local tribes, in its view, then formed part of the "Bilad Shinguitti" or Mauritanian entity. Any conclusions that the Court may reach with respect to either of these points of view cannot change the negative character of the answer which, for other reasons already set out, it has found that it must give to Question I.

83. The Court's answer to Question I is, therefore, in the negative and, in accordance with the terms of the request, it will now turn to Question II.

84. Question II asks the Court to state "what were the legal ties between this territory"—that is, Western Sahara—"and the Kingdom of Morocco and the Mauritanian entity." The scope of this question depends upon the meaning to be attached to the expression "legal ties" in the context of the time of the colonization of the territory by Spain. That expression, however, unlike "*terra nullius*" in Question I, was not a term having in itself a very precise meaning. Accordingly, in the view of the Court, the meaning of the expression "legal ties" in Question II has to be found rather in the object and purpose of General Assembly

resolution 3292 (XXIX), by which it was decided to request the present advisory opinion of the Court.

85. Analysis of this resolution, as the Court has already pointed out, shows that the two questions contained in the request have been put to the Court in the context of proceedings in the General Assembly directed to the decolonization of Western Sahara in conformity with resolution 1514 (XV) of 14 December 1960. During the discussion of this item, according to resolution 3292 (XXIX), a legal controversy arose over the status of Western Sahara at the time of its colonization by Spain; and the records of the proceedings make it plain that the "legal controversy" in question concerned pretensions put forward, on the one hand, by Morocco that the territory was then a part of the Sherifian State and, on the other, by Mauritania that the territory then formed part of the Bilad Shinguitti or Mauritanian entity. Accordingly, it appears to the Court that in Question II the words "legal ties between this territory and the Kingdom of Morocco and the Mauritanian entity" must be understood as referring to such "legal ties" as may affect the policy to be followed in the decolonization of Western Sahara. In this connection, the Court cannot accept the view that the legal ties the General Assembly had in mind in framing Question II were limited to ties established directly with the territory and without reference to the people who may be found in it. Such an interpretation would unduly restrict the scope of the question, since legal ties are normally established in relation to people.

86. The Court further observes that, inasmuch as Question II had its origin in the contentions of Morocco and Mauritania, it was for them to satisfy the Court in the present proceedings that legal ties existed between Western Sahara and the Kingdom of Morocco or the Mauritanian entity at the time of the colonization of the territory by Spain.

87. Western Sahara (Río de Oro and Sakiet El Hamra) is a territory having very special characteristics which, at the time of colonization by Spain, largely determined the way of life and social and political organization of the people inhabiting it. In consequence, the legal régime of Western Sahara, including its legal relations with neighbouring territories, cannot properly be appreciated without reference to these special characteristics. The territory forms part of the great Sahara desert which extends from the Atlantic coast of Africa to Egypt and the Sudan. At the time of its colonization by Spain, the area of this desert with which the Court is concerned was being exploited, because of its low and spasmodic rainfall, almost exclusively by nomads, pasturing their animals or growing crops as and where conditions were favourable. It may be said that the territory, at the time of its colonization, had a sparse population that, for the most part, consisted of nomadic tribes the members of which traversed the desert on more or less regular routes dictated by the seasons and the wells or water-holes available to them. In general, the Court was informed, the right of pasture was enjoyed in common by these tribes; some areas suitable for cultivation, on the other hand, were subject to a greater degree to separate rights. Perennial

water-holes were in principle considered the property of the tribe which put them into commission, though their use also was open to all, subject to certain customs as to priorities and the amount of water taken. Similarly, many tribes were said to have their recognized burial grounds, which constituted a rallying point for themselves and for allied tribes. Another feature of life in the region, according to the information before the Court, was that inter-tribal conflict was not infrequent.

88. These various points of attraction of a tribe to particular localities were reflected in its nomadic routes. But what is important for present purposes is the fact that the sparsity of the resources and the spasmodic character of the rainfall compelled all those nomadic tribes to traverse very wide areas of the desert. In consequence, the nomadic routes of none of them were confined to Western Sahara; some passed also through areas of southern Morocco, or of present-day Mauritania or Algeria, and some even through further countries. All the tribes were of the Islamic faith and the whole territory lay within the Dar al–Islam. In general, authority in the tribe was vested in a sheikh, subject to the assent of the "Juma'a," that is, of an assembly of its leading members, and the tribe had its own customary law applicable in conjunction with the Koranic law. Not infrequently one tribe had ties with another, either of dependence or of alliance, which were essentially tribal rather than territorial, ties of allegiance or vassalage. * * *

90. Morocco's claim to "legal ties" with Western Sahara at the time of colonization by Spain has been put to the Court as a claim to ties of sovereignty on the ground of an alleged immemorial possession of the territory. This immemorial possession, it maintains, was based not on an isolated act of occupation but on the public display of sovereignty, uninterrupted and uncontested, for centuries.

91. In support of this claim Morocco refers to a series of events stretching back to the Arab conquest of North Africa in the seventh century A.D., the evidence of which is, understandably, for the most part taken from historical works. The far-flung, spasmodic and often transitory character of many of these events renders the historical material somewhat equivocal as evidence of possession of the territory now in question. Morocco, however, invokes *inter alia* the decision of the Permanent Court of International Justice in the *Legal Status of Eastern Greenland* case (*P.C.I.J., Series A/B, No. 53*). Stressing that during a long period Morocco was the only independent State which existed in the north-west of Africa, it points to the geographical contiguity of Western Sahara to Morocco and the desert character of the territory. In the light of these considerations, it maintains that the historical material suffices to establish Morocco's claim to a title based "upon continued display of authority" on the same principles as those applied by the Permanent Court in upholding Denmark's claim to possession of the whole of Greenland.

92. This method of formulating Morocco's claims to ties of sovereignty with Western Sahara encounters certain difficulties. As the Per-

manent Court stated in the case concerning the *Legal Status of Eastern Greenland*, a claim to sovereignty based upon continued display of authority involves "two elements each of which must be shown to exist: the intention and will to act as sovereign, and some actual exercise or display of such authority." True, the Permanent Court recognized that in the case of claims to sovereignty over areas in thinly populated or unsettled countries, "very little in the way of actual exercise of sovereign rights" might be sufficient in the absence of a competing claim. But, in the present instance, Western Sahara, if somewhat sparsely populated, was a territory across which socially and politically organized tribes were in constant movement and where armed incidents between these tribes were frequent. In the particular circumstances outlined in paragraphs 87 and 88 above, the paucity of evidence of actual display of authority unambiguously relating to Western Sahara renders it difficult to consider the Moroccan claim as on all fours with that of Denmark in the *Eastern Greenland* case. Nor is the difficulty cured by introducing the argument of geographical unity or contiguity. In fact, the information before the Court shows that the geographical unity of Western Sahara with Morocco is somewhat debatable, which also militates against giving effect to the concept of contiguity. Even if the geographical contiguity of Western Sahara with Morocco could be taken into account in the present connection, it would only make the paucity of evidence of unambiguous display of authority with respect to Western Sahara more difficult to reconcile with Morocco's claim to immemorial possession. * * *

94. Morocco requests that, in appreciating the evidence, the Court should take account of the special structure of the Sherifian State. No rule of international law, in the view of the Court, requires the structure of a State to follow any particular pattern, as is evident from the diversity of the forms of State found in the world today. Morocco's request is therefore justified. At the same time, where sovereignty over territory is claimed, the particular structure of a State may be a relevant element in appreciating the reality or otherwise of a display of State activity adduced as evidence of that sovereignty.

95. That the Sherifian State at the time of the Spanish colonization of Western Sahara was a State of a special character is certain. Its special character consisted in the fact that it was founded on the common religious bond of Islam existing among the peoples and on the allegiance of various tribes to the Sultan, through their caids or sheikhs, rather than on the notion of territory. Common religious links have, of course, existed in many parts of the world without signifying a legal tie of sovereignty or subordination to a ruler. Even the Dar al–Islam, as Morocco itself pointed out in its oral statement, knows and then knew separate States within the common religious bond of Islam. Political ties of allegiance to a ruler, on the other hand, have frequently formed a major element in the composition of a State. Such an allegiance, however, if it is to afford indications of the ruler's sovereignty, must clearly be real and manifested in acts evidencing acceptance of his political authority. Otherwise, there will be no genuine display or exercise of State

authority. It follows that the special character of the Moroccan State and the special forms in which its exercise of sovereignty may, in consequence, have expressed itself, do not dispense the Court from appreciating whether at the relevant time Moroccan sovereignty was effectively exercised or displayed in Western Sahara. * * *

98.   As evidence of its display of sovereignty in Western Sahara, Morocco has invoked alleged acts of internal display of Moroccan authority and also certain international acts said to constitute recognition by other States of its sovereignty over the whole or part of the territory.

99.   The principal indications of "internal" display of authority invoked by Morocco consist of evidence alleged to show the allegiance of Saharan caids to the Sultan, including dahirs and other documents concerning the appointment of caids, the alleged imposition of Koranic and other taxes, and what were referred to as "military decisions" said to constitute acts of resistance to foreign penetration of the territory. In particular, the allegiance is claimed of the confederation of Tekna tribes, together with its allies, one part of which was stated to be established in the Noun and another part to lead a nomadic life the route of which traversed areas of Western Sahara: through Tekna caids, Morocco claims, the Sultan's authority and influence were exercised on the nomad tribes pasturing in Western Sahara. Moreover, Morocco alleges that, after the marabout Ma ul–'Aineen established himself at Smara in the Sakiet El Hamra in the late 1890s, much of the territory came under the direct authority of this sheikh, and that he himself was the personal representative of the Sultan. Emphasis is also placed by Morocco on two visits of Sultan Hassan I in person to the southern area of the Souss in 1882 and 1886 to maintain and strengthen his authority in the southern part of his realm, and on the despatch of arms by the Sultan to Ma ul–'Aineen and others in the south to reinforce their resistance to foreign penetration. In general, it is urged that Western Sahara has always been linked to the interior of Morocco by common ethnological, cultural and religious ties, and that the Sakiet El Hamra was artificially separated from the Moroccan territory of the Noun by colonization.

100.   Spain, on the other hand, maintains that there is a striking absence of any documentary evidence or other traces of a display of political authority by Morocco with respect to Western Sahara. The acts of appointment of caids produced by Morocco, whether dahirs or official correspondence, do not in Spain's view relate to Western Sahara but to areas within southern Morocco such as the Noun and the Dra'a; nor has any document of acceptance by the recipients been adduced. Furthermore, according to Spain, these alleged appointments as caid were conferred on sheikhs already elected by their own tribes and were, in truth, only titles of honour bestowed on existing and *de facto* independent local rulers. As to the Tekna confederation, its two parts are said to have been in quite different relations to the Sultan: only the settled Tekna, established in southern Morocco, acknowledged their political allegiance to the Sultan, while the nomadic septs of the tribe who traversed the Western Sahara were "free" Tekna, autonomous and

independent of the Sultan. Nor was Ma ul–'Aineen, according to Spain, at any time the personal representative of the Sultan's authority in Western Sahara; on the contrary, he exercised his authority to the south of the Dra'a in complete independence of the Sultan; his relations with the Sultan were based on mutual respect and a common interest in resisting French expansion from the south; they were relations of equality, not political ties of allegiance or of sovereignty.

101. Further, Spain invokes the absence of any evidence of the payment of taxes by tribes of Western Sahara and denies all possibility of such evidence being adduced; according to Spain, it was a characteristic even of the Bled Siba that the tribes refused to be taxed, and in Western Sahara there was no question of taxes having been paid to the Makhzen. As to the Sultan's expeditions of 1882 and 1886, these, according to Spain, are shown by the historical evidence never to have reached Western Sahara or even the Dra'a, but only the Souss and the Noun; nor did they succeed in completely subjecting even those areas; and they cannot therefore constitute evidence of display of authority with respect to Western Sahara. Their purpose, Spain maintains, was to prevent commerce between Europeans and the tribes of the Souss and Noun, and this purpose was unrelated to Western Sahara. Again, the alleged acts of resistance in Western Sahara to foreign penetration are said by Spain to have been nothing more than occasional raids to obtain booty or hostages for ransom and to have nothing to do with display of Moroccan authority. In general, both on geographical and on other grounds, Spain questions the unity of the Saharan region with the regions of southern Morocco. * * *

103. The Court does not overlook the position of the Sultan of Morocco as a religious leader. In the view of the Court, however, the information and arguments invoked by Morocco cannot, for the most part, be considered as disposing of the difficulties in the way of its claim to have exercised effectively internal sovereignty over Western Sahara. The material before the Court appears to support the view that almost all the dahirs and other acts concerning caids relate to areas situated within present-day Morocco itself and do not in themselves provide evidence of effective display of Moroccan authority in Western Sahara. Nor can the information furnished by Morocco be said to provide convincing evidence of the imposition or levying of Moroccan taxes with respect to the territory. As to Sheikh Ma ul–'Aineen, the complexities of his career may leave doubts as to the precise nature of his relations with the Sultan, and different interpretations have been put upon them. The material before the Court, taken as a whole, does not suffice to convince it that the activities of this sheikh should be considered as having constituted a display of the Sultan's authority in Western Sahara at the time of its colonization.

[The Court reviews other evidence relating to possible acts of sovereignty relating to the Western Sahara.]

150. In the light of the above considerations, the Court must conclude that at the time of colonization by Spain there did not exist between the territory of Western Sahara and the Mauritanian entity any tie of sovereignty, or of allegiance of tribes, or of "simple inclusion" in the same legal entity. * * *

162. The materials and information presented to the Court show the existence, at the time of Spanish colonization, of legal ties of allegiance between the Sultan of Morocco and some of the tribes living in the territory of Western Sahara. They equally show the existence of rights, including some rights relating to the land, which constituted legal ties between the Mauritanian entity, as understood by the Court, and the territory of Western Sahara. On the other hand, the Court's conclusion is that the materials and information presented to it do not establish any tie of territorial sovereignty between the territory of Western Sahara and the Kingdom of Morocco or the Muaritanian entity. Thus the Court has not found legal ties of such a nature as might affect the application of resolution 1514 (XV) in the decolonization of Western Sahara and, in particular, of the principle of self-determination through the free and genuine expression of the will of the peoples of the Territory * * *.

163. For these reasons,

THE COURT DECIDES,

with regard to Question I,

by 13 votes to 3,

and with regard to Question II,

by 14 votes to 2,

to comply with the request for an advisory opinion;

THE COURT IS OF OPINION,

with regard to Question I,

unanimously,

that Western Sahara (Río de Oro and Sakiet El Hamra) at the time of colonization by Spain was not a territory belonging to no-one (*terra nullius*);

with regard to Question II,

by 14 votes to 2,

that there were legal ties between this territory and the Kingdom of Morocco of the kinds indicated in paragraph 162 of this Opinion;

by 15 votes to 1,

that there were legal ties between this territory and the Mauritanian entity of the kinds indicated in paragraph 162 of this Opinion.

Notes and Questions

1. *A Contentious Case?* Was the Court's advisory opinion in *Western Sahara* really a contentious case submitted to the ICJ via the General Assembly after Spain refused Morocco's request to accept judicial settlement of the dispute? Why did Morocco want to go to the Court? Note that Morocco would have formulated the question on which an advisory opinion was sought differently from the way the General Assembly eventually phrased the question; Morocco proposed that the question to be resolved was whether the Western Sahara had, at the time of colonization, been *terra nullius* or under Moroccan sovereignty. See Malcolm Shaw, "The *Western Sahara* Case," 49 *British Yearbook of International Law* 119, 124 (1978). Did the ICJ adequately justify its decision to render an advisory opinion?

2. *Answering the Referendum Question.* Why did the ICJ answer the "unasked question," *i.e.*, whether the peoples of the Western Sahara are entitled to a referendum about their future? Did the Court stress the need for a referendum because it took account of its role as an organ of the United Nations? Or because it anticipated that Morocco would greet its opinion as a victory for Morocco and invade the Western Sahara?

3. *The Political Aftermath.* Morocco indeed did invade the Western Sahara in November 1975. By the mid–1980's, Morocco was spending some $17 million a day to prosecute its war efforts against the nationalist Polisario Front there. Morocco built a 1243–mile–long wall in the Western Sahara costing billions of dollars and equipped with radar and alarm systems, to keep the Polisario away from valuable land and Moroccan fishing boats. See Louise Lief, "Saudi King Intervenes in Western Sahara in Bid to Stem Conflict," *The Christian Science Monitor*, May 8, 1987, at 11. Following a cease-fire, a United Nations peace-keeping force entered the Western Sahara in 1991, charged with implementing a referendum as suggested by the ICJ. Yet, the dispute in the Western Sahara carries on. In 1995, Morocco was blamed for attempting to block the U.N.–sponsored referendum on sovereignty in the territory. Chris Hedges, "Morocco, Defending Claim in the Desert, Exerts a Hand on Neighbor's Vote," *New York Times,* Mar. 5, 1995, § 1, at 5. The stalemate continues. The Western Sahara is still classified by the United Nations as awaiting "decolonization." John F. Burns, "Sahara Impasse: Line in the Sand or National Boundary?," *New York Times*, June 16, 1999, at A10. In October 2000, U.N. Secretary–General Kofi Annan "came close to admitting that the plebiscite was unlikely ever to take place." "Triumph for Procrastination," *The Economist*, Nov. 4, 2000, at 52.

4. *Respecting Advisory Opinions.* How similar is an advisory opinion like that in *Western Sahara* to a judgment in a contentious case like *Diplomatic and Consular Staff*? Neither case was particularly well-respected in practice. Is the Court's prestige less damaged by a disregarded advisory opinion, where there is no legal obligation to obey the opinion, than by a disregarded judgment in a contentious case? Do both serve the same marshalling of public opinion and generation of law functions?

4. CHAMBERS AT THE INTERNATIONAL COURT

Lately, the Court has been willing to hear cases submitted to it via chambers pursuant to Article 26 of its Statute. One of these chambers cases, *ELSI*, is excerpted below. Ask whether the chambers procedure makes it more likely that states will turn to the ICJ.

STATUTE OF THE INTERNATIONAL COURT OF JUSTICE, ARTICLE 26

June 26, 1945, 59 Stat. 1031, T.S. No. 993.

1.   The Court may from time to time form one or more chambers, composed of three or more judges as the Court may determine, for dealing with particular categories of cases; for example, labor cases and cases relating to transit and communications.

2.   The Court may at any time form a chamber for dealing with a particular case. The number of judges to constitute such a chamber shall be determined by the Court with the approval of the parties.

3.   Cases shall be heard and determined by the chambers provided for in this Article if the parties so request.

THE ELSI CASE

United States v. Italy,
1989 I.C.J. 15, 1989 WL 139016.

1.   By a letter dated 6 February 1987, filed in the Registry of the Court the same day, the Secretary of State of the United States of America transmitted to the Court an Application instituting proceedings against the Republic of Italy in respect of a dispute arising out of the requisition by the Government of Italy of the plant and related assets of Raytheon–Elsi S.p.A., previously known as Elettronica Sicula S.p.A. (ELSI), an Italian company which was stated to have been 100 per cent owned by two United States corporations. By the same letter, the Secretary of State informed the Court that the Government of the United States requested, pursuant to Article 26 of the Statute of the Court, that the dispute be resolved by a Chamber of the Court.

2.   Pursuant to Article 40, paragraph 2, of the Statute, the Application was at once communicated to the Government of the Republic of Italy. In accordance with paragraph 3 of that Article, all other States entitled to appear before the Court were notified of the Application.

3.   By a telegram dated 13 February 1987 the Minister for Foreign Affairs of Italy informed the Court that his Government accepted the proposal put forward by the Government of the United States that the case be heard by a Chamber composed in accordance with Article 26 of the Statute; this acceptance was confirmed by a letter dated 13 February 1987 from the Agent of Italy.

4.   By an Order dated 2 March 1987, the Court, after recalling the request for a Chamber and reciting that the Parties had been duly consulted as to the composition of the proposed Chamber in accordance with Article 26, paragraph 2, of the Statute * * * decided to accede to the request of the Governments of the United States of America and

Italy to form a special Chamber of five judges to deal with the case, declared that at an election held on that day President Nagendra Singh and Judges Oda, Ago, Schwebel and Sir Robert Jennings had been elected to the Chamber, and declared a Chamber to deal with the case to have been duly constituted by the Order, with the composition indicated. * * *

6.   On 11 December 1988 Judge Nagendra Singh, President of the Chamber, died. Following further consultations with the Parties * * *, the Court, by Order dated 20 December 1988, declared that Judge Ruda, President of the Court, had that day been elected a Member of the Chamber to fill the vacancy left by the death of Judge Nagendra Singh. * * * President Ruda became President of the Chamber. * * *

12.   The claim of the United States in the present case is that Italy has violated the international legal obligations which it undertook by the Treaty of Friendship, Commerce and Navigation between the two countries concluded on 2 February 1948 ("the FCN Treaty") and the Supplementary Agreement thereto concluded on 26 September 1951, by reason of its acts and omissions in relation to, and its treatment of, two United States corporations, the Raytheon Company ("Raytheon") and The Machlett Laboratories Incorporated ("Machlett"), in relation to the Italian corporation Raytheon–Elsi S.p.A. (previously Elettronica Sicula S.p.A. (ELSI)), which was wholly owned by the two United States corporations. Italy contests certain of the facts alleged by the United States, denies that there has been any violation of the FCN Treaty, and contends, on a subsidiary and alternative basis, that if there was any such violation, no injury was caused for which payment of any indemnity would be justified.

13.   In 1955, Raytheon (then known as Raytheon Manufacturing Company) agreed to subscribe for 14 per cent of the shares in Elettronica Sicula S.p.A. Over the period 1956–1967, Raytheon successively increased its holding of ELSI shares (as well as investing capital in the company in other ways) to a total holding of 99.16 per cent of its shares. In April 1963 the name of the company was changed from Elettronica Sicula S.p.A. to "Raytheon–Elsi S.p.A."; it will however be referred to hereafter as "ELSI." The remaining shares (0.84 per cent) in ELSI were acquired in April 1967 by Machlett, which was a wholly-owned subsidiary of Raytheon. ELSI was established in Palermo, Sicily, where it had a plant for the production of electronic components; in 1967 it had a workforce of slightly under 900 employees. Its five major product lines were microwave tubes, cathode-ray tubes, semiconductor rectifiers, X-ray tubes and surge arresters.

14.   During the fiscal years 1964 to 1966 inclusive, ELSI made an operating profit, but this profit was insufficient to offset its debt expense or accumulated losses, and no dividends were ever paid to its shareholders. * * * In February 1967, according to the United States, Raytheon began taking steps to endeavour to make ELSI self-sufficient. Raytheon and Machlett designated a number of highly-qualified personnel to provide financial, managerial and technical expertise, and Raytheon

provided a total of over 4,000 million lire in recapitalization and guaranteed credit. By December 1967, according to the United States, major steps had been taken to upgrade plant facilities and operations. * * *

16.   The management of ELSI took the view that one of the reasons for its lack of success was that it had trained and was employing an excessively large labour force. In June 1967 it was decided to dismiss some 300 employees; under an Italian union agreement this involved a procedure of notifications and negotiations. * * * [A]n alternative plan was agreed to whereby 168 workers would be suspended from 10 July 1967, with limited pay by ELSI for a period not exceeding six weeks. After a training programme during which the workers were paid by the Sicilian Government, it was contemplated that ELSI would endeavor to reemploy the suspended employees. The necessary additional business to make this possible was not forthcoming, and the suspended employees were dismissed early in March 1968. * * *

17.   When it became apparent that the discussions with Italian officials and companies were unlikely to lead to a mutually satisfactory arrangement to resolve ELSI's difficulties, Raytheon and Machlett, as shareholders in ELSI, began seriously to plan to close and liquidate ELSI to minimize their losses. General planning for the potential liquidation of ELSI began in the latter part of 1967, and in early 1968 detailed plans were made for a shut-down and liquidation at any time after 16 March 1968. * * *

25.   In the view of ELSI's legal counsel at the time * * * and of Italian lawyers consulted by the United States, ELSI was in March 1968 entitled to engage in orderly liquidation of its assets, was under no obligation to file a petition in bankruptcy, and was never in jeopardy of compulsory dissolution under Article 2447 of the Italian Civil Code, and was at all times in compliance with Article 2446 of the Code. It has however been contended by Italy that ELSI was in March 1968 unable to pay its debts, and its capital of 4,000 million lire was completely lost; accordingly, an orderly liquidation was not available to it, but as an insolvent debtor it was under an obligation to file a petition in bankruptcy. * * *

30.   On 1 April 1968 the Mayor of Palermo issued an order, effective immediately, requisitioning ELSI's plant and related assets for a period of six months. The text of this order, in the translation supplied by the United States, was as follows:

> *"The Mayor of the Municipality of Palermo,*
>
> *Taking into consideration* that Raytheon–Elsi of Palermo has decided to close its plant located in this city at Via Villagrazia, 79, because of market difficulties and lack of orders;
>
> *That* the company has furthermore decided to send dismissal letters to the personnel consisting of about 1,000 persons;
>
> *Taking notice* that ELSI's actions, besides provoking the reaction of the workers and of the unions giving rise to strikes (both

general and sectional) has caused a wide and general movement of solidarity of all public opinion which has strongly stigmatized the action taken considering that about 1,000 families are suddenly destituted;

That, considering the fact that ELSI is the second firm in order of importance in the District, because of the shutdown of the plant a serious damage will be caused to the District, which has been so severely tried by the earthquakes had during the month of January 1968;

Considering also that the local press is taking a great interest in the situation and that the press is being very critical toward the authorities and is accusing them of indifference to this serious civic problem;

That, furthermore, the present situation is particularly touchy and unforeseeable disturbances of public order could take place;

Taking into consideration that in this particular instance there is sufficient ground for holding that there is a grave public necessity and urgency to protect the general economic public interest (already seriously compromised) and public order, and that these reasons justify requisitioning the plant and all equipment owned by Raytheon–Elsi located here at Via Villagrazia 79; * * *

Orders

the requisition, with immediate effect and for the duration of six months, except as may be necessary to extend such period, and without prejudice for the rights of the parties and of third parties, of the plant and relative equipment owned by Raytheon–Elsi of Palermo.

With a subsequent decree, the indemnification to be paid to said company for the requisition will be established.''

The order was served on the company on 2 April 1968.

31. On 6 April 1968 the Mayor issued an order entrusting the management of the requisitioned plant to Mr. Aldo Profumo, the Managing Director of ELSI, for the purpose, *inter alia*, of "avoiding any damage to the equipment and machinery due to the abandoning of all activity, including maintenance." Mr. Profumo declined to accept this appointment, and on 16 April 1968 the Mayor wrote to Mr. Silvio Laurin, the senior director, appointing him temporarily to replace Mr. Profumo "in the same capacity, with the same powers, functions and limitations," and Mr. Laurin accepted this appointment. The company management requested another of its directors, Mr. Rico Merluzzo, to stay at the plant night and day "to preclude local authorities from somehow asserting that the plant had been 'abandoned' by ELSI."

32. On 9 April 1968 ELSI addressed a telegram to the Mayor of Palermo, with copies to other Government authorities, claiming *(inter alia)* that the requisition was illegal and expressing the company's

intention to take all legal steps to have it revoked and to claim damages. On 12 April 1968 the company served on the Mayor a formal document dated 11 April 1968 inviting him to revoke the requisition order. The Mayor did not respond and the order was not revoked, and on 19 April 1968 ELSI brought an administrative appeal against it to the Prefect of Palermo, who was empowered to hear appeals against decisions by local governmental officials. The decision on that appeal was not given until 22 August 1969 * * * ; in the meantime however the requisition was not formally prolonged, and therefore ceased to have legal effect after six months, more than four months after the bankruptcy of ELSI had been declared * * *. * * *

44. In the bankruptcy proceedings, creditors presented claims against ELSI totalling some 13,000 million lire; these did not include amounts due to Raytheon and Raytheon Service Company * * *. The bankruptcy proceedings closed in November 1985. According to the bankruptcy reports, the bankruptcy realized only some 6,370 million lire for ELSI's assets, as compared with the minimum liquidation value estimated by ELSI's management in March 1968 at 10,840 million lire. Of the amount realized, some 6,080 million lire went to pay banks, employees, and other creditors. The remainder went to pay bankruptcy administration, tax, registry, and customs charges. All of the secured and preferred creditors who filed claims in the bankruptcy were paid in full. The unsecured creditors received less than one per cent of their claims; accordingly no surplus remained for distribution to the shareholders, Raytheon and Machlett.

45. Raytheon had guaranteed the indebtedness of ELSI to a number of banks, and on the bankruptcy of ELSI it was accordingly liable for, and paid, the sum of 5,787.6 million lire to the banks in accordance with the terms of the guarantees. * * *

46. On 7 February 1974, the Embassy in Rome of the United States transmitted to the Italian Ministry of Foreign Affairs a note enclosing the "claim of the Government of the United States of America on behalf of Raytheon Company and Machlett Laboratories, Incorporated." * * *

48. It is common ground between the Parties that the Court has jurisdiction in the present case, under Article 36, paragraph 1, of its Statute, and Article XXVI of the Treaty of Friendship, Commerce and Navigation, of 2 June 1948 ("the FCN Treaty"), between Italy and the United States; which Article reads:

> "Any dispute between the High Contracting Parties as to the interpretation or the application of this Treaty, which the High Contracting Parties shall not satisfactorily adjust by diplomacy, shall be submitted to the International Court of Justice, unless the High Contracting Parties shall agree to settlement by some other pacific means." * * *

56. The damage claimed in this case to have been caused to Raytheon and Machlett is said to have resulted from the "losses incurred

by ELSI's owners as a result of the involuntary change in the manner of disposing of ELSI's assets'': and it is the requisition order that is said to have caused this change, and which is therefore at the core of the United States complaint. * * *

65.   The acts of the Respondent which are thus alleged to violate its treaty obligations were described by the Applicant's counsel in terms which it is convenient to cite here:

> "First, the Respondent violated its legal obligations when it unlawfully requisitioned the ELSI plant on 1 April 1968 which denied the ELSI stockholders their direct right to liquidate the ELSI assets in an orderly fashion. Second, the Respondent violated its obligations when it allowed ELSI workers to occupy the plant. Third, the Respondent violated its obligations when it unreasonably delayed ruling on the lawfulness of the requisition for 16 months until immediately after the ELSI plant, equipment and work-in-process had all been acquired by ELTEL. Fourth and finally, the Respondent violated its obligations when it interfered with the ELSI bankruptcy proceedings, which allowed the Respondent to realize its previously expressed intention of acquiring ELSI for a price far less than its fair market value." * * *

67.   The Chamber is faced with a situation of mixed fact and law of considerable complexity, wherein several different strands of fact and law have to be examined both separately and for their effect on each other: the meaning and effect of the relevant Articles of the FCN Treaty and Supplementary Agreement; the legal status of the Mayor's requisition of ELSI's plant and assets; and the legal and practical significance of the financial position of ELSI at material times, and its effect, if any, upon ELSI's plan for orderly liquidation of the company. It will be convenient to begin by examining these considerations in relation to the Applicant's claim that the requisition order was a violation of Article III of the FCN Treaty.

68.   Article III of the FCN Treaty is in two paragraphs. Paragraph 1 provides for rights of participation of nationals of one High Contracting Party, in corporations and associations of the other High Contracting Party, and for the exercise by such corporations and associations of their functions. Since there is no allegation of treatment less favourable than is required according to the standards set by this paragraph, it need not detain the Chamber. Paragraph 2 of Article III is however important for the Applicant's claim; it provides:

> "The nationals, corporations and associations of either High Contracting Party shall be permitted, in conformity with the applicable laws and regulations within the territories of the other High Contracting Party, to organize, control and manage corporations and associations of such other High Contracting Party for engaging in commercial, manufacturing, processing, mining, educational, philanthropic, religious and scientific activities. Corporations and asso-

ciations, controlled by nationals, corporations and associations of either High Contracting Party and created or organized under the applicable laws and regulations within the territories of the other High Contracting Party, shall be permitted to engage in the afore-mentioned activities therein, in conformity with the applicable laws and regulations, upon terms no less favorable than those now or hereafter accorded to corporations and associations of such other High Contracting Party controlled by its own nationals, corporations and associations."

Again there is no allegation of treatment of ELSI according to standards less favourable than those laid down in the second sentence of the paragraph: the allegation by the United States of a violation of this paragraph by Italy relates to the first sentence.

69.   In terms of the present case, the effect of the first sentence of this paragraph is that Raytheon and Machlett are to be permitted, in conformity with the applicable laws and regulations within the territory of Italy, to organize, control and manage ELSI. The claim of the United States focuses on the right to "control and manage"; the right to "organize," apparently in the sense of the creation of a corporation, is not in question in this case. Is there, then, a violation of this Article if, as the United States alleges, the requisition had the effect of depriving ELSI of both the right and practical possibility of selling off its plant and assets for satisfaction of its liabilities to its creditors and satisfaction of its shareholders? * * *

85.   Did ELSI, in this precarious position at the end of March 1968, still have the practical possibility to proceed with an orderly liquidation plan? The successful implementation of a plan of orderly liquidation would have depended upon a number of factors not under the control of ELSI's management. Since the company's coffers were dangerously low, funds had to be forthcoming to maintain the cash flow necessary while the plan was being carried out. Evidence has been produced by the Applicant that Raytheon was prepared to supply cash flow and other assistance necessary to effect the orderly liquidation, and the Chamber sees no reason to question that Raytheon had entered or was ready to enter into such a commitment. Other factors governing the matter however give rise to some doubt.

86.   First, for the success of the plan it was necessary that the major creditors (i.e., the banks) would be willing to wait for payment of their claims until the sale of the assets released funds to settle them: and this applied not only to the capital sums outstanding, which may not at the time have yet been legally due for repayment, but also the agreed payments of interest or installments of capital. Though the Chamber has been given no specific information on the point, this is of the essence of such a liquidation plan: the creditors had to be asked to give the company time. If ELSI had been confident of continuing to meet all its obligations promptly and regularly while seeking a buyer for its assets, no negotiations with creditors, and no elaborate calculations of division

of the proceeds, on different hypotheses, such as have been produced to the Chamber, would have been needed.

87. Secondly, the management were by no means certain that the sale of the assets would realize enough to pay all creditors in full; in fact, the existence of the calculation of a "quick-sale value" suggests perhaps more than uncertainty. Thus the creditors had to be asked to give time in return for an assurance, not that 100 per cent would be paid, but that a minimum of 50 per cent would be paid. While in general it might be in the creditors' interest to agree to such a proposal, this does not mean in this case that ELSI could count on such agreement. * * *

88. Nor should it be overlooked that the dismissed employees of ELSI ranked as preferential creditors for such sums as might be due to them for severance pay or arrears. In this respect Italy has drawn attention to the Sicilian regional law of 13 May 1968, providing for the payment

> "for the months of March, April and May 1968, to the dismissed employees of Raytheon–Elsi of Palermo of a special monthly indemnity equal to the actual monthly pay received until the month of February 1968."

From this it could be inferred, said Italy, that ELSI did not pay its employees for the month of March 1968. Further it was conceded by the former Chairman of ELSI, when he appeared as a witness and was cross-examined, that the cash available at 31 March 1968 ("22 million in the kitty"), would have been insufficient to meet the payroll of the full staff even for the first week of April ("at least 25 million"). The suggestion that ELSI did not meet its March 1968 payroll was not put to the witness; and counsel for the United States later stated that the assertion that "ELSI could not make its March payroll," was "simply wrong." It is in any event certain that when the company ceased activity there were still severance payments due to the dismissed staff; those, the Applicant suggested, would have been covered by funds to be provided by Raytheon * * *. They could not have been met from the money still remaining in ELSI's coffers at the time.

89. Thirdly, the plan as formulated by ELSI's management involved a potential inequality among creditors: unless enough was realized to cover the liabilities fully, the major creditors were to be content with some 50 per cent of their claims; but the smaller creditors were still to be paid in full. * * * [This] was an additional factor which might have caused a major creditor to hesitate to agree. According to the evidence, when in late March 1968 ELSI started using funds made available by Raytheon to pay off the small creditors in full, "the banks intervened and said that they did not want that to happen as that was showing preference." Once the banks adopted this attitude, the whole orderly liquidation plan was jeopardized, because a purpose of the settlement with small creditors was, according to the 1974 diplomatic claim, "to eliminate the risk that a small irresponsible creditor would take precipi-

tous action which would raise formidable obstacles in the way of orderly liquidation."

90. Fourthly, the assets of the company had to be sold with the minimum delay and at the best price obtainable—desiderata which are often in practice irreconcilable. The United States has emphasized the damaging effect of the requisition on attempts to realize the assets; after the requisition it was no longer possible for prospective buyers to view the plant, nor to assure them that if they bought they would obtain immediate possession. It is however not at all certain that the company could have counted on unfettered access to its premises and plant, and the opportunity of showing it to buyers without disturbance, even if the requisition had not been made. There has been argument between the Parties on the question whether and to what extent the plant was occupied by employees of ELSI both before and after the requisition; but what is clear is that the company was expecting trouble at the plant when its closure plans became known: the books had been removed to Milan, according to the evidence given at the hearings, "so that if we did have problems we could at least control the books" and "we had moved quite a lot of inventory [to Milan] so that we could sell it from there if we had to."

91. Fifthly, there was the attitude of the Sicilian administration: the company was well aware that the administration was strongly opposed to a closure of the plant, or more specifically, to a dismissal of the workers. True, the measure used to try to prevent this—the requisition order—was found by the Prefect to have lacked the "juridical cause which might justify it and make it operative" * * *. But ELSI's management in March 1968 could not have been certain that the hostility of the local authorities to their plan of closure and dismissals would not take practical form in a legal manner. The company's management had been told before the staff dismissal letters were sent out that such dismissals would lead to a requisition of the plant.

92. All these factors point towards a conclusion that the feasibility at 31 March 1968 of a plan of orderly liquidation, an essential link in the chain of reasoning upon the United States claim rests, has not been sufficiently established. * * *

137. For these reasons,

THE CHAMBER, * * *

(2) By four votes to one,

Finds that the Italian Republic has not committed any of the breaches, alleged in the said Application, of the Treaty of Friendship, Commerce and Navigation between the Parties signed at Rome on 2 February 1948, or of the Agreement Supplementing that Treaty signed by the Parties at Washington on 26 September 1951.

IN FAVOUR: *President* Ruda; *Judges* Oda, Ago and Sir Robert Jennings;

AGAINST: *Judge* Schwebel. * * *

DISSENTING OPINION OF JUDGE SCHWEBEL * * *

The Chamber's Judgment concludes that "the possibility" of an orderly liquidation by ELSI "is purely a matter of speculation." I agree that an orderly liquidation would have been beset with uncertainties, but those uncertainties go not so much to ELSI's ability and entitlement to liquidate its assets as to the calculability of the damages which may be found to flow from the denial of that ability and entitlement by the requisition imposed upon ELSI.

In my view, it is unpersuasive for the Chamber to say, in effect, that ELSI would have gone into bankruptcy later if not sooner, and accordingly that the requisition did not matter. It is in this respect that I believe that the Chamber muddles what it finds to be the facts with time factors. At the time the requisition took place, it did matter, it did have the economic effects, or some of the economic effects, just described; and at the time it took place, it deprived Raytheon and Machlett of their right to control and manage and hence liquidate ELSI and it deprived ELSI of its right to be liquidated by a management responsible to Raytheon and Machlett. Accordingly the requisition placed Italy in violation of its obligation under Article III of the Treaty to permit Raytheon and Machlett to "control and manage" ELSI.

This conclusion is the more compelling when the meaning of the Treaty is interpreted in the light of the provisions and ratification processes set out in this opinion. Can it be said that the requisition, imposed as it was when it was, comported with the "full rights" of Raytheon and Machlett to "organize, direct and control" ELSI, that it comported with their "unobstructed control" and "maximum freedom of choice"? Was it consistent with "the principles of equitable treatment" which the Preamble to the Supplementary Agreement describes the Treaty as containing? Was the requisition consonant with assuring to Raytheon "the most liberal treatment practicable" in respect of the repatriation of its invested capital? Did it respect "the guaranty against political risks" which the Treaty as a whole was designed to provide? Not in my view.

Notes and Questions

1. *The Decision to Use Chambers.* The United States brought the *ELSI Case* with Italy to the ICJ shortly after the U.S. backed away from participating in the merits stage of the *Nicaragua Case* and after it withdrew its consent to the Court's Article 36(2) compulsory jurisdiction, events that are chronicled in Chapter 9. Previously, the United States and Italy had been planning to take the ELSI dispute to an arbitral tribunal. See W. Michael Reisman, *Systems of Control in International Adjudication and Arbitration* 43 (1992). Having decided to go to the International Court, why would the United States and Italy choose to employ a five-judge chamber? Why would the Court have agreed to proceedings by a chamber rather than by its full membership?

2. *Fact or Law?* Rather than a legal problem, was it the facts that lost the case for Raytheon and the United States? Did they fail to establish that ELSI was sufficiently financed at the time of the requisition to permit an orderly liquidation of its assets? See Sean D. Murphy, "The ELSI Case: An Investment Dispute at the International Court of Justice," 16 *Yale Journal of International Law* 391 (1991). Was the *ELSI* chamber realistic in expecting that the course of any international bankruptcy could be accurately foreseen?

3. *Access to the International Court.* Note that Raytheon itself had no standing to bring suit in the ICJ. The Statute of the ICJ provides that "only states may be parties in cases before the Court." Why was the U.S. government willing to forward Raytheon's case to The Hague Court? What would be objections the U.S. government might have had to so "internationalizing" the ELSI dispute? Certainly, if private litigants like Raytheon could bring cases themselves to the ICJ, there would be far more cases for the ICJ. Is this an argument for or against a right of private parties to sue in the ICJ? Could there be a half-way house, where municipal courts could refer international legal issues to the ICJ? There is such a mechanism, called a Preliminary Ruling, already in European law: Article 177 of the EEC Treaty permits domestic judges to ask the European Court of Justice in Luxembourg for their advice relating to the Treaty.

4. *The ICJ and Other International Courts and Tribunals.* Nowadays the International Court has been joined by many other international courts and tribunals. We explore several of them in this book: the European Court of Human Rights in Chapters 1, 2, and 6, the European Court of Justice in Chapter 3, the dispute settlement panels of the World Trade Organization in Chapter 10, the International Tribunal for the Law of the Sea in Chapter 11, various forms of international arbitration here in Chapter 5, as well as in Chapters 3, 9, 10, 11, and 12, and the Nuremberg Tribunal and the proposed International Criminal Court in Chapter 6.

What roles should the ICJ play now that there are so many other international courts and tribunals? How should this new panoply of international dispute-settlement procedures be made to work together effectively and efficiently? See *International Courts for the Twenty–First Century* (Mark W. Janis ed. 1992). What can be done to make the ICJ more up-to-date? Modernizing the Court's antiquated procedures has been termed the ICJ's "foremost challenge" by its new President, Gilbert Guillaume of France. "Press Conference of Judge Gilbert Guillaume, President of the International Court Of Justice," *ICJ Communiqué* No. 2000/5, Feb. 16, 2000. Presently the Court has about 24 cases pending, a "negligible" number when compared to other international tribunals like the European Court of Human Rights and the European Court of Justice. However, even that small amount of pending work has led to enormous delays. *Id.*

Chapter 6

INDIVIDUALS
AND INTERNATIONAL LAW

The legal status of individuals has been a controversial topic in international law. The classical law of nations of the 17th and 18th centuries gave individuals legal rights and duties, but, as we explore in Part A below, the narrow positivist doctrine of the 19th and early 20th centuries treated individuals as mere objects of international law. Part B introduces the modern concept of individuals as subjects of international law, a theme developed in Part C, which provides an overview of the development of international human rights law in the later 20th century. Finally follow cases and commentary on two of the most important modern aspects of the rights and duties of individuals in international law: European human rights law in Part D and the International Criminal Court in Part E.

A. INDIVIDUALS AS OBJECTS
OF INTERNATIONAL LAW

In the traditional positivistic international law of the 19th and early 20th centuries, individuals were viewed as "objects" of international law. Although individuals were not deemed to be "subjects" of international law (and so had neither international legal rights nor duties), they could be objects of state versus state litigation. So grew up doctrines of state protection of individuals and state responsibility for injuries done to individuals. However, the traditional doctrines of state protection and state responsibility have at least three significant limitations. First, as we see in *Nottebohm* below, individuals may only be protected by their national states; national links may be elusive. Second, when the notion of national links is extended to corporations, even more confusion can result, as *Barcelona Traction* illustrates. Finally, the objective view of individuals leaves nationals open to abuse by their own states, since it is impractical to conceive of a state protecting its own national against itself in international law.

THE NOTTEBOHM CASE

Liechtenstein v. Guatemala, 1955 I.C.J. 4, 1955 WL 1.

[Nottebohm, born German, obtained Liechtenstein citizenship in 1939, but nonetheless was subject to Guatemalan penalties as a German enemy alien during the Second World War. Liechtenstein sued Guatemala on Nottebohm's behalf in the ICJ, but Guatemala objected that Liechtenstein was not a state that might legitimately protect Nottebohm before the Court.]

Nottebohm was born at Hamburg on September 16th, 1881. He was German by birth, and still possessed German nationality when, in October 1939, he applied for naturalization in Liechtenstein.

In 1905 he went to Guatemala. He took up residence there and made that country the headquarters of his business activities, which increased and prospered; these activities developed in the field of commerce, banking and plantations. Having been an employee in the firm of Nottebohm Hermanos, which had been founded by his brothers Juan and Arturo, he became their partner in 1912 and later, in 1937, he was made head of the firm. After 1905 he sometimes went to Germany on business and to other countries for holidays. He continued to have business connections in Germany. He paid a few visits to a brother who had lived in Liechtenstein since 1931. Some of his other brothers, relatives and friends were in Germany, others in Guatemala. He himself continued to have his fixed abode in Guatemala until 1943, that is to say, until the occurrence of the events which constitute the basis of the present dispute.

In 1939, after having provided for the safeguarding of his interests in Guatemala by a power of attorney given to the firm of Nottebohm Hermanos on March 22nd, he left that country at a date fixed by Counsel for Liechtenstein as at approximately the end of March or the beginning of April, when he seems to have gone to Hamburg, and later to have paid a few brief visits to Vaduz where he was at the beginning of October 1939. It was then, on October 9th, a little more than a month after the opening of the second World War marked by Germany's attack on Poland, that his attorney, Dr. Marxer, submitted an application for naturalization on behalf of Nottebohm.

The Liechtenstein Law of January 4th, 1934, lays down the conditions for the naturalization of foreigners, specifies the supporting documents to be submitted and the undertakings to be given and defines the competent organs for giving a decision and the procedure to be followed. The Law specifies certain mandatory requirements, namely, that the applicant for naturalization should prove: (1) "that the acceptance into the Home Corporation (*Heimatverband*) of a Liechtenstein commune has been promised to him in case of acquisition of the nationality of the State"; (2) that he will lose his former nationality as a result of naturalization, although this requirement may be waived under stated conditions. It further makes naturalization conditional upon compliance with the requirement of residence for at least three years in the territory of the Principality, although it is provided that "this requirement can be dispensed with in circumstances deserving special consideration and by way of exception." In addition, the applicant for naturalization is required to submit a number of documents, such as evidence of his residence in the territory of the Principality, a certificate of good conduct issued by the competent authority of the place of residence, documents relating to his property and income and, if he is not a resident in the Principality, proof that he has concluded an agreement with the Revenue authorities, "subsequent to the revenue commission of the presumptive home commune having been heard." The Law further provides for the payment by the applicant of a naturalization fee, which is fixed by the Princely Government and amounts to at least one half of the sum payable by the applicant for reception into the Home Corporation of a Liechtenstein commune, the promise of such reception constituting a condition under the Law for the grant of naturalization. * * *

On October 9th, 1939, Nottebohm, "resident in Guatemala since 1905 (at present residing as a visitor with his brother, Hermann Nottebohm, in Vaduz)," applied for admission as a national of Liechtenstein and, at the same time, for the previous conferment of citizenship in the Commune of Mauren. He sought dispensation from the condition of three years' residence as prescribed by law, without indicating the special circumstances warranting such waiver. He submitted a statement of the *Crédit Suisse* in Zurich concerning his assets, and undertook to pay 25,000 Swiss francs to the Commune of Mauren, 12,500 Swiss francs to the State, to which was to be added the payment of dues in connection with the proceedings. He further stated that he had made "arrangements with the Revenue Authorities of the Government of Liechtenstein for the conclusion of a formal agreement to the effect that he will pay an annual tax of naturalization amounting to Swiss francs 1,000 of which Swiss francs 600 are payable to the Commune of Mauren and Swiss francs 400 are payable to the Principality of Liechtenstein, subject to the proviso that the payments of these taxes will be set off against ordinary taxes which will fall due if the applicant takes up residence in one of the Communes of the Principality." He further undertook to deposit as security a sum of 30,000 Swiss francs. He also gave certain general information as to his financial position and indicated that he would never become a burden to the Commune whose citizenship he was seeking.

Lastly, he requested "that naturalization proceedings be initiated and concluded before the Government of the Principality and before the Commune of Mauren without delay, that the application be then placed before the Diet with a favourable recommendation and, finally, that it be submitted with all necessary expedition to His Highness the Reigning Prince."

On the original typewritten application which has been produced in a photostatic copy, it can be seen that the name of the Commune of

Mauren and the amounts to be paid were added by hand, a fact which gave rise to some argument on the part of Counsel for the Parties. There is also a reference to the *"Vorausverständnis"* of the Reigning Prince obtained on October 13th, 1939, which Liechtenstein interprets as showing the decision to grant naturalization, which interpretation has, however, been questioned. Finally, there is annexed to the application an otherwise blank sheet bearing the signature of the Reigning Prince, "Franz Josef," but without any date or other explanation.

A document dated October 15th, 1939, certifies that on that date the Commune of Mauren conferred the privilege of its citizenship upon Mr. Nottebohm and requested the Government to transmit it to the Diet for approval. A certificate of October 17th, 1939, evidences the payment of the taxes required to be paid by Mr. Nottebohm. On October 20th, 1939, Mr. Nottebohm took the oath of allegiance and a final arrangement concerning liability to taxation was concluded on October 23rd.

This was the procedure followed in the case of the naturalization of Nottebohm.

A certificate of nationality has also been produced, signed on behalf of the Government of the Principality and dated October 20th, 1939, to the effect that Nottebohm was naturalized by Supreme Resolution of the Reigning Prince dated October 13th, 1939.

Having obtained a Liechtenstein passport, Nottebohm had it visa-ed by the Consul General of Guatemala in Zurich on December 1st, 1939, and returned to Guatemala at the beginning of 1940, where he resumed his former business activities and in particular the management of the firm of Nottebohm Hermanos.

Relying on the nationality thus conferred on Nottebohm, Liechtenstein considers itself entitled to seize the Court of its claim on his behalf, and its Final Conclusions contain two submissions in this connection. Liechtenstein requests the Court to find and declare, first, "that the naturalization of Mr. Frederic Nottebohm in Liechtenstein on October 13th, 1939, was not contrary to international law," and secondly, "that Liechtenstein's claim on behalf of Mr. Nottebohm as a national of Liechtenstein is admissible before the Court."

The Final Conclusions of Guatemala, on the other hand, request the Court "to declare that the claim of the Principality of Liechtenstein is inadmissible," and set forth a number of grounds relating to the nationality of Liechtenstein granted to Nottebohm by naturalization.

Thus, the real issue before the Court is the admissibility of the claim of Liechtenstein in respect of Nottebohm. * * *

In order to decide upon the admissibility of the Application, the Court must ascertain whether the nationality conferred on Nottebohm by Liechtenstein by means of a naturalization which took place in the circumstances which have been described, can be validly invoked as against Guatemala, whether it bestows upon Liechtenstein a sufficient title to the exercise of protection in respect of Nottebohm as against

Guatemala and therefore entitles it to seize the Court of a claim relating to him. * * *

Since no proof has been adduced that Guatemala has recognized the title to the exercise of protection relied upon by Liechtenstein as being derived from the naturalization which it granted to Nottebohm, the Court must consider whether such an act of granting nationality by Liechtenstein directly entails an obligation on the part of Guatemala to recognize its effect, namely, Liechtenstein's right to exercise its protection. In other words, it must be determined whether that unilateral act by Liechtenstein is one which can be relied upon against Guatemala in regard to the exercise of protection. The Court will deal with this question without considering that of the validity of Nottebohm's naturalization according to the law of Liechtenstein.

It is for Liechtenstein, as it is for every sovereign State, to settle by its own legislation the rules relating to the acquisition of its nationality, and to confer that nationality by naturalization granted by its own organs in accordance with that legislation. It is not necessary to determine whether international law imposes any limitations on its freedom of decision in this domain. Furthermore, nationality has its most immediate, its most far-reaching and, for most people, its only effects within the legal system of the State conferring it. Nationality serves above all to determine that the person upon whom it is conferred enjoys the rights and is bound by the obligations which the law of the State in question grants to or imposes on its nationals. This is implied in the wider concept that nationality is within the domestic jurisdiction of the State.

But the issue which the Court must decide is not one which pertains to the legal system of Liechtenstein. It does not depend on the law or on the decision of Liechtenstein whether that State is entitled to exercise its protection, in the case under consideration. To exercise protection, to apply to the Court, is to place oneself on the plane of international law. It is international law which determines whether a State is entitled to exercise protection and to seize the Court.

The naturalization of Nottebohm was an act performed by Liechtenstein in the exercise of its domestic jurisdiction. The question to be decided is whether that act has the international effect here under consideration.

International practice provides many examples of acts performed by States in the exercise of their domestic jurisdiction which do not necessarily or automatically have international effect, which are not necessarily and automatically binding on other States or which are binding on them only subject to certain conditions: this is the case, for instance, of a judgment given by the competent court of a State which it is sought to invoke in another state.

In the present case it is necessary to determine whether the naturalization conferred on Nottebohm can be successfully invoked against Guatemala, whether, as has already been stated, it can be relied upon as against that State, so that Liechtenstein is thereby entitled to exercise its protection in favour of Nottebohm against Guatemala. * * *

International arbitrators have decided * * * numerous cases of dual nationality, where the question arose with regard to the exercise of protection. They have given their preference to the real and effective nationality, that which accorded with the facts, that based on stronger factual ties between the person concerned and one of the States whose nationality is involved. Different factors are taken into consideration, and their importance will vary from one case to the next: the habitual residence of the individual concerned is an important factor, but there are other factors such as the centre of his interests, his family ties, his participation in public life, attachment shown by him for a given country and inculcated in his children, etc.

Similarly, the courts of third States, when they have before them an individual whom two other States hold to be their national, seek to resolve the conflict by having recourse to international criteria and their prevailing tendency is to prefer the real and effective nationality.

The same tendency prevails in the writings of publicists and in practice. This notion is inherent in the provisions of Article 3, paragraph 2, of the Statute of the Court. National laws reflect this tendency when, *inter alia*, they make naturalization dependent on conditions indicating the existence of a link, which may vary in their purpose or in their nature but which are essentially concerned with this idea. The Liechtenstein Law of January 4th, 1934, is a good example.

The practice of certain States which refrain from exercising protection in favour of a naturalized person when the latter has in fact, by his prolonged absence, severed his links with what is no longer for him anything but his nominal country, manifests the view of these States that, in order to be capable of being invoked against another State, nationality must correspond with the factual situation. A similar view is manifested in the relevant provisions of the bilateral nationality treaties concluded between the United States of America and other States since 1868, such as those sometimes referred to as the Bancroft Treaties, and in the Pan–American Convention, signed at Rio de Janeiro on August 13th, 1906, on the status of naturalized citizens who resume residence in their country of origin.

The character thus recognized on the international level as pertaining to nationality is in no way inconsistent with the fact that international law leaves it to each State to lay down the rules governing the grant of its own nationality. The reason for this is that the diversity of demographic conditions has thus far made it impossible for any general agreement to be reached on the rules relating to nationality, although the latter by its very nature affects international relations. It has been considered that the best way of making such rules accord with the varying demographic conditions in different countries is to leave the fixing of such rules to the competence of each State. On the other hand, a State cannot claim that the rules it has thus laid down are entitled to recognition by another State unless it has acted in conformity with this general aim of making the legal bond of nationality accord with the individual's genuine connection with the State which assumes the defence of its citizens by means of protection as against other States. * * *

According to the practice of States, to arbitral and judicial decisions and to the opinions of writers, nationality is a legal bond having as its basis a social fact of attachment, a genuine connection of existence, interests and sentiments, together with the existence of reciprocal rights and duties. It may be said to constitute the juridical expression of the fact that the individual upon whom it is conferred, either directly by the law or as the result of an act of the authorities, is in fact more closely connected with the population of the State conferring nationality than with that of any other State. Conferred by a State, it only entitles that State to exercise protection vis-à-vis another State, if it constitutes a translation into juridical terms of the individual's connection with the State which has made him its national.

Diplomatic protection and protection by means of international judicial proceedings constitute measures for the defence of the rights of the State. As the Permanent Court of International Justice has said and has repeated, "by taking up the case of one of its subjects and by resorting to diplomatic action or international judicial proceedings on his behalf, a State is in reality asserting its own rights—its right to ensure, in the person of its subjects, respect for the rules of international law."

Since this is the character which nationality must present when it is invoked to furnish the State which has granted it with a title to the exercise of protection and to the institution of international judicial proceedings, the Court must ascertain whether the nationality granted to Nottebohm by means of naturalization is of this character or, in other words, whether the factual connection between Nottebohm and Liechtenstein in the period preceding, contemporaneous with and following his naturalization appears to be sufficiently close, so preponderant in relation to any connection which may have existed between him and any other State, that it is possible to regard the nationality conferred upon him as real and effective, as the exact juridical expression of a social fact of a connection which existed previously or came into existence thereafter.

Naturalization is not a matter to be taken lightly. To seek and to obtain it is not something that happens frequently in the life of a human being. It involves his breaking a bond of allegiance and his establishment of a new bond of allegiance. It may have far-reaching consequences and involve profound changes in the destiny of the individual who obtains it. It concerns him personally, and to consider it only from the point of view of its repercussions with regard to his property would be to misunderstand its profound significance. In order to appraise its international effect, it is impossible to disregard the circumstances in which it was conferred, the serious character which attaches to it, the real and effective, and not merely the verbal preference of the individual seeking it for the country which grants it to him.

At the time of his naturalization does Nottebohm appear to have been more closely attached by his tradition, his establishment, his interests, his activities, his family ties, his intentions for the near future to Liechtenstein than to any other State? * * *

The essential facts are as follows:

At the date when he applied for naturalization Nottebohm had been a German national from the time of his birth. He had always retained his connections with members of his family who had remained in Germany and he had always had business connections with that country. His country had been at war for more than a month, and there is nothing to indicate that the application for naturalization then made by Nottebohm was motivated by any desire to dissociate himself from the Government of his country.

He had been settled in Guatemala for 34 years. He had carried on his activities there. It was the main seat of his interests. He returned there shortly after his naturalization, and it remained the centre of his interests and of his business activities. He stayed there until his removal as a result of war measures in 1943. He subsequently attempted to return there, and he now complains of Guatemala's refusal to admit him. There, too, were several members of his family who sought to safeguard his interests.

In contrast, his actual connections with Liechtenstein were extremely tenuous. No settled abode, no prolonged residence in that country at the time of his application for naturalization: the application indicates that he was paying a visit there and confirms the transient character of this visit by its request that the naturalization proceedings should be initiated and concluded without delay. No intention of settling there was shown at that time or realized in the ensuing weeks, months or years— on the contrary, he returned to Guatemala very shortly after his naturalization and showed every intention of remaining there. If Nottebohm went to Liechtenstein in 1946, this was because of the refusal of Guatemala to admit him. No indication is given of the grounds warranting the waiver of the condition of residence, required by the 1934 Nationality Law, which waiver was implicitly granted to him. There is no allegation of any economic interests or of any activities exercised or to be exercised in Liechtenstein, and no manifestation of any intention whatsoever to transfer all or some of his interests and his business activities to Liechtenstein. It is unnecessary in this connection to attribute much importance to the promise to pay the taxes levied at the time of his naturalization. The only links to be discovered between the Principality and Nottebohm are the short sojourns already referred to and the presence in Vaduz of one of his brothers: but his brother's presence is referred to in his application for naturalization only as a reference to his good conduct. Furthermore, other members of his family have asserted Nottebohm's desire to spend his old age in Guatemala.

These facts clearly establish, on the one hand, the absence of any bond of attachment between Nottebohm and Liechtenstein and, on the other hand, the existence of a long-standing and close connection between him and Guatemala, a link which his naturalization in no way weakened. That naturalization was not based on any real prior connection with Liechtenstein, nor did it in any way alter the manner of life of the person upon whom it was conferred in exceptional circumstances of speed and accommodation. In both respects, it was lacking in the genuineness requisite to an act of such importance, if it is to be entitled to be respected by a State in the position of Guatemala. It was granted without regard to the concept of nationality adopted in international relations.

Naturalization was asked for not so much for the purpose of obtaining a legal recognition of Nottebohm's membership in fact in the population of Liechtenstein, as it was to enable him to substitute for his status as a national of a belligerent State that of a national of a neutral State, with the sole aim of thus coming within the protection of Liechtenstein but not of becoming wedded to its traditions, its interests, its way of life or of assuming the obligations—other than fiscal obligations—and exercising the rights pertaining to the status thus acquired.

Guatemala is under no obligation to recognize a nationality granted in such circumstances. Liechtenstein consequently is not entitled to extend its protection to Nottebohm vis-à-vis Guatemala and its claim must, for this reason, be held to be inadmissible.

The Court is not therefore called upon to deal with the other pleas in bar put forward by Guatemala or the Conclusions of the Parties other than those on which it is adjudicating in accordance with the reasons indicated above.

For these reasons,

THE COURT,

by eleven votes to three,

Holds that the claim submitted by the Government of the Principality of Liechtenstein is inadmissible.

Notes and Questions

1. *State Responsibility.* Much of the international law of state responsibility developed from state practice and tribunal decisions relating to states taking up the claims of their citizens for harm done to those citizens by another state; the *Nottebohm Case* is an example. In the *Mavrommatis Palestine Concessions Case*, 1924 P.C.I.J., Ser. A, No. 2, the Greek government sued the United Kingdom for denial of contractual rights of a Greek national to operate public works in Jerusalem and Jaffa in the British mandate of Palestine. Answering the British objection that Mavrommatis was merely a private person, the Permanent Court of International Justice held:

[I]t is true that the dispute was at first between a private person and a State—i.e. between M. Mavrommatis and Great Britain. Subsequently the Greek Government took up the case. The dispute then entered upon a new phase; it entered into the domain of international law, and became a dispute between two States.

Id. at 12. In the latter part of the 20th century, new procedural mechanisms developed allowing individuals to pursue claims at international law against states directly on their own behalf. We have already seen several examples, *e.g., Filartiga* and *Golder* in Chapter 1, *Belilos* in Chapter 2, and the *Texaco/Libya Arbitration* in Chapter 3. We see more examples later in this chapter.

Issues of state responsibility also arise in contexts other than cases of injuries to aliens. States may be responsible for violating the territorial integrity of other states, as in the *Rainbow Warrior Case* in Chapter 5, or for unlawfully using force against another state (Chapter 9). States may be responsible for harm to the environment (Chapter 10) or for breaching their treaty obligations, as in the *Gabcíkovo–Nagymaros Case* in Chapter 2. And states now may be responsible for violating the rights of their own citizens, *e.g.,* when states breach certain *erga omnes* obligations (Chapter 3), or when they violate international conventions, *e.g.,* the European Human Rights Convention below.

Since 1949, the International Law Commission, an expert body operating within the United Nations system, has engaged in extensive studies in an effort to codify basic principles of the law of state responsibility. The Commission's recent work on state responsibility is found in International Law Commission, *Report on the Work of Its Fifty-second Session (1 May–9 June and 10 July–18 August 2000)* 10–140, General Assembly Official Records, 55th Sess., Supp. No. 10 (A/55/10) (2000).

2. *Attribution.* For whose acts is a state responsible? The case law illustrates the considerable reach of the state responsibility doctrine. The United Kingdom was held responsible in the Union Bridge Co. Case (1924), 6 U.N.R.I.A.A. 138, for the acts of a low-level railway official in South Africa who wrongly interfered with property belonging to a U.S. citizen in 1900 when the U.S. was a neutral during the Anglo–Boer War. The International Law Commission, after surveying state practice, judicial decisions, and the writings of publicists, has concluded that a state may be held responsible for the acts of all of its organs—executive, legislative, and judicial. International Law Commission, 2 *Yearbook of the International Law Commission* 194–95 (1973).

Some cases pose difficult questions about whether the actions of individuals or groups may be attributed to a state. In Yeager v. Iran, 17 Iran–U.S. Claims Tribunal Reports 92 (1987), Iran was held responsible for the actions of Revolutionary Guards when they harassed U.S. citizens out of their employment in the country. Tribunals sometimes have relied on notions of "due diligence" to find states responsible for failing to prevent individuals from harming foreign nationals, or for failing to apprehend or punish the perpetrators. For example, in Janes (U.S.A.) v. United Mexican States (1925), 4 U.N.R.I.A.A. 82, an international arbitral tribunal found Mexico responsible for the failure of Mexican authorities to exercise due diligence in their efforts to apprehend a mine company employee who in 1918 shot and killed Byron Janes, a U.S. citizen who was a superintendent of mines.

3. *State Protection.* A counterpart of state responsibility is state protection, a doctrine permitting a state to protect its nationals. A state, however, has no legal obligation to espouse the claims of its nationals. In one recent case, a U.S. national sued for a writ of mandamus to require the U.S. State Department to press Brazil for redress for the alleged torture and death of a U.S. spouse. The U.S. District Court for the Southern District of Florida granted the government's motion to dismiss because the decision whether to espouse private claims against a foreign state is a matter of discretion. Brown v. Christopher, No. 93–1375–CIV (S.D. Fla. Nov. 18, 1993).

Given that Liechtenstein in the *Nottebohm Case* was under no legal obligation to protect Nottebohm, what reasons would there have been for Liechtenstein to go to the trouble and expense of suing Guatemala in the International Court? Was it because of the government's concern for Nottebohm? Because of the threat to Liechtenstein's reputation as a safe haven? If Liechtenstein had refused to pursue Nottebohm's claim, how else could Nottebohm have sought redress? What were his chances for real success in Guatemala's courts? Liechtenstein's courts? Diplomatic negotiations? International arbitration?

The ICJ was careful to state that Nottebohm's Liechtenstein nationality was not "opposable" to Guatemala, and that Liechtenstein could not "extend its protection to Nottebohm *vis-à-vis* Guatemala." Did this leave open the possibility that Liechtenstein might have effectively espoused Nottebohm's claims against other states?

4. *Reparation.* Every breach of a state's legal obligations gives rise to a duty to make reparation. Reparation may take the form of guarantees against repetition of the illegal conduct, and, alternatively or in combination, restitution, compensation, or satisfaction. As we saw in the *Rainbow Warrior Case* in Chapter 5, satisfaction may take different forms, including apology and a declaration that a responsible state engaged in wrongdoing. For discussion of reparation, see, *e.g.*, International Law Commission, *Report on the Work of Its Fifty-second Session, supra* Note 1, at 48–73; Christine Gray, *Judicial Remedies in International Law* (1987).

When one state successfully claims that another state is responsible for injuring the claimant state's national, does the notion that the claimant state is "in reality asserting its own right" extend to issues of reparation? For example, if Liechtenstein had been successful in obtaining compensation from Guatemala for injuries done to Nottebohm, should Liechtenstein have had to turn the proceeds it obtained over to Nottebohm?

5. *Stateless Persons.* Do stateless people have rights? How can stateless individuals pursue claims against states for violating their rights? In Trop v. Dulles, 356 U.S. 86, 78 S.Ct. 590, 2 L.Ed.2d 630 (1958), the U.S. Supreme Court found that depriving a military deserter of his U.S. citizenship was a violation of the Eighth Amendment's protection against cruel and unusual punishment:

> There may be involved no physical mistreatment, no primitive torture. There is instead the total destruction of the individual's status in

organized society. It is a form of punishment more primitive than torture, for it destroys for the individual the political existence that was centuries in the development. The punishment strips the citizen of his status in the national and international political community. His very existence is at the sufferance of the country in which he happens to find himself. * * * In short, the expatriate has lost the right to have rights.

This punishment * * * subjects the individual to a fate of ever-increasing fear and distress. He knows not what discriminations may be established against him, what proscriptions may be directed against him, and when and for what cause his existence in his native land may be terminated. He may be subject to banishment, a fate universally decried by civilized people. He is stateless, a condition deplored in the international community of democracies. * * *

The civilized nations of the world are in virtual unanimity that statelessness is not to be imposed as punishment for crime.

Id. at 101–02, 78 S.Ct. at 598–99, 2 L.Ed.2d at 642–43.

As reproduced at page 354, in 1948, the U.N. General Assembly resolved in Article 15 of the Universal Declaration of Human Rights that "[e]veryone has the right to a nationality" and that "[n]o one shall be arbitrarily deprived of his nationality nor denied the right to change his nationality."

THE BARCELONA TRACTION CASE

Case Concerning the Barcelona Traction, Light and Power Co., Limited,
Second Phase, Belgium v. Spain, 1970 I.C.J. 3, 1970 WL 1.

8.   The Barcelona Traction, Light and Power Company, Limited, is a holding company incorporated in 1911 in Toronto (Canada), where it has its head office. For the purpose of creating and developing an electric power production and distribution system in Catalonia (Spain), it formed a number of operating, financing, and concession-holding subsidiary companies. Three of these companies, whose shares it owned wholly or almost wholly, were incorporated under Canadian law and had their registered offices in Canada (Ebro Irrigation and Power Company, Limited, Catalonian Land Company, Limited and International Utilities Finance Corporation, Limited); the others were incorporated under Spanish law and had their registered offices in Spain. At the time of the outbreak of the Spanish Civil War the group, through its operating subsidiaries, supplied the major part of Catalonia's electricity requirements.

9.   According to the Belgian Government, some years after the First World War Barcelona Traction's share capital came to be very largely held by Belgian nationals—natural or juristic persons—and a very high percentage of the shares has since then continuously belonged to Belgian nationals, particularly the Société Internationale d'Energie Hydro–Electrique (Sidro), whose principal shareholder, the Société Financière de Transports et D'Entreprises Industrieles (Sofina), is itself a company in which Belgian interests are preponderant. The fact that large blocks of shares were for certain periods transferred to American nominees, to

protect these securities in the event of invasion of Belgian territory during the Second World War, is not, according to the Belgian contention, of any relevance in this connection, as it was Belgian nationals, particularly Sidro, who continued to be the real owners. For a time the shares were vested in a trustee, but the Belgian Government maintains that the trust terminated in 1946. The Spanish Government contends, on the contrary, that the Belgian nationality of the shareholders is not proven and that the trustee or the nominees must be regarded as the true shareholders in the case of the shares concerned.

[Barcelona Traction issued bonds, most in pounds sterling. It serviced the bonds through funds transferred to it from its subsidiaries operating in Spain. Interest payments were disrupted in 1936 by the Spanish Civil War. The Spanish Government refused to allow transfers of foreign currency, and interest payments on the sterling bonds were never resumed. Three Spanish holders of Barcelona Traction bonds obtained a bankruptcy declaration against Barcelona Traction in Spanish court because of its failure to pay interest on the bonds. A bankruptcy receiver seized the assets of Barcelona Traction, Ebro, and a Spanish subsidiary. Barcelona Traction, which did not receive proper notice of the proceedings, failed to enter a plea opposing the bankruptcy judgment, as was required under Spanish law, within the requisite time period. In 1949, trustees in bankruptcy created new shares of the subsidiaries, cancelled the shares located outside Spain, and decreed that the head offices of Ebro and Catalonian Land were in Barcelona rather than Toronto. In 1952, the trustees, operating under court authorization, sold all the shares of the subsidiaries at public auction.]

20. The British Government made representations to the Spanish Government on 23 February 1948 concerning the bankruptcy of Barcelona Traction and the seizure of its assets as well as those of Ebro and Barcelonesa, stating its interest in the situation of the bondholders resident in United Kingdom. It subsequently supported the representations made by the Canadian Government.

21. The Canadian Government made representations to the Spanish Government in a series of diplomatic notes, the first being dated 27 March 1948 and the last 21 April 1952; in addition, approaches were made on a less official level in July 1954 and March 1955. The Canadian Government first complained of the denials of justice said to have been committed in Spain towards Barcelona Traction, Ebro and National Trust, but it subsequently based its complaints more particularly on conduct towards the Ebro company said to be in breach of certain treaty provisions applicable between Spain and Canada. The Spanish Government did not respond to a Canadian proposal for the submission of the dispute to arbitration and the Canadian Government subsequently confined itself, until the time when its interposition entirely ceased, to endeavoring to promote a settlement by agreement between the private groups concerned.

22. The United States Government made representations to the Spanish Government on behalf of Barcelona Traction in a note of 22 July 1949, in support of a note submitted by the Canadian Government the previous day. It subsequently continued its interposition through the diplomatic channel and by other means. Since references were made by the United States Government in these representations to the presence of American interests in Barcelona Traction, the Spanish Government draws the conclusion that, in the light of the customary practice of the United States Government to protect only substantial American investments abroad, the existence must be presumed of such large American interests as to rule out a preponderance of Belgian interests. The Belgian Government considers that the United States Government was motivated by a more general concern to secure equitable treatment of foreign investments in Spain, and in this context cites, *inter alia*, a note of 5 June 1967 from the United States Government.

23. The Spanish Government having stated in a note of 26 September 1949 that Ebro had not furnished proof as to the origin and genuineness of the bond debts, which justified the refusal of foreign currency transfers, the Belgian and Canadian Governments considered proposing to the Spanish Government the establishment of a tripartite committee to study the question. Before this proposal was made, the Spanish Government suggested in March 1950 the creation of a committee on which, in addition to Spain, only Canada and the United Kingdom would be represented. This proposal was accepted by the United Kingdom and Canadian Governments. The work of the committee led to a joint statement of 11 June 1951 by the three Governments to the effect, *inter alia*, that the attitude of the Spanish administration in not authorizing the transfers of foreign currency was fully justified. The Belgian Government protested against the fact that it had not been invited to nominate an expert to take part in the enquiry, and reserved its rights; in the proceedings before the Court it contended that the joint statement of 1951, which was based on the work of the committee, could not be set up against it, being *res inter alios acta*.

24. The Belgian Government made representations to the Spanish Government on the same day as the Canadian Government, in a note of 27 March 1948. It continued its diplomatic intervention until the rejection by the Spanish Government of a Belgian proposal for submission to arbitration (end of 1951). After the admission of Spain to membership in the United Nations (1955), which, as found by the Court in 1964, rendered operative again the clause of compulsory jurisdiction contained in the 1927 Hispano–Belgian Treaty of Conciliation, Judicial Settlement and Arbitration, the Belgian Government attempted further representations. After the rejection of a proposal for a special agreement, it decided to refer the dispute unilaterally to this Court.

[The Spanish Government objected, *inter alia*, that the Belgian Government "lacked capacity to submit any claim in respect of wrongs done to a Canadian company, even if the shareholders were Belgian." The Court joined that objection to the merits.]

28. * * * The claim is presented on behalf of natural and juristic persons, alleged to be Belgian nationals and shareholders in the Barcelona Traction, Light and Power Company, Limited. The submissions of the Belgian Government make it clear that the object of its Application is reparation for damage allegedly caused to these persons by the conduct, said to be contrary to international law, of various organs of the Spanish State towards that company and various other companies in the same group. * * *

30. The States which the present case principally concerns are Belgium, the national State of the alleged shareholders, Spain, the State whose organs are alleged to have committed the unlawful acts complained of, and Canada, the State under whose law Barcelona Traction was incorporated and in whose territory it has its registered office ("head office" in the terms of the by-laws of Barcelona Traction). * * *

32. In these circumstances it is logical that the Court should first address itself to what was originally presented as the subject-matter of the third preliminary objection: namely the question of the right of Belgium to exercise diplomatic protection of Belgian shareholders in a company which is a juristic entity incorporated in Canada, the measures complained of having been taken in relation not to any Belgian national but to the company itself.

33. When a State admits into its territory foreign investments or foreign nationals, whether natural or juristic persons, it is bound to extend to them the protection of the law and assumes obligations concerning the treatment to be afforded them. These obligations, however, are neither absolute nor unqualified. In particular, an essential distinction should be drawn between the obligations of a State towards the international community as a whole, and those arising vis-à-vis another State in the field of diplomatic protection. By their very nature the former are the concern of all States. In view of the importance of the rights involved, all States can be held to have a legal interest in their protection; they are obligations *erga omnes*.

34. Such obligations derive, for example, in contemporary international law, from the outlawing of acts of aggression, and of genocide, as also from the principles and rules concerning the basic rights of the human person, including protection from slavery and racial discrimination. Some of the corresponding rights of protection have entered into the body of general international law (*Reservations to the Convention on the Prevention and Punishment of the Crime of Genocide, Advisory Opinion, I.C.J. Reports 1951*, p. 23); others are conferred by international instruments of a universal or quasi-universal character.

35. Obligations the performance of which is the subject of diplomatic protection are not of the same category. It cannot be held, when one such obligation in particular is in question, in a specific case, that all States have a legal interest in its observance. * * * In the present case it is therefore essential to establish whether the losses allegedly suffered by Belgian shareholders in Barcelona Traction were the consequence of the

violation of obligations of which they were the beneficiaries. In other words: has a right of Belgium been violated on account of its nationals' having suffered infringement of their rights as shareholders in a company not of Belgian nationality?

36. Thus it is the existence or absence of a right, belonging to Belgium and recognized as such by international law, which is decisive for the problem of Belgium's capacity.

"This right is necessarily limited to intervention [by a State] on behalf of its own nationals because, in the absence of a special agreement, it is the bond of nationality between the State and the individual which alone confers upon the State the right of diplomatic protection, and it is as a part of the function of diplomatic protection that the right to take up a claim and to ensure respect for the rules of international law must be envisaged." (*Panevezys-Saldutiskis Railway, Judgment, 1939, P.C.I.J., Series A/B, No. 76,* p. 16.)

It follows that the same question is determinant in respect of Spain's responsibility towards Belgium. Responsibility is the necessary corollary of a right. In the absence of any treaty on the subject between the Parties, this essential issue has to be decided in the light of the general rules of diplomatic protection. * * *

38. In this field international law is called upon to recognize institutions of municipal law that have an important and extensive role in the international field. This does not necessarily imply drawing any analogy between its own institutions and those of municipal law, nor does it amount to making rules of international law dependent upon categories of municipal law. All it means is that international law has had to recognize the corporate entity as an institution created by States in a domain essentially within their domestic jurisdiction. This in turn requires that, whenever legal issues arise concerning the rights of States with regard to the treatment of companies and shareholders, as to which rights international law has not established its own rules, it has to refer to the relevant rules of municipal law. Consequently, in view of the relevance to the present case of the rights of the corporate entity and its shareholders under municipal law, the Court must devote attention to the nature and interrelation of those rights.

39. Seen in historical perspective, the corporate personality represents a development brought about by new and expanding requirements in the economic field, an entity which in particular allows of operation in circumstances which exceed the normal capacity of individuals. As such it has become a powerful factor in the economic life of nations. Of this, municipal law has had to take due account, whence the increasing volume of rules governing the creation and operation of corporate entities, endowed with a specific status. These entities have rights and obligations peculiar to themselves. * * *

41. Municipal law determines the legal situation not only of such limited liability companies but also of those persons who hold shares in them. Separated from the company by numerous barriers, the sharehold-

er cannot be identified with it. The concept and structure of the company are founded on and determined by a firm distinction between the separate entity of the company and that of the shareholder, each with a distinct set of rights. The separation of property rights as between company and shareholder is an important manifestation of this distinction. So long as the company is in existence the shareholder has no right to the corporate assets.

42. It is a basic characteristic of the corporate structure that the company alone, through its directors or management acting in its name, can take action in respect of matters that are of a corporate character. The underlying justification for this is that, in seeking to serve its own best interests, the company will serve those of the shareholder too. Ordinarily, no individual shareholder can take legal steps, either in the name of the company or in his own name. If the shareholders disagree with the decisions taken on behalf of the company they may, in accordance with its articles or the relevant provisions of the law, change them or replace its officers, or take such action as is provided by law. Thus to protect the company against abuse by its management or the majority of shareholders, several municipal legal systems have vested in shareholders (sometimes a particular number is specified) the right to bring an action for the defence of the company, and conferred upon the minority of shareholders certain rights to guard against decisions affecting the rights of the company vis-à-vis its management or controlling shareholders. Nonetheless the shareholders' rights in relation to the company and its assets remain limited, this being, moreover, a corollary of the limited nature of their liability. * * *

44. Notwithstanding the separate corporate personality, a wrong done to the company frequently causes prejudice to its shareholders. But the mere fact that damage is sustained by both company and shareholder does not imply that both are entitled to claim compensation. * * * Thus whenever a shareholder's interests are harmed by an act done to the company, it is to the latter that he must look to institute appropriate action; for although two separate entities may have suffered from the same wrong, it is only one entity whose rights have been infringed. * * *

47. The situation is different if the act complained of is aimed at the direct rights of the shareholder as such. It is well known that there are rights which municipal law confers upon the latter distinct from those of the company, including the right to any declared dividend, the right to attend and vote at general meetings, the right to share in the residual assets of the company on liquidation. Whenever one of his direct rights is infringed, the shareholder has an independent right of action. * * *

48. The Belgian Government claims that shareholders of Belgian nationality suffered damage in consequence of unlawful acts of the Spanish authorities and, in particular, that the Barcelona Traction shares, though they did not cease to exist, were emptied of all real economic content. It accordingly contends that the shareholders had an

independent right to redress, notwithstanding the fact that the acts complained of were directed against the company as such. Thus the legal issue is reducible to the question of whether it is legitimate to identify an attack on company rights, resulting in damage to shareholders, with the violation of their direct rights. * * *

50. In turning now to the international legal aspects of the case, the Court must, as already indicated, start from the fact that the present case essentially involves factors derived from municipal law—the distinction and the community between the company and the shareholder—which the Parties, however widely their interpretations may differ, each take as the point of departure of their reasoning. If the Court were to decide the case in disregard of the relevant institutions of municipal law it would, without justification, invite serious legal difficulties. It would lose touch with reality, for there are no corresponding institutions of international law to which the Court could resort. Thus the Court has, as indicated, not only to take cognizance of municipal law but also to refer to it. It is to rules generally accepted by municipal legal systems which recognize the limited company whose capital is represented by shares, and not to the municipal law of a particular State, that international law refers. * * *

52. International law may not, in some fields, provide specific rules in particular cases. In the concrete situation, the company against which allegedly unlawful acts were directed is expressly vested with a right, whereas no such right is specifically provided for the shareholder in respect of those acts. Thus the position of the company rests on a positive rule of both municipal and international law. As to the shareholder, while he has certain rights expressly provided for him by municipal law * * *, appeal can, in the circumstances of the present case, only be made to the silence of international law. Such silence scarcely admits of interpretation in favour of the shareholder. * * *

56. * * * [Municipal] law, confronted with economic realities, has had to provide protective measures and remedies in the interests of those within the corporate entity as well as of those outside who have dealings with it: the law has recognized that the independent existence of the legal entity cannot be treated as an absolute. It is in this context that the process of "lifting the corporate veil" or "disregarding the legal entity" has been found justified and equitable in certain circumstances. * * *

64. * * * In this connection two particular situations must be studied: the case of the company having ceased to exist and the case of the company's national State lacking capacity to take action on its behalf.

65. As regards the first of these possibilities the Court observes that * * * Barcelona Traction has lost all its assets in Spain, and was placed in receivership in Canada, a receiver and manager having been appointed. * * * [F]rom the economic viewpoint the company has been entirely paralyzed. It has been deprived of all its Spanish sources of income, and the Belgian Government has asserted that the company

could no longer find the funds for its legal defence, so that these had to be supplied by the shareholders.

66. It cannot however, be contended that the corporate entity of the company has ceased to exist, or that it has lost its capacity to take corporate action. * * * [A] precarious financial situation cannot be equated with the demise of the corporate entity, which is the hypothesis under consideration: the company's status in law is alone relevant, and not its economic condition * * *. Only in the event of the legal demise of the company are the shareholders deprived of the possibility of a remedy available through the company; it is only if they became deprived of all such possibility that an independent right of action for them and their government could arise.

67. In the present case, Barcelona Traction is in receivership in the country of incorporation. Far from implying the demise of the entity or of its rights, this much rather denotes that those rights are preserved for so long as no liquidation has ensued. Though in receivership, the company continues to exist. Moreover, it is a matter of public record that the company's shares were quoted on the stock-market at a recent date.

68. * * * [E]ven if the company is limited in its activity after being placed in receivership, there can be no doubt that it has retained its legal capacity and that the power to exercise it is vested in the manager appointed by the Canadian courts. The Court is thus not confronted with the first hypothesis contemplated in paragraph 64, and need not pronounce upon it.

69. The Court will now turn to the second possibility, that of the lack of capacity of the company's national State to act on its behalf. The first question which must be asked here is whether Canada—the third apex of the triangular relationship—is, in law, the national State of Barcelona Traction.

70. In allocating corporate entities to States for purposes of diplomatic protection, international law is based, but only to a limited extent, on an analogy with the rules governing the nationality of individuals. The traditional rule attributes the right of diplomatic protection of a corporate entity to the State under the laws of which it is incorporated and in whose territory it has its registered office. These two criteria have been confirmed by long practice and by numerous international instruments. This notwithstanding, further or different links are at times said to be required in order that a right of diplomatic protection should exist. Indeed, it has been the practice of some States to give a company incorporated under their law diplomatic protection solely when it has its seat (*siège social*) or management or centre of control in their territory, or when a majority or a substantial proportion of the shares has been owned by nationals of the State concerned. Only then, it has been held, does there exist between the corporation and the State in question a genuine connection of the kind familiar from other branches of international law. However, in the particular field of the diplomatic protection of corporate entities, no absolute test of the "genuine connection" has

found general acceptance. Such tests as have been applied are of a relative nature, and sometimes links with one State have had to be weighed against those with another. In this connection reference has been made to the *Nottebohm* case. * * * However, given both the legal and factual aspects of protection in the present case the Court is of the opinion that there can be no analogy with the issues raised or the decision given in that case.

71.   In the present case, it is not disputed that the company was incorporated in Canada and has its registered office in that country. The incorporation of the company under the law of Canada was an act of free choice. Not only did the founders of the company seek its incorporation under Canadian law but it has remained under that law for a period of over 50 years. It has maintained in Canada its registered office, its accounts and its share registers. Board meetings were held there for many years; it has been listed in the records of the Canadian tax authorities. Thus a close and permanent connection has been established, fortified by the passage of over half a century. This connection is in no way weakened by the fact that the company engaged from the very outset in commercial activities outside Canada, for that was its declared object. Barcelona Traction's links with Canada are thus manifold.

72.   Furthermore, the Canadian nationality of the company has received general recognition. Prior to the institution of proceedings before the Court, three other governments apart from that of Canada (those of the United Kingdom, the United States and Belgium) made representations concerning the treatment accorded to Barcelona Traction by the Spanish authorities. The United Kingdom Government intervened on behalf of bondholders and of shareholders. Several representations were also made by the United States Government, but not on behalf of the Barcelona Traction company as such. * * *

74.   * * * The Belgian Government admitted the Canadian character of the company in the course of the present proceedings. It explicitly stated that Barcelona Traction was a company of neither Spanish nor Belgian nationality but a Canadian company incorporated in Canada. The Belgian Government has even conceded that it was not concerned with the injury suffered by Barcelona Traction itself, since that was Canada's affair.

76.   * * * [F]rom 1948 onwards the Canadian Government made to the Spanish Government numerous representations which cannot be viewed otherwise than as the exercise of diplomatic protection in respect of the Barcelona Traction company. Therefore this was not a case where diplomatic protection was refused or remained in the sphere of fiction. It is also clear that over the whole period of its diplomatic activity the Canadian Government proceeded in full knowledge of the Belgian attitude and activity.

77.   It is true that at a certain point the Canadian Government ceased to act on behalf of Barcelona Traction, for reasons which have not been fully revealed, though a statement made in a letter of 19 July 1955

by the Canadian Secretary of State for External Affairs suggests that it felt the matter should be settled by means of private negotiations. The Canadian Government has nonetheless retained its capacity to exercise diplomatic protection; no legal impediment has prevented it from doing so: no fact has arisen to render this protection impossible. It has discontinued its action of its own free will.

78. The Court would here observe that, within the limits prescribed by international law, a State may exercise diplomatic protection by whatever means and to whatever extent it thinks fit, for it is its own right that the State is asserting. Should the natural or legal persons on whose behalf it is acting consider that their rights are not adequately protected, they have no remedy in international law. All they can do is to resort to municipal law, if means are available, with a view to furthering their cause or obtaining redress. The municipal legislator may lay upon the State an obligation to protect its citizens abroad, and may also confer upon the national a right to demand the performance of that obligation, and clothe the right with corresponding sanctions. However, all these questions remain within the province of municipal law and do not affect the position internationally.

79. The State must be viewed as the sole judge to decide whether its protection will be granted, to what extent it is granted, and when it will cease. It retains in this respect a discretionary power the exercise of which may be determined by considerations of a political or other nature, unrelated to the particular case. Since the claim of the State is not identical with that of the individual or corporate person whose cause is espoused, the State enjoys complete freedom of action. Whatever the reasons for any change of attitude, the fact cannot in itself constitute a justification for the exercise of diplomatic protection by another government, unless there is some independent and otherwise valid ground for that.

80. This cannot be regarded as amounting to a situation where a violation of law remains without remedy: in short, a legal vacuum. There is no obligation upon the possessors of rights to exercise them. Sometimes no remedy is sought, though rights are infringed. To equate this with the creation of a vacuum would be to equate a right with an obligation. * * *

92. Since the general rule on the subject does not entitle the Belgian Government to put forward a claim in this case, the question remains to be considered whether nonetheless, as the Belgian Government has contended during the proceedings, considerations of equity do not require that it be held to possess a right of protection. * * * [A] theory has been developed to the effect that the State of the shareholders has a right of diplomatic protection when the State whose responsibility is invoked is the national State of the company. Whatever the validity of this theory may be, it is certainly not applicable to the present case, since Spain is not the national State of Barcelona Traction.

93. On the other hand, the Court considers that, in the field of diplomatic protection as in all other fields of international law, it is necessary that the law be applied reasonably. It has been suggested that if in a given case it is not possible to apply the general rule that the right of diplomatic protection of a company belongs to its national State, considerations of equity might call for the possibility of protection of the shareholders in question by their own national State. This hypothesis does not correspond to the circumstances of the present case.

94. In view, however, of the discretionary nature of diplomatic protection, considerations of equity cannot require more than the possibility for some protector State to intervene, whether it be the national State of the company, by virtue of the general rule mentioned above, or, in a secondary capacity, the national State of the shareholders who claim protection. In this connection, account should also be taken of the practical effects of deducing from considerations of equity any broader right of protection for the national State of the shareholders. It must first of all be observed that it would be difficult on an equitable basis to make distinctions according to any quantitative test: it would seem that the owner of 1 per cent. and the owner of 90 per cent. of the share-capital should have the same possibility of enjoying the benefit of diplomatic protection. The protector State may, of course, be disinclined to take up the case of the single small shareholder, but it could scarcely be denied the right to do so in the name of equitable considerations. In that field, protection by the national State of the shareholders can hardly be graduated according to the absolute or relative size of the shareholding involved.

95. The Belgian Government, it is true, has also contended that as high a proportion as 88 per cent. of the shares in Barcelona Traction belonged to natural or juristic persons of Belgian nationality, and it has used this as an argument for the purpose not only of determining the amount of the damages which it claims, but also of establishing its right of action on behalf of the Belgian shareholders. Nevertheless, this does not alter the Belgian Government's position * * * which implies, in the last analysis, that it might be sufficient for one single share to belong to a national of a given State for the latter to be entitled to exercise its diplomatic protection.

96. The Court considers that the adoption of the theory of diplomatic protection of shareholders as such, by opening the door to competing diplomatic claims, could create an atmosphere of confusion and insecurity in international economic relations. The danger would be all the greater inasmuch as the shares of companies whose activity is international are widely scattered and frequently change hands. It might perhaps be claimed that, if the right of protection belonging to the national States of the shareholders were considered as only secondary to that of the national State of the company, there would be less danger of difficulties of the kind contemplated. However, the Court must state that the essence of a secondary right is that it only comes into existence at the time when the original right ceases to exist. As the right of protec-

tion vested in the national State of the company cannot be regarded as extinguished because it is not exercised, it is not possible to accept the proposition that in case of its non-exercise the national States of the shareholders have a right of protection secondary to that of the national State of the company. * * *

99. * * * [T]he promoters of a company whose operations will be international must take into account the fact that States have, with regard to their nationals, a discretionary power to grant diplomatic protection or to refuse it. When establishing a company in a foreign country, its promoters are normally impelled by particular considerations; it is often a question of tax or other advantages offered by the host State. It does not seem to be in any way inequitable that the advantages thus obtained should be balanced by the risks arising from the fact that the protection of the company and hence of its shareholders is thus entrusted to a State other than the national State of the shareholders.

100. In the present case, it is clear from what has been said above that Barcelona Traction was never reduced to a position of impotence such that it could not have approached its national State, Canada, to ask for its diplomatic protection, and that, as far as appeared to the Court, there was nothing to prevent Canada from continuing to grant its diplomatic protection to Barcelona Traction if it had considered that it should do so.

101. For the above reasons, the Court is not of the opinion that, in the particular circumstances of the present case, *jus standi* is conferred on the Belgian Government by considerations of equity. * * *

102. * * * The Court fully appreciates the importance of the legal problems raised by the allegation, which is at the root of the Belgian claim for reparation, concerning the denials of justice allegedly committed by organs of the Spanish State. However, the possession by the Belgian Government of a right of protection is a prerequisite for the examination of these problems. Since no *jus standi* before the Court has been established, it is not for the Court in its Judgment to pronounce upon any other aspect of the case, on which it should take a decision only if the Belgian Government had a right of protection in respect of its nationals, shareholders in Barcelona Traction.

103. Accordingly,

THE COURT rejects the Belgian Government's claim by fifteen votes to one, twelve votes of the majority being based on the reasons set out in the present Judgment.

Notes and Questions

1. *Expropriation. Barcelona Traction* illustrated some of the problems involved in protecting a foreign branch or subsidiary from discriminatory treatment by the host country, even from out-right expropriation. A foreign expropriation can be blatant, for example, the expropriation by Libya in the

Texaco/Libya Case in Chapter 3 or by Cuba of United States sugar interests in *Banco Nacional de Cuba v. Sabbatino*, which we explore in Chapter 12.

A tale of *Barcelona Traction* put a face to a more subtle expropriation: "Juan March—the former smuggler who in the nineteen-twenties had become one of the richest men in Spain and in the nineteen-thirties had been the chief private financier of the counter-revolution that had put Francisco Franco in power." John Brooks, "Annals of Finance: Privateer—II," *The New Yorker*, May 28, 1979, at 42. Juan March's maneuvers led a court in a small town in Spain to declare the Barcelona Traction Company bankrupt, in 1948, despite the fact that the company had shown net profits of $3.7 million in the previous year and had sufficient cash on hand to pay off its debts. "[L]ater evidence strongly suggested [that] the complainants, the trustees in bankruptcy, and the judge himself were all allies of the man seeking to seize the company, Juan March." John Brooks, "Annals of Finance: Privateer—I," *The New Yorker*, May 21, 1979, at 42, 42–43.

2. *Diplomatic Protection.* The Barcelona Traction, Light and Power Co., Limited, was incorporated in Canada, as were some, though not all, of its subsidiaries. Its operating assets were, however, virtually all in Spain. What were the advantages and disadvantages of Canadian incorporation for foreign investors? Certainly, one advantage would be the possibility of triggering the diplomatic intercession of the Canadian government in any investment dispute with Spain. How did Canada actually come to the aid of the expropriated company?

3. *The Jurisdiction of the ICJ.* Unlike Belgium, which could rely on a treaty with Spain providing for the submission of disputes to the International Court of Justice, Canada had no way to bring Spain before the ICJ. See Chapter 5's discussion of grounds for ICJ jurisdiction. Was it any wonder that Spain would not agree to an *ad hoc* case between it and Canada? Can the Belgian suit in the ICJ be viewed as a way to circumvent the obstacle posed by Spain's unwillingness to litigate with Canada? Did the ICJ's judgment take this obstacle of non-consent at all into account?

4. *Obtaining Justice for Barcelona Traction.* Was it equitable for Spain to, first, prevent a solvent Spanish company from paying its obligations denominated in foreign currency, second, through its judicial process declare the company bankrupt, and, third, sell the company's assets to domestic purchasers, thereby depriving the foreign shareholders of their stake in the company? Besides going to the ICJ, how did the foreign shareholders complain both inside and outside Spain? What other avenues of protest, legal or political, might they have followed? Would Barcelona Traction have been better served with a bilateral treaty protecting foreign investment like that in *ELSI* in Chapter 5?

5. *Genuine Link.* Should the ICJ have adopted a *Nottebohm* genuine link requirement with respect to corporations? Some corporations are only technically incorporated in one state. They may have their headquarters and many operations in a second state, with shareholders and managers domiciled there. Which state should be able to pursue an international claim on the corporation's behalf for injury caused by a third state?

Judge Jessup, who wrote a concurring opinion in *Barcelona Traction*, accepted the genuine link theory, and rejected Great Britain, the United

States, and Canada as claimants because their connections with Barcelona Traction were transitory and nominal. Belgium, he found, might have had a "genuine link" with the company because Belgian nationals beneficially owned 88 per cent of the company's shares. Nevertheless, Belgium's claim failed because there was no continuous Belgian interest between the time injury was inflicted and the date Belgium espoused the claim. See 1970 I.C.J. at 200, 203. On the date of injury—which Judge Jessup deemed to be February 12, 1948, the date of the bankruptcy decree—the Belgian shares were still held in trust by a U.S. corporation, which had legal title to and full control of the shares. He therefore concluded that the claim was not Belgian in character on the critical date of injury. Does this suggest a flaw in the use of a "genuine link" approach? Are the problems with allowing all interested states—the state of incorporation and the states of any shareholders—to exercise rights of protection before the Court in fact insoluble?

Note that in some other forms of international legal process, no "genuine link" between a state and a private party is required. In European human rights law, for example, states may protect private parties against other states regardless of the nationality of the victim. See Part D below.

B. INDIVIDUALS AS SUBJECTS OF INTERNATIONAL LAW

MARK W. JANIS, "INDIVIDUALS AS SUBJECTS OF INTERNATIONAL LAW"

17 *Cornell International Law Journal* 61 (1984).

Legal positivism has long provided the usual theory for comprehending international law. The typical positivist definition of international law is grounded on a subject-based differentiation between international and municipal rules. Positivism views international law as a set of rules with states as its subjects. Municipal law is thought of as pertaining to individuals who are subjects of a single state. * * *

Before positivism, there was no theoretical insistence that the rules of the law of nations applied only to states. William Blackstone reflected the sentiment of the middle eighteenth century. For Blackstone, individuals and states were both proper subjects of the law of nations. He drew no dividing line between what later came to be called public and private international law. Blackstone distinguished his law of nations from other sorts of law not on the basis of its subjects but because of its sources. He saw the rules of the law of nations as universal, emanating either from natural justice or from the practice of many states. Municipal legal rules, however, emanated from a single state.

In 1789, Jeremy Bentham created the term "international law" in his *Introduction to the Principles of Morals and Legislation*. Bentham defined the new concept as the law which relates to "the mutual transactions between sovereigns as such." He thought that "as to any transactions which may take place between individuals who are subjects of different states, these are regulated by the internal laws, and decided upon by the internal tribunals" of individual sovereign states. Categorizing laws on the basis of "the persons whose conduct is the object of the law," Bentham concluded that international law had only states as its subjects. While categorizing rules on the basis of the subjects to be governed is logical enough, it plainly was wrong for Bentham to assume that international law so defined was equivalent to the traditional law of nations. There were significant differences between the two.

Two early nineteenth century positivists promoted the notion that the individual was not a proper subject of international law. Joseph Story, complaining that no treatises existed on the subject, crafted "private" international law to parallel Bentham's "public" international law. Public international law went to international matters affecting states, while private international law concerned international matters between individuals. John Austin argued that because public international law claimed to regulate matters between sovereign states which as sovereigns could not be regulated by any outside authority, international law was just a form of "positive morality" and not really law at all.

Legal positivism had taken the eighteenth century law of nations, a law common to individuals and states, and transformed it into public and private international law. The former was deemed to apply to states, the latter to individuals. Positivists scorned both sides of the discipline. Public international law was "international" but not really "law." Private international law was "law" but not really "international." Even so insightful a modern positivist as H.L.A. Hart assumed that the essence of international law was that it addressed states. Although Hart saw persuasive similarities between international and municipal law, he accepted uncritically Bentham's subject-based approach to the field.

The positivist definition of international law has had an enormous impact on modern perceptions concerning the individual and international law. With few exceptions, the theory rejects the notion that individuals are proper subjects of public international law. Originally, the subject-based approach was merely Bentham's attempt to provide a rational way of explaining that law may have different subjects: individuals and states. While law can be categorized on the basis of its subjects, in practice the law of nations and international law have concerned more than the legal rights of states. * * *

A prominent example of the failure of positivism to describe adequately the reality of the individual as a subject of international law comes from the time of Bentham himself. In *Respublica v. De Longchamps*, an American municipal court indicted the defendant for assaulting the Consul General of France to the new United States. It was held that the case "must be determined on the principles of the laws of nations." There was, following Blackstone, no doubt that an individual could be guilty of an infraction of the law of nations. De Longchamps, for his violation of the law of nations, was ordered to pay a fine of one hundred French crowns to the Commonwealth of Pennsylvania and to be imprisoned for "a little more" than two years.

Even during the high tide of positivism, the United States Supreme Court had no difficulty seeing individuals as subjects of international law. In *The Paquete Habana*, the United States Navy had seized two Cuban fishing smacks in the opening days of the Spanish–American War. A lower federal court condemned the boats as prizes of war. The masters for themselves, their crews, and their owners, argued before the Supreme Court that peaceful fishing craft were exempt from seizure under the rules of international law. In perhaps the most famous statement ever made about international law by a United States court, the Supreme Court held that "[i]nternational law is part of our law, and must be ascertained and administered by the courts of justice of appropriate jurisdiction, as often as questions of right depending upon it are duly presented for their determination." The Court held that:

> By an ancient usage among civilized nations, beginning centuries ago, and gradually ripening into a rule of international law, coast fishing vessels, pursuing their vocation of catching and bringing in fresh fish, have been recognized as exempt, with their cargoes and crews, from capture as prize of war.

Individuals had a right to rely on this rule as against the United States. The Court ordered the government to pay over the proceeds of the sale of the vessels and their cargoes to the individual claimants.

However inadequately subject-based theory accounted for individual rights and obligations in international law in the eighteenth and nineteenth centuries, positivism has done an even poorer job in explaining the practices of the twentieth century. The trials of Nazi war criminals after the Second World War highlighted the limitations of positivism. Faced with the excesses of a seemingly "civilized" state, those formulating and applying international law discarded any pretense that international rules applied only to state behavior.

The Charter of the International Military Tribunal at Nuremberg explicitly made individuals subject to international rules relating to crimes against peace, war crimes, and crimes against humanity. At Nuremberg and in other war trials, thousands of individuals were tried and convicted; hundreds were executed. Nuremberg re-established plainly and forcefully that the rules of international law should and do apply to individuals. The Nuremberg Tribunal held that "[c]rimes against international law are committed by men, not by abstract entities, and only by punishing individuals who commit such crimes can the provisions of international law be enforced." * * *

All of these examples—*De Longchamps, Paquete Habana*, the Nuremberg trials, the European and American human rights systems, the European Economic Community, and *Filartiga*—demonstrate that a large and important part of international law practice establishes individual rights and obligations and provides international and municipal procedures for enforcing these rights and obligations. The reality of practice contradicts the positivist insistence that international law applies only to relations among states. Insofar as the purpose of theory is to describe reality, the positivist, subject-based theory is inadequate.

Furthermore, restricting international law to states fails a second test by which positivism may be measured—its prescriptive worth. Surely, it is counter to the proper values of international law to prescribe that individuals may not be the subjects of international law. It was, at the time of the Nuremberg trials, politically and morally unacceptable to say that individuals within the German State between 1933 and 1945 were subjects only of German law to whom international rights and obligations could not pertain. In light of the atrocities of Nazi Germany, it would have been reprehensible to leave victims without legal rights and perpetrators without legal obligations. The lesson of Nuremberg is that there are individual international rights and obligations that transcend state boundaries.

Similar considerations pertain to international communities such as the Council of Europe and the European Economic Community. These groups have recognized the need to extend certain basic human and economic rights and obligations directly to individuals even though these rights and obligations emanate not from municipal law but from international law. Given the difficulty of addressing some issues, such as human rights and economic development, through municipal legal systems alone, such an extension of international law rules to individuals makes sense. It is impressive that, with the European Human Rights system and the legal system of the E.E.C., the Europeans have begun to open international legal processes to individuals.

It is wrong, both in terms of describing reality and in terms of preferential expression, for the theory of international law to hold that individuals are outside the ambit of international law rules. Individuals are and should be within this realm. The positivist notion that individuals are not fit subjects for international law springs not from a description of reality, but from a jurisprudential philosophy most concerned with a subject-based categorization of types of law. In so categorizing international law, the positivist theorists simply discarded the more inclusive notions of the law of nations. Whatever the impact of positivist theory, it never absolutely represented the practice of any time. Today, reality and preference have so revealed the weakness and obsolescence of subject-based theory that the sooner we rid ourselves of it the better.
* * *

If we reject the positivist's subject-based definition of international law, then what should be our new concept of the nature of international law? What are the objections to reverting to Blackstone's understanding that the discipline should be characterized by its reliance on universal and multinational sources?

One might say that, so characterized, international law is not properly "inter-national," but this is a rather superficial problem. Bentham supposed international law to be the equivalent of the law of nations, but it was not. So, the fault, if any, in matching the term and the content of international law must rest with its creator. We could easily use the old term, law of nations, and eliminate the linguistic quibble. But the term "international law" is too much in use to abandon it now. I suggest that we continue using the word international but understand "nation" to mean not only the national state but also the individuals who are the nationals of state. This meaning is both true to the word "nation" and finally makes sense of Bentham's equivalence between the law of nations and international law.

C. INTERNATIONAL HUMAN RIGHTS LAW

The concept that individuals can be subjects, as well as objects, of international law logically divides into individual *rights* at international law and individual *duties*. The next two parts primarily explore individual human rights—Part C looks at international human rights law and the United Nations, and Part D addresses the particularly successful European regional international human rights legal system. Part E then turns to individual duties with an introduction to international criminal law. Note how much progress has been made over the last six decades in establishing individuals as true subjects of international law.

Part C's Section 1 is a short introduction to the antecedents of international human rights law in municipal (domestic) human rights law. Section 2 examines the Nuremberg Trial and the Universal Declaration of Human Rights, which inaugurated modern international human rights law in the 1940's. Section 3 discusses the evolution of international human rights law, using a sample case, *Damian Thomas*, before the U.N. Human Rights Committee to show some of the strengths and weaknesses of general international human rights law under the auspices of the United Nations.

1. HUMAN RIGHTS AND MUNICIPAL LAW

The principle that law should protect the rights of individuals against the abuses of governments can at least be dated back to John Locke's *Two Treatises of Government* published in 1690. Locke believed that human rights, not governments, came first in the natural order of things:

> If Man in the State of Nature be so free, as has been said; If he be absolute Lord of his own Person and Possessions, equal to the greatest, and subject to no Body, why will he part with his Freedom? Why will he give up this Empire, and subject himself to the Dominion and Controul of any other Power? To which 'tis obvious to Answer, that though in the state of Nature he hath such a right, yet the Enjoyment of it is very uncertain, and constantly exposed to the Invasion of others. For all being Kings as much as he, every Man his Equal, and the greater part no strict Observers of Equity and Justice, the enjoyment of the property he has in this state is very unsafe, very unsecure. This makes him willing to quit a Condition, which however free, is full of fears and continual dangers: And 'tis

not without reason, that he seeks out, and is willing to joyn in Society with others who are already united, or have a mind to unite for the mutual *Preservation* of their Lives, Liberties and Estates.

John Locke, *Two Treatises of Government*, Book II, Chapter IX, section 123, at 395 (Peter Laslett rev.ed. 1963).

Locke's prose celebrated the rights to life, liberty, and property of the English under the limited government won by the Glorious Revolution of 1688. The particular advantages of England's unwritten constitution in the 18th century, especially the separation and balance of powers among the executive, legislative and judicial branches of government, were elaborated and popularized by the French political philosopher, Montesquieu, in the *Spirit of the Laws* in 1748. In 1762, the revolutionary potential of human rights—"Man is born free; and everywhere he is in chains"—was proclaimed by Jean Jacques Rousseau. Democratic revolutions soon followed in America and throughout Europe.

On July 4, 1776, the American Declaration of Independence issued from Philadelphia. The intellectual influences of Locke, Montesquieu, and Rousseau on Thomas Jefferson's document were plain to see. In a ringing affirmation of human rights and the duty of governments to protect them, the delegates of the 13 United States of America proclaimed:

We hold these truths to be self-evident, that all men are created equal, that they are endowed by their Creator with certain unalienable Rights, that among these are Life, Liberty and the pursuit of Happiness. That to secure these rights, Governments are instituted among Men, deriving their just powers from the consent of the governed. That whenever any Form of Government becomes destructive of these ends, it is the Right of the People to alter or to abolish it, and to institute new Government, laying its foundation on such principles and organizing its powers in such form, as to them shall seem most likely to effect their Safety and Happiness.

The last decades of the 18th century were a good time for political affirmations of human rights. As the constitutions of the newly independent American states were drafted in 1776, bills of rights enumerating specific rights were directly incorporated therein, even, as for Virginia, making up its first part. The fashion of bills of rights spread to Europe. Jefferson wrote James Madison from Paris on January 12, 1789: "Everybody here is trying their hands at forming declarations of rights." Thomas Jefferson, Letter of Jan. 12, 1789, 14 *The Papers of Thomas Jefferson* 436, 437 (Julian P. Boyd ed. 1958). Jefferson continued to play his part, reading and critiquing Lafayette's draft of what on August 27, 1789, a few weeks after the fall of the Bastille, would become the National Assembly's Declaration of the Rights of Man and Citizen. Thomas Jefferson, Letter of June 3, 1789, to Rabaut de St. Etienne, 15 *id.* at 166. The French Declaration's indebtedness to Rousseau's philosophy and Philadelphia's practice was widely acknowledged.

On September 25, 1789, less than a month after the promulgation of the French Declaration, the first Congress of the new Federal Government of the United States of America proposed the first ten amendments to the United States Constitution. These amendments, which are reproduced in the Appendix, came into force following the tenth state ratification (Virginia's) on December 15, 1791.

Many of the rights enunciated in the French Declaration and the U.S. Bill of Rights are similar. For example, Article 11 of the French Declaration reads: "Free communication of ideas and opinions is one of the most precious of the rights of man. Consequently, every citizen may speak, write, and print freely subject to responsibility for the abuse of such liberty in the cases determined by law;" while Article 1 of the U.S. Bill of Rights provides: "Congress shall make no law * * * abridging the freedom of speech, or of the press * * *."

Close in kinship, the American Declaration of Independence, the French Declaration of the Rights of Man and Citizen, and the U.S. Bill of Rights make up the 18th-century documentary foundation on which two centuries of legal protection of human rights in municipal law have been built. Constitutional guarantees of human rights are now widespread. In many countries, such as the United Kingdom, the principal responsibility for protecting human rights has ordinarily been vested in a democratically elected legislature. In others, such as the United States, that role has been assumed by the courts.

2. THE NUREMBERG TRIAL AND THE UNIVERSAL DECLARATION OF HUMAN RIGHTS

The idea that human rights could be protected by international, as well as municipal, law developed slowly. Throughout the 19th and early 20th centuries, the conception of state sovereignty then prevalent proved a stumbling block to efforts to impose international legal obligations on states to protect individuals. Instead, the doctrine of state responsibility examined above provided partial protection, but only so long as a foreign national injured by a state was effectively protected at the international level by that individual's national state. However, neither the doctrine of state sovereignty nor its counterpart, the doctrine of state protection, could shield individuals from abuses committed by their own governments. In practice, this fault excluded international review of most instances of governmental violations of human rights.

The turning point for this traditional approach in international law came in the 1940's in the midst of the extreme human rights abuses in war-torn Europe. In the Moscow Declaration of German Atrocities of October 30, 1943, the United States, the United Kingdom, France, and the Soviet Union declared that individual Germans would be held responsible for their violations of international law. U.N. Doc. A/CN.4/5, at 87–88 (1949). In the August 8, 1945, Charter of the International Military Tribunal, the same four Allies established the Nuremberg Tribunal.

THE NUREMBERG JUDGMENT

The United States of America, the French Republic,
the United Kingdom of Great Britain and Northern Ireland,
and the Union of Soviet Socialist Republics v. Hermann Wilhelm Goering,
Rudolf Hess, Joachim von Ribbentrop, [and 24 Other Named Defendants],
6 F.R.D. 69 (1946).

The Court:

On the 8th August 1945, the Government of the United Kingdom of Great Britain and Northern Ireland, the Government of the United States of America, the Provisional Government of the French Republic, and the Government of the Union of Soviet Socialist Republics entered into an agreement establishing this Tribunal for the trial of War Criminals whose offences have no particular geographical location. In accordance with Article 5, the following Governments of the United Nations have expressed their adherence to the Agreement:

Greece, Denmark, Yugoslavia, the Netherlands,

Czechoslovakia, Poland, Belgium, Ethiopia, Australia,

Honduras, Norway, Panama, Luxemburg, Haiti, New Zealand,

India, Venezuela, Uruguay, and Paraguay.

By the Charter annexed to the Agreement, the constitution, jurisdiction and functions of the Tribunal were defined.

The Tribunal was invested with power to try and punish persons who had committed crimes against peace, war crimes and crimes against humanity as defined in the Charter.

The Charter also provided that at the trial of any individual member of any group or organization the Tribunal may declare (in connection with any act of which the individual may be convicted) that the group or organization of which the individual was a member was a criminal organization.

In Berlin, on the 18th October 1945, in accordance with Article 14 of the Charter, an indictment was lodged against the defendants named in the caption above, who had been designated by the Committee of the Chief Prosecutors of the signatory Powers as major war criminals.

A copy of the indictment in the German language was served upon each defendant in custody at least thirty days before the Trial opened.

This indictment charges the defendants with crimes against peace by the planning, preparation, initiation and waging of wars of aggression, which were also wars in violation of international treaties, agreements and assurances; with war crimes; and with crimes against humanity. The defendants are also charged with participating in the formulation or execution of a common plan or conspiracy to commit all these crimes. The Tribunal was further asked by the Prosecution to declare all the named groups or organizations to be criminal within the meaning of the Charter.

The defendant Robert Ley committed suicide in prison on the 25th October 1945. On the 15th November 1945 the Tribunal decided that the defendant Gustav Krupp von Bohlen und Halbach could not then be tried because of his physical and mental condition, but that the charges against him in the indictment should be retained for trial thereafter, if the physical and mental condition of the defendant should permit. On the 17th November 1945 the Tribunal decided to try the defendant Bormann in his absence under the provisions of Article 12 of the Charter. After argument, and consideration of full medical reports, and a statement from the defendant himself, the Tribunal decided on the 1st December 1945 that no grounds existed for a postponement of the trial against the defendant Hess because of his mental condition. A similar decision was made in the case of the defendant Streicher.

In accordance with Articles 16 and 23 of the Charter, Counsel were either chosen by the defendants in custody themselves, or at their request were appointed by the Tribunal. In his absence the Tribunal appointed Counsel for the defendant Bormann, and also assigned Counsel to represent the named groups or organizations.

The trial which was conducted in four languages—English, Russian, French and German—began on the 20th November 1945, and pleas of "Not Guilty" were made by all the defendants except Bormann.

The hearing of evidence and the speeches of Counsel concluded on 31st August 1946.

403 open sessions of the Tribunal have been held. 33 witnesses gave evidence orally for the Prosecution against the individual defendants, and 61 witnesses, in addition to 19 of the defendants, gave evidence for the Defense.

A further 143 witnesses gave evidence for the Defense by means of written answers to interrogatories.

The Tribunal appointed Commissioners to hear evidence relating to the organizations, and 101 witnesses were heard for the Defense before the Commissioners, and 1,809 affidavits from other witnesses were submitted. Six reports were also submitted, summarizing the contents of a great number of further affidavits.

38,000 affidavits signed by 155,000 people were submitted on behalf of the Political Leaders, 136,213 on behalf of the SS, 10,000 on behalf of the SA, 7,000 on behalf of the SD, 3,000 on behalf of the General Staff and OKW, and 2,000 on behalf of the Gestapo.

The Tribunal itself heard 22 witnesses for the organizations. The documents tendered in evidence for the prosecution of the individual defendants and the organizations numbered several thousands. A complete stenographic record of everything said in court has been made, as well as an electrical recording of all the proceedings.

Copies of all the documents put in evidence by the Prosecution have been supplied to the Defense in the German language. The applications made by the defendants for the production of witnesses and documents raised serious problems in some instances, on account of the unsettled state of the country. It was also necessary to limit the number of witnesses to be called, in order to have an expeditious hearing, in accordance with Article 18(c) of the Charter. The Tribunal after examination, granted all those applications which in their opinion were relevant to the defense of any defendant or named group or organization, and were not cumulative. Facilities were provided for obtaining those witnesses and documents granted through the office of the General Secretary established by the Tribunal.

Much of the evidence presented to the Tribunal on behalf of the Prosecution was documentary evidence, captured by the Allied armies in German army headquarters, Government buildings, and elsewhere. Some of the documents were found in salt mines, buried in the ground, hidden behind false walls and in other places thought to be secure from discovery. The case, therefore against the defendants rests in a large measure on documents of their own making, the authenticity of which has not been challenged except in one or two cases.

The Charter Provisions

The individual defendants are indicted under Article 6 of the Charter, which is as follows:

"Article 6. The Tribunal established by the Agreement referred to in Article 1 hereof for the trial and punishment of the major war criminals of the European Axis countries shall have the power to try and punish persons who, acting in the interests of the European Axis countries, whether as individuals or as members of organizations, committed any of the following crimes.

"The following acts, or any of them, are crimes coming within the jurisdiction of the Tribunal for which there shall be individual responsibility;

"(a) Crimes Against Peace: namely planning, preparation, initiation or waging a war of aggression, or a war in violation of international treaties, agreements or assurances, or participation in a common plan or conspiracy for the accomplishment of any of the foregoing:

"(b) War Crimes: namely, violations of the laws or customs of war. Such violations shall include, but not be limited to, murder, ill-treatment or deportation to slave labor or for any other purpose of civilian population of or in occupied territory, murder or ill-treatment of prisoners of war or persons on the seas, killing of hostages, plunder of public or private property, wanton destruction of cities, towns or villages, or devastation not justified by military necessity;

"(c) Crimes Against Humanity: namely, murder, extermination, enslavement, deportation, and other inhumane acts committed against any civilian population, before or during the war, or persecutions on political, racial or religious grounds in execution of or in connection with any crime within the jurisdiction of the Tribunal, whether or not in violation of the domestic law of the country where perpetrated.

"Leaders, organizers, instigators and accomplices participating in the formulation or execution of a common plan or conspiracy to commit any of the foregoing crimes are responsible for all acts performed by any persons in execution of such plan." * * *

THE LAW OF THE CHARTER

The jurisdiction of the Tribunal is defined in the Agreement and Charter, and the crimes coming within the jurisdiction of the Tribunal, for which there shall be individual responsibility, are set out in Article 6. The law of the Charter is decisive, and binding upon the Tribunal.

The making of the Charter was the exercise of the sovereign legislative power by the countries to which the German Reich unconditionally surrendered; and the undoubted right of these countries to legislate for the occupied territories has been recognized by the civilized world. The Charter is not an arbitrary exercise of power on the part of the victorious nations, but in the view of the Tribunal, as will be shown, it is the expression of international law existing at the time of its creation; and to that extent is itself a contribution to international law.

The Signatory Powers created this Tribunal, defined the law it was to administer, and made regulations for the proper conduct of the Trial. In doing so, they have done together what any one of them might have done singly; for it is not to be doubted that any nation has the right thus to set up special courts to administer law. With regard to the constitution of the court, all that the defendants are entitled to ask is to receive a fair trial on the facts and the law.

The Charter makes the planning or waging of a war of aggression or a war in violation of international treaties a crime; and it is therefore not strictly necessary to consider whether and to what extent aggressive war was a crime before the execution of the London Agreement. But in view of the great importance of the questions of law involved, the Tribunal has heard full argument from the Prosecution and the Defense, and will express its view on the matter.

It was urged on behalf of the defendants that a fundamental principle of all law—international and domestic—is that there can be no punishment of crime without a pre-existing law. *Nullum crimen sine lege, nulla poena sine lege.* It was submitted that *ex post facto* punishment is abhorrent to the law of all civilized nations, that no sovereign power had made aggressive war a crime at the time the alleged criminal acts were committed, that no statute had defined aggressive war, that no penalty had been fixed for its commission, and no court had been created to try and punish offenders.

In the first place, it is to be observed that the maxim *nullum crimen sine lege* is not a limitation of sovereignty, but is in general a principle of justice. To assert that it is unjust to punish those who in defiance of treaties and assurances have attacked neighboring states without warning is obviously untrue, for in such circumstances the attacker must know that he is doing wrong, and so far from it being unjust to punish him, it would be unjust if his wrong were allowed to go unpunished. Occupying the positions they did in the government of Germany, the defendants, or at least some of them must have known of the treaties signed by Germany, outlawing recourse to war for the settlement of international disputes; they must have known that they were acting in defiance of all international law when in complete deliberation they carried out their designs of invasion and aggression. On this view of the case alone, it would appear that the maxim has no application to the present facts.

This view is strongly reinforced by a consideration of the state of international law in 1939, so far as aggressive war is concerned. The General Treaty for the Renunciation of War of August 27th 1928, more generally known as the Pact of Paris or the Kellogg–Briand Pact, was binding on sixty-three nations, including Germany, Italy and Japan at the outbreak of war in 1939. In the preamble, the signatories declared that they were:—

> "Deeply sensible of their solemn duty to promote the welfare of mankind; persuaded that the time has come when a frank renunciation of war as an instrument of national policy should be made to the end that the peaceful and friendly relations now existing between their peoples should be perpetuated ... all changes in their relations with one another should be sought only be pacific means ... thus uniting civilised nations of the world in a common renunciation of war as an instrument of their national policy ..."

The first two articles are as follows:

> "Article I: the High Contracting Parties solemnly declare in the names of their respective peoples that they condemn recourse to war for the solution of international controversies and renounce it as an instrument of national policy in their relations to one another."

> "Article II: The High Contracting Parties agree that the settlement or solution of all disputes or conflicts of whatever nature or of whatever origin they may be, which may arrive among them, shall never be sought except by pacific means."

The question is, what was the legal effect of this pact? The nations who signed the pact or adhered to it unconditionally condemned recourse to war for the future as an instrument of policy, and expressly renounced it. After the signing of the pact, any nation resorting to war as an instrument of national policy breaks the pact. In the opinion of the

Tribunal, the solemn renunciation of war as an instrument of national policy necessarily involves the proposition that such a war is illegal in international law and that those who plan and wage such a war, with its inevitable and terrible consequences, are committing a crime in so doing. War for the solution of international controversies undertaken as an instrument of national policy certainly includes a war of aggression, and such a war is therefore outlawed by the pact. As Mr. Henry L. Stimson, then Secretary of State of the United States, said in 1932:

> "War between nations was renounced by the signatories of the Kellogg–Briand Treaty. This means that it has become throughout practically the entire world ... an illegal thing. Hereafter, when nations engage in armed conflict, either one or both of them must be termed violators of this general treaty law.... We denounce them as law breakers."

But it is argued that the pact does not expressly enact that such wars are crimes, or set up courts to try those who make such wars. To that extent the same is true with regard to the laws of war contained in the Hague Convention. The Hague Convention of 1907 prohibited resort to certain methods of waging war. These included the inhumane treatment of prisoners, the employment of poisoned weapons, the improper use of flags of truce, and similar matters. Many of these prohibitions had been enforced long before the date of the Convention; but since 1907 they have certainly been crimes, punishable as offences against the laws of war; yet the Hague Convention nowhere designates such practices as criminal, nor is any sentence prescribed, nor any mention made of a court to try and punish offenders. For many years past, however, military tribunals have tried and punished individuals guilty of violating the rules of land warfare laid down by this Convention. In the opinion of the Tribunal, those who wage aggressive war are doing that which is equally illegal, and of much greater moment than a breach of one of the rules of the Hague Convention. In interpreting the words of the Pact, it must be remembered that international law is not the product of an international legislature, and that such international agreements as the Pact of Paris have to deal with general principles of law, and not with administrative matters of procedure. The law of war is to be found not only in treaties, but in the customs and practices of states which gradually obtained universal recognition and from the general principles of justice applied by jurists and practised by military courts. This law is not static, but by continual adaptation follows the needs of a changing world. Indeed, in many cases treaties do no more than express and define for more accurate reference the principles of law already existing.
* * *

It was submitted that international law is concerned with the actions of sovereign states, and provides no punishment for individuals; and further, that where the act in question is an act of state, those who carry it out are not personally responsible, but are protected by the doctrine of the sovereignty of the State. In the opinion of the Tribunal, both these submissions must be rejected. That international law imposes duties and liabilities upon individuals as well as upon states has long been recognized. In the recent case of Ex Parte Quirin (1942, 317 U.S. 1, 63 S.Ct. 2, 87 L.Ed.3), before the Supreme Court of the United States, persons were charged during the war with landing in the United States for purposes of spying and sabotage. The late Chief Justice Stone, speaking for the Court, said:

> "From the very beginning of its history this Court has applied the law of war as including that part of the law of nations which prescribes for the conduct of war, the status, rights and duties of enemy nations as well as enemy individuals."

He went on to give a list of cases tried by the Courts, where individual offenders were charged with offences against the laws of nations, and particularly the laws of war. Many other authorities could be cited, but enough has been said to show that individuals can be punished for violations of international law. Crimes against international law are committed by men, not by abstract entities, and only by punishing individuals who commit such crimes can the provisions of international law be enforced.

The provisions of Article 228 of the Treaty of Versailles * * * illustrate and enforce this view of individual responsibility.

The principle of international law, which under certain circumstances, protects the representatives of a state, cannot be applied to acts which are condemned as criminal by international law. The authors of these acts cannot shelter themselves behind their official position in order to be freed from punishment in appropriate proceedings. Article 7 of the Charter expressly declares:

> "The official position of defendants, whether as heads of state, or responsible officials in government departments, shall not be considered as freeing them from responsibility, or mitigating punishment."

On the other hand the very essence of the Charter is that individuals have international duties which transcend the national obligations of obedience imposed by the individual state. He who violates the laws of war cannot obtain immunity while acting in pursuance of the authority of the state if the state in authorizing action moves outside its competence under International Law.

It was also submitted on behalf of most of these defendants that in doing what they did they were acting under the orders of Hitler, and therefore cannot be held responsible for the acts committed by them in carrying out these orders. The Charter specifically provides in Article 3:

> "The fact that the defendant acted pursuant to orders of his Government or of a superior shall not free him from responsibility, but may be considered in mitigation of punishment."

The provisions of this article are in conformity with the law of all nations. That a soldier was ordered to kill or torture in violation of the international law of war has never been recognized as a defense to such acts of brutality, though, as the Charter here provides, the order may be urged in mitigation of the punishment. The true test, which is found in varying degrees in the criminal law of most nations, is not the existence of the order, but whether moral choice was in fact possible.

Notes and Questions

1. *The Nuremberg Judgment.* The 1946 judgment of the Nuremberg Tribunal confirmed the classical norm that individuals, as well as states, were proper subjects of international law. The Nuremberg judgment has come to stand not only for the moral and political imperative that individuals be made legally responsible for violations of international law but also for the proposition that individual human rights ought to be protected at the level of international law. In the words of Professor Henry King, one of the prosecuting attorneys at Nuremberg: "Nuremberg was designed to change the anarchic context in which the nations and peoples of the world related to one another." Henry T. King, "The Meaning of Nuremberg," 30 *Case Western Journal of International Law* 143, 143–44 (1998).

2. *Human Rights and the U.N. Charter.* In the Preamble of the 1945 Charter of the United Nations, the People of the United Nations reaffirm their "faith in fundamental human rights." Charter Article 55 calls on the Organization to promote "universal respect for, and observance of, human rights and fundamental freedoms for all without distinction as to race, sex, language, or religion." We saw that these norms were held not self-executing in U.S. law by the California Supreme Court in *Sei Fujii* in Chapter 4.

The transformation of the substantive norms of human rights law from national to international law was made complete in 1948 in the Universal Declaration of Human Rights, where the United Nations General Assembly followed in the footsteps of Jefferson and the drafters of the French Declaration of the Rights of Man and Citizen and the U.S. Bill of Rights. The Universal Declaration, parts of which appear below, is generally said to enumerate human rights norms at the level of international law. Among the sources of international law surveyed in Chapters 2 and 3, which would most strongly support the assertion that the various articles in the Universal Declaration constitute international legal norms? Is the fact that the norms are embodied in a General Assembly resolution that was adopted unanimously (the vote was 48 states in favor, none against, and 8 abstaining) itself sufficient? Does every article of the Universal Declaration have an equal claim to be an international legal norm?

THE UNIVERSAL DECLARATION OF HUMAN RIGHTS
G.A. Resolution 217A (III), U.N. Doc. A/810, at 71 (1948).

Article 3

Everyone has the right to life, liberty and the security of person.

Article 4

No one shall be held in slavery or servitude; slavery and the slave trade shall be prohibited in all their forms.

Article 5

No one shall be subjected to torture or to cruel, inhuman or degrading treatment or punishment.

Article 6

Everyone has the right to recognition everywhere as a person before the law.

Article 7

All are equal before the law and are entitled without any discrimination to equal protection of the law. All are entitled to equal protection against any discrimination in violation of this Declaration and against any incitement to such discrimination.

Article 8

Everyone has the right to an effective remedy by the competent national tribunals for acts violating the fundamental rights granted him by the constitution or by law.

Article 9

No one shall be subjected to arbitrary arrest, detention or exile.

Article 10

Everyone is entitled in full equality to a fair and public hearing by an independent and impartial tribunal, in the determination of his rights and obligations and of any criminal charge against him.

Article 11

1. Everyone charged with a penal offence has the right to be presumed innocent until proved guilty according to law in a public trial at which he has had all the guarantees necessary for his defence.

2. No one shall be held guilty of any penal offence on account of any act or omission which did not constitute a penal offence, under national or international law, at the time when it was committed. Nor shall a heavier penalty be imposed than the one that was applicable at the time the penal offence was committed.

Article 12

No one shall be subjected to arbitrary interference with his privacy, family, home or correspondence, nor to attacks upon his honour and reputation. Everyone has the right to the protection of the law against such interference or attacks.

Article 13

1. Everyone has the right to freedom of movement and residence within the borders of each State.

2. Everyone has the right to leave any country, including his own, and to return to his country.

Article 14

1. Everyone has the right to seek and to enjoy in other countries asylum from persecution.

2. This right may not be invoked in the case of prosecutions genuinely arising from nonpolitical crimes or from acts contrary to the purposes and principles of the United Nations.

Article 15

1. Everyone has the right to a nationality.

2. No one shall be arbitrarily deprived of his nationality nor denied the right to change his nationality.

Article 16

1. Men and women of full age, without any limitation due to race, nationality or religion, have the right to marry and to found a family. They are entitled to equal rights as to marriage, during marriage and at its dissolution.

2. Marriage shall be entered into only with the free and full consent of the intending spouses.

3. The family is the natural and fundamental group unit of society and is entitled to protection by society and the State.

Article 17

1. Everyone has the right to own property alone as well as in association with others.

2. No one shall be arbitrarily deprived of his property.

Article 18

Everyone has the right to freedom of thought, conscience and religion; this right includes freedom to change his religion or belief, and freedom, either alone or in community with others and in public or private, to manifest his religion or belief in teaching, practice, worship and observance.

Article 19

Everyone has the right to freedom of opinion and expression; this right includes freedom to hold opinions without interference and to seek, receive and impart information and ideas through any media and regardless of frontiers.

Article 20

1. Everyone has the right to freedom of peaceful assembly and association.

2. No on may be compelled to belong to an association.

Article 21

1. Everyone has the right to take part in the government of his country, directly or through freely chosen representatives.

2. Everyone has the right of equal access to public service in his country.

3. The will of the people shall be the basis of the authority of government; this will shall be expressed in periodic and genuine elections which shall be by universal and equal suffrage and shall be held by secret vote or by equivalent free voting procedures.

Notes and Questions

1. *State Sovereignty.* The emergence of international human rights law in the mid-20th century has been described as the most "radical development in the whole history of international law" since it so speedily established individuals as well as states as subjects of international law. John P. Humphrey, "The Revolution in the International Law of Human Rights," 4 *Human Rights* 205, 208 (1975). Why did it take so long for international law to protect human rights? Certainly, part of the answer lies in the idea of state sovereignty, one of the fundamental principles of international law since its modern emergence in the 17th century. Insofar as international law is meant to protect states from the interference of other states, international human rights law still poses a real conflict. When does a state's treatment of individuals within its own boundaries go so far wrong as to permit the interference—even the intervention—of other states? Is it any surprise that it was the experience of Nazi-occupied Europe that destroyed the moral foundations of the positivist theory that international law and legal process should not be available to individuals?

2. *International Legal Machinery.* However rapid the emergence of the rules of international human rights law, the development of effective international human rights legal process has been much more gradual. Need there necessarily be a greater political consensus to create effective legal machinery than to promulgate rules of substantive law? In cases where there is no formal international legal process, *i.e.*, no court or executive to enforce international human rights law, how is international human rights law to be made efficacious? What is the influence of public pronouncements by critical governments or private groups? How can such pronouncements be made more forceful, *e.g.*, by economic or political sanctions? As we see below, some progress has been made in creating enforcement mechanisms at the level of the United Nations. More progress, however, is to be seen in regional human rights systems, especially in Europe.

3. THE UNITED NATIONS AND HUMAN RIGHTS LAW

The system of human rights law at the United Nations has evolved from a preoccupation with the development of norms to an emphasis on procedures for implementing those norms, an evolution traced in the first excerpt in this Section. Following this excerpt is an opinion in the

Damian Thomas Case brought before the U.N. Human Rights Committee, one of the forums available at the United Nations for pursuing complaints of human rights abuses, along with discussion of some of the effects of the Committee's work.

THOMAS BUERGENTHAL, "THE NORMATIVE AND INSTITUTIONAL EVOLUTION OF INTERNATIONAL HUMAN RIGHTS"

19 *Human Rights Quarterly* 703 (1997).

I. INTRODUCTION * * *

The starting point of this analysis is the Charter of the United Nations (Charter), which laid the foundation of modern international human rights law. While it is true that international law recognized some forms of international human rights protection prior to the [1945] entry into force of the UN Charter, "the internationalization of human rights and the humanizaton of international law" begins with the establishment of the United Nations. The Charter ushered in a worldwide movement in which states, intergovernmental, and nongovernmental organizations are the principal players in an ongoing struggle over the role the international community should play in promoting and protecting human rights. * * *

II. STAGE ONE: THE NORMATIVE FOUNDATION

The first stage in this process begins with the entry into force of the UN Charter and continues at least through the adoption in 1966 of the International Covenants on Human Rights. By this time, the Universal Declaration of Human Rights had been adopted by the United Nations, as had the Genocide Convention and the Convention on the Elimination of All Forms of Racial Discrimination, to mention only the principal human rights instruments. During this same period, the European Convention on Human Rights entered into force; the Organization of American States proclaimed the American Declaration on the Rights and Duties of Man; and UNESCO [the United Nations Educational, Social and Cultural Organization] and the ILO [International Labor Organization], respectively, promulgated the Convention against Discrimination in Education and the Convention Concerning Discrimination in Respect of Employment and Occupation.

This period, in short, witnessed the normative consolidation of international human rights law. It is true, of course, that this process continues to this day. It is equally true, however, that in these first 20 years following the establishment of the UN the process had become irreversible. * * *

III. STAGE TWO: INSTITUTION BUILDING

The second stage in the evolution of international human rights begins in the late 1960s and continues for the next fifteen to twenty years. This is the era of institution building. During these years we find two distinct developments taking place within the UN framework. The first focused on the nature or scope of the human rights obligations that Articles 55 and 56 imposed on the Member States. Only after this issue had been resolved could the UN begin to create institutions and mechanisms to enforce their obligations. * * *

The period here under consideration also saw the emergence and consolidation of universal and regional treaty-based institutions for the protection of human rights. In the mid to late 1970s the UN Human Rights Committee and the Committee on the Elimination of Racial Discrimination (CERD) came into being with the entry into force of the International Covenant on Civil and Political Rights and the International Convention on the Elimination of All Forms of Racial Discrimination. The entry into force in 1978 of the American Convention on Human Rights brought with it the establishment of the Inter–American Commission and Court of Human Rights. Although the European Convention of Human Rights came into effect as early as 1953, it was not until the late 1960s and early 1970s that the institutions it created, particularly the Court, began to play an important role in the implementation of the Convention. In 1978, moreover, UNESCO adopted a special mechanism for dealing with human rights violations falling within its sphere of competence. ILO institutions for dealing with human rights issues predate those referred to above, whereas those established under the African Charter on Human and Peoples' Rights did not come into being until after the entry into force of that instrument in 1986. * * *

IV.   STAGE THREE: IMPLEMENTATION
IN THE POST COLD WAR ERA

The institutions referred to in the preceding section did not come fully into their own until the mid to late 1980s when they could begin to focus on adopting effective measures to ensure state compliance with their international obligations. This process continues to this day. It is one thing to establish institutions on the international plane to promote and protect human rights, it is quite another to give them the authority and tools they need to achieve their objective. States are more likely to agree to the creation of human rights institutions than to cooperate with these institutions when they or their allies are charged with human rights violations. It must be recognized, however, that the political factors which contributed in large measure to the creation of human rights institutions in the first place—the ideas that inspired the international human rights movement and captured the imagination of mankind—make it increasingly more difficult for states not to comply with their human rights obligations.

During the period here under consideration, the world underwent dramatic changes to which the human rights revolution contributed significantly and from which the revolution also benefitted significantly. The end of the Cold War freed many nations in Europe from Communist rule, permitting them to embark on a process of democratic transformation. What is more, it liberated international efforts to promote human rights from the debilitating ideological conflicts and political sloganeering of the past. These developments have enabled the UN to focus increasingly on obstacles to the implementation of human rights. * * *

In some regions of the world considerable progress has * * * been made in the implementation of human rights. During the period here under consideration the human rights system established under the European Convention of Human Rights gained institutional maturity. In fact, by the time the Soviet Union collapsed, the European Court of Human Rights had for all practical purposes become the constitutional court of Western Europe. The recent accession to the European Convention of the former Eastern and Central European allies of the Soviet Union as well as some of the new Soviet Republics has the potential of transforming the Court into the constitutional court of all Europe. This process may take longer, however, than one might assume at first glance because the newer members face many serious political, economic and social problems that few, if any, of the Western European members confronted when they first joined the Convention system.

The inter-American human rights system, which came into being later than its European counterpart, was unable for many years to play a major role in improving the human rights situation in the Americas. For decades the region was in the grips of oppressive regimes that engaged in massive violations of human rights behind a veil of impunity sustained at the height of the Cold War by superpower protection. With the onset of the process of transition to democracy in that region, which began in the mid–1980s, the inter-American human rights system could finally focus on implementation. The judgments of the Inter–American Court of Human Rights in the late 1980s, exposing the heinous practice of disappearances for all the world to see, opened the way for the Court and the Inter–American Commission on Human Rights to play a much more active role in protecting human rights in the Americas. Unlike Western Europe, however, the Americas is a region still very much in the process of development, with serious social and economic problems, poverty, and corruption. Moreover, there are some countries where the military, while ostensibly no longer in power, remains a real force to be reckoned with. Transition to democracy has a long way to go in the region, despite the impressive progress made in the past few years. It is clear, though, that those who believed in the 1960s and 1970s that oppressive military regimes were the only obstacle to the effective protection of human rights and genuine democracy in the region proved to be only partially right. By the same token, it is probably true that the process of democratization is now irreversible. Moreover, while the human rights problems of the region cannot be solved by merely substituting a freely elected government for a military regime, the inter-American human rights system has in recent years been able to point to some real successes.

The same cannot be said as yet of the African human rights system. It still faces many of the problems that afflicted the inter-American system two decades ago as far as repressive regimes are concerned and even greater economic, social, and political obstacles. The poverty, corruption, underdevelopment, disease, tribal conflicts, and many other scourges that affect African society today make the task of the African Commission on Human and Peoples' Rights extremely difficult. The liberation of South Africa from apartheid—in itself probably the greatest victory to date of the human rights revolution—and that country's emergence as the foremost democratic nation on the African continent, as well as some promising trends towards democracy in the region, cannot in the long run do anything but strengthen the role of the African Commission.

The African Commission, the human rights organs of the inter-American system, and the treaty bodies established within the UN framework all suffer from a very serious lack of financial resources. This fact has very harmful consequences for their ability to discharge their responsibilities. The real tragedy here is that at precisely the moment in history when conditions are, on the whole, more favorable than ever before for the implementation of human rights on the global and regional levels, the institutions assigned the task of promoting and supervising this process are for financial reasons not able to do so satisfactorily. Here it should be said that while resources are scarce everywhere, the real reasons for at least some budget-cutting activities affecting human rights bodies have more to do with a desire of certain governments to limit the power of these institutions than with genuine budgetary concerns. Given the contemporary human rights revolution, it is politically easier today to cut the budget of a human rights body by pointing to a lack of funds than by suggesting that its activities are not important.

DAMIAN THOMAS v. JAMAICA

U.N. Human Rights Committee Communication No. 800/1998,
U.N. Doc. CCPR/65/D/800/1998,
7 *International Human Rights Report* 326 (2000).

The Human Rights Committee, established under article 28 of the International Covenant on Civil and Political Rights, [m]eeting on 8 April 1999 * * * [a]dopts the following:

VIEWS UNDER ARTICLE 5, PARAGRAPH 4, OF THE OPTIONAL PROTOCOL

1. The author of the communication is Damian Thomas, a Jamaican minor (16 years old at the time of submission of the communication), currently at St. Catherine's District Prison, Jamaica. The author was born on 21 November 1980. * * * He is not represented by counsel.

2.1 The author was arrested on 9 May 1995 and convicted on 3 May 1996. On 5 May 1996 he was placed in the General Penitentiary, Kingston.

2.2 By a further submission the author informed the Committee that he was 15 years old when he was arrested. He was brought before the

Gun Court for two murders, where only one of those allegations was sent to trial. He was tried before the Home Circuit Court, convicted and sentenced to be detained during her Majesty's pleasure. * * *

3. While at the General Penitentiary, the author wrote to the Commissioner for Prisons requesting that he be removed from the adult prison. It appears that someone within the prison system, one Mr. Dawkins, informed him that he was to be moved to a juvenile institution. However, when the author was moved it was to St. Catherine District Prison, once again among adults. The author claims that he is being held in a prison with adult inmates in violation of the Covenant.

4.1 By submission dated 23 March 1998, the State party contends that the circumstances under which the author is being held are not clear. It requests that the author provide information on the offence for which he was convicted, as well as any other relevant information, e.g. how old was he at the time of his sentence and whether the judicial authorities were made aware of his age.

4.2 It undertakes to investigate the circumstances of the author's detention and would advise the Committee as soon as the results were available.

5.1 The author in a letter dated 11 May 1998, informed the Committee that he was tried at the Gun Court for two murders, that he lost his appeal, being sentenced to detention during her Majesty's pleasure. He informs the Committee that he was born on 21 November 1980, and was only 15 at the time of his arrest.

5.2 He further submits that since he has been in detention both at the General Penitentiary and at St. Catherine District Prison he has been systematically beaten by warders. He refers to several incidents; one on 8 November 1996, where he was kicked by several warders; Mr. Norris, Mr. Dwight and Sergeant Brown. On 20 March 1997 a warder called Mr. Waugh boxed him round the ears and threatened him. On 16 December 1997 he was thumped on the back and beaten by a Mr. Campbell and a corporal Ferguson while taking him to the overseer's office. They told the overseer that they were taking him to the hospital allegedly because he had lice. He was never taken to the hospital but rather he was beaten and kicked about by the warders and a warder called Mr. Mcdermatt cut off his Rastafarian hair. On 20 July 1997, he was beaten by several warders including a Mr. Gardener allegedly because the author was from the same area where the warder's aunt had been killed.

5.3 These new allegations were transmitted to the State party with a request that any comments be submitted to the Committee before 30 January 1999, since the case would be put before the Committee at its 65th session. To date, 25 March 1999, no response has been received from the State party.

6.1 Before considering any claim contained in a communication, the Human Rights Committee must, in accordance with rule 87 of its procedure, decide whether or not it is admissible under the Optional Protocol to the Covenant.

6.2   The Committee has ascertained as required under article 5 paragraph 2(a) of the Optional Protocol that the same matter is not being examined under another procedure of international investigation or settlement.

6.3   With regard to the author's alleged ill-treatment at the General Penitentiary and St. Catherine District Prison, the Committee notes that the author has made precise allegations that he was brutalized by several wardens on 8 November 1996; 20 March 1997; 16 December 1997 and 20 July 1997. The Committee also notes that the author has complained to the prison authorities. His claims have not been refuted by the State party, which has promised to investigate these, but has failed to forward to the Committee its findings, eleven months after promising to do so, in spite of a reminder sent on 30 October 1998. The Committee recalls that a State party is under the obligation to investigate seriously allegations of violations of the Covenant made under the Optional Protocol. However, in the present case the Committee notes that these allegations were transmitted to the State party after Jamaica's denunciation of the Optional Protocol came into force on 23 January 1998. Consequently, the Committee considers that these claims are inadmissible under article 1 of the Optional Protocol.

6.4   With respect to the remaining allegations the Committee observes that the State party has not raised objections to the admissibility of the communication. It further observes that, given the name, date of birth, date of arrest and of conviction and the location in 1998 in St. Catherine's District Prison, all in relation to the author, the State party should have no difficulty in identifying the details relevant to this matter. Accordingly the Committee decides that the remaining allegations are admissible and proceeds, without further delay, to an examination of the substance of the author's claims, in the light of all the information made available to it by the parties, as required by article 5, paragraph 1 of the Optional Protocol.

6.5   With respect to the non segregation of the author from adult prisoners both at the General Penitentiary and at St. Catherine's District Prison, the Committee once again regrets the State party's lack of cooperation in this matter. The Committee considers that it is incumbent upon the State party where a complaint such as this is submitted to it in respect of a serving prisoner, to verify whether that prisoner is, or has at any relevant stage, been a minor. The Committee notes from the information before it and not refuted by the State party, that the author was born in November 1980, making him seventeen years old when his communication was submitted to the Committee and 15, when he was sentenced. The Committee considers that the State party has failed to discharge its obligations under the Covenant in respect of Damian Thomas, in so far as he has been kept among adult prisoners when still a minor, and consequently, finds that there has been a violation of article 10, paragraphs 2 and 3.

6.6 The Committee further observes that the facts as described in the present case, also constitute a violation of article 24 of the Covenant, since the State party has failed to provide to Damian Thomas such measures of protection as are required by his status as a minor.

7. The Human Rights Committee, acting under article 5, paragraph 4, of the Optional Protocol to the International Covenant on Civil and Political Rights, is of the view that the facts before it disclose a violation of articles 10, paragraphs 2 and 3, and 24 of the Covenant.

8. In accordance with article 2, paragraph 3(a), of the Covenant, the State party is under an obligation to provide Mr. Thomas with an effective remedy, entailing his placement in a juvenile institution, separated from adult prisoners if Jamaican legislation authorises it, and including compensation for his non segregation from adult prisoners while a minor. The State party is under an obligation to ensure that similar violations do not occur in the future.

9. On becoming a State party to the Optional Protocol, Jamaica recognized the competence of the Committee to determine whether there has been a violation of the Covenant or not. This case was submitted for consideration before Jamaica's denunciation of the Optional Protocol became effective on 23 January 1998; in accordance with article 12(2) of the Optional Protocol it is subject to the continued application of the Optional Protocol. Pursuant to article 2 of the Covenant, the State party has undertaken to ensure to all individuals within its territory or subject to its jurisdiction the rights recognized in the Covenant and to provide an effective and enforceable remedy in case a violation has been established. The Committee wishes to receive from the State party, within 90 days, information about the measures taken to give effect to the Committee's views.

NATALIA SCHIFFRIN, "JAMAICA WITHDRAWS THE RIGHT OF INDIVIDUAL PETITION UNDER THE INTERNATIONAL COVENANT ON CIVIL AND POLITICAL RIGHTS"

92 *American Journal of International Law* 563 (1998).

In October 1997, a little-noticed event took place at the United Nations that may roll back the international legal protection of human rights. Jamaica became the first country to denounce the Optional Protocol to the International Covenant on Civil and Political Rights (ICCPR), and thus withdrew the right of individual petition to the UN Human Rights Committee (Committee). Although it is provided for under the Protocol's Article 12, no state has previously made such a denunciation.[3]

3. North Korea withdrew from the Covenant itself in August 1997. Shortly after its withdrawal, the UN Human Rights Committee adopted General Comment No.

Jamaica's action runs counter to the steady growth in ratifications of the Optional Protocol, expanding from twenty-two nations (including Jamaica) on the day it entered into force of March 23, 1976, to ninety-two by the time of denunciation this past fall. In the more than twenty years since the Committee has been rendering decisions (or "adopting views") under the Optional Protocol, hundreds of decisions have been issued concerning a vast array of human rights issues across the globe.

Jamaica's decision is particularly troublesome because, it is feared in some quarters, this action may serve as a catalyst for other countries in the Commonwealth Caribbean and elsewhere to follow suit. It is no secret that several other nations have been considering the same move.
* * *

The background to Jamaica's unprecedented move is complex. The story begins in the late 1980's, when lawyers representing death row litigants in Jamaica started making petitions to the Committee as an integral part of a campaign against the use of capital punishment. This legal maneuver contributed to the success of that campaign; though the death penalty is considered to enjoy wide public support in Jamaica, there have been no executions on the island since 1988.

The first case against Jamaica before the Committee was filed in 1984, the 165th case received by that body. At that time, communications had been filed against only a few states, with Uruguay and Canada receiving the most complaints. In the late 1980s and 1990s, an ever-growing number of cases were filed against Jamaica concerning the death penalty, eventually rendering that state one of the most frequent respondents before the Committee. Many of the Committee's most important judgments in the field of liberty and security of the person have been adopted in relation to Jamaica, exposing various serious human rights violations left unremedied by the domestic courts. In terms of the death penalty, the Committee has principally ruled against it on the grounds that execution of an individual when the Covenant's fair trial guarantees (contained in Article 14) have not been met violates the Covenant's guarantee of the right to life (contained in Article 6). Without review by the Committee, for example, individuals in Jamaica could be sentenced to death without the benefit of counsel present at trial, with only a few moments to consult counsel before trial, and without a written judgment upon which to base an appeal.

At first, the strategy of taking cases to the Committee worked as well in Jamaica as it does in most countries. In other words, it was hard to say exactly how effective the strategy was. Since its inception, enforcement of the Covenant, like that of all international human rights agreements, has been problematic. Some countries file the required

26 on issues relating to the continuity of obligations to the International Covenant on Civil and Political Rights, UN Doc. CCPR/C/21/Rev.1/Add.9 (1997). The com- ment states that withdrawals and denunciations are not permitted under the Covenant, and thus throws into question the status of North Korea's withdrawal.

periodic state reports years late,[10] while others never file at all.[11] The individual petition system is considered to be one of the most effective enforcement mechanisms within the international human rights legal framework, and yet even it boasts a state compliance rate of only about 25 percent. Jamaica, like most states, does not readily admit when an action is taken directly in response to a decision by the Committee, but, on the other hand, Jamaica has never executed an individual where the Committee has recommended that it should not.[13] * * *

Resuming capital punishment in a manner consistent with Jamaica's legal obligations is no easy task. Jamaica's decision to pull out of the Optional Protocol will not of itself achieve this goal, while it will potentially cause great harm. Jamaica's action has taken away an important avenue of redress and may encourage other states to follow suit. Until now, the individual petitions procedure has worked at least to some extent because it represents an attempt by state parties to participate in a growing community of nations trying to create and adhere to a universal set of human rights standards, irrespective of whether it suits those nations on a case-by-case basis. The system is only as strong as its members. Its effectiveness will be significantly reduced if countries pull out whenever they perceive the Committee as posing an obstacle to domestic practice. When Jamaica withdrew from the Optional Protocol, it was thus, in the words of the Human Rights Committee member Christine Chanet of France, a sad day for human rights and a sad day for the community of nations that adhere to the Covenant.

To be sure, Jamaica remains a party to the Covenant itself, and to that end the rights enshrined in it are still guaranteed to its people. But without the right of individual petition, enforcement will be even more difficult than it has been thus far. And, clearly, without the Optional Protocol, an important avenue of redress has been shut off. Its absence will be felt especially by the residents of death row in St. Catherine's district prison.

Notes and Questions

1. *Human Rights Norms, Institutions, and Implementation.* Professor Buergenthal, now the U.S. judge on the International Court of Justice, divides the history of international human rights law into three eras: norm-building between 1945 and 1966, institution-building between 1966 and 1989, and implementation-building since 1989. Of course, not all international human rights systems have developed at the same pace. On the one hand,

10. For example, Cyprus, Mali, Jamaica and Vietnam have all been half a dozen years late or more in the submission of their state reports to the Human Rights Committee.

11. For example, Equatorial Guinea, Gabon and Somalia.

13. Unfortunately, this cannot be said of two of Jamaica's Commonwealth Carib-bean neighbors. Trinidad and Tobago executed Glen Ashby in 1994 despite a request by the Committee under Rule 86 of its Rules of Procedure for an interim stay of execution pending consideration of Mr. Ashby's application to the Committee. Shortly after acceding to the Optional Protocol, Guyana executed Rockliffe Ross in 1996 under similar circumstances.

the most effective system of all, European human rights law, explored in Section D below, was effectively implementing the European Human Rights Convention at least by the 1970s. On the other hand, most U.N.-based human rights systems, the Human Rights Committee being just one example, seem to be still well short of effective implementation.

2. *Accounting for the Weakness of the U.N. Human Rights System.* Professor Mutua has criticized "official international human rights bodies such as the Human Rights Committee * * * [as] basically weak and ineffectual." Makau wa Mutua, "Looking Past the Human Rights Committee: An Argument for De–Marginalizing Enforcement," 4 *Buffalo Human Rights Law Review* 211, 211 (1998). The causes are many, including poor funding, "organizational and bureaucratic constraints," and a choice of "the UN institutional culture which emphasizes compromise, consensus and diplomacy" rather than a disinterested "application of norm to fact." *Id.* at 223. But does the fault really rest with either the United Nations or the U.N. Human Rights Committee? Can a more or less universal institution really be expected to surmount the ideological and cultural divides among states with at all as much success as regional institutions such as the Council of Europe and the European Court of Human Rights explored below?

Moreover, it is important to note that unlike some of the regional human rights systems, most U.N.-based bodies lack any enforcement power; their decisions are not even legally binding. The U.N. Human Rights Committee can only hope to "shame" a government with bad publicity. See Markus Schmidt, "Treaty–Based Human Rights Complaints Procedures in the UN–Remedy or Mirage for Victims of Human Rights Violations?," 1998 *Human Rights*, No. 2, at 13, 15–16.

3. *"Shaming" Jamaica.* "Shaming" a government can, however, sometimes be an important goal in human rights litigation, as we saw in *Filartiga* in Chapter 1. When might a government be more or less susceptible to pressure from an adverse opinion of an international body such as the U.N. Human Rights Committee? What has Jamaica lost by repudiating the right of individual petition to the U.N. Human Rights Committee? Will criticism, such as that from Natalia Schiffrin, Senior Legal Officer at the International Centre for the Legal Protection of Human Rights (Interights), a nongovernmental organization based in London, have an international economic or political impact? Will it encourage domestic dissatisfaction with government policies?

4. *A Confusion of Norms and Institutions.* Is it fair to say that the United Nations has too often substituted words and bureaucracies for action on human rights? There are "literally several hundred" U.N. human rights treaties and, besides the U.N. Human Rights Committee, tens of U.N. institutions charged with monitoring human rights. See Gudmundur Alfredsson, "The United Nations and Human Rights," 25 *International Journal of Legal Information* 17 (1998). For discussion of possible steps to improve the effectiveness of U.N. human rights efforts, see American Bar Association Working Group on Improving the Effectiveness of the United Nations, "Recommendation and Report on the International Protection of Human Rights," in *The United Nations at 50: Proposals for Improving Its*

Effectiveness 63 (John E. Noyes ed. 1997). For more on the origins and structure of the United Nations, see Chapter 8.

D. EUROPEAN HUMAN RIGHTS LAW

The proceedings at Nuremberg had special meaning for those who had witnessed the awful abuses of human rights in Nazi-occupied Europe. For the Europeans pressing for political union, human rights became an important priority. The European Convention for the Protection of Human Rights and Fundamental Freedoms was signed on November 4, 1950, and came into force on September 3, 1953. Merely as a European bill of rights, the Convention provided little exceptional on the international scene. The heart of the Convention rested in what were, until 1998, two optional clauses, the crucial aspects of the system's enforcement machinery: Article 25 (now mandatory Article 34) gave individuals as well as states the right to petition the European human rights system, and Article 46 (now mandatory Article 32) gave the European Court of Human Rights jurisdiction to hear and try cases already reported on by the Commission.

Historically, the Europeans were familiar with bills of rights, but they were unfamiliar with judicial enforcement of those rights. Domestically, they trusted the legislative and executive branches of government rather than the judiciary to protect fundamental freedoms. Only over time have they been willing to empower international institutions to safeguard the Convention's rights.

Looking at the history of the system, it can be said that each of the five decades of the European Convention on Human Rights has told its own distinctive tale. The 1950's spoke of institutional development but had little actual case law about which to boast. The Convention was signed in 1950 and, ratified by eight states, came into force in 1953. In 1955 the Commission was granted the right to hear individual petitions against consenting states. The Court was constituted in 1958. Only on June 2, 1956, was an application declared admissible by the Commission (by Greece against the United Kingdom respecting Cyprus). Altogether only five applications (two government, three individual) were deemed admissible in the 1950's. No case was heard by the Court.

The 1960's saw both modest triumph and disquieting disobedience. There were some 54 applications admitted by the Commission (five government and 49 individual), and the Court rendered its first ten decisions in seven cases. However, in 1969, following adverse reports by the Commission, Greece withdrew from the Council of Europe and denounced the European Convention on Human Rights. This reduced the total membership in the system from 16 to 15 at the end of the decade. The number of states accepting the right of individual petition had grown to 11. The same number (though not always the same states) accepted the jurisdiction of the Court.

The 1970's showed a solid maturation of the system. Greece rejoined the Convention in 1974. By the end of the decade some 20 countries belonged, 14 accepting individual petition and 17 consenting to the jurisdiction of the Court. One hundred sixty-eight applications (five government, 163 individual) were deemed admissible by the Commission. Twenty-four cases were decided by the Court.

The 1980's witnessed an explosion of activity under the Convention. As of December 31, 1989, 22 states were parties to the Convention. All had accepted the right of individual petition and the jurisdiction of the Court. Four hundred and fifty-five applications were deemed admissible by the Commission. One hundred and sixty-nine cases were decided by the Court.

The 1990's evidenced the continuing growth of the system. As of November 1, 2000, 41 countries had ratified the European Human Rights Convention and thus accept the Convention's now mandatory right of individual petition and jurisdiction of the Court. The member states now include many nations from the former Communist bloc: Hungary, Bulgaria, Poland, Romania, Slovenia, the Czech Republic, Slovakia, Slovenia, Lithuania, Estonia, Albania, the former Yugoslav Republic of Macedonia, Ukraine, Latvia, Moldova, Croatia, Russia, and Georgia. In the first eight years of the decade (1990–1997), the Commission admitted 3,491 applications. Between 1990 and 1998, the Court delivered 818 judgments, more in those nine years than in the previous four decades. On November 1, 1998, the Convention was significantly amended by Protocol No. 11, which not only transformed the two critical optional clauses into mandatory provisions, but merged the part-time European Commission and Court of Human Rights into a single full-time European Court of Human Rights.

The story of the success of the European human rights law system is the story of what were the two optional clauses. In 1950, it may have seemed that opponents had "gutted" the Convention by making the right of individual petition and the jurisdiction of the Court optional, but, over time, the nations "opted into" both procedures. What strategies did the Commission and the Court use to induce states to accept the optional clauses and to maintain their acceptances? Did the example of some European governments accepting the optional clauses make it difficult for other European governments to opt out? Were European governments influenced by human rights abuses in other parts of the world, and did they seek to underline their own commitments to human rights? See Mark W. Janis, Richard S. Kay & Anthony W. Bradley, *European Human Rights Law* 16–26, 80–83 (2d ed. 2000).

THE SUNDAY TIMES CASE
European Court of Human Rights,
Judgment of 26 April 1979, Series A, Vol. 30, 1979 WL 68905.

8.   Between 1958 and 1961 Distillers Company (Biochemicals) Limited ("Distillers") manufactured and marketed under license in the

United Kingdom drugs containing an ingredient initially developed in the Federal Republic of Germany and known as thalidomide. The drugs were prescribed as sedatives for, in particular, expectant mothers. In 1961 a number of women who had taken the drugs during pregnancy gave birth to children suffering from severe deformities; in the course of time there were some 250 such births in all. Distillers withdrew all drugs containing thalidomide from the British market in November of the same year. * * *

10. * * * [B]y 1971, three hundred and eighty-nine claims in all were pending against Distillers. Apart from a statement of claim in one case and a defence delivered in 1969, no further steps were taken in those actions where writs had been issued. Distillers had announced in February 1968 that they would provide a substantial sum for the benefit of the remaining three hundred and eighty-nine claimants and both sides were anxious to arrive at a settlement out of court. The case in fact raised legal issues of considerable difficulty under English law. Had any of the actions come on for trial, they would have been heard by a professional judge sitting without a jury.

In 1971 negotiations began on a proposal by Distillers to establish a charitable trust fund for all the deformed children other than those covered by the 1968 settlement. The proposal was made subject to the condition that all parents accepted but five refused, one, at least, because payments out of the fund would have been based on need. An application, on behalf of the parents who would have accepted, to replace those five by the Official Solicitor as next friend was refused by the Court of Appeal in April 1972. During subsequent negotiations, the original condition was replaced by a requirement that "a substantial majority" of the parents consented. By September 1972 a settlement involving the setting-up of a £3,250,000 trust fund had been worked out and was expected to be submitted in October to the court for approval.

11. Reports concerning the deformed children had appeared regularly in *The Sunday Times* since 1967 and in 1968 it had ventured some criticism of the settlement concluded in that year. There had also been comment on the children's circumstances in other newspapers and on television. In particular, in December 1971, the *Daily Mail* published an article which prompted complaints from parents that it might jeopardize the settlement negotiations in hand; the *Daily Mail* was "warned off" by the Attorney–General in a formal letter threatening sanctions under the law of contempt of court but contempt proceedings were not actually instituted. On 24 September 1972, *The Sunday Times* carried an article entitled "Our Thalidomide Children: A Cause for National Shame": this examined the settlement proposals then under consideration, describing them as "grotesquely out of proportion to the injuries suffered," criticized various aspects of English law on the recovery and assessment of damages in personal injury cases, complained of the delay that had elapsed since the births and appealed to Distillers to make a more generous offer. The article contained the following passage:

"... the thalidomide children shame Distillers ... there are times when to insist on the letter of the law is as exposed to criticism as infringement of another's legal rights. The figure in the proposed settlement is to be £3.25 million, spread over 10 years. This does not shine as a beacon against pre-tax profits last year of £64.8 million and company assets worth £421 million. Without in any way surrendering on negligence, Distillers could and should think again."

A footnote in the article announced that "in a future article *The Sunday Times* [would] trace how the tragedy occurred." On 17 November 1972, the Divisional Court of the Queen's Bench Division granted the Attorney–General's application for an injunction restraining publication of this future article on the ground that it would constitute contempt of court * * *. * * *

17. The unpublished article which was the subject of the injunction opened with a suggestion that the manner of marketing thalidomide in Britain left a lot to be desired. It stated that Distillers:

"—relied heavily on the German tests and had not completed full trials of its own *before* marketing the drug;

—failed to uncover in its research into medical and scientific literature the fact that a drug related to thalidomide could cause monster births;

—before marketing the drug did no animal tests to determine the drug's effect on the foetus;

—accelerated the marketing of the drug for commercial reasons. Were not deflected by a warning from one of its own staff that thalidomide was far more dangerous than had been supposed;

—were not deflected by the discovery that thalidomide could damage the nervous system, in itself a hint that it might damage the foetus;

—continued to advertise the drug as safe for pregnant women up to a month from when it was withdrawn."

The body of the article described how, after their apparently disappointing initial ventures into pharmaceutics, Distillers learned in 1956 that the German firm of *Chemie Gruenenthal* had developed a sedative considered harmless and unique—thalidomide. The very large market existing at the time for sedatives was becoming overcrowded and Distillers thought it necessary to act quickly. Their decision to market the drug was taken before they had seen technical information, other than the transcript of a German symposium, and before carrying out independent tests. Indeed, they seemed to believe that thalidomide would not need elaborate tests. Distillers put in hand a search of scientific literature but failed to discover the results of research in 1950 by a Dr. Thiersch showing that a chemical related to thalidomide could cause monster births; opinions differed as to whether his work should have been found.

Sales of thalidomide began in Germany in October 1957 and Distillers were committed under their licensing agreement to commence marketing in April 1958. They put the programme for the drug's launch in hand even though clinical trials were behind. Results of the first British trials were published in January 1958: it had been found that thalidomide suppressed the work of the thyroid gland and that its method of action was unknown; the researcher warned that more tests were needed. Distillers did not rely on this advice, basing their decision on "flimsy" evidence, namely other trials in the United Kingdom and assurances concerning the results of research in Germany. The warning about anti-thyroid effects was particularly relevant since it was known that drugs affecting the thyroid could affect unborn children; it was reasonable to argue that Distillers should have delayed launching the drug pending further tests.

On 14 April 1958, continued the article, thalidomide went on sale in Britain, advertised as "completely safe." At the end of 1959, Distillers' pharmacologist discovered that thalidomide in liquid form was highly poisonous and that an overdose might be lethal, but his report was never published and the liquid product went on sale in July 1961. In December 1960, it was reported that patients who had taken thalidomide in the tablet form in which it had firstly been on sale showed symptoms of peripheral neuritis; this news had the result of holding up an application to market thalidomide in the United States of America where it was, in fact, never sold. Further cases of peripheral neuritis were reported in 1961 but Distillers' advertising continued to stress the drug's safety.

Early in 1961 children were born in the United Kingdom with deformities, but there was at the time nothing to connect them with thalidomide. However, between May and October, a doctor in Australia discovered that the common factor in a number of monster births was that the mothers had taken thalidomide during pregnancy. This was reported to *Chemie Gruenenthal* on 24 November who withdrew the drug two days later following newspaper disclosures. Distillers ended the public sale of thalidomide immediately afterwards. Tests on animals, published in April 1962, confirmed that thalidomide caused deformities, but sales to hospitals were not ended until December 1962.

The draft article concluded as follows:

> "So the burden of making certain that thalidomide was safe fell squarely on [Distillers]. How did the company measure up to this heavy responsibility? It can be argued that:
>
> 1. [Distillers] should have found all the scientific literature about drugs related to thalidomide. It did not.
>
> 2. It should have read Thiersch's work on the effects on the nervous system of drugs related to thalidomide, have suspected the possible action on unborn babies and therefore have done tests on animals for teratogenic effect. It did not.

3. It should have done further tests when it discovered that the drug had anti-thyroid activity and unsuspected toxicity. It did not.

4. It should have had proof before advertising the drug as safe for pregnant women that this was in fact so. It did not.

For [Distillers] it could be argued that it sincerely believed that thalidomide was free from any toxicity at the time it was first put on the market in Britain; that peripheral neuritis did not emerge as a side effect until the drug had been on sale in Britain for two years; that testing for teratogenic effects was not general in 1958; that if tests had been done on the usual laboratory animals nothing would have shown because it is only in the New Zealand white rabbit that thalidomide produces the same effects as in human beings; and, finally, that in the one clinical report of thalidomide being given to pregnant women no serious results followed (because thalidomide is dangerous only during the first 12 weeks of pregnancy). * * *

There appears to be no neat set of answers. . . ." * * *

21. Distillers made a formal complaint to the Attorney–General that the *Sunday Times* article of 24 September 1972 constituted contempt of court in view of the litigation still outstanding and, on 27 September, the Solicitor–General, in the absence of the Attorney–General, wrote to the editor of *The Sunday Times* to ask him for his observations. The editor, in his reply, justified that article and also submitted the draft of the proposed future article for which he claimed complete factual accuracy. The Solicitor–General enquired whether the draft had been seen by any of the parties to the litigation, as a consequence of which a copy of the draft was sent by *The Sunday Times* to Distillers on 10 October. On the previous day, *The Sunday Times* had been advised that the Attorney–General had decided to take no action in respect of the matter already published in September and October; Distillers also took no action. On 11 October, the Attorney–General's Office informed *The Sunday Times* that, following representations by Distillers, the Attorney–General had decided to apply to the High Court in order to obtain a judicial decision on the legality of the publication of the proposed article. On the following day, he issued a writ against Times Newspapers Ltd. in which he claimed an injunction "to restrain the defendants . . . by themselves, their servants or agents or otherwise, from publishing or causing or authorizing to be published or printed an article in draft dealing, *inter alia*, with the development, distribution and use of the drug thalidomide, a copy of which article had been supplied to the Attorney–General by the defendants."

22. The Attorney–General's application was heard by three judges of the Queen's Bench Division from 7 to 9 November 1972; on 17 November the court granted the injunction.

In its judgment the court remarked:

"the article does not purport to express any views as to the legal responsibility of Distillers ... but ... is in many respects critical of Distillers and charges them with neglect in regard to their own failure to test the product, or their failure to react sufficiently sharply to warning signs obtained from the tests by others. No one reading the article could ... fail to gain the impression that the case against Distillers on the footing of negligence was a substantial one."

The editor of the *Sunday Times* had indicated that any libel proceedings following publication would be defended by a plea that the contents of the article were true and the court approached the article on the footing that it was factually accurate.

23.   The reasoning in the court's judgment may be summarised as follows. The objection to unilateral comment, prior to conclusion of the court hearing, was that it might prevent the due and impartial administration of justice by affecting and prejudicing the mind of the tribunal itself, by affecting witnesses who were to be called or by prejudicing the free choice and conduct of a party to the litigation. It was the third form of prejudice that was relevant to the present case. * * *

24.   An appeal by Times Newspapers Ltd. against the Divisional Court's decision was heard by the Court of Appeal from 30 January to 2 February 1973. The court had before it an affidavit by the editor of the Sunday Times setting out developments in the intervening period both in the case itself and in public discussion thereof. With the leave of the court, counsel for Distillers made submissions on the contents of the proposed article, pointing to errors he said it contained. On 16 February, the Court of Appeal discharged the injunction. * * *

25.   Lord Denning said that the proposed article:

"... contains a detailed analysis of the evidence against Distillers. It marshals forcibly the arguments for saying that Distillers did not measure up to their responsibility. Though, to be fair, it does summarise the arguments which could be made for Distillers." * * *

"Trial by newspaper," continued Lord Denning, must not be allowed. However, the public interest in a matter of national concern had to be balanced against the interest of the parties in a fair trial or settlement; in the present case the public interest in discussion outweighed the potential prejudice to a party. The law did not prevent comment when litigation was dormant and not being actively pursued. * * *

28.   Following the Court of Appeal's decision, the *Sunday Times* refrained from publishing the proposed article so as to enable the Attorney–General to appeal. The Court of Appeal refused him leave to appeal but this was granted by the House of Lords on 1 March 1973. The hearing before the House of Lords was held in May 1973. On 18 July 1973, the House gave judgment unanimously allowing the appeal and

subsequently directed the Divisional Court to grant an injunction in the terms set out in paragraph 34 below. * * *

29. Lord Reid said that the House must try to remove the uncertainty which was the main objection to the present law. The law of contempt had to be founded entirely on public policy; it was not there to protect the rights of parties to a litigation but to prevent interference with the administration of justice and should be limited to what was reasonably necessary for the purpose. Freedom of speech should not be limited more than was necessary but it could not be allowed where there would be real prejudice to the administration of justice. * * *

The Court of Appeal had wrongly described the actions as "dormant" since settlement negotiations were in hand and improper pressure on a litigant to settle could constitute contempt. As for the Court of Appeal's balancing of competing interests, Lord Reid said:

"... contempt of court has nothing to do with the private interests of litigants. I have already indicated the way in which I think that a balance must be struck between the public interest in freedom of speech and the public interest in protecting the administration of justice from interference. I do not see why there should be any difference in principle between a case which is thought to have news value and one which is not. Protection of the administration of justice is equally important whether or not the case involves important general issues."

Lord Reid concluded that publication of the article should be postponed for the time being in the light of the circumstances then prevailing; however, if things dragged on indefinitely, there would have to be a reassessment of the public interest in a unique situation.

[A summary of the concurring opinion of Lord Morris of Booth-y-Gest in the English House of Lords is omitted.]

31. Lord Diplock said that contempt of court was punishable because it undermined the confidence of the parties and of the public in the due administration of justice. The due administration of justice required that all citizens should have unhindered access to the courts; that they should be able to rely on an unbiased decision based only on facts proved in accordance with the rules of evidence; that, once a case was submitted to a court, they should be able to rely upon there being no usurpation by any other person, for example in the form of "trial by newspaper," of the function of the court. Conduct calculated to prejudice any of these requirements or to undermine public confidence that they would be observed was contempt of court.

[Summaries of the concurring opinions of Lord Simon of Glaisdale and Lord Cross of Chelsea in the English House of Lords are omitted.]

34. On 25 July 1973, the House of Lords ordered that the cause be remitted to the Divisional Court with a direction to grant the following injunction:

"That ... Times Newspapers Ltd., by themselves, their servants, agents or otherwise, be restrained from publishing, or causing or authorising or procuring to be published or printed, any article or matter which prejudges the issues of negligence, breach of contract or breach of duty, or deals with the evidence relating to any of the said issues arising in any actions pending or imminent against Distillers ... in respect of the development, distribution or use of the drug 'thalidomide.' "

The defendants were granted liberty to apply to the Divisional Court for discharge of the injunction.

The Divisional Court implemented the above direction on 24 August 1973.

35.   On 23 June 1976, the Divisional Court heard an application by the Attorney–General for the discharge of the injunction. It was said on behalf of the Attorney–General that the need for the injunction no longer arose: most of the claims against Distillers had been settled and there were only four extant actions which could by then have been brought before the courts if they had been pursued diligently. As there was a conflicting public interest in the *Sunday Times* being allowed to publish "at the earliest possible date," the Attorney–General submitted the matter to the court as one where the public interest no longer required the restraint. The court, considering that the possibility of pressure on Distillers had completely evaporated, granted the application.

[A discussion of the Phillimore Report on the Law of Contempt, issued in December 1974, is omitted.]

38.   In their application, lodged with the Commission on 19 January 1974, the applicants claimed that the injunction, issued by the High Court and upheld by the House of Lords, to restrain them from publishing an article in the *Sunday Times* dealing with thalidomide children and the settlement of their compensation claims in the United Kingdom constituted a breach of Article 10 of the Convention. They further alleged that the principles upon which the decision of the House of Lords was founded amounted to a violation of Article 10 and asked the Commission to direct or, alternatively, to request the Government to introduce legislation overruling the decision of the House of Lords and bringing the law of contempt of court into line with the Convention.

39.   In its decision of 21 March 1975, the Commission, after describing the question before it as "whether the rules of contempt of court as applied in the decision of the House of Lords granting the injunction are a ground justifying the restriction under Article 10 § 2," declared admissible and accepted the application.

[Additional allegations were made by the applicant under Articles 14 and 18 of the Convention; though considered by the Commission and by the Court, neither additional allegation is held by either body to have demonstrated a violation of the Convention.]

41. In its report of 18 May 1977, the Commission * * * expressed the opinion:

—by eight votes to five, that the restriction imposed on the applicant's right to freedom of expression was in breach of Article 10 of the Convention * * *. * * *

42. The applicants claim to be the victims of a violation of Article 10 of the Convention which provides:

"1. Everyone has the right to freedom of expression. This right shall include freedom to hold opinions and to receive and impart information and ideas without interference by public authority and regardless of frontiers. This Article shall not prevent States from requiring the licensing of broadcasting, television or cinema enterprises.

2. The exercise of these freedoms, since it carries with it duties and responsibilities, may be subject to such formalities, conditions, restrictions or penalties as are prescribed by law and are necessary in a democratic society, in the interests of national security, territorial integrity or public safety, for the prevention of disorder or crime, for the protection of health or morals, for the protection of the reputation or rights of others, for preventing the disclosure of information received in confidence, or for maintaining the authority and impartiality of the judiciary." * * *

45. It is clear that there was an "interference by public authority" in the exercise of the applicants' freedom of expression which is guaranteed by paragraph 1 of Article 10. Such an interference entails a "violation" of Article 10 if it does not fall within one of the exceptions provided for in paragraph 2. The Court, therefore, has to examine in turn whether the interference in the present case was "prescribed by law," whether it had an aim or aims that is or are legitimate under Article 10 § 2 and whether it was "necessary in a democratic society" for the aforesaid aim or aims.

[The European Court holds that there had been an "interference with the applicants' freedom of expression," that it was "prescribed by law," and that "the interference with the applicants' freedom of expression had an aim that is legitimate under Article 10 § 2." The crucial part of the case then follows: "Was the interference 'necessary in a democratic society' for maintaining the authority of the judiciary?"]

65. * * * As the Court remarked in its Handyside judgment, freedom of expression constitutes one of the essential foundations of a democratic society; subject to paragraph 2 of Article 10, it is applicable not only to information or ideas that are favourably received or regarded as inoffensive or as a matter of indifference, but also to those that offend, shock or disturb the State or any sector of the population.

These principles are of particular importance as far as the press is concerned. They are equally applicable to the field of the administration of justice, which serves the interests of the community at large and requires the co-operation of an enlightened public. There is general recognition of the fact that the courts cannot operate in a vacuum. Whilst they are the forum for the settlement of disputes, this does not mean that there can be no prior discussion of disputes elsewhere, be it in specialized journals, in the general press or amongst the public at large. Furthermore, whilst the mass media must not overstep the bounds imposed in the interests of the proper administration of justice, it is incumbent on them to impart information and ideas concerning matters that come before the courts just as in other areas of public interest. Not only do the media have the task of imparting such information and ideas: the public also has a right to receive them.

To assess whether the interference complained of was based on "sufficient" reasons which rendered it "necessary in a democratic society," account must thus be taken of any public interest aspect of the case. The Court observes in this connection that, following a balancing of the conflicting interests involved, an absolute rule was formulated by certain of the Law Lords to the effect that it was not permissible to prejudge issues in pending cases: it was considered that the law would be too uncertain if the balance were to be struck anew in each case. Whilst emphasising that it is not its function to pronounce itself on an interpretation of English law adopted in the House of Lords, the Court points out that it has to take a different approach. The Court is faced not with a choice between two conflicting principles but with a principle of freedom of expression that is subject to a number of exceptions which must be narrowly interpreted. In the second place, the Court's supervision under Article 10 covers not only the basic legislation but also the decision applying it. It is not sufficient that the interference involved belongs to that class of the exceptions listed in Article 10 § 2 which has been invoked; neither is it sufficient that the interference was imposed because its subject-matter fell within a particular category or was caught by a legal rule formulated in general or absolute terms: the Court has to be satisfied that the interference was necessary having regard to the facts and circumstances prevailing in the specific case before it.

66.   The thalidomide disaster was a matter of undisputed public concern. It posed the question whether the powerful company which had marketed the drug bore legal or moral responsibility towards hundreds of individuals experiencing an appalling personal tragedy or whether the victims could demand or hope for indemnification only from the community as a whole; fundamental issues concerning protection against and compensation for injuries resulting from scientific developments were raised and many facets of the existing law on these subjects were called in question.

As the Court has already observed, Article 10 guarantees not only the freedom of the press to inform the public but also the right of the public to be properly informed * * *.

In the present case, the families of numerous victims of the tragedy, who were unaware of the legal difficulties involved, had a vital interest in knowing all the underlying facts and the various possible solutions. They could be deprived of this information, which was crucially important for them, only if it appeared absolutely certain that its diffusion would have presented a threat to the "authority of the judiciary."

Being called upon to weigh the interests involved and assess their respective force, the Court makes the following observations:

In September 1972, the case had, in the words of the applicants, been in a "legal cocoon" for several years and it was, at the very least, far from certain that the parents' actions would have come on for trial. There had also been no public enquiry * * *.

The Government and the minority of the Commission point out that there was no prohibition on discussion of the "wider issues," such as the principles of the English law of negligence, and indeed it is true that there had been extensive discussion in various circles especially after, but also before, the Divisional Court's initial decision * * *. However, the Court considers it rather artificial to attempt to divide the "wider issues" and the negligence issue. The question of where responsibility for a tragedy of this kind actually lies is also a matter of public interest.

It is true that, if the *Sunday Times* article had appeared at the intended time, Distillers might have felt obliged to develop in public, and in advance of any trial, their arguments on the facts of the case * * *; however, those facts did not cease to be a matter of public interest merely because they formed the background to pending litigation. By bringing to light certain facts, the article might have served as a brake on speculative and unenlightened discussion.

67. Having regard to all the circumstances of the case on the basis of the approach described in paragraph 65 above, the Court concludes that the interference complained of did not correspond to a social need sufficiently pressing to outweigh the public interest in freedom of expression within the meaning of the Convention. The Court therefore finds the reasons for the restraint imposed on the applicants not to be sufficient under Article 10 § 2. That restraint proves not to be proportionate to the legitimate aim pursued; it was not necessary in a democratic society for maintaining the authority of the judiciary.

68. There has accordingly been a violation of Article 10. * * *

FOR THESE REASONS, THE COURT

1. *holds* by eleven votes to nine that there has been a breach of Article 10 of the Convention * * *.

Notes and Questions

1. *Balancing the Issues.* In *Sunday Times*, there was no doubt that the balancing of the legal issues—weighing the public's right to know and the *Sunday Times'* right to freedom of expression against Distillers' right to a trial by the courts, not by the media, and the interest of the English government in the integrity of the judicial process—was a very close one.

Eight English judges (three at the trial level and five in the House of Lords), five European Human Rights Commissioners, and nine European Human Rights Judges felt that the scales tilted toward granting an injunction against the *Sunday Times*. Three English judges (in the Court of Appeal), eight European Human Rights Commissioners, and eleven European Human Rights Judges felt that the balance went for permitting the *Sunday Times* to publish the thalidomide article. Of 44 judges and commissioners who considered the case, half went one way and half the other. Reasonable men and women could and did differ. What is the difference between the standards applied in English law and those in European human rights law?

2. *The Boldness of the Court.* A distinguished British international lawyer, F.A. Mann, felt that the European Court of Human Rights had gone too far:

> However uncertain its definition and scope may be in some respects, contempt of court is undoubtedly one of the great contributions the common law has made to the civilised behaviour of a large part of the world beyond the continent of Europe where the institution is unknown. * * * Yet it is that very branch of the law which the European Court of Human Rights has seriously undermined by, in effect, overturning the unanimous decision of the House of Lords in the *Sunday Times* case—a unique event in the history of English law. In fact it is probably no exaggeration to say that the gravest blow to the fabric of English law has been dealt by the majority of eleven judges coming from Cyprus, Denmark, Eire, France, Germany, Greece, Italy, Portugal, Spain, Sweden and Turkey, who, over the dissent of nine judges from Austria, Belgium, Holland, Iceland, Luxembourg, Malta, Norway, Switzerland and the United Kingdom, decided in favor of the *Sunday Times*. * * *

> The reader will have to make up his or her own mind * * * whether the Strasbourg Court arrogated to itself powers of factual appreciation which it cannot possibly exercise convincingly * * * and ask whether according to the standards and traditions of English law and English public life it is the decision of the House of Lords or that of the European Court of Human Rights which more correctly assesses the "social need" and "the legitimate aim" of a civilised society * * * and whether the level of judicial reasoning is higher in London or Strasbourg.

F.A. Mann, "Contempt of Court in the House of Lords and the European Court of Human Rights," 95 *Law Quarterly Review* 348, 348–49, 352 (1979).

One can understand Mann's discomfort with the "overturning" of the House of Lords by the Strasbourg Court, but did *Sunday Times* really raise the question of which court's "judicial reasoning" was "higher"? As another observer remarked about another judgment against the U.K., the *Golder Case* in Chapter 1: "Membership of a European institution, and submission to the jurisdiction of its organs, means the acceptance of a European way of thinking. The European Commission and Court of Human Rights are likely to construe texts in the 'continental,' not the common law, manner." William Dale, "Human Rights in the United Kingdom—International Standards," 25 *International and Comparative Law Quarterly* 292, 302 (1976).

3. *Continued Acceptance of the Optional Clauses.* The United Kingdom was at the time not obliged to accept forever "a European way of thinking." However, states continued to accept both Article 25 and Article 46. At the time of the *Sunday Times Case* 14 of the 21 Council of Europe states had already accepted Article 25 individual petition, and 16 had consented to Article 46 jurisdiction of the Court. Not only did the United Kingdom continue to renew its pledges to both Article 25 and Article 46, but so did the other then-consenting states. Now, the once optional clauses are mandatory. Far from discouraging governments, the *Sunday Times* judgment and cases like it did not slow the accession of states to the legal machinery of European human rights law.

4. *The Efficacy of European Human Rights Law.* How far can the Court go without upsetting the apple cart of state consent? Writing just after the *Sunday Times Case*, Ralph Beddard remarked on the caution exercised by the system's institutions up to that time:

> It is, and always has been, obvious that winning the confidence of the parties and the public was a first step in any attempt to establish judicial determination of the protection of human rights. The last 27 years have not been free of difficulties, however, and the confidence of the parties was won, particularly in the early days, by very careful treading on the part of the Commission. There are cases which, if presented to the Commission today, would probably make greater progress than they did at the time of application. However, a Commission leaning heavily in favor of governments would have lost the confidence of the public.

Ralph Beddard, *Human Rights and Europe* 4 (1980).

Such caution paid off. In 1980, Sir Humphrey Waldock, then President of the International Court of Justice but previously President of both the European Commission and the European Court of Human Rights, could conclude that "the system set up by the European Convention on Human Rights is, in general, effective is not, I believe, today open to serious question." Humphrey Waldock, "The Effectiveness of the System Set Up by the European Convention on Human Rights," 1 *Human Rights Law Journal* 1, 1 (1980).

How easy is it to judge the "efficacy" of law? Does it matter whether one is testing (1) the efficacy of a particular legal decision, (2) the efficacy of legal rules in practice, or (3) the efficacy of the legal system in the society in general? Most studies evaluating the "efficacy" of European human rights law focus on the efficacy of the judgments of the European Court of Human Rights, but avoid broader efficacy questions. See Mark W. Janis, "The Efficacy of Strasbourg Law," 15 *Connecticut Journal of International Law* 39 (2000).

5. *The Efficacy of International Law.* Regional international law, and especially judgments of regional international courts like the European Court of Human Rights or the European Union's European Court of Justice, can become so effective that some commentators unused to a really efficacious system of international law may think it has become a form of municipal law. Some, for example, view the law of the European Union as "federal" law. See John Bridge, "American Analogues in the Law of the

European Community," 11 *Anglo–American Law Review* 130 (1982). Others feel European Union law is still fundamentally international law. See Derrick Wyatt, "New Legal Order or Old," 7 *European Law Review* 147 (1982). Does it really matter whether a legal system is denominated "federal law" or "regional international law"? Does one or the other have a more impressive connotation?

THE SOERING CASE

European Court of Human Rights,
Judgment of 7 July 1989, Series A, Vol. 161, 1989 WL 650110.

AS TO THE FACTS

I. *Particular circumstances of the case*

11.   The applicant, Mr. Jens Soering, was born on 1 August 1966 and is a German national. He is currently detained in prison in England pending extradition to the United States of America to face charges of murder in the Commonwealth of Virginia.

12.   The homicides in question were committed in Bedford County, Virginia, in March 1985. The victims, William Reginald Haysom (aged 72) and Nancy Astor Haysom (aged 53), were the parents of the applicant's girlfriend, Elizabeth Haysom, who is a Canadian national. Death in each case was the result of multiple and massive stab and slash wounds to the neck, throat and body. At the time the applicant and Elizabeth Haysom, aged 18 and 20 respectively, were students at the University of Virginia. They disappeared together from Virginia in October 1985, but were arrested in England in April 1986 in connection with cheque fraud.

13.   The applicant was interviewed in England between 5 and 8 June 1986 by a police investigator from the Sheriff's Department of Bedford County. In a sworn affidavit dated 24 July 1986 the investigator recorded the applicant as having admitted to killings in his presence and in that of two United Kingdom police officers. The applicant had stated that he was in love with Miss Haysom but that her parents were opposed to the relationship. He and Miss Haysom had therefore planned to kill them. They rented a car in Charlottesville and traveled to Washington where they set up an alibi. The applicant then went to the parents' house, discussed the relationship with them and, when they told him they would do anything to prevent it, a row developed during which he killed them with a knife.

On 13 June 1986 a grand jury of the Circuit Court of Bedford County indicted him on charges of murdering the Haysom parents. The charges alleged capital murder of both of them and the separate non-capital murders of each.

14.   On 11 August 1986 the Government of the United States of America requested the applicant's and Miss Haysom's extradition under the terms of the Extradition Treaty of 1972 between the United States and the United Kingdom * * *. On 12 September a Magistrate at Bow

Street Magistrates' Court was required by the Secretary of State for Home Affairs to issue a warrant for the applicant's arrest under the provisions of section 8 of the Extradition Act 1870 * * *. The applicant was subsequently arrested on 30 December at HM Prison Chelmsford after serving a prison sentence for cheque fraud.

15.   On 29 October 1986 the British Embassy in Washington addressed a request to the United States' authorities in the following terms:

> "Because the death penalty has been abolished in Great Britain, the Embassy has been instructed to seek an assurance, in accordance with the terms of ... the Extradition Treaty, that, in the event of Mr. Soering being surrendered and being convicted of the crimes for which he has been indicted ..., the death penalty, if imposed, will not be carried out.
>
> Should it not be possible on constitutional grounds for the United States Government to give such an assurance, the United Kingdom authorities ask that the United States Government undertake to recommend to the appropriate authorities that the death penalty should not be imposed or, if imposed, should not be executed."

16.   On 30 December 1986 the applicant was interviewed in prison by a German prosecutor (*Staatsanwalt*) from Bonn. In a sworn witness statement the prosecutor recorded the applicant as having said, *inter alia*, that "he had never had the intention of killing Mr. and Mrs. Haysom and ... he could only remember having inflicted wounds at the neck on Mr. and Mrs. Haysom which must have had something to do with their dying later;" and that in the immediately preceding days "there had been no talk whatsoever [between him and Elizabeth Haysom] about killing Elizabeth's parents." * * *

On 11 February 1987 the local court in Bonn issued a warrant for the applicant's arrest in respect of the alleged murders. On 11 March the Government of the Federal Republic of Germany requested his extradition to the Federal Republic under the Extradition Treaty of 1872 between the Federal Republic and the United Kingdom * * *. The Secretary of State was then advised by the Director of Public Prosecutions that, although the German request contained proof that German courts had jurisdiction to try the applicant, the evidence submitted, since it consisted solely of the admissions made by the applicant to the Bonn prosecutor in the absence of a caution, did not amount to a *prima facie* case against him and that a magistrate would not be able under the Extradition Act 1870 * * * to commit him to await extradition to Germany on the strength of admissions obtained in such circumstances.

17.   In a letter dated 20 April 1987 to the Director of the Office of International Affairs, Criminal Division, United States Department of Justice, the Attorney for Bedford County, Virginia (Mr. James W. Updike, Jr.) stated that, on the assumption that the applicant could not be tried in Germany on the basis of admissions alone, there was no

means of compelling witnesses from the United States to appear in a criminal court in Germany. On 23 April the United States, by diplomatic note, requested the applicant's extradition to the United States in preference to the Federal Republic of Germany.

18.   On 8 May 1987 Elizabeth Haysom was surrendered for extradition to the United States. After pleading guilty on 22 August as an accessory to the murder of her parents, she was sentenced on 6 October to 90 years' imprisonment (45 years on each count of murder).

19.   On 20 May 1987 the Government of the United Kingdom informed the Federal Republic of Germany that the United States had earlier "submitted a request, supported by *prima facie* evidence, for the extradition of Mr. Soering." The United Kingdom Government notified the Federal Republic that they had "concluded that, having regard to all the circumstances of the case, the court should continue to consider in the normal way the United States' request." They further indicated that they had sought an assurance from the United States' authorities on the question of the death penalty and that "in the event that the court commits Mr. Soering, his surrender to the United States' authorities would be subject to the receipt of satisfactory assurances on this matter."

20.   On 1 June 1987 Mr. Updike swore an affidavit in his capacity as Attorney for Bedford County, in which he certified as follows:

> "I hereby certify that should Jens Soering be convicted of the offence of capital murder as charged in Bedford County, Virginia ... a representation will be made in the name of the United Kingdom to the judge at the time of sentencing that it is the wish of the United Kingdom that the death penalty should not be imposed or carried out."

This assurance was transmitted to the United Kingdom Government under cover of a diplomatic note on 8 June. It was repeated in the same terms in a further affidavit from Mr. Updike sworn on 16 February 1988 and forwarded to the United Kingdom by diplomatic note on 17 May 1988. In the same note the Federal Government of the United States undertook to ensure that the commitment of the appropriate authorities of the Commonwealth of Virginia to make representations on behalf of the United Kingdom would be honored.

During the course of the present proceedings the Virginia authorities have informed the United Kingdom Government that Mr. Updike was not planning to provide any further assurances and intended to seek the death penalty in Mr. Soering's case because the evidence, in his determination, supported such action.

21.   On 16 June 1987 at the Bow Street Magistrates' Court committal proceedings took place before the Chief Stipendiary Magistrate.

The Government of the United States adduced evidence that on the night of 30 March 1985 the applicant killed William and Nancy Haysom at their home in Bedford County, Virginia. In particular, evidence was given of the applicant's own admissions as recorded in the affidavit of the Bedford County police investigator (see paragraph 13 above).

On behalf of the applicant psychiatric evidence was adduced from a consultant forensic psychiatrist (report dated 15 December 1986 by Dr. Henrietta Bullard) that he was immature and inexperienced and had lost his personal identity in a symbiotic relationship with his girlfriend—a powerful, persuasive and disturbed young woman. * * *

22. On 29 June 1987 Mr. Soering applied to the Divisional Court for a writ of habeas corpus in respect of his committal and for leave to apply for judicial review. On 11 December both applications were refused by the Divisional Court (Lord Justice Lloyd and Mr. Justice Macpherson).

In support of his application for leave to apply for judicial review, Mr. Soering had submitted that the assurance received from the United States' authorities was so worthless that no reasonable Secretary of State could regard it as satisfactory under Article IV of the Extradition Treaty between the United Kingdom and the United States * * *. In his judgment Lord Justice Lloyd agreed that "the assurance leaves something to be desired":

> "Article IV of the Treaty contemplates an assurance that the death penalty will not be carried out. That must presumably mean an assurance by or on behalf of the Executive Branch of Government, which in this case would be the Governor of the Commonwealth of Virginia. The certificate sworn by Mr. Updike, far from being an assurance on behalf of the Executive, is nothing more than an undertaking to make representations on behalf of the United Kingdom to the judge. I cannot believe that this is what was intended when the Treaty was signed. But I can understand that there may well be difficulties in obtaining more by way of assurance in view of the federal nature of the United States Constitution."
>
> * * *

23. On 30 June 1988 the House of Lords rejected the applicant's petition for leave to appeal against the decision of the Divisional Court.

24. On 14 July 1988 the applicant petitioned the Secretary of State, requesting him to exercise his discretion not to make an order for the applicant's surrender under section 11 of the Extradition Act 1870 * * *.

This request was rejected, and on 3 August 1988 the Secretary of State signed a warrant ordering the applicant's surrender to the United States' authorities. However, the applicant has not been transferred to the United States by virtue of the interim measures indicated in the present proceedings firstly by the European Commission and then by the European Court * * *.

[The European Court of Human Rights reviews the laws relating to murder in England and Virginia and then turns to the prison conditions in Virginia facing Soering.]

61. There are currently 40 people under sentence of death in Virginia. The majority are detained in Mecklenburg Correctional Center, which is a modern maximum security institution with a total capacity of 335 inmates. Institutional Operating Procedures (IOP 821.1) establish uniform operating procedures for the administration, security, control and delivery of necessary services to death row in Mecklenburg. In addition conditions of confinement are governed by a comprehensive consent decree handed down by the United States District Court in Richmond in the case of *Alan Brown et al. v. Allyn R. Sielaff et al.* (5 April 1985). Both the Virginia Department of Corrections and the American Civil Liberties Union monitor compliance with the terms of the consent decree. The United States District Court also retains jurisdiction to enforce compliance with the decree. * * *

63. The size of a death row inmate's cell is 3m by 2.2m. Prisoners have an opportunity for approximately 7 1/2 hours' recreation per week in summer and approximately 6 hours' per week, weather permitting, in winter. The death row area has two recreation yards, both of which are equipped with basketball courts and one of which is equipped with weights and weight benches. Inmates are also permitted to leave their cells on other occasions, such as to receive visits, to visit the law library or to attend the prison infirmary. In addition, death row inmates are given one hour out-of-cell time in the morning in a common area. Each death row inmate is eligible for work assignments, such as cleaning duties. When prisoners move around the prison they are handcuffed with special shackles around the waist.

When not in their cells, death row inmates are housed in a common area called "the pod." The guards are not within this area and remain in a box outside. In the event of disturbance or inter-inmate assault, the guards are not allowed to intervene until instructed to do so by the ranking officer present.

64. The applicant adduced much evidence of extreme stress, psychological deterioration and risk of homosexual abuse and physical attack undergone by prisoners on death row, including Mecklenburg Correctional Center. This evidence was strongly contested by the United Kingdom Government on the basis of affidavits sworn by administrators from the Virginia Department of Corrections. * * *

68. A death row prisoner is moved to the death house 15 days before he is due to be executed. The death house is next to the death chamber where the electric chair is situated. Whilst a prisoner is in the death house he is watched 24 hours a day. He is isolated and has no light in his cell. The lights outside are permanently lit. A prisoner who utilizes the appeals process can be placed in the death house several times. * * *

As to the Law

I. *Alleged Breach of Article 3*

80. The applicant alleged that the decision by the Secretary of State for the Home Department to surrender him to the authorities of

the United States of America would, if implemented, give rise to a breach by the United Kingdom of Article 3 of the Convention, which provides:

> "No one shall be subjected to torture or to inhuman or degrading treatment or punishment."

A. Applicability of Article 3 in cases of extradition

81. The alleged breach derives from the applicant's exposure to the so-called "death row phenomenon." This phenomenon may be described as consisting in a combination of circumstances to which the applicant would be exposed if, after having been extradited to Virginia to face a capital murder charge, he was sentenced to death.

82. In its report (at paragraph 94) the Commission reaffirmed "its case-law that a person's deportation or extradition may give rise to an issue under Article 3 of the Convention where there are serious reasons to believe that the individual will be subjected, in the receiving State, to treatment contrary to that Article."

The Government of the Federal Republic of Germany supported the approach of the Commission, pointing to a similar approach in the case-law of the German courts.

The applicant likewise submitted that Article 3 not only prohibits the Contracting States from causing inhuman or degrading treatment or punishment to occur within their jurisdiction but also embodies an associated obligation not to put a person in a position where he will or may suffer such treatment or punishment at the hands of other States. For the applicant, at least as far as Article 3 is concerned, an individual may not be surrendered out of the protective zone of the Convention without the certainty that the safeguards which he would enjoy are as effective as the Convention standard.

83. The United Kingdom Government, on the other hand, contended that Article 3 should not be interpreted so as to impose responsibility on a Contracting State for acts which occur outside its jurisdiction. In particular, in their submission, extradition does not involve the responsibility of the extraditing State for inhuman or degrading treatment or punishment which the extradited person may suffer outside the State's jurisdiction. To begin with, they maintained, it would be straining the language of Article 3 intolerably to hold that by surrendering a fugitive criminal the extraditing State has "subjected" him to any treatment or punishment that he will receive following conviction and sentence in the receiving State. Further arguments advanced against the approach of the Commission were that it interferes with international treaty rights; it leads to a conflict with the norms of international judicial process, in that it in effect involves adjudication on the internal affairs of foreign States not Parties to the Convention or to the proceedings before the Convention institutions; it entails grave difficulties of evaluation and proof in requiring the examination of alien systems of law and of conditions in foreign States; the practice of national courts and the international community cannot reasonably be invoked to support it; it

causes a serious risk of harm in the Contracting State which is obliged to harbour the protected person, and leaves criminals untried, at large and unpunished.

In the alternative, the United Kingdom Government submitted that the application of Article 3 in extradition cases should be limited to those occasions in which the treatment or punishment abroad is certain, imminent and serious. In their view, the fact that by definition the matters complained of are only anticipated, together with the common and legitimate interest of all States in bringing fugitive criminals to justice, requires a very high degree of risk, proved beyond reasonable doubt, that ill-treatment will actually occur.

84. The Court will approach the matter on the basis of the following considerations.

85. As results from Article 5 § 1(f), which permits "the lawful . . . detention of a person against whom action is being taken with a view to . . . extradition," no right not to be extradited is as such protected by the Convention. Nevertheless, in so far as a measure of extradition has consequences adversely affecting the enjoyment of a Convention right, it may, assuming that the consequences are not too remote, attract the obligations of a Contracting State under the relevant Convention guarantee. What is at issue in the present case is whether Article 3 can be applicable when the adverse consequences of extradition are, or may be, suffered outside the jurisdiction of the extraditing State as a result of treatment or punishment administered in the receiving State.

86. Article 1 of the Convention, which provides that "the High Contracting Parties shall secure to everyone within their jurisdiction the rights and freedoms defined in Section I," sets a limit, notably territorial, on the reach of the Convention. In particular, the engagement undertaken by a Contracting State is confined to "securing" ("*reconnaître*" in the French text) the listed rights and freedoms to persons within its own "jurisdiction." Further, the Convention does not govern the actions of States not Parties to it, nor does it purport to be a means of requiring the Contracting States to impose Convention standards on other States. Article 1 cannot be read as justifying a general principle to the effect that, notwithstanding its extradition obligations, a Contracting State may not surrender an individual unless satisfied that the conditions awaiting him in the country of destination are in full accord with each of the safeguards of the Convention. Indeed, as the United Kingdom Government stressed, the beneficial purpose of extradition in preventing fugitive offenders from evading justice cannot be ignored in determining the scope of application of the Convention and of Article 3 in particular.

In the instant case it is common ground that the United Kingdom has no power over the practices and arrangements of the Virginia authorities which are the subject of the applicant's complaints. It is also true that in other international instruments cited by the United Kingdom Government—for example the 1951 United Nations Convention relating to the Status of Refugees (Article 33), the 1957 European

Convention on Extradition (Article 11) and the 1984 United Nations Convention against Torture and Other Cruel, Inhuman and Degrading Treatment or Punishment (Article 3)—the problems of removing a person to another jurisdiction where unwanted consequences may follow are addressed expressly and specifically.

These considerations cannot, however, absolve the Contracting Parties from responsibility under Article 3 for all and any foreseeable consequences of extradition suffered outside their jurisdiction.

87. In interpreting the Convention regard must be had to its special character as a treaty for the collective enforcement of human rights and fundamental freedoms. Thus, the object and purpose of the Convention as an instrument for the protection of individual human beings require that its provisions be interpreted and applied so as to make its safeguards practical and effective. In addition, any interpretation of the rights and freedoms guaranteed has to be consistent with "the general spirit of the Convention, an instrument designed to maintain and promote the ideals and values of a democratic society."

88. Article 3 makes no provision for exceptions and no derogation from it is permissible under Article 15 in time of war or other national emergency. This absolute prohibition of torture and of inhuman or degrading treatment or punishment under the terms of the Convention shows that Article 3 enshrines one of the fundamental values of the democratic societies making up the Council of Europe. It is also to be found in similar terms in other international instruments such as the 1966 International Covenant on Civil and Political Rights and the 1969 American Convention on Human Rights and is generally recognised as an internationally accepted standard.

The question remains whether the extradition of a fugitive to another State where he would be subjected or be likely to be subjected to torture or to inhuman or degrading treatment or punishment would itself engage the responsibility of a Contracting State under Article 3. That the abhorrence of torture has such implications is recognised in Article 3 of the United Nations Convention Against Torture and Other Cruel, Inhuman or Degrading Treatment or Punishment, which provides that "no State Party shall ... extradite a person where there are substantial grounds for believing that he would be in danger of being subjected to torture." The fact that a specialised treaty should spell out in detail a specific obligation attaching to the prohibition of torture does not mean that an essentially similar obligation is not already inherent in the general terms of Article 3 of the European Convention. It would hardly be compatible with the underlying values of the Convention, that "common heritage of political traditions, ideals, freedom and the rule of law" to which the Preamble refers, were a Contracting State knowingly to surrender a fugitive to another State where there were substantial grounds for believing that he would be in danger of being subjected to torture, however heinous the crime allegedly committed. Extradition in such circumstances, while not explicitly referred to in the brief and general wording of Article 3, would plainly be contrary to the spirit and intendment of the Article, and in the Court's view this inherent obligation not to extradite also extends to cases in which the fugitive would be faced in the receiving State by a real risk of exposure to inhuman or degrading treatment or punishment proscribed by that Article.

89. What amounts to "inhuman or degrading treatment or punishment" depends on all the circumstances of the case (see paragraph 100 below). Furthermore, inherent in the whole of the Convention is a search for a fair balance between the demands of the general interest of the community and the requirements of the protection of the individual's fundamental rights. As movement about the world becomes easier and crime takes on a larger international dimension, it is increasingly in the interest of all nations that suspected offenders who flee abroad should be brought to justice. Conversely, the establishment of safe havens for fugitives would not only result in danger for the State obliged to harbour the protected person but also tend to undermine the foundations of extradition. These considerations must also be included among the factors to be taken into account in the interpretation and application of the notions of inhuman and degrading treatment or punishment in extradition cases.

90. It is not normally for the Convention institutions to pronounce on the existence or otherwise of potential violations of the Convention. However, where an applicant claims that a decision to extradite him would, if implemented, be contrary to Article 3 by reason of its foreseeable consequences in the requesting country, a departure from this principle is necessary, in view of the serious and irreparable nature of the alleged suffering risked, in order to ensure the effectiveness of the safeguard provided by that Article (see paragraph 87 above).

91. In sum, the decision by a Contracting State to extradite a fugitive may give rise to an issue under Article 3, and hence engage the responsibility of that State under the Convention, where substantial grounds have been shown for believing that the person concerned, if extradited, faces a real risk of being subjected to torture or to inhuman or degrading treatment or punishment in the requesting country. The establishment of such responsibility inevitably involves an assessment of conditions in the requesting country against the standards of Article 3 of the Convention. Nonetheless, there is no question of adjudicating on or establishing the responsibility of the receiving country, whether under general international law, under the Convention or otherwise. In so far as any liability under the Convention is or may be incurred, it is liability incurred by the extraditing Contracting State by reason of its having taken action which has as a direct consequence the exposure of an individual to proscribed ill-treatment.

B. Application of Article 3 in the particular circumstances of the present case

[The Court first determines that it was not unlikely that Soering would be charged with and convicted of a crime that would expose him to the "death row phenomenon."]

2. Whether in the circumstances the risk of exposure to the "death row phenomenon" would make extradition a breach of Article 3

(a) General considerations

100. As is established in the Court's case-law, ill-treatment, including punishment, must attain a minimum level of severity if it is to fall within the scope of Article 3. The assessment of this minimum is, in the nature of things, relative; it depends on all the circumstances of the case, such as the nature and context of the treatment or punishment, the manner and method of its execution, its duration, its physical or mental effects and, in some instances, the sex, age and state of health of the victim.

Treatment has been held by the Court to be both "inhuman" because it was premeditated, was applied for hours at a stretch and "caused, if not actual bodily injury, at least intense physical and mental suffering," and also, "degrading" because it was "such as to arouse in [its] victims feelings of fear, anguish and inferiority capable of humiliating and debasing them and possibly breaking their physical or moral resistance." In order for a punishment or treatment associated with it to be "inhuman" or "degrading," the suffering or humiliation involved must in any event go beyond that inevitable element of suffering or humiliation connected with a given form of legitimate punishment. In this connection, account is to be taken not only of the physical pain experienced but also, where there is a considerable delay before execution of the punishment, of the sentenced person's mental anguish of anticipating the violence he is to have inflicted on him.

101. Capital punishment is permitted under certain conditions by Article 2 § 1 of the Convention, which reads:

> "Everyone's right to life shall be protected by law. No one shall be deprived of his life intentionally save in the execution of a sentence of a court following his conviction of a crime for which this penalty is provided by law."

In view of this wording, the applicant did not suggest that the death penalty *per se* violated Article 3. He, like the two Government Parties, agreed with the Commission that the extradition of a person to a country where he risks the death penalty does not in itself raise an issue under either Article 2 or Article 3. On the other hand, Amnesty International in their written comments * * * argued that the evolving standards in Western Europe regarding the existence and use of the death penalty required that the death penalty should now be considered as an inhuman and degrading punishment within the meaning of Article 3.

102. Certainly, "the Convention is a living instrument which ... must be interpreted in the light of present-day conditions;" and, in assessing whether a given treatment or punishment is to be regarded as

inhuman or degrading for the purposes of Article 3, "the Court cannot but be influenced by the developments and commonly accepted standards in the penal policy of the member States of the Council of Europe in this field." *De facto* the death penalty no longer exists in time of peace in the Contracting States to the Convention. In the few Contracting States which retain the death penalty in law for some peacetime offences, death sentences, if ever imposed, are nowadays not carried out. This "virtual consensus in Western European legal systems that the death penalty is, under current circumstances, no longer consistent with regional standards of justice," to use the words of Amnesty International, is reflected in Protocol No. 6 to the Convention, which provides for the abolition of the death penalty in time of peace. Protocol No. 6 was opened for signature in April 1983, which in the practice of the Council of Europe indicates the absence of objection on the part of any of the Member States of the Organization; it came into force in March 1985 and to date has been ratified by thirteen Contracting States to the Convention, not however including the United Kingdom.

Whether these marked changes have the effect of bringing the death penalty *per se* within the prohibition of ill-treatment under Article 3 must be determined on the principles governing the interpretation of the Convention.

103.   The Convention is to be read as a whole and Article 3 should therefore be construed in harmony with the provisions of Article 2. On this basis Article 3 evidently cannot have been intended by the drafters of the Convention to include a general prohibition of the death penalty since that would nullify the clear wording of Article 2 § 1.

Subsequent practice in national penal policy, in the form of a generalized abolition of capital punishment, could be taken as establishing the agreement of the Contracting States to abrogate the exception provided for under Article 2 § 1 and hence to remove a textual limit on the scope for evolutive interpretation of Article 3. However, Protocol No. 6, as a subsequent written agreement, shows that the intention of the Contracting Parties as recently as 1983 was to adopt the normal method of amendment of the text in order to introduce a new obligation to abolish capital punishment in time of peace and, what is more, to do so by an optional instrument allowing each State to choose the moment when to undertake such an engagement. In these conditions, notwithstanding the special character of the Convention (see paragraph 87 above), Article 3 cannot be interpreted as generally prohibiting the death penalty.

104.   That does not mean however that circumstances relating to a death sentence can never give rise to an issue under Article 3. The manner in which it is imposed or executed, the personal circumstances of the condemned person and a disproportionality to the gravity of the crime committed, as well as the conditions of detention awaiting execution, are examples of factors capable of bringing the treatment or punishment received by the condemned person within the proscription

under Article 3. Present-day attitudes in the Contracting States to capital punishment are relevant for the assessment whether the acceptable threshold of suffering or degradation has been exceeded.

(b) The particular circumstances

105. The applicant submitted that the circumstances to which he would be exposed as a consequence of the implementation of the Secretary of State's decision to return him to the United States, namely the "death row phenomenon," cumulatively constitute such serious treatment that his extradition would be contrary to Article 3. He cited in particular the delays in the appeal and review procedures following a death sentence, during which time he would be subject to increasing tension and psychological trauma; the fact, so he said, that the judge or jury in determining sentence is not obliged to take into account the defendant's age and mental state at the time of the offence; the extreme conditions of his future detention on "death row" in Mecklenburg Correctional Center, where he expects to be the victim of violence and sexual abuse because of his age, color and nationality; and the constant spectre of the execution itself, including the ritual of execution. He also relied on the possibility of extradition or deportation, which he would not oppose, to the Federal Republic of Germany as accentuating the disproportionality of the Secretary of State's decision.

The Government of the Federal Republic of Germany took the view that, taking all the circumstances together, the treatment awaiting the applicant in Virginia would go so far beyond treatment inevitably connected with the imposition and execution of a death penalty as to be "inhuman" within the meaning of Article 3.

On the other hand, the conclusion expressed by the Commission was that the degree of severity contemplated by Article 3 would not be attained.

The United Kingdom Government shared this opinion. In particular, they disputed many of the applicant's factual allegations as to the conditions on death row in Mecklenburg and his expected fate there.

i. Length of detention prior to execution

106. The period that a condemned prisoner can expect to spend on death row in Virginia before being executed is on average six to eight years * * *. This length of time awaiting death is, as the Commission and the United Kingdom Government noted, in a sense largely of the prisoner's own making in that he takes advantage of all avenues of appeal which are offered to him by Virginia law. The automatic appeal to the Supreme Court of Virginia normally takes no more than six months * * *. The remaining time is accounted for by collateral attacks mounted by the prisoner himself in habeas corpus proceedings before both the State and Federal courts and in applications to the Supreme Court of the United States for certiorari review, the prisoner at each stage being able to seek a stay of execution * * *. The remedies available under Virginia

law serve the purpose of ensuring that the ultimate sanction of death is not unlawfully or arbitrarily imposed.

Nevertheless, just as some lapse of time between sentence and execution is inevitable if appeal safeguards are to be provided to the condemned person, so it is equally part of human nature that the person will cling to life by exploiting those safeguards to the full. However well-intentioned and even potentially beneficial is the provision of the complex of post-sentence procedures in Virginia, the consequence is that the condemned prisoner has to endure for many years the conditions on death row and the anguish and mounting tension of living in the ever-present shadow of death.

ii. Conditions on death row

107. As to conditions in Mecklenburg Correctional Center, where the applicant could expect to be held if sentenced to death, the Court bases itself on the facts which were uncontested by the United Kingdom Government, without finding it necessary to determine the reliability of the additional evidence adduced by the applicant, notably as to the risk of homosexual abuse and physical attack undergone by prisoners on death row (see paragraph 64 above).

The stringency of the custodial regime in Mecklenburg, as well as the services (medical, legal and social) and the controls (legislative, judicial and administrative) provided for inmates, are described in some detail above (see paragraphs 61–63 and 65–68). In this connection, the United Kingdom Government drew attention to the necessary requirement of extra security for the safe custody of prisoners condemned to death for murder. Whilst it might thus well be justifiable in principle, the severity of a special regime such as that operated on death row in Mecklenburg is compounded by the fact of inmates being subject to it for a protracted period lasting on average six to eight years.

iii. The applicant's age and mental state

108. At the time of the killings, the applicant was only 18 years old and there is some psychiatric evidence, which was not contested as such, that he "was suffering from [such] an abnormality of mind ... as substantially impaired his mental responsibility for his acts" (see paragraphs 11, 12 and 21 above).

Unlike Article 2 of the Convention, Article 6 of the 1966 International Covenant on Civil and Political Rights and Article 4 of the 1969 American Convention on Human Rights expressly prohibit the death penalty from being imposed on persons aged less than 18 at the time of commission of the offence. Whether or not such a prohibition be inherent in the brief and general language of Article 2 of the European Convention, its explicit enunciation in other, later international instruments, the former of which has been ratified by a large number of States Parties to the European Convention, at the very least indicates that as a general principle the youth of the person concerned is a circumstance which is liable, with others, to put in question the compatibility with Article 3 of measures connected with a death sentence.

It is in line with the Court's case-law (as summarised above at paragraph 100) to treat disturbed mental health as having the same effect for the application of Article 3.

109.   Virginia law, as the United Kingdom Government and the Commission emphasised, certainly does not ignore these two factors. Under the Virginia Code account has to be taken of mental disturbance in a defendant, either as an absolute bar to conviction if it is judged to be sufficient to amount to insanity or, like age, as a fact in mitigation at the sentencing stage * * *. Additionally, indigent capital murder defendants are entitled to the appointment of a qualified mental health expert to assist in the preparation of their submissions at the separate sentencing proceedings * * *. These provisions in the Virginia Code undoubtedly serve, as the American courts have stated, to prevent the arbitrary or capricious imposition of the death penalty and narrowly to channel the sentencer's discretion * * *. They do not however remove the relevance of age and mental condition in relation to the acceptability, under Article 3, of the "death row phenomenon" for a given individual once condemned to death.

Although it is not for this Court to prejudge issues of criminal responsibility and appropriate sentence, the applicant's youth at the time of the offence and his then mental state, on the psychiatric evidence as it stands, are therefore to be taken into consideration as contributory factors tending, in his case, to bring the treatment on death row within the terms of Article 3.

iv.   Possibility of extradition to the Federal Republic of Germany

110.   For the United Kingdom Government and the majority of the Commission, the possibility of extraditing or deporting the applicant to face trial in the Federal Republic of Germany (see paragraphs 16, 19, 26, 38 and 71–74 above), where the death penalty has been abolished under the Constitution * * *, is not material for the present purposes. Any other approach, the United Kingdom Government submitted, would lead to a "dual standard" affording the protection of the Convention to extraditable persons fortunate enough to have such an alternative destination available but refusing it to others not so fortunate.

This argument is not without weight. Furthermore, the Court cannot overlook either the horrible nature of the murders with which Mr. Soering is charged or the legitimate and beneficial role of extradition arrangements in combating crime. The purpose for which his removal to the United States was sought, in accordance with the Extradition Treaty between the United Kingdom and the United States, is undoubtedly a legitimate one. However, sending Mr. Soering to be tried in his own country would remove the danger of a fugitive criminal going unpunished as well as the risk of intense and protracted suffering on death row. It is therefore a circumstance of relevance for the overall assessment under Article 3 in that it goes to the search for the requisite fair balance of interests and to the proportionality of the contested extradition decision in the particular case (see paragraphs 89 and 104 above).

(c) Conclusion

111.   For any prisoner condemned to death, some element of delay between imposition and execution of the sentence and the experience of severe stress in conditions necessary for strict incarceration are inevitable. The democratic character of the Virginia legal system in general and the positive features of Virginia trial, sentencing and appeal procedures in particular are beyond doubt. The Court agrees with the Commission that the machinery of justice to which the applicant would be subject in the United States is in itself neither arbitrary nor unreasonable, but, rather, respects the rule of law and affords not inconsiderable procedural safeguards to the defendant in a capital trial. Facilities are available on death row for the assistance of inmates, notably through provision of psychological and psychiatric services * * *.

However, in the Court's view, having regard to the very long period of time spent on death row in such extreme conditions, with the ever present and mounting anguish of awaiting execution of the death penalty, and to the personal circumstances of the applicant, especially his age and mental state at the time of the offence, the applicant's extradition to the United States would expose him to a real risk of treatment going beyond the threshold set by Article 3. A further consideration of relevance is that in the particular instance the legitimate purpose of extradition could be achieved by another means which would not involve suffering of such exceptional intensity or duration.

Accordingly, the Secretary of State's decision to extradite the applicant to the United States would, if implemented, give rise to a breach of Article 3.

This finding in no way puts in question the good faith of the United Kingdom Government, who have from the outset of the present proceedings demonstrated their desire to abide by their Convention obligations, firstly by staying the applicant's surrender to the United States authorities in accord with the interim measures indicated by the Convention institutions and secondly by themselves referring the case to the Court for a judicial ruling (see paragraphs 1, 4, 24 and 77 above). * * *

FOR THESE REASONS, THE COURT UNANIMOUSLY

1.   *Holds* that, in the event of the Secretary of State's decision to extradite the applicant to the United States of America being implemented, there would be a violation of Article 3 * * *.

Notes and Questions

1.   *Soering's Fate.* Soon after the judgment of the Court, the United States represented to the United Kingdom that Soering would not be tried for a crime for which the death penalty could be imposed. Soering was then extradited to the United States, tried in Virginia, and found guilty on two

counts of first-degree murder; it was recommended by the jury that he serve two life terms. Richard Lillich & Hurst Hannum, *International Human Rights* 768 (3d ed. 1995). Might the Court have differed from the Commission because it thought that Virginia would be willing to reduce the charge only if the United Kingdom were ordered *not* to extradite Soering otherwise?

2. *The United Kingdom's Predicament*. If Virginia had refused to try Soering for a charge where the death penalty could not be imposed, then the United Kingdom would have been caught between a rock and a hard place in international law. By the terms of the U.K.–U.S. extradition treaty it seemed clear that the United Kingdom was bound to extradite Soering, but by the terms of the European Convention for the Protection of Human Rights and Fundamental Freedoms, the United Kingdom was obligated to follow the judgment of the European Court of Human Rights. If the conflict had persisted in practice, what should the United Kingdom have done? Should the U.K. government follow the extradition treaty because it is the international agreement later in time? Or should the U.K. government follow the European Human Rights Convention because the Convention concerns more fundamental rights? Is the answer linked to notions about *jus cogens*? See Chapter 3 and look back to *Filartiga* in Chapter 1. As it turned out, Virginia let the United Kingdom off the hook. There is more about international conflict of laws in general in Chapter 12 and about the specific conflict in *Soering* in Stephan Breitenmoser & Gunter Wilms, "Human Rights v. Extradition: The *Soering* Case," 11 *Michigan Journal of International Law* 845 (1990).

3. *The Extraterritorial Effect of the* Soering *Judgment*. Is it fair to impose the human rights obligations of the European Convention on a nonparty such as the United States? See Christine Van den Wyngaert, "Applying the European Convention on Human Rights to Extradition: Opening Pandora's Box?" 39 *International & Comparative Law Quarterly* 757 (1990). According to one extradition expert, the *Soering* decision "is having an impact on U.S. domestic criminal procedure at a very basic level;" officials of U.S. states seeking to extradite from Europe a fugitive accused of murder must essentially "prove to the Departments of State and Justice that the document [seeking extradition] is signed by the state official who has authority to bind the state to the commitment not to pursue or impose the death penalty." Christopher L. Blakesley, "The *Pinochet Extradition Case* and Beyond: Human Rights Clauses Compared to Traditional Derivative Protections Such as Double Criminality," 1999–2000 *Proceedings of the American Branch of the International Law Association* 370, 402. Why should U.S. death row conditions be a fit topic for consideration by the Strasbourg Court? The aftermath of *Soering* is treated in John Dugard & Christine Van den Wyngaert, "Reconciling Extradition with Human Rights," 92 *American Journal of International Law* 187 (1998).

E. INTERNATIONAL CRIMINAL LAW

Besides *rights* individuals may also have *duties* at international law. Indeed, as we have seen, the modern transformation of the role of individuals in international law began after World War II with the Nuremberg criminal trials of individual defendants. Since Nuremberg, it has been the hope of many to establish a permanent international criminal tribunal. The reading below shows the progress so far. Following are some notes about the ad hoc international criminal tribunals established in the 1990's for the Former Yugoslavia and Rwanda. International criminal law is a field just emerging.

LEILA NADYA SADAT & S. RICHARD CARDEN, "THE NEW INTERNATIONAL CRIMINAL COURT: AN UNEASY REVOLUTION"

88 *Georgetown Law Journal* 381 (2000).

I. PROLOGUE: THE LAST INTERNATIONAL INSTITUTION OF THE TWENTIETH CENTURY

From June 15 through July 17, 1998, representatives of 160 countries,[14] closely watched by 250 non-governmental organizations (NGOs), met in Rome to negotiate a Treaty that would establish a permanent international criminal court. The Conference was held in the United Nations Food and Agricultural Organization building ("la FAO" in Italian), a large, rather plebeian structure from the Mussolini period, with a splendid view of *Il Palatino* from the top floor terrace. The weather was hot, the mood alternated between exhilaration and anxiety, the work was hard. Issues that had been debated for more than two years during the Preparatory Committee meetings leading up to the Rome Conference (PrepComI) remained on the table unresolved. The starting point of the negotiations was a complex consolidated text containing 116 articles, including some 1300 phrases in brackets. It was extremely difficult to read, let alone understand. As is by now well known, after five weeks of grueling negotiations, the Diplomatic Conference adopted a Statute for the Court in an emotional vote of 120 to 7, with 21 countries abstaining. The United States, whose delegation was instrumental in the development of the Statute throughout the PrepComI meetings and the Rome Conference, was one of the seven countries voting against the Treaty.

The adoption of the International Criminal Court (ICC) Statute is the result of more than seventy-five years of hard work and false starts. As the Preamble to the Treaty notes, the purpose of the Court is to end impunity for the perpetrators of "atrocities that deeply shock the conscience of humanity." And the Twentieth Century witnessed atrocities on a truly unprecedented scale. The estimate of 170 million dead in 250 conflicts that have occurred since World War II is a grim testament to the failure of the international community to create a viable mechanism to prevent aggression and enforce international humanitarian law.

---

14. *See Rome Statute of the International Criminal Court*, United Nations Diplomatic Conference of Plenipotentiaries on the Establishment of an International Criminal Court, July 17, 1998, Annex II, U.N. Doc. A/CONF.183/9 (1998). This article is based on the Statute as of July 18, 1998. * * *

It was thus appropriate and somehow fortuitous that the Diplomatic Conference was held in Rome. Once the center of an empire that stretched, during the Hadrianic period, across an area the size of the Continental United States and Alaska, Rome is a city rich in historic and cultural treasures. It has also been repeatedly devastated by war. And what delegate, gazing out over *Il Palatino* and the ruins of the Forum, or seeing *Castel Sant'Angelo*, where Pope Clement was besieged for months while soldiers looted the city and tormented and killed its inhabitants, could not feel the weight of history upon him or her, or understand the historic purpose for which all were gathered? Indeed, what better place in which to argue, on behalf of humanity, that the excesses of war should be restrained by the Rule of Law?

The International Criminal Court is the last great international institution of the Twentieth Century. It is no exaggeration to suggest that its creation has the potential to reshape our thinking about international law. For if many aspects of the Rome Treaty demonstrate the tenacity of traditional Westphalian notions of State sovereignty, there are nonetheless elements of supranationalism and efficacy (in spite of the complementarity principle [under which states may try individuals for crimes within the ICC's jurisdiction, in place of the ICC]) in the Statute that could prove extremely powerful. Not only does the Statute place State and non-State actors side-by-side in the international arena, but the Court will put real people in real jails. Indeed, the establishment of the Court raises hopes that the lines between international law on the one hand, and world order, on the other, are blurring and that the normative structure being created by international law might influence or even restrain the Hobbesian order established by the politics of States.

Given the unsuccessful history of previous efforts to establish an international criminal court, and the tepid support of many of the major powers during the Preparatory Committee meetings leading up to the Diplomatic Conference, the adoption of the Statute by the Diplomatic Conference comes as a surprise. It can be credited at least in part, to the enormous lobbying and informational efforts of NGO's, which conducted a tireless campaign in support of the Court and came together as new evidence of global civil society. Another important factor was the emergence of a so-called "like-minded" group of States, which, although individually holding quite divergent views on many issues, were united in their view that the Court's ultimate establishment was a priority. Moreover, strong support from European countries and other traditional U.S. allies rallied the West behind the Court even without U.S. participation. * * *

But classic ideas about sovereignty die hard, and if the road to Rome was long and difficult, the journey to the seat of the Court at the Hague may be even more arduous. First, sixty States must ratify the Treaty before the Court can come into existence. In addition, before the Court can exercise its functions, the Preparatory Commission, established by the Diplomatic Conference at Rome (PrepComII), must prepare draft texts of Rules of Procedure and Evidence (RPE), Elements of Crimes, a relationship agreement between the Court and the United Nations, basic principles of the headquarters agreement, financial regulations and rules, an agreement on the privileges and immunities of the Court, a budget for the first financial year, and the rules of procedure for the Assembly of States Parties. Much of this work will be the subject of Preparatory Commission meetings held over the next two years.

Notes and Questions

1. *The Utility of International Criminal Courts.* There seem to be four kinds of goals advanced for the creation of international criminal courts: (1) justice and punishment, (2) deterrence, (3) record-keeping, and (4) the progressive development of international law. So far, practice shows that achievement of the first two goals—justice/punishment and deterrence—has been spotty at best. However, the utility of the international criminal courts has been surer for the other two aims—record-keeping and the progressive development of international law. See Mark W. Janis, "The Utility of International Criminal Courts," 12 *Connecticut Journal of International Law* 161 (1997). If the new permanent International Criminal Court is finally created, will it improve the justice/punishment and deterrence functions? What will be likely to account for its eventual success or failure?

2. Ad Hoc *International Criminal Tribunals.* Besides the Nuremberg trials, there have been *ad hoc* international criminal tribunals in Tokyo for the trial of Japanese World War II war criminals, in The Hague (beginning in 1993) for crimes in the former Yugoslavia, and in Arusha (beginning in 1994) for crimes in Rwanda. There are significant differences among the four proceedings. Among other things, the Nuremberg and Tokyo trials, following the Allied defeat of Germany and Japan, proceeded against the principal leaders of those governments; the Hague and Arusha trials, with no conquests in hand, have had to proceed against figures of lesser consequence. Louis B. Sohn, "From Nazi Germany and Japan to Yugoslavia and Rwanda: Similarities and Differences," 12 *Connecticut Journal of International Law* 209 (1997).

However, some have argued that criminal process, *e.g.*, "the standard of proof beyond reasonable doubt, the weighing of evidence, and the development of transparent and consistent rules in the treatment of evidence," has been fairer at The Hague and Arusha. Richard May & Marieke Wierda, "Trends in International Criminal Evidence: Nuremberg, Tokyo, The Hague, and Arusha," 37 *Columbia Journal of Transnational Law* 725, 764 (1999). A more critical view of procedure in the modern tribunals is to be found in José E. Alvarez, "Rush to Closure: Lessons of the Tadić Judgment," 96 *Michigan Law Review* 2031 (1998).

3. Ad Hoc *v. Permanent International Criminal Courts.* One of the central debates surrounding the proposed new International Criminal Court has been about the control of such a court. The *ad hoc* courts in The Hague and Arusha were created by the U.N. Security Council and thus much more effectively controlled by great powers like the United States, Russia, and China than would be a permanent court. Should powerful states be willing to

surrender authority to the International Criminal Court? At first, the United States was unwilling to sign, much less ratify, the treaty establishing the permanent International Criminal Court, an echo of U.S. concerns surrounding the International Court of Justice, see Chapter 5 and Chapter 9, and legitimacy of the United Nations in Chapter 8.

Despite U.S. concerns, President Clinton, in his last weeks in office, did finally sign the Convention. U.S. ratification is, however, still unlikely. Meantimes, the International Criminal Court has already garnered considerable support among other states. As of November 1, 2000, 115 states had signed the treaty containing the ICC Statute and 22 had ratified it. For updates on the status of the ICC, see <http://www.un.org/law/icc/statute/status.htm>. For more background on the ICC, see "Association of American Law Schools Panel on the International Criminal Court," 36 *American Criminal Law Review* 223 (1999).

Chapter 7

STATES AND INTERNATIONAL LAW

Although individuals and a variety of non-state entities shape and are affected by international law, states have been central components of the international legal system, at least since the Peace of Westphalia in 1648. But just what is a "state"? In Part A of this chapter, we introduce the ways in which international law helps define the sovereign state.

Part B explores questions involving the transformation of states and governments. What are the legal effects of the succession of states or governments? Do the legal obligations of a state continue when its government changes radically, or when the state breaks apart? What is the significance, in municipal legal systems, of the recognition of a new state or government?

Finally, in Part C, we examine the international law relating to self-determination. To what groups of peoples does the concept apply? When it does apply, what are the consequences? Self-determination is important both in its own right and because it can contribute to our understanding of the sovereign state and its place in the international legal system.

A. THE SOVEREIGN STATE

This Part explores several questions about the sovereign state, which has played a central role in international law over the past several centuries. Do states merely create international legal rules and procedural mechanisms, or is state sovereignty itself a product of international law? Does a state's existence depend on recognition by other states or international organizations? We look first at an excerpt from the work of Jean Bodin, who sought to conceptualize the sovereign state when the state system was beginning to develop in Europe, and then consider several articles from the Montevideo Convention, a 20th-century effort to codify basic precepts about states.

JEAN BODIN, THE SIX BOOKES
OF A COMMONWEALE

1606 English translation of Jean Bodin, *République* (1576)
(Kenneth Douglas McRae ed. 1962), excerpts from Book I.

Majestie or Soveraigntie is the most high, absolute, and perpetuall
power over the citisens and subjects in a Commonweale: * * * that is to
say, The greatest power to command. * * *

* * * But as for the lawes of God and nature, all princes and people
of the world are unto them subject: neither is it in their power to
impugne them, if will not be guiltie of high treason to the divine
maiestie, making warre against God; under the greatnesse of whome all
monarches of the world ought to beare the yoke, and to bow their heads
in all feare and reverence. Wherefore in that wee said the soveraigne
power in a Commonweale to be free from all lawes, concerneth nothing
the lawes of God and nature. * * *

* * * It is also evill done, to say, that a soveraigne prince hath
power by violence to take away another mans goods, to rob, to commit
adulterie, or to do evill, seeing that so to doe, is rather an impotencie, or
feeblenes, proceeding from a weake mind overcome with impotent lust
and desire, rather than any soveraignty. Now then if a soveraigne prince
may not remove the bounds which almightie God (of whom he is the
living & breathing image) hath prefined unto the everlasting lawes of
nature: neither may he take from another man that which is his, without
iust cause * * *. * * *

Now * * * I say that the first and chiefe marke of Soveraigntie is for
the prince to be of power to give lawes unto all his subjects in generall,
and to everie one of them in particular. * * *

But forasmuch as the word *Law*, is too general a marke, it is the
more expedient particularly to specifie the rights of Soveraigntie, * * *
as to denounce warre, or treat of peace, one of the greatest points of
soveraigne maiestie.

[Other "markes of Soveraignetie" include the right of "liege fealtie
and homage," and the powers to name magistrates, hear final appeals,
grant pardons, coin money, set weights and measures, and impose taxes
(albeit consent of subjects to new taxes is generally required).]

Notes and Questions

1. *Jean Bodin and Sovereignty.* Jean Bodin, a 16th-century French
philosopher and lawyer, was one of the first scholars to develop a theory of
sovereignty. France organized as a centralized state before most other parts
of Europe, and Bodin's views supported the French monarchy of the day.
Nevertheless, Bodin sought to develop a theory applicable to systems of
government generally. For Bodin, sovereignty had to be unified in one place
in each state. Sovereignty was also "absolute," by which Bodin meant that
the sovereign had no human superior in its territory. But Bodin, who put a

premium on preservation of social order and who saw a universe ordered by God, did envision some limits on the sovereign's authority. In addition to the limits noted in the excerpt above, Bodin accepted the immutability of French laws governing succession to the throne, and of laws forbidding the king from disposing of the public domain (thus insuring sources of revenue for the king and his successors). Bodin also acknowledged that governments could limit their freedom of action by treaty. In Books I and V of *République*, he discussed treaties at length, finding the marks of sovereignty preserved when governments entered into conventions or alliances.

Bodin's insistence that sovereignty must be unified in one body or person and his affinity for monarchy certainly date his theory. But Bodin's effort to ascertain generally applicable "marks" of sovereignty, his view that the core of sovereign authority is the power to make laws and not just to administer or judge, and his struggle to articulate limits on sovereignty at least preview modern concerns. In the words of one commentator, Bodin's "theory of sovereignty was the proximate source of the idea that there must exist in every legal system an ultimate legal norm or set of procedures by which all decisions are coordinated." Julian H. Franklin, *Jean Bodin and the Rise of Absolutist Theory* 108 (1973).

2. *Sovereignty and International Law*. Review the Peace of Westphalia and the notes on Hobbes, Grotius, and the Thirty Years War in Chapter 2. What measures of autonomy and authority did the Peace of Westphalia grant to states? Is state sovereignty consistent with the notion that international law can provide rules concerning, for example, how a state treats individuals or uses force against another state? Does the acquiescence of each state in rules of international law concerning territorial integrity, jurisdictional authority, and protections for citizens travelling abroad help to establish and preserve the "rights" of every other state? According to Martti Koskenniemi:

> [W]e cannot deduce the extent of a state's freedom of action from the mere fact of its statehood. Sovereignty is, as the Permanent Court of International Justice noted in 1923, an "essentially relative question"— dependent on whatever law there is to curtail it.
>
> Any international conflict juxtaposes the freedom of action of two or more states. All conflict resolution involves boundary determination, or the delimitation of one sovereign's freedom of action against that of another. We cannot look for justification in statehood because our task consists precisely of giving statehood some normative sense. To decide boundary disputes without violating sovereign equality, we are limited to criteria that are hierarchically more important than statehood to provide a justification for drawing its limit in some particular way.

Martti Koskenniemi, "The Future of Statehood," 32 *Harvard International Law Journal* 397, 408 (1991).

3. *The Development of the State System*. Following the Peace of Westphalia, states with defined boundaries became the predominant form of political organization in Europe. Outside of Europe, states also evolved from other forms of political relationships. In some regions, territorially bounded states are modern phenomena. Until the late 19th century, for example, the rulers of Siam (Thailand):

controlled a set of specific, non-adjacent places according to their proximity and usefulness to Bangkok; [rulers] controlled specific resources, trade routes or populations [but] did not conceive of * * * authority in terms of territory. * * * Hierarchical relations between various rulers and subjects, not control over continuous territory, defined Siam. * * *

* * *[B]oundaries were not thin demarcating lines but rather substantial regions or zones. Moreover, boundaries were indeterminate, even potentially mobile.

Richard T. Ford, "Law's Territory (A History of Jurisdiction)," 97 *Michigan Law Review* 843, 868–69 (1999), *citing* Thongchai Winichakul, *Siam Mapped: A History of the Geo–Body of a Nation* (1994). Decolonization in the 20th century also led to the creation of many states; we explore decolonization and self-determination in Part C of this chapter. For discussion of the spread of the European model of statehood to other parts of the world, see Robert H. Jackson, *Quasi-states: Sovereignty, International Relations, and the Third World* 59–81 (1990).

4. *"Civilized" States.* Recall from Chapter 3 that the ICJ Statute, echoing language in the 1920 Statute of the Permanent Court of International Justice, lists as a source of law "general principles of law recognized by civilized nations." The "civilized" limitation is not invoked today. In the 19th and early 20th centuries, however, European international law doctrine generally considered that the "family of nations" was open only to European states and to those entities outside Europe that achieved a certain degree of civilization and of interaction with states that were already part of the "family." How could an entity join the family of nations? According to the British scholar Lassa Oppenheim, "a new State before its recognition cannot claim any right which a member of the Family of Nations has towards other members. * * * Through recognition only and exclusively a State becomes an International Person and a subject of International Law." 1 Lassa Oppenheim, *International Law* § 71 (1905). Contrast Oppenheim's view of recognition's "constitutive" role with the "declaratory" treatment of recognition in the Montevideo Convention below.

THE MONTEVIDEO CONVENTION
Convention on Rights and Duties of States,
Dec. 26, 1933, 49 Stat. 3097, 165 L.N.T.S. 19.

Article 1
The state as a person of international law should possess the following qualifications: *a)* a permanent population; *b)* a defined territory; *c)* government; and *d)* capacity to enter into relations with the other states.

Article 2
The federal state shall constitute a sole person in the eyes of international law.

Article 3
The political existence of the state is independent of recognition by the other states. Even before recognition the state has the right to

defend its integrity and independence, to provide for its conservation and prosperity, and consequently to organize itself as it sees fit, to legislate upon its interests, administer its services, and to define the jurisdiction and competence of its courts.

The exercise of these rights has no other limitation than the exercise of the rights of other states according to international law.

Article 4

States are juridically equal, enjoy the same rights, and have equal capacity in their exercise. The rights of each one do not depend upon the power which it possesses to assure its exercise, but upon the simple fact of its existence as a person under international law.

Article 5

The fundamental rights of states are not susceptible of being affected in any manner whatsoever.

Article 6

The recognition of a state merely signifies that the state which recognizes it accepts the personality of the other with all the rights and duties determined by international law. Recognition is unconditional and irrevocable.

Article 7

The recognition of a state may be express or tacit. The latter results from any act which implies the intention of recognizing the new state.

Article 8

No state has the right to intervene in the internal or external affairs of another.

Notes and Questions

1. *The Montevideo Convention in Historical Context.* The years after World War I saw a growth in multilateral codification efforts promoting broad principles of interstate relations. See Thomas D. Grant, "Defining Statehood: The Montevideo Convention and its Discontents," 37 *Columbia Journal of International Law* 403, 447–48 (1999), and recall the Kellogg–Briand Pact in Chapter 2. The Montevideo Convention was adopted in 1933 at the 7th International Conference of American States. The Convention reflected Latin American concerns with the intervention of major powers in the internal and external affairs of Latin American states. In a similar vein, the 1930 "Estrada Doctrine," proclaimed by Mexico's Secretary of Foreign Relations, provided that Mexico would end the "insulting practice" of recognizing new governments:

> [I]n addition to the fact that it offends the sovereignty of other nations, [this practice] implies that judgment of some sort may be passed upon

the internal affairs of those nations by other governments, inasmuch as the latter assume, in effect, an attitude of criticism, when they decide, favorably or unfavorably, as to the legal qualifications of foreign régimes.

2 Marjorie Whiteman, *Digest of International Law* 85 (1963). The United States, for its part, was turning away from interventionism in Central America and South America when the Convention was concluded. See E.H. Carr, *International Relations Between the Two World Wars* 250–51 (1966). The United States and 15 Latin American states accepted the Montevideo Convention.

2. *The Montevideo Convention's Definition of "State."* The definition of "state" in Article 1 of the Montevideo Convention, which continues to be widely cited, restated ideas prevalent when it was drafted. See Grant, *supra,* at 416–18. Is the definition overinclusive? For example, is the "capacity to enter relations with other states" an effect, rather than a prerequisite, of statehood? Is the definition underinclusive? For example, should an entity such as Taiwan have to claim statehood before it can be a state?

3. *The Constitutive and Declaratory Theories of Recognition.* Is recognition by already existing states a condition of statehood? For example, what was the status of The Former Yugoslav Republic of Macedonia when it declared its independence during the dissolution of Yugoslavia in the early 1990s? Very few states initially recognized the Republic, their reluctance probably reflecting Greece's complaints over Macedonia's use of the name of Greece's northern region. See Paul C. Szasz, "Introductory Note," 34 I.L.M. 1461 (1995). Would the view that recognition is "constitutive" of statehood mean, for example, that international law rules forbidding transborder use of force do not apply to invasions of unrecognized "states"? How many existing states need to recognize an entity before it legally becomes a state? An alternative to the constitutive view is to consider recognition as merely "declaratory" of statehood, a position reflected in Articles 3 and 6 of the Montevideo Convention. But who determines whether an entity is a state? If an existing state is the decision-maker, would not its recognition or nonrecognition of statehood shape its conclusion as to whether a state exists?

Even if formal recognition is not a prerequisite of statehood, why might a new state—even one whose government appears stable and in control of the population—care about recognition? How well can a new state function if other states refuse to acknowledge its existence or enter into relations with it?

There are also constitutive and declaratory theories about the recognition of governments. See the *Tinoco Arbitration* in Part B below.

4. *The Equality of States.* Article 4 of the Montevideo Convention provides that each state has the same legal rights as other states. This principle of juridical equality of states is enshrined in Article 2(1) of the United Nations Charter and is often described as one of the hallmarks of state sovereignty. According to Chief Justice Marshall of the U.S. Supreme Court, "No principle of general law is more universally acknowledged, than the perfect equality of nations." The Antelope, 23 U.S. (10 Wheat.) 66, 122, 6 L.Ed. 268, 282 (1825). Should this fundamental principle ever be varied? If so, when and why? For example, how well does the principle of equality of

states fit with the right of the five permanent members at the United Nations Security Council to veto resolutions? See Chapter 8.

5. *The Variety of "States."* Do the following examples suggest that a state's sovereignty is a variable bundle of rights and duties, with some states being "more sovereign" than others? Or does every state today possess some inviolable marks of sovereignty? What distinguishes a state from a non-state?

a. *Micro-states.* The Republic of Nauru, an eight-square-mile South Pacific island with a population of 8,000, joined the United Nations in 1999. The Principality of Liechtenstein, which was admitted to the United Nations in 1990, has delegated to Switzerland much responsibility for its defense, custom affairs, and diplomatic relations with other states.

b. *Subjugated "States."* Is the Navajo Nation a state? Approximately 200,000 Navajos live within a large, clearly bounded territory in the southwestern United States. In 1849, the Navajos acknowledged that the tribe "was lawfully placed under the exclusive jurisdiction and protection" of the United States. Treaty between the United States of America and the Navajo Tribe of Indians, Sept. 9, 1849, art. I, 9 Stat. 974. The Navajo Nation has its own constitution, however, and exercises domestic self-governance within boundaries set by an 1868 treaty. Treaty Between the United States of America and the Navajo Tribe of Indians, June 1, 1868, 15 Stat. 667.

Compare the status of Kuwait after it was overrun by Iraq in 1990. See the discussion of U.N. Charter proscriptions against the use of force in Chapter 9. Compare too the status of colonies, whose transition to full independence may be more or less gradual. See the discussion of self-determination in Part C of this chapter.

c. *"Failed States."* In 1991, Somalia's central government collapsed, contributing to widespread pillage and fighting among rival clans. In 1992, the United States and other states sent troops to Somalia. These troops were sent, pursuant to U.N. Security Council Resolution 794, to provide humanitarian relief to displaced persons, to help restore peace and stability, and to act with "a view to facilitating the process of a political settlement under the auspices of the United Nations." Efforts to negotiate an end to this civil war proved unavailing during the 1990s, and the involvement of the United Nations and other non-Somali entities in efforts to rebuild Somalia has been controversial. See Ruth Gordon, "Saving Failed States: Sometimes a Neocolonialist Notion," 12 *American University Journal of International Law and Policy* 903 (1997); Gerald B. Helman & Steven R. Ratner, "Saving Failed States," 89 *Foreign Policy*, Winter 1992–1993, at 3; Nii Lante Wallace-Bruce, "Of Collapsed, Dysfunctional and Disoriented States: Challenges to International Law," 47 *Netherlands International Law Review* 53 (2000).

d. *States in Economic and Strategic Unions.* The best known example of a functioning, highly integrated economic union of states is the European Union, but numerous other looser unions also exist. For instance, the Commonwealth of Independent States, formed in 1991 when the Soviet Union disintegrated, is composed of Azerbaijan, Armenia, Belarus, Georgia, Kazakhstan, Kyrgystan, Moldova, the Russian Federation, Tajikistan, Turkmenistan, Uzbekistan, and Ukraine. The C.I.S. contemplates unified command of strategic military forces, joint control over nuclear weapons, joint decisions on military training and the use of peace-keeping forces, and an economic union. See the Alma Alta Declaration, Dec. 21, 1991, 31 I.L.M. 138 (1992); C.I.S. Charter, June 22, 1993, 34 I.L.M. 1279 (1995); C.I.S. Treaty on Creation of Economic Union, Sept. 24, 1993, 34 I.L.M. 1298 (1995); C.I.S. Council of Heads of State Decisions on Settlement of Conflicts, Peace-keeping Forces and Military Training, Jan. 19, 1996, 35 I.L.M. 783 (1996). According to the Alma Alta Declaration, the C.I.S. itself "is neither a State nor a supra-State entity." Belarus and the Russian Federation, however, have supported even closer political and economic ties than those contemplated under C.I.S. instruments. See Steven Erlanger, "Yeltsin Finds Success in Tiny Belarus," *New York Times*, May 27, 1995, at 5; Treaty on the Formation of the Community of Belarus and Russia, Apr. 2, 1996, 35 I.L.M. 1190 (1996).

e. *Federal States.* Australia, Brazil, Canada, Germany, India, the Russian Federation, Switzerland, and the United States are examples of federal states. Can the components of a federal state themselves be states under international law? Consider the Republic of Tatarstan, which is one of the 21 component republics of the Russian Federation. Tatarstan has an area of over 26,000 miles and is home to approximately four million predominantly Muslim people. In March 1992, over 60 per cent of voters in a referendum in Tatarstan agreed "that the Republic of Tatarstan is a sovereign state, a subject of international law, developing its relations with the Russian federation and other republics and states on the basis of equal treaties." *The Economist*, Mar. 28, 1992, at 49. Under a February 1994 treaty between Russia and Tatarstan, Tatarstan acknowledged it was "united" with Russia. *The Economist*, Jan. 14, 1995, at 43–44. Nevertheless, Tatarstan retains its own constitution, passes legislation that sometimes contradicts federal law, and maintains its own diplomatic ties with over 15 foreign governments. See Sam Nunn & Adam Stulberg, "The Many Faces of Modern Russia," 79 *Foreign Affairs*, Mar./Apr. 2000, at 48; Brian R. Opeskin, "Federal States in the International Legal Order," 43 *Netherlands International Law Review* 353 (1996).

6. *States and Admission to the United Nations.* Is admission to the United Nations a proxy for statehood? "States" cannot unilaterally accede to the U.N. Charter. According to Article 4 of the U.N. Charter, "peace-loving states" which accept the Charter's obligations and "are able and willing to carry out" those obligations may be admitted by action of the U.N. Security Council and General Assembly. Virtually every state belongs to the United Nations, which as of November 1, 2000, had 189 members. Does U.N. membership assure statehood status? Were the Byelorussian S.S.R. and the Ukrainian S.S.R.—Union Republics in the Soviet Union that were also members of the United Nations—really states? The Soviet Constitution did formally accord Union Republics "the right to enter into relations with

foreign states, conclude treaties with them, exchange diplomatic and consular representatives, and to be part in the work of international organizations." John N. Hazard, *Constitutions of the Countries of the World: Union of Soviet Socialist Republics* 33 (1978). See Henn–Jüri Uibopuu, "International Legal Personality of Union Republics of U.S.S.R.," 24 *International and Comparative Law Quarterly* 811 (1975). Does nonmembership in the United Nations necessarily mean that an entity is not a state? Note that Switzerland has not yet joined the United Nations, though it is contemplating membership.

7. *Statehood and Compliance with International Legal Norms.* Should recognition of statehood depend on a potential state's respecting borders with its neighbors or accepting arms control commitments? Should recognition of statehood depend on internal compliance with norms concerning human rights and the protection of minorities? In 1991 the European Community adopted "Guidelines on the Recognition of New States in Eastern Europe and in the Soviet Union," 31 I.L.M. 1455 (1992). The Guidelines provide that new states should demonstrate the following characteristics, inter alia, before being recognized: respect for provisions of the U.N. Charter and for European commitments "with regard to the rule of law, democracy and human rights;" "guarantees for the rights of ethnic and national groups and minorities;" "respect for the inviolability of all frontiers which can only be changed by peaceful means and by common agreement;" and "acceptance of all relevant commitments with regard to disarmament and nuclear non-proliferation as well as to security and regional stability." See Roland Bieber, "European Community Recognition of Eastern European States: A New Perspective for International Law?," 1992 *American Society of International Law Proceedings* 374.

B. THE RECOGNITION AND SUCCESSION OF STATES AND GOVERNMENTS

At times in history, changes in states have been dramatic. As recently as between 1990 and 1993, for example, East and West Germany united, as did North and South Yemen; Eritrea seceded from Ethiopia; Czechoslovakia split in two; and Yugoslavia and the Soviet Union each broke apart into several new states. Namibia also gained full independence during this period, and a United Nations Trusteeship over the Marshall Islands ended. Changes in governments are even more common than changes in states. New governments may be radically different from their predecessors when, for example, new constitutions are adopted or governments fall in coups.

International lawyers must grapple with legal issues related to the transformation of states and governments. In this Part we examine four cases—the first an international arbitral decision, followed by three decisions from municipal courts—in which problems related to recognition and succession are prominent.

THE TINOCO ARBITRATION

Arbitration Between Great Britain and Costa Rica, Opinion and Award of
William H. Taft, Sole Arbitrator, Washington, D.C., Oct. 18, 1923,
18 *American Journal of International Law* 147 (1924), 1 U.N.R.I.A.A. 369 (1923).

This is a proceeding under a treaty of arbitration between Great Britain and Costa Rica. * * *

In January, 1917, the Government of Costa Rica, under President Alfredo Gonzalez, was overthrown by Frederico Tinoco, the Secretary of War. Gonzalez fled. Tinoco assumed power, called an election, and established a new constitution in June, 1917. His government continued until August, 1919, when Tinoco retired, and left the country. His government fell in September following. After a provisional government under one Barquero, the old constitution was restored and elections held under it. The restored government is a signatory to this treaty of arbitration.

On the 22nd of August, 1922, the Constitutional Congress of the restored Costa Rican Government passed a law known as Law of Nullities No. 41. It invalidated all contracts between the executive power and private persons, made with or without approval of the legislative power between January 27, 1917 and September 2, 1919, covering the period of the Tinoco government. It also nullified the legislative decree No. 12 of the Tinoco government, dated June 28, 1919, authorizing the issue of the 15 million colones currency notes. The colon is a Costa Rican gold coin or standard nominally equal to 46½ cents of an American dollar, but it is uncoined and the exchange value of the paper colon actually in circulation is much less. The Nullities Law also invalidated the legislative decree of the Tinoco government of July 8, 1919, authorizing the circulation of notes of the nomination of 1000 colones, and annulled all transactions with such colones bills between holders and the state, directly or indirectly, by means of negotiation or contract, if thereby the holders received value as if they were ordinary bills of current issue.

The claim of Great Britain is that the Royal Bank of Canada and the Central Costa Rica Petroleum Company are Britain corporations whose shares are owned by British subjects; that the Banco Internacional of Costa Rica and the Government of Costa Rica are both indebted to the Royal Bank in the sum of 998,000 colones, evidenced by 998 one thousand colones bills held by the Bank; that the Central Costa Rica Petroleum Company owns, by due assignment, a grant by the Tinoco government in 1918 of the right to explore for and exploit oil deposits in Costa Rica, and that both the indebtedness and the concession have been annulled without right by the Law of Nullities and should be excepted from its operation. She asks an award that she is entitled on behalf of her subjects to have the claim of the bank paid, and the concession recognized and given effect by the Costa Rican Government.

The Government of Costa Rica denies its liability for the acts or obligations of the Tinoco government and maintains that the Law of Nullities was a legitimate exercise of its legislative governing power. It further denies the validity of such claims on the merits, unaffected by the Law of Nullities.

It is convenient to consider first the general objections to both claims of Great Britain, urged by Costa Rica, and then if such general objections cannot prevail, to consider the merits of each claim and Costa Rica's special defenses to it.

Coming now to the general issues applicable to both claims, Great Britain contends, first, that the Tinoco government was the only government of Costa Rica *de facto* and *de jure* for two years and nine months; that during that time there is no other government disputing its sovereignty, that it was in peaceful administration of the whole country, with the acquiescence of its people.

Second, that the succeeding government could not by legislative decree avoid responsibility for acts of that government affecting British subjects, or appropriate or confiscate rights and property by that government except in violation of international law; that the act of Nullities is as to British interests, therefore itself a nullity, and is to be disregarded, with the consequence that the contracts validly made with the Tinoco government must be performed by the present Costa Rican Government, and that the property which has been invaded or the rights nullified must be restored.

To these contentions the Costa Rican Government answers: First, that the Tinoco government was not a *de facto* or *de jure* government according to the rules of international law. This raises an issue of fact.

Second, that the contracts and obligations of the Tinoco government, set up by Great Britain on behalf of its subjects, are void, and do not create a legal obligation, because the government of Tinoco and its acts were in violation of the constitution of Costa Rica of 1871.

Third, that Great Britain is stopped by the fact that it did not recognize the Tinoco government during its incumbency, to claim on behalf of its subjects that Tinoco's was a government which could confer rights binding on its successor.

Fourth, that the subjects of Great Britain, whose claims are here in controversy, were either by contract or the law of Costa Rica bound to pursue their remedies before the courts of Costa Rica and not to seek diplomatic interference on the part of their home government.

Dr. John Bassett Moore, now a member of the Permanent Court of International Justice, in his *Digest of International Law*, Volume I, p. 249, announces the general principle which has had such universal acquiescence as to become well settled international law:

> Changes in the government or the international policy of a state do not as a rule affect its position in international law. A monarchy may be transformed into a republic or a republic into a monarchy;

absolute principles may be substituted for constitutional, or the reverse; but though the government changes, the nation remains, with rights and obligations unimpaired. . . .

The principle of the continuity of states has important results. The state is bound by engagements entered into by governments that have ceased to exist; the restored government is generally liable for the acts of the usurper. The governments of Louis XVIII and Louis Philippe so far as practicable indemnified the citizens of foreign states for losses caused by the government of Napoleon; and the King of the Two Cicilies made compensation to citizens of the United States for the wrongful acts of Murat.

Again Dr. Moore says:

The origin and organization of government are questions generally of internal discussion and decision. Foreign powers deal with the existing *de facto* government, when sufficiently established to give reasonable assurance of its permanence, and of the acquiescence of those who constitute the state in its ability to maintain itself, and discharge its internal duties and its external obligations.
* * *

First, what are the facts to be gathered from the documents and evidence submitted by the two parties as to the *de facto* character of the Tinoco government?

In January, 1917, Frederico A. Tinoco was Secretary of War under Alfredo Gonzalez, the then President of Costa Rica. On the ground that Gonzalez was seeking reelection as President in violation of a constitutional limitation, Tinoco used the army and navy to seize the government, assume the provisional headship of the Republic and become Commander-in-Chief of the army. Gonzalez took refuge in the American Legation, thence escaping to the United States. Tinoco constituted a provisional government at once and summoned the people to an election for deputies to a constituent assembly on the first of May, 1917. At the same time he directed an election to take place for the Presidency and himself became a candidate. An election was held. Some 61,000 votes were cast for Tinoco and 259 for another candidate. Tinoco then was inaugurated as the President to administer his powers under the former constitution until the creation of a new one. A new constitution was adopted June 8, 1917, supplanting the constitution of 1871. For a full two years Tinoco and the legislative assembly under him peaceably administered the affairs of the Government of Costa Rica, and there was no disorder of a revolutionary character during that interval. No other government of any kind asserted power in the country. The courts sat, Congress legislated, and the government was duly administered. Its power was fully established and peaceably exercised. The people seemed to have accepted Tinoco's government with great good will when it came in, and to have welcomed the change. * * * [T]hroughout the record as made by the case and counter case, there is no substantial evidence that Tinoco was not in actual and peaceable administration without resistance or conflict or contest by anyone until a few months before the time when he retired and resigned.

Speaking of the resumption of the present government, this passage occurs in the argument on behalf of Costa Rica:

> Powerful forces in Costa Rica were opposed to Tinoco from the outset, but his overthrow by ballot or unarmed opposition was impossible and it was equally impossible to organize armed opposition against him in Costa Rican territory.

It is true that action of the supporters of those seeking to restore the former government was somewhat delayed by the influence of the United States with Gonzalez and his friends against armed action, on the ground that military disturbances in Central America during the World War would be prejudicial to the interests of the Allied Powers. It is not important, however, what were the causes that enabled Tinoco to carry on his government effectively and peaceably. The question is, must his government be considered a link in the continuity of the Government of Costa Rica? I must hold that from the evidence that the Tinoco government was an actual sovereign government.

But it is urged that many leading Powers refused to recognize the Tinoco government, and that recognition by other nations is the chief and best evidence of the birth, existence and continuity of succession of a government. Undoubtedly recognition by other Powers is an important evidential factor in establishing proof of the existence of a government in the society of nations. What are the facts as to this? The Tinoco government was recognized by Bolivia on May 17, 1917; by Argentina on May 22, 1917; by Chile on May 22, 1917; by Haiti on May 22, 1917; by Guatemala on May 28, 1917; by Switzerland on June 1, 1917; by Germany on June 10, 1917; by Denmark on June 18, 1917; by Spain on June 18, 1917; by Mexico on July 1, 1917; by Holland on July 11, 1917; by the Vatican on June 9, 1917; by Colombia on August 9, 1917; by Austria on August 10, 1917; by Portugal on August 14, 1917; by El Salvador on September 12, 1917; by Romania on November 15, 1917; by Brazil on November 28, 1917; by Peru on December 15, 1917; and by Ecuador on April 23, 1917.

What were the circumstances as to the other nations?

The United States, on February 9, 1917, two weeks after Tinoco had assumed power, took this action:

> The Government of the United States has viewed the recent overthrow of the established government in Costa Rica with the gravest concern and considers that illegal acts of this character tend to disturb the peace of Central America and to disrupt the unity of the American continent. In view of its policy in regard to the assumption of power through illegal methods, clearly enunciated by it on several occasions during the past four years, the Government of the United States desires to set forth in an emphatic and distinct manner its present position in regard to the actual situation in

Costa Rica which is that it will not give recognition or support to any government which may be established unless it is clearly proven that it is elected by legal and constitutional means.

And again on February 24, 1917:

In order that citizens of the United States may have definite information as to the position of this Government in regard to any financial aid which they may give to, or any business transaction which they may have with those persons who overthrew the constitutional Government of Costa Rica by an act of armed rebellion, the Government of the United States desires to advise them that it will not consider any claims which may in the future arise from such dealings, worthy of its diplomatic support.

[The U.S. State Department reaffirmed its nonrecognition of the Tinoco regime in April 1918.]

Probably because of the leadership of the United States in respect to a matter of this kind, her then Allies in the war, Great Britain, France and Italy, declined to recognize the Tinoco government. Costa Rica was, therefore, not permitted to sign the Treaty of Peace at Versailles, although the Tinoco government had declared war against Germany.

The merits of the policy of the United States in this non-recognition it is not for the arbitrator to discuss, for the reason that in his consideration of this case, he is necessarily controlled by principles of international law, and however justified as a national policy non-recognition on such a ground may be, it certainly has not been acquiesced in by all the nations of the world, which is a condition precedent to considering it as a postulate of international law.

The non-recognition by other nations of a government claiming to be a national personality, is usually appropriate evidence that it has not attained the independence and control entitling it by international law to be classed as such. But when recognition *vel non* of a government is by such nations determined by inquiry, not into its *de facto* sovereignty and complete governmental control, but into its illegitimacy or irregularity of origin, their non-recognition loses something of evidential weight on the issue with which those applying the rules of international law are alone concerned. What is true of the non-recognition of the United States in its bearing upon the existence of a *de facto* government under Tinoco for thirty months is probably in a measure true of the non-recognition by her Allies in the European War. Such non-recognition for any reason, however, cannot outweigh the evidence disclosed by this record before me as to the *de facto* character of Tinoco's government, according to the standard set by international law.

Second. It is ably and earnestly argued on behalf of Costa Rica that the Tinoco government cannot be considered a *de facto* government, because it was not established and maintained in accord with the constitution of Costa Rica of 1871. To hold that a government which establishes itself and maintains a peaceful administration, with the acquiescence of the people for a substantial period of time, does not become a *de facto* government unless it conforms to a previous constitution would be to hold that within the rules of international law a revolution contrary to the fundamental law of the existing government cannot establish a new government. This cannot be, and is not, true. The change by revolution upsets the rule of the authorities in power under the then existing fundamental law, and sets aside the fundamental law in so far as the change of rule makes it necessary. To speak of a revolution creating a *de facto* government, which conforms to the limitations of the old constitution is to use a contradiction in terms. The same government continues internationally, but not the internal law of its being. The issue is not whether the new government assumes power or conducts its administration under constitutional limitations established by the people during the incumbency of the government it has overthrown. The question is, has it really established itself in such a way that all within its influence recognize its control, and that there is no opposing force assuming to be a government in its place? Is it discharging its functions as a government usually does, respected within its own jurisdiction? * * *

Third. It is further objected by Costa Rica that Great Britain by her failure to recognize the Tinoco government is estopped now to urge claims of her subjects dependent upon the acts and contracts of the Tinoco government. The evidential weight of such non-recognition against the claim of its *de facto* character I have already considered and admitted. The contention here goes further and precludes a government which did not recognize a *de facto* government from appearing in an international tribunal in behalf of its nationals to claim any rights based on the acts of such government.

To sustain this view a great number of decisions in English and American courts are cited to the point that a municipal court cannot, in litigation before it, recognize or assume the *de facto* character of a foreign government which the executive department of foreign affairs of the government of which the court is a branch has not recognized. This is clearly true. It is for the executive to decide questions of foreign policy and not courts. It would be most unseemly to have a conflict of opinion in respect to foreign relations of a nation between its department charged with the conduct of its foreign affairs and its judicial branch. But such cases have no bearing on the point before us. Here the executive of Great Britain takes the position that the Tinoco government which it did not recognize, was nevertheless a *de facto* government that could create rights in British subjects which it now seeks to protect. Of course, as already emphasized, its failure to recognize the *de facto* government can be used against it as evidence to disprove the character it now attributes to that government, but this does not bar it from changing its position. Should a case arise in one of its own courts after it has changed its position, doubtless that court would feel it incumbent upon it to note the change in its further rulings.

Precedents in American arbitrations are cited to show that an estoppel like the one urged does arise. They are Schultz's case (Moore, *International Arbitrations*, Vol. 3, 2973), Janson's case (*ibidem*, 2902), and Jarvis's case (Ralston, *Venezuela Arbitrations*, 150). In the opinions of these cases delivered by American commissioners, there are expressions sustaining the view that the bar of an estoppel exists, but an examination shows that no authorities are cited and no arguments are made in support of the view. Moreover, the array of facts in the cases was conclusive against the existence of a *de facto* government, and the expressions were unnecessary to the conclusion. * * *

I do not understand the arguments on which an equitable estoppel in such case can rest. The failure to recognize the *de facto* government did not lead the succeeding government to change its position in any way upon the faith of it. Non-recognition may have aided the succeeding government to come into power; but subsequent presentation of claims based on the *de facto* existence of the previous government and its dealings does not work an injury to the succeeding government in the nature of a fraud or breach of faith. An equitable estoppel to prove the truth must rest on previous conduct of the person to be estopped, which has led the person claiming the estoppel into a position in which the truth will injure him. There is no such case here.

* * * It may be urged that it would be in the interest of the stability of governments and the orderly adjustment of international relations, and so a proper rule of international law, that a government in recognizing or refusing to recognize a government claiming admission to the society of nations should thereafter be held to an attitude consistent with its deliberate conclusion on this issue. Arguments for and against such a rule occur to me; but it suffices to say that I have not been cited to text writers of authority or to decisions of significance indicating a general acquiescence of nations in such a rule. Without this, it cannot be applied here as a principle of international law.

It is urged that the subjects of Great Britain knew of the policy of their home government in refusing to recognize the Tinoco régime and cannot now rely on protection by Great Britain. This is a question solely between the home government and its subjects. That government may take the course which the United States had done and refuse to use any diplomatic offices to promote such claims and thus to leave its nationals to depend upon the sense of justice of the existing Costa Rican Government, as they were warned in advance would be its policy, or it may change its conclusion as to the *de facto* existence of the Tinoco government and offer its subjects the protection of its diplomatic intervention. It is entirely a question between the claimants and their own government. It should be noted that Great Britain issued no such warning to its subjects as did the United States to its citizens in this matter.

The fourth point made on behalf of Costa Rica against the claims here pressed is that both claimants are bound either by their own contractual obligation entered into with the Government of Costa Rica, or by the laws of Costa Rica, to which they subscribed, not to present their claims by way of diplomatic intervention of their home government, but to submit their claims to the courts of Costa Rica. [The arbitrator concludes that Costa Rica's claim of failure to exhaust local remedies was not well founded.]

A consideration of the issues before us, therefore, recurs to the merits of the two claims. The decision of them must be governed by the answer to the question whether the claims would have been good against the Tinoco government as a government, unaffected by the Law of Nullities, and unaffected by the Costa Rican Constitution of 1871. [The arbitrator examines the complex banking arrangements related to the claim of the Royal Bank of Canada, and finds in favor of Great Britain on behalf of the Royal Bank. With respect to the issue of the petroleum concession, however, the arbitrator disallows recovery because the concession violated Costa Rica's 1917 constitution. Because of this violation, even Tinoco's government could have defeated the concession. Thus, when the Law of Nullities deemed the concession to be invalid, it worked no injury to the British companies of which Great Britain could complain.]

Notes and Questions

1. *The Arbitrator in the* Tinoco *Case.* William Howard Taft, the sole arbitrator in the *Tinoco Case*, was President of the United States during 1909–1913 and Chief Justice of the U.S. Supreme Court during 1921–1930. As President, he, along with other leading public figures, supported treaties of general arbitration, applicable even to questions of "vital interests" and "national honor." See Henry F. Pringle, 2 *The Life and Times of William Howard Taft* 737–39 (1939).

2. *Government Succession to Obligations.* Taft held that, by international law, a new government is bound by the legal commitments of an old government. Could there be any practical alternative to this rule? It is difficult to see how there could be any legally binding commitments of states if international obligations could be repudiated simply by forming or declaring a new government. Should an exception be made to permit the repudiation of national commitments when there has been a radical change in government? If so, who determines whether the change is radical enough? Today, should the contracts of a government that seized control in an extraconstitutional coup, in violation of the wishes of the people who are governed, be considered binding? Professor Reisman has suggested that the *Tinoco* decision, although "consistent with the law of its time" and supported by "policy reasons * * * which may still have some cogency," is now "anachronistic, for it stands in stark contradiction to the new constitutive, human rights-based conception of popular sovereignty." W. Michael Reisman, "Sovereignty and Human Rights in Contemporary International Law," in *Democratic Governance and International Law* 239, 244 (Gregory H. Fox & Brad R. Roth eds. 2000).

3. De Facto *and* De Jure *Governments.* Taft was concerned to establish that the Tinoco regime was the actual government of Costa Rica when it

entered into the banking and oil concession arrangements with the British companies. He discussed the categories of *de facto* and *de jure* governments. What is the difference between them? Taft seemed to look most at the factor of popular acquiescence to determine whether the Tinoco regime was the *de facto* government of Costa Rica. What evidences would a judge or lawyer consider in evaluating the popular support for a government? If Taft had found that the Tinoco regime lacked popular support, would he necessarily have concluded it was not the *de facto* government?

There were about 50 governments world-wide in 1917; the Tinoco regime was recognized by 20 of them. Was this number of recognitions enough to establish Tinoco as the *de jure* government of Costa Rica? Would the answer depend on the degree to which nonrecognizing foreign governments opposed the Tinoco regime and still supported the old Gonzalez regime?

4. *The Relative Importance of* De Facto *Control and* De Jure *Recognition.* What if the evidences of *de facto* control conflict with the evidences of *de jure* recognition? Which should govern in determining the legitimate government of a state? Could there be different answers to this question depending on the forum and depending on whether the forum looks to an answer in international law or one or another municipal law? Is the distinction between *de facto* and *de jure* governments another way of stating the conflict between declaratory and constitutive theories of recognition?

5. *Estoppel.* How persuasive was Taft in his estoppel argument? Should Great Britain have been permitted to insist that the Tinoco regime was the government of Costa Rica when it had failed to recognize the Tinoco regime? The Tinoco regime probably could not have availed itself of the British courts because it was unrecognized. Should there be one answer as to the status of the Tinoco regime vis-à-vis Great Britain in British municipal courts and another in an international tribunal?

6. *Comparing the Succession of States and the Succession of Governments.* Is it always easy to distinguish changes in states from changes in governments? Should different consequences attach to changes in governments and changes in states? In the view of Professor O'Connell,

> the solution of the problem raised by political change cannot be left to the hazard of characterizing the event as a succession of States or a succession of governments. There is evident at the present time a developing pressure in the direction of assimilating these two categories of events, and as the nineteenth-century theory of the State, with its concomitant metaphysics of political personality, loses its cogency, legal theory will tend more and more to return to its eighteenth-century position.

D.P. O'Connell, 1 *State Succession in Municipal Law and International Law* 7 (1967). The 18th-century position to which O'Connell referred called for a succession to commitments without drawing a distinction between states and governments.

AUTOCEPHALOUS GREEK–ORTHODOX CHURCH OF CYPRUS v. GOLDBERG & FELDMAN FINE ARTS, INC.

917 F.2d 278 (7th Cir.1990), *cert. denied,*
502 U.S. 941, 112 S.Ct. 377, 116 L.Ed.2d 329 (1991).

BAUER, CHIEF JUDGE. * * *

* * * In this appeal, we consider the fate of several tangible victims of Cyprus' turbulent history: specifically, four Byzantine mosaics created over 1400 years ago. The district court awarded possession of these extremely valuable mosaics to plaintiff-appellee, the Autocephalous Greek–Orthodox Church of Cyprus ("Church of Cyprus" or "Church"). *Autocephalous Greek–Orthodox Church of Cyprus v. Goldberg & Feldman Fine Arts, Inc.,* 717 F.Supp. 1374 (S.D.Ind.1989). Defendants-appellants, Peg Goldberg and Goldberg & Feldman Fine Arts, Inc. (collectively "Goldberg"), claim that in so doing, the court committed various reversible errors. We affirm.

I. BACKGROUND

In the early sixth century, A.D., a large mosaic was affixed to the apse of the Church of the Panagia Kanakaria ("Kanakaria Church") in the village of Lythrankomi, Cyprus. The mosaic, made of small bits of colored glass, depicted Jesus Christ as a young boy in the lap of his mother, the Virgin Mary, who was seated on a throne. Jesus and Mary were attended by two archangels and surrounded by a frieze depicting the twelve apostles. The mosaic was displayed in the Kanakaria Church for centuries, where it became, under the practices of Eastern Orthodox Christianity, sanctified as a holy relic. It survived both the vicissitudes of history, *see Autocephalous,* 717 F.Supp. at 1377 (discussing the period of Iconoclasm during which many religious artifacts were destroyed), and, thanks to restoration efforts, the ravages of time.

Testimony before Judge Noland established that the Kanakaria mosaic was one of only a handful of such holy Byzantine relics to survive into the twentieth century. Sadly, however, war came to Cyprus in the 1970s, from which the mosaic could not be spared.

The Cypriot people have long been a divided people, approximately three-fourths being of Greek descent and Greek–Orthodox faith, the other quarter of Turkish descent and Muslim [sic] faith. No sooner had Cyprus gained independence from British rule in 1960 than this bitter division surfaced. Civil disturbances erupted between Greek and Turkish Cypriots, necessitating the introduction of United Nations peacekeeping forces in 1964. (U.N. forces still remain in Cyprus.) Through the 1960s, the Greek Cypriots, concentrated in the southern part of the island, became increasingly estranged from the Turkish Cypriots, concentrated in the north.

The tensions erupted again in 1974, this time with more violent results. In July, 1974, the civil government of the Republic of Cyprus was replaced by a government controlled by the Greek Cypriot military. In apparent response, on July 20, 1974, Turkey invaded Cyprus from the north. By late August, the Turkish military forces had advanced to occupy approximately the northern third of the island. The point at which the invading forces stopped is called the "Green Line." To this day, the heavily-guarded Green Line bisects Nicosia, the capital of the Republic, and splits the island from east to west.

The Turkish forces quickly established their own "government" north of the Green Line. In 1975, they formed what they called the "Turkish Federated State of Cyprus" ("TFSC"). In 1983, that administration was dissolved, and the "Turkish Republic of Northern Cyprus" ("TRNC") was formed. These "governments" were recognized immediately by Turkey, but all other nations in the world—including the United States—have never recognized them, and continue to recognize the Republic of Cyprus ("Republic"), plaintiff-appellee in this action, as the only legitimate government for all Cypriot people.

The Turkish invasion led to the forced southern exodus of over 100,000 Greek Cypriots who lived in northern Cyprus. Turkish Cypriots living in southern Cyprus (and tens of thousands of settlers from mainland Turkey) likewise flooded into northern Cyprus, resulting in a massive exchange of populations.

Lythrankomi is in the northern portion of Cyprus that came under Turkish rule. Although the village and the Kanakaria Church were untouched by the invading forces in 1974, the villagers of Greek ancestry were soon thereafter "enclaved" by the Turkish military. Despite the hostile environment, the pastor and priests of the Kanakaria Church continued for two years to conduct religious services for the Greek Cypriots who remained in Lythrankomi. Hardy as they must have been, these clerics, and virtually all remaining Greek Cypriots, were forced to flee to southern Cyprus in the summer of 1976. Church of Cyprus officials testified that they intend to re-establish the congregation at the Kanakaria Church as soon as Greek Cypriots are permitted to return safely to Lythrankomi. (Thirty-five thousand Turkish troops remain in northern Cyprus.)

When the priests evacuated the Kanakaria Church in 1976, the mosaic was still intact. In the late 1970s, however, Church of Cyprus officials received increasing reports that Greek Cypriot churches and monuments in northern Cyprus were being attacked and vandalized, their contents stolen or destroyed. * * * In November, 1979, a resident of northern Cyprus brought word to the Republic's Department of Antiquities that this fate had also befallen the Kanakaria Church and its mosaic. Vandals had plundered the church, removing anything of value from its interior. The mosaic, or at least its most recognizable and valuable parts, had been forcibly ripped from the apse of the church.

Once a place of worship, the Kanakaria Church had been reduced to a stable for farm animals.

Upon learning of the looting of the Kanakaria Church and the loss of its mosaics (made plural by the vandals' axes), the Republic of Cyprus took immediate steps to recover them. As discussed in greater detail in Judge Noland's opinion, these efforts took the form of contacting and seeking assistance from many organizations and individuals, including the United Nations Educational, Scientific and Cultural Organization ("UNESCO"); the International Council of Museums; the International Council of Museums and Sites; Europa Nostra (an organization devoted to the conservation of the architectural heritage of Europe); the Council of Europe; international auction houses such as Christie's and Sotheby's; Harvard University's Dumbarton Oaks Institute for Byzantine Studies; and the foremost museums, curators and Byzantine scholars throughout the world. The Republic's United States Embassy also routinely disseminated information about lost cultural properties to journalists, U.S. officials and scores of scholars, architects and collectors in this country, asking for assistance in recovering the mosaics. The overall strategy behind these efforts was to get word to the experts and scholars who would probably be involved in any ultimate sale of the mosaics. These individuals, it was hoped, would be the most likely (only?) actors in the chain of custody of stolen cultural properties who would be interested in helping the Republic and Church of Cyprus recover them.

The Republic's efforts have paid off. In recent years, the Republic has recovered and returned to the Church of Cyprus several stolen relics and antiquities. The Republic has even located frescoes and other works taken from the Kanakaria Church, including the four mosaics at issue here. These four mosaics, each measuring about two feet square, depict the figure of Jesus, the busts of one of the attending archangels, the apostle Matthew and the apostle James.

To understand how these pieces of the Kanakaria mosaic resurfaced, we must trace the actions of appellant Peg Goldberg and the other principals through whose hands they passed in 1988.

Peg Goldberg is an art dealer and gallery operator. Goldberg and Feldman Fine Arts, Inc., is the Indiana corporation that owns her gallery in Carmel, Indiana. In the summer of 1988, Peg Goldberg went to Europe to shop for works for her gallery. Although her main interest is 20th century paintings, etchings and sculptures, Goldberg was enticed while in The Netherlands by Robert Fitzgerald, another Indiana art dealer and "casual friend" of hers, to consider the purchase of "four early Christian mosaics." [The court details Goldberg's efforts to buy the mosaics. The sale was concluded by the exchange of the mosaics for $1,080,000 in $100 bills at the airport in Geneva, Switzerland.]

Peg Goldberg's efforts soon turned to * * * the resale of these valuable mosaics. She worked up sales brochures about them, and contacted several other dealers to help her find a buyer. Two of these dealers' searches led them both to Dr. Marion True of the Getty Museum in California. When told of these mosaics and their likely origin, the aptly-named Dr. True explained to the dealers that she had a working relationship with the Republic of Cyprus and that she was duty-bound to contact Cypriot officials about them. Dr. True called Dr. Vassos Karageorghis, the Director of the Republic's Department of Antiquities and one of the primary Cypriot officials involved in the worldwide search for the mosaics. Dr. Karageorghis verified that the Republic was in fact hunting for the mosaics that had been described to Dr. True, and he set in motion the investigative and legal machinery that ultimately resulted in the Republic learning that they were in Goldberg's possession in Indianapolis.

After their request for the return of the mosaics was refused by Goldberg, the Republic of Cyprus and the Church of Cyprus (collectively "Cyprus") brought this suit in the Southern District of Indiana for the recovery of the mosaics. * * * Judge Noland awarded possession of the mosaics to the Church of Cyprus. Goldberg filed a timely appeal.

II. ANALYSIS * * *

[The court concludes that there is no statute of limitations bar to the action, and that applicable rules of replevin allow the plaintiff Church to recover the mosaics.]

Finally, Goldberg argues that several decrees of the TFSC (the entity established in northern Cyprus by the Turkish military immediately after the 1974 invasion) divested the Church of title to the mosaics. Goldberg asks us to honor these decrees under the notion that in some instances courts in the United States can give effect to the acts of nonrecognized but *"de facto"* regimes if the acts relate to purely local matters. *See Restatement (Third) of the Foreign Relations Law of the United States ("Third Restatement")* § 205(3) (1987);[15] *Salimoff v. Standard Oil Co.*, 262 N.Y. 220, 186 N.E. 679 (1933) (under Soviet law, U.S.S.R. nationalization decree effective to pass title to oil within Russia despite fact that U.S.S.R. was not yet recognized by the U.S.). The TFSC decrees at issue, all propagated in 1975, are principally these: 1) the "Abandoned Movable Property Law," which provided that all movable property within the boundaries of the TFSC abandoned by its owner because of the owner's "departure" from northern Cyprus "as a result of the situation after 20th July 1974" now belongs to the TFSC "in the name of the Turkish Community" and that the TFSC "is responsible for the possession and control of such property;" and 2) the "Antiquities Ordinance," which provided that all religious buildings and antiquities, including specifically "synagogues, basilicas, churches, monasteries and the like," located north of the Green Line, as well as any and all "movable antiquities" contained therein, are now the property of the

---

15. This Restatement section provides: [C]ourts in the United States ordinarily give effect to acts of a regime representing an entity not recognized as a state, or of a regime not recognized as the government of a state, if those acts apply to territory under the control of that regime and relate to domestic matters only.

TFSC.[16] Because these decrees were enacted before the Kanakaria Church was looted and its mosaics stolen, the argument concludes, the Church cannot here claim to hold title to the mosaics.

It is helpful to note at the outset what is *not* being claimed here. First, Goldberg does not (and cannot) suggest that this court should pass on the validity of the Turkish administration in northern Cyprus. We repeat here precepts that are well-established in the law of this country:

> [T]he conduct of foreign relations was committed by the Constitution to the political departments of the government, and the propriety of what may be done in the exercise of this political power [is] not subject to judicial inquiry or decision, ... [and] who is the sovereign of a territory is not a judicial question, but one the determination of which by the political departments conclusively binds the courts[.]

United States v. Belmont, 301 U.S. 324, 328, 57 S.Ct. 758, 759–60, 81 L.Ed. 1134 (1937) (*citing Oetjen v. Central Leather Co.*, 246 U.S. 297, 38 S.Ct. 309, 62 L.Ed. 726 (1918)). Indeed, Goldberg herself supports the district court's decision to deny the TRNC's motion to intervene in this case, which decision was based on the TRNC's continued status as a nonrecognized entity. *See Third Restatement* § 205(1) (entity not recognized as a state ordinarily denied access to U.S. courts); *Republic of Vietnam v. Pfizer, Inc.*, 556 F.2d 892 (8th Cir.1977).

Second, this is not a case in which one party is claiming title under the laws of a state that has been entirely displaced, and the other is claiming title under the laws of the new, displacing regime. All Goldberg can hope to gain from the invocation of these TFSC edicts is a finding that the Church's claim of title is defective; she has no plausible claim of valid title in herself based on these edicts. This fact sets this case apart from the cases cited by Goldberg, including *Salimoff*, 186 N.E. 679 (plaintiff Russian nationals claimed title to property under laws of the old Russian Empire and defendant U.S. companies claimed title due to purchase from Soviet government, which seized the property pursuant to nationalization decree); and *The Denny*, 127 F.2d 404 (3d Cir.1942) (dispute between Lithuanian citizens wherein both claimed right to possess property as agents under Lithuanian law, one relying on the effect of nationalization decrees of the Lithuanian Soviet Socialist Republic, the other on pre-nationalization law).

What Goldberg is claiming is that the TFSC's confiscatory decrees, adopted only one year after the Turkish invasion, should be given effect by this court because the TFSC and its successor TRNC should now be viewed as the "*de facto*" government north of the Green Line. This we are unwilling to do. We draw on two lines of precedent as support for our

16. We note that Cyprus has raised arguments that cast substantial doubt on the actual meaning and effect of these and other TFSC decrees, even should we decide to apply them. For the purposes of disposing of Goldberg's argument, however, we will assume that the TFSC decrees actually mean what Goldberg represents them to mean.

decision. First, we note that, contrary to the New York court's decision in *Salimoff*, several courts of the same era refused to give effect to the nationalization decrees of the as-yet-unrecognized Soviet Republics. These courts relied on a variety of grounds, including especially the fact that the political branches of our government still refused to recognize these entities. *See, e.g., Latvian State Cargo & Passenger S.S. Line v. McGrath*, 188 F.2d 1000, 1002–04 (D.C.Cir.1951) (also stating as a possible alternative ground the following view: "since the nationalization decrees here involved were confiscatory and thus contrary to the public policy of this country, our courts would in no event give them effect," and citing cases); *The Maret*, 145 F.2d 431, 442 (3d Cir.1944) ("[N]o valid distinction can be drawn between the political or diplomatic act of nonrecognition of a sovereign and nonrecognition of the decrees or acts of that sovereign.... Nonrecognition of a foreign sovereign and nonrecognition of its decrees are to be deemed to be as essential a part of the power confided by the Constitution to the Executive for the conduct of foreign affairs as recognition."). Similarly, as regards the Turkish administration in northern Cyprus, the United States government (like the rest of the non-Turkish world) has not recognized its legitimacy, nor does our government "recognize that [the Turkish administration] has functioned as a de facto or quasi government ..., ruling within its own borders."

Second, we are guided in part by the post-Civil War cases in which courts refused to give effect to property-affecting acts of the Confederate state legislatures. In one such case, *Williams v. Bruffy*, 96 U.S. 176, 24 L.Ed. 716 (1878), the Supreme Court drew a helpful distinction between two kinds of "*de facto*" governments. The first kind "is such as exists after it has expelled the regularly constituted authorities from the seats of power and the public offices, and established its own functionaries in their places, so as to represent in fact the sovereignty of the nation." This kind of *de facto* government, the Court explained, "is treated as in most respects possessing rightful authority, ... [and] its legislation is in general recognized." The second kind of *de facto* government "is such as exists where a portion of the inhabitants of a country have separated themselves from the parent State and established an independent government. The validity of its acts, both against the parent State and its citizens or subjects, depends entirely upon its ultimate success.... If it succeed, and become recognized, its acts from the commencement of its existence are upheld as those of an independent nation." (The Court held that the Confederacy was a government of the second type that ultimately failed.) Goldberg argues that the TFSC and its successor TRNC have achieved the level of "ultimate success" contemplated by this standard, because they have maintained control of the territory north of the Green Line for over fifteen years. We will not thus equate simple longevity of control with "ultimate success." The Turkish forces, despite their best efforts, did not completely supplant the Republic nor its officers. Instead, the TFSC and the TRNC, neither of which has ever been recognized by the non-Turkish world, only acceded to the control of the northern portion of Cyprus. The Republic of Cyprus remains the only recognized Cypriot government, the sovereign nation for the entire island. * * * [W]e conclude that the confiscatory decrees proffered by Goldberg do not divest the Church of its claim of title.

III. Conclusion

* * * Those who plundered the churches and monuments of war-torn Cyprus, hoarded their relics away, and are now smuggling and selling them for large sums, are * * * blackguards. The Republic of Cyprus, with diligent effort and the help of friends like Dr. True, has been able to locate several of these stolen antiquities; items of vast cultural, religious (and, as this case demonstrates, monetary) value. Among such finds are the pieces of the Kanakaria mosaic at issue in this case. Unfortunately, when these mosaics surfaced they were in the hands not of the most guilty parties, but of Peg Goldberg and her gallery. Correctly applying Indiana law, the district court determined that Goldberg must return the mosaics to their rightful owner: the Church of Cyprus. Goldberg's tireless attacks have not established reversible error in that determination, and thus, for the reasons discussed above, the district court's judgment is Affirmed.

Lest this result seem too harsh, we should note that those who wish to purchase art work on the international market, undoubtedly a ticklish business, are not without means by which to protect themselves. Especially when circumstances are as suspicious as those that faced Peg Goldberg, prospective purchasers would do best to do more than make a few last-minute phone calls. * * * In such cases, dealers can (and probably should) take steps such as a formal IFAR [International Foundation for Art Research] search; a documented authenticity check by disinterested experts; a full background search of the seller and his claim of title; insurance protection and a contingency sales contract; and the like. If Goldberg would have pursued such methods, perhaps she would have discovered in time what she has now discovered too late: the Church has a valid, superior and enforceable claim to these Byzantine treasures, which therefore must be returned to it.

Cudahy, Circuit Judge, concurring * * *

A second * * * aspect of this case involves the treatment of the cultural heritage of foreign nations under international and United States law. The United States has both acceded to international agreements and enacted its own statutes regarding the importation of cultural property. These regulatory efforts have encompassed transfers of property during both wartime and peacetime and apply whether the property was originally stolen or "merely" illegally exported from the country of origin. The two most significant international agreements that attempt to protect cultural property are the 1954 Convention on the Protection of Cultural Property in the Event of Armed Conflict (the "1954 Hague Convention"), 249 U.N.T.S. 215 (1956), and the UNESCO Convention on the Means of Prohibiting and Preventing the Illicit Transport, Export and Transfer of Ownership of Cultural Property (the "UNESCO Convention"), 823 U.N.T.S. 231 (1972). Under both these multinational treaties, as well as under the United States' Convention on Cultural Property Implementation Act, 19 U.S.C. § 2601 *et seq.* (1983), the Cypriot mosaics would be considered cultural property warranting international protection. * * *

The 1954 Hague Convention may be applicable to the case before us given the incursion of Turkish armed forces into Cyprus in 1974 and our ongoing refusal to recognize the government established in the northern part of Cyprus. The 1954 Hague Convention, which is but the most recent multilateral agreement in a 200–year history of international attempts to protect cultural property during wartime, prohibits the destruction or seizure of cultural property during armed conflict, whether international or civil in nature, and during periods of belligerent occupation. The Hague Convention also applies to international trafficking during peacetime in cultural property unlawfully seized during an armed conflict. The attempt of the government established in northern Cyprus by the Turkish military to divest the Greek Cypriot church of ownership of the mosaics might be viewed as an interference of the sort contemplated by the 1954 Hague Convention. If this were the case, the acts and decrees of the northern Cyprus government divesting title to this cultural property would not demand the deference of American courts.

The second international agreement, the UNESCO Convention, focuses on private conduct, primarily during peacetime, and thus is also applicable to the theft and removal of the mosaics from Cyprus. Article 7 of that Convention requires signatory nations:

(a) To take the necessary measures, consistent with national legislation, to prevent museums and similar institutions within their territories from acquiring cultural property originating in another State Party which has been illegally exported . . .;

(b)(i) to prohibit the import of cultural property stolen from a museum or a religious or secular public monument or similar institution in another State Party . . ., provided that such property is documented as appertaining to the inventory of that institution;

(ii) at the request of the State Party of origin, to take appropriate steps to recover and return any such cultural property . . ., provided, however, that the requesting State shall pay just compensation to an innocent purchaser or to a person who has valid title to that property. . . .

It is clear that the mosaics in the case before us were stolen (under any reasonable definition of that word) from a religious institution and that the mosaics were extensively documented by the Dumbarton Oaks publication as belonging to the Kanakaria Church. While the UNESCO Convention seems to contemplate primarily measures to be implemented by the executive branch of a government through its import and export rules and policies, the judicial branch should certainly attempt to reflect in its decisionmaking the spirit as well as the letter of an international agreement to which the United States is a party.

Notes and Questions

1. *International Law and the Protection of Cultural Property.* The *Goldberg* opinions addressed international legal efforts to protect cultural property as well as recognition issues. Illegal trade in art and antiquities is big business; in dollar terms, it is larger than every area of international crime except the arms trade and narcotics trafficking. 1993 estimates of annual international art crime ranged from $3 billion to $6 billion. Only approximately 12 per cent of stolen art is recovered, and those who steal antiquities often destroy archaeological information. See Note, Lisa J. Borodkin, "The Economics of Antiquities Looting and a Proposed Legal Alternative," 95 *Columbia Law Review* 377, 377–78 (1995). The *Goldberg Case* and international trade in cultural property are explored in Dan Hofstadter, *Goldberg's Angel* (1994).

2. *Nonrecognition and the Use of Force.* The widespread refusal of states to recognize the Turkish Federated State of Cyprus (TFSC) or the Turkish Republic of Northern Cyprus (TRNC) has been explained as a reaction to Turkey's unlawful use of force in Northern Cyprus. See Ian Brownlie, "The United Nations Charter and the Use of Force, 1945–1985," in *The Current Legal Regulation of the Use of Force* 491, 492 (A. Cassese ed. 1986). Efforts to end the division of Cyprus have been unsuccessful. See "Cyprus: Talks About Talks," *The Economist*, Dec. 4, 1999, at 49. We consider international law and the use of force in Chapter 9.

3. *Giving Effect to the Laws of Unrecognized States and Governments.* In the *Goldberg Case* a U.S. court refused to give effect to a law of an entity that the United States had not recognized as a state. If the TFSC and the TRNC had been recognized by many states, but not by the United States, would the court have scrutinized the decrees concerning the mosaics, because made by a *de jure* government? Did the *Goldberg* court refuse to consider the TFSC's decrees concerning the mosaics because the court found the decrees objectionable? Should acts taken under *un*objectionable laws of an unrecognized state—such as laws specifying when marriages and divorces are valid—be denied effect in U.S. courts?

4. *Access of Unrecognized States and Governments to U.S. Courts.* The *Goldberg* district court also refused to allow the TRNC to intervene directly in the case, stating that to do so "would create the incongruous result of having the Judicial Branch implicitly recognize that entity as a legitimate government in the face of explicit nonrecognition by the Executive Branch." Autocephalous Greek–Orthodox Church of Cyprus v. Goldberg & Feldman Fine Arts, Inc., No. IP 89–304–C (S.D.Ind. May 31, 1989), *quoted in* 86 *American Journal of International Law* 128, 129 (1992). Other decisions also have denied unrecognized states or governments access to U.S. courts. In Russian Socialist Federated Soviet Republic v. Cibrario, 235 N.Y. 255, 139 N.E. 259 (1923), the court concluded that foreign powers appeared in U.S. courts only as a matter of comity. The court defined comity as "that reciprocal courtesy which one member of the family of nations owes to the

others," a concept that presupposed friendship. No comity was due a foreign government appearing as a plaintiff in U.S. court, the *Cibrario* court found, unless the United States had recognized that government. For a critique of the role of comity in U.S. courts, see Joel Paul, "Comity in International Law," 32 *Harvard International Law Journal* 1 (1991).

U.S. courts have not always refused to allow unrecognized entities to pursue their claims. In National Petrochemical Co. v. M/T Stolt Sheaf, 860 F.2d 551 (2d Cir.1988), *cert. denied*, 489 U.S. 1081, 109 S.Ct. 1535, 103 L.Ed.2d 840 (1989), the Second Circuit reversed the district court's dismissal of a suit brought by a corporation wholly owned by the government of Iran. Although the United States did not recognize Iran at the time, the court accepted the view of the U.S. Justice and State Departments, which argued in an *amicus* brief that this plaintiff should have access to U.S. courts:

> Two reasons support this holding. First, as this century draws to a close, the practice of extending formal recognition to new governments has altered: The United States Department of State has sometimes refrained from announcing recognition of a new government because grants of recognition have been misinterpreted as pronouncements of approval. As a result, the absence of formal recognition cannot serve as the touchstone for determining whether the Executive Branch has "recognized" a foreign nation for the purpose of granting that government access to United States courts.
>
> Second, the power to deal with foreign nations outside the bounds of formal recognition is essential to a president's implied power to maintain international relations. *Cf. United States v. Curtiss–Wright Export Corp.*, 299 U.S. 304, 318–20, 57 S.Ct. 216, 220–21, 81 L.Ed. 255 (1936). As part of this power, the Executive Branch must have the latitude to permit a foreign nation access to U.S. courts, even if that nation is not formally recognized by the U.S. government.

Id. at 554–55. Would it be preferable to allow unrecognized governments access to U.S. courts unless the executive branch expressly objects?

5. *Comparing Recognition and the Establishment of Diplomatic Relations*. Recognition by the executive branch is ordinarily a prerequisite for the establishment of diplomatic relations. As noted above, nonrecognition traditionally meant that the unrecognized state or government could not sue in U.S. court. Should a government with which the United States does not maintain diplomatic relations be similarly barred? The U.S. Supreme Court addressed the issue in Banco Nacional de Cuba v. Sabbatino, 376 U.S. 398, 410, 84 S.Ct. 923, 930–31, 11 L.Ed.2d 804, 819 (1964):

> Respondents, pointing to the severance of diplomatic relations, commercial embargo, and freezing of Cuban assets in this country, contend that relations between the United States and Cuba manifest such animosity that unfriendliness is clear, and that the courts should be closed to the Cuban Government. We do not agree. This Court would hardly be competent to undertake assessments of varying degrees of friendliness or its absence, and, lacking some definite touchstone for determination, we are constrained to consider any relationship, short of war, with a recognized sovereign power as embracing the privilege of resorting to United States courts. Although the severance of diplomatic

relations is an overt act with objective significance in the dealings of sovereign states, we are unwilling to say that it should inevitably result in the withdrawal of the privilege of bringing suit. Severance may take place for any number of political reasons, its duration is unpredictable, and whatever expression of animosity it may imply does not approach that implicit in a declaration of war.

Is it sensible to treat the effects of nonrecognition and severance of diplomatic relations differently? Do recognition and the establishment of diplomatic relations serve different functions?

KADIC v. KARADZIC

70 F.3d 232 (2d Cir.1995), *cert. denied*, 518 U.S. 1005,
116 S.Ct. 2524, 135 L.Ed.2d 1048 (1996).

Jon O. Newman, Chief Judge:

Most Americans would probably be surprised to learn that victims of atrocities committed in Bosnia are suing the leader of the insurgent Bosnia–Serb forces in a United States District Court in Manhattan. Their claims seek to build upon the foundation of this Court's decision in *Filartiga v. Pena–Irala*, 630 F.2d 876 (2d Cir.1980), which recognized the important principle that the venerable Alien Tort Act, 28 U.S.C. § 1350 (1988), enacted in 1789 but rarely invoked since then, validly creates federal court jurisdiction for suits alleging torts committed anywhere in the world against aliens in violation of the law of nations. * * *

These issues arise on appeals by two groups of plaintiffs-appellants from the November 19, 1994, judgment of the United States District Court for the Southern District of New York (Peter K. Leisure, Judge), dismissing, for lack of subject matter jurisdiction, their suits against defendant-appellee Radovan Karadžić, President of the self-proclaimed Bosnian–Serb republic of "Srpska." For reasons set forth below, we hold that subject matter jurisdiction exists, that Karadžić may be found liable for genocide, war crimes, and crimes against humanity in his private capacity and for other violations in his capacity as a state actor, and that he is not immune from service of process. We therefore reverse and remand.

The plaintiffs-appellants are Croat and Muslim citizens of the internationally recognized nation of Bosnia–Herzegovina, formerly a republic of Yugoslavia. Their complaints, which we accept as true for purposes of this appeal, allege that they are victims, and representatives of victims, of various atrocities, including brutal acts of rape, forced prostitution, forced impregnation, torture, and summary execution, carried out by Bosnian–Serb military forces as part of a genocidal campaign conducted in the course of the Bosnian civil war. Karadžić, formerly a citizen of Yugoslavia and now a citizen of Bosnia–Herzegovina, is the President of a three-man presidency of the self-proclaimed Bosnian–Serb republic within Bosnia–Herzegovina, sometimes referred to as "Srpska," which claims to exercise lawful authority, and does in fact exercise actual control, over large parts of the territory of Bosnia–Herzegovina. In his capacity as President, Karadžić possesses ultimate command authority over the Bosnian–Serb military forces, and the injuries perpetrated upon plaintiffs were committed as part of a pattern of systematic human rights violations that was directed by Karadžić and carried out by the military forces under his command. The complaints allege that Karadžić acted in an official capacity either as the titular head of Srpska or in collaboration with the government of the recognized nation of the former Yugoslavia and its dominant constituent republic, Serbia.

The two groups of plaintiffs asserted causes of action for genocide, rape, forced prostitution and impregnation, torture and other cruel, inhuman, and degrading treatment, assault and battery, sex and ethnic inequality, summary execution, and wrongful death. They sought compensatory and punitive damages, attorney's fees, and, in one of the cases, injunctive relief. * * *

* * * Our decision in *Filartiga* established that [the Alien Tort Act] offers federal subject-matter jurisdiction when the following three conditions are satisfied: (1) an alien sues (2) for a tort (3) committed in violation of the law of nations (*i.e.*, international law). The first two requirements are plainly satisfied here, and the only disputed issue is whether plaintiffs have pleaded violations of international law. * * *

We do not agree that the law of nations, as understood in the modern era, confines its reach to state action. Instead, we hold that certain forms of conduct violate the law of nations whether undertaken by those acting under the auspices of a state or only as private individuals. [The court concludes that genocide and war crimes are violations of international law that may be committed by individuals and may give rise to Alien Tort Act claims against individuals.]

* * * However, torture and summary execution—when not perpetrated in the course of genocide or war crimes—are proscribed by international law only when committed by state officials or under color of law. *See* Declaration on Torture art. 1 (defining torture as being "inflicted by or at the instigation of a public official"); Convention Against Torture and Other Cruel, Inhuman, or Degrading Treatment or Punishment pt. I, art. 1, 23 I.L.M. 1027 (1984), *as modified*, 24 I.L.M. 535 (1985), *entered into force* June 26, 1987, *ratified by United States* Oct. 21, 1994, 34 I.L.M. 590, 591 (1995) (defining torture as "inflicted by or at the instigation of or with the consent or acquiescence of a public official or other person acting in an official capacity"); Torture Victim [Protection] Act [of 1991, Pub. L. No. 102–256, 106 Stat. 73 (1992), *codified at* 28 U.S.C. § 1350 note,] § 2(a) (imposing liability on individuals acting "under actual or apparent authority, or color of law, of any foreign nation").

* * * The definition of a state is well established in international law:

> Under international law, a state is an entity that has a defined territory and permanent population, under the control of its own

government, and that engages in, or has the capacity to engage in, formal relations with other such entities.

Restatement (Third) [of the Foreign Relations Law of the United States] § 201. * * *

The customary international law of human rights, such as the proscription of official torture, applies to states without distinction between recognized and unrecognized states. *See Restatement (Third)* §§ 207, 702. It would be anomalous indeed if non-recognition by the United States, which typically reflects disfavor with a foreign regime— sometimes due to human rights abuses—had the perverse effect of shielding officials of the unrecognized regime from liability for those violations of international law norms that apply only to state actors.

Appellants' allegations entitle them to prove that Karadžić's regime satisfies the criteria for a state, for purposes of those international law violations requiring state action. Srpska is alleged to control defined territory, control populations within its power, and to have entered into agreements with other governments. It has a president, a legislature, and its own currency. These circumstances readily appear to satisfy the criteria for a state in all aspects of international law. Moreover, it is likely that the state action concept, where applicable for some violations like "official" torture, requires merely the semblance of official authority. The inquiry, after all, is whether a person purporting to wield official power has exceeded internationally recognized standards of civilized conduct, not whether statehood in all its formal aspects exists.

* * * Appellants also sufficiently alleged that Karadžić acted under color of law insofar as they claimed that he acted in concert with the former Yugoslavia, the statehood of which is not disputed. The "color of law" jurisprudence of 42 U.S.C. § 1983 is a relevant guide to whether a defendant has engaged in official action for purposes of jurisdiction under the Alien Tort Act. A private individual acts under color of law within the meaning of section 1983 when he acts together with state officials or with significant state aid. The appellants are entitled to prove their allegations that Karadžić acted under color of law of Yugoslavia by acting in concert with Yugoslav officials or with significant Yugoslavian aid.

REPUBLIC OF CROATIA ET AL. v. GIROCREDIT BANK A.G. DER SPARKASSEN

Supreme Court of Austria, Dec. 17, 1996,
36 *International Legal Materials* 1520 (1997).

The Supreme Court, * * * in the cause of the Plaintiffs (1) Republic of Croatia, (2) National Bank of Croatia, * * * (3) Republic of Macedonia, (4) National Bank of Macedonia, * * * versus the Defendant Giro-Credit Bank Aktiengesellschaft der Sparkassen, Schubertring 5, Vienna, * * * to cease and desist and render accounts * * *.

On the appeal of the Defendant against the decision of the Higher Provincial Court of Vienna as the Court of Appeal, of 29 July 1996, upholding the decision of the Vienna Commercial Court of 16 January 1996, has taken the following Decision: * * * With respect to the first and third Plaintiffs the decision is upheld. * * *

The National Bank of the Socialist Federal Republic of Yugoslavia (hereinafter SFRY) had concluded banking contracts with the Defendant, on the basis of which funds were invested upon interest in Austria and assets were deposited.

The SFRY has been dissolved by "dismembratio." The successor States of Croatia, Macedonia, Slovenia, Bosnia–Herzegovina and the Federal Republic of Yugoslavia have so far not reached any agreement on the distribution of the assets and liabilities of the SFRY. The National Bank of the Federal Republic of Yugoslavia, founded in 1993, claims to be the sole lawful successor to the former National Bank of the SFRY. * * *

In order to secure their claims made * * * to cease and desist and to render accounts, the Plaintiffs applied for an interim injunction * * *. [Plaintiffs obtained an injunction in Austria's Court of First Instance, which was upheld by the Court of Appeal.]

While the rights and obligations resulting from the banking contract itself are to be judged under the law of the place of the establishment of the credit institution, *i.e.*, under Austrian law, the question as to whether the assets invested by the National Bank of the SFRY in Austria were held by the National Bank as an independent legal entity or constituted State property (in terms of international law) are to be assessed according to the then domestic law of the SFRY.

It is in this sense that Art. 8 of the 1983 "Vienna Convention on Succession of States in Respect of State Property, Archives and Debts," prepared by the International Law Commission, defines "State property of the predecessor State" as property and rights which, at the date of the succession of States, were, according to the internal law of the predecessor State, owned by that State. The purpose of this codification was to formulate existing customary international law. * * *

[The court discusses various provisions of the National Bank Act of the SFRY.] The legal personality of the National Bank of the SFRY is defined in Art. 91 of said Act. It was a "socialized" legal person, which is to be seen in contrast to a legal person under private law. Its organs were appointed by the Federal Parliament and responsible to it. The Parliament also adopted the Statutes of the National Bank as the basis of its organization (Art. 93 and Art. 96). The National Bank performed its activities in political dependence, it had no political autonomy. It was directly subject to political influence.

All these provisions taken together show that the assets of the National Bank of the SFRY—although it enjoyed legal personality as a "socialized company"—formed part of State property of the SFRY according to international law, which in the case of a "dismembratio" has to be distributed among the successor States. * * *

While the Federal Republic of Yugoslavia considers itself to be the sole successor State to the SFRY and identical with it, the international community unanimously views the disintegration of the SFRY as a case of "dismembratio." In international law this means the complete dissolution of the predecessor State and replacement by several successor States.

The opinion of the international community is expressed in the following documents:

In Security Council Resolution 757 (1992) it was stated that the claim of the successor States of Serbia and Montenegro to continue automatically the membership of the former SFRY in the United Nations was not recognized.

In Security Council Resolution 777 (1992) the view was expressed that the SFRY had ceased to exist, that there was no identity of the Federal Republic of Yugoslavia, consisting of Serbia and Montenegro, with the former State of the SFRY. The Federal Republic of Yugoslavia could not participate in the General Assembly of the United Nations and would have first to apply for membership.

Pursuant to a recommendation of the Security Council, the General Assembly of the United Nations decided in a Resolution of 22 September 1992 that the Federal Republic of Yugoslavia should apply for membership and could not participate in the work of the General Assembly.

The Arbitration Commission set up by the Members of the European Community and chaired by Badinter also dealt with the question of State succession and in its Opinions No. 1, 8 and 10 (1992) held the view that the SFRY had been dissolved and had ceased to exist, that the Federal Republic of Yugoslavia was one of the successor States and not the sole legal successor. This view was also supported in a declaration of the European Political Cooperation of 20 July 1992 as well as the EU Declaration of 9 April 1996 on the Recognition of the Federal Republic of Yugoslavia as a successor State.

On the basis of this, Austria recognized the Federal Republic of Yugoslavia as one of the successor States of the SFRY and as an independent and sovereign Member of the community of States (Note of the Federal Minister for Foreign Affairs of the Republic of Austria of 17 April 1996, presented to the Federal Republic of Yugoslavia on 25 April 1996).

In terms of international law, the disintegration of the SFRY therefore is to be regarded as a case of "dismembratio." The SFRY as a subject of international law has ceased to exist, its State territory has been divided among five successor States, which have in the meantime been recognized by Austria.

Under customary international law, in the case of "dismembratio," State property is to be distributed according to the international principle of "equity." In such a case Art. 18 of the "Vienna Convention on Succession of States in Respect of State Property, Archives and Debts" of 1983 prepared by the International Law Commission provides for the passing of movable State property to the successor States in "equitable proportions." Thus, the successor States have an international law title to distribution recognized by the community of States.

Resolution 1022 of the [Security Council] of the United Nations, leaving it to the Member States to release funds and assets frozen pursuant to Security Council Resolutions 757 and 820, specifically points out in operative paragraph 6 that these funds and assets had to be released without prejudice to claims of the successor States to such property. Moreover, operative paragraph 5 provides (this being binding on Members) that property being subject to legal action shall remain frozen until released in accordance with applicable law.

Also the EU Arbitration Commission chaired by Badinter states in its Opinion No. 9 that State property of the SFRY located in third countries must be distributed equitably among the successor States in accordance with an agreement to be reached among them.

The requirement of an agreement among the successor States on the distribution [of assets] is also evident from the EU Declaration of 9 April 1996.

The question of whether this international law title to distribution held by the successor States can be secured by an interim injunction by Austrian courts according to § 381(1) of the [Austrian] Enforcement Code need not be decided as in view of the assets invested in Austria the first and third Plaintiffs in any case hold securable private law claims in their capacity as members of the resulting joint-ownership community.

The theory of "communio incidens" developed by the Supreme Court for cases of extinction of the legal personality of a foreign corporation is also to be applied to the matter under consideration.

As a result of the disintegration of the SFRY by "dismembratio," the legal personalities of that State and its National Bank ceased to exist. The property attributable to the State (of the SFRY) is to be distributed among the successor States in accordance with international agreements still to be concluded. As far as funds and assets deposited with Austrian banks are concerned, surrendering the joint property to only one of the successor States—ignoring the claims of the other members of such a community—would even more amount to the recognition of an expropriation without compensation in the State of the actual administrative seat, as the Federal Republic of Yugoslavia claims to be the sole successor State to the SFRY, if not identical with it. As the confiscation of property, being contrary to *ordre public*, does not extend to property located in Austria of a legal person the extinction of which has to be recognized in Austria under § 12 of the [Austrian] Federal Statute on Private International Law, such property constitutes a "communio incidens," *i.e.*, a joint-ownership community of all successor States. Each member of this community thus has only a joint-ownership claim vis-a-vis the Defendant, which would be—illegally—infringed upon by any unilateral acts of disposal by one of them. Hence, each member of this community has a private law claim to the maintenance of the status quo, thus also a legal claim against the Defendant to desist from any disposal of such property as long as the successor States do not jointly dispose of such funds and assets.

This right can be secured by an interim injunction according to § 381(1) of the [Austrian] Enforcement Code.

In view of the position of the National Bank of the Federal Republic of Yugoslavia claiming to be the sole legal successor to the National Bank of the SFRY and thus exclusively entitled to dispose of the accounts administered by the Defendant, in view of the efforts made by the Federal Republic of Yugoslavia to gain access to the funds and assets of the former SFRY everywhere in Europe, evidenced by the affidavit of 11 January 1996, as well as in view of the content of the correspondence between the Plaintiffs and the Defendant, the Court of Appeal was right in assuming an actual risk to the claims of the first and third Plaintiffs as members of the communio incidens. It is a fact that the Defendant had, by reference to the existing banking contracts, refused to (continue to) freeze the accounts and deposits as demanded by the Plaintiffs and had thus made payments to the Federal Republic of Yugoslavia appear probable as soon as the latter would raise such claims based on the banking contracts concluded between the former National Bank of the SFRY and the Defendant * * *.

However, only the first and third Plaintiffs [the Republic of Croatia and the Republic of Macedonia] in their capacity as legitimate successor States to the SFRY are to be regarded as members of this joint-ownership community. * * * Opinion No. 15 of the Arbitration Commission of the European Union chaired by Badinter was not adequate to prove a claim for an injunction on the part of the second and fourth Plaintiffs [the National Bank of Croatia and the National Bank of Macedonia]. This Opinion does specifically state (Question 5b) that the respective successor States will have to determine whether the rights and obligations to be assumed by them will be taken over by the State itself or its National Bank. Proof of the fact that the National Banks of Croatia and Macedonia are entitled to bring a claim against said funds and assets was, however, not submitted by the Plaintiffs.

Notes and Questions

1. *The Break-up of Yugoslavia.* Both *GiroCredit Bank* and *Kadic* arose in the context of the break-up of Yugoslavia. Yugoslavia originally known as the "Serb–Croat–Slovene State," was recognized as independent in treaties following World War I. It was composed of Macedonia, Croatia, Slovenia, and Bosnia and Herzegovina, all of which had been under the control of the Austrian–Hungarian Empire, and of independent Serbia and nominally independent Montenegro. Following World War II, the government of Marshall Tito headed the Socialist Federal Republic of Yugoslavia (SFRY) for

many years. During 1991–1992, the SFRY broke up into what are now generally recognized as Croatia, Bosnia–Herzegovina, Slovenia, and The Former Yugoslav Republic of Macedonia; two other components of the SFRY, Serbia and Montenegro, form the Federal Republic of Yugoslavia. Since 1991–1992, fighting among ethnic groups has plagued the region.

The European Community, now known as the European Union, and its member states convened a Yugoslav peace conference in 1991. As part of its peace efforts, the EC established an Arbitration Commission to engage in fact-finding and render legal opinions concerning aspects of the Yugoslav crisis. Beginning in August 1992, the Conference on the Former Yugoslavia, co-chaired by the Secretary–General of the United Nations and the head of the state holding the Presidency of the EC Council of Ministers, served as a forum for discussions and proposals concerning sanctions, cessation of violence, transit, humanitarian aid, and compliance with United Nations resolutions. The Conference structure was terminated in January 1996, and efforts toward peace in the former Yugoslavia were pursued through the 1995 General Framework Agreement for Peace in Bosnia and Herzegovina (the Dayton Accords) and initiatives involving the United Nations and the North Atlantic Treaty Organization. We revisit the situation in the former Yugoslavia at the end of this Chapter and again in Chapter 9, when we examine the role of the United Nations and regional organizations in efforts to settle armed conflicts.

2. *Human Rights, Recognition, and Succession.* The *Kadic Case* serves as a reminder that municipal courts may decide cases involving international human rights law, a topic explored in Chapter 6. Should a U.S. court find Srpska to be a successor state to the former Yugoslavia, even though the United States government has not recognized Srpska? Would other forums also consider Srpska to be a state? Is it likely that Srpska would be regarded as a state with respect to issues other than those being litigated in the *Kadic Case,* such as admission to the United Nations or entitlement to share in Yugoslav accounts in an Austrian bank? Is it appropriate for the same entity to be considered a state for some purposes and not others?

3. *The Interplay of International and Municipal Law.* The court in the *GiroCredit Bank Case* used Austrian law to judge rights and obligations under the banking contract. In order to determine whether the Austrian assets of the National Bank of the SFRY were "state property," however, the court referred to a 1983 treaty, which in turn defined state property of a predecessor state in terms of the municipal law of the predecessor state, thus requiring the court to look to the law of the SFRY. When it came to determining the appropriate remedy for the plaintiff successor states, the court relied on Austrian law and its theory of *communio incidens,* although a similar remedy could have been identified in international law and applied in the case in accordance with Austria's constitutional law principles regarding the use of international law. See Konrad G. Bühler, "Two Recent Austrian Supreme Court Decisions on State Succession from an International Law Perspective," 2 *Austrian Review of International and European Law* 213, 233–38 (1997).

Austria's implementation of United Nations Security Council decisions affected the timing of the lawsuit. The National Bank had deposited funds with Austrian commercial banks before the break-up of Yugoslavia began in 1991. Yet Croatia and Macedonia did not seek an injunction to keep the National Bank from turning over the funds to the Serbian-dominated Federal Republic of Yugoslavia until February 1996. Before then Austria had frozen Yugoslav accounts in Austria in accordance with U.N. Security Council Resolutions 757 (1992), 31 I.L.M. 1453 (1992), and 820 (1993), 47 U.N.Y.B. 471 (1993), resolutions adopted to reduce the amount of hard currency available to Yugoslav President Milosevic. Just prior to this lawsuit, Austria had repealed its freezing orders by implementing Security Council Resolution 1022 (1995), 35 I.L.M. 259 (1996), which endorsed the results of the Dayton Accords. More on the legal effect of U.N. Security Council decisions appears in Chapters 8 and 9.

Finally, the Austrian court looked to international legal sources to determine the critical issue of whether Yugoslavia had dissolved into entirely new states, or whether the Federal Republic of Yugoslavia was the successor state to the SFRY. What was the significance of recognition with respect to this conclusion? Should the court have considered the objective characteristics stressed by the Federal Republic, and asked whether the Federal Republic retained a substantial percentage of the SFRY's territory, resources, and population, as well as its seat of government?

4. *Succession to Assets and the Use of Equity.* The *GiroCredit Bank* court concluded that, following the dissolution of the SFRY, international law required the National Bank's accounts to be distributed equitably among the successor states pursuant to agreement. What is the meaning of equity in this context? What factors ought to be taken into account in negotiating an agreement? Should state property be divided on a per capita basis, or according to historical shares of tax revenues received from different regions of the predecessor state? Should property that can be placed within the territory of the predecessor state be allocated based on its physical location? Equity is also invoked with respect to other succession issues, such as succession in respect of debt. See Daniel S. Blum, "The Apportionment of Public Debt and Assets During State Secession," 29 *Case Western Reserve Journal of International Law* 263 (1997); and see the *North Sea Cases* and the accompanying Notes in Chapter 3 for discussion of various meanings of equity in international law.

5. *The Variety of Succession Issues.* According to one court, "[t]he problem of State succession is one of the most disputed areas of international law." Espionage Prosecution Case (Case No. 2 BGs 38/91), 94 Int'l L. Rep. 68, 77–78 (Ger. Fed. Sup. Ct., 1991). The variety of state succession issues makes generalizations about this area of law difficult. Succession may affect contract obligations (as in the *Tinoco Arbitration*, albeit that case involved a succession of governments), state property (as in the *GiroCredit Bank Case*), archives and cultural heritage, treaties, membership in international organizations, and nationality of citizens. Part of the complexity also stems from the various ways in which states may appear, disappear, or change. Sometimes states dissolve into entirely new states, as the *GiroCredit Bank* court concluded was true of the SFRY, and sometimes states secede from a state that continues in existence. If states merge, they may form an entirely new state, or one state may absorb another. Sometimes a state grows when a neighboring state cedes some of its territory or loses it in a war. Particularly

in the absence of agreements addressing succession issues, the applicable legal rules may be much debated. Municipal courts provide guidance on some succession issues, as in the *GiroCredit Bank Case*, but the issues frequently arise in diplomatic or other political contexts.

6. *Succession to Treaties.* Agreements may address what is to become of treaty obligations when new states emerge as a result of secession, the disintegration of existing states, or independence from a colonial power. See, *e.g.,* Marian Nash (Leich), "Contemporary Practice of the United States Relating to International Law: Succession of States," 89 *American Journal of International Law* 761 (1995). Sometimes, however, as in the break-up of Yugoslavia, successor states make no agreements concerning preexisting treaties. Should the emergence of a new state always be considered a "fundamental change of circumstances," under which the new state could avoid its treaty obligations? See Chapter 2, and especially Note 3, page 79. The Vienna Convention on Succession of States in Respect of Treaties, arts. 2(f), 16, Aug. 23, 1978, 17 I.L.M. 1488 (1978), takes the position that a "newly independent" state, defined as a previously dependent territory "for the international relations of which the predecessor state was responsible," is entitled to begin life with a "clean slate," not bound by its predecessor's treaties. When parts of the territory of an existing state separate to form one or more new states, however, many treaties are said to continue in force. See *id.* art. 34. Is it sensible to distinguish among types of new states for the purpose of succession of treaty obligations? What practical reasons support a general presumption that treaties should continue in force for all successor states?

Should distinctions be made among types of treaties for the purpose of succession? Treaties that establish international boundaries or other territorial regimes generally continue in existence in cases of state succession. See Case Concerning the Gabcíkovo-Nagymaros Project (Hungary/Slovakia), 1997 I.C.J. 3, 1997 WL 289957 (1997). What about human rights treaties, which provide rights for individuals? Treaties concerning alliances and diplomatic exchanges? Commercial and extradition treaties? Should the same general presumptions concerning succession apply to bilateral and multilateral treaties?

7. *Succession to Membership in International Organizations.* Succession to membership in an international organization requires satisfying its membership standards, as revealed in the organization's charter and practice. The *GiroCredit Bank* court described the United Nations' treatment of the membership of the Federal Republic of Yugoslavia. What explains the U.N. action, given that Russia was allowed to retain the U.N. membership of the Soviet Union when it broke apart, and India was permitted to keep the U.N. membership of British India when Pakistan and India separated in 1947? Note that the Federal Republic of Yugoslavia was the subject of U.N. Security Council sanctions for its aggressive actions in Croatia and Bosnia–Herzegovina. Also, unlike the cases of Russia and India, no devolution agreement specified the entity entitled to continuing U.N. membership. Furthermore, Russia and India, unlike the Federal Republic of Yugoslavia, each had a majority of the predecessor state's territory, population, and resources. See Michael P. Scharf, "Musical Chairs: The Dissolution of States and Membership in the United Nations," 28 *Cornell International Law*

Journal 29 (1995). Croatia, Bosnia–Herzegovina, Slovenia, and The Former Yugoslav Republic of Macedonia were all admitted as U.N. members in 1992 and 1993. On November 1, 2000, the Federal Republic of Yugoslavia was admitted to the United Nations, when Yugoslav President Slobadan Milosevic was voted out of office.

8. *New States and Customary International Law.* Decision-makers typically consider new states to be bound by customary international law. Why should Srpska or the Federal Republic of Yugoslavia, if they are new states, be bound by customary rules that were formed before they came into existence? Customary international law is considered in Chapter 3.

C. SELF–DETERMINATION

The meaning of "self-determination" is much debated in international law. Although it is clear that the concept of self-determination relates to group rather than individual rights, what groups comprise the relevant "self"? And once consensus develops that some group is entitled to self-determination, what legal consequences follow? How should the wishes of a group that is entitled to self-determination be determined and implemented?

The principle of self-determination gained prominence in international relations at the Paris Peace Conference at the end of World War I. U.S. President Woodrow Wilson believed that national self-determination was important in maintaining a peaceful international society. For Wilson, self-determination had both an "external" aspect (freedom from alien rule) and an "internal" aspect (promotion of democratic institutions). In an address to the Senate in 1917, Wilson said: "No peace can last, or ought to last, which does not recognize and accept the principle that governments derive all their just powers from the consent of the governed, and that no right anywhere exists to hand peoples about from sovereignty to sovereignty as if they were property." Sen. Doc. No. 685, 64th Cong., 2d Sess. 6. Wilson particularly championed self-determination in regulating the break-up of the Austro–Hungarian and Ottoman Empires. The Soviet leader at the time, Vladimir Lenin, also forcefully espoused, at least on the international level, a right of self-determination. Lenin's view of self-determination contained an anti-colonial emphasis. He argued that peoples under colonial rule had the right to gain their independence, a position that was closely tied to his more fundamental goal of achieving socialism on a global basis. While Wilson also thought that self-determination should be taken into account in settling colonial claims, he sought to balance self-determination concerns with the interests of the colonial powers, and to implement claims to self-determination in an orderly, nonviolent manner.

This Part examines changing conceptions of self-determination in international law. We start with a decision of the League of Nations' Committee of Jurists, which concluded that self-determination posed an international legal question in the particular context of the claims of the Aaland Islanders following World War I. Following this decision is a case addressing whether Quebec has a legal right to secede from Canada. The case reviews the legal significance of self-determination in the decolonization movement after World War II. Nowadays, claims for self-determination are raised outside the decolonization context, as ethnic, cultural, linguistic, and religious groups seek to break away from existing states or to conclude special autonomy relationships with them.

REPORT OF THE INTERNATIONAL COMMITTEE OF JURISTS ON THE LEGAL ASPECTS OF THE AALAND ISLANDS QUESTION

League of Nations Official Journal, Special Supp. No. 3 (1920).

At a meeting held on the 12th July, 1920, the Council of the League of Nations, assembled at London, unanimously adopted with the assent of Finland and Sweden, the opposing parties in a dispute as to whether the inhabitants of the Aaland Islands should "be authorized to determine forthwith by plebiscite whether the archipelago should remain under Finnish sovereignty or be incorporated in the kingdom of Sweden," the following resolution:

"An International Commission of three jurists shall be appointed for the purpose of submitting to the Council, with the least possible delay, their opinion on the following points:

(1) Whether, within the meaning of paragraph 8 of Article 15 of the Covenant, the case presented by Sweden to the Council with reference to the Aaland Islands deals with a question that should, according to International Law, be entirely left to the domestic jurisdiction of Finland. * * *" * * *

THE PRINCIPLE OF SELF-DETERMINATION AND THE RIGHTS OF PEOPLE.

Although the principle of self-determination of peoples plays an important part in modern political thought, especially since the Great War, it must be pointed out that there is no mention of it in the Covenant of the League of Nations. The recognition of this principle in a certain number of international treaties cannot be considered as sufficient to put it upon the same footing as a positive rule of the Law of Nations.

On the contrary, in the absence of express provisions in international treaties, the right of disposing of national territory is essentially an attribute of the sovereignty of every State. Positive International Law does not recognize the right of national groups, as such, to separate themselves from the State of which they form part by the simple expression of a wish, any more than it recognizes the right of other States to claim such a separation. Generally speaking, the grant or refusal of the right to a portion of its population of determining its own political fate by plebiscite or by some other method, is, exclusively, an attribute of the sovereignty of every State which is definitively constituted. A dispute between two States concerning such a question, under normal conditions therefore, bears upon a question which International Law leaves entirely to the domestic jurisdiction of one of the States concerned. Any other solution would amount to an infringement of sovereign rights of a State and would involve the risk of creating difficulties and a lack of stability which would not only be contrary to the very idea embodied in term "State," but would also endanger the interests of the international community. If this right is not possessed by a large or small section of a nation, neither can it be held by the State to which the National group wishes to be attached, nor by any other State.

The Commission, in affirming these principles, does not give an opinion concerning the question as to whether a manifest and continued abuse of sovereign power, to the detriment of a section of the population of a State, would, if such circumstances arose, give to an international dispute, arising therefrom, such a character that its object should be considered as one which is not confined to the domestic jurisdiction of the State concerned, but comes within the sphere of action of the League of Nations. Such a supposition certainly does not apply to the case under consideration, and has not been put forward by either of the parties to the dispute.

De facto and *de jure* Considerations. Their International Character.

3. It must, however, be observed that all that has been said concerning the attributes of the sovereignty of a State, generally speaking, only applies to a nation which is definitively constituted as a sovereign State and an independent member of the international community, and so long as it continues to possess these characteristics. From the point of view of both domestic and international law, the formation, transformation and dismemberment of States as a result of revolutions and wars create situations of fact which, to a large extent, cannot be met by the application of the normal rules of positive law. This amounts to a statement that if the essential basis of these rules, that is to say, territorial sovereignty, is lacking, either because the State is not yet fully formed or because it is undergoing transformation or dissolution, the situation is obscure and uncertain from a legal point of view, and will not become clear until the period of development is completed and a definite new situation, which is normal in respect to territorial sovereignty, has been established.

This transition from a *de facto* situation to a normal situation *de jure* cannot be considered as one confined entirely within the domestic jurisdiction of a State. It tends to lead to readjustments between the members of the international community and to alterations in their territorial and legal status; consequently, this transition interests the community of States very deeply both from political and legal standpoints.

Self-Determination as Applied to *de facto* Situations. Its Forms.

Under such circumstances, the principle of self-determination of peoples may be called into play. New aspirations of certain sections of a nation, which are sometimes based on old traditions or on a common language and civilisation, may come to the surface and produce effects which must be taken into account in the interests of the internal and external peace of nations.

The principle recognising the rights of peoples to determine their political fate may be applied in various ways; the most important of these are, on the one hand the formation of an independent State, and on the other hand the right of choice between two existing States. This principle, however, must be brought into line with that of the protection of minorities; both have a common object—to assure to some national Group the maintenance and free development of its social, ethnical or religious characteristics.

The protection of minorities is already provided for, to a very varying extent, in a fairly large number of constitutions. This principle appears to be one of the essential characteristics of liberty at the present time. Under certain circumstances, however, it has been thought necessary to go further, and to guarantee, by international treaties, some particular situation to certain racial or religious minorities. Thus, in some recent treaties a special legal régime, under the control and guarantee of the League of Nations, has been established for certain sections of the population of a State.

The fact must, however, not be lost sight of that the principle that nations must have the right of self-determination is not the only one to be taken into account. Even though it be regarded as the most important of the principles governing the formation of States, geographical, economic and other similar considerations may put obstacles in the way of its complete recognition. Under such circumstances, a solution in the nature of a compromise, based on an extensive grant of liberty to minorities, may appear necessary according to international legal conception and may even be dictated by the interests of peace.

HISTORICAL DEVELOPMENT OF FINLAND.

4. In the light of the foregoing, the question has to be decided as to whether, from the standpoint of territorial sovereignty, the situation of the Aaland Islands in the independent State of Finland is of a definite and normal character, or whether it is a transitory or not fully developed situation. * * *

* * * [T]he State of Finland, which since 1899 was in fact treated by the Russian Government as an ordinary province, had not and also never claimed to have an independent legal existence in external affairs and was indissolubly bound to Russia. * * *

DECLARATION OF INDEPENDENCE.

* * * [T]he Finnish Diet, on the 15th November, 1917, assumed the supreme power and constituted a national Government which, on the 4th December, 1917, sent forth an appeal to the Finnish people exhorting them to make every effort to enable Finland to take her place as an

independent nation among the other nations. During the events which followed, this object was ultimately attained. * * *

INTERNAL SITUATION OF FINLAND.

In addition to these facts which bear upon the external relations of Finland, the very abnormal character of her internal situation must be brought out. This situation was such that, for a considerable time, the conditions required for the formation of a sovereign State did not exist.

In the midst of revolution and anarchy, certain elements essential to the existence of a State, even some elements of fact, were lacking for a fairly considerable period. Political and social life was disorganized; the authorities were not strong enough to assert themselves; civil war was rife; further, the Diet, the legality of which had been disputed by a large section of the people, had been dispersed by the revolutionary party, and the Government had been chased from the capital and forcibly prevented from carrying out its duties; the armed camps and the police were divided into two opposing forces, and Russian troops, and after a time Germans also, took part in the civil war between the inhabitants and between the Red and White Finnish troops.

It is, therefore, difficult to say at what exact date the Finnish Republic, in the legal sense of the term, actually became a definitely constituted sovereign State. * * * It would appear that it was in May, 1918, that the civil war ended and that the foreign troops began to leave the country, so that from that time onwards it was possible to reestablish order and normal political and social life, little by little.

It follows from all these facts that the formation of an independent State of Finland in 1917 and 1918, whatever may have been the legal status of Finland formerly under the Russian Empire, must be considered, at any rate in several aspects, as a new political phenomenon and not as a mere continuation of a previously existing political entity. * * *

THE PURPORT OF THE FINNISH DECLARATION OF INDEPENDENCE.

The Aaland Islands were undoubtedly part of Finland during the period of Russian rule. Must they, for this reason alone, be considered as definitely incorporated *de jure* in the State of Finland which was formed as a result of the events described above?

The Commission finds it impossible to admit this. The extent and nature of the political changes, which take place as facts and outside the domain of law, are necessarily limited by the results actually produced. These results alone form the basis of the new legal entity which is about to be formed, and it is they which will determine its essential characteristics. If one part of a State actually separates itself from that State, the separation is necessarily limited in its effect to the population of the territory which has taken part in the act of separation. Though the political projects leading to the separation may be manifested in different ways in different parts of the territory, nevertheless these projects all have an equal value as a foundation for the new legal order, though of course only in so far as those who adopt them are able to maintain them. It may even be said that if a separation occurs from a political organism which is more or less autonomous, and which is itself *de facto* in process of political transformation, this organism cannot at the very moment when it transforms itself outside the domain of positive law invoke the principles of this law in order to force upon a national group a political status which the latter refuses to accept. * * *

COMPARISON BETWEEN THE POLITICAL ATTITUDE ON THE MAINLAND OF FINLAND AND ON THE ISLANDS. * * *

* * * The Aaland Islands agitation originated at a time when Finland was undergoing a process of transformation. The fact that Finland was eventually reconstituted as an independent State is not sufficient to efface the conditions which gave rise to the aspirations of the Aaland Islanders and to cause these conditions to be regarded as if they had never arisen. These arguments are emphasized by the fact that the population of the Islands, which is very homogeneous, inhabits a territory which is more or less geographically distinct; further, the population is united by ties of race, language and traditions to the Swedish race, from which it was only separated by force, whereas the population of the Finnish mainland is, for the most part, of Finnish origin, and the small portion of Swedish which has become mingled with it to a large extent shares the ideal of the majority with regard to an independent State of Finland. It must be added that the population of the Islands had no means of asserting its nationalist aspirations during the period of Russian rule. * * *

CONCLUSIONS.

The Commission, after consideration of the arguments set out and developed in the preceding report, have arrived at the following conclusions:—

(1) The dispute between Sweden and Finland does not refer to a definitive established political situation, depending exclusively upon the territorial sovereignty of a State.

(2) On the contrary, the dispute arose from a *de facto* situation caused by the political transformation of the Aaland Islands, which transformation was caused by and originated in the separatist movement among the inhabitants, who quoted the principle of national self-determination, and certain military events which accompanied and followed the separation of Finland from the Russian Empire at a time when Finland had not yet acquired the character of a definitively constituted State.

(3) It follows from the above that the dispute does not refer to a question which is left by International Law to the domestic jurisdiction of Finland.

(4) The Council of the League of Nations, therefore, is competent, under paragraph 4 of Article 15, to make any recommendations which it deems just and proper in the case.

Notes and Questions

1. *Self-determination and the Paris Peace Conference.* At the end of World War I, the Paris Peace Conference consulted with numerous European groups seeking self-determination. In some cases, such as those populations along the border between Germany and Denmark, the Conference agreed to allow local residents to hold plebiscites to help determine border changes. The attention given to self-determination promoted the establishment of Poland and Czechoslovakia as independent states. Talk of self-determination also encouraged the inclusion of formal guarantees for minority rights in peace treaties among the victorious powers and new states. Nevertheless, it is only fair to say that economic, strategic, and geopolitical interests of the Allies proved to be, overall, more important than self-determination in decisions about the shape of Europe after World War I. For additional discussion of the concept of self-determination used at the end of World War I, see Anthony Whelan, "Wilsonian Self-determination and the Versailles Settlement," 43 *International and Comparative Law Quarterly* 99 (1994).

2. *The Aaland Islands Question.* The Aaland Islands question occupied delegates to the Paris Peace Conference. The Aaland Islanders apparently wanted to unite with Sweden, a desire in accord with notions of self-determination. Sweden stressed the Islanders' racial, linguistic, and historical ties to Sweden. Yet, Britain wondered whether Swedish or Finnish control of the Islands would be the greater deterrent to their occupation by a great power, and France thought Finland a better buffer between Bolshevist Russia and Europe than historically neutral Sweden. See James Barros, *The Aaland Islands Question: Its Settlement by the League of Nations* 163, 215 (1968).

When the Aaland Islands question was not resolved at the Peace Conference, the League of Nations took it up, with the result being the first instance of an intergovernmental organization's involvement in structuring an autonomy relationship. After the Committee of Jurists concluded that the League's Council was legally competent to address the politically sensitive question, the Council established a new Commission of Inquiry. This Commission favored continuing Finnish control over the Aaland Islands, citing the Islands' geographical ties to the Finnish mainland and a range of Finnish and international political considerations. League of Nations, *The Aaland Islands Question: Report Submitted to the Council of the League of Nations by the Commission of Rapporteurs* (Doc. B 7.21/68/106) (1921). The League's Council ultimately accepted Finnish sovereignty over the Aaland Islands, but also sought guarantees concerning demilitarization of the Islands (see the Convention Relating to the Non–Fortification and Neutralization of the Aaland Islands, Oct. 21, 1921, 9 L.N.T.S. 211) and autonomy for the Islanders. Finland agreed to support Swedish language schools for the Aaland Islanders, a preemptive right for the Islanders when outsiders sought to buy land, restrictions on the voting rights of immigrants to the Islands, and a say for the citizens of Aaland in the appointment of their governor. See Barros, *supra*, at 330–33. Today, the 25,000 Aaland Islanders retain a significant degree of autonomy. The Islanders separately approved, by referendum, joining with Finland when it acceded to the European Union, and the Islands maintain direct relations with the EU. See *Autonomy and Demilitarisation in International Law: The Aaland Islands in a Changing Europe* (Lauri Hannikainen & Frank Horn eds. 1997).

3. *The Committee of Jurists and the International Legal Right to Self–Determination.* In the view of the Committee of Jurists, the self-determination claim of the Aaland Islanders was not, under international law, reserved to Finland's domestic jurisdiction. Why was this so if, as the Committee says, the principle of self-determination is not "upon the same footing as a positive rule of the Law of Nations"?

4. *Self-determination and the Protection of Minorities.* What should be the relationship between the principle of self-determination and the principle of protection of minorities?

5. *Autonomy and Self-determination.* Autonomy of a group is one possible outcome of applying a right to self-determination. In many ways, the situation of the Aaland Islanders is conducive to arrangements for autonomy. The Aaland Islands are geographically separate from the rest of Finland; their boundaries are definite. The Islanders are homogeneous, overwhelmingly viewing themselves as Swedish. If a distinct group is not confined within clear territorial borders, or if a population within such borders is not homogeneous, should that preclude a legal right to self-determination?

6. *The League of Nations and "Internationalized" Territories.* The League of Nations itself was directly involved in governing certain "internationalized" territories. For example, the League, by virtue of Article 102 of the Versailles Peace Treaty, exercised protection over the Free City of Danzig. Poland conducted Danzig's foreign relations, and Polish customs regulations applied there; Poland also, jointly with Danzig, administered Danzig's port and waterways. The League, however, appointed a High Commissioner who could decide all disputes with respect to the Treaty of Versailles; appeals went to the League's Council, whose decisions were binding on Danzig and Poland. The High Commissioner also could veto any Polish treaty applying to Danzig that he regarded as inconsistent with its "Free City" status, and revisions to Danzig's constitution could enter into force only when the League of Nations declared that it had no objections to them. For discussion of Danzig, other "internationalized" territories, and intellectual conceptions of these new international legal forms, see Nathaniel Berman, " 'But the Alternative is Despair:' Nationalism and the Modernist Renewal of International Law," 106 *Harvard Law Review* 1792, 1874–98 (1993).

7. *The United Nations and Self-determination.* Unlike the Covenant of the League of Nations, the Charter of the United Nations specifically refers to self-determination. Article 1(2) of the Charter provides that one of the purposes of the Organization is "to develop friendly relations among nations based on respect for the principle of equal rights and self-determination of peoples, and to take other appropriate measures to strengthen universal

peace." Article 1(2) is phrased as a general goal, seemingly linked to the more fundamental goal of furthering friendly, peaceful relations among states. The principle of self-determination has also been developed in subsequent widely accepted treaties and in U.N. General Assembly declarations, especially those related to decolonization. Important U.N. instruments are noted in the following case.

REFERENCE RE SECESSION OF QUEBEC

Supreme Court of Canada, Aug. 20, 1998,
37 *International Legal Materials* 1340 (1998).

[The Canadian Supreme Court finds that a "reference," or request for an advisory opinion, from the Canadian Governor in Council was proper with respect to questions relating to the potential secession of Quebec from Canada. The Court first determines that Canadian constitutional law did not permit unilateral secession, although a constitutional duty to negotiate about the issue would arise if Quebecers voted for secession by "a clear majority on a clear question." The Court then turns to the second question the Governor in Council addressed to it:

> Does international law give the National Assembly, legislature or government of Quebec the right to effect the secession of Quebec from Canada unilaterally? In this regard, is there a right to self-determination under international law that would give the National Assembly, legislature or government of Quebec the right to effect the secession of Quebec from Canada unilaterally?]

(1) *Secession at International Law*

111. It is clear that international law does not specifically grant component parts of sovereign states the legal right to secede unilaterally from their "parent" state. * * * Given the lack of specific authorization for unilateral secession, proponents of the existence of such a right at international law are therefore left to attempt to found their argument (i) on the proposition that unilateral secession is not specifically prohibited and that what is not specifically prohibited is inferentially permitted; or (ii) on the implied duty of states to recognize the legitimacy of secession brought about by the exercise of the well-established international law right of "a people" to self-determination. * * *

(a) *Absence of a Specific Prohibition*

112. International law contains neither a right of unilateral secession nor the explicit denial of such a right, although such a denial is, to some extent, implicit in the exceptional circumstances required for secession to be permitted under the right of a people to self-determination, e.g., the right of secession that arises in the exceptional situation of an oppressed or colonial people, discussed below. As will be seen, international law places great importance on the territorial integrity of nation states and, by and large, leaves the creation of a new state to be determined by the domestic law of the existing state of which the seceding entity presently forms a part. Where, as here, unilateral seces-

sion would be incompatible with the domestic Constitution, international law is likely to accept that conclusion subject to the right of peoples to self-determination, a topic to which we now turn.

(b) *The Right of a People to Self-determination*

113. While international law generally regulates the conduct of nation states, it does, in some specific circumstances, also recognize the "rights" of entities other than nation states—such as the right of a *people* to self-determination.

114. The existence of the right of a people to self-determination is now so widely recognized in international conventions that the principle has acquired a status beyond "convention" and is considered a general principle of international law (A. Cassese, *Self-determination of peoples: A legal reappraisal* (1995), at pp. 171–72; K. Doehring, "Self–Determination," in B. Simma, ed., *The Charter of the United Nations: A Commentary* (1994), at p. 70).

115. Article 1[(2)] of the *Charter of the United Nations* states in part that one of the purposes of the United Nations (U.N.) is:

> To develop friendly relations among nations based on respect for the principle of equal rights and self-determination of peoples, and to take other appropriate measures to strengthen universal peace[.]

116. Article 55 of the U.N. *Charter* further states that the U.N. shall promote goals such as higher standards of living, full employment and human rights "[w]ith a view to the creation of conditions of stability and well-being which are necessary for peaceful and friendly relations among nations based on respect for the principle of equal rights and self-determination of peoples." * * *

118. * * * Article 1 of both the U.N.'s *International Covenant on Civil and Political Rights*, 999 U.N.T.S. 171, and its *International Covenant on Economic, Social and Cultural Rights*, 993 U.N.T.S. 3, states:

> All peoples have the right of self-determination. By virtue of that right they freely determine their political status and freely pursue their economic, social and cultural development.

119. Similarly, the U.N. General Assembly's *Declaration on Principles of International Law Concerning Friendly Relations and Co-operation Among States in Accordance with the Charter of the United Nations*, GA Res. 2625 (XXV), 24 October 1970, states:

> By virtue of the principle of equal rights and self-determination of peoples enshrined in the Charter of the United Nations, all peoples have the right freely to determine, without external interference, their political status and to pursue their economic, social and cultural development, and every State has the duty to respect this right in accordance with the provisions of the Charter.

120. In 1993, the U.N. World Conference on Human Rights adopted the *Vienna Declaration and Programme of Action*, A/Conf.

157/24, 25 June 1993, that reaffirmed Article 1 of the two above-mentioned covenants. The U.N. General Assembly's *Declaration on the Occasion of the Fiftieth Anniversary of the United Nations*, GA Res. 50/6 [para. 1], 9 November 1995, also emphasizes the right to self-determination by providing that the U.N.'s member states will:

> Continue to reaffirm the right of *self-determination of all peoples*, taking into account the particular situation of peoples under colonial or other forms of alien domination or foreign occupation, and recognize the right of peoples to take legitimate action in accordance with the Charter of the United Nations to realize their inalienable right of self-determination. *This shall not be construed as authorizing* or encouraging any action that would dismember or impair, totally or in part, the *territorial integrity or political unity of sovereign and independent States* conducting themselves in compliance with the principle of equal rights and self-determination of peoples and thus possessed of a Government representing the whole people belonging to the territory without distinction of any kind. . . . (Emphasis added.)

121. The right to self-determination is also recognized in other international legal documents. For example, the *Final Act of the Conference on Security and Co-operation in Europe*, 14 I.L.M. 1292 (1975) (*Helsinki Final Act*), states (in Part VIII):

> The participating States will respect the equal rights of peoples and their *right to self-determination*, acting at all times in conformity with the purposes and principles of the Charter of the United Nations and with the relevant norms of international law, including those relating to territorial integrity of States.

> By virtue of the principle of equal rights and self-determination of peoples, all peoples always have the right, in full freedom, to determine, when and as they wish, their internal and external political status, without external interference, and to pursue as they wish their political, economic, social and cultural development. (Emphasis added.)

122. As will be seen, international law expects that the right to self-determination will be exercised by peoples within the framework of existing sovereign states and consistently with the maintenance of the territorial integrity of those states. Where this is not possible, in the exceptional circumstances discussed below, a right of secession may arise.

(i) Defining "Peoples"

123. International law grants the right to self-determination to "peoples." Accordingly, access to the right requires the threshold step of characterizing as a people the group seeking self-determination. However, * * * the precise meaning of the term "people" remains somewhat uncertain.

124. It is clear that "a people" may include only a portion of the population of an existing state. The right to self-determination has developed largely as a human right, and is generally used in documents that simultaneously contain references to "nation" and "state." The juxtaposition of these terms is indicative that the reference to "people" does not necessarily mean the entirety of a state's population. To restrict the definition of the term to the population of existing states would render the granting of a right to self-determination largely duplicative, given the parallel emphasis within the majority of the source documents on the need to protect the territorial integrity of existing states, and would frustrate its remedial purpose.

125. While much of the Quebec population certainly shares many of the characteristics (such as a common language and culture) that would be considered in determining whether a specific group is a "people," as do other groups within Quebec and/or Canada, it is not necessary to explore this legal characterization to resolve Question 2 appropriately. Similarly, it is not necessary for the Court to determine whether, should a Quebec people exist within the definition of public international law, such a people encompasses the entirety of the provincial population or just a portion thereof. Nor is it necessary to examine the position of the aboriginal population within Quebec. As the following discussion of the scope of the right to self-determination will make clear, whatever be the correct application of the definition of people(s) in this context, their right of self-determination cannot in the present circumstances be said to ground a right to unilateral secession.

(ii) Scope of the Right to Self-determination

126. The recognized sources of international law establish that the right to self-determination of a people is normally fulfilled through *internal* self-determination—a people's pursuit of its political, economic, social and cultural development within the framework of an existing state. A right to *external* self-determination (which in this case potentially takes the form of the assertion of a right to unilateral secession) arises in only the most extreme of cases and, even then, under carefully defined circumstances. *External* self-determination can be defined as in the following statement from the *Declaration on Friendly Relations, supra,* as

> The establishment of a sovereign and independent State, the free association or integration with an independent State or the emergence into any other political status freely determined by a *people* constitute modes of implementing the right of self-determination by *that people*. (Emphasis added.)

127. The international law principle of self-determination has evolved within a framework of respect for the territorial integrity of existing states. The various international documents that support the existence of a people's right to self-determination also contain parallel statements supportive of the conclusion that the exercise of such a right

must be sufficiently limited to prevent threats to an existing state's territorial integrity or the stability of relations between sovereign states.

128. The *Declaration on Friendly Relations, supra, Vienna Declaration, supra,* and *Declaration on the Occasion of the Fiftieth Anniversary of the United Nations, supra,* are specific. They state, immediately after affirming a people's right to determine political, economic, social and cultural issues, that such rights are *not* to ["]be construed as authorizing or encouraging any action which would dismember or *impair, totally or in part, the territorial integrity or political unity of sovereign and independent States conducting themselves in compliance with the principle of equal rights and self-determination of peoples* as described above and thus possessed of a government representing the whole people belonging to the territory without distinction...." (Emphasis added.)

129. Similarly, while the concluding document of the Vienna Meeting in 1989 of the Conference on Security and Co-operation in Europe on the follow-up to the *Helsinki Final Act* again refers to peoples having the right to determine "their internal and *external* political status" (emphasis added), that statement is immediately followed by express recognition that the participating states will at all times act, as stated in the *Helsinki Final Act,* "in conformity with the purposes and principles of the Charter of the United Nations and with the relevant norms of international law, *including those relating to territorial integrity of states*" (emphasis added). * * *

* * * [T]he reference in the *Helsinki Final Act* to a people determining its external political status is interpreted to mean the expression of a people's external political status through the government of the existing state, save in the exceptional circumstances discussed below. As noted by Cassese, *supra,* at p. 287, given the history and textual structure of this document, its reference to external self-determination simply means that "no territorial or other change can be brought about by the central authorities of a State that is contrary to the will of the whole people of that State."

130. While the *International Covenant on Economic, Social and Cultural Rights, supra,* and the *International Covenant on Civil and Political Rights, supra,* do not specifically refer to the protection of territorial integrity, they both define the ambit of the right to self-determination in terms that are normally attainable within the framework of an existing state. There is no necessary incompatibility between the maintenance of the territorial integrity of existing states, including Canada, and the right of a "people" to achieve a full measure of self-determination. A state whose government represents the whole of the people or peoples resident within its territory, on a basis of equality and without discrimination, and respects the principles of self-determination in its own internal arrangements, is entitled to the protection under international law of its territorial integrity.

(iii) Colonial and Oppressed Peoples

131. Accordingly, the general state of international law with respect to the right to self-determination is that the right operates within the overriding protection granted to the territorial integrity of "parent" states. However, as noted by Cassese, *supra*, at p. 334, there are certain defined contexts within which the right to the self-determination of peoples does allow that right to be exercised "externally," which, in the context of this Reference, would potentially mean secession:

> . . . the right to external self-determination, which entails the possibility of choosing (or restoring) independence, has only been bestowed upon two classes of peoples (those under colonial rule or foreign occupation), based upon the assumption that both classes make up entities that are inherently distinct from the colonialist Power and the occupant Power and that their "territorial integrity," all but destroyed by the colonialist or occupying Power, should be fully restored[.]

132. The right of colonial peoples to exercise their right to self-determination by breaking away from the "imperial" power is now undisputed, but is irrelevant to this Reference.

133. The other clear case where a right to external self-determination accrues is where a people is subject to alien subjugation, domination or exploitation outside a colonial context. This recognition finds its roots in the *Declaration on Friendly Relations, supra*:

> . . . Every State has the duty to promote, through joint and separate action, the realization of the principle of equal rights and self-determination of peoples, in accordance with the provisions of the Charter, and to render assistance to the United Nations in carrying out the responsibilities entrusted to it by the Charter regarding the implementation of the principle, in order:
>
> (a) To promote friendly relations and co-operation among States; and
>
> (b) To bring a speedy end to colonialism, having due regard to the freely expressed will of the peoples concerned;
>
> and bearing in mind that subjection of peoples to alien subjugation, domination and exploitation constitutes a violation of the principle, as well as a denial of fundamental human rights, and is contrary to the Charter. * * *

134. A number of commentators have further asserted that the right to self-determination may ground a right to unilateral secession in a third circumstance. Although this third circumstance has been described in several ways, the underlying proposition is that, when a people is blocked from the meaningful exercise of its right to self-determination internally, it is entitled, as a last resort, to exercise it by secession. The *Vienna Declaration, supra*, requirement that governments represent "the whole people belonging to the territory without distinction of any kind" adds credence to the assertion that such a complete blockage may potentially give rise to a right of secession.

135. * * * Even assuming that the third circumstance is sufficient to create a right to unilateral secession under international law, the current Quebec context cannot be said to approach such a threshold. * * *

136. The population of Quebec cannot plausibly be said to be denied access to government. Quebecers occupy prominent positions within the government of Canada. Residents of the province freely make political choices and pursue economic, social and cultural development within Quebec, across Canada, and throughout the world. The population of Quebec is equitably represented in legislative, executive and judicial institutions. In short, to reflect the phraseology of the international documents that address the right to self-determination of peoples, Canada is a "sovereign and independent state conducting itself in compliance with the principle of equal rights and self-determination of peoples and thus possessed of a government representing the whole people belonging to the territory without distinction."

137. * * * [W]e cannot conclude under current circumstances that [the Canadian constitutional arrangements presently in effect] place Quebecers in a disadvantaged position within the scope of the international law rule.

138. In summary, the international law right to self-determination only generates, at best, a right to external self-determination in situations of former colonies; where a people is oppressed, as for example under foreign military occupation; or where a definable group is denied meaningful access to government to pursue their political, economic, social and cultural development. In all three situations, the people in question are entitled to a right to external self-determination because they have been denied the ability to exert internally their right to self-determination. Such exceptional circumstances are manifestly inapplicable to Quebec under existing conditions. Accordingly, neither the population of the province of Quebec, even if characterized in terms of "people" or "peoples," nor its representative institutions, the National Assembly, the legislature or government of Quebec, possess a right, under international law, to secede unilaterally from Canada.

139. We would not wish to leave this aspect of our answer to Question 2 without acknowledging the importance of the submissions made to us respecting the rights and concerns of aboriginal peoples in the event of a unilateral secession, as well as the appropriate means of defining the boundaries of a seceding Quebec with particular regard to the northern lands occupied largely by aboriginal peoples. However, the concern of aboriginal peoples is precipitated by the asserted right of Quebec to unilateral secession. In light of our finding that there is no such right applicable to the population of Quebec, either under the Constitution of Canada or at international law, but that on the contrary a clear democratic expression of support for secession would lead under the Constitution to negotiations in which aboriginal interests would be

taken into account, it becomes unnecessary to explore further the concerns of the aboriginal peoples in this Reference.

(2) *Recognition of a Factual/Political Reality: the "Effectivity" Principle*

140. * * * [A]n argument advanced by the *amicus curiae* * * * was that, while international law may not ground a positive right to unilateral secession in the context of Quebec, international law equally does not prohibit secession and, in fact, international recognition would be conferred on such a political reality if it emerged, for example, via effective control of the territory of what is now the province of Quebec.

141. It is true that international law may well, depending on the circumstances, adapt to recognize a political and/or factual reality, regardless of the legality of the steps leading to its creation. However, * * * effectivity, as such, does not have any real applicability to Question 2, which asks whether a right to unilateral secession exists.

142. No one doubts that legal consequences may flow from political facts * * *. Secession of a province from Canada, if successful in the streets, might well lead to the creation of a new state. Although recognition by other states is not, at least as a matter of theory, necessary to achieve statehood, the viability of a would-be state in the international community depends, as a practical matter, upon recognition by other states. * * * However, international recognition * * * does not relate back to the date of secession to serve retroactively as a source of a "legal" right to secede in the first place. Recognition occurs only after a territorial unit has been successful, as a political fact, in achieving secession.

143. * * * [O]ne of the legal norms which may be recognized by states in granting or withholding recognition of emergent states is the legitimacy of the process by which the *de facto* secession is, or was, being pursued. The process of recognition, once considered to be an exercise of pure sovereign discretion, has come to be associated with legal norms. See, e.g., *European Community Declaration on the Guidelines on the Recognition of New States in Eastern Europe and in the Soviet Union*, 31 I.L.M. 1485 (1992), at p. 1487. While national interest and perceived political advantage to the recognizing state obviously play an important role, foreign states may also take into account their view as to the existence of a right to self-determination on the part of the population of the putative state, and * * * an examination of the legality of the secession according to the law of the state from which the territorial unit purports to have seceded. * * * [A]n emergent state that has disregarded legitimate obligations arising out of its previous situation can potentially expect to be hindered by that disregard in achieving international recognition, at least with respect to the timing of that recognition. * * * The notion that what is not explicitly prohibited is implicitly permitted has little relevance where (as here) international law refers the legality of secession to the domestic law of the seceding state and the law of that state holds unilateral secession to be unconstitutional. * * *

146. The principle of effectivity * * * proclaims that an illegal act may eventually acquire legal status if, as a matter of empirical fact, it is recognized on the international plane. Our law has long recognized that through a combination of acquiescence and prescription, an illegal act may at some later point be accorded some form of legal status. In the law of property, for example, it is well-known that a squatter on land may ultimately become the owner if the true owner sleeps on his or her right to repossess the land. In this way, a change in the factual circumstances may subsequently be reflected in a change in legal status. It is, however, quite another matter to suggest that a subsequent condonation of an initially illegal act retroactively creates a legal right to engage in the act in the first place. The broader contention is not supported by the international principle of effectivity or otherwise and must be rejected.

Notes and Questions

1. *The* Secession of Quebec Case *in Context.* In October 1995, federalist supporters narrowly defeated a referendum in Quebec calling for the province's secession from Canada. National government leaders, upset at the close vote, determined they had been insufficiently attentive to the arguments of Quebec separatists. The national government decided to counter separatist arguments aggressively, by stressing the social and economic downsides of secession and questioning whether a referendum on the future of Canada in which only Quebecers could vote would be legitimate. The request for an advisory opinion on the legality of Quebec's secession was part of the national government's strategy. "[T]he federal Government wanted to reassert the relevance of law to the shaping of democratic governance within Canada. Less charitably, the Government may also have hoped that Quebecers"—who showed little sympathy for revolutionary movements—would "be frightened by a judicial declaration that secession by the province would be an 'illegal' act." Stephen J. Troope, "International Decision," 93 *American Journal of International Law* 519, 520 (1999). Quebec's Attorney General refused to participate in the case, and the Court appointed a separatist lawyer as an *amicus curiae.* For additional background on the case, see Anne F. Bayefsky, "Introduction," in *Self-determination in International Law: Quebec and Lessons Learned* 1 (Anne F. Bayefsky ed. 2000).

Note the phrasing of the international law questions that the Court addressed. How might the Court have dealt with the question, "If Quebec were to secede from Canada, would it be a state in international law?" Or with the question suggested by Professor Troope, "According to prevailing normative criteria, would a unilateral secession attract the recognition of Quebec by the international community as a sovereign state?" Troope, *supra*, at 522. In light of the Court's determination that Quebec had no right to secede under either Canadian constitutional law or international law, the Court did not address another question that was posed to it: would the Canadian Constitution or international law have priority in case of a conflict?

2. *Self-determination and the United Nations.* It should not be surprising that the United Nations, whose membership is open only to states, would emphasize the importance of the territorial integrity of states. Yet there also has been tremendous support at the United Nations for the right of self-determination of "peoples." The 1970 Declaration on Friendly Relations, cited in the *Secession of Quebec Case*, was adopted without a vote. Another significant General Assembly resolution, the Declaration on the Granting of Independence to Colonial Countries and Peoples, G.A. Res. 1514 (XV) (1960), which was adopted with no dissenting votes, declares that "subjection of peoples to alien subjugation, domination and exploitation" violates the U.N. Charter, and that "[a]ll peoples have the right to self-determination." Resolution 1514 also declares that "[i]mmediate steps shall be taken" in "territories which have not yet attained independence, to transfer all powers to the peoples of those territories, without any conditions or reservations, in accordance with their freely expressed will and desire * * * in order to enable them to enjoy complete independence and freedom." Another General Assembly resolution established a mechanism under which the General Assembly could designate a colony to be a "non-self-governing territory," if it were shown that the territory in question was both geographically separate and ethnically or culturally distinct from its administering power. G.A. Res. 1541 (XV) (1960).

The International Court of Justice has stressed that "the right of peoples to self-determination, as it evolved from the Charter and from United Nations practice, has an *erga omnes* character." Case Concerning East Timor (Portugal v. Australia), 1995 I.C.J. 90, 102, 1995 WL 688255. See Chapter 3 for discussion of obligations *erga omnes*. The ICJ has also emphasized that self-determination "requires a free and genuine expression of the will of the peoples concerned." Advisory Opinion on the Western Sahara, 1975 I.C.J. 12, 32, 1975 WL 5, discussed in Chapter 5.

What "peoples" have a right of "external" self-determination? Certainly, the populations of non-self-governing territories are among those legally entitled to external self-determination. The result of applying the principle of self-determination to such peoples most often led to independence—70 such territories gained independence between 1945 and 1979, with a few more becoming independent since then—although some territories chose to associate with or integrate into another state. Do minority groups within former non-self-governing territories have a right of external self-determination as it has developed in U.N. practice? Does the principle of self-determination reinforce state sovereignty?

3. *Implementing the Right to Self-determination.* How should the will of peoples in non-self-governing territories with respect to external self-determination be ascertained? Since 1954, the United Nations has often organized and supervised plebiscites or elections in such territories. The importance of referendums is discussed in the *Western Sahara Case* in Chapter 5.

A U.N. Trusteeship Council also helped promote self-government or independence for territories that were run by "administering authorities" pursuant to the U.N. Charter's International Trusteeship System. Trust territories included some former Italian and Japanese colonies, as well as territories previously administered under League of Nations mandates. (Pursuant to Article 22 of the League's Covenant, colonies that had been governed by states defeated in World War I and that were "inhabited by peoples not yet able to stand by themselves under the strenuous conditions of the modern world" could be administered under a mandates system, subject to "the principle that the well-being and development of such peoples form a sacred trust of civilization.") Several Pacific Island and African states were once trust territories. When Palau became independent in 1994, the last U.N. Trusteeship was dissolved; the U.N. Trusteeship Council is now dormant. See also Note 5 below and the *South West Africa Cases* in Chapter 3.

4. *Self-determination and the Boundaries of States.* Almost all non-self-governing territories that achieved independence did so without any changes in their territorial boundaries. As a result, several groups with different ethnic backgrounds have found themselves in the same state. Tensions among ethnic groups have sometimes led to horrific violence or genocide, as in Rwanda in the 1990s. Should the United Nations have sought changes in existing international boundaries in conjunction with its promotion of self-determination? After all, many of these boundaries were drawn by European powers in the late nineteenth century. Or, should the United Nations have more actively promoted autonomy for sub-state ethnic groups within newly independent states?

5. *Consequences of Interfering with the Right to Self-determination.* What have been the responses when a state has violated the principle of self-determination with respect to non-self-governing territories? When a colony did not gain its independence peacefully, the colonial power could be condemned for illegally using force against liberation forces—despite what had been the widely accepted view that a state's decision to use force inside its own borders was a matter reserved to the domestic jurisdiction of that state. For example, when local liberation forces in Portuguese Guinea declared independence in 1973 in the face of continued Portuguese opposition, the U.N. General Assembly invoked the right of self-determination, welcomed the independence of "the sovereign State of the Republic of Guinea–Bissau," and strongly condemned Portugal for its "illegal occupation of certain sectors of the Republic of Guinea–Bissau and the repeated acts of aggression committed by its armed forces against the people of Guinea–Bissau." G.A. Res. 3061 (XXVIII). Many states recognized Guinea–Bissau even before this General Assembly resolution. In the 1970 Declaration on Friendly Relations, the General Assembly also referred to the duty of every state "to refrain from any forcible action which deprives peoples * * * of their right to self-determination and freedom and independence." We take up the international law on the use of force in Chapter 9.

Following the U.N.'s decision to terminate apartheid South Africa's Mandate to administer Namibia (South West Africa), the U.N. Security Council declared that South Africa's continued presence in Namibia and South Africa's acts "on behalf of or concerning Namibia after the termination of the Mandate" were illegal. The Council called on all states "to refrain from any dealings" with South Africa that were inconsistent with this declaration of illegality. S.C. Res. 276 (1970). In Legal Consequences for States of the Continued Presence of South Africa in Namibia (South West Africa) Notwithstanding Security Council Resolution 276 (1970), 1971 I.C.J.

16, 1971 WL 8, the International Court of Justice emphasized that states legally could not enter numerous types of treaty, diplomatic, and economic relationships with South Africa, because those relationships might imply recognition of the legality of South Africa's presence and administration in Namibia.

6. *The Helsinki Accords.* Should the *Secession of Quebec* court have given equal weight to all the sources it cited to interpret the meaning of "self-determination"? For example, what treatment should the Helsinki Accords (see paragraphs 121 and 129 of the court's opinion) have received? The Accords were the Final Act of the Conference on Security and Cooperation in Europe, 14 I.L.M. 1292 (1975), negotiated over a two-year period and signed in 1975 by leaders of the United States, Canada, the Soviet Union, and 32 states in Eastern and Western Europe. The Final Act addresses not only self-determination, but human rights, a particular concern of Western European states, and the need to respect states' territorial integrity, which was a politically important point for Eastern European states whose legitimacy the West had challenged. Concluded during the Cold War, the Helsinki Accords represented a significant political bargain. But the states that signed them did not regard them as legally binding. What, then, is their legal significance? See the discussion of customary law in Chapter 3.

7. *Self-determination and the Rights of Indigenous Peoples.* Should the aboriginal peoples of northern Quebec, which the Canadian Supreme Court mentioned in paragraph 139 of its opinion, have a right of self-determination? If so, how should such a right be implemented? The international status and rights of indigenous peoples have been the subject of negotiations in the U.N. Human Rights Commission and other international organizations. The Draft U.N. Declaration on the Rights of Indigenous Peoples, Oct. 28, 1994, 34 I.L.M 541 (1995), is significant as the first attempt to develop a body of group rights in international law for indigenous peoples. Drafts of the Declaration were circulated annually to the governing bodies of indigenous groups and to human rights experts, and nongovernmental organizations and representatives of indigenous peoples openly participated as observers at sessions of the Working Group on Indigenous Populations of the U.N. Subcommission on the Prevention of Discrimination and Protection of Minorities. The Declaration was adopted by the Subcommission, which is an expert body within the United Nations system, in 1994 and submitted to the U.N. Commission on Human Rights in 1995 for further action. See also International Labour Organization: Convention Concerning Indigenous and Tribal Peoples in Independent Countries, June 27, 1989, 28 I.L.M. 1382 (1989).

8. *Expanding the Scope of Self-determination.* Did the Court in the *Secession of Quebec Case* take too restrictive a view of the scope of the legal right to self-determination? Should this right apply only to peoples in non-self-governing territories and to peoples under foreign domination? Should it apply when a group whose cultural survival is threatened expresses its desire for external self-determination? Are there drawbacks to accepting an expansive scope for external self-determination? The following Note considers claims of self-determination with respect to the situation in the former Yugoslavia and, more broadly, challenges to the sovereign state.

Note: Self-determination and Challenges to the Sovereign State

During the break-up of Yugoslavia in the early 1990s, various ethnic groups asserted a right to self-determination. The 1991 European Community Guidelines on Recognition of New States (see Note 7, page 408) and opinions of the Conference on Yugoslavia's Arbitration Commission suggested that self-determination had legal significance, and perhaps pointed to future development of the concept. In the preamble of its Recognition Guidelines, the European Community and its member states confirmed "their attachment to * * * the principle of self-determination." What did this attachment mean in the context of the break-up of the SFRY?

First, the EC appeared concerned with internal self-determination. The Recognition Guidelines emphasized that recognition was contingent on the various successor states respecting democracy and guaranteeing "the rights of ethnic and national groups and minorities in accordance with the commitments subscribed to in the framework of" the Conference on Security and Cooperation in Europe. The EC did not always strictly follow its own Guidelines; for example, the EC decided to recognize Croatia despite an Arbitration Commission opinion finding that Croatia had not taken sufficient steps to protect its minority Serb population. See Arbitration Commission Opinion No. 5, 31 I.L.M. 1503 (1992). This lapse aside, the EC seemed ready to reinforce the notion that recognition for new states depended on their demonstrating commitment to internal self-determination. The EC was "prepared to endorse the achievement of independent statehood, i.e., external self-determination, only on condition that the breakaway Republics fully respected the principle of representative democracy, i.e., internal self-determination." Antonio Cassese, "Self–Determination of Peoples and the Recent Break–Up of USSR and Yugoslavia," in *Essays in Honour of Wang Tieya* 131, 140 (Ronald St. John MacDonald ed. 1994).

Second, the Arbitration Commission was unwilling to accept that minority populations in the successor states themselves could legally establish new states. When asked whether "the Serbian population in Croatia and Bosnia–Hercegovina, as one of the constituent peoples of Yugoslavia, [had] a right to self-determination," the Arbitration Commission found that the right to self-determination "must not involve changes to existing frontiers at the time of independence * * * except where the States concerned agree otherwise." Arbitration Commission Opinion No. 2, 31 I.L.M. 1497 (1992). (In its Opinion No. 3, the Commission confirmed that the former internal Yugoslav boundaries between Croatia and Serbia, and between Bosnia–Herzegovina and Serbia, "become frontiers protected by international law." 31 I.L.M. 1499, 1500 (1992).) In Opinion No. 2, the Commission stressed the importance of human rights and the rights of minority and ethnic groups under international law, but did not proclaim a right to external self-determination for the groups.

What are the implications of these opinions for Albanians in Kosovo, a region within the Serb-dominated Federal Republic of Yugoslavia in which there has been intense fighting among ethnic groups? If basic requirements of internal self-determination are not in fact satisfied, should ethnic Albanians be legally entitled at least to operate under autonomy arrangements?

One can envision a range of possible self-determination remedies. See Paul H. Brietzke, "Self–Determination, or Jurisprudential Confusion: Exacerbating Political Conflict," 14 *Wisconsin International Law Journal* 69, 122–23 (1995). The ideas that a "people" or "nation" may have some right to be governed with its consent—a "democratic entitlement"—and even some justifiable claim to secession if its fundamental rights are systematically denied pose a challenge to traditional notions of state sovereignty. See Universal Declaration of Human Rights, art. 21(3); Thomas M. Franck, "The Emerging Right to Democratic Governance," 86 *American Journal of International Law* 46 (1992); Diane F. Orentlicher, "Separation Anxiety: International Responses to Ethno–Separatist Claims," 23 *Yale Journal of International Law* 1, 44–62 (1998).

Third, the situation in the former Yugoslavia prompts one to consider how claims for self-determination should be authoritatively resolved. The legal procedures used to determine the status of Bosnia–Herzegovina, Croatia, Slovenia, and The Former Yugoslav Republic of Macedonia tracked procedures that had been used to implement the right of self-determination elsewhere. Referendums, often employed in decolonization situations, were conducted to determine the wishes of the populations of the new republics. The EC's Arbitration Commission in fact attempted to monitor whether each republic had held referendums on independence, as well as to ascertain whether each republic had implemented measures to respect individual, group, and minority rights. See Arbitration Commission Opinions Nos. 4–7, 31 I.L.M. 1501, 1503, 1507, 1511 (1992). What more effective international responses to the dissolution of Yugoslavia could have been devised? Is it appropriate for international organizations to take an active role in mediating and resolving ethno-separatist claims, *à la* the League of Nations in the Aaland Islands dispute? Does the involvement of international organizations in devising and implementing mechanisms to help peacefully resolve separatist claims challenge traditional notions of state sovereignty? See Orentlicher, *supra*, at 62–78. We look more closely at international organizations in the next chapter.

What other challenges to traditional conceptions of state sovereignty does international law pose today? Certainly, the development of individual human rights (see Chapter 6) counters the notion that states enjoy legally untrammeled freedom of action even with respect to their own citizens. The sovereign state has also been subject to attacks on other fronts. Some, for example, stress the importance of economics in the modern world and see states as imposing artificial boundaries that impede the efficient operation of markets. Others argue that states are either too large or too small to respond well to current challenges; management problems may require structures larger than the state, even while entities smaller than the state may more effectively produce political legitimacy. In light of such criticisms of the state, what justifies its continuing central role in international law? See "Theoretical Perspectives on the Transformation of Sovereignty," 1994 *American Society of International Law Proceedings* 1. And if non-state entities—individuals, peoples, and regional and international organizations—as well as states have rights and obligations under international law, how should international lawyers today conceptualize their discipline?

Chapter 8

INTERNATIONAL ORGANIZATIONS AND INTERNATIONAL LAW

Along with states and individuals, international organizations are active participants in the international legal arena. Part A of this chapter examines intergovernmental organizations, which are created by treaties among states, employing the United Nations as our focus. Part B introduces nongovernmental organizations. NGOs, organized or chartered under municipal laws, increasingly influence international law and process.

A. INTERGOVERNMENTAL ORGANIZATIONS

Multilateral treaties, an innovation of the 19th century, were an indispensable prerequisite to the formation of intergovernmental organizations, created to achieve common ends. Among the precursors to intergovernmental organizations were conferences among states, such as the 1815 Congress of Vienna. When conferences met at periodic intervals, states sometimes created intergovernmental organizations to fulfill administrative roles. For example, the International Union of American Republics was established in 1890 to hold periodic conferences to discuss and negotiate treaties concerning such issues as arbitration, the extradition of criminals, the codification of intellectual property law, and the status of diplomats and aliens. The Union's Commercial Bureau and a political organ formed in 1896 prepared conference agendas, collected and published commercial information, and helped to implement measures adopted at the conferences. Out of this Pan–American system grew the Organization of American States, established in 1948. Numerous regional intergovernmental organizations now exist, including the Council of Europe, which, among other things, addresses human rights issues (see Chapter 6), and the institutions of the European Union, notably the Parliament, Council, Commission, and European Court of Justice, which regulate a wide range of economic, social, and political matters. We saw an ECJ case, *AM & S*, in Chapter 3.

Early intergovernmental organizations were often designed to develop and administer common standards for specialized and largely technical matters. Among the several such organizations created in the 19th century were the 1856 European Danube Commission, the 1865 Universal Telegraphic Union (now the International Telecommunications Union), and the 1874 Universal Postal Union. Many of the hundreds of intergovernmental organizations existing today focus on technical, specialized subject areas, providing continuity and expertise with respect to the issues within their mandate.

Global intergovernmental organizations designed to address broader issues, such as social welfare and the use of force, were in practice if not in theory slower to develop than were specialized organizations. Ideas about peaceful universal unions of people can be found in the writings of ancient Greek and Roman thinkers. European political philosophers, including Erasmus, Thomas More, Jean–Jacques Rousseau, Immanuel Kant, and Jeremy Bentham also devised and espoused utopian proposals involving international organizations. The League of Nations, formed in 1919 after World War I, was the first general association of states concerned with social welfare issues, dispute settlement, the development of international law, and the promotion of peace.

In this chapter, we use the United Nations, the successor organization to the League of Nations, as our primary example of an intergovernmental organization. Section 1 of this Part A includes background on the League of Nations and the United Nations, while Section 2 introduces the concept of "international personality" that is associated with intergovernmental organizations and some other non-state entities. Section 3 then explores changes in the functions of some of the various U.N. organs as well as the limits that exist on the authority of U.N. organs.

1. AN OVERVIEW OF INTERGOVERNMENTAL ORGANIZATIONS AND THE UNITED NATIONS

MARK W. JANIS, AN INTRODUCTION TO INTERNATIONAL LAW

201–204 (3d ed. 1999).

In the nineteenth century, alongside the movement for an international court, there emerged a popular enthusiasm for an international government. One of the most important publications promoting the idea was the *Essay on a Congress of Nations*, written in 1840 by the president of the American Peace Society, William Ladd (1778–1841). * * * Reviewing Ladd's *Essay*, Georg Schwarzenberger in 1935 decided that there was "a direct line" in the history of ideas about international organization "from Ladd to the achievements of Geneva, and even further, on the foundations of his Equity Tribunal, to a real League of Nations."

American enthusiasm for international government, at least in theory, ran high in the early years of the twentieth century. The onset of the Great War in 1914 only quickened the pace. Notables at a meeting of the First Annual National Assemblage of the League to Enforce Peace in Washington, D.C., in 1916 included the former President of the United States, William Howard Taft; the president of Harvard, A. Lawrence

Lowell; the director of the Chamber of Commerce of the United States, Edward Filene; the president of the American Federation of Labor, Samuel Gompers; the senator from Massachusetts, Henry Cabot Lodge; the president of the Federal Council of Churches of Christ in America, Shailer Matthews; and the former president of Princeton and the then-President of the United States, Woodrow Wilson. It was Wilson who put the longstanding aspirations for international government into concrete form, proposing in the last of his Fourteen Points on January 8, 1918, that "[a] general association of nations must be formed under specific covenants for the purpose of affording mutual guarantees of political independence and territorial integrity to great and small States alike." Wilson and others believed that an international organization devoted to collective security could better guarantee the peace than could tradition-al balance-of-power politics, which not only had failed to prevent the outbreak of war in 1914, but also, because of its triggering system of alliances, had contributed to the expansion of the conflict.

The Versailles Treaty establishing the League "had been construct-ed on the assumption that the United States would be not merely a contracting but an actively executant party." Unfortunately, or as put politely by a Frenchman, "by a strange paradox," the U.S. Senate refused to consent to the ratification of the Treaty, and the United States stayed out of its own plan to keep the peace.

For a decade, from 1920 to 1930, the League, based in Geneva, even without the United States and also without the new Soviet Union, made real contributions to international law, world health, the protection of minorities, and the settlement of international disputes (for example, the pacific settlement of the dispute between Greece and Bulgaria in 1925). Unfortunately, the next decade was disastrous for the League. The turning point was probably the Japanese invasion of Manchuria on September 18, 1931, which the League proved powerless to stop. The League finally condemned the Japanese occupation of Manchuria on February 24, 1933, and Japan simply left the League the next month. Dedicated to the prevention of aggression, the League watched helplessly as Italy invaded Ethiopia in 1934 and as Germany marched into the Rhineland, Austria, and Czechoslovakia between 1936 and 1938. Finally, when Germany and Russia attacked Poland in 1939, Britain and France took action, but it was too late. Poland was lost, then France itself, and the nations descended into the twentieth century's second world war.

By the time of the invasion of Poland in 1939, the League was, in large measure, already a forgotten institution. Poland, France, and Great Britain made no attempt to involve the League in the new world war. For a year, the functionaries of the League carried on in Geneva, a situation described by the Deputy Secretary–General of the League as a "situation of abnormal normality." In the summer and autumn of 1940, the League's officials departed Geneva, where they feared a German or Italian invasion, for safer locations. A large part of the Secretariat was based at Princeton University, a fitting, if ironic, twist on the origins of the League with Woodrow Wilson. Almost a year after the foundation of the United Nations in June 1945, diplomats reconvened at Geneva, where on April 8, 1946, Lord Robert Cecil closed his speech to the League Assembly as follows: "The League is dead, Long live the United Nations." Ten days later, the Assembly unanimously voted to dissolve the League and to transfer its powers, functions, buildings, library, and archives to the United Nations.

ADAM ROBERTS & BENEDICT KINGSBURY, "INTRODUCTION: THE UN'S ROLES IN INTERNATIONAL SOCIETY SINCE 1945"

United Nations, Divided World 1 (2d rev. ed. 1996).

The origins of the term "United Nations" are to be found in the events surrounding the Washington Declaration of 1 January 1942, in which twenty-six Allied countries, which came to be called the "United Nations," pledged themselves to employ their full resources against Germany, Italy, and Japan; and the Moscow Four–Nation Declaration of 30 October 1943, which frequently called the Allies "the United Nations." * * * The term "the United Nations" has long since been effectively appropriated by the international organization created in 1945.

The first blueprints for the UN were drafted by the USA, the UK, the USSR, and their allies during World War II, reflecting their conceptions of the post-war international order. The Charter was finally adopted by fifty states meeting at San Francisco in June 1945. Although the nature and work of the UN has evolved considerably, the Charter has remained virtually unchanged. The UN was formally established on 24 October 1945, when its basic constitutive instrument, the UN Charter, entered into force.

In the years since 1945 the number of member states of the UN has steadily increased, due mainly to the effects of successive waves of decolonization and disintegration of states. In 1945 the UN had fifty-one original members; by September 1961, one hundred; by the end of 1984, one hundred and fifty-nine; and by July 1993, one hundred and eighty-four.[†] Throughout its history, the UN has had as members the great majority of states. Despite trends towards regional integration, there have only exceptionally been enduring cases of UN member states unifying to form a single larger state: Tanzania (1964), Yemen (1990), and Germany (1990).

The most conspicuous case of non-membership was the People's Republic of China from the revolution in 1949 until 1971, during which period China was represented by the regime in Taiwan. Since 1971 the UN's claims to near-universalism have had real substance. Its members include virtually all the states of the contemporary world. No member state has ever left the UN * * * [although] in 1965–6 Indonesia temporarily withdrew from the UN. In some cases the credentials of particular

[†] As of November 1, 2000, U.N. membership stood at 189.—Eds.

authorities to represent their state have not been accepted and the Federal Republic of Yugoslavia (Serbia and Montenegro) was advised in 1992 by the Security Council and by the General Assembly that it could not continue the membership of the former Socialist Federal Republic of Yugoslavia, although it was able to continue participation in some UN bodies.

Six "principal organs" of the UN were established by the Charter: the General Assembly, the Security Council, the Secretariat, the International Court of Justice (ICJ), the Trusteeship Council, and the Economic and Social Council (ECOSOC).

The *General Assembly* as the plenary body controls much of the work of the UN. It meets in regular session for approximately the last quarter of every year (with sessions spilling over well into the new year), and occasionally holds special or emergency sessions to consider specific issues. The General Assembly approves the budget, adopts priorities, calls international conferences, superintends the operations of the Secretariat and of numerous committees and subsidiary organs, and debates and adopts resolutions on diverse issues. It played a major role in supervising European decolonization, and has also become involved in human rights supervision and election-monitoring in independent countries. The many subsidiary bodies created by the General Assembly include the United Nations Children's Fund (UNICEF), the Office of the United Nations High Commissioner for Refugees (UNHCR), the United Nations Conference on Trade and Development (UNCTAD), the United Nations Development Programme (UNDP), and the United Nations Environment Programme (UNEP). Much of the work of the General Assembly is done in permanent or ad hoc committees responsible for particular fields of UN activity or deliberation. * * *

The fifteen-member *Security Council* is dominated by its five Permanent Members (China, France, Russia, the UK, and the USA), each of which has power to veto any draft resolution on substantive matters. The ten non-permanent members (six until a Charter amendment came into force in 1965) are elected for two-year periods by the General Assembly. The Security Council has primary responsibility for the maintenance of international peace and security, and unlike the General Assembly is able to take decisions which are supposed to be binding on all members of the UN. It meets almost continuously throughout the year, mainly to consider armed conflicts and other situations or disputes where international peace and security are threatened. It is empowered to order mandatory sanctions, call for cease-fires, and even to authorize military action on behalf of the UN.

The Security Council has also had a central role in the development of the institution of UN peacekeeping forces, which were not envisaged at all in the Charter. The blue berets or helmets worn by members of national military units working in the service of the UN have become a well-known symbol. UN peacekeeping forces, ranging from small observer units to larger forces for purposes of interposition, policing, and humanitarian assistance, have been established by the Security Council in numerous countries. On a few occasions, it has been the General Assembly rather than the Security Council which has initiated the use of such forces. * * * However, control of peacekeeping has now returned firmly to the Security Council.

The Security Council has played an important role in easing or containing numerous crises, and it provides a high-level forum for diplomatic contact and negotiation. The Security Council also has a role, with the General Assembly, in the admission of new members to the UN, the appointment of the Secretary–General, and the election of judges to the ICJ.

The Charter provision that the Council must operate on the basis of unanimity of its Permanent Members was not the product of impractical idealism: the memoirs of some of those who helped frame the Charter confirm that they knew what they were doing in this as in many other respects. The provision, which has been interpreted in practice to mean that any one of the Permanent Members has to vote against a resolution in order to veto it, reflects a highly realistic belief that UN action will not be possible if one of the great powers seriously dissents from it.

Both the actual use of the veto, and the constant possibility of its use, have been central features of the functioning of the Security Council throughout the UN's history. In the period from 1945 to the end of 1992 [234] vetoes were cast * * *.[††]

* * * [A] Permanent Member of the Security Council can avoid having to make direct use of the veto power if it is sure that the proposal in question will not in any event obtain the requisite three-fifths majority. The Western states, in particular, were frequently able to use this tactic in the early years of the UN, the Soviet Union in the 1970s and 1980s. To some extent the use of the veto has reflected a degree of diplomatic isolation of the vetoing state(s) on the particular issue. Forcing such resolutions to a vote has been a diplomatic strategy to demonstrate the isolation of particular states. The period from 31 May 1990 (when the USA vetoed a resolution on the Israeli-occupied territories) to 11 May 1993 (when Russia vetoed a resolution on the financing of the peacekeeping force in Cyprus) was notable as the longest without use of the veto in the history of the UN.

Because of the veto, the Security Council could contribute little to the amelioration of armed conflicts in which its Permanent Members were directly involved * * *. Since the mid–1980s the Security Council has had a more central role in international security * * *.

The *UN Secretariat*, which is headed by the Secretary–General, comprises some 14,000 people at UN Headquarters in New York and at other UN offices (the largest of which is Geneva). * * * While the nature and quality of the UN's work depends greatly on the comparatively

[††] From 1993 through November 1, 2000, only seven vetoes were cast. See <http:// www.globalpolicy.org/security/membship/ veto.htm>.—Eds.

"faceless" Secretariat, the Secretary–General is also a significant figure in international diplomacy.

The role of the Secretary–General has developed very significantly since 1945. The * * * Secretary–General has taken on—or has had forced upon him—a wide range of functions: fact-finding, mediating in disputes between states, and responding to rapidly moving crises in which other UN bodies, because of disagreement among members or the sheer pace of events, have only limited possibilities of doing anything.

The *International Court of Justice* (ICJ) is the successor to the Permanent Court of International Justice, which had been established at The Hague in 1922. The ICJ's Statute was adopted in 1945 at the same time as the UN Charter, and all UN member states are parties, as are certain other states. * * *

The *Trusteeship Council* superintended the transition of trust territories to self-government. * * *

The *Economic and Social Council* comprises fifty-four states elected by the General Assembly. Many non-governmental organizations also participate in its proceedings. It supervises the work of numerous commissions, committees, and expert bodies in the economic and social fields, and endeavours, so far with only limited success, to coordinate the efforts of the many UN specialized agencies in this area.

The UN system extends beyond the six UN organs created by the Charter, and the various subsidiary bodies established subsequently by the UN, to include also a host of specialized agencies with their own separate constitutions, memberships, and budgets. These agencies constitute a distinct part of the UN system. In the words of Article 57 of the UN Charter, they are "established by intergovernmental agreement" and have "wide international responsibilities, as defined in their basic instruments, in economic, social, cultural, educational, health, and related fields." There are sixteen such specialized agencies associated with the UN: apart from the financial agencies—the main ones being the International Monetary Fund (IMF) and the World Bank (IBRD)—the "big four" are the International Labour Organization (ILO); the Food and Agriculture Organization (FAO); the United Nations Educational, Scientific and Cultural Organization (UNESCO); and the World Health Organization (WHO). * * *

* * * [M]ore than half of the UN budget is financed by voluntary contributions, with most of the remainder contributed by member states in accordance with binding assessments based mainly on gross and per capita national incomes. Some costs, particularly some of those for peacekeeping, are absorbed directly by member states. * * * The UN has been in financial difficulties arising from non-payment of assessed contributions since the early 1960s, and the deficit increased sharply in the 1980s. * * *

The UN is too often evaluated by standards unrelated to its actual capacities. Some have judged the UN against the standard of a prototype world government; or at least as a means of eliminating completely one of the plagues of international life, namely war. Such expectations were built up at the time of the UN's foundation. Even now, many see the organization in idealistic terms (sometimes reflecting the language of the Charter) as standing on a higher moral plane than the states of which it is composed, especially because of its advocacy of such principles as human rights, non-use of force, and disarmament. Others have used the non-fulfillment of these highly idealistic expectations as a starting-point for bitter criticism. The UN is all talk and no action; it is an arena in which governments hypocritically proclaim one set of values while themselves practising another; it is a vehicle for the pursuit of power politics in disguise, not for their replacement. In the late 1970s and early 1980s these critical views became more prevalent and more influential, especially in that country where idealism about the UN had once been particularly strong—the USA. Such views, idealistic or dismissive, evaluated the UN in simple terms, assumed that the UN must be judged by the aspirational standards set for it in the Charter, and made few distinctions between the UN's numerous different roles. * * *

A general inter-governmental organization, be it regional or global, cannot be evaluated in quite the same terms as governments: its decision-making and implementation powers are limited, it lacks the boundaries which define and distinguish a territorial entity, and it is always operating concurrently with governments and other entities which it does not control. Such results as are achieved are often difficult to attribute to any single body. * * *

When the United Nations was established in the immediate aftermath of the Second World War, it was viewed similarly as being concerned above all with the maintenance of peace. However, in the years of East–West rivalry its role in this area sometimes seemed marginal. * * *

Against this background, it is not surprising that the UN's contribution came to be seen by many as being less in the field of peace between the major powers than in other areas: defusing certain regional conflicts, advocating self-determination, assisting decolonization, codifying international law, protecting human rights, and providing a possible framework for social and economic improvement, even for redistribution of wealth on a global scale. * * *

There is a complex relation between the UN's attempts to fulfil the terms of its innumerable express mandates and its more abstract role as a symbol of both the constraints and the possibilities of international society. The UN should be judged, not just by what it does in particular fields of activity, or in particular crises, but also by the way in which, through its very existence, through the influence of its Charter, through the questions it addresses, and through its diplomatic rituals, it proclaims certain values and sets the terms of international debates.

Notes and Questions

1. *The Variety of U.N. Activities.* We have already referred to various activities of U.N. organs in previous chapters. Recall the debate over General Assembly resolutions as a potential source of international law (Chapter 3), the Secretary–General's role in helping to settle the *Rainbow Warrior* dispute (Chapter 5), the decisions of the International Court of Justice (Chapter 5 and elsewhere), the U.N.'s work with respect to human rights and international criminal law (Chapter 6), and the Organization's efforts concerning decolonization (Chapter 7 and the *Western Sahara Case* in Chapter 5). The International Law Commission, a body of legal experts appointed by the General Assembly pursuant to Article 13 of the U.N. Charter, helps to codify international law (*e.g.*, by preparing drafts of Vienna Convention on the Law of Treaties, considered in Chapter 2). The relationship between the United Nations and the use of force is introduced in this chapter and explored more thoroughly in Chapter 9. The United Nations has also contributed significantly to international environmental law and the international law of the sea, topics we consider in Chapters 10 and 11.

2. *The U.N. Budget.* The United Nations has reduced its personnel and budget in recent years. As of 1999, approximately 8,600 people from 170 states worked for the Secretariat under the U.N.'s regular budget. See <http://www.un.org/documents/st.htm>. The U.N. budget, which is proposed by the Secretary–General, reviewed by budgetary committees, and approved by the General Assembly pursuant to Article 17 of the U.N. Charter, was set at $2.535 billion for the 2000–2001 fiscal year; this figure is approximately $100 million less than the U.N.'s budget for 1994–1995. "Statement on United Nations Programme Budget for 2000–2001," Press Release GA/9695 (1999). Expenses for the entire U.N. system (including the U.N. itself, the various U.N. programs and funds, and the U.N. specialized agencies, but excluding the World Bank, the IMF, and the International Fund for Agricultural Development) amount to approximately $10 billion annually, two-thirds of which is derived from Member States' voluntary contributions. See <http://www.un.org/geninfo/ir/ch6/ch6_txt.htm>. For discussion of issues related to nonpayment of U.N. assessments, see Note 3, page 481 below.

3. *Changes to the U.N. Charter.* It is possible to amend the U.N. Charter pursuant to Articles 108 or 109, and—as indicated by footnotes to Charter articles in the Appendix—a few amendments have been adopted. Consistent practice may also effectively change the Charter. For example, as Professors Roberts and Kingsbury pointed out, an abstention by a permanent member of the Security Council is not now regarded as a veto of a Council decision, despite the literal language of Article 27(3) of the Charter. How else do changes in the interpretation of the Charter or the relationships of the U.N.'s principal organs occur? One of the themes in the cases and readings in the next two sections of this Part A is the constitutional evolution of the United Nations. Constitutional law is always a complex subject. It becomes even more so in an international context when many states and legal cultures are involved.

2. INTERNATIONAL PERSONALITY

In this Section we explore some fundamental questions about intergovernmental organizations. Does an organization such as the United Nations have "international personality" of its own? Or are its powers limited to those expressly delegated by Member States in the U.N. Charter? Is it international law or municipal law that answers such questions? The International Court of Justice addressed these concerns in its advisory opinion in the *Reparation Case* which follows. The case specifically involved the capacity of the United Nations to bring an international claim for reparations when a U.N. agent was injured due to the responsibility of a state. May the United Nations itself bring such a claim? Or must such a claim be pursued, if at all, in traditional fashion by the state of the agent's nationality?

THE REPARATION CASE

Reparation for Injuries Suffered in the Service of the United Nations,
1949 I.C.J. 174, 1949 WL 3.

On December 3rd, 1948, the General Assembly of the United Nations adopted the following Resolution:

"Whereas the series of tragic events which have lately befallen agents of the United Nations engaged in the performance of their duties raises, with greater urgency than ever, the question of the arrangements to be made by the United Nations with a view to ensuring to its agents the fullest measure of protection in the future and ensuring that reparation be made for the injuries suffered; and

Whereas it is highly desirable that the Secretary–General should be able to act without question as efficaciously as possible with a view to obtaining any reparation due; therefore

The General Assembly

Decides to submit the following legal questions to the International Court of Justice for an advisory opinion:

I. In the event of an agent of the United Nations in the performance of his duties suffering injury in circumstances involving the responsibility of a State, has the United Nations, as an Organization, the capacity to bring an international claim against the responsible *de jure* or *de facto* government with a view to obtaining the reparation due in respect of the damage caused (*a*) to the United Nations, (*b*) to the victim or to persons entitled through him?
* * *." * * *

Competence to bring an international claim is, for those possessing it, the capacity to resort to the customary methods recognized by international law for the establishment, the presentation and the settlement of claims. Among these methods may be mentioned protest, request for an enquiry, negotiation, and request for submission to an arbitral tribunal or to the Court in so far as this may be authorized by the Statute. * * *

But, in the international sphere, has the Organization such a nature as involves the capacity to bring an international claim? In order to answer this question, the Court must first enquire whether the Charter has given the Organization such a position that it possesses, in regard to its Members, rights which it is entitled to ask them to respect. In other words, does the Organization possess international personality? This is no doubt a doctrinal expression, which has sometimes given rise to controversy. But it will be used here to mean that if the Organization is recognized as having that personality, it is an entity capable of availing itself of obligations incumbent upon its Members.

To answer this question, which is not settled by the actual terms of the Charter, we must consider what characteristics it was intended thereby to give to the Organization.

The subjects of law in any legal system are not necessarily identical in their nature or in the extent of their rights, and their nature depends upon the needs of the community. Throughout its history, the development of international law has been influenced by the requirements of international life, and the progressive increase in the collective activities of States has already given rise to instances of action upon the international plane by certain entities which are not States. This development culminated in the establishment in June 1945 of an international organization whose purposes and principles are specified in the Charter of the United Nations. But to achieve these ends the attribution of international personality is indispensable.

The Charter has not been content to make the Organization created by it merely a centre "for harmonizing the actions of nations in the attainment of these common ends" (Article I, para. 4). It has equipped that centre with organs, and has given it special tasks. It has defined the position of the Members in relation to the Organization by requiring them to give it every assistance in any action undertaken by it (Article 2, para. 5), and to accept and carry out the decisions of the Security Council; by authorizing the General Assembly to make recommendations to the Members; by giving the Organization legal capacity and privileges and immunities in the territory of each of its Members; and by providing for the conclusion of agreements between the Organization and its Members. Practice—in particular the conclusion of conventions to which the Organization is a party—has confirmed this character of the Organization, which occupies a position in certain respects in detachment from its Members, and which is under a duty to remind them, if need be, of certain obligations. It must be added that the Organization is a political body, charged with political tasks of an important character, and covering a wide field namely, the maintenance of international peace and security, the development of friendly relations among nations, and the achievement of international co-operation in the solution of problems of an economic, social, cultural or humanitarian character (Article I); and in dealing with its Members it employs political means. The "Convention on the Privileges and Immunities of the United Nations" of 1946 creates rights and duties between each of the signatories and the Organization (see, in particular, Section 35). It is difficult to see how such a convention could operate except upon the international plane and as between parties possessing international personality.

In the opinion of the Court, the Organization was intended to exercise and enjoy, and is in fact exercising and enjoying, functions and rights which can only be explained on the basis of the possession of a large measure of international personality and the capacity to operate upon an international plane. It is at present the supreme type of international organization, and it could not carry out the intentions of its founders if it was devoid of international personality. It must be acknowledged that its Members, by entrusting certain functions to it, with the attendant duties and responsibilities, have clothed it with the competence required to enable those functions to be effectively discharged.

Accordingly, the Court has come to the conclusion that the Organization is an international person. That is not the same thing as saying that it is a State, which it certainly is not, or that its legal personality and rights and duties are the same as those of a State. Still less is it the same thing as saying that it is "a super–State," whatever that expression may mean. It does not even imply that all its rights and duties must be upon the international plane, any more than all the rights and duties of a State must be upon that plane. What it does mean is that it is a subject of international law and capable of possessing international rights and duties, and that it has capacity to maintain its rights by bringing international claims.

The next question is whether the sum of the international rights of the Organization comprises the right to bring the kind of international claim described in the Request for this Opinion. That is a claim against a State to obtain reparation in respect of the damage caused by the injury of an agent of the Organization in the course of the performance of his duties. Whereas a State possesses the totality of international rights and duties recognized by international law, the rights and duties of an entity such as the Organization must depend upon its purposes and functions as specified or implied in its constituent documents and developed in practice. The functions of the Organization are of such a character that they could not be effectively discharged if they involved the concurrent action, on the international plane, of fifty-eight or more Foreign Offices, and the Court concludes that the Members have endowed the Organization with capacity to bring international claims when necessitated by the discharge of its functions.

What is the position as regards the claims mentioned in the request for an opinion? Question I is divided into two points, which must be considered in turn. * * *

* * * It cannot be doubted that the Organization has the capacity to bring an international claim against one of its Members which has caused injury to it by a breach of its international obligations towards it. The damage specified in Question I (*a*) means exclusively damage caused to the interests of the Organization itself, to its administrative machine, to its property and assets, and to the interests of which it is the guardian. It is clear that the Organization has the capacity to bring a claim for this damage. As the claim is based on the breach of an international obligation on the part of the Member held responsible by the Organization, the Member cannot contend that this obligation is governed by municipal law, and the Organization is justified in giving its claim the character of an international claim.

When the Organization has sustained damage resulting from a breach by a Member of its international obligations, it is impossible to see how it can obtain reparation unless it possesses capacity to bring an international claim. It cannot be supposed that in such an event all the Members of the Organization, save the defendant State, must combine to bring a claim against the defendant for the damage suffered by the Organization. * * *

Question I (*b*) is as follows:

... "has the United Nations, as an Organization, the capacity to bring an international claim ... in respect of the damage caused ... (*b*) to the victim or to persons entitled through him?" * * *

The traditional rule that diplomatic protection is exercised by the national State does not involve the giving of a negative answer to Question I (*b*). * * *

The Court is here faced with a new situation. The questions to which it gives rise can only be solved by realizing that the situation is dominated by the provisions of the Charter considered in the light of the principles of international law.

The question lies within the limits already established; that is to say it presupposes that the injury for which the reparation is demanded arises from a breach of an obligation designed to help an agent of the Organization in the performance of his duties. It is not a case in which the wrongful act or omission would merely constitute a breach of the general obligations of a State concerning the position of aliens; claims made under this head would be within the competence of the national State and not, as a general rule, within that of the Organization.

The Charter does not expressly confer upon the Organization the capacity to include, in its claim for reparation, damage caused to the victim or to persons entitled through him. The Court must therefore begin by enquiring whether the provisions of the Charter concerning the functions of the Organization, and the part played by its agents in the performance of those functions, imply for the Organization power to afford its agents the limited protection that would consist in the bringing of a claim on their behalf for reparation for damage suffered in such circumstances. Under international law, the Organization must be deemed to have those powers which, though not expressly provided in the Charter, are conferred upon it by necessary implication as being essential to the performance of its duties. * * *

Having regard to its purposes and functions already referred to, the Organization may find it necessary, and has in fact found it necessary, to entrust its agents with important missions to be performed in disturbed parts of the world. Many missions, from their very nature, involve the agents in unusual dangers to which ordinary persons are not exposed. For the same reason, the injuries suffered by its agents in these circumstances will sometimes have occurred in such a manner that their national State would not be justified in bringing a claim for reparation on the ground of diplomatic protection, or, at any rate, would not feel disposed to do so. Both to ensure the efficient and independent performance of these missions and to afford effective support to its agents, the Organization must provide them with adequate protection. * * *

For this purpose, the Members of the Organization have entered into certain undertakings, some of which are in the Charter and others in complementary agreements. The content of these undertakings need not be described here; but the Court must stress the importance of the duty to render to the Organization "every assistance" which is accepted by the Members in Article 2, paragraph 5, of the Charter. It must be noted that the effective working of the Organization—the accomplishment of its task, and the independence and effectiveness of the work of its agents—require that these undertakings should be strictly observed. For that purpose, it is necessary that, when an infringement occurs, the Organization should be able to call upon the responsible State to remedy its default, and, in particular, to obtain from the State reparation for the damage that the default may have caused to its agent.

In order that the agent may perform his duties satisfactorily, he must feel that this protection is assured to him by the Organization, and that he may count on it. To ensure the independence of the agent, and, consequently, the independent action of the Organization itself, it is essential that in performing his duties he need not have to rely on any other protection than that of the Organization (save of course for the more direct and immediate protection due from the State in whose territory he may be). In particular, he should not have to rely on the protection of his own State. If he had to rely on that State, his independence might well be compromised, contrary to the principle applied by Article 100 of the Charter. And lastly, it is essential that— whether the agent belongs to a powerful or to a weak State; to one more affected or less affected by the complications of international life; to one in sympathy or not in sympathy with the mission of the agent—he should know that in the performance of his duties he is under the protection of the Organization. This assurance is even more necessary when the agent is stateless.

Upon examination of the character of the functions entrusted to the Organization and of the nature of the missions of its agents, it becomes clear that the capacity of the Organization to exercise a measure of functional protection of its agents arises by necessary intendment out of the Charter.

The obligations entered into by States to enable the agents of the Organization to perform their duties are undertaken not in the interest of the agents, but in that of the Organization. When it claims redress for a breach of these obligations, the Organization is invoking its own right, the right that the obligations due to it should be respected. On this ground, it asks for reparation of the injury suffered, for "it is a principle of international law that the breach of an engagement involves an obligation to make reparation in an adequate form;" as was stated by the Permanent Court in its Judgment No. 8 of July 26th, 1927. In claiming reparation based on the injury suffered by its agent, the Organization does not represent the agent, but is asserting its own right, the right to secure respect for undertakings entered into towards the Organization.

Having regard to the foregoing considerations, and to the undeniable right of the Organization to demand that its Members shall fulfill the obligations entered into by them in the interest of the good working of the Organization, the Court is of the opinion that, in the case of a breach of these obligations, the Organization has the capacity to claim adequate reparation, and that in assessing this reparation it is authorized to include the damage suffered by the victim or by persons entitled through him.

The question remains whether the Organization has "the capacity to bring an international claim against the responsible *de jure* or *de facto* government with a view to obtaining the reparation due in respect of the damage caused (*a*) to the United Nations, (*b*) to the victim or to persons entitled through him" when the defendant State is not a member of the Organization.

In considering this aspect of Question I (*a*) and (*b*), it is necessary to keep in mind the reasons which have led the Court to given an affirmative answer to it when the defendant State is a Member of the Organization. It has now been established that the Organization has capacity to bring claims on the international plane, and that it possesses a right of functional protection in respect of its agents. Here again the Court is authorized to assume that the damage suffered involves the responsibility of a State, and it is not called upon to express an opinion upon the various ways in which that responsibility might be engaged. Accordingly the question is whether the Organization has capacity to bring a claim against the defendant State to recover reparation in respect of that damage or whether, on the contrary, the defendant State, not being a member, is justified in raising the objection that the Organization lacks the capacity to bring an international claim. On this point, the Court's opinion is that fifty States, representing the vast majority of the members of the international community, had the power, in conformity with international law, to bring into being an entity possessing objective international personality, and not merely personality recognized by them alone, together with capacity to bring international claims.

Accordingly, the Court arrives at the conclusion that an affirmative answer should be given to Question I (*a*) and (*b*) whether or not the defendant State is a Member of the United Nations. * * *

FOR THESE REASONS,

The Court is of opinion

On Question I (a):

(i) unanimously,

That, in the event of an agent of the United Nations in the performance of his duties suffering injury in circumstances involving the responsibility of a Member State, the United Nations as an Organization has the capacity to bring an international claim against the responsible *de jure* or *de facto* government with a view to obtaining the reparation due in respect of the damage caused to the United Nations.

(ii) unanimously,

That, in the event of an agent of the United Nations in the performance of his duties suffering injury in circumstances involving the responsibility of a State which is not a member, the United Nations as an Organization has the capacity to bring an international claim against the responsible *de jure* or *de facto* government with a view to obtaining the reparation due in respect of the damage caused to the United Nations.

On Question I (b):

(i) by eleven votes against four,

That, in the event of an agent of the United Nations in the performance of his duties suffering injury in circumstances involving the responsibility of a Member State, the United Nations as an Organization has the capacity to bring an international claim against the responsible *de jure* or *de facto* government with a view to obtaining the reparation due in respect of the damage caused to the victim or to persons entitled through him.

(ii) by eleven votes against four,

That, in the event of an agent of the United Nations in the performance of his duties suffering injury in circumstances involving the responsibility of a State which is not a member, the United Nations as an Organization has the capacity to bring an international claim against the responsible *de jure* or *de facto* government with a view to obtaining the reparation due in respect of the damage caused to the victim or to persons entitled through him.

Notes and Questions

1. *Background.* The events leading the General Assembly to request an advisory opinion in the *Reparation Case* stemmed from the U.N.'s involvement in Palestine. In April 1947, Great Britain, which administered a League of Nations Mandate over Palestine (formerly part of the Ottoman Empire), asked the U.N. General Assembly to consider the Palestine situation. The General Assembly recommended that Palestine be divided into independent Arab and Jewish states; Jerusalem was to be administered under international control. Resulting skirmishes in the region led the U.N. Security Council, in April 1948, to call for a truce in Palestine and to establish a Truce Commission. See S.C. Res. S/273, S/727. The U.N. General Assembly appointed Count Folke Bernadotte, a Swedish national, to be U.N. Mediator in Palestine. On September 17, 1948, several months after the Provisional Government of Israel proclaimed Israel to be a state, Count Bernadotte and another U.N. observer, Colonel Serot of France, were assassinated in the Israeli-held zone of Jerusalem by men in Israeli uniform. 1 *Public Papers of the Secretaries–General of the United Nations* 163 (1969). The General Assembly asked whether the United Nations could seek reparations with respect to these assassinations.

Following the ICJ's opinion in the *Reparation Case*, the U.N. General Assembly authorized the Secretary–General to bring a claim for reparations against allegedly responsible states for injuries incurred in the service of the United Nations. Arbitration was called for if negotiation did not lead to a settlement. G.A. Res. 365 (IV) (1949). Israel paid $50,000 in reparations for the deaths of Count Bernadotte and Colonel Serot. 1 *Public Papers of the Secretaries–General of the United Nations* 228 (1969); Ralph Hewins, *Count Folke Bernadotte: His Life and Work* 239 (1950).

2. *International Personality.* Why did the Court find that the United Nations had "international personality"? What are the implications of this finding? Is it sensible to maintain that the United Nations (or other intergovernmental organizations, or, indeed, other entities) have international legal rights and obligations only if such rights and obligations are specified or authorized by states? According to Professor Bederman, the opinion in the *Reparation Case*:

> conclusively ushered in a new era of international law, fully diversified with multiple subjects and objects. Indeed, what the *Reparation* opinion achieved was a fusion between the subjects and objects of international law. Any entity, thing or person bound by international legal rules was an international legal person. The distinction between active subjects and passive objects of the law was no longer relevant.

David J. Bederman, "The Souls of International Organizations: Legal Personality and the Lighthouse at Cape Spartel," 36 *Virginia Journal of International Law* 275, 367 (1996).

3. *Capacity of the United Nations to Bring International Claims.* In the *Reparation Case*, the capacity of the United Nations to bring a claim for the death of Count Bernadotte did not follow automatically once the Court concluded the Organization had international personality. The Court sepa-

rately found that the United Nations could bring an international claim against a responsible government to obtain reparations on behalf of a U.N. employee or his survivors. Why did the Court reach this result? Was the Court persuasive in arguing that the intention of Article 100 of the U.N. Charter (see Appendix) would be compromised if the employee must rely only on protection from his own state?

Judge Hackworth dissented from the part of the Court's opinion finding that the United Nations had the capacity to sponsor an international claim on behalf of one of its agents. He said in part:

> [T]he Organization is one of delegated and enumerated powers. It is to be presumed that such powers as the Member States desired to confer upon it are stated either in the Charter or in complementary agreements concluded by them. Powers not expressed cannot freely be implied. Implied powers flow from a grant of expressed powers, and are limited to those that are "necessary" to the exercise of powers expressly granted. No necessity for the exercise of the power here in question has been shown to exist. There is no impelling reason, if any at all, why the Organization should become the sponsor of claims on behalf of its employees, even though limited to those arising while the employee is in line of duty. These employees are still nationals of their respective countries, and the customary methods of handling such claims are still available in full vigour.

1949 I.C.J. at 196, 198. Should the Court have required that the U.N. Charter be amended to authorize the United Nations to espouse claims on behalf of nationals of Member States in service of the Organization?

4. *Other Types of Legal Capacity.* What other international legal rights does the United Nations have, in addition to the right to make claims for injuries to the Organization and its agents? Although Articles 1 and 2 of Vienna Convention on the Law of Treaties (see Appendix) do not define "treaties" to include agreements made by international organizations, it seems clear that the U.N. can enter into treaties. For example, as discussed in the following Note, the United States and the United Nations have entered into a Headquarters Agreement. There is in fact a Vienna Convention on the Law of Treaties between States and International Organizations or between International Organizations, Mar. 21, 1986, 25 I.L.M. 543 (1986), modeled after the Vienna Convention on the Law of Treaties. However, the U.N. does not have all the rights of a state. For example, the Organization cannot be a party in contentious cases before the International Court of Justice.

Should the United Nations itself be legally responsible if its agents cause harm, or should the agent's own state bear responsibility? The Secretary–General in 1999 instructed forces under U.N. command and control to respect international humanitarian law. The Organization also accepts responsibility, subject to certain temporal and financial limitations, for tortious damage caused by U.N. peacekeeping forces while performing their official duties. See Daphna Shraga, "UN Peacekeeping Operations: Applicability of International Humanitarian Law and Responsibility for Operations–Related Damage," 94 *American Journal of International Law* 406 (2000).

Does every intergovernmental organization have the same legal attributes? The Permanent Court of International Justice, in its *Advisory Opinion of February 7, 1923, on Nationality Decrees in Tunis and Morocco*, suggested that the legal authority of apparently similar entities may differ. The Court, while noting some common features of protectorates under international law, also stressed that "they have individual legal characteristics resulting from the special conditions under which they were created, and the stage of their development." 1923 P.C.I.J., Ser. B, No. 4, at 27.

5. *The United Nations and Municipal Legal Systems*. The United Nations relies on its Member States to accord the Organization and its employees and agents certain rights, privileges, and immunities. On the international level, these measures are furthered by treaties, such as Articles 104 and 105 of the U.N. Charter and the Convention on the Privileges and Immunities of the United Nations, Feb. 13, 1946, 21 U.S.T. 1418, 1 U.N.T.S. 16. On the municipal level, a state defines the "legal personality" of international organizations for municipal legal purposes. States enact legislation to provide privileges, immunities, and protections to U.N. missions, to U.N. officials, and to diplomats representing their states at U.N. offices. The United States, for example, enacted the International Organizations Immunities Act, 22 U.S.C. §§ 288–288f, in 1945, and the Act for the Prevention and Punishment of Crimes Against Internationally Protected Persons, codified at 18 U.S.C. § 112, in 1976 (implementing a convention that addresses such crimes). The bilateral U.S.–U.N. Agreement Regarding the Headquarters of the United Nations, June 26, 1947, 61 Stat. 3416, 11 U.N.T.S. 11, was implemented by a 1947 joint Congressional resolution.

A state may not always take the same view of its obligations *vis-à-vis* U.N. officials as does the United Nations. Consider the case of Dato Param Cumaraswamy, a Malaysian jurist, who was named in 1994 as Special Rapporteur on the Independence of Judges and Lawyers by the U.N. Commission on Human Rights (a subsidiary organ of ECOSOC) to investigate the independence of judges, lawyers, and court officials in Malaysia. Cumaraswamy was sued for defamation in Malaysian court for his comments during an interview about matters relating to judicial corruption, that were published in an article in a 1995 issue of the magazine *International Commercial Litigation*. Despite the U.N. Secretary–General's finding that Cumaraswamy spoke in his official capacity as Special Rapporteur during the interview, and that he therefore was immune from legal process pursuant to Article VI, Section 22 of the Convention on Privileges and Immunities of the United Nations, the Malaysian High Court for Kuala Lumpur rejected Cumaraswamy's absolute immunity in June 1997. ECOSOC then requested an advisory opinion from the International Court of Justice, which ruled in April 1999 that Cumaraswamy was "entitled to immunity from legal process of every kind" for his words during the interview in question. Difference Relating to Immunity from Legal Process of a Special Rapporteur of the Commission on Human Rights (Advisory Opinion), 1999 I.C.J. 1, 1999 WL 1693056. Article VIII, Section 30 of the Privileges and Immunities Convention varies the normal rule that ICJ advisory opinions are not legally binding, by providing that advisory opinions concerning the Convention "shall be accepted as decisive by the parties." Counsel for plaintiffs argued to the Malaysian High Court, however, that the ICJ's decision was not binding in a defamation case between private litigants, that the ICJ did not consider all the relevant issues in making its ruling, and that the ICJ's decision breached "rules of natural justice." "Counsel: ICJ's Decision Was in Breach of the Rules of Natural Justice," *New Straits Times (Malaysia)*, May 12, 2000, at 19. In July 2000, the Malaysian High Court noted with "great concern that Param * * * was able to make damaging statements of the plaintiffs" and opined that the defendant had "shown a total disregard to the meaning of the word impartial" with respect to his views concerning the Malaysian legal system. The High Court nevertheless ruled that Malaysia's agreement to be bound by the ICJ's advisory opinion required that the defendant be accorded immunity from all legal process. Sujatani Poosparajah, "Param Is Immune, Rules High Court," *New Straits Times (Malaysia)*, July 8, 2000, at 6.

3. THE CONSTITUTIONAL STRUCTURE AND LEGITIMACY OF THE UNITED NATIONS

Questions about the relationship among the different organs of the United Nations, and about limits on their authority, have arisen on several occasions. The International Court, in its 1962 advisory opinion in the *Certain Expenses Case* excerpted below, addressed limits on the authority of the General Assembly. The specific issue in the case related to General Assembly-authorized expenses for activities that the Security Council had not approved, but that some states believed the Council should have approved. According to Article 24 of the U.N. Charter, Member States "confer on the Security Council primary responsibility for the maintenance of international peace and security." During the Cold War, however, one or another of the Council's five permanent members—China, France, the Soviet Union, the United Kingdom, and the United States—often vetoed proposed Security Council decisions relating to peace and security. When the General Assembly side-stepped the Security Council and approved "peacekeeping" operations, voting to assess Member States for the costs, some states refused to pay, and the ICJ was called on to give an advisory opinion.

When the Security Council does make decisions, Articles 25 and 103 of the U.N. Charter, reproduced below, apparently give such decisions powerful legal effect. What constrains the Security Council? What kinds of constitutional changes might improve the legitimacy and efficacy of Security Council decisions? The article and notes at the end of this Section explore these questions.

THE CERTAIN EXPENSES CASE

Certain Expenses of the United Nations (Article 17, Paragraph 2 of the Charter),
Advisory Opinion of 20 July 1962, 1962 I.C.J. 151, 1962 WL 4.

The question on which the Court is asked to give its opinion is whether certain expenditures which were authorized by the General Assembly to cover the costs of the United Nations operations in the Congo (hereinafter referred to as ONUC) and of the operations of the United Nations Emergency Force in the Middle East (hereinafter referred to as UNEF), "constitute 'expenses of the Organization' within the meaning of Article 17, paragraph 2, of the Charter of the United Nations." * * *

* * * In determining whether the actual expenditures authorized constitute "expenses of the Organization within the meaning of Article 17, paragraph 2, of the Charter," the Court agrees that such expenditures must be tested by their relationship to the purposes of the United Nations in the sense that if an expenditure were made for a purpose which is not one of the purposes of the United Nations, it could not be considered an "expense of the Organization."

The purposes of the United Nations are set forth in Article 1 of the Charter. The first two purposes as stated in paragraphs 1 and 2, may be summarily described as pointing to the goal of international peace and security and friendly relations. The third purpose is the achievement of economic, social, cultural and humanitarian goals and respect for human rights. The fourth and last purpose is: "To be a center for harmonizing the actions of nations in the attainment of these common ends."

The primary place ascribed to international peace and security is natural, since the fulfilment of the other purposes will be dependent upon the attainment of that basic condition. These purposes are broad indeed, but neither they nor the powers conferred to effectuate them are unlimited. Save as they have entrusted the Organization with the attainment of these common ends, the Member States retain their freedom of action. But when the Organization takes action which warrants the assertion that it was appropriate for the fulfilment of one of the stated purposes of the United Nations, the presumption is that such action is not *ultra vires* the Organization.

If it is agreed that the action in question is within the scope of the functions of the Organization but it is alleged that it has been initiated or carried out in a manner not in conformity with the division of functions among the several organs which the Charter prescribes, one moves to the internal plane, to the internal structure of the Organization. If the action was taken by the wrong organ, it was irregular as a matter of that internal structure, but this would not necessarily mean that the expense incurred was not an expense of the Organization. Both national and international law contemplate cases in which the body corporate or politic may be bound, as to third parties, by an *ultra vires* act of an agent.

In the legal systems of States, there is often some procedure for determining the validity of even a legislative or governmental act, but no analogous procedure is to be found in the structure of the United Nations. Proposals made during the drafting of the Charter to place the ultimate authority to interpret the Charter in the International Court of Justice were not accepted; the opinion which the Court is in course of rendering is an *advisory* opinion. As anticipated in 1945, therefore, each organ must, in the first place at least, determine its own jurisdiction. * * *

* * * [I]t is apparent that the operations were undertaken to fulfil a prime purpose of the United Nations, that is, to promote and to maintain a peaceful settlement of the situation. This being true, the Secretary–General properly exercised the authority given him to incur financial obligations of the Organization and expenses resulting from such obligations must be considered "expenses of the Organization within the meaning of Article 17, paragraph 2."

Notes and Questions

1. *Interpreting the U.N. Charter.* Does the U.N. Charter merely assign functions to different U.N. organs, or does it, in addition, establish limits illegal for organs to transcend? Is it appropriate, as the ICJ suggested in the *Certain Expenses Case*, to adopt a presumption against *ultra vires* U.N. action "when the Organization takes action which warrants the assertion that it was appropriate for the fulfillment of one of the stated purposes of the United Nations"? Should the Court have refused to rule on this matter of Charter interpretation at all, on the grounds that it was a "political question" better left to other U.N. organs?

In the *Certain Expenses Case*, the Court contrasted the constitutional structure of the United Nations with the legal systems of states. In general, how analogous is the U.N. Charter to municipal constitutions? What differences are explained by the fact that most municipal constitutions draw their authority from the people, while the U.N.'s constitution is based on authority given by states?

2. *Peacekeeping and Chapter VII Enforcement Actions.* In portions of the *Certain Expenses Case* not reproduced above, the International Court articulated a distinction between "Chapter VII enforcement actions," which the Security Council alone could take, and other measures relating to international peace and security, such as the authorization of peacekeeping operations. The General Assembly has sometimes recommended peacekeeping operations when the Security Council has refused to act, although in recent decades the Council has asserted full control over the approval of peacekeeping operations. We explore peacekeeping and Chapter VII enforcement actions more fully in Chapter 9.

3. *Paying for U.N. Expenses.* Following the *Certain Expenses Case*, the General Assembly voted to "accept" the ICJ's advisory opinion, but France, the Soviet Union, and Soviet bloc states still refused to pay their shares of peacekeeping assessments. What can the United Nations do when Member States are seriously in arrears in their payments? The United States argued at the time that the "shall have no vote" sanction specified in Article 19 of the U.N. Charter (see Appendix) should apply automatically when a Member State fell two years in arrears in its payments to the U.N. See Office of the Legal Adviser, U.S. Dep't of State, "Article 19 of the Charter of the United Nations, Memorandum of Law," *reprinted in* 58 *American Journal of International Law* 753 (1964). Other states, however, maintained that under U.N. rules, suspending the right to vote required a two-thirds decision of the General Assembly. In order to avoid a confrontation, the General Assembly went through its 1964–1965 session by dealing only with matters that could

be acted on by consensus. The United States and other proponents of the view that voting rights of delinquent states should be automatically suspended relented in 1965, however, and Article 19 was not enforced. France paid the amounts it had withheld several years later, and the Soviet Union made substantial payments beginning in the late 1980s.

Funding for the U.N. peacekeeping and regular budgets has remained a problem, despite U.N. budget cuts in the late 1990s. According to the United Nations, as of September 30, 2000, "Member States owed the United Nations over $3 billion for current and past assessments—$2.5 billion for peacekeeping, $533 million for the regular UN budget, and $54 million for international tribunals. The largest debtor, the United States, owes the UN $1.9 billion for past and current assessments, two-thirds of the total due." "The UN Financial Crisis," U.N. Dep't of Public Information, DPI/1815/ Rev.18 (Oct. 2000), available at < http://www.un.org/News/facts/finance.htm >. Nonpayment of dues has limited U.N. operations and caused the Organization to postpone payments to states contributing troops and equipment for peacekeeping. In late 1999 the United States at least temporarily avoided loss of its vote in the General Assembly when Congress passed legislation authorizing payment of a portion of the U.S. arrears. However, the legislation provided that the United Nations must meet several conditions, including agreeing to reduce the U.S. share of the U.N.'s regular budget from 25 to 22 percent and the U.S. share of the peacekeeping budget from 31 to 25 percent, before the United States would pay in full. See Michael P. Scharf, "A Joint Report of the International Institutions Committee and the U.N. Affairs Coordinating Committee on the Helms–Biden Law Concerning Payment of U.S. Arrears to the UN," in ABA Section of International Law and Practice, *International Law News*, Vol. 29, No. 2, at 9 (Spring 2000). In December 2000 the United Nations agreed to reduce the U.S. share of the U.N.'s regular budget to 22 percent and the U.S. share for peacekeeping to 27 per cent, with additional cuts in the U.S. peacekeeping share to be phased in gradually. The U.S. Senate approved the payment of the bulk of the dues owed by the United States. See Barbara Crossette, "After Long Fight, U.N. Agrees to Cut Dues Paid by U.S.," *New York Times*, Dec. 23, 2000, at A1; Lizette Alvarez, "Senate Ends Bitter Dispute With the U.N. on U.S. Dues," *New York Times*, Feb. 8, 2001, at A9.

In order to comply with its legal obligations, must each U.N. Member State pay its General Assembly assessments in full and without attaching conditions? Are there any legal alternatives? See Francesco Francioni, "Multilateralism à la Carte: The Limits to Unilateral Withholdings of Assessed Contributions to the UN Budget," 11 *European Journal of International Law* 43 (2000).

4. *The Legal Effect of Security Council Decisions.* The phrasing of U.N. Security Council resolutions can have legal significance. Note the formal legal effect of Security Council "decisions" according to Articles 25 and 103 of the U.N. Charter, reproduced below. See also Article 48 of the Charter.

UNITED NATIONS CHARTER, ARTICLES 25, 27(3), 103

June 26, 1945, 59 Stat. 1031, T.S. No. 993, 3 Bevans 1153, 1976 Y.B.U.N. 1043.

Article 25

The Members of the United Nations agree to accept and carry out the decisions of the Security Council in accordance with the present Charter.

Article 27(3)

Decisions of the Security Council on [non-procedural] matters shall be made by an affirmative vote of nine [of the Council's fifteen] members including the concurring votes of the permanent members * * *.

Article 103

In the event of a conflict between the obligations of the Members of the United Nations under the present Charter and their obligations under any other international agreement, their obligations under the present Charter shall prevail.

JOSE E. ALVAREZ, "THE ONCE AND FUTURE SECURITY COUNCIL"

18 *The Washington Quarterly*, No. 2, at 3 (Spring 1995).

The post-cold war revival of the United Nations (UN) Security Council has come with a price: many UN members are questioning the Council's legitimacy and calling for its restructuring. * * *

IS THE COUNCIL OUT OF CONTROL? * * *

* * * Today the almost defunct organ largely unable to react to the most direct breaches of the international peace during the Cold War has become an entity capable of finding an "international threat to the peace" or "breach of the peace" in unexpected, not to say strange, places: in the context of conflicts *within* states (e.g., Somalia and, some would say, at least initially in the former Yugoslavia); because of ostensible threats to the human rights of a state's own citizens (e.g., the Kurds in Iraq); because of a state's refusal to surrender its own nationals accused of terrorism (Libya); or because a military elite has failed to respect the results of a UN–supervised election (Haiti). Further, the entity that had only rarely in 45 years authorized the use of force, has now, in the few years since the end of the Cold War, managed to delegate away the authority to use force in its name on several occasions— explicitly in Haiti and on the occasion of the Persian Gulf War—and implicitly in Somalia, post–Gulf war Iraq, and the former Yugoslavia. Yet, despite the increasing resort to force and its variants (such as the use of "peacekeepers" to track down a warlord in Somalia), articles 43 to 45 in the Charter remain effectively unimplemented: special agreements to allocate forces to the organization are not in place and neither is there an effective Military Staff Committee to oversee UN use of force. * * *

Although some have questioned aspects of the Council's initial authorization to use force in defense of Kuwait, more widespread have been the doubts evoked by the Council's actions since the end of the Gulf war. Serious doubts began with resolution 687 of April 3, 1991, the "mother of all resolutions" and the most complex adopted in the Council's history. In this resolution, and in many since relating to Iraq, the Council exercised sweeping powers over a defeated aggressor state. Ostensibly licensed by its power to "restore" international peace and security (article 39), the Council effectively put Iraqi sovereignty under UN receivership. For the first time, the UN told a supposedly sovereign state what its borders are supposed to be, what proportion of its export earnings it is entitled to keep, what financial liability it has incurred and to whom, what kinds of observers it must admit into its militarily most sensitive areas, what types of weapons it may possess, and even what treaties it must ratify.

These determinations have been imposed as if by a legislature or a court, subject to no time constraint and indeed, some of them, such as with respect to boundaries, presumably to apply in perpetuity. * * * There are doubts about the Council's good faith. It is suspected that the post-Gulf war resolutions were in reality attempts to bring down a particular regime in pursuit of well-known U.S. foreign policy goals (i.e., to stifle a powerful regional enemy of democracy, encourage nuclear non-proliferation, and secure regional stability).

Others have questioned the Iraqi sanctions on moral or humanitarian grounds. Under existing Council decisions, Iraq remains liable, for example, for all Gulf war liabilities as determined by the Council and the Compensation Commission it has created to deal with claims against Iraq. Unless these Council resolutions are modified or terminated, in principle the people of Iraq remain liable, if necessary in perpetuity, for what is estimated to be over $170 billion to cover the 2,335,000 claims filed to date. The Council has presumably decided that a "just" peace in the region requires the infliction of economic pain on a people living within a totalitarian state not amenable to bottom-up pressures for change. One need not be a friend of Iraq to be troubled by the Council's assumption of a judicial power purportedly more vast than any wielded by any national or international court in history. Doubts about the wisdom of such a course are only heightened by the suspicion that, unlike any court, the Council has not established any clear rules of general applicability on when comparable actions will be taken for other culprits or the scope of the precedents being set. Certainly the Council has not visited such a plight on all those who have violated the Charter or international law.

Council resolution 688 of April 5, 1991, another in the line of post-Gulf war resolutions, whereby the Council compelled Iraq to grant access to international humanitarian organizations to assist its internal Kurdish population, illustrates another set of concerns about legitimacy. Advocates of self-determination for the Kurdish people as well as others have criticized this institutional innovation, considered by many international lawyers to be the UN's first real attempt to legitimize the doctrine of humanitarian intervention. Advocates of Kurdish self-determination note that this resolution fell far short of the Council's full-throttle response to Iraq's invasion of Kuwait and was a betrayal of the UN's responsibilities to a population that had been encouraged to put itself at risk by the organization's own actions. On the other hand, there were those, such as Chinese representatives to the UN, who were reluctant to establish even this modest precedent, arguing that a state's treatment of its own nationals lies at the heart of a member's untrammeled "domestic jurisdiction."[18] Both sides see the Council's resolution as legally incoherent: it bows to the principle of noninterference in domestic jurisdiction in article 2(7) but then proceeds to interfere, without making an explicit determination that the situation constitutes a breach of the international peace. * * *

The Council's recent authorization to use force to dislodge the military regime in Haiti has prompted concerns both within the United States and in the greater membership of the UN. * * * [The Council] delegat[ed] to the United States the role of coordinating and undertaking military action. Although this delegation was arguably permissible under the Charter, doubts remain. Is it tactically wise to cast the military action of select states charged with doing the UN's bidding as UN action? What is the cost to the organization's future ability to collectively legitimize such actions? Does the UN want to be held accountable for all that is done in its name, especially when the Council delegation is given in such expansive terms ("all necessary means")?

Further, although the cases of Korea and Iraq were relatively easy to portray as "aggression," posing clear threats to the international peace and therefore licensed under chapter VII, just exactly what was the "threat to the international peace and security" posed by Haiti? If waves of refugees, standing alone, are enough, the Council's license to authorize force has now expanded exponentially. * * * [Alternatively,] [t]hat a military coup, because of its threat to an emerging right to democratic governance, is sufficient to trigger chapter VII action is not comforting to those states whose histories are strewn with the wrecks of successful and unsuccessful coups. It is an especially questionable precedent to establish in the context of Haiti, a country whose history of "established democracy" is essentially limited to one presidential election. It is also not a precedent that the UN is likely to follow with any lawyerly consistency—as is suggested by the Council's total inaction with respect to Alberto Fujimori's undemocratic actions within Peru. * * *

THE UN'S EMERGING DEMOCRATIC DEFICIT

Joseph Weiler has suggested that the making of law by international bodies, as in the European Union, appears to follow a peculiar dynamic:

---

18. Article 2(7) provides that "[n]othing in the present Charter shall authorize the United Nations to intervene in matters which are essentially within the domestic jurisdiction of any state or shall require the Members to submit such matters to settlement under the present Charter, but this principle shall not prejudice the application of enforcement measures under Chapter VII."

successful international organizations evolve into effective lawmaking institutions when members forgo their sovereign option to "exit" (either totally or selectively) and opt instead to correct the organization's inadequacies by exercising a greater "voice" in that organization's decision-making processes. Weiler argues that the more an international organization successfully "legislates," in the sense of the promulgation of rules that are binding both on and within states, the more members become conscious of the need to assert themselves in the organization's ways of making law, for instance, by keeping tighter "democratic" control over their executive branch representatives to that organization.[30]

Although the UN is a long way from becoming the effective lawmaking institution that the European Union now is, the Council is issuing purportedly binding edicts on a regular basis and other parts of the UN are also showing signs of waking up from their cold war quiescence. And the more the organization "legislates," the more its members, particularly those without the veto, see possible threats to their "sovereignty." Recent claims within the UN for greater "democratic accountability" replicate, at a modest level, Weiler's exit and voice dynamic. Such demands, like those from states whose economies are dramatically affected by the UN's penchant for economic sanctions targeting their trading partners, stem from an increased realization that what the organization, and especially the Council, is doing *matters* to them.

Such demands also originate from pressures internal to governments—from nongovernmental interest groups and others affected by UN action. Council decisions are beginning to have a direct impact on individuals and corporations and not merely on their governments. An individual charged with a crime before an international tribunal created by the Council, the business whose contract for exports of goods to Iraq or Libya is breached at the Council's direction, the consumer who cannot get an imported product because of a decision by a sanctions committee, or the corporation whose claim against Iraq is dismissed because of a decision by the Compensation Commission, all have an interest in the Council's decisions and are beginning to articulate those interests * * *. * * *

Amelioration of the emerging democratic deficit problems will, over the long term, require something more than the addition of two or three members to the Council. * * * General Assembly * * * proposals for greater coordination and consultation with the Assembly both prior to and after significant Council action * * * have a respectable lineage. * * *

One approach, suggested by Michael Reisman, would be the formation of a "Chapter VII Consultation Committee" of 21 members of the Assembly. Under Reisman's proposal, the Council would immediately notify this committee whenever it planned to move into a chapter VII

---

30. This vastly oversimplifies a rich and complex argument. See J.H.H. Weiler, "The Transformation of Europe," *Yale Law Journal* 100 (June 1991).

mode. The secretary general and the president of the Council would promptly meet with the committee to share information and solicit its views. Throughout the crisis, the Council and committee would remain in constant contact in the best tradition of "consultation" as understood in international law and practice. The Assembly would not have a veto over Council action, but at the same time its participation would extend beyond a right to mere notification. Such institutionalized give-and-take would facilitate a greater sense of participation and endow final Council decisions with the imprimatur, the legitimacy, of the larger world community. * * *

Less radical but no less useful may be more modest changes to the Council's now overly secretive "informal consultations." The Council, which did not hold a single meeting during the first four weeks of the 1991 air war over Iraq, needs to consider, as do all public bodies, the need for public accountability. Although much that goes on within the Council may need to remain confidential, especially in the midst of an ongoing crisis, at a minimum, states particularly affected by the imposition of economic sanctions or states that would be expected to contribute troops to a contemplated mission should be invited to Council deliberations before decisions are made—as is anticipated in articles 44 and 50 of the Charter. The Council also needs to take more seriously its duty to report to the Assembly; such reports should be more timely and include substantive discussions of the issues. They should not merely list Council decisions. After a crisis is over, the Council could seek the advice of others as to controversial issues likely to arise again.

The Security Council's Normative Deficits

But the Security Council and the United States need to address not only *how* the Council undertakes decisions, but *what* decisions it undertakes. What is in doubt is the substance of its decisions, not only the procedures behind them.

The purported legal justifications offered for the Council's involvement in the Haiti situation suggest one major substantive issue: the Council has not come up with an alternative to interstate aggression as a raison d'être likely to be coherent over the long term. To date it has given no principled answer—apart from realpolitik—to those who would ask why the Council chose to act in some cases falling short of manifest interstate aggression but not in other cases of arguable violation of the Charter. Why Libya and Haiti but not Israel, Cuba, or North Korea? Particularly to those unable to exercise a veto over these decisions, these Council actions—not to mention cases of Council inaction—pose increasingly difficult issues of normative justification.

The scope of recent peace operations suggests another set of normative gaps. * * * [As] UN operations in Somalia showed, increasingly today "peacekeepers" are being sent where there is no peace to keep, where there is no host state to give consent to their presence, and where the rules of engagement anticipate the use of force in instances other than self-defense.

* * * [T]he Council is a lawmaking institution * * *. When it acts under chapter VII, the Council is authorized to make binding law that can be invoked against members of the UN and even non-members. In the cases discussed above and in others the Council purports to act to enforce the rule of law and purports to be subject to the rule of law. It also purports to act in a judicial manner. Council decisions "determine" that Iraq, Libya, Serbia, and Montenegro have violated international law in specific ways, invoke treaty authority to render judgment, and invite the international community to judge the Council as if it were a court or legislature. States are encouraged to judge the Council's actions—which after all constitute precedents for the interpretation of the Charter—in the same way all laws are judged: by their textual clarity, consonance with other rules of general application, the match between deed and sanction, and the impartiality of application. When on close examination the Council's actions fail to meet these requisites, when no rule emerges to explain what the Council is doing or how its action comports with the Charter, including its principles, states are entitled to legalistic doubts. * * *

Today the Council sometimes goes beyond the immediate need to defuse a threat to international peace and security. At times it is attempting to adjudicate legal disputes and impose long-term legal solutions (as with Iraq on weapons, financial liability, and boundaries); trying to alter (or progressively develop) established law (as with the regime to "extradite or prosecute" terrorists and possibly with respect to war crimes); or trying itself to apply (or create) principles of international law (as through its delegated body to adjudicate claims against Iraq). Arguably nothing in the Charter precludes these actions. Indeed, back in 1945, the United States argued that the Council had two functions: the "political function" of taking enforcement action and a "quasi-judicial" function of settling disputes. It argued that the veto applied only to the first type of action and that every nation "large or small" should abstain from voting on disputes to which it was a party. Although the United States' promise not to deploy its veto and to abstain from voting all but died with the Cold War, the premise that the Council can successfully carry out this dual role is with us yet again.

Revival of the no-veto/abstention promise might yet make the Council's claim to "quasi-judicial" status credible, but this is dubious. The Council is preeminently a reactive, political forum apt to act on the basis of short-term needs, not long-term judicious (or judicial) perspective. Council representatives do not necessarily consider the broader legal consequences of what they do. This is probably as it must and should be, because the enforcer of the international peace must be political. A decision to act or to refuse to act in a case like Bosnia needs to consider factors other than the establishment of legal precedents pleasing to law professors. Council decisions are often the product of political horse-trading and compromise. No amount of tinkering in its membership is likely to turn the Council into an impartial court or a deliberative "lawmaking" body like the International Law Commission.

Yet, if at least some of the doubts now entertained about the Council are due to its tendency to assume a greater quasi-judicial role than is warranted by the existing threat to the peace, there are ways to defuse these doubts. The Council cannot and should not avoid taking legally binding decisions. The Council's legal determination that Iraq's purported annexation of Kuwait is "null and void," for instance, is part of its job. It can, however, consciously exercise some restraint and leave to more appropriate bodies the task of defining and applying the law. In other instances, when the Council has either no or only a dubious normative justification for doing what it is doing, it should reconsider the wisdom of doing it. * * *

Conclusion

UN Security Council decisions, like all of international law, are ultimately made effective by collective legitimation. Council sanctions have not always been faithfully enforced, and unless measures are taken to expand the sense of participation there may well be a progressive deterioration in the effectiveness of these and other Council decisions or, at a minimum, direct conflict between institutional organs—as is suggested by General Assembly resolutions that have criticized the Council's continued arms embargo for Bosnia. To avoid the fate of its illustrious but failed predecessor, the League of Nations, the UN needs to shore up its floundering legitimacy. Restructuring the Council is part of that task, but such restructuring must be pursued with a broader vision of the final goal.

From a Western lawyer's perspective, the Council's current dilemma is predictable. A Charter that puts at the helm unreviewable political authority with no competing political or judicial check may indeed be the basis of a workable system but it is not, as has been suggested, a constitution worthy of the name. Yet if there is to be a "new world order" based on the rule of law, it is difficult to see how that world can come about except through some approximation of such a constitutional system.

In its stead, the Council is flexing its legal muscles, and no other entity—certainly not the General Assembly and not the ICJ—has yet emerged as an acceptable check or balance on Council action.

Notes and Questions

1. *Security Council Resolution 687.* One of the examples of bold Security Council action cited by Professor Alvarez is Resolution 687, 30 I.L.M. 846 (1991), a follow-up to Iraq's 1990 invasion of Kuwait, more about which appears in Chapter 9. The Security Council's actions with respect, for example, to the Iraq–Kuwait boundary were dramatic. Iraq contested the validity of the Iraq–Kuwait Agreed Minutes, Oct. 4, 1963, 485 U.N.T.S. 321, which related to the boundary between the two states, and questioned the

boundary demarcation. Drawing international boundaries is a sensitive matter; states normally set them by agreement or by authorizing a tribunal to decide them. But in Resolution 687, the Security Council itself seemed to impose a settlement to an international boundary dispute by deciding to guarantee this 1963 boundary. In Resolution 833 of May 1993, the Security Council "reaffirmed" its guarantee of the inviolability of the Iraq–Kuwait border and "welcomed" the decisions of a Demarcation Commission established pursuant to Resolution 687.

Resolution 687 also contemplated a compensation commission to assess Iraq's liability for losses suffered because of its invasion of Kuwait. In May 1991 the Security Council formally created the U.N. Compensation Commission, a subsidiary organ of the Security Council under Article 29 of the U.N. Charter. S.C. Res. 692 (1991). The Compensation Commission, whose procedures are supervised by a Governing Council composed of Security Council members' representatives acting in their governmental capacities, can resolve disputed claims, assess damages, and review damage assessments through an appellate mechanism. Successful claimants are compensated from a fund created by taking certain proceeds of Iraq's sales of its oil exports. See S.C. Res. 705 (1991), 706 (1991), 778 (1992). Was it appropriate for the Security Council to create and supervise an adjudicatory commission, to determine who was to receive compensation, and to sequester the natural resource wealth of a state to insure that the Commission's awards would be paid?

In Resolution 687, the Security Council also directly spoke to litigation in municipal courts. Paragraph 29 effectively required all states to apply a *force majeure* defense to Iraqi claims in connection with otherwise valid transactions that were not carried out because of the Security Council's economic sanctions against Iraq. Should the Security Council legislate on *force majeure* in municipal courts?

Some paragraphs of Resolution 687 related to humanitarian measures, as did Security Council Resolution 688, which condemned Iraq's repression of Kurds in northern Iraq. Resolution 688 characterized the flow of Kurdish refugees "towards and across international frontiers" as a threat to international peace and security, "insisted" that Iraq allow international humanitarian organizations immediate access to those in need of aid, requested the U.N. Secretary–General to pursue humanitarian efforts in Iraq, and demanded Iraqi cooperation with the Secretary–General on humanitarian measures. See Jane E. Stromseth, "Iraq's Repression of Its Civilian Population: Collective Responses and Continuing Challenges," in *Enforcing Restraint* 77 (Lori Fisler Damrosch ed. 1993). Iraq consented to a U.N. humanitarian presence within Iraq in April 1991, and eventually asked the United Nations to take responsibility for Kurdish relief efforts.

Was Resolution 687 illegitimate, or did it serve a proper legal function? Was the Security Council, although a political institution, providing "institutionalized countermeasures" as a means of responding to Iraq's illegal actions and thus enforcing international law? See Vera Gowlland–Debbas, "Security Council Enforcement Action and Issues of State Responsibility," 43 *International and Comparative Law Quarterly* 55 (1994).

2. *Terminating Security Council Decisions.* Security Council Resolution 687 provided that some Council sanctions imposed against Iraq were to continue in effect "until a further decision is taken by the Security Council." Since one of the Security Council's permanent members could veto any proposal to lift sanctions, should the Council require that any sanctions it imposes expire if they are not renewed by some date certain? Or require that an initial sanctions resolution include a modified voting procedure to determine when the sanctions can be lifted? See David D. Caron, "The Legitimacy of the Collective Authority of the Security Council," 87 *American Journal of International Law* 552, 577–88 (1994).

3. *Changes Affecting the Security Council.* World politics has changed dramatically since 1945, when the United Nations was formed with the United States, Great Britain, France, China, and the Soviet Union as permanent members of the Security Council. Japan and Germany, in ruins after their defeat in World War II, have emerged as major economic and political powers. Many new states have gained independence: the United Nations began with 51 Member States; as of November 1, 2000, U.N. membership stood at 189.

Since 1945, however, only a few changes have affected the structure and composition of the Security Council. In 1971, the government of the People's Republic of China replaced that of the government of the Republic of China (Taiwan) in the United Nations, the PRC taking the "Chinese seat" on the Security Council. The Russian Federation took over the seat of the Soviet Union in 1991, following the break-up of the Soviet Union. The U.N. Charter was amended in 1965, so that the membership of the Security Council now totals 15 states, rather than the original 11; nine votes are now required to adopt resolutions, rather than seven. There have been no changes, however, in the permanent member veto system.

4. *Enhancing the Legitimacy of the Security Council.* Would changes in the composition of the Security Council enhance its legitimacy? Should the veto power be changed? Should more states become members of the Security Council? If so, how many? Should any new members, say Germany and Japan, be made permanent members, with or without a veto? Would any such changes cause the Security Council to act more or less effectively than it now does to help maintain international peace and security?

What nonstructural changes with respect to Security Council actions might enhance the Council's legitimacy? One of the criticisms of the Security Council has been that too many of its deliberations are carried out in secret, and that Security Council decision-making should become more "transparent." What are the prospects for enhancing the legitimacy of Security Council actions through greater transparency, more consultations with the General Assembly or with states affected by Security Council actions, or other nonstructural changes? See Michael C. Wood, "Security Council Working Methods and Procedure: Recent Developments," 45 *International & Comparative Law Quarterly* 150 (1996). Complaints about a lack of transparency are sometimes lodged by the Security Council's nonpermanent members against its permanent members. For example, the representative of the Netherlands, commenting on the slow pace and the secrecy of deliberations among the five permanent members concerning Iraqi sanctions, complained:

"But we, the elected members [of the Council], simply cannot go on telling the other United Nations members who have elected us that we are content to sit and wait for smoke to emerge from the H–5—the P–5—chamber. I use the word H–5 because in my delegation we have started to call the permanent five the 'hereditary five.' " *Quoted in* Barbara Crosette, "Tempers Flare in the U.N. Council Over Stalemate on Iraq Issue," *New York Times*, Nov. 20, 1999, at A4.

For more on the concept of legitimacy, see Thomas M. Franck, *The Power of Legitimacy Among Nations* (1990).

5. *Judicial Review of Security Council Decisions?* Should the ICJ exercise any power of judicial review over Security Council decisions, and, if so, what form should it take? The issue has been discussed in connection with the Case Concerning Questions of Interpretation and Application of the 1971 Montreal Convention Arising From the Aerial Incident at Lockerbie (Libya v. United States), 1992 I.C.J. 114, 1992 WL 190214 (Request for Provisional Measures). On March 3, 1992, Libya sought provisional measures (see Article 41 of the Court's Statute, in the Appendix) against the United States. Libya claimed that the United States violated the 1971 Montreal Convention for the Suppression of Unlawful Acts Against the Safety of Civil Aviation when it sought the extradition of Libyan nationals suspected of bombing a Pan Am flight that crashed in Lockerbie, Scotland. On March 31, 1992, the Security Council, acting under Chapter VII of the U.N. Charter, decided in Resolution 748 that Libya was required to extradite two of its nationals to the United States or the United Kingdom. The Court refused to indicate provisional measures, noting that:

> both Libya and the United States, as Members of the United Nations, are obliged to accept and carry out the decisions of the Security Council in accordance with article 25 of the Charter; [that] the Court, which is at the stage of proceedings on provisional measures, considers that prima facie this obligation extends to the decision contained in resolution 748 (1992); and [that], in accordance with Article 103 of the Charter, the obligations of the Parties in that respect prevail over their obligations under any other international agreement, including the Montreal Convention[.]

Id. at 126. Some of the separate and dissenting opinions raised at least the possibility of judicial review in an appropriate case. For example, Judge Shahabuddeen wondered whether there was "any conceivable point beyond which a legal issue may properly arise as to the competence of the Security Council to produce" overriding results, and if there are any limits, "what are those limits and what body, if other than the Security Council, is competent to say what those limits are." *Id.* at 142. For discussion, see José E. Alvarez, "Judging the Security Council," 90 *American Journal of International Law* 1 (1996); Bernd Martenczuk, "The Security Council, the International Court and Judicial Review: What Lessons from Lockerbie?," 10 *European Journal of International Law* 517 (1999). As part of an effort to resolve the Lockerbie situation, there has now been a trial of the Libyan suspects in the Netherlands under Scottish law, resulting in the conviction of one of the suspects. See Agreement Concerning a Scottish Trial in the Netherlands, Neth.-U.K., Sept. 18, 1998, 38 I.L.M. 926 (1999); Micheal P. Scharf, "A Preview of the

Lockerbie Case"(May 2000), and "The Lockerbie Trial Verdict" (Feb. 2001), both available at <http://www.asil.org/insights.htm>.

6. *Other Modes of Promoting Legitimacy.* If legitimacy concerns arise because of a democratic deficit, is it wrong to look for a cure at the level of the Security Council? Should the powers of the U.N. General Assembly instead be increased, because that body is more representative? Or should an altogether new institution—a global democratic assembly with elected individual representatives—be created, in order to help contribute to legal solutions to international problems? How would such an assembly be organized, and what powers should it have? See Richard Falk & Andrew Strauss, "On the Creation of a Global Peoples Assembly: Legitimacy and the Power of Popular Sovereignty," 36 *Stanford Journal of International Law* 191 (2000). In the European Union, the European Parliament, popularly elected since 1979, has "co-decision" authority with the European Council, an authority that allows the Parliament to veto or amend European legislation in specified issue areas. The Parliament also has powers with respect to the EU budget, approval of the nominee for the Presidency of the European Commission, approval of treaties between the EU and third states, and approval of accession of new states to membership in the EU. See Treaty of Amsterdam amending the Treaty on European Union, the Treaties Establishing the European Communities and Certain Related Acts, Nov. 10, 1997, 1997 O.J. (C 340) 1; *Foundations of Democracy in the European Union: From the Genesis of Parliamentary Democracy to the European Parliament* (John Pinder ed. 1999).

B. NONGOVERNMENTAL ORGANIZATIONS

Non-governmental organizations (NGOs) are created under municipal law rather than by interstate agreement. There are thousands of "international NGOs," which work on a wide range of economic, social, human rights, and environmental issues of international concern. Although some NGOs have links to governments or receive government grants, most are private, not-for-profit entities, receiving all their support from individual members or private contributions. As we saw in the *Texaco–Libya Arbitration* in Chapter 3 and the *Barcelona Traction Case* in Chapter 6, business corporations, which are also creatures of municipal law, may use international law and international legal process to try to obtain redress in specific cases of harm to their economic interests. International NGOs, by contrast, often have as primary goals the development of international legal norms and the implementation and enforcement of those norms on the international and municipal levels.

In this Part, we consider some of the roles of NGOs in international law and process. The first reading below examines some of the functions of the International Committee of the Red Cross, a private NGO formed in 1863 and headquartered in Geneva, Switzerland. Although its governing body is composed of Swiss nationals, the ICRC employs non-Swiss nationals and is active in many states, providing relief services in situations of armed conflict. The second reading concerns actual and potential functions of NGOs in developing and enforcing international environmental law. These materials explore questions about the international legal personality of NGOs, their recognition by other entities, and their legitimacy.

DAVID P. FORSYTHE, "WHO GUARDS THE GUARDIANS: THIRD PARTIES AND THE LAW OF ARMED CONFLICT"

70 *American Journal of International Law* 41 (1976).

The Geneva Diplomatic Conference on the Reaffirmation and Development of International Humanitarian Law in Armed Conflicts continues its attempts to supplement the 1949 Geneva Conventions. [The Geneva Diplomatic Conference was charged with negotiating protocols to the four 1949 Geneva Conventions. These Conventions are: the Convention for the Amelioration of the Condition of the Wounded and Sick in Armed Forces in the Field, Aug. 12, 1949, 3 U.S.T. 3114, 75 U.N.T.S. 31 (First Convention); the Convention for the Amelioration of the Condition of the Wounded, Sick, and Shipwrecked Members of the Armed Forces at Sea, Aug. 12, 1949, 3 U.S.T. 3217, 75 U.N.T.S. 85 (Second Convention); the Convention Relative to the Treatment of Prisoners of War, Aug. 12, 1949, 3 U.S.T. 3316, 75 U.N.T.S. 135 (Third Convention); and the Convention Relative to the Protection of Civilian Persons in Time of War, Aug. 12, 1949, 3 U.S.T. 3516, 75 U.N.T.S. 287 (Fourth Convention). During 1975 the Conference reviewed and adopted some of the 137 draft articles] presented to the Conference by the International Committee of the Red Cross (ICRC).[1] * * *

Also among the subjects provisionally treated by the 1975 session was that of the Protecting Power system—the rights and duties of neutral states or their substitutes to supervise the implementation of the law of international armed conflict. This is a crucial part of the law. The debate at the 1975 session on the Protecting Power system is one indication of the strength of the movement to guarantee that the law on the books does indeed become the applied law in war. That debate also reflects the strength of the movement to give nonstate third parties, such as the ICRC or the United Nations, the right to supervise application of the law. These are two sides of the same coin. * * *

[In the 1949 Conventions,] aside from the tasks assigned to Protecting Powers and their official substitutes, the ICRC was authorized to carry out its traditional tasks with the consent of the parties. Article 9 of the Prisoners of War Convention reads:

The provisions of the present Convention constitute no obstacle to the humanitarian activities which the International Committee of the Red Cross or any other impartial humanitarian organization

---

1. The ICRC drew up, in consultation with individuals and governments, two draft protocols to the 1949 Conventions, the first pertaining to international armed conflict, the second to noninternational armed conflict. * * *

may, subject to the consent of the parties to the conflict concerned, undertake for the protection of prisoners of war and their relief.[†]

Moreover, the ICRC was authorized by the 1949 Conventions not only to become an official substitute [for a Protecting Power] under certain conditions (Article 10/10/10/11) and an unofficial substitute (Article 9/9/9/10) but also to engage in such specific tasks as operating the Central Information Agency under Article 140 of the Civilians Convention. Among its functions was the *right* to visit places of detention, whether or not a Protecting Power or official substitute was designated by belligerents (Article 126 of the Prisoners of War Convention; Article 143 of the Civilians Convention). These ICRC visits were to occur *automatically,* subject only to the detaining state's consent to the particular ICRC delegate, but not to the visits in principle. * * *

[During the 1975 negotiations, the] formulations by the ICRC and its statements on the subject of the Protecting Power system were extremely important. The ICRC took a highly active role in the negotiations, departing from its more usual role of being a technical drafting secretariat. This change was explained by the head of the ICRC delegation:

> While the ICRC was pleased to place the technical skill of its experts at the Diplomatic Conference's disposal, it did not consider that it should take a stand on provisions which mainly concerned governments. * * * In the article at present under discussion, however, special functions of great importance were envisaged for the ICRC, and it would therefore be useful for delegations to know its views on the subject.

What the ICRC wanted, which was implicit in its texts and made clear by the statements of its representatives, was the *nonautomatic* introduction of itself as a substitute for Protecting Powers in certain situations. It did not wish to be thrust upon a belligerent against its or the belligerent's wishes. * * *

Despite the fact that no one could name any organization other than the ICRC that might serve as a formal substitute, there was compromise on this point * * *. As reported out by [the Working] Group, paragraph 4 of Article 5 reads:

> If, despite the foregoing, there is no Protecting Power, the Parties to the conflict shall accept without delay an offer which may be made by the International Committee of the Red Cross or by any other organization which offers all guarantees of impartiality and efficacy, after due consultations with the said Parties and taking into account the result of these consultations, to act as a substitute. The function of such a substitute is subject to the consent of the Parties to a conflict; all efforts shall be made by the Parties to facilitate the

[†] Similar language appears in Article 9 of the First Convention, Article 9 of the Second Convention, and Article 10 of the Fourth Convention.—Eds.

operation of a substitute in fulfilling its tasks under the Conventions and Protocol.†† * * *

Common Article 9/9/9/10 of the Geneva Conventions, pertaining to the traditional humanitarian tasks, remains unchanged. Moreover, both the general and the specific functions of the ICRC, already found in the 1949 treaties, appear to be strengthened by new Article 70–bis:

> The Parties to the conflict shall grant to the International Committee of the Red Cross all facilities within their power so as to enable it to carry out the humanitarian role assigned to it by the Conventions and the present Protocol in order to ensure protection and assistance to the victims of conflicts; the International Committee of the Red Cross may also carry out any other humanitarian activities in favor of these victims, subject to the consent of the Parties to the conflict concerned.†††

Therefore, the specific tasks of the ICRC and their automatic nature are reaffirmed in Protocol I—as well as the general humanitarian functions of that organization. The parties "shall grant" to the ICRC what is needed for the exercise or the specific functions of humanitarian protection and assistance.

Article 70 bis conveys the expectation that the ICRC will be functioning. While Red Cross protection and assistance is undefined in law and perhaps undefinable in practice, surely that protection and assistance includes most of the Protecting Power's tasks. The ICRC has stated that it performs "many of the functions of substitutes for Protecting Powers as part of its traditional activities." * * *

Thus a minimally adequate supervision would seem to be assured in the future through ICRC action, regardless of the disposition of new Article 5. Whether or not the introduction of the ICRC is automatic may become an academic question, if there is a general expectation that the ICRC will become systematically involved in armed conflicts in order to assure that humanitarian needs are met.

A "minimally adequate supervision" involves two things. One is the ability to identify humanitarian need and to respond to it logistically and technically and in terms of material goods. The long record of the ICRC in this regard and its recent efforts in the Middle East and Sub–Continent, not to mention Cyprus, suggest clearly that the ICRC is able to provide effective protection and assistance, which is precisely the meaning of implementing the law. A second dimension to adequate supervision is the ability to get states to change their policies when such policies are outside the rules. The ICRC has taken the approach of a "friendly legal adviser" rather than a "policeman." The results are inconclusive historically. All that can be said is that the ICRC has had

†† This text became, with minor drafting changes, Article 5(4) of Protocol I, the Protocol Additional (No. I) to the Geneva Conventions of August 12, 1949, and Relating to the Protection of Victims of International Armed Conflicts, June 8, 1977, 1125 U.N.T.S. 3.—Eds.

††† This text became, with minor drafting changes, Article 81 of Protocol I.—Eds.

some success in this matter and that "public finger shaking" and reprisals have not proven any more effective. In historical perspective, * * * the ICRC may have more capacity for effective supervising of the law than have governments that have assumed the role of Protecting Power.

Notes and Questions

1. *The ICRC and the International Red Cross and Red Crescent Movement.* The International Committee of the Red Cross is one component of what is known as the International Red Cross and Red Crescent Movement. Another part is the International Federation of Red Cross and Red Crescent Societies (formerly the League of Red Cross Societies), an NGO founded in 1919 and, like the ICRC, headquartered in Geneva. The Federation supports the activities of national societies, promoting aid for development and coordinating relief operations for natural or technological disasters. There are approximately 175 national Red Cross and Red Crescent societies, of which the American Red Cross—a corporation formed and supported by the U.S. government (see 36 U.S.C. §§ 300101–300111)—is one example. The ICRC itself has multiple functions: assessing whether new national societies meet conditions for recognition and, if so, recognizing them; providing international relief services to soldiers and civilians in armed conflicts; assisting national societies in such situations; and educating people about international humanitarian law. Professor Forsythe has described the "International Red Cross" as "a transnational movement with two heads and many arms. * * * [T]he heads do not control the arms, and the heads are not always looking in the same direction." David P. Forsythe, *Humanitarian Politics: The International Committee of the Red Cross* 5 (1977).

2. *The ICRC as an "International Person."* Do the ICRC's roles in formulating and enforcing international legal rules suggest that it is a subject of international law with international personality? Consider the various ICRC functions in the excerpt above. The Committee provided the draft of a treaty that served as the basis for negotiating the final treaty text, and then itself participated along with governments in the negotiations. Treaty articles specifically name the ICRC, some providing that the Committee has the right to act if governments accept its offer of services and others providing that the Committee has specified mandatory rights. The ICRC may also serve as an official substitute "Protecting Power" or, as Professor Forsythe noted, may unofficially carry out "Protecting Power" functions. Why might governments prefer to have the ICRC, as opposed to a neutral government or the United Nations, act as a Protecting Power?

The ICRC has also entered into headquarters agreements with approximately 50 states where the Committee conducts its activities. These agreements give the ICRC much the same sorts of privileges and immunities that intergovernmental organizations enjoy pursuant to agreement. For example, the Agreement Between the International Committee of the Red Cross and the Swiss Federal Council To Determine the Legal Status of the Committee in Switzerland, Mar. 1, 1993, *reprinted in International Review of the Red Cross*, No. 293, at 152, provides that the ICRC's premises and archives are inviolable and that the ICRC is, with certain exceptions, immune from legal process and execution. According to Article 1 of the Agreement, Switzerland "recognizes the international juridical personality and the legal capacity in Switzerland" of the ICRC.

3. *International Humanitarian Law*. International humanitarian law relates to the protection and humane treatment of combatants and noncombatants during armed conflicts. It historically falls under the heading of *jus in bello*, rather than *jus ad bellum* (the law governing when force may legally be used), which we consider in Chapter 9. Core humanitarian law treaties include the four 1949 Geneva Conventions (applicable to international armed conflicts) and two 1977 Additional Protocols (one concerning the protection of victims of international armed conflicts, and one concerning the protection of victims of non-international armed conflicts). As of September 2000, 189 states were parties to the Geneva Conventions, 157 states had accepted Additional Protocol I, and 150 had accepted Additional Protocol II. See also the discussion in Chapter 6 of rules and procedures concerning individual responsibility for crimes committed during times of armed conflict.

4. *The Contribution of NGOs to International Governance*. NGOs engage in a wide range of functions that relate to the development and implementation of treaties and other international legal norms, to the work of intergovernmental organizations, and to the international legal activities of national governments. NGOs gather facts, lobby, and provide technical expertise. See Steve Charnovitz, "Two Centuries of Participation: NGOs and International Governance," 18 *Michigan Journal of International Law* 183 (1997). Treaties occasionally specify a direct role for NGOs in intergovernmental organizations. For example, the Constitution of the International Labor Organization, which was established in 1919, provides for direct NGO participation. Each ILO member state is represented by four delegates at the ILO's plenary body: two representatives from government, one representative from management, and one from labor. For the United States, the United States Council for International Business represents employers, and the AFL–CIO represents workers. This tripartite ILO structure can facilitate the formulation of consensus positions, although each delegate votes independently, and the votes of the employer, labor, and government representatives from the same state may differ. See Recommendation and Report on the International Labor Organization, in *The United Nations at 50: Proposals for Improving Its Effectiveness* 107 (John E. Noyes ed. 1997). The following excerpt suggests some other roles for NGOs in international legal process.

PHILIPPE J. SANDS, "THE ENVIRONMENT, COMMUNITY AND INTERNATIONAL LAW"

30 *Harvard International Law Journal* 393 (1988).

The problem of transboundary pollution demonstrates how states have failed to take effective international enforcement measures to protect the environment from degradation. In attempting to fill this void, NGOs have become the environment's moral, if not legal, guardians.

Experience both in national and international fora suggests that NGOs will have a useful and increasingly pivotal role to play. And the NGOs, with their multinational membership and resources, are slowly discovering that international law might provide a tool with which to challenge the degradation of the environment.

NGOs have traditionally been handicapped in this regard by their lack of standing under general international law. NGOs * * * cannot act as legal guardians under international law because they cannot pursue legal claims on the international plane.

Nonetheless, many NGOs have legal personality in national law, a prerequisite to the grant of personality and status in international law. In an article published in 1972, Professor Christopher Stone proposed that American law "give legal rights to forests, oceans, rivers and other so called 'natural objects' in the environment—indeed to the natural environment as a whole." Professor Stone's article had considerable influence on the development of environmental protection litigation in the United States. * * *

While international responses to environmental concerns lag somewhat behind developments in the United States, there are indications that similar developments are taking place. There is now a considerable body of international treaty law which expressly or implicitly seeks to protect the environment. Moreover, NGOs have been recognized as having a legal personality within regional "international" legal systems, such as the European Community and the Nordic Community.

In many respects the 1974 Nordic Convention is unique in establishing a comprehensive regime for the protection of the environment.[87] It allows any person who is or may be affected by a nuisance caused by "environmentally harmful activities" in another contracting state to challenge the activity before the appropriate court or administrative authority ("examining authority") of the state and to seek compensation. Sovereign immunity from suit is not a possibility. * * *

The Convention, which grants individuals, groups, and non-governmental organizations access to a legal system under international law, recognizes the right and the interest of such persons in the protection of the environment. It treats such persons as members of a community and gives expression to their concerns, interests and rights.

The 1987 amendments to the EEC Treaty have brought environmental protection within the Community's jurisdiction. The amendments were preceded by a large body of secondary legislation enforceable by the Commission of the EEC against member states before the European Court of Justice, and by private citizens and groups against offending public (and sometimes private) bodies in the national courts of the member states. As a result of these amendments, NGOs are able to

---

87. Nordic Convention on the Protection of the Environment, Feb. 19, 1974 (*entered into force* Oct. 5, 1976), 1092 U.N.T.S. 279 (1978) *reprinted in* 13 I.L.M. 591 (1974).

initiate proceedings against the Community directly before the European Court of Justice; to inform the EEC Commission of breaches of Community environmental laws by individual member states; and to intervene as interested parties in certain cases before the European Court in which environmental issues are at stake.

Political integration in the European and Nordic Communities has been accompanied by more flexible standing requirements in relation to the enforcement of supranational rules. While neither the European nor the Nordic Community has gone so far as to establish the notion of "environmental rights," both developments mark a considerable step forward for individuals who wish to enforce environmental regulations under international treaties.

Greater action by NGOs in this "watchdog" capacity—identifying rules of international law and highlighting breaches by states—might in itself contribute to the further development of the law, by publicizing the existing shortcomings and by bringing pressure to bear from citizens on governments to remedy the wrongs.

Some NGOs have been granted observer or consultative status in certain international institutions, a recognition of their legitimate interest in certain fields of international affairs. Consultative status at the International Atomic Energy Agency, for example, may be granted to organizations "having special competence in the field." Organizations so designated may be represented by an observer at sessions of the General Conference and at public meetings of the Board of Governors; submit certain written statements; make certain brief oral statements; and have access to some of the Agency's documentation. NGOs not qualified for consultative status but nonetheless recognized as "concerned with developing uses of nuclear energy for peaceful purposes" may be represented by observers at regular sessions of the General Conference.

As NGOs become more ambitious, they may attempt to litigate breaches of environmental standards, either in national courts or perhaps before international tribunals. They might do this in their own name or on behalf of interested and affected persons. They might also provide assistance to poorer states which themselves seek to litigate against other states. * * *

Any objective of such judicial efforts must be twofold: to establish that the environmental issues are susceptible of international legal clarification (that is to say, that international law provides methods and means for ascertaining rules and their meaning and enforcement); and to establish the significant contribution that can be made by non-state actors once they are given the right to assert their interests. * * *

* * * [N]ew treaties and intergovernmental agencies are being proposed to deal with the environment. Such instruments could be rendered more effective by establishing a formal legal role for NGOs as "guardians" of the environment. At a minimum, NGOs should be given wider consultative status, with the right to make representations and participate in the development of environmental standards.

In the event that a new international agency were created with the power to investigate breaches of environmental standards, it should be able to receive information and petitions from NGOs and individuals. If such an agency were to be endowed with the right to make requests for Advisory Opinions from the ICJ or some other tribunal, NGOs should be entitled to intervene as interested parties.

* * * [T]he time has come to expand the role of NGOs under general international law by giving their guardianship role formal legal expression. Unless and until such groups, or individuals or corporations, are given standing under general international law, so that their voices are not only heard but their actions felt, the role of international law in environmental protection will be limited and considerably less effective than it could be.

Notes and Questions

1. *Legitimacy and Recognition of NGOs.* Should NGOs be able to pursue claims before tribunals addressing international matters, *e.g.*, questions relating to the environment or human rights law, and otherwise actively participate in making and implementing international law? Do NGOs face concerns about legitimacy as they take on roles related to international law? It is often easy to form an NGO—a step typically accomplished by satisfying one state's requirements for forming a not-for-profit entity—and a small group of individuals may make decisions on behalf of an NGO. Are concerns about input from members, accuracy and impartiality of positions espoused, and transparency in decision-making assuaged because of competition from other groups and individuals? Are such concerns assuaged because an NGO must be "recognized" by an international legal person with which it has dealings? As Professor Sands noted, the International Atomic Energy Agency may grant consultative status to NGOs that have special competence. Other formal mechanisms also address relationships between NGOs and intergovernmental organizations, such as the practice of NGO accreditation to an international conference that an intergovernmental organization has organized.

The U.N. Economic and Social Council, acting pursuant to Article 71 of the U.N. Charter, has adopted criteria for establishing consultative relationships with NGOs. ECOSOC Res. 1996/31. Under these criteria, an NGO must focus on matters within ECOSOC's competence, have purposes in conformity with those of the U.N. Charter, and disclose its sources of revenue to ECOSOC. Furthermore:

The organization shall be of recognized standing within the particular field of its competence or of a representative character. Where there exist a number of organizations with similar objectives, interests and basic views in a given field, they may, for the purposes of consultation with the Council, form a joint committee or other body authorized to carry on such consultation for the group as a whole.

The organization * * * shall have a democratically adopted constitution, * * * which shall provide for the determination of policy by a conference, congress or other representative body, and for an executive organ responsible to the policy-making body. * * *

The organization shall have a representative structure and possess appropriate mechanisms of accountability to its members, who shall exercise effective control over its policies and actions through the exercise of voting rights or other appropriate democratic and transparent decision-making processes.

Id. ¶ ¶ 9–10, 12. Consultative status with ECOSOC will be suspended or withdrawn:

(a) If an organization, either directly or through its affiliates or representatives acting on its behalf, clearly abuses its status by engaging in a pattern of acts contrary to the purposes and principles of the Charter of the United Nations including unsubstantiated or politically motivated acts against Member States of the United Nations incompatible with those purposes and principles;

(b) If there exists substantiated evidence of influence from proceeds resulting from internationally recognized criminal activities such as the illicit drugs trade, money-laundering or the illegal arms trade;

(c) If, within the preceding three years, an organization did not make any positive or effective contribution to the work of the United Nations and, in particular, of the Council or its commissions or other subsidiary organs.

Id. ¶ 57. Almost 2000 NGOs have entered into consultative status with ECOSOC. See <http://www.un.org/esa/coordination/ngo>.

2. *NGOs and International Law Litigation in Municipal Courts.* Human rights NGOs, such as Human Rights Watch, Amnesty International, and the Lawyers Committee for Human Rights, have participated in many cases in municipal courts in which issues of international human rights law arise. Such groups may file *amicus curiae* briefs, and courts have on occasion cited these briefs as persuasive in their rulings on issues of international law. See, *e.g.*, Ma v. Reno, 208 F.3d 815, 829–30 (9th Cir.2000). In some municipal legal systems, NGOs may be allowed to intervene in lawsuits. For example, Amnesty International was allowed to intervene in a case before the British House of Lords, in support of Spain's effort to extradite Chile's former dictator, General Augusto Pinochet, in order to prosecute him for human rights offenses. The House of Lords' 1998 decision denying Pinochet immunity with respect to alleged instances of torture and hostage-taking was, however, set aside when it was discovered that one of the Law Lords sitting on the case had links to Amnesty International (as chair and a director of a separate organization, Amnesty International Charity Limited). Following hearings before a new panel of judges, the House of Lords ruled that Pinochet could be extradited to stand trial for limited alleged offenses. See William J. Aceves, "Liberalism and International Legal Scholarship: The Pinochet Case and the Move Toward a Universal System of Transnational Law Litigation," 41 *Harvard Journal of International Law* 129 (2000).

3. *Transnational Civil Society.* Do the activities of NGOs suggest that our conception of international law and legal process should take account of the input of a wide variety of entities? Some have argued that NGOs

contribute to the development of a "transnational civil society," a concept that, in general, competes with a state-centric view of international law and relations. According to one study:

> Global civil society is best expressed in the global non-governmental movement. * * *
>
> Global governance, once viewed primarily as concerned with intergovernmental relationships, now involves not only governments and intergovernmental institutions but also * * * NGOs, citizens' movements, transnational corporations, academia, and the mass media. The emergence of a global civil society, with many movements reinforcing a sense of human solidarity, reflects a large increase in the capacity and will of people to take control of their own lives.
>
> States remain primary actors but have to work with others. The United Nations must play a vital role, but it cannot do all the work. Global governance does not imply world governance or world federalism. * * * It requires a strong commitment to democracy grounded in civil society.

Our Global Neighborhood: The Report of the Commission on Global Governance 254, 335–36 (1995).

NGOs often interact with each other and with other entities, forming networks of advocacy groups. As noted in Chapter 6, NGOs collaborated to promote the new International Criminal Court. Networking has been aided by developments in information technology. Web sites facilitate communication and cooperative endeavors among numerous groups, especially with respect to human rights and environmental issues. See, *e.g.*, <http://www.derechos.net>. For thoughtful discussions of advocacy networks and the possibilities for various types of entities to contribute to the formation and implementation of international law norms, see Margaret E. Keck & Kathryn Sikkink, *Activists Beyond Borders* (1998); Julie Mertus, "Considering Nonstate Actors in the New Millenium: Toward Expanded Participation in Norm Generation and Norm Application," 32 *New York University Journal of International Law and Politics* 537 (2000).

Chapter 9

INTERNATIONAL LAW AND
THE USE OF FORCE

Rules relating to the use of force are among the traditional concerns of international law. Although nowadays provisions of the United Nations Charter mark the starting point in debates about the legality of use of force under international law, we begin this chapter in Part A with an introduction to pre-Charter law, aspects of which still remain relevant. Part B explores when states may legally use force under the U.N. Charter absent the authorization of the U.N. Security Council. Part C then addresses the roles of the United Nations and regional organizations in using force or authorizing its use.

A. THE TRADITIONAL LAWS OF WAR

For centuries, theologians and international law theorists worked to define limits on permissible uses of force. St. Augustine, writing in the 5th century, developed a concept of *just war*, war pursued to avenge injuries against an enemy that "has neglected either to punish wrongs committed by its own citizens or to restore what has been unjustly taken by it. Further that kind of war is undoubtedly just which God Himself ordains." *Quoted in* Ian Brownlie, *International Law and the Use of Force by States* 5 (1963). The 16th-century Spanish Catholic jurists Vitoria and Suarez, along with the Dutch theorist Hugo Grotius, who wrote at the time of the Thirty Years War (1618–1648), were among those who refined the just war doctrine, stressing the need for both humane means and right ends in the prosecution of war.

The just war doctrine, however, fell into disfavor in international legal circles. In the 19th and early 20th centuries, international law commentators regarded interstate war—a formal status that depended on the declaration or intention of one of the parties—as a legitimate exercise of sovereign power. Writing in the late 19th century, William Hall claimed that international law has "no alternative but to accept war, independently of the justice of its origin, as a relation which the parties to it may set up, if they choose." W.E. Hall, *A Treatise on International Law* § 16, at 64–65 (4th ed. 1895). According to Charles Hyde, "[i]t always lies within the power of a State to endeavor to obtain

504

redress for wrongs, or to gain political or other advantages over another, not merely by the employment of force, but also by direct recourse to war." 2 *International Law Chiefly as Interpreted and Applied by the United States* § 597, at 189 (1922). Indeed, a traditional way for a state to acquire territory was by conquest followed by occupation and effective control, a method consistent with discretionary unilateral use of force.

Yet some limitations related to the use of force were accepted, even when recourse to war was generally regarded as legal. A *jus in bello*, or international humanitarian law, developed, addressing the methods soldiers could use against other soldiers, civilians, or prisoners during interstate hostilities (in contrast to the *jus ad bellum*, which concerned the decision to resort to force in the first place). Before the 20th century, customary international law rules called for armies to protect civilian populations. Conventions proscribing certain conduct during hostilities were also negotiated and adopted. Many conventions specifying protections both for civilians and for enemy combatants were products of the Hague Peace Conferences of 1899 and 1906. The 1949 Geneva Conventions noted in Chapter 8 also contributed significantly to international humanitarian law, which today links conceptually to international human rights law.

Our primary concern in this chapter is with legal constraints on states resorting to force, rather than with international humanitarian law. Some such constraints developed in two forms during the 19th and early 20th centuries. First, treaties relating to specific situations constrained states in their use of force. For example, parties to the 1907 Hague Convention No. II agreed "not to have recourse to armed force for the recovery of contract debts claimed from the Government of one country by the Government of another country as being due to its nationals," although the limitation was not applicable if the debtor state refused to submit to arbitration or to comply with a resulting arbitral award. Art. 1, 36 Stat. 2241, 2251 (1907). Other agreements limited the size of forces that could be placed along borders, while still others protected neutral states.

Second, significant authority suggested that general international law limited the use of force short of war. If war was legal, rules limiting the use of lower levels of force could in theory be circumvented, just by one of the states involved moving to a state of war. Nonetheless, states were often reluctant to take the serious political step of declaring war. The arbitral tribunal in the *Naulilaa Case*, excerpted below, discussed limits on the use of force involving an alleged reprisal, or act of self-help by an injured state, that took place in 1914. The second reading in this Part, about a 19th-century diplomatic exchange between the United States and Great Britain, concerns limits on the use of force in self-defense.

THE NAULILAA CASE

Portugal v. Germany, Special Arbitral Tribunal, Judgment of 31 July 1928,
8 *Recueil des Décisions des Tribunaux Arbitrales Mixtes* 409,
2 *United Nations Reports of International Arbitral Awards* 1012 (1949)
(authors' translation from the French).

[In October 1914, a German delegation from the German colony of Southwest Africa (present-day Namibia) visited the border post of Naulilaa in Angola, then a Portuguese colony, to discuss importing food into Southwest Africa. A series of misunderstandings, originating with translation difficulties on the part of the German interpreter, led the Portuguese garrison to kill three Germans and to confine two others. In retaliation, the German authorities in Southwest Africa sent German troops to attack Naulilaa and other Portuguese outposts in Angola, resulting in casualties and serious property damage. The Portuguese retreated to the north, the Germans withdrew back into Southwest Africa, and the indigenous Cuanhama peoples then pillaged the evacuated region. Portugal recaptured the territory it had evacuated in the spring of 1915. An arbitral tribunal, composed of three Swiss arbiters, was constituted to judge Portugal's claim for the damages resulting from Germany's attack.]

The arbitrators conclude as follows:

a) The Naulilaa incident was not the result of acts contrary to the law of nations imputable to German or Portuguese civil or military authorities. In particular, it is necessary to rule out, on the part of the [German] Schultze–Jena mission, any intentional penetration of Portuguese territory with the secret goal of beginning or preparing an invasion, and on the part of the regional Portuguese military authorities, any premeditated intention to lure the German detachment to Naulilaa in order to destroy or capture it.

b) The deplorable occurrence, which took place at the fort itself, was clearly fortuitous. It was the result of a series of misunderstandings, due initially to the inadequacy of the interpreter Jensen, next to some imprudence on the part of Dr. Schultze–Jena, and lastly to an unfortunate gesture, perhaps wrongly interpreted, which could have led [Portuguese] Lieutenant Sereno to believe that he was being threatened and that he found himself in a condition calling for legitimate defense.

THE QUESTION OF REPRISALS

The most recent doctrine, notably German doctrine, defines a reprisal in these terms:

The *reprisal* is an act of self-help (*Selbsthilfehandlung*) on the part of the injured state—*after an unsatisfied demand*—responding to an act contrary to the law of nations on the part of the offending state. [The reprisal] has the effect of momentarily suspending, in the relations of the two states, the observance of one or another rule of international law. It is *limited* by considerations of humanity and rules of good faith, applicable in interstate relations. *It would be illegal if a prior act, contrary to international law, had not furnished the reason for it.* It tends to impose, on the offending state, the duty to make reparation for the offense or to return to legality, while avoiding new offenses.

This definition does not require that a reprisal be *proportionate* to the offense. On this point, authors, unanimous until a few years ago, are beginning to be divided in their opinions. Most take the view that a certain proportionality between offense and reprisal is necessary for the legitimacy of the latter. Others, among the most modern, no longer demand this condition. As for international law, presently developing in the light of the last war, it certainly seems to restrict the notion of legitimate reprisal and to prohibit excess. * * *

* * * [T]he deaths of Dr. Schultze–Jena and the two officers who accompanied him were not the result of any act contrary to the law of nations by the Portuguese authorities.

A neutral state has the right to disarm and to intern armed belligerents who enter its territory. The internment of the interpreter Jensen and the soldier Kimmel were thus, in principle, authorized by the positive law of nations. * * * The German authorities * * * could not * * * consider such internment or its continuance as an act contrary to the law of nations, giving them a fair motive to conduct armed reprisals.

[The German vice-consul Schoess was expelled from Portuguese territory after the German attacks.] Furthermore, expulsion of a consular agent, against whom a state believes it has a complaint, may constitute an "unfriendly" act, giving rise to diplomatic representations[.] [B]ut [such an expulsion] cannot be, in similar circumstances where the sovereign authority of a neutral state is asserted, an act contrary to the law of nations, justifying, in the name of reprisal, an attack accompanied by all the severities of war.

The first condition—*sine qua non*—of the right to take reprisals is a reason furnished by a prior act contrary to the law of nations. This condition—the necessity of which is acknowledged by Germany—is lacking * * *.

Even if the arbitrators had found that the Portuguese authorities had acted contrary to the law of nations, providing, in principle, justification for reprisals, the German case would nevertheless fail for two other reasons, each of them decisive:

1. A reprisal is only lawful when it has been preceded by an unsatisfied *demand*. The use of force is justified, indeed, only by its character of necessity. * * * There was, on the part of the authorities of [German] South–West Africa, resort to force, without a prior attempt to obtain satisfaction by way of legal means, which, again, precludes the legality of the reprisals taken.

2. The necessity of *proportionality* between the reprisal and the offense seems to be recognized in the German response. Even if one were to admit that the law of nations required that a reprisal correlate only

approximately to an offense, one certainly ought to consider as excessive, and hence illegal, reprisals beyond all proportion with the act that motivated them. * * * [T]here was evident disproportion between the incident at Naulilaa and the 6 acts of reprisals that followed it.

The arbitrators thus reach the conclusion that the German aggressions in October, November and December 1914 at the Angolan border cannot be considered as legal reprisals for the Naulilaa incident or for the subsequent acts of the Portuguese authorities, because of the lack of a prior demand and of acceptable proportionality between the alleged offense and the reprisals taken. * * *

Some of the damages for which Portugal demands reparation are the immediate consequence of the unjustified acts of aggression committed by Germany: soldiers or civilians killed or wounded in the fighting with the German troops, destruction by enemy fire of forts or outposts and all they contained, supplies, war material, etc. * * *

As for the remainder [of the damages], the Portuguese claims relate to damages for which the German attacks are not in all cases the sole cause. The Portuguese troops having fallen back after the battle of Naulilaa, and the forts and outposts of the Cunene line having been evacuated, the indigenous peoples rebelled. [The tribunal determines that the cause of the damage that occurred during this rebellion was attributable in part to Germany, in part to Portugal, whose local commander decided to evacuate a wide area although not under immediate pressure from German forces, and in part to the indigenous Cuanhama peoples.]

In conclusion, it is necessary to distinguish two categories of damages: the immediate damages caused by the German attacks, for which the respondent state is held fully liable, * * * and other damages which * * * the arbitrators will take into account, in a very limited measure, by fixing a supplemental equitable indemnity, noting the greater part of the causes foreign to Germany.

Notes and Questions

1. *The Naulilaa Arbitral Tribunal.* To establish the tribunal, Portugal invoked paragraph 4 of the Annex to Articles 297 and 298 of the Treaty of Versailles, concluded at the end of World War I. June 28, 1919, 225 Consolidated Treaty Series 189, 332. This paragraph concerned, *inter alia*, claims of nationals of Allied or Associated Powers, of which Portugal was one, "growing out of acts committed by" Germany after July 31, 1914, but before the Allied or Associated Power in question entered World War I. The paragraph provided a mechanism that assured arbitration to assess unsatisfied claims. Although most disputes relating to the use of force are not the subject of adjudication or arbitration, there have been notable exceptions. The International Court of Justice, for example, has heard cases relating to the use of force; we examine one such case in Part B. We also have looked at an arbitration pertaining to the use of force before the Permanent Court of Arbitration—the *Dogger Bank Case* in Chapter 5.

2. *Neutrality.* Although World War I was underway during the Naulilaa incident, Portugal was neutral at the time. Portugal and Germany did not officially go to war with each other until 1916. The arbitrators refer to some rights of neutral states. A detailed body of international law historically has addressed the rights and obligations of neutral states. See generally Rudolf L. Bindschedler, "Neutrality, Concept and General Rules," in 4 *Encyclopedia of Public International Law* 9 (1982). How much these traditional rules are still in play is not so sure. See Mark W. Janis, "Neutrality," in *The Law of Naval Operations* 148 (Horace B. Robertson, Jr., ed. 1991).

3. *Reprisals and Other Forms of Self–Help.* Reprisals, retorsions, and countermeasures are all measures of self-help taken by states. A reprisal is a state act taken in response to another state's internationally wrongful act. Reprisals would themselves be illegal acts, except for the prior illegality of the other state. Reprisals traditionally might (as in the *Naulilaa Case*) or might not involve the use of force; as we shall see in Part B, provisions of the U.N. Charter today call into question the legality of reprisals involving the use of force. Detentions of foreign vessels in port, pacific blockades against the movement of foreign vessels, and seizures of foreign vessels or their cargoes on the high seas were typical forms of reprisals. The early practice of "special reprisal," whereby a state would issue a "letter of marque" to one of its citizens who was wronged by another state, authorizing that citizen to seize property of citizens of the wrongdoing state, has long been discontinued.

In contrast to a reprisal, a retorsion is an act that, though unfriendly, would have been entirely legal even if not taken in response to another state's action. For example, if one state cut off longstanding economic assistance to another state or publicly condemned certain political practices of that other state, the offended state might reply by withdrawing its ambassador from the first state. Other traditional measures of self-help included intervention, which is addressed in the Notes following the *Nicaragua Case* in Part B, and self-defense, which is the subject of the next excerpt in this Part.

International lawyers today often use the term "countermeasures" instead of referring to reprisals or retorsions. A countermeasure was at issue in the Case Concerning the Air Services Agreement of 27 March 1946 (U.S.-France), 54 Int'l L. Rep. 304 (1978). France had refused to allow passengers travelling to Paris on a U.S. airline to disembark because the airline had switched them to a smaller plane in London en route from the U.S. west coast. The United States believed that this "change in gauge" was legal, and France's action illegal, under a 1946 U.S.-French Air Services Agreement, 139 U.N.T.S. 253, and a 1960 U.S.-French Exchange of Notes, 458 U.N.T.S. 292. Responding to France's refusal to allow passengers to disembark in Paris, the United States took steps to prohibit certain flights by French carriers to the U.S. west coast. This U.S. move would have been illegal under the 1946 Agreement, but the United States argued that it was a valid countermeasure. The arbitral tribunal first ruled that the U.S. carrier had the right to operate its U.S. west coast-Paris service with a change in gauge in London, and then turned to the U.S. countermeasure. In line with the decision in the *Naulilaa Case*, the tribunal emphasized that a countermeasure must be proportionate to the prior illegal act, both in terms of the damages it causes and in terms of the importance of the principle at stake. What is the relationship between the law concerning countermeasures and the law governing termination or suspension of treaties in the event of material breach (see Chapter 2)? Are the bodies of law consistent?

Should a party have to make use of dispute settlement mechanisms, such as available arbitration, before taking countermeasures? The *Air Services Agreement* tribunal found that the United States was not precluded from taking countermeasures before concluding an arbitral *compromis*. The International Law Commission, in its studies of state responsibility, has debated a proposal that would condition the lawfulness of countermeasures on recourse to international dispute settlement procedures. See Oscar Schachter, "Dispute Settlement and Countermeasures in the International Law Commission," 88 *American Journal of International Law* 471 (1994). See generally Elisabeth Zoller, *Peacetime Unilateral Remedies* (1984).

THE CAROLINE DISPUTE

29 *British Foreign and State Papers* 1129;
30 *British Foreign and State Papers* 195.

[During an 1837 Canadian insurrection against the British government, the rebels urged Americans to help their cause. Despite the efforts of U.S. authorities to prevent U.S. citizens from cooperating with the rebels, many volunteers from the Buffalo, NY area were recruited. In December 1837 a force of about 1000 men, mostly U.S. citizens, took possession of Navy Island, in Canadian waters. This base was used to raid the Canadian shore and to fire on British ships. The *Caroline*, a privately owned American ship, delivered ammunition and supplies from U.S. territory to Navy Island. One night in late December 1837, the British attacked the *Caroline*, which at the time was docked in U.S. port. At least one American was killed during the attack, and the British set the ship on fire and then set it loose in the river, where it drifted over Niagara Falls. This incident gave rise to a diplomatic exchange between the U.S. and British governments in early 1838. The following excerpts are from correspondence after the 1840 arrest in New York of a British citizen, Alexander McLeod, who was charged with murder and arson for his alleged participation in the attack on the *Caroline*. U.S. Secretary of State Daniel Webster sent his April 1841 letter to Henry Fox, the British Minister in Washington. The second excerpt below is from the reply of Lord Ashburton to a note from Daniel Webster dated July 27, 1842, with which Webster enclosed a copy of his April 1841 letter. Lord Ashburton had been sent from Britain to the United States as a special minister to address several outstanding disputes between the two countries.]

Mr. Webster to Mr. Fox. Washington, April 24, 1841. * * *

* * * [T]he act of destroying the *Caroline* [cannot] be justified by any reasonable application or construction of the right of self-defence under the laws of nations. It is admitted that a just right of self-defence attaches always to nations as well as to individuals, and is equally necessary for the preservation of both. But the extent of this right is a

question to be judged of by the circumstances of each particular case, and when its alleged exercise has led to the commission of hostile acts within the territory of a Power at peace, nothing less than a clear and absolute necessity can afford ground of justification. * * *

* * * [I]t will be for Her Majesty's Government * * * to show a necessity of self-defence, instant, overwhelming, leaving no choice of means, and no moment for deliberation. It will be for it to show, also, that the local authorities of Canada, even supposing the necessity of the moment authorized them to enter the territories of The United States at all, did nothing unreasonable or excessive; since the act, justified by the necessity of self-defence, must be limited by that necessity, and kept clearly within it. It must be shown that admonition or remonstrance to the person on board the *Caroline* was impracticable, or would have been unavailing; it must be shown that day-light could not be waited for; that there could be no attempt at discrimination between the innocent and the guilty; that it would not have been enough to seize and detain the vessel; but that there was a necessity, present and inevitable, for attacking her in the darkness of the night, while moored to the shore, and while unarmed men were asleep on board, killing some and wounding others, and then drawing her into the current, above the cataract, setting her on fire, and, careless to know whether there might not be in her the innocent with the guilty, or the living with the dead, committing her to a fate which fills the imagination with horror. A necessity for all this, the Government of The United States cannot believe to have existed.

Lord Ashburton to Mr. Webster. Washington, July 28, 1842. * * *

It is so far satisfactory to perceive that we are perfectly agreed as to the general principles of international law applicable to this unfortunate case. Respect for the inviolable character of the territory of independent nations is the most essential foundation of civilization. It is useless to strengthen a principle so generally acknowledged by any appeal to authorities on international law, and you may be assured, Sir, that Her Majesty's Government set the highest possible value on this principle, and are sensible of their duty to support it by their conduct and example for the maintenance of peace and order in the world.

Notes and Questions

1. *The Outcome of the* Caroline *Dispute.* In parts of his July 1842 letter not reproduced above, Lord Ashburton attempted, in good lawyerly fashion, to justify the attack on the *Caroline* within the framework of the rules Webster had set forth. Ashburton also expressed regret for the need to violate U.S. territory, and apologized for not expressing that regret earlier. Webster replied on August 6, 1842. He accepted the apology, noting "with pleasure that your Lordship fully admits those great principles of public law, applicable to cases of this kind, which this government has expressed; and that on your part, as on ours, respect for the inviolable character of the territory of independent states is the most essential foundation of civiliza-

tion." *Quoted in* 2 John Bassett Moore, *Digest of International Law* § 217, at 412 (1906). President Tyler found Ashburton's letter "sufficient to warrant forbearance from any further remonstrance against what took place * * *." *Quoted in id.* at 413.

What of Alexander McLeod? Webster agreed with the British that, on the facts, McLeod should not be individually responsible if he was following British orders to attack the *Caroline.* Nevertheless, Webster thought that any defenses had to be raised in McLeod's criminal trial. McLeod was in fact tried in New York state court. He was acquitted in 1841 for "lack of evidence even to show that he had been present at the destruction of the *Caroline*," and released after spending about 11 months in jail. R.Y. Jennings, "The *Caroline* and McLeod Cases," 32 *American Journal of International Law* 82, 95 (1938). In response to McLeod's case, Congress enacted a statute providing that the federal courts could hear *habeas corpus* petitions from foreigners who were in custody for acts done under orders "of any foreign State or Sovereignty, the validity and effect whereof depend upon the law of nations * * *." Act of Aug. 29, 1842, 5 Stat. 539 (now codified, as amended, at 28 U.S.C. § 2241(c)(4)). McLeod, for his part, sought compensation for his imprisonment and trial. An 1853 U.S.-British treaty established a binational claims mechanism to consider outstanding claims of U.S. citizens against the British government, and of British citizens against the United States. 10 Stat. 988. The two claims commissioners and the umpire considered the McLeod claim, but ruled, by a vote of 2 to 1, that they could not proceed to the merits of the claim. The 1853 treaty only authorized decisions with respect to "unsettled" claims, and one commissioner and the umpire believed that matters related to the *Caroline* affair had been settled by the diplomatic exchanges of 1841–1842. See 3 John Bassett Moore, *History and Digest of the International Arbitrations to Which the United States Has Been a Party* 2419–28 (1898; reprinted 1995).

2.   *Self-defense.* The *Caroline* formulation has often been cited in elaborating traditional international law rules governing the legality of a state's use of force in self-defense. For example, the Nuremberg Tribunal invoked the rule in *Caroline* when rejecting Germany's arguments that it had been entitled to attack Norway in self-defense. International Military Tribunal (Nuremberg), Judgment and Sentences, Oct. 1, 1946, *reprinted in* 41 *American Journal of International Law* 172, 205–07 (1947). Which aspects, if any, of the *Caroline* rule are ill suited to today's world? We examine some modern arguments about the scope of self-defense in the next Parts of this chapter.

B.   ARTICLE 2(4) AND THE USE OF FORCE BY STATES

States reacted to the excesses of World War I by adopting new legal constraints on the use of force. For example, the Kellogg–Briand Pact, which is reproduced in Chapter 2, condemned "recourse to war for the solution of international controversies" and renounced war "as an instrument of national policy." The Covenant of the League of Nations provided procedural mechanisms encouraging a cooling-off period before hostilities could commence. Members of the League agreed to submit "any dispute likely to lead to a rupture" to arbitration or judicial settlement, or to the League's Council for inquiry. Members agreed "in no case to resort to war until three months after the award by the arbitrators or the judicial decision, or the report by the Council." League of Nations Covenant, art. 12, para. 1; art. 15, para. 1.

Following the carnage of World War II, the United Nations Charter in 1945 introduced the notion of a general prohibition on the unilateral use of force by states. Articles 2(3) and 33 of the Charter impose obligations on Member States to settle their disputes by peaceful means. Article 2(4), which limits the threat or use of force by states, and Article 51, which preserves a right of self-defense, are set out below. Also reproduced are portions of articles by Professors Louis Henkin and Michael Reisman, who take different views of the meaning of Article 2(4) and its importance in a world armed with weapons of mass destruction. This Part concludes with a Note about the International Court of Justice's opinion in *Nicaragua v. United States*, an important judicial analysis of the international law concerning intervention and the use of force, and an excerpt from that case.

UNITED NATIONS CHARTER, ARTICLES 2(4), 51
June 26, 1945, 59 Stat. 1031, T.S. No. 993, 3 Bevans 1153, 1976 Y.B.U.N. 1043.

Article 2(4)

All Members shall refrain in their international relations from the threat or use of force against the territorial integrity or political independence of any state, or in any manner inconsistent with the Purposes of the United Nations.

Article 51

Nothing in the present Charter shall impair the inherent right of individual or collective self-defense if an armed attack occurs against a Member of the United Nations until the Security Council has taken the measures necessary to maintain international peace and security. Measures taken by Members in the exercise of this right of self-defense shall be immediately reported to the Security Council and shall not in any way affect the authority and responsibility of the Security Council under the present Charter to take at any time such action as it deems necessary in order to maintain or restore international peace and security.

LOUIS HENKIN, "THE USE OF FORCE: LAW AND U.S. POLICY"
Right v. Might: International Law and the Use of Force 37 (1989).

* * * The Charter remains the authoritative statement of the law on the use of force. It is the principal norm of international law of this century.

The crucial norm is set forth in article 2(4). * * *

The Charter reflected universal agreement that the status quo prevailing at the end of World War II was not to be changed by force. Even justified grievances and a sincere concern for "national security" or other "vital interests" would not warrant any nation's initiating war. Peace was the paramount value. The Charter and the organization were dedicated to realizing other values as well—self-determination, respect for human rights, economic and social development, justice, and a just international order. But those purposes could not justify the use of force between states to achieve them; they would have to be pursued by other means. Peace was more important than progress and more important than justice. The purposes of the United Nations could not in fact be achieved by war. War inflicted the greatest injustice, the most serious violations of human rights, and the most violence to self-determination and to economic and social development. War was inherently unjust. In the future, the only "just war" would be war against an aggressor—in self-defense by the victim, in collective defense of the victim by others, or by all. Nations would be assured independence, the undisturbed enjoyment of autonomy within their territory, and their right to be let alone. Change—other than internal change through internal forces—would have to be achieved peacefully by international agreement. Henceforth there would be order so that international society could concentrate on meeting better the needs of justice and human welfare.

Efforts to Reconstrue the Charter

During the early postwar years there was general agreement as to what the prescriptions of article 2(4) meant. Clearly, the article outlaws war and other acts of armed aggression by one state against another; it also forbids lesser forms of intervention by force by one state in the territory of another. Apart from collective action under the auspices of the United Nations to enforce the peace, the only lawful use of force by a state is that contemplated under the limited exception in article 51 permitting the use of force in self-defense against an armed attack. In time, the language of article 2(4) proved to be not without ambiguities and not invulnerable to claims that intervention by force is permitted for certain "benign" purposes.

One initial ambiguity appears on the face of article 2(4). Does the prohibition of the use of force against "the territorial integrity" of another state forbid only a use of force designed to deprive that state of territory, or does it also prohibit force that violates the territorial borders of that state, however temporarily and for whatever purpose? Does the prohibition of the use of force against "the political independence" of another state outlaw only a use of force that aims to end that state's political independence by annexing it or rendering it a puppet, or does it also prohibit force designed to coerce that state to follow a particular policy or take a particular decisions? In what other circumstances would a use or threat of force be "inconsistent with the purposes of the United Nations"? Another debate concerned whether economic pressure—an oil embargo, a boycott, or other sanctions—designed to derogate from a state's territorial integrity or political independence is a "use of force" prohibited by article 2(4).

An effective United Nations system, or a court with comprehensive jurisdiction and recognized authority, might have answered these and other questions by developing the law of the Charter through construction and case-by-case application. In the absence of such authoritative interpretation, the meaning of the Charter has been shaped by the actions and reactions of states and by the opinions of publicists and scholars. Scholars have debated the ambiguities of the Charter that I have cited and other questions of interpretation; a government occasionally has sought to shape the law to justify an action it has taken. But governments generally have insisted on the interpretations most restrictive of the use of force: the Charter outlaws war for any reason; it prohibits the use of armed force by one state on the territory of another or against the forces, vessels, or other public property of another state located anywhere, for any purpose, in any circumstances. Virtually every use of force in the years since the Charter was signed has been clearly condemned by virtually all states. Virtually every putative justification of a use of force has been rejected. Over the years since the Charter's adoption, even states that have perpetrated acts of force, when seeking to justify their acts, have not commonly urged a relaxed interpretation of the prohibition. Rather, they have asserted facts and circumstances that might have rendered their actions not unlawful. For example, in 1950, North Korea claimed that the South Korean army had initiated hostilities, permitting North Korea to act in self-defense; in Czechoslovakia in 1948 and 1968, and in Hungary in 1956, the USSR claimed that its troops had been invited by the legitimate authorities to help preserve order.

Indeed, the community of states has acted formally to tighten the Charter's restrictions. The Declaration on Principles of International Law concerning Friendly Relations and Cooperation among States in Accordance with the Charter of the United Nations, adopted by consensus in the General Assembly in 1970, and the Definition of Aggression, adopted by consensus in 1974, have restated and expanded the law of the Charter as prohibiting armed intervention and aggression, broadly conceived. The resolution defining aggression made it clear that prohibited forms of aggression include not only invasion, but also attack or military occupation, however temporary; sending armed bands or mercenaries that carry out grave acts of armed force; bombarding a state's territory; blocking its ports; and attacking the forces of another state (wherever they are).

SUGGESTED EXCEPTIONS TO THE PROHIBITIONS OF ARTICLE 2(4)

In time, however, some states claimed exceptions to the absolute prohibitions of article 2(4), as permitting intervention by force for certain "benign" purposes (in addition to the self-defense exception under article 51). None of the "benign exceptions" has been formally accepted; only one has brought wide acquiescence.

Humanitarian intervention. On several occasions states have claimed the right to use force in "humanitarian intervention." The paradigmatic case was the action of Israel in 1976 to extricate hostages held on a hijacked plane at Entebbe (Uganda). The United States claimed its unsuccessful attempt in 1980 to liberate the diplomatic hostages held in Teheran also came within the exception. States have been reluctant to adopt this exception to article 2(4) formally, but the legal community has widely accepted that the Charter does not prohibit humanitarian intervention by use of force strictly limited to what is necessary to save lives.

The exception, I believe, is not restricted to actions by a state on behalf of its own nationals. But it is a right to liberate hostages if the territorial state cannot or will not do so. It has not been accepted, however, that a state has a right to intervene by force to topple a government or occupy its territory even if that were necessary to terminate atrocities or to liberate detainees. Entebbe was acceptable, but the occupation of Cambodia by Vietnam was not. The U.S. invasion and occupation of Grenada, even if in fact designed to protect the lives of U.S. nationals, also was widely challenged.

Intervention to support self-determination. The suggestion that a state may intervene by force to help a people achieve "self-determination" in some circumstances has received some support.

Self-determination is a powerful political dogma that has been accepted as a principle of international law. It is incorporated in widely accepted treaties, including both the International Covenant on Civil and Political Rights and the International Covenant on Economic, Social and Cultural Rights. The concept of self-determination cries for definition, and few agree on its content, but all agree that it includes at least the right of peoples in Asia and Africa to be free from colonial domination, Western style.

Neither article 2(4) of the Charter nor any other provision of international law forbids authentic revolution and wars of independence. Indeed, there is a strong case that it is now unlawful for a state to maintain an unwilling people in colonial status, and such unlawfulness is compounded if a colony is maintained by force. A very different question, however, is whether an external power is permitted to intervene by force to help expel the colonial power or hasten its departure.

On various theories, many states have supported the right to intervene by force to help an entity achieve independence from colonial rule. The United States has firmly rejected any such right. In addressing India's invasion and occupation of Goa (Portuguese India) in 1961, Ambassador Adlai Stevenson said:

> What is at stake today is not colonialism; it is a bold violation of one of the most basic principles in the United Nations Charter. . . . But if our Charter means anything, it means that states are obligated to renounce the use of force, are obligated to seek a solution of their differences by peaceful means.

India used force to end Portuguese control in Goa and claimed the territory for itself; later, other states asserted a general right to intervene by force to help a people achieve independence. In a famous statement, attributed to Leonid Brezhnev, defending the Soviet invasion of Czechoslovakia in 1968, the USSR decried those who "regard the notion of sovereignty as prohibiting support for the struggle of progressive forces." He added: "Genuine revolutionaries, being internationalists, cannot but support progressive forces in their just struggle for national and social liberation."

The world rejected Brezhnev's invasion of Czechoslovakia; even the Third World was not persuaded by the "national liberation" justification. General Assembly resolutions, however, have confirmed the right of colonial peoples to achieve independence by force if necessary and included ambiguous declarations that suggested a right of other states to intervene to help them.

With colonialism no longer an important concern, the pressure for a "self-determination exception" to the law of the Charter has subsided, and the potential significance of such an exception, if recognized, is sharply reduced.

Intervention for socialism: The Brezhnev Doctrine. The Brezhnev regime also asserted generally the right of any socialist state to intervene in another when socialism there is threatened. It said:

> Just as, in Lenin's words, a man living in a society cannot be free from the society, a particular socialist state, staying in a system of other states composing the socialist community, cannot be free from the common interests of that community.
>
> The sovereignty of each socialist country cannot be opposed to the interests of the world of socialism, of the world revolutionary movement....
>
> Discharging their internationalist duty toward the fraternal peoples of Czechoslovakia and defending their own socialist gains, the U.S.S.R. and other socialist states had to act decisively and they did act against the antisocialist forces in Czechoslovakia.

The Brezhnev Doctrine has been generally condemned. The USSR itself appears to have disavowed it in the Helsinki accords.

Intervention for democracy. Self-determination as a justification for the use of force to end colonialism has lost its raison d'être, but some have invoked a people's right to "internal self-determination" to support the use of force by one state to preserve or impose democracy in another. One suggestion, for example, is that article 2(4) permits the use of force to "enhance opportunities of ongoing self-determination ... to increase the probability of the free choice of peoples about their government and political structure." Some see this view as the foundation of the so-called Reagan Doctrine, construed as including a claim of the right to intervene by force in another state to preserve or impose democracy.

The claim has received no support by any other government. Like the use of force to impose or maintain socialism or any other ideology, the use of force for democracy clearly would be contrary to the language of article 2(4), to the intent of its framers, and to the construction long given to that article by the United States.

At bottom, all suggestions for exceptions to article 2(4) imply that, contrary to the assumptions of the Charter's framers, there are universally recognized values higher than peace and the autonomy of states. In general, the claims of peace and state autonomy have prevailed.

SELF-DEFENSE UNDER THE CHARTER * * *

The original intent of article 51 seems clear: despite the prohibition on the unilateral use of force in article 2(4), a victim of an armed attack may use force to defend itself, and others may join to use force in collective self-defense of the victim, pending action by the Security Council. No one has doubted that the right of individual or collective self-defense against armed attack continues to apply if the Security Council does not act, or if—as later proved to be the case—the Security Council becomes generally incapable of acting. It has also been accepted that the right of self-defense, individual or collective, is subject to limitations of "necessity" and "proportionality," but that self-defense includes a right both to repel the armed attack and to take the war to the aggressor state in order effectively to terminate the attack and prevent a recurrence. It is generally accepted, too, that states are permitted to organize themselves in advance in bona fide collective self-defense arrangements (such as the North Atlantic Treaty Organization) for possible response if one of the members should become the victim of an armed attack.

The right of self-defense is available "if an armed attack occurs." In the wake of Suez–Sinai (1956), however, some publicists began to argue that the "inherent right of self-defense" recognized by article 51 is the traditional right of self-defense, predating the Charter, which was not limited to defense against "armed attack." They argued that the right of self-defense "if an armed attack occurs" does not mean "only if an armed attack occurs." The only limitation on self-defense, they said, was that implied in the famous *Caroline* dictum: that the right of self-defense was available only when "the necessity of that self-defense is instant, overwhelming, and leaving no choice of means, and no moment for deliberation."

This more permissive interpretation of article 51 found favor with some commentators, but little with governments. The United States rejected it when its allies in effect invoked it at Suez (1956). During the Cuban missile crisis (1962), the United States, though eager to justify its blockade of Cuba, pointedly refrained from adopting the "loose" construction of article 51 and did not claim as justification a right to act in "inherent self-defense." To this day, the United States has not claimed a right to act in self-defense where no armed attack has occurred. In 1985, however, the United States interpreted the concept of armed attack to include certain terrorist activities. Declaring the Libyan government responsible for terrorist acts in Europe, including the bombing of a Berlin nightclub frequented by U.S. servicemen in which one was killed and many wounded, the United States launched a bomb attack on targets in Libyan territory. President Reagan described the attack as "fully consistent with Article 51 of the UN Charter," presumably because, in the American view, the terrorist act was an "armed attack" justifying the bombing as a use of force in self-defense.

In that case, the United States also referred to its attack as a "preemptive action." The legal implication of that phrase was not elaborated. Publicists have debated whether, under article 51, a state may use force in "preemptive," or "anticipatory," self-defense, particularly in the context of nuclear strategy. Some have suggested that if a state has strong reasons to believe it is about to be the target of a nuclear strike, the "armed attack has occurred" and the victim need not wait but may "respond" in "anticipatory self-defense." Fortunately, that issue has remained academic. The justification for the attack on Libya, however, apparently was using "preemptive action" in a different sense. The action was not designed to "beat Libya to the punch," but, President Reagan said, it "will not only diminish Colonel Quadhafi's capacity to export terror, it will provide him with incentives and reasons to alter his criminal behavior."

The bombing of Libya by the United States was widely condemned and the claimed justification widely rejected.

Intervention and Counterintervention

Before the UN Charter, the law seemed to be that a state may provide military assistance to the government of another state, even to help it suppress rebellion, but a state could not assist rebels against the incumbent government of another state. If rebellion succeeded sufficiently to achieve the status of "belligerent" and constitute a civil war, the law probably forbade assistance to either side. That law, confirmed by special Non–Intervention Agreements in the 1930s, was battered during the Spanish Civil War as states intervened on both sides. The United States, however, honored the principle of nonintervention, helping neither side.

The United Nations Charter did not expressly address intervention in civil wars. Nothing in article 2(4) forbids sending military assistance to an incumbent government, but the use of force in support of rebels against an incumbent government would be a use of force against the territorial integrity of the state and, presumably, against its political independence. Under the Charter, a state probably may not send troops into the territory of another state to support either side in a civil war, since that too would violate the latter's territorial integrity and compromise its political independence. Assistance not involving the use of force, however—for example, providing advice, selling arms, or giving financial assistance to one (or both) sides in a civil war—seems not to be covered by article 2(4), but may violate norms against nonintervention that predate the Charter and have been strongly restated in numerous General Assembly resolutions.

W. MICHAEL REISMAN, "CRITERIA FOR THE LAWFUL USE OF FORCE IN INTERNATIONAL LAW"

10 *Yale Journal of International Law* 279 (1985).

Law includes a system of authorized coercion in which force is used to maintain and enhance public order objectives and in which unauthorized coercions are prohibited. * * * Law acknowledges the utility and the inescapability of the use of coercion in social processes, but seeks to organize, monopolize, and economize it.

The international legal system diverges from these general legal features only in terms of degree of organization and centralization of the use of coercion. In national systems, coercion is organized, relatively centralized, and, for the most part, monopolized by the apparatus of the state. In the international system, it is not. Individual actors historically have reserved the right to use force unilaterally to protect and vindicate legal entitlements.

Political and jurisprudential principles such as these must be kept in mind in an examination and rational interpretation of Article 2(4) of the United Nations Charter. Its sweeping prohibition of the threat or use of force in international politics was not an autonomous ethical affirmation of nonviolence * * *. Article 2(4) was embedded in and made initially plausible by a complex security scheme, established and spelled out in the United Nations Charter. If the scheme had operated, it would have obviated the need for the unilateral use of force. States with a grievance could have repaired to the Security Council, which could then apply the appropriate quantum and form of authoritative coercion and thereby vindicate collectively the rights it found had been violated. Under these circumstances, the need for and justification of a unilateral resort to force ceased. Even then, * * * the Charter acknowledged the inherent limits of its structures in the prevailing international politics by reserving to states the right of self-defense.

But the security system of the United Nations was premised on a consensus between the permanent members of the Security Council. Lamentably, that consensus dissolved early in the history of the organization. Thereafter, for almost all cases but those in which there was a short-term interest in collaboration, the Security Council could not operate as originally planned. Part of the systemic justification for the theory of Article 2(4) disappeared. At the same time, the Soviet Union announced, in effect, that it did not accept Article 2(4): "Wars of national liberation," an open-textured conception essentially meaning wars the Soviets supported, were not, in the Soviet conception, violations of Article 2(4). * * *

The international political system has largely accommodated itself to the indispensability of coercion in a legal system, on the one hand, and the deterioration of the Charter system, on the other, by developing a nuanced code for appraising the lawfulness of individual unilateral uses of force. The net result is not the value sterility of nineteenth century international legal conceptions of coercion, but neither is it Article 2(4). Some sense of the complexity of the code can be gained by examining, in a single time period, 1979, forceful unilateral interventions without the prior authorization of the United Nations.

In 1979, forces of Tanzania invaded Uganda, expelled the government of Idi Amin, and ultimately restored the government of Milton Obote. In the same year, French forces, in a quick and bloodless coup, expelled the government of Jean–Bedel Bokassa from the Central African Republic and installed a different president. In the same year, forces of the government of Vietnam entered Cambodia and sought to unseat the Pol Pot government and to replace it with a Vietnamese-backed government led by Heng Samrin. And in the same year, Soviet forces entered Afghanistan to support a government which, it seemed, would not have survived had it not been for the timely intervention and continued presence and operation of a foreign military force. * * *

Although efforts were made to arouse the United Nations to criticize the first two of these interventions, the organization resisted. But the organization condemned the latter two. Since all of these interventions, like all unilateral actions, were motivated in key part by the self-interest of the actors concerned, we must assume that there were some additional ingredients that rendered some of them internationally acceptable. I submit that it is in the identification of those factors that one can begin to describe the contemporary international law on the use of force.

The deterioration of the Charter security regime has stimulated a partial revival of a type of unilateral *jus ad bellum*. But in sharp contrast to the nineteenth century conception, which was value-neutral and ultimately power-based, the contemporary doctrine relates only to the vindication of rights which the international community recognizes but has, in general or in a particular case, demonstrated an inability to secure or guarantee. Hence, appraisals of state resort to coercion can no longer simply condemn them by invoking Article 2(4), but must test permissibility or lawfulness by reference to a number of factors, including the objective and the contingency for which coercion is being applied.

Nine basic categories appear to have emerged in which one finds varying support for unilateral uses of force. They are self-defense, which has been construed quite broadly; self-determination and decolonization; humanitarian intervention by the military instrument to replace an elite in another state; uses of the military instrument within spheres of influence and critical defense zones; treaty-sanctioned interventions within the territory of another state; use of the military instrument for the gathering of evidence in international proceedings; use of the military instrument to enforce international judgments; and counter-measures such as reprisals and retorsions. The categories themselves, however, are not determinative. * * *

In the determination of any action, a key and constant factor—less a criterion of lawfulness and more a sine qua non of survival—is the need for the maintenance of minimum order in a precarious international system. Will a particular use of force, whatever its justification otherwise, enhance or undermine world order?

When this requirement is met, attention may be directed to the fundamental principle of political legitimacy in contemporary international politics. It is, as anyone familiar with the UN Charter and with such key constitutive decisions as *Namibia* and *Western Sahara* knows, the enhancement of the ongoing right of peoples to determine their own political destinies. That obvious point bears renewed emphasis, for it is, in my view, the main purpose of contemporary international law: Article 2(4) is the means. The basic policy of contemporary international law has been to maintain the political independence of territorial communities so that they can continue to be able to express their ongoing desire for political organization in a form appropriate to them. Article 2(4), like so much in the Charter and in contemporary international politics, supports and must be interpreted in terms of this key postulate. Each application of Article 2(4) must enhance opportunities for ongoing self-determination. Though all interventions are lamentable, the fact is that some may serve, in terms of aggregate consequences, to increase the probability of the free choice of peoples about their government and political structure. Others have the manifest objective and consequence of doing exactly the opposite.

There is, thus, neither need nor justification for treating in a mechanically equal fashion, Tanzania's intervention in Uganda to overthrow the Amin despotism, on the one hand, and Soviet intervention in Hungary or Czechoslovakia to overthrow popular governments and to impose an undesired regime on a coerced population, on the other. Nor should the different appraisal of these cases by the international legal system occasion any surprise.

It is important to remember that norms are instruments devised by human beings to precipitate desired social consequences. One should not seek a point-for-point conformity to a rule without constant regard for the policy or principle that animated its prescription, with appropriate regard for the factual constellation in the minds of the drafters. Legal statements, like all others, are made in a context whose features are part of the expectations of speaker and audience. The expression of Article 2(4), in the form of a rule, is premised, I submit, on a political context and a technological environment which has been changing inexorably since the end of the nineteenth century. The rule assumes that the only threat to or usurpation of the right of political independence of a people within a particular territorial community is from external and overt invasion. It makes a historicist assumption as well: internal changes are deemed to be personnel changes in the composition of an elite which do not bring about basic changes in systems of public order within the country or in its external political alignments; governments come and go but the life of the people continues in its traditional fashion. Most important, it does not presuppose division, maintained by a precarious nuclear equipoise, between two contending public order systems, either of which might find itself substantially disadvantaged and pressed to intense coercion by the defection of a particular community from its own critical defense zone.

The rule-formulation of Article 2(4) is oblivious to these factors. * * *

The net effect of a mechanical interpretation of Article 2(4) may be to superimpose on an unwilling polity an elite, an ideology, and an external alignment alien to its wishes. This may entail far-reaching social and economic changes and grave deprivations of human rights for substantial numbers and strata of the population. * * *

Notes and Questions

1. *Contrasting Views of Article 2(4).* Contrast the views of Professors Henkin and Reisman concerning the international law governing the use of force. What for each is the role of Article 2(4)? What are the permissible exceptions to 2(4)? What instances of the use of force would both regard as illegal? How does each explain the fact that the world has seen many examples of the use of force involving territorial incursions since World War II?

The excerpts from Henkin and Reisman were both written during the Cold War. The United Nations Security Council has become more directly involved in authorizing the use of force since 1989. Recent developments in the United Nations are addressed in Part C of this chapter.

2. *The Relevance of International Law.* When is the international law relating to the use of force really taken into account? Debates over the use of force are often carried out in diplomatic or political fora, with states making opposing assertions about the legality of each other's recourse to armed force. In such highly political contexts, is the law on the use of force irrelevant? Are the legal rules too indeterminate to matter? Do they sometimes provide at least a framework for debate and perhaps a structure for the formulation of policy positions?

How else might the international law relating to the use of force be relevant? As suggested in the Notes and Questions following the *Goldberg Case* in Chapter 7, states sometimes have refused to recognize a government that they believe has come into existence because of an illegal use of force. Professor Brownlie believes that the international law on the use of force has influenced such varied matters as the law of treaties, the content of treaties, rules of engagement written by states for their armed forces, and the content of municipal laws and constitutions. See Ian Brownlie, "The United Nations Charter and the Use of Force, 1945–1985," in *The Current Legal Regulation of the Use of Force* 491 (A. Cassese ed. 1986). Furthermore, as we shall see in

Part C of this chapter, a state's illegal use of force also may affect the response of the U.N. Security Council towards that state.

3. *The Legality of the Use of Nuclear Weapons.* When, if ever, should it be permissible for a state to use nuclear weapons? In Legality of the Threat or Use of Nuclear Weapons (Request by the General Assembly), 1996 I.C.J. 226, 1996 WL 939337, the International Court issued an advisory opinion responding to a question posed by the U.N. General Assembly: "Is the threat or use of nuclear weapons in any circumstance permitted under international law?" The Court concluded in part:

> [T]he threat or use of nuclear weapons would generally be contrary to the rules of international law applicable in armed conflict, and in particular the principles and rules of humanitarian law;
>
> However, in view of the current state of international law, and of the elements of fact at its disposal, the Court cannot conclude definitely whether the threat or use of nuclear weapons would be lawful or unlawful in an extreme circumstance of self-defence, in which the very survival of a State would be at stake[.]

Id. at 266. Many of the issues concerning the legality of using nuclear weapons fall within the field of international humanitarian law.

4. *International Judicial Pronouncements on the Use of Force.* On occasion, international tribunals have pronounced on the legality of the use of force. The International Court of Justice addressed use of force issues in the Corfu Channel Case (U.K. v. Albania), 1949 I.C.J. 4, 1949 WL 1, as well as in the *Nuclear Weapons Case* referenced in the preceding Note. In the *Nicaragua Case*, the ICJ squarely faced arguments about the legality of one state's use of force against another. The following Note sets out the background to this case. The excerpt from the *Nicaragua Case* itself, which follows the summary Note, addresses the issues of use of force and collective self-defense, and the Notes following the excerpt summarize the Court's treatment of the principle of non-intervention.

Note: The Nicaragua Case

In 1984 Nicaragua filed an application against the United States with the International Court of Justice. Nicaragua contested the legality of U.S. support for rebels attacking the Nicaraguan government (the *contras*), as well as such U.S. acts as laying mines in Nicaraguan territorial waters and attacking Nicaraguan ports and oil installations. Nicaragua claimed, *inter alia*, that the behavior of the United States amounted to both an illegal intervention in Nicaragua's internal affairs and an illegal use of force against Nicaragua. The case raised legal issues that international lawyers had long debated: what assistance may one state give to rebels fighting against another state, and what assistance may one state give another state that is attempting to suppress rebels aided by a third state. The latter issue arose in the case because the United States claimed that its challenged actions could be justified as collective self-defense, assisting the governments of Honduras, Costa Rica, and El Salvador in fighting Nicaragua-backed rebels.

Before reaching the merits of Nicaragua's case, the International Court of Justice faced difficult questions about its jurisdiction. In 1946, the United

States had accepted the Court's jurisdiction under Article 36(2) of the ICJ Statute, albeit with several reservations. When the United States learned that Nicaragua was about to file a claim in the International Court of Justice, the United States attempted to modify its acceptance of Article 36(2) jurisdiction with respect to disputes related to events in Central America. The United States made this attempt just three days before the claim was filed. The Court ruled that this purported withdrawal of jurisdiction was invalid because the United States had not provided six months' notice as specified in its 1946 declaration. (The United States subsequently withdrew its Article 36(2) acceptance of the Court's jurisdiction altogether.) In response to a U.S. argument that mutual consent to jurisdiction was lacking because Nicaragua itself had not accepted the Court's jurisdiction, the ICJ ruled that Nicaragua had accepted the jurisdiction of the Permanent Court of International Justice, an acceptance that continued to apply to the ICJ by virtue of Article 36(5) of the Court's Statute. The United States unsuccessfully raised other jurisdictional and preliminary objections, including objections to jurisdiction asserted under a compromissory clause in a bilateral U.S.–Nicaragua Friendship, Commerce and Navigation Treaty. See Case Concerning Military and Paramilitary Activities In and Against Nicaragua (Nicaragua v. United States), 1984 I.C.J. 392, 1984 WL 501 (Jurisdiction of the Court and Admissibility of the Application); D.W. Greig, "Nicaragua and the United States: Confrontation Over the Jurisdiction of the International Court," 62 *British Yearbook of International Law* 119 (1991). We have looked at the jurisdiction of the I.C.J more broadly in Chapter 5.

Having lost its jurisdictional arguments, the United States refused to appear in the merits phase of the *Nicaragua Case*, Case Concerning Military and Paramilitary Activities In and Against Nicaragua (Nicaragua v. United States), 1986 I.C.J. 14, 1986 WL 522 (Merits). In accordance with Article 53 of the ICJ's Statute (see the Appendix), the Court nevertheless proceeded to reach a judgment on the merits. Should the United States have appeared, in order to stress particular facts and legal arguments? The Court raised many of these issues itself, as it was obliged by its Statute to satisfy itself that Nicaragua's claim was "well founded in fact and law." ICJ Statute, Article 53(2). In Chapter 5, we saw that the Court responded similarly when Iran refused to appear in the *Diplomatic and Consular Staff Case*.

A U.S. reservation to its 1946 acceptance of the Court's jurisdiction excluded multilateral treaties from the scope of the Court's jurisdiction. Because of this reservation, the International Court of Justice decided that it could not rely directly on Article 2(4) of the U.N. Charter or on the Charter of the Organization of American States in the merits phase of the *Nicaragua Case*. For this reason, many of Nicaragua's claims and the United States' defenses were analyzed under customary international law. The multilateral treaty reservation did not affect Nicaragua's arguments that the United States had breached its obligations under a bilateral U.S.–Nicaragua Friendship, Commerce and Navigation Treaty. In portions of the *Nicaragua* judgment not considered here, the Court found the United States in breach of its obligations under this bilateral treaty.

Among the customary international law issues addressed in the merits phase of the *Nicaragua Case* were claims relating to the use of force and to intervention. As we shall see in the case excerpt and Notes below, the Court ruled that the United States in several respects illegally used force against Nicaragua and illegally intervened in the affairs of Nicaragua, and that those U.S. actions could not be justified as collective self-defense or on other grounds.

The Court found that the United States had an obligation to make reparation to Nicaragua for injury caused by the U.S. breaches, but decided to leave the issue of reparation for a subsequent procedure, "failing agreement between the Parties." Nicaragua presented a claim for $12 billion to the ICJ in September 1987. Following a change in government in Nicaragua, however, Nicaragua opted, in September 1991, to discontinue the ICJ proceedings. See Order on the Discontinuance and Removal from the List in the Case Concerning Military and Paramilitary Activities In and Against Nicaragua (Nicaragua v. United States), 1991 I.C.J. 47, 1991 WL 287867. The United States reportedly made it clear that trade and foreign aid packages to Nicaragua depended on Nicaragua's dropping its ICJ reparations claim. Tim Coone, "Nicaragua Renews Drive to Unblock Credit Pipeline," *Financial Times*, Dec. 5, 1990, at 6; Mark A. Uhlig, "U.S. Urges Nicaragua to Forgive Legal Claim," *New York Times*, Sept. 26, 1990, at 18. Had Nicaragua pursued its claim for reparations to a successful conclusion at the ICJ, could the Court's award have been enforced through any judicial process? See Mary Ellen O'Connell, "The Prospect of Enforcing Monetary Judgments of the International Court of Justice: A Study of Nicaragua's Judgment Against the United States," 30 *Virginia Journal of International Law* 891 (1990).

THE NICARAGUA CASE

Case Concerning Military and Paramilitary Activities In and Against Nicaragua, Nicaragua v. United States, 1986 I.C.J. 14, 1986 WL 522 (Merits).

176. * * * [T]he Court observes that the United Nations Charter * * * by no means covers the whole area of the regulation of the use of force in international relations. On one essential point, this treaty itself refers to pre-existing customary international law; this reference to customary law is contained in the actual text of Article 51, which mentions the "inherent right" * * * of individual or collective self-defence, which "nothing in the present Charter shall impair" and which applies in the event of an armed attack. The Court therefore finds that Article 51 of the Charter is only meaningful on the basis that there is a "natural" or "inherent" right of self-defence, and it is hard to see how this can be other than of a customary nature, even if its present content has been confirmed and influenced by the Charter. Moreover, the Charter having itself recognized the existence of this right, does not go on to regulate directly all aspects of its content. For example, it does not contain any specific rule whereby self-defence would warrant only measures which are proportional to the armed attack and necessary to respond to it, a rule well established in customary international law. Moreover, a definition of the "armed attack" which, if found to exist, authorizes the exercise of the "inherent right" of self-defence, is not provided in the Charter, and is not part of treaty law. * * *

186. It is not to be expected that in the practice of States the application of the rules in question should have been perfect, in the sense that States should have refrained, with complete consistency, from the use of force or from intervention in each other's internal affairs. The Court does not consider that, for a rule to be established as customary, the corresponding practice must be in absolutely rigorous conformity with the rule. In order to deduce the existence of customary rules, the Court deems it sufficient that the conduct of States should, in general, be consistent with such rules, and that instances of State conduct inconsistent with a given rule should generally have been treated as breaches of that rule, not as indications of the recognition of a new rule. If a State acts in a way prima facie incompatible with a recognized rule, but defends its conduct by appealing to exceptions or justifications contained within the rule itself, then whether or not the State's conduct is in fact justifiable on that basis, the significance of that attitude is to confirm rather than to weaken the rule.

187. The Court must therefore determine, first, the substance of the customary rules relating to the use of force in international relations, applicable to the dispute submitted to it. * * *

188. The Court thus finds that both Parties take the view that the principles as to the use of force incorporated in the United Nations Charter correspond, in essentials, to those found in customary international law. The Parties thus both take the view that the fundamental principle in this area is expressed in the terms employed in Article 2, paragraph 4, of the United Nations Charter. They therefore accept a treaty-law obligation to refrain in their international relations from the threat or use of force against the territorial integrity or political independence of any State, or in any other manner inconsistent with the purposes of the United Nations. The Court has however to be satisfied that there exists in customary international law an *opinio juris* as to the binding character of such abstention. This *opinio juris* may, though with all due caution, be deduced from, *inter alia*, the attitude of the Parties and the attitude of States towards certain General Assembly resolutions, and particularly resolution 2625 (XXV) entitled "Declaration on Principles of International Law concerning Friendly Relations and Co-operation among States in accordance with the Charter of the United Nations." The effect of consent to the text of such resolutions cannot be understood as merely that of a "reiteration or elucidation" of the treaty commitment undertaken in the Charter. On the contrary, it may be understood as an acceptance of the validity of the rule or set of rules declared by the resolution by themselves. The principle of non-use of force, for example, may thus be regarded as a principle of customary international law * * *. * * *

189. As regards the United States in particular, the weight of an expression of *opinio juris* can similarly be attached to its support of the resolution of the Sixth International Conference of American States condemning aggression (18 February 1928) and ratification of the Montevideo Convention on Rights and Duties of States (26 December 1933),

Article 11 of which imposes the obligation not to recognize territorial acquisitions or special advantages which have been obtained by force. Also significant is United States acceptance of the principle of the prohibition of the use of force which is contained in the declaration on principles governing the mutual relations of States participating in the Conference on Security and Co-operation in Europe (Helsinki, 1 August 1975), whereby the participating States undertake to "refrain in their mutual relations, *as well as in their international relations in general*," (emphasis added) from the threat or use of force. Acceptance of a text in these terms confirms the existence of an *opinio juris* of the participating States prohibiting the use of force in international relations.

190.   A further confirmation of the validity as customary international law of the principle of the prohibition of the use of force expressed in Article 2, paragraph 4, of the Charter of the United Nations may be found in the fact that it is frequently referred to in statements by State representatives as being not only a principle of customary international law but also a fundamental or cardinal principle of such law. The International Law Commission, in the course of its work on the codification of the law of treaties, expressed the view that "the law of the Charter concerning the prohibition of the use of force in itself constitutes a conspicuous example of a rule in international law having the character of *jus cogens*." Nicaragua in its Memorial on the Merits submitted in the present case states that the principle prohibiting the use of force embodied in Article 2, paragraph 4, of the Charter of the United Nations "has come to be recognized as *jus cogens*." The United States, in its Counter–Memorial on the questions of jurisdiction and admissibility, found it material to quote the views of scholars that this principle is a "universal norm," a "universal international law," a "universally recognized principle of international law," and a "principle of *jus cogens*."

191.   As regards certain particular aspects of the principle in question, it will be necessary to distinguish the most grave forms of the use of force (those constituting an armed attack) from other less grave forms. In determining the legal rule which applies to these latter forms, the Court can again draw on the formulations contained in the Declaration on Principles of International Law concerning Friendly Relations and Co-operation among States in accordance with the Charter of the United Nations (General Assembly resolution 2625 (XXV), referred to above). As already observed, the adoption by States of this text affords an indication of their *opinio juris* as to customary international law on the question. Alongside certain descriptions which may refer to aggression, this text includes others which refer only to less grave forms of the use of force. In particular, according to this resolution:

> "Every State has the duty to refrain from the threat or use of force to violate the existing international boundaries of another State or as a means of solving international disputes, including territorial disputes and problems concerning frontiers of States...."

States have a duty to refrain from acts of reprisal involving the use of force. . . .

Every State has the duty to refrain from any forcible action which deprives peoples referred to in the elaboration of the principle of equal rights and self-determination of that right to self-determination and freedom and independence.

Every State has the duty to refrain from organizing or encouraging the organization of irregular forces or armed bands, including mercenaries, for incursion into the territory of another State.

Every State has the duty to refrain from organizing, instigating, assisting or participating in acts of civil strife or terrorist acts in another State or acquiescing in organized activities within its territory directed towards the commission of such acts, when the acts referred to in the present paragraph involve a threat or use of force." * * *

193. The general rule prohibiting force allows for certain exceptions. In view of the arguments advanced by the United States to justify the acts of which it is accused by Nicaragua, the Court must express a view on the content of the right of self-defence, and more particularly the right of collective self-defence. First, with regard to the existence of this right, it notes that in the language of Article 51 of the United Nations Charter, the inherent right (or "droit naturel") which any State possesses in the event of an armed attack, covers both collective and individual self-defence. Thus, the Charter itself testifies to the existence of the right of collective self-defence in customary international law. Moreover, just as the wording of certain General Assembly declarations adopted by States demonstrates their recognition of the principle of prohibition of force as definitely a matter of customary international law, some of the wording in those declarations operates similarly in respect of the right of self-defence (both collective and individual). * * *

194. With regard to the characteristics governing the right of self-defence, since the Parties consider the existence of this right to be established as a matter of customary international law, they have concentrated on the conditions governing its use. In view of the circumstances in which the dispute has arisen, reliance is placed by the Parties only on the right of self-defence in the case of an armed attack which has already occurred, and the issue of the lawfulness of a response to the imminent threat of armed attack has not been raised. Accordingly the Court expresses no view on that issue. The Parties also agree in holding that whether the response to the attack is lawful depends on observance of the criteria of the necessity and the proportionality of the measures taken in self-defence. Since the existence of the right of collective self-defence is established in customary international law, the Court must define the specific conditions which may have to be met for its exercise, in addition to the conditions of necessity and proportionality to which the Parties have referred.

195. In the case of individual self-defence, the exercise of this right is subject to the State concerned having been the victim of an armed attack. Reliance on collective self-defence of course does not remove the need for this. There appears now to be general agreement on the nature of the acts which can be treated as constituting armed attacks. In particular, it may be considered to be agreed that an armed attack must be understood as including not merely action by regular armed forces across an international border, but also "the sending by or on behalf of a State of armed bands, groups, irregulars or mercenaries, which carry out acts of armed force against another State of such gravity as to amount to" (*inter alia*) an actual armed attack conducted by regular forces, "or its substantial involvement therein." This description contained in Article 3, paragraph (g), of the Definition of Aggression annexed to General Assembly resolution 3314 (XXIX), may be taken to reflect customary international law. The Court sees no reason to deny that, in customary law, the prohibition of armed attacks may apply to the sending by a State of armed bands to the territory of another State, if such an operation, because of its scale and effects, would have been classified as an armed attack rather than as a mere frontier incident had it been carried out by regular armed forces. But the Court does not believe that the concept of "armed attack" includes not only acts by armed bands where such acts occur on a significant scale but also assistance to rebels in the form of the provision of weapons or logistical or other support. Such assistance may be regarded as a threat or use of force, or amount to intervention in the internal or external affairs of other States. It is also clear that it is the State which is the victim of an armed attack which must form and declare the view that it has been so attacked. There is no rule in customary international law permitting another State to exercise the right of collective self-defence on the basis of its own assessment of the situation. Where collective self-defence is invoked, it is to be expected that the State for whose benefit this right is used will have declared itself to be the victim of an armed attack. * * *

199. * * * [T]he Court finds that in customary international law, whether of a general kind or that particular to the inter–American legal system, there is no rule permitting the exercise of collective self-defence in the absence of a request by the State which regards itself as the victim of an armed attack. The Court concludes that the requirement of a request by the State which is the victim of the alleged attack is additional to the requirement that such a State should have declared itself to have been attacked. * * *

226. The Court, having outlined both the facts of the case as proved by the evidence before it, and the general rules of international law which appear to it to be in issue as a result of these facts, * * * has now to appraise the facts in relation to the legal rules applicable. * * *

227. The Court will first appraise the facts in the light of the principle of the non-use of force, examined in paragraphs 187 to 200 above. What is unlawful, in accordance with that principle, is recourse to either the threat or the use of force against the territorial integrity or

political independence of any State. For the most part, the complaints by Nicaragua are of the actual use of force against it by the United States. Of the acts which the Court has found imputable to the Government of the United States, the following are relevant in this respect:

> —the laying of mines in Nicaraguan internal or territorial waters in early 1984 * * *;

> —certain attacks on Nicaraguan ports, oil installations and a naval base * * *.

These activities constitute infringements of the principle of the prohibition of the use of force, defined earlier, unless they are justified by circumstances which exclude their unlawfulness, a question now to be examined. The Court has also found * * * the existence of military manoeuvres held by the United States near the Nicaraguan borders; and Nicaragua has made some suggestion that this constituted a "threat of force," which is equally forbidden by the principle of non-use of force. The Court is however not satisfied that the manoeuvres complained of, in the circumstances in which they were held, constituted on the part of the United States a breach, as against Nicaragua, of the principle forbidding recourse to the threat or use of force.

228. Nicaragua has also claimed that the United States * * * used force against Nicaragua in breach of its obligation under customary international law in as much as it has engaged in

> "recruiting, training, arming, equipping, financing, supplying and otherwise encouraging, supporting, aiding, and directing military and paramilitary actions in and against Nicaragua" * * *. * * *

[T]he Court finds that, subject to the question whether the action of the United States might be justified as an exercise of the right of self-defence, the United States has committed a prima facie violation of that principle by its assistance to the *contras* in Nicaragua, by "organizing or encouraging the organization of irregular forces or armed bands … for the incursion into the territory of another State," and "participating in acts of civil strife … in another State," in the terms of General Assembly resolution 2625 (XXV). According to that resolution, participation of this kind is contrary to the principle of the prohibition of the use of force when the acts of civil strife referred to "involve a threat or use of force." In the view of the Court, while the arming and training of the *contras* can certainly be said to involve the threat or use of force against Nicaragua, this is not necessarily so in respect of all the assistance given by the United States Government. In particular, the Court considers that the mere supply of funds to the *contras*, while undoubtedly an act of intervention in the internal affairs of Nicaragua, as will be explained below, does not in itself amount to a use of force.

229. The Court must thus consider whether, as the Respondent claims, the acts in question of the United States are justified by the exercise of its right of collective self-defence against an armed attack. * * * For the Court to conclude that the United States was lawfully

exercising its right of collective self-defence, it must first find that Nicaragua engaged in an armed attack against El Salvador, Honduras or Costa Rica.

230. As regards El Salvador, the Court has found * * * that it is satisfied that between July 1979 and the early months of 1981, an intermittent flow of arms was routed via the territory of Nicaragua to the armed opposition in that country. The Court was not however satisfied that assistance has reached the Salvadorian armed opposition, on a scale of any significance, since the early months of 1981, or that the Government of Nicaragua was responsible for any flow of arms at either period. Even assuming that the supply of arms to the opposition in El Salvador could be treated as imputable to the Government of Nicaragua, to justify invocation of the right of collective self-defence in customary international law, it would have to be equated with an armed attack by Nicaragua on El Salvador. As stated above, the Court is unable to consider that, in customary international law, the provision of arms to the opposition in another State constitutes an armed attack on that State. Even at a time when the arms flow was at its peak, and again assuming the participation of the Nicaraguan Government, that would not constitute such armed attack.

231. Turning to Honduras and Costa Rica, the Court has also stated * * * that it should find established that certain trans-border incursions into the territory of those two States, in 1982, 1983 and 1984, were imputable to the Government of Nicaragua. Very little information is however available to the Court as to the circumstances of these incursions or their possible motivations, which renders it difficult to decide whether they may be treated for legal purposes as amounting, singly or collectively, to an "armed attack" by Nicaragua on either or both States. * * * There are however other considerations which justify the Court in finding that neither these incursions, nor the alleged supply of arms to the opposition in El Salvador, may be relied on as justifying the exercise of the right of collective self-defence.

232. The exercise of the right of collective self-defence presupposes that an armed attack has occurred; and it is evident that it is the victim State, being the most directly aware of that fact, which is likely to draw general attention to its plight. It is also evident that if the victim State wishes another State to come to its help in the exercise of the right of collective self-defence, it will normally make an express request to that effect. Thus in the present instance, the Court is entitled to take account, in judging the asserted justification of the exercise of collective self-defence by the United States, of the actual conduct of El Salvador, Honduras and Costa Rica at the relevant time, as indicative of a belief by the State in question that it was the victim of an armed attack by Nicaragua, and of the making of a request by the victim State to the United States for help in the exercise of collective self-defence.

233. The Court has seen no evidence that the conduct of those States was consistent with such a situation, either at the time when the

United States first embarked on the activities which were allegedly justified by self-defence, or indeed for a long period subsequently. So far as El Salvador is concerned, it appears to the Court that while El Salvador did in fact officially declare itself the victim of an armed attack, and did ask for the United States to exercise its right of collective self-defence, this occurred only on a date much later than the commencement of the United States activities which were allegedly justified by this request. The Court notes that on 3 April 1984, the representative of El Salvador before the United Nations Security Council, while complaining of the "open foreign intervention practiced by Nicaragua in our internal affairs," refrained from stating that El Salvador had been subjected to armed attack, and made no mention of the right of collective self-defence which it had supposedly asked the United States to exercise. Nor was this mentioned when El Salvador addressed a letter to the Court in April 1984, in connection with Nicaragua's complaint against the United States. It was only in its Declaration of Intervention filed on 15 August 1984, that El Salvador referred to requests addressed at various dates to the United States for the latter to exercise its right of collective self-defence, asserting on this occasion that it had been the victim of aggression from Nicaragua "since at least 1980." In that Declaration, El Salvador affirmed that initially it had "not wanted to present any accusation or allegation [against Nicaragua] to any of the jurisdictions to which we have a right to apply," since it sought "a solution of understanding and mutual respect."

234. As to Honduras and Costa Rica, they also were prompted by the institution of proceedings in this case to address communications to the Court; in neither of these is there mention of armed attack or collective self-defence. * * *

235. There is also an aspect of the conduct of the United States which the Court is entitled to take into account as indicative of the view of that State on the question of the existence of an armed attack. At no time, up to the present, has the United States Government addressed to the Security Council, in connection with the matters the subject of the present case, the report which is required by Article 51 of the United Nations Charter in respect of measures which a State believes itself bound to take when it exercises the right of individual or collective self-defence. The Court, whose decision has to be made on the basis of customary international law, has already observed that in the context of that law, the reporting obligation enshrined in Article 51 of the Charter of the United Nations does not exist. It does not therefore treat the absence of a report on the part of the United States as the breach of an undertaking forming part of the customary international law applicable to the present dispute. But the Court is justified in observing that this conduct of the United States hardly conforms with the latter's avowed conviction that it was acting in the context of collective self-defence as consecrated by Article 51 of the Charter. This fact is all the more noteworthy because, in the Security Council, the United States has itself taken the view that failure to observe the requirement to make a report

contradicted a State's claim to be acting on the basis of collective self-defence. * * *

237. Since the Court has found that the condition *sine qua non* required for the exercise of the right of collective self-defence by the United States is not fulfilled in this case, the appraisal of the United States activities in relation to the criteria of necessity and proportionality takes on a different significance. * * * [E]ven if the United States activities in question had been carried on in strict compliance with the canons of necessity and proportionality, they would not thereby become lawful. If however they were not, it may constitute an additional ground of wrongfulness. On the question of necessity, the Court observes that the United States measures taken in December 1981 (or, at the earliest, March of that year * * *) cannot be said to correspond to a "necessity" justifying the United States action against Nicaragua on the basis of assistance given by Nicaragua to the armed opposition in El Salvador. First, these measures were only taken, and began to produce their effects, several months after the major offensive of the armed opposition against the Government of El Salvador had been completely repulsed (January 1981), and the actions of the opposition considerably reduced in consequence. Thus it was possible to eliminate the main danger to the Salvadorian Government without the United States embarking on activities in and against Nicaragua. Accordingly, it cannot be held that these activities were undertaken in the light of necessity. Whether or not the assistance to the *contras* might meet the criterion of proportionality, the Court cannot regard the United States activities * * * relating to the mining of the Nicaraguan ports and the attacks on ports, oil installations, etc., as satisfying that criterion. Whatever uncertainty may exist as to the exact scale of the aid received by the Salvadorian armed opposition from Nicaragua, it is clear that these latter United States activities in question could not have been proportionate to that aid. Finally on this point, the Court must also observe that the reaction of the United States in the context of what it regarded as self-defence was continued long after the period in which any presumed armed attack by Nicaragua could reasonably be contemplated.

238. Accordingly, the Court concludes that the plea of collective self-defence against an alleged armed attack on El Salvador, Honduras or Costa Rica, advanced by the United States to justify its conduct toward Nicaragua, cannot be upheld; and accordingly that the United States has violated the principle prohibiting recourse to the threat or use of force by the acts listed in paragraph 227 above, and by its assistance to the *contras* to the extent that this assistance "involve[s] a threat or use of force" (paragraph 228 above). * * *

249. * * * While an armed attack would give rise to an entitlement to collective self-defence, a use of force of a lesser degree of gravity cannot produce any entitlement to take collective counter-measures involving the use of force. The acts of which Nicaragua is accused, even assuming them to have been established and imputable to that State, could only have proportionate counter-measures on the part of the State

which had been the victim of these acts, namely El Salvador, Honduras or Costa Rica. They could not justify counter-measures taken by a third State, the United States, and particularly could not justify intervention involving the use of force. * * *

290.   * * * The Court has * * * also to recall the principle that the parties to any dispute, particularly any dispute the continuance of which is likely to endanger the maintenance of international peace and security, should seek a solution by peaceful means. Enshrined in Article 33 of the United Nations Charter, which also indicates a number of peaceful means which are available, this principle has also the status of customary law. * * *

292.   For these reasons:

THE COURT * * *

(2) By twelve votes to three,

Rejects the justification of collective self-defence maintained by the United States of America in connection with the military and paramilitary activities in and against Nicaragua the subject of this case; * * *

(4) By twelve votes to three,

Decides that the United States of America, by certain attacks on Nicaraguan territory in 1983–1984, namely attacks on Peurto Sandino on 13 September and 14 October 1983; an attack on Corinto on 10 October 1983; an attack on Potosi Naval Base on 4/5 January 1984; an attack on San Juan del Sur on 7 March 1984; attacks on patrol boats at Puerto Sandino on 28 and 30 March 1984; and an attack on San Juan del Norte on 9 April 1984; and further by [specified] acts of intervention * * * which involve the use of force, has acted, against the Republic of Nicaragua, in breach of its obligation under customary international law not to use force against another State; * * *

(6) By twelve votes to three,

Decides that, by laying mines in the internal or territorial waters of the Republic of Nicaragua during the first months of 1984, the United States of America has acted, against the Republic of Nicaragua, in breach of its obligations under customary international law not to use force against another State, not to intervene in its affairs, not to violate its sovereignty, and not to interrupt peaceful maritime commerce; * * *

(12) By twelve votes to three,

Decides that the United States of America is under a duty immediately to cease and to refrain from all such acts as may constitute breaches of the foregoing legal obligations; * * *

(16) Unanimously,

Recalls to both Parties their obligation to seek a solution to their disputes by peaceful means in accordance with international law.

Notes and Questions

1. *The International Court of Justice and Cases Involving the Use of Force.* What are the advantages and disadvantages of the International Court of Justice hearing and deciding cases involving the use of force and intervention? Compare the *Nicaragua Case* with the ICJ decisions in Chapter 5, as well as with the PCA's *Dogger Bank Case* in the same chapter. For reactions to the ICJ's decision, see "Appraisals of the ICJ's Decision: Nicaragua vs. United States," 81 *American Journal of International Law* 77 (1987). Other states have also recently used the ICJ as a forum in which to allege illegal military actions. Several such cases were on the Court's docket as of November 1, 2000: the United States and Iran each claimed that the other's military activities during 1987–1988 violated a bilateral Friendship, Commerce and Navigation Treaty (the *Oil Platforms Case*); the Federal Republic of Yugoslavia alleged that member states of NATO had illegally bombed the Yugoslav province of Kosovo during 1999 (see Part C below); and in 1999 the Democratic Republic of the Congo filed claims against Burundi, Rwanda, and Uganda for their ongoing armed activities in the territory of the Congo. See <www.icj-cij.org>.

2. *Customary International Law and the Use of Force.* In the *Nicaragua Case*, the ICJ was precluded from relying directly on the U.N. Charter because of the multilateral treaty reservation attached to the U.S. acceptance of the Court's jurisdiction. Is it possible for the content of Charter and post-Charter customary norms to differ with respect to the legality of the use of force? Assess the methodology the Court used to determine customary or general international law on the use of force and collective self-defense. How did the Court determine that the requirement of an "armed attack" was a prerequisite to the use of self-defense in customary international law as well as under the U.N. Charter? How did the Court determine the meaning of "armed attack"? More generally, how did the Court explain the existence of customary rules when states so often use force against other states? If state practice generally proscribes the use of force against the territorial integrity of other states, why does that practice not indicate state compliance with a treaty obligation (the U.N. Charter) rather than with a customary legal obligation? Did the ICJ, at least implicitly, accept the view that prohibitions on the use of force were *jus cogens*? See John Tasioulas, "In Defence of Relative Normativity: Communitarian Values and the *Nicaragua Case*," 16 *Oxford Journal of Legal Studies* 85 (1996), and the discussion of *jus cogens* in Chapter 3.

3. *Non-intervention.* In addition to considering arguments on the use of force and collective self-defense, the Court in the *Nicaragua Case* addressed the international law relating to intervention and the right of third states to take countermeasures in response to intervention not amounting to an armed attack. In particular, the Court considered the argument that U.S. actions were legitimate responses to Nicaragua's own acts in support of insurgents in El Salvador, though Nicaragua's acts did not amount to armed attacks. The Court first defined the principle of non-intervention, saying that the principle:

forbids all States or groups of States to intervene directly or indirectly in internal or external affairs of other States. A prohibited intervention must accordingly be one bearing on matters in which each State is permitted, by the principle of State sovereignty, to decide freely. One of these is the choice of a political, economic, social and cultural system, and the formulation of foreign policy. Intervention is wrongful when it uses methods of coercion in regard to such choices, which must remain free ones. The element of coercion, which defines, and indeed forms the very essence of, prohibited intervention, is particularly obvious in the case of an intervention which uses force, either in the direct form of military action, or in the indirect form of support for subversive or terrorist armed activities within another State.

1986 I.C.J. at 108. The principle of non-intervention, the Court concluded, was established as a matter of customary international law. The Court found no exception in favor of a right of intervention to support "an internal opposition in another State, whose cause appear[s] particularly worthy by reason of the political and moral values with which it was identified." *Id*. Compare the debate between Professors Henkin and Reisman above. Applying the principle of non-intervention to the facts of the case, the Court concluded that U.S. support for "the military and paramilitary activities of the *contras* in Nicaragua by financial support, training, supply of weapons, intelligence and logistic support, constitutes a clear breach of the principle of non-intervention." *Id*. at 124. See also paragraph 249 in the Court's opinion above.

4. *Dissenting Opinions*. Judges Oda of Japan, Jennings of the United Kingdom, and Schwebel of the United States dissented from most of the Court's particular holdings. The tenor of Judge Schwebel's view of the *Nicaragua Case* is suggested by the first paragraph of his lengthy opinion:

To say that I dissent from the Court's Judgment is to understate the depth of my differences with it. I agree with the Court's finding that the United States, by failing to make known the existence and location of the mines laid by it, acted in violation of customary international law (in relation to the shipping of third States); I agree that the CIA's causing publication of a manual advocating acts in violation of the law of war is indefensible; and I agree with some other elements of the Judgment as well. Nevertheless, in my view the Judgment misperceives and misconstrues essential facts—not so much the facts concerning the actions of the United States of which Nicaragua complains as the facts concerning the actions of Nicaragua of which the United States complains. It misconceives and misapplies the law—not in all respects, on some of which the whole Court is agreed, but in paramount respects: particularly in its interpretation of what is an "armed attack" within the meaning of the United Nations Charter and customary international law; * * * and in nearly all of its holdings as to which Party to this case has acted in violation of its international responsibilities and which, because it has acted defensively, has not. * * * [T]his Judgment asserts a jurisdiction which in my view the Court properly lacks, and it adjudges a vital question which, I believe, is not justiciable. And, I am profoundly pained to say, I dissent from this Judgment because I believe that, in effect, it adopts the false testimony of representatives of the Government of the Republic of Nicaragua on a matter which, in my view, is essential to the disposition of this case and which, on any view, is material to its disposition.

Id. at 249, 256.

5. *Modifying Legal Proscriptions Against the Use of Force.* If you find that legal standards relating to use of force, intervention, and countermeasures are either inappropriate or inappropriately vague, how should they be changed or clarified? Is it desirable for states to act unilaterally in this area, thus providing examples of "state practice" useful for the formation of customary international law? What are the prospects for bilateral agreements restricting intervention or the use of force? For regional understandings? For steps by the United Nations?

C. THE UNITED NATIONS AND THE USE OF FORCE

The first and probably most important aim of United Nations, as set forth in the Preamble to the U.N. Charter, is to "save succeeding generations from the scourge of war." The Organization's first purpose, listed in Article 1, is "to maintain international peace and security." Various U.N. organs have addressed use of force issues. The General Assembly, for example, has adopted important resolutions relating to the use of force, such as the Definition of Aggression considered in the *Nicaragua Case* above. According to Article 24 of the U.N. Charter, however, the Security Council has "primary responsibility for the maintenance of international peace and security." Under Chapter VII of the Charter, the Security Council is charged with taking action with respect to threats to the peace, breaches of the peace, and acts of aggression. As we saw in Chapter 8, U.N. Member States are legally obligated to accept and carry out Security Council "decisions."

Cold War politics often led Security Council permanent members to veto proposed Security Council measures. The Council became much more active with respect to matters affecting international peace and security after 1989. In this Part, we look first at Chapter VII of the U.N. Charter and the Security Council's responses to Iraq's 1990 invasion of Kuwait. In Section 2, we explore how the United Nations has acted in response to fighting or instability within a state's borders. Section 3 addresses the actions of the United Nations and regional organizations in the Balkans.

1. THE UNITED NATIONS, CHAPTER VII, AND THE INVASION OF KUWAIT

On August 2, 1990, over 100,000 Iraqi troops attacked neighboring Kuwait. The greatly outnumbered Kuwaiti forces were routed, and the Emir of Kuwait fled the country. Iraq alleged that Kuwait's government was corrupt and had violated the rights of the Kuwaiti peoples; that Kuwait had violated the production quota of the Organization of Petroleum Exporting Countries; that Kuwait had been taking more than its share of oil from a huge oil field that straddled the Iraq–Kuwait border; and that Iraq had never agreed to its border with Kuwait, which the British had set in 1922. The invasion followed the collapse of talks in which Iraq had asserted financial and territorial claims. On the same day as the invasion, the U.N. Security Council voted 14–0, with Yemen abstaining, to condemn the invasion and to demand immediate and unconditional withdrawal of all Iraq forces. S.C. Res. 660 (1990). One week later, the Security Council voted unanimously to declare Iraq's asserted "annexation" of Kuwait null and void. S.C. Res. 662 (1990).

The readings in this section illustrate the scope of Security Council actions under Chapter VII of the U.N. Charter. We begin with excerpts from Chapter VII and two of the Security Council's resolutions responding to Iraq's invasion of Kuwait. The second of these, Resolution 678, followed a massive buildup of U.S. military forces in Saudi Arabia and the region, and the deployment of many non-U.S. troops as well. Beginning on January 16, 1991, after Iraq refused to comply with a U.S. deadline for withdrawing from Kuwait, the air strikes and ground assault of "Operation Desert Storm" began. These led, by the end of February, to the restoration of Kuwaiti sovereignty within the territory of Kuwait. Was Operation Desert Storm an exercise of collective self-defense or a proper exercise of Security Council authority under Chapter VII of the U.N. Charter? The readings that follow Resolutions 661 and 678 debate the question. The U.N. Security Council has continued to sanction Iraq, as explored in the Notes at the end of this Section.

UNITED NATIONS CHARTER, ARTICLES 39–43, 48
June 26, 1945, 59 Stat. 1031, T.S. No. 993, 3 Bevans 1153, 1976 Y.B.U.N. 1043.

CHAPTER VII: ACTION WITH RESPECT TO THREATS TO THE PEACE, BREACHES OF THE PEACE, AND ACTS OF AGGRESSION

Article 39

The Security Council shall determine the existence of any threat to the peace, breach of the peace, or act of aggression and shall make recommendations, or decide what measures shall be taken in accordance with Articles 41 and 42, to maintain or restore international peace and security.

Article 40

In order to prevent an aggravation of the situation, the Security Council may, before making the recommendations or deciding upon the measures provided for in Article 39, call upon the parties concerned to comply with such provisional measures as it deems necessary or desirable. Such provisional measures shall be without prejudice to the rights, claims, or position of the parties concerned. The Security Council shall duly take account of failure to comply with such provisional measures.

Article 41

The Security Council may decide what measures not involving the use of armed force are to be employed to give effect to its decisions, and it may call upon the Members of the United Nations to apply such measures. These may include complete or partial interruption of economic relations and of rail, sea, air, postal, telegraphic, radio, and other means of communication, and the severance of diplomatic relations.

Article 42

Should the Security Council consider that measures provided for in Article 41 would be inadequate or have proved to be inadequate, it may take such action by air, sea, or land forces as may be necessary to maintain or restore international peace and security. Such action may include demonstrations, blockage, and other operations by air, sea, or land forces of Members of the United Nations.

Article 43

1. All Members of the United Nations, in order to contribute to the maintenance of international peace and security, undertake to make available to the Security Council, on its call and in accordance with a special agreement or agreements, armed forces, assistance, and facilities, including rights of passage, necessary for the purpose of maintaining international peace and security.

2. Such agreement or agreements shall govern the numbers and types of forces, their degree of readiness and general location, and the nature of the facilities and assistance to be provided.

3. The agreement or agreements shall be negotiated as soon as possible on the initiative of the Security Council. They shall be concluded between the Security Council and Members or between the Security Council and groups of Members and shall be subject to ratification by the signatory states in accordance with their respective constitutional processes. * * *

Article 48

1. The action required to carry out the decisions of the Security Council for the maintenance of international peace and security shall be taken by all the Members of the United Nations or by some of them, as the Security Council may determine.

2. Such decisions shall be carried out by the Members of the United Nations directly and through their action in the appropriate international agencies of which they are members.

SECURITY COUNCIL RESOLUTION 661

S/RES/661 (1990), Aug. 6, 1990, 29 *International Legal Materials* 1325 (1990).

The Security Council

Reaffirming its resolution 660 (1990) of 2 August 1990,

Deeply concerned that resolution has not been implemented and that the invasion by Iraq of Kuwait continues with further loss of human life and material destruction,

Determined to bring the invasion and occupation of Kuwait by Iraq to an end and to restore the sovereignty, independence and territorial integrity of Kuwait, * * *

Mindful of its responsibilities under the Charter of the United Nations for the maintenance of international peace and security,

Affirming the inherent right of individual or collective self-defense, in response to the armed attack by Iraq against Kuwait, in accordance with Article 51 of the Charter,

Acting under Chapter VII of the Charter of the United Nations, * * *

3. *Decides* that all States shall prevent:

(a) The import into their territories of all commodities and products originating in Iraq or Kuwait exported therefrom after the date of the present resolution;

(b) Any activities by their nationals or in their territories which would promote or are calculated to promote the export or trans-shipment of any commodities or products from Iraq or Kuwait; and any dealings by their flag vessels or in their territories in any commodities or products originating in Iraq or Kuwait and exported therefrom after the date of the present resolution, including in particular any transfer of funds to Iraq or Kuwait for the purposes of such activities or dealings;

(c) The sale or supply by their nationals or from their territories or using their flag vessels of any commodities or products, including weapons or any other military equipment, whether or not originating in their territories but not including supplies intended strictly for medical purposes, and, in humanitarian circumstances, foodstuffs, to any person or body in Iraq or Kuwait or to any person or body for the purposes of any business carried on or operated from Iraq or Kuwait, and any activities by their nationals or in their territories which promote or are calculated to promote such sale or supply of such commodities or products;

4. *Decides* that all States shall not make available to the Government of Iraq or to any commercial, industrial or public utility undertaking in Iraq or Kuwait, any funds or any other financial or economic resources and shall prevent their nationals and any persons within their territories from removing from their territories or otherwise making available to that Government or to any such undertaking any such funds or resources and from remitting any other funds to persons or bodies within Iraq or Kuwait, except payments exclusively for strictly medical or humanitarian purposes and, in humanitarian circumstances, foodstuffs;

5. *Calls upon* all States, including States non-members of the United Nations, to act strictly in accordance with the provisions of the present resolution notwithstanding any contract entered into or license granted before the date of the present resolution; * * *

9. *Decides* that, notwithstanding paragraphs 4 through 8 above, nothing in the present resolution shall prohibit assistance to the legitimate Government of Kuwait, and *calls upon* all States:

(a) To take appropriate measures to protect assets of the legitimate Government of Kuwait and its agencies;

(b) Not to recognize any régime set up by the occupying Power; * * *.

SECURITY COUNCIL RESOLUTION 678

S/RES/678 (1990), Nov. 28, 1990, 29 *International Legal Materials* 1565 (1990).

The Security Council,

Recalling, and reaffirming its resolutions 660 (1990) of 2 August 1990, 661 (1990) of 6 August 1990, 662 (1990) of 9 August 1990, 664 (1990) of 18 August 1990, 665 (1990) of 25 August, 1990, 666 (1990) of 13 September 1990, 667 (1990) of 16 September 1990, 669 (1990) of 24 September 1990, 670 (1990) of 25 September 1990, 674 (1990) of 29 October 1990 and 677 (1990) of 28 November 1990,

Noting that, despite all efforts by the United Nations, Iraq refuses to comply with its obligation to implement resolution 660 (1990) and the above mentioned subsequent relevant resolutions, in flagrant contempt of the Security Council,

Mindful of its duties and responsibilities under the Charter of the United Nations for the maintenance and preservation of international peace and security,

Determined to secure full compliance with its decisions,

Acting under Chapter VII of the Charter,

1. *Demands* that Iraq comply fully with resolution 660 (1990) and all subsequent relevant resolutions, and decides, while maintaining all its decisions, to allow Iraq one final opportunity, as a pause of goodwill, to do so;

2. *Authorizes* Member States co-operating with the government of Kuwait, unless Iraq on or before 15 January 1991 fully implements, as set forth in paragraph 1 above, the foregoing resolutions, to use all necessary means to uphold and implement resolution 660 (1990) and all subsequent relevant resolutions and to restore international peace and security in the area;

3. *Requests* all States to provide appropriate support for the actions undertaken in pursuance of paragraph 2 of the present resolution; * * *.

THOMAS M. FRANCK & FAIZA PATEL,
"UN POLICE ACTION IN LIEU OF WAR:
'THE OLD ORDER CHANGETH' "

85 *American Journal of International Law* 63 (1991).

The United Nations system is an elegant, carefully crafted instrument to make war illegal and unnecessary. To this end, in Article 2(4) of the UN Charter, members are required to "refrain . . . from the threat or use of force against the territorial integrity or political independence of any state." * * *

The new alternative to traditional wars of self-defense is collective police actions by the members of the international community. Exceptionally, these could be implemented by regional organizations. Usually, they would take the form of global action. Either way, the police action must be authorized specifically by the Security Council under Article 53 (for regional action) or Article 42 (for global action).

If states use armed force under the self-defense rubric of Article 51, their individual activities are subsumed by, or incorporated into, the global police response once it is activated. That is, the old way is licensed only until the new way begins to work: "until," in the words of Article 51, "the Security Council has taken the necessary measures to maintain international peace and security." * * *

* * * [T]he argument that the *war* power of member states was not intended to be restricted, but only augmented, by the Charter's creation of a new *police* power [is erroneous]. This interpretation flies in the face of common sense and the literal text. A new-style, UN-authorized police action functioning alongside a traditional sovereign exercise of war powers is conceptually and operationally untenable, the more so when states seeking the freedom to act unilaterally have forces committed alongside others in a Security Council police action. As a textual matter, it is obvious on its face that the Charter, in creating the new police power, intended to establish an exclusive alternative to the old war system. The old system was retained only as a fallback, available when the new system could not be made to work; not as an equal alternative, to be chosen at the sole discretion of the members. * * *

The delegates to the San Francisco Conference recognized that the enforcement provisions of chapter VII of the Charter provided "the teeth of the United Nations." The committee considering its military enforcement measures adopted Article 42 unanimously. In so doing, delegates intended to give the Security Council "the power, when diplomatic, economic, or other measures are considered by the Council to be inadequate, to undertake such aerial, naval, or other operations as may be necessary to maintain or restore international peace and security." This article was thought to remedy the principal defect of the League Covenant and the committee's rapporteur observed that "this unanimous vote ... renders sacred the obligation of all states to participate in the operations." Thus, "[m]ilitary assistance, in case of aggression, ceases to be a *recommendation* made to member states; it becomes for us an *obligation* which none can shirk."

This record is entirely inconsistent with the notion that, once the Security Council has taken measures, individual members are supposed to remain free to design their own military responses. * * *

Any effort to ascertain the intent of the drafters is somewhat clouded by the large amount of attention given by the drafters and ratifiers of the Charter to one provision pertaining to police action, which, historically, has proven to be something of a red herring. Just as Congress nowadays does not grant letters of marque and reprisal (Constitution, Article I, section 8(11)) or establish post roads (Article I, section 8(7)), so the Security Council has not made use of Article 43 of the Charter, which authorizes it to negotiate agreements with consenting member states that, preemptively, would have placed designated national military contingents at the Council's disposal. That no such agreements were made, owing to the Cold War, does not signify a lapse in the Organization's general police power, set out in Article 42, any more than the abstinence by Congress in matters of post roads signifies a lapse in its power to legislate on other matters pertaining to the Postal Service. Rather, the practice of the Security Council has evolved other means for taking coercive measures, including the use of police forces raised ad hoc in response to a specific threat to the peace. Both the Korean and the Kuwaiti situations are examples. What emerges from the institutional history of the years of stasis is not evidence that the Council's policing functions have fallen into desuetude but, on the contrary, that the central idea of a globally sanctioned police action was never abandoned; that the failure to implement Article 43 merely led to organic growth and the alternative creation of police action through invocation of Article 42, which does not require special agreements.

This is as one would expect. The UN Charter is not merely a treaty, but also the constitutive instrument of a living global organization. Its organs were designed both to implement important tasks and to interpret their own authority. Such organic growth is desirable and inevitable.

EUGENE V. ROSTOW, "UNTIL WHAT? ENFORCEMENT ACTION OR COLLECTIVE SELF–DEFENSE?"

85 *American Journal of International Law* 506 (1991).

Should the Persian Gulf war of 1990–1991 be characterized as an "international enforcement action" of the United Nations Security Council or as a campaign of collective self-defense approved, encouraged, and blessed by the Security Council?

This is not simply a nice and rather metaphysical legal issue, but an extremely practical one. The question it presents is whether the control and direction of hostilities in the gulf, their termination, and the substance of the settlement they produce were handled by the Council as the Korean War was handled, that is, as a campaign of collective self-defense, or as the United Nations' first "international enforcement action." * * *

On paper, the powers of the UN Security Council go beyond those possessed by the League of Nations. The Council can call on the members to apply measures not involving the use of armed force in order to deal with situations of aggression, and, if such measures are deemed inadequate, it "may take such action by air, sea, or land forces as may be necessary to maintain or restore international peace and security." Provision was made for the formation of a standing United Nations force, and of a Military Staff Committee to advise and assist the Security Council on these and cognate questions. The Military Staff Committee exists in a state of suspended animation at the present time, although it may be revived. Military actions to restore peace taken under Article 42 and 43 of the Charter are called "international enforcement actions."

Finally, after the Charter outlined the peacekeeping procedures of the Security Council under chapter VII in Articles 39–50, it provided in Article 51 that "[n]othing in the present Charter shall impair the inherent right of individual or collective self-defense if an armed attack occurs ... until the Security Council has taken measures necessary to maintain international peace and security." In the narrowest sense, the present controversy is about the meaning of the word "until" in Article 51.

The coercive powers conferred on the Security Council have not yet become a working part of the process for managing the state system. The fate of these coercive powers thus far reflects the nature of the United Nations as a hybrid political entity superimposed on the system of sovereign states: not a superpower or a world government, but an instrumentality for achieving cooperation among the nations in the interest of peace; an instrumentality, a catalyst, to which certain powers have been tentatively delegated by those nations. Diplomacy and conciliation are the normal methods of the Security Council. * * *

While some eminent authorities consider the Korean War to have been a Security Council "enforcement action," they press the term too hard. In the Korean episode, the Security Council was able to function for two months because the Soviet Union was boycotting the Organization at the time. Even under those circumstances, however, the Council did not use the language of "decision" which would have activated Article 25. The Council's resolutions simply recommended that the members refrain from helping North Korea and urged them to "furnish such assistance to the Republic of Korea as may be necessary to repel the armed attack and to restore international peace and security in the area." For all their symbolic panoply of the United Nations flag and other emblems, the forces which finally prevailed in Korea were national forces carrying out a mission of collective self-defense under American direction, not a Security Council enforcement action. * * *

In the Persian Gulf crisis, Security Council Resolution 678 "[*a*]*uthorizes* Member States co-operating with the Government of Kuwait ... to use all necessary means to uphold [the earlier resolutions] and to restore international peace and security in the area." Except for the word "authorizes," the resolution is clearly one designed to encourage and support a campaign of collective self-defense, and therefore not a Security Council enforcement action. Instead of attempting to direct such an operation itself, the Council "requests the States concerned" to keep it regularly informed about their progress. The Security Council held no meetings on the gulf crisis between November 29, 1990, when Resolution 678 was adopted, and February 14, 1991, when it met in secret session to discuss the political aspects of the end of the war. And the initial cease-fire in the gulf war was achieved as a practical matter not by an agreed Security Council resolution but by President Bush's ultimatum of February 28, 1991. * * *

During the period of active hostilities, neither the Secretary–General nor any other part of the United Nations Secretariat attempted to exercise control over military operations, although a committee of the Council actively supervised the program of economic sanctions.

Thus, the practice followed in implementing Resolution 678 and in terminating hostilities has been that of an allied military campaign in defense of Kuwait directed by officers of the United States and the associated nations. Does the word "authorized" in Resolution 678 mean that the member states which cooperated with Kuwait in driving Iraq out of that country could not have done so without the Council's "authority"? As Professor Glennon points out, Resolution 678 is in fact permissive, like Resolution 83 of June 27, 1950, adopted by the Security Council during the Korean War. It imposes no legally binding obligation under Article 25 of the Charter. In Glennon's words, it "merely exhorts, authorizes or recommends," leaving to the member states the decision whether to cooperate in the effort of the allied coalition to liberate Kuwait. The word "authorizes" in Resolution 678 should not therefore be considered to transform a military campaign of self-defense into an enforcement action.

Thus far, the nominal authority of the Security Council to engage in military "enforcement actions" has not been tested. This is not a state of affairs to be deplored. Political relations among the members of the Council—permanent and temporary alike—are not sufficiently stable to make so radical a step politically feasible or desirable. Although the diplomacy of the gulf crisis in 1990 and 1991 has shown some movement in a promising direction, it remains to be seen whether these hints of progress are followed by more substantial changes.

Notes and Questions

1. *The Structure of Chapter VII.* What were the legal grounds for the Security Council's resolutions related to the Gulf War? According to Resolution 661, the Security Council acted generally under Chapter VII of the United Nations Charter. Must the Security Council find explicit authority to justify its Chapter VII actions?

In evaluating the structure of Chapter VII, see—in addition to Charter Articles 39–43 and 48 reproduced above—Articles 44–47, 49–51, and 106 in the Appendix. Note also that Chapter VI of the U.N. Charter, entitled "Pacific Settlement of Disputes," contemplates Security Council investigations and recommendations related to the peaceful settlement of interstate disputes.

2. *Article 43 Agreements.* No Article 43 special agreements have ever been concluded, leading some observers to contend the Security Council's authorization of the use of force in Resolution 678 fell within some penumbra of powers that the Council has assumed under Chapter VII—an "Article 42½" power. U.N. Secretary–General Boutros–Ghali reintroduced the possibility of concluding Article 43 agreements in 1992:

It is the essence of the concept of collective security as contained in the Charter that if peaceful means fail, the measures provided in Chapter VII should be used on the decision of the Security Council, to maintain or restore international peace and security in the face of a "threat to the peace, breach of the peace, or act of aggression." * * *

Under Article 42 of the Charter, the Security Council has the authority to take military action to maintain or restore international peace and security. While such action should only be taken when all peaceful means have failed, the option of taking it is essential to the credibility of the United Nations as a guarantor of international security. This will require bringing into being, through negotiations, the special agreements foreseen in Article 43 of the Charter, whereby Member States undertake to make armed forces, assistance and facilities available to the Security Council for the purposes stated in Article 42, not only on an ad hoc basis but on a permanent basis. * * * I recommend that the Security Council initiate negotiations in accordance with Article 43, supported by the Military Staff Committee * * *.

"An Agenda for Peace: Preventive diplomacy, peacemaking and peace-keeping," Report of the Secretary–General pursuant to the statement adopted by the Summit Meeting of the Security Council on 31 January 1992, A/47/277–S/24111, 17 June 1992, in *An Agenda for Peace 1995*, at 39, 55–56 (2d ed. 1995) (U.N. Sales No. E.95.I.15). Why have states been so reluctant to accept Article 43 agreements to make forces permanently available to the United Nations? What alternatives to Article 43 arrangements could make some forces available to the United Nations for use in crises? For example, could the Security Council itself establish a globally recruited volunteer force, using its authority under Article 29 of the U.N. Charter? See Thomas Franck, "The United Nations as Guarantor of International Peace and

Security: Past, Present and Future," in *The United Nations at Age Fifty*: *A Legal Perspective* 25, 33–35 (Christian Tomuschat ed. 1995).

3. *Collective Self-defense vs. Chapter VII Enforcement Action.* Did Security Council Resolution 678 authorize a type of Chapter VII enforcement action, as Franck and Patel suggest? Or was the use of force against Iraq an exercise of collective self-defense in accordance with Article 51 of the U.N. Charter? If the use of force against Iraq was an exercise of collective self-defense, why did the United States and other members of the Security Council find it necessary to approve Resolution 678?

According to Article 51 of the U.N. Charter, the right of self-defense is preserved "until the Security Council has taken measures necessary to maintain international peace and security." When is the right of states to use force in self-defense suspended? When the Security Council passes any resolutions under Chapter VII? When the Security Council decides U.N. Member States should impose comprehensive mandatory sanctions against a state that has used force? Once the Security Council has taken measures sufficient to suspend the right of self-defense, how long should the suspension continue? Note that the Security Council in Resolution 661 explicitly affirmed "the inherent right of individual or collective self-defense, in response to the armed attack by Iraq against Kuwait, in accordance with Article 51 of the Charter." But what if references to Article 51 were absent in a comprehensive sanctions resolution? May the Security Council explicitly prohibit all military action by a state, including defensive action? Who decides whether any Security Council measures satisfy the "necessary to maintain international peace and security" clause of Article 51?

4. *The Aftermath.* Resolutions 661 and 678, reproduced above, were only two in a series of Security Council resolutions responding to Iraq's invasion of Kuwait. Some resolutions attempted to redress damage caused by Iraq, to require U.N. inspections inside Iraq in order to prevent Iraq from rebuilding certain weapons systems, and to provide humanitarian relief for segments of the Iraqi population. One of the most significant was Resolution 687 of April 1991. For a summary of Resolution 687, see Note 1, page 489, and for an overview of the efficacy of U.N. sanctions against Iraq, see David Cartright & George A. Lopez, *The Sanctions Decade: Assessing UN Strategies in the 1990s* 37–61 (2000). As of November 1, 2000, Security Council-mandated sanctions against Iraq continued in effect. In 1996, the Security Council allowed Iraq to increase its oil exports, in order to provide funds to purchase medicine, food, and other civilian necessities for Iraqi citizens. See Barbara Crossette, "Security Council Extends Oil-for-Food Program Allowing Iraq to Import Necessities," *New York Times*, June 10, 2000, at A7. The U.N. Compensation Commission, established pursuant to Security Council Resolutions 687 and 692 and based in Switzerland, has awarded payments derived from the sale of a percentage of supervised Iraqi oil exports to claimants damaged by Iraq's invasion. By September 2000, over $8 billion had been awarded. See Barbara Crossette, "A U.N. Compromise on Iraqi Money Matters," *New York Times*, Sept. 28, 2000, at A6.

The effectiveness of some sanctions has been called into question. Iraq expelled U.N. weapons inspectors in 1998 and has resisted allowing a new team of inspectors to return, even under a revised inspection regime. See

S.C. Res. 1284 (1999), 39 I.L.M. 760 (2000); Barbara Crossette, "Split U.N. Creates a New Inspection for Iraqi Weapons," *New York Times*, Dec. 18, 1999, at 1; Barbara Crossette & Steven Lee Myers, "U.N. Readies Team to Check Weapons Held by the Iraqis," *New York Times*, Aug. 22, 2000, at 1. Some states have resumed civilian air travel to Iraq, avoiding sanctions imposed by the Security Council. See Barbara Crossette, "French Flight Tests Ban Against Iraq," *New York Times*, Sept. 23, 2000, at A7.

5. *The Effect of Sanctions on Non–Target States.* Economic sanctions can be a double-edged sword. If sanctions under Chapter VII prohibit imports into a target country, exporters in other states and the economies of other states may be harmed. What mechanisms are available to mitigate the hardships of sanctions in non-target states? See Article 50 of the U.N. Charter, which is reproduced in the Appendix, and Jeremy Carver & Jenine Hulsmann, "The Role of Article 50 of the UN Charter in the Search for International Peace and Security," 49 *International and Comparative Law Quarterly* 528 (2000).

6. *The Role of the U.N. Secretary–General in Maintaining Peace and Security.* The Secretary–General of the United Nations has authority under Article 99 of the Charter to "bring to the attention of the Security Council any matter which in his opinion may threaten the maintenance of international peace and security." The U.N. Secretariat, administered by the Secretary–General, helps to organize and supervise peacekeeping operations, which are considered in the next section. The Secretary–General also from time to time has served as a mediator and has undertaken other efforts to resolve international disputes. Recall the Secretary–General's role in the *Rainbow Warrior Case* in Chapter 5.

2. THE UNITED NATIONS AND PEACEKEEPING

The United Nations has been involved in many "peacekeeping" operations that are not Chapter VII enforcement actions. U.N. Member States contribute peacekeeping troops who may play major roles in situations of internal unrest within states. The first reading in this section examines traditional uses of peacekeeping forces and explores the relationship between the General Assembly and the Security Council with respect to peace and security issues. The second reading, which is taken from a report by the U.N. Secretary–General, addresses the expanded functions of peacekeeping forces in recent years.

THOMAS M. FRANCK, NATION AGAINST NATION
38–42 (1985).

* * * [T]he Korean conflict * * * eventually prompted a significant shift in responsibility for collective security from the Security Council to the General Assembly. This occurred when, after the Inchon landing, United Nations forces appeared to have routed the North. New instructions were needed as General Douglas MacArthur's army neared the 38th parallel. But, with the Russians back at the circular table, instructions could not come from the veto-bound Council.

Washington wanted to pursue the remnants of the Northern army beyond the 38th parallel, despite serious misgivings among allies with contingents under MacArthur's command. On October 7, 1950, at U.S. insistence, the General Assembly authorized the pursuit of the aggressor into its own territory. The resolution passed on that date by a vote of 47 to 5, with seven abstentions, approving "[a]ll appropriate steps ... to ensure stability throughout Korea ... including the holding of elections, under the auspices of the United Nations, for the establishment of a unified, independent and democratic government in the sovereign State of Korea ...[,]" also authorized the U.N. forces to occupy as much of Korea "as necessary for achieving the objectives specified...." Dean Acheson thought that this "might be construed to mean something more than the prevention of a new attack."

This new and wider mandate for the U.N. force replaced the earlier one spelled out in the Security Council resolution of June 25, which had only called for pushing North Korean forces back to the 38th parallel. Whatever its tactical wisdom, the resolution of October 7 had the most far-reaching implications for the distribution of functions and powers within the U.N.: the Assembly had been used to circumvent the Council. This was fully understood by Secretary–General Lie, who declared himself elated at the ability of the organization to neutralize obstacles: "This was Korea, not Manchuria," he wrote; "this was the United Nations, not the League of Nations." To make sure that this was not an isolated victory, Washington, with the Secretary–General's support, persuaded the Assembly to establish simplified procedures for convening that body to sidestep the Council in future.

The British had not been nearly as enthusiastic as Trygve Lie. Wiser heads at the Foreign Office had correctly prophesied, in a warning to the U.S. Department of State, that any move to increase the power of the General Assembly would present dangers to the West once its majority gave way before the surge of new nations being created in Africa and Asia. Acheson disagreed, arguing that "present difficulties outweighed possible future ones, and we pressed on." The U.S. proceeded at full speed to secure the Assembly's adoption of what became known as the Uniting for Peace resolution, or Acheson Plan. Acheson personally introduced it, claiming it would increase the effectiveness of the United Nations against aggression. He urged the Assembly not to allow the Soviet veto to render the organization impotent. In good lawyerly fashion he argued that articles 10, 11, and 14 of the Charter made the Assembly the Council's partner in wielding "authority and responsibility for matters affecting international peace." The U.S.'s ambassador Benjamin Cohen added the uniquely American argument that the U.N. should follow our Supreme Court's practice of construing the Constitution flexibly, allowing the system to invent new ways of overcoming unanticipated difficulties without formal amendment of the basic compact. He cited the invention of the Presidential "executive agreement" as an example of how the U.S. had worked around the awkward constitutional requirement of a two-thirds Senatorial majority for the ratification of treaties, and urged the undoubtedly bemused Assembly delegates to study the creative U.S. Supreme Court decision in *McCulloch v. Mary-*

land. There the Justices had inferred from the Constitution's enumerated federal powers certain additional "implied" powers not spelled out in the text.

Advocates of the Acheson Plan pointed out that it meticulously adhered to the fundamental difference between the powers of the General Assembly—which may only *recommend* collective action—and those of the Security Council—which may *order* member states to participate in enforcing collective security. Even so, the Uniting for Peace resolution does envisage circumstances in which the Assembly, convened on 24 hours' notice after a veto in the Council, would step in to organize the collective use of force against an aggressor. Such was certainly not the intent of the drafters at San Francisco. Article 10 allows the Assembly to discuss "any questions or any matters within the scope of the present Charter" and "make recommendations to the Members" except when the matter is being considered by the Security Council. But this is qualified by article 11, which says that when the issue relates "to the maintenance of peace and security" and "action is necessary," the matter "shall be referred to the Security Council." U.S. Ambassador Ernest Gross has rightly written that the effect of the Acheson Plan is to transfer to the Assembly "major, rather than merely 'residual ...'" authority "in relation to peace and security."

Eventually, the International Court [in the *Certain Expenses Case*] declared, in effect, that the Acheson Plan was a lawful interpretation of the Charter. Although the Uniting for Peace resolution had formalized the new rules, they had been evolving almost from the first, when it became clear that optimistic prophecies about Soviet restraint in using the veto were wrong. In 1946, the first Assembly had called on members to implement diplomatic sanctions against Franco's Spain, after the sanctions had drawn a veto in the Council. In 1949, in response to another veto, the Assembly had asked its members to embargo military supplies for communist guerrillas in Greece. Even the Assembly's resolution of October 7, 1950, redefining the mission of U.N. forces in Korea, antedated the Acheson Plan. * * *

* * * Uniting for Peace was adopted on November 3, 1950, by a handy 40-to-5 (with 12 abstentions, including India and Argentina) * * * . * * *

The Israeli, British, and French invasion of Egypt, late in 1956, led to the formation of the United Nations Emergency Force (UNEF). Unlike U.N. contingents in Korea, UNEF was not created to repel an ongoing breach of the peace with a collective use of armed might, but as a legion of peacekeepers to oversee a decision of the combatants to disengage. Unlike the Korean force, UNEF was genuinely international, commanded by an officer appointed on the initiative of the Secretary-General. It deliberately excluded contributions from any of the Big Five. Instead, UNEF was made up of small units from a broad assortment of states. * * * UNEF was authorized not by the Security Council, but by the General Assembly acting on the basis of the Uniting for Peace resolution.

The Suez crisis began when Egypt's President Gamal Abdel Nasser nationalized the Suez Canal Company on July 26, 1956. After inconclusive negotiations to establish international guarantees for unfettered use of the Canal, Israel attacked Egypt on October 29. The next day a prearranged British and French ultimatum demanded that Egypt and Israel both withdraw from the area of the Canal. When Egypt demurred, British aircraft stationed in Cyprus began bombing Egyptian targets. On November 5 British and French paratroops were dropped near Port Said.

British and French vetoes effectively immobilized the Security Council, but not the Soviets, who began threatening direct retaliation against London and Paris. * * *

With matters approaching [a] dangerous pass, the Yugoslav member of the Security Council, specifically invoking the Uniting for Peace resolution, introduced a resolution to convene an Emergency Session of the General Assembly. Since the resolution was procedural, the negative British and French votes did not constitute a veto. The Soviets, who had bitterly opposed the Acheson Plan, now voted with the U.S. to implement it.

After much behind-the-scenes maneuvering—in which Canada's foreign minister Lester B. Pearson and Secretary–General Dag Hammarskjold played leading roles—an agreement was reached. British, French, and—somewhat later—Israeli forces were to withdraw from the Canal and be replaced by UNEF. A few weeks later, the Assembly authorized UNEF "to assist in achieving situations conducive to the maintenance of peaceful conditions in the area" and gave the Secretary–General wide discretion "to take steps to carry out these measures." Hammarskjold negotiated personally with President Nasser to create the agreed framework for UNEF's operations in Egypt, which was duly approved by the Assembly.

At its zenith the UNEF force, with contingents from ten nations chosen by the Secretary–General after consulting with Egypt, consisted of some 6000 officers and men. Stationed along the Egyptian side of the armistice line, the force became a major factor in preventing the renewal of fedayeen raids from Egypt into Israel and in maintaining peace along that previously afflicted boundary. Not only did the Suez crisis further enhance the peacekeeping and conflict-resolving role of the General Assembly, but it also thrust forward Hammarskjold, whose skill in setting up UNEF earned him the respect of world leaders, including President Eisenhower and Secretary of State Dulles.

The Suez crisis thus confirmed the United Nations in its most fruitful line of endeavor: the stationing of international peacekeeping forces between mutually hostile antagonists at that crucial moment in a dispute when both sides perceive disengagement as preferable to continued hostilities.

SUPPLEMENT TO AN AGENDA FOR PEACE

Position Paper of the Secretary–General on the Occasion of the Fiftieth
Anniversary of the United Nations A/50/60–S/1995/1, 3 January 1995,
in *An Agenda for Peace 1995*, at 5 (2d ed. 1995) (U.N. Sales No. E.95.I.15).

[Since the end of the Cold War, U.N. activities related to the
maintenance of peace and security have increased dramatically. For
example, as of January 31, 1988, the Security Council had adopted 15
resolutions in the preceding 12 months, and as of December 31, 1994, it
had adopted 78 in the preceding 12 months. As of January 31, 1988, the
United Nations had been actively involved in preventive diplomacy or
peacemaking in 11 disputes and conflicts during the preceding 12
months, and as of December 16, 1994, the number was 28 for the
preceding 12 months. The number of military personnel deployed increased from 9,570 to 73,393 between January 31, 1988, and December
16, 1994, and the number of civilian police increased from 35 to 2,130.
Over the same period, the number of states contributing military and
police personnel rose from 26 to 76, and the annual U.N. budget for
peacekeeping grew from $230.4 million to a projected $3.61 billion.]

II. Quantitative and Qualitative Changes * * *

9. This increased volume of activity would have strained the Organization even if the nature of the activity had remained unchanged. It
has not remained unchanged, however: there have been qualitative
changes even more significant than the quantitative ones.

10. One is the fact that so many of today's conflicts are within
States rather than between States. The end of the Cold War removed
constraints that had inhibited conflict in the former Soviet Union and
elsewhere. As a result there has been a rash of wars within newly
independent States, often of a religious or ethnic character and often
involving unusual violence and cruelty. The end of the cold war seems
also to have contributed to an outbreak of such wars in Africa. In
addition, some of the proxy wars fueled by the cold war within States
remain unresolved. Inter–State wars, by contrast, have become infrequent.

11. Of the five peace-keeping operations that existed in early 1988,
four related to inter–State wars and only one (20 per cent of the total) to
an intra–State conflict. Of the 21 operations established since then, only
8 have related to inter–State wars, whereas 13 (62 per cent) have related
to intra–State conflicts, though some of them, especially those in former
Yugoslavia, have some inter–State dimensions also. Of the 11 operations
established since January 1992, all but 2 (82 per cent) related to intra–
State conflicts.

12. The new breed of intra–State conflicts * * * are usually fought
not only by regular armies but also by militias and armed civilians with
little discipline and with ill-defined chains of command. They are often
guerrilla wars without clear front lines. Civilians are the main victims

and often the main targets. Humanitarian emergencies are commonplace and the combatant authorities, in so far as they can be called authorities, lack the capacity to cope with them. The number of refugees registered with the Office of the United Nations High Commissioner for Refugees (UNHCR) has increased from 13 million at the end of 1987 to 26 million at the end of 1994. The number of internally displaced persons has increased even more dramatically.

13.   Another feature of such conflicts is the collapse of State institutions, especially the police and judiciary, with resulting paralysis of governance, a breakdown of law and order, and general banditry and chaos. Not only are the functions of government suspended, its assets are destroyed or looted and experienced officials are killed or flee the country. This is rarely the case in inter–State wars. It means that international intervention must extend beyond military and humanitarian tasks and must include the promotion of national reconciliation and the re-establishment of effective government. * * *

15.   Peace-keeping in such contexts is far more complex and more expensive than when its tasks were mainly to monitor cease-fires and control buffer zones with the consent of the States involved in the conflict. * * *

18.   A second qualitative change is the use of United Nations forces to protect humanitarian operations. Humanitarian agencies endeavour to provide succor to civilian victims of war wherever they may be. Too often the warring parties make it difficult or impossible for them to do so. This is sometimes because of the exigencies of war but more often because the relief of a particular population is contrary to the war aims of one or other of the parties. There is also a growing tendency for the combatants to divert relief supplies for their own purposes. Because the wars are intra–State conflicts, the humanitarian agencies often have to undertake their tasks in the chaotic and lawless conditions described above. * * *

20.   A third change has been in the nature of the United Nations operations in the field. During the cold war United Nations peace-keeping operations were largely military in character and were usually deployed after a cease-fire but before a settlement of the conflict in question had been negotiated. Indeed one of their main purposes was to create conditions in which negotiations for a settlement could take place. In the late 1980s a new kind of peace-keeping operation evolved. It was established after negotiations had succeeded, with the mandate of helping the parties implement the comprehensive settlement they had negotiated. Such operations have been deployed in Namibia, Angola, El Salvador, Cambodia and Mozambique. In most cases they have been conspicuously successful.

21.   The negotiated settlements involved not only military arrangements but also a wide range of civilian matters. As a result, the United Nations found itself asked to undertake an unprecedented variety of functions: the supervision of cease-fires, the regroupment and demobili-

zation of forces, their reintegration into civilian life and the destruction
of their weapons; the design and implementation of de-mining programmes; the return of refugees and displaced persons; the provision of
humanitarian assistance; the supervision of existing administrative
structures; the establishment of new police forces; the verification of
respect for human rights; the design and supervision of constitutional,
judicial and electoral reforms; the observation, supervision and even
organization and conduct of elections; and the coordination of support
for economic rehabilitation and reconstruction.

22. Fourthly, these multifunctional peace-keeping operations have
highlighted the role the United Nations can play after a negotiated
settlement has been implemented. It is now recognized that implementation of the settlement in the time prescribed may not be enough to
guarantee that the conflict will not revive. Coordinated programmes are
required, over a number of years and in various fields, to ensure that the
original causes of war are eradicated. This involves the building up of
national institutions, the promotion of human rights, the creation of
civilian police forces and other actions in the political field. * * *

III. INSTRUMENTS FOR PEACE AND SECURITY

23. The United Nations has developed a range of instruments for
controlling and resolving conflicts between and within States. The most
important of them are preventive diplomacy and peacemaking; peacekeeping; peace-building; disarmament; sanctions; and peace enforcement. The first three can be employed only with the consent of the
parties to the conflict. Sanctions and enforcement, on the other hand,
are coercive measures and thus, by definition, do not require the consent
of the party concerned. Disarmament can take place on an agreed basis
or in the context of coercive action under Chapter VII. * * *

A. *Preventive diplomacy and peacemaking*

26. It is evidently better to prevent conflicts through early warning, quiet diplomacy and, in some cases, preventive deployment than to
have to undertake major politico-military efforts to resolve them after
they have broken out. * * *

27. Experience has shown that the greatest obstacle to success in
these endeavours is not, as is widely supposed, lack of information,
analytical capacity or ideas for United Nations initiatives. Success is
often blocked at the outset by the reluctance of one or other of the
parties to accept United Nations help. * * *

31. * * * Although special envoys can achieve much on a visiting
basis, their capacity is greatly enhanced if continuity can be assured by
the presence on the ground of a small support mission on a full-time
basis. * * *

B. *Peace-keeping* * * *

33. * * * [R]espect for certain basic principles of peace-keeping [is]
essential to its success. Three particularly important principles are the

consent of the parties, impartiality and the non-use of force except in self-defence. Analysis of recent successes and failures shows that in all the successes those principles were respected and in most of the less successful operations one or other of them was not.

34.   There are three aspects of recent mandates that, in particular, have led peace-keeping operations to forfeit the consent of the parties, to behave in a way that was perceived to be partial and/or to use force other than in self-defence. These have been the tasks of protecting humanitarian operations during continuing warfare, protecting civilian populations in designated safe areas and pressing the parties to achieve national reconciliation at a pace faster than they were ready to accept. The cases of Somalia and of Bosnia and Herzegovina are instructive in this respect.
* * *

43.   As regards the availability of troops and equipment, problems have become steadily more serious. Availability has palpably declined as measured against the Organization's requirements. A considerable effort has been made to expand and refine stand-by arrangements, but these provide no guarantee that troops will be provided for a specific operation. For example, when in May 1994 the Security Council decided to expand the United Nations Assistance Mission for Rwanda (UNAMIR), not one of the 19 Governments that at that time had undertaken to have troops on stand-by agreed to contribute.

44.   In these circumstances, I have come to the conclusion that the United Nations does need to give serious thought to the idea of a rapid reaction force. Such a force would be the Security Council's strategic reserve for deployment when there was an emergency need for peace-keeping troops. It might comprise battalion-sized units from a number of countries. These units would be trained to the same standards, use the same operating procedures, be equipped with integrated communications equipment and take part in joint exercises at regular intervals. They would be stationed in their home countries but maintained at a high state of readiness. * * *

[The Secretary–General also reports on practical difficulties with peacekeeping related to command and control, the level of equipment and training provided by contributing states, and the need for peace-keepers to provide effective information to the population about their mandate.]

C.   *Post-conflict peace-building*

47.   The validity of the concept of post-conflict peace-building has received wide recognition. The measures it can use—and they are many—can also support preventive diplomacy. Demilitarization, the control of small arms, institutional reform, improved police and judicial systems, the monitoring of human rights, electoral reform and social and economic development can be as valuable in preventing conflict as in healing the wounds after conflict has occurred.

48. The implementation of post-conflict peace-building can, however, be complicated. It requires integrated action and delicate dealings between the United Nations and the parties to the conflict in respect of which peace-building activities are to be undertaken. * * *

51. * * * [P]olitical elements who dislike the peace agreement concluded by their Government (and the United Nations verification provided for therein) may resent the United Nations presence and be waiting impatiently for it to leave. Their concerns may find an echo among Member States who fear that the United Nations is in danger of slipping into a role prejudicial to the sovereignty of the country in question and among others who may be uneasy about the resource implications of a long-term peace-building commitment. * * *

53. Most of the activities that together constitute peace-building fall within the mandates of the various programmes, funds, offices and agencies of the United Nations system with responsibilities in the economic, social, humanitarian and human rights fields. In a country ruined by war, resumption of such activities may initially have to be entrusted to, or at least coordinated by, a multifunctional peace-keeping operation, but as that operation succeeds in restoring normal conditions, the programmes, funds, offices and agencies can re-establish themselves and gradually take over responsibility from the peace-keepers, with the resident coordinator in due course assuming the coordination functions temporarily entrusted to the special representative of the Secretary–General. * * *

V. Financial Resources

97. None of the instruments discussed in the present paper can be used unless Governments provide the necessary financial resources. There is no other source of funds. The failure of Member States to pay their assessed contributions for activities they themselves have voted into being makes it impossible to carry out those activities to the standard expected. It also calls in question the credibility of those who have willed the ends but not the means—and who then criticize the United Nations for its failures. * * *

98. The financial crisis is particularly debilitating as regards peace-keeping. The shortage of funds, in particular for reconnaissance and planning, for the start-up of operations and for the recruitment and training of personnel imposes severe constraints on the Organization's ability to deploy, with the desired speed, newly approved operations. Peace-keeping is also afflicted by Member States' difficulties in providing troops, police and equipment on the scale required by the current volume of peace-keeping activity.

Notes and Questions

1. *Traditional Peacekeeping.* Does the U.N. Charter clearly authorize the Security Council, if not the General Assembly, to establish peacekeeping operations? According to a former U.N. Under–Secretary–General for Politi-

cal Affairs, "[t]he technique of peacekeeping is a distinctive innovation by the United Nations. The Charter does not mention it. It was discovered, like penicillin. We came across it, while looking for something else, during an investigation of the guerrilla fighting in northern Greece in 1947." Brian Urquhart, "The United Nations, Collective Security, and International Peacekeeping," in *Negotiating World Order: The Artisanship and Architecture of Global Diplomacy* 59, 62 (Alan K. Henrikson ed. 1986), *quoted in* Frederic L. Kirgis, Jr., "The Security Council's First Fifty Years," 89 *American Journal of International Law* 506, 532 (1995). Some observers find sufficient Charter authority for peacekeeping operations in Chapter VII's Article 40, under which the Security Council may call on states to comply with "provisional measures." Others analogize peacekeeping to "peacemaking" and point to Charter provisions in Chapter VI, which concerns the pacific settlement of disputes. See John F. Murphy, "Force and Arms," in 1 *United Nations Legal Order* 247, 294 (Oscar Schachter & Christopher C. Joyner eds. 1995). U.N. Secretary–General Dag Hammerskjold said that, in truth, peacekeeping derived from a Chapter "six-and-a-half" of the Charter, since it bridged Chapter VII, dealing with enforcement measures, and Chapter VI. Is it important to identify specific authority for peacekeeping in the text of the Charter?

Between 1948 and 1978, the United Nations authorized 13 peacekeeping bodies, which, since there was and is no standing U.N. army, utilized forces contributed by U.N. Member States. Early peacekeeping operations followed a traditional pattern: U.N. peacekeepers were stationed along a cease-fire line, interposed between belligerents, or assigned to observe boundaries; they could use force only to defend themselves or to remain in positions taken in accordance with U.N. authorization; they operated under U.N. command; and they included no representatives from any of the permanent members of the Security Council. UNEF was an example of U.N. peacekeepers undertaking traditional functions. Such peacekeeping operations were established only with the consent of the states in which they were to be deployed. Is such consent important legally or politically? Does such consent necessarily signal a willingness to support the operations of peacekeepers?

2. *The Security Council, the General Assembly, and Peacekeeping.* In the 1950 Uniting for Peace Resolution, the General Assembly asserted its responsibility to help maintain international peace and security if the Security Council failed "to discharge its responsibilities." The International Court of Justice, in the *Certain Expenses Case* (see Chapter 8), essentially found that the General Assembly could take "measures" involving peacekeeping forces, as it did in the case of UNEF, thus affirming a role for the Assembly with respect to international peace and security. Since the 1970s, the Security Council has exercised firm control over the authorization of peacekeeping operations. What limits the General Assembly's power with respect to peacekeeping? Echoing Article 12 of the U.N. Charter, the ICJ in the *Certain Expenses Case* ruled that "the Assembly should not recommend measures while the Security Council is dealing with the same matter unless the Council requests it to do so." *Id.* at 163. Furthermore, the Court emphasized that the Council had exclusive authority over "coercive" or "enforcement actions" under Chapter VII of the Charter.

3. *Peacekeeping, Peacemaking, and Peacebuilding since the End of the Cold War.* As Secretary–General Boutros–Ghali noted, some of the peacekeeping, preventive diplomacy (also known as "peacemaking"), and peacebuilding operations approved by the U.N. Security Council since the end of the Cold War have involved the United Nations in functions far different from monitoring cease-fires or observing boundary lines. One extensive operation was the U.N. Transitional Authority in Cambodia. UNTAC was contemplated by the 1991 Agreements on a Comprehensive Political Settlement of the Cambodian Conflict (the Paris Agreements), a pact entered into by warring factions in Cambodia and supported by the five permanent members of the U.N. Security Council. In addition to undertaking traditional peacekeeping functions, UNTAC, along with the U.N. High Commissioner for Refugees, coordinated the repatriation of more than 360,000 refugees living in camps in Thailand. UNTAC also was charged with controlling the civil administration of Cambodia's government (in particular in the areas of defense, public security, finance, information, and foreign affairs), developing a civilian police force, and organizing and monitoring free elections. With respect to military issues, UNTAC's mandate included the demobilization and disarming of the armed forces of the various Cambodian factions. Over its 18 months of operation, UNTAC employed about 22,000 international personnel and cost about $1.7 billion. For assessments of UNTAC's successes and failures, see Michael W. Doyle, *UN Peacekeeping in Cambodia: UNTAC's Civil Mandate* (1995), and Steven R. Ratner, *The New UN Peacekeeping* 135–206 (1995). For more information on peacekeeping and proposals for changes in the existing system, see Report of the Panel on United Nations Peace Operations, 39 I.L.M. 1432 (2000); <http://www.globalpolicy.org/security/peacekpg>; <http://www.un.org/Depts/DPKO>.

3. THE UNITED NATIONS, REGIONAL ORGANIZATIONS, AND THE CONFLICT IN THE BALKANS

The United Nations has been involved with conflicts in the Balkans since the early 1990s. The first Note in this section provides background on the region and on the roles of the U.N. and regional organizations in Bosnia. Later readings examine regional agencies recognized in Chapter VIII of the U.N. Charter, regional collective self-defense organizations, and legal issues related to NATO's use of force in the Federal Republic of Yugoslavia during 1999.

Note: Bosnia and the Dayton Accords

Bosnia–Herzegovina, one of the regions of Yugoslavia, became an independent state when Yugoslavia disintegrated in the early 1990s. In a referendum held in February–March 1992, Bosnia's Slavic Muslims, representing 43 percent of the population, and Croats (17 percent) voted overwhelmingly for independence. The Bosnian Serbs, constituting 31 percent of the population, resisted separation from the Serb-dominated Federal Republic of Yugoslavia (FRY). The United States, the European Union, and other states recognized Bosnia–Herzegovina in April 1992. The Bosnian Serbs, supported by the FRY's Yugoslav National Army, proclaimed their own Respublika Srpska and gained control over two-thirds of Bosnia's territory.

Although the FRY officially withdrew the Yugoslav National Army from Bosnia in May 1992, it left behind army equipment and "demobilized" officers and soldiers; the FRY continued to provide assistance to the Bosnian Serbs.

The Security Council, concluding that the crisis in the former Yugoslavia had an international dimension and acting under Chapter VII, adopted many resolutions related to Bosnia and Herzegovina. Before the 1995 General Framework Agreement for Peace in Bosnia and Herzegovina (the Dayton Accords), the Security Council imposed an arms embargo, restricted flights over Bosnian airspace, imposed economic sanctions against the Federal Republic of Yugoslavia (Serbia and Montenegro) and Serb-controlled territory in Bosnia, and froze overseas assets of the Federal Republic. See S.C. Res. 713 (1991), 757 (1992), 781 (1992), 820 (1993), 824 (1993), 942 (1994). The Council, in a step unprecedented under Chapter VII of the Charter, created a judicial organ, the International Criminal Tribunal for the Former Yugoslavia, to try individuals for violating international criminal law. S.C. Res. 808 (1993), 827 (1993). See Chapter 6.

The Security Council also authorized a peacekeeping operation, the U.N. Protection Forces (UNPROFOR). Its mandate included facilitating the delivery of humanitarian aid to civilians, protecting U.N.–declared safe areas, and engaging in preventive diplomacy functions before the outbreak of conflict in particular areas. Other U.N. bodies have been involved in Bosnia as well, including the U.N. Human Rights Commission, the U.N. High Commissioner for Refugees, other U.N. agencies that have provided aid to some of Bosnia's two million displaced persons, and the U.N. Secretary–General, who was involved in mediation efforts.

The crisis in the former Yugoslavia also shows how the United Nations may cooperate with regional international organizations in efforts to maintain peace and security. At the request of the U.N. Security Council, the North Atlantic Treaty Organization (NATO) was actively involved in enforcing the U.N. arms embargo, ensuring the ban on flights in Bosnian airspace, and carrying out air operations to support UNPROFOR safe areas. NATO also played a significant role in implementing the Dayton Accords.

The Dayton Accords are complex, and the General Framework Agreement itself was at the center of other intricate arrangements involving international organizations and states. The state of Bosnia and Herzegovina, the Federation of Bosnia and Herzegovina (which is the product of an agreement between Bosnian Croats and Bosnian Muslims), and the Republika Srpska (the Bosnian Serb entity) concluded Annexes to the General Framework Agreement that relate to military matters, monitoring of the peace settlement, boundaries between entities within Bosnia and Herzegovina, a complex constitution for Bosnia and Herzegovina, elections, human rights, refugees, and binding arbitration of disputes. The Annexes contemplate, and constitute the parties' consent to, numerous roles for international organizations. See Bosnia and Herzegovina–Croatia–Yugoslavia: General Framework Agreement for Peace in Bosnia and Herzegovina with Annexes, Dec. 14, 1995, 35 I.L.M. 75 (1996). The following excerpt is from a report of the U.N. Secretary–General addressing U.N. activities in Bosnia and the creation of an Implementation Force (IFOR) (since December 1996, the

Stabilization Force (SFOR)), which was designed to monitor and, if necessary, use force to enforce the peace settlement.

REPORT OF THE SECRETARY–GENERAL PURSUANT TO SECURITY COUNCIL RESOLUTION 1026

S/1995/1031, Dec. 13, 1995, 35 *International Legal Materials* 237 (1996).

7. In * * * the Agreement on the Military Aspects of the Peace Settlement * * * the Security Council is invited to authorize Member States or regional organizations or arrangements to establish a multinational military Implementation Force (IFOR), which will be composed of ground, air and maritime units from the members of the North Atlantic Treaty Organization (NATO) and from non-NATO States. The parties to the Agreement understand and agree that IFOR will begin implementation of the military aspects of the Peace Agreement upon the transfer of authority for the forces deployed in Bosnia and Herzegovina from the UNPROFOR Commander to the IFOR Commander. * * * [T]he parties understand and agree that NATO may establish such a force, which will operate under the authority and subject to the direction and political control of the North Atlantic Council through the NATO chain of command. The modalities of the participation of non-NATO States in IFOR are to be agreed between those States and NATO. * * *

47. I welcome these * * * agreements because, if the parties will allow them to be implemented, they will end the terrible suffering inflicted on the people of those two Member States for so many years and a major source of instability in Europe will be removed. I also welcome them because of their implications for the United Nations. It is widely held that the United Nations' involvement in the former Yugoslavia has not been a success. I strongly dispute that allegation. The original and primary purpose in deploying United Nations peace-keepers in Bosnia and Herzegovina after war broke out there was to protect humanitarian activities. That mission has been successfully carried out, thanks to the courage and dedication of the civilian workers concerned but also thanks to the protection, logistics support and other services afforded to them by UNPROFOR. UNPROFOR also deserves credit for its successes in negotiating and helping to implement cease-fires and other military arrangements, often of a local nature, without which many people alive today would be dead and material destruction would have been even greater. I also count it a gain that the United Nations, Member States and Secretariat alike, have learnt many lessons in Bosnia and Herzegovina whose benefit will become apparent in our future peacemaking and peace-keeping endeavours.

48. The price for the United Nations has, however, been high. Too many United Nations personnel have been killed or suffered crippling injuries. The conflicts in the former Yugoslavia have dominated the Organization's agenda in the peace and security field in recent years and

have distorted its peacemaking and peace-keeping efforts at the expense of other parts of the world. At the time of peak deployment, in August 1995, the former Yugoslavia accounted for nearly 70 per cent of peace-keepers world wide and over two thirds of peace-keeping cost. I therefore welcome the fact the Member States have decided that the vast task of helping to implement the Peace Agreement in Bosnia and Herzegovina should not be entrusted to the United Nations alone. Only a cooperative effort between many international organizations and Member States can generate the skills and resources and, above all, the political will required to end the fighting and start building the peace in Bosnia and Herzegovina.

49.   In the present report, as requested by the Security Council, I have set out proposals concerning a variety of ways in which the United Nations can make its contribution to this common effort. The most important of them are in the fields of humanitarian relief and return of refugees, where UNHCR is well placed to continue and develop the work it has been doing from the outset, and civilian police, where the parties have asked the United Nations to deploy a United Nations civilian police force greater than any previously seen. In both cases, I am confident that the United Nations has the ability to perform the tasks assigned to it, provided that the parties cooperate and provided that Member States make available the resources that will be necessary. In the case of UNHCR, that will primarily mean financial resources, voluntarily contributed. In case of the International Police Task Force, it will mean not only financial resources, which will have to be obtained through assessed contributions if the Force is to be deployed in time, but also human resources in the form of trained and experienced police officers. I urge Member States to respond promptly and generously to these requirements.

Notes and Questions

1.   *International vs. Internal Conflicts.* According to Article 2(7) of the U.N. Charter, nothing in the Charter

> shall authorize the United Nations to intervene in matters which are essentially within the domestic jurisdiction of any state or shall require the Members to submit such matters to settlement under the present Charter; but this principle shall not prejudice the application of enforcement measures under Chapter VII.

What is the dividing line between "international" and "internal" conflicts? What factors may convince members of the Security Council that a particular conflict is a sufficient threat to "*international* peace and security" to warrant Security Council measures under Chapter VII? The support of the Federal Republic of Yugoslavia for Serbians in Bosnia–Herzegovina added an international dimension to that conflict. What other factors may influence the Security Council? The size and intensity of a purportedly domestic conflict? A flow of refugees across international borders? Significant human rights violations?

2. *After the Dayton Accords.* Following the Dayton Accords, the United Nations was to continue its participation in Bosnia, particularly by providing humanitarian assistance and exercising such peacekeeping functions as monitoring, observing, and giving advice. Why, however, was the United Nations itself not given the military role that IFOR assumed, a role that was considered necessary as part of the peace accords? Did a lack of assertiveness by U.N. officials in previous peacekeeping operations explain, in part, the decision to utilize NATO and IFOR? Or did the reluctance of states to make peacekeeping forces available in timely fashion necessitate the recourse to regional efforts? The United Nations reported that in 1994, when the U.N. Secretary–General "informed the Security Council that peacekeeping commanders would need 35,000 troops to deter attacks" on Security Council-created safe areas in Bosnia and Herzegovina, "Member States authorized 7,600 troops and took a year to provide them." <http://www.un.org/News/facts/peacefct.htm>. For a criticism of the U.N.'s and Europe's pre-Dayton "attempt at limited but impartial involvement" in Bosnia, see Richard K. Betts, "The Delusion of Impartial Intervention," 73 *Foreign Affairs*, Nov./Dec. 1994, at 20.

For analyses of the Dayton Accords, see "Symposium: The Dayton Agreements: A Breakthrough for Peace and Justice?," 7 *European Journal of International Law* 147 (1996). For discussion of ongoing efforts to build a functioning multi-ethnic state under the Dayton constitution, to ensure peace and stability, to stabilize the economy, and to solve problems of refugees and displaced persons, see Declaration of the Bosnia Peace Implementation Council with Annex (Peace Implementation Agenda), Dec. 16, 1998, 38 I.L.M. 484 (1999); Marcus Cox, "The Dayton Agreement in Bosnia and Herzegovina: A Study of Implementation Strategies," 69 *British Yearbook of International Law* 201 (1999); Robert M. Hayden, "Bosnia: The Contradictions of 'Democracy' Without Consent," *East European Constitutional Review*, Spring 1998, at 47.

3. *International Involvement in Bosnia.* One is struck by the variety of states and international organizations involved in what might be regarded primarily as a tragic domestic civil war in Bosnia. In addition to the United Nations and its various agencies, NATO, the International Conference on the Former Yugoslavia, the Organization for Security and Cooperation in Europe, the European Union, the Council of Europe, the European Bank for Reconstruction and Development, and the World Bank all have played roles in the Bosnian conflict and settlement. Even the European Court of Human Rights had a part: the Court's President named three of the nine members of a Bosnian constitutional court created under the Dayton Accords. Diplomats from several states also have been involved in mediation efforts, and approximately two dozen states from different parts of the world contributed troops to UNPROFOR. How should the policies and activities of these various entities be coordinated? See generally Abram Chayes & Antonia Handler Chayes, *Planning for Intervention: International Cooperation in Conflict Management* (1999).

4. *The Security Council, Regional Organizations, and the Use of Force.* Annex 1–A of the General Framework Agreement for Peace in Bosnia and

Herzegovina "invited" the U.N. Security Council to adopt a resolution authorizing Member States to establish IFOR. The Council, acting under Chapter VII of the U.N. Charter, then authorized Member States to cooperate with NATO "to establish a multinational implementation force (IFOR) under unified command and control," to "take all necessary measures" to implement and insure compliance with the Annex, and to "take all necessary measures, at the request of IFOR, either in defense of IFOR or to assist the force in carrying out its mission." S.C. Res. 1031 (1995), 35 I.L.M. 251, 253 (1996). Why was Security Council authorization of IFOR deemed necessary? The readings below explore the relationship between the United Nations and regional organizations with respect to peace and security matters.

UNITED NATIONS CHARTER, ARTICLES 52–54

June 26, 1945, 59 Stat. 1031, T.S. No. 993, 3 Bevans 1153, 1976 Y.B.U.N. 1043.

CHAPTER VIII: REGIONAL ARRANGEMENTS

Article 52

1. Nothing in the present Charter precludes the existence of regional arrangements or agencies for dealing with such matters relating to the maintenance of international peace and security as are appropriate for regional action, provided that such arrangements or agencies and their activities are consistent with the Purposes and Principles of the United Nations.

2. The Members of the United Nations entering into such arrangements or constituting such agencies shall make every effort to achieve pacific settlement of local disputes through such regional arrangements or by such regional agencies before referring them to the Security Council.

3. The Security Council shall encourage the development of pacific settlement of local disputes through such regional arrangements or by such regional agencies either on the initiative of the states concerned or by reference from the Security Council. * * *

Article 53

1. The Security Council shall, where appropriate, utilize such regional arrangements or agencies for enforcement action under its authority. But no enforcement action shall be taken under regional arrangements or by regional agencies without the authorization of the Security Council * * *. * * *

Article 54

The Security Council shall at all times be kept fully informed of activities undertaken or in contemplation under regional arrangements or by regional agencies for the maintenance of international peace and security.

SUPPLEMENT TO AN AGENDA FOR PEACE

Position Paper of the Secretary–General on the Occasion of the Fiftieth
Anniversary of the United Nations A/50/60–S/1995/1, 3 January 1995,
in *An Agenda for Peace 1995*, at 5 (2d ed. 1995) (U.N. Sales No. E.95.I.15).

86.   Cooperation between the United Nations and regional organizations takes a number of forms * * * :

(a) *Consultation*: this has been well-established for some time. In some cases it is governed by formal agreements and reports are made to the General Assembly; in other cases it is less formal. The purpose is to exchange views on conflicts that both the United Nations and regional organization may be trying to solve;

(b) *Diplomatic support*: the regional organization participates in the peacemaking activities of the United Nations and supports them by diplomatic initiatives * * * and/or by providing technical input * * *. In the same way, the United Nations can support the regional organization in its efforts * * *;

(c) *Operational support*: the most developed example is the provision by NATO of air power to support the United Nations Protection Force (UNPROFOR) in the former Yugoslavia. For its part, the United Nations can provide technical advice to regional organizations that undertake peace-keeping operations of their own;

(d) *Co-deployment*: United Nations field missions have been deployed in conjunction with the Economic Community of West African States (ECOWAS) in Liberia and with the Commonwealth of Independent States (CIS) in Georgia. If those experiments succeed, they may herald a new division of labor between the United Nations and regional organizations, under which the regional organization carries the main burden but a small United Nations operation supports it and verifies that it is functioning in a manner consistent with positions adopted by the Security Council. The political, operational and financial aspects of the arrangement give rise to questions of some delicacy * * *;

(e) *Joint operations*: the example is the United Nations Mission in Haiti, the staffing, direction and financing of which are shared between the United Nations and the Organization of American States (OAS). This arrangement * * * too is a possible model for the future that will need careful assessment.

NORTH ATLANTIC TREATY

Apr. 4, 1949, 34 U.N.T.S. 244.

Article 1

The Parties undertake, as set forth in the Charter of the United Nations, to settle any international disputes in which they may be involved by peaceful means in such a manner that international peace and security, and justice, are not endangered, and to refrain in their international relations from the threat or use of force in any manner inconsistent with the purposes of the United Nations. * * *

Article 3

In order more effectively to achieve the objectives of this Treaty, the Parties, separately and jointly, by means of continuous and effective self-help and mutual aid, will maintain and develop their individual and collective capacity to resist armed attack.

Article 4

The Parties will consult together whenever, in the opinion of any of them, the territorial integrity, political independence or security of any of the Parties is threatened.

Article 5

The Parties agree that an armed attack against one or more of them in Europe or North America shall be considered an attack against them all; and consequently they agree that, if such an armed attack occurs, each of them in exercise of the right of individual or collective self-defense recognized by Article 51 of the Charter of the United Nations, will assist the Party or Parties so attacked by taking forthwith, individually and in concert with the other Parties, such action as it deems necessary, including the use of armed force, to restore and maintain the security of the North Atlantic area.

Any such armed attack and all measures taken as a result thereof shall immediately be reported to the Security Council. Such measures shall be terminated when the Security Council has taken the measures necessary to restore and maintain international peace and security.
* * *

Article 7

This Treaty does not affect, and shall not be interpreted as affecting, in any way the rights and obligations under the Charter of the Parties which are members of the United Nations, or the primary responsibility of the Security Council for the maintenance of international peace and security. * * *

Article 9

The Parties hereby establish a council, on which each of them shall be represented, to consider matters concerning the implementation of this Treaty. The council shall be so organized as to be able to meet promptly at any time. The council shall set up such subsidiary bodies as may be necessary; in particular it shall establish immediately a defense committee which shall recommend measures for the implementation of Articles 3 and 5.

Notes and Questions

1. *Chapter VIII Organizations.* Chapter VIII of the U.N. Charter reflects a 1945 compromise between proponents of a universal security organization and those, primarily from Latin America, who favored the use of regional arrangements to help maintain international peace and security.

The United Nations has never defined "regional arrangements or agencies," and neither the International Court of Justice nor any other U.N. organ has provided comprehensive guidelines concerning when regional organizations legally may use force. Some organizations—the Organization of American States, the Organization for Security and Cooperation in Europe, and the Commonwealth of Independent States—have declared themselves to be Chapter VIII organizations. The U.N. Security Council has treated several other organizations—the Organization of African Unity, the League of Arab States, and the Economic Community of West African States—as regional agencies or arrangements. See Mary Ellen O'Connell, "The UN, NATO, and International Law After Kosovo," 22 *Human Rights Quarterly* 57, 62–67 (2000).

2. *NATO.* NATO was formed in 1949 as a collective self-defense organization, with the goal of protecting its members from attack by the then Communist Soviet Union and the states of Eastern Europe. There were 12 original parties: Belgium, Canada, Denmark, France, Iceland, Italy, Luxembourg, the Netherlands, Norway, Portugal, the United Kingdom, and the United States. NATO's membership expanded to include Germany, Greece, Spain, and Turkey, and, in 1998, the Czech Republic, Hungary, and Poland. How different in kind is the NATO agreement from the self-defense alliance of the Romans and Jews 2000 years ago, set out in Chapter 2?

In 1992, the U.N. Security Council referred to Chapter VIII regional agencies and arrangements in resolutions relating to no-fly zones over Bosnia–Herzegovina and to an embargo of Yugoslavia—measures that NATO helped to enforce. See S.C. Res. 781 (1992), 787 (1992). Nevertheless, NATO has never declared itself to be a Chapter VIII organization, and there is now significant doubt that the Security Council regards NATO as such an organization. It is clear, however, that with the end of the Cold War NATO has sought new tasks that expand on its traditional role as a collective self-defense organization. See Lawrence S. Kaplan, *The Long Entanglement: NATO's First Fifty Years* (1999); Robert B. McCalla, "NATO's Persistence After the Cold War," 50 *International Organization* 445 (1996).

DICK A. LEURDIJK, "NATO'S DECISIONMAKING TOWARDS AIR STRIKES ON KOSOVO"

International Peacekeeping, Nov.-Dec. 1999, at 193.

The issue of Kosovo was on the agenda of the international community at an early stage, well before the outbreak of hostilities in the first week of March 1998. * * * NATO's concern about the "potentially explosive" situation in Kosovo, in particular, was both inspired by fear of a possible "spillover" into neighbouring countries, such as Albania and Macedonia, and by the possible occurrence of negative consequences for the consolidation of the peace implementation process in Bosnia and Herzegovina. * * * The recognition that NATO had "a legitimate interest in developments in Kosovo" was the starting point for a discussion at NATO's headquarters in Brussels on the modalities of possible military intervention by NATO along its periphery * * *. The issue of the international legal basis for such action, including the question whether explicit authorisation by the Security Council would be needed, led to extensive discussions and difference of opinion among the allies. * * * The US Secretary of Defence, William Cohen, * * * thought it unnecessary for NATO to subordinate its security to the UN, emphasizing NATO's own autonomy in taking decisions. The US position, however, was not shared by all within NATO. Others said that they would not approve the use of force by NATO without a UN mandate, fearing both the risk of alienating the Russians, among others, and the consequences such a precedent could set for others (the Russians, among others) in the future. The differences of opinion on this issue among NATO's sixteen nations were reflected in official consecutive NATO statements by stressing the need for a "relevant," and "appropriate," a "sufficient" or a "sound legal base," while avoiding references to the need for an explicit UN mandate. For the rest of the year, the issue would remain on the Alliance's table and become more relevant to policy than ever.

* * * In the fall of 1998, two considerations started to play a crucial role for NATO in re-assessing its posture with respect to Kosovo: (a) the coming winter and the impending humanitarian disaster, taking into account the large number of displaced people, who found themselves in the mountains without shelter as a consequence of the continuing hostilities, and (b) NATO's own credibility, considering how many times the use of force had been threatened by the Alliance since May—threats never followed up, notwithstanding the many cases of defiance by Belgrade of the demands of the international community. In the new political climate of mid-September, the Security Council adopted resolution 1199 * * *. * * * [T]he Council * * * repeated demands made three months before[,] concern[ing] a series of measures, including ceasing of hostilities, the maintenance of a cease-fire, the withdrawal of troops and special police forces, the return of refugees and displaced persons, access for humanitarian organisations and international monitoring in Kosovo. At NATO, the procedure was set in motion that would culminate, mid-October, in the issuance of two so-called Activation Orders, for both a limited air operation and a phased air campaign in Kosovo. At the same time, it was clear to all concerned that a resolution authorising the use of force in Kosovo would be vetoed in the Security Council by, among others, the Russian Federation. This made the need for a sound legal base for military action all the more acute. Ultimately, NATO members could not agree on an official, common position in this respect, divided as they were on the question whether NATO by definition needed the explicit authorisation of the Security Council for the use of force. * * * The European partners of the US, while insisting on the need for UN authorisation, contended that Kosovo was an exceptional case because of the impending, potential humanitarian catastrophe. By recognising that NATO was unable to come up with a common declaration * * * the Alliance left it to each individual Member State to give its own, separate legal justification of the ACTORD. The use of the notion of a "sufficient legal base," thus, had two functions: it covered the

recognition both of the lack of explicit UN authorisation and of the inability of NATO to formulate an official, common legal basis for the planned air operations—thereby withdrawing its, until then, habitual and explicit acceptance of the political primacy of the Security Council.

The ACTORD, in the meantime, functioned as the ultimate leverage for US diplomat Richard Holbrooke in his negotiations with President Milosevic. The talks ultimately led to the so-called Milosevic–Holbrooke agreement, in which the former committed himself to implementing the demands laid down in Security Council resolution 1199. * * *

* * * [T]wo further agreements [were] directed at the establishment of a verification regime, consisting of two components: an OSCE [Organization for Security and Cooperation in Europe] mission on the ground, and a NATO verification mission in the air. The aim of both missions was the verification of compliance by the Federal Republic of Yugoslavia and "all others concerned in Kosovo" with the demands of the international community, as laid down in the resolutions the Security Council adopted with respect to the situation in Kosovo: 1160 (March 1998), 1199 (September 1998) and 1203 (October 1998).[†] The reference to "all others concerned" (diplomatic language for the ethnic Albanians, comprising Rugova and co. and the Kosovo Liberation Army) is derived from Security Council resolution 1203, * * * in which the Council formally authorised both verification missions. The compliance requirements were thus explicitly directed at both parties to the conflict. * * * [T]he [OSCE] mission * * * had a typical "peacekeeping" character being unarmed and functioning with the consent of the government of the "host" country * * *. [The verifiers] were not in a position to stop violence, they could not safeguard the respect for the rules of international humanitarian law, they were just "verifiers," there to verify compliance with international demands, but without any enforcement powers whatsoever. * * * [W]ith the experience with UNPROFOR in Bosnia–Herzegovina still fresh in their minds, some governments wanted additional security guarantees for the verifiers, unarmed as they would be, operating in a potentially violent environment and vulnerable as potential targets for hostage-taking or use as human shields. * * * NATO, in an effort to provide extra security and in close consultation with the OSCE, established a separate, so-called Extraction Force, aimed at the evacuation of the verifiers in an emergency, i.e. most probably under "hostile conditions." While in Western capitals it was believed that both the establishment of the "Extraction Force" and its use of force were authorised by resolution 1203, this argument was heavily contested, both on legal and political grounds, by members of the Security Council, including Costa Rica, Brazil and the Russian Federation. * * * President Milosevic denied that the deployment of the "Extraction Force" was part of his 13 October "agreement" with Holbrooke,

[†] In each of these resolutions, the Security Council indicated that it was "[a]cting under Chapter VII of the Charter of the United Nations."—Eds.

and warned that action by the force on the territory of Kosovo would be considered "an act of aggression," provoking retaliatory action by his forces. * * *

* * * [A] massacre in Racak on 15 January [1999], in which 45 Kosovar Albanians died[,] * * * forced the international community both to acknowledge that hardly any progress had been made, since mid-October, in the implementation of its demands as laid down in the relevant Security Council resolutions, and that it had to step up its efforts again, both diplomatically and militarily. * * * NATO gave its full support to th[e] strategy [of setting a deadline for a political settlement, which would entail "substantial autonomy for Kosovo" and still insure the Federal Republic's territorial integrity] by fortifying the political initiative with the threat of using force, in line with its Activation Orders of mid-October. In an official statement, it said it was ready "to take whatever measures are necessary in the light of both parties' compliance with international commitments and requirements." The Council thus authorised [NATO] Secretary–General Solana to order air strikes against targets on FRY territory, adding that it would take "all appropriate measures" in case of non-compliance by the Kosovar Albanian side, without, however, giving further details. Responding to NATO's decision to empower its Secretary–General to authorise air strikes, the government in Belgrade, describing the authorisation as "an open threat of aggression" against its sovereignty and territorial integrity, warned that it would "protect resolutely its legitimate State and national interests." Against this background of two similar warnings from Belgrade on retaliatory action against NATO, the Alliance's military authorities started contingency planning on the modalities of the "international presence," * * * in anticipation of a positive outcome of the Rambouillet talks. The concept of * * * a force "to help the parties implement a settlement" * * * was heavily contested by Belgrade, which refused the deployment of foreign troops on its territory, arguing that it would be an infringement on its national sovereignty * * *. [Following the breakdown of negotiations,] NATO in the night of 24 March 1999 decided to start operation "Allied Force"—the execution of air strikes along the lines of the Activation Orders, as adopted five months earlier. It was only then, that the public debate started on the political, military and international legal implications of the use of force by NATO, in terms of its legitimacy, proportionality, and effectiveness. At that time already, it was clear that the operation would have far-reaching consequences for the functioning of the international political system as set up after the Second World War. As one German cabinet minister declared one month before the start of the air strikes: "Any way you look at it, if NATO attacks a sovereign country it will create a historical precedent that will have unforeseen consequences for the alliance and all of its members." One can easily add: and for the rest of the world.

BRUNO SIMMA, "NATO, THE UN AND THE USE OF FORCE: LEGAL ASPECTS"

10 *European Journal of International Law* 1 (1999).

[Professor Simma concludes that NATO is not a Chapter VIII regional organization, and that the U.N. Security Council neither explicitly nor implicitly, authorized NATO's use of force against the Federal Republic of Yugoslavia].

* * * [T]he Parliament of the Federal Republic of Germany (*Bundestag*) in mid-October 1998 [deliberated about] German participation in NATO air strikes. In these debates, the international legal issues involved were discussed at great length and in considerable depth. The respect for UN Charter law demonstrated throughout the debates was remarkable. Such deference became particularly apparent in the critical discussion of the absence of a Security Council authorization. The German Federal Government, while recognizing this legal flaw, argued that the situation in Kosovo was so desperate as to justify the NATO threat, even without UN authorization, in a state of humanitarian necessity leaving no choice of other means. In this regard, differently from the NATO Secretary–General, the Government * * * spoke of the NATO threat as an instance of "humanitarian intervention." The *Bundestag* finally gave its approval to German participation in the NATO action. But it was stressed by all voices in favour of such participation, in particular by the Federal Government, that German agreement with the legal position taken by the Alliance in the specific instance of Kosovo was not to be regarded as "green light" for similar NATO interventions in general.

[Professor Simma reviews a November 1998 NATO resolution addressing the use of force in "non-Article 5 missions" such as in the Federal Republic of Yugoslavia. He concludes that NATO's purported expansion of the right of individual or collective self-defense to include the defense "of common interests and values" is "intolerable, indeed absurd, from a legal point of view." He also criticizes a second NATO argument, that NATO must "stand ready to act should the UN Security Council be prevented from discharging its purpose of maintaining international peace and security."]

* * * It is probably no coincidence that NATO's wording is similar to that of the "Uniting for Peace" Resolution of the UN General Assembly of 3 November 1950 * * *. But of course, according to "Uniting for Peace," it was the General Assembly, as a UN organ comprising all Member States, that was to shoulder the burden of maintaining or restoring international peace and security in lieu of the Security Council, not an extraneous, regional organization comprising only about 10 per cent of UN membership. * * *

* * * In most quarters of the world, including Germany, it is accepted that the UN Charter is not just one multilateral treaty among

others but an instrument of singular legal weight, something akin to a "constitution" of the international community. This status of the Charter should not be prejudiced by NATO. * * *

* * * [T]he capacity of NATO to absorb * * * new roles and missions without any formal changes considered necessary to the original founding treaty [is] astonishing * * *. Thus, quite aptly, some members of the German Federal Constitutional Court once spoke of the NATO Treaty as "a treaty on wheels."

* * * In the Federal Republic of Germany [the question of legal limits on the transformation of NATO] has been at the heart of several great constitutional controversies ultimately resolved by the Federal Constitutional Court (*Bundesverfassungsgericht*). In these cases, one of the decisive issues was the extent to which alterations of existing [NATO Treaty] obligations * * * could be [brought about] by way of "soft law," for instance by decisions of the North Atlantic Council, while still being covered by the *Bundestag*'s original approval of the NATO Treaty almost half a century ago. The Court was prepared to go quite far in allowing the dynamic evolution of NATO to escape the prerequisite of new parliamentary approval, but it did indicate certain [limits. These limits, reflected in the Court's] 1994 judgment on the constitutionality of German participation in NATO/WEU action against the FRY in the Mediterranean and in UNOSOM II, [included] the conformity of all these activities with the rules and procedures of the UN Charter as the overarching, universal system of collective security. Hence, in view of the strong emphasis placed by the German Government as well as the *Bundestag* on the singular, exceptional character of, and the express denial of precedential value to, the threat of force by NATO against Yugoslavia expressed in the fall of 1998, a general authorization for a "new" NATO to proceed to military enforcement out of area without UN Security Council assent * * * might well transcend the limits set up by the German Basic Law. The German Constitution provides for several procedures to have this question adjudicated by the Karlsruhe Court. * * * [T]he *Bundesverfassungsgericht* has demonstrated its willingness to uphold the constitutional requirements for German participation in international organizations and supranational integration even against heavy political headwinds. * * *

* * * NATO action has moved from full collaboration with the UN in both peacekeeping and enforcement in Bosnia to enforcement action in place of the UN, albeit still authorized by the Security Council to implement the Dayton Agreement[. Now in] Kosovo it has shifted to enforcement in place of the UN without such authorization. * * *

* * * If we agree that the NATO Treaty does have a hard legal core which even the most dynamic and innovative (re-)interpretation cannot erode, it is NATO's subordination to the principles of the United Nations Charter.

Notes and Questions

1. *The Aftermath*. NATO's 1999 bombing of Yugoslavia lasted for 78 days. The U.N. Security Council, acting under Chapter VII of the U.N. Charter, has authorized Member States and NATO to establish an "international security presence" in Kosovo and authorized the Secretary–General "to establish an international civil presence in Kosovo in order to provide an interim administration for Kosovo under which the people of Kosovo can enjoy substantial autonomy within the Federal Republic of Yugoslavia." S.C. Res. 1244 (1999). NATO forces have occupied Kosovo, which has been plagued by a breakdown in governmental services, the destruction of infrastructure, and retaliations by ethnic Albanians against ethnic Serbs. The Federal Republic of Yugoslavia, for its part, challenged the legality of NATO's bombing, filing claims against NATO members in the International Court of Justice. Some of these cases were dismissed for clear lack of jurisdiction, but, as of November 1, 2000, the cases against Belgium, Canada, France, Germany, Italy, the Netherlands, Portugal, and the United Kingdom remained on the Court's docket. See <http://www.icj-cij.org>. For background on Kosovo, see Julie A. Mertus, *Kosovo: How Myths and Truths Started a War* (1999).

2. *Collective Security and the Use of Force by Regional Organizations.* Was it only the severe violations of the human rights of the Kosovars that led NATO to ignore the requirements of the U.N. Charter and the North Atlantic Treaty that Security Council approval for the use of force be obtained? Was NATO's use of force a sign of the break-down of the collective security system of the United Nations? What standards and processes now define the legality of unilateral or regional recourse to the use of force? See W. Michael Reisman, "Unilateral Action and the Transformations of the World Constitutive Process: The Special Problem of Humanitarian Intervention," 11 *European Journal of International Law* 3 (2000). What could be done to bolster the efficacy and legitimacy of the U.N.'s collective security system? See the discussion of U.N. legitimacy in Chapter 8.

3. *Municipal Legal Systems and Limits on the Use of Force.* What are the prospects that municipal legal systems can limit the use of force by regional international organizations in the future? Note Professor Simma's discussion of the debates within Germany concerning a legal basis for NATO's actions.

4. *Humanitarian Intervention.* Can NATO's bombing of Serbia and Kosovo be justified as an instance of humanitarian intervention? Or should the bombing instead be seen as a reprisal responding to Yugoslavia's lack of compliance with U.N. Security Council resolutions and to the commission of human rights violations in Kosovo—a reprisal that was illegal because it involved the use of force, violating Articles 2(4) and 2(7) of the U.N. Charter? Recall Professor Henkin's views on the restrictive scope of a humanitarian intervention exception to the prohibition on the use of force, in Part B above. What are the dangers of giving a broad scope to this exception? When, if ever, should the use of force be permitted in the interest of humanitarian intervention? What conditions should have to be satisfied? For example, how extensive should human rights violations have to be in

order to justify a humanitarian intervention? Should humanitarian intervention be precluded if intervening states also have significant interests of their own that would be furthered by the intervention? Does humanitarian intervention gain legitimacy when undertaken by a group of states, rather than by a single state? More legitimacy if the states are democratic? Does a requirement of proportionality make sense, and was NATO's bombing a proportionate response? Should any humanitarian intervention have to have a reasonable chance of correcting the violation? For discussion of humanitarian intervention, see, *e.g.*, Bartram S. Brown, "Humanitarian Intervention at a Crossroads," 41 *William and Mary Law Review* 1683 (2000); Dino Kritsiotis, "Reappraising Policy Objections to Humanitarian Intervention," 19 *Michigan Journal of International Law* 1005 (1998); James A.R. Nafziger, "Self–Determination and Humanitarian Intervention in a Community of Power," 20 *Denver Journal of International Law and Policy* 9 (1991), and *id.* "Part II," 22 *Denver Journal of International Law and Policy* 219 (1994).

Chapter 10

INTERNATIONAL LAW, THE ENVIRONMENT, AND COMMON SPACES

Harm to the environment has been a concern for many years, and the subject of international cases and treaties. During the late 1970s and the 1980s, environmental disasters in Bhopal, Chernobyl, and Basel, confirmation of the ozone hole over Antarctica, and damaging maritime oil spills helped make the international environment a more significant world political and legal issue than it had been in the past. The international environment and international common spaces are nowadays regarded as objects of international law.

International lawyers frequently refer to "regimes" when discussing international legal arrangements respecting the environment and common spaces. International regimes encompass the various rules, policies, and international institutions related to an international area.[†] An international regime relating to a common space, for example, typically involves a treaty-based settlement that defines the common space's status for treaty parties, and has implications for other international entities as well. International organizations often have roles in regimes.

Part B of this chapter considers multilateral treaty-based regimes that have addressed environmental degradation. Part C then examines the international legal regimes for Antarctica and outer space. Questions about how to manage and conserve the environment in those regions are part of a broader inquiry into governance and resource allocation in international common spaces. We start, however, in Part A with a traditional topic—the law of state responsibility—and look at the development of principles of state responsibility applicable to environmental harm.

[†] One standard source defines "regimes" as "sets of implicit or explicit principles, norms, rules, and decision-making procedures around which actors' expectations converge in a given area of international relations." Stephen D. Krasner, "Structural Causes and Regime Consequences: Regimes as Intervening Variables," in *International Regimes* 1, 2 (Stephen D. Krasner ed. 1992).

A. STATE RESPONSIBILITY AND THE ENVIRONMENT

The first excerpt in this Part is an influential arbitral decision concerning transboundary environmental harm. The *Trail Smelter Case* raises questions about one way—a liability regime based on notions of state responsibility—in which international law and process might address damage to the environment. The materials following the *Trail Smelter Case* address changes in concepts of state responsibility that accommodate concerns with environmental degradation on a global scale.

THE TRAIL SMELTER CASE

United States v. Canada, 1941, U.N. Rep. Int'l Arb. Awards 1905, 1938 (1949).

This Tribunal is constituted under, and its powers are derived from and limited by, the Convention between the United States of America and the Dominion of Canada signed at Ottawa, April 15 1935, duly ratified by the two parties, and ratifications exchanged at Ottawa, August 3, 1935 (hereinafter termed "the Convention").

By Article II of the Convention, each Government was to choose one member of the Tribunal and the two Governments were to choose jointly a chairman who should be neither a British subject nor a citizen of the United States. The members of the Tribunal were chosen as follows: by the United States of America, Charles Warren of Massachusetts; by the Dominion of Canada, Robert A.E. Greenshields of the Province of Quebec; by the two Governments jointly, Jan Frans Hostie of Belgium.

Article II, paragraph 4, of the Convention provided that "the Governments may each designate a scientist to assist the tribunal"; and the scientists were designated * * *. * * *

The controversy is between two Governments involving damage occurring or having occurred, in the territory of one of them (the United States of America) and alleged to be due to an agency situated in the territory of the other (the Dominion of Canada). In this controversy, the Tribunal did not sit and is not sitting to pass upon claims presented by individuals or on behalf of one or more individuals by their Government, although individuals may come within the meaning of "parties concerned," in Article IV * * * of the Convention and although the damage suffered by individuals did, in part, "afford a convenient scale for the calculation of the reparation due to the State." * * *

As between the two countries involved, each has an equal interest that if a nuisance is proved, the indemnity to damaged parties for proven damage shall be just and adequate and each has also an equal interest that unproven or unwarranted claims shall not be allowed. For, while the United States' interests may now be claimed to be injured by the operations of a Canadian corporation, it is equally possible that at some time in the future Canadian interests might be claimed to be injured by an American corporation. As has well been said: "It would not be to the advantage of the two countries concerned that industrial effort should be prevented by exaggerating the interests of the agricultural community. Equally, it would not be to the advantage of the two countries that the agricultural community should be oppressed to advance the interest of industry."

Considerations like the above are reflected in the provisions of the Convention in Article IV, that "the desire of the high contracting parties" is "to reach a solution just to all parties concerned." And the phraseology of the questions submitted to the Tribunal clearly evinces a desire and an intention that, to some extent, in making its answers to the questions, the Tribunal should endeavor to adjust the conflicting interests by some "just solution" which would allow the continuance of the operation of the Trail Smelter but under such restrictions and limitations as would, as far as foreseeable, prevent damage in the United States, and as would enable indemnity to be obtained, if in spite of such restrictions and limitations, damage should occur in the future in the United States.

In arriving at its decision, the Tribunal has had always to bear in mind the further fact that in the preamble to the Convention, it is stated that it is concluded with the recognition of "the desirability and necessity of effecting a permanent settlement."

The duty imposed upon the Tribunal by [Article III of] the Convention was to "finally decide" the following questions:

(1) Whether damage caused by the Trail Smelter in the State of Washington has occurred since the first day of January, 1932, and, if so, what indemnity should be paid therefor?

(2) In the event of the answer to the first part of the preceding question being in the affirmative, whether the Trail Smelter should be required to refrain from causing damage in the State of Washington in the future and, if so, to what extent?

(3) In the light of the answer to the preceding question, what measures or regime, if any, should be adopted or maintained by the Trail Smelter?

(4) What indemnity or compensation, if any, should be paid on account of any decision or decisions rendered by the Tribunal pursuant to the next two preceding questions? * * *

On April 16, 1938, the Tribunal reported its "final decision" on Question No. 1, as well as its temporary decisions on Questions No. 2 and No. 3, and provided for a temporary régime thereunder. The decision reported on April 16, 1938, will be referred to hereinafter as the "previous decision." * * *

In conclusion (end of Part Two of the previous decision), the Tribunal answered Question No. 1 as follows:

Damage caused by the Trail Smelter in the State of Washington has occurred since the first day of January, 1932, and up to October 1, 1937, and the indemnity to be paid therefore is seventy-eight thousand dollars ($78,000), and is to be complete and final indemnity and compensation for all damage which occurred between such dates. * * *

Answering Questions No. 2 and No. 3, the Tribunal decided that, until a final decision should be made, the Trail Smelter should be subject to a temporary régime (described more in detail in Part Four of the present decision) and a trial period was established to a date not later than October 1, 1940, in order to enable the Tribunal to establish a permanent régime based on a "more adequate and intensive study" * * * * * *

The period within which the Tribunal shall report its final decisions was extended by agreement of the two Governments until March 12, 1941. * * *

In 1896, a smelter was started under American auspices near the locality known as Trail, B.C. In 1906, the Consolidated Mining and Smelting Company of Canada, Limited, obtained a charter of incorporation from the Canadian authorities, and that company acquired the smelter plant at Trail as it then existed. Since that time, the Canadian company, without interruption, has operated the Smelter, and from time to time has greatly added to the plant until it has become one of the best and largest equipped smelting plants on the American continent. In 1925 and 1927, two stacks of the plant were erected to 409 feet in height and the Smelter greatly increased its daily smelting of zinc and lead ores. This increased production resulted in more sulphur dioxide fumes and higher concentrations being emitted into the air. In 1916, about 5,000 tons of sulphur per month were emitted; in 1924, about 4,700 tons; in 1926, about 9,000 tons—an amount which rose near to 10,000 tons per month in 1930. In other words, about 300–350 tons of sulphur were being emitted daily in 1930. * * *

From 1925, at least, to 1937, damage occurred in the State of Washington, resulting from the sulphur dioxide emitted from the Trail Smelter * * *.

The subject of fumigations and damage claimed to result from them was referred by the two Governments on August 7, 1928, to the International Joint Commission, United States and Canada, under Article IX of the Convention of January 11, 1909, between the United States and Great Britain, providing that the high contracting parties might agree that "any other question or matters of difference arising between them involving the rights, obligations or interests of either in relation to the other, or to the inhabitants of the other, along the common frontier between the United States and the Dominion of Canada shall be referred from time to time to the International Joint Commission for examination and report. Such reports shall not be regarded as decisions of the question or matters so submitted either on the facts or on the law, and shall not, in any way, have the character of an arbitral award.''

[The Joint Commission's 1931 report recommended that steps be taken to reduce sulphur dioxide fumes from the Trail Smelter "to a point where it will do no damage in the United States." The Commission also held that damages to the United States caused by pollution from the Trail Smelter through January 1, 1932, amounted to $350,000.]

This report failed to secure the acceptance of both Governments. A sum of $350,000 has, however, been paid by the Dominion of Canada to the United States.

Two years after the filing of the above report, the United States Government, on February 17, 1933, made representations to the Canadian Government that existing conditions were entirely unsatisfactory and that damage was still occurring and diplomatic negotiations were entered into which resulted in the signing of the present Convention.

The Consolidated Mining and Smelting Company of Canada, Limited, proceeded after 1930 to make certain changes and additions in its plant, with the intention and purpose of lessening the sulphur contents of the fumes, and in an attempt to lessen injurious fumigations, a new system of control over the emission of fumes during the crop growing season came into operation about 1934. * * *

The tons of sulphur emitted into the air from the Trail Smelter fell from about 10,000 tons per month in 1930 to about 7,200 tons in 1931 and 3,400 tons in 1932 as a result both of sulphur dioxide beginning to be absorbed and of depressed business conditions. As depression receded, this monthly average rose in 1933 to 4,000 tons, in 1934 to nearly 6,300 tons and in 1935 to 6,800 tons. In 1936, however, it had fallen to 5,600 tons; in 1937, if further fell to 4,850 tons; in 1938, still further to 4,230 tons to reach 3,250 tons in 1939. It rose again, however, to 3,875 tons in 1940. * * *

PART TWO. * * *

Since the Tribunal has, in its previous decision, answered Question No. 1 with respect to the period from the first day of January, 1932, to the first day of October, 1937, it now answers Question No. 1 with respect to the period from the first day of October, 1937, to the first day of October, 1940, as follows:

(1) No damage caused by the Trail Smelter in the State of Washington has occurred since the first day of October, 1937, and prior to the first day of October, 1940, and hence no indemnity shall be paid therefor.

PART THREE.

The second question under Article III of the Convention is as follows:

In the event of the answer to the first part of the preceding question being in the affirmative, whether the Trail Smelter should be required to refrain from causing damage in the State of Washington in the future and, if so, to what extent?

Damage has occurred since January 1, 1932, as fully set forth in the previous decision. To that extent, the first part of the preceding question has thus been answered in the affirmative. * * *

The first problem which arises is whether the question should be answered on the basis of the law followed in the United States or on the basis of international law. The Tribunal, however, finds that this problem need not be solved here as the law followed in the United States in dealing with the quasi-sovereign rights of the States of the Union, in the matter of air pollution, whilst more definite, is in conformity with the general rules of international law.

Particularly in reaching its conclusions as regards this question as well as the next, the Tribunal has given consideration to the desire of the high contracting parties "to reach a solution just to all parties concerned."

As Professor Eagleton puts it (*Responsibility of States in International Law*, 1928, p. 80): "A State owes at all times a duty to protect other States against injurious acts by individuals from within its jurisdiction." A great number of such general pronouncements by leading authorities concerning the duty of a State to respect other States and their territory have been presented to the Tribunal. These and many others have been carefully examined. International decisions, in various matters, from the Alabama case onward, and also earlier ones, are based on the same general principle, and, indeed, this principle, as such, has not been questioned by Canada. But the real difficulty often arises rather when it comes to determine what, *pro subjecta materie*, is deemed to constitute an injurious act. * * *

No case of air pollution dealt with by an international tribunal has been brought to the attention of the Tribunal nor does the Tribunal know of any such case. The nearest analogy is that of water pollution. But, here also, no decision of an international tribunal has been cited or has been found.

There are, however, as regards both air pollution and water pollution, certain decisions of the Supreme Court of the United States which may legitimately be taken as a guide in this field of international law, for it is reasonable to follow by analogy, in international cases, precedents established by that court in dealing with controversies between States of the Union or with other controversies concerning the quasi-sovereign rights of such States, where no contrary rule prevails in international law and no reason for rejecting such precedents can be adduced from the limitations of sovereignty inherent in the Constitution of the United States. * * *

In * * * the State of New York against the State of New Jersey (256 U.S. 296, 309), concerning the pollution of New York Bay, the injunction was also refused for lack of proof * * *. The court * * * said: "... the burden on the State of New York of sustaining the allegations of its bill is much greater than that imposed upon a complainant in an ordinary suit between private parties. Before this court can be moved to exercise its extraordinary power under the Constitution to control the conduct of one State at the suit of another, the threatened invasion of rights must be of serious magnitude and it must be established by clear and convincing evidence."

What the Supreme Court says there of its power under the Constitution equally applies to the extraordinary power granted this Tribunal under the Convention. What is true between States of the Union is, at least, equally true concerning the relations between the United States and the Dominion of Canada. [The Tribunal summarizes other U.S. Supreme Court decisions.]

On the question whether an injunction should be granted or not [in *Georgia v. Tennessee Copper Co.*], the court said (206 U.S. 230):

> It (the State) has the last word as to whether its mountains shall be stripped of their forests and its inhabitants shall breathe pure air.... It is not lightly to be presumed to give up quasi-sovereign rights for pay and ... if that be its choice, it may insist that an infraction of them shall be stopped. This court has not quite the same freedom to balance the harm that will be done by an injunction against that of which the plaintiff complains, that it would have in deciding between two subjects of a single political power. Without excluding the considerations that equity always takes into account ... it is a fair and reasonable demand on the part of a sovereign that the air over its territory should not be polluted on a great scale by sulfurous acid gas, that the forests on its mountains, be they better or worse, and whatever domestic destruction they may have suffered, should not be further destroyed or threatened by the act of persons beyond its control, that the crops and orchards on its hills should not be endangered from the same source.... Whether Georgia, by insisting upon this claim, is doing more harm than good to her own citizens, is for her to determine. The possible disaster to those outside the State must be accepted as a consequence of her standing upon her extreme rights.

Later on, however, when the court actually framed an injunction, in the case of the Ducktown Company (237 U.S. 474, 477) (an agreement on the basis of an annual compensation was reached with the most important of the two smelters, the Tennessee Copper Company), they did not go beyond a decree "adequate to diminish materially the present probability of damage to its (Georgia's) citizens." * * *

The Tribunal, therefore, finds that the above decisions, taken as a whole, constitute an adequate basis for its conclusions, namely, that, under the principles of international law, as well as of the law of the United States, no State has the right to use or permit the use of its territory in such a manner as to cause injury by fumes in or to the territory of another or the properties or persons therein, when the case is of serious consequence and the injury is established by clear and convincing evidence.

The decisions of the Supreme Court of the United States which are the basis of these conclusions are decisions in equity and a solution inspired by them, together with the régime hereinafter prescribed, will, in the opinion of the Tribunal, be "just to all parties concerned," as long, at least, as the present conditions in the Columbia River Valley continue to prevail.

Considering the circumstances of the case, the Tribunal holds that the Dominion of Canada is responsible in international law for the conduct of the Trail Smelter. Apart from the undertakings in the Convention, it is, therefore, the duty of the Government of the Dominion of Canada to see to it that this conduct should be in conformity with the obligation of the Dominion under international law as herein determined.

The Tribunal, therefore, answers Question No. 2 as follows: (2) So long as the present conditions in the Columbia River Valley prevail, the Trail Smelter shall be required to refrain from causing any damage through fumes in the State of Washington; the damage herein referred to and its extent being such as would be recoverable under the decisions of the courts of the United States in suits between private individuals. The indemnity for such damage should be fixed in such manner as the Governments * * * should agree upon.

PART FOUR.

The third question under Article III of the Convention is as follows: "In the light of the answer to the preceding question, what measures or régime, if any, should be adopted and maintained by the Trail Smelter?"

Answering this question in the light of the preceding one, since the Tribunal has, in its previous decision, found that damage caused by the Trail Smelter has occurred in the State of Washington since January 1, 1932, and since the Tribunal is of opinion that damage may occur in the future unless the operations of the Smelter shall be subject to some control, in order to avoid damage occurring, the Tribunal now decides that a régime or measure of control shall be applied to the operations of the Smelter and shall remain in full force unless and until modified in accordance with the provisions hereinafter set forth * * *.

[The Tribunal establishes a highly technical regime of pollution abatement. In response to Question 4, concerning additional compensation or indemnity, the Tribunal states that "the prescribed régime * * * will probably result in preventing any damage of a material nature occurring in the State of Washington in the future." The Tribunal nevertheless calls for the payment of certain indemnities and costs should the Trail Smelter cause damage in the state of Washington in the future.]

Notes and Questions

1. *The Use of Public International Arbitration to Resolve Environmental Disputes.* Is international arbitration based on principles of state responsibility an efficacious way to deter and remedy instances of transboundary environmental harm? The *Trail Smelter Case* was a lengthy and expensive process, requiring six years of fact-finding. The Tribunal not only heard detailed oral and documentary evidence, but its three members personally examined many damaged farms and orchards in Washington. In addition, each government, in accordance with the Tribunal's 1935 constitution, appointed a scientist to assist in the process. The scientists heard all the witnesses and arguments, examined all the documents, consulted with the Tribunal, inspected the Trail Smelter and areas of alleged injury, and administered a trial regime for the operation of the smelter. Would it be better to hear such cases under some simplified procedure, or with some relaxation in required burdens of proof?

2. *Compliance with the Arbitral Decision.* It cost Consolidated Mining and Smelting Co., the company responsible for operating the Trail Smelter, approximately $20 million to comply with the Tribunal's pollution abatement regime. The company's willingness to bear these costs may, at least in part, have been due to the fact that it was involved in all stages of the arbitration. The company participated with the Government of Canada in negotiating the 1935 Convention, and both company and Canadian Government lawyers were actively involved in all aspects of the proceedings. See John E. Read, "The Trail Smelter Dispute," 1 *Canadian Yearbook of International Law* 213, 227–28 (1963).

3. *The Governing Law.* Article IV of the 1935 Convention directed the Tribunal to "apply the law and practice followed in dealing with cognate questions in the United States of America as well as international law and practice, and to give consideration to the desire of the high contracting parties to reach a solution just to all parties concerned." Why did the United States and Canada authorize the Tribunal, an international institution, to apply the law of the United States? Was the Tribunal's use of U.S. law appropriate?

4. *State Responsibility and "International Liability" for Material Transboundary Environmental Harm.* As a matter of state responsibility, what obligation did Canada breach in the *Trail Smelter Case*? The government was not running the polluting facility. Had it failed to exercise due diligence to prevent the harm to U.S. territory? Although the decision might have been viewed as providing little support for an international law rule concerning state responsibility for transboundary harm, because the Tribunal relied on municipal practice as authority and because the terms of the *compromis* seemed to assume Canadian responsibility, other authorities have affirmed an international legal norm limiting material transboundary environmental damage. See, *e.g.*, Brian D. Smith, *State Responsibility and the Marine Environment* 73–76 (1988); Advisory Opinion on the Legality of the Threat or Use of Nuclear Weapons, 1996 I.C.J. 226, 241, 1996 WL 939337.

The International Law Commission, which has been working to develop general rules of state responsibility, believed that its rules could apply to cases of material transboundary environmental harm attributable to a state that was at fault or engaged in an ultrahazardous activity. If a state was acting reasonably, however, it seemed unfair to call that state "responsible" under international law, since "responsibility" meant the state's behavior was "wrongful," and "wrongfulness" meant the injurious conduct should be prohibited. Yet a conclusion of "no responsibility" would mean that the injured state would have to bear the loss or injury, and that seemed unfair too. In 1978 the ILC decided to address this dilemma by studying the topic of "International Liability for Injurious Consequences Arising out of Acts Not Prohibited by International Law." See Daniel Barstow Magraw, "Transboundary Harm: The International Law Commission's Study of 'International Liability,'" 80 *American Journal of International Law* 305 (1986); Alan Khee–Jin Tan, "Forest Fires of Indonesia: State Responsibility and International Liability," 48 *International and Comparative Law Quarterly* 826 (1999). Is this ILC endeavor necessary? As a doctrinal matter, why not resolve the dilemma by providing that the consequences of state responsibility in the problematic environmental cases should be compensation or satisfaction, rather than, invariably, prohibition of the wrongful injury? See Smith, *supra*, at 124.

5. *Alternative Fora.* Could Washington landowners who claimed damage have pursued Consolidated Mining and Smelting Co. directly? They would have faced hurdles had they sued Consolidated in British Columbia, not the least of which was the likelihood that a court in British Columbia would find it could not exercise jurisdiction in a suit based on damage to land located outside the province. See British South Africa Co. v. Companhia de Moçambique, [1893] A.C. 602. A plausible solution under the laws of Washington would have led Consolidated to purchase smoke easements from landowners threatened or affected by fumes, but Washington's constitution prohibited any alien person or corporation from holding interests in land in the state. Should individual landowners have access to an international tribunal to pursue their claims? Should nongovernmental environmental organizations be able to pursue claims in an international tribunal? More generally, what mechanisms, in addition to or in place of lawsuits or arbitral proceedings, should be used to address international environmental degradation?

6. *Bilateral Efforts to Combat Acid Rain.* The United States and Canada conducted negotiations during the 1970s and 1980s concerning control of "acid rain" caused by sulfer dioxide (the pollutant involved in the *Trail Smelter Arbitration*) and nitrogen oxides. The U.S.-Canada Bilateral Air Quality Agreement, Mar. 13, 1991, 30 I.L.M. 676 (1991), commits each state to specific emission reduction objectives. Under this Agreement, an International Joint Commission, originally established in the Boundary Waters Treaty, U.S.-Gr. Brit., Jan. 11. 1909, 36 Stat. 2448, T.S. No. 548, oversees a bilateral Air Quality Committee. This Committee, as part of a review and assessment procedure, reports to the governments and the public on progress in implementing the Agreement's specific objectives. See Jeffrey L. Roelofs, "United States–Canada Air Quality Agreement: A Framework for Addressing Transboundary Air Pollution Problems," 26 *Cornell International Law Journal* 421 (1993).

Multilateral conferences in Stockholm (1972) and Rio de Janeiro (1992) increased awareness of environmental problems affecting many states and international common spaces. We consider some of the principles fashioned at Stockholm and Rio next.

STOCKHOLM DECLARATION OF THE UNITED NATIONS CONFERENCE ON THE HUMAN ENVIRONMENT

Adopted by the U.N. Conference on the Human Environment at Stockholm, 16 June 1972, U.N. Doc. A/CONF.48/14/Rev.1 at 3 (1973), U.N. Doc. A/CONF.48/14 at 2–65, and Corr.1 (1972), 11 *International Legal Materials* 1416 (1972).

Principle 6

The discharge of toxic substances or of other substances and the release of heat, in such quantities or concentrations as to exceed the capacity of the environment to render them harmless, must be halted in order to ensure that serious or irreversible damage is not inflicted upon ecosystems. The just struggle of the peoples of all countries against pollution should be supported. * * *

Principle 21

States have, in accordance with the Charter of the United Nations and the principles of international law, the sovereign right to exploit their own resources pursuant to their own environmental policies, and the responsibility to ensure that activities within their jurisdiction or control do not cause damage to the environment of other States or of areas beyond the limits of national jurisdiction.

Principle 22

States shall co-operate to develop further the international law regarding liability and compensation for the victims of pollution and other environmental damage caused by activities within the jurisdiction or control of such States to areas beyond their jurisdiction.

RIO DECLARATION ON ENVIRONMENT AND DEVELOPMENT

Adopted by the United Nations Conference on Environment and Development, June 14, 1992, UNCED Doc. A/CONF.151/5/Rev.1, 31 *International Legal Materials* 874 (1992).

Principle 1

Human beings are at the centre of concerns for sustainable development. They are entitled to a healthy and productive life in harmony with nature.

Principle 2

States have, in accordance with the Charter of the United Nations and the principles of international law, the sovereign right to exploit their own resources pursuant to their own environmental and developmental policies, and the responsibility to ensure that activities within their jurisdiction or control do not cause damage to the environment of other States or of areas beyond the limits of national jurisdiction.

Principle 3

The right to development must be fulfilled so as to equitably meet developmental and environmental needs of present and future generations.

Principle 4

In order to achieve sustainable development, environmental protection shall constitute an integral part of the development process and cannot be considered in isolation from it.

Principle 5

All States and all people shall cooperate in the essential task of eradicating poverty as an indispensable requirement for sustainable development, in order to decrease the disparities in standards of living and better meet the needs of the majority of the people of the world.

Principle 6

The special situation and needs of developing countries, particularly the least developed and those most environmentally vulnerable, shall be given special priority. International actions in the field of environment and development should also address the interests and needs of all countries.

Principle 7

States shall cooperate in a spirit of global partnership to conserve, protect and restore the health and integrity of the Earth's ecosystem. In view of the different contributions to global environmental degradation, States have common but differentiated responsibilities. The developed countries acknowledge the responsibility that they bear in the international pursuit of sustainable development in view of the pressures their societies place on the global environment and of the technologies and financial resources they command.

Principle 8

To achieve sustainable development and a higher quality of life for all people, States should reduce and eliminate unsustainable patterns of production and consumption and promote appropriate demographic policies.

Principle 9

States should cooperate to strengthen endogenous capacity-building for sustainable development by improving scientific understanding through exchanges of scientific and technological knowledge, and by enhancing the development, adaptation, diffusion and transfer of technologies, including new and innovative technologies.

Principle 10

Environmental issues are best handled with the participation of all concerned citizens, at the relevant level. At the national level, each individual shall have appropriate access to information concerning the environment that is held by public authorities, including information on hazardous materials and activities in their communities, and the opportunity to participate in decision-making processes. States shall facilitate and encourage public awareness and participation by making information widely available. Effective access to judicial and administrative proceedings, including redress and remedy, shall be provided.

Principle 11

States shall enact effective environmental legislation. Environmental standards, management objectives and priorities should reflect the environmental and developmental context to which they apply. Standards applied by some countries may be inappropriate and of unwarranted economic and social cost to other countries, in particular developing countries.

Principle 12

States should cooperate to promote a supportive and open international economic system that would lead to economic growth and sustainable development in all countries, to better address the problems of environmental degradation. Trade policy measures for environmental purposes should not constitute a means of arbitrary or unjustifiable discrimination or a disguised restriction on international trade. Unilateral actions to deal with environmental challenges outside the jurisdiction of the importing country should be avoided. Environmental measures addressing transboundary or global environmental problems should, as far as possible, be based on an international consensus.

Principle 13

States shall develop national law regarding liability and compensation for the victims of pollution and other environmental damage. States shall also cooperate in an expeditious and more determined manner to develop further international law regarding liability and compensation for adverse effects of environmental damage caused by activities within their jurisdiction or control to areas beyond their jurisdiction.

Principle 14

States should effectively cooperate to discourage or prevent the relocation and transfer to other States of any activities and substances that cause severe environmental degradation or are found to be harmful to human health.

Principle 15

In order to protect the environment, the precautionary approach shall be widely applied by States according to their capabilities. Where there are threats of serious or irreversible damage, lack of full scientific certainty shall not be used as a reason for postponing cost-effective measures to prevent environmental degradation.

Principle 16

National authorities should endeavor to promote the internalization of environmental costs and the use of economic instruments, taking into account the approach that the polluter should, in principle, bear the cost of pollution, with due regard to the public interest and without distorting international trade and investment.

Principle 17

Environmental impact assessment, as a national instrument, shall be undertaken for proposed activities that are likely to have a significant adverse impact on the environment and are subject to a decision of a competent national authority.

Principle 18

States shall immediately notify other States of any natural disasters or other emergencies that are likely to produce sudden harmful effects on the environment of those States. Every effort shall be made by the international community to help States so afflicted.

Principle 19

States shall provide prior and timely notification and relevant information to potentially affected States on activities that may have a significant adverse transboundary environmental effect and shall consult with those States at an early stage and in good faith.

Notes and Questions

1. *The Stockholm and Rio Declarations.* The Stockholm Declaration and the Rio Declaration are examples of "soft law," declarations that the adopting states do not regard as creating legally binding obligations at international law. The Stockholm Declaration emerged from the 1972 Stockholm Conference on the Human Environment, the first major intergovernmental conference to address environmental issues in a comprehensive fashion. The Rio Declaration was adopted at the United Nations Conference on Environment and Development, the "Earth Summit," in Rio de Janeiro, Brazil in June 1992. It was attended by approximately 4000 delegates from over 170 states, as well as by 30,000 representatives of nongovernmental organizations, and followed numerous preparatory committee meetings held over a two-year period. If states do not generally regard such instruments as the Stockholm Declaration and the Rio Declaration as legally binding, what is their significance for international law? Are the Stockholm and Rio

Declarations similar in kind to the aspirational Kellogg–Briand Pact we saw in Chapter 2?

2. *State Responsibility and Guiding Principles of International Environmental Law*. International lawyers look for evidence of the content of principles of state responsibility for environmental harm in a variety of declarations and instances of state practice. Some commentators suggest that Principle 21 of the Stockholm Declaration deserves acceptance as a rule of customary law. How do Principle 21 of the Stockholm Declaration and Principle 2 of the Rio Declaration differ from the rules of state responsibility for environmental harm stated in the *Trail Smelter Case*?

Also of particular note as key concepts in international environmental law are the "precautionary principle," one version of which appears in Principle 15 of the Rio Declaration, and "sustainable development," which, as noted in several Rio Principles, suggests that economic development should be pursued only with concern for environmental protection. Numerous declarations and treaties now incorporate these concepts. An extensive literature examines their meaning in various contexts, and explores how the concepts relate to fundamental purposes of environmental protection. See, *e.g.*, Case Concerning the Gabcíkovo-Nagymaros Project (Hungary/Slovakia), 1997 I.C.J. 3, 85, 85–111, 1997 WL 289957 (separate opinion of Vice–President Weeramantry); David Freestone, *The Precautionary Principle in International Environmental Law* (1996).

3. *Obligations* Erga Omnes. If one state has polluted the international commons, should that state be responsible under international law? The International Law Commission has endorsed the idea that obligations *erga omnes*, which we considered in Chapter 3, include obligations "of essential importance for the safeguarding and preservation of the human environment, such as those prohibiting massive pollution of the atmosphere or of the sea." U.N. GAOR, 31st Sess., Supp. No. 10, at 170, U.N. Doc. A/31/10 (1976), art. 19(3), *reprinted in* 2 *Yearbook of the International Law Commission* 73, U.N. Doc. A/CN.4/Ser.A/1976/Add.1 (1976). Does the concept of obligations *erga omnes*, proscribing massive pollution of the global commons, suggest that any state should be allowed to pursue a claim before a tribunal against the state or entity responsible? Should an international legal "guardian"—an intergovernmental or nongovernmental international organization—be empowered to intervene, or even initiate an action, on behalf of the natural environment? See Christopher D. Stone, "Defending the Global Commons," in *Greening International Law* 50 (Philippe Sands ed. 1994), and the article by Philippe Sands in Chapter 8.

4. *Multiple State Responsibility*. Several states may act in concert or independently to cause environmental harm in a neighboring state or in the global commons. State responsibility doctrine holds that the breach of any international obligation gives rise to a duty to make reparation. When reparation takes the form of compensation, should multiple responsible states be jointly and severally liable? In what circumstances?

* * * Even in the simple case [in which the actions of a few states violate their international obligations with regard to indivisible injury],

the nature of international legal process, including the difficulty of insuring contribution among wrongdoing states, explains why joint and several liability is not currently widespread in international practice. The absence of an international legislative authority also impedes the widespread adoption of such a rule. A legislative authority could more easily make the difficult policy choices necessary to formulate a detailed comprehensive legal regime in this area. * * *

Despite procedural and political reasons that may impede the acceptance or limit the scope of application of joint and several liability, many considerations support its recognition as an international law rule governing the consequences of multiple state responsibility. The international community's concern with deterring wrongful conduct by channeling the cost of an injury to its author and with making an injured party whole through pecuniary compensation for loss is well reflected in international law rules of reparation. Municipal analogies, viewed either as general principles of law or as tools in the progressive development of international law, suggest that joint and several liability is the most appropriate method to achieve these objectives. Finally, state practice, although limited, evidences that joint and several liability has achieved a measure of acceptance in international law, demonstrates that tribunals deciding international cases have the requisite will and capacity to allocate the burden of compensation among multiple responsible states, and points toward favorable international reception of a principle of joint and several liability.

John E. Noyes & Brian D. Smith, "State Responsibility and the Principle of Joint and Several Liability," 13 *Yale Journal of International Law* 225, 266–67 (1988).

5. *Procedural Obligations.* States are obliged to notify other states of activities that may cause environmental harm, and to consult about matters that may cause such harm. See, *e.g.*, Principle 19 of the Rio Declaration; Lac Lanoux Arbitration (Spain v. France), 12 R. Int'l Arb. Awards 281 (1957); Brian D. Smith, *State Responsibility and the Marine Environment* 80–83 (1988). If these procedural obligations are breached, what consequences follow? Are procedural duties so general in nature that they provide "only a superficial gloss of international consensus," emphasize "form over substance," and steer international environmental law "toward irrelevance"? "Developments in the Law: International Environmental Law," 104 *Harvard Law Review* 1484, 1493 (1991). More generally, if broad principles of state responsibility and occasional international cases are not themselves likely to protect the international environment effectively, how should the hard work of developing workable regimes be done? What can lawyers, better than diplomats, scientists, or economists, contribute in developing effective regimes?

6. *Contributions of the Stockholm and Rio Conferences to International Regulatory Regimes.* International information-gathering and regulatory regimes may serve as alternatives or supplements to processes designed to hold states responsible for environmental harm. The Stockholm and Rio Confer-

ences, in addition to contributing the declarations excerpted above, also produced new institutions and legal instruments relating to the international environment. The United Nations Environment Programme (UNEP) was established at the Stockholm Conference to coordinate efforts to protect the international environment. UNEP has initiated workshops and multilateral treaty negotiations, leading, for example, to the 1985 Convention for the Protection of the Ozone Layer (considered in Part B) and the 1989 Basel Convention on the Control of Transboundary Movements of Hazardous Wastes and their Disposal. The Rio Earth Summit produced a Framework Convention on Climate Change, a Convention on Biological Diversity, and a statement of principles on forest conservation. The Rio Conference also produced Agenda 21, an approximately 800–page document that sets priorities and details steps for achieving sustainable growth, protecting human health, promoting urban habitability, encouraging efficient resource use, protecting the atmosphere and the oceans, and managing chemicals and hazardous and nuclear wastes.

B. TREATY REGIMES AND PROTECTION OF THE ENVIRONMENT

International environmental problems are often addressed in regulatory regimes. The first excerpt below explores the treaty regime designed to limit the production and consumption of chlorofluorocarbons (CFCs) and other ozone-depleting substances. Scientists have concluded that the release of such substances, which were used in refrigerants, air conditioners, aerosol cans, and fire extinguishers, has resulted in the destruction of ozone in the stratosphere. Ozone in the stratosphere filters out shortwave ultraviolet radiation, so when the amount of ozone diminishes, more ultraviolet radiation reaches the earth. Increased ultraviolet radiation may lead to, among other things, increased incidence of skin cancer, cataracts, suppression of the immune system, stunted crop growth, and a drop in the productivity of phytoplankton, an important marine food source. Scientists first postulated the process of ozone depletion in 1974. Huge losses in the ozone layer over Antarctica were documented in 1985; ozone depletion now affects the middle and high latitudes of both hemispheres as well. The ozone treaty regime adopts a "framework convention-protocol" approach, and uses some other techniques designed to encourage widespread participation in a regime that, in order to be effective, requires near-universal participation.

The second reading in this Part, the *Shrimp-Turtle Case*, decided pursuant to the World Trade Organization's dispute settlement system, illustrates how some treaty regimes not originally designed to address international environmental matters, may still sometimes face them. This case raises questions about how existing non-environmental treaty regimes can accommodate environmental concerns and take account of new international legal developments relating to the environment.

DAVID D. CARON, "PROTECTION OF THE STRATOSPHERIC OZONE LAYER AND THE STRUCTURE OF INTERNATIONAL ENVIRONMENTAL LAWMAKING"

14 *Hastings International and Comparative Law Review* 755 (1991).

II. STRATOSPHERIC OZONE DEPLETION:
THE PROBLEM AND A BRIEF HISTORY OF THE INTERNATIONAL RESPONSE * * *

C. UNEP and the 1985 Vienna Framework Convention

Even as the national debates proceeded, the groundwork for an international approach was laid. The United Nations Environmental Programme (UNEP) in 1977 convened a meeting to begin the international process. The meeting resulted in the adoption of the "World Plan of Action on the Ozone Layer" and the establishment of a Global Coordinating Committee on the Ozone Layer.

* * * In 1981 UNEP established an Ad Hoc Working Group of Legal and Technical Experts charged with the task of drafting a framework convention for the protection of the ozone layer. A framework convention is a document that aims not at substantive norms, but rather at establishment of the institutional framework that will result in such norms. * * * [S]everal * * * drafts were produced prior to the Vienna Conference in March 1985, which ultimately adopted a framework convention.

Adoption of the Vienna Convention was bittersweet, however, because several states had sought more from the Conference. * * * Ultimately a compromise was reached in the form of a Resolution of the Conference calling for the states to reassemble for the purpose of concluding a protocol regulating CFCs.

D. A Growing Sense of Urgency and the 1987 Montreal Protocol

Even as work proceeded in anticipation of a second meeting to adopt a protocol, two important trends were occurring. First, a British research group in May 1985 announced that huge losses in Antarctic ozone had occurred in the springs of 1982, 1983, and 1984. By late summer 1985 American satellite measurements, free of certain previous interpretational errors, confirmed the British findings. * * * [T]he Antarctic hole was significant because, even before the scientific community could confirm that chlorine was responsible for the hole, the public had what in its view was tangible and comprehensible evidence that humanity could fundamentally alter the Earth's atmosphere. As the public increasingly voiced its concern, the states participating in the international negotiations became increasingly receptive not only to a ban on aerosol use, but, more generally, to across the board phased reductions in CFC and halon consumption and production.

The second trend also facilitated the inclination to adopt across the board phased reductions. Specifically, the major producers of CFCs had come to believe that environmentally safe substitutes for CFSs existed, and that it was for each of them in their individual interest to be the first to develop and offer such substitutes. Although it was thought that such substitutes would be several times more expensive than CFCs, it was also thought that there would be a market for them in a world that called for limits on the use of CFCs. Simultaneously, numerous large users of CFCs moved to eliminate their reliance on such substances.

For these reasons, the Montreal meeting was quite different from the one held only two years earlier in Vienna in that virtually all of the interested parties were now in agreement that some amount of phased reductions was appropriate. Thus, even though the final report of the international study of the Antarctic hole was not yet released, a Protocol to the Vienna Convention calling for a 50 percent reduction in the production and consumption of specified CFCs over an approximately ten year period was adopted in Montreal in September 1987.

E. The Antarctic Ozone Hole and the Race to 1990 London Adjustments and Amendments

But even as states adopted the Montreal Protocol in September 1987, two major concerns were present regarding the instrument. First, the startling findings regarding the Antarctic ozone hole, officially confirmed only after the meeting in Montreal, had not been taken fully into account in the Protocol. The negotiators were frustrated by their apparent inability to draft regimes that kept up with the revelations emerging from the scientific community. They had taken a step forward in Montreal, but they felt that they were always two steps behind in their own understanding of the problem, and at least two steps behind in their response to the problem. Thus, there was a widespread feeling that the Protocol was inadequate and would require revision.

Second, the early indications by China and India, representing over one-third of humanity, that they would not become parties to the Protocol because of its failure to provide adequate assistance to developing countries, suggested that the international community might not be sufficiently cohesive to comprehensively regulate the matter. * * * It was apparent that any regime relating to protection of the ozone layer must include highly populated states, whether or not they presently were significant consumers or producers of ozone-depleting substances. This development was particularly important because it marked one of the few times that the industrialized world needed the cooperation and participation of the Third World. This need allowed the Third World to raise development and international equity concerns they believed had been unaddressed for too long.

As to the adequacy of the Montreal Protocol, planning for its adjustment and amendment began almost immediately. The political focus on the global environment in general, and on the protection of the ozone layer in particular, was intense from the 1987 Montreal Conference of Parties to the 1990 London Meeting of the Parties to the Montreal Protocol. Of particular importance at this time, although less publicly dramatic than the Antarctic ozone hole, was the release of a study by the U.S. Environmental Protection Agency asserting that even assuming 100 percent global participation in the Protocol, the presence of chlorine in the stratosphere would, by the year 2075, increase by a factor of three.

Amidst these new revelations, the entry into force of the Montreal Protocol on January 1, 1989, was anticlimactic and hardly noticed. At that time, one nation after another was calling for swifter and deeper cuts in the production and consumption of ozone-depleting substances, and in some cases unilaterally adopting such measures. By the opening of the London Meeting in June 1990, the negotiating parties were in agreement not merely on accelerating the phased reductions, but on phasing out entirely the substances specified by the Montreal Protocol. The primary issue was whether this phase out should be accomplished by the year 1997 or the year 2000, the latter representing the adjustment ultimately made to the Montreal schedules. Simultaneously, evolving scientific knowledge regarding the threat posed by other substances led to the consensus to amend the Protocol so that it would require phase outs of other fully halogenated CFCs and carbon tetrachloride by the year 2000, and a phaseout of methyl chloroform by the year 2005. Increased understanding that the substitutes thought to exist at the time of the Montreal Protocol might also be ozone-depleting and significant contributors to the greenhouse effect, resulted in the designation of these substitutes as "transitional ozone-depleting substances," and in the conclusion that the transitional substances should be phased out by the year 2040, or, if possible, by the year 2020.

The apparent willingness of nonparticipating countries such as China and India to operate outside of what they perceived to be an unjust regime, was pitted against the reluctance of some developed countries such as the United States, to construct new international structures, to recognize a right of such countries to assistance and technology transfer, and to encourage linkages between participation in regimes like the Protocol and recognition of the special situation of developing countries. This reluctance was particularly strong since, at this same time, the developing world was making analogous demands for a global climate change fund. * * * Ultimately, the London meeting adopted amendments to the Protocol that provided for technology transfer, and established a fund under the supervision of a fourteen member committee drawn from the developed and developing world. At the conclusion of the London Meeting, the representatives of China and India indicated their countries would sign the Protocol in 1992. * * *

F. The Task Ahead

* * * Although the list of controlled substances has been increased and, for the most part, total phaseouts have been called for, an observer group at the London Meeting noted that the phaseout periods—generally

of ten years—will allow the production of another 17 million tons of ozone-depleting substances. Such arguments arise amidst continued findings by the scientific community that the ozone layer continues to deteriorate over Antarctica, the Arctic, and generally, and increasing evidence that the same substances that deplete ozone are major contributors to global warming. * * *

III. A Restatement of the Regime

A. *The Organization of the Regime*

There are two main strands to the international organizational scheme created by the Vienna Convention and the Montreal Protocol, as amended and adjusted. First, there are state parties (to the Convention, to the Protocol, and to the Protocol as amended) who meet on a regular basis and who in smaller groups meet more regularly for particular tasks. Second, there is a Secretariat which fulfills a number of duties, occasionally through ad hoc working groups, assigned to it by the state parties in the Convention and Protocol.

* * * Inasmuch as a party to the [Montreal] Protocol or the Protocol as amended must also be a party to the Convention, the parties to the Protocol or the Protocol as amended are subgroups of the "Conference of the Parties" to the Convention.

* * * [O]nly Parties to the Protocol, and not those who are solely members of the Conference of the Parties to the Convention, can vote on amendments to the Protocol. Similarly, membership on the Executive Committee, which is responsible for the Multilateral Fund established by the London Amendments to the Protocol is limited to Parties to the Protocol as amended. * * *

Finally, the organizational structure created by the Convention and Protocol necessarily has extensive relations with two other organizational clusters. First, in order to provide a better foundation for the timely making of policy, there are relations with the public international scientific community (namely, the World Meteorological Organization and the World Health Organization), leading national scientific agencies, and private international scientific organizations. Second, in order to provide financial and technical assistance, there are relations with organizations such as the World Bank.

B. *The Lawmaking Process*

A number of innovative steps in lawmaking are contained in the Montreal Protocol. * * *

The Protocol anticipates that continued revision may be necessary, and calls for the Parties periodically to assess the adequacy of the measures taken in the Protocol. The Protocol provides that the parties, on the basis of such an assessment, may decide to adjust the reductions called for in the controlled substances, and if the parties are unable to reach agreement on such adjustments, two-thirds majority adoption of adjustments shall be binding upon all Parties to the Protocol. Thus, the

Parties to the Protocol have limited legislative power in this area with an objector's recourse being withdrawal generally from the Protocol. Some of the actions taken at the London Meeting were adjustments.

In contrast to this legislative-like adjustment process, there is also the more commonly encountered amendment process that becomes binding only upon those states who accept such amendments. In this regard, it is particularly important to see that although the parties may make adjustments to the controlled substances already designated, they cannot use an adjustment to designate a new controlled substance. As a consequence, the actions taken at the London Meeting were in part also amendments. Many of the amendments relate to the creation of a financial mechanism, but many others relate to the addition of new controlled substances. The crucial implication, however, is that since amendments must be consented to in order to have application to any particular party, a confusing array of regimes may arise.

C. The Normative Scheme

1. The Obligation to Phase Out Designated Ozone–Depleting Chemicals

The basic regulatory approach of the Montreal Protocol in 1987 was to require the Parties to the Protocol to reduce their production and consumption of five chlorofluorocarbons * * * and three halons * * *. The London Adjustments to the Protocol accelerated this timetable and deepened the cuts by requiring the parties to phase out production and consumption entirely by the year 2000. * * *

The London Amendments to the Protocol added new chemicals to the regulatory scheme * * *. * * *

* * * [T]he scheduled reductions, leading ultimately to phaseouts, are expressed in terms of percentages of calculated national levels of consumption and production in either 1986, in the case of the substances originally regulated by the Protocol, or in 1989, for the substances added to the scope of the Protocol by the London Amendments. * * *

The use of national calculated levels is * * * significant because it inherently gives value to historical usage and avoids the difficult issue of equitably allocating between states a limited resource, the right to emit ozone-depleting substances. Thus, the United States could be viewed as particularly advantaged under the Montreal Protocol since a fifty percent reduction in its production and consumption would still leave it with a disproportionate per capita share of such use. This significance of course diminished greatly when the Protocol was adjusted and amended so as to require phaseouts rather than mere reductions. * * *

2. Recognition of the Special Situation of Developing Countries

The special situation of certain developing countries is recognized through the possibility of a delayed phaseout schedule for such countries. These special provisions apply to any party "that is a developing country and whose annual calculated level of consumption ... is less than 0.3 kilograms per capita...." The delay works in two ways. First, these parties are allowed to exceed the target percentage reduction at any point in the schedule by a specified percentage of their initial calculated level if such action is necessary in order to satisfy "basic domestic needs." Second, such developing countries, in order to meet basic domestic needs, also are entitled to delay at every point their compliance with the schedule of reductions leading to phase outs by a period of ten years.

3. The Resolution of States to Act Beyond the Requirements of the Protocol as Adjusted and Amended

It is important to recognize that the reduction schedule set forth in the Protocol as adjusted and amended represents only the baseline. A number of states have accepted greater obligations, and the Protocol urges the parties to act with greater dispatch when possible. * * *

D. Encouraging Participation and Facilitating Implementation

From the beginning, it was recognized that the shared nature of the ozone-depletion problem required widespread participation in the regime to be established by the Convention and Protocol. Encouragement of participation by developing countries, in particular India and China, required mechanisms to aid implementation of the regime by those countries. Thus, encouragement of participation and facilitation of implementation were and remain linked.

The regime encourages participation in a number of ways. First, because the reduction schedules are tied to either 1986 or 1989 levels of consumption and production, there is no advantage to waiting to join the regime. Second, although the parties to the regime during the phaseout periods may trade the controlled substances with one another, the Protocol, as adjusted and amended, progressively restricts trade involving controlled substances between parties and nonparties. Thus, for example, by January 1, 1993, the parties, having agreed upon a list of products containing the controlled substances specified in the Montreal Protocol, shall bar the import of those products from any state not party to the Protocol.

Third, the Protocol not only attempts to limit the advantages of remaining outside, but for developing countries, also provides incentives to join. * * * In response to the positions of India and China in particular, more specific and detailed provisions for financial assistance and technology transfer were adopted at the London Meeting.

E. Noncompliance, Enforcement, and Dispute Settlement

Thus far, the Parties to the Convention and the Protocol have been concerned primarily with elaboration of and formal participation in the regime. As a result, enforcement procedures at this point are not particularly developed.

The key monitoring and enforcement device at present is the requirement for parties to provide to the Secretariat statistics on production, on imports and exports to parties and nonparties, and on amounts destroyed or recycled as feedstocks. Such reports will aid Secretariat and party monitoring, and will also further nongovernmental organization involvement since such data is not regarded as confidential. Unfortunately, not all parties have made such reports, or have submitted incomplete reports. The London meeting of the parties, noting these reporting difficulties, established an ad hoc group of experts to consider the reasons for the difficulties and to recommend solutions.

Investigatory and dispute settlement provisions are quite limited. The Convention, with application to the Protocol, provides that in the event of a dispute concerning interpretation or application of a provision, the parties (1) shall negotiate; (2) failing that, seek the good offices of, or request mediation by, a third party; and (3) failing that, submit the dispute to conciliation. The parties, in accepting the Convention also may declare that they accept as a means of dispute settlement either arbitration or submission to the International Court of Justice, or both. Against that backdrop, the Parties to the Protocol have been considering procedures and institutional mechanisms for determining noncompliance and for treatment of parties found to be in noncompliance. Interim noncompliance provisions adopted at the London Meeting essentially provide for parties with reservations regarding implementation by other parties to report such concerns in writing to the Secretariat. The Secretariat shall transmit the submission to a Implementation Committee established by these same interim procedures, and that Committee shall consider the record with a view to securing an amicable resolution. The Committee shall report on its work to the Meeting of the Parties and the parties "may . . . decide upon and call for steps to bring about full compliance . . . including measures to assist the Party's compliance. . . ."

IV. THE EVOLVING STRUCTURE OF INTERNATIONAL ENVIRONMENTAL LAWMAKING

Reflection on the international effort to protect the stratospheric ozone layer illuminates the emerging structure of international environmental lawmaking. * * *

A. *Lawmaking Amidst Uncertainty: The Process as the Solution * * ***

In the case of stratospheric ozone depletion, the international community initially confronted great debate as to whether there was a problem at all, followed by debate regarding the extent of the problem. * * * [T]he nature of many environmental problems requires action by the relevant community before it has proof of the theory. In other words, the international community, despite uncertainty about the theory, must act to confront the danger indicated by the theory. Moreover, it must act knowing that its knowledge will continue to evolve and suggest further actions. These aspects of uncertainty and evolving knowledge lead to two major differences in international environmental lawmaking efforts from lawmaking efforts generally. Both of these differences evidence an emphasis on an ongoing process of lawmaking rather than, as ordinarily the case, the one time negotiation of a treaty at a particular conference.

The first difference is the explicit incorporation of scientific inquiry into the lawmaking process. Dealing with the uncertainty necessarily present in environmental problems requires that the process not only increase the shared knowledge of the parties, but that such knowledge also accurately reflect the state of scientific understanding of the problem. This requires much greater cooperation between the lawmaking community attempting to draft a response and the scientific community seeking to understand the phenomena. Imbedding this scientific effort in an international organizational structure or in international efforts that coordinate national efforts increases the perceived legitimacy, and hence shared nature, of the resulting description of the problem. Making the scientific inquiry an integral part of an ongoing lawmaking process serves both to educate the lawmakers and to speed up the incorporation of such knowledge into the process. In the case of the ozone regime, the Protocol institutionalizes this cooperation by requiring the convening of "appropriate panels of experts" (scientific, environmental, technical, and economic) at least one year before the parties meet to reassess the sufficiency of the Protocol's controls on ozone-depleting substances.

The second major difference is that the lawmaking effort that accommodates evolving knowledge through the establishment of an ongoing process of lawmaking continuously incorporates new knowledge and revises previous responses. In this sense, the Protocol calls for the parties to periodically "assess the control measures provided for in Article 2 on the basis of available scientific, environmental, technical, and economic information." Thus, we see a transition from a one-conference effort to an ongoing process, and from "two steps behind" to action on the basis of evolving knowledge. In this sense, cooperation and education are recognized as important aspects of the lawmaking process in the environmental area. For all these reasons, the solution to a threat such as ozone depletion is not the particular requirements of the Montreal Protocol or the London Adjustments and Amendments to the Protocol. Rather, the solution is the process which yielded the Protocol and which already looks ahead to the next adjustments and amendments.

B. *Consensual Lawmaking on Transcendent Problems*

International environmental lawmaking is also distinct in that the nature of many environmental problems requires that at least those countries primarily contributing, or potentially contributing, to the problem participate in the regime. * * *

In encouraging participation, the tools of the lawmaker are sticks and carrots. In other words, states either may be penalized for not joining the regime or rewarded for doing so. In the ozone protection regime, developing countries were encouraged to join through the recognition of their special needs. Moreover, although there are no sticks per se, the treaty does attempt to prevent those who remain outside from benefitting by doing so. First, there is no advantage in waiting to join the treaty since the baseline calculation from which reductions are to be made is fixed. Second, there is no trade advantage in remaining outside the convention since it restricts members from trading in areas involving the regulated substances with those outside the regime.

The more subtle implication of needing widespread participation, as discussed above, was the demand by China, India, and others for a linkage between their agreement to participate in the regime and satisfaction of other concerns, particularly, development assistance for the Third World. In the case of stratospheric ozone protection, linkage ultimately was made in the London amendments. The amendments provide for technology transfer and establish a fund to aid implementation of the Protocol by facilitating nonozone-depleting paths for growth in developing countries. * * *

C.   The Tension Between Manageability of Negotiations and Systemic Thinking

One of the first lessons of environmental studies is the need to approach the environment as a system, an indivisible process. The lawmaker, however, cannot approach the development of an environmentally sound relationship between humanity and the world all at once. Rather, negotiations must be limited so that the number of issues and interests involved remain at a manageable level. The danger with the slicing off of what appears to be a somewhat separable and manageable problem, however, is that systemic thinking may be lost. The question thus becomes how to best reconcile the need for manageable negotiations with the need for holistic thinking.

Notes and Questions

1. *The Framework Convention–Protocol Approach.* The Vienna Convention on Substances that Deplete the Ozone Layer, Mar. 22, 1985, 26 I.L.M. 1529 (1987), and its 1987 Montreal Protocol exemplify a framework convention-protocol approach to regulating behavior affecting the environment. What are the advantages and disadvantages of such an approach compared to negotiating a single comprehensive convention? As of November 1, 2000, 176 states had ratified the Vienna Convention and 175 the Montreal Protocol. In addition, 146 states had accepted the 1990 London Amendment to the Montreal Protocol, June 29, 1990, 30 I.L.M. 537 (1991). Additional amendments to the Montreal Protocol were adopted in Copenhagen in November 1992, 32 I.L.M. 874 (1993), in Montreal in 1997, and in Beijing in 1999. Is the ozone regime's distinction between "adjustments" and "amendments" sensible? Would it be desirable to increase the scope of the decisions that parties to the Montreal Protocol can, by majority or supermajority vote, make binding on all parties? See Geoffrey Palmer, "New Ways to Make International Environmental Law," 86 *American Journal of International Law* 259 (1992).

2. *Environmental Lawmaking in Areas of Scientific Uncertainty.* With respect to many issues—such as global warming—scientific evidence of the extent, rate, or effects of environmental degradation is not so clear as it was with respect to the ozone hole. How should states make use of scientists and

equivocal scientific evidence? This issue was addressed in general terms in Principle 15 of the Rio Declaration, which sets out one version of the "precautionary principle." Would any variation in the framework convention-protocol approach better take account of uncertain scientific evidence?

3. *Encouraging Widespread Participation in the Ozone Regime.* Note the various incentives that the Vienna Convention and the Montreal Protocol provide to encourage participation by many states. What other techniques could be used to prevent states from becoming "free riders," benefitting from widespread implementation of the Convention, the Protocol, and various amendments and adjustments without themselves becoming parties?

4. *Developing States and the Ozone Regime.* What is the nature of the "special status" accorded developing states in the ozone regime? What practical and conceptual arguments support differentiated responsibilities for developing states? Recall Principle 7 of the Rio Declaration, and see Duncan French, "Developing States and International Environmental Law: The Importance of Differentiated Responsibilities," 49 *International and Comparative Law Quarterly* 35 (2000).

Some 1990 amendments to the Montreal Protocol reflect the concerns of developing states. For example, states agreed to establish a Multilateral Fund, to be funded by developed states. Developing states that submit a detailed program for reducing their production and consumption of ozone-depleting substances may receive grants and technical assistance to help them switch to safer substances and technologies. The Fund is administered by an Executive Committee on which developing and developed states are equally represented. London Amendment, 30 I.L.M. at 549–51. Establishing this Fund helped persuade China and India to accept the Vienna Convention and the Montreal Protocol. Since its inception, 32 industrialized states have contributed over $1 billion to the Fund. See <http://www.unmfs.org>.

5. *A Liability Regime?* Would it be equitable to require that developing states be compensated for damage caused by CFC emissions, in accordance with the "polluter pays" principle (see Principle 16 of the Rio Declaration)? More generally, should there be an international liability regime to provide compensation for damage caused by the release of CFCs and other harmful substances into the environment, either in addition to or in place of the Vienna Convention/Montreal Protocol system? Some international environmental treaties require that states impose liability—even strict liability—on private entities that cause harm, with states becoming liable in the event a private entity cannot pay. See International Convention for Civil Liability for Oil Pollution Damage, Nov. 29, 1969, 9 I.L.M. 45 (1970); Vienna Convention on Civil Liability for Nuclear Damage, May 21, 1963, 2 I.L.M. 727 (1963).

6. *The Role of Intergovernmental Organizations.* How well could the ozone regime function if the only entities involved were states? Note the range of roles that intergovernmental organizations play in the ozone regime. UNEP helped in negotiating the regime, and the United Nations and its specialized agencies participate as observers at meetings of the Conference of the Parties. Vienna Convention, art. 6(5), 26 I.L.M. at 1532. As Professor Caron noted, there are links with international scientific organizations such as the World Health Organization and international financial

organizations such as the World Bank. The Vienna Convention itself creates an institution, the Secretariat, which is headquartered at UNEP offices in Nairobi, Kenya, and carries out various duties specified in the Vienna Convention and the Montreal Protocol. These duties include arranging meetings of parties, arranging for the implementation of decisions reached at meetings, monitoring and reporting on implementation of the Convention and Protocol, providing information, and analyzing data. See <http://www.unep.ch/ozone>. The Multilateral Fund (see Note 4 above) also is administered under the UNEP umbrella.

7. *The Role of Nongovernmental Organizations.* Nongovernmental organizations have provided scientific advice and gathered information important in the negotiation of environmental treaties. What other roles do and should NGOs play with regard to international environmental treaties? Article 6(5) of the Vienna Convention allows NGOs "qualified in fields relating to the protection of the ozone layer" to sit as observers at a meeting of the Conference of the Parties "unless at least one-third of the Parties present object." 26 I.L.M. at 1532. NGOs can also obtain reports that are submitted to an Implementation Committee (see Note 8 below), allowing them to monitor states' compliance with the ozone regime. For more on NGOs, see Chapter 8.

8. *Encouraging Compliance with the Ozone Regime.* What mechanisms should be used to promote compliance with the Montreal Protocol to the Vienna Convention? In addition to providing for dispute settlement mechanisms, states have now implemented a non-compliance procedure. See Copenhagen Amendments, Annex IV, 32 I.L.M. 874 (1995). As David Hunter, James Salzman, and Durwood Zaelke have written, the non-compliance procedure "facilitates compliance by encouraging Parties to self-police themselves. By coming to the Implementation Committee, Parties can ask for assistance from other parties. Facilitating compliance as opposed to mandating it through sanctions is a growing trend in international environmental law." *International Environmental Law and Policy* 586 (1998). Should the ozone regime instead emphasize sanctions? Or should an institutional monitoring system be mandated, in order to determine instances of non-compliance? Monitoring was discussed at the 1990 London conference, but was not implemented.

9. *Efforts to Build Other Multilateral Environmental Regimes.* As evidence of global warming became increasingly clear during the 1990s, states and NGOs proceeded to fashion an international legal regime to address that problem. A Framework Convention on Climate Change, May 9, 1992, 31 I.L.M. 849 (1992), which was signed by over 150 states, was followed by periodic meetings of the Framework Convention's Conference of the Parties, which has reviewed implementation of states' commitments in the Framework Convention, facilitated cooperative measures, and spurred scientific assessment of climate change. One product of the Conference of the Parties was the Kyoto Protocol, Dec. 10, 1997, 37 I.L.M. 22 (1998), which contemplates a complicated regime, potentially involving emissions trading, to limit greenhouse gases. For an overview of the Kyoto Protocol, see Clare Breidenich et al., "The Kyoto Protocol to the United Nations Framework Convention on Climate Change," 92 *American Journal of International Law* 315 (1998), and for discussion of the role of conferences of the parties in this

and other environmental regimes, see Robin R. Churchill & Geir Ulfstein, "Autonomous Institutional Arrangements in Multilateral Environmental Agreements: A Little–Noticed Phenomenon in International Law," 94 *American Journal of International Law* 623 (2000). Optimism about the success of a legal solution respecting global climate change may be premature: agreement on the precise details necessary for an operational climate change regime has been difficult, and prospects for acceptance of the regime in many states remain uncertain. See "Hotting up in The Hague," *The Economist*, Nov. 18, 2000, at 81.

What factors are likely to contribute to the success of efforts to build regimes to remedy an environmental problem? For example, is a regime more likely if there is some clear environmental crisis, such as the Chernobyl nuclear catastrophe or the ozone hole, rather than gradual degradation, as many argue is happening with global warming? Are the internal dynamics among entities at treaty-making conferences, and at subsequent meetings of treaty parties, more relevant to understanding the content and efficacy of international environmental regimes than are external factors? See Thomas Gehring, "International Environmental Regimes: Dynamic Sectoral Legal Systems," 1 *Yearbook of International Environmental Law* 35 (1990); Oran R. Young, "The Politics of International Regime Formation: Managing Natural Resources and the Environment," 43 *International Organization* 349 (1989).

10. *A Comprehensive Environmental Treaty?* Threats to the environment are interrelated. For example, as Professor Caron noted, certain substitutes for CFCs are also greenhouse gases that may contribute to global warming. More broadly, atmospheric pollution affects the oceans and land resources, which in turn affect the atmosphere. As we see in Chapter 11, virtually all issues relating to the oceans were addressed in a comprehensive U.N. Conference on the Law of the Sea, which led to the now widely accepted 1982 Convention on the Law of the Sea. Should a comprehensive treaty-making conference be convened to address all issues relating to the use and pollution of the atmosphere?

THE SHRIMP–TURTLE CASE

United States–Import Prohibition of Certain Shrimp and Shrimp Products,
World Trade Organization, Report of the Appellate Body, AB–1998–4 (1998),
38 *International Legal Materials* 121 (1999).

[The United States, in section 609 of Public Law 101–162 (1997), imposed an import ban on shrimp harvested in ways that could damage sea turtles. A harvesting state could receive an annual certification allowing imports if it could show either (a) that its shrimp harvesting environment posed no threat to the incidental taking of sea turtles, or (b) that the harvesting state required Turtle Exclusion Devices (TEDs) comparable in effectiveness to those required to be used in the United States. Several states—India, Pakistan, Thailand, Malaysia, Australia, Ecuador, the European Communities, Hong Kong, and Nigeria—claimed that the U.S. policy was an illegal restraint on trade that violated the General Agreement on Tariffs and Trade (GATT), and challenged the policy before a panel established under the 1994 GATT/World Trade Organization (WTO) Dispute Settlement Understanding. The panel decided that the U.S. program violated Article XI(1) of GATT 1994, which prohibits quantitative barriers to trade, and was not justified under exceptions contained in Article XX. The United States appealed to the WTO's Appellate Body, a permanent quasi-judicial body composed of seven members broadly representing WTO membership. The U.S. appeal focused on Article XX.]

IV. ISSUES RAISED IN THIS APPEAL

1. The issues raised in this appeal by the appellant, the United States, are the following: * * *

(b) whether the Panel erred in finding that the measure at issue constitutes unjustifiable discrimination between countries where the same conditions prevail and thus is not within the scope of measures permitted under Article XX of the GATT 1994. * * *

VI. APPRAISING SECTION 609 UNDER ARTICLE XX OF THE GATT 1994 * * *

A. *The Panel's Findings and Interpretative Analysis* * * *

113. Article XX of the GATT 1994 reads, in its relevant parts:

ARTICLE XX

General Exceptions

Subject to the requirement that such measures are not applied in a manner which would constitute a means of arbitrary or unjustifiable discrimination between countries where the same conditions prevail, or a disguised restriction on international trade, nothing in this Agreement shall be construed to prevent the adoption or enforcement by any Member of measures: ...

(b) necessary to protect human, animal or plant life or health; ...

(g) relating to the conservation of exhaustible natural resources if such measures are made effective in conjunction with restrictions on domestic production or consumption; * * *.

116. * * * Maintaining, rather than undermining, the multilateral trading system is necessarily a fundamental and pervasive premise underlying the *WTO Agreement*; but it is not a right or an obligation, nor is it an interpretative rule which can be employed in the appraisal of a given measure under the chapeau of Article XX. * * *

118. In *United States—Gasoline*, we enunciated the appropriate method for applying Article XX of the GATT 1994:

In order that the justifying protection of Article XX may be extended to it, the measure at issue must not only come under one or another of the particular exceptions—paragraphs (a) to (j)—listed under Article XX; it must also satisfy the requirements imposed by the opening clauses of Article XX. *The analysis is*, in other words, *two-*

tiered: first, provisional justification by reason of characterization of the measure under XX(g); second, further appraisal of the same measure under the introductory clauses of Article XX. (emphasis added)

[The Appellate Body concludes that the panel did not follow this methodology.]

B. *Article XX(g): Provisional Justification of Section 609*

125. In claiming justification for its measure, the United States primarily invokes Article XX(g). * * *

1. *"Exhaustible Natural Resources"* * * *

128. * * * Textually, Article XX(g) is not limited to the conservation of "mineral" or "non-living" natural resources. * * * We do not believe that "exhaustible" natural resources and "renewable" natural resources are mutually exclusive. One lesson that modern biological sciences teach us is that living species, though in principle, capable of reproduction and, in that sense, "renewable," are in certain circumstances indeed susceptible of depletion, exhaustion and extinction, frequently because of human activities. Living resources are just as "finite" as petroleum, iron ore and other non-living resources.

129. The words of Article XX(g), "exhaustible natural resources," were actually crafted more than 50 years ago. They must be read by a treaty interpreter in the light of contemporary concerns of the community of nations about the protection and conservation of the environment. While Article XX was not modified in the Uruguay Round, the preamble attached to the *WTO Agreement* shows that the signatories to that Agreement were, in 1994, fully aware of the importance and legitimacy of environmental protection as a goal of national and international policy. The preamble of the *WTO Agreement*—which informs not only the GATT 1994, but also the other covered agreements—explicitly acknowledges "the objective of *sustainable development*"[107] * * *.

130. From the perspective embodied in the preamble of the *WTO Agreement*, we note that the generic term "natural resources" in Article XX(g) is not "static" in its content or reference but is rather "by definition, evolutionary."[109] It is, therefore, pertinent to note that modern international conventions and declarations make frequent references to natural resources as embracing both living and non-living resources. [The Appellate Body reviews various sources that refer to the conserva-

107. This concept has been generally accepted as integrating economic and social development and environmental protection. See e.g., G. Handl, "Sustainable Development: General Rules versus Specific Obligations," in *Sustainable Development and International Law* (ed. W. Lang, 1995), p. 35; World Commission on Environment and Development, *Our Common Future* (Oxford University Press, 1987), p. 43.

109. See *Namibia (Legal Consequences) Advisory Opinion* (1971) I.C.J. Rep., p. 31. The International Court of Justice stated that where concepts embodied in a treaty are "by definition, evolutionary," their "interpretation cannot remain unaffected by the subsequent development of law.... Moreover, an international instrument has to be interpreted and applied within the framework of the entire legal system prevailing at the time of the interpretation."

tion and management of living resources, including the 1982 United Nations Convention on the Law of the Sea, the Convention on Biological Diversity, Agenda 21 adopted at the 1992 Rio Conference, the Resolution on Assistance to Developing Countries adopted in conjunction with the Convention on the Conservation of Migratory Species of Wild Animals, and GATT panel reports.]

131. * * * We hold that * * * measures to conserve exhaustible natural resources, whether *living or non-living*, may fall within Article XX(g).

132. We turn next to the issue of whether the living natural resources sought to be conserved by the measure are "exhaustible" under Article XX(g). That this element is present in respect of the five species of sea turtles here involved appears to be conceded by all the participants and third participants in this case. The exhaustibility of sea turtles would in fact have been very difficult to controvert since all of the seven recognized species of sea turtles are today listed in Appendix 1 of the Convention on International Trade in Endangered Species of Wild Fauna and Flora ("CITES"). The list in Appendix 1 includes "all species *threatened with extinction* which are or may be affected by trade." (emphasis added)

133. Finally, we observe that sea turtles are highly migratory animals, passing in and out of waters subject to the rights of jurisdiction of various coastal states and the high seas. * * * The sea turtle species here at stake, i.e., covered by Section 609, are all known to occur in waters over which the United States exercises jurisdiction. Of course, it is not claimed that *all* populations of these species migrate to, or traverse, at one time or another, waters subject to United States jurisdiction. Neither the appellant nor any of the appellees claims any rights of exclusive ownership over the sea turtles, at least not while they are swimming freely in their natural habitat—the oceans. We do not pass upon the question of whether there is an implied jurisdictional limitation in Article XX(g), and if so, the nature or extent of that limitation. We note only that in the specific circumstances of the case before us, there is a sufficient nexus between the migratory and endangered marine populations involved and the United States for purposes of Article XX(g).

134. For all the foregoing reasons, we find that the sea turtles here involved constitute "exhaustible natural resources" for purposes of Article XX(g) of the GATT 1994.

2. *"Relating to the Conservation of [Exhaustible Natural Resources]"*

135. Article XX(g) requires that the measure sought to be justified be one which "relat[es] to" the conservation of exhaustible natural resources. * * *

137. In the present case, we must examine the relationship between the general structure and design of the measure here at stake,

Section 609, and the policy goal it purports to serve, that is, the conservation of sea turtles. * * *

142. In our view, * * * Section 609 is a measure "relating to" the conservation of an exhaustible natural resource within the meaning of Article XX(g) of the GATT 1994.

3. *"If Such Measures are Made Effective in conjunction with Restrictions on Domestic Production or Consumption"* * * *

144. * * * [U.S. regulations] require United States shrimp trawlers to use approved TEDs "in areas and at times when there is a likelihood of intercepting sea turtles," with certain limited exceptions. Penalties for violation of the Endangered Species Act, or the regulations issued thereunder, include civil and criminal sanctions. The United States government currently relies on monetary sanctions and civil penalties for enforcement. The government has the ability to seize shrimp catch from trawl vessels fishing in United States waters and has done so in cases of egregious violations. We believe that, in principle, Section 609 is an even-handed measure.

145. Accordingly, we hold that Section 609 is a measure made effective in conjunction with the restrictions on domestic harvesting of shrimp, as required by Article XX(g).

C. *The Introductory Clauses of Article XX: Characterizing Section 609 under the Chapeau's Standards* * * *

147. Although provisionally justified under Article XX(g), Section 609, if it is ultimately to be justified as an exception under Article XX, must also satisfy the requirements of the introductory clauses—the "chapeau"—of Article XX, that is,

ARTICLE XX

General Exceptions

Subject to the requirement that such measures are *not applied in a manner which would constitute a means of arbitrary or unjustifiable discrimination between countries where the same conditions prevail, or a disguised restriction on international trade*, nothing in this Agreement shall be construed to prevent the adoption or enforcement by any Member of measures: (emphasis added)

We turn, hence, to the task of appraising Section 609, and specifically the manner in which it is applied under the chapeau of Article XX; that is, to the second part of the two-tier analysis required under Article XX.

1. *General Considerations* * * *

155. * * * Pending any specific recommendations by the [WTO's Committee on Trade and Environment] to WTO Members on the issues raised in its terms of reference, and in the absence up to now of any agreed amendments or modifications to the substantive provisions of the GATT 1994 and the *WTO Agreement* generally, we must fulfill our responsibility in this specific case, which is to interpret the existing

language of the chapeau of Article XX by examining its ordinary meaning, in light of its context and object and purpose in order to determine whether the United States measure at issue qualifies for justification under Article XX. It is proper for us to take into account, as part of the context of the chapeau, the specific language of the preamble to the *WTO Agreement*, which [recognizes the objective of sustainable development and] gives colour, texture and shading to the rights and obligations of Members under the *WTO Agreement*, generally, and under GATT 1994, in particular.

156.   * * * [T]he chapeau of Article XX * * * embodies the recognition on the part of WTO Members of the need to maintain a balance of rights and obligations between the right of a Member to invoke one or another of the exceptions of Article XX, specified in paragraphs (a) to (j), on the one hand, and the substantive rights of the other Members under the GATT 1994, on the other hand. * * * [A] balance must be struck between the *right* of a Member to invoke an exception under Article XX and the *duty* of that same Member to respect the treaty rights of the other Members. To permit one Member to abuse or misuse its right to invoke an exception would be effectively to allow that Member to degrade its own treaty obligations as well as to devalue the treaty rights of other Members. If the abuse or misuse is sufficiently grave or extensive, the Member, in effect, reduces its treaty obligation to a merely facultative one and dissolves its juridical character, and, in so doing, negates altogether the treaty rights of other Members. The chapeau was installed at the head of the list of "General Exceptions" in Article XX to prevent such far-reaching consequences.

157.   In our view, the language of the chapeau makes clear that each of the exceptions in paragraphs (a) to (j) of Article XX is a *limited and conditional* exception from the substantive obligations contained in the other provisions of the GATT 1994, that is to say, the ultimate availability of the exception is subject to the compliance by the invoking Member with the requirements of the chapeau. This interpretation of the chapeau is confirmed by its negotiating history. * * *

158.   The chapeau of Article XX is, in fact, but one expression of the principle of good faith. * * * One application of this general principle, the application widely known as the doctrine of *abus de droit*, prohibits the abusive exercise of a state's rights and enjoins that whenever the assertion of a right "impinges on the field covered by [a] treaty obligation, it must be exercised bona fide, that is to say, reasonably."
* * *

159.   The task of interpreting and applying the chapeau is, hence, essentially the delicate one of locating and marking out a line of equilibrium between the right of a Member to invoke an exception under Article XX and the rights of the other Members under varying substantive provisions (e.g., Article XI) of the GATT 1994, so that neither of the competing rights will cancel out the other and thereby distort and nullify or impair the balance of rights and obligations constructed by the

Members themselves in that Agreement. The location of the line of equilibrium, as expressed in the chapeau, is not fixed and unchanging; the line moves as the kind and the shape of the measures at stake vary and as the facts making up specific cases differ.

160. With these general considerations in mind, we address now the issue of whether the *application* of the United States measure, although the measure itself falls within the terms of Article XX(g), nevertheless constitutes "a means of arbitrary or unjustifiable discrimination between countries where the same conditions prevail" or "a disguised restriction on international trade." We address, in other words, whether the application of this measure constitutes an abuse or misuse of the provisional justification made available by Article XX(g). We note, preliminarily, that the application of a measure may be characterized as amounting to an abuse or misuse of an exception of Article XX not only when the detailed operating provisions of the measure prescribe the arbitrary or unjustifiable activity, but also where a measure, otherwise fair and just on its face, is actually applied in an arbitrary or unjustifiable manner. The standards of the chapeau, in our view, project both substantive and procedural requirements.

2. *"Unjustifiable Discrimination"*

161. We scrutinize first whether Section 609 has been applied in a manner constituting "unjustifiable discrimination between countries where the same conditions prevail." Perhaps the most conspicuous flaw in this measure's application relates to its intended and actual coercive effect on the specific policy decisions made by foreign governments, Members of the WTO. * * *

163. The actual *application* of the measure, through the implementation of the 1996 Guidelines and the regulatory practice of administrators, *requires* other WTO Members to adopt a regulatory program that is not merely *comparable*, but rather *essentially the same*, as that applied to the United States shrimp trawl vessels. Thus, the effect of the application of Section 609 is to establish a rigid and unbending standard by which United States officials determine whether or not countries will be certified, thus granting or refusing other countries the right to export shrimp to the United States. Other specific policies and measures that an exporting country may have adopted for the protection and conservation of sea turtles are not taken into account, in practice, by the administrators making the comparability determination.

164. We understand that the United States also applies a uniform standard throughout its territory, regardless of the particular conditions existing in certain parts of the country. * * * However, it is not acceptable, in international trade relations, for one WTO Member to use an economic embargo to *require* other Members to adopt essentially the same comprehensive regulatory program, to achieve a certain policy goal, as that in force within that Member's territory, *without* taking into consideration different conditions which may occur in the territories of those other Members.

165. Furthermore, when this dispute was before the Panel and before us, the United States did not permit imports of shrimp harvested by commercial shrimp trawl vessels using TEDs comparable in effectiveness to those required in the United States if those shrimp originated in waters of countries not certified under Section 609. In other words, *shrimp caught using methods identical to those employed in the United States* have been excluded from the United States market solely because they have been caught in waters of *countries that have not been certified by the United States.* The resulting situation is difficult to reconcile with the declared policy objective of protecting and conserving sea turtles. This suggests to us that this measure, in its application, is more concerned with effectively influencing WTO Members to adopt essentially the same comprehensive regulatory regime as that applied by the United States to its domestic shrimp trawlers, even though many of those Members may be differently situated. We believe that discrimination results not only when countries in which the same conditions prevail are differently treated, but also when the application of the measure at issue does not allow for any inquiry into the appropriateness of the regulatory program for the conditions prevailing in those exporting countries.

166. Another aspect of the application of Section 609 that bears heavily in any appraisal of justifiable or unjustifiable discrimination is the failure of the United States to engage the appellees, as well as other Members exporting shrimp to the United States, in serious, across-the-board negotiations with the objective of concluding bilateral or multilateral agreements for the protection and conservation of sea turtles, before enforcing the import prohibition against the shrimp exports of those other Members. * * *

167. * * * First, * * * [a]part from the negotiation of the Inter–American Convention for the Protection and Conservation of Sea Turtles (the "Inter–American Convention") which concluded in 1996, the record before the Panel does not indicate any serious, substantial efforts to carry out [the] express directions of Congress [to initiate negotiations with other states to develop treaties protecting sea turtles].

168. Second, the protection and conservation of highly migratory species of sea turtles, that is, the very policy objective of the measure, demands concerted and cooperative efforts on the part of the many countries whose waters are traversed in the course of recurrent sea turtle migrations. The need for, and the appropriateness of, such efforts have been recognized in the WTO itself as well as in a significant number of other international instruments and declarations. * * * Of particular relevance is Principle 12 of the Rio Declaration on Environment and Development, which states, in part:

> Unilateral actions to deal with environmental challenges outside the jurisdiction of the importing country should be avoided. *Environmental measures addressing transboundary or global environmental*

problems should, as far as possible, be based on international consensus. (emphasis added)

[The Appellate Body notes similar language in Agenda 21, the Convention on Biological Diversity, the Convention on the Conservation of Migratory Species of Wild Animals, and a 1996 Report of the WTO's Committee on Trade and Environment.]

171. * * * [T]he record does not, however, show that serious efforts were made by the United States to negotiate similar agreements with any other country or group of countries before (and, as far as the record shows, after) Section 609 was enforced on a world-wide basis on 1 May 1996. Finally, the record also does not show that the appellant, the United States, attempted to have recourse to such international mechanisms as exist to achieve cooperative efforts to protect and conserve sea turtles[174] before imposing the import ban.

172. Clearly, the United States negotiated seriously with some, but not with other Members (including the appellees), that export shrimp to the United States. The effect is plainly discriminatory and, in our view, unjustifiable. * * * [T]he policies relating to the necessity for use of particular kinds of TEDs in various maritime areas, and the operating details of these policies, are all shaped by the Department of State, without the participation of the exporting Members. The system and processes of certification are established and administered by the United States agencies alone. The decision-making involved in the grant, denial or withdrawal of certification to the exporting Members, is, accordingly, also unilateral. The unilateral character of the application of Section 609 heightens the disruptive and discriminatory influence of the import prohibition and underscores its unjustifiability.

173. The application of Section 609, through the implementing guidelines together with administrative practice, also resulted in other differential treatment among various countries desiring certification. Under the 1991 and 1993 Guidelines, to be certifiable, fourteen countries in the wider Caribbean/western Atlantic region had to commit themselves to require the use of TEDs on all commercial shrimp trawling vessels by 1 May 1994. These fourteen countries had a "phase-in" period of three years during which their respective shrimp trawling sectors could adjust to the requirement of the use of TEDs. With respect to all other countries exporting shrimp to the United States (including the appellees, India, Malaysia, Pakistan and Thailand), on 29 December 1995, the United States Court of International Trade directed the Department of State to apply the import ban on a world-wide basis not later than 1 May 1996. * * * Thus, all countries that were not among the fourteen in the wider Caribbean/western Atlantic region had only

174. While the United States is a party to CITES, it did not make any attempt to raise the issue of sea turtle mortality due to shrimp trawling in the CITES Standing Committee as a subject requiring concerted action by states. In this context, we note that the United States, for example, has not signed the Convention on the Conservation of Migratory Species of Wild Animals or UNCLOS, and has not ratified the Convention on Biological Diversity.

four months to implement the requirement of compulsory use of TEDs. We acknowledge that the greatly differing periods for putting into operation the requirement for use of TEDs resulted from decisions of the Court of International Trade. Even so, this does not relieve the United States of the legal consequences of the discriminatory impact of the decisions of that Court. The United States, like all other Members of the WTO and of the general community of states, bears responsibility for acts of all its departments of government, including its judiciary.

174. The length of the "phase-in" period is not inconsequential for exporting countries desiring certification. That period relates directly to the onerousness of the burdens of complying with the requisites of certification and the practical feasibility of locating and developing alternative export markets for shrimp. The shorter that period, the heavier the burdens of compliance, particularly where an applicant has a large number of trawler vessels, and the greater the difficulties of re-orienting the harvesting country's shrimp exports. The shorter that period, in net effect, the heavier the influence of the import ban. * * *

175. Differing treatment of different countries desiring certification is also observable in the differences in the levels of effort made by the United States in transferring the required TED technology to specific countries. Far greater efforts to transfer that technology success-fully were made to certain exporting countries—basically the fourteen wider Caribbean/western Atlantic countries cited earlier—than to other exporting countries, including the appellees. * * * Because compliance with the requirements of certification realistically assumes successful TED technology transfer, low or merely nominal efforts at achieving that transfer will, in all probability, result in fewer countries being able to satisfy the certification requirements under Section 609, within the very limited "phase-in" periods allowed them.

176. When the foregoing differences in the means of application of Section 609 to various shrimp exporting countries are considered in their cumulative effect, we find, and so hold, that those differences in treat-ment constitute "unjustifiable discrimination" between exporting coun-tries desiring certification in order to gain access to the United States shrimp market within the meaning of the chapeau of Article XX.

3. *"Arbitrary Discrimination"*

177. We next consider whether Section 609 has been applied in a manner constituting "arbitrary discrimination between countries where the same conditions prevail." * * *

180. * * * The certification processes under Section 609 consist principally of administrative *ex parte* inquiry or verification by staff of the Office of Marine Conservation in the Department of State with staff of the United States National Marine Fisheries Service. * * * [T]here is no formal opportunity for an applicant country to be heard, or to respond to any arguments that may be made against it, in the course of the certification process before a decision to grant or to deny certification is made. Moreover, no formal written, reasoned decision, whether of

acceptance or rejection, is rendered on applications for * * * certification * * *. Countries which are granted certification are included in a list of approved applications published in the Federal Register; however, they are not notified specifically. Countries whose applications are denied also do not receive notice of such denial (other than by omission from the list of approved applications) or of the reasons for the denial. No procedure for review of, or appeal from, a denial of an application is provided.

181. The certification processes followed by the United States thus appear to be singularly informal and casual, and to be conducted in a manner such that these processes could result in the negation of rights of Members. There appears to be no way that exporting Members can be certain whether the terms of Section 609, in particular, the 1996 Guidelines, are being applied in a fair and just manner by the appropriate governmental agencies of the United States. It appears to us that, effectively, exporting Members applying for certification whose applications are rejected are denied basic fairness and due process, and are discriminated against, *vis-à-vis* those Members which are granted certification.

182. The provisions of Article X:3[191] of the GATT 1994 bear upon this matter. In our view, Section 609 falls within the "laws, regulations, judicial decisions and administrative rulings of general application" described in Article X:1. Inasmuch as there are due process requirements generally for measures that are otherwise imposed in compliance with WTO obligations, it is only reasonable that rigorous compliance with the fundamental requirements of due process should be required in the application and administration of a measure which purports to be an exception to the treaty obligations of the Member imposing the measure and which effectively results in a suspension *pro hac vice* of the treaty rights of other Members.

183. It is also clear to us that Article X:3 of the GATT 1994 establishes certain minimum standards for transparency and procedural fairness in the administration of trade regulations which, in our view, are not met here. The non-transparent and *ex parte* nature of the internal governmental procedures applied by the competent officials in the Office of Marine Conservation, the Department of State, and the United States National Marine Fisheries Service throughout the certification processes under Section 609, as well as the fact that countries whose applications are denied do not receive formal notice of such denial, nor of the reasons for the denial, and the fact, too, that there is no formal legal procedure for review of, or appeal from, a denial of an

---

191. Article X:3 states, in part:

(a) Each Member shall administer in a uniform, impartial and reasonable manner all its laws, regulations, decisions and rulings of the kind described in paragraph 1 of this Article.

(b) Each Member shall maintain, or institute as soon as practicable, judicial, arbitral or administrative tribunals or procedures for the purpose, inter alia, of the prompt review and correction of administrative action relating to customs matters. . . .

application, are all contrary to the spirit, if not the letter, of Article X:3 of the GATT 1994.

184. We find, accordingly, that the United States measure is applied in a manner which amounts to a means not just of "unjustifiable discrimination," but also of "arbitrary discrimination" between countries where the same conditions prevail, contrary to the requirements of the chapeau of Article XX. The measure, therefore, is not entitled to the justifying protection of Article XX of the GATT 1994. Having made this finding, it is not necessary for us to examine also whether the United States measure is applied in a manner that constitutes a "disguised restriction on international trade" under the chapeau of Article XX.

185. In reaching these conclusions, we wish to underscore what we have not decided in this appeal. We have *not* decided that the protection and preservation of the environment is of no significance to the Members of the WTO. Clearly, it is. We have *not* decided that the sovereign nations that are Members of the WTO cannot adopt effective measures to protect endangered species, such as sea turtles. Clearly, they can and should. And we have *not* decided that sovereign states should not act together bilaterally, plurilaterally or multilaterally, either within the WTO or in other international fora, to protect endangered species or to otherwise protect the environment. Clearly, they should and do.

186. What we *have* decided in this appeal is simply this: although the measure of the United States in dispute in this appeal serves an environmental objective that is recognized as legitimate under paragraph (g) of Article XX of the GATT 1994, this measure has been applied by the United States in a manner which constitutes arbitrary and unjustifiable discrimination between Members of the WTO, contrary to the requirements of the chapeau of Article XX. For all of the specific reasons outlined in this Report, this measure does not qualify for the exemption that Article XX of the GATT 1994 affords to measures which serve certain recognized, legitimate environmental purposes but which, at the same time, are not applied in a manner that constitutes a means of arbitrary or unjustifiable discrimination between countries where the same conditions prevail or a disguised restriction on international trade. * * * WTO Members are free to adopt their own policies aimed at protecting the environment as long as, in so doing, they fulfill their obligations and respect the rights of other Members under the *WTO Agreement.* * * *

188. The Appellate Body *recommends* that the DSB request the United States to bring its measure found in the Panel Report to be inconsistent with Article XI of the GATT 1994, and found in this Report to be not justified under Article XX of the GATT 1994, into conformity with the obligations of the United States under that Agreement.

Notes and Questions

1. *The GATT and the WTO.* The General Agreement on Tariffs and Trade, Oct. 30, 1947, T.I.A.S. No. 1700, 55 U.N.T.S. 187, a multilateral treaty adopted to further the goal of reducing tariffs and other barriers to trade, was one of several post-World War II initiatives relating to trade and development. The International Monetary Fund and the World Bank were also created in the 1940s as institutions designed to promote investment and economic growth. One guiding principle of the GATT is "national treatment," which provides for equal treatment of foreign and domestic goods after foreign goods have been imported. Another guiding principle is "non-discrimination," embodied especially in the GATT's Most Favored Nation (MFN) clause, which requires a state that provides a trade benefit to one party to extend it to all GATT Contracting Parties; one exception is the 1979 GATT Generalized System of Preferences (GSP), which gives temporary preferences to specific goods imported from developing states whose trading prospects were disadvantaged by application of the MFN provision. GATT Article XI(1), which the complaining states argued was violated in the *Shrimp-Turtle Case*, prohibits discriminatory restrictions on imports that are based on standards related to the means of producing a product. Tariffs and various non-tariff trade barriers have been progressively lowered or eliminated in a series of GATT negotiating "Rounds" held since 1947.

The World Trade Organization was established on January 1, 1995, one product of the Uruguay Round of GATT negotiations. Unlike the original GATT, the WTO is an intergovernmental organization, headquartered in Switzerland and charged with administering WTO trade agreements. It serves as a forum for trade negotiations, provides technical assistance to developing states, and addresses trade disputes. As of November 1, 2000, there were 138 members of the WTO. Other products of the Uruguay Round include an updated version of the GATT (GATT–1994), a General Agreement on Trade in Services (GATS), and an agreement on Trade–Related Aspects of Intellectual Property Rights (TRIPS).

2. *The WTO and Dispute Settlement.* The agreement establishing the WTO also provided for a formal dispute settlement mechanism. Agreement Establishing the World Trade Organization, Annex 2, Understanding on Rules and Procedures Governing the Settlement of Disputes, in GATT Multilateral Trade Negotiations Final Act Embodying the Results of the Uruguay Round of Trade Negotiations, 33 I.L.M. 1125, 1216 (1994). The original GATT contemplated that consultation, good offices, or conciliation would resolve many disputes. In case such informal mechanisms proved unavailing, many GATT disputes could be submitted to a panel selected by the parties, which would issue a report containing recommendations for the parties. Although a panel report could be submitted to the Council of the GATT Contracting Parties in an effort to have it adopted as an authoritative ruling, a party to a dispute that felt itself disadvantaged by a panel report could block its adoption by the Council.

The WTO's Dispute Settlement Understanding (DSU) replaced the GATT panel process with a more formal third-party mechanism that can lead to legally binding decisions. A party to a dispute may appeal the panel report to a standing Appellate Body. A panel report (including any changes made by the Appellate Body) is adopted by the WTO's Dispute Settlement Body (DSB) unless that Body decides by consensus not to adopt it. A disadvantaged party can no longer unilaterally block a report from being adopted. The DSU also specifies dispute settlement deadlines and procedures in much detail. The WTO's caseload of trade disputes has been heavy. During the first six years of the WTO's existence, over 200 complaints were notified to the WTO, and over 40 Appellate Body and panel reports have been adopted. See "Overview of the State-of-Play of WTO Disputes," <http://www.wto.org/english/tratop_e/dispu_e/stplay_e.doc>. What has been gained by making the WTO's dispute settlement mechanism more formal? Has anything been lost? Should the process be made more formal still, *e.g.*, by creating a standing judicial body to decide trade disputes? See "Presentation Summary and Comments," 32 *International Lawyer* 883 (1998); Alan Wm. Wolff, "Reflections on WTO Dispute Settlement," 32 *International Lawyer* 95 (1998). Should nongovernmental organizations be entitled to participate in the process of deciding WTO disputes, and, if so, in what capacity? This question was at issue in portions of the *Shrimp–Turtle* decision not reproduced above.

3. *The Aftermath of the* Shrimp–Turtle Case. In November 1998 the WTO's DSB formally adopted the Appellate Body's report in the *Shrimp-Turtle Case*, and issued corresponding recommendations and rulings. What must the United States do to implement the Appellate Body's findings that application of the U.S. law failed to satisfy the requirements of the chapeau of Article XX? The WTO's DSU includes detailed enforcement provisions. These concern surveillance of compliance by the DSB, a call for negotiated compensation, and a provision under which parties to a dispute that are affected by an illegal trade measure ultimately may suspend trade concessions or other GATT obligations towards the violating WTO member.

Would you expect the United States to comply with the DSB's rulings? Following the DSB's adoption of the *Shrimp-Turtle* report, the U.S. State Department, "in response to recommendations of the Dispute Settlement Body of the World Trade Association," adopted new shrimp import certification guidelines. These new guidelines were intended to "introduc[e] greater flexibility in considering the comparability of foreign programs and the U.S. programs," and to set out procedures designed "to increase the transparency and predictability of the certification process and to afford foreign governments seeking certification a greater degree of due process." 64 *Federal Register* 36946, 36996 (1999). The United States also announced that it had undertaken steps to begin negotiations with governments in the Indian Ocean region to protect sea turtles there, and that it offered to supply TEDs and technical training to states affected by the U.S. shrimp ban. In October 2000, at Malaysia's request, the DSB asked the original *Shrimp-Turtle* panel to consider whether the United States had taken sufficient steps to comply with the DSB's rulings. See "WTO Panel Sets Up Panel to Rule on Compliance by United States with Shrimp–Turtle Ruling," 23 *BNA International Environment Reporter* No. 22, at 821 (2000); "Overview of the State-of-Play of WTO Disputes," <http://www.wto.org/english/tratop_e/dispu_e/stplay_e.doc>.

4. *Compatibility of Unilateral and Multilateral Environmental Measures with the GATT.* The WTO's establishment of a Committee on Trade and Environment and the *Shrimp-Turtle* Appellate Body's willingness at least to consider evolving environmental norms represent changes from the GATT being viewed as a self-contained legal regime concerned exclusively with GATT trade standards. See Richard J. McLaughlin, "Sovereignty, Utility, and Fairness: Using U.S. Takings Law to Guide the Evolving Utilitarian Balancing Approach to Global Environmental Disputes in the WTO," 78 *Oregon Law Review* 855, 869–74 (1999). What environmental measures will be upheld as compatible with the GATT? What distinguishes "acceptable" from "unacceptable" unilateral measures? Should the United States unilaterally be able to impose environmental measures respecting sea turtles found beyond its boundaries and in the international commons? Are unilateral import bans more acceptable when they are imposed to protect species such as sea turtles that have been recognized as endangered in an international treaty (*i.e.*, CITES, noted in the *Shrimp-Turtle Case*), even though no international agreement requires that shrimp be harvested in ways safe for sea turtles? See Jeffrey Atik, "Two Hopeful Readings of *Shrimp-Turtle*," 9 *Yearbook of International Environmental Law* 6 (1998); Daniel Bodansky, "What's So Bad About Unilateral Action to Protect the Environment?," 11 *European Journal of International Law* 339 (2000); Thomas M. Franck, *Fairness in International Law and Institutions* 376–79 (1995).

Should a GATT panel, following the *Shrimp-Turtle Case*, give effect to any environmental measure authorized by a multilateral agreement, even if the measure results in trade restrictions? Over 20 multilateral environmental treaties contain restraint-of-trade measures. Should a WTO panel necessarily reject a trade-restrictive measure imposed pursuant to a multilateral environmental agreement if the measure is challenged by a state that is not party to the environmental agreement? Should a panel be less deferential to a trade-restrictive measure used to persuade states to join a multilateral environmental agreement and thus to make it more effective—recall the Montreal Protocol's measures banning trade in ozone-depleting substances—than to a measure designed to restrict trade that itself is perceived to cause environmental damage? What should be done to increase the compatibility of multilateral environmental agreements with the GATT? See Duncan Brack, "The *Shrimp–Turtle* Case: Implications for the Multilateral Environmental Agreement—World Trade Organization Debate," 9 *Yearbook of International Environmental Law* 13 (1998).

5. *Conflicts of Jurisdiction and the Coherence of International Law.* Is a WTO panel, which will focus its analysis primarily on the GATT itself, the best forum to address the full range of legal issues presented in a dispute such as the *Shrimp-Turtle Case*? As Professor Trachtman has noted, "[t]he WTO dispute resolution system is clearly not a court of general jurisdiction, competent to apply all applicable international law. * * * There is no mechanism for integrating diverse legal rules, that is, for determining which law takes precedence when diverse laws conflict." Joel P. Trachtman, "The Domain of WTO Dispute Resolution," 40 *Harvard International Law Journal* 333, 338 (1999).

Article 23 of the WTO's Dispute Settlement Understanding provides that when members seek to redress an alleged GATT violation, "they shall have recourse to, and abide by, the rules and procedures of this Understanding." Are WTO members therefore precluded from pursuing a trade-related dispute in the International Court of Justice or another international tribunal if the rules of that forum provide jurisdiction? Would the ICJ be more willing than a WTO panel to find that U.S. shrimp import restrictions were not wrongful under the law of state responsibility, given the threat to sea turtles? See David D. Caron & Hans Rudolf Trüeb, "Protecting Trade and Turtles: The WTO and the Coherency of International Law," *Translex*, Vol. 1, No. 5, at 3, 5 (Dec. 1998). More generally, does the proliferation of international tribunals threaten the coherence and legitimacy of international law? See Jonathan I. Charney, "Is International Law Threatened by Multiple International Tribunals?," 271 *Recueil des Cours* 101 (1998); John E. Noyes, "The International Tribunal for the Law of the Sea," 32 *Cornell International Law Journal* 110, 173–81 (1998).

C. INTERNATIONAL COMMON SPACES

Common spaces are jurisdictions regulated by many or all states, in which all states have similar rights and duties. This Part examines international legal arrangements respecting Antarctica and outer space. As you read these materials, consider how and why these regimes evolved, their effectiveness, and any potential alternatives. Note too how these regimes regulate activities that sometimes may have harmful environmental effects.

1. ANTARCTICA

Ice-covered Antarctica, with its harsh and bitterly cold climate, has no indigenous human population. In the 19th and early 20th centuries, European explorers engaged in surveying and conducting scientific investigations laid claim to parts of Antarctica on behalf of their states. For example, a 1929 royal commission by Great Britain's King George to explorer Douglas Mawson instructed him "to take possession in Our name, during the course of the expedition presently to be conducted to the Antarctic regions * * * of such territories now unknown as may be discovered in the course of the aforesaid expedition, and further of certain territories not under the sovereignty of any other State which have been discovered in the past by subjects of Our Royal Predecessors or of Ourself * * *." Mawson was to "plant the British flag wherever * * * practicable to do so, * * * read the proclamation of annexation * * *, attach a copy of the proclamation to the flagstaff, and place a second copy of the proclamation in a tin at the foot of the flagstaff." *Reprinted in* A. Grenfell Price, *The Winning of Australian Antarctica: Maws ı's B.A.N.Z.A.R.E. Voyages 1929–31*, at 22–24 (1962).

After states laid claim to portions of Antarctica, governments occasionally debated the nature and validity of their asserted sovereignty. For example, the British ambassador in Washington and the U.S. Secretary of State exchanged diplomatic notes on the issue in 1934 and 1935.

1 Green Haywood Hackworth, *Digest of International Law* 457–59 (1940). Initially, Britain expressed concern about U.S. airplane flights over, and the establishment of a wireless station and postal facilities in, the Ross Dependency, now an area of Antarctica claimed by New Zealand. If the United States were to establish a post office in this area or to sanction the use of U.S. postage stamps there without permission, the British ambassador claimed, "such acts could not be regarded otherwise than as infringing the British sovereignty and New Zealand administrative rights in the dependency as well as the laws there in force." The United States responded that discovery—the basis of the British Antarctic claim—could not, "unaccompanied by occupancy and use," lead to sovereignty. The British replied that they had no objection to a U.S. expedition to the Antarctic and its associated commemorative postal activities. The United States in turn "noted that His Majesty's Government in New Zealand have no objection to the proposed visit" and stated that it "reserves all rights which this country or its citizens may have with respect to the matter." Is this diplomatic exchange part of the claim-counterclaim process used in the formation of customary international law?

Some disputes over territory in Antarctica led to tense incidents. The claims of Argentina, Chile, and the United Kingdom overlap, and in the areas of overlapping claims there were occasional displays of naval power and even the firing of shots by military personnel. The Antarctic Treaty, below, helped stabilize the situation on the continent, providing the foundation of the current Antarctic regime.

THE ANTARCTIC TREATY
Dec. 1, 1959, 12 U.S.T. 794, 402 U.N.T.S. 71.

The Governments of Argentina, Australia, Belgium, Chile, the French Republic, Japan, New Zealand, Norway, the Union of South Africa, the Union of Soviet Socialist Republics, the United Kingdom of Great Britain and Northern Ireland, and the United States of America,

Recognizing that it is in the best interest of all mankind that Antarctica shall continue forever to be used exclusively for peaceful purposes and shall not become the scene or object of international discord;

Acknowledging the substantial contributions to scientific knowledge resulting from international cooperation in scientific investigation in Antarctica;

Convinced that the establishment of a firm foundation for the continuation and development of such cooperation on the basis of freedom of scientific investigation in Antarctica as applied during the International Geophysical Year accords with the interests of science and progress of all mankind;

Convinced also that a treaty ensuring the use of Antarctica for peaceful purposes only and the continuance of international harmony in

Antarctica will further the purposes and principles embodied in the Charter of the United Nations;

Have agreed as follows:

Article I

1. Antarctica shall be used for peaceful purposes only. There shall be prohibited, *inter alia*, any measures of a military nature, such as the establishment of military bases and fortifications, the carrying out of military maneuvers, as well as the testing of any type of weapons.

2. The present Treaty shall not prevent the use of military personnel or equipment for scientific research or for any other peaceful purpose.

Article II

Freedom of scientific investigation in Antarctica and cooperation toward that end, as applied during the International Geophysical Year, shall continue, subject to the provisions of the present Treaty.

Article III

1. In order to promote international cooperation in scientific investigation in Antarctica, as provided for in Article II of the present Treaty, the Contracting Parties agree that, to the greatest extent feasible and practicable:

(a) information regarding plans for scientific programs in Antarctica shall be exchanged to permit maximum economy and efficiency of operations;

(b) scientific personnel shall be exchanged in Antarctica between expeditions and stations;

(c) scientific observations and results from Antarctica shall be exchanged and made freely available.

2. In implementing this Article, every encouragement shall be given to the establishment of cooperative working relations with those Specialized Agencies of the United Nations and other international organizations having a scientific or technical interest in Antarctica.

Article IV

1. Nothing contained in the present Treaty shall be interpreted as:

(a) a renunciation by any Contracting Party of previously asserted rights of or claims to territorial sovereignty in Antarctica;

(b) a renunciation or diminution by any Contracting Party of any basis of claim to territorial sovereignty in Antarctica which it may have whether as a result of its activities or those of its nationals in Antarctica, or otherwise;

(c) prejudicing the position of any Contracting Party as regards its recognition or nonrecognition of any other State's right of or claim or basis of claim to territorial sovereignty in Antarctica.

2. No acts or activities taking place while the present Treaty is in force shall constitute a basis for asserting, supporting or denying a claim to territorial sovereignty in Antarctica or create any rights of sovereignty in Antarctica. No new claim, or enlargement of an existing claim, to territorial sovereignty in Antarctica shall be asserted while the present Treaty is in force.

Article V

1. Any nuclear explosions in Antarctica and the disposal there of radioactive waste material shall be prohibited.

2. In the event of the conclusion of international agreements concerning the use of nuclear energy, including nuclear explosions and the disposal of radioactive waste material, to which all of the Contracting Parties whose representatives are entitled to participate in the meetings provided for under Article IX are parties, the rules established under such agreements shall apply in Antarctica.

Article VI

The provisions of the present Treaty shall apply to the area south of 60° South Latitude, including all ice shelves, but nothing in the present Treaty shall prejudice or in any way affect the rights, or the exercise of the rights, of any State under international law with regard to the high seas within that area.

Article VII

1. In order to promote the objectives and ensure the observance of the provisions of the present Treaty, each Contracting Party whose representatives are entitled to participate in the meetings referred to in Article IX of the Treaty shall have the right to designate observers to carry out any inspection provided for by the present Article. Observers shall be nationals of the Contracting Parties which designate them. The names of observers shall be communicated to every other Contracting Party having the right to designate observers, and like notice shall be given of the termination of their appointment.

2. Each observer designated in accordance with the provisions of paragraph 1 of this Article shall have complete freedom of access at any time to any or all areas of Antarctica.

3. All areas of Antarctica, including all stations, installations and equipment within those areas, and all ships and aircraft at points of discharging or embarking cargoes or personnel in Antarctica, shall be open at all times to inspection by any observers designated in accordance with paragraph 1 of this Article.

4. Aerial observation may be carried out at any time over any or all areas of Antarctica by any of the Contracting Parties having the right to designate obser— —s.

5. Each Contracting Party shall, at the time when the present Treaty enters into force for it, inform the other Contracting Parties, and thereafter shall give them notice in advance, of

(a) all expeditions to and within Antarctica, on the part of its ships or nationals, and all expeditions to Antarctica organized in or proceeding from its territory;

(b) all stations in Antarctica occupied by its nationals; and

(c) any military personnel or equipment intended to be introduced by it into Antarctica subject to the conditions prescribed in paragraph 2 of Article I of the present Treaty.

Article VIII

1. In order to facilitate the exercise of their functions under the present Treaty, and without prejudice to the respective positions of the Contracting Parties relating to jurisdiction over all other persons in Antarctica, observers designated under paragraph 1 of Article VII and scientific personnel exchanged under subparagraph 1(b) of Article III of the Treaty, and members of the staffs accompanying any such persons, shall be subject only to the jurisdiction of the Contracting Party of which they are nationals in respect of all acts or omissions occurring while they are in Antarctica for the purpose of exercising their functions.

2. Without prejudice to the provisions of paragraph 1 of this Article, and pending the adoption of measures in pursuance of subparagraph 1(e) of Article IX, the Contracting Parties concerned in any case of dispute with regard to the exercise of jurisdiction in Antarctica shall immediately consult together with a view to reaching a mutually acceptable solution.

Article IX

1. Representatives of the Contracting Parties named in the preamble to the present Treaty shall meet at the City of Canberra within two months after the date of entry into force of the Treaty, and thereafter at suitable intervals and places, for the purpose of exchanging information, consulting together on matters of common interest pertaining to Antarctica, and formulating and considering, and recommending to their Governments, measures in furtherance of the principles and objectives of the Treaty, including measures regarding:

(a) use of Antarctica for peaceful purposes only;

(b) facilitation of scientific research in Antarctica;

(c) facilitation of international scientific cooperation in Antarctica;

(d) facilitation of the exercise of the rights of inspection provided for in Article VII of the Treaty;

(e) questions relating to the exercise of jurisdiction in Antarctica;

(f) preservation and conservation of living resources in Antarctica.

2. Each Contracting Party which has become a party to the present Treaty by accession under Article XIII shall be entitled to appoint representatives to participate in the meetings referred to in paragraph 1 of the present Article, during such time as that Contracting Party demonstrates its interest in Antarctica by conducting substantial scientific research activity there, such as the establishment of a scientific station or the despatch of a scientific expedition.

3. Reports from the observers referred to in Article VII of the present Treaty shall be transmitted to the representatives of the Contracting Parties participating in the meetings referred to in paragraph 1 of the present Article.

4. The measures referred to in paragraph 1 of this Article shall become effective when approved by all the Contracting Parties whose representatives were entitled to participate in the meetings held to consider those measures. * * *

Article X

Each of the Contracting Parties undertakes to exert appropriate efforts, consistent with the Charter of the United Nations, to the end that no one engages in any activity in Antarctica contrary to the principles or purposes of the present Treaty.

Article XI

1. If any dispute arises between two or more of the Contracting Parties concerning the interpretation or application of the present Treaty, those Contracting Parties shall consult among themselves with a view to having the dispute resolved by negotiation, inquiry, mediation, conciliation, arbitration, judicial settlement or other peaceful means of their own choice.

2. Any dispute of this character not so resolved shall, with the consent, in each case, of all parties to the dispute, be referred to the International Court of Justice for settlement; but failure to reach agreement on reference to the International Court shall not absolve parties to the dispute from the responsibility of continuing to seek to resolve it by any of the various peaceful means referred to in paragraph 1 of this Article. * * *

Article XIII

1. The present Treaty shall be subject to ratification by the signatory States. It shall be open for accession by any State which is a

Member of the United Nations, or by any other State which may be invited to accede to the Treaty with the consent of all the Contracting Parties whose representatives are entitled to participate in the meetings provided for under Article IX of the Treaty.

Notes and Questions

1. *Acquisition of Territory.* A generally accepted way for states to acquire new territory is by discovery and occupation of *terra nullius*, a label used to describe uninhabited territory, including new islands. Writers in the early 20th century considered that discovery alone provided only an "inchoate" title, which in order to become effective against other states had to be followed by occupation and concrete acts exercising authority. See, *e.g.*, T.J. Lawrence, *The Principles of International Law* § 74 (1915). In light of the practical difficulties of establishing permanent settlements in Antarctica, should discovery alone have sufficed to establish state sovereignty?

More controversial than discovery plus effective occupation as grounds for asserting sovereignty over portions of Antarctica are the contiguity theory, propounded by several states geographically close to Antarctica, and the sector theory. Under the sector theory, Antarctic territorial boundaries correspond to longitudinal lines that converge on the South Pole. The longitudinal lines either are extensions of the mainland boundaries of a nearby claimant state, or are drawn from the ends of a stretch of coast claimed by the state. By the 1950s, Argentina, Australia, Chile, France, New Zealand, Norway, and the United Kingdom exercised or claimed territorial sovereignty over "pie slice" sectors of Antarctica that meet at the South Pole. The United States and the Soviet Union made no claims to territory in Antarctica but reserved their right to assert claims in the future. These "nonclaimant states" also refused to recognize the territorial claims of other states. As shown in Figure 9.1, one area of Antarctica was (and still is) unclaimed.

Other traditional ways for a state to acquire territory have not been applicable to Antarctica. These include cession from another state, accretion (the increase of land, as through new geological formations), prescription (a continuous, uncontested display of control), and subjugation (conquest followed by annexation, the legality of which as a way to acquire territory today runs afoul of the proscriptions on the use of force in the United Nations Charter). See 1 *Oppenheim's International Law* §§ 241–275 (9th ed., Robert Jennings & Arthur Watts eds. 1992), and the discussion of use of force in Chapter 9.

Figure 9.1. Map of national claims in Antarctica

2. *The International Geophysical Year.* The shape of the current legal regime governing Antarctica was influenced by the 1957 International Geophysical Year (IGY), a cooperative effort by 66 states including all the major powers except the People's Republic of China. One of the IGY's scientific projects involved Antarctica. Scientists meeting during the IGY allocated scientific stations in Antarctica to states and arranged cooperative ventures concerning mapping, collection of weather data, and exchanges of scientific personnel. The entry of the Soviet Union into Antarctic activities beginning in 1955 contributed to efforts to specify an international arrangement for Antarctica that would help preserve the continent as a laboratory for cooperative scientific research and as a region to be used only for peaceful purposes.

Following the IGY, representatives of the 12 states active in the Antarctic work of the IGY met regularly in Washington, D.C., for preparatory treaty talks and a formal negotiating conference. The Antarctic Treaty was signed in Washington on December 1, 1959, and entered into force June 23, 1961. See Christopher C. Joyner, "U.S.–Soviet Cooperative Diplomacy: The Case of Antarctica," in *U.S.–Soviet Cooperation* 39 (Nish Jamgotch ed. 1989); Walter Sullivan, "Antarctica," in *The International Geophysical Year* 318 (International Conciliation No. 521, Jan. 1959).

3. *Freezing Territorial Claims.* Article IV of the Antarctic Treaty "freezes" territorial and sovereignty claims. Why have states found this arrangement acceptable? What problems might be anticipated under this arrangement?

4. *Effect on Nonparties.* Does the Antarctic Treaty create legal obligations for nonparties? Does the Treaty thus create international obligations *erga omnes*? See Chapter 3. What would be the reaction if a nonparty to the Antarctic Treaty were to claim sovereignty over the "unclaimed sector" or some other portion of Antarctica? To dispose of radioactive waste anywhere on the continent? See Article X of the Treaty.

5. *Jurisdiction Over Activities in Antarctica.* What laws govern individuals' activities in Antarctica? Article VIII of the Antarctic Treaty provides at best a partial answer. Some of the issues relating to the assertion of "legislative jurisdiction" over crimes and torts in Antarctica are explored in Beverly May Carl, "The Need for a Private International Law Regime in Antarctica," in *The Antarctic Legal Regime* 65 (Christopher C. Joyner & Sudhir K. Chopra eds. 1988), and in Comment, Jonathan Blum, "The Deep Freeze: Torts, Choice of Law, and the Antarctic Treaty Regime," 8 *Emory International Law Review* 667 (1994).

6. *Classes of Parties to the Antarctic Treaty.* The Antarctic Treaty distinguishes between Consultative Parties and other parties. The 12 original parties to the Antarctic Treaty joined as Consultative Parties, entitled to decision-making roles in periodic international meetings. As of November 1, 2000, 44 states were parties to the Antarctic Treaty, but only 27 of them were Consultative Parties. What justifies the Treaty's two-tiered system? Among the Consultative Parties, should some special status be accorded those states that have asserted territorial claims? The following excerpt addresses some of these concerns.

UNITED NATIONS GENERAL ASSEMBLY
DEBATES ON ANTARCTICA

A/C.1/38/PV.42 (1983), Thirty–Eighth Session, First Committee, Summary Record
of the 42nd Meeting, Nov. 28, 1983; A/C.1/38/PV.44 (1983), Thirty–Eighth Session,
First Committee, Summary Record of the 44th Meeting, Nov. 29, 1983;
A/C.1/38/PV.5 (1984), Thirty–Eighth Session, First Committee, Verbatim Record of
the 45th Meeting, Nov. 30, 1983; A/C.1/39/PV.54 (1984), Thirty–Ninth Session,
First Committee, Verbatim Record of the 54th Meeting, Nov. 30, 1984.

MR. ZAINAL ABIDIN (Malaysia) * * *

* * * The [Antarctic] Treaty at its inception could have been
considered as an unusually enlightened experiment in international cooperation.

In our view, however, the Treaty and its system have become mired
in the obsession to maintain a *status quo* régime advantageous to the
privileged few. * * * My delegation would like to draw the attention of
the Committee to two crucial areas in which the Treaty has not kept
pace with current international reality.

My delegation would like first to address the obvious structural flaw
inherent in the Treaty system. The Treaty provides for a two-tier
membership structure, characterized by gross inequality. This is evident
from the relevant Treaty articles pertaining to membership [Articles
XIII(1) and IX(2)]. * * *

This means that while every State is welcome and encouraged to
accede to the Treaty only the original 12 can participate in decision-
making, along with such other States as, in the unanimous judgement of
the original Contracting Parties, have demonstrated significant interest
in Antarctica by conducting substantial scientific research activity there.
Thus, a State acceding to the Treaty formalizes its willingness to abide
by the Treaty provisions without any role to play whatsoever, as voting
and regulatory control are reserved for the full—or "consultative"—
members only. States are, in actual fact, called upon to accede to the
Treaty without any right to participate in the decision-making process. It
is clear that this undemocratic arrangement which the Treaty perpetu-
ates goes against the grain of current international reality. Most States
would find accession without representation extremely difficult to accept,
while the representation requirement of a significant capacity for research would be beyond their means. They are thus effectively frozen out
of meaningful participation in the Antarctic Treaty system.

The second major flaw of the Treaty system, in the view of my
delegation, pertains to the limitations on its efficacy. The Treaty purports to be an international régime that serves the interests of all
mankind, yet it benefits only the few. * * * [Despite Article III(2) of the
Antarctic Treaty, which encourages cooperative working relations with
international organizations,] the Consultative Parties have actually rejected co-operation with the Food and Agriculture Organization of the

United Nations (FAO), the United Nations Environment Programme (UNEP), the Committee on Natural Resources and other international organizations. Furthermore, the * * * flow of information about Antarctica * * * is very much limited to the Consultative Parties and is not even made available to ordinary parties of the Treaty, let alone the international community at large.

The efficacy of the Treaty system is especially questionable with regard to environmental and ecological management. * * * [T]o forestall any destruction of Antarctica's invaluable and irreplaceable endowments, environmentalists world-wide have advocated the designation of Antarctica as a world park. [Because international nongovernmental organizations are denied access,] even as observers, to ATCP [Antarctic Treaty Consultative Party] meetings * * *, the world community is entitled to entertain serious doubts on the effective management of Antarctica's present and future environment, especially as the Treaty system lacks a centralized environmental review body and enforcement is left to individual States. * * *

We note that several closed-door meetings have been held to devise a new and exclusive minerals régime in Antarctica among the few parties enjoying consultative status within the Antarctic Treaty framework. * * *

* * * [S]afeguarding of the interests of all mankind * * * requires the creation of international mechanisms that are not only truly representative in membership but also truly committed to serving all of its constituents. The philosophy that guides those mechanisms must be such as to command unquestioned moral authority amongst the nations of the world. In this respect the concepts of common benefit and common heritage come to mind.

The common heritage approach * * * should be considered in a future international design for Antarctica. The elements of the common heritage concept—peaceful use, non-appropriation, preservation for future generations, including environmental protection and conservation of resources, international management and benefit-sharing—are of great relevance to Antarctica. * * *

In conclusion, may I be permitted to sum up the conviction of my delegation as follows. First, the world is in a process of evolution and there is an urgent need for all to display the necessary political will to make adaptations and adjustments to rapidly changing circumstances in order to build a structure of international peace and a just international order.

Secondly, the world of 1959, when the Antarctic Treaty was first formulated, is different from that of 1983. There are now 158 States Members of the United Nations, most of which are categorized as developing countries. Their rights, interests, aspirations and, not least, their views have to be accommodated by any purportedly international régime on Antarctica.

Thirdly, there is a growing and an inexorable demand by this articulate and growing majority for greater involvement in international decision-making. No longer can a handful of countries arrogate unto themselves the prerogative of representing humanity in matters of common concern when the majority of humanity is not directly involved.

Fourthly, the movement for a just and a balanced world order for the cause of mankind is irresistible. Significant areas of the world beyond national jurisdiction, and the celestial bodies in outer space, must be viewed in the context of the common heritage of mankind, and for the benefit of mankind as a whole.

And, fifth, Antarctica constitutes one such significant and vital area, because what happens in this region will have a direct effect on the rest of the world. * * * It is time that a proper and representative international régime beyond the Antarctic Treaty be explored within the framework of the United Nations.

Mr. Heap (United Kingdom) * * *

* * * [T]he Antarctic Treaty system was an exercise in prudent forethought. [A] number of notable "firsts" * * * have been achieved by agreement between States within the Treaty system. The Antarctic Treaty was the first international agreement to demilitarize a whole continent, to provide for on-site inspection of all activities on a continent, to outlaw nuclear explosions or the dumping of radioactive waste, to ensure freedom of scientific investigation and require that the results be freely available and to set aside, in favour of co-operation, conflicting views about the legal basis which should underlie the management of affairs over a whole continent.

* * * [T]hese firsts * * * are totally consistent with the Charter of the United Nations.

Since the Antarctic Treaty came into force in 1961 the development of a large number of agreements through its consultative mechanism has given rise to a number of other "firsts," among which are: the Agreed Measures for the Conservation of Antarctic Fauna and Flora, the first international agreement to prohibit the killing of any native mammal or native bird in Antarctica without a permit and to arrange for details on the permits issued to be internationally exchanged; the Convention for the Conservation of Antarctic Seals, the first and, I believe, so far the only international agreement to regulate the utilization of a living resource before any industry has developed to exploit it; the Convention for the Conservation of Antarctic Marine Living Resources, the first international agreement to require that regulation of the utilization of target species shall have regard to the effect that utilization has on the ecosystem as a whole. More generally, certain pioneering recommendations of the Treaty's consultative procedures require that the first consideration to be applied to a new activity in Antarctica is not whether it is profitable or in the interests of one or more Governments. Instead, prior consideration has to be given to whether or not it will have adverse effects on the Antarctic environment. This test, itself a notable first, is unparalleled anywhere else in the world.

* * * [A]ll these "firsts," and note especially those measures taken to protect Antarctic marine living resources, are in marked contrast to what happened before the Treaty system came into being. * * *

None of these "firsts" give substantive rights to the parties to the agreements. They all circumscribe the freedom of action of all parties. Overwhelmingly, they consist of obligations and not of rights. This record of achievement should go far to put right the misconception that the Antarctic Treaty Consultative Parties are carving up Antarctica for their own benefit.

Mr. Woolcott (Australia) * * *

* * * There seems to be a desire, at least on the part of some delegations, to have Antarctic resources, whatever these are or may be, declared the common heritage of mankind, like those of outer space and the deep sea-bed, beyond national jurisdiction. Australia is, of course, in favour of this principle in the Law-of-the-Sea context, but we do not consider it relevant or appropriate in Antarctica. First, for Australia and six other countries that maintain national territorial claims and, let me add, national settlements, Antarctica is not beyond national jurisdiction. Antarctica has instead been the subject of exploration, settlement and claims to sovereignty by a number of countries over many years. So there can be no international consensus that a common-heritage approach to Antarctica is acceptable.

Secondly, the common-heritage concept embodies a developmental purpose, which is not now, and we hope will never be, dominant in Antarctica, where the environment is, as some of the sponsors of this draft resolution have stressed, extremely vulnerable to the activity of man and must be safeguarded by those pursuing activity there in the interest of all mankind. * * *

* * * The Treaty is not exclusive. Any State may join, and 28 countries with diverse economic and political interests have already done so. In 1983, two new members, China and India, joined the Treaty, and Finland only yesterday signified its intention to do so. * * *

What about the status of Consultative Parties? Claims have been made here which reveal a misunderstanding of the operation of the Treaty. Any State carrying out substantial scientific activities may become a Consultative Party to the Treaty. In 1983 Brazil and India took this step. There are now 16 Treaty members that are also Consultative Parties.

It is not unnatural that those heavily involved in scientific research should wish to consult together and then to make available to the international community the fruits of their consultations.

Claims that the deliberations of the Consultative Parties are conducted in secret and that consultative Parties meet as a cabal to take secret decisions, sometimes contrary to the interest of the acceding parties and the international community are quite simply untrue. Acceding parties, for their own good reasons, have presumably wished to limit their commitment to the Antarctic, short of that implied by consultative status. * * *

It is relevant that at the last meeting of the Consultative Parties in Canberra as recently as in September of this year, all members of the Antarctic Treaty, acceding as well as Consultative, participated in the deliberations. The results of the discussions at the meeting are before the Committee today, in the Final Report of the Twelfth Antarctic Treaty Consultative Meeting. * * *

Australia, when it determines its approach to a regional question, invariably gives weight to the views of the regional countries closest to, and most directly concerned with, the particular issue under consideration. * * * A glance at the map will show that Antarctica lies to Australia's immediate south. This is the basis of our own clear and legitimate concern that the present satisfactory situation there should not be disturbed. * * *

In current international circumstances it would simply, in the view of my delegation, not be realistic to expect that a new instrument could have the same provisions for total demilitarization of the region, verified by on-site inspection, for the setting aside of potential disputes over territorial sovereignty and for harmonious international co-operation in scientific research and environmental protection. In short, any new instrument would not as effectively protect important international interests in the Antarctic as does the current Treaty, and any attempt to revise this situation would, in our view, risk reopening the very contention and competition which the Treaty was created to do away with.

Mr. Jesus (Cape Verde) * * *

* * * During this debate I have not heard anybody question the principles established in the Antarctic Treaty relating to the peaceful use of Antarctica, the preservation of flora, fauna and the environment in general or its declaration as an area free from military activities, or even the freedom of scientific research. In this respect, it seems to my delegation that we are all in agreement with one another. What therefore, we, the majority of members of the international community, are in disagreement with is the fact that a few countries which have consultative status, however powerful they might be, can ascribe to themselves the right to decide what is right or wrong for the whole of mankind. * * *

* * * [O]nly a party to the Treaty which demonstrates its interest in Antarctica by conducting substantial scientific research activity there, such as the establishment of a scientific station or the dispatch of a scientific expedition, is entitled to become a Consultative Party.

In other words, the majority of third world countries, even if they became parties to the Antarctic Treaty, would not be able to participate fully on an equal footing with any other State Consultative Party in establishing the policies for the activities of Antarctica for the simple reason that they cannot afford to send a scientific expedition to Antarctica or to establish a scientific station there. It is evident that the principle of equality of States established in the Charter, upon which the Antarctic Treaty is said to be based, cannot allow that its observance be limited with regard to co-operation on Antarctica merely because of lack of resources of third world countries.

The Antarctic Treaty can become a basis for universal co-operation in Antarctica, subject to the following provisos: the extension of the right of equal treatment to all States parties, irrespective of their conduct of substantial scientific research activity in Antarctica; that in all activities related to Antarctica decisions be taken by all States parties on the basis of one State, one vote; that provision be made to make it plain that Antarctica is free from national appropriation and therefore no territorial claim there should ever be recognized.

Notes and Questions

1. *The Common Heritage Principle.* Mr. Abidin listed in summary fashion features of the common heritage principle, a principle that has also been associated with the international law governing outer space and the deep sea bed. According to typical formulations, the common heritage principle requires: that no state appropriate an area or its resources; a common management system with universal participation; equitable sharing of economic benefits, with particular attention to the needs of states with developing economies; the conservation of the area and its resources, a feature which requires that regard be given to environmental protection and the interests of future generations; and the peaceful use of the area. See Sudhir K. Chopra, "Antarctica as a Commons Regime: A Conceptual Framework for Cooperation and Coexistence," in *The Antarctic Legal Regime* 163, 172–74 (Christopher C. Joyner & Sudhir K. Chopra eds. 1988); Christopher C. Joyner, "Legal Implications of the Concept of the Common Heritage of Mankind," 35 *International and Comparative Law Quarterly* 190 (1986). Should the U.N. General Assembly resolve that Antarctica is the "common heritage of mankind"? What would be the legal implications of such a resolution? Would it be effective?

2. *The United Nations and Antarctica.* The issue of U.N. involvement with Antarctica was first posed shortly after World War II. India raised the question again in 1956, and Malaysia brought the issue before the U.N. General Assembly in 1982. In 1989, the General Assembly called on the Antarctic Treaty Consultative Parties to invite the U.N. Secretary–General to ATCP meetings, expressing the conviction that regimes to protect the Antarctic environment "must be negotiated with the full participation of all members of the international community," urging bans on prospecting and mining in Antarctica, and asking all members of the international community to ensure that activities in Antarctica "are for the benefit of all mankind." G.A. Res. 44/124 (1989) (adopted by a vote of 108 states in favor, 0 opposed, and 6 abstaining).

3. *Governing Antarctica*. The basic structure for the Antarctic regime was laid out in the 1959 Antarctic Treaty. Additional treaties regulating activities in Antarctica have been negotiated. The Treaty's Consultative Parties have also issued approximately 200 Recommendations on such topics as meteorology, the environment, natural resources, tourism, and telecommunications, Recommendations that become formally effective once the ATCPs ratify them.

One can envision a number of alternatives either to the current system or to international administration of Antarctica as a common heritage regime. What would be the advantages and disadvantages of, for example, a territorial regime in which claimant states asserted absolute control over their pie-shaped claims? Of a condominium regime, pursuant to which the Antarctic Treaty parties establish a system of joint sovereignty over the continent? Assuming that no fundamental change is made to the framework established by the Antarctic Treaty, what steps could be taken to respond to increased international interest in Antarctica?

Note: The Antarctic Environment and Mineral Resources

States, scientists, and nongovernmental organizations have been concerned about protecting the fragile Antarctic environment. Antarctica's seas are home to numerous birds, fish, whales, and seals. Antarctica's environment also affects the Earth's ocean circulation and weather patterns. The Antarctic Treaty itself contains several provisions relating to the environment, notably Article V's prohibition on nuclear explosions and the disposal of radioactive waste and Article IX(1)(f)'s call for consultations on the preservation and conservation of living resources. Approximately half of the many Recommendations adopted by the Antarctic Treaty Consultative Parties have related to protection of the environment. Notable environmental instruments include the Agreed Measures for the Conservation of Antarctic Flora and Fauna, June 13, 1964, 17 U.S.T. 441, the Convention for the Conservation of Antarctic Seals, Feb. 11, 1972, 29 U.S.T. 441, 11 I.L.M. 251 (1972), and the Convention for the Conservation of Antarctic Marine Living Resources (CCAMLR), May 20, 1980, 33 U.S.T. 3476, 19 I.L.M. 841 (1980).

The CCAMLR has as its goal a comprehensive management scheme that seeks to maintain ecological relationships among all populations of Antarctic living resources. Whereas many fisheries treaties seek to insure the maximum sustainable yield of a particular species, the CCAMLR (which applies to birds and other organisms as well as to fish) follows an "ecosystem approach." Under the CCAMLR, a Commission composed of Contracting States to the Convention is to gather data, study environmental issues, and formulate and adopt conservation measures "on the basis of the best scientific evidence available." Reviews of the contributions of the CCAMLR to protecting the environment have been mixed. See Stuart B. Kaye, "Legal Approaches to Polar Fisheries Regimes: A Comparative Analysis of the Convention for the Conservation of Antarctic Marine Living Resources and the Bering Sea Doughnut Hole Convention," 26 *California Western International Law Journal* 75, 87–97 (1995); Deborah H. Overholt, "Environmental Protection in the Antarctic: Past, Present, and Future," 1992 *Canadian Yearbook of International Law* 227, 238–45, 250–52. Cutting against the adoption and implementation of strong environmental measures have been the requirement that the CCAMLR Commission adopt conservation measures by consensus, the fact that the CCAMLR leaves it up to each Contracting State to "take appropriate measures within its competence to ensure compliance," and the possibility that nonparties to the CCAMLR may take detrimental actions.

Environmental considerations have also been important in negotiations relating to the use of mineral resources in Antarctica. Between 1982 and 1988—not coincidentally, a period of great interest in Antarctica at the United Nations—the ATCPs negotiated a regime to regulate mineral exploration and exploitation. The product of these negotiations, the Convention on the Regulation of Antarctic Mineral Resource Activities (CRAMRA), June 2, 1988, 27 I.L.M. 859 (1988), called for a regulatory framework to govern minerals activities. It provided for inspection, monitoring, reporting, obligatory dispute settlement, and the suspension of any activities that caused unacceptable damage to the environment. A new international institution, the Antarctic Minerals Resources Commission, was to decide whether to open an area for minerals exploration and development, and any activities were to be overseen by a Regulatory Committee.

In the summer of 1989, however, Australia and France announced they would not sign the CRAMRA, and it did not enter into force. Contributing to the demise of the CRAMRA were the efforts of international nongovernmental organizations concerned about the environment. They argued the Convention would promote prospecting and eventual exploitation, criticized the fact that enforcement ultimately remained with individual governments, and objected to the structure and powers of some of the proposed new institutions. Sovereignty concerns also contributed to the CRAMRA's demise. Australia feared that agreeing to a treaty-based Antarctica minerals arrangement would be viewed as an admission that Australia's "claim of sovereignty was soft and could be compromised." Furthermore, CRAMRA's failure "to provide any royalties to claimant states for other states' exploration or exploitation activities in claimed sectors * * * could be read as tacit admission that claimant states were willing to give up full administrative control over *their* territory." Christopher C. Joyner, "Antarctic Treaty Diplomacy: Problems, Prospects, and Policy Implications," in *The Diplomatic Record 1989–1990*, at 155, 163 (David D. Newsom ed. 1991).

Following adverse reactions to CRAMRA, states negotiated the Madrid Protocol on Environmental Protection, Oct. 4, 1991, 30 I.L.M. 1455 (1991). The Madrid Protocol prohibits "[a]ny activity relating to mineral resources, other than scientific research," for at least 50 years. Its focus is thus on preventing environmental harm by banning mining, rather than, as under the CRAMRA, on permitting activities but protecting against harm. The Protocol also creates a Committee on Environmental Protection that advises the ATCPs on implementing the Protocol, provides for mandatory dispute settlement, and authorizes any party to inspect, unannounced, any area of the continent. Five detailed Annexes to the Madrid Protocol also address other environmental issues: (1) environmental impact assessments must be prepared in advance of almost all activity in Antarctica; (2) the 1964 Agreed Measures for Flora and Fauna is strengthened; (3) the production, storage, and disposal of wastes are regulated, and the introduction of pesticides and other chemicals into Antarctica is prohibited; (4) ship discharges of oil, other noxious substances, garbage, and sewage are regulated according to standards based on the International Convention for the Prevention of Pollution from Ships (MARPOL 73/78); and (5) sites of "outstanding environmental, scientific, historic, aesthetic and/or wilderness values" are protected. The Madrid Protocol entered into force in January 1998, following its acceptance by all states that were ATCPs when Protocol negotiations concluded in 1991. The ATCP governments must implement the Protocol in their municipal laws.

Negotiations for a treaty on liability for environmental damage in Antarctica have yet to be successfully concluded. Many issues have proven controversial, including how natural resource damages should be measured, the standard for liability, financial limits on liability, whether damages caused by certain scientific activities or other causes should be excluded from the scope of a liability regime, how response actions should be coordinated and funded, how a liability regime should be administered, and the shape of a dispute settlement system. The ATCPs are divided about whether all issues should be addressed together in a comprehensive treaty, or whether to develop a series of texts that address particular liability issues. How should this last issue be resolved? Is negotiation of a liability regime intrinsically more difficult that negotiation of a regulatory regime?

Environmental and mineral resource issues lead one to wonder how adaptable the Antarctic legal regime will prove to be. Is it possible to achieve a satisfactory system of environmental protection in Antarctica by leaving so much control with states, some of which claim sovereignty over portions of the continent? Can states effectively regulate the Antarctic environment and mineral resources without a significant restructuring of the existing Antarctic Treaty regime?

2. OUTER SPACE

International legal arrangements for outer space differ from the regime governing the airspace between the earth and outer space. The airspace regime is premised on notions of territorial sovereignty. For example, Article 1 of the Convention on International Civil Aviation, Dec. 7, 1944, T.I.A.S. No. 1591, 15 U.N.T.S. 295, to which over 185 states are parties, provides that "every State has complete and exclusive sovereignty over the airspace above its territory." International aviation thus has developed on the basis of treaties among states, rather than on a principle of airspace freedom. Although the precise location of the boundary separating outer space from domestic airspace has never been explicitly demarcated, it is clear that principles of state territorial sovereignty have not been extended skyward into outer space. For discussion of the boundary between airspace and outer space, see Bin Cheng, *Studies in International Space Law* 81–84, 393–97, 425–61, 645–48 (1997), and I.H. Ph. Diederiks–Verschoor, *An Introduction to Space Law* 15–19 (1993).

What legal regimes do apply above national airspace? The United Nations and its agencies have played dominant roles in developing the international law of outer space. In 1959—two years after the launch of

Sputnik I, the first satellite to orbit Earth—the United Nations General Assembly established the Committee for Peaceful Uses of Outer Space (COPUOS). The Committee's work led to the widely accepted Treaty on Principles Governing the Activities of States in the Exploration and Use of Outer Space, Including the Moon and Other Celestial Bodies (the Outer Space Treaty), Jan. 27, 1967, 18 U.S.T. 2410, 610 U.N.T.S. 205. According to Article II of this Treaty, "[o]uter space, including the moon and other celestial bodies, is not subject to national appropriation." Article I sets out other basic principles:

> The exploration and use of outer space, including the moon and other celestial bodies, shall be carried out for the benefit and in the interests of all countries, irrespective of their degree of economic or scientific development, and shall be the province of all mankind.

> Outer space, including the moon and other celestial bodies, shall be free for exploration and use by all States without discrimination of any kind, on a basis of equality and in accordance with international law, and there shall be free access to all areas of celestial bodies.

> There shall be freedom of scientific investigation in outer space, including the moon and other celestial bodies, and States shall facilitate and encourage international co-operation in such investigation.

COPUOS, the primary forum for discussing international space law issues, has also drafted treaties that have added specific content to some issues covered in the Outer Space Treaty. See Agreement on the Rescue of Astronauts, the Return of Astronauts and the Return of Objects Launched into Outer Space, Apr. 22, 1968, 19 U.S.T. 7570, 672 U.N.T.S. 119; Convention on International Liability for Damage Caused by Space Objects, Mar. 29, 1972, 24 U.S.T. 2389, 961 U.N.T.S. 187; Convention on Registration of Objects Launched into Outer Space, Jan. 14, 1975, 28 U.S.T. 695, 1023 U.N.T.S. 15.

The Outer Space Treaty does not explicitly provide that outer space is subject to the common heritage principle, which some states espoused in the U.N. General Assembly debates concerning Antarctica. The common heritage principle is, however, mentioned in Article 11 of another treaty, the Agreement Governing the Activities of States on the Moon and Other Celestial Bodies, Dec. 18, 1979, U.N. Doc. A/RES/34/68 (Moon Treaty). Article 11 calls for "equitable sharing by all States Parties" of benefits derived from the moon's resources, and the Treaty authorizes states parties to establish an international regime governing exploitation of the moon's resources when exploitation is about to become feasible. As of February 1, 2000, however, only nine states had accepted the Moon Treaty, and neither the United States nor Russia, which have carried on most space activities, are parties. See also the Bogotá Declaration, ITU Broadcasting Satellite Conference, Doc. No. 81–E (Jan. 17, 1977), Annex 4, *reprinted in* 2 *Manual on Space Law* 383 (Nandasiri Jasentuliyan & Roy S.K. Lee eds. 1979) (signed in 1976 by eight equatorial developing states and asserting, *inter alia*, that "[t]he segments of the [geostationary] orbit corresponding to the open sea * * * beyond the national jurisdiction of states will be considered as common heritage of mankind").

As the use of outer space for broadcasting and other commercial purposes has increased, operative regimes have developed. For example, one currently important issue regarding the use of outer space is access to geostationary orbit, the circular orbit approximately 22,300 miles above the Earth's equator. A satellite placed in this orbit will rotate at the same speed as the Earth, allowing transmitting and receiving equipment to remain directed at the same spot in outer space, and thus avoiding the expense of having continually to redirect the equipment. The geostationary orbit is a finite resource, the number of spots limited by the fact that electronic signals from satellites whose orbits are too close together can interfere with each other.

The legal regime that evolved to govern access to the geostationary orbit has depended on regulations of the International Telecommunication Union (ITU), one of the specialized agencies of the United Nations. Traditionally, access to the geostationary orbit has been governed by a "first come, first served" principle. With respect to proposed satellite services (which use the radio spectrum), the International Frequency Registration Board (IFRB), an organ of the ITU, records radio frequency assignments made by member states and recommends solutions when coordination with other assignments is needed. The IFRB currently registers frequencies and coordinates orbital positions for states, but not for business entities or international organizations.

As the space powers began to occupy the geostationary orbit with their satellites, developing states became concerned that no room would be left in the geostationary orbit by the time they acquired space technology. They objected to Article 33(2) of the 1973 ITU Convention, which provided that states had access to frequencies and to the geostationary orbit in conformity with the ITU's regulations and "according to their needs and the technical facilities at their disposal." International Telecommunication Convention, Oct. 25, 1973, art. 33(2), 28 U.S.T. 2495, 2530, 1209 U.N.T.S. 32, 268. Concerns of developing states were acknowledged in the 1980s. Article 33(2) of the ITU Convention was revised in 1982 to take into account "the special needs of the developing countries and the special geographical situation of particular countries." More significantly, a 1985–1988 World Administrative Radio Conference (WARC-ORB), which had the authority under the ITU Convention to adopt regulations having the same legal status as the ITU Convention itself, approved an allotment plan that effectively guarantees each state at least one geostationary orbital position, regardless of national ability to place a satellite into orbit. Orbital positions not allocated under this plan, and allocated positions not yet claimed, remain available for use through the IFRB's normal notification and coordination procedures. See Francis Lyall, "Posts and Telecommunications," in 2 *United Nations Legal Order* 789, 796–822 (Oscar Schachter & Christopher C. Joyner eds.

1995); Milton L. Smith, "The Space WARC Concludes," 83 *American Journal of International Law* 596 (1989); Farhad Talaie, "Legal Issues Concerning the Radio Frequency Spectrum and Geostationary Satellite Orbit," 1998 *Australian International Law Journal* 28. In 1990 Tonga, complying with the IFRB's standard procedures, filed a claim for several orbital slots on behalf of TONGASAT, an entity owned by members of Tonga's ruling family and a U.S. entrepreneur; some of Tonga's reserved slots have subsequently been leased to commercial enterprises. See Comment, Jannat C. Thompson, "Space for Rent: The International Telecommunications Union, Space Law, and Orbit/Spectrum Leasing," 62 *Journal of Air Law and Commerce* 279 (1996). How does the regime for allocating geostationary orbital positions compare with the international legal system governing Antarctica? How does it compare with the regimes governing the high seas and the sea bed beyond the limits of national jurisdiction, which we examine in Chapter 11? What are the advantages and disadvantages of each arrangement?

Outer space environmental issues have received attention in recent years. Do nuclear power sources used in spacecraft operating systems, and possible collisions with space debris from damaged or abandoned man-made objects in heavily used earth orbits, pose significant environmental risks? See David Tan, "Towards a New Regime for the Protection of Outer Space as the 'Province of All Mankind,' " 25 *Yale Journal of International Law* 145 (2000). Tan has proposed a new regime to address outer space pollution, building on the precautionary principle and concepts of sustainable development and intergenerational equity. These concepts are recognized in the Rio Declaration (see Part A of this chapter). Professor Edith Brown Weiss has developed the principle of intergenerational equity, which is premised on the notion of a "planetary trust," requiring one generation to pass along the planet to the next without worsening its condition. Basic principles underlying intergenerational equity include the "conservation of options," the "conservation of access," and the "conservation of quality." See generally Edith Brown Weiss, *In Fairness to Future Generations: International Law, Common Patrimony, and Intergenerational Equity* (1989). How should a regime to address the environmental problems facing outer space be structured?

Chapter 11

THE LAW OF THE SEA

From at least the 18th century, vast areas of the oceans—the high seas—have been generally regarded as common space, not subject to the sovereignty or exclusive control of any state. On the high seas, the flag state of a vessel has the right to regulate the vessel's activities. By contrast, in internal waters, such as ports, and in a narrow band of oceans near the coast known as the territorial sea, coastal states exercise sovereign rights. Rights of flag states are limited in these zones.

In the mid-20th century, what had been a relatively stable legal system for the oceans began to disintegrate. Some states made claims over broad coastal zones, assertions of jurisdiction largely stimulated by changes in technology, permitting mining or drilling for oil and gas on the continental shelf. The ability of foreign trawlers and factory ships to capture and process huge quantities of fish near the shores of coastal states also contributed to proclamations of wide coastal fisheries zones. Assertions of coastal state control over broad zones disquieted maritime powers, which feared infringements on traditional navigational freedoms.

The modern law of the sea has been fundamentally shaped by the Third United Nations Conference on the Law of the Sea (UNCLOS III). UNCLOS III formally convened in 1973, following six years of studies and preparatory work by United Nations bodies. Following numerous formal negotiating sessions and intersessional meetings, the Conference produced the 1982 United Nations Convention on the Law of the Sea. The Convention codified many principles that had previously been generally accepted in customary and treaty law. It also introduced or affirmed new concepts, concerning the exclusive economic zone, fishing rights, the continental shelf, marine scientific research, pollution, transit passage through straits, the breadth of the territorial sea, and rights of landlocked states. Controversial provisions concerning mining the sea bed beyond national jurisdiction, an issue explored in Part E, delayed the entry into force of the Convention until November 1994, but 135 states, including most developed states, are now parties.

The concept of regimes, introduced in Chapter 10, is useful in thinking about the law of the sea. International lawyers do not usually speak of one regime governing the oceans, for law of the sea issues are so diverse. It probably is more helpful to think about one regime governing warships, for example, and another governing sea-bed mining. In each, the forums available to address legal issues and the relative importance of municipal and international law may vary. The 1982 Convention, customary international law, other treaties, and regulations of many international organizations (*e.g.*, the International Maritime Organization) shape the law in many issue areas. In addition, state agencies, including municipal courts, regularly address law of the sea matters.

This chapter begins with a look at two traditional law of the sea topics—the high seas and vessels. Part C then explores assertions of coastal state jurisdiction over parts of the commons and over resources on the continental shelf, in exclusive economic zones, and in fisheries zones. Part D addresses the territorial sea and straits, and Part E the regime governing deep sea-bed mining.

A. THE HIGH SEAS

The high seas have traditionally been regarded as international common space, open to all vessels and subject to the sovereignty of no state. The readings in this Part are separated by a period of 350 years. Hugo Grotius's 1633 treatise was influential in shaping conceptions of the legal status of the high seas. The excerpts from the 1982 U.N. Convention on the Law of the Sea provide a modern vantage point from which to assess some of the changes in the law governing the high seas.

HUGO GROTIUS, THE FREEDOM OF THE SEAS (1633)

Ralph van Deman Magoffin trans. & James Brown Scott ed. 1916.

My intention is to demonstrate briefly and clearly that the Dutch—that is to say, the subjects of the United Netherlands—have the right to sail to the East Indies, as they are now doing, and to engage in trade with the people there. I shall base my argument on the following most specific and unimpeachable axiom of the Law of Nations, called a primary rule or first principle, the spirit of which is self-evident and immutable, to wit; Every nation is free to travel to every other nation, and to trade with it.

God Himself says this speaking through the voice of nature; and inasmuch as it is not His will to have Nature supply every place with all the necessaries of life, He ordains that some nations excel in one art and others in another. Why is this His will, except it be that He wished human friendships to be engendered by mutual needs and resources, lest individuals deeming themselves entirely sufficient unto themselves should for that very reason be rendered unsociable? * * * Those therefore who deny this law, destroy this most praiseworthy bond of human fellowship, remove the opportunities for doing mutual service, in a word do violence to Nature herself. For do not the ocean[s], navigable in every direction with which God has encompassed all the earth, and the regular and the occasional winds which blow now from one quarter and now from another, offer sufficient proof that Nature has given to all peoples a right of access to all other peoples? * * *

If therefore the Portuguese have acquired no legal right over the nations of the East Indies, and their territory and sovereignty, let us consider whether they have been able to obtain exclusive jurisdiction over the sea and its navigation or over trade. Let us first consider the case of the sea.

Now, in the legal phraseology of the Law of Nations, the sea is called indifferently the property of no one (*res nullius*), or a common possession (*res communis*), or public property (*res publica*). It will be most convenient to explain the signification of these terms if we follow the practice of all the poets since Hesiod, of the philosophers and jurists of the past, and distinguish certain epochs, the divisions of which are marked off perhaps not so much by intervals of time as by obvious logic and essential character. And we ought not to be criticized if in our explanation of a law deriving from nature, we use the authority and definition of those whose natural judgment admittedly is held in the highest esteem. * * *

* * * [C]ommon possession relates to use, as is seen from a quotation from Seneca:

"Every path was free, All things were used in common."

According to his reasoning there was a kind of sovereignty, but it was universal and unlimited. For God had not given all things to this individual or to that, but to the entire human race, and thus a number of persons, as it were *en masse*, were not debarred from being substantially sovereigns or owners of the same thing, which is quite contradictory to our modern meaning of sovereignty. For it now implies particular or private ownership, a thing which no one then had. * * *

It seems certain that the transition to the present distinction of ownerships did not come violently, but gradually, nature herself pointing out the way. For since there are some things, the use of which consists in their being used up, either because having become part of the very substance of the user they can never be used again, or because by use they become less fit for future use, it has become apparent, especially in dealing with the first category, such things as food and drink for example, that a certain kind of ownership is inseparable from use. For "own" implies that a thing belongs to some one person, in such a way that it cannot belong to any other person. By the process of reasoning this was next extended to things of the second category, such as clothes and movables and some living things. * * *

This occupation or possession, however, in the case of things which resist seizure, like wild animals for example, must be uninterrupted or perpetually maintained, but in the case of other things it is sufficient if after physical possession is once taken the intention to possess is maintained. Possession of movables implies seizure, and possession of immovables either the erection of buildings or some determination of boundaries, such as fencing in. * * *

Two conclusions may be drawn from what has thus far been said. The first is, that which cannot be occupied, or which never has been occupied, cannot be the property of any one, because all property has arisen from occupation. The second is, that all that which has been so constituted by nature that although serving some one person it still suffices for the common use of all other persons, is today and ought in perpetuity to remain in the same condition as when it was first created by nature. * * *

The air * * * is not susceptible of occupation; and * * * its common use is destined for all men. For the same reasons the sea is common to all, because it is so limitless that it cannot become a possession of any one, and because it is adapted for the use of all, whether we consider it from the point of view of navigation or of fisheries. * * *

These things therefore are what the Romans call "common" to all men by natural law, or as we have said, "public" according to the law of nations; and indeed they call their use sometimes common, sometimes public. Nevertheless, although those things are with reason said to be *res nullius*, so far as private ownership is concerned, still they differ very much from those things which, though also *res nullius*, have not been marked out for common use, such for example as wild animals, fish, and birds. For if any one seizes those things and assumes possession of them, they can become objects of private ownership, but the things in the former category by the consensus of opinion of all mankind are forever exempt from such private ownership on account of their susceptibility to universal use; and as they belong to all they cannot be taken away from all by any one person any more than what is mine can be taken away from me by you. * * *

The nature of the sea * * * differs from that of the shore, because the sea, except for a very restricted space, can neither easily be built upon, nor inclosed; if the contrary were true yet this could hardly happen without hindrance to the general use. Nevertheless, if any small portion of the sea can be thus occupied, the occupation is recognized. * * *

Now Celsus holds that piles driven into the sea belong to the man who drove them. But such an act is not permissible if the use of the sea be thereby impaired. * * * Labeo * * * holds that in case any * * * construction should be made in the sea, the following injunction is to be enforced: "Nothing may be built in the sea whereby the harbor, the roadstead, or the channel be rendered less safe for navigation."

Now the same principle which applies to navigation applies also to fishing, namely, that it remains free and open to all. Nevertheless there shall be no prejudice if any one shall by fencing off with stakes an inlet of the sea make a fish pond for himself, and so establish a private preserve. * * *

* * * But outside of an inlet this will not hold, for then the common use of the sea might be hindered. * * *

* * * The Portuguese claim as their own the whole expanse of the sea which separates two parts of the world so far distant the one from the other, that in all the preceding centuries neither one has so much as heard of the other. Indeed, if we take into account the share of the Spaniards, whose claim is the same as that of the Portuguese, only a little less than the whole ocean is found to be subject to two nations, while all the rest of the peoples in the world are restricted to the narrow bounds of the northern seas. * * * If in a thing so vast as the sea a man were to reserve to himself from general use nothing more than mere sovereignty, still he would be considered a seeker after unreasonable power. If a man were to enjoin other people from fishing, he would not escape the reproach of monstrous greed. But the man who even prevents navigation, a thing which means no loss to himself, what are we to say of him? * * *

* * * For it is most outrageous for you to appropriate a thing, which both by ordinance of nature and by common consent is as much mine as yours, so exclusively that you will not grant me a right of use in it which leaves it no less yours than it was before. * * *

The last defense of injustice is usually a claim or plea based on prescription or on custom. To this defense therefore the Portuguese have resorted. But the best established reasoning of the law precludes them from enjoying the protection of either plea. * * *

* * * [I]t is impossible to acquire by usucaption or prescription things which cannot become property, that is, which are not susceptible of possession or of quasi-possession, and which cannot be alienated. All of which is true of the sea and its use. * * *

* * * [S]ince the law of nature arises out of Divine Providence, it is immutable; but a part of this natural law is the primary or primitive law of nations, differing from the secondary or positive law of nations, which is mutable. For if there are customs incompatible with the primary law of nations, then, according to the judgment of Vasquez, they are not customs belonging to men, but to wild beasts, customs which are corruptions and abuses, not laws and usages. Therefore those customs cannot become prescriptions by mere lapse of time, cannot be justified by the passage of any law, cannot be established by the consent, the protection, or the practice even of many nations. * * *

The conclusion of the whole matter therefore is that the Portuguese are in possession of no right whereby they may interdict to any nation whatsoever the navigation of the Ocean to the East Indies.

UNITED NATIONS CONVENTION ON THE LAW OF THE SEA, ARTICLES 86–90, 301

Dec. 10, 1982, 1833 U.N.T.S. 3.

High Seas

Article 86

Application of the provisions of this Part

The provisions of this Part apply to all parts of the sea that are not included in the exclusive economic zone, in the territorial sea or in the internal waters of a State, or in the archipelagic waters of an archipelagic State. This article does not entail any abridgement of the freedoms enjoyed by all States in the exclusive economic zone in accordance with article 58.

Article 87

Freedom of the high seas

1. The high seas are open to all States, whether coastal or land-locked. Freedom of the high seas is exercised under the conditions laid down by this Convention and by other rules of international law. It comprises, *inter alia*, both for coastal and land-locked States:

(a) freedom of navigation;

(b) freedom of overflight;

(c) freedom to lay submarine cables and pipelines, subject to Part VI;

(d) freedom to construct artificial islands and other installations permitted under international law, subject to Part VI;

(e) freedom of fishing, subject to the conditions laid down in section 2;

(f) freedom of scientific research, subject to Parts VI and XIII.

2. These freedoms shall be exercised by all States with due regard for the interests of other States in their exercise of the freedom of the high seas, and also with due regard for the rights under this Convention with respect to activities in the Area.

Article 88

Reservation of the high seas for peaceful purposes

The high seas shall be reserved for peaceful purposes.

Article 89

Invalidity of claims of sovereignty over the high seas

No State may validly purport to subject any part of the high seas to its sovereignty.

Article 90

Right of navigation

Every State, whether coastal or land-locked, has the right to sail ships flying its flag on the high seas.

General Provisions * * *

Article 301

Peaceful uses of the seas

In exercising their rights and performing their duties under this Convention, States Parties shall refrain from any threat or use of force against the territorial integrity or political independence of any State, or in any other manner inconsistent with the principles of international law embodied in the Charter of the United Nations.

Notes and Questions

1. *Hugo Grotius.* Hugo Grotius was a prodigy. He knew Latin and Greek by age 8, entered university at age 11, edited an encyclopedia at 15, was a lawyer pleading cases in the highest court of the Netherlands at 16, and became Attorney General of the Netherlands by the time he was 24. Grotius gained fame not only as a lawyer, but as a diplomat and a political and legal theorist. He is one of the most important figures in the history of international law. His *De Mare Liberum* was originally a chapter of *De Iure Praede* (*Commentary on the Law of Prize and Booty*), a work written in 1604–1605. Grotius's most famous work, *De Jure Belli ac Pacis* (*On the Law of War and Peace*), was published in 1625.

2. *Grotius and High Seas Freedoms.* Grotius wrote *De Iure Praede* to support Dutch access to the East Indian trade and to dispute Portugal's claims over the high seas. *De Mare Liberum* was separately published in 1609, probably in anticipation of a proclamation by King James I of England which prohibited foreigners from fishing in "British seas" unless they obtained a British license. How did Grotius envision the legal regime of the high seas? How did he support his position?

3. *John Selden and Closed Seas.* Grotius's views did not go unchallenged. The best-known response is that of the Englishman John Selden, who published *Mare Clausum sive De Domino Maris* in 1635. Selden argued that the seas could be appropriated, and that various uses of the oceans could diminish the owner's rights. Selden's work supported such British practices as requiring foreigners to obtain fishing licenses, demanding that foreign ships strike their flags in salute to British ships in "British seas," stopping hostilities by foreign ships in those seas, and imposing certain tolls on the passage of foreign vessels. See Ruth Lapidoth, "Freedom of Navigation—Its Legal History and Its Normative Basis," 6 *Journal of Maritime Law and Commerce* 259 (1975).

4. *British Sea Power and High Seas Freedoms.* Grotius's notion of the high seas as not subject to exclusive sovereignty came to be generally accepted:

During the 19th century, British sea power, then supreme, helped consolidate an international maritime regime based on the freedoms of the high seas, freedoms to travel and to fish without coastal state regulation outside a 3–mile territorial sea. This was a customary legal regime, not written in any convention or treaty. It was, however, remarkably effective, respected by most states in times of peace from the end of the Napoleonic Wars in 1815 to the end of World War II in 1945. As a result, for over a century, navies and other users of the oceans could sail freely on seas covering some 70 percent of the earth's surface. Only within a narrow band of 3 miles, the territorial sea, did coastal states put some legal limits on the mobility of naval forces.

Mark W. Janis, *Sea Power and the Law of the Sea* xiii-xiv (1976).

5. *20th-century Conceptions of High Seas Freedoms.* Article 2 of the 1958 Geneva Convention on the High Seas explicitly named navigation, fishing, overflight, and the laying of submarine cables and pipelines as high seas freedoms. These are repeated in Article 87 of the 1982 Convention on the Law of the Sea, which added the freedom of scientific research and the freedom to build artificial islands and other installations permitted under international law to the list of high seas freedoms. Are other, unenumerated uses legitimate? For example, states have, from time to time, used the high seas for military purposes. Would it be legitimate for a state to declare a military test site in the oceans? To place weapons or military detection devices on the sea bed, invoking traditional high seas freedoms? What do you make of Articles 88 and 301 of the 1982 Convention? For discussion of some military activities on the high seas, see the *Amerada Hess* case in Chapter 4. Overall, what modifications of the Grotian conception of *mare liberum* do Articles 86–90 of the 1982 United Nations Convention on the Law of the Sea reflect?

6. *Controlling Activities on the High Seas.* If the high seas are generally open to ships for a variety of purposes, who is responsible for maintaining order there? What if a vessel is in an unsafe operating condition, or threatens other vessels or the environment? What if a ship engages in such egregious practices as slave trading, piracy, or the dumping of dangerous chemicals? The next Part addresses the system of control over activities on the high seas.

B. VESSELS

Jurisdiction and control over the actions of and activities on board vessels on the high seas have traditionally been left to the vessel's "flag state," the state of the vessel's nationality. The first reading in this Part, an excerpt from a 1905 arbitral decision, explores the concept of vessel nationality. Both that decision and the second reading, taken from a British government report about oil spills from vessels, also suggest some of the problems that arise when some flag states do not effectively exercise control over their vessels. What steps have and should be taken to address these problems? The Notes and the last two readings—from a recent decision by the International Tribunal for the Law of the Sea and from the 1982 Law of the Sea Convention—explore that question.

CASE OF THE MUSCAT DHOWS

France–Great Britain, 1905, in *The Hague Arbitration
Cases* 64 (George G. Wilson ed. 1915).

The Tribunal of Arbitration constituted in virtue of the Compromis concluded at London on October 13, 1904 between Great Britain and France;

Whereas the Government of His Britannic Majesty and that of the French Republic have thought it right by the Declaration of March 10, 1862 "to engage reciprocally to respect the independence" of His Highness the Sultan of Muscat,

Whereas difficulties as to the scope of that Declaration have arisen in relation to the issue, by the French Republic, to certain subjects of His Highness the Sultan of Muscat of papers authorizing them to fly the French flag, and also as to the nature of the privileges and immunities claimed by subjects of His Highness who are owners or masters of dhows and in possession of such papers or are members of the crew of such dhows and their families, especially as to the manner in which such privileges and immunities affect the jurisdiction of His Highness the Sultan over his said subjects,

Whereas the two Governments have agreed by the Compromis of October 13, 1904 that these questions shall be determined by reference to arbitration * * *;

AS TO THE FIRST QUESTION:

Whereas generally speaking it belongs to every Sovereign to decide to whom he will accord the right to fly his flag and to prescribe the rules governing such grants, and whereas therefore the granting of the French flag to subjects of His Highness the Sultan of Muscat in itself constitutes no attack on the independence of the Sultan,

Whereas nevertheless a Sovereign may be limited by treaties in the exercise of this right, and * * * whereas therefore the question arises, under what conditions Powers which have acceded to the General Act of the Brussels Conference of July 2, 1890 relative to the African Slave Trade, especially to article 32 of this Act, are entitled to authorize native vessels to fly their flags,

Whereas by article 32 of this Act the faculty of the Signatory Powers to grant their flag to native vessels has been limited for the purpose of suppressing slave trading and in the general interests of humanity, irrespective of whether the applicant for the flag may belong to a state signatory of this Act or not, and whereas at any rate France is in relation to Great Britain bound to grant her flag only under the conditions prescribed by this Act,

Whereas in order to attain the above mentioned purpose, the Signatory Powers of the Brussels Act have agreed in its article 32 that the authority to fly the flag of one of the Signatory Powers shall in future only be granted to such native vessels, which shall satisfy all the three following conditions:

1.   Their fitters-out or owners must be either subjects of or persons protected by [protégés] the Power whose flag they claim to fly,

2.   They must furnish proof that they possess real estate situated in the district of the authority to whom their application is addressed, or supply a solvent security as a guarantee for any fines to which they may eventually become liable,

3.   Such fitters-out or owners, as well as the captain of the vessel, must furnish proof that they enjoy a good reputation, and especially that they have never been condemned for acts of slave trade,

Whereas in default of a definition of the term "protégé" in the General Act of the Brussels Conference this term must be understood in the sense which corresponds best as well to the elevated aims of the Conference and its Final Act, as to the principles of the law of nations, as they have been expressed in treaties existing at that time, in internationally recognized legislation and in international practice,

Whereas the aim of the said article 32 is to admit to navigation in the seas infested by slave trade only those native vessels which are under the strictest surveillance of the Signatory Powers, a condition which can only be secured if the owners, fitters-out and crews of such vessels are exclusively subjected to the sovereignty and jurisdiction of the State, under whose flag they are sailing,

[The tribunal examines the meaning of the term "protégé." It reviews several instruments, including an 1863 French treaty and an 1863 municipal statute that limited France's rights to create new "protégés."]

Whereas the fact of having granted before the ratification of the Brussels Act on January 2, 1892 authorizations to fly the French flag to native vessels not satisfying the conditions prescribed by article 32 of this Act was not in contradiction with any international obligation of France,

FOR THESE REASONS,

decides and pronounces as follows:

1.   *before the 2nd of January 1892 France was entitled to authorize vessels belonging to subjects of His Highness the Sultan of Muscat to fly the French flag, only bound by her own legislation and administrative rules;*

2.   *owners of dhows, who before 1892 have been authorized by France to fly the French flag, retain this authorization as long as France renews it to the grantee;*

3.   *after January 2, 1892 France was not entitled to authorize vessels belonging to subjects of His Highness the Sultan of Muscat to fly the*

French flag, except on condition that their owners or fitters-out had established or should establish that they had been considered and treated by France as her "protégés" before the year 1863;

AS TO THE 2ND QUESTION:

Whereas the legal situation of vessels flying foreign flags and of the owners of such vessels in the territorial waters of an Oriental State is determined by the general principles of jurisdiction, by * * * treaties and by the practice resulting therefrom,

Whereas the terms of the Treaty of Friendship and Commerce between France and the Iman of Muscat of November 17, 1844, [preclude visits by the authorities of the Sultan to French vessels without the consent of such vessels],

Whereas, although it cannot be denied that by admitting the right of France to grant under certain circumstances her flag to native vessels and to have these vessels exempted from visitation by the authorities of the Sultan or in his name, slave trade is facilitated, because slave traders may easily abuse the French flag, for the purpose of escaping from search, the possibility of this abuse, which can be entirely suppressed by the accession of all Powers to article 42 of the Brussels Convention, cannot affect the decision of this case, which must only rest on juridical grounds, * * *

FOR THESE REASONS,

decides and pronounces as follows:

*1. dhows of Muscat authorized as aforesaid to fly the French flag are entitled in the territorial waters of Muscat to the inviolability provided by the French–Muscat Treaty of November 17, 1844; * * *.*

Done at The Hague, in the Permanent Court of Arbitration, August 8, 1905.

SAFER SHIPS, CLEANER SEAS

Report of Lord Donaldson's Inquiry Into the Prevention of Pollution From Merchant Shipping, Cm. 2560 (1994).

1.1 On 5 January 1993 one of the Shetland Islanders' worst nightmares became a reality. The MV *BRAER* went onto the rocks at Garths Ness. She was fully laden with 84,700 tonnes of Norwegian Gullfaks crude oil and some 1,600 tonnes of heavy fuel oil bunkers. The weather was atrocious—storm force winds and mountainous seas. There were all the makings of a major economic and ecological disaster for the local community.

1.2 In the event the consequences were serious but miraculously less catastrophic than might have been expected. * * *

1.29 * * * [T]he *BRAER* was registered in Liberia * * *. * * *

1.31 It must not be forgotten that on 3 December 1992, only a month before the *BRAER* was wrecked off Shetland, the tanker *AEGEAN SEA* was wrecked off La Coruña in northern Spain. * * *

6.1 In an ideal world Flag States, whose flags are worn by the world's shipping, would lay down, and enforce upon their own shipowners, standards of design, maintenance and operation which would ensure a very high standard of safety at sea. Coastal States, along whose coasts shipping passes, and Port States, at whose ports or anchorages shipping calls, would have no cause to concern themselves with the maintenance of such standards.

6.2 The present system of Flag State Control falls well short of this ideal. At any one time the fleet of any Flag State will be scattered throughout the world. No Flag State has the resources to police its fleet on a continuous and all-embracing basis. The most that it can do is to insist upon periodic surveys and to undertake *ad hoc* inspection if it learns that a ship has suffered a casualty or, for some other reason such as a Port State Control inspection, it suspects that its ship no longer complies with internationally agreed standards. Good shipowners will maintain the seaworthiness of their ships regardless of whether a Flag State periodical survey is imminent. Regrettably, bad shipowners regard the imminence of such a survey as the only reason for spending money on maintenance or repairs and then only if satisfied that the survey will be thorough.

6.3 In this situation, even if Flag States were to comply to the full with their responsibilities, Coastal and Port States would have a part to play. They would, in their own interests, be concerned to detect the few unseaworthy ships which had escaped the Flag State net. Their role would be to supplement and support Flag State Control, but not to substitute for it.

6.4 Regrettably it is beyond argument that not all Flag States live up to their responsibilities. Figures for deficiencies and detections revealed by Port State Control inspections show that, for example, of 61 Indian registered ships inspected over one in four were so seriously deficient that they had to be detained in port. Over 85 per cent of the inspections of Indian registered ships uncovered deficiencies. India, although a striking example, is by no means alone and a number of other Flag States also have a poor record.

[The Report demonstrates that the United Kingdom's percentage of the world's shipping has declined significantly, and that the U.K. depends heavily on foreign-flag vessels to move its goods.]

6.8 A State which confers its nationality upon a ship, and thus authorizes it to fly its flag, has an unfettered right to subject that ship to its laws. This enables it to impose and maintain standards of design, construction, equipment, maintenance and operation. Whilst there is no upper limit to these standards, there are lower limits. These stem from the various international Conventions to which Flag States are parties, such as the SOLAS, MARPOL 73/78 and Load Line Conventions, under which Flag States are required to establish that ships flying their flags comply with the provisions of those Conventions and to issue the necessary certificates of compliance. * * *

6.9 Economic and competitive considerations effectively prevent Flag States from imposing standards which are higher than those internationally agreed and any improvement in standards is thus only achievable by international agreement. The machinery for such agreement is provided by the International Maritime Organization (IMO). * * *

6.12 It is for Flag States individually to decide how to give effect to their international obligations. In some cases the international Conventions specify precise requirements. SOLAS, for example, requires minimum pressures at fire hydrants and MARPOL includes precise formulae for the calculation of positions of ballast tanks. But in other cases, the Conventions merely specify that equipment must be "approved" by the Flag State or be "to the satisfaction of the Flag State." Sometimes such lack of precision is necessary for technical reasons or to allow for innovation. Regrettably in others it is merely designed to conceal differences of view between the members of IMO. * * *

6.18 When the international Conventions were originally drafted, most of the world's merchant fleet was owned by, and flew the flags of, the world's major maritime and trading powers. These States had already established survey and inspection of their ships as a matter of public policy aimed at protecting the safety of crews and passengers. While the setting of such standards was not immune from commercial pressures from shipowning interests, their enforcement was not subject to such pressures. This was presumably in reflection of the fact that in the UK, for example, there had been a long history of regulation through the Board of Trade and the fact that most UK trade was carried in UK ships which were subject to the same standards and accordingly competed fairly with one another. States had little or no direct financial interest in shipping and could apply and enforce standards in the interests of public policy without feeling any pressure to maintain or enhance their merchant fleets.

6.19 All that has changed. Today few States regard it as consistent with their national status and dignity to be without a register of national shipping of as large a size as possible. Some also regard such a register as a useful source of income. In seeking to achieve this aim, some see no need to limit eligibility to ships whose owners or operators have any connection with the State. They maintain what are called "open" registers. A few such States are landlocked and have no connection with the sea. Rather more include ships which are never likely to call at a national port. Perhaps in recognition of this fact one of the largest and, it has to be said, one of the most efficient, Liberia, maintains its register and discharges its responsibilities from an office in the USA. Relatively few Liberian ships ever call at Monrovia, their usual port of registry. Another example is Vanuatu, which has few foreign exports and whose register is run from the USA and London.

6.20 All this might be unobjectionable if, despite the very considerable difficulties in enforcing standards on ships (and shipowners) which have no real connection with the State whose flag the ships fly, agreed international standards were universally enforced. However they are not. The vice of "open" registers is twofold. First, in practice they lead to varying standards of safety. This is easily demonstrated by [statistics on] the incidence of total losses by flag. Second, the existence of "open" registers and the consequent ease with which ships can be transferred to a different register and flag has led to some shipowners shopping around for the registers which have the lowest standards of enforcement and which, in consequence, involve them in the least expense. This is positively encouraged by some of the Flag States concerned which have even been known to advertise competitive "prices" for their survey and certification work.

Notes and Questions

1. *The* Muscat Dhows *Arbitration.* The *Muscat Dhows Case* was conducted before the Permanent Court of Arbitration, which is discussed in Chapter 5. The case arose after the British captured, at the request of the Sultan of Oman, five Omani subjects holding French papers. Britain agreed to advise the Sultan to release the men if France agreed to arbitrate the question of the rights of French flag holders in the area. The arbitration was set against the backdrop of competing French and British efforts to assert authority in the Persian Gulf, with French influence on the wane. Also important were a series of French–British treaties on which the British had relied to exercise limited rights with respect to vessels flying the French flag that were suspected of engaging in the slave trade.

Note that Muscat (Oman) was not a party to the arbitration. The Sultan was reportedly dissuaded from sending an Omani representative to The Hague because of the cost involved, and he asked Britain to act on Oman's behalf. France was not willing to accept this arrangement, however, and Oman was left out of the case. Following the arbitral decision, it took France and Britain over three years to agree on which particular French protégés and dhows were "grandfathered" under the French flag. For accounts of the arbitration and events leading up to it, see Briton Cooper Busch, *Britain and the Persian Gulf, 1894–1914*, at 154–86 (1967), and Charles Brunet–Millon, *Les Boutriers de la Mer des Indes* (1910).

2. *The Nationality of Ships.* During the *Muscat Dhows* arbitration, Great Britain argued that "Frenchifying" the dhows infringed on the independence of the Sultan of Muscat, because dhows owned by Muscat nationals were "thereby withdrawn from their natural jurisdiction" and could not be searched by Muscat warships. *The Times (London)*, July 25, 1905, at 5. The arbitral tribunal, however, affirmed the general rule that a state may authorize any vessel to fly its flag. The flag that a ship is entitled to fly is a symbol of its nationality. States normally register ships to establish their nationality, issuing documents that those ships can use as proof of their nationality. See Article 91 of the 1982 U.N. Convention on the Law of the Sea.

3. *Flag State Authority and the Nationality of Ships.* Why is it important for ships to have nationality? Consider the following passage from

United States v. Marino–Garcia, 679 F.2d 1373, 1382 (11th Cir.1982), in which the court addresses the nature of stateless vessels:

> * * * Vessels without nationality are international pariahs. They have no internationally recognized right to navigate freely on the high seas. Moreover, flagless vessels are frequently not subject to the laws of a flag-state. As such they represent "floating sanctuaries from authority" and constitute a potential threat to the order and stability of navigation on the high seas.
>
> The absence of any right to navigate freely on the high seas coupled with the potential threat to order on international waterways has led various courts to conclude that international law places no restrictions upon a nation's right to subject stateless vessels to its jurisdiction.

On the high seas, a ship is generally immune from the exercise of jurisdiction except by the authorities of the ship's flag state. See Article 92 of the U.N. Convention on the Law of the Sea. There are limited exceptions to the principle of exclusive flag state jurisdiction and control on the high seas. For example, as we saw in *United States v. Smith* in Chapter 3, any state may exercise jurisdiction in cases of piracy.

4. *Coastal State Control of Foreign Flag Vessels.* The second question discussed in the *Muscat Dhows Case* suggests that a coastal state may visit foreign flag vessels while they are in the territorial sea, a zone of coastal state sovereignty that today may extend up to 12 miles from a state's coastal baselines. The coastal state may by treaty limit its rights in this regard, as Muscat had done in this case. We further address coastal state jurisdiction in the territorial sea, as well as the right of foreign flag vessels to "innocent passage" through the territorial sea, in Part D of this chapter.

With respect to pollution issues, coastal states today have considerable rights to set standards and to take enforcement measures in their offshore zones. These measures may affect foreign flag ships. See Articles 220–221 of the U.N. Convention on the Law of the Sea. Should coastal states have the right to take steps to prevent pollution from foreign flag ships on the high seas?

5. *Open Registry.* A system of flag state control poses particular difficulties if a flag state cannot or will not control its ships. The *Muscat Dhows* tribunal expressed concern that "slavetraders may easily abuse the French flag, for the purpose of escaping from search." Similar concerns have been raised, more recently, with respect to unsafe labor conditions on board ships and threats of oil spills. Almost 90 years after the *Muscat Dhows* decision, the Liberian-flag *Braer* spilled huge quantities of crude oil when it ran aground off the Shetlands. The *Braer*'s largely Filipino crew told the International Transport Workers' Federation in 1992 that the aging ship was undermanned. Jason Benetto, "The Cut-price Recipe for Catastrophe," *Independent on Sunday*, Jan. 10, 1993, at 22. Although vessels registered in "open registry" (also known as "flag of convenience") states certainly are not responsible for all vessel safety and pollution problems—the *Exxon Valdez*, which caused a massive oil spill off Alaska in 1989, was registered in the United States—the safety record of many such vessels has been questionable.

A 1970 British committee headed by Lord Rochdale identified six features common to open registry:

(i) The country of registry allows ownership and/or control of its merchant vessels by non-citizens;

(ii) Access to the registry is easy. A ship may usually be registered at a consul's office abroad. Equally important, transfer from the registry at the owner's option is not restricted;

(iii) Taxes on the income from the ships are not levied locally or are low. A registry fee and an annual fee, based on tonnage, are normally the only charges made. A guarantee or acceptable understanding regarding future freedom from taxation may also be given;

(iv) The country of registry is a small power with no national requirement under any foreseeable circumstances for all the shipping registered, but receipts from very small charges on a large tonnage may produce a substantial effect on its national income and balance of payments;

(v) Manning of ships by non-nationals is freely permitted; and

(vi) The country of registry has neither the power nor the administrative machinery effectively to impose any government or international regulations; nor has the country the wish or the power to control the companies themselves.

Committee of Inquiry into Shipping, *Report* 51, Cmnd. 4337 (1970). As of 1996, according to one study, flag of convenience vessels, registered in such states as the Bahamas, Honduras, Liberia, Malta, Panama, Saint Vincent and the Grenadines, and Vanuatu, accounted for approximately 20 per cent of the world's total number of ships and over 45 per cent of the world's total of shipping tons. K.X. Li & J. Wonham, "New Developments in Ship Registration," 14 *International Journal of Marine and Coastal Law* 137, 144–45 (1999).

6. *Limiting Flag State Grants of Nationality.* In the *Muscat Dhows Case*, should France have had an unqualified right to determine the conditions under which a vessel was entitled to fly the French flag? Would conditions such as those set forth in Article 32 of the General Act of the Brussels Conference of 1890 make sense today? States generally have not accepted significant limitations on their right to grant nationality to vessels. One limited response to open registry is the "genuine link" requirement, explored in the next excerpt.

THE M/V "SAIGA" (NO. 2)

Saint Vincent and the Grenadines v. Guinea,
International Tribunal for the Law of the Sea,
38 *International Legal Materials* 1323 (1999).

[The *Saiga*, a tanker flying the flag of Saint Vincent and the Grenadines, was engaged in supplying fuel oil to fishing vessels in Guinea's exclusive economic zone, an area we discuss in Part C. On October 28, 1997, a Guinean patrol boat attacked the *Saiga*, arrested it, and brought the vessel and its crew to port in Conkary, Guinea, where the master was detained and the cargo of fuel oil was discharged. Guinea claimed the *Saiga*'s supplying of fuel to fishing vessels violated Guinean customs laws and filed criminal charges against the master, who received a suspended sentence of six months imprisonment and a fine. In this case, Saint Vincent and the Grenadines claimed, *inter alia*, that Guinea interfered with the navigation rights of a Vincentian vessel and used excessive force in stopping and arresting the vessel. The International Tribunal for the Law of the Sea, in this judgment of July 1, 1999, ultimately rules in favor of Saint Vincent and the Grenadines on several issues, and awards that state $2,123,357 as compensation.

The Tribunal also addresses arguments raised by Guinea urging that, as a threshold matter, the claims of Saint Vincent and the Grenadines were inadmissible. One of the admissibility arguments, concerning the issue of "genuine link," is considered in the excerpt below.]

75. The next objection to admissibility raised by Guinea is that there was no genuine link between the *Saiga* and Saint Vincent and the Grenadines. Guinea contends that "without a genuine link between Saint Vincent and the Grenadines and the M/V 'Saiga,' Saint Vincent and the Grenadines' claim concerning a violation of its right of navigation and the status of the ship is not admissible before the Tribunal *vis-à-vis* Guinea, because Guinea is not bound to recognize the Vincentian nationality of the M/V 'Saiga,' which forms a prerequisite for the mentioned claim in international law."

76. Guinea further argues that a State cannot fulfill its obligations as a flag State under the [1982 United Nations] Convention [on the Law of the Sea] with regard to a ship unless it exercises prescriptive and enforcement jurisdiction over the owner or, as the case may be, the operator of the ship. Guinea contends that, in the absence of such jurisdiction, there is no genuine link between the ship and Saint Vincent and the Grenadines and that, accordingly, it is not obliged to recognize the claims of Saint Vincent and the Grenadines in relation to the ship.

77. Saint Vincent and the Grenadines maintains that there is nothing in the Convention to support the contention that the existence of a genuine link between a ship and a State is a necessary precondition for the grant of nationality to the ship, or that the absence of such a genuine link deprives a flag State of the right to bring an international claim against another State in respect of illegal measures taken against the ship.

78. Saint Vincent and the Grenadines also challenges the assertion of Guinea that there was no genuine link between the *Saiga* and Saint Vincent and the Grenadines. It claims that the requisite genuine link existed between it and the ship. Saint Vincent and the Grenadines calls attention to various facts which, according to it, provide evidence of this link. These include the fact that the owner of the *Saiga* is represented in Saint Vincent and the Grenadines by a company formed and established

in that State and the fact that the *Saiga* is subject to the supervision of the Vincentian authorities to secure compliance with the International Convention for the Safety of Life at Sea (SOLAS), 1960 and 1974, the International Convention for the Prevention of Pollution from Ships, 1973, as modified by the Protocol of 1978 relating thereto (MARPOL 73/78), and other conventions of the International Maritime Organization to which Saint Vincent and the Grenadines is a party. In addition, Saint Vincent and the Grenadines maintains that arrangements have been made to secure regular supervision of the vessel's seaworthiness through surveys, on at least an annual basis, conducted by reputable classification societies authorized for that purpose by Saint Vincent and the Grenadines. Saint Vincent and the Grenadines also points out that, under its laws, preference is given to Vincentian nationals in the manning of ships flying its flag. It further draws attention to the vigorous efforts made by its authorities to secure the protection of the *Saiga* on the international plane before and throughout the present dispute.

79. Article 91, paragraph 1, of the [1982 Law of the Sea] Convention provides: "There must exist a genuine link between the State and the ship." Two questions need to be addressed in this connection. The first is whether the absence of a genuine link between a flag State and a ship entitles another State to refuse to recognize the nationality of the ship. The second question is whether or not a genuine link existed between the *Saiga* and Saint Vincent and the Grenadines at the time of the incident.

80. With regard to the first question, the Tribunal notes that the provision in article 91, paragraph 1, of the Convention, requiring a genuine link between the State and the ship, does not provide the answer. Nor do articles 92 and 94 of the Convention, which together with article 91 constitute the context of the provision, provide the answer. The Tribunal, however, recalls that the International Law Commission, in article 29 of the Draft Articles on the Law of the Sea adopted by it in 1956, proposed the concept of a "genuine link" as a criterion not only for the attribution of nationality to a ship but also for the recognition by other States of such nationality. After providing that "ships have the nationality of the State whose flag they are entitled to fly," the draft article continued: "Nevertheless, for purposes of recognition of the national character of the ship by other States, there must exist a genuine link between the State and the ship." This sentence was not included in article 5, paragraph 1, of the Convention on the High Seas of 29 April 1958 (hereinafter "the 1958 Convention"), which reads, in part, as follows:

> There must exist a genuine link between the State and the ship; in particular, the State must effectively exercise its jurisdiction and control in administrative, technical and social matters over ships flying its flag.

Thus, while the obligation regarding a genuine link was maintained in the 1958 Convention, the proposal that the existence of a genuine link should be a basis for the recognition of nationality was not adopted.

81. The [1982] Convention follows the approach of the 1958 Convention. Article 91 retains the part of the third sentence of article 5, paragraph 1, of the 1958 Convention which provides that there must be a genuine link between the State and the ship. The other part of that sentence, stating that the flag State shall effectively exercise its jurisdiction and control in administrative, technical and social matters over ships flying its flag, is reflected in article 94 of the Convention, dealing with the duties of the flag State.

82. Paragraphs 2 to 5 of article 94 of the Convention outline the measures that a flag State is required to take to exercise effective jurisdiction as envisaged in paragraph 1. Paragraph 6 sets out the procedure to be followed where another State has "clear grounds to believe that proper jurisdiction and control with respect to a ship have not been exercised." That State is entitled to report the facts to the flag State which is then obliged to "investigate the matter and, if appropriate, take any action necessary to remedy the situation." There is nothing in article 94 to permit a State which discovers evidence indicating the absence of proper jurisdiction and control by a flag State over a ship to refuse to recognize the right of the ship to fly the flag of the flag State.

83. The conclusion of the Tribunal is that the purpose of the provisions of the Convention on the need for a genuine link between a ship and its flag State is to secure more effective implementation of the duties of the flag State, and not to establish criteria by reference to which the validity of the registration of ships in a flag State may be challenged by other States. * * *

86. In the light of the above considerations, the Tribunal concludes that there is no legal basis for the claim of Guinea that it can refuse to recognize the right of the *Saiga* to fly the flag of Saint Vincent and the Grenadines on the ground that there was no genuine link between the ship and Saint Vincent and the Grenadines.

87. With regard to the second question, the Tribunal finds that, in any case, the evidence adduced by Guinea is not sufficient to justify its contention that there was no genuine link between the ship and Saint Vincent and the Grenadines at the material time. * * *

183. For the above reasons, the Tribunal * * *

(4) By 18 votes to 2,

> *Rejects* the objection to the admissibility of the claims of Saint Vincent and the Grenadines based on Guinea's contention that there was no genuine link between Saint Vincent and the Grenadines and the *Saiga* at the time of its arrest[.]

UNITED NATIONS CONVENTION ON THE LAW OF THE SEA, ARTICLE 94

Dec. 10, 1982, 1833 U.N.T.S. 3.

Duties of the flag state

1. Every State shall effectively exercise its jurisdiction and control in administrative, technical and social matters over ships flying its flag.

2. In particular, every State shall:

(a) maintain a register of ships containing the names and particulars of ships flying its flag, except those which are excluded from generally accepted international regulations on account of their small size; and

(b) assume jurisdiction under its internal law over each ship flying its flag and its master, officers and crew in respect of administrative, technical and social matters concerning the ship.

3. Every State shall take such measures for ships flying its flag as are necessary to ensure safety at sea with regard, *inter alia*, to:

(a) the construction, equipment and seaworthiness of ships;

(b) the manning of ships, labour conditions and the training of crews, taking into account the applicable international instruments;

(c) the use of signals, the maintenance of communications and the prevention of collisions.

4. Such measures shall include those necessary to ensure:

(a) that each ship, before registration and thereafter at appropriate intervals, is surveyed by a qualified surveyor of ships, and has on board such charts, nautical publications and navigational equipment and instruments as are appropriate for the safe navigation of the ship;

(b) that each ship is in the charge of a master and officers who possess appropriate qualifications, in particular in seamanship, navigation, communications and marine engineering, and that the crew is appropriate in qualifications and numbers for the type, size, machinery and equipment of the ship;

(c) that the master, officers and, to the extent appropriate, the crew are fully conversant with and required to observe the applicable international regulations concerning the safety of life at sea, the prevention of collisions, the prevention, reduction and control of marine pollution, and the maintenance of communications by radio.

5. In taking the measures called for in paragraphs 3 and 4 each State is required to conform to generally accepted international regula-

tions, procedures and practices and to take any steps which may be necessary to secure their observance.

6. A State which has clear grounds to believe that proper jurisdiction and control with respect to a ship have not been exercised may report the facts to the flag State. Upon receiving such a report, the flag State shall investigate the matter and, if appropriate, take any action necessary to remedy the situation.

7. Each State shall cause an inquiry to be held by or before a suitably qualified person or persons into every marine casualty or incident of navigation on the high seas involving a ship flying its flag and causing loss of life or serious injury to nationals of another State or serious damage to ships or installations of another State or to the marine environment. The flag State and the other State shall co-operate in the conduct of any inquiry held by that other State into any such marine casualty or incident of navigation.

Notes and Questions

1. *The International Tribunal for the Law of the Sea.* Part XV of the 1982 Convention on the Law of the Sea provides for obligatory reference of certain disputes to third-party tribunals if negotiated settlements fail. Parties may choose among different fora, including the International Tribunal for the Law of the Sea (ITLOS), which decided the *Saiga Case.* The ITLOS is located in Hamburg, Germany; its 21 judges were elected after the Convention entered into force in November 1994.

If states parties to a dispute do not agree on the same forum, or fail to indicate a preferred forum, the dispute will usually be referred to binding arbitration. However, when a flag state seeks only the prompt release of a vessel and crew being detained by a coastal state under specific circumstances, or when provisional relief is sought, the ITLOS has residual compulsory jurisdiction. The *Saiga* dispute led to three different decisions by the ITLOS. First, on December 4, 1997, the ITLOS ordered the prompt release of the *Saiga* and its crew on the posting of a $400,000 bond. Second, on March 11, 1998, the Tribunal prescribed provisional measures, ordering Guinea to refrain from taking certain enforcement measures. Third, the Tribunal decided the merits of the case, in the decision excerpted above; jurisdiction at this stage was pursuant to a special agreement concluded between Guinea and Saint Vincent and the Grenadines. For an overview of the ITLOS, see John E. Noyes, "The International Tribunal for the Law of the Sea," 28 *Cornell International Law Journal* 109 (1998).

2. *The "Genuine Link" Requirement.* What does the "genuine link" requirement mean? Is this requirement a type of "soft law"? Compare the Kellogg–Briand Agreement in Chapter 2. Should a lack of a genuine link between a flag state and a vessel allow one state to refuse to recognize the nationality of that vessel? Compare the *Nottebohm Case* in Chapter 6.

3. *Specifying the Responsibilities of Flag States.* States have accepted treaty provisions insisting that each flag state exercise administrative and supervisory responsibilities with respect to ships flying its flag. Article 94 of

the 1982 Convention on the Law of the Sea is one example. Does this article provide a reasonable approach to the challenges posed by open registry states? How else should international law and process respond to those challenges? Would a system of inspections and approvals of ship safety by an international regulatory body be preferable?

4. *Multiple Treaty Obligations.* Besides the 1982 U.N. Convention on the Law of the Sea, numerous other treaties set rules governing ships and shipboard activities. Many contain specific substantive standards. The Law of the Sea Tribunal in the *Saiga Case* and Lord Donaldson's Report mentioned a few examples: the Convention on Safety of Life at Sea, Nov. 1, 1974, 32 U.S.T. 47, 1184 U.N.T.S. 2 (SOLAS); the International Convention on the Prevention of Pollution from Ships, Nov. 2 1973, 13 I.L.M. 605 (1974), and its 1978 Protocol, Feb. 17, 1978, 17 I.L.M. 548 (1978) (MARPOL 73/78); and the International Convention on Load Lines, Apr. 5, 1966, 18 U.S.T. 1857, 640 U.N.T.S. 133.

In taking the measures listed in Article 94(3) and (4) of the 1982 Law of the Sea Convention, a flag state must "conform to generally accepted international regulations, procedures and practices." Such regulations may be embodied in a growing number of international conventions adopted primarily under the auspices of the International Maritime Organization (IMO). The reference to "generally accepted" standards, which also appears elsewhere in the 1982 Convention (*e.g.*, Article 21, reproduced at page 696 below), apparently means that a State Party to the Convention may be legally obligated to apply detailed standards developed by the IMO even if that state is not a party to the specific treaty that sets the standards. But what determines whether a regulation has been "generally accepted"? Is the inquiry identical to whether the standard has been accepted as customary international law? Is the practice of ship owners or other private entities relevant in determining "general acceptance"? For discussion, see Bernard H. Oxman, "The Duty to Respect Generally Accepted International Standards," 24 *New York University Journal of International Law and Politics* 109, 149–58 (1991).

5. *Nationality of Claims.* If a vessel's crew members, ship owners, and cargo interests suffer injury through actions of a non-flag state, may the vessel's flag state represent those various entities if they are not of the same nationality as the flag state? In the *Saiga Case*, Saint Vincent and the Grenadines alleged that Guinea had illegally seized the vessel and used excessive force against it, resulting in damage to the vessel and its cargo and injury to some of those on board. Although the *Saiga* was flying the flag of Saint Vincent and the Grenadines, a corporation from Cyprus owned the vessel, a Scottish corporation managed it, a Swiss corporation chartered it, its master and crew were Ukrainians, and some Senegalese nationals were employed on board. Guinea argued that Saint Vincent and the Grenadines was not entitled to represent the interests of the *Saiga*'s employees, crew, or cargo owners. The ITLOS disagreed:

106. * * * [T]he [1982 Law of the Sea] Convention considers a ship as a unit, as regards the obligations of the flag State with respect to

the ship and the right of a flag State to seek reparation for loss or damage. * * * Thus the ship, every thing on it, and every person involved or interested in its operations are treated as an entity linked to the flag State. The nationalities of these persons are not relevant.

107. The Tribunal must * * * call attention to * * * two basic characteristics of modern maritime transport: the transient and multi-national composition of ships' crews and the multiplicity of interests that may be involved in the cargo on board a single ship. A container vessel carries a large number of containers, and the persons with interests in them may be of many different nationalities. This may also be true in relation to cargo on board a break-bulk carrier. Any of these ships could have a crew comprising persons of several nationalities. If each person sustaining damage were obliged to look for protection from the State of which such person is a national, undue hardship would ensue.

38 I.L.M. at 1347. What if a crew member or cargo interest preferred to pursue its own claim, either before the ITLOS or in another international or municipal forum? If the flag state is unwilling or unable to pursue a claim, should the state of nationality of a crew member, cargo interest, or vessel owner then have standing to espouse a claim? Compare the *Barcelona Traction Case* in Chapter 6, and see generally Bernard H. Oxman, "Human Rights and the United Nations Convention on the Law of the Sea," 36 *Columbia Journal of Transnational Law* 399 (1997).

C. THE CONTINENTAL SHELF, FISHERIES ZONES, AND THE EXCLUSIVE ECONOMIC ZONE

In the middle of the 20th century, coastal states began to make claims with respect to zones of the oceans beyond the narrow "territorial sea" over which states traditionally had asserted sovereignty. In this section, we first examine the regime of the continental shelf, developed as treaty law in the Convention on the Continental Shelf, Apr. 29, 1958, 15 U.S.T. 471, 499 U.N.T.S. 311, and in Part VI of the 1982 U.N. Convention on the Law of the Sea. We then look at coastal state claims to fisheries zones. These claims contributed to acceptance of preferential coastal state rights over fisheries in the exclusive economic zone (EEZ), a legal construct now set out in Part V of the 1982 Convention.

The seaward extension of national jurisdiction has affected both access to and management of ocean resources. The materials at the end of this Part explore attempts to devise international legal regimes to manage "straddling stocks" of fish that range beyond national zones of authority.

THE TRUMAN PROCLAMATION

Proclamation 2667, Policy of the United States With Respect to the Natural
Resources of the Subsoil and Sea Bed of the Continental Shelf,
Sept. 28, 1945 3 C.F.R. 67 (1943–1948 Compilation).

WHEREAS the Government of the United States of America, aware
of the long range world-wide need for new sources of petroleum and
other minerals, holds the view that efforts to discover and make available
new supplies of these sources should be encouraged; and

WHEREAS its competent experts are of the opinion that such
resources underlie many parts of the continental shelf off the coasts of
the United States of America, and that with modern technological
progress their utilization is already practicable or will become so at an
early date; and

WHEREAS recognized jurisdiction over these resources is required
in the interest of their conservation and prudent utilization when and as
development is undertaken; and

WHEREAS it is the view of the Government of the United States
that the exercise of jurisdiction over the natural resources of the subsoil
and sea bed of the continental shelf by the contiguous nation is reasonable
and just, since the effectiveness of measures to utilize or conserve
those resources would be contingent upon cooperation and protection
from the shore, since the continental shelf may be regarded as an
extension of the land-mass of the coastal nation and thus naturally
appurtenant to it, since these resources frequently form a seaward
extension of a pool or deposit lying within the territory, and since self-
protection compels the coastal nation to keep close watch over activities
off its shores which are of the nature necessary for utilization of these
resources;

NOW, THEREFORE, I, HARRY S. TRUMAN, President of the
United States of America, do hereby proclaim the following policy of the
United States of America with respect to the natural resources of the
subsoil and sea bed of the continental shelf.

Having concern for the urgency of conserving and prudently utilizing
its natural resources, the Government of the United States regards
the natural resources of the subsoil and sea bed of the continental shelf
beneath the high seas but contiguous to the coasts of the United States
as appertaining to the United States, subject to its jurisdiction and
control. In cases where the continental shelf extends to the shores of
another State, or is shared with an adjacent State, the boundary shall be
determined by the United States and the State concerned in accordance
with equitable principles. The character as high seas of the waters above
the continental shelf and the right to their free and unimpeded navigation
are in no way thus affected.

UNITED NATIONS CONVENTION ON THE LAW OF THE SEA, ARTICLES 77–78

Dec. 10, 1982, 1833 U.N.T.S. 3.

Article 77

Rights of the coastal State over the continental shelf

1. The coastal State exercises over the continental shelf sovereign rights for the purpose of exploring it and exploiting its natural resources.

2. The rights referred to in paragraph 1 are exclusive in the sense that if the coastal State does not explore the continental shelf or exploit its natural resources, no one may undertake these activities without the express consent of the coastal State.

3. The rights of the coastal State over the continental shelf do not depend on occupation, effective or notional, or on any express proclamation.

4. The natural resources referred to in this Part consist of the mineral and other non-living resources of the sea-bed and subsoil together with living organisms belonging to sedentary species, that is to say, organisms which, at the harvestable stage, either are immobile on or under the sea-bed or are unable to move except in constant physical contact with the sea-bed or the subsoil.

Article 78

*Legal status of the superjacent waters and airspace
and the rights and freedoms of other States*

1. The rights of the coastal State over the continental shelf do not affect the legal status of the superjacent waters or of the air space above those waters.

2. The exercise of the rights of the coastal State over the continental shelf must not infringe or result in any unjustifiable interference with navigation and other rights and freedoms of other States as provided for in this Convention.

Notes and Questions

1. *The Truman Proclamation on the Continental Shelf.* The Truman Proclamation on the continental shelf was a significant event in the 20th-century movement toward extended coastal state jurisdiction. In June 1943, U.S. Secretary of the Interior Harold Ickes wrote to President Franklin Roosevelt:

> The war has impressed us with the necessity for an augmented supply of natural resources. In this connection I draw your attention to the importance of the Continental Shelf not only to the defence of our country, but more particularly as a storehouse of natural resources. The extent of these resources can only be guessed at and needs careful investigation.

The Continental Shelf extending some 100 or 150 miles from our shores forms a fine breeding place for fish of all kinds; it is an excellent hiding-place for submarines; and since it is a continuation of our continent, it probably contains oil and other resources similar to those found in our States.

I suggest the advisability of laying the ground work now for availing ourselves fully of the riches in this submerged land and in the waters over them. The legal and policy problems involved, both international and domestic, are many and complex. In the international field, it may be necessary to evolve new concepts of maritime territorial limits beyond three miles, and of rights to occupy and exploit the surface and the subsoil of the open sea.

Quoted in Donald Cameron Watt, "First steps in enclosure of the oceans: The origins of Truman's proclamation on the resources of the continental shelf, 28 September 1945," 3 *Marine Policy* 211, 212 (1979). Ickes referred to "maritime territorial limits beyond three miles," because the United States, like many other states, already claimed sovereignty over a three-mile territorial sea. In 1988 the United States extended its territorial sea to 12 nautical miles, a step consistent with Article 3 of the 1982 U.N. Convention on the Law of the Sea. See John E. Noyes, "United States of America Presidential Proclamation No. 5298: A 12–Mile U.S. Territorial Sea," 4 *International Journal of Estuarine and Coastal Law* 142 (1989).

President Roosevelt reacted favorably to Ickes's suggestion regarding the continental shelf when he forwarded Ickes's letter to Secretary of State Cordell Hull:

I think Harold Ickes has the right slant on this. For many years I have felt that the old three-mile limit . . . should be superseded by a rule of common sense. For instance the Gulf of Mexico is bounded on the South by Mexico and on the North by the United States. In parts of the Gulf, shallow water extends very many miles offshore. It seems to me that the Mexican Government should be entitled to drill for oil in the Southern half of the Gulf and we in the Northern half of the Gulf. That would be far more sensible than allowing some European nation, for example, to come in there and drill.

Quoted in Watt, *supra*, at 213. The State Department's Office of Economic Affairs, reviewing Ickes's proposal and another proposal to establish U.S. fisheries conservation zones, argued that the proposals "constituted 'so significant a departure from past practices under the law of nations' that 'if proper precautions were not taken' they could lead to 'misunderstanding, suspicions and opposition on the part of many nations.'" *Id.* at 214. The Office argued for international consultation with, and the "concurrence" of, various states. The U.S. proposals were in fact informally communicated to Canada, Cuba, Mexico, Newfoundland, the Soviet Union, and the United Kingdom. Some states raised the possibility of negotiating international agreements concerning resources outside the territorial sea, but the United States proceeded unilaterally. Was it appropriate for the United States unilaterally to extend its authority over the continental shelf?

2. *Latin American Coastal Zones.* Following the Truman Proclamation, Mexico issued a proclamation claiming the adjacent continental shelf and its

superjacent resources. Several other Latin American states, including Argentina, Chile, Costa Rica, El Salvador, and Peru, soon claimed sovereign rights up to 200 miles from their coasts. Although other states cited U.S. action as precedent for their assertions of authority over broad coastal zones, each responded to its own set of national goals. Chile, for example, was particularly concerned to protect its new offshore whaling industry when it issued its proclamation, and Peru sought primarily to reserve rich offshore fisheries for its own citizens. See Ann Hollick, "The Origins of 200–Mile Offshore Zones," 71 *American Journal of International Law* 994 (1977). The states making these various claims typically disavowed any intention of interfering with freedom of navigation. After the Truman Proclamation, could the United States effectively object to assertions by other coastal states of extensive authority over coastal zones?

3. *Evolution of the Legal Concept of the Continental Shelf.* The several unilateral proclamations contributed to a process by which the regime of the continental shelf came ultimately to be considered customary international law. In Petroleum Dev't Ltd. v. Abu Dhabi, 18 Int'l L. Rep. 144, 155 (1951), the arbitrator concluded "that in no form can the doctrine [of the continental shelf] claim as yet to have assumed * * * the hard lineaments or the definitive status of an established rule of International Law." Also in 1951, however, the International Law Commission adopted draft articles on the continental shelf, work that contributed significantly to the 1958 Geneva Convention on the Continental Shelf, Apr. 29, 1958, 15 U.S.T. 471, 499 U.N.T.S. 311. The contribution of the 1958 Convention to the crystallization of customary international law was addressed by the International Court of Justice in the 1969 *North Sea Continental Shelf Cases*, which appear in Chapter 3. The ICJ's decisions also emphasized that the continental shelf was to be considered the "natural prolongation" of the land territory of a state.

4. *The Continental Shelf and the U.N. Convention on the Law of the Sea.* The legal status of the continental shelf was one of many issues addressed during the Third United Nations Conference on the Law of the Sea, which led to the 1982 U.N. Convention on the Law of the Sea. Under the 1982 Convention, what is the balance struck between coastal state rights and the rights of other states, with regard to the continental shelf and activities on and above it?

5. *The Definition of the Continental Shelf.* What exactly is the continental shelf, and how far from shore does it extend? A White House press release accompanying President Truman's Proclamation No. 2667 stated that "[g]enerally, submerged land which is contiguous to the continent and which is covered by no more than 100 fathoms (600 feet) of water is considered as the continental shelf." Article 1 of the 1958 Convention on the Continental Shelf refers to the continental shelf as:

> the seabed and subsoil of the submarine areas adjacent to the coast but outside the area of the territorial sea, to a depth of 200 metres or, beyond that limit, to where the depth of the superjacent waters admits of the exploitation of the natural resources of the said areas * * *.

Article 76 of the 1982 U.N. Convention on the Law of the Sea, in contrast, uses a complex geographical formula to determine the outer limit of a state's continental shelf; a Continental Shelf Commission, established by the Convention, is to review coastal state claims to continental shelf limits extending more than 200 nautical miles from a state's baselines. Under Article 76, every state is guaranteed a continental shelf of at least 200 miles. Why the changes in definition?

6. *Baselines*. The lines from which the breadth of a state's continental shelf and its other coastal zones is measured are known as "baselines." In general, the baseline follows the low-water line along the coast. See Article 3 of the 1958 Convention on the Territorial Sea and Contiguous Zone; Article 5 of the 1982 Convention on the Law of the Sea.

Some states have proclaimed lengthy straight baselines rather than baselines that closely follow the low water marks of the coastline. In 1951 the International Court of Justice approved Norway's decision to draw a straight baseline along a fringe of islands and rocks, known as the skjærgaard, that generally followed the direction of the coast. "Where a coast is deeply indented and cut into, as is that of Eastern Finnmark," the Court stated, "or where it is bordered by an archipelago such as in the 'skjærgaard' * * *, the base line becomes independent of the low-water mark, and can only be determined by means of a geometric construction." Anglo–Norwegian Fisheries Case, 1951 I.C.J. 116, 128–29, 1951 WL 12. The Court also suggested that important economic interests in a region, "clearly evidenced by a long usage," were a relevant consideration supporting straight baselines, in addition to geographical factors. *Id.* at 133. Article 7 of the 1982 U.N. Convention on the Law of the Sea describes conditions under which a state may draw straight baselines.

Approximately 80 states have drawn straight baselines along all or part of their coasts since 1951. Some of these baselines are many miles distant from the coast. See W. Michael Reisman & Gayle S. Westerman, *Straight Baselines in International Maritime Boundary Delimitation* (1992). What are the implications of the practice of drawing straight baselines? What mechanisms are available to challenge assertions of straight baselines?

7. *United States Fisheries Zones*. A companion to President Truman's continental shelf proclamation was Proclamation No. 2668, Policy of the United States With Respect to Coastal Fisheries in Certain Areas of the High Seas, Sept. 28, 1945, 3 C.F.R. 68 (1943–1948 Compilation). The fisheries proclamation asserted sole U.S. authority to conserve and manage fisheries in areas where U.S. nationals historically had fished exclusively, and called for joint arrangements in areas where both U.S. and foreign nationals had fished. The United States, however, never established conservation zones under this proclamation. The Exclusive Fisheries Zone Act of 1966, 16 U.S.C. §§ 1091–1094, established a 12–mile exclusive U.S. fisheries zone. That statute was repealed by the 1976 Fishery Conservation and Management Act, 16 U.S.C. §§ 1801–1882, which established a 200–mile fisheries conservation zone. The American Fisheries Promotion Act of 1980, 16 U.S.C. § 1821(e), phased out foreign fishing in this 200–mile zone. The following case excerpt and set of Notes refer to some of the features of the expansion of coastal fishing zones in international law.

THE FISHERIES JURISDICTION CASE

United Kingdom v. Iceland, 1974 I.C.J. 3, 1974 WL 1 (Merits).

[In 1948, Iceland's Parliament passed a law authorizing the Ministry of Fisheries to set "conservation zones within the limits of the continental shelf of Iceland; wherein all fisheries shall be subject to Icelandic rules and control." In 1952, Iceland established a fisheries zone extending four miles from straight baselines and prohibiting foreign fishing within the zone. In 1958, Iceland proclaimed a 12–mile fisheries zone, again prohibiting foreign fishing within the new limit. British efforts to continue fishing in the 12–mile zone led to "incidents on the fishing grounds" and a 1959 Icelandic parliamentary resolution emphasizing Iceland's objective to extend a fisheries zone "over the whole of the continental shelf area." In a 1960 exchange of notes, the United Kingdom acknowledged Iceland's dependence on coastal fisheries for its livelihood and economic development and agreed not to object to the 12– mile zone. Iceland, for its part, agreed to give the United Kingdom six months' notice of any further extension of Icelandic fisheries jurisdiction and agreed to refer any dispute over such an extension to the International Court of Justice. When Iceland extended its fisheries jurisdiction to 50 miles in 1972, the United Kingdom brought a claim to the Court. Iceland refused to appear before the Court.]

11.   In the course of the written proceedings, the following submissions were presented on behalf of the Government of the United Kingdom: * * *

"The United Kingdom asks the Court to adjudge and declare:

(a) That there is no foundation in international law for the claim by Iceland to be entitled to extend its fisheries jurisdiction by establishing a zone of exclusive fisheries jurisdiction extending to 50 nautical miles from the baselines * * *; and that its claim is therefore invalid; and

(b) that questions concerning the conservation of fish stocks in the waters around Iceland are not susceptible in international law to regulation by the unilateral extension by Iceland of its exclusive fisheries jurisdiction to 50 nautical miles from the aforesaid baselines but are matters that may be regulated, as between Iceland and the United Kingdom, by arrangements agreed between those two countries * * *." * * *

50.   The Geneva Convention on the High Seas of 1958, which was adopted "as generally declaratory of established principles of international law," defines in Article 1 the term "high seas" as "all parts of the sea that are not included in the territorial sea or in the internal waters of a State." Article 2 then declares that "The high seas being open to all nations, no State may validly purport to subject any part of them to its sovereignty" and goes on to provide that the freedom of the high seas comprises, *inter alia*, both for coastal and non-coastal States, freedom of

navigation and freedom of fishing. The freedoms of the high seas are however made subject to the consideration that they "shall be exercised by all States with reasonable regard to the interests of other States in their exercise of the freedom of the high seas."

51. * * * At the 1958 Conference, the main differences on the breadth of the territorial sea were limited at the time to disagreements as to what limit, not exceeding 12 miles, was the appropriate one. The question of the breadth of the territorial sea and that of the extent of the coastal State's fishery jurisdiction were left unsettled at the 1958 conference. These questions were referred to the Second Conference on the Law of the Sea, held in 1960. Furthermore, the question of the extent of the fisheries jurisdiction of the coastal State, which had constituted a serious obstacle to the reaching of an agreement at the 1958 Conference, became gradually separated from the notion of the territorial sea. This was a development which reflected the increasing importance of fishery resources for all States.

52. The 1960 Conference failed by one vote to adopt a text governing the two questions of the breadth of the territorial sea and the extent of fishery rights. However, after that Conference the law evolved through the practice of States on the basis of the debates and near-agreements at the Conference. Two concepts have crystallized as customary law in recent years arising out of the general consensus revealed at that Conference. The first is the concept of the fishery zone, the area in which a State may claim exclusive fishery jurisdiction independently of its territorial sea; the extension of that fishery zone up to a 12–mile limit from the baselines appears now to be generally accepted. The second is the concept of preferential rights of fishing in adjacent waters in favour of the coastal State in a situation of special dependence on its coastal fisheries, this preference operating in regard to other States concerned in the exploitation of the same fisheries, and to be implemented in the way indicated in paragraph 57 below.

53. In recent years the question of extending the coastal State's fisheries jurisdiction has come increasingly to the forefront. The Court is aware that a number of States has asserted an extension of fishery limits. The Court is also aware of present endeavours, pursued under the auspices of the United Nations, to achieve in a third Conference on the Law of the Sea the further codification and progressive development of this branch of the law, as it is of various proposals and preparatory documents produced in this framework, which must be regarded as manifestations of the views and opinions of individual States and as vehicles of their aspirations, rather than as expressing principles of existing law. The very fact of convening the third Conference on the Law of the Sea evidences a manifest desire on the part of all States to proceed to the codification of that law on a universal basis, including the question of fisheries and conservation of the living resources of the sea. * * * In the circumstances, the Court, as a court of law, cannot render judgment *sub specie legis ferendae*, or anticipate the law before the legislator has laid it down.

54.   The concept of a 12–mile fishery zone * * * has been accepted with regard to Iceland in the substantive provisions of the 1961 Exchange of Notes, and the United Kingdom has also applied the same fishery limit to its own coastal waters since 1964; therefore this matter is no longer in dispute between the Parties. At the same time, * * * the Applicant has expressly recognized Iceland's preferential rights in the disputed waters and at the same time has invoked its own historic fishing rights in these same waters, on the ground that reasonable regard must be had to such traditional rights by the coastal State, in accordance with the generally recognized principles embodied in Article 2 of the High Seas Convention. * * *

57.   * * * The contemporary practice of States leads to the conclusion that the preferential rights of the coastal State in a special situation are to be implemented by agreement between the States concerned, either bilateral or multilateral, and, in case of disagreement, through the means for the peaceful settlement of disputes provided for in Article 33 of the Charter of the United Nations. * * *

58.   State practice on the subject of fisheries reveals an increasing and widespread acceptance of the concept of preferential rights for coastal States, particularly in favour of countries or territories in a situation of special dependence on coastal fisheries. Both [a resolution at the 1958 conference] and [a] 1960 joint amendment concerning preferential rights were approved by a large majority of the Conferences, thus showing overwhelming support for the idea that in certain special situations it was fair to recognize that the coastal State had preferential fishing rights. After these Conferences, the preferential rights of the coastal State were recognized in various bilateral and multilateral international agreements. * * *

59.   There can be no doubt of the exceptional dependence of Iceland on its fisheries. That exceptional dependence was explicitly recognized by the Applicant in the Exchange of Notes of 11 March 1961, and the Court has also taken judicial notice of such recognition * * *.

60.   The preferential rights of the coastal State come into play only at the moment when an intensification in the exploitation of fishery resources makes it imperative to introduce some system of catch-limitation and sharing of those resources, to preserve the fish stocks in the interests of their rational and economic exploitation. This situation appears to have been reached in the present case. * * *

61.   The Icelandic regulations challenged before the Court have been issued and applied by the Icelandic authorities as a claim to exclusive rights thus going beyond the concept of preferential rights. Article 2 of the Icelandic Regulations of 14 July 1972 states:

"Within the fishery limits all fishing activities by foreign vessels shall be prohibited in accordance with the provisions of Law No. 33 of 19 June 1922, concerning Fishing inside the Fishery Limits."

Article 1 of the 1922 Law provides: "Only Icelandic citizens may engage in fishing in the territorial waters of Iceland, and only Icelandic boats or ships may be used for such fishing." * * *

62. The concept of preferential rights is not compatible with the exclusion of all fishing activities of other States. A coastal State entitled to preferential rights is not free, unilaterally and according to its own uncontrolled discretion, to determine the extent of those rights. The characterization of the coastal State's rights as preferential implies a certain priority, but cannot imply the extinction of the concurrent rights of other States, and particularly of a State which, like the Applicant, has for many years been engaged in fishing in the waters in question, such fishing activity being important to the economy of the country concerned. * * *

63. In this case, the Applicant has pointed out that its vessels have been fishing in Icelandic waters for centuries and that they have done so in a manner comparable with their present activities for upwards of 50 years. Published statistics indicate that from 1920 onwards, fishing of demersal species by United Kingdom vessels in the disputed area has taken place on a continuous basis from year to year, and that, except for the period of the Second World War, the total catch of those vessels has been remarkably steady. Similar statistics indicate that the waters in question constitute the most important of the Applicant's distant-water fishing grounds for demersal species.

64. The Applicant further states that in view of the present situation of fisheries in the North Atlantic, which has demanded the establishment of agreed catch-limitations of cod and haddock in various areas, it would not be possible for the fishing effort of United Kingdom vessels displaced from the Icelandic area to be diverted at economic levels to other fishing grounds in the North Atlantic. Given the lack of alternative fishing opportunity, it is further contended, the exclusion of British fishing vessels from the Icelandic area would have very serious adverse consequences, with immediate results for the affected vessels and with damage extending over a wide range of supporting and related industries. It is pointed out in particular that wide-spread unemployment would be caused among all sections of the British fishing industry and in ancillary industries and that certain ports—Hull, Grimsby and Fleetwood—specially reliant on fishing in the Icelandic area, would be seriously affected. * * *

67. The provisions of the Icelandic Regulations of 14 July 1972 and the manner of their implementation disregard the fishing rights of the Applicant. Iceland's unilateral action thus constitutes an infringement of the principle enshrined in Article 2 of the 1958 Geneva Convention on the High Seas which requires that all States, including coastal States, in exercising their freedom of fishing, pay reasonable regard to the interests of other States. It also disregards the rights of the Applicant as they result from the Exchange of Notes of 1961. The Applicant is therefore justified in asking the Court to give all necessary protection to its own

rights, while at the same time agreeing to recognize Iceland's preferential position. Accordingly, the Court is bound to conclude that the Icelandic Regulations of 14 July 1972 establishing a zone of exclusive fisheries jurisdiction extending to 50 nautical miles from baselines around the coast of Iceland, are not opposable to the United Kingdom, and the latter is under no obligation to accept the unilateral termination by Iceland of United Kingdom fishery rights in the area. * * *

71.   * * * Due recognition must be given to the rights of both Parties, namely the rights of the United Kingdom to fish in the waters in dispute, and the preferential rights of Iceland. Neither right is an absolute one: the preferential rights of a coastal State are limited according to the extent of its special dependence on the fisheries and by its obligation to take account of the rights of other States and the needs of conservation; the established rights of other fishing States are in turn limited by reason of the coastal State's special dependence on the fisheries and its own obligation to take account of the rights of other States, including the coastal State, and of the needs of conservation.

72.   It follows that even if the court holds that Iceland's extension of its fishery limits is not opposable to the Applicant, this does not mean that the Applicant is under no obligation to Iceland with respect to fishing in the disputed waters in the 12–mile to 50–mile zone. On the contrary, both States have an obligation to take full account of each other's rights and of any fishery conservation measures the necessity of which is shown to exist in those waters. It is one of the advances in maritime international law, resulting from the intensification of fishing, that the former *laissez-faire* treatment of the living resources of the sea in the high seas has been replaced by a recognition of a duty to have due regard to the rights of other States and the needs of conservation for the benefit of all. Consequently, both Parties have the obligation to keep under review the fishery resources in the disputed waters and to examine together, in the light of scientific and other available information, the measures required for the conservation and development, and equitable exploitation, of those resources, taking into account any international agreement in force between them, such as the North–East Atlantic Fisheries Convention of 24 January 1959, as well as such other agreements as may be reached in the matter in the course of further negotiation.

73.   The most appropriate method for the solution of the dispute is clearly that of negotiation. Its objectives should be the delimitation of the rights and interests of the Parties, the preferential rights of the coastal State on the one hand and the rights of the Applicant on the other, to balance and regulate equitably questions such as those of catch-limitation, share allocations and "related restrictions concerning areas closed to fishing, number and type of vessels allowed and forms of control of the agreed provisions" (*Fisheries Jurisdiction (United Kingdom v. Iceland), Interim Measures, Order of 12 July 1973, I.C.J. Reports 1973*, p. 303, para. 7). This necessitates detailed scientific knowledge of the fishing grounds. It is obvious that the relevant information and

expertise would be mainly in the possession of the Parties. The Court would, for this reason, meet with difficulties if it were itself to attempt to lay down a precise scheme for an equitable adjustment of the rights involved. * * *

78.   In the fresh negotiations which are to take place on the basis of the present Judgment, the Parties will have the benefit of the above appraisal of their respective rights, and of certain guidelines defining their scope. The task before them will be to conduct their negotiations on the basis that each must in good faith pay reasonable regard to the legal rights of the other in the waters around Iceland outside the 12–mile limit, thus bringing about an equitable apportionment of the fishing resources based on the facts of the particular situation, and having regard to the interests of other States which have established fishing rights in the area. It is not a matter of finding simply an equitable solution, but an equitable solution derived from the applicable law. * * *

79.   For these reasons,

THE COURT,

by ten votes to four,

(1) finds that the Regulations concerning the Fishery Limits off Iceland * * * promulgated by the Government of Iceland on 14 July 1972 and constituting a unilateral extension of the exclusive fishing rights of Iceland to 50 nautical miles from the baselines specified therein are not opposable to the Government of the United Kingdom;

(2) finds that, in consequence, the Government of Iceland is not entitled unilaterally to exclude United Kingdom fishing vessels from areas between the fishery limits agreed to in the Exchange of Notes of 11 March 1961 and the limits specified in the Icelandic Regulations of 14 July 1972, or unilaterally to impose restrictions on the activities of those vessels in such areas;

by ten votes to four,

(3) holds that the Government of Iceland and the Government of the United Kingdom are under mutual obligations to undertake negotiations in good faith for the equitable solution of their differences concerning their respective fishery rights in the areas specified in subparagraph 2;

(4) holds that in these negotiations the Parties are to take into account, *inter alia*:

(a) that in the distribution of the fishing resources in the areas specified in subparagraph 2 Iceland is entitled to a preferential share to the extent of the special dependence of its people upon the fisheries in the seas around its coasts for their livelihood and economic development;

(b) that by reason of its fishing activities in the areas specified in subparagraph 2, the United Kingdom also has established rights in the fishery resources of the said areas on which elements of its people depend for their livelihood and economic well-being;

(c) the obligation to pay due regard to the interests of other States in the conservation and equitable exploitation of these resources;

(d) that the above-mentioned rights of Iceland and of the United Kingdom should each be given effect to the extent compatible with the conservation and development of the fishery resources in the areas specified in subparagraph 2 and with the interests of other States in their conservation and equitable exploitation;

(e) their obligation to keep under review those resources and to examine together, in the light of scientific and other available information, such measures as may be required for the conservation and development, and equitable exploitation, of those resources, making use of the machinery established by the North–East Atlantic Fisheries Convention or such other means as may be agreed upon as a result of international negotiations.

Notes and Questions

1. *The Cod Wars.* During the "Cod Wars," Iceland boarded British vessels, arrested British fishermen, and cut the nets of British trawlers. The British sent frigates to escort and protect British trawlers off Iceland. There were shooting and ramming incidents. Tensions were particularly high during 1958–1961, after Iceland extended its fisheries zone from four to 12 miles, and during 1972–1973, after Iceland declared a 50–mile fisheries zone. Iceland's 1972 decisions to extend its fisheries zone and to denounce its 1961 agreement with Great Britain followed the 1971 Icelandic election, in which the Agrarian Progressive Party, which had made fisheries jurisdiction a major campaign issue, emerged as the head of a new coalition government.

Rejecting the decision in the *Fisheries Jurisdiction Case,* Iceland extended its fishing limits from 50 to 200 miles in 1975. Regulations Concerning the Fishery Limits off Iceland, July 15, 1975, 14 I.L.M. 1282 (1975). This extension resulted in further clashes involving British and Icelandic naval units. Other states became concerned the controversy might lead Iceland to withdraw from the North Atlantic Treaty Organization and to shut down a NATO military base in Iceland that was used to monitor Soviet vessels. In June 1976, Iceland and the United Kingdom finally reached an agreement allowing British fishing within the 200–mile limit, but at a substantially reduced level. Iceland–United Kingdom: Agreement Concerning British Fishing in Icelandic Waters, June 1, 1976, 15 I.L.M. 878 (1976). Iceland also concluded bilateral fishing agreements with Belgium, the Federal Republic of Germany, and Norway. Fisheries Agreement, Nov. 28, 1975, Ice.–Belg., 15 I.L.M. 1 (1976); Fisheries Agreement, Nov. 28, 1975, Ice.–F.R.G., 15 I.L.M. 43 (1976); Fisheries Agreement, Mar. 10, 1976, Ice.–Nor., 15 I.L.M. 875 (1976).

2. *The ICJ's View of Rights to Fisheries.* Since the ICJ concluded that Iceland had disregarded British fishing rights, why did the ICJ not grant the relief the British sought? How does the Court's invocation of equity compare

with its use of equity in the *North Sea Continental Shelf Cases* in Chapter 3? The Court concluded that Iceland and the United Kingdom should negotiate a settlement of their differences over rights to fisheries. Did this recourse to procedure as a way to deal with conflict suggest that, at base, there was a lack of consensus on the substantive values that would shape any norm of international law on this issue? Was the Court more concerned to try to help Britain and Iceland resolve this particular dispute, rather than to arrive at general rules of law?

3. *Customary International Law and Coastal State Fisheries Jurisdiction.* Judges Forster, Bengzon, Jimenez de Arechaga, Nagendra Singh, and Ruda concurred separately in the *Fisheries Jurisdiction Case.* Although the judges agreed with the result in the majority opinion and found that a 12–mile fisheries zone was generally accepted in international law, they felt that no general rule of customary international law established 12 miles as the obligatory maximum limit. The judges argued that 30 to 35 coastal states had extended their fisheries jurisdiction beyond 12 miles, and noted the general lack of protests to such extensions and the existence of public pronouncements inconsistent with making any protest. The concurring judges also cited declarations and proposals made at the then-ongoing Third United Nations Conference on the Law of the Sea. They questioned whether, on "a subject where practice was contradictory and lacks precision," it was "reasonable to discard entirely as irrelevant the evidence of what States are prepared to claim and to acquiesce in, as gathered from the positions taken by them in view of or in preparation for a conference for the codification and progressive development of the law on the subject." 1974 I.C.J. at 48. Finally, the judges lamented the legal uncertainty at the time regarding the maximum limit of coastal state fisheries jurisdiction, and expressed the hope that the matter would be clarified at UNCLOS III.

4. *Multilateral Efforts to Codify the Law of the Sea.* The *Fisheries Jurisdiction* decision noted multilateral efforts prior to UNCLOS III to codify the international law of the sea. The excerpt above refers specifically to two of the four 1958 Geneva Conventions concluded at the First United Nations Conference on the Law of the Sea: the Convention on the High Seas, Apr. 29, 1958, 13 U.S.T. 2312, 450 U.N.T.S. 82, and the Convention on the Territorial Sea and the Contiguous Zone, Apr. 29, 1958, 15 U.S.T. 1606, 516 U.N.T.S. 205. The other two 1958 conventions are the Convention on the Continental Shelf, Apr. 29, 1958, 15 U.S.T. 471, 499 U.N.T.S. 311, and the Convention on Fishing and Conservation of the Living Resources of the High Seas, Apr. 29, 1958, 17 U.S.T. 138, 559 U.N.T.S. 285. The United Kingdom, but not Iceland, was party to those four conventions.

Note: UNCLOS III Negotiations Concerning the Exclusive Economic Zone

At the 1974 Caracas session of UNCLOS III, over 100 states spoke in favor of a 200–mile coastal state exclusive economic zone (EEZ). That is not to say that all issues relating to the EEZ were resolved early in the Conference. With regard to many such issues—concerning the legal status of the EEZ, the applicability of the EEZ to archipelagic states and small islands, the relationship between the EEZ and the continental shelf, boundary delimitation, dispute settlement, and coastal state responsibilities concerning fish in their EEZs—it took years to negotiate the language eventually contained in the 1982 United Nations Convention on the Law of the Sea.

The 1974 debates in the Second Committee of UNCLOS III revealed considerable variety in the positions of states. To pick just a few examples: Honduras's delegate claimed "inherent rights" over resources in its adjacent zones, and argued that foreign states had no competence there absent agreement with the coastal state. UNCLOS III, 2nd Sess., 2nd Comm., 22nd Mtg., July 31, 1974, in 2 *UNCLOS III Official Records* 171 (U.N. Sales No. E.75.V.4). The delegates of Kenya and Ecuador were among the many developing states that favored complete coastal state sovereignty in the EEZ, and suggested the desirability of 200–mile territorial seas. Somalia's delegate thought that the traditional law of the sea favored the major maritime powers, and that developing coastal states should not "sign away their territorial sovereignty in exchange for lesser rights." *Id.* at 210 (26th Mtg., Aug. 5, 1974).

Island states and archipelagic states had particular interests in fisheries. New Zealand's delegate criticized a suggestion that the economic zone of islands should be restricted. Archipelagic states also strongly supported the concept of an EEZ, but did not necessarily favor complete coastal state "sovereignty" over the EEZ.

For other states, the EEZ concept represented a significant concession. Mr. Ogiso, Japan's delegate, argued that "[f]reedom of access to fishery resources, if it was retained only beyond 200 miles, would become practically meaningless." *Id.* at 217 (28th Mtg., Aug. 6, 1974). He urged respect for traditional distant water fishing states whose economies were dependent on fishing.

Maritime powers, including states in the Soviet bloc, also stressed the importance of coastal states not exercising rights in their EEZs that would interfere with navigational freedoms. The concern was that extensive coastal state EEZ rights or 200–mile territorial seas might well allow coastal states to interfere with navigational freedoms by exercising control over pollution, scientific research, or customs, fiscal, immigration, and health matters. The delegate of the Ukrainian Soviet Socialist Republic stated that "[u]nder the pretext of exercising such controls, a coastal State might at any time detain a foreign vessel and reduce to nothing the freedom of navigation in the zone." *Id.* at 201 (25th Mtg., Aug. 5, 1974).

Land-locked and geographically disadvantaged states also voiced concerns. Upper Volta's delegate argued for assured access to the sea by land-locked countries and for their right to participate in the exploitation of EEZ resources. Mr. Ballah, the delegate from Trinidad and Tobago, said his state "conditioned its acceptance of the concept of the 200–mile exclusive economic zone on recognition by the Conference of preferential or equal rights for every State within a region or subregion to the living resources of the economic zones of the other States of the region." *Id.* at 179 (22nd Mtg., July 31, 1974). Turkey noted that, although it was surrounded on three sides by seas, those seas were semi-enclosed and not well stocked with fish. The delegate of the Federal Republic of Germany stressed dual needs: for effective conservation of fisheries and for equitable allocation of those resources, finding "no justification for the reallocation of available resources for the benefit of a limited number of geographically advantaged States." *Id.* at 192 (24th Mtg., Aug. 1, 1974). Germany was one of several states stressing the importance of an obligatory dispute settlement mechanism to review the actions of coastal states.

UNITED NATIONS CONVENTION ON THE LAW OF THE SEA, ARTICLES 55–59, 61–62, 121

Dec. 10, 1982, 1833 U.N.T.S. 3.

Exclusive Economic Zone

Article 55

Specific legal regime of the exclusive economic zone

The exclusive economic zone is an area beyond and adjacent to the territorial sea, subject to the specific legal regime established in this Part, under which the rights and jurisdiction of the coastal State and the rights and freedoms of other States are governed by the relevant provisions of this Convention.

Article 56

Rights, jurisdiction and duties of the coastal State in the exclusive economic zone

1.   In the exclusive economic zone, the coastal State has:

(a) sovereign rights for the purpose of exploring and exploiting, conserving and managing the natural resources, whether living or non-living, of the waters superjacent to the sea-bed and of the sea-bed and its subsoil, and with regard to other activities for the economic exploitation and exploration of the zone, such as the production of energy from the water, currents and winds;

(b) jurisdiction as provided for in the relevant provisions of this Convention with regard to:

(i) the establishment and use of artificial islands, installations and structures;

(ii) marine scientific research;

(iii) the protection and preservation of the marine environment;

(c) other rights and duties provided for in this Convention.

2.   In exercising its rights and performing its duties under this Convention in the exclusive economic zone, the coastal State shall have due regard to the rights and duties of other States and shall act in a manner compatible with the provisions of this Convention.

3.   The rights set out in this article with respect to the sea-bed and subsoil shall be exercised in accordance with Part VI.

Article 57

Breadth of the exclusive economic zone

The exclusive economic zone shall not extend beyond 200 nautical miles from the baselines from which the breadth of the territorial sea is measured.

Article 58

Rights and duties of other States in the exclusive economic zone

1. In the exclusive economic zone, all States, whether coastal or land-locked, enjoy, subject to the relevant provisions of this Convention, the freedoms referred to in article 87 of navigation and overflight and of the laying of submarine cables and pipelines, and other internationally lawful uses of the sea related to these freedoms, such as those associated with the operation of ships, aircraft and submarine cables and pipelines, and compatible with the other provisions of this Convention.

2. Articles 88 to 115 and other pertinent rules of international law apply to the exclusive economic zone in so far as they are not incompatible with this Part.

3. In exercising their rights and performing their duties under this Convention in the exclusive economic zone, States shall have due regard to the rights and duties of the coastal State and shall comply with the laws and regulations adopted by the coastal State in accordance with the provisions of this Convention and other rules of international law in so far as they are not incompatible with this Part.

Article 59

Basis for the resolution of conflicts regarding the attribution of rights and jurisdiction in the exclusive economic zone

In cases where this Convention does not attribute rights or jurisdiction to the coastal State or to other States within the exclusive economic zone, and a conflict arises between the interests of the coastal State and any other State or States, the conflict should be resolved on the basis of equity and in the light of all the relevant circumstances, taking into account the respective importance of the interests involved to the parties as well as to the international community as a whole.

Article 61

Conservation of the living resources

1. The coastal State shall determine the allowable catch of the living resources in its exclusive economic zone.

2. The coastal State, taking into account the best scientific evidence available to it, shall ensure through proper conservation and management measures that the maintenance of the living resources in the exclusive economic zone is not endangered by over-exploitation. As appropriate, the coastal State and competent international organiza-

tions, whether subregional, regional or global, shall co-operate to this end.

3. Such measures shall also be designed to maintain or restore populations of harvested species at levels which can produce the maximum sustainable yield, as qualified by relevant environmental and economic factors, including the economic needs of coastal fishing communities and the special requirements of developing States, and taking into account fishing patterns, the interdependence of stocks and any generally recommended international minimum standards, whether subregional, regional or global. * * *

Article 62

Utilization of the living resources

1. The coastal State shall promote the objective of optimum utilization of the living resources in the exclusive economic zone without prejudice to article 61.

2. The coastal State shall determine its capacity to harvest the living resources of the exclusive economic zone. Where the coastal State does not have the capacity to harvest the entire allowable catch, it shall, through agreements or other arrangements and pursuant to the terms, conditions, laws and regulations referred to in paragraph 4, give other States access to the surplus of the allowable catch, having particular regard to the provisions of articles 69 and 70,[†] especially in relation to the developing States mentioned therein.

3. In giving access to other States to its exclusive economic zone under this article, the coastal State shall take into account all relevant factors, including, *inter alia,* the significance of the living resources of the area to the economy of the coastal State concerned and its other national interests, the provisions of articles 69 and 70, the requirements of developing States in the subregion or region in harvesting part of the surplus and the need to minimize economic dislocation in States whose nationals have habitually fished in the zone or which have made substantial efforts in research and identification of stocks.

4. Nationals of other States fishing in the exclusive economic zone shall comply with the conservation measures and with the other terms and conditions established in the laws and regulations of the coastal State. These laws and regulations shall be consistent with this Convention and may relate, *inter alia,* to the following:

    (a) licensing of fishermen, fishing vessels and equipment, including payment of fees and other forms of remuneration, which, in the case of developing coastal States, may consist of adequate compensation

---

† These articles concern the rights of land-locked and geographically disadvantaged states "to participate, on an equitable basis, in the exploitation of an appropriate part of the surplus" of EEZ fisheries, pursuant to bilateral or regional agreements.— Eds.

in the field of financing, equipment and technology relating to the fishing industry;

(b) determining the species which may be caught, and fixing quotas of catch, whether in relation to particular stocks or groups of stocks or catch per vessel over a period of time or to the catch by nationals of any State during a specified period;

(c) regulating seasons and areas of fishing, the types, sizes and amount of gear, and the types, sizes and number of fishing vessels that may be used;

(d) fixing the age and size of fish and other species that may be caught;

(e) specifying information required of fishing vessels, including catch and effort statistics and vessel position reports;

(f) requiring, under the authorization and control of the coastal State, the conduct of specified fisheries research programmes and regulating the conduct of such research, including the sampling of catches, disposition of samples and reporting of associated scientific data;

(g) the placing of observers or trainees on board such vessels by the coastal State;

(h) the landing of all or any part of the catch by such vessels in the ports of the coastal State;

(i) terms and conditions relating to joint ventures or other co-operative arrangements;

(j) requirements for the training of personnel and the transfer of fisheries technology, including enhancement of the coastal State's capability of undertaking fisheries research;

(k) enforcement procedures.

5. Coastal States shall give due notice of conservation and management laws and regulations.

Regime of Islands

Article 121

Regime of islands

1. An island is a naturally formed area of land, surrounded by water, which is above water at high tide.

2. Except as provided for in paragraph 3, the territorial sea, the contiguous zone, the exclusive economic zone and the continental shelf of an island are determined in accordance with the provisions of this Convention applicable to other land territory.

3. Rocks which cannot sustain human habitation or economic life of their own shall have no exclusive economic zone or continental shelf.

Notes and Questions

1. *Acceptance of the EEZ as Customary International Law.* As of January 1993, according to the United Nations Division for Ocean Affairs and Law of the Sea Office of Legal Affairs, 89 states had claimed a 200–mile exclusive economic zone (or one up to a median line with opposite states), and an additional 17 states had claimed a 200–mile fisheries zone (or one up to a median line with opposite states). Eleven states claimed a 200–mile territorial sea. In 1985 the International Court of Justice found it "incontestable that * * * the institution of the exclusive economic zone * * * is shown by the practice of states to have become part of customary law." Continental Shelf (Libya v. Malta) Case, 1985 I.C.J. 13, 33, 1985 WL 138. Had the 1982 Convention's EEZ regime gained general acceptance as customary international law even before the Convention entered into force in November 1994? What additional information, if any, is needed to answer the question?

2. *High Seas Freedoms in the EEZ.* How does the Law of the Sea Convention resolve the Grotius/Selden *mare liberum/mare clausum* debate with regard to the 200–mile EEZ? In light of Article 58, is the EEZ really still a part of the high seas?

3. *Conflicting Interests in the EEZ.* Access to and control over coastal fisheries was an issue of tremendous importance in the debate over the EEZ. Does the 1982 Convention follow the same conception of rights concerning fisheries that the ICJ articulated in the *Fisheries Jurisdiction Case*? Under Articles 61 and 62 of the Convention, is a coastal state's role better described as a steward, to protect fisheries resources, or as a proprietor?

How satisfied do you think each of the states whose position on the EEZ is outlined in the Note above entitled "UNCLOS III Negotiations Concerning the Exclusive Economic Zone" was with the final text of Part V of the 1982 U.N. Convention on the Law of the Sea? To the extent some states' concerns were not satisfied, why would those states accept the Convention? With regard to land-locked states, note that their concerns with a right of access to the sea were separately addressed in another Part of the Convention. Separate Parts of the Convention also concern protection of the marine environment in the EEZ and elsewhere, and marine scientific research in the EEZ and on the continental shelf.

4. *Obligatory Third-party Dispute Resolution.* Among the few categories of disputes excluded from obligatory third-party arbitration or adjudication under the Law of the Sea Convention's dispute settlement provisions are disputes relating to a coastal state's "sovereign rights with respect to the living resources in the exclusive economic zone or their exercise, including its discretionary powers for determining allowable catch, its harvesting capacity, the allocation of surpluses to other States and the terms and conditions established in its conservation and management laws and regulations." Article 297(3). Certain categories of EEZ fisheries disputes may be referred to a compulsory conciliation procedure. Why did states seek provisions for obligatory binding procedures in the Convention, and why did they exclude certain fisheries disputes? What are the implications of the Article

297(3) exclusion for the balance of rights and obligations set out in Part V? For more on obligatory dispute settlement, see John E. Noyes, "Compulsory Third–Party Adjudication and the 1982 United Nations Convention on the Law of the Sea," 4 *Connecticut Journal of International Law* 675 (1989).

5. *Comparing the EEZ and the Continental Shelf.* Article 56 of the 1982 Convention, which is contained in Part V on the EEZ, refers to sovereign rights of coastal states to explore, exploit, conserve, and manage non-living, as well as living, natural resources. Why, then, does the Convention include a separate Part VI on the continental shelf?

6. *Comparing the EEZ and the Contiguous Zone.* The 1958 Convention on the Territorial Sea and the Contiguous Zone provided that states could assert a zone contiguous to the territorial sea. This contiguous zone could extend 12 miles from the baseline; Article 33 of the 1982 Convention increased the limit to 24 miles. Within this zone, according to Article 33, a coastal state "may exercise the control necessary to (a) prevent infringement of its customs, fiscal, immigration or sanitary laws and regulations within its territory or territorial sea; (b) punish infringement of the above laws and regulations committed within its territory or territorial sea." Does the EEZ render the concept of the contiguous zone superfluous?

In the *Saiga Case* excerpted above, Guinea attempted to justify its arrest of a foreign-flag vessel outside a 24–mile zone. Guinea argued that the vessel's actions in Guinea's EEZ—supplying fuel oil to fishing vessels ("bunkering")—circumvented Guinean customs laws, and that arrest of the vessel was consistent with Article 58(3) of the Law of the Sea Convention. The International Tribunal for the Law of the Sea rejected Guinea's assertion:

> 130. The main public interest which Guinea claims to be protecting by applying its customs laws to the exclusive economic zone is said to be the "considerable fiscal losses a developing country like Guinea is suffering from illegal off-shore bunkering in its exclusive economic zone." * * * In effect, Guinea's contention is that the customary international law principle of "public interest" gives it the power to impede "economic activities that are undertaken [in its EEZ] under the guise of navigation but are different from communication."

> 131. According to article 58, paragraph 3, of the Convention, the "other rules of international law" which a coastal State is entitled to apply in the exclusive economic zone are those which are not incompatible with Part V of the Convention. In the view of the Tribunal, recourse to the principle of "public interest," as invoked by Guinea, would entitle a coastal State to prohibit any activities in the exclusive economic zone which it decides to characterize as activities which affect its economic "public interest" or entail "fiscal losses" for it. This would curtail the rights of other States in the exclusive economic zone. The Tribunal is satisfied that this would be incompatible with the provisions of articles 56 and 58 of the Convention regarding the rights of the coastal State in the exclusive economic zone.

38 I.L.M. at 1351. An arrest of a foreign flag vessel in the EEZ for customs violations may, however, be valid under international law if the arrest

follows "hot pursuit" from the territorial sea or the contiguous zone. See Article 111 of the U.N. Convention on the Law of the Sea.

7. *Straddling Stocks and Highly Migratory Species.* Some species of fish do not live exclusively in the EEZs of just one state. They swim into neighboring states' EEZs or into the high seas beyond the EEZ. What sort of international legal regime regulates the exploitation of such species? Is further extension of coastal state authority beyond the EEZ desirable to promote the effective management of straddling stocks? The next two readings and accompanying notes examine these questions.

UNITED NATIONS CONVENTION ON THE LAW OF THE SEA, ARTICLES 63(2), 116–119

Dec. 10, 1982, 1833 U.N.T.S. 3.

*Exclusive Economic Zone * * ***

Article 63

*Stocks occurring within the exclusive economic zones of two or more coastal States or both within the exclusive economic zone and in an area beyond and adjacent to it * * ***

2.   Where the same stock or stocks of associated species occur both within the exclusive economic zone and in an area beyond and adjacent to the zone, the coastal State and the States fishing for such stocks in the adjacent area shall seek, either directly or through appropriate subregional or regional organizations, to agree upon the measures necessary for the conservation of these stocks in the adjacent area.

*High Seas * * ***

Article 116

Right to fish on the high seas

All States have the right for their nationals to engage in fishing on the high seas subject to:

(a) their treaty obligations;

(b) the rights and duties as well as the interests of coastal States provided for, *inter alia*, in article 63, paragraph 2, and articles 64 to 67; and

(c) the provisions of this section.

Article 117

Duty of States to adopt with respect to their nationals measures for the conservation of the living resources of the high seas

All States have the duty to take, or to co-operate with other States in taking, such measures for their respective nationals as may be necessary for the conservation of the living resources of the high seas.

Article 118

*Co-operation of States in the conservation
and management of living resources*

States shall co-operate with each other in the conservation and management of living resources in the areas of the high seas. States whose nationals exploit identical living resources, or different living resources in the same area, shall enter into negotiations with a view to taking the measures necessary for the conservation of the living resources concerned. They shall, as appropriate, cooperate to establish subregional or regional fisheries organizations to this end.

Article 119

Conservation of the living resources of the high seas

1.   In determining the allowable catch and establishing other conservation measures for the living resources in the high seas, States shall:

(a) take measures which are designed, on the best scientific evidence available to the state concerned, to maintain or restore populations of harvested species at levels which can produce the maximum sustainable yield, as qualified by relevant environmental and economic factors, including the special requirements of developing States, and taking into account fishing patterns, the interdependence of stocks and any generally recommended international minimum standards, whether subregional, regional or global;

(b) take into consideration the effects on species associated with or dependent upon harvested species with a view to maintaining or restoring populations of such associated or dependent species above levels at which their reproduction may become seriously threatened.

2.   Available scientific information, catch and fishing effort statistics, and other data relevant to the conservation of fish stocks shall be contributed and exchanged on a regular basis through competent international organizations, whether subregional, regional or global, where appropriate and with participation by all States concerned.

3.   States concerned shall ensure that conservation measures and their implementation do not discriminate in form or in fact against the fishermen of any State.

"GLOBAL SOLUTION MUST BE FOUND TO PROBLEMS OF MANAGEMENT, CONSERVATION, CHAIRMAN TELLS STRADDLING AND HIGHLY MIGRATORY FISH STOCKS CONFERENCE"

Conference on Straddling and Highly Migratory Fish Stocks,
58th Meeting (AM), SEA/1475, 27 Mar. 1995.

[The United Nations Conference on Environment and Development, held in Rio de Janeiro in 1992, called for U.N. negotiations to implement the general provisions of the 1982 Convention on the Law of the Sea concerning straddling stocks and highly migratory species.]

The United Nations Conference on Straddling Fish Stocks and Highly Migratory Fish Stocks, which began its fifth session this morning, is expected to discuss a draft agreement * * * which could lead to a global treaty on the long-term conservation and sustainable use of those stocks. * * *

SATYA N. NANDAN (Fiji), Chairman of the Conference, said that a recent report by the Food and Agriculture Organization (FAO) indicated that the volume of marine and fresh water fish catches has continued to decline since its peak in 1989. Since the beginning of the 1990s, about 70 per cent of the world's conventional species of fish were fully exploited, over-exploited, depleted, or were in the process of being regenerated following depletion.

He said action was needed in the following areas: control of fishing effort and the reduction in the fishing industry's over-capacity; resource-allocation decisions and improved decision-making on resource use; and the adoption of precautionary approaches to fisheries conservation and management, among others. * * * The Conference must establish a sound legal framework consistent with the 1982 United Nations Convention on the Law of the Sea, in order to promote effective conservation and management measures so that fisheries resources could be utilized in a sustainable manner. * * *

BRIAN TOBIN, Minister for Fisheries of Canada, said the conditions of the world's fisheries had worsened in the last year. Despite the large number of distant-water vessels still operating, their catches on the high seas had continued to fall from 9.1 million metric tons in 1989 to 4.7 million tons in 1993. Some countries, like Japan, had made the necessary transition and operated reasonable distant-water fleets, which were not a threat to straddling and highly migratory stocks. "Other distant-water vessels were not operating in the same responsible manner." They had become increasingly desperate, fishing whatever, wherever and however they could, heedless of the consequences. "These fleets, from countries like Spain, fish today and forget tomorrow," he said. Such ecological disaster could not continue. It could have only one outcome—depletion and, in some cases, destruction of fish stocks.

Spanish vessels were not the only ones taking 10 or 20 times their cod and flounder quotas, under the terms of the North–West Atlantic Fisheries Organization. Canadians also took too much fish in the 1970s and 1980s, but it had faced up to those mistakes and implemented strong conservation and enforcement measures to protect the commercial extinction of straddling stocks. However, sacrifices made by fishermen in Atlantic Canada and their communities would all be in vain unless there was effective conservation and enforcement outside the 200–mile exclusive economic zones.

He stressed that an effective system of international control of high-seas fisheries included these elements: a legally binding United Nations treaty; a precautionary approach to conservation; compatibility between conservation measures inside and outside the 200–mile economic zones; binding and compulsory dispute settlement; and high-seas enforcement. While some progress had been made in the first four elements, work must still be done during the Conference in the area of high-seas enforcement. Everything accomplished by the Conference, the Law of the Sea Convention and the 1992 United Nations Conference on the Environment and Development (UNCED) would be rendered meaningless without effective high-seas enforcement.

* * * He stressed that Canada was not seeking an extension of the jurisdiction of the 200–mile exclusive economic zone, nor was it seeking authority for the kind of measures it had taken recently against a Spanish vessel. Canada * * * wished to help prevent overfishing and avoid the kind of conflict that Canada was now involved in against Spain.

EMMA BONINO, Commissioner for Fisheries of the European Community, said * * * [e]ffective conservation could only be achieved by ensuring compatibility between measures taken on the high seas and inside national waters. Measures which were taken under different legal regimes should not undermine each other. When dealing with fish stocks which involved the rights of more than one State, sound and effective conservation could only be achieved through effective cooperation between those States. That implied due regard to the rights and obligations of others and must rest on transparent and objective procedures and criteria.

She stressed that if States asserted unilateral jurisdiction on the high seas, it would seriously undermine the Law of the Sea Convention and would have adverse repercussions on other issues governed by the Convention, not only fisheries. * * * Coastal States were much to blame for the problems of the migratory and straddling fish stocks, as the larger part of those fish stocks lived within the exclusive economic zones of coastal States. Distant-water-fishing States must assume their responsibilities, but could not be made "the scapegoat for the management faults committed by others."

The only remaining disagreement concerning fishing in the northwest Atlantic concerned the sharing of the total allowable catch among the fleets operating in the region, she continued. "It is inconceivable to pretend that where the coastal State catches the main portion of a stock, this is to be viewed as a responsible and ecological fishing activity, whereas if others claim to have the right to fish a part of that stock in the high seas, they plunder the seas." Claims of a purely economic interest could not be concealed behind a veil of ecological and humanitarian appearance.

Once the necessary conservation rules had been agreed on, there were two possibilities to accommodate economic interest at the international level: negotiations within a bilateral or multilateral framework could be held with a view to arriving at equitable solutions, while taking into account the interests of others; if negotiations failed to yield satisfactory results, any responsible party would be bound to accept international arbitration. She regretted that some chose to withdraw from international arbitration in the field of fisheries while knowing perfectly well that, in accordance with the procedures of international law, the lawlessness of their actions would have been established.

Notes and Questions

1. *The Depletion of Fisheries and the Case for International Management Regimes.* Grotius considered the supply of fish to be inexhaustible. "Freedoms of the high seas" implied open access to fisheries. Today, however, the depletion of fisheries to which Ambassador Nandan referred has been well documented. Why has the operation of market forces not served to protect fisheries? If a fisheries management regime is necessary, how should it be structured? Between 85 and 90 per cent of the world's commercial fisheries are found in states' coastal zones, and each state decides how to manage fish in its own EEZ. The case for international management regimes becomes stronger, however, when one considers species of fish that swim between the EEZs of two or more coastal states, or that divide their lives inside and outside EEZs. See William T. Burke, *The New International Law of Fisheries* (1994).

2. *Unilateral Coastal State Action to Conserve Straddling Stocks.* Greenland halibut is a "straddling stock" in the northwest Atlantic, with a fishing ground both within Canada's EEZ and on the Grand Banks just outside the EEZ. Depletion of Greenland halibut led Canada to impose severe catch restrictions on Canadians; Canada also, in May 1994, enacted unilateral legislation authorizing conservation and management measures, as well as enforcement measures, with respect to non-Canadian ships fishing for straddling stocks outside Canada's 200–mile EEZ. Coastal Fisheries Protection Act, *entered into force* May 25, 1994, 33 I.L.M. 1383 (1994). Canada initially directed its attention to stateless and flag-of-convenience vessels, several of which were fishing in the high seas area affected by the legislation. In March 1995, Canada extended its regulations to prohibit Spanish and Portuguese vessels from fishing for Greenland halibut on the Grand Banks outside Canada's 200–mile EEZ. On March 9, 1995, Canada boarded and seized the Spanish trawler *Estai,* and, a few weeks later, used a giant scissors-like device to cut the nets of another Spanish trawler fishing

on the Grand Banks. The European Union called Canadian officials "pirates"; Canada accused EU fishermen of being "conservation criminals." Lisa Anderson, "Depleted Fish Stocks Spark Canada's Turbot War with Spain," *Chicago Tribune*, Mar. 19, 1995, at 4.

Canada could not point to clear support in international practice for its high seas measures. What are the problems with unilateral assertions of coastal state jurisdiction beyond the 200–mile EEZ?

3. *The Role of Regional Organizations*. Article 63 of the 1982 U.N. Convention on the Law of the Sea refers to a role for regional organizations with regard to straddling stocks. The Northwest Atlantic Fisheries Organization (NAFO), established by the Convention on Future Multilateral Cooperation in the Northwest Atlantic Fisheries, Oct. 24, 1978, Sen. Exec. Doc. T, 96th Cong., 1st Sess., has regulatory powers in the Northwest Atlantic outside coastal states' EEZs. From Canada's perspective, NAFO's conservation and management efforts have been largely ineffective. Although NAFO's Fisheries Commission does have the authority to set catch quotas in its Regulatory Area, the Convention authorizes parties to veto these quotas. The European Union, one of the parties to the Convention, rejected a 12 per cent share of a 27,000–ton Greenland halibut catch quota that NAFO set for 1995—not the first time the EU had rejected a NAFO quota. NAFO also leaves enforcement of catch quotas and other conservation measures to flag states, and fishing vessels registered in states that are not members of NAFO are not bound by its regulations.

The crisis over Canada's seizure of Spanish vessels was defused when Canada and the EU agreed to propose to NAFO a reallocation of fishing quotas for Greenland halibut. Agreed Minute on the Conservation and Management of Fish Stocks, Can.–Eur. Community, Apr. 20, 1995, 34 I.L.M. 1260 (1995). The Agreed Minute also provides for independent onboard observers, improved NAFO inspection procedures, and increased satellite surveillance of fishing vessels, and it allows Canada to inspect fishing vessels that call at Canadian ports.

4. *Multilateral Agreement on Conservation and Enforcement Measures*. The U.N. negotiations led to the 1995 Agreement Relating to the Conservation and Management of Straddling Fish Stocks and Highly Migratory Fish Stocks, Sept. 8, 1995, A/CONF.167/37, 34 I.L.M. 1542 (1995), which had been accepted by 27 states as of December 31, 2000, and which will enter into force after 30 states accept it. This Agreement requires that conservation and management regimes applicable to areas under national jurisdiction and to the high seas be coordinated. The Agreement calls for the collection, compilation, and exchange of data related to covered fish stocks; it also mandates use of the "precautionary approach" in an effort to insure that lack of firm scientific data does not preclude conservation efforts. See Principle 15 of the Rio Declaration, at page 588.

What should be done to prevent fishing vessels flying the flag of a state not a member of a regional organization such as NAFO from undermining NAFO's conservation measures? The Straddling Stocks Agreement requires States Parties to cooperate in regional conservation and management measures even if they are not members of the regional organization. Under Article 8(4), furthermore, only members of regional organizations or states agreeing to apply regional conservation and management measures are to have access to the fisheries to which the measures apply. The Agreement also contains innovative enforcement mechanisms. A State Party that also is a member of a regional fisheries organization may board and inspect vessels flying the flag of another State Party, even if the latter is not a member of the regional organization, to check whether the vessels comply with regional conservation and management measures. Should the flag state fail to respond when notified of a violation or fail to take enforcement action with respect to its vessel, the boarding state may secure evidence, bring the vessel into port, or take other steps proportionate to the seriousness of the violation. See also Agreement to Promote Compliance with International Conservation and Management Measures by Fishing Vessels on the High Seas, Nov. 24, 1993, 33 I.L.M. 968 (1994), a treaty directed at flag state obligations.

5. *Third-party Adjudication of High Seas Fishing Disputes.* What are the prospects for international adjudication of disputes over straddling stocks or highly migratory species? When Canada enacted its Coastal Fisheries Protection Act in June 1994, it amended its acceptance of the compulsory jurisdiction of the International Court of Justice to exclude the Court's jurisdiction over disputes arising from Canadian management, conservation, and enforcement measures concerning fishing in the NAFO Regulatory Area. Spain nevertheless instituted proceedings in the ICJ in March 1995, challenging the legality of the Canadian legislation and of Canada's boarding Spanish vessels on the high seas. In December 1998, the International Court ruled that it lacked jurisdiction to adjudicate the dispute. Fisheries Jurisdiction (Spain v. Canada), 1998 I.C.J. No. 96 (Dec. 4).

Among States Parties to the 1982 U.N. Convention on the Law of the Sea, the provisions in Part XV of the Convention concerning the obligatory submission of disputes to a third-party tribunal apply. (Spain ratified the Convention in January 1997, but Canada is not a party.) The 1995 Straddling Stocks Agreement also incorporates the 1982 Convention's third-party dispute settlement mechanisms; when the 1995 Agreement enters into force, these mechanisms will apply to parties to the Straddling Stocks Agreement even if they are not parties to the 1982 Convention.

Some disputes related to high seas fisheries have been litigated in international tribunals. In August 1999, the International Tribunal for the Law of the Sea prescribed provisional measures (see Note 1, page 659) in the Southern Bluefin Tuna Cases (Australia and New Zealand v. Japan), 38 I.L.M. 1624 (1999), *revoked by* Arbitral Award on Jurisdiction and Admissibility, 39 I.L.M. 1359 (2000). Pending before a chamber of the ITLOS as of late 2000 is the *Case on Conservation of Swordfish Stocks*, submitted pursuant to a special agreement between Chile and the European Community. The dispute in that case involves the EC's obligations to insure that vessels flying the flag of EC member states conserve swordfish in the high seas adjacent to Chile's EEZ, as well as the application of Chilean conservation measures outside Chile's EEZ. See <http://www.un.org/Depts/los/IT-LOS/ITLOShome.htm>.

D. THE TERRITORIAL SEA AND STRAITS

International law has long provided that a coastal state has sovereignty over a narrow band of waters adjacent to its coastline, known as the territorial sea. More controversial, however, have been the relative rights and responsibilities of coastal states and flag states there. The readings in this Part explore those issues. We start with a case and a treaty excerpt relating to the exercise of criminal jurisdiction by a coastal state over a person on board a foreign flag vessel in the territorial sea. Subsequent excerpts concern the rights of vessels to innocent passage through the territorial sea and to transit passage through straits, issues that have been particularly controversial with respect to warships.

REGINA v. KEYN

Great Britain, Court for Crown Cases Reserved,
2 Law Reports (Exchequer Division) 63 (1876).

[The *Franconia*, a German merchant ship, accidentally struck and sunk the *Strathclyde*, a British vessel, less than three miles from the British coast, resulting in the drowning of a woman aboard the *Strathclyde*. Ferdinand Keyn, the German captain of the *Franconia*, was tried for manslaughter in a British criminal court and convicted. The Court for Crown Cases Reserved then addressed the issue of the jurisdiction of British courts over acts by foreign nationals aboard foreign vessels in British coastal waters. The Court's 13 judges voted, 7 to 6, that British courts had no jurisdiction. The majority held that Parliament could grant the courts jurisdiction over acts committed in a marginal belt of the oceans, but concluded that Parliament had not yet done so. The following excerpt contains brief excerpts from two of the lengthy opinions in this case.]

Sir R. Phillimore * * *

The question as to dominion over portions of the seas inclosed within headlands or contiguous shores * * * is not now under consideration. It is enough to say that within [the] term "territory" are certainly comprised the ports and harbours, and the space between the flux and reflux of tide, or the land up to the furthest point at which the tide recedes. But it is at this point that the difficulty presented by the case before us begins, and here the following questions present themselves for solution:

1. Is a state entitled to any extension of dominion beyond low-water mark?

2. If so, how far does this territory, or do these territorial waters, as they are usually called, extend?

3. Has a state the same dominion over these territorial waters as over the territory of her soil and in her ports, or is it of a more limited character and confined to certain purposes?

With respect to the first of these questions the answer may be given without doubt or hesitation, namely, that a state is entitled to a certain extension of territory, in a certain sense of that word, beyond low-water mark.

With respect to the second question, the distance to which the territorial waters extend, it appears on an examination of the authorities that the distance has varied (setting aside even more extravagant claims) from 100 to 3 miles, the present limit. * * *

The third question * * * remains to be substantively considered; it is one of much importance, viz., whether, admitting that the state has a dominion over three miles of adjacent water, it is the same dominion which the possessor has over her land and her ports, or is it of a more limited character—limited to the purpose of protecting the adjacent shore, for which it was granted, and not extending to a general sovereignty over all passing vessels * * *. * * *

The consensus of civilised independent states has recognised a maritime extension of frontier to the distance of three miles from low-water mark, because such a frontier or belt of water is necessary for the defence and security of the adjacent state.

It is for the attainment of these particular objects that a dominium has been granted over this portion of the high seas.

This proposition is materially different from the proposition contended for, namely, that it is competent to a state to exercise within these waters the same rights of jurisdiction and property which appertain to it in respect to its lands and its ports. There is one obvious test by which the two sovereignties may be distinguished.

According to modern international law, it is certainly a right incident to each state to refuse a passage to foreigners over its territory by land, whether in time of peace or war. But it does not appear to have the same right with respect to preventing the passage of foreign ships over this portion of the high seas.

In the former case there is no jus transitus; in the latter case there is.

The reason of the thing, that is, the defence and security of the state, does not require or warrant the exclusion of peaceable foreign vessels from passing over these waters; and the custom and usage of nations has not sanctioned it.

Consequences fraught with mischief and injustice might flow from the opposite doctrine, which would render applicable to a foreign vessel while in itinere from one foreign port to another, passing over these waters, all the criminal law of the adjacent territory. No single instance has been brought to our notice of the practical exercise by any nation of this jurisdiction.

The authorities cited in order to shew that a foreign vessel is subject to the laws of the foreign port which she enters appear to me inapplicable to the present case.

A foreign merchant vessel going into the port of a foreign state subjects herself to the ordinary law of the place during the period of her commorancy [*i.e.,* stopping] there; she is as much a subditus temporaneus as the individual who visits the interior of the country for the purposes of pleasure or business. * * *

If, indeed, as has been contended, there be no difference between the jurisdiction by the adjacent state over vessels in ports and over passing and commorant vessels, then the whole criminal law of England was applicable to the crew and those on board the German vessel, so long as she was within a marine league of the English shore.

The consequences of such a position of law appear to me, especially in the absence of any precedent, sufficient to render it untenable.

There is yet another argument, already partially adverted to, which appears to me entitled to great weight in an English court of justice.

Upon the subject of the three-miles belt of territorial water, Parliament has frequently legislated. It might perhaps be not impertinently asked, why, if these waters are territorial in the same sense as the land, and those who traverse them are already subject to the law. But, passing by this observation, it will be found on examination of the statutes that the provisions in them are either framed exclusively for British subjects and ships, or that they relate to the protection and peace of the state. * * *

Upon the whole, I am of opinion that the Court had no jurisdiction over this foreigner for an offence committed on board a foreign ship on the high seas, though within three miles of the coast; that he is governed by the law of the state to which his flag belongs; and that the conviction cannot be sustained. * * *

Cockburn, C.J. * * *

* * * There can be no doubt that the suggestion of Bynkershoek, that the sea surrounding the coast to the extent of cannon-range should be treated as belonging to the state owning the coast, has, with but very few exceptions, been accepted and adopted by the publicists who have followed him during the last two centuries. But it is equally clear that, in the practical application of the rule, in respect of the particular of distance, as also in the still more essential particular of the character and degree of sovereignty and dominion to be exercised, great difference of opinion and uncertainty have prevailed, and still continue to exist. * * *

One set of writers * * * ascribe to the state territorial property and sovereignty over the three miles of sea, to the extent of the right of excluding the ships of all other nations, even for the purpose of passage—a doctrine flowing immediately from the principle of territorial property, but which is too monstrous to be admitted. Another set concede territorial property and sovereignty, but make it subject to the right of other nations to use these waters for the purpose of navigation. Others * * * deny any right of territorial property, but concede "jurisdiction;" by which I understand them to mean the power of applying the law, applicable to persons on the land, to all who are within the territorial water, and the power of legislating in respect of it, so as to bind every one who comes within the jurisdiction, whether subjects or foreigners. Some * * * would confine this jurisdiction to purposes of "safety and police"—by which I should be disposed to understand measures for the protection of the territory, and for the regulation of the navigation, and the use of harbours and roadsteads, and the maintenance of order among the shipping therein, rather than the general application of the criminal law.

Other authors * * * would restrict the jurisdiction to certain specified purposes in which the local state has an immediate interest, namely, the protection of its revenue and fisheries, the exacting of harbour and light dues, and the protection of its coasts in time of war.

Some of these authors * * * make a most important distinction between a commorant and a passing ship. According to [one] author, while the commorant ship is subject to the general law of the local state, the passing ship is liable to the local jurisdiction only in matters of "military and police regulations, made for the safety of the territory and population of the coast." None of these writers, it should be noted, discuss the question, or go the length of asserting that a foreigner in a foreign ship, using the waters in question for the purpose of navigation solely, on its way to another country, is liable to the criminal law of the adjoining country for an offence committed on board.

Now, when it is remembered that it is mainly on the statements and authority of these writers, and to opinions founded upon them, that we are called upon to hold that foreigners on the so-called territorial sea are subject to the general law of this country, the discrepancy of opinion which I have been pointing out becomes very material. * * *

* * * This unanimity of opinion that the littoral sea is, at all events for some purposes, subject to the dominion of the local state, may go far to shew that, by the concurrence of other nations, such a state may deal with these waters as subject to its legislation. But it wholly fails to show that, in the absence of such legislation, the ordinary law of the local state will extend over the waters in question—which is the point which we have to determine.

UNITED NATIONS CONVENTION ON THE LAW OF THE SEA, ARTICLE 27

Dec. 10, 1982, 1833 U.N.T.S. 3.

Criminal jurisdiction on board a foreign ship

1. The criminal jurisdiction of the coastal State should not be exercised on board a foreign ship passing through the territorial sea to

arrest any person or to conduct any investigation in connection with any crime committed on board the ship during its passage, save only in the following cases:

(a) if the consequences of the crime extend to the coastal State;

(b) if the crime is of a kind to disturb the peace of the country or the good order of the territorial sea;

(c) if the assistance of the local authorities has been requested by the master of the ship or by a diplomatic agent or consular officer of the flag State; or

(d) if such measures are necessary for the suppression of illicit traffic in narcotic drugs or psychotropic substances.

2. The above provisions do not affect the right of the coastal State to take any steps authorized by its laws for the purpose of an arrest or investigation on board a foreign ship passing through the territorial sea after leaving internal waters.

3. In the cases provided for in paragraphs 1 and 2, the coastal State shall, if the master so requests, notify a diplomatic agent or consular officer of the flag State before taking any steps, and shall facilitate contact between such agent or officer and the ship's crew. In cases of emergency this notification may be communicated while the measures are being taken.

4. In considering whether or in what manner an arrest should be made, the local authorities shall have due regard to the interests of navigation.

5. Except as provided in Part XII [concerning protection of the marine environment] or with respect to violations of laws and regulations adopted in accordance with Part V [concerning the exclusive economic zone], the coastal State may not take any steps on board a foreign ship passing through the territorial sea to arrest any person or to conduct any investigation in connection with any crime committed before the ship entered the territorial sea, if the ship, proceeding from a foreign port, is only passing through the territorial sea without entering internal waters.

Notes and Questions

1. *Municipal Courts and the Law of the Sea. Regina v. Keyn* is but one of many examples of municipal courts deciding issues related to the international law of the sea. Municipal courts may apply customary law (*e.g.,* *Paquete Habana* in Chapter 3 and *Amerada Hess* in Chapter 4), law of the sea treaties (see generally Chapter 4), or municipal statutes embodying maritime treaties or custom. Municipal courts traditionally have been a force in developing and articulating a uniform maritime law, applicable to a wide range of issues. Indeed, the law of the sea was one of the principal topics of the law of nations applied by municipal courts for centuries.

2. *Coastal State Sovereignty and Exercise of Criminal Jurisdiction on Board Foreign Ships in the Territorial Sea.* What supports coastal state

sovereignty over the territorial sea? Are there justifications for sovereign authority valid today that were not present or not recognized in 1876?

Who exercises jurisdiction over criminal activity in the territorial sea? Coastal states may defer to a flag state's exercise of jurisdiction with respect to criminal activities on board a foreign flag vessel. The circumstances in which such deference is appropriate are debatable. The narrow reason precluding the British courts from prosecuting Captain Keyn was cured within two years, when Parliament enacted a law authorizing, *inter alia*, Britain's exercise of criminal jurisdiction over acts in a marginal sea. Territorial Waters Jurisdiction Act, 41 and 42 Victoria, c. 73 (1878). Would Britain's exercise of criminal jurisdiction over Keyn have been appropriate under Article 27 of the 1982 Law of the Sea Convention? Is it sensible, for purposes of the exercise of a coastal state's criminal jurisdiction, to distinguish among vessels passing through the territorial sea on their way to or from one of the coastal state's ports, vessels simply passing by the coastal state's shores, and vessels stopping in the territorial sea?

3. *The Breadth of the Territorial Sea.* As the opinions in *Regina v. Keyn* indicate, the permissible breadth of the territorial sea has historically been the subject of disagreement. In the mid-20th century, some Latin American states unilaterally asserted 200–mile territorial seas, and the delegates to the 1958 First United Nations Conference on the Law of the Sea could reach no agreement on the permissible breadth of the territorial sea. In 1960, the Second United Nations Conference on the Law of the Sea failed by one vote to adopt a proposal for a six-mile territorial sea and an additional six-mile fisheries zone. Now, almost all states accept that the territorial sea may extend only up to 12 miles from a state's baselines, which is the width specified in Article 3 of the 1982 United Nations Convention; states favoring very broad territorial seas in order to protect their access to living resources were largely satisfied by the acceptance of a 200–mile EEZ in the 1982 Convention.

4. *Internal Waters.* Ports and other waters landward of a state's baselines (see Note 6, page 666) are internal waters, unambiguously within a state's sovereignty. A foreign merchant vessel in internal waters, in Phillimore's words, "subjects herself to the ordinary law of the place during the period of her commorancy there." This not to say, however, that international law is irrelevant in internal waters. For example, Articles 218 and 219 of the 1982 Law of the Sea Convention specify the enforcement measures port states may take with respect to foreign flag vessels that are voluntarily in port. Port states, through so-called Memoranda of Understanding, have agreed on collaborative efforts to inspect foreign flag vessels while in port, to help promote their compliance with international safety and environmental treaties and regulations. See, *e.g.*, Tatjana Keselj, "Port State Jurisdiction in Respect of Pollution from Ships: The 1982 United Nations Convention on the Law of the Sea and the Memoranda of Understanding," 30 *Ocean Development and International Law* 127 (1999).

International law may limit or specify port state rights with respect to other issues as well. For example, many have argued that international law provides a right of access to ports for foreign flag vessels, subject to those vessels' compliance with port state laws and regulations relating to health or security. See Saudi Arabia v. Aramco, 27 Int'l L. Rep. 117 (1963); *Restatement (Third) of the Foreign Relations Law of the United States* § 512, Reporter's Note 3 (1988); A.V. Lowe, "The Right of Entry into Maritime Ports in International Law," 14 *San Diego Law Review* 597 (1977). And port states often refrain from exercising their jurisdiction with regard to shipboard matters that do not "disturb the public tranquility," leaving such matters to flag state authorities. The "peace of the port" doctrine may be regulated by bilateral treaties. See Wildenhus's Case, 120 U.S. 1, 7 S.Ct. 385, 30 L.Ed. 565 (1887). Conflicts of jurisdiction between flag states and coastal or port states are an aspect of international conflict of laws, a topic we explore in general in Chapter 12.

UNITED NATIONS CONVENTION ON THE LAW OF THE SEA, ARTICLES 17, 19–21, 24–26

Dec. 10, 1982, 1833 U.N.T.S. 3.

Article 17

Right of innocent passage

Subject to this Convention, ships of all States, whether coastal or land-locked, enjoy the right of innocent passage through the territorial sea.

Article 19

Meaning of innocent passage

1. Passage is innocent so long as it is not prejudicial to the peace, good order or security of the coastal State. Such passage shall take place in conformity with this Convention and with other rules of international law.

2. Passage of a foreign ship shall be considered to be prejudicial to the peace, good order or security of the coastal state if in the territorial sea it engages in any of the following activities:

(a) any threat or use of force against the sovereignty, territorial integrity or political independence of the coastal state, or in any other manner in violation of the principles of international law embodied in the Charter of the United Nations;

(b) any exercise or practice with weapons of any kind;

(c) any act aimed at collecting information to the prejudice of the defence or security of the coastal State;

(d) any act of propaganda aimed at affecting the defence or security of the coastal State;

(e) the launching, landing or taking on board of any aircraft;

(f) the launching, landing or taking on board of any military device;

(g) the loading or unloading of any commodity, currency or person contrary to the customs, fiscal, immigration or sanitary laws and regulations of the coastal State;

(h) any act of wilful and serious pollution contrary to this Convention;

(i) any fishing activities;

(j) the carrying out of research or survey activities;

(k) any act aimed at interfering with any systems of communication or any other facilities or installations of the coastal State;

(*l*) any other activity not having a direct bearing on passage.

Article 20

Submarines and other underwater vehicles

In the territorial sea, submarines and other underwater vehicles are required to navigate on the surface and to show their flag.

Article 21

Laws and regulations of the coastal state relating to innocent passage

1.   The coastal State may adopt laws and regulations, in conformity with the provisions of this Convention and other rules of international law, relating to innocent passage through the territorial sea, in respect of all or any of the following:

(a) the safety of navigation and the regulation of maritime traffic;

(b) the protection of navigational aids and facilities and other facilities or installations;

(c) the protection of cables and pipelines;

(d) the conservation of the living resources of the sea;

(e) the prevention of infringement of the fisheries laws and regulations of the coastal State;

(f) the preservation of the environment of the coastal state and the prevention, reduction and control of pollution thereof;

(g) marine scientific research and hydrographic surveys;

(h) the prevention of infringement of the customs, fiscal, immigration or sanitary laws and regulations of the coastal State.

2.   Such laws and regulations shall not apply to the design, construction, manning or equipment of foreign ships unless they are giving effect to generally accepted international rules or standards.

3.   The coastal State shall give due publicity to all such laws and regulations.

4.   Foreign ships exercising the right of innocent passage through the territorial sea shall comply with all such laws and regulations and all

generally accepted international regulations relating to the prevention of collisions at sea.

Article 24

Duties of the coastal State

1. The coastal State shall not hamper the innocent passage of foreign ships through the territorial sea except in accordance with this Convention. In particular, in the application of this Convention or of any laws or regulations adopted in conformity with this Convention, the coastal State shall not:

   (a) impose requirements on foreign ships which have the practical effect of denying or impairing the right of innocent passage; or

   (b) discriminate in form or in fact against the ships of any State or against ships carrying cargoes to, from or on behalf of any State.

2. The coastal State shall give appropriate publicity to any danger to navigation, of which it has knowledge, within its territorial sea.

Article 25

Rights of protection of the coastal State

1. The coastal State may take the necessary steps in its territorial sea to prevent passage which is not innocent.

2. In the case of ships proceeding to internal waters or a call at a port facility outside internal waters, the coastal State also has the right to take the necessary steps to prevent any breach of the conditions to which admission of those ships to internal waters or such a call is subject.

3. The coastal State may, without discrimination in form or in fact among foreign ships, suspend temporarily in specified areas of its territorial sea the innocent passage of foreign ships if such suspension is essential for the protection of its security, including weapons exercises. Such suspension shall take effect only after having been duly published.

Article 26

Charges which may be levied upon foreign ships

1. No charge may be levied upon foreign ships by reason only of their passage through the territorial sea.

2. Charges may be levied upon a foreign ship passing through the territorial sea as payment only for specific services rendered to the ship. These charges shall be levied without discrimination.

R.P. ANAND, "TRANSIT PASSAGE AND OVERFLIGHT IN INTERNATIONAL STRAITS"

26 *Indian Journal of International Law* 72 (1986).

Since the doctrine of innocent passage came to be established in the middle of the nineteenth century, the question of right of passage of warships has remained controversial and coastal states have been reluctant to permit passage without previous authorization or at least notification. * * * At the [Hague Codification] Conference in 1930, * * * the United States, for one, bluntly denied that there was such a right, because innocent passage existed primarily for commerce, and, so far as warships were concerned, it was wholly a question of usage and comity. * * *

The International Law Commission, in its 1956 draft presented to the 1958 UN Conference on the Law of the Sea, suggested that:

> The coastal state may make the passage of warships through the territorial sea subject to previous authorization or notification. Normally it shall grant innocent passage * * *. * * * *

The International Law Commission's text, as it was presented to the conference, favoured the policies of the Soviet bloc. However, the United States, which until the Second World War was always opposed to the passage of warships through [the] territorial sea without authorization, had changed its stance. Having emerged as the greatest maritime power, it was now interested in the widest freedom of navigation even for its warships. The United States and its allies in NATO were strongly opposed to any limitation on the freedom of the seas, whether in the form of an extension of the territorial sea or a limitation on the passage of warships. Such a limitation, they thought, favoured the Soviet Union which possessed the largest fleet of submarines which could operate undetected for long periods in neutral states' territorial waters without surfacing. Extension of territorial waters coupled with restrictions on free passage of warships, they felt, would have the effect of exposing the mobility of NATO warships and aircraft to crippling jurisdictional restrictions.

[Anand traces diplomatic maneuvering at the 1958 Conference, related to the adoption of the ILC's proposed article.]

The bizarre result of this diplomatic struggle at Geneva was that the 1958 Convention contains no provision on the subject of passage of warships through the territorial sea, but includes Article 23 as suggested by the International Law Commission, which states that if a warship does not comply with the regulations of the coastal state, the latter may require it to leave the territorial sea. This provision survived because the Commission had fortuitously made it a separate article rather than a part of the composite article on straits.

The absence of an article on innocent passage of warships is sometimes interpreted by scholars and diplomats to mean that no restrictions are permissible on the passage of warships. This is said to be supported by Article 14 in which "all ships," including warships, it is asserted, are given the right of innocent passage. Furthermore, Article 23 is said to permit the coastal state to regulate the use of the territorial sea by foreign warships, but not to require previous permission for their transit.

On the other hand, it is argued by some countries and publicists that the expression "ships" in Article 14 means merchant ships because the inclusion of warships, in the light of long-standing customary law, would have required express provision; that Article 23 authorized the coastal state to insist on prior permission as part of its regulatory competence; and that this interpretation is supported by customary law which authorized the coastal state to exclude foreign warships from the territorial sea at will. * * *

With this historical record, it is difficult to conclude that warships have an untrammeled right of innocent passage through territorial waters. Because the 1958 Convention is silent on the subject, it must be interpreted in the light of customary law * * * which did permit coastal states to require notification and authorization before such passage was permitted. * * *

During the Third UN Conference on the Law of the Sea (UNCLOS III), the Soviet Union and its allies quietly dropped their strong objections to innocent passage of warships through territorial waters. The new identity of interest among the major naval powers led to substantially identical proposals by NATO and Warsaw Pact countries to include warships in the rules relating to innocent passage. * * *

The opposition to the right of innocent passage of warships shifted during the Conference from the Soviet bloc to a few Third World countries which were both afraid of the super powers and wanted to protect their coastal areas from becoming involved with their military maneuvers. * * *

* * * [A]lthough the 1982 Convention defines innocent passage in the same terms as the 1958 Convention as a passage that "is not prejudicial to the peace, good order or security of the coastal state" (Article 19(1)), unlike the 1958 Convention, it contains a catalogue of actions, applicable to all ships, that render the passage non-innocent. * * * The adoption of this catalogue to some extent presumes the right of innocent passage for warships, because the activities generally concern the mode of passage of warships. * * *

* * * [T]he 1958 Convention, like past practice dealt with the question of straits in the context of innocent passage in the territorial sea. * * *

The assimilation of the regime of straits with that of the territorial sea in the 1958 Convention was a step backward for all those supporting a special regime for straits. * * *

After the failure of the 1958 and 1960 Conferences to reach an agreement on the limits of the territorial sea, extension by many states of coastal state maritime zone jurisdiction to 12 miles threatened to enclose within * * * territorial sea limits another 116 straits. The three mile rule would have left a strip of high seas between them. Freedom of navigation through several strategic straits, such as the Dover Strait, the Strait of Gibraltar, the Bering Straits, Babel–Mandeb, the Strait of Hormuz, became more precarious, because they came under the coastal states' problematic territorial sea jurisdiction and discretion. The territorial seas regime requires submarines to come up to the surface and show their flag, and there is no right of innocent passage for aircraft through the airspace above the territorial sea. This regime thus leaves the coastal state with wide discretion to declare any particular passage as non-innocent, the passage of nuclear-powered ships, for instance, or big oil tankers.

It is also important to recall the changed political environment after the two UN Conferences on the Law of the Sea. Before the Second World War, most of the strategic and vital straits, especially in Asia and the Middle East, were under the control of the maritime power interested in keeping them open (and claiming narrow territorial sea of three miles). With the collapse of colonialism, new states emerged which were more concerned about their own security and economic interests and were not enamored by the "freedom of the seas" doctrine which had for a long time been used and abused to their disadvantage. Indeed, feeling that unlimited freedom of the seas was against their interests, they wanted to curb it. Some of these newly independent states were strait states now able and willing to control these important waterways to protect their vital interests. The threat of oil spills, dumping on the high seas, and other sources of pollution in a period of growing ecological concern, added still another reason for expanded jurisdictional claims by coastal states. As the trend to extend territorial waters gathered momentum after 1960, most of these straits became part of the territorial seas subject to numerous controls and limitations imposed by the coastal states. In fact, some of these states went further and sought to make certain important straits internal waters subject to their absolute sovereignty. * * * Indonesia enjoys a monopoly over all deep water straits between the Asian mainland and Australia connecting the Pacific and the Indian Oceans. The closure of those straits like Sunda, Lombok, Ombai–Wetar or Macassar would necessitate a diversion of traffic around Australia or through the Panama Canal resulting in time delays, higher consumer prices, and the reduced mobility and flexibility of naval forces.

This trend was totally unacceptable to the maritime powers. * * *

As the Seabed Committee (established by the General Assembly to prepare for the Third UN Conference on the Law of the Sea) started functioning, the maritime powers made clear their intention to keep the straits open. * * * The maritime powers realized, however, that in spite of their strong intention to retain a three-mile limit, they could not force others to roll back their territorial seas. * * *

The United States representative said in Sub-committee of the Seabed Committee that "in addition to the importance of sea navigation for their international trade, many states depended upon air and sea mobility in order to exercise their inherent right of individual and collective self-defence." He pointed out that "the security of the United States and its allies depended to a very large extent on the freedom of navigation and on the overflight of the high seas. More extensive territorial seas, without the right to free transit of straits, would threaten that security." The United States maintained that the invulnerability of its nuclear missile submarines (SSBNs)—currently the Polaris/Poseidon fleet—and hence their indispensable role in an adequate second strike force depended on their right to pass through straits submerged and unannounced. In the U.S. view, the right of free transit through straits was "an indispensable adjunct to the freedom of navigation and that of overflight on the high seas themselves." Moreover, the regime of innocent passage provided for in the 1958 Convention on the Territorial Sea was "inadequate when applied to international straits" because it was a subjective standard subject to abuse. Some states, he said, had in fact claimed that certain types of passage—by nuclear-powered ships and super tankers—should be considered as non-innocent *per se.*

The United States made it clear time and again that it would not accept any extension of the territorial sea from three miles to twelve miles unless the right of *free passage* through international straits was accepted. It demanded freedom of unobstructed passage for warships, including nuclear submarines, on the surface or submerged, without notification and irrespective of mission. Further, it wanted freedom of civilian and military flights through the superjacent airspace. All these rights were claimed not only in those straits that were wider than six miles and were supposed to have, at least theoretically, a corridor of high seas in their midst, but in *all straits irrespective of their breadth or importance.*

The United States was willing to accept and "observe reasonable traffic safety and marine pollution regulations," that is to say, regulations that were "consistent with the basic right of transit." The safety standards to be applied in straits, however, should be established by international agreement and should not be unilaterally imposed by the coastal state.

As to the free transit of aircraft, the United States stated that civil aircraft already enjoyed transit rights over national territory of other states, under the Convention on International Civil Aviation and the International Air Service Transit Agreement. But such rights were not available to state aircraft. The United States demanded a right of free transit for all aircraft over straits, but also stated that such aircraft need not be routed over the strait itself but, at the coastal state's discretion, could be directed through "suitable corridors over land areas."

The United States was supported on this issue not only by the western maritime powers, like the United Kingdom, France, West Germany and others but also by the Soviet Union and Communist bloc countries which also insisted that the limited right of "innocent passage" was not sufficient and "had never been and could never be applied to such straits as those of Gibraltar, Dover, Malacca, Singapore and Bab-el-Mandeb, where freedom of navigation had always been enjoyed." * * *

* * * Refusal to recognize the principle of free passage would mean, according to the Soviet Union, "establishing the domination of only 12 to 15 states adjacent to straits over the passage of vessels of some 130 states of the world." The reversal of the Soviet Policy from its stand in 1958 was, of course, the result of the emergence of the Soviet military capability—naval, fishing and merchant marine—during the subsequent two decades.

Skeptical of the true intentions of the maritime powers and fearful for their own security and sovereignty, the small coastal and strait states strongly objected to the right of "free passage" (instead of "innocent passage") through international straits. By "championing a superficial freedom of navigation," their representatives decried, the big powers were actually seeking authority to "interfere in the domestic affairs of states situated thousands of miles away from their shores." * * *

The principle of "free transit," they contended, might lead to a variety of unfortunate results. For instance, coastal state patrols might misinterpret the presence of military vessels and become involved in a confrontation. Foreign warships might meet other unfriendly warships with results detrimental to the coastal state. Moreover, a foreign military presence could cause domestic consternation and political upheaval, or create misunderstandings between the coastal state and its neighbors. If warships and submarines are engaged in harmless innocent passage there should be no reason for them not to let the coastal state know of their presence. If free transit were permitted, it was contended, military vessels and aircraft passing through international straits would enjoy freedom from law or regulation, a status never enjoyed by any navigator.

Despite all the misgivings and apprehensions of the smaller coastal and strait states * * *, the maritime powers * * * left no one in doubt that "unless unimpeded passage on, over and under straits used for international navigation was conceded to all commercial vessels and warships, including submarines, there was simply no possibility of coming to an agreement on the subject of national jurisdiction and other issues." They were prepared to make concessions on other issues, e.g., the exploitation of deep seabed resources and to accept wide coastal jurisdiction, even the claims of archipelagic states, provided their naval mobility was not affected.

* * * As finally adopted, the Convention provides for a guaranteed non-suspendable transit passage through straits and archipelagic waters, subject only to the power of the coastal state to make certain rules related to navigational safety, pollution, and fishing. For the first time the Convention provides separate regimes for "innocent passage" through [the] territorial sea, laid down in Part II, Section 3 (Articles 17 to 32), and "Transit Passage," through International Straits, laid down in Part III, Section 2 (Articles 37 to 44), and Section 3 (Article 45), the latter applicable only to special straits. The right of transit passage applies to "straits which are used for international navigation between one part of the high seas or an exclusive economic zone and another part of the high seas or an exclusive economic zone" [Article 37]. But transit passage does not apply to:

(1) Straits formed by an island of a state bordering the strait and its mainland if there exists seaward of the island a route through the high seas or through an EEZ of similar convenience with respect to navigational and hydrographical characteristics [Article 38(1)].

(2) Straits used for international navigation between one area of the high seas or an EEZ and the territorial sea of a foreign state [Article 45(1)(b)].

For these two categories the right of "innocent passage" is deemed sufficient which however cannot be suspended [Article 45(2)].

Transit passage is defined as:

the exercise in accordance with this part of the freedom of navigation and overflight solely for the purpose of continuous and expeditious transit of the strait between one part of the high seas or an EEZ and another part of the high seas or an EEZ. However, the requirement of continuous and expeditious transit does not preclude passage through the strait for the purpose of entering, leaving or returning from a state bordering the strait, subject to the conditions of entry to that state [Art. 38(2)].

Article 39 lays down the duties of ships and aircraft while exercising the right of transit passage, such as, [(1)] to proceed without delay through or over the strait; (2) refrain from use of force against the sovereignty, integrity or independence of the bordering states, or in any manner in violation of the principles of international law; (3) refrain from any activities other than those incidental to their normal modes of continuous and expeditious transit unless rendered necessary by *force majeure* or by distress. The ships and aircraft are also expected to comply with the generally accepted international regulations, procedures, and practices for preventing collision and avoiding collisions and aircraft must comply with the rules of the air established by ICAO or otherwise [Article 34(2)(3)].

The coastal states have been authorized under Article 41 to designate sealanes and prescribe traffic separation schemes for navigation after receiving the approval of the IMO. They may also adopt rules and regulations regarding navigation, pollution, fishing, and loading and unloading in transit.

Notes and Questions

1. *Innocent Passage.* The existence of a right of innocent passage demonstrates that a coastal state's sovereignty over its territorial sea is not absolute in international law. The coastal state has no right to exclude foreign vessels engaged in innocent passage. The innocent passage articles of the 1982 Convention reflect an effort to make the standards for innocent passage more objective than was the case under the 1958 Convention on the Territorial Sea and Contiguous Zone. That Convention, in Article 14(4), simply defined innocent passage in the same terms that were later repeated in Article 19(1) of the 1982 Convention. The 1982 Convention articles certainly are more detailed than those in earlier treaties. In addition to the articles reproduced above, the Convention defines "passage," which must be "continuous and expeditious" (Article 18), allows the coastal state to designate sea lanes and traffic separation schemes in the territorial sea (Article 22), and authorizes special precautionary measures with respect to nuclear-powered ships or ships with particularly dangerous cargoes (Article 28). But are the 1982 Convention's standards for innocent passage all that objective? Who decides whether passage is innocent?

Does the 1982 Convention treat the passage of foreign warships through the territorial sea, as opposed to the passage of merchant ships, as "innocent"? Is a coastal state legally entitled to be notified, or to give its authorization, before a foreign warship may pass through its territorial sea? In 1989, the United States and the former Soviet Union concluded a bilateral agreement providing that "neither prior notification or authorization" is a precondition to warships' enjoying the right of innocent passage. Uniform Interpretation of Norms of International Law Governing Innocent Passage, Sept. 23, 1989, 28 I.L.M. 1444 (1989). However, several states maintain that passage of warships through the territorial sea requires the prior consent of the coastal state. See 1 E.D. Brown, *The International Law of the Sea* 66–71 (1994).

2. *The* Corfu Channel Case. As R.P. Anand indicated, maritime powers tried to assure free navigation of their warships in territorial seas and through straits well before UNCLOS III. State practice and treaty negotiations largely shaped the law in this area, but an early decision by the International Court of Justice also was influential. In the Corfu Channel Case (U.K. v. Albania), 1949 I.C.J. 4, 1949 WL 1, the Court found Albania responsible for damage done to British warships by mines in the Corfu Strait, a strait 31 miles long between Albania and the Greek island of Corfu. The Court held:

> * * * States in time of peace have a right to send their warships through straits used for international navigation between two parts of the high seas without the previous authorization of a coastal State,

provided that the passage is *innocent*. Unless otherwise prescribed in an international convention, there is no right for a coastal State to prohibit such passage through straits in time of peace. * * *

It may be asked whether the test is to be found in the volume of traffic passing through the Strait or in its greater or lesser importance for international navigation. But in the opinion of the Court the decisive criterion is rather its geographical situation as connecting two parts of the high seas and the fact of its being used for international navigation. Nor can it be decisive that this Strait is not a necessary route between two parts of the high seas, but only an alternative passage between the Ægean and the Adriatic Seas. It has nevertheless been a useful route for international maritime traffic. * * *

Having regard to these various considerations, the Court has arrived at the conclusion that the North Corfu Channel should be considered as belonging to the class of international highways through which passage cannot be prohibited by a coastal State in time of peace.

On the other hand, it is a fact that the two coastal States did not maintain normal relations, that Greece had made territorial claims precisely with regard to a part of Albanian territory bordering on the Channel, that Greece had declared that she considered herself technically in a state of war with Albania, and that Albania, invoking the danger of Greek incursions, had considered it necessary to take certain measures of vigilance in this region. The Court is of opinion that Albania, in view of these exceptional circumstances, would have been justified in issuing regulations in respect of the passage of warships through the Strait, but not in prohibiting such passage or in subjecting it to the requirement of special authorization.

Id. at 28–29.

3. *Transit Passage Through Straits*. How does the right of transit passage through straits, as set out in the 1982 Convention on the Law of the Sea, differ from the right of innocent passage? How, with respect to the issue of transit passage through straits, does the Convention strike a balance between coastal states' claims of sovereignty and maritime powers' claims of high seas freedoms? How can compliance with Convention provisions on transit passage through straits best be assured? For different views of the provisions on transit passage through straits, compare John Norton Moore, "The Regime of Straits and the Third United Nations Conference on the Law of the Sea," 74 *American Journal of International Law* 77 (1980), with W. Michael Reisman, "The Regime of Straits and National Security: An Appraisal of International Lawmaking," 74 *American Journal of International Law* 48 (1980).

4. *The Regime of Warships*. The ability of warships to navigate or conduct exercises in zones of the oceans other than the territorial sea and straits has been also, of course, of concern to maritime powers. Professor Oxman found "nothing surprisingly new in the regime of warships under the 1982 Convention":

The demilitarization pressures were deflected by liberal use of "peaceful purposes" clauses and cross-references to the prohibitions on the threat or use of force in the U.N. Charter that have little, if any, effect on the legal regime. With respect to all the new regimes or geographical expansions of existing regimes, effects on activities of warships are expressly eliminated or mitigated in each case:

—there is a liberal right of archipelagic sea lanes passage in broad sealanes traversing the newly recognized archipelagic waters;

—the regime of innocent passage in the expanded territorial sea is made more objective and is replaced by a more liberal regime of transit passage in straits;

—high seas freedoms of navigation, overflight and the laying of submarine cables and pipelines, and other internationally lawful uses of the sea related to those freedoms, are expressly preserved in the economic zone;

—high seas freedoms are given more explicit protection from infringement by the coastal State in its exercise of continental shelf rights;

—warships are excluded from all environmental provisions;

—regulation of the deep seabeds depends on a definition of the term "activities in the Area" that does not cover military activities or marine scientific research.

Bernard H. Oxman, "The Regime of Warships Under the United Nations Convention on the Law of the Sea," 24 *Virginia Journal of International Law* 809, 861–62 (1984).

5. *A Package Deal?* International lawyers debate whether the various new provisions in the 1982 Convention amount to customary international law, or whether they are binding only as treaty law. Some argue that acceptance of provisions at UNCLOS III, coupled with state practice, provide the necessary consensus for the bulk of the Convention to be considered customary international law. Others argue that the Convention is a "package deal," the product of numerous compromises and trade-offs, and that a state cannot claim particular rights concerning the oceans while rejecting certain obligations. Which approach is the more sensible?

Indeed, UNCLOS III negotiations concerning innocent passage and transit passage through straits were not carried out in isolation from negotiations on other issues. Some maritime powers, whose interests, according to many observers, were well-served by the outcome of the negotiations on transit passage through straits, were less pleased by other negotiated compromises. In particular, some developed states criticized the regime for mining the deep sea bed that evolved at UNCLOS III. That regime is explored in the next section.

E. THE DEEP SEA BED

The contours of a legal regime to govern the sea bed beyond the limits of national jurisdiction have taken shape only in recent decades. In 1967, Arvid Pardo, Malta's Ambassador to the United Nations, addressed the General Assembly on the uses and resources of the sea bed. In his noteworthy speech, he touched on such varied matters as underseas archaeological treasures, offshore natural gas and petroleum, mineral deposits, ocean floor sediments, oceanographic research, missile systems and other fixed military installations, and pollution. He stirred the most interest, however, when he "conservatively" projected net annual revenues of at least $5 billion from the exploitation of nonliving resources on the ocean floor beyond the boundaries of national jurisdiction. Pardo assumed these boundaries would be set at approximately the 200–meter isobath or 12 miles from the nearest coast. U.N. Doc. A/C.1/PV1515 (1967) (speech by Dr. Pardo in U.N. General Assembly, First Committee, Nov. 1, 1967). Although Pardo greatly underestimated the extent of national jurisdiction over the continental shelf that came to be accepted, during the negotiations at UNCLOS III many states shared his vision of great deep sea-bed wealth. Much attention focused on nodules rich in manganese, nickel, copper, and cobalt that are scattered over about 15 per cent of the sea bed at depths of 3000 to 6000 meters. Current technology allows recovery of these nodules, although such recovery has to date not been economically viable.

Pardo referred to the sea bed beyond the limits of national jurisdiction as the "common heritage of mankind" which "should be used and exploited for peaceful purposes and for the exclusive benefit of mankind as a whole." Pardo argued that developing states, "representing that part of mankind which is most in need of assistance, should receive preferential consideration" in the distribution of revenues derived from the exploitation of the sea bed, an argument reflected in the following U.N. General Assembly resolution.

THE DECLARATION OF PRINCIPLES GOVERNING THE SEA–BED AND THE OCEAN FLOOR, AND THE SUBSOIL THEREOF, BEYOND THE LIMITS OF NATIONAL JURISDICTION

G.A. Res. 2749 (XXV), 25 U.N. GAOR Supp.
(No. 28), at 24, U.N. Doc. A/8028 (1970).

The General Assembly, * * *

Affirming that there is an area of the sea-bed and the ocean floor, and the subsoil thereof, beyond the limits of national jurisdiction, the precise limits of which are yet to be determined,

Recognizing that the existing legal régime of the high seas does not provide substantive rules for regulating the exploration of the aforesaid area and the exploitation of its resources,

Convinced that the area shall be reserved exclusively for peaceful purposes and that the exploration of the area and the exploitation of its resources shall be carried out for the benefit of mankind as a whole,

Believing it essential that an international régime applying to the area and its resources and including appropriate international machinery should be established as soon as possible,

Bearing in mind that the development and use of the area and its resources shall be undertaken in such a manner as to foster the healthy development of the world economy and balanced growth of international trade, and to minimize any adverse economic effects caused by fluctuation of prices of raw materials resulting from such activities,

Solemnly declares that:

1. The sea-bed and ocean floor, and the subsoil thereof, beyond the limits of national jurisdiction (hereinafter referred to as the area), as well as the resources of the area, are the common heritage of mankind.

2. The area shall not be subject to appropriation by any means by States or persons, natural or juridical, and no State shall claim or exercise sovereignty or sovereign rights over any part thereof.

3. No State or person, natural or juridical, shall claim, exercise or acquire rights with respect to the area or its resources incompatible with the international régime to be established and the principles of this Declaration.

4. All activities regarding the exploration and exploitation of the resources of the area and other related activities shall be governed by the international régime to be established.

5. The area shall be open to use exclusively for peaceful purposes by all States, whether coastal or land-locked, without discrimination, in accordance with the international régime to be established.

6. States shall act in the area in accordance with the applicable principles and rules of international law, including the Charter of the United Nations and the Declaration on Principles of International Law concerning Friendly Relations and Co-operation among States in accordance with the Charter of the United Nations, adopted by the General Assembly on 24 October 1970, in the interests of maintaining international peace and security and promoting international co-operation and mutual understanding.

7. The exploration of the area and the exploitation of its resources shall be carried out for the benefit of mankind as a whole, irrespective of the geographical location of States, whether land-locked or coastal, and taking into particular consideration the interests and needs of the developing countries.

8. The area shall be reserved exclusively for peaceful purposes, without prejudice to any measures which have been or may be agreed upon in the context of international negotiations undertaken in the field of disarmament and which may be applicable to a broader area. One or more international agreements shall be concluded as soon as possible in order to implement effectively this principle and to constitute a step towards the exclusion of the sea-bed, the ocean floor and the subsoil thereof from the arms race.

9. On the basis of the principles of this Declaration, an international régime applying to the area and its resources and including appropri-

ate international machinery to give effect to its provisions shall be established by an international treaty of a universal character, generally agreed upon. The régime shall, *inter alia*, provide for the orderly and safe development and rational management of the area and its resources and for expanding opportunities in the use thereof, and ensure the equitable sharing by States in the benefits derived therefrom, taking into particular consideration the interests and needs of the developing countries, whether land-locked or coastal.

10.   States shall promote international co-operation in scientific research exclusively for peaceful purposes:

(*a*) By participation in international programmes and by encouraging co-operation in scientific research by personnel of different countries;

(*b*) Through effective publication of research programmes and dissemination of the results of research through international channels;

(*c*) By co-operation in measures to strengthen research capabilities of developing countries, including the participation of their nationals in research programmes.

No such activity shall form the legal basis for any claims with respect to any part of the area or its resources.

11.   With respect to activities in the area and acting in conformity with the international régime to be established, States shall take appropriate measures for and shall co-operate in the adoption and implementation of international rules, standards and procedures for, *inter alia*:

(*a*) The prevention of pollution and contamination, and other hazards to the marine environment, including the coastline, and of interference with the ecological balance of the marine environment;

(*b*) The protection and conservation of the natural resources of the area and prevention of damage to the flora and fauna of the marine environment.

12.   In their activities in the area, including those relating to its resources, States shall pay due regard to the rights and legitimate interests of coastal States in the region of such activities, as well as of all other States which may be affected by such activities. Consultations shall be maintained with the coastal States concerned with respect to activities relating to the exploration of the area and the exploitation of its resources with a view to avoiding infringement of such rights and interests.

13.   Nothing herein shall affect:

(*a*) The legal status of the waters superjacent to the area or that of the air space above those waters;

(*b*) The rights of coastal States with respect to measures to prevent, mitigate or eliminate grave and imminent danger to their coastline or related interests from pollution or threat thereof or from other hazardous occurrences resulting from or caused by any activities in the area, subject to the international régime to be established.

14. Every State shall have the responsibility to ensure that activities in the area, including those relating to its resources, whether undertaken by governmental agencies, or non-governmental entities or persons under its jurisdiction, or acting on its behalf, shall be carried out in conformity with the international régime to be established. The same responsibility applies to international organizations and their members for activities undertaken by such organizations or on their behalf. Damage caused by such activities shall entail liability.

15. The parties to any dispute relating to activities in the area and its resources shall resolve such dispute by the measures mentioned in Article 33 of the Charter of the United Nations and such procedures for settling disputes as may be agreed upon in the international régime to be established.

Notes and Questions

1. *The Legal Effect of U.N. General Assembly Resolutions.* The 1970 Declaration of Principles was adopted without opposition. What legal effect should be given to it? Compare the U.N. resolutions considered by Professor Dupuy in the *Texaco/Libya Case* in Chapter 3. Also important was the Moratorium Resolution, G.A. Res. 2574–D (XXIV), Dec. 15, 1969, which declared that pending the establishment of an international regime, no state or person was to exploit the resources of the sea bed beyond the limits of national jurisdiction, and that no claim to the deep sea bed or its resources would be recognized.

2. *Differing Legal Conceptions of the Deep Sea Bed.* Before UNCLOS III, views of the legal nature of the deep sea bed differed widely. Some argued that the sea bed beyond the limits of national jurisdiction was *res nullius,* a conception that would allow unilateral claims of title or sovereignty. Others termed the deep sea bed *res communis* and thus not subject to expropriation. Note how Grotius was already distinguishing these concepts in the 1633 excerpt in Part A above. The General Assembly's 1970 Declaration of Principles proclaimed the deep sea bed and its resources to be the common heritage of mankind. In response to a 1974 claim by Deepsea Ventures, Inc. seeking U.S. recognition of "exclusive rights to develop, evaluate and mine" a claim in the deep sea bed, the U.S. State Department stated that it did not grant or recognize exclusive mining rights in the deep sea bed, but that "the mining of the seabed beyond the limits of national jurisdiction may proceed as a freedom of the high seas under existing international law." *Digest of U.S. Practice in International Law* § 5, at 342–43 (1974). Diplomats generally agreed UNCLOS III was the appropriate forum to develop a legal regime to govern the deep sea bed.

3. *International Institutions for the Deep Sea Bed.* Even before UNCLOS III was formally convened, debate centered on the appropriate structure of an international sea-bed authority. Some favored an authority that itself would engage in exploitation, others proposed an authority that would license private claims to blocks of the sea bed, and still others conceived of the authority as a supervisory and consultative body. Many developing states favored a body that would be able to profit from mining and redistribute the

wealth to the developing states. The call for an international regime providing economic assistance to developing states was not restricted to developing states. President Richard Nixon endorsed that goal in his statement on U.S. sea-bed policy on May 23, 1970:

> that all nations adopt as soon as possible a treaty under which they would renounce all national claims over the natural resources of the seabed beyond the point where the high seas reach a depth of 200 meters (218.8 yards) and would agree to regard these resources as the common heritage of mankind.
>
> The treaty should establish an international regime for the exploitation of seabed resources beyond this limit. The regime should include the collection of substantial mineral royalties to be used for international community purposes, particularly economic assistance to developing countries. * * *
>
> * * * [A]greed international machinery would authorize and regulate exploration and use of seabed resources beyond the continental margins.

"United States Oceans Policy: Statement by the President," 6 *Weekly Compilation of Presidential Documents* 667, 667–68 (1970).

4. *The Sea-bed Mining Regime of the U.N. Convention on the Law of the Sea.* Part XI of the 1982 U.N. Convention on the Law of the Sea contains detailed rules and procedures concerning sea-bed mining beyond the limits of national jurisdiction. Article 136 of the Convention sets out the basic principle that the sea bed beyond the limits of national jurisdiction and its resources are the "common heritage of mankind." Part XI also provides for new international institutions. These include the Authority, which is to regulate and govern sea-bed mining primarily through rules, regulations, and procedures adopted by an Assembly and Council. The Enterprise is the mining arm of the Authority, and a Sea–Bed Disputes Chamber of the new International Tribunal for the Law of the Sea is available for compulsory third-party adjudication. Part XI contemplates a "parallel system," under which both the Enterprise and other actors (states and commercial entities) that pay fees and royalties to, and register with, the Authority will mine sea-bed minerals; the benefits received by the Authority from activities in the deep sea bed are to be equitably shared. See Convention on the Law of the Sea, Article 140. Part XI also contains production limits, included to assuage the concerns of land-based producers of minerals that feared the economic impact of an influx of sea-bed minerals onto world markets. Was it wise to provide such detail in the Convention? What exactly is "equitable sharing"? See Note 11 below.

5. *U.S. Objections to the U.N. Convention's Sea-bed Mining Regime.* In 1981, near the end of the UNCLOS III negotiations, the United States during the Reagan Administration announced that it would not support the U.N. Convention on the Law of the Sea, objecting to certain provisions in Part XI. Articles requiring payments from miners, limits on production, and the transfer of technology to the Enterprise were seen as incompatible with the operation of market forces. The United States also sought a greater role in the decision-making bodies of the Authority, and objected to provisions for a Review Conference, which could adopt amendments to Part XI binding on

all states regardless of their concurrence. The United States, the Federal Republic of Germany, and the United Kingdom did not sign the Convention; other developed states signed but did not ratify. On November 16, 1993, when the Convention received its 60th acceptance—the number necessary for its entry into force a year later—virtually all ratifications were by developing states.

Efforts to accommodate the U.S. objections, and to provide for a regime to govern sea-bed mining, followed three different tracks outside UNCLOS III. We consider these tracks in the next three notes.

6. *Unilateral Sea-bed Mining Legislation and "Reciprocating States" Treaties.* One track involved municipal legislation. Legislation authorizing unilateral licensing of certain deep sea-bed mining activities was enacted in the United States. Deep Seabed Hard Minerals Resource Act of 1980, 30 U.S.C. §§ 1401–1473 (1994). By 1985, the Federal Republic of Germany, France, Japan, Italy, the Soviet Union, and the United Kingdom also had adopted unilateral legislation. Each piece of legislation proclaimed that deep sea-bed mining conducted with due regard for the interests of other states was a high seas freedom; the legislation did not claim sovereignty or sovereign rights over any portion of the deep sea bed or its resources. The governments of the states enacting the legislation claimed that it was interim in nature, to be in effect pending agreement on a satisfactory Convention text. Developed states also entered into "reciprocating states" treaties designed to respect licenses issued under national laws and to avoid overlaps in mining claims. See Agreement Concerning Interim Arrangements Relating to Polymetallic Nodules of the Deep Sea Bed, Sept. 2, 1982, 21 I.L.M. 950 (1982). The prospect of unilateral legislation had provoked debate at UNCLOS III, with developing states arguing that unilateral exploitation would be contrary to the Declaration of Principles and "a clear violation of international law." See UNCLOS III, Resumed 7th Sess., Plenary, 109th Mtg., Sept. 15, 1978, in 9 *UNCLOS III Official Records* 103–08 (U.N. Sales No. E.79.V.3). Could a unilateral mining state still claim the benefit of other provisions of the 1982 Convention, *e.g.*, transit passage through straits?

7. *The Preparatory Commission.* The second track towards providing a workable regime to govern sea-bed mining involved the Preparatory Commission for the International Sea–Bed Authority and for the International Tribunal for the Law of the Sea (Prepcom), established pursuant to Resolution I of UNCLOS III. Prepcom had two broad mandates. First, it was to plan for the international institutions and arrangements that would operate under Part XI when the 1982 Convention entered into force, making budget and agenda recommendations and preparing draft rules, regulations, and procedures for the Authority. Second, Prepcom exercised significant administrative power of its own, in regards to registering the deep sea-bed exploration activities of certain states and multinational mining consortia as "pioneer investors." While condemning as "wholly illegal" any mining-related activities incompatible with the 1982 Convention, U.N. Doc. LOS/PCN/72 (1985), Prepcom displayed a flexible attitude with regard to the "reciprocating states" regime discussed in Note 6. In particular, Prepcom supported agreements to resolve overlapping claims to mine sites in the Pacific as a precondition to the registration of four pioneer investor states; these included agreements with the United States and other nonsignatories of the

Convention. See Statement on the Implementation of Resolution II, Aug. 11–Sept. 5, 1986, 25 I.L.M. 1326 (1986).

8. *The 1994 Agreement Modifying the Law of the Sea Convention's Sea-bed Mining Regime*. The third track addressing difficulties with the Law of the Sea Convention's sea-bed mining regime resulted in a compromise agreement. Proposals to modify or set aside Part XI of the 1982 Convention were discussed in a series of informal meetings beginning in July 1990, undertaken at the initiative of the U.N. Secretary–General. The result of these meetings was the detailed Agreement Relating to the Implementation of Part XI, 1836 U.N.T.S. 3, which was opened for signature on July 29, 1994, less than four months before the Law of the Sea Convention entered into force. This Agreement dispenses with large annual fees for miners, production limitations, and the requirement that States Parties fund the Enterprise's mining operations. Part XI requirements concerning the transfer of private technology are not implemented; a mandate that the Enterprise and developing states "seek to obtain such technology on fair and reasonable commercial terms and conditions on the open market, or through joint venture arrangements" applies instead. Multinational consortia previously licensed under municipal legislation are guaranteed access to sea-bed mining on terms "no less favorable than" terms given to entities whose mine site claims had been registered by Prepcom. With respect to several other issues, general principles, to guide the formulation of more specific rules, regulations, and procedures the Authority is to adopt when commercial production is imminent, will be used in place of detailed provisions of Part XI.

The 1994 Agreement also revises procedural aspects of Part XI. For example, any of four chambers—including a chamber representing the industrialized states—may now block important substantive decisions of the Council, including decisions on the sharing of benefits derived from sea-bed mining. Furthermore, provisions relating to the Review Conference "shall not apply," so no amendments to the sea-bed mining regime can apply to any state that does not accept them.

The 1994 Agreement contains provisions to help insure that the 1982 Convention is implemented along with the Agreement. States accepting the 1982 Convention after July 29, 1994, must also accept the Agreement, which is to be interpreted and applied together with the Convention as a single instrument. In addition, no state may accept the Part XI Agreement without also accepting the Convention. States that accepted the Convention prior to July 29, 1994, can become bound by the Agreement merely by signing it, unless they take affirmative steps to indicate their intent not to be bound. The Part XI Agreement entered into force on July 28, 1996.

9. *The International Sea-bed Authority*. The International Sea-bed Authority, created pursuant to the 1982 Law of the Sea Convention as modified by the 1994 Part XI Agreement, is operational, headquartered in Kingston, Jamaica. In 1997 the Authority approved "plans of work" for seven registered pioneer investors (see Note 7), some of which are private and some of which are governmental entities. The sponsoring states are China, France, India, Japan, Russia, South Korea, and a group of six states (Cuba and five Eastern European states). In July 2000, the Authority adopted "Regulations

on Prospecting and Exploration for Polymetallic Nodules," which constitute the first part of what is contemplated to be a detailed sea-bed mining code. See <www.isa.org.jm>.

10. *The Impact of International Law on Deep Sea-bed Mining.* Suppose a company or consortium were authorized under national legislation to exploit manganese nodules on the deep sea bed beyond the limits of national jurisdiction, and suppose the authorizing state is not a party to the U.N. Convention on the Law of the Sea. How would international law affect any decision to exploit nodules pursuant to such legislation? Are the 1982 Convention's deep sea-bed mining provisions an international legal obligation *erga omnes*?

11. *Equitable Sharing of Revenues From Mining the Continental Shelf.* Under Article 82 of the U.N. Convention on the Law of the Sea, each coastal state (with the exception of certain developing states) must pay a portion of its revenues from its exploitation of the nonliving resources of the continental shelf beyond 200 miles from its baselines. The Authority, established to regulate deep sea-bed mining, is to receive such payments. The Authority will then distribute them to parties to the Convention "on the basis of equitable sharing criteria, taking into account the interests and needs of developing States, particularly the least developed and the land-locked among them." Does the reference to "equitable sharing" have a definite meaning, or is it merely a grant of discretion to the Authority? See Chapter 3.

Chapter 12

INTERNATIONAL CONFLICT OF LAWS

The anticipation and resolution of international legal disputes is often made more complex by the fundamental contradictions that exist between the realities of international transactions and the artifices of law. A basic fact of international relations is that private, as well as public, transactions abound which overleap national boundaries. No such overleapings, however, characterize the ordinary allocation and exercise of legal authority. These remain predominately vested in sovereign states. Hence, a dispute involving a single international transaction typically triggers responses from two or more national legal systems.

The intellectual discipline concerning the international interface of municipal legal systems has no satisfactory denomination. In civil law nations the field is usually called *private international law*, even though it concerns the international relations of national courts, legislatures, and administrations, surely a matter of public concern. In the United States and some other common law countries, the subject's customary appellation is *conflict of laws*, even though the relevant laws and processes have much more to do with conflict-avoidance and international legal cooperation. What is agreed is that the substance of the discipline includes topics such as jurisdiction, foreign sovereign immunity, and act of state. All are examined below. In practical terms, anticipating and solving problems of international conflict of laws constitutes a large fraction of the work of most international lawyers.

A. THE PRINCIPLES OF JURISDICTION

In studying the complex world of international conflict of laws, a reasonable point of first contact is the description and analysis of the authority (sometimes called power or competence) of different states to determine and affect the legal relationships of private parties. This topic is usually denoted by the term *jurisdiction*. Legislative jurisdiction, adjudicatory jurisdiction, and executive jurisdiction are more specific terms used to describe the power of states to make laws, to have their

715

courts render authoritative judgments, and to enforce laws and the decisions of courts. Almost invariably in international transactions, any one nation's exercise of any sort of jurisdiction conflicts, at least in principle and often in practice, with the jurisdictional realm of another state. The problems of jurisdiction, be they legislative, judicial, or executive, usually involve both describing and justifying permissible forms of national legal authority and explicating the means, municipal and international, of reconciling conflicts among such municipal assertions of legal competence.

1. THE TERRITORIAL PRINCIPLE

AMERICAN BANANA CO. v. UNITED FRUIT CO.

213 U.S. 347, 29 S.Ct. 511, 53 L.Ed. 826 (1909).

Mr. Justice Holmes delivered the opinion of the Court.

The allegations of the complaint may be summed up as follows: The plaintiff is an Alabama corporation, organized in 1904. The defendant is a New Jersey corporation, organized in 1899. Long before the plaintiff was formed, the defendant, with intent to prevent competition and to control and monopolize the banana trade, bought the property and business of several of its previous competitors, with provision against their resuming the trade, made contracts with others, including a majority of the most important, regulating the quantity to be purchased and the price to be paid, and acquired a controlling amount of stock in still others. For the same purpose it organized a selling company, of which it held the stock, that by agreement sold at fixed prices all the bananas of the bringing parties. By this and other means it did monopolize and restrain the trade and maintained unreasonable prices. The defendant being in this ominous attitude, one McConnell in 1903 started a banana plantation in Panama, then part of the United States of Colombia, and began to build a railway (which would afford his only means of export), both in accordance with the laws of the United States of Columbia. He was notified by the defendant that he must either combine or stop. Two months later, it is believed at the defendant's instigation, the governor of Panama recommended to his national government that Costa Rica be allowed to administer the territory through which the railroad was to run, and this although that territory had been awarded to Colombia under an arbitration agreed to by treaty. The defendant, and afterwards, in September, the government of Costa Rica, it is believed by the inducement of the defendant, interfered with McConnell. In November, 1903, Panama revolted and became an independent republic, declaring its boundary to be settled by the award. In June, 1904, the plaintiff bought out McConnell and went on with the work, as it had a right to do under the laws of Panama. But in July, Costa Rican soldiers and officials, instigated by the defendant, seized a part of the plantation and a cargo of supplies and have held them ever since, and stopped the construction and operation of the plantation and railway. In August one Astua, by *ex parte* proceedings, got a judgment from a Costa Rican court, declaring the plantation to be his, although, it is alleged, the proceedings were not within the jurisdiction of Costa Rica, and were contrary to its laws and void. Agents of the defendant then bought the lands from Astua. The plaintiff has tried to induce the government of Costa Rica to withdraw its soldiers and also has tried to persuade the United States to interfere, but has been thwarted in both by the defendant and has failed. The government of Costa Rica remained in possession down to the bringing of the suit.

As a result of the defendant's acts the plaintiff has been deprived of the use of the plantation, and the railway, the plantation and supplies have been injured. The defendant also, by outbidding, has driven purchasers out of the market and has compelled producers to come to its terms, and it has prevented the plaintiff from buying for export and sale. This is the substantial damage alleged. * * *

It is obvious that, however stated, the plaintiff's case depended on several rather startling propositions. In the first place the acts causing the damage were done, so far as appears, outside the jurisdiction of the United States and within that of other states. It is surprising to hear it argued that they were governed by the act of Congress.

No doubt in regions subject to no sovereign, like the high seas, or to no law that civilized countries would recognize as adequate, such countries may treat some relations between their citizens as governed by their own law, and keep to some extent the old notion of personal sovereignty alive. They go further, at times, and declare that they will punish any one, subject or not, who shall do certain things, if they can catch him, as in the case of pirates on the high seas. In cases immediately affecting national interests they may go further still and may make, and, if they get the chance, execute similar threats as to acts done within another recognized jurisdiction. An illustration from our statutes is found with regard to criminal correspondence with foreign governments. And the notion that English statutes bind British subjects everywhere has found expression in modern times and has had some startling applications. But the general and almost universal rule is that the character of an act as lawful or unlawful must be determined wholly by the law of the country where the act is done. * * * For another jurisdiction, if it should happen to lay hold of the actor, to treat him according to its own notions rather than those of the place where he did the acts, not only would be unjust, but would be an interference with the authority of another sovereign, contrary to the comity of nations, which the other state concerned justly might resent.

Law is a statement of the circumstances in which the public force will be brought to bear upon men through the courts. But the word commonly is confined to such prophecies or threats when addressed to persons living with the power of the courts. A threat that depends upon the choice of the party affected to bring himself within that power hardly would be called law in the ordinary sense. We do not speak of blockade running by neutrals as unlawful. And the usages of speech correspond to the limit of the attempts of the lawmaker, except in extraordinary cases. It is true that domestic corporations remain always with the power of the domestic law, but in the present case, at least, there is not ground for distinguishing between corporations and men.

The foregoing considerations would lead in case of doubt to a construction of any statute as intended to be confined in its operation and effect to the territorial limits over which the lawmaker has general and legitimate power. "All legislation is *prima facie* territorial." Words having universal scope, such as "Every contract in restraint of trade," "Every person who shall monopolize," etc., will be taken as a matter of course to mean only every one subject to such legislation, not all that the legislator subsequently may be able to catch. In the case of the present statute the improbability of the United States attempting to make acts done in Panama or Costa Rica criminal is obvious, yet the law begins by making criminal the acts for which it gives a right to sue. We think it entirely plain that what the defendant did in Panama or Costa Rica is not within the scope of the statute so far as the present suit is concerned. Other objections of a serious nature are urged but need not be discussed.

For again, not only were the acts of the defendant in Panama or Costa Rica not within the Sherman Act, but they were not torts by the law of the place and therefore were not torts at all, however contrary to the ethical and economic postulates of the statute. * * * Giving to this complaint every reasonable latitude of interpretation we are of opinion that it alleges no case under the act of Congress and discloses nothing that we can suppose to have been a tort where it was done. A conspiracy in this country to do acts in another jurisdiction does not draw to itself those acts and make them unlawful, if they are permitted by the local law.

Notes and Questions

1. *The Territorial Principle.* In *American Banana* Justice Holmes maintained that "the general and almost universal rule is that the character of an act as lawful or unlawful must be determined wholly by the law of the country where the act is done." Did he explain if this was a jurisdictional rule based on U.S. law, Panamanian or Costa Rican law, or international law? What if the Court had found that Congress indeed had intended to prohibit U.S. companies from conspiring in the United States to restrain imports to the U.S.? Could international law or the law of Panama or that of Costa Rica have limited the extraterritorial reach of the U.S. statute? If so, in what court(s) could those limiting laws have been applied? If acts facilitating a restraint of trade had been done in the United States, *e.g.*, by corporate officers of United Fruit, would the Supreme Court necessarily have had to construe the statute as reaching outside U.S. territory?

2. *Holmes and Legal Realism.* Holmes's reasoning in *American Banana* reflected his well-known version of American legal realism: "Law is a

statement of the circumstances in which the public force will be brought to bear upon men through the courts." Holmes employed his realism to argue that it would be unusual to use the term "law" to describe one nation's prescription of rules on another nation's territory: "But the word commonly is confined to such prophecies or threats when addressed to persons living within the power of the courts. A threat that depends upon the choice of the party affected to bring himself within that power hardly would be called law in the ordinary sense."

3. *Competing Principles of Jurisdiction.* Nowadays, U.S. courts ordinarily recognize forms of extraterritorial jurisdiction that severely limit *American Banana.* In the 1990 *Kirkpatrick* case, Justice Scalia, delivering the opinion of the Supreme Court, wrote that *American Banana's* proposition "that the antitrust laws had no extraterritorial application" had been "substantially overruled," *e.g.*, by Continental Ore Co. v. Union Carbide & Carbon Corp., 370 U.S. 690, 704–05, 82 S.Ct. 1404, 1413–14, 8 L.Ed.2d 777, 787–88 (1962). W.S. Kirkpatrick & Co. v. Environmental Tectonics Corp., 493 U.S. 400, 407, 110 S.Ct. 701, 705–06, 107 L.Ed.2d 816, 824 (1990). For more on the "erosion" of the authority of *American Banana*, see the review of authority in Zenith Radio Corp. v. Matsushita Elec. Indus. Co., 494 F.Supp. 1161, 1181–86 (E.D.Pa.1980). Nonetheless, though *American Banana* may no longer be good law respecting the exclusive potency of the territorial principle, it still can be used to support the territorial principle as one basis, albeit among several, for a state's assertion of legislative, judicial, or executive jurisdiction.

4. *Choice-of-Law Considerations. American Banana* may also be seen to reflect policy preferences justifying the act of state doctrine, a topic explored in Part D below. That is, instead of viewing *American Banana* as a case about adjudicatory jurisdiction, why not see it as a case about choice of law? Holmes could be said to have chosen to respect a foreign law that permitted the company's alleged activities rather than a U.S. law that outlawed them.

5. *Statutory Interpretation.* One of the reasons why U.S. courts have treated cases like *American Banana* as adjudicatory jurisdiction cases rather than choice-of-law cases has been that U.S. judges have traditionally seen their role as construing a federal statute, *e.g.*, asking whether Congress "meant" to regulate the matter in controversy. Is this too artificial an inquiry? Does Congress ordinarily "mean" anything about the reach of a statute outside the U.S.? Would it not make more sense and lead to a fairer evaluation if U.S. courts simply acknowledged that they were choosing among possible laws, each of which had a valid claim to regulate the transaction? We see a more sophisticated analysis of conflicts of jurisdiction in *Timberlane* below.

That the courts have never totally abandoned *American Banana's* presumption against the extraterritorial application of U.S. law can be seen in E.E.O.C. v. Arabian American Oil Co., 499 U.S. 244, 111 S.Ct. 1227, 113 L.Ed.2d 274 (1991). In that case, Chief Justice Rehnquist refused to extend U.S. anti-discrimination legislation to protect a U.S. citizen employed by a U.S. oil company in Saudi Arabia: "It is a longstanding principle of American law 'that legislation of Congress, unless a contrary intent appears, is meant to apply only within the territorial jurisdiction of the United States.' " *Id.* at 248, 111 S.Ct. at 1230, 113 L.Ed.2d at 282, *quoting* Foley Bros. v. Filardo, 336 U.S. 281, 285, 69 S.Ct. 575, 577, 93 L.Ed. 680, 683.

2. THE NATIONALITY PRINCIPLE

BLACKMER v. UNITED STATES

284 U.S. 421, 52 S.Ct. 252, 76 L.Ed. 375 (1932).

MR. CHIEF JUSTICE HUGHES delivered the opinion of the Court.

The petitioner, Harry M. Blackmer, a citizen of the United States resident of Paris, France, was adjudged guilty of contempt of the Supreme Court of the District of Columbia for failure to respond to subpoenas served upon him in France and requiring him to appear as a witness on behalf of the United States at a criminal trial in that court. Two subpoenas were issued, for appearances at different times, and there was a separate proceeding with respect to each. The two cases were heard together, and a fine of $30,000 with costs was imposed in each case, to be satisfied out of the property of the petitioner which had been seized by order of the court. The decrees were affirmed by the Court of Appeals of the District, and this Court granted writs of certiorari. * * *

While it appears that the petitioner removed his residence to France in the year 1924, it is undisputed that he was, and continued to be, a citizen of the United States. He continued to owe allegiance to the United States. By virtue of the obligations of citizenship, the United States retained its authority over him, and he was bound by its laws made applicable to him in a foreign country. Thus, although resident abroad, the petitioner remained subject to the taxing power of the United States. For disobedience to its laws through conduct abroad he was subject to punishment in the courts of the United States. *United States v. Bowman*, 260 U.S. 94, 102. With respect to such an exercise of authority, there is no question of international law, but solely of the purport of the municipal law which establishes the duties of the citizen in relation to his own government. While the legislation of the Congress, unless the contrary intent appears, is construed to apply only within the territorial jurisdiction of the United States, the question of its application, so far as citizens of the United States in foreign countries are concerned, is one of construction, not of legislative power. *American Banana Co. v. United Fruit Co.*, 213 U.S. 347, 357; *United States* v. *Bowman, supra.* Nor can it be doubted that the United States possesses the power inherent in sovereignty to require the return to this country of a citizen, resident elsewhere, whenever the public interest requires it, and to penalize him in case of refusal. What in England was the prerogative of the sovereign in this respect, pertains under our constitutional system to the national authority which may be exercised by the Congress by virtue of the legislative power to prescribe the duties of the citizens of the United States. It is also beyond controversy that one of the duties which the citizen owes to his government is to support the administration of justice by attending its courts and giving his testimony whenever he is properly summoned. And the Congress may provide for the performance of this duty and prescribe penalties for disobedience.

In the present instance, the question concerns only the method of enforcing the obligation. The jurisdiction of the United States over its absent citizen, so far as the binding effect of its legislation is concerned, is a jurisdiction *in personam*, as he is personally bound to take notice of the laws that are applicable to him and to obey them. *United States* v. *Bowman*, supra. But, for the exercise of judicial jurisdiction *in personam*, there must be due process, which requires appropriate notice of the judicial action and an opportunity to be heard. For this notice and opportunity the statute provides. The authority to require the absent citizen to return and testify necessarily implies the authority to give him notice of the requirement. As his attendance is needed in court, it is appropriate that the Congress should authorize the court to direct the notice to be given and that it should be in the customary form of a subpoena. Obviously, the requirement would be nugatory, if provision could not be made for its communication to the witness in the foreign country. The efficacy of an attempt to provide constructive service in this country would rest upon the presumption that the notice would be given in a manner calculated to reach the witness abroad. The question of the validity of the provision for actual service of the subpoena in a foreign country is one that arises solely between the Government of the United States and the citizen. The mere giving of such a notice to the citizen in the foreign country of the requirement of his government that he shall return is in no sense an invasion of any right of the foreign government; and the citizen has no standing to invoke any such supposed right. While consular privileges in foreign countries are the appropriate subjects of treaties, it does not follow that every act of a consul, as, *e.g.*, in communicating with citizens of his country, must be predicated upon a specific provision of a treaty. The intercourse of friendly nations, permitting travel and residence of the citizens of each in the territory of the other, presupposes and facilitates such communications. In selecting the consul for the service of the subpoena, the Congress merely prescribed a method deemed to assure the desired result but in no sense essential. The consul was not directed to perform any function involving consular privileges or depending upon any treaty relating to them, but simply to act as any designated person might act for the Government in conveying to the citizen the actual notice of the requirement of his attendance. The point raised by the petitioner with respect to the provision for the service of the subpoena abroad is without merit.

Notes and Questions

1. *The Nationality Principle. Blackmer* is a classic example of jurisdiction based on the principle of nationality, but did the *Blackmer* Court fail to recognize that the case raised rather different questions, *e.g.*, about legislative and judicial jurisdiction on the one hand and executive jurisdiction on

the other? Chief Justice Hughes thoroughly explained why Blackmer as a U.S. citizen was subject to the laws and courts of the United States, but how effectively did Hughes ever grapple with the question of whether the U.S. had jurisdiction to serve process on *Blackmer* in France and the related question about the reconciliation of U.S. executive jurisdiction with the executive jurisdiction of France?

Territoriality and nationality are the two most commonly accepted bases for jurisdiction, but, taken together, they immediately raise problems of conflicts, for example, in *Blackmer* of conflicts between the territorial jurisdiction of France and the nationality jurisdiction of the United States. After territoriality, all other bases of jurisdiction are more or less extraterritorial. In 19th and early 20th century China, extraterritorial nationality jurisdiction went so far as to exclude the territorial jurisdiction of China over foreign nationals of the Great Powers, who were subject only to the laws and courts of their national governments, a fact keenly resented by many Chinese. E.H. Carr, *International Relations Since the Peace Treaties* 156 (1941 rev. ed.).

2. *Executive Acts on Foreign Soil*. The United States employed the U.S. consul in Paris to serve process on Blackmer. Should the United States instead have used the French courts or French administrative officers? What responses might any country, including the United States, have to the exercise of executive jurisdiction within its territorial boundaries by a foreign country, even against a foreign citizen? Remember the outrage in Mexico over the kidnapping of one of its citizens in Mexico by the United States in *Alvarez–Machain* in Chapter 4. If France was theoretically or actually offended by the exercise of U.S. jurisdiction in the case, should Blackmer himself have had standing to complain? How would the French government itself object?

Should U.S. courts use cases like *Blackmer* to limit assertions of U.S. governmental power in foreign countries, or would that be too politically risky? Should U.S. courts be more ready to limit their own judicial jurisdiction in cases of international conflicts than they ought to be to limit extraterritorial assertions of U.S. legislative or executive power? In *Blackmer* and *Alvarez–Machain* the Supreme Court chose not to restrain the extraterritorial reach of the U.S. executive branch.

3. *Other Bases of Jurisdiction*. While territory and nationality are the two most important traditional bases of jurisdiction, others have also appeared. Besides effects jurisdiction, explored in *Aluminum* immediately below, there are:

> —the protective principle, guarding the security or the central interests of the state;

> —the universality principle, giving any state the right to extend its jurisdiction to certain sorts of offenders, *e.g.*, pirates and war criminals; and

> —the passive personality principle, protecting nationals even when abroad.

See Mark W. Janis, *An Introduction to International Law* 329–30 (3d ed. 1999).

It is important to remember that the various principles of jurisdiction do not constitute hard and fast discrete categories, but are often blended together in judicial discussions about jurisdiction in specific cases. For example, in United States v. Bowman, 260 U.S. 94, 43 S.Ct. 39, 67 L.Ed. 149 (1922), a case cited in *Blackmer*, the offense was defrauding the U.S. government by claiming payment for 1000 tons of fuel oil delivered to a U.S.–operated vessel when the ship had really taken on and paid for only 600 tons. Since three of the four malfeasors were U.S. citizens, *Bowman* could certainly be read as the *Blackmer* Court read it, *i.e.*, that a U.S. citizen "was subject to punishment in the courts of the United States" for "disobedience to its laws through conduct abroad." Yet, the actual language in *Bowman* seemed to mix nationality with protective principles. Respecting criminal statutes, at least, *Bowman* held that there is a "right of the Government to defend itself against obstruction, or fraud whenever perpetrated, especially if committed by its own citizens, officers or agents." 260 U.S. at 98, 43 S.Ct. at 41, 67 L.Ed. at 151.

3. THE EFFECTS PRINCIPLE

UNITED STATES v. ALUMINUM CO. OF AMERICA

148 F.2d 416 (2d Cir.1945).

L. Hand, Circuit Judge

[The case concerns the application of U.S. antitrust laws to "Limited," a Canadian company, spun off from "Alcoa," a U.S. company.]

"Limited" was incorporated in Canada on May 31, 1928, to take over those properties of "Alcoa" which were outside the United States. * * * [F]ormally at any rate, the separation between the two companies was complete. At the conclusion of the transfers a majority, though only a bare majority, of the common shares of "Alcoa" was in the hands of three persons: Andrew W. Mellon, Richard B. Mellon, his brother, and Arthur V. Davis. Richard Mellon died in 1933, and Andrew in 1937, and their shares passed to their families; but in January, 1939, the Davises, the officers and directors of "Alcoa" and the Mellon families—eleven individuals in all—collectively still held 48.9 per cent of "Alcoa's" shares, and 48.5 per cent of "Limited's"; and Arthur V. Davis was then the largest shareholder in both companies.

[The court finds that "Alcoa" had not been party to the "Alliance," a foreign cartel fixing the price of aluminum world-wide].

Whether "Limited" itself violated [Section 1 of the Sherman Act] depends upon the character of the "Alliance." It was a Swiss corporation, created in pursuance of an agreement entered into on July 3, 1931, the signatories to which were a French corporation, two German, one Swiss, a British, and "Limited." The original agreement, or "cartel," provided for the formation of a corporation in Switzerland which should issue shares, to be taken up by the signatories. This corporation was from time to time to fix a quota of production for each share, and each shareholder was to be limited to the quantity measured by the number of shares it held, but was free to sell at any price it chose. The corporation fixed a price every year at which it would take off any shareholder's hands any part of its quota which it did not sell. No shareholder was to "buy, borrow, fabricate or sell" aluminum produced by anyone not a shareholder except with the consent of the board of governors, but that must not be "unreasonably withheld." Nothing was said as to whether the arrangement extended to sales in the United States; but Article X, known as the "Conversion Clause," provided that any shareholder might exceed his quota to the extent that he converted into aluminum in the United States or Canada any ores delivered to him in either of those countries by persons situated in the United States. This was confessedly put in to allow "Limited" to receive bauxite or alumina from "Alcoa," to smelt it into aluminum and to deliver the aluminum to "Alcoa." * * *

The agreement of 1936 abandoned the system of unconditional quotas, and substituted a system of royalties. Each shareholder was to have a fixed free quota for every share it held, but as its production exceeded the sum of its quotas, it was to pay a royalty, graduated progressively in proportion to the excess; and these royalties the "Alliance" divided among the shareholders in proportion to their shares. * * * Although this agreement, like its predecessor, was silent as to imports into the United States, when that question arose during its preparation, as it did, all the shareholders agreed that such imports should be included in the quotas. * * *

Did either the agreement of 1931 or that of 1936 violate § 1 of the Act? The answer does not depend upon whether we shall recognize as a source of liability a liability imposed by another state. On the contrary we are concerned only with whether Congress chose to attach liability to the conduct outside the United States of persons not in allegiance to it. That being so, the only question open is whether Congress intended to impose the liability, and whether our own Constitution permitted it to do so: as a court of the United States, we cannot look beyond our own law. Nevertheless, it is quite true that we are not to read general words, such as those in this Act, without regard to the limitations customarily observed by nations upon the exercise of their powers; limitations which generally correspond to those fixed by the "Conflict of Laws." We should not impute to Congress an intent to punish all whom its courts can catch, for conduct which has no consequences within the United States. American Banana Co. v. United Fruit Co., 213 U.S. 347, 357, 29 S.Ct. 511, 53 L.Ed. 826; United States v. Bowman, 260 U.S. 94, 98, 43 S.Ct. 39, 67, L.Ed. 149; Blackmer v. United States, 284 U.S. 421, 437, 52 S.Ct. 252, 76 L.Ed. 375. On the other hand, it is settled—as "Limited" itself agrees—that any state may impose liabilities, even upon persons not within its allegiance, for conduct outside its borders that has consequences within its borders which the state reprehends; and these liabilities other states will ordinarily recognize. Strassheim v. Daily, 221 U.S. 280, 284, 285, 31 S.Ct. 558, 55 L.Ed. 735; Lamar v. United States, 240 U.S. 60, 65, 66, 36 S.Ct. 255, 60 L.Ed. 526; Ford v. United States, 273

U.S. 593, 620, 621, 47 S.Ct. 531, 71 L.Ed. 793; Restatement of Conflict of Laws § 65. It may be argued that this Act extends further. Two situations are possible. There may be agreements made beyond our borders not intended to affect imports, which do affect them, or which affect exports. Almost any limitation of the supply of goods in Europe, for example, or in South America, may have repercussions in the United States if there is trade between the two. Yet when one considers the international complications likely to arise from an effort in this country to treat such agreements as unlawful, it is safe to assume that Congress certainly did not intend the Act to cover them. Such agreements may on the other hand intend to include imports into the United States, and yet it may appear that they have had no effect upon them. That situation might be thought to fall within the doctrine that intent may be a substitute for performance in the case of a contract made within the United States; or it might be thought to fall within the doctrine that a statute should not be interpreted to cover acts abroad which have no consequence here. We shall not choose between these alternatives; but for argument we shall assume that the Act does not cover agreements, even though intended to affect imports or exports, unless its performance is shown actually to have had some effect upon them.

Both agreements would clearly have been unlawful, had they been made within the United States; and it follows from what we have just said that both were unlawful, though made abroad, if they were intended to affect imports and did affect them. Since the shareholders almost at once agreed that the agreement of 1931 should not cover imports, we may ignore it and confine our discussion to that of 1936: indeed that we should have to do anyway, since it superseded the earlier agreement. The judge found that it was not the purpose of the agreement to "suppress or restrain the exportation of aluminum to the United States for sale in competition with["] "Alcoa." By that we understand that he meant that the agreement was not specifically directed to "Alcoa," because it only applied generally to the production of the shareholders. If he meant that it was not expected that the general restriction upon production would have an effect upon imports, we cannot agree, for the change made in 1936 was deliberate and was expressly made to accomplish just that. It would have been an idle gesture, unless the shareholders had supposed that it would, or at least might, have that effect. The first of the conditions which we mentioned was therefore satisfied; the intent was to set up a quota system for imports.

The judge also found that the 1936 agreement did not "materially affect the * * * foreign trade or commerce of the United States"; apparently because the imported ingot was greater in 1936 and 1937 than in earlier years. We cannot accept this finding, based as it was upon the fact that, in 1936, 1937 and the first quarter of 1938, the gross imports of ingot increased. It by no means follows from such an increase that the agreement did not restrict imports; and incidentally it so happens that in those years such inference as is possible at all, leads to the opposite conclusion. It is true that the average imports—including

"Alcoa's"—for the years 1932–1935 inclusive were about 15 million pounds, and that for 1936, 1937 and one-fourth of 1938 they were about 33 million pounds; but the average domestic ingot manufacture in the first period was about 96 million and in the second about 262 million; so that the proportion of imports to domestic ingot was about 15.6 per cent for the first period and about 12.6 per cent for the second. We do not mean to infer from this that the quota system of 1936 did in fact restrain imports, as these figures might suggest; but we do mean that nothing is to be inferred from the gross increase of imports. We shall dispose of the matter therefore upon the assumption that, although the shareholders intended to restrict imports, it does not appear whether in fact they did so. Upon our hypothesis the plaintiff would therefore fail, if it carried the burden of proof upon this issue as upon others. We think, however, that, after the intent to affect imports was proved, the burden of proof shifted to "Limited." In the first place a depressant upon production which applies generally may be assumed, ceteris paribus, to distribute its effect evenly upon all markets. Again, when the parties took the trouble specifically to make the depressant apply to a given market, there is reason to suppose that they expected that it would have some effect, which it could have only by lessening what would otherwise have been imported. If the motive they introduced was over-balanced in all instances by motives which induced the shareholders to import, if the United States market became so attractive that the royalties did not count at all and their expectations were in fact defeated, they to whom the facts were more accessible than to the plaintiff ought to prove it, for a prima facie case had been made. Moreover, there is an especial propriety in demanding this of "Limited," because it was "Limited" which procured the inclusion in the agreement of 1936 imports in the quotas.

There remains only the question whether this assumed restriction had any influence upon prices. To that United States v. Socony–Vacuum Oil Co., 310 U.S. 150, 60 S.Ct. 811, 84 L.Ed. 1129, is an entire answer. It will be remembered that, when the defendants in that case protested that the prosecution had not proved that the "distress" gasoline had affected prices, the court answered that that was not necessary, because an agreement to withdraw any substantial part of the supply from a market would, if carried out, have some effect upon prices, and was as unlawful as an agreement expressly to fix prices. The underlying doctrine was that all factors which contribute to determine prices, must be kept free to operate unhampered by agreements. For these reasons we think that the agreement of 1936 violated § 1 of the Act.

Notes and Questions

1. *Determining Legislative Jurisdiction.* Albeit the *Aluminum* analysis of legislative jurisdiction over an international transaction was more sophisticated than that of *American Banana* or *Blackmer*, was it thorough enough? Learned Hand pronounced that he was "concerned only with whether Congress chose to attach liability to the conduct outside the United States of

persons not in allegiance to it." This avowal to look only at the intent of Congress was remarkably narrow and probably fictitious. Interpreting congressional intent as to extraterritorial reach usually leaves courts a great deal of latitude. Happily, Hand quickly circumvented his self-imposed obstacle and paid attention to "limitations customarily observed by nations upon the exercise of their powers; limitations which generally correspond to those fixed by the 'Conflict of Laws.'" However, rather than simply elaborating how Limited's participation in the foreign cartel was justifiably within the legislative jurisdiction of the United States, why did he not attempt to determine whether the U.S., or Switzerland, or some other country had the better right to regulate Limited's conduct? The explicit reason given was that "as a court of the United States, we cannot look beyond our own law." How can this be true, when for centuries common law courts in England and America have routinely reviewed, incorporated, and applied rules of both foreign and international law?

2. *Origins and Implications of the Effects Doctrine.* When anyone, even Learned Hand, calls the extraterritorial assertion of jurisdiction by the United States "settled" law, the reader should be just as much on guard as when a lawyer or a judge reassuringly calls facts or law "clear" or "plain." There was then and is now no "settled" law clearly or plainly establishing what is sometimes called "effects" or "objective territorial" jurisdiction. Did the *Aluminum* court demonstrate that it understood that U.S. jurisdiction based on the effects of foreign conduct in the United States would necessarily overlap and conflict with the territorial jurisdiction of foreign countries, *e.g.*, Canada, France, Germany, Great Britain, and Switzerland? Did Learned Hand really grapple with the problem identified by Justice Holmes in *American Banana*, that U.S. antitrust law may attempt to make illegal overseas acts that are legal by the law of the foreign state in which they take place?

3. *Reconciling the Effects Doctrine and the Presumption Against Extraterritoriality.* Notwithstanding *Aluminum*, the Supreme Court, as noted above, has recently held that there "is a longstanding principle of American law" that the statutes of Congress are to apply only within the United States unless a contrary intent is shown. EEOC v. Arabian American Oil Co., 499 U.S. 244, 248, 111 S.Ct. 1227, 113 L.Ed.2d 274 (1991). How does one reconcile the effects doctrine with this presumption against extraterritoriality? Looking at the case law, Professor Dodge argued that the two can be made to fit together if one accepts that Congress is presumed to intend that its laws "should be applied to conduct that affects [domestic] conditions, regardless of where that conduct occurs." William S. Dodge, "Understanding the Presumption Against Extraterritoriality," 16 *Berkeley Journal of International Law* 85, 124 (1998). Such an approach makes sense of *Aluminum* and its progeny, *e.g.*, United States v. Nippon Paper Industries Co., Ltd., 109 F.3d 1 (1st Cir.1997), *cert. denied*, 522 U.S. 1044, 118 S.Ct. 685, 139 L.Ed.2d 632 (1998), where the First Circuit held that a U.S. criminal antitrust prosecution could be based on entirely extraterritorial conduct in Japan, so long as the conduct had an intended and substantial effect on the United States.

4. *Jurisdiction and Choice of Forum.* The variety of bases for jurisdiction leads inevitably to jurisdictional conflicts, as well as to practical ques-

tions about where to bring suit. As Professor Vagts has pointed out, in "An Introduction to International Civil Practice," 17 *Vanderbilt Journal of Transnational Law* 1, 6 (1984):

> Counsel must recommend whether to bring a suit and where it should be brought. The latter decision can be a complex one. First, the question of in personam jurisdiction must be considered. The bases for jurisdiction in the United States (from doing business, to mere presence, to long-arm statutes) vary from those recognized in Europe. Each system has some type of jurisdictional claim that others regard as "exorbitant." France allows suit by virtue of a plaintiff's nationality. Germany sustains a suit if some of the defendant's property is present; in one case, a skier's underwear provided the necessary property. Other nations may find it strange that jurisdiction can arise under United States law merely because the sheriff was able to catch the defendant in transit within United States borders.

Did Hand in *Aluminum* give us any useful guidance about how clashes between U.S. and foreign law and process ought to be settled? See the discussion in *Timberlane* and *Hartford Fire* below.

5. *Jurisdiction Over Corporations.* Note how Alcoa used the formalities of corporate law to try to avoid having its cartel activities caught up by U.S. antitrust law. Could the court have better regulated Alcoa simply by piercing the corporate veil between Alcoa and Limited? After all, Hand found as facts that "in January, 1939, the Davises, the officers and directors of 'Alcoa,' and the Mellon families—eleven individuals in all—collectively still held 48.9 per cent of 'Alcoa's' shares, and 48.5 per cent of Limited's; and Arthur V. Davis was then the largest shareholder in both countries." The shareholders in *Barcelona Traction*, reproduced in Chapter 6, asked the International Court of Justice to disregard the corporate form and look at the real owners of the company, an unsuccessful argument. In *Aluminum*, the shareholders argued successfully that the corporate form should be respected. See Phillip I. Blumberg, *The Law of Corporate Groups: Procedural Problems in the Law of Parent and Subsidiary Corporations* (1983).

B. RESOLVING CONFLICTS OF JURISDICTION

Since the time of cases such as *American Banana, Blackmer,* and *Aluminum*, U.S. courts have attempted to develop more sophisticated approaches for recognizing and resolving international conflicts of jurisdiction. The cases in this part of the chapter illustrate four different modern approaches to conflict resolution: party choice, the balancing test, international comity, and *forum non conveniens*. Two other somewhat older approaches, foreign sovereign immunity and act of state, are treated in Parts C and D.

1. PARTY CHOICE

An apparently simple way to resolve jurisdictional conflicts is for the parties to agree where disputes will be settled and what law will be applied. Traditionally, U.S. courts looked suspiciously on such party choice agreements, fearing that private parties were usurping judicial functions. Nowadays, judicial suspicion of party choice has been largely abandoned, especially for international transactions, thanks to the pair of Supreme Court cases examined below.

THE BREMEN v. ZAPATA OFF–SHORE CO.

407 U.S. 1, 92 S.Ct. 1907, 32 L.Ed.2d 513 (1972).

MR. CHIEF JUSTICE BURGER delivered the opinion of the Court.

We granted certiorari to review a judgment of the United States Court of Appeals for the Fifth Circuit declining to enforce a forum-selection clause governing disputes arising under an international towage contract between petitioners and respondent. The circuits have differed in their approach to such clauses. For the reasons stated hereafter, we vacate the judgment of the Court of Appeals.

In November 1967, respondent Zapata, a Houston-based American corporation, contracted with petitioner Unterweser, a German corporation, to tow Zapata's ocean-going, self-elevating drilling rig *Chaparral* from Louisiana to a point off Ravenna, Italy, in the Adriatic Sea, where Zapata had agreed to drill certain wells.

Zapata had solicited bids for the towage, and several companies including Unterweser had responded. Unterweser was the low bidder and Zapata requested it to submit a contract, which it did. The contract submitted by Unterweser contained the following provision, which is at issue in this case:

"Any dispute arising must be treated before the London Court of Justice."

In addition the contract contained two clauses purporting to exculpate Unterweser from liability for damages to the towed barge.[2]

After reviewing the contract and making several changes, but without any alteration in the forum-selection or exculpatory clauses, a Zapata vice president executed the contract and forwarded it to Unterweser in Germany, where Unterweser accepted the changes, and the contract became effective.

On January 5, 1968, Unterweser's deep sea tug *Bremen* departed Venice, Louisiana, with the *Chaparral* in tow bound for Italy. On

2. The General Towage Conditions of the contract included the following:

"1. ... [Unterweser and its] masters and crews are not responsible for defaults and/or errors in the navigation of the tow.

"2. ...

"b) Damages suffered by the towed object are in any case for account of its Owners."

In addition, the contract provided that any insurance of the *Chaparral* was to be "for account of" Zapata. Unterweser's initial telegraphic bid had also offered to "arrange insurance covering towage risk for rig if desired." As Zapata had chosen to be self-insured on all its rigs, the loss in this case was not compensated by insurance.

January 9, while the flotilla was in international waters in the middle of the Gulf of Mexico, a severe storm arose. The sharp roll of the *Chaparral* in Gulf waters caused its elevator legs, which had been raised for the voyage, to break off and fall into the sea, seriously damaging the *Chaparral*. In this emergency situation Zapata instructed the *Bremen* to tow its damaged rig to Tampa, Florida, the nearest port of refuge.

On January 12, Zapata, ignoring its contract promise to litigate "any dispute arising" in the English courts, commenced a suit in admiralty in the United States District Court at Tampa, seeking $3,500,000 damages against Unterweser *in personam* and the *Bremen in rem*, alleging negligent towage and breach of contract. Unterweser responded by invoking the forum clause of the towage contract, and moved to dismiss for lack of jurisdiction or on *forum non conveniens* grounds, or in the alternative to stay the action pending submission of the dispute to the "London Court of Justice." Shortly thereafter, in February, before the District Court had ruled on its motion to stay or dismiss the United States action, Unterweser commenced an action against Zapata seeking damages for breach of the towage contract in the High Court of Justice in London, as the contract provided. Zapata appeared in that court to contest jurisdiction, but its challenge was rejected, the English courts holding that the contractual forum provision conferred jurisdiction.

In the meantime, Unterweser was faced with a dilemma in the pending action in the United States court at Tampa. The six-month period for filing action to limit its liability to Zapata and other potential claimants was about to expire, but the United States District Court in Tampa had not yet ruled on Unterweser's motion to dismiss or stay Zapata's action. On July 2, 1968, confronted with difficult alternatives, Unterweser filed an action to limit its liability in the District Court in Tampa. That court entered the customary injunction against proceedings outside the limitation court, and Zapata refiled its initial claim in the limitation action.

It was only at this juncture, on July 29, after the six-month period for filing the limitation action had run, that the District Court denied Unterweser's January motion to dismiss or stay Zapata's initial action. In denying the motion, that court relied on the prior decision of the Court of Appeals in *Carbon Black Export, Inc. v. The Monrosa*, 254 F.2d 297 (CA5 1958), cert. dismissed, 359 U.S. 180 (1959). In that case the Court of Appeals had held a forum-selection clause unenforceable, reiterating the traditional view of many American courts that "agreements in advance of controversy whose object is to oust the jurisdiction of the courts are contrary to public policy and will not be enforced." Apparently concluding that it was bound by the *Carbon Black* case, the District Court gave the forum-selection clause little, if any, weight. Instead, the Court treated the motion to dismiss under normal *forum non conveniens* doctrine applicable in the absence of such a clause, citing *Gulf Oil Corp., v. Gilbert*, 330 U.S. 501 (1947). Under that doctrine "unless the balance is strongly in favor of the defendant, the plaintiff's choice of forum should rarely be disturbed." The District Court concluded: "The balance of conveniences here is not strongly in favor of [Unterweser] and [Zapata's] choice of forum should not be disturbed."

Thereafter, on January 21, 1969, the District Court denied another motion by Unterweser to stay the limitation action pending determination of the controversy in the High Court of Justice in London and granted Zapata's motion to restrain Unterweser from litigating further in the London court. * * *

On appeal, a divided panel of the Court of Appeals affirmed, and on rehearing *en banc* the panel opinion was adopted, with six of the 14 *en banc* judges dissenting. As had the District Court, the majority rested on the *Carbon Black* decision, concluding that " 'at the very least' " that case stood for the proposition that a forum-selection clause " 'will not be enforced unless the selected state would provide a more convenient forum than the state in which suit is brought.' " From that premise the Court of Appeals proceeded to conclude that, apart from the forum-selection clause, the District Court did not abuse its discretion in refusing to decline jurisdiction on the basis of *forum non conveniens*. It noted that (1) the flotilla never "escaped the Fifth Circuit's mare nostrum, and the casualty occurred in close proximity to the district court"; (2) a considerable number of potential witnesses, including Zapata crewmen, resided in the Gulf Coast area; (3) preparation for the voyage and inspection and repair work had been performed in the Gulf area; (4) the testimony of the *Bremen* crew was available by way of deposition; (5) England had no interest in or contact with the controversy other than the forum-selection clause. The Court of Appeals majority further noted that Zapata was a United States citizen and "[t]he discretion of the district court to remand the case to a foreign forum was consequently limited"—especially since it appeared likely that the English courts would enforce the exculpatory clauses.[8] In the Court of Appeals' view, enforcement of such clauses would be contrary to public policy in American courts under *Bisso v. Inland Waterways Corp.*, 349 U.S. 85 (1955), and *Dixilyn Drilling Corp. v. Crescent Towing & Salvage Co.*, 372 U. S. 697 (1963). Therefore, "[t]he district court was entitled to consider that remanding Zapata to a foreign forum, with no practical contact with the controversy, could raise a bar to recovery by a United States citizen which its own convenient courts would not countenance."[9]

8. The record contains an undisputed affidavit of a British solicitor stating an opinion that the exculpatory clauses of the contract would be held "prima facie valid and enforceable" against Zapata in any action maintained in England in which Zapata alleged that defaults or errors in Unterweser's tow caused the casualty and damage to the *Chaparral*.

In addition, it is not disputed that while the limitation fund in the District Court in Tampa amounts to $1,390,000, the limita-tion fund in England would be only slightly in excess of $80,000 under English law.

9. The Court of Appeals also indicated in passing that even if it took the view that choice-of-forum clauses were enforceable unless "unreasonable" it was "doubtful" that enforcement would be proper here because the exculpatory clauses would deny Zapata relief to which it was "entitled" and because England was "seriously inconvenient" for trial of the action.

We hold, with the six dissenting members of the Court of Appeals, that far too little weight and effect were given to the forum clause in resolving this controversy. For at least two decades we have witnessed an expansion of overseas commercial activities by business enterprises based in the United States. The barrier of distance that once tended to confine a business concern to a modest territory no longer does so. Here we see an American company with special expertise contracting with a foreign company to tow a complex machine thousands of miles across seas and oceans. The expansion of American business and industry will hardly be encouraged if, notwithstanding solemn contracts, we insist on a parochial concept that all disputes must be resolved under our laws and in our courts. Absent a contract forum, the considerations relied on by the Court of Appeals would be persuasive reasons for holding an American forum convenient in the traditional sense, but in an era of expanding world trade and commerce, the absolute aspects of the doctrine of the *Carbon Black* case have little place and would be a heavy hand indeed on the future development of international commercial dealings by Americans. We cannot have trade and commerce in world markets and international waters exclusively on our terms, governed by our laws, and resolved in our courts.

Forum-selection clauses have historically not been favored by American courts. Many courts, federal and state, have declined to enforce such clauses on the ground that they were "contrary to public policy," or that their effect was to "oust the jurisdiction" of the court. Although this view apparently still has considerable acceptance, other courts are tending to adopt a more hospitable attitude toward forum-selection clauses. This view, advanced in the well-reasoned dissenting opinion in the instant case, is that such clauses are prima facie valid and should be enforced unless enforcement is shown by the resisting party to be "unreasonable" under the circumstances. We believe this is the correct doctrine to be followed by federal district courts sitting in admiralty. It is merely the other side of the proposition recognized by this Court in *National Equipment Rental, Ltd.* v. *Szukhent*, 375 U.S. 311 (1964), holding that in federal courts a party may validly consent to be sued in a jurisdiction where he cannot be found for service of process through contractual designation of an "agent" for receipt of process in that jurisdiction. In so holding, the Court stated:

> "[I]t is settled . . . that parties to a contract may agree in advance to submit to the jurisdiction of a given court, to permit notice to be served by the opposing party, or even to waive notice altogether."

This approach is substantially that followed in other common-law countries including England. It is the view advanced by noted scholars and that adopted by the Restatement of the Conflict of Laws. It accords with ancient concepts of freedom of contract and reflects an appreciation of the expanding horizons of American contractors who seek business in all parts of the world. Not surprisingly, foreign businessmen prefer, as do we, to have disputes resolved in their own courts, but if that choice is not available, then in a neutral forum with expertise in the subject matter.

Plainly, the courts of England meet the standards of neutrality and long experience in admiralty litigation. The choice of that forum was made in an arm's-length negotiation by experienced and sophisticated businessmen, and absent some compelling and countervailing reason it should be honored by the parties and enforced by the courts.

The argument that such clauses are improper because they tend to "oust" a court of jurisdiction is hardly more than a vestigial legal fiction. It appears to rest at core on historical judicial resistance to any attempt to reduce the power and business of a particular court and has little place in an era when all courts are overloaded and when businesses once essentially local now operate in world markets. It reflects something of a provincial attitude regarding the fairness of other tribunals. No one seriously contends in this case that the forum-selection clause "ousted" the District Court of jurisdiction over Zapata's action. The threshold question is whether that court should have exercised its jurisdiction to do more than give effect to the legitimate expectations of the parties, manifested in their freely negotiated agreement, by specifically enforcing the forum clause.

There are compelling reasons why a freely negotiated private international agreement, unaffected by fraud, undue influence, or overweening bargaining power,[14] such as that involved here, should be given full effect. In this case, for example, we are concerned with a far from routine transaction between companies of two different nations contemplating the tow of an extremely costly piece of equipment from Louisiana across the Gulf of Mexico and the Atlantic Ocean, through the Mediterranean Sea to its final destination in the Adriatic sea. In the course of its voyage, it was to traverse the waters of many jurisdictions. The *Chaparral* could have been damaged at any point along the route, and there were countless possible ports of refuge. That the accident occurred in the Gulf of Mexico and the barge was towed to Tampa in an emergency were mere fortuities. It cannot be doubted for a moment that the parties sought to provide for a neutral forum for the resolution of any disputes arising during the tow. Manifestly much uncertainty and possibly great inconvenience to both parties could arise if a suit could be maintained in any jurisdiction in which an accident might occur or if jurisdiction were left to any place where the *Bremen* or Unterweser might happen to be found. The elimination of all such uncertainties by agreeing in advance

---

14. The record here refutes any notion of overweening bargaining power. Judge Wisdom, dissenting, in the Court of Appeals noted:

"Zapata has neither presented evidence of nor alleged fraud or undue bargaining power in the agreement. Unterweser was only one of several companies bidding on the project. No evidence contradicts its Managing Director's affidavit that it specified English courts 'in an effort to meet Zapata Off–Shore company half way.' Zapata's Vice President has declared by affidavit that no specific negotiations concerning the forum clause took place. But his was not simply a form contract with boilerplate language that Zapata had no power to alter. The towing of an oil rig across the Atlantic was a new business. Zapata did make alterations to the contract submitted by Unterweser. The forum clause could hardly be ignored. It is the final sentence of the agreement, immediately preceding the date and the parties' signatures...."

on a forum acceptable to both parties is an indispensable element in international trade, commerce, and contracting. There is strong evidence that the forum clause was a vital part of the agreement, and it would be unrealistic to think that the parties did not conduct their negotiations, including fixing the monetary terms, with the consequences of the forum clause figuring prominently in their calculations. Under these circumstances, as Justice Karminski reasoned in sustaining jurisdiction over Zapata in the High Court of Justice, "[t]he force of an agreement for litigation in this country, freely entered into between two competent parties seems to me to be very powerful."

Thus, in the light of present-day commercial realities and expanding international trade we conclude that the forum clause should control absent a strong showing that it should be set aside. Although their opinions are not altogether explicit, it seems reasonably clear that the District Court and the Court of Appeals placed the burden on Unterweser to show that London would be a more convenient forum than Tampa, although the contract expressly resolved that issue. The correct approach would have been to enforce the forum clause specifically unless Zapata could clearly show that enforcement would be unreasonable and unjust, or that the clause was invalid for such reasons as fraud or overreaching. Accordingly, the case must be remanded for reconsideration.

We note, however, that there is nothing in the record presently before us that would support a refusal to enforce the forum clause. * * *

This case, however, involves a freely negotiated international commercial transaction between a German and an American corporation for towage of a vessel from the Gulf of Mexico to the Adriatic Sea. As noted, selection of a London forum was clearly a reasonable effort to bring vital certainty to this international transaction and to provide a neutral forum experienced and capable in the resolution of admiralty litigation. Whatever "inconvenience" Zapata would suffer by being forced to litigate in the contractual forum as it agreed to do was clearly foreseeable at the time of contracting. In such circumstances it should be incumbent on the party seeking to escape his contract to show that trial in the contractual forum will be so gravely difficult and inconvenient that he will for all practical purposes be deprived of his day in court. Absent that, there is no basis for concluding that it would be unfair, unjust, or unreasonable to hold that party to his bargain.

Notes and Questions

1. *Bremen's Rationale. Bremen* was the first in a series of important U.S. Supreme Court decisions favoring forum-selection clauses in international contracts. In *Bremen* the Court enforced a choice-of-forum clause and sent the case abroad, reasoning in part that Zapata had fairly bargained away its access to U.S. courts in the course of its international contract negotiations. Did the Supreme Court in *Bremen* rely mostly on freedom-of-contract arguments in reaching its decision? Or was it more persuaded by other policy factors? For example, did the Court attempt to protect the

negotiating position of U.S. companies by enforcing forum-selection clauses? If the clause in *Bremen* had been held unenforceable, would U.S. businesses simply not be believed if in the future they promised to trade off a forum-selection clause for some other benefit in a contract because they could always find U.S. judicial support to renege on their deal?

2. *Lower Court Discretion.* It is important to remember that *Bremen* did not entirely eliminate the discretion of the trial court to decide whether to respect a choice-of-forum clause in an international contract. This discretionary principle was reinforced in Lauro Lines v. Chasser, 490 U.S. 495, 109 S.Ct. 1976, 104 L.Ed 2d 548 (1989), where the end result was that a choice-of-forum clause was not enforced. In *Lauro Lines* the Supreme Court decided that an interlocutory order of a U.S. district court denying a defendant's motion to dismiss a damages action on the basis of a contractual forum-selection clause was not immediately appealable:

> The individual respondents were, or represent the estates of persons who were, passengers aboard the cruise ship Achille Lauro when it was hijacked by terrorists in the Mediterranean in October 1985. Petitioner Lauro Lines s.r.l., an Italian company, owns the Achille Lauro. Respondents filed suits against Lauro Lines in the District Court for the Southern District of New York to recover damages for injuries sustained as a result of the hijacking, and for the wrongful death of passenger Leon Klinghoffer. Lauro Lines moved before trial to dismiss the actions, citing the forum-selection clause printed on each passenger ticket. This clause purported to obligate the passenger to institute any suit arising in connection with the contract in Naples, Italy, and to renounce the right to sue elsewhere.

> The District Court denied petitioner's motions to dismiss, holding that the ticket as a whole did not give reasonable notice to passengers that they were waiving the opportunity to sue in a domestic forum.

Id. at 496–97, 109 S.Ct. at 1977, 104 L.Ed.2d at 552. Justice Scalia observed in his concurring opinion:

> While it is true, therefore, that the "right not to be sued elsewhere than in Naples" is not fully vindicated—indeed, to be utterly frank, is positively destroyed—by permitting the trial to occur and reversing its outcome, that is vindication enough because the right is not sufficiently important to overcome the policies militating against interlocutory appeals.

Id. at 502–03, 109 S.Ct. at 1980, 104 L.Ed.2d at 556.

Has *Lauro Lines* diminished the force of *Bremen*? See also Carnival Cruise Lines v. Shute, 499 U.S. 585, 111 S.Ct. 1522, 113 L.Ed.2d 622 (1991), in which the Supreme Court upheld a forum-selection clause in a passenger ticket that specified a U.S. forum different from the one in which the U.S. plaintiff had sued the U.S. corporate defendant.

3. *Choice of Law as a Factor.* What difference should choice-of-law considerations make when deciding whether to enforce a contractual choice-of-forum clause? In *Bremen*, the Supreme Court noted:

> The record contains an undisputed affidavit of a British solicitor stating an opinion that the exculpatory clauses of the contract would be

held "prima facie valid and enforceable" against Zapata in any action maintained in England in which Zapata alleged that defaults or errors in Unterweser's tow caused the casualty and damage to the *Chaparral.*

407 U.S. at 8 n.8, 92 S.Ct. at 1912 n.8, 32 L.Ed.2d at 519 n.8.

The court of appeals in *Bremen* felt that enforcement of the exculpatory clauses would be contrary to U.S. public policy and that a U.S. court presumably would have voided them. The Supreme Court, as we have seen, preferred to weigh other factors more heavily. How far must a conflicting substantive law go to trigger a U.S. public policy objection? In *Bremen* it seemed that the choice-of-law decision about the validity of the exculpatory clauses would virtually decide the case. Was the explicit battle between the parties about choice of forum simply a surrogate for the real battle between them about choice of law? Why did the parties not also include a choice-of-law clause in their contract?

4.   Bremen *and State Law.* The *Bremen* rule, which is technically a rule binding federal courts exercising admiralty jurisdiction, has moved into some state law. In Manrique v. Fabbri, 493 So.2d 437 (Fla.1986), the Florida Supreme Court reversed Florida precedent and enforced a clause selecting the courts and laws of the Netherlands Antilles in a contractual dispute between a Netherlands Antilles company and an Italian national living in Argentina. The *Manrique* court observed that "[b]ecause the *Zapata* rule is based on a realistic assessment of modern commercial culture, and because the rule enhances contractual predictability with that culture, it is not surprising that it is rapidly becoming a majority view." *Id.* at 439.

5.   *The Interests of the Chosen Forum.* The British courts accepted jurisdiction in the *Bremen* dispute, allowing Unterweser to proceed on a claim for damages there. Unterweser Reederei G.M.B.H. v. Zapata Off-shore Co., [1968] 2 Lloyd's L. Rep. 158 (U.K. Court of Appeal). Why should a British court have heard a dispute between a U.S. and a German company, with respect to a transaction that did not touch British ports or waters? When, if ever, will a court refuse to hear a case if the parties to a dispute have freely selected that court in a forum-selection clause? See also the discussion of *forum non conveniens* below.

6.   Bremen *and International Lawyering.* Note that although *Bremen* concerned a choice-of-forum clause, at bottom it was a battle about which set of legal rules, English or American, to apply to the substantive issues of the case. In a litigation setting, international lawyers know which legal rules will most benefit their clients. Moreover, this wisdom is part of the background that international lawyers bring to international negotiations. Cases like *Bremen* provide international lawyers with considerable flexibility and power in structuring transactions, concerning both the rules to be applied and the legal processes to be made available. Because of the variety of laws and legal processes, international transactions often give lawyers greater authority than they would have in a domestic context.

SCHERK v. ALBERTO–CULVER CO.

417 U.S. 506, 94 S.Ct. 2449, 41 L.Ed.2d 270 (1974).

MR. JUSTICE STEWART delivered the opinion of the Court.

Alberto–Culver Co., the respondent, is an American company incorporated in Delaware with its principal office in Illinois. It manufactures and distributes toiletries and hair products in this country and abroad. During the 1960's Alberto–Culver decided to expand its overseas operations, and as part of this program it approached the petitioner Fritz Scherk, a German citizen residing at the time of trial in Switzerland. Scherk was the owner of three interrelated business entities, organized under the laws of Germany and Liechtenstein, that were engaged in the manufacture of toiletries and the licensing of trademarks for such toiletries. An initial contact with Scherk was made by a representative of Alberto–Culver in Germany in June 1967, and negotiations followed at further meetings in both Europe and the United States during 1967 and 1968. In February 1969 a contract was signed in Vienna, Austria, which provided for the transfer of the ownership of Scherk's enterprises to Alberto–Culver, along with all rights held by these enterprises to trademarks in cosmetic goods. The contract contained a number of express warranties whereby Scherk guaranteed the sole and unencumbered ownership of these trademarks. In addition, the contract contained an arbitration clause providing that "any controversy or claim [that] shall arise out of this agreement or the breach thereof" would be referred to arbitration before the International Chamber of Commerce in Paris, France, and that "[t]he laws of the State of Illinois, U.S.A. shall apply to and govern this agreement, its interpretation and performance."[1]

The closing of the transaction took place in Geneva, Switzerland, in June 1969. Nearly one year later Alberto–Culver allegedly discovered that the trademark rights purchased under the contract were subject to substantial encumbrances that threatened to give others superior rights to the trademarks and to restrict or preclude Alberto–Culver's use of them. Alberto–Culver thereupon tendered back to Scherk the property that had been transferred to it and offered to rescind the contract. Upon Scherk's refusal, Alberto–Culver commenced this action for damages and

---

1. The arbitration clause relating to the transfer of one of Scherk's business entities, similar to the clauses covering the other two, reads in its entirety as follows:

"The parties agree that if any controversy or claim shall arise out of this agreement or the breach thereof and either party shall request that the matter shall be settled by arbitration, the matter shall be settled exclusively by arbitration in accordance with the rules then obtaining of the International Chamber of Commerce, Paris, France, by a single arbitrator, if the parties shall agree upon one, or by one arbitrator appointed by each party and a third arbitrator appointed by the other arbitrators. In case of any failure of a party to make an appointment referred to above within four weeks after notice of the controversy, such appointment shall be made by said Chamber. All arbitration proceedings shall be held in Paris, France, and each party agrees to comply in all respects with any award made in any such proceeding and to the entry of a judgment in any jurisdiction upon any award rendered in such proceeding. The laws of the State of Illinois, U.S.A. shall apply to and govern this agreement, its interpretation and performance."

other relief in a Federal District Court in Illinois, contending that Scherk's fraudulent representations concerning the status of the trademark rights constituted violations of § 10(b) of the Securities Exchange Act of 1934 and Rule 10b–5 promulgated thereunder.

In response, Scherk filed a motion to dismiss the action for want of personal and subject-matter jurisdiction as well as on the basis of *forum non conveniens*, or, alternatively, to stay the action pending arbitration in Paris pursuant to the agreement of the parties. Alberto–Culver, in turn, opposed this motion and sought a preliminary injunction restraining the prosecution of arbitration proceedings.[2] On December 2, 1971, the District Court denied Scherk's motion to dismiss, and, on January 14, 1972, it granted a preliminary order enjoining Scherk from proceeding with arbitration. In taking these actions the court relied entirely on this Court's decision in *Wilko v. Swan*, 346 U.S. 427, which held that an agreement to arbitrate could not preclude a buyer of a security from seeking a judicial remedy under the Securities Act of 1933, in view of the language of § 14 of that Act, barring "[a]ny condition, stipulation, or provision binding any person acquiring any security to waive compliance with any provision of this subchapter...." The Court of Appeals for the Seventh Circuit, with one judge dissenting, affirmed, upon what it considered the controlling authority of the *Wilko* decision. Because of the importance of the question presented we granted Scherk's petition for a writ of certiorari.

The United States Arbitration Act, now 9 U.S.C. § 1 *et seq.*, reversing centuries of judicial hostility to arbitration agreements,[4] was designed to allow parties to avoid "the costliness and delays of litigation," and to place arbitration agreements "upon the same footing as other contracts...." Accordingly, the Act provides that an arbitration agreement such as is here involved "shall be valid, irrevocable, and enforceable, save upon such grounds as exist at law or in equity for the revocation of any contract." The Act also provides in § 3 for a stay of proceedings in a case where a court is satisfied that the issue before it is arbitrable under the agreement, and § 4 of the Act directs a federal court to order parties to proceed to arbitration if there has been a "failure, neglect, or refusal" of any party to honor an agreement to arbitrate.

In *Wilko v. Swan, supra,* this Court acknowledged that the Act reflects a legislative recognition of the "desirability of arbitration as an alternative to the complications of litigation," but nonetheless declined to apply the Act's provisions. That case involved an agreement between Anthony Wilko and Hayden, Stone & Co., a large brokerage firm, under

2. Scherk had taken steps to initiate arbitration in Paris in early 1971. He did not, however, file a formal request for arbitration with the International Chamber of Commerce until November 9, 1971, almost five months after the filing of Alberto–Culver's complaint in the Illinois federal court.

4. English courts traditionally considered irrevocable arbitration agreements as "ousting" the courts of jurisdiction, and refused to enforce such agreements for this reason. This view was adopted by American courts as part of the common law up to the time of the adoption of the Arbitration Act.

which Wilko agreed to purchase on margin a number of shares of a corporation's common stock. Wilko alleged that his purchase of the stock was induced by false representations on the part of the defendant concerning the value of the shares, and he brought suit for damages under § 12(2) of the Securities Act of 1933. The defendant responded that Wilko had agreed to submit all controversies arising out of the purchase to arbitration, and that this agreement, contained in a written margin contract between the parties, should be given full effect under the Arbitration Act.

The Court found that "[t]wo policies, not easily reconcilable, are involved in this case." On the one hand, the Arbitration Act stressed "the need for avoiding the delay and expense of litigation," and directed that such agreements be "valid, irrevocable, and enforceable" in federal courts. On the other hand, the Securities Act of 1933 was "[d]esigned to protect investors" and to require "issuers, underwriters, and dealers to make full and fair disclosure of the character of securities sold in interstate and foreign commerce and to prevent fraud in their sale," by creating "a special right to recover for misrepresentation. . . ." In particular, the Court noted that § 14 of the Securities Act provides:

> "Any condition, stipulation, or provision binding any person acquiring any security to waive compliance with any provision of this subchapter or of the rules and regulations of the Commission shall be void."

The Court ruled that an agreement to arbitrate "is a 'stipulation,' and [that] the right to select the judicial forum is the kind of 'provision' that cannot be waived under § 14 of the Securities Act." Thus, Wilko's advance agreement to arbitrate any disputes subsequently arising out of his contract to purchase the securities was unenforceable under the terms of § 14 of the Securities Act of 1933.

Alberto–Culver, relying on this precedent, contends that the District Court and Court of Appeals were correct in holding that its agreement to arbitrate disputes arising under the contract with Scherk is similarly unenforceable in view of its contentions that Scherk's conduct constituted violations of the Securities Exchange Act of 1934 and rules promulgated thereunder. For the reasons that follow, we reject this contention and hold that the provisions of the Arbitration Act cannot be ignored in this case.

At the outset, a colorable argument could be made that even the semantic reasoning of the *Wilko* opinion does not control the case before us. * * *

Accepting the premise, however, that the operative portions of the language of the 1933 Act relied upon in *Wilko* are contained in the Securities Exchange Act of 1934, the respondent's reliance on *Wilko* in this case ignores the significant and, we find, crucial differences between the agreement involved in *Wilko* and the one signed by the parties here. Alberto–Culver's contract to purchase the business entities belonging to Scherk was a truly international agreement. Albeto-Culver is an Ameri-

can corporation with its principal place of business and the vast bulk of
its activity in this country, while Scherk is a citizen of Germany whose
companies were organized under the laws of Germany and Liechtenstein.
The negotiations leading to the signing of the contract in Austria and to
the closing in Switzerland took place in the United States, England, and
Germany, and involved consultations with legal and trademark experts
from each of those countries and from Liechtenstein. Finally, and most
significantly, the subject matter of the contract concerned the sale of
business enterprises organized under the laws of and primarily situated
in European countries, whose activities were largely, if not entirely,
directed to European markets.

Such a contract involves considerations and policies significantly
different from those found controlling in *Wilko*. In *Wilko*, quite apart
from the arbitration provision, there was no question but that the laws
of the United States generally, and the federal securities laws in particular, would govern disputes arising out of the stock-purchase agreement.
The parties, the negotiations, and the subject matter of the contract
were all situated in this country, and no credible claim could have been
entertained that any international conflict-of-laws problems would arise.
In this case, by contrast, in the absence of the arbitration provision
considerable uncertainty existed at the time of the agreement, and still
exists, concerning the law applicable to the resolution of disputes arising
out of the contract.

Such uncertainty will almost inevitably exist with respect to any
contract touching two or more countries, each with its own substantive
laws and conflict-of-laws rules. A contractual provision specifying in
advance the forum in which disputes shall be litigated and the law to be
applied is, therefore, an almost indispensable precondition to achievement of the orderliness and predictability essential to any international
business transaction. Furthermore, such a provision obviates the danger
that a dispute under the agreement might be submitted to a forum
hostile to the interests of one of the parties or unfamiliar with the
problem area involved.

A parochial refusal by the courts of one country to enforce an
international arbitration agreement would not only frustrate these purposes, but would invite unseemly and mutually destructive jockeying by
the parties to secure tactical litigation advantages. In the present case,
for example, it is not inconceivable that if Scherk had anticipated that
Alberto–Culver would be able in this country to enjoin resort to arbitration he might have sought an order in France or some other country
enjoining Alberto–Culver from proceeding with its litigation in the
United States. Whatever recognition the courts of this country might
ultimately have granted to the order of the foreign court, the dicey
atmosphere of such a legal no-man's-land would surely damage the
fabric of international commerce and trade, and imperil the willingness
and ability of businessmen to enter into international commercial agreements.

The exception to the clear provisions of the Arbitration Act carved out by *Wilko* is simply inapposite to a case such as the one before us. In *Wilko* the Court reasoned that "[w]hen the security buyer, prior to any violation of the Securities Act, waives his right to sue in courts, he gives up more than would a participant in other business transactions. The security buyer has a wider choice of courts and venue. He thus surrenders one of the advantages the Act gives him...." In the context of an international contract, however, these advantages become chimerical since, as indicated above, an opposing party may by speedy resort to a foreign court block or hinder access to the American court of the purchaser's choice.

Two Terms ago in *The Bremen v. Zapata Off–Shore Co.*, we rejected the doctrine that a forum-selection clause of a contract, although voluntarily adopted by the parties, will not be respected in a suit brought in the United States " 'unless the selected state would provide a more convenient forum than the state in which suit is brought.' " Rather, we concluded that a "forum clause should control absent a strong showing that it should be set aside." We noted that "much uncertainty and possibly great inconvenience to both parties could arise if a suit could be maintained in any jurisdiction in which an accident might occur or if jurisdiction were left to any place [where personal or *in rem* jurisdiction might be established]. The elimination of all such uncertainties by agreeing in advance on a forum acceptable to both parties is an indispensable element in international trade, commerce, and contracting."

An agreement to arbitrate before a specified tribunal is, in effect, a specialized kind of forum-selection clause that posits not only the situs of suit but also the procedure to be used in resolving the dispute.[13] The invalidation of such an agreement in the case before us would not only allow the respondent to repudiate its solemn promise but would, as well, reflect a "parochial concept that all disputes must be resolved under our laws and in our courts.... We cannot have trade and commerce in world markets and international waters exclusively on our terms, governed by our laws, and resolved in our courts." [14]

---

13. Under some circumstances, the designation of arbitration in a certain place might also be viewed as implicitly selecting the law of that place to apply to that transaction. In this case, however, "[t]he laws of the State of Illinois" were explicitly made applicable by the arbitration agreement. See n. 1, *supra*.

14. In *The Bremen* we noted that forum-selection clauses "should be given full effect" when "a freely negotiated private international agreement [is] unaffected by fraud...." This qualification does not mean that any time a dispute arising out of a transaction is based upon an allegation of fraud, as in this case, the clause is unenforceable. Rather, it means that an arbitration or forum-selection clause in a contract is not enforceable if the *inclusion of that clause in the contract* was the product of fraud or coercion.

Although we do not decide the question, presumably the type of fraud alleged here could be raised, under Art. V of the Convention on the Recognition and Enforcement of Foreign Arbitral Awards, see n. 15, *infra*, in challenging the enforcement of whatever arbitral award is produced through arbitration. Article V(2)(b) of the Convention provides that a country may refuse recognition and enforcement of an award if "recognition or enforcement of the award would be contrary to the public policy of that country."

For all these reasons we hold that the agreement of the parties in this case to arbitrate any dispute arising out of their international commercial transaction is to be respected and enforced by the federal courts in accord with the explicit provisions of the Arbitration Act.[15]

Accordingly, the judgment of the Court of Appeals is reversed and the case is remanded to that court with directions to remand to the District Court for further proceedings consistent with this opinion.

It is so ordered.

Notes and Questions

1. *Party Choice: A Sensible Approach.* Note the number of countries connected with the transaction in *Scherk*: at least the United States, Germany, Switzerland, Liechtenstein, Austria, England, and France. Given that courts in each of these states might have jurisdiction to adjudicate a case arising out of the transaction, why did it make sense for Alberto–Culver and Scherk to settle contractually the forum for any future dispute settlement procedure? Under what circumstances might it have been in the interests of either party *not* to agree in advance as to the place and form of dispute settlement? Using the phrase of the Supreme Court, might "a legal no-man's-land" favor a party that expected to run a significant risk of breaching the contract? Should the other party be alert to a significant risk of noncompliance when there is difficulty in reaching agreement upon a choice-of-forum clause?

---

15. Our conclusion today is confirmed by international developments and domestic legislation in the area of commercial arbitration subsequent to the *Wilko* decision. On June 10, 1958, a special conference of the United Nations Economic and Social Council adopted the Convention on the Recognition and Enforcement of Foreign Arbitral Awards. In 1970 the United States acceded to the treaty, [1970] 3 U.S.T. 2517, T.I.A.S. No. 6997, and Congress passed Chapter 2 of the United States Arbitration Act, 9 U.S.C. § 201 *et seq.*, in order to implement the Convention. Section 1 of the new chapter, 9 U.S.C. § 201, provides unequivocally that the Convention "shall be enforced in United States courts in accordance with this chapter."

The goal of the Convention, and the principal purpose underlying American adoption and implementation of it, was to encourage the recognition and enforcement of commercial arbitration agreements in international contracts and to unify the standards by which agreements to arbitrate are observed and arbitral awards are enforced in the signatory countries. Article II(1) of the convention provides:

"Each Contracting State shall recognize an agreement in writing under which the parties undertake to submit to arbitration all or any differences which have arisen or which may arise between them in respect of a defined legal relationship, whether contractual or not, concerning a subject matter capable of settlement by arbitration."

In their discussion of this Article, the delegates to the Convention voiced frequent concern that courts of signatory countries in which an agreement to arbitrate is sought to be enforced should not be permitted to decline enforcement of such agreements on the basis of parochial views of their desirability or in a manner that would diminish the mutually binding nature of the agreements.

Without reaching the issue of whether the Convention, apart from the considerations expressed in this opinion, would require of its own force that the agreement to arbitrate be enforced in the present case, we think that this country's adoption and ratification of the Convention and the passage of Chapter 2 of the United States Arbitration Act provide strongly persuasive evidence of congressional policy consistent with the decision we reach today.

2. *Mixing Forum and Law.* The contract in *Scherk* included an arbitration clause that selected International Chamber of Commerce arbitration in Paris as a choice of forum and Illinois law as a choice of law. Why "mix" the forum (and thus much of the procedural law) and substantive law? Was it a result of compromise? What did the two parties each gain and lose when they agreed to such an arbitration clause?

3. *The Chicago Suit.* Why did Alberto–Culver decide to sue in Chicago? Could the company offer only technical reasons justifying why it should be permitted to avoid living up to its promise to arbitrate in Paris? Could one argue that fraud voided not only the contract but also the choice-of-forum clause? Was the Chicago suit merely a means of harassing Scherk? If Alberto–Culver were to win its suit in Chicago, what obstacles might there have been in enforcing the U.S. judgment in Europe? See Note 5 below.

4. *The Rationale of the Court.* Did it make a difference to the Court that Alberto–Culver was the larger entity and that it had chosen to go to Europe to seek out acquisitions? What difference might it have made if Scherk had come to Chicago to peddle his companies? In Mitsubishi Motors Corp. v. Soler Chrysler–Plymouth, Inc., 473 U.S. 614, 105 S.Ct. 3346, 87 L.Ed.2d 444 (1985), the Supreme Court enforced an agreement to arbitrate in Japan against the less powerful party, a Puerto Rican car dealer, to the advantage of the larger party, a Japanese auto manufacturer.

Was the Court protecting the honor of U.S. companies by making Alberto–Culver stick to its agreement to arbitrate? What would be the value of a U.S. company's promise to arbitrate abroad if such promises were *not* enforced by the U.S. legal system? Would this scenario put U.S. companies at a relative disadvantage *vis-à-vis* foreign companies, the promises of which to arbitrate might be upheld by their home courts? Compare the *Scherk* case to *Bremen* above. Should the same rationale apply to enforcing choice-of-forum clauses selecting foreign arbitration as to enforcing choice-of-forum clauses selecting foreign municipal courts?

5. *The New York Convention.* Without the New York Convention on the Recognition and Enforcement of Foreign Arbitral Awards, discussed in footnote 15 of the *Scherk* opinion, the recognition of arbitral agreements and the enforcement of foreign arbitral awards would depend on international comity and the municipal law of each country. What are the advantages to the Convention framework? There is no comparable "full faith and credit" treaty to which the United States is a party to promote the recognition and enforcement of foreign judicial awards. Why should nations have found it easier to agree on a treaty to facilitate the enforcement of awards of foreign arbitral tribunals—as of June 2000, 123 states were parties to the New York Convention—than to agree on a treaty to facilitate the enforcement of judgments of foreign courts? Is it because the jurisdiction of arbitral tribunals is based on consent and tends to be less controversial than the jurisdictional assertions of municipal courts? Is it because arbitral panels are regarded as more neutral than municipal courts?

Why did the Court in *Scherk* not rely on the New York Convention? Was it because Alberto–Culver's agreement with Scherk was made before the Convention came into force in the U.S.? Would the agreement to arbitrate have been enforced under the New York Convention? Article II of the

Convention provides for the recognition of written agreements to arbitrate disputes "concerning a subject matter capable of settlement by arbitration." Article II(3) reads that the court of a state that has accepted the New York Convention "shall, at the request of one of the parties [to a dispute], refer the parties to arbitration, unless it finds that the said agreement is null and void, inoperative or incapable of being performed." Would this Article II(3) limitation have prevented a court from giving effect to the choice-of-forum clause in *Scherk*?

As noted in footnote 14 of *Scherk*, another provision of the New York Convention, Article V, governs judicial recognition and enforcement of awards granted by arbitral tribunals. Without the recognition and enforcement of arbitral awards by municipal courts, what would be the likelihood of such awards being respected in business practice? Would simply the desire to continue doing business after the dispute is arbitrated serve as something of an enforcement mechanism? Even when arbitral awards are honored without recourse to municipal legal systems, how much does the potential for municipal enforcement loom as a threat to noncompliance?

6. *Arbitral Institutes.* The parties in *Scherk* chose to go to the ICC in Paris. There is a fierce competition among different arbitral institutes for business. How do factors of convenience, cost, efficiency, and rules governing arbitral procedures influence party choice? See David J. Branson, *Selecting an Arbitral Forum : A Guide to Cost Effective International Law* 917, 919–21 (1984); Samuel V. Goekjian, "ICC Arbitration from a Practitioner's Perspective," 14 *Journal of International Law and Economics* 407 (1980).

Parties may also decide to resolve disputes outside the established arbitral institutes. Such *ad hoc* arbitration necessitates special agreement, *e.g.*, about the arbitrator(s), venue, language, applicable law, procedural rules, and costs. There may be advantages to *ad hoc* arbitration, *e.g.*, possibly lower costs, greater speed, acceptance by parties wary of arbitral institutes, and greater flexibility. See Harry L. Arkin, "International Ad Hoc Arbitration: A Practical Alternative," 15 *International Business Lawyer* 5 (1987). Compare the relative advantages of *ad hoc* and institutional arbitration. For more on the history of international commercial arbitration, see Sir Michael J. Mustill, "Arbitration: History and Background," 6 *Journal of International Arbitration*, No. 2, at 43 (1989).

2. THE BALANCING TEST

TIMBERLANE LUMBER CO. v. BANK OF AMERICA
549 F.2d 597 (9th Cir.1976).

Choy, Circuit Judge * * *

Cast of Characters

There are three affiliated plaintiffs in the Timberlane action. Timberlane Lumber Company is an Oregon partnership principally involved in the purchase and distribution of lumber at wholesale in the United States and the importation of lumber into the United States for sale and use. Danli Industrial, S.A., and Maya Lumber Company, S. de R.L., are both Honduras corporations, incorporated and principally owned by the general partners of Timberlane. Danli held contracts to purchase timber in Honduras, and Maya was to conduct the milling operations to produce the lumber for export. (Timberlane, Danli, and Maya will be collectively referred to as "Timberlane.")

The primary defendants are Bank of America Corporation (Bank), a California corporation, and its wholly-owned subsidiary, Bank of America National Trust and Savings Association, which operates a branch in Tegucigalpa, Honduras. Several employees of the Bank have also been named and served as defendants. * * *

Other defendants have been named, but have not been served. * * * Also unserved are two Honduras corporations, Pedro Casanova e Hijos, S.A., and Importadore Mayorista, S. de R.L., and Michael Casanova, a citizen of Honduras (together referred to as "Casanova"), who together represent one of the two main competitors to Timberlane and its predecessor in the Honduran lumber business. * * *

The Timberlane complaint identified two co-conspirators not named as defendants. Jose Lamas, S. de R.L. (Lamas), a Honduran corporation, is the second major competitor in the lumber business. Jose Caminals Galegro (Caminals), a citizen of Spain, is described as an agent or employee of the Bank of Tegucigalpa.

FACTS AS ALLEGED

The conspiracy sketched by Timberlane actually started before the plaintiffs entered the scene. The Lima family operated a lumber mill in Honduras, competing with Lamas and Casanova, in both of which the Bank had significant financial interests. The Lima enterprise was also indebted to the Bank. By 1971, however, the Lima business was in financial trouble. Timberlane alleges that driving Lima under was the first step in the conspiracy which eventually crippled Timberlane's efforts, but the particulars do not matter for this appeal. What does matter is that various interests in the Lima assets, including its milling plant, passed to Lima's creditors: Casanova, the Bank, and the group of Lima employees who had not been paid the wages and severance pay due them. Under Honduran law, the employees' claim had priority.

Enter Timberlane, with a long history in the lumber business, in search of alternative sources of lumber for delivery to its distribution system on the East Coast of the United States. After study, it decided to try Honduras. In 1971, Danli was formed, tracts of forest land were acquired, plans for a modern log-processing plant were prepared, and equipment was purchased and assembled for shipment from the United States to Danli in Honduras. Timberlane became aware that the Lima plant might be available and began negotiating for its acquisition. Maya was formed, purchased the Lima employees' interest in the machinery and equipment in January 1972, despite opposition from the conspirators, and re-activated the Lima mill.

Realizing that they were faced with better-financed and more vigorous competition from Timberlane and its Honduran subsidiaries, the defendants and others extended the anti–Lima conspiracy to disrupt Timberlane's efforts. The primary weapons employed by the conspirators were the claim still held by the Bank in the remaining assets of the Lima enterprise under the all-inclusive mortgage Lima had been forced to sign and another claim held by Casanova. Maya made a substantial cash offer for the Bank's interest in an effort to clear its title, but the Bank refused to sell. Instead, the Bank surreptitiously conveyed the mortgage to Casanova for questionable consideration, Casanova paying nothing and agreeing only to pay the Bank a portion of what it collected. Casanova immediately assigned the Bank's claim and its own on similar terms to Caminals, who promptly set out to disrupt the Timberlane operation.

Caminals is characterized as the "front man" in the campaign to drive Timberlane out of Honduras, with the Bank and other defendants intending and carrying responsibility for his actions. Having acquired the claims of Casanova and the Bank, Caminals went to court to enforce them, ignoring throughout Timberlane's offers to purchase or settle them. Under the laws of Honduras, an "embargo" on property is a court-ordered attachment, registered with the Public Registry, which precludes the sale of that property without a court order. Honduran law provides, upon embargo, that the court appoint a judicial officer, called an "interventor" to ensure against any diminution in the value of the property. In order to paralyze the Timberlane operation, Caminals obtained embargoes against Maya and Danli. Acting through the interventor, since accused of being on the payroll of the Bank, guards and troops were used to cripple and, for a time, completely shut down Timberlane's milling operation. The harassment took other forms as well: the conspirators caused the manager of Timberlane's Honduras operations, Gordon Sloan Smith, to be falsely arrested and imprisoned and were responsible for the publication of several defamatory articles about Timberlane in the Honduran press.

As a result of the conspiracy, Timberlane's complaint claimed damages then estimated in excess of $5,000,000. Plaintiffs also allege that there has been a direct and substantial effect on United States foreign commerce, and that defendants intended the results of the conspiracy, including the impact on United States commerce.

[The court reviews and rejects the application of the act of state doctrine. The act of state doctrine is explored in Part D below.]

There is no doubt that American antitrust laws extend over some conduct in other nations. There was language in the first Supreme Court case in point, *American Banana Co. v. United Fruit Co.,* 213 U.S. 347, 29 S.Ct. 511, 53 L.Ed. 826 (1909), casting doubt on the extension of the Sherman Act to acts outside United States territory. But subsequent cases have limited *American Banana* to its particular facts, and the Sherman Act—and with it other antitrust laws—has been applied to extraterritorial conduct. *See, e.g., Continental Ore Co. v. Union Carbide*

& Carbon Corp., 370 U.S. 690, 82 S.Ct. 1404, 8 L.Ed.2d 777 (1962); *United States v. Sisal Sales Corp.*, 274 U.S. 268, 47 S.Ct. 592, 71 L.Ed. 1042 (1927); *United States v. Aluminum Co. of America*, 148 F.2d 416 (2d Cir.1945) (the *"Alcoa"* case). The act may encompass the foreign activities of aliens as well as American citizens.

That American law covers some conduct beyond this nation's borders does not mean that it embraces all, however. Extraterritorial application is understandably a matter of concern for the other countries involved. Those nations have sometimes resented and protested, as excessive intrusions into their own spheres, broad assertions of authority by American courts. Our courts have recognized this concern and have, at times, responded to it, even if not always enough to satisfy all the foreign critics. In any event, it is evident that at some point the interests of the United States are too weak and the foreign harmony incentive for restraint too strong to justify an extraterritorial assertion of jurisdiction. * * *

A tripartite analysis seems to be indicated. As acknowledged above, the antitrust laws require in the first instance that there be *some* effect—actual or intended—on American foreign commerce before the federal courts may legitimately exercise subject matter jurisdiction under those statutes. Second, a greater showing of burden or restraint may be necessary to demonstrate that the effect is sufficiently large to present a cognizable injury to the plaintiffs and, therefore, a civil *violation* of the antitrust laws. Third, there is the additional question which is unique to the international setting of whether the interests of, and links to, the United States—including the magnitude of the effect on American foreign commerce—are sufficiently strong, vis-à-vis those of other nations, to justify an assertion of extraterritorial authority. * * *

What we prefer is an evaluation and balancing of the relevant considerations in each case—in the words of Kingman Brewster, a "jurisdictional rule of reason." Balancing of the foreign interests involved was the approach taken by the Supreme Court in *Continental Ore Co. v. Union Carbide & Carbon Corp.*, 370 U.S. 690, 82 S.Ct. 1404, 8 L.Ed.2d 777 (1962), where the involvement of the Canadian government in the alleged monopolization was held not to require dismissal. The Court stressed that there was no indication that the Canadian authorities approved or would have approved of the monopolization, meaning that the Canadian interest, if any, was slight and was outweighed by the American interest in condemning the restraint. Similarly, in *Lauritzen v. Larsen*, 345 U.S. 571, 73 S.Ct. 921, 97 L.Ed. 1254 (1953), the Court used a like approach in declining to apply the Jones Act to a Danish seaman, injured in Havana on a Danish ship, although he had signed on to the ship in New York.

The elements to be weighed include the degree of conflict with foreign law or policy, the nationality or allegiance of the parties and the locations or principal places of business of corporations, the extent to which enforcement by either state can be expected to achieve compliance, the relative significance of effects on the United States as compared with those elsewhere, the extent to which there is explicit purpose to harm or affect American commerce, the foreseeability of such effect, and the relative importance to the violations charged of conduct with the United States as compared with conduct abroad. A court evaluating these factors should identify the potential degree of conflict if American authority is asserted. A difference in law or policy is one likely sore spot, though one which may not always be present. Nationality is another; though foreign governments may have some concern for the treatment of American citizens and business residing there, they primarily care about their own nationals. Having assessed the conflict, the court should then determine whether in the face of it the contacts and interests of the United States are sufficient to support the exercise of extraterritorial jurisdiction. * * *

The Sherman Act is not limited to trade restraints which have both a direct and substantial effect on our foreign commerce. Timberlane has alleged that the complained of activities were intended to, and did, affect the export of lumber from Honduras to the United States—the flow of United States foreign commerce, and as such they are within the jurisdiction of the federal courts under the Sherman Act. Moreover, the magnitude of the effect alleged would appear to be sufficient to state a claim.

The comity question is more complicated. From Timberlane's complaint it is evident that there are grounds for concern as to at least a few of the defendants, for some are identified as foreign citizens: Laureano Gutierrez Falla, Michael Casanova and the Casanova firms of Honduras, and Patrick Byrne, of Canada. Moreover, it is clear that most of the activity took place in Honduras, though the conspiracy may have been directed from San Francisco, and that the most direct economic effect was probably on Honduras. However, there has been no indication of any conflict with the law or policy of the Honduran government, nor any comprehensive analysis of the relative connections and interests of Honduras and the United States. Under these circumstances, the dismissal by the district court cannot be sustained on jurisdictional grounds.

We, therefore, vacate the dismissal, and remand the Timberlane action.

Notes and Questions

1. Banana *Revisited.* Note how the *Timberlane* court returned to a premise of the much-derided *American Banana* case, albeit taking extraterritorial jurisdiction doctrine into account: "That American law covers some conduct beyond this nation's borders does not mean that it embraces all, however." *American Banana* simply restricted U.S. jurisdiction to the water's edge. *Blackmer* and *Aluminum* equally simplistically looked only to the reach of U.S. law. The *Timberlane* court, like Justice Holmes in *American Banana*, was willing to limit U.S. jurisdiction, but it refused to do so by

holding that U.S. law was not meant to apply. Rather, *Timberlane* held that U.S. law sometimes *ought* not to be employed even if it might apply. *Timberlane* reached this result by acknowledging that, in many international cases, laws of two or more countries govern transactions concurrently. Hence, Judge Choy's working assumption: "[I]t is evident that at some point the interests of the United States are too weak and the foreign harmony incentive for restraint too strong to justify an extraterritorial assertion of jurisdiction." Should a court therefore have discretion to weigh U.S. and foreign interests to find a balance in each individual case? If the court finds the balance tilts toward the interests of the foreign state, should the result be deemed a denial of U.S. jurisdiction or simply a choice of foreign law?

2. *Balancing Factors.* Given the recurrent problem of concurrent jurisdiction in international transactions, how should courts structure their analyses to best balance and reconcile competing national interests? Professor Lea Brilmayer has identified five "considerations" U.S. courts have taken into account when deciding whether to apply U.S. law extraterritorially: the legislative intent of the Congress, the presumptive "reach" of the statute, the limits imposed by international law, judicial doctrines of discretion like comity, and the U.S. Constitution. Lea Brilmayer, "The Extraterritorial Application of American Law: A Methodological and Constitutional Approach," 50 *Law and Contemporary Problems*, Summer 1987, at 11, 14–16. In a rebuttal, Professor Friedrich Juenger argued that "the solution to the problem of extraterritoriality will remain elusive as long as the clash of regulatory policies is analyzed in terms of legislative jurisdiction," a choice-of-law analysis that he felt masked real conflicts of substantive policy. Friedrich K. Juenger, "Constitutional Control of Extraterritoriality?: A Comment on Professor Brilmayer's Appraisal," 50 *Law and Contemporary Problems*, Summer 1987, at 39, 46. For other formulations of the balancing test, see *Restatement (Third) of the Foreign Relations Law of the United States* § 403 and Mannington Mills, Inc. v. Congoleum Corp., 595 F.2d 1287 (3d Cir.1979).

3. *The Role of Case Law.* Granting that there may always be conflicts of substantive national policies in problems of transnational litigation, why should the courts not try to resolve such conflicts as clearly and fairly as possible? Can a consistent pattern of court decisions help bolster international comity and help develop rules of international law respecting jurisdiction? Should U.S. courts look not only to their own judgments, but also to judgments made by foreign and international courts to develop such rules?

3. INTERNATIONAL COMITY

HILTON v. GUYOT

159 U.S. 113, 16 S.Ct. 139, 40 L.Ed. 95 (1895).

MR. JUSTICE GRAY * * *

International law, in its widest and most comprehensive sense—including not only questions of right between nations, governed by what has been appropriately called the law of nations, but also questions arising under what is usually called private international law, or the conflict of laws, and concerning the rights of persons within the territory and dominion of one nation, by reason of acts, private or public, done within the dominions of another nation—is part of our law, and must be ascertained and administered by the courts of justice, as often as such questions are presented in litigation between man and man, duly submitted to their determination. * * *

No law has any effect, of its own force, beyond the limits of the sovereignty from which its authority is derived. The extent to which the law of one nation, as put in force within its territory, whether by executive order, by legislative act, or by judicial decree, shall be allowed to operate within the dominion of another nation, depends upon what our greatest jurists have been content to call "the comity of nations." Although the phrase has been often criticised, no satisfactory substitute has been suggested.

"Comity," in the legal sense, is neither a matter of absolute obligation, on the one hand, nor of mere courtesy and good will, upon the other. But it is the recognition which one nation allows within its territory to the legislative, executive or judicial acts of another nation, having due regard both to international duty and convenience, and to the rights of its own citizens or of other persons who are under the protection of its laws. * * *

Chief Justice Taney, * * * speaking for this court while Mr. Justice Story was a member of it, and largely adopting his words, said: * * * "The comity thus extended to other nations is no impeachment of sovereignty. It is the voluntary act of the nation by which it is offered, and is inadmissible when contrary to its policy, or prejudicial to its interests. But it contributes so largely to promote justice between individuals, and to produce a friendly intercourse between the sovereignties to which they belong, that courts of justice have continually acted upon it, as a part of the voluntary law of nations." "It is not the comity of the courts, but the comity of the nation, which is administered and ascertained in the same way, and guided by the same reasoning, by which all other principles of municipal law are ascertained and guided." *Bank v. Earle*, (1839) 13 Pet. 519, 589; Story's, Conflict of Laws, § 38.

HARTFORD FIRE INSURANCE CO. v. CALIFORNIA

509 U.S. 764, 113 S.Ct. 2891, 125 L.Ed.2d 612 (1993).

JUSTICE SOUTER announced the judgment of the Court and delivered the opinion of the Court with respect to Parts I, II(A), III, and IV, and an opinion [concurring in the judgment with respect to Part II(B)].

The Sherman Act makes every contract, combination, or conspiracy in unreasonable restraint of interstate or foreign commerce illegal. 15 U.S.C. § 1. These consolidated cases present questions about the application of that Act to the insurance industry, both here and abroad. The plaintiffs (respondents here) allege that both domestic and foreign defendants (petitioners here) violated the Sherman Act by engaging in various conspiracies to affect the American insurance market. A group of domestic defendants argues that the McCarran–Ferguson Act, 15 U.S.C. § 1011 *et seq.*, precludes application of the Sherman Act to the conduct alleged; a group of foreign defendants argues that the principle of international comity requires the District Court to refrain from exercising jurisdiction over certain claims against it. We hold that most of the domestic defendants' alleged conduct is not immunized from antitrust liability by the McCarran–Ferguson Act, and that, even assuming it applies, the principle of international comity does not preclude District Court jurisdiction over the foreign conduct alleged.

I

The two petitions before us stem from consolidated litigation comprising the complaints of 19 States and many private plaintiffs alleging that the defendants, members of the insurance industry, conspired in violation of § 1 of the Sherman Act to restrict the terms of coverage of commercial general liability (CGL) insurance available in the United States. Because the cases come to us on motions to dismiss, we take the allegations of the complaints as true.

A

According to the complaints, the object of the conspiracies was to force certain primary insurers (insurers who sell insurance directly to consumers) to change the terms of their standard CGL insurance policies to conform with the policies the defendant insurers wanted to sell. The defendants wanted four changes.

First, CGL insurance has traditionally been sold in the United States on an "occurrence" basis, through a policy obligating the insurer "to pay or defend claims, whenever made, resulting from an accident or 'injurious exposure to conditions' that occurred during the [specific time] period the policy was in effect." In place of this traditional "occurrence" trigger of coverage, the defendants wanted a "claims-made" trigger, obligating the insurer to pay or defend only those claims made during the policy period. Such a policy has the distinct advantage for the insurer that when the policy period ends without a claim having been made, the insurer can be certain that the policy will not expose it to any further liability. Second, the defendants wanted the "claims-made" policy to have a "retroactive date" provision, which would further restrict coverage to claims based on incidents that occurred after a certain date. Such a provision eliminates the risk that an insurer, by issuing a claims-made policy, would assume liability arising from incidents that occurred before the policy's effective date, but remained undiscovered or caused no immediate harm. Third, CGL insurance has traditionally covered "sudden and accidental" pollution; the defendants wanted to eliminate that coverage. Finally, CGL insurance has traditionally provided that the insurer would bear the legal costs of defending covered claims against the insured without regard to the policy's stated limits of coverage; the defendants wanted legal defense costs to be counted against the stated limits (providing a "legal defense cost cap"). * * *

<h1 style="text-align:center">III</h1>

Finally, we take up the question * * * whether certain claims against the London reinsurers should have been dismissed as improper applications of the Sherman Act to foreign conduct. The Fifth Claim for Relief of the California Complaint alleges a violation of § 1 of the Sherman Act by certain London reinsurers who conspired to coerce primary insurers in the United States to offer CGL coverage on a claims-made basis, thereby making "occurrence CGL coverage ... unavailable in the State of California for many risks." The Sixth Claim for Relief of the California Complaint alleges that the London reinsurers violated § 1 by a conspiracy to limit coverage of pollution risks in North America, thereby rendering "pollution liability coverage ... almost entirely unavailable for the vast majority of casualty insurance purchasers in the State of California." The Eighth Claim for Relief of the California Complaint alleges a further § 1 violation by the London reinsurers who, along with domestic retrocessional reinsurers, conspired to limit coverage of seepage, pollution, and property contamination risks in North America, thereby eliminating such coverage in the State of California.

At the outset, we note that the District Court undoubtedly had jurisdiction of these Sherman Act claims, as the London reinsurers apparently concede. ("Our position is not that the Sherman Act does not apply in the sense that a minimal basis for the exercise of jurisdiction doesn't exist here. Our position is that there are certain circumstances, and that this is one of them, in which the interests of another State are sufficient that the exercise of that jurisdiction should be restrained.") Although the proposition was perhaps not always free from doubt, see *American Banana Co. v. United Fruit Co.*, 213 U.S. 347 (1909), it is well established by now that the Sherman Act applies to foreign conduct that was meant to produce and did in fact produce some substantial effect in the United States.[22] Such is the conduct alleged here: that the London reinsurers engaged in unlawful conspiracies to affect the market for insurance in the United States and that their conduct in fact produced substantial effect.

According to the London reinsurers, the District Court should have declined to exercise such jurisdiction under the principle of international comity.[24] The Court of Appeals agreed that courts should look to that

22. JUSTICE SCALIA believes that what is at issue in this case is prescriptive, as opposed to subject-matter, jurisdiction. The parties do not question prescriptive jurisdiction, however, and for good reason: it is well established that Congress has exercised such jurisdiction under the Sherman Act. See G. Born & D. Westin, International Civil Litigation in United States Courts 542, n.5 (2d ed. 1992) (Sherman Act is a

"prime exampl[e] of the simultaneous exercise of prescriptive jurisdiction and grant of subject matter jurisdiction").

24. JUSTICE SCALIA contends that comity concerns figure into the prior analysis whether jurisdiction exists under the Sherman Act. This contention is inconsistent with the general understanding that the Sherman Act covers foreign conduct producing a substantial intended effect in the principle in deciding whether to exercise jurisdiction under the Sherman Act. This availed the London reinsurers nothing, however. To be sure, the Court of Appeals believed that "application of [American] antitrust laws to the London reinsurance market 'would lead to significant conflict with English law and policy,'" and that "[s]uch a conflict, unless outweighed by other factors, would by itself be reason to decline exercise of jurisdiction." But other factors, in the court's view, including the London reinsurers' express purpose to affect United States commerce and the substantial nature of the effect produced, outweighed the supposed conflict and required the exercise of jurisdiction in this case.

When it enacted the Foreign Trade Antitrust Improvements Act of 1982 (FTAIA), 15 U.S.C. § 6a, Congress expressed no view on the question whether a court with Sherman Act jurisdiction should ever decline to exercise such jurisdiction on grounds of international comity. See H.R. Rep. No. 97–686, p. 13 (1982) ("If a court determines that the requirements for subject matter jurisdiction are met, [the FTAIA] would have no effect on the court['s] ability to employ notions of comity ... or otherwise to take account of the international character of the transaction") (citing *Timberlane*). We need not decide that question here, however, for even assuming that in a proper case a court may decline to exercise Sherman Act jurisdiction over foreign conduct (or, as JUSTICE SCALIA would put it, may conclude by the employment of comity analysis in the first instance that there is no jurisdiction), international comity would not counsel against exercising jurisdiction in the circumstances alleged here.

The only substantial question in this case is whether "there is in fact a true conflict between domestic and foreign law." *Societe Nationale Industrielle Aerospatiale v. United States District Court*, 482 U.S. 522, 555 (1987) (BLACKMUN, J., concurring in part and dissenting in part). The London reinsurers contend that applying the Act to their conduct would conflict significantly with British law, and the British Government, appearing before us as *amicus curiae,* concurs. They assert that Parliament has established a comprehensive regulatory regime over the London reinsurance market and that the conduct alleged here was perfectly consistent with British law and policy. But this is not to state a conflict. "[T]he fact that conduct is lawful in the state in which it took place will not, of itself, bar application of the United States antitrust laws," even where the foreign state has a strong policy to permit or encourage such conduct. Restatement (Third) Foreign Relations Law § 415, Comment *j*;

United States, and that concerns of comity come into play, if at all, only after a court has determined that the acts complained of are subject to Sherman Act jurisdiction. See *United States v. Aluminum Co. of America*, 148 F.2d 416, 444 (C.A.2 1945) ("it follows from what we have ... said that [the agreements at issue] were unlawful [under the Sherman Act], though made abroad, if they were intended to affect imports and did affect them"); *Mannington Mills, Inc. v.* *Congoleum Corp.*, 595 F.2d 1287, 1294 (C.A.3 1979) (once court determines that jurisdiction exists under the Sherman Act, question remains whether comity precludes its exercise); H.R. Rep. No. 97–686, p. 13 (1982). But cf. *Timberlane Lumber Co. v. Bank of America, N. T. & S. A.*, 549 F.2d 597, 613 (C.A.9 1976). In any event, the parties conceded jurisdiction at oral argument, and we see no need to address this contention here.

see *Continental Ore Co., supra*, at 706–707. No conflict exists, for these purposes, "where a person subject to regulation by two states can comply with the laws of both." Restatement (Third) Foreign Relations Law § 403, Comment *e*.[25] Since the London reinsurers do not argue that British law requires them to act in some fashion prohibited by the law of the United States, or claim that their compliance with the laws of both countries is otherwise impossible, we see no conflict with British law. We have no need in this case to address other considerations that might inform a decision to refrain from the exercise of jurisdiction on grounds of international comity. * * *

JUSTICE SCALIA * * * delivered a dissenting opinion with respect to Part II [in which JUSTICE O'CONNOR, JUSTICE KENNEDY, and JUSTICE THOMAS join]. * * *

II

The petitioners in No. 91–1128, various British corporations and other British subjects, argue that certain of the claims against them constitute an inappropriate extraterritorial application of the Sherman Act. It is important to distinguish two distinct questions raised by this petition: whether the District Court had jurisdiction, and whether the Sherman Act reaches the extraterritorial conduct alleged here. On the first question, I believe that the District Court had subject-matter jurisdiction over the Sherman Act claims against all the defendants (personal jurisdiction is not contested). The respondents asserted non-frivolous claims under the Sherman Act, and 28 U.S.C. § 1331 vests district courts with subject-matter jurisdiction over cases "arising under" federal statutes. As precedents such as *Lauritzen v. Larsen*, 345 U.S. 571 (1953), make clear, that is sufficient to establish the District Court's jurisdiction over these claims. *Lauritzen* involved a Jones Act claim brought by a foreign sailor against a foreign shipowner. The shipowner contested the District Court's jurisdiction, apparently on the grounds that the Jones Act did not govern the dispute between the foreign parties to the action. Though ultimately agreeing with the shipowner that the Jones Act did not apply, the Court held that the District Court had jurisdiction.

> "As frequently happens, a contention that there is some barrier to granting plaintiff's claim is cast in terms of an exception to jurisdiction of subject matter. A cause of action under our law was asserted here, and the court had power to determine whether it was or was not founded in law and in fact."

The second question—the extraterritorial reach of the Sherman Act—has nothing to do with the jurisdiction of the courts. It is a question of substantive law turning on whether, in enacting the Sherman Act, Congress asserted regulatory power over the challenged con-

25. JUSTICE SCALIA says that we put the cart before the horse in citing this authority, for he argues it may be apposite only after a determination that jurisdiction over the foreign acts is reasonable. But whatever the order of cart and horse, conflict in this sense is the only substantial issue before the Court.

duct. See *EEOC v. Arabian American Oil Co.*, 499 U.S. 244, 248 (1991) (*Aramco*) ("It is our task to determine whether Congress intended the protections of Title VII to apply to United States citizens employed by American employers outside of the United States"). If a plaintiff fails to prevail on this issue, the court does not dismiss the claim for want of subject-matter jurisdiction—want of power to adjudicate; rather, it decides the claim, ruling on the merits that the plaintiff has failed to state a cause of action under the relevant statute. See *American Banana Co. v. United Fruit Co.*, 213 U.S. 347, 359 (1909) (holding that complaint based upon foreign conduct "alleges no case under the [Sherman Act]").

There is, however, a type of "jurisdiction" relevant to determining the extraterritorial reach of a statute; it is known as "legislative jurisdiction" or "jurisdiction to prescribe." This refers to "the authority of a state to make its law applicable to persons or activities," and is quite a separate matter from "jurisdiction to adjudicate." There is no doubt, of course, that Congress possesses legislative jurisdiction over the acts alleged in this complaint: Congress has broad power under Article I, § 8, cl. 3 "[t]o regulate Commerce with foreign Nations," and this Court has repeatedly upheld its power to make laws applicable to persons or activities beyond our territorial boundaries where United States interests are affected. But the question in this case is whether, and to what extent, Congress *has* exercised that undoubted legislative jurisdiction in enacting the Sherman Act.

Two canons of statutory construction are relevant in this inquiry. The first is the "long-standing principle of American law 'that legislation of Congress, unless a contrary intent appears, is meant to apply only within the territorial jurisdiction of the United States.' " *Aramco, supra,* at 253 (quoting *Foley Bros., Inc. v. Filardo*, 336 U.S. 281, 285 (1949)). * * * We, have, however, found the presumption to be overcome with respect to our antitrust laws; it is now well established that the Sherman Act applies extraterritorially.

But if the presumption against extraterritoriality has been overcome or is otherwise inapplicable, a second canon of statutory construction becomes relevant: "[A]n act of congress ought never to be construed to violate the law of nations if any other possible construction remains." *Murray v. The Charming Betsy*, 2 Cranch 64, 118 (1804) (Marshall, C.J.). This canon is "wholly independent" of the presumption against extraterritoriality. It is relevant to determining the substantive reach of a statute because "the law of nations," or customary international law, includes limitations on a nation's exercise of its jurisdiction to prescribe. Though it clearly has constitutional authority to do so, Congress is generally presumed not to have exceeded those customary international-law limits on jurisdiction to prescribe.

Consistent with that presumption, this and other courts have frequently recognized that, even where the presumption against extraterritoriality does not apply, statutes should not be interpreted to regulate foreign persons or conduct if that regulation would conflict with principles of international law. For example, in *Romero v. International Terminal Operating Co.*, 358 U.S. 354 (1959), the plaintiff, a Spanish sailor who had been injured while working aboard a Spanish-flag and Spanish-owned vessel, filed a Jones Act claim against his Spanish employer. The presumption against extraterritorial application of federal statutes was inapplicable to the case, as the actionable tort had occurred in American waters. The Court nonetheless stated that, "in the absence of contrary congressional direction," it would apply "principles of choice of law that are consonant with the needs of a general federal maritime law and with due recognition of our self-regarding respect for the relevant interests of foreign nations in the regulation of maritime commerce as part of the legitimate concern of the international community." "The controlling considerations" in this choice-of-law analysis were "the interacting interests of the United States and of foreign countries."

Romero referred to, and followed, the choice-of-law analysis set forth in *Lauritzen v. Larsen*, 345 U.S. 571 (1953). As previously mentioned, *Lauritzen* also involved a Jones Act claim brought by a foreign sailor against a foreign employer. The *Lauritzen* Court recognized the basic problem: "If [the Jones Act were] read literally, Congress has conferred an American right of action which requires nothing more than that plaintiff be 'any seaman who shall suffer personal injury in the course of his employment.' "The solution it adopted was to construe the statute "to apply only to areas and transactions in which *American law would be considered operative under prevalent doctrines of international law.*" To support application of international law to limit the facial breadth of the statute, the Court relied upon—of course—Chief Justice Marshall's statement in *The Charming Betsy* quoted *supra*. See also *McCulloch v. Sociedad Nacional de Marineros de Honduras*, 372 U.S. 10, 21–22 (1963) (applying *The Charming Betsy* principle to restrict application of National Labor Relations Act to foreign-flag vessels).

Lauritzen, Romero, and *McCulloch* were maritime cases, but we have recognized the principle that the scope of generally worded statutes must be construed in light of international law in other areas as well. More specifically, the principle was expressed in *United States v. Aluminum Co. of America*, 148 F.2d 416 (C.A.2 1945), the decision that established the extraterritorial reach of the Sherman Act. In his opinion for the court, Judge Learned Hand cautioned "we are not to read general words, such as those in [the Sherman] Act, without regard to the limitations customarily observed by nations upon the exercise of their powers; limitations which generally correspond to those fixed by the 'Conflict of Laws.' "

More recent lower court precedent has also tempered the extraterritorial application of the Sherman Act with considerations of "international comity." See *Timberlane Lumber Co. v. Bank of America, N.T & S.A.*, 549 F.2d 597, 608–615 (C.A.9 1976); *Mannington Mills, Inc. v. Congoleum Corp.*, 595 F.2d 1287, 1294–1298 (C.A.3 1979). The "comity" they refer to is not the comity of courts, whereby judges decline to exercise jurisdiction over matters more appropriately adjudged elsewhere, but rather what might be termed "prescriptive comity": the respect sovereign nations afford each other by limiting the reach of their laws. That comity is exercised by legislatures when they enact laws, and courts assume it has been exercised when they come to interpreting the scope of laws their legislatures have enacted. It is a traditional component of choice-of-law theory. See J. Story, Commentaries on the Conflict of Laws § 38 (1834) (distinguishing between the "comity of the courts" and the "comity of nations," and defining the latter as "the true foundation and extent of the obligation of the laws of one nation within the territories of another"). Comity in this sense includes the choice-of-law principles that, "in the absence of contrary congressional direction," are assumed to be incorporated into our substantive laws having extraterritorial reach. Considering comity in this way is just part of determining whether the Sherman Act prohibits the conduct at issue.

In sum, the practice of using international law to limit the extraterritorial reach of statutes is firmly established in our jurisprudence. In proceeding to apply that practice to the present case, I shall rely on the Restatement (Third) of Foreign Relations Law for the relevant principles of international law. Its standards appear fairly supported in the decisions of this Court construing international choice-of-law principles (*Lauritzen, Romero*, and *McCulloch)* and in the decisions of other federal courts, especially *Timberlane*. Whether the Restatement precisely reflects international law in every detail matters little here, as I believe this case would be resolved the same way under virtually any conceivable test that takes account of foreign regulatory interests.

Under the Restatement, a nation having some "basis" for jurisdiction to prescribe law should nonetheless refrain from exercising that jurisdiction "with respect to a person or activity having connections with another state when the exercise of such jurisdiction is unreasonable." Restatement (Third) § 403(l). The "reasonableness" inquiry turns on a number of factors including, but not limited to: "the extent to which the activity takes place within the territory [of the regulating state]," § 403(2)(a); "the connections, such as nationality, residence, or economic activity, between the regulating state and the person principally responsible for the activity to be regulated," § 403(2)(b); "the character of the activity to be regulated, the importance of regulation to the regulating state, the extent to which other states regulate such activities, and the degree to which the desirability of such regulation is generally accepted," § 403(2)(c); "the extent to which another state may have an interest in regulating the activity," § 403(2)(g); and "the likelihood of conflict with regulation by another state," § 403(2)(h). Rarely would these factors point more clearly against application of United States law. The activity relevant to the counts at issue here took place primarily in the United Kingdom, and the defendants in these counts are British corporations and British subjects having their principal place of business or residence outside the United States. Great Britain has established a comprehensive regulatory scheme governing the London reinsurance markets, and clearly has a heavy "interest in regulating the activity." Finally, § 2(b) of the McCarran–Ferguson Act allows state regulatory statutes to override the Sherman Act in the insurance field, subject only to the narrow "boycott" exception set forth in § 3(b)—suggesting that "the importance of regulation to the [United States]" is slight. Considering these factors, I think it unimaginable that an assertion of legislative jurisdiction by the United States would be considered reasonable, and therefore it is inappropriate to assume, in the absence of statutory indication to the contrary, that Congress has made such an assertion.

It is evident from what I have said that the Court's comity analysis, which proceeds as though the issue is whether the courts should "decline to exercise ... jurisdiction," rather than whether the Sherman Act covers this conduct, is simply misdirected. I do not at all agree, moreover, with the Court's conclusion that the issue of the substantive scope of the Sherman Act is not in the case. To be sure, the parties did not make a clear distinction between adjudicative jurisdiction and the scope of the statute. Parties often do not, as we have observed (and have declined to punish with procedural default) before. It is not realistic, and also not helpful, to pretend that the only really relevant issue in this case is not before us. In any event, if one erroneously chooses, as the Court does, to make adjudicative jurisdiction (or, more precisely, abstention) the vehicle for taking account of the needs of prescriptive comity, the Court still gets it wrong. It concludes that no "true conflict" counseling nonapplication of United States law (or rather, as it thinks, United States judicial jurisdiction) exists unless compliance with United States law would constitute a *violation* of another country's law. That breathtakingly broad proposition, which contradicts the many cases discussed earlier, will bring the Sherman Act and other laws into sharp and unnecessary conflict with the legitimate interests of other countries—particularly our closest trading partners.

In the sense in which the term "conflic[t]" was used in *Lauritzen,* and is generally understood in the field of conflicts of laws, there is clearly a conflict in this case. The petitioners here, like the defendant in *Lauritzen,* were not compelled by any foreign law to take their allegedly wrongful actions, but that no more precludes a conflict-of-laws analysis here than it did there. Where applicable foreign and domestic law provide different substantive rules of decision to govern the parties' dispute, a conflict-of-laws analysis is necessary.

Literally the *only* support that the Court adduces for its position is § 403 of the Restatement (Third) of Foreign Relations Law—or more precisely Comment *e* to that provision, which states:

> "Subsection (3) [which says that a state should defer to another state if that state's interest is clearly greater] applies only when one state requires what another prohibits, or where compliance with the regulations of two states exercising jurisdiction consistently with this section is otherwise impossible. It does not apply where a person

subject to regulation by two states can comply with the laws of both...."

The Court has completely misinterpreted this provision. Subsection (3) of § 403 (requiring one State to defer to another in the limited circumstances just described) comes into play only after subsection (1) of § 403 has been complied with—*i.e.*, after it has been determined that the exercise of jurisdiction by *both* of the two States is not "unreasonable." That prior question is answered by applying the factors (*inter alia*) set forth in subsection (2) of § 403, that is, precisely the factors that I have discussed in text and that the Court rejects.

Notes and Questions

1. *The Classical Definition of Comity.* In an interesting modern example of *Hilton's* classical definition of comity, Laker Airways v. Sabena, Belgian World Airlines, 731 F.2d 909, 937 (D.C.Cir.1984), Judge Wilkey addressed arguments that a U.S. anti-suit injunction "violates the crucial principles of comity that regulate and moderate the social and economic intercourse between independent nations":

[C]omity serves our international system like the mortar which cements together a brick house. No one would willingly permit the mortar to crumble or be chipped away for fear of compromising the entire structure.

"Comity" summarizes in a brief word a complex and elusive concept—the degree of deference that a domestic forum must pay to the act of a foreign government not otherwise binding on the forum. Since comity varies according to the factual circumstances surrounding each claim for its recognition, the absolute boundaries of the duties it imposes are inherently uncertain. However, the central precept of comity teaches that, when possible, the decisions of foreign tribunals should be given effect in domestic courts, since recognition fosters international cooperation and encourages reciprocity, thereby promoting predictability and stability through satisfaction of mutual expectations. The interests of both forums are advanced—the foreign court because its laws and policies have been vindicated; the domestic country because international cooperation and ties have been strengthened. The rule of law is also encouraged, which benefits all nations.

Comity is a necessary outgrowth of our international system of politically independent, socio-economically interdependent nation states. As surely as people, products and problems move freely among adjoining countries, so national interests cross territorial borders. * * * Every nation must often rely on other countries to help it achieve its regulatory expectations. Thus, comity compels national courts to act at all times to increase the international legal ties that advance the rule of law within and among nations.

However, there are limitations to the application of comity. When the foreign act is inherently inconsistent with the policies underlying comity, domestic recognition could tend either to legitimize the aberration or to encourage retaliation, undercutting the realization of the goals served by comity. No nation is under an unremitting obligation to enforce foreign interests which are fundamentally prejudicial to those of the domestic forum. Thus, from the earliest times, authorities have recognized that the obligation of comity expires when the strong public policies of the forum are vitiated by the foreign act.

2. *Comity in* Hartford Fire. Does Justice Souter's conception of comity in *Hartford Fire* differ from the more traditional notion set out in *Hilton* and *Laker Airways*? According to Justice Souter, the assertion "that Parliament has established a comprehensive regulatory regime over the London reinsurance market and that the conduct alleged here was perfectly consistent with British law and policy" did not "state a conflict" with U.S. law. Professor Dam criticized the majority opinion in *Hartford Fire* for "plung[ing] forward in applying the Sherman Act extraterritorially, whatever the foreign interests involved." Kenneth W. Dam, "Extraterritoriality in an Age of Globalization: The Hartford Fire Case," 1993 *Supreme Court Review* 289, 294. Did Justice Souter in essence make what had been called the "foreign compulsion defense" the centerpiece of his comity inquiry? Or is it more plausible that, as Professor Weintraub has stated, "Justice Souter is saying that it would be a waste of time in such an egregious case, a conspiracy abroad solely intended to cause anticompetitive effects in the United States, to wade through the comity analysis"? Russell J. Weintraub, *Commentary on the Conflict of Laws* 713 (4th ed. 2001).

Even U.S. courts that have limited the application of U.S. law have not often relied directly on the traditional comity doctrine when faced with foreign conflicts. Instead, U.S. courts have tended to look to some other kind of justification for limiting the application of U.S. law or legal process, *e.g.*, the choice-of-law limitations posed by territorialism in *American Banana* or the abstention doctrines of *forum non conveniens*, foreign sovereign immunity, or act of state, all explored below. Note, however, that U.S. courts often employ *Hilton*'s traditional comity test when deciding whether to recognize foreign court judgments.

3. Hartford Fire *and the Balancing Test*. Did *Hartford Fire* repudiate the balancing test of *Timberlane*? Demetriou and Robertson thought so: "[T]he balancing test [is] meaningless. So long as the conduct concerned 'was meant to produce and did in fact produce some substantial effect in the United States,' then jurisdiction is established." Marie Demetriou & Aidan Robertson, "US Extra-territorial Jurisdiction in Anti–Trust Matters: Recent Developments," 8 *European Competition Law Review* 461, 465 (1995). Unlike Justice Souter's majority opinion, Justice Scalia's dissent explicitly relied on *Timberlane* and other formulations of the balancing test.

Should *Hartford Fire* be narrowly construed? In Sterling Drug, Inc. v. Bayer USA Inc., 14 F.3d 733 (2d Cir.1994), the Second Circuit considered the extraterritorial application of an injunction restraining violations of the Lanham Act's trademark protection provisions. The court found that even after *Hartford Fire*, the traditional notion of international comity remained an appropriate concern: "[T]he [*Hartford Fire*] Court's approach to the comity issue . . . is not automatically transferable to the trademark context, especially where the contending parties both hold rights in the same mark under the respective laws of their countries." *Id.* at 746. In the court's view, the extraterritorial aspects of a trademark infringement injunction needed to be "carefully crafted to prohibit only those foreign uses of the mark * * * that are likely to have significant trademark-impairing effects on United States commerce." *Id.* at 747. The Ninth Circuit has also addressed the implications of *Hartford Fire*. In Metro Indus., Inc. v. Sammi Corp., 82 F.3d 839 (9th Cir.1996), the court upheld a summary judgment for the defendant, finding Metro had not presented evidence sufficient to allow a rational fact finder to decide in Metro's favor on its Sherman Act claim against a Korean exporting company and two of its U.S. subsidiaries. In the course of its opinion, the court found a traditional comity analysis relevant in deciding it had jurisdiction to rule on Metro's antitrust suit. According to the Ninth Circuit, although *Hartford Fire* held "that a foreign government's encouragement of conduct which the United States prohibits [could not] amount to a conflict of law, it did not question the propriety of the jurisdictional rule of reason or the seven comity factors set forth in *Timberlane*." *Id.* at 846 n.5.

4. Hartford Fire *and the Global Economy*. Does the U.S.-centric approach of *Hartford Fire* fail to respond to modern international economic needs? Professor Dam believed that the judgment sounded "a discordant note in an increasingly globalized economy in an era when the need for more outward-looking and cooperative economic policy measures has become increasingly obvious." Dam, *supra*, at 297. Professor Waller has contended that though nowadays in antitrust litigation "comity is no longer important" both because the U.S. government is more restrained in attempting unilaterally to govern extraterritorial anticompetitive conduct and because U.S. courts are not required to do a balancing analysis, the global economy will be protected by thoughtful cooperation between U.S. and foreign regulators. Spencer Weber Waller, "The Twilight of Comity," 38 *Columbia Journal of Transnational Law* 563, 565–66 (2000).

5. *Reactions to* Hartford Fire *from Abroad*. One British commentator called the *Hartford Fire* decision a "staggeringly blinkered approach" that in effect means that the United States will respect

> only * * * the laws of those foreign States which actually legislate in favour of monopolistic, price-fixing or other anti-competitive practices. The sovereign interests of those States which actually share US free-market principles but do not regulate anti-competition with the aggression or exorbitant reach of the US can be ignored. Under this approach, greater consideration would be due to the laws of an old-style Soviet State than those of a European trading partner.

Julian Wilson, "US exports in anti-trust: the primacy of economic muscle over international law," *International Litigation News*, July 1995, at 3, 4. Will Justice Souter's narrow definition of comity encourage other states to take actions that more directly challenge the applicability of U.S. law? Might some states be tempted to enact countermeasures, making it illegal under their laws to comply with U.S. laws, refusing enforcement of U.S. judgments, or providing a cause of action allowing the recovery of damages paid as a result of a U.S. court's finding of liability? For discussion of legislative responses abroad to what have been regarded as overbroad assertions of U.S. antitrust jurisdiction, see, *e.g.*, A.V. Lowe, "Blocking Extraterritorial Jurisdiction: The British Protection of Trading Interests Acts, 1980," 75 *American Journal of International Law* 257 (1981).

4. FORUM NON CONVENIENS

PIPER AIRCRAFT CO. v. REYNO
454 U.S. 235, 102 S.Ct. 252, 70 L.Ed.2d 419 (1981).

JUSTICE MARSHALL delivered the opinion of the Court. * * *

I

A

In July 1976, a small commercial aircraft crashed in the Scottish highlands during the course of a charter flight from Blackpool to Perth. The pilot and five passengers were killed instantly. The decedents were all Scottish subjects and residents, as are their heirs and next of kin. There were no eyewitnesses to the accident. At the time of the crash the plane was subject to Scottish air traffic control.

The aircraft, a twin-engine Piper Aztec, was manufactured in Pennsylvania by petitioner Piper Aircraft Co. (Piper). The propellers were manufactured in Ohio by petitioner Hartzell Propeller, Inc. (Hartzell). At the time of the crash the aircraft was registered in Great Britain and was owned and maintained by Air Navigation and Trading Co., Ltd. (Air Navigation). It was operated by McDonald Aviation, Ltd. (McDonald), a Scottish air taxi service. Both Air Navigation and McDonald were organized in the United Kingdom. The wreckage of the plane is now in a hanger in Farnsborough, England.

The British Department of Trade investigated the accident shortly after it occurred. A preliminary report found that the plane crashed after developing a spin, and suggested that mechanical failure in the plane or the propeller was responsible. At Hartzell's request, this report was reviewed by a three-member Review Board, which held a 9–day adversary hearing attended by all interested parties. The Review Board found no evidence of defective equipment and indicated that pilot error may have contributed to the accident. The pilot, who had obtained his commercial pilot's license only three months earlier, was flying over high ground at an altitude considerably lower than the minimum height required by his company's operations manual.

In July 1977, a California probate court appointed respondent Gaynell Reyno administratrix of the estates of the five passengers. Reyno is not related to and does not know any of the decedents or their survivors; she was a legal secretary to the attorney who filed this lawsuit. Several days after her appointment, Reyno commenced separate wrongful-death actions against Piper and Hartzell in the Superior Court of California, claiming negligence and strict liability. Air Navigation, McDonald, and the estate of the pilot are not parties to this litigation. The survivors of the five passengers whose estates are represented by Reyno filed a separate action in the United Kingdom against Air Navigation, Mc-Donald, and the pilot's estate. Reyno candidly admits that the action against Piper and Hartzell was filed in the United States because its laws regarding liability, capacity to sue, and damages are more favorable to her position than are those of Scotland. Scottish law does not recognize strict liability in tort. Moreover, it permits wrongful-death actions only when brought by a decedent's relatives. The relatives may sue only for "loss of support and society."

On petitioners' motion, the suit was removed to the United States District Court for the Central District of California. Piper then moved for transfer to the United States District Court for the Middle District of Pennsylvania, pursuant to 28 U.S.C. § 1404(a). Hartzell moved to dismiss for lack of personal jurisdiction, or in the alternative, to transfer. In December 1977, the District Court quashed service on Hartzell and transferred the case to the Middle District of Pennsylvania. Respondent then properly served process on Hartzell.

B

In May 1978, after the suit had been transferred, both Hartzell and Piper moved to dismiss the action on the ground of *forum non conveniens*. The District Court granted these motions in October 1979. It relied on the balancing test set forth by this Court in *Gulf Oil Corp. v. Gilbert*, 330 U.S. 501 (1947), and its companion case, *Koster v. Lumbermens Mut. Cas. Co.*, 330 U.S. 518 (1947). In those decisions, the Court stated that a plaintiff's choice of forum should rarely be disturbed. However, when an alternative forum has jurisdiction to hear the case, and when trial in the chosen forum would "establish ... oppressiveness and vexation to a defendant ... out of all proportion to plaintiff's convenience," or when the "chosen forum [is] inappropriate because of considerations affecting the court's own administrative and legal problems," the court may, in the exercise of its sound discretion, dismiss the case. To guide trial court discretion, the Court provided a list of "private interest factors" affecting the convenience of the litigants, and a list of "public interest factors" affecting the convenience of the forum.[6]

On appeal, the United States Court of Appeals for the Third Circuit reversed and remanded for trial. The decision to reverse appears to be based on two alternative grounds. First, the Court held that the District Court abused its discretion in conducting the *Gilbert* analysis. Second,

---

6. The factors pertaining to the private interests of the litigants included the "relative ease of access to sources of proof; availability of compulsory process for attendance of unwilling, and the cost of obtaining attendance of willing, witnesses; possibility of view of premises, if view would be appropriate to the action; and all other practical problems that make trial of a case easy, expeditious and inexpensive." *Gilbert*, 330 U.S., at 508. The public factors bearing on the question included the administrative difficulties flowing from court congestion; the "local interest in having localized controversies decided at home"; the interest in having the trial of a diversity case in a forum that is at home with the law that must govern the action; the avoidance of unnecessary problems in conflict of laws, or in the application of foreign law; and the unfairness of burdening citizens in an unrelated forum with jury duty.

the Court held that dismissal is never appropriate where the law of the alternative forum is less favorable to the plaintiff. * * *

II

The Court of Appeals erred in holding that plaintiffs may defeat a motion to dismiss on the ground of *forum non conveniens* merely by showing that the substantive law that would be applied in the alternative forum is less favorable to the plaintiffs than that of the present forum. The possibility of a change in substantive law should ordinarily not be given conclusive or even substantial weight in the *forum non conveniens* inquiry.

We expressly rejected the position adopted by the Court of Appeals in our decision in *Canada Malting Co. v. Paterson Steamships, Ltd.*, 285 U.S. 413 (1932). That case arose out of a collision between two vessels in American waters. The Canadian owners of cargo lost in the accident sued the Canadian owners of one of the vessels in Federal District Court. The cargo owners chose an American court in large part because the relevant American liability rules were more favorable than the Canadian rules. The District Court dismissed on grounds of *forum non conveniens*. The plaintiffs argued that dismissal was inappropriate because Canadian laws were less favorable to them. This Court nonetheless affirmed:

> "We have no occasion to enquire by what law the rights of the parties are governed, as we are of the opinion that, under any view of that question, it lay within the discretion of the District Court to decline to assume jurisdiction over the controversy. . . . '[The] court will not take cognizance of the case if justice would be as well done by remitting the parties to their home forum.' "

The Court further stated that "[t]here was no basis for the contention that the District Court abused its discretion."

It is true that *Canada Malting* was decided before *Gilbert*, and that the doctrine of *forum non conveniens* was not fully crystallized until our decision in that case. However, *Gilbert* in no way affects the validity of *Canada Malting*. Indeed, by holding that the central focus of the *forum non conveniens* inquiry is convenience, *Gilbert* implicitly recognized that dismissal may not be barred solely because of the possibility of an unfavorable change in law. Under *Gilbert*, dismissal will ordinarily be appropriate where trial in the plaintiff's chosen forum imposes a heavy burden on the defendant or the court, and where the plaintiff is unable to offer any specific reasons of convenience supporting his choice. If substantial weight were given to the possibility of an unfavorable change in law, however, dismissal might be barred even where trial in the chosen forum was plainly inconvenient.

The Court of Appeals' decision is inconsistent with this Court's earlier *forum non conveniens* decisions in another respect. Those decisions have repeatedly emphasized the need to retain flexibility. In *Gilbert*, the Court refused to identify specific circumstances "which will justify or require either grant or denial of remedy." * * * If central emphasis were placed on any one factor, the *forum non conveniens* doctrine would lose much of the very flexibility that makes it so valuable.

In fact, if conclusive or substantial weight were given to the possibility of a change in law, the *forum non conveniens* doctrine would become virtually useless. Jurisdiction and venue requirements are often easily satisfied. As a result, many plaintiffs are able to choose from among several forums. Ordinarily, these plaintiffs will select that forum whose choice-of-law rules are most advantageous. Thus, if the possibility of an unfavorable change in substantive law is given substantial weight in the *forum non conveniens* inquiry, dismissal would rarely be proper. * * *

The Court of Appeals' approach is not only inconsistent with the purpose of the *forum non conveniens* doctrine, but also poses substantial practical problems. If the possibility of a change in law were given substantial weight, deciding motions to dismiss on the ground of *forum non conveniens* would become quite difficult. Choice-of-law analysis would become extremely important, and the courts would frequently be required to interpret the law of foreign jurisdictions. First, the trial court would have to determine what law would apply if the case were tried in the chosen forum, and what law would apply if the case were tried in the alternative forum. It would then have to compare the rights, remedies, and procedures available under the law that would be applied in each forum. Dismissal would be appropriate only if the court concluded that the law applied by the alternative forum is as favorable to the plaintiff as that of the chosen forum. The doctrine of *forum non conveniens*, however, is designed in part to help courts avoid conducting complex exercises in comparative law. As we stated in *Gilbert*, the public interest factors point towards dismissal where the court would be required to "untangle problems in conflict of laws, and in law foreign to itself."

Upholding the decision of the Court of Appeals would result in other practical problems. At least where the foreign plaintiff named an American manufacturer as defendant, a court could not dismiss the case on grounds of *forum non conveniens* where dismissal might lead to an unfavorable change in law. The American courts, which are already extremely attractive to foreign plaintiffs, would become even more attractive. The flow of litigation into the United States would increase and further congest already crowded courts.

The Court of Appeals based its decision, at least in part, on an analogy between dismissals on grounds of *forum non conveniens* and transfers between federal courts pursuant to § 1404(a). In *Van Dusen v. Barrack*, 376 U.S. 612 (1964), this Court ruled that a § 1404(a) transfer should not result in a change in the applicable law. Relying on dictum in an earlier Third Circuit opinion interpreting *Van Dusen*, the court below held that that principle is also applicable to a dismissal on *forum non conveniens* grounds. However, § 1404(a) transfers are different than dismissals on the ground of *forum non conveniens*.

Congress enacted § 1404(a) to permit change of venue between federal courts. Although the statute was drafted in accordance with the doctrine of *forum non conveniens*, it was intended to be a revision rather than a codification of the common law. District courts were given more discretion to transfer under § 1404(a) than they had to dismiss on grounds of *forum non conveniens*.

The reasoning employed in *Van Dusen v. Barrack* is simply inapplicable to dismissals on grounds of *forum non conveniens*. That case did not discuss the common-law doctrine. Rather, it focused on "the construction and application" of § 1404(a). Emphasizing the remedial purpose of the statute, *Barrack* concluded that Congress could not have intended a transfer to be accompanied by a change in law. The statute was designed as a "federal housekeeping measure," allowing easy change of venue within a unified federal system. The Court feared that if a change in venue were accompanied by a change in law, forum-shopping parties would take unfair advantage of the relaxed standards for transfer. The rule was necessary to ensure the just and efficient operation of the statute.

We do not hold that the possibility of an unfavorable change in law should *never* be a relevant consideration in a *forum non conveniens* inquiry. Of course, if the remedy provided by the alternative forum is so clearly inadequate or unsatisfactory that it is no remedy at all, the unfavorable change in law may be given substantial weight; the district court may conclude that dismissal would not be in the interest of justice.[22] In these cases, however, the remedies that would be provided by the Scottish courts do not fall within this category. Although the relatives of the decedents may not be able to rely on a strict liability theory, and although their potential damages award may be smaller, there is no danger that they will be deprived of any remedy or treated unfairly.

III

The Court of Appeals also erred in rejecting the District Court's *Gilbert* analysis. The Court of Appeals stated that more weight should have been given to the plaintiff's choice of forum, and criticized the District Court's analysis of the private and public interests. However, the District Court's decision regarding the deference due plaintiff's choice of forum was appropriate. Furthermore, we do not believe that the District Court abused its discretion in weighing the private and public interests.

---

22. At the outset of any *forum non conveniens* inquiry, the court must determine whether there exists an alternative forum. Ordinarily, this requirement will be satisfied when the defendant is "amenable to process" in the other jurisdiction. *Gilbert,* 330 U.S., at 506–507. In rare circumstances, however, where the remedy offered by the other forum is clearly unsatisfactory, the other forum may not be an adequate alternative, and the initial requirement may not be satisfied. Thus, for example, dismissal would not be appropriate where the alternative forum does not permit litigation of the subject matter of the dispute. Cf. *Phoenix Canada Oil Co. Ltd. v. Texaco, Inc.,* 78 F.R.D. 445 (Del.1978) (court refuses to dismiss, where alternative forum is Ecuador, it is unclear whether Ecuadorean tribunal will hear the case, and there is no generally codified Ecuadorean legal remedy for the unjust enrichment and tort claims asserted).

A

The District Court acknowledged that there is ordinarily a strong presumption in favor of the plaintiff's choice of forum, which may be overcome only when the private and public interest factors clearly point towards trial in the alternative forum. It held, however, that the presumption applied with less force when the plaintiff or real parties in interest are foreign.

The District Court's distinction between resident or citizen plaintiffs and foreign plaintiffs is fully justified. In *Koster*, the Court indicated that a plaintiff's choice of forum is entitled to greater deference when the plaintiff has chosen the home forum. When the home forum has been chosen, it is reasonable to assume that this choice is convenient. When the plaintiff is foreign, however, this assumption is much less reasonable. Because the central purpose of any *forum non conveniens* inquiry is to ensure that the trial is convenient, a foreign plaintiff's choice deserves less deference.

B

The *forum non conveniens* determination is committed to the sound discretion of the trial court. It may be reversed only when there has been a clear abuse of discretion; where the court has considered all relevant public and private interest factors, and where its balancing of these factors is reasonable, its decision deserves substantial deference. Here, the Court of Appeals expressly acknowledged that the standard of review was one of abuse of discretion. In examining the District Court's analysis of the public and private interests, however, the Court of Appeals seems to have lost sight of this rule, and substituted its own judgment for that of the District Court.

(1)

In analyzing the private interest factors, the District Court stated that the connections with Scotland are "overwhelming." This characterization may be somewhat exaggerated. Particularly with respect to the question of relative ease of access to sources of proof, the private interests point in both directions. As respondent emphasizes, records concerning the design, manufacture, and testing of the propeller and plane are located in the United States. She would have greater access to sources of proof relevant to her strict liability and negligence theories if trial were held here. However, the District Court did not act unreasonably in concluding that fewer evidentiary problems would be posed if the trial were held in Scotland. A large proportion of the relevant evidence is located in Great Britain.

The Court of Appeals found that the problems of proof could not be given any weight because Piper and Hartzell failed to describe with specificity the evidence they would not be able to obtain if trial were held in the United States. It suggested that defendants seeking *forum non conveniens* dismissal must submit affidavits identifying the witnesses they would call and the testimony these witnesses would provide if the trial were held in the alternative forum. Such detail is not necessary. Piper and Hartzell have moved for dismissal precisely because many crucial witnesses are located beyond the reach of compulsory process, and thus are difficult to identify or interview. Requiring extensive investigation would defeat the purpose of their motion. Of course, defendants must provide enough information to enable the District Court to balance the parties' interests. Our examination of the record convinces us that sufficient information was provided here. Both Piper and Hartzell submitted affidavits describing the evidentiary problems they would face if the trial were held in the United States.

The District Court correctly concluded that the problems posed by the inability to implead potential third-party defendants clearly supported holding the trial in Scotland. Joinder of the pilot's estate, Air Navigation, and McDonald is critical to the presentation of petitioners' defense. If Piper and Hartzell can show that the accident was caused not by a design defect, but rather by the negligence of the pilot, the plane's owners, or the charter company, they will be relieved of all liability. It is true, of course, that if Hartzell and Piper were found liable after a trial in the United States, they could institute an action for indemnity or contribution against these parties in Scotland. It would be far more convenient, however, to resolve all claims in one trial. The Court of Appeals rejected this argument. Forcing petitioners to rely on actions for indemnity or contributions would be "burdensome" but not "unfair." Finding that trial in the plaintiff's chosen forum would be burdensome, however, is sufficient to support dismissal on grounds of *forum non conveniens*.

(2)

The District Court's review of the factors relating to the public interest was also reasonable. On the basis of its choice-of-law analysis, it concluded that if the case were tried in the Middle District of Pennsylvania, Pennsylvania law would apply to Piper and Scottish law to Hartzell. It stated that a trial involving two sets of laws would be confusing to the jury. It also noted its own lack of familiarity with Scottish law. Consideration of these problems was clearly appropriate under *Gilbert*; in that case we explicitly held that the need to apply foreign law pointed towards dismissal. The Court of Appeals found that the District Court's choice-of-law analysis was incorrect, and that American law would apply to both Hartzell and Piper. Thus, lack of familiarity with foreign law would not be a problem. Even if the Court of Appeals' conclusion is correct, however, all other public interest factors favored trial in Scotland.

Scotland has a very strong interest in this litigation. The accident occurred in its airspace. All of the decedents were Scottish. Apart from Piper and Hartzell, all potential plaintiffs and defendants are either Scottish or English. As we stated in *Gilbert*, there is "a local interest in having localized controversies decided at home." Respondent argues that

American citizens have an interest in ensuring that American manufacturers are deterred from producing defective products, and that additional deterrence must be obtained if Piper and Hartzell were tried in the United States, where they could be sued on the basis of both negligence and strict liability. However, the incremental deterrence that would be gained if this trial were held in an American court is likely to be insignificant. The American interest in this accident is simply not sufficient to justify the enormous commitment of judicial time and resources that would inevitably be required if the case were to be tried here.

IV

The Court of Appeals erred in holding that the possibility of an unfavorable change in law bars dismissal on the ground of *forum non conveniens*. It also erred in rejecting the District Court's *Gilbert* analysis. The District Court properly decided that the presumption in favor of the respondent's forum choice applied with less than maximum force because the real parties in interest are foreign. It did not act unreasonably in deciding that the private interests pointed towards trial in Scotland. Nor did it act unreasonably in deciding that the public interests favored trial in Scotland. Thus, the judgment of the Court of Appeals is

Reversed.

Notes and Questions

1. Forum Non Conveniens *and Reasonable Jurisdiction.* The *forum non conveniens* doctrine is an important tool for courts faced with problems of concurrent jurisdiction. Rather than employ the restrictive statutory analysis of *American Banana* or the jurisdictional balancing test of *Timberlane*, *Piper* used *forum non conveniens* as a factually-oriented test to evaluate the reasonableness of one jurisdiction against another. Note that there was no doubt in *Piper* that the federal court in Pennsylvania had adjudicatory jurisdiction over both Piper and Hartzell. Piper and Hartzell (though apparently not the pilot's estate, A.V. Navigation, and McDonald) could be sued in Pennsylvania. The question in the case was whether, in the trial court's opinion, it was unreasonable to try them there.

2. Forum Non Conveniens *and Judicial Discretion.* *Piper* established how discretionary may be a trial court's power to dismiss on *forum non conveniens* grounds. In effect the Supreme Court asks a trial court to weigh public and private interests reasonably and to determine the existence of an adequate alternative forum. Under what circumstances may an appeals court review and reverse a trial court's decision which is so based on the fact-specific nature of a particular case? *In re* Disaster at Riyadh Airport, Saudi Arabia, 540 F.Supp. 1141 (D.D.C.1982), and Nai–Chao v. Boeing Co., 555 F.Supp. 9 (N.D.Cal.1982), show trial courts willing to dismiss cases involving foreign plaintiffs where an alternative forum is adequate and where no overwhelming U.S. forum interest outweighs the problems of federal court congestion and overrides local interests in the case at hand. However, in *In re* Air Disaster Near Bombay, India on January 1, 1978, 531 F.Supp. 1175

(W.D.Wash.1982), the trial court denied a motion for a *forum non conveniens* dismissal, ruling there was no adequate alternative forum.

3. *The Foreign Plaintiff. Forum non conveniens* cases are sometimes ironic. In a typical case, a "far-away" foreign plaintiff chooses voluntarily to bring an action in the United States. The U.S. defendant then asserts that the U.S. court is not a "convenient" site for the action, even though it is the foreign plaintiff who chose the "inconvenient" forum otherwise apparently "home" to the defendant. Does the irony demonstrate the importance of public interest factors when a court decides a *forum non conveniens* request?

Piper held that less deference should be granted to a plaintiff's choice of a U.S. forum when the plaintiff is foreign. However, does it matter that *Piper* "did not consider the jurisdictional provisions of various FCN [friendship, commerce, and navigation] treaties which grant foreign plaintiffs equal access to American courts and apply with the force of statutory law"? Note, Maria A. Mazzola, "*Forum Non Conveniens* and Foreign Plaintiffs: Addressing the Unanswered Questions of *Reyno*," 6 *Fordham Journal of International Law* 577, 604 (1983).

Should U.S. courts be more ready to hear a foreigner's complaint if the allegation involves a violation of international human rights law? See Kathryn Lee Boyd, "The Inconvenience of Victims: Abolishing Forum Non Conveniens in U.S. Human Rights Litigation," 39 *Virginia Journal of International Law* 41 (1998).

4. Forum Non Conveniens *and International Lawyering Tactics.* Look, too, at *Piper* as a good example of lawyering tactics in international litigation. Plaintiffs' lawyer made the first move, using his secretary to commence the action in a California state court on her home turf far away from the accident, the families of the decedents, and most, if not all, possible defendants. From then on, the tactical moves were those of defendants' lawyers. First, the case was removed to federal court in California where service on Hartzell was quashed. Second, the case was transferred to federal court in Pennsylvania, nearer Piper and Hartzell and farther from plaintiffs' attorney. Third, defendants persuaded the trial court and the Supreme Court to dismiss the case on *forum non conveniens* grounds. What likelihood was there that the California lawyer who initiated the action in California state court would follow the case all the way back to Scotland? Could the California attorney even have hoped to litigate the case in the United Kingdom? From a lawyering point of view, can the *Piper* case be viewed as the attempt of a California lawyer to use liberal U.S. jurisdictional rules to "capture" a litigation with little California connection being blocked by lawyers for Piper and Hartzell who use removal, transfer, and *forum non conveniens* rules as a way to "return" the case to Scotland where the case is most intimately connected? How much more "advanced" is this procedure than what went on in *American Banana* 72 years before?

5. *The States and* Forum Non Conveniens. The Texas Supreme Court has held that the Texas legislature abolished the doctrine of *forum non conveniens* as long ago as 1913. Dow Chemical Co. v. Castro Alfaro, 786 S.W.2d 674 (Tex.1990), *cert. denied,* 498 U.S. 1024, 111 S.Ct. 671, 112 L.Ed.2d 663 (1991). This curious judgment evoked four vigorous dissents, one by Justice Cook:

Like turn-of-the century wildcatters, the plaintiffs in this case searched all across the nation for a place to make their claims. Through three courts they moved, filing their lawsuits on one coast and then on the other. By each of those courts the plaintiffs were rejected, and so they continued their search for a more willing forum. Their efforts are finally rewarded. Today they hit pay dirt in Texas.

No reason exists, in law or in policy, to support their presence in this state. The legislature adopted within the statute the phrase "may be enforced" to permit plaintiffs to sue in Texas, irrespective of where they live or where the cause of action arose. The legislature did not adopt this statute, however, to remove from our courts all discretion to dismiss. To use the statute to sweep away, completely and finally, a common law doctrine painstakingly developed over the years is to infuse the statute with a power not contained in the words. Properly read, the statute is asymmetrical. Although it confers upon the plaintiffs an absolute right to bring claims in our courts, it does not impose upon our courts an absolute responsibility to entertain those claims.

Even if the statute supported the court's interpretation, however, I would remain unwilling to join in the opinion. The decision places too great a burden on defendants who are citizens of our state because, by abolishing *forum non conveniens*, the decision exposes our citizens to the claims of any plaintiff, no matter how distant from Texas is that plaintiff's home or cause of action. The interest of Texas in these disputes is likely to be as slight as the relationship of the plaintiffs to Texas. The interest of other nations, on the other hand, is likely to be substantial. For these reasons, I fear the decision allows assertions of jurisdiction by Texas courts that are so unfair and unreasonable as to violate the due process clause of the federal constitution.

Id. at 697. The Texas legislature responded to *Dow Chemical* by enacting a limited *forum non conveniens* statute in 1993. See Louise Ellen Teitz, *Transnational Litigation* § 3–5, at 123–25 (1996).

Not only the due process clause, but also federal common law might pose a problem for the majority in *Dow Chemical*. As we see below in the *Sabbatino Case*, the federal courts are able to elaborate a federal common law in certain areas of special concern to national interests such as foreign affairs. See Gary Born, "Forum Non Conveniens Held Unavailable Under Texas Law," 18 *International Business Lawyer* 392 (1990). Moreover, in diversity cases, the federal courts will apply the federal *forum non conveniens* doctrine, even in Texas. See Villar v. Crowley Maritime Corp., 780 F.Supp. 1467, 1483–85 (S.D.Tex.1992). However, in American Dredging Co. v. Miller, 510 U.S. 443, 114 S.Ct. 981, 127 L.Ed.2d 285 (1994), the Supreme Court passed by an opportunity to help nationalize the doctrine, holding that in admiralty cases states acting under the Jones Act and the "savings to suiters clause," which gives concurrent jurisdiction to U.S. state courts in certain admiralty actions, do not have to apply the federal *forum non conveniens* doctrine. Justice Scalia's majority opinion concluded that "maritime commerce in general does not require a uniform rule of *forum non conveniens*." *Id.* at 456, 114 S.Ct. at 990, 127 L.Ed.2d at 299. In dissent, Justice Kennedy for himself and Justice Thomas disapproved, believing "that *forum non conveniens* is an established feature of the general maritime law." *Id.* at 466, 114 S.Ct. at 993, 127 L.Ed.2d at 305. *American Dredging* involved only U.S. actors, however, and the Supreme Court might reach "a different result if those who raise the *forum non conveniens* objection are of foreign nationality." *Id.* at 469, 114 S.Ct. at 996, 127 L.Ed.2d at 307.

MARK W. JANIS, "THE DOCTRINE OF FORUM NON CONVENIENS AND THE BHOPAL CASE"

34 *Netherlands International Law Review* 192 (1987).

1. The Doctrine of *Forum Non Conveniens*

It is generally acknowledged that a law review article by Paxton Blair in 1929,[3] popularized the term *forum non conveniens* in American law. To what degree the term denominated an already extant practice is not an easy question. Characterizing the existing American cases, Blair referred to Moliere's M. Jourdain: "he had been speaking prose all his life without knowing it." Subsequent commentators have argued, however, that Blair overestimated the foundation laid by the early case law.

Blair relied heavily on a 1926 Scottish case heard in the House of Lords, *Société du Gaz Paris v. Société Anonyme de Navigation "Les Armateurs Français."* There the court held:

> If in the whole circumstances of the case it be discovered that there is a real unfairness to one of the suitors in permitting the choice of a forum which is not the natural or proper forum, either on the ground of convenience of trial or the residence or domicile of parties, or of its being either the *locus contractus,* or the *locus solutionis,* then the doctrine of *forum non conveniens* is properly applied.

Despite the term's Latin rendering, it does not seem that Scots law borrowed the term from the Continent. It is possible that the ancestor of *forum non conveniens* may be the Scottish doctrine of *forum non competens*, a plea used as long ago as 1610, "which normally was directed to a lack of jurisdiction, [but which] was [also] sustained in cases where the jurisdiction seemed clear but the parties were non-residents and trial in Scotland would have been inconvenient." In any event, *forum non conveniens* appears to have first entered modern cases in 1873 in the Scots case, *Macadam v. Macadam*. Within a few years, the term was also to be seen, albeit infrequently, in English cases where it was viewed as a development in the procedural law concerning abuse of process. * * *

The settled establishment of the doctrine of *forum non conveniens* in American law came in 1947, in a pair of United States Supreme Court decisions: *Gulf Oil Corp. v. Gilbert* and *Koster v. Lumbermens Mutual Casualty Co.* * * *

3. P. Blair, "The Doctrine of Forum Non Conveniens in Anglo–American Law", 29 Columbia LR (1929) p. 1.

The *forum non conveniens* doctrine was partly transformed into United States federal law not long after the *Gilbert* and *Koster* cases. In 1948 Congress enacted the federal transfer statute which provides: "For the convenience of parties and witnesses, in the interest of justice, a district court may transfer any civil action to any other district or division where it might have been brought." So, in cases on facts like *Gilbert* and *Koster* where suit has been brought in one federal district court and the defendant wishes to move the action to another federal district court, the federal transfer statute rather than the judicial doctrine of *forum non conveniens* ought to be employed.

However, the federal transfer statute applies only to the transfer of cases within the United States federal judicial system. So, when defendants seek to move from one state court to another state court, or from a United States state or federal court to the court of a foreign country, reliance upon the judicial doctrine of *forum non conveniens* is still appropriate. This was, for example, true in the most important United States Supreme Court case to be decided on *forum non conveniens* grounds since the *Gilbert/Koster* pair of cases in 1947, i.e., *Piper Aircraft Co. v. Reyno.* * * *

* * * It is against the background of *Gilbert* and *Koster* and, especially *Piper*, that the employment of *forum non conveniens* in *Bhopal* must be surveyed.

2.   The Bhopal Case

The industrial accident at the Union Carbide plant in Bhopal, India on December 3, 1984, released methyl isocyanate gas which killed more than 2,000 people and injured about 200,000. Newspaper investigations of the tragedy indicated that there were numerous violations of the operating codes established both by the company operating the plant, Union Carbide India Limited, and its parent company, Union Carbide Corporation. There may well have been negligence not only by those engaged in making the lethal chemical used in pesticides but also by the Indian governmental bodies charged with setting and enforcing safety standards. The factual pattern of the disaster and the allocation of legal responsibility for it are incredibly tangled webs.

Immediately after the accident, some American lawyers made an unseemly rush to Bhopal. As the *New York Times* reported: "Right behind the stream of scientists, executives, officials, aid givers, and others who have come to this central Indian city after the gas leak last week are American lawyers, members of a breed of legal specialists seen by some as ambulance chasers and by others as champions of the individual against the corporation and of industrial safety and consumer protection." * * *

However, not only American lawyers were interested in suing Union Carbide in American courts. On March 9, 1985, the *New York Times* reported that the Indian Government had also decided to sue on behalf of the Indian victims in United States courts in order "to secure higher compensation and also because Union Carbide has to share responsibility for the gas leak at its Indian subsidiary." On March 29, 1985, the Indian Government enacted the Bhopal Gas Leak Disaster (Processing of Claims) Act, a statute which vested in the Indian Government the exclusive right to represent the Indian plaintiffs in the Bhopal case in India and elsewhere. On April 8, 1985, pursuant to the Act, the Indian Government filed its own claims against Union Carbide in the American courts.

The Indian Government claims, along with some 144 lawsuits brought privately, were all consolidated on June 28, 1985, in a consolidated complaint filed in the federal district court for the Southern District of New York. * * *

With the filing of the Indian Government claims, the *Bhopal* case showed the peculiar circumstance of a government arguing that its own courts were less preferable than those of a foreign State for the resolution of disputes touching on both legal systems. When the defendant, Union Carbide, raised the *forum non conveniens* argument, the Indian Government was in the even more awkward posture of contending (as part of the Plaintiffs' Executive Committee) that the Indian courts were actually inadequate for handling the Bhopal claims. Although both the trial court and the appeals court recognized that their *forum non conveniens* analysis was to be conducted pursuant to the holdings in *Gilbert* and *Piper*, neither the 1947 cases nor the 1981 case faced the question of whether the arguably more convenient forum was up to the task of adequately adjudicating the dispute at hand. It had been assumed that the courts of Virginia (in *Gilbert*), Illinois (in *Koster*), and the United Kingdom (in *Piper*), were just as sophisticated as the courts in which the *forum non conveniens* dismissal was sought.

In *Bhopal*, both the District Court and the Court of Appeals concluded that the Indian courts could properly adjudicate the accident cases. Moreover, while the District Court imposed certain United States procedural guarantees on the Indian litigation, the Court of Appeals, even more respectful towards the foreign proceedings, modified the trial court's order and imposed none.

In reviewing the competence of the Indian courts, the District Court weighed the testimony of an American law professor, Marc Galanter, an expert on Indian law opposing the adequacy of the Indian legal system against the testimony of two senior Indian advocates, N. A. Palkhivala, formerly Ambassador of India to the United States, and J. B. Dadachanji arguing in favor of the Indian system. The court thought the conclusions of Professor Galanter "far less persuasive than those of" the two Indian lawyers. The District Court's opinion was summarized and approved by the Court of Appeal:

> The Indian judiciary was found by the court to be a developed, independent and progressive one, which has demonstrated its capability of circumventing long delays and backlogs prevalent in the Indian courts' handling of ordinary cases by devising special expediting procedures in extraordinary cases, such as by directing its High

Court to hear them on a daily basis, appointing special tribunals to handle them, and assigning daily hearing duties to a single judge. [The District Court judge] found that Indian courts have competently dealt with complex technological issues. Since the Bhopal Act provides that the case may be treated speedily, effectively and to the best advantage of the claimants, and since the Union of India represents the claimants, the prosecution of the claims is expected to be adequately staffed by the Attorney General or Solicitor General of India.

The tort law of India, which is derived from common law and British precedent, was found to be suitable for resolution of legal issues arising in cases involving highly complex technology. Moreover, Indian courts would be in a superior position to construe and apply applicable Indian laws and standards than would courts of the United States. Third parties may be interpleaded under Order 1, Rule 10(2) of the Indian Code of Civil Procedure, and defendants may seek contribution from third parties. The absence in India of a class action procedure comparable to that in federal courts here was found not to deprive the plaintiffs of a remedy, in view of existing Indian legal authorization for "representative" suits under Order 1, Rule 8 of the Indian Code of Civil Procedure, which would permit an Indian court to create representative classes. Judge Keenan further found that the absence of juries and contingent fee arrangements in India would not deprive the claimants of an adequate remedy. * * *

Having determined that Indian courts were an acceptable alternative to American courts for the adjudication of the Bhopal suits, the District and Circuit Courts turned to the weighing of private and public interest factors at the heart of any *forum non conveniens* inquiry. Both courts follow *Piper* in holding that since the plaintiffs in *Bhopal* were foreign, their choice of an American court was due less deference than had they been United States citizens seeking to sue at home. Given the factual situation surrounding the Bhopal accident, the courts had little difficulty in deciding that the claims arising from it should be decided in India, not America.

Looking first at the private interest factors, the District Court compared *Bhopal* to *Piper* where private interests pointed in two ways: "By contrast, this Court finds that the private interests point strongly one way"—India. The Circuit Court agreed:

> In short, the plant has been constructed and managed by Indians in India. No Americans were employed at the plant at the time of the accident. In the five years from 1980 to 1984, although there were more than 1,000 Indians employed at the plant, only one American was employed there and he left in 1982. No Americans visited the plant for more than one year prior to the accident, and during the 5–year period before the accident the communications between the plant and the United States were almost non-existent.

The vast majority of material witnesses and documentary proof bearing on causation of and liability for the accident is located in India, not the United States, and would be more accessible to an Indian court than to a United States court. The records are almost entirely in Hindi or other Indian languages, understandable to an Indian court without translation. The witnesses for the most part do not speak English but Indian languages, understood by an Indian court but not by an American court. These witnesses could be required to appear in an Indian court but not in a court of the United States. Although witnesses in the United States could not be subpoenaed to appear in India, they are comparatively few in number and most are employed by [Union Carbide Corporation] which, as a party would produce them in India, with lower overall transportation costs than if the parties were to attempt to bring hundreds of Indian witnesses to the United States. Lastly, Judge Keenan properly concluded that an Indian court would be in a better position to direct and supervise a viewing of the Bhopal plant, which was sealed after the accident. Such a viewing could be of help to a court in determining liability issues.

Similarly, both courts decided that public interest factors tilted towards trying the case in India. Endorsing the findings of the District Court, the Circuit Court ruled:

After a thorough review, the district court concluded that the public interest concerns, like the private ones, also weigh heavily in favor of India as the situs for trial and disposition of the cases. The accident and all the relevant events occurred in India. The victims, over 200,000 in number, are citizens of India and located there. The witnesses are almost entirely Indian citizens. The Union of India has a greater interest than does the United States in facilitating the trial and adjudication of the victims' claims. Despite the contentions of plaintiffs and amici that it would be in the public interest to avoid a "double standard" by requiring an American parent corporation (UCC) to submit to the jurisdiction of American courts, India has a stronger countervailing interest in adjudicating the claims in its courts according to its standards rather than having American values and standards of care imposed upon it.

India's interest is increased by the fact that it has for years treated UCIL as an Indian national, subjecting it to intensive regulations and governmental supervision of the construction, development and operation of the Bhopal plant, its emissions, water and air pollution, and safety precautions. Numerous Indian government officials have regularly conducted on-site inspections of the plant and approved its machinery and equipment, including its facilities for storage of the lethal methyl isocyanate gas that escaped and caused the disaster giving rise to the claims. Thus India has considered the plant to be an Indian one and the disaster to be an Indian problem. It therefore has a deep interest in ensuring compliance with its safety standards. Moreover, plaintiffs have conceded that in view of India's strong interest and its greater contacts with the plant, its operation, its employees, and the victims of the accident, the law of India, as the place where the tort occurred, will undoubtedly govern. In contrast, the American interests are relatively minor. Indeed, a long trial of the 145 cases here would unduly burden an already overburdened court, involving both jury hardship and heavy expense. It would face the court with numerous practical difficulties, including the most impossible task of attempting to understand extensive relevant Indian regulations published in a foreign language and the slow process of receiving testimony of scores of witnesses through interpreters.

The incongruity of finding that the public interest of India called for trying the *Bhopal* case in India even when the Indian Government sought to have it tried in America was rectified between the District Court opinion and that of the Circuit Court. The Government of India decided to support the judgment of the District Court. The private plaintiffs, however, continued in their opposition to the *forum non conveniens* dismissal. * * *

In a world increasingly filled with transactions and, sadly, accidents touching on more than one country, the need to properly allocate international judicial business becomes even more pressing. In time perhaps, public international law will help provide more answers to questions about the allocation of judicial competence between nations by the framing and application of international conventions. Until then, and, of course, in some cases even thereafter, States will have to moderate their extensions of jurisdiction to matters involving foreign countries by employing notions of comity and good sense. *Forum non conveniens* is one such useful notion, and it was rightly applied in the United States in the case of *Bhopal*.

Notes and Questions

1. *The Aftermath of the* Bhopal Case. Bi v. Union Carbide Chemicals & Plastics Co., 984 F.2d 582 (2d Cir.1993), an action brought by individual Indian victims of the Bhopal tragedy who sought to supplement the relief they ultimately won in the Indian courts, contained an interesting account of the aftermath of the *Bhopal Case*. In 1989, the Indian Supreme Court approved a settlement between the government of India representing all the victims and Union Carbide for $470 million. The Indian Supreme Court in a related decision that year also "upheld the constitutional validity of the Bhopal Act and confirmed the Indian Government's exclusive authority to compromise all claims arising out of the Bhopal disaster." *Id.* at 584. In 1990, Bi and another, class representatives for some of the Indian victims, filed suits against Union Carbide in Texas state court, arguing that the Indian government had a conflict of interest in trying to represent victims and that the settlement in India was too low. Union Carbide removed the suits to U.S. federal court in Texas, and the suits were then transferred to U.S. federal court in New York. The Southern District dismissed both

actions under *forum non conveniens,* and the Second Circuit affirmed: "We hold that when a recognized democracy determines that the interests of the victims of a mass tort that occurred within its borders will be best served if the foreign government exclusively represents the victims in courts around the world, we will not pass judgment on that determination * * * ." *Id.* at 586.

2. *The Adequacy of the Foreign Legal System.* The U.S. Supreme Court chose not to review *Bhopal,* Executive Committee Members v. Union of India, 484 U.S. 871, 108 S.Ct. 199, 98 L.Ed.2d 150 (1987), letting stand the opinion of the Second Circuit. Thus, the Supreme Court did not consider the adequacy of the foreign legal system, a consideration also left unaddressed in its two key *forum non conveniens* decisions, *Gilbert* and *Piper.* Looking at the opinions of the trial court and the appellate court in *Bhopal,* we can see that they at least used another balancing test to evaluate the plausibility of justice being done in a foreign court, weighing here the testimony of conflicting expert witnesses. Is this an example, once again, of the judicial discretion built into *forum non conveniens*? In Bhatnagar v. Surrendra Overseas Ltd., 52 F.3d 1220 (3d Cir.1995), the Third Circuit held that the potential for long delay in the Indian legal system was a permissible ground for denying a motion of *forum non conveniens.*

3. Forum Non Conveniens *and* International Shoe. Note that in the United States *forum non conveniens* is considered only if the court already has personal and subject matter jurisdiction over the defendants and the transaction. It is no coincidence that *forum non conveniens* formally entered into federal law in 1947, two years after International Shoe Co. v. State of Washington, 326 U.S. 310, 66 S.Ct. 154, 90 L.Ed. 95 (1945), extended the jurisdictional reach of state courts. After *International Shoe* plaintiffs had more choice about their courts. *Forum non conveniens* and the federal transfer statute moderated the new power of plaintiffs over forum selection.

Forum non conveniens and the federal transfer statute are also used in some U.S. cases where adjudicatory jurisdiction is not based on a specific activity in the forum related to the cause of action (as in *International Shoe*), but instead is based on "systematic and continuous" activities of a corporate defendant at a place other than its headquarters or place of incorporation. Thus, in *Piper,* Reyno obtained jurisdiction in California over Piper Aircraft Co., a Pennsylvania corporation, and was able to serve process in Pennsylvania on Hartzell Propeller, Inc., an Ohio corporation.

4. *Judge-made Procedural Law.* In *Gilbert* the Supreme Court rested the doctrine of *forum non conveniens* on the foundations of a court's "inherent power." *Forum non conveniens* is an excellent example of a procedure-facilitating rule based on judge-made common law. Contrast the source of the *forum non conveniens* doctrine with the statutory source of a rule achieving similar goals: the 1948 federal transfer statute, 28 U.S.C. § 1404(a). Would anything be gained (or lost) if *forum non conveniens* were codified? Is a judge-made rule more responsive to changing notions of comity, *e.g.,* able to respond more readily to the development of case law in other countries accommodating (or not) conflicts of jurisdiction?

5. *International Mechanisms for the Resolution of Jurisdictional Conflicts.* Could a treaty or even an international court or panel help reconcile

conflicts of jurisdiction better than *ad hoc* national judicial decision making? How might such a treaty or court be fashioned?

C. FOREIGN SOVEREIGN IMMUNITY

A variety of legal rules shield foreign sovereigns and their acts from the scrutiny of national courts. Although less pervasive nowadays than before, these rules generally have been grounded on the principle or policy that to implead foreign sovereigns before local courts or to challenge the legality of foreign sovereign acts could upset friendly relations between states. It has been reckoned that questions relating to the jurisdictional immunities of foreign sovereigns figure more before national courts than do any other questions of international law. Leo J. Bouchez, "The Nature and Scope of State Immunity from Jurisdiction and Execution," 10 *Netherlands Yearbook of International Law* 3, 4 (1979). In 1989, "a fairly ordinary year" for foreign sovereign immunities litigation in the United States, there were altogether one Supreme Court decision, 19 reported judgments of federal appeals courts, 20 reported and seven unpublished but computer-available federal district court decisions, and one published state appellate court judgment relating to questions of foreign sovereign immunity. ABA Section of International Law and Practice, *Suing Foreign States: Newsletter of the Committee on Foreign Sovereign Immunity*, Vol. 1, No. 1, at 1, 10–15 (Spring 1990). In the United States, both the doctrine of sovereign immunity and the act of state doctrine examined in Part D may be said to be grounded on the judgment in 1812 of Chief Justice John Marshall in the case of *The Schooner Exchange*.

THE SCHOONER EXCHANGE v. MCFADDON

11 U.S. (7 Cranch) 116, 3 L.Ed. 287 (1812).

This being a cause in which the sovereign right claimed by Napoleon, the reigning emperor of the French, and the political relations between the United States and France, were involved, it was, upon the suggestion of the Attorney General, ordered to a hearing in preference to other causes which stood before it on the docket.

It was an appeal from the sentence of the Circuit Court of the United States, for the district of Pennsylvania, which reversed the sentence of the District Court, and ordered the vessel to be restored to the libellants.

The case was this—on the 24th of August, 1811, *John McFaddon & William Greetham*, of the State of Maryland, filed their libel in the District Court of the United States, for the District of Pennsylvania, against the *Schooner Exchange*, setting forth that they were her sole owners, on the 27th of October, 1809, when she sailed from Baltimore, bound to St. Sebastians, in Spain. That while lawfully and peaceably pursuing her voyage, she was on the 30th of December, 1810, violently and forcibly taken by certain persons, acting under the decrees and orders of Napoleon, *Emperor of the French*, out of the custody of the libellants, and of their captain and agent, and was disposed of by those persons, or some of them, in violation of the rights of the libellants, and of the law of nations in that behalf. That she had been brought into the port of Philadelphia, and was then in the jurisdiction of that court, in possession of a certain *Dennis M. Begon*, her reputed captain or master. That no sentence or decree of condemnation had been pronounced against her, by any court of competent jurisdiction; but that the property of the libellants in her, remained unchanged and in full force. They therefore prayed the usual process of the court, to attach the vessel, and that she might be restored to them.

MARSHALL, *CH. J.*, delivered the opinion of the Court as follows:

This case involves the very delicate and important inquiry, whether an American citizen can assert, in an American court, a title to an armed national vessel found within the waters of the United States. * * *

The jurisdiction of courts is a branch of that which is possessed by the nation as an independent sovereign power.

The jurisdiction of the nation within its own territory is necessarily exclusive and absolute. It is susceptible of no limitation not imposed by itself. Any restriction upon it, deriving validity from an external source, would imply a diminution of its sovereignty to the extent of the restriction, and an investment of that sovereignty to the same extent in that power which could impose such restrictions.

All exceptions, therefore, to the full and complete power of a nation within its own territories, must be traced up to the consent of the nation itself. They can flow from no other legitimate source.

This consent may be either express or implied. In the latter case, it is less determinate, exposed more to the uncertainties of construction; but, if understood, not less obligatory.

The world being composed of distinct sovereignties, possessing equal rights and equal independence, whose mutual benefit is promoted by intercourse with each other, and by an interchange of those good offices which humanity dictates and its wants require, all sovereigns have consented to a relaxation in practice, in cases under certain peculiar circumstances, of that absolute and complete jurisdiction within their respective territories which sovereignty confers. * * *

A nation would justly be considered as violating its faith, although that faith might not be expressly plighted, which should suddenly and without previous notice, exercise its territorial powers in a manner not consonant to the usages and received obligations of the civilized world.

This full and absolute territorial jurisdiction being alike the attribute of every sovereign, and being incapable of conferring extra-territorial power, would not seem to contemplate foreign sovereigns nor their sovereign rights as its objects. One sovereign being in no respect amenable to another; and being bound by obligations of the highest character not to degrade the dignity of his nation, by placing himself or its sovereign rights within the jurisdiction of another, can be supposed to enter a foreign territory only under an express license, or in the confidence that the immunities belonging to his independent sovereign station, though not expressly stipulated, are reserved by implication and will be extended to him.

This perfect equality and absolute independence of sovereigns, and this common interest impelling them to mutual intercourse, and an interchange of good offices with each other, have given rise to a class of cases in which every sovereign is understood to waive the exercise of a part of that complete exclusive territorial jurisdiction, which has been stated to be the attribute of every nation. * * *

When private individuals of one nation spread themselves through another as business or caprice may direct, mingling indiscriminately with the inhabitants of that other, or when merchant vessels enter for the purposes of trade, it would be obviously inconvenient and dangerous to society, and would subject the laws to continual infraction, and the government to degradation, if such individuals or merchants did not owe temporary and local allegiance, and were not amenable to the jurisdiction of the country. Nor can the foreign sovereign have any motive for wishing such exemption. His subjects thus passing into foreign countries, are not employed by him, nor are they engaged in national pursuits. Consequently there are powerful motives for not exempting persons of this description from the jurisdiction of the country in which they are found, and no one motive for requiring it. The implied license, therefore, under which they enter can never be construed to grant such exemption.

But in all respects different is the situation of a public armed ship. She constitutes a part of the military force of her nation; acts under the immediate and direct command of the sovereign; is employed by him in national objects. He has many and powerful motives for preventing those objects from being defeated by the interference of a foreign state. Such interference cannot take place without affecting his power and his dignity. The implied license therefore under which such vessel enters a friendly port, may reasonably be construed, and it seems to the Court, ought to be construed, as containing an exemption from the jurisdiction of the sovereign, within whose territory she claims the rites of hospitality.

Upon these principles, by the unanimous consent of nations, a foreigner is amenable to the laws of the place; but certainly in practice, nations have not yet asserted their jurisdiction over the public armed ships of a foreign sovereign entering a port open for their reception. * * *

* * * [T]here is a manifest distinction between the private property of the person who happens to be a prince, and that military force which supports the sovereign power, and maintains the dignity and the independence of a nation. A prince, by acquiring private property in a foreign country, may possibly be considered as subjecting that property to the territorial jurisdiction; he may be considered as so far laying down the

prince, and assuming the character of a private individual; but this he cannot be presumed to do, with respect to any portion of that armed force, which upholds his crown, and the nation he is intrusted to govern. * * *

It seems, then, to the court, to be a principle of public law, that national ships of war, entering the port of a friendly power open for their reception are to be considered as exempted by the consent of that power from its jurisdiction. * * *

If the preceding reasoning be correct, the Exchange, being a public armed ship, in the service of a foreign sovereign, with whom the government of the United States is at peace, having entered an American port open for her reception, on the terms on which ships of war are generally permitted to enter the ports of a friendly power, must be considered as having come into the American territory, under an implied promise, that while necessarily within it, and demeaning herself in a friendly manner, she should be exempt from the jurisdiction of the country.

Notes and Questions

1. *The Historical Context.* In 1812, how anxious would Chief Justice Marshall have been to have the U.S. legal system seize a French warship for the benefit of a private litigant? This was the very year the United States went to war with Great Britain, France's enemy in the Napoleonic Wars. France and England were blockading each other's ports, and American merchant shipping was reaping large profits (and incurring considerable risks) in blockade running. Was it the mission of Marshall both to protect the dignity of France and to bolster the sovereignty of the United States? Notice Marshall's insistence on how "distinct sovereignties" have "equal rights and equal independence."

2. *Sovereigns and the Forms of Jurisdiction.* Note that Marshall distinguished between "the jurisdiction of the courts" and the general jurisdiction "possessed by the nation as an independent sovereign power." Was this distinction an early sign of the development of what we would now call adjudicatory jurisdiction? Was the French government being protected just from the jurisdiction of the courts? Was Marshall's judgment broad enough to encompass protection from U.S. legislative and executive jurisdiction as well?

How similar was Marshall's belief in the "full and absolute territorial jurisdiction" of "every sovereign" to Holmes's belief a century later, in *American Banana* above, that "all legislation is *prima facie* territorial"? Both approaches certainly appear to limit extraterritorial jurisdiction. Why did Marshall make the territorial case so strongly when he meant to upset it with an exception for the warships of foreign sovereigns?

3. *U.S. Law or International Law?* When Marshall wrote that it seems "to be a principle of public law, that national ships of war, entering the port of a friendly power open for their reception, are to be considered as exempted by the consent of that power from its jurisdiction," was he

referring to a "principle" of U.S. law or of international law or of both? A similar confusion or conflation exists in the language of the Foreign Sovereign Immunities Act of 1976 considered below. First, though, is *Victory Transport*, a case that shows development of the foreign sovereign immunity doctrine in the United States between *Schooner Exchange* and the 1976 Act.

VICTORY TRANSPORT, INC. v. COMISARIA GENERAL

336 F.2d 354 (2d Cir.1964), *cert. denied*,
381 U.S. 934, 85 S.Ct. 1763, 14 L.Ed.2d 698 (1965).

J. JOSEPH SMITH, CIRCUIT JUDGE: * * *

The appellant, a branch of the Spanish Ministry of Commerce, voyage-chartered the S.S. Hudson from its owner, the appellee, to transport a cargo of surplus wheat, purchased pursuant to the Agricultural Trade Development and Assistance Act, 7 U.S.C. § 1691 et seq., from Mobile, Alabama to one or two safe Spanish ports. * * *

Appellant's primary contention is that as an arm of the sovereign Government of Spain, it cannot be sued in the courts of the United States without its consent, which it declines to accord in this case. There is certainly a great deal of impressive precedent to support this contention, for the doctrine of the immunity of foreign sovereigns from the jurisdiction of our courts was early entrenched in our law by Chief Justice Marshall's historic decision in The Schooner Exchange v. McFaddon. The doctrine originated in an era of personal sovereignty, when kings could theoretically do no wrong and when the exercise of authority by one sovereign over another indicated hostility or superiority. With the passing of that era, sovereign immunity has been retained by the courts chiefly to avoid possible embarrassment to those responsible for the conduct of the nation's foreign relations. However, because of the dramatic changes in the nature and functioning of sovereigns, particularly in the last half century, the wisdom of retaining the doctrine has been cogently questioned. Growing concern for individual rights and public morality, coupled with the increasing entry of governments into what had previously been regarded as private pursuits, has led a substantial number of nations to abandon the absolute theory of sovereign immunity in favor of a restrictive theory.

Meeting in Brussels in 1926, representatives of twenty nations, including all the major powers except the United States and Russia, signed a convention limiting sovereign immunity in the area of maritime commerce to ships and cargoes employed exclusively for public and non-commercial purposes. After World War II the United States began to restrict immunity by negotiating treaties obligating each contracting party to waive its sovereign immunity for state-controlled enterprises engaged in business activities within the territory of the other party. Fourteen such treaties were negotiated by our State Department in the decade 1948 to 1958. And in 1952 our State Department, in a widely publicized letter from Acting Legal Adviser Jack B. Tate to the Acting Attorney General Philip B. Perlman, announced that the Department would generally adhere to the restrictive theory of sovereign immunity, recognizing immunity for a foreign state's public or sovereign acts (*jure imperii*) but denying immunity to a foreign state's private or commercial acts (*jure gestionis*). * * *

Through the "Tate letter" the State Department has made it clear that its policy is to decline immunity to friendly foreign sovereigns in suits arising from private or commercial activity. But the "Tate letter" offers no guide-lines or criteria for differentiating between a sovereign's private and public acts. Nor have the courts or commentators suggested any satisfactory test. Some have looked to the nature of the transaction, categorizing as sovereign acts only activity which could not be performed by individuals. While this criterion is relatively easy to apply, it ofttimes produces rather astonishing results, such as the holdings of some European courts that purchases of bullets or shoes for the army, the erection of fortifications for defense, or the rental of a house for an embassy, are private acts. Furthermore, this test merely postpones the difficulty, for particular contracts in some instances may be made only by states. Others have looked to the purpose of the transaction, categorizing as *jure imperii* all activities in which the object of performance is public in character. But this test is even more unsatisfactory, for conceptually the modern sovereign always acts for a public purpose. Functionally the criterion is purely arbitrary and necessarily involves the court in projecting personal notions about the proper realm of state functioning. * * *

The purpose of the restrictive theory of sovereign immunity is to try to accommodate the interest of individuals doing business with foreign governments in having their legal rights determined by the courts, with the interest of foreign governments in being free to perform certain political acts without undergoing the embarrassment or hindrance of defending the propriety of such acts before foreign courts. Sovereign immunity is a derogation from the normal exercise of jurisdiction by the courts and should be accorded only in clear cases. Since the State Department's failure or refusal to suggest immunity is significant, we are disposed to deny a claim of sovereign immunity that has not been "recognized and allowed" by the State Department unless it is plain that the activity in question falls within one of the categories of strictly political or public acts about which sovereigns have traditionally been quite sensitive. Such acts are generally limited to the following categories:

    (1) internal administrative acts, such as expulsion of an alien.

    (2) legislative acts, such as nationalization.

    (3) acts concerning the armed forces.

    (4) acts concerning diplomatic activity.

    (5) public loans.

We do not think that the restrictive theory adopted by the State Department requires sacrificing the interests of private litigants to international comity in other than these limited categories. Should diplomacy require enlargement of these categories, the State Department can file a suggestion of immunity with the court. Should diplomacy require contraction of these categories, the State Department can issue a new or clarifying policy pronouncement.

The Comisaría General's chartering of the appellee's ship to transport a purchase of wheat is not a strictly public or political act. Indeed, it partakes far more of the character of a private commercial act than a public or political act.

The charter party has all the earmarks of a typical commercial transaction. It was executed for the Comisaría General by "El Jefe del Servicio Commercial," the head of its commercial division. The wheat was consigned to and shipped by a private commercial concern. And one of the most significant indicators of the private commercial nature of this charter is the inclusion of the arbitration clause. The French Court of Appeal, in dismissing a claim of sovereign immunity where the governmental charterer had agreed to arbitration, pointed out:

> A contract relating to maritime transport is a private contract where the owner merely puts his ship and the ship's crew at the disposal of the State and does not take a direct part in the performance of the public service undertaken by the State in the latter's capacity as a charterer. The charter party does not contain any clause peculiar to public law or unusual in private law. It provides for a time charter of the vessel which is put at the disposal of the State chartering it. The insertion of the arbitration clause underlines the intention of the parties to make their agreement subject to private law.

Maritime transport has been included among the commercial or business activities specifically mentioned in recent United States treaties restricting sovereign immunity. And the 1926 Brussels Convention, the first major international attempt to restrict sovereign immunity, which Spain signed but never ratified, denied immunity to all maritime governmental activities except vessels operated exclusively on non-commercial service, such as warships, patrol vessels, or hospital ships.

Even if we take a broader view of the transaction to encompass the purchase of wheat pursuant to the Surplus Agricultural Commodities Agreement to help feed the people of Spain, the activity of the Comisaría General remains more in the commercial than political realm. Appellant does not claim that the wheat will be used for the public services of Spain; presumptively the wheat will be resold to Spanish nationals. Whether the Comisaría General loses money or makes a profit on the sale, this purchasing activity has been conducted through private channels of trade. Except for United States financing, permitting payment in pesetas, the Comisaría General acted much like any private purchaser of wheat.

Our conclusion that the Comisaría General's activity is more properly labeled an act *jure gestionis* than *jure imperii* is supported by the practice of those countries which have adopted the restrictive theory of sovereign immunity. Thus the Commercial Tribunal of Alexandria declined to grant immunity to this same Spanish instrumentality in a more difficult case—a suit arising from the Comisaría's purchase of rice to help feed the people of neutral Spain during wartime.

It is not contended in the present case that the rice in question was bought by the *Comisaría General* for the needs of the Spanish public services. On the contrary, it seems clearly established that the rice was bought for the feeding of the Spanish population during a difficult period. In negotiating this purchase herself, instead of leaving the matter to private enterprise, Spain proceeded in much the same manner as any other Spanish trader would have done who wanted to buy rice in Egypt; that is to say, she got it out of Egypt with the necessary permits and carried it to Spain in a Spanish ship in order to re-sell it on the usual commercial lines. This being so, the *Comisaría General* cannot claim immunity from jurisdiction, and the judgment entered against it must be confirmed.

Though there are a few inconsistencies, the courts in those countries which have adopted the restrictive theory have generally considered purchasing activity by a state instrumentality, particularly for resale to nationals, as commercial or private activity.

Finally, our conclusion that the Comisaría General's claim of sovereign immunity should be denied finds support in the State Department's communication to the court in New York and Cuba Mail S. S. Co. v. Republic of Korea, 132 F.Supp. 684, 685 (S.D.N.Y.1955). There the Republic of Korea was allegedly responsible for damaging a ship while assisting in the unloading of a cargo of rice for distribution without charge to its civilian and military personnel during the Korean War. Though suggesting that Korea's property was immune from attachment, the State Department refused to suggest immunity "inasmuch as the particular acts out of which the cause of action arose are not shown to be of a purely governmental character." If the wartime transportation of rice to civilian and military personnel is not an act *jure imperii, a fortiori* the peacetime transportation of wheat for presumptive resale is not an act *jure imperii*.

Notes and Questions

1. *The Origins of the Absolute Sovereign Immunity Doctrine. Victory Transport* dated *Schooner Exchange* by observing that Marshall's "doctrine originated in an era of personal sovereignty, when kings could theoretically do no wrong and when the exercise of authority by one sovereign over another indicated hostility or superiority." Can *Schooner Exchange* really be read so broadly? After all, Marshall carefully delineated his issue as involving only "the very delicate and important inquiry, whether an American citizen can assert, in an American court, a title to an armed national vessel,

found within the waters of the United States." Presumably, the answer to this specific inquiry has remained "no" over two centuries of U.S. practice. Is the doctrine of absolute sovereign immunity properly attributable to *Schooner Exchange*? Did Marshall say anything at all about the commercial activities of states that would be helpful in deciding *Victory Transport*?

2. *The Tate Letter.* Whatever the theoretical or practical soundness of the old doctrine of absolute sovereign immunity, the Tate letter, 26 *Department of State Bulletin* 984 (1952), inaugurated the restrictive doctrine in U.S. law. What exactly was the authority of Acting Legal Adviser to the State Department Jack Tate to suggest changing U.S. common law by way of a letter to the Acting Attorney General? Did the real authority belong to the federal courts, which merely responded to the Executive Branch's "suggestion" and which then authoritatively reversed old and set new precedent?

3. *Sovereign Immunity and Foreign Law.* How did foreign practice, *e.g.*, the decisions of French and Egyptian courts, help the U.S. court determine what are and are not "commercial activities" of foreign governments? U.S. courts not only watch foreign courts, but they are also watched by them. Looking at judicial cross-fertilization, Professor Riesenfeld wrote that *Schooner Exchange* has been recognized as the "earliest judicial pronouncement of the doctrine of sovereign immunity by the highest court of a nation." Stefan A. Riesenfeld, "Sovereign Immunity in Perspective," 19 *Vanderbilt Journal of Transnational Law* 1, 2 (1986). *Schooner Exchange* was soon followed by lower French courts, though not confirmed by the Cour de Cassation (the highest French civil court) until 1849. *Id.* at 2–4. Riesenfeld dated other early lower court decisions on sovereign immunity to 1819 in Germany and to the early 19th century in Italy. *Id.* at 8–12. Such borrowing of rules among municipal legal systems is an example of what might be thought of as "international common law."

4. *Codifying Sovereign Immunity.* Absolute U.S. judicial deference toward foreign governments began to be turned back in the Tate letter in 1952. *Victory Transport* in 1965 showed how exceptions to sovereign immunity were beginning to overwhelm the rule of deference. The exceptions were codified in the Foreign Sovereign Immunities Act of 1976.

THE FOREIGN SOVEREIGN IMMUNITIES ACT OF 1976
28 U.S.C. §§ 1602–1605.

CHAPTER 97. JURISDICTIONAL IMMUNITIES OF FOREIGN STATES

§ 1602. Findings and declaration of purpose

The Congress finds that the determination by the United States courts of the claims of foreign states to immunity from the jurisdiction of such courts would serve the interests of justice and would protect the rights of both foreign states and litigants in United States courts. Under international law, states are not immune from the jurisdiction of foreign courts insofar as their commercial activities are concerned, and their commercial property may be levied upon for the satisfaction of judgments rendered against them in connection with their commercial activities. Claims of foreign states to immunity should henceforth be decided by courts of the United States and of the States in conformity with the principles set forth in this chapter.

§ 1603. Definitions

For purposes of this chapter—

(a) A "foreign state" * * * includes a political subdivision of a foreign state or an agency or instrumentality of a foreign state as defined in subsection (b).

(b) An "agency or instrumentality of a foreign state" means any entity—

(1) which is a separate legal person, corporate or otherwise, and

(2) which is an organ of a foreign state or political subdivision thereof, or a majority of whose shares or other ownership interest is owned by a foreign state or political subdivision thereof, and

(3) which is neither a citizen of a State of the United States as defined in section 1332(c) and (d) of this title, nor created under the laws of any third country.

(c) The "United States" includes all territory and waters, continental or insular, subject to the jurisdiction of the United States.

(d) A "commercial activity" means either a regular course of commercial conduct or a particular commercial transaction or act. The commercial character of an activity shall be determined by reference to the nature of the course of conduct or particular transaction or act, rather than by reference to its purpose.

(e) A "commercial activity carried on in the United States by a foreign state" means commercial activity carried on by such state and having substantial contact with the United States.

§ 1604. Immunity of a foreign state from jurisdiction

Subject to existing international agreements to which the United States is a party at the time of enactment of this Act a foreign state shall be immune from the jurisdiction of the courts of the United States and of the States except as provided in sections 1605 to 1607 of this chapter.

§ 1605. General exceptions to the jurisdictional immunity of a foreign state

(a) A foreign state shall not be immune from the jurisdiction of courts of the United States or of the States in any case—

(1) in which the foreign state has waived its immunity either explicitly or by implication, notwithstanding any withdrawal of the waiver which the foreign state may purport to effect except in accordance with the terms of the waiver;

(2) in which the action is based upon a commercial activity carried on in the United States by the foreign state; or upon an act

performed in the United States in connection with a commercial activity of the foreign state elsewhere; or upon an act outside the territory of the United States in connection with a commercial activity of the foreign state elsewhere and that act causes a direct effect in the United States;

(3) in which rights in property taken in violation of international law are in issue and that property or any property exchanged for such property is present in the United States in connection with a commercial activity carried on in the United States by the foreign state; or that property or any property exchanged for such property is owned or operated by an agency or instrumentality of the foreign state and that agency or instrumentality is engaged in a commercial activity in the United States;

(4) in which rights in property in the United States acquired by succession or gift or rights in immovable property situated in the United States are in issue;

(5) not otherwise encompassed in paragraph (2) above, in which money damages are sought against a foreign state for personal injury or death, or damage to or loss of property, occurring in the United States and caused by the tortious act or omission of that foreign state or of any official or employee of that foreign state while acting within the scope of his office or employment; except this paragraph shall not apply to—

(A) any claim based upon the exercise or performance or the failure to exercise or perform a discretionary function regardless of whether the discretion be abused, or

(B) any claim arising out of malicious prosecution, abuse of process, libel, slander, misrepresentation, deceit, or interference with contract rights;

(6) in which the action is brought, either to enforce an agreement made by the foreign state with or for the benefit of a private party to submit to arbitration all or any differences which have arisen or which may arise between the parties with respect to a defined legal relationship, whether contractual or not, concerning a subject matter capable of settlement by arbitration under the laws of the United States, or to confirm an award made pursuant to such an agreement to arbitrate, if (A) the arbitration takes place or is intended to take place in the United States, (B) the agreement or award is or may be governed by a treaty or other international agreement in force for the United States calling for the recognition and enforcement of arbitral awards, (C) the underlying claim, save for the agreement to arbitrate, could have been brought in a United States court under this section or section 1607, or (D) paragraph (1) of this subsection is otherwise applicable; or

(7) not otherwise covered by paragraph (2), in which money damages are sought against a foreign state for personal injury or

death that was caused by an act of torture, extrajudicial killing, aircraft sabotage, hostage taking, or the provision of material support or resources (as defined in section 2339A of title 18) for such an act if such act or provision of material support is engaged in by an official, employee, or agent of such foreign state while acting within the scope of his or her office, employment, or agency, except that the court shall decline to hear a claim under this paragraph—

    (A) if the foreign state was not designated as a state sponsor of terrorism under section 6(j) of the Export Administration Act of 1979 (50 U.S.C. App. 2405(j)) or section 620A of the Foreign Assistance Act or 1961 (22 U.S.C. 2371) at the time the act occurred, unless later so designated as a result of such an act; and

    (B) even if the foreign state is or was so designated, if—

        (i) the act occurred in the foreign state against which the claim has been brought and the claimant has not afforded the foreign state a reasonable opportunity to arbitrate the claim in accordance with accepted international rules of arbitration; or

        (ii) neither the claimant nor the victim was a national of the United States (as that term is defined in section 101(a)(22) of the Immigration and Nationality Act) when the act upon which the claim is based occurred. * * *

(e) For purposes of paragraph (7) of subsection (a)—

    (1) the terms "torture" and "extrajudicial killing" have the meaning given those terms in section 3 of the Torture Victim Protection Act of 1991;

    (2) the term "hostage taking" has the meaning given that term in Article 1 of the International Convention Against the Taking of Hostages; and

    (3) the term "aircraft sabotage" has the meaning given that term in Article 1 of the Convention for the Suppression of Unlawful Acts Against the Safety of Civil Aviation.

Notes and Questions

    1. *Case Law, International Law, and the Foreign Sovereign Immunities Act.* Note how Section 1602, "Findings and declaration of purpose," mixes possible sources of law. The first sentence seems to entrust the courts with power to decide questions of foreign sovereign immunity. The second sentence appears to incorporate rules from international law. The third instructs that the courts decide "in conformity with the principles set forth in" the statute. Deciding cases involving claims of foreign sovereign immunity has come to mean using material evidences from all three sources: case law, international law, and statute. We have, of course, studied international law as a source of law in Chapters 1, 2, and 3 above.

2. *The Presumption of Immunity.* Note that a presumption in *Victory Transport* was reversed in the FSIA. *Victory Transport* presumed to deny immunity unless the state proved it deserved to be protected. Section 1604, on the other hand, presumes to grant immunity unless a private plaintiff shows an exception. As we see in *Amerada Hess* below, this reversal can make a decisive effect in practice. If the main purpose of the FSIA was to codify the commercial activities exception, was it necessary to codify other exceptions as an exclusive list? Why not leave some flexibility for the courts to develop exceptions?

3. *The 1996 Antiterrorism Amendment.* In 1996, the FSIA was amended by the Anti-Terrorism and Death Penalty Act, which added the seventh exception to foreign sovereign immunity in "any case * * * in which money damages are sought against a foreign state for personal injury or death that was caused by an act of torture, extrajudicial killing, aircraft sabotage, hostage taking, or the provision of material support or resources * * * for such an act * * * ." This exception applies only if the foreign state has been designated a state sponsor of terrorism by the U.S. Secretary of State and if the claimant or victim was a national of the United States when the act occurred. Unlike other exceptions, the seventh exception permits state-owned property unrelated to the claim to be executed against to satisfy a judgment based on its terms. See Monroe Leigh, "1996 Amendments to the Foreign Sovereign Immunities Act with Respect to Terrorist Activities," 91 *American Journal of International Law* 187 (1997).

Cases applying the FSIA's anti-terrorism exception include Flatow v. Islamic Republic of Iran, 999 F.Supp. 1 (D.D.C.1998), involving a terrorist bombing in Israel killing a U.S. student, and Alejandre v. Republic of Cuba, 996 F.Supp. 1239 (S.D.Fla.1997), respecting an attack on three unarmed civilian planes over international waters killing three U.S. pilots. The secondary literature has raised questions about the constitutionality of the jurisdictional provisions of the seventh exception as applied by the lower courts. See Keith E. Sealing, "State Sponsors of Terrorism are Entitled to Due Process Too: The Amended Foreign Sovereign Immunities Act is Unconstitutional," 15 *American University International Law Review* 395 (1999); Joseph W. Glannon & Jeffrey Atik, "Politics and Personal Jurisdiction: Suing State Sponsors of Terrorism Under the 1996 Amendments of the Foreign Sovereign Immunities Act," 87 *Georgetown Law Journal* 675 (1999).

TEXAS TRADING & MILLING CORP. v. FEDERAL REPUBLIC OF NIGERIA

647 F.2d 300 (2d Cir.1981), *cert. denied*,
454 U.S. 1148, 102 S.Ct. 1012, 71 L.Ed.2d 301 (1982).

Irving R. Kaufman, Circuit Judge:

These four appeals grow out of one of the most enormous commercial disputes in history, and present questions which strike to the very heart of the modern international economic order. An African nation, developing at breakneck speed by virtue of huge exports of high-grade oil, contracted to buy huge quantities of Portland cement, a commodity crucial to the construction of its infrastructure. It overbought, and the country's docks and harbors became clogged with ships waiting to unload. Imports of other goods ground to a halt. More vessels carrying cement arrived daily; still others were steaming toward the port. Unable to accept delivery of the cement it had bought, the nation repudiated its contracts. In response to suits brought by disgruntled suppliers, it now seeks to invoke an ancient maxim of sovereign immunity—*par in parem imperium non habet*—to insulate itself from liability. But Latin phrases speak with a hoary simplicity inappropriate to the modern financial world. For the ruling principles here, we must look instead to a new and vaguely-worded statute, the Foreign Sovereign Immunities Act of 1976 ("FSIA" or "Act")—a law described by its draftsmen as providing only "very modest guidance" on issues of preeminent importance. For answers to those most difficult questions, the authors of the law "decided to put [their] faith in the U.S. courts." Guided by reason, precedent, and equity, we have attempted to give form and substance to the legislative intent. Accordingly, we find that the defense of sovereign immunity is not available in any of these four cases.

I.

The facts of the four appeals are remarkably parallel, and can be stated in somewhat consolidated form. Early in 1975, the Federal Military Government of the Federal Republic of Nigeria ("Nigeria") embarked on an ambitious program to purchase immense amounts of cement. We have already had occasion in another case to call the program "incredible," but the statistics speak for themselves. Nigeria executed 109 contracts, with 68 suppliers. It purchased, in all, over sixteen million metric tons of cement. The price was close to one billion dollars.

A.

Four of the 109 contracts were made with American companies that were plaintiffs below in the cases now before us: Texas Trading & Milling Corp. ("Texas Trading"), Decor by Nikkei International, Inc. ("Nikkei"), East Europe Import–Export, Inc. ("East Europe"), and Chenax Majesty, Inc. ("Chenax"). The four plaintiffs are not industrial corporations; they are, instead, "trading companies," which buy from one person and sell to another in hopes of making a profit on the differential. Each of the plaintiffs is a New York corporation.

The contracts at issue were signed early in 1975. Each is substantially similar; indeed, Nigeria seems to have mimeographed them in blank, and filled in details with individual suppliers. Overall, each contract called for the sale by the supplier to Nigeria of 240,000 metric tons of Portland cement. Specifically, the contracts required Nigeria, within a time certain after execution, to establish in the seller's favor "an Irrevocable, Transferable abroad, Divisible and Confirmed letter of credit" for the total amount due under the particular contract, slightly over $14 million in each case. The contract also named the bank through which the letter of credit was to be made payable. Nikkei and East

Europe named First National City Bank in New York, and Texas Trading specified Fidelity International Bank, also in New York. Chenax denominated Schroeder, Muenchmeyer, Hengst & Co. of Hamburg, West Germany. Drafts under the letters of credit were to be "payable at sight, on presentation" of certain documents to the specified bank.

Within a time certain after establishment and receipt of the letter of credit, each seller was to start shipping cement to Nigeria. The cement was to be bagged, and was to meet certain chemical specifications. Shipments were to be from ports named in the contracts, mostly Spanish, and were to proceed at approximately 20,000 tons per month. Delivery was to the port of Lagos/Apapa, Nigeria, and the seller was obligated to insure the freight to the Nigerian quay. Each contract also provided for demurrage. The Nikkei and East Europe contracts provided they were to be governed by the laws of the United States. The Chenax contract specified the law of Switzerland, and the Texas Trading contract named the law of Nigeria. * * *

The actual financial arrangements differed from those set forth in the cement contracts. Instead of establishing "confirmed" letters of credit with the banks named, Nigeria established what it called "irrevocable" letters of credit with the Central Bank of Nigeria ("Central Bank"), an instrumentality of the Nigerian government, and advised those letters of credit through the Morgan Guaranty Trust Company ("Morgan") of New York. That is, under the letters of credit as established, each seller was to present appropriate documents not to the named bank, but to Morgan. And, since the letters were not "confirmed," Morgan did not promise to pay "on sight"; it assumed no independent liability. Each of the letters of credit provided it was to be governed by the Uniform Customs and Practice for Documentary Credits ("UCP") (1962 Revision), as set forth in Brochure No. 222 of the International Chamber of Commerce. * * *

After receiving notice that the letters of credit had been established, the suppliers set out to secure subcontracts to procure the cement, and shipping contracts to transport it. They, through their subcontractors, began to bag the cement and load it on ships, as suppliers across the globe were doing the same. Hundreds of ships arrived in Lagos/Apapa in the summer of 1975, and most were carrying cement. Nigeria's port facilities could accept only one to five million tons of cement per year; at any rate, they could not begin to unload the over sixteen million tons Nigeria had slated for delivery in eighteen short months. Based on prior experience, Nigeria had made the contracts expecting only twenty percent of the suppliers to be able to perform. By July, when the harbor held over 400 ships waiting to unload—260 of them carrying cement— Nigeria realized it had misjudged the market considerably.

C.

With demurrage piling up at astronomical rates, and suppliers, hiring, loading, and dispatching more ships daily, Nigeria decided to act.

On August 9, 1975, Nigeria caused its Ports Authority to issue Government Notice No. 1434, a regulation which stated that, effective August 18, all ships destined for Lagos/Apapa would be required to convey to the Ports Authority, two months before sailing, certain information concerning their time of arrival in the port. The regulation also stated vaguely that the Ports Authority would "co-ordinate all sailing," and that it would "refus[e] service" to vessels which did not comply with the regulation. Then, on August 18, Nigeria cabled its suppliers and asked them to stop sending cement, and to cease loading or even chartering ships. In late September, Nigeria took the crucial step: Central Bank instructed Morgan not to pay under the letters of credit unless the supplier submitted—in addition to the documents required by the letter of credit as written—a statement from Central Bank that payment ought to be made. Morgan notified each supplier of Nigeria's instructions, and Morgan commenced refusing to make payment under the letters of credit as written. Almost three months later, on December 19, 1975, Nigeria promulgated Decree No. 40, a law prohibiting entry into a Nigerian port to any ship which had not secured two months' prior approval, and imposing criminal penalties for unauthorized entry. * * *

II.

The law before us is complex and largely unconstrued, and has introduced sweeping changes in some areas of prior law. In structure, the FSIA is a marvel of compression. Within the bounds of a few tersely-worded sections, it purports to provide answers to three crucial questions in a suit against a foreign state: the availability of sovereign immunity as a defense, the presence of subject matter jurisdiction over the claim, and the propriety of personal jurisdiction over the defendant. Through a series of intricately coordinated provisions, the FSIA seems at first glance to make the answer to one of the questions, subject matter jurisdiction, dispositive of all three. * * *

A.

Turning to the specific provisions of the law, a description of the FSIA's analytic structure is helpful. The jurisdiction-conferring provision of the Act, 28 U.S.C. § 1330(a), creates in the district courts:

> original jurisdiction without regard to amount in controversy of any nonjury civil action against a foreign state as defined in section 1603(a) of this title as to any claim for relief in personam with respect to which the foreign state is not entitled to immunity either under sections 1605–1607 of this title or any applicable international agreement.

Although § 1330(a) refers to sections 1605–1607, the section most frequently relevant, and the one applicable here, is § 1605. It provides, in part:

> (a) A foreign state shall not be immune from the jurisdiction of courts of the United States or of the States in any case—* * *

(2) in which the action is based upon a commercial activity carried on in the United States by the foreign state; or upon an act performed in the United States in connection with a commercial activity of the foreign state elsewhere; or upon an act outside the territory of the United States in connection with a commercial activity of the foreign state elsewhere and that act causes a direct effect in the United States.

Crucial to each of the three clauses of § 1605(a)(2) is the phrase "commercial activity." In it is lodged centuries of Anglo–American and civil law precedent construing the term "sovereign immunity." If the activity is not "commercial," but, rather, is "governmental," then the foreign state is entitled to immunity under section 1605, and "original jurisdiction" is not present under § 1330(a).

For the definition of "commercial activity," we turn to subsection 1603(d), which provides:

(d) A "commercial activity" means either a regular course of commercial conduct or a particular commercial transaction or act. The commercial character of an activity shall be determined by reference to the nature of the course of conduct or particular transaction or act, rather than by references to its purpose.

If "commercial activity" under § 1603(d) is present, and if it bears the relation to the United States required by § 1605(a)(2), then the foreign state is "not entitled to immunity," and the district court has statutory subject matter jurisdiction over the claim through § 1330(a). And, if the exercise of that jurisdiction falls within the judicial power set forth by Article III of the Constitution, subject matter jurisdiction over the claim exists. * * *

B.   * * *

The determination of whether particular behavior is "commercial" is perhaps the most important decision a court faces in an FSIA suit. This problem is significant because the primary purpose of the Act is to "restrict" the immunity of a foreign state to suits involving a foreign state's public acts. If the activity is not "commercial," it satisfies none of the three clauses of § 1605(a)(2), and the foreign state is (at least under that subsection) immune from suit. Unfortunately, the definition of "commercial" is the one issue on which the Act provides almost no guidance at all. Subsection 1603(d) advances the inquiry somewhat, for it provides: "The commercial character of an activity shall be determined by reference to the nature of the course of conduct or particular transaction or act, rather than by reference to its purpose." No provision of the Act, however, defines "commercial." Congress deliberately left the meaning open and * * * "put [its] faith in the U.S. courts to work out progressively, on a case-by-case basis ... the distinction between commercial and governmental." We are referred to no less than three separate sources of authority to resolve this fundamental definitional question.

The first source is statements contained in the legislative history itself. Perhaps the clearest of them was made by Bruno Ristau, then Chief of the Foreign Litigation Section of the Civil Division, Department of Justice. Ristau stated: "[I]f a government enters into a contract to purchase goods and services, that is considered a commercial activity. It avails itself of the ordinary contract machinery. It bargains and negotiates. It accepts an offer. It enters into a written contract and the contract is to be performed." The House Report seems to conclude that a contract or series of contracts for the purchase of goods would be *per se* a "commercial activity," and the illustrations cited by experts who testified on the bill—contracts, for example, for the sale of army boots or grain—support such a rule. Or, put another way, if the activity is one in which a private person could engage, it is not entitled to immunity.

The second source for interpreting the phrase "commercial activity" is the "very large body of case law which exist[ed]" in American law upon passage of the Act in 1976. Testifying on an earlier version of the bill, Charles N. Brower, then Legal Adviser of the Department of State, stated:

> [T]he restrictive theory of sovereign immunity from jurisdiction, which has been followed by the Department of State and the courts since it was articulated in the familiar letter of Acting Legal Adviser Jack B. Tate of May 29, 1952, would be incorporated into statutory law. This theory limits immunity to public acts, leaving so-called private acts subject to suit. The proposed legislation would make it clear that immunity cannot be claimed with respect to acts or transactions that are commercial in nature, regardless of their underlying purpose.

Finally, current standards of international law concerning sovereign immunity add content to the "commercial activity" phrase of the FSIA. Section 1602 of the Act, entitled "Findings and declaration of purpose," contains a cryptic reference to international law, but fails wholly to adopt it. The legislative history states that the Act "incorporates standards recognized under international law," and the drafters seem to have intended rather generally to bring American sovereign immunity practice into line with that of other nations. At this point, there can be little doubt that international law follows the restrictive theory of sovereign immunity.

Under each of these three standards, Nigeria's cement contracts and letters of credit qualify as "commercial activity." Lord Denning, writing in *Trendtex Trading Corp. v. Central Bank of Nigeria*, [1977] 2 W.L.R. 356, 369, 1 All E.R. 881, with his usual erudition and clarity, stated: "If a government department goes into the market places of the world and buys boots or cement—as a commercial transaction—that government department should be subject to all the rules of the marketplace." Nigeria's activity here is in the nature of a private contract for the purchase of goods. Its purpose—to build roads, army barracks, whatever—is irrelevant. Accordingly, courts in other nations have uniformly held Nigeria's 1975 cement purchase program and appurtenant letters of credit to be "commercial activity," and have denied the defense of sovereign immunity. [The Court cites decisions from the United Kingdom and Germany, as well as an International Chamber of Commerce arbitral award.] We find defendants' activity here to constitute "commercial activity" * * *.

[The Court finds there is jurisdiction over Nigeria.]

Notes and Questions

1. *Proving "Commercial Activities."* Section 1602 of the FSIA refers to the commercial activities exception as being part of international law and also instructs courts to decide sovereign immunity cases in accordance with the statute. How well did the *Texas Trading* court employ both international law and statutory analysis to decide whether Nigeria was protected by the commercial activities exception? Did the FSIA much change the exercise of line-drawing between "public" and "private" acts as done before 1976, *e.g.*, in *Victory Transport*?

2. *Direct Effect in the United States.* Note how the *Texas Trading* court found "direct effect in the United States":

> [T]he financial loss in these cases occurred "in the United States" for two * * * simple[ ] reasons. First, the cement suppliers were to present documents and collect money in the United States, and the breaches precluded their doing so. Second, each of the plaintiffs is an American corporation. Whether a failure to pay a foreign corporation in the United States or to pay an American corporation overseas creates an effect "in the United States" under § 1605(a)(2) is not before us. Both factors are present here and the subsection is clearly satisfied.

647 F.2d at 312.

In Martin v. Republic of South Africa, 836 F.2d 91 (2d Cir.1987), the Second Circuit ruled that an African American could not sue the government of South Africa in U.S. courts for a delay in providing him with medical treatment following an automobile accident in South Africa. A member of a U.S. dance company performing in South Africa, Martin had to wait longer for care than did a white companion also in the car. Citing *Texas Trading*, *inter alia*, Martin argued that for the court to refuse to find "direct effect" in his case would create an "anomaly between the treatment of corporations and the treatment of individuals." How persuasive was the court's rejection of Martin's claim?:

> We do not believe that such a distinction exists, nor do we create one here. Appellant was not in the United States at the time of the accident. He was in South Africa. Indeed, he did not return to the United States until more than a year after the date of the accident. Application of the plain language of § 1605(a)(2) leads us to conclude that South Africa's conduct did not cause a direct effect in the United States.

Id. at 95.

In Republic of Argentina v. Weltover, Inc., 504 U.S. 607, 112 S.Ct. 2160, 119 L.Ed.2d 394 (1992), Justice Scalia, writing for a unanimous Supreme Court, held that Argentina's reschedulings of debt payments had a "direct effect" in the United States since New York was the place where the debts had to be repaid. *Id.* at 617, 112 S.Ct. at 2168, 119 L.Ed.2d at 407. Did *Weltover* set too low a threshold for direct effect and open the door too wide for suits against foreign sovereigns in U.S. courts?

In Voest–Alpine Trading USA Corp. v. Bank of China, 142 F.3d 887 (5th Cir.1998), *cert. denied*, 525 U.S. 1041, 119 S.Ct. 591, 142 L.Ed.2d 534 (1998), the Fifth Circuit held that the Bank of China, an instrumentality of the People's Republic of China, was open to suit in federal district court in Texas for failure to pay under a letter of credit issued to protect a U.S. seller *vis-à-vis* a Chinese buyer. The letter of credit, though telexed to the United States, did not designate a particular place of payment. Nonetheless, the Fifth Circuit ruled "that a financial loss incurred in the United States by an American plaintiff, if it is an immediate consequence of the defendant's activity, constitutes a direct effect sufficient to support jurisdiction under the third clause of the commercial activity exception to the FSIA." *Id.* at 897.

Is a U.S. court or the FSIA itself limited by jurisdictional rules of international law in determining whether an activity has "a direct effect in the United States"? Should the jurisdictional practice of other countries be taken into account? As one observer noted: "[A]ll States have a strong incentive to make reasonable rules of immunity. They know that the rules applied to other States in their national courts can be applied to them in the courts of other countries." Mark B. Feldman, "The United States Foreign Sovereign Immunities Act of 1976 in Perspective: A Founder's View," 35 *International and Comparative Law Quarterly* 302, 303 (1986).

3. *Sovereign Immunity and the Executive Branch.* What should be the role of the executive branch *vis-à-vis* the courts and the legislature in making sovereign immunity determinations? Before the Foreign Sovereign Immunity Act was enacted in 1976, the State Department recommended what position the courts should take on a case-by-case basis. An internal memo to the Legal Adviser of the State Department in 1966 commented on the "plainly unsatisfactory" state of the law of sovereign immunity:

1. The determination by the State Department, though generally considered conclusive by the courts, is made without clear guidelines or procedures. It is in part a "legal" determination, though it is held not to be reviewable; and in part a political determination, though made by lawyers. The determination is sometimes made after a kind of hearing, sometimes not, and there is virtually never an articulation of the reasons for the determination.

2. The courts, when asked to rule in the absence of a State Department suggestion, have no satisfactory distinctions to follow, and reach inconsistent results.

3. There is no consistency between the policy of the United States Government in defending suits abroad and in recognition by the Executive Branch of claims of immunity of foreign governments in the United States.

Quoted in Andreas F. Lowenfeld, *International Litigation and Arbitration* 588 (1993). The Foreign Sovereign Immunities Act places the burden of determining sovereign immunity with the federal courts. Was the statutory solution necessary, or could the courts have accomplished the same result simply through case law? Or would it have been wiser to leave the development of sovereign immunity to periodic executive pronouncement?

ARGENTINE REPUBLIC v. AMERADA HESS SHIPPING CORP.

488 U.S. 428, 109 S.Ct. 683, 102 L.Ed.2d 818 (1989).

CHIEF JUSTICE REHNQUIST delivered the opinion of the Court.

Two Liberian corporations sued the Argentine Republic in a United States District Court to recover damages for a tort allegedly committed by its armed forces on the high seas in violation of international law. We hold that the District Court correctly dismissed the action, because the Foreign Sovereign Immunities Act of 1976 (FSIA), 29 U.S.C. § 1330 *et seq.*, does not authorize jurisdiction over a foreign state in this situation.

Respondents alleged the following facts in their complaints. Respondent United Carriers, Inc., a Liberian corporation, chartered one of its oil tankers, the Hercules, to respondent Amerada Hess Shipping Corporation, also a Liberian corporation. The contract was executed in New York City. Amerada Hess used the Hercules to transport crude oil from the southern terminus of the Trans–Alaska Pipeline in Valdez, Alaska, around Cape Horn in South America, to the Hess refinery in the United States Virgin Islands. On May 25, 1982, the Hercules began a return voyage, without cargo but fully fueled, from the Virgin Islands to Alaska. At that time, Great Britain and petitioner Argentine Republic were at war over an archipelago of some 200 islands—the Falkland Islands to the British, and the Islas Malvinas to the Argentineans—in the South Atlantic off the Argentine coast. On June 3, United States officials informed the two belligerents of the location of United States vessels and Liberian tankers owned by United States interests then traversing the South Atlantic, including the Hercules, to avoid any attacks on neutral shipping.

By June 8, 1982, after a stop in Brazil, the Hercules was in international waters about 600 nautical miles from Argentina and 500 miles from the Falklands; she was outside the "war zones" designated by Britain and Argentina. At 12:15 Greenwich mean time, the ship's master made a routine report by radio to Argentina officials, providing the ship's name, international call sign, registry, position, course, speed, and voyage description. About 45 minutes later, an Argentine military aircraft began to circle the Hercules. The ship's master repeated his earlier message by radio to Argentine officials, who acknowledged receiving it. Six minutes later, without provocation, another Argentine military plane began to bomb the Hercules; the master immediately hoisted a white flag. A second bombing soon followed, and a third attack came about two hours later, when an Argentine jet struck the ship with an air-to-surface rocket. Disabled but not destroyed, the Hercules reversed course and sailed to Rio de Janeiro, the nearest safe port. At Rio de Janeiro, respondent United Carriers determined that the ship had suffered extensive deck and hull damage, and that an undetonated bomb remained lodged in her No. 2 tank. After an investigation by the Brazilian Navy, United Carriers decided that it would be too hazardous to remove the undetonated bomb, and on July 20, 1978, the Hercules was scuttled 250 miles off the Brazilian coast.

Following unsuccessful attempts to obtain relief in Argentina, respondents commenced this action in the United States District Court for the Southern District of New York for the damage that they sustained from the attack. United Carriers sought $10 million in damages for the loss of the ship; Amerada Hess sought $1.9 million in damages for the fuel that went down with the ship. Respondents alleged that petitioner's attack on the neutral Hercules violated international law. They invoked the District Court's jurisdiction under the Alien Tort Statute, 28 U.S.C. § 1350, which provides that "[t]he district courts shall have original jurisdiction of any civil action by an alien for a tort only, committed in violation of the law of nations or a treaty of the United States." Amerada Hess also brought suit under the general admiralty and maritime jurisdiction, 28 U.S.C. § 1333, and "the principle of universal jurisdiction, recognized in customary international law." The District Court dismissed both complaints for lack of subject-matter jurisdiction, ruling that respondents' suits were barred by the FSIA.

A divided panel of the United States Court of Appeals for the Second Circuit reversed. * * *

We think that the text and structure of the FSIA demonstrate Congress' intention that the FSIA be the sole basis for obtaining jurisdiction over a foreign state in our courts. Section 1604 and § 1330(a) work in tandem; § 1604 bars federal and state courts from exercising jurisdiction when a foreign state is entitled to immunity, and § 1330(a) confers jurisdiction on district courts to hear suits brought by United States citizens and by aliens when a foreign state is *not* entitled to immunity. As we said in *Verlinden,* the FSIA "must be applied by the district courts in every action against a foreign sovereign, since subject-matter jurisdiction in any such action depends on the existence of one of the specified exceptions to foreign sovereign immunity." *Verlinden B.V. v. Central Bank of Nigeria,* 461 U.S. 480, 493 (1983).

The Court of Appeals acknowledged that the FSIA's language and legislative history support the "general rule" that the Act governs the immunity of foreign states in federal court. The Court of Appeals, however, thought that the FSIA's "focus on commercial concerns" and Congress' failure to "repeal" the Alien Tort Statute indicated Congress' intention that federal courts continue to exercise jurisdiction over foreign states in suits alleging violations of international law outside the confines of the FSIA. The Court of Appeals also believed that to construe the FSIA to bar the instant suit would "fly in the face" of Congress' intention that the FSIA be interpreted pursuant to "standards recognized under international law."

Taking the last of these points first, Congress had violations of international law by foreign states in mind when it enacted the FSIA. For example, the FSIA specifically denies foreign states immunity in suits "in which rights in property taken in violation of international law are in issue." 28 U.S.C. § 1605(a)(3). Congress also rested the FSIA in part on its power under Art. I., § 8, cl. 10, of the Constitution "[t]o define and punish Piracies and Felonies committed on the high Seas, and Offenses against the Law of Nations." From Congress' decision to deny immunity to foreign states in the class of cases just mentioned, we draw the plain implication that immunity is granted in those cases involving alleged violations of international law that do not come within one of the FSIA's exceptions.

As to the other point made by the Court of Appeals, Congress' failure to enact a *pro tanto* repealer of the Alien Tort Statute when it passed the FSIA in 1976 may be explained at least in part by the lack of certainty as to whether the Alien Tort Statute conferred jurisdiction in suits against foreign states. Enacted by the First Congress in 1789, the Alien Tort Statute provides that "[t]he district courts shall have original jurisdiction of any civil action by an alien for a tort only, committed in violation of the law of nations or a treaty of the United States." 28 U.S.C. § 1350. The Court of Appeals did not cite any decision in which a United States court exercised jurisdiction over a foreign state under the Alien Tort Statute, and only one such case has come to our attention— one which was decided after the enactment of the FSIA. * * *

We think that Congress' failure in the FSIA to enact an express *pro tanto* repealer of the Alien Tort Statute speaks only faintly, if at all, to the issue involved in this case. In light of the comprehensiveness of the statutory scheme in the FSIA, we doubt that even the most meticulous draftsman would have concluded that Congress also needed to amend *pro tanto* the Alien Tort Statute and presumably such other grants of subject-matter jurisdiction in Title 28 as § 1331 (federal question), § 1333 (admiralty), § 1335 (interpleader), § 1337 (commerce and antitrust), and § 1338 (patents, copyrights, and trademarks). Congress provided in § 1602 of the FSIA that "[c]laims of foreign states to immunity should *henceforth* be decided by courts of the United States in conformity with the principles set forth in this chapter," and very likely it thought that should be sufficient. * * *

Having determined that the FSIA provides the sole basis for obtaining jurisdiction over a foreign state in federal court, we turn to whether any of the exceptions enumerated in the Act apply here. These exceptions include cases involving the waiver of immunity, commercial activities occurring in the United States or causing a direct effect in this country, property expropriated in violation of international law, inherited, gift, or immovable property located in the United States, noncommercial torts occurring in the United States, and maritime liens. We agree with the District Court that none of the FSIA's exceptions applies on these facts.

Respondents assert that FSIA exception for noncommercial torts, § 1605(a)(5), is most in point. This provision denies immunity in a case

"in which money damages are sought against a foreign state for personal injury or death, or damage to or loss of property, occurring in the United States and caused by the tortious act or omission of that foreign state or of any official or employee of that foreign state while acting within the scope of his office or employment."

Section 1605(a)(5) is limited by its terms, however, to those cases in which the damage to or loss of property occurs *in the United States*. Congress' primary purpose in enacting § 1605(a)(5) was to eliminate a foreign state's immunity for traffic accidents and other torts committed in the United States, for which liability is imposed under domestic tort law.

In this case, the injury to respondents' ship occurred on the high seas some 5,000 miles off the nearest shores of the United States. Despite these telling facts, respondents nonetheless claim that the tortious attack on the Hercules occurred "in the United States." They point out that the FSIA defines "United States" as including all "territory and waters, continental and insular, subject to the jurisdiction of the United States," and that their injury occurred on the high seas, which is within the admiralty jurisdiction of the United States, see *The Plymouth*, 3 Wall. 20, 36 (1866). They reason, therefore, that "by statutory definition" petitioner's attack occurred in the United States.

We find this logic unpersuasive. We construe the modifying phrase "continental and insular" to restrict the definition of United States to the continental United States and those islands that are part of the United States or its possessions; any other reading would render this phrase nugatory. Likewise, the term "waters" in § 1603(c) cannot reasonably be read to cover all waters over which United States courts might exercise jurisdiction. When it desires to do so, Congress knows how to place the high seas within the jurisdiction reach of a statute. We thus apply "[t]he canon of construction which teaches that legislation of Congress, unless contrary intent appears, is meant to apply only within the territorial jurisdiction of the United States." Because respondents' injury unquestionably occurred well outside the 3–mile limit then in effect for the territorial waters of the United States, the exception for noncommercial torts cannot apply.

The result in this case is not altered by the fact that petitioner's alleged tort may have had effects in the United States. Respondents state, for example, that the Hercules was transporting oil intended for use in this country and that the loss of the ship disrupted contractual payments due in New York. Under the commercial activity exception to the FSIA, § 1605(a)(2), a foreign state may be liable for its commercial activities "outside the territory of the United States" having a "direct effect" inside the United States. But the noncommercial tort exception,

§ 1605(a)(5), upon which respondents rely, makes no mention of "territory outside the United States" or of "direct effects" in the United States. Congress' decision to use explicit language in § 1605(a)(2), and not to do so in § 1605(a)(5), indicates that the exception in § 1605(a)(5) covers only torts occurring within the territorial jurisdiction of the United States. Respondents do not claim that § 1605(a)(2) covers these facts.

We also disagree with respondents' claim that certain international agreements entered into by petitioner and by the United States create an exception to the FSIA here. As noted, the FSIA was adopted "[s]ubject to international agreements to which the United States [was] a party at the time of [its] enactment." This exception applies when international agreements "expressly conflic[t]" with the immunity provisions of the FSIA, hardly the circumstances in this case. Respondents point to the Geneva Convention on the High Seas, Apr. 29, 1958, [1962] 13 U.S.T. 2312, T.I.A.S. No. 5200, and the Pan–American Maritime Neutrality Convention, Feb. 20, 1928, 47 Stat. 1989, 1990–1991, T.S. No. 845. These conventions, however, only set forth substantive rules of conduct and state that compensation shall be paid for certain wrongs. They do not create private rights of action for foreign corporations to recover compensation from foreign states in United States courts. Nor do we see how a foreign state can waive its immunity under § 1605(a)(1) by signing an international agreement that contains no mention of a waiver of immunity to suit in United States courts or even the availability of a cause of action in the United States. We find similarly unpersuasive the argument of respondent and *Amicus Curiae* Republic of Liberia that the Treaty of Friendship, Commerce and Navigation, Aug. 8, 1938, United States–Liberia, 54 Stat. 1739, T.S. No. 956, carves out an exception to the FSIA. Article I of this Treaty provides, in pertinent part, that the nationals of the United States and Liberia "shall enjoy freedom of access to the courts of justice of the other on conforming to the local laws." The FSIA is clearly one of the "local laws" to which respondents must "conform" before bringing suit in United States courts.

We hold that the FSIA provides the sole basis for obtaining jurisdiction over a foreign state in the courts of this country, and that none of the enumerated exceptions to the Act applies to the facts of this case. The judgment of the Court of Appeals is therefore

Reversed.

Notes and Questions

1. *The Alleged Violation of International Law.* In *Amerada Hess* the Supreme Court did not reach the issue of Argentina's alleged violation of international law. The Court of Appeals believed that "[t]he facts alleged by [Amerada Hess and United Carriers], if proven, would constitute a clear violation of international law." Amerada Hess Shipping Corp. v. Argentine Republic, 830 F.2d 421, 423 (2d Cir.1987). Looking to treaties dating from the Declaration of Paris of 1856 to the United Nations Law of the Sea

Convention of 1982, the Second Circuit ruled that "it is beyond controversy that attacking a neutral ship in international waters, without proper cause for suspicion or investigation, violates international law." *Id.* at 424. See Chapter 4.

Whatever the possibility of an international law violation, the Supreme Court ruled that the Liberian shipping companies could not sue the Argentine government in a U.S. court. Where could the companies then go for redress? What was the potential for other legal procedures, *e.g.*, litigation in Argentina or international arbitration? Were there political or economic avenues open to the companies, *e.g.*, diplomatic protest or economic reprisals?

2. *The Alien Tort Statute.* The Supreme Court in *Amerada Hess* was careful not to decide questions relating to the 1789 Alien Tort Statute and non-governmental defendants: "The Alien Tort Statute by its terms does not distinguish among classes of defendants, and it of course has the same effect after the passage of the FSIA as before with respect to defendants other than foreign states." With respect to government defendants, given the *Amerada Hess* decision, does the Alien Tort Statute add anything to the arsenal of a plaintiff's lawyer that is not already there courtesy of the Foreign Sovereign Immunity Act?

3. *Foreign Parties in U.S. Courts.* In *Amerada Hess* a foreign plaintiff sued a foreign state in U.S. federal court. In Verlinden B.V. v. Central Bank of Nigeria, 461 U.S. 480, 103 S.Ct. 1962, 76 L.Ed.2d 81 (1983), the Supreme Court considered whether the requirements of Article III of the U.S. Constitution were met when a foreign plaintiff sued a foreign defendant in federal court on a nonfederal, breach-of-contract cause of action. The Supreme Court found that jurisdiction was constitutional:

> By reason of its authority over foreign commerce and foreign relations, Congress has the undisputed power to decide, as a matter of federal law, whether and under what circumstances foreign nations should be amenable to suit in the United States. Actions against foreign sovereigns in our courts raise sensitive issues concerning the foreign relations of the United States, and the primacy of federal concerns is evident.

> To promote these federal interests, Congress exercised its Art. I powers by enacting a statute comprehensively regulating the amenability of foreign nations to suit in the United States. The statute must be applied by the district court in every action against a foreign sovereign, since subject-matter jurisdiction in any such action depends on the existence of one of the specified exceptions to foreign sovereign immunity, 28 US.C. § 1330(a). At the threshold of every action in a district court against a foreign state, therefore, the court must satisfy itself that one of the exceptions applies—and in doing so it must apply the detailed federal law standards set forth in the [FSIA]. Accordingly, an action against a foreign sovereign arises under federal law, for purposes of Art. III jurisdiction.

Id. at 493–94, 103 S.Ct. at 1971, 76 L.Ed.2d at 92.

4. *Exceptions to Immunity.* After ruling that the FSIA provided the only way to sue foreign governments, the Supreme Court in *Amerada Hess* considered whether any section 1605 exceptions to immunity existed. Justices Blackmun and Marshall dissented from this part of the judgment, arguing that the question of the FSIA's exceptions had not been fully briefed in the case. They preferred to remand. However, Justice Rehnquist and the majority rejected the possibility that there was a section 1605(a)(5) tort "occurring in the United States." Could it have been shown that Argentina had made some sort of implicit waiver in customary international law under section 1605(a)(1)?

Justice Rehnquist also observed that the companies did not make a claim under section 1605(a)(2) for an exception based on "an act outside the territory of the United States in connection with a commercial activity of the foreign state elsewhere and that act causes a direct effect in the United States." What sort of a "commercial activities" exception claim could have been made in *Amerada Hess*? In Republic of Argentina v. Weltover, Inc., 504 U.S. 607, 112 S.Ct. 2160, 119 L.Ed.2d 394 (1992), the Supreme Court decided that the Argentine government's issuance of bonds to protect foreign creditors did qualify as "commercial": "[T]hey are in almost all respects garden-variety debt instruments: They may be held by private parties; they are negotiable and may be traded on the international market (except in Argentina); and they promise a future stream of cash income." *Id.* at 615, 112 S.Ct. at 2166, 119 L.Ed.2d at 405. In Cicippio v. Islamic Republic of Iran, 30 F.3d 164 (D.C.Cir.1994), however, the D.C. Circuit held that kidnapping even for monetary ransom could not be characterized as "commercial" for the purpose of the FSIA. In Saudi Arabia v. Nelson, 507 U.S. 349, 113 S.Ct. 1471, 123 L.Ed.2d 47 (1993), the Supreme Court considered whether a U.S. citizen's alleged detention and torture by the Saudi government were so intertwined with his recruitment and hiring to work in a Saudi hospital as to bring into play the "commercial activity" exception of section 1605(a)(2). The Court found the exception to immunity inapplicable.

5. *The Presumption of Immunity.* Is the *Amerada Hess Case* a good example of the shift in presumption made, perhaps unwittingly, by the drafters of the FSIA? How might the Court's analysis in *Amerada Hess* have been changed if, as in *Victory Transport*, it was incumbent on Argentina to prove that immunity ought to be granted rather than on plaintiffs to show that an exception to immunity existed?

6. *The Definition of "Foreign State."* In *Amerada Hess* there was no question that the defendant, the Argentine Republic, was a foreign state for the purposes of the FSIA, but in other cases the definition of "foreign state" may be more perplexing. The FSIA designates that a "foreign state" includes not only the state itself but both "a political subdivision of a foreign state" and "an agency or instrumentality of a foreign state [including] a separate legal person, corporate or otherwise * * * a majority of whose shares or other ownership interest is owned by a foreign state or a political subdivision thereof." 28 U.S.C. § 1603(a), (b).

When must that majority ownership interest be owned in order for an entity to be deemed a state for purposes of the FSIA? In Pere v. Nuovo Pignone, Inc., 150 F.3d 477 (5th Cir.1998), *cert. denied*, 525 U.S. 1141, 119

S.Ct. 1033, 143 L.Ed.2d 42 (1999), the Fifth Circuit held that an Italian company, Nuovo Pignone, was entitled to be protected by the doctrine of sovereign immunity because, when one of its turbine engines exploded off the coast of West Africa, it was majority-owned by an instrumentality of the Italian government. The court chose to reject plaintiff's argument that, since at the time of suit a majority of the ownership of Nuovo Pignone had been transferred to private companies, the Italian company should no longer be given the protections afforded foreign states: "The foreign policy concerns underlying foreign sovereign immunity do not necessarily disappear when a defendant loses its [governmental] status before suit is filed." *Id.* at 481. Working within the confines of the FSIA, the Fifth Circuit then ruled that plaintiff failed to show the necessary connections between the defendant or its conduct and the United States to establish a commercial activities exception. *Id.* at 481–82. On the definition of "foreign state" in *Pere* and other cases, see Amber L. Cottle, "Foreign Sovereign Immunity and the Foreign Sovereign Immunities Act," 33 *International Lawyer* 409, 410–11 (1999).

7. *The Responsibility of Foreign States for State–owned Enterprises.* A related problem concerns the responsibility of a state that is sued under the FSIA for the acts of a state-owned enterprise, especially when that owned enterprise is no longer able to pay its own debts. Here the legal issues may revolve around the control of the enterprise and raise questions similar to those touching on corporate groups in general. See Philip I. Blumberg, *The Law of Corporate Groups: Problems in the Bankruptcy or Reorganization of Parent and Subsidiary Corporations, Including the Law of Corporate Guaranties* (1985). In Transamerica Leasing, Inc. v. La Republica de Venezuela, 200 F.3d 843 (D.C.Cir.2000), Argentina was held not responsible to answer for a breach of contract claim under the FSIA (commercial activities exception) for the acts of a defunct Argentine shipping company, Compania Anonima Venezolana de Navegacion, that had been 99.86% owned by an instrumentality of the Venezuelan government created to help restructure and privatize Venezuelan state enterprises. The D.C. Circuit held that the facts of *Transamerica Leasing* established neither actual nor apparent Venezuelan government control over the defunct company.

8. *International Codification of Sovereign Immunity.* Might sovereign immunity be ripe for international codification? At least six national sovereign immunity statutes—in Australia, Canada, Pakistan, Singapore, South Africa, and the United Kingdom—have been enacted since 1976 when the FSIA became law in the United States. Whatever the virtues of domestic legislation, might not international legislation better suit this field? If possible, why should not there be a treaty providing common rules for different states? For information about efforts to draft an international sovereign immunity convention, see Virginia Morris, "The International Law Commission's Draft Convention on the Jurisdictional Immunities of States and Their Property," 17 *Denver Journal of International Law and Policy* 395 (1989).

D. THE ACT OF STATE DOCTRINE

Also rooted in *The Schooner Exchange*, the act of state doctrine can be easily confused with the doctrine of foreign sovereign immunity. To make an easy distinction, note that act of state does not provide a jurisdictional immunity. Rather, it serves as a principle of choice of law, instructing a court to apply the law of a foreign state respecting an act made by the foreign government in its own territory. The act of state doctrine does share with the doctrine of foreign sovereign immunity (and indeed with the doctrine of *forum non conveniens*) the notion of comity; all in one way or another defer to foreign governments.

There is antique support for the act of state doctrine. In Blad v. Bamfield, 3 Swans. 605 (Chancery, 1674), Blad, a Danish subject, sued Bamfield and others, English subjects, in Chancery for an injunction to stay several actions Bamfield had commenced in the English law courts. Blad had a monopoly for certain trade in Iceland, which was Danish territory, and had seized Bamfield's goods brought to Iceland in contravention of Blad's rights. In Law, Bamfield argued that the Danish royal grants to Blad violated the free-trading terms of an English–Danish treaty. In issuing a perpetual injunction against Bamfield's legal action, Lord Nottingham ruled in Chancery:

> [C]ertainly no case [Blad's] was ever better proved; for the Plaintiff hath proved letters patent from the King of Denmark for the sole trade of Iceland; a seizure by virtue of that patent; a sentence upon that seizure; a confirmation of that sentence by the Chancellor of Denmark; an execution of that sentence after confirmation; and a payment of two thirds to the King of Denmark after that execution. Now, after all this, to send it to a trial at law, where either the Court must pretend to judge of the validity of the King's letters patent in Denmark, or of the exposition and meaning of the articles of peace; or that a common jury should try whether the English have a right to trade in Iceland, is monstrous and absurd.

Id. at 606–07.

In the United States, the act of state doctrine is usually thought to have been first separately elaborated in 1897 in *Underhill v. Hernandez* and to have reached its pinnacle in 1964 in *Banco Nacional de Cuba v. Sabbatino*. Both cases follow.

UNDERHILL v. HERNANDEZ
168 U.S. 250, 18 S.Ct. 83, 42 L.Ed. 456 (1897).

In the early part of 1892 a revolution was initiated in Venezuela against the administration thereof, which the revolutionists claimed had ceased to be the legitimate government. The principal parties to this conflict were those who recognized Palacio as their head and those who followed the leadership of Crespo. General Hernandez belonged to the anti-administration party, and commanded its forces in the vicinity of

Ciudad Bolivar. On the 8th of August 1892, an engagement took place between the armies of the two parties at Buena Vista, some seven miles from Bolivar, in which the troops under Hernandez prevailed, and on the 13th of August, Hernandez entered Bolivar and assumed command of the city. All of the local officials had in the meantime left, and the vacant positions were filled by General Hernandez, who from that date and during the period of the transactions complained of was the civil and military chief of the city and district. In October the party in revolt had achieved success generally, taking possession of the capital of Venezuela, October 6, and on October 23, 1892, the Crespo government, so called, was formally recognized as the legitimate government of Venezuela by the United States.

George F. Underhill was a citizen of the United States, who had constructed a waterworks system for the city of Bolivar under a contract with the government, and was engaged in supplying the place with water, and he also carried on a machinery-repair business. Some time after the entry of General Hernandez, Underhill applied to him as the officer in command for a passport to leave the city. Hernandez refused this request, and requests made by others in Underhill's behalf, until October 18, when a passport was given and Underhill left the country.

This action was brought to recover damages for the detention caused by reason of the refusal to grant the passport; for the alleged confinement of Underhill to his own house; and for certain alleged assaults and affronts by the soldiers of Hernandez' army.

MR. CHIEF JUSTICE FULLER, after stating the case, delivered the opinion of the court.

Every sovereign State is bound to respect the independence of every other sovereign State, and the courts of one country will not sit in judgment on the acts of the government of another done within its own territory. Redress of grievances by reason of such acts must be obtained through the means open to be availed of by sovereign powers as between themselves.

Nor can the principle be confined to lawful or recognized governments, or to cases where redress can manifestly be had through public channels. The immunity of individuals from suits brought in foreign tribunals for acts done within their own States, in the exercise of governmental authority, whether as civil officers or as military commanders, must necessarily extend to the agents of governments ruling by paramount force as matter of fact. Where a civil war prevails, that is where the people of a country are divided into two hostile parties, who take up arms and oppose one another by military force, generally speaking foreign nations do not assume to judge of the merits of the quarrel. If the party seeking to dislodge the existing government succeeds, and the independence of the government it has set up is recognized, then the acts of such government from the commencement of its existence are regarded as those of an independent nation. If the political revolt fails of success, still if actual war has been waged, acts of legitimate warfare cannot be made the basis of individual liability. * * *

We entertain no doubt upon the evidence that Hernandez was carrying on military operations in support of the revolutionary party. It may be that adherents of the side of the controversy in the particular locality where Hernandez was the leader of the movement entertained a preference for him as the future executive head of the nation, but that is beside the question. The acts complained of were the acts of a military commander representing the authority of the revolutionary party as a government, which afterwards succeeded and was recognized by the United States. We think the Circuit Court of Appeals was justified in concluding "that the acts of the defendant were the acts of the government of Venezuela, and as such are not properly the subject of adjudication in the courts of another government."

The decisions cited on plaintiff's behalf are not in point. Cases respecting arrest by military authority in the absence of the prevalence of war; or the validity of contracts between individuals entered into in aid of insurrection; or the right of revolutionary bodies to vex the commerce of the world on its common highway without incurring the penalties denounced on piracy; and the like, do not involve the questions presented here.

We agree with Circuit Court of Appeals, that "the evidence upon the trial indicated that the purpose of the defendant in his treatment of the plaintiff was to coerce the plaintiff to operate his waterworks and his repair works for the benefit of the community and the revolutionary forces," and that "it was not sufficient to have warranted a finding by the jury that the defendant was actuated by malice or any personal or private motive"; and we concur in its disposition of the rulings below. The decree of the Circuit Court is

Affirmed.

BANCO NACIONAL DE CUBA v. SABBATINO

376 U.S. 398, 84 S.Ct. 923, 11 L.Ed.2d 804 (1964).

MR. JUSTICE HARLAN delivered the opinion of the Court.

The question which brought this case here, and is now found to be the dispositive issue, is whether the so-called act of state doctrine serves to sustain petitioner's claims in this litigation. Such claims are ultimately found on a decree of the Government of Cuba expropriating certain property, the right to the proceeds of which is here in controversy. The act of state doctrine in its traditional formulation precludes the courts of this country from inquiring into the validity of the public acts a recognized foreign sovereign power committed within its own territory.

I.

In February and July of 1960, respondent Farr, Whitlock & Co., an American commodity broker, contracted to purchase Cuban sugar, free alongside the streamer, from a wholly owned subsidiary of Compania Azucarera Vertientes–Camaguey de Cuba (C. A. V.), a corporation organized under Cuban law whose capital stock was owned principally by United States residents. Farr, Whitlock agreed to pay for the sugar in New York upon presentation of the shipping documents and a sight draft.

On July 6, 1960, the Congress of the United States amended the Sugar Act of 1948 to permit a presidentially directed reduction of the sugar quota for Cuba. On the same day President Eisenhower exercised the granted power. The day of the congressional enactment, the Cuban Council of Ministers adopted "Law No. 851," which characterized this reduction in the Cuban sugar quota as an act of "aggression, for political purposes" on the part of the United States, justifying the taking of countermeasures by Cuba. The law gave the Cuban President and Prime Minister discretionary power to nationalize by forced expropriation property or enterprises in which American nationals had an interest. Although a system of compensation was formally provided, the possibility of payment under it may well be deemed illusory. Our State Department has described the Cuban law as "manifestly in violation of those principles of international law which have long been accepted by the free countries of the West. It is in its essence discriminatory, arbitrary and confiscatory."

Between August 6 and August 9, 1960, the sugar covered by the contract between Farr, Whitlock and C. A. V. was loaded, destined for Morocco, onto the S. S. *Hornfels*, which was standing offshore at the Cuban port of Jucaro (Santa Maria). On the day loading commenced, the Cuban President and Prime Minister, acting pursuant to Law No. 851, issued Executive Power Resolution No. 1. It provided for the compulsory expropriation of all property and enterprises, and of rights and interests arising therefrom, of certain listed companies, including C. A. V., wholly or principally owned by American nationals. The preamble reiterated the alleged injustice of the American reduction of the Cuban sugar quota and emphasized the importance of Cuba's serving as an example for other countries to follow "in their struggle to free themselves from the brutal claws of Imperialism." In consequence of the resolution, the consent of the Cuban Government was necessary before a ship carrying sugar of a named company could leave Cuban waters. In order to obtain this consent, Farr, Whitlock, on August 11, entered into contracts, identical to those it had made with C. A. V., with the Banco Para el Comercio Exterior de Cuba, an instrumentality of the Cuban Government. The S. S. *Hornfels* sailed for Morocco on August 12.

Banco Exterior assigned the bills of lading to petitioner, also an instrumentality of the Cuban Government, which instructed its agent in New York, Société Génerale, to deliver the bills and a sight draft in the sum of $175,250.69 to Farr, Whitlock in return for payment. Société Génerale's initial tender of the documents was refused by Farr, Whitlock, which on the same day was notified of C. A. V.'s claim that as rightful owner of the sugar it was entitled to the proceeds. In return for a promise not to turn the funds over to petitioner or its agent, C. A. V. agreed to indemnify Farr, Whitlock for any loss. Farr, Whitlock subsequently accepted the shipping documents, negotiated the bills of lading to its customer, and received payment for the sugar. It refused, however, to hand over the proceeds to Société Génerale. Shortly thereafter, Farr, Whitlock was served with an order of the New York Supreme Court, which had appointed Sabbatino as Temporary Receiver of C. A. V.'s New York assets, enjoining it from taking any action in regard to the money claimed by C. A. V. that might result in its removal from the State. Following this, Farr, Whitlock, pursuant to court order, transferred the funds to Sabbatino, to abide the event of a judicial determination as to their ownership.

[The Court decides that Cuba could still sue in the United States though it was an unfriendly power, rejects the contention that the case should be decided by New York law, then turns to the act of state doctrine.]

IV.

The classic American statement of the act of state doctrine, which appears to have taken root in England as early as 1674, *Blad v. Bamfield*, 3 Swans. 604, 36 Eng.Rep. 992, and began to emerge in the jurisprudence of this country in the late eighteenth and early nineteenth centuries, see *e.g., Ware v. Hylton*, 3 Dall, 199, 230; *The Schooner Exchange v. M'Faddon*, 7 Cranch 116, 135, 136, is found in *Underhill v. Hernandez*, where Chief Justice Fuller said for a unanimous Court:

> "Every sovereign State is bound to respect the independence of every other sovereign State, and the courts of one country will not sit in judgment on the acts of the government of another done within its own territory. Redress of grievances by reason of such acts must be obtained through the means open to be availed of by sovereign powers as between themselves."

Following this precept the Court in that case refused to inquire into acts of Hernandez, a revolutionary Venezuelan military commander whose government had been later recognized by the United States, which were made the basis of a damage action in this country by Underhill, an American citizen, who claimed that he had been unlawfully assaulted, coerced, and detained in Venezuela by Hernandez.

None of this Court's subsequent cases in which the act of state doctrine was directly or peripherally involved manifest any retreat from *Underhill*. * * *

V.

Preliminarily, we discuss the foundations on which we deem the act of state doctrine to rest, and more particularly the question of whether state or federal law governs its application in a federal diversity case.

We do not believe that this doctrine is compelled either by the inherent nature of sovereign authority, as some of the earlier decisions seem to imply, or by some principle of international law. If a transaction takes place in one jurisdiction and the forum is in another, the forum does not by dismissing an action or by applying its own law purport to divest the first jurisdiction of its territorial sovereignty; it merely declines to adjudicate or makes applicable its own law to parties or property before it. The refusal of one country to enforce the penal laws of another is a typical example of an instance when a court will not entertain a cause of action arising in another jurisdiction. While historic notions of sovereign authority do bear upon the wisdom of employing the act of state doctrine, they do not dictate its existence.

That international law does not require application of the doctrine is evidenced by the practice of nations. Most of the countries rendering decisions on the subject fail to follow the rule rigidly. [The Court cites authorities from France, Germany, Greece, Italy, Japan, the Netherlands, Switzerland, and the United Kingdom.] No international arbitral or judicial decision discovered suggests that international law prescribes recognition of sovereign acts of foreign governments, and apparently no claim has ever been raised before an international tribunal that failure to apply the act of state doctrine constitutes a breach of international obligation. If international law does not prescribe use of the doctrine, neither does it forbid application of the rule even if it is claimed that the act of state in question violated international law. The traditional view of international law is that it establishes substantive principles for determining whether one country has wronged another. Because of its peculiar nation-to-nation character the usual method for an individual to seek relief is to exhaust local remedies and then repair to the executive authorities of his own state to persuade them to champion his claim in diplomacy or before an international tribunal. Although it is, of course, true that United States courts apply international law as a part of our own in appropriate circumstances, the public law of nations can hardly dictate to a country which is in theory wronged how to treat that wrong within its domestic borders.

Despite the broad statement in *Oetjen* [*v. Central Leather Co.*, 246 U.S. 297, 38 S.Ct. 309, 62 L.Ed. 726 (1918),] that "The conduct of the foreign relations of our Government is committed by the Constitution to the Executive and Legislative ... Departments," it cannot of course be thought that "every case or controversy which touches foreign relations lies beyond judicial cognizance." *Baker v. Carr*, 369 U.S. 186, 211. The text of the Constitution does not require the act of state doctrine; it does not irrevocably remove from the judiciary the capacity to review the validity of foreign acts of state.

The act of state doctrine does, however, have "constitutional" underpinnings. It arises out of the basic relationships between branches of government in a system of separation of powers. It concerns the competency of dissimilar institutions to make and implement particular kinds of decisions in the area of international relations. The doctrine as formulated in past decisions expresses the strong sense of the Judicial Branch that its engagement in the task of passing on the validity of foreign acts of state may hinder rather than further this country's pursuit of goals both for itself and for the community of nations as a whole in the international sphere. Many commentators disagree with this view; they have striven by means of distinguishing and limiting past decisions and by advancing various considerations of policy to stimulate a narrowing of the apparent scope of the rule. Whatever considerations are thought to predominate, it is plain that the problems involved are uniquely federal in nature. If federal authority, in this instance this Court, orders the field of judicial competence in this area for the federal courts, and the state courts are left free to formulate their own rules, the purposes behind the doctrine could be as effectively undermined as if there had been no federal pronouncement on the subject.

We could perhaps in this diversity action avoid the question of deciding whether federal or state law is applicable to this aspect of the litigation. New York has enunciated the act of state doctrine in terms that echo those of federal decisions decided during the reign of *Swift v. Tyson*, 16 Pet. 1. * * *

However, we are constrained to make it clear that an issue concerned with a basic choice regarding the competence and function of the Judiciary and the National Executive in ordering our relationships with other members of the international community must be treated exclusively as an aspect of federal law. It seems fair to assume that the Court did not have rules like the act of state doctrine in mind when it decided *Erie R. Co. v. Tompkins*. Soon thereafter, Professor Philip C. Jessup, now a judge of the International Court of Justice, recognized the potential dangers were *Erie* extended to legal problems affecting international relations. He cautioned that rules of international law should not be left to divergent and perhaps parochial state interpretations. His basic rationale is equally applicable to the act of state doctrine. * * *

VI.

If the act of state doctrine is a principle of decision binding on federal and state courts alike but compelled by neither international law nor the Constitution, its continuing vitality depends on its capacity to reflect the proper distribution of functions between the judicial and political branches of the Government on matters bearing upon foreign affairs. It should be apparent that the greater the degree of codification or consensus concerning a particular area of international law, the more appropriate it is for the judiciary to render decisions regarding it, since the courts can then focus on the application of an agreed principle to circumstances of fact rather than on the sensitive task of establishing a principle not inconsistent with the national interest or with international justice. It is also evident that some aspects of international law touch much more sharply on national nerves than do others; the less important the implications of an issue are for our foreign relations, the weaker the justification of exclusivity in the political branches. The balance of relevant considerations may also be shifted if the government which perpetrated the challenged act of state is no longer in existence, * * * for the political interest of this country may, as a result, be measurably altered. Therefore, rather than laying down or reaffirming an inflexible and all-encompassing rule in this case, we decide only that the Judicial Branch will not examine the validity of a taking of property within its own territory by a foreign sovereign government, extant and recognized by this country at the time of suit, in the absence of a treaty or other unambiguous agreement regarding controlling legal principles, even if the complaint alleges that the taking violates customary international law.

There are few if any issues in international law today on which opinion seems to be so divided as the limitations on a state's power to expropriate the property of aliens. There is, of course, authority, in international judicial and arbitral decisions, in the expressions of national governments, and among commentators for the view that a taking is improper under international law if it is not for a public purpose, is discriminatory, or is without provision for prompt, adequate, and effective compensation. However, Communist countries, although they have in fact provided a degree of compensation after diplomatic efforts, commonly recognize no obligation on the part of the taking country. Certain representatives of the newly independent and underdeveloped countries have questioned whether rules of state responsibility toward aliens can bind nations that have not consented to them and it is argued that the traditionally articulated standards governing expropriation of property reflect "imperialist" interests and are inappropriate to the circumstances of emergent states.

The disagreement as to relevant international law standards reflects an even more basic divergence between the national interests of capital importing and capital exporting nations and between the social ideologies of those countries that favor state control of a considerable portion of the means of production and those that adhere to a free enterprise system. It is difficult to imagine the courts of this country embarking on adjudication in an area which touches more sensitively the practical and ideological goals of the various members of the community of nations.

When we consider the prospect of the courts characterizing foreign expropriations, however justifiably, as invalid under international law and ineffective to pass title, the wisdom of the precedents is confirmed.
* * *

The possible adverse consequences of a conclusion to the contrary of that implicit in these cases is highlighted by contrasting that practices of the political branch with the limitations of the judicial process in matters of this kind. Following an expropriation of any significance, the Executive engages in diplomacy aimed to assure that United States citizens who are harmed are compensated fairly. Representing all claimants of this country, it will often be able, either by bilateral or multilateral talks, by submission to the United Nations, or by the employment of economic and political sanctions, to achieve some degree of general redress. Judicial determinations of invalidity of title can, on the other hand, have only an occasional impact, since they depend on the fortuitous circumstance of the property in question being brought into this country. Such decisions would, if the acts involved were declared invalid, often be likely to give offense to the expropriating country; since the concept of territorial sovereignty is so deep seated, any state may resent the refusal of the courts of another sovereign to accord validity to acts within its territorial borders. Piecemeal dispositions of this sort involving the probability of affront to another state could seriously interfere with negotiations being carried on by the Executive Branch and might prevent or render less favorable the terms of an agreement that could otherwise be reached. Relations with third countries which have engaged in similar expropriations would not be immune from effect.

The dangers of such adjudication are present regardless of whether the State Department has, as it did in this case, asserted that the relevant act violated international law. If the Executive Branch has undertaken negotiations with an expropriating country, but has refrained from claims of violation of the law of nations, a determination to that effect by a court might be regarded as a serious insult, while a finding of compliance with international law would greatly strengthen the bargaining hand of the other state with consequent detriment to American interests.

Even if the State Department has proclaimed the impropriety of the expropriation, the stamp of approval of its view by a judicial tribunal, however impartial, might increase any affront and the judicial decision might occur at a time, almost always well after the taking, when such an impact would be contrary to our national interest. Considerably more serious and far-reaching consequences would flow from a judicial finding that international law standards had been met if that determination flew in the face of a State Department proclamation to the contrary. When articulating principles of international law in its relations with other states, the Executive Branch speaks not only as an interpreter of generally accepted and traditional rules, as would the courts, but also as an advocate of standards it believes desirable for the community of nations and protective of national concerns. In short, whatever way the matter is cut, the possibility of conflict between the Judicial and Executive Branches could hardly be avoided. * * *

However offensive to the public policy of this country and its constituent States an expropriation of this kind may be, we conclude that both the national interest and progress toward the goal of establishing the rule of law among nations are best served by maintaining intact the act of state doctrine in this realm of its application.

Notes and Questions

1. *The* Underhill *Doctrine.* The famous line in *Underhill,* even reaching the *New York Times,* "Underhill's Suit Dismissed: No Judicial Remedy for His Detention in Venezuela," *New York Times,* Nov. 30, 1897, at 10, was the first one in Chief Justice Fuller's opinion: "Every sovereign State is bound

to respect the independence of every other sovereign State, and the courts of one country will not sit in judgment on the acts of the government done within its own territory." Though first enunciating the act of state doctrine, could *Underhill* have also been decided simply by treating General Hernandez as an agent of the Venezuelan government and then by protecting both from the jurisdiction of U.S. courts by way of the doctrine of sovereign immunity? After all, the opinion went on to say: "The acts complained of were the acts of a military commander representing the authority of the revolutionary party as a government, which afterwards succeeded and was recognized by the United States."

2. *The Background to* Sabbatino. The political events leading to the *Sabbatino Case* were front-page news in the United States. On June 23, 1960, "Premier Fidel Castro threatened * * * to meet 'economic aggression' by the United States with the seizure of all American-owned property and business interests in Cuba." "U.S. Holdings to Be Taken If Sugar Is Cut, Castro Says," *New York Times*, June 24, 1960, at 1. On July 6, 1960, President Eisenhower "virtually ended * * * Cuba's sugar sales to the United States for this year." Tad Szulc, "U.S. Cuts Cuba Sugar Sale By 95% for Rest of Year; President Cites Hostility," *New York Times*, July 7, 1960, at 1, 9. The next day, Castro "whipped [a] crowd of several thousand into displays of frenzied anger against the United States." R. Hart Phillips, "Castro Attacks Sugar Quota as 'Imperialism,'" *New York Times*, July 8, 1960, at 1. And on August 7, 1960, the Cuban Premier proclaimed the "forcible expropriation" of all U.S.-owned companies in his country. R. Hart Phillips, "Castro Decrees Seizure of Rest of U.S. Property; Cites Cut in Sugar Quota," *New York Times*, Aug. 7, 1960, at 1. The *Sabbatino* decision of the U.S. Supreme Court also took on a high political profile. The Court's reaffirmation of the act of state doctrine itself achieved front-page status. Anthony Lewis, "High Court Bars Judging of Cuba on Expropriation," *New York Times*, Mar. 24, 1964, at 1.

3. *The Reaction to* Sabbatino. It should be no surprise that the *Sabbatino* judgment evoked an uproar in the U.S. Congress, which promptly passed what became known as the *Sabbatino* or Second Hickenlooper Amendment to the Foreign Assistance Act of 1964. The amendment includes the following language:

> Notwithstanding any other provision of law, no court in the United States shall decline on the ground of the federal act of state doctrine to make a determination on the merits giving effect to the principles of international law in a case in which a claim of title or other right to property is asserted by any party including a foreign state (or a party claiming through such state) based upon (or traced through) a confiscation or other taking after January 1, 1959, by an act of that state in violation of the principles of international law, including the principles of compensation and the other standards set out in this subsection: *Provided,* That this subparagraph shall not be applicable (1) in any case in which an act of a foreign state is not contrary to international law or with respect to a claim of title or other right acquired pursuant to an irrevocable letter of credit of not more than 180 days duration issued in good faith prior to the time of confiscation or other taking, or (2) in any case with respect to which the President determines the application of

the act of state doctrine is required in that particular case by the foreign policy interests of the United States and a suggestion to this effect is filed on his behalf in that case with the court.

22 U.S.C. § 2370(e)(2).

On remand, the Southern District Court in New York followed the dictate of the *Sabbatino* Amendment and dismissed plaintiff's complaint. The Second Circuit affirmed, while the Supreme Court denied *certiorari*, effectively permitting itself to be reversed by Congress. Banco Nacional de Cuba v. Farr, 243 F.Supp. 957 (S.D.N.Y.1965), *aff'd*, 383 F.2d 166 (2d Cir.1967), *cert. denied*, 390 U.S. 956, 88 S.Ct. 1038, 19 L.Ed.2d 1151 (1968). See Richard A. Falk, *The Aftermath of Sabbatino* (Lyman M. Tondel, Jr. ed. 1965). What is the authority of the *Sabbatino Case* as precedent following Congress's *Sabbatino* Amendment? Do the decisions in the follow-up case affect its precedential value?

4. Sabbatino *and the Role of the Courts.* Was the Supreme Court too deferential in principle to the legislative and executive branches in *Sabbatino*? After all, the Court was reluctant to decide a case involving an uncertain point of international law apparently for fear of reaching a conflicting opinion with that of the President or Congress. Is not the Court the branch of the U.S. government best positioned to discover and elaborate international law? Here the international law rule could be used to trump the rule of the foreign state in U.S. litigation. When should the Court turn to the executive or legislative branches for their advice as to whether such a trumping would upset U.S. foreign relations? Compare the reasoning of the Court in *Dames & Moore v. Regan* in Chapter 4.

W.S. KIRKPATRICK & CO. v. ENVIRONMENTAL TECTONICS CORP. INTERNATIONAL

493 U.S. 400, 110 S.Ct. 701, 107 L.Ed.2d 816 (1990).

JUSTICE SCALIA delivered the opinion of the Court.

In this case we must decide whether the act of state doctrine bars a court in the United States from entertaining a cause of action that does not rest upon the asserted invalidity of an official act of a foreign sovereign, but that does require imputing to foreign officials an unlawful motivation (the obtaining of bribes) in the performance of such an official act.

I

The facts as alleged in respondent's complaint are as follows: In 1981, Harry Carpenter, who was then Chairman of the Board and Chief Executive Officer of petitioner W. S. Kirkpatrick & Co., Inc. (Kirkpatrick), learned that the Republic of Nigeria was interested in contracting for the construction and equipment of an aeromedical center at Kaduna Air Force Base in Nigeria. He made arrangements with Benson "Tunde" Akindele, a Nigerian citizen whereby Akindele would endeavor to secure the contract for Kirkpatrick. It was agreed that, in the event the contract was awarded to Kirkpatrick, Kirkpatrick would pay to two

Panamanian entities controlled by Akindele a "commission" equal to 20% of the contract price, which would in turn be given as a bribe to officials of the Nigerian Government. In accordance with this plan, the contract was awarded to petitioner W. S. Kirkpatrick & Co., International (Kirkpatrick International), a wholly owned subsidiary of Kirkpatrick; Kirkpatrick paid the promised "commission" to the appointed Panamanian entities; and those funds were disbursed as bribes. All parties agree that Nigerian law prohibits both the payment and the receipt of bribes in connection with the award of a government contract.

Respondent Environmental Tectonics Corporation, International, an unsuccessful bidder for the Kaduna contract, learned of the 20% "commission" and brought the matter to the attention of the Nigerian Air Force and the United States Embassy in Lagos. Following an investigation by the Federal Bureau of Investigation, the United States Attorney for the District of New Jersey brought charges against both Kirkpatrick and Carpenter for violations of the Foreign Corrupt Practices Act of 1977, 15 U.S.C. § 78dd–1 *et seq.*, and both pleaded guilty.

Respondent then brought this civil action in the United States District Court for District of New Jersey against Carpenter, Akindele, petitioners, and others, seeking damages under the Racketeer Influenced and Corrupt Organizations Act, 18 U.S.C. § 1961 *et seq.*, the Robinson–Patman Act, 15 U.S.C. § 13 *et seq.*, and the New Jersey Anti–Racketeering Act N.J. Stat. Ann. § 2C:41–2 *et seq.* (West 1982). The defendants moved to dismiss the complaint under Rule 12(b)(6) of the Federal Rules of Civil Procedure on the ground that the action was barred by the act of state doctrine.

The District Court, having requested and received a letter expressing the views of the legal adviser to the United States Department of State as to the applicability of the act of state doctrine, treated the motion as one for summary judgment under Rule 56 of the Federal Rules of Civil Procedure and granted the motion. The District Court concluded that the act of state doctrine applies "if the inquiry presented for judicial determination includes the motivation of a sovereign act which would result in embarrassment to the sovereign or constitute interference in the conduct of foreign policy of the United States." Applying that principle to the facts at hand, the court held that respondent's suit had to be dismissed because in order to prevail respondent would have to show that "the defendants or certain of them intended to wrongfully influence the decision to award the Nigerian Contract by payment of a bribe, that the Government of Nigeria, its officials or other representatives knew of the offered consideration for awarding the Nigerian Contract to Kirkpatrick, that the bribe was actually received or anticipated and that 'but for' the payment or anticipation of the payment of the bribe, ETC would have been awarded the Nigerian Contract."

The Court of Appeals for the Third Circuit reversed. Although agreeing with the District Court that "the award of a military procurement contract can be, in certain circumstances, a sufficiently formal expression of a government's public interests to trigger application" of the act of state doctrine, it found application of the doctrine unwarranted on the facts of this case. The Court of Appeals found particularly persuasive the letter to the District Court from the legal adviser to the Department of State, which had stated that in the opinion of the Department judicial inquiry into the purpose behind the act of a foreign sovereign would not produce the "unique embarrassment, and the particular interference with the conduct of foreign affairs, that may result from the judicial determination that a foreign sovereign's acts are invalid." In light of the Department's view that the interests of the Executive Branch would not be harmed by prosecution of the action, the Court of Appeals held that Kirkpatrick had not met its burden of showing that the case should not go forward; accordingly, it reversed the judgment of the District Court and remanded the case for trial. We granted certiorari.

II

This Court's description of the jurisprudential foundation for the act of state doctrine has undergone some evolution over the years. We once viewed the doctrine as an expression of international law, resting upon "the highest considerations of international comity and expediency," *Oetjen v. Central Leather Co.*, 246 U.S. 297, 303–304 (1918). We have more recently described it, however, as a consequence of domestic separation of powers, reflecting "the strong sense of the Judicial Branch that its engagement in the task of passing on the validity of foreign acts of state may hinder" the conduct of foreign affairs, *Banco Nacional de Cuba v. Sabbatino*, 376 U.S. 398, 423 (1964). Some Justices have suggested possible exceptions to application of the doctrine, where one or both of the foregoing policies would seemingly not be served: an exception, for example, for acts of state that consist of commercial transactions, since neither modern international comity nor the current position of our Executive Branch accorded sovereign immunity to such acts; or an exception for cases in which the Executive Branch has represented that it has no objection to denying validity to the foreign sovereign act, since then the courts would be impeding no foreign policy goals.

The parties have argued at length about the applicability of these possible exceptions, and, more generally, about whether the purpose of the act of state doctrine would be furthered by its application in this case. We find it unnecessary, however, to pursue those inquiries, since the factual predicate for application of the act of state doctrine does not exist. Nothing in the present suit requires the Court to declare invalid, and thus ineffective as "a rule of decision for the courts of this country," *Ricaud v. American Metal Co.*, 246 U.S. 304, 310 (1918), the official act of a foreign sovereign.

In every case in which we have held the act of state doctrine applicable, the relief sought or the defense interposed would have required a court in the United States to declare invalid the official act of a foreign sovereign performed within its own territory. In *Underhill v.*

Hernandez, 168 U.S. 250, 254 (1897), holding the defendant's detention of the plaintiff to be tortious would have required denying legal effect to "acts of a military commander representing the authority of the revolutionary party as government, which afterwards succeeded and was recognized by the United States." In *Oetjen v. Central Leather Co.* and in *Ricaud v. American Metal Co.*, denying title to the party who claimed through purchase from Mexico would have required declaring that government's prior seizure of the property, within its own territory, legally ineffective. In *Sabbatino,* upholding the defendant's claim to the funds would have required a holding that Cuba's expropriation of goods located in Havana was null and void. In the present case, by contrast, neither the claim nor any asserted defense requires a determination that Nigeria's contract with Kirkpatrick International was, or was not, effective.

Petitioners point out, however, that the facts necessary to establish respondent's claim will also establish that the contract was unlawful. Specifically, they note that in order to prevail respondent must prove that petitioner Kirkpatrick made, and Nigerian officials received, payments that violate Nigerian law, which would, they assert, support a finding that the contract is invalid under Nigerian law. Assuming that to be true, it still does not suffice. The act of state doctrine is not some vague doctrine of abstention but a *"principle of decision* binding on federal and state courts alike." *Sabbatino* (emphasis added). As we said in *Ricaud,* "the act within its own boundaries of one sovereign State . . . becomes . . . a rule of decision for the courts of this country." Act of state issues only arise when a court *must decide*—that is, when the outcome of the case turns upon—the effect of official action by a foreign sovereign. When that question is not the case, neither is the act of state doctrine. That is the situation here. Regardless of what the court's factual findings may suggest as to the legality of the Nigerian contract, its legality is simply not a question to be decided in the present suit, and there is thus no occasion to apply the rule of decision that the act of state doctrine requires.

In support of their position that the act of state doctrine bars any factual findings that may cast doubt upon the validity of foreign sovereign acts, petitioners cite Justice Holmes' opinion for the Court in *American Banana Co. v. United Fruit Co.*, 213 U.S. 347 (1909). That was a suit under the United States antitrust laws, alleging that Costa Rica's seizure of the plaintiff's property had been induced by an unlawful conspiracy. In the course of a lengthy opinion Justice Holmes observed, citing *Underhill,* that "a seizure by a state is not a thing that can be complained of elsewhere in the courts." The statement is concededly puzzling. *Underhill* does indeed stand for the proposition that a seizure by a state cannot be complained of elsewhere—in the sense of being sought to be declared *ineffective* elsewhere. The plaintiff in *American Banana*, however, like the plaintiff here, was not trying to undo or disregard the governmental action, but only to obtain damages from private parties who had procured it. Arguably, then, the statement did imply that suit would not lie if a foreign state's actions would be, though not invalidated, impugned.

Whatever Justice Holmes may have had in mind, his statement lends inadequate support to petitioners' position here, for two reasons. First, it was a brief aside, entirely unnecessary to the decision. *American Banana* was squarely decided on the ground (later substantially overruled, see *Continental Ore Co. v. Union Carbide & Carbon Corp.*, 370 U.S. 690, 704–705 (1962)) that the antitrust laws had no extraterritorial application, so that "what the defendant did in Panama or Costa Rica is not within the scope of the statute." Second, whatever support the dictum might provide for petitioners' position is more than overcome by our later holding in *United States v. Sisal Sales Corp.*, 274 U.S. 268 (1927). There we held that, *American Banana* notwithstanding, the defendant's actions in obtaining Mexico's enactment of "discriminating legislation" could form part of the basis for suit under the United States antitrust laws. Simply put, *American Banana* was not an act of state case; and whatever it said by way of dictum that might be relevant to the present case has not survived *Sisal Sales*.

Petitioners insist, however, that the policies underlying our act of state cases—international comity, respect for the sovereignty of foreign nations on their own territory, and the avoidance of embarrassment to the Executive Branch in its conduct of foreign relations—are implicated in the present case because, as the District Court found, a determination that Nigerian officials demanded and accepted a bribe "would impugn or question the nobility of a foreign nation's motivations," and would "result in embarrassment to the sovereign or constitute interference in the conduct of foreign policy of the United States." The United States, as *amicus curiae*, favors the same approach to the act of state doctrine, though disagreeing with petitioners as to the outcome it produces in the present case. We should not, the United States urges, "attach dispositive significance to the fact that this suit involves only the 'motivation' for, rather than the 'validity' of, a foreign sovereign act," and should eschew "any rigid formula for the resolution of act of state cases generally." In some future case, perhaps, "litigation . . . based on alleged corruption in the award of contracts or other commercially oriented activities of foreign governments could sufficiently touch on 'national nerves' that the act of state doctrine or related principles of abstention would appropriately be found to bar the suit," and we should therefore resolve this case on the narrowest possible ground, viz., that the letter from the legal adviser to the District Court gives sufficient indication that, "in the setting of this case," the act of state doctrine poses no bar to adjudication.

These urgings are deceptively similar to what we said in *Sabbatino*, where we observed that sometimes, even though the validity of the act of a foreign sovereign within its own territory is called into question, the policies underlying the act of state doctrine may not justify its application. We suggested that a sort of balancing approach could be applied— the balance shifting against application of the doctrine, for example, if the government that committed the "challenged act of state" is no longer in existence. But what is appropriate in order to avoid unquestioning judicial acceptance of the acts of foreign sovereigns is not similarly appropriate for the quite opposite purpose of expanding judicial incapacities where such acts are not directly (or even indirectly) involved. It is one thing to suggest, as we have, that the policies underlying the act of state doctrine should be considered in deciding whether, despite the doctrine's technical availability, it should nonetheless not be invoked; it is something quite different to suggest that those underlying policies are a doctrine unto themselves, justifying expansion of the act of state doctrine (or, as the United States puts it, unspecified "related principles of abstention") into new and uncharted fields.

The short of the matter is this: Courts in the United States have the power, and ordinarily the obligation, to decide cases and controversies properly presented to them. The act of state doctrine does not establish an exception for cases and controversies that may embarrass foreign governments, but merely requires that, in the process of deciding, the acts of foreign sovereigns taken within their own jurisdictions shall be deemed valid. That doctrine has no application to the present case because the validity of no foreign sovereign act is at issue.

The judgment of the Court of Appeals for the Third Circuit is affirmed.

It is so ordered.

Notes and Questions

1. *The Act of State Doctrine as a Principle of Decision.* In *Kirkpatrick*, a unanimous opinion, Justice Scalia wrote that the act of state doctrine "is not some vague doctrine of abstention but a *principle of decision* binding on federal and state courts alike." Did this decision then repudiate the separation of powers rationale of *Sabbatino* and move act of state more to a choice-of-law rationale? One observer noted that *Kirkpatrick* "has sharply circumscribed the reach of the doctrine." Mark Feldman, "Supreme Court Limits the Act of State Doctrine," ABA Section of International Law and Practice, *Suing Foreign States: Newsletter of the Committee on Foreign Sovereign Immunity*, Vol. 1, No. 1, at 1 (Spring 1990).

2. *Abolish the Act of State Doctrine?* Should *Sabbatino* and the act of state doctrine simply be eliminated from the common law of the United States? True, the doctrine "is being referred to repeatedly in court decisions in the United States and is used in different ways by different courts." Donald W. Hoagland, "The Act of State Doctrine: Abandon It," 14 *Denver Journal of International Law and Policy* 317, 317 (1986). However, Hoagland, a former Assistant Administrator of the U.S. Agency for International Development, argued that there are by now so many exceptions to the doctrine and it has been applied so confusingly, that act of state has little "integrity" left. *Id.* at 333. As an example of an exception, consider Roxas v. Marcos, 89 Haw. 91, 969 P.2d 1209 (1998), in which the Supreme Court of Hawaii refused to apply the act of state doctrine to acts of President Marcos

in the Philippines seizing buried World War II treasure, holding that the acts were "carried out for Ferdinand [Marcos]'s personal benefit and were therefore a violation of international law." *Id.* at 1251. In general, as Professor Ramsey has concluded, "[d]iscontent with the act of state doctrine is widespread." Michael D. Ramsey, "Acts of State and Foreign Sovereign Obligations," 39 *Harvard International Law Journal* 1, 99 (1998).

Would it make more sense simply to use ordinary conflict-of-laws rules to determine whether foreign law, U.S. law, or international law applies in cases where the act of state doctrine might otherwise be employed? Could *Underhill*, *Sabbatino*, and *Kirkpatrick* all have been answered in more or less the way they were with choice-of-law techniques and without employing the act of state doctrine?

Is the act of state doctrine more trouble than it is worth? Monroe Leigh, formerly Legal Adviser to the U.S. Department of State, thought not, believing the act of state doctrine should be retained, but that "the doctrine needs to be properly defined and limited," a task not accomplished, in his view, by the 1987 *Restatement (Third) of the Foreign Relations Law of the United States*. Monroe Leigh, "*Sabbatino*'s Silver Anniversary and the Restatement: No Cause for Celebration," 24 *International Lawyer* 1, 20 (1990). Another sympathetic account of the act of state doctrine concluded that the doctrine "is in great need of reform." Daniel C.K. Chow, "Rethinking the Act of State Doctrine: An Analysis in Terms of Jurisdiction to Prescribe," 62 *Washington Law Review* 397, 475 (1987). For further discussion, see Gregory H. Fox, "Reexamining the Act of State Doctrine: An Integrated Conflicts Analysis," 33 *Harvard International Law Journal* 521 (1992).

APPENDIX

CONSTITUTION OF THE UNITED STATES OF AMERICA

ARTICLE I

SECTION 8. The Congress shall have Power * * *

To regulate Commerce with foreign Nations, and among the several States, and with the Indian Tribes;

To establish an uniform Rule of Naturalization, and uniform Laws on the subject of Bankruptcies throughout the United States; * * *

To constitute Tribunals inferior to the supreme Court;

To define and punish Piracies and Felonies committed on the high Seas, and Offences against the Law of Nations;

To declare War, grant Letters of Marque and Reprisal, and make Rules concerning Captures on Land and Water;

To raise and support Armies, but no Appropriation of Money to that Use shall be for a longer Term than two Years;

To provide and maintain a Navy;

To make Rules for the Government and Regulation of the land and naval Forces;

To provide for calling forth the Militia to execute the Laws of the Union, suppress Insurrections and repel Invasions;

To provide for organizing, arming, and disciplining, the Militia, and for governing such Part of them as may be employed in the Service of the United States, reserving to the States respectively, the Appointment of the Officers, and the Authority of training the Militia according to the discipline prescribed by Congress; * * *

To make all Laws which shall be necessary and proper for carrying into Execution the foregoing Powers, and all other Powers vested by this Constitution in the Government of the United States, or in any Department or Officer thereof. * * *

SECTION 10. No State shall enter into any Treaty, Alliance, or Confederation; grant Letters of Marque and Reprisal; coin Money; emit Bills of Credit; make any Thing but gold and silver Coin a Tender in Payment of Debts; pass any Bill of Attainder, ex post facto Law, or Law impairing the Obligation of Contracts, or grant any Title of Nobility.

No State shall, without the Consent of the Congress, lay any Imposts or Duties on Imports or Exports, except what may be absolutely necessary for executing its inspection Laws; and the net Produce of all Duties and Imposts, laid by any State on Imports or Exports, shall be for the Use of the Treasury of the United States; and all such Laws shall be subject to the Revision and Controul of the Congress.

No State shall, without the Consent of Congress, lay any Duty of Tonnage, keep Troops, or Ships of War in time of Peace, enter into any Agreement or Compact with another State, or with a foreign Power, or engage in War, unless actually invaded, or in such imminent Danger as will not admit of delay.

ARTICLE II

SECTION 1. The executive Power shall be vested in a President of the United States of America. * * *

SECTION 2. The President shall be Commander in Chief of the Army and Navy of the United States, and of the Militia of the several States, when called into the actual Service of the United States * * *.

He shall have Power, by and with the Advice and Consent of the Senate, to make Treaties, provided two thirds of the Senators present concur; and he shall nominate, and by and with the Advice and Consent of the Senate, shall appoint Ambassadors, other public Ministers and Consuls * * *.

ARTICLE III

SECTION 1. The judicial Power of the United States, shall be vested in one supreme Court, and in such inferior Courts as the Congress may from time to time ordain and establish. * * *

SECTION 2. The judicial Power shall extend to all Cases, in Law and Equity, arising under this Constitution, the Laws of the United States, and Treaties made, or which shall be made, under their Authority;—to all Cases affecting Ambassadors, other public Ministers and Consuls;—to all Cases of admiralty and maritime Jurisdiction;—to Controversies to which the United States shall be a Party;—to Controversies between two or more States;—between a State and Citizens of another State;—between Citizens of different States;—between Citizens of the same State claiming Lands under Grants of different States, and between a State, or the Citizens thereof, and foreign States, Citizens or Subjects.

In all Cases affecting Ambassadors, other public Ministers and Consuls, and those in which a State shall be Party, the supreme Court shall have original Jurisdiction. In all the other Cases before mentioned, the supreme Court shall have appellate Jurisdiction, both as to Law and Fact, with such Exceptions, and under such Regulations as the Congress shall make. * * *

ARTICLE VI

All Debts contracted and Engagements entered into, before the Adoption of this Constitution, shall be as valid against the United States under this Constitution, as under the Confederation.

This Constitution, and the Laws of the United States which shall be made in Pursuance thereof; and all Treaties made, or which shall be made, under the Authority of the United States, shall be the supreme Law of the Land; and the Judges in every State shall be bound thereby, any Thing in the Constitution or Laws of any State to the Contrary notwithstanding. * * *

AMENDMENT I

Congress shall make no law respecting an establishment of religion, or prohibiting the free exercise thereof; or abridging the freedom of speech, or of the press; or of the right of the people peaceably to assemble, and to petition the Government for a redress of grievances.

AMENDMENT II

A well regulated Militia, being necessary to the security of a free State, the right of the people to keep and bear Arms, shall not be infringed.

AMENDMENT III

No Soldier shall, in time of peace be quartered in any house, without the consent of the Owner, nor in time of war, but in a manner to be prescribed by law.

AMENDMENT IV

The right of the people to be secure in their persons, houses, papers, and effects, against unreasonable searches and seizures, shall not be violated, and no Warrants shall issue, but upon probable cause, supported by Oath or affirmation, and particularly describing the place to be searched, and the persons or things to be seized.

AMENDMENT V

No person shall be held to answer for a capital, or otherwise infamous crime, unless on a presentment or indictment of a Grand Jury, except in cases arising in the land or naval forces, or in the Militia, when in actual service in time of War or public danger; nor shall any person be subject for the same offence to be twice put in jeopardy of life or limb; nor shall be compelled in any criminal case to be a witness against himself, nor be deprived of life, liberty, or property, without due process of law; nor shall private property be taken for public use, without just compensation.

AMENDMENT VI

In all criminal prosecutions, the accused shall enjoy the right to a speedy and public trial, by an impartial jury of the State and district wherein the crime shall have been committed, which district shall have been previously ascertained by law, and to be informed of the nature and cause of the accusation; to be confronted with the witnesses against him; to have compulsory process for obtaining witnesses in his favor, and to have the Assistance of Counsel for his defence.

AMENDMENT VII

In suits at common law, where the value in controversy shall exceed twenty dollars, the right of trial by jury shall be preserved, and no fact tried by a jury, shall be otherwise reexamined in any Court of the United States, than according to the rules of the common law.

AMENDMENT VIII

Excessive bail shall not be required, nor excessive fines imposed, nor cruel and unusual punishments inflicted.

AMENDMENT IX

The enumeration in the Constitution, of certain rights, shall not be construed to deny or disparage others retained by the people.

AMENDMENT X

The powers not delegated to the United States by the Constitution, nor prohibited by it to the States, are reserved to the States respectively, or to the people. * * *

AMENDMENT XIV

SECTION 1. All persons born or naturalized in the United States, and subject to the jurisdiction thereof, are citizens of the United States and of the State wherein they reside. No State shall make or enforce any law which shall abridge the privileges or immunities of citizens of the United States; nor shall any State deprive any person of life, liberty, or property, without due process of law; nor deny to any person within its jurisdiction the equal protection of the laws. * * *

CHARTER OF THE UNITED NATIONS

June 26, 1945, 59 Stat. 1031, T.S. No. 993, 3 Bevans 1153, 1976 Y.B.U.N. 1043.

WE THE PEOPLES OF THE UNITED NATIONS DETERMINED

to save succeeding generations from the scourge of war, which twice in our lifetime has brought untold sorrow to mankind, and

to reaffirm faith in fundamental human rights, in the dignity and worth of the human person, in the equal rights of men and women and of nations large and small, and

to establish conditions under which justice and respect for the obligations arising from treaties and other sources of international law can be maintained, and

to promote social progress and better standards of life in larger freedom,

AND FOR THESE ENDS

to practice tolerance and live together in peace with one another as good neighbors, and

to unite our strength to maintain international peace and security, and

to ensure, by the acceptance of principles and the institution of methods, that armed force shall not be used, save in the common interest, and

to employ international machinery for the promotion of the economic and social advancement of all peoples,

HAVE RESOLVED TO COMBINE OUR EFFORTS TO ACCOMPLISH THESE AIMS.

Accordingly, our respective Governments, through representatives assembled in the city of San Francisco, who have exhibited their full powers found to be in good and due form, have agreed to the present Charter of the United Nations and do hereby establish an international organization to be known as the United Nations.

CHAPTER I

PURPOSES AND PRINCIPLES

Article 1

The Purposes of the United Nations are:

1. To maintain international peace and security, and to that end: to take effective collective measures for the prevention and removal of threats to the peace, and for the suppression of acts of aggression or other breaches of the peace, and to bring about by peaceful means, and in conformity with the principles of justice and international law, adjustment or settlement of international disputes or situations which might lead to a breach of the peace;

2. To develop friendly relations among nations based on respect for the principle of equal rights and self-determination of peoples, and to take other appropriate measures to strengthen universal peace;

3. To achieve international cooperation in solving international problems of an economic, social, cultural, or humanitarian character, and in promoting and encouraging respect for human rights and for fundamental freedoms for all without distinction as to race, sex, language, or religion; and

4. To be a center for harmonizing the actions of nations in the attainment of these common ends.

Article 2

The Organization and its Members, in pursuit of the Purposes stated in Article 1, shall act in accordance with the following Principles.

1. The Organization is based on the principle of the sovereign equality of all its Members.

2. All Members, in order to ensure to all of them the rights and benefits resulting from membership, shall fulfil in good faith the obligations assumed by them in accordance with the present Charter.

3. All Members shall settle their international disputes by peaceful means in such a manner that international peace and security, and justice, are not endangered.

4. All Members shall refrain in their international relations from the threat or use of force against the territorial integrity or political independence of any state, or in any other manner inconsistent with the Purposes of the United Nations.

5. All Members shall give the United Nations every assistance in any action it takes in accordance with the present Charter, and shall refrain from giving assistance to any state against which the United Nations is taking preventive or enforcement action.

6. The Organization shall ensure that states which are not Members of the United Nations act in accordance with these Principles so far as may be necessary for the maintenance of international peace and security.

7. Nothing contained in the present Charter shall authorize the United Nations to intervene in matters which are essentially within the domestic jurisdiction of any state or shall require the Members to submit such matters to settlement under the present Charter; but this principle shall not prejudice the application of enforcement measures under Chapter VII.

CHAPTER II

MEMBERSHIP

Article 3

The original Members of the United Nations shall be the states which, having participated in the United Nations Conference on International Organization at San Francisco, or having previously signed the Declaration by United Nations of January 1, 1942, sign the present Charter and ratify it in accordance with Article 110.

Article 4

1. Membership in the United Nations is open to all other peace-loving states which accept the obligations contained in the present Charter and, in the judgment of the Organization, are able and willing to carry out these obligations.

2. The admission of any such state to membership in the United Nations will be effected by a decision of the General Assembly upon the recommendation of the Security Council.

Article 5

A Member of the United Nations against which preventive or enforcement action has been taken by the Security Council may be suspended from the exercise of the rights and privileges of membership by the General Assembly upon the recommendation of the Security Council. The exercise of these rights and privileges may be restored by the Security Council.

Article 6

A Member of the United Nations which has persistently violated the Principles contained in the present Charter may be expelled from the Organization by the General Assembly upon the recommendation of the Security Council.

CHAPTER III

ORGANS

Article 7

1. There are established as the principal organs of the United Nations: a General Assembly, a Security Council, an Economic and Social Council, a Trusteeship Council, an International Court of Justice, and a Secretariat.

2. Such subsidiary organs as may be found necessary may be established in accordance with the present Charter.

Article 8

The United Nations shall place no restrictions on the eligibility of men and women to participate in any capacity and under conditions of equality in its principal and subsidiary organs.

CHAPTER IV

THE GENERAL ASSEMBLY

Composition

Article 9

1. The General Assembly shall consist of all the Members of the United Nations.

2. Each Member shall have not more than five representatives in the General Assembly.

Functions and Powers

Article 10

The General Assembly may discuss any questions or any matters within the scope of the present Charter or relating to the powers and functions of any organs provided for in the present Charter, and, except as provided in Article 12, may make recommendations to the Members of the United Nations or to the Security Council or to both on any such questions or matters.

Article 11

1. The General Assembly may consider the general principles of cooperation in the maintenance of international peace and security, including the principles governing disarmament and the regulation of armaments, and may make recommendations with regard to such principles to the Members or to the Security Council or to both.

2. The General Assembly may discuss any questions relating to the maintenance of international peace and security brought before it by any Member of the United Nations, or by the Security Council, or by a state which is not a Member of the United Nations in accordance with Article 35, paragraph 2, and, except as provided in Article 12, may make recommendations with regard to any such questions to the state or states concerned or to the Security Council or to both. Any such question on which action is necessary shall be referred to the Security Council by the General Assembly either before or after discussion.

3. The General Assembly may call the attention of the Security Council to situations which are likely to endanger international peace and security.

4. The powers of the General Assembly set forth in this Article shall not limit the general scope of Article 10.

Article 12

1. While the Security Council is exercising in respect of any dispute or situation the functions assigned to it in the present Charter, the General Assembly shall not make any recommendation with regard to that dispute or situation unless the Security Council so requests.

2. The Secretary–General, with the consent of the Security Council, shall notify the General Assembly at each session of any matters relative to the maintenance of international peace and security which are being dealt with by the Security Council and shall similarly notify the

General Assembly, or the Members of the United Nations if the General Assembly is not in session, immediately the Security Council ceases to deal with such matters.

Article 13

1.   The General Assembly shall initiate studies and make recommendations for the purpose of:

a.   promoting international cooperation in the political field and encouraging the progressive development of international law and its codification;

b.   promoting international cooperation in the economic, social, cultural, educational, and health fields, and assisting in the realization of human rights and fundamental freedoms for all without distinction as to race, sex, language, or religion.

2.   The further responsibilities, functions, and powers of the General Assembly with respect to matters mentioned in paragraph 1(b) above are set forth in Chapters IX and X.

Article 14

Subject to the provisions of Article 12, the General Assembly may recommend measures for the peaceful adjustment of any situation, regardless of origin, which it deems likely to impair the general welfare or friendly relations among nations, including situations resulting from a violation of the provisions of the present Charter setting forth the Purposes and Principles of the United Nations.

Article 15

1.   The General Assembly shall receive and consider annual and special reports from the Security Council; these reports shall include an account of the measures that the Security Council has decided upon or taken to maintain international peace and security.

2.   The General Assembly shall receive and consider reports from the other organs of the United Nations.

Article 16

The General Assembly shall perform such functions with respect to the international trusteeship system as are assigned to it under Chapters XII and XIII, including the approval of the trusteeship agreements for areas not designated as strategic.

Article 17

1.   The General Assembly shall consider and approve the budget of the Organization.

2.   The expenses of the Organization shall be borne by the Members as apportioned by the General Assembly.

3.   The General Assembly shall consider and approve any financial and budgetary arrangements with specialized agencies referred to in

Article 57 and shall examine the administrative budgets of such specialized agencies with a view to making recommendations to the agencies concerned.

Voting

Article 18

1. Each member of the General Assembly shall have one vote.

2. Decisions of the General Assembly on important questions shall be made by a two-thirds majority of the members present and voting. These questions shall include: recommendations with respect to the maintenance of international peace and security, the election of the non-permanent members of the Security Council, the election of the members of the Economic and Social Council, the election of the members of the Trusteeship Council in accordance with paragraph 1(c) of Article 86, the admission of new Members to the United Nations, the suspension of the rights and privileges of membership, the expulsion of Members, questions relating to the operation of the trusteeship system, and budgetary questions.

3. Decisions on other questions, including the determination of additional categories of questions to be decided by a two-thirds majority, shall be made by a majority of the members present and voting.

Article 19

A Member of the United Nations which is in arrears in the payment of its financial contributions to the Organization shall have no vote in the General Assembly if the amount of its arrears equals or exceeds the amount of the contributions due from it for the preceding two full years. The General Assembly may, nevertheless, permit such a Member to vote if it is satisfied that the failure to pay is due to conditions beyond the control of the Member.

Procedure

Article 20

The General Assembly shall meet in regular annual sessions and in such special sessions as occasion may require. Special sessions shall be convoked by the Secretary–General at the request of the Security Council or of a majority of the Members of the United Nations.

Article 21

The General Assembly shall adopt its own rules of procedure. It shall elect its President for each session.

Article 22

The General Assembly may establish such subsidiary organs as it deems necessary for the performance of its functions.

CHAPTER V

THE SECURITY COUNCIL

Composition

Article 23[a]

1. The Security Council shall consist of fifteen Members of the United Nations. The Republic of China, France, the Union of Soviet Socialist Republics, the United Kingdom of Great Britain and Northern Ireland, and the United States of America shall be permanent members of the Security Council. The General Assembly shall elect ten other Members of the United Nations to be non-permanent members of the Security Council, due regard being specially paid, in the first instance to the contribution of Members of the United Nations to the maintenance of international peace and security and to the other purposes of the Organization, and also to equitable geographical distribution.

2. The non-permanent members of the Security Council shall be elected for a term of two years. In the first election of the non-permanent members after the increase of the membership of the Security Council from eleven to fifteen, two of the four additional members shall be chosen for a term of one year. A retiring member shall not be eligible for immediate re-election.

3. Each member of the Security Council shall have one representative.

Functions and Powers

Article 24

1. In order to ensure prompt and effective action by the United Nations, its Members confer on the Security Council primary responsibility for the maintenance of international peace and security, and agree that in carrying out its duties under this responsibility the Security Council acts on their behalf.

2. In discharging these duties the Security Council shall act in accordance with the Purposes and Principles of the United Nations. The specific powers granted to the Security Council for the discharge of these duties are laid down in Chapters VI, VII, VIII, and XII.

3. The Security Council shall submit annual and, when necessary, special reports to the General Assembly for its consideration.

Article 25

The Members of the United Nations agree to accept and carry out the decisions of the Security Council in accordance with the present Charter.

a. Amended text of Article 23 that came into force August 31, 1965.

Article 26

In order to promote the establishment and maintenance of international peace and security with the least diversion for armaments of the world's human and economic resources, the Security Council shall be responsible for formulating, with the assistance of the Military Staff Committee referred to in article 47, plans to be submitted to the Members of the United Nations for the establishment of a system for the regulation of armaments.

Voting

Article 27[b]

1.   Each member of the Security Council shall have one vote.

2.   Decisions of the Security Council on procedural matters shall be made by an affirmative vote of nine members.

3.   Decisions of the Security Council on all other matters shall be made by an affirmative vote of nine members including the concurring votes of the permanent members; provided that, in decisions under Chapter VI, and under paragraph 3 of Article 52, a party to a dispute shall abstain from voting.

Procedure

Article 28

1.   The Security Council shall be so organized as to be able to function continuously. Each member of the Security Council shall for this purpose be represented at all times at the seat of the Organization.

2.   The Security Council shall hold periodic meetings at which each of its members may, if it so desires, be represented by a member of the government or by some other specially designated representative.

3.   The Security Council may hold meetings at such places other than the seat of the Organization as in its judgment will best facilitate its work.

Article 29

The Security Council may establish such subsidiary organs as it deems necessary for the performance of its functions.

Article 30

The Security Council shall adopt its own rules of procedure, including the method of selecting its President.

Article 31

Any Member of the United Nations which is not a member of the Security Council may participate, without vote, in the discussion of any question brought before the Security Council whenever the latter considers that the interests of that Member are specially affected.

b.   Amended text of Article 27 that came
into force August 31, 1965.

Article 32

Any Member of the United Nations which is not a member of the Security Council or any state which is not a Member of the United Nations, if it is a party to a dispute under consideration by the Security Council, shall be invited to participate, without vote, in the discussion relating to the dispute. The Security Council shall lay down such conditions as it deems just for the participation of a state which is not a Member of the United Nations.

CHAPTER VI

PACIFIC SETTLEMENT OF DISPUTES

Article 33

1. The parties to any dispute, the continuance of which is likely to endanger the maintenance of international peace and security, shall, first of all, seek a solution by negotiation, enquiry, mediation, conciliation, arbitration, judicial settlement, resort to regional agencies or arrangements, or other peaceful means of their own choice.

2. The Security Council shall, when it deems necessary, call upon the parties to settle their dispute by such means.

Article 34

The Security Council may investigate any dispute, or any situation which might lead to international friction or give rise to a dispute, in order to determine whether the continuance of the dispute or situation is likely to endanger the maintenance of international peace and security.

Article 35

1. Any Member of the United Nations may bring any dispute, or any situation of the nature referred to in Article 34, to the attention of the Security Council or of the General Assembly.

2. A state which is not a Member of the United Nations may bring to the attention of the Security Council or of the General Assembly any dispute to which it is a party if it accepts in advance, for the purposes of the dispute, the obligations of pacific settlement provided in the present Charter.

3. The proceedings of the General Assembly in respect of matters brought to its attention under this Article will be subject to the provisions of Articles 11 and 12.

Article 36

1. The Security Council may, at any stage of a dispute of the nature referred to in Article 33 or of a situation of like nature, recommend appropriate procedures or methods of adjustment.

2. The Security Council should take into consideration any procedures for the settlement of the dispute which have already been adopted by the parties.

3. In making recommendations under this Article the Security Council should also take into consideration that legal disputes should as a general rule be referred by the parties to the International Court of Justice in accordance with the provisions of the Statute of the Court.

Article 37

1. Should the parties to a dispute of the nature referred to in Article 33 fail to settle it by the means indicated in that Article, they shall refer it to the Security Council.

2. If the Security Council deems that the continuance of the dispute is in fact likely to endanger the maintenance of international peace and security, it shall decide whether to take action under Article 36 or to recommend such terms of settlement as it may consider appropriate.

Article 38

Without prejudice to the provisions of Articles 33 to 37, the Security Council may, if all the parties to any dispute so request, make recommendations to the parties with a view to a pacific settlement of the dispute.

CHAPTER VII

ACTION WITH RESPECT TO THREATS TO THE PEACE, BREACHES OF THE PEACE, AND ACTS OF AGGRESSION

Article 39

The Security Council shall determine the existence of any threat to the peace, breach of the peace, or act of aggression and shall make recommendations, or decide what measures shall be taken in accordance with Articles 41 and 42, to maintain or restore international peace and security.

Article 40

In order to prevent an aggravation of the situation, the Security Council may, before making the recommendations or deciding upon the measures provided for in Article 39, call upon the parties concerned to comply with such provisional measures as it deems necessary or desirable. Such provisional measures shall be without prejudice to the rights, claims, or position of the parties concerned. The Security Council shall duly take account of failure to comply with such provisional measures.

Article 41

The Security Council may decide what measures not involving the use of armed force are to be employed to give effect to its decisions, and it may call upon the Members of the United Nations to apply such measures. These may include complete or partial interruption of economic relations and of rail, sea, air, postal, telegraphic, radio, and other means of communication, and the severance of diplomatic relations.

Article 42

Should the Security Council consider that measures provided for in Article 41 would be inadequate or have proved to be inadequate, it may take such action by air, sea, or land forces as may be necessary to maintain or restore international peace and security. Such action may include demonstrations, blockage, and other operations by air, sea, or land forces of Members of the United Nations.

Article 43

1.   All Members of the United Nations, in order to contribute to the maintenance of international peace and security, undertake to make available to the Security Council, on its call and in accordance with a special agreement or agreements, armed forces, assistance, and facilities, including rights of passage, necessary for the purpose of maintaining international peace and security.

2.   Such agreement or agreements shall govern the numbers and types of forces, their degree of readiness and general location, and the nature of the facilities and assistance to be provided.

3.   The agreement or agreements shall be negotiated as soon as possible on the initiative of the Security Council. They shall be concluded between the Security Council and Members or between the Security Council and groups of Members and shall be subject to ratification by the signatory states in accordance with their respective constitutional processes.

Article 44

When the Security Council has decided to use force it shall, before calling upon a Member not represented on it to provide armed forces in fulfillment of the obligations assumed under Article 43, invite that Member, if the Member so desires, to participate in the decisions of the Security Council concerning the employment of contingents of that Member's armed forces.

Article 45

In order to enable the United Nations to take urgent military measures, Members shall hold immediately available national air-force contingents for combined international enforcement action. The strength and degree of readiness of these contingents and plans for their combined action shall be determined, within the limits laid down in the special agreement or agreements referred to in Article 43, by the Security Council with the assistance of the Military Staff Committee.

Article 46

Plans for the application of armed force shall be made by the Security Council with the assistance of the Military Staff Committee.

Article 47

1. There shall be established a Military Staff Committee to advise and assist the Security Council on all questions relating to the Security Council's military requirements for the maintenance of international peace and security, the employment and command of forces placed at its disposal, the regulation of armaments, and possible disarmament.

2. The Military Staff Committee shall consist of the Chiefs of Staff of the permanent members of the Security Council or their representatives. Any Member of the United Nations not permanently represented on the Committee shall be invited by the Committee to be associated with it when the efficient discharge of the Committee's responsibilities requires the participation of that Member in its work.

3. The Military Staff Committee shall be responsible under the Security Council for the strategic direction of any armed forces placed at the disposal of the Security Council. Questions relating to the command of such forces shall be worked out subsequently.

4. The Military Staff Committee, with the authorization of the Security Council and after consultation with appropriate regional agencies, may establish regional subcommittees.

Article 48

1. The action required to carry out the decisions of the Security Council for the maintenance of international peace and security shall be taken by all the Members of the United Nations or by some of them, as the Security Council may determine.

2. Such decisions shall be carried out by the Members of the United Nations directly and through their action in the appropriate international agencies of which they are members.

Article 49

The Members of the United Nations shall join in affording mutual assistance in carrying out the measures decided upon by the Security Council.

Article 50

If preventive or enforcement measures against any state are taken by the Security Council, any other state, whether a Member of the United Nations or not, which finds itself confronted with special economic problems arising from the carrying out of those measures shall have the right to consult the Security Council with regard to a solution of those problems.

Article 51

Nothing in the present Charter shall impair the inherent right of individual or collective self-defense if an armed attack occurs against a Member of the United Nations, until the Security Council has taken measures necessary to maintain international peace and security. Measures taken by Members in the exercise of this right of self-defense shall be immediately reported to the Security Council and shall not in any way affect the authority and responsibility of the Security Council under the present Charter to take at any time such action as it deems necessary in order to maintain or restore international peace and security.

CHAPTER VIII

REGIONAL ARRANGEMENTS

Article 52

1.   Nothing in the present Charter precludes the existence of regional arrangements or agencies for dealing with such matters relating to the maintenance of international peace and security as are appropriate for regional action, provided that such arrangements or agencies and their activities are consistent with the Purposes and Principles of the United Nations.

2.   The Members of the United Nations entering into such arrangements or constituting such agencies shall make every effort to achieve pacific settlement of local disputes through such regional arrangements or by such regional agencies before referring them to the Security Council.

3.   The Security Council shall encourage the development of pacific settlement of local disputes through such regional arrangements or by such regional agencies either on the initiative of the states concerned or by reference from the Security Council.

4.   This Article in no way impairs the application of Articles 34 and 35.

Article 53

1.   The Security Council shall, where appropriate, utilize such regional arrangements or agencies for enforcement action under its authority. But no enforcement action shall be taken under regional arrangements or by regional agencies without the authorization of the Security Council, with the exception of measures against any enemy state, as defined in paragraph 2 of this Article, provided for pursuant to Article 107 or in regional arrangements directed against renewal of aggressive policy on the part of any such state, until such time as the Organization may, on request of the Governments concerned, be charged with the responsibility for preventing further aggression by such a state.

2.   The term enemy state as used in paragraph 1 of this Article applies to any state which during the Second World War has been an enemy of any signatory of the present Charter.

Article 54

The Security Council shall at all times be kept fully informed of activities undertaken or in contemplation under regional arrangements or by regional agencies for the maintenance of international peace and security.

CHAPTER IX

INTERNATIONAL ECONOMIC AND SOCIAL COOPERATION

Article 55

With a view to the creation of conditions of stability and well-being which are necessary for peaceful and friendly relations among nations based on respect for the principle of equal rights and self-determination of peoples, the United Nations shall promote:

　　a.　higher standards of living, full employment, and conditions of economic and social progress and development;

　　b.　solutions of international economic, social, health, and related problems; and international cultural and educational cooperation; and

　　c.　universal respect for, and observance of, human rights and fundamental freedoms for all without distinction as to race, sex, language, or religion.

Article 56

All Members pledge themselves to take joint and separate action in cooperation with the Organization for the achievement of the purposes set forth in Article 55.

Article 57

　　1.　The various specialized agencies, established by intergovernmental agreement and having wide international responsibilities, as defined in their basic instruments, in economic, social, cultural, educational, health, and related fields, shall be brought into relationship with the United Nations in accordance with the provisions of Article 63.

　　2.　Such agencies thus brought into relationship with the United Nations are hereinafter referred to as specialized agencies.

Article 58

The Organization shall make recommendations for the coordination of the policies and activities of the specialized agencies.

Article 59

The Organization shall, where appropriate, initiate negotiations among the states concerned for the creation of any new specialized agencies required for the accomplishment of the purposes set forth in Article 55.

Article 60

Responsibility for the discharge of the functions of the Organization set forth in this Chapter shall be vested in the General Assembly and, under the authority of the General Assembly, in the Economic and Social Council, which shall have for this purpose the powers set forth in Chapter X.

CHAPTER X

THE ECONOMIC AND SOCIAL COUNCIL

Composition

Article 61

1.   The Economic and Social Council shall consist of eighteen Members of the United Nations elected by the General Assembly.

2.   Subject to the provisions of paragraph 3, six members of the Economic and Social Council shall be elected each year for a term of three years. A retiring member shall be eligible for immediate re-election.

3.   At the first election, eighteen members of the Economic and Social Council shall be chosen. The term of office of six members so chosen shall expire at the end of one year, and of six other members at the end of two years, in accordance with arrangements made by the General Assembly.

4.   Each member of the Economic and Social Council shall have one representative.

Functions and Powers

Article 62

1.   The Economic and Social Council may make or initiate studies and reports with respect to international economic, social, cultural, educational, health, and related matters and may make recommendations with respect to any such matters to the General Assembly, to the Members of the United Nations, and to the specialized agencies concerned.

2.   It may make recommendations for the purpose of promoting respect for, and observance of, human rights and fundamental freedoms for all.

3.   It may prepare draft conventions for submission to the General Assembly, with respect to matters falling within its competence.

4.   It may call, in accordance with the rules prescribed by the United Nations, international conferences on matters falling within its competence.

Article 63

1. The Economic and Social Council may enter into agreements with any of the agencies referred to in Article 57, defining the terms on which the agency concerned shall be brought into relationship with the United Nations. Such agreement shall be subject to approval by the General Assembly.

2. It may coordinate the activities of the specialized agencies through consultation with and recommendations to such agencies and through recommendations to the General Assembly and to the Members of the United Nations.

Article 64

1. The Economic and Social Council may take appropriate steps to obtain regular reports from the specialized agencies. It may make arrangements with the Members of the United Nations and with the specialized agencies to obtain reports on the steps taken to give effect to its own recommendations and to recommendations on matters falling within its competence made by the General Assembly.

2. It may communicate its observations on these reports to the General Assembly.

Article 65

The Economic and Social Council may furnish information to the Security Council and shall assist the Security Council upon its request.

Article 66

1. The Economic and Social Council shall perform such functions as fall within its competence in connection with the carrying out of the recommendations of the General Assembly.

2. It may, with the approval of the General Assembly, perform services at the request of specialized agencies.

3. It shall perform such other functions as are specified elsewhere in the present Charter or as may be assigned to it by the General Assembly.

Voting

Article 67

1. Each member of the Economic and Social Council shall have one vote.

2. Decisions of the Economic and Social Council shall be made by a majority of the members present and voting.

Procedure

Article 68

The Economic and Social Council shall set up commissions in economic and social fields and for the promotion of human rights, and such other commissions as may be required for the performance of its functions.

Article 69

The Economic and Social Council shall invite any Member of the United Nations to participate, without vote, in its deliberations on any matter of particular concern to that Member.

Article 70

The Economic and Social Council may make arrangements for representatives of the specialized agencies to participate, without vote, in its deliberations and in those of the commissions established by it, and for its representatives to participate in the deliberations of the specialized agencies.

Article 71

The Economic and Social Council may make suitable arrangements for consultation with non-governmental organizations which are concerned with matters within its competence. Such arrangements may be made with international organizations and, where appropriate, with national organizations after consultation with the Member of the United Nations concerned.

Article 72

1. The Economic and Social Council shall adopt its own rules of procedure, including the method of selecting its President.

2. The Economic and Social Council shall meet as required in accordance with its rules, which shall include provision for the convening of meetings on the request of a majority of its members.

CHAPTER XI

DECLARATION REGARDING NON–SELF–GOVERNING TERRITORIES

Article 73

Members of the United Nations which have or assume responsibilities for the administration of territories whose peoples have not yet attained a full measure of self-government recognize the principle that the interests of the inhabitants of these territories are paramount, and accept as a sacred trust the obligation to promote to the utmost, within the system of international peace and security established by the present Charter, the well-being of the inhabitants of these territories, and, to this end:

a. to ensure, with due respect for the culture of the peoples concerned, their political, economic, social, and educational advancement, their just treatment, and their protection against abuses;

b. to develop self-government, to take due account of the political aspirations of the peoples, and to assist them in the progressive development of their free political institutions, according to the particular circumstances of each territory and its peoples and their varying stages of advancement;

c. to further international peace and security;

d. to promote constructive measures of development, to encourage research, and to cooperate with one another and, when and where appropriate, with specialized international bodies with a view to the practical achievement of the social, economic, and scientific purposes set forth in this Article; and

e. to transmit regularly to the Secretary–General for information purposes, subject to such limitation as security and constitutional considerations may require, statistical and other information of a technical nature relating to economic, social, and educational conditions in the territories for which they are respectively responsible other than those territories to which Chapters XII and XIII apply.

Article 74

Members of the United Nations also agree that their policy in respect of the territories to which this Chapter applies, no less than in respect of their metropolitan areas, must be based on the general principle of good-neighborliness, due account being taken of the interests and well-being of the rest of the world, in social, economic, and commercial matters.

CHAPTER XII

INTERNATIONAL TRUSTEESHIP SYSTEM

Article 75

The United Nations shall establish under its authority an international trusteeship system for the administration and supervision of such territories as may be placed thereunder by subsequent individual agreements. These territories are hereinafter referred to as trust territories.

Article 76

The basic objectives of the trusteeship system, in accordance with the Purposes of the United Nations laid down in Article I of the present Charter, shall be:

a. to further international peace and security;

b. to promote the political, economic, social, and educational advancement of the inhabitants of the trust territories, and their progressive development towards self-government or independence as may be appropriate to the particular circumstances of each territory and its peoples and the freely expressed wishes of the peoples concerned, and as may be provided by the terms of each trusteeship agreement;

c. to encourage respect for human rights and for fundamental freedoms for all without distinction as to race, sex, language, or religion, and to encourage recognition of the interdependence of the peoples of the world; and

d. to ensure equal treatment in social, economic, and commercial matters for all Members of the United Nations and their nationals, and also equal treatment for the latter in the administration of justice, without prejudice to the attainment of the foregoing objectives and subject to the provisions of Article 80.

Article 77

1. The trusteeship system shall apply to such territories in the following categories as may be placed thereunder by means of trusteeship agreements:

a. territories now held under mandate;

b. territories which may be detached from enemy states as a result of the Second World War; and

c. territories voluntarily placed under the system by states responsible for their administration.

2. It will be a matter for subsequent agreement as to which territories in the foregoing categories will be brought under the trusteeship system and upon what terms.

Article 78

The trusteeship system shall not apply to territories which have become Members of the United Nations, relationship among which shall be based on respect for the principle of sovereign equality.

Article 79

The terms of trusteeship for each territory to be placed under the trusteeship system, including any alteration or amendment, shall he agreed upon by the states directly concerned, including the mandatory power in the case of territories held under mandate by a Member of the United Nations, and shall be approved as provided for in Articles 83 and 85.

Article 80

1. Except as may be agreed upon in individual trusteeship agreements, made under Articles 77, 79, and 81, placing each territory under the trusteeship system, and until such agreements have been concluded, nothing in this Chapter shall be construed in or of itself to alter in any manner the rights whatsoever of any states or any peoples or the terms of existing international instruments to which Members of the United Nations may respectively be parties.

2. Paragraph 1 of this Article shall not be interpreted as giving grounds for delay or postponement of the negotiation and conclusion of agreements for placing mandated and other territories under the trusteeship system as provided for in Article 77.

Article 81

The trusteeship agreement shall in each case include the terms under which the trust territory will be administered and designate the authority which will exercise the administration of the trust territory. Such authority, hereinafter called the administering authority, may be one or more states or the Organization itself.

Article 82

There may be designated, in any trusteeship agreement, a strategic area or areas which may include part or all of the trust territory to which the agreement applies, without prejudice to any special agreement or agreements made under Article 43.

Article 83

1. All functions of the United Nations relating to strategic areas, including the approval of the terms of the trusteeship agreements and of their alteration or amendment, shall be exercised by the Security Council.

2. The basic objectives set forth in Article 76 shall be applicable to the people of each strategic area.

3. The Security Council shall, subject to the provisions of the trusteeship agreements and without prejudice to security considerations, avail itself of the assistance of the Trusteeship Council to perform those functions of the United Nations under the trusteeship system relating to political, economic, social, and educational matters in the strategic areas.

Article 84

It shall be the duty of the administering authority to ensure that the trust territory shall play its part in the maintenance of international peace and security. To this end the administering authority may make use of volunteer forces, facilities, and assistance from the trust territory in carrying the obligations towards the Security Council undertaken in this regard by the administering authority, as well as for local defense and the maintenance of law and order within the trust territory.

Article 85

1. The functions of the United Nations with regard to trusteeship agreements for all areas not designated as strategic, including the approval of the terms of the trusteeship agreements and of their alteration or amendment, shall be exercised by the General Assembly.

2. The Trusteeship Council, operating under the authority of the General Assembly, shall assist the General Assembly in carrying out these functions.

CHAPTER XIII

THE TRUSTEESHIP COUNCIL

Composition

Article 86

1. The Trusteeship Council shall consist of the following Members of the United Nations:

    a. those Members administering trust territories;

    b. such of those Members mentioned by name in Article 23 as are not administering trust territories; and

    c. as many other Members elected for three-year terms by the General Assembly as may be necessary to ensure that the total number of members of the Trusteeship Council is equally divided between those Members of the United Nations which administer trust territories and those which do not.

2. Each member of the Trusteeship Council shall designate one specially qualified person to represent it therein.

Functions and Powers

Article 87

The General Assembly and, under its authority, the Trusteeship Council, in carrying out their functions, may:

    a. consider reports submitted by the administering authority;

    b. accept petitions and examine them in consultation with the administering authority;

    c. provide for periodic visits to the respective trust territories at times agreed upon with the administering authority; and

    d. take these and other actions in conformity with the terms of the trusteeship agreements.

Article 88

The Trusteeship Council shall formulate a questionnaire on the political, economic, social, and educational advancement of the inhabitants of each trust territory, and the administering authority for each trust territory within the competency of the General Assembly shall make an annual report to the General Assembly upon the basis of such questionnaire.

Voting

Article 89

1. Each member of the Trusteeship Council shall have one vote.

2.   Decisions of the Trusteeship Council shall be made by a majority of the members present and voting.

Procedure

Article 90

1.   The Trusteeship Council shall adopt its own rules of procedure, including the method of selecting its President.

2.   The Trusteeship Council shall meet as required in accordance with its rules, which shall include provision for the convening of meetings on the request of a majority of its members.

Article 91

The Trusteeship Council shall, when appropriate, avail itself of the assistance of the Economic and Social Council and of the specialized agencies in regard to matters with which they are respectively concerned.

CHAPTER XIV

THE INTERNATIONAL COURT OF JUSTICE

Article 92

The International Court of Justice shall be the principal judicial organ of the United Nations. It shall function in accordance with the annexed Statute, which is based upon the Statute of the Permanent Court of International Justice and forms an integral part of the present Charter.

Article 93

1.   All Members of the United Nations are *ipso facto* parties to the Statute of the International Court of Justice.

2.   A state which is not a Member of the United Nations may become a party to the Statute of the International Court of Justice on conditions to be determined in each case by the General Assembly upon the recommendation of the Security Council.

Article 94

1.   Each Member of the United Nations undertakes to comply with the decision of the International Court of Justice in any case to which it is a party.

2.   If any party to a case fails to perform the obligations incumbent upon it under a judgment rendered by the Court, the other party may have recourse to the Security Council, which may, if it deems necessary, make recommendations or decide upon measures to be taken to give effect to the judgment.

Article 95

Nothing in the present Charter shall prevent Members of the United Nations from entrusting the solution of their differences to other tribunals by virtue of agreements already in existence or which may be concluded in the future.

Article 96

1. The General Assembly or the Security Council may request the International Court of Justice to give an advisory opinion on any legal question.

2. Other organs of the United Nations and specialized agencies, which may at any time be so authorized by the General Assembly, may also request advisory opinions of the Court on legal questions arising within the scope of their activities.

CHAPTER XV

THE SECRETARIAT

Article 97

The Secretariat shall comprise a Secretary–General and such staff as the Organization may require. The Secretary–General shall be appointed by the General Assembly upon the recommendation of the Security Council. He shall be the chief administrative officer of the Organization.

Article 98

The Secretary–General shall act in that capacity in all meetings of the General Assembly, of the Security Council, of the Economic and Social Council, and of the Trusteeship Council, and shall perform such other functions as are entrusted to him by these organs. The Secretary–General shall make an annual report to the General Assembly on the work of the Organization.

Article 99

The Secretary–General may bring to the attention of the Security Council any matter which in his opinion may threaten the maintenance of international peace and security.

Article 100

1. In the performance of their duties the Secretary–General and the staff shall not seek or receive instructions from any government or from any other authority external to the Organization. They shall refrain from any action which might reflect on their position as international officials responsible only to the Organization.

2. Each Member of the United Nations undertakes to respect the exclusively international character of the responsibilities of the Secretary–General and the staff and not to seek to influence them in the discharge of their responsibilities.

Article 101

1. The staff shall be appointed by the Secretary–General under regulations established by the General Assembly.

2. Appropriate staffs shall be permanently assigned to the Economic and Social Council, the Trusteeship Council, and, as required, to other organs of the United Nations. These staffs shall form a part of the Secretariat.

3. The paramount consideration in the employment of the staff and in the determination of the conditions of service shall be the necessity of securing the highest standards of efficiency, competence, and integrity. Due regard shall be paid to the importance of recruiting the staff on as wide a geographical basis as possible.

CHAPTER XVI

MISCELLANEOUS PROVISIONS

Article 102

1. Every treaty and every international agreement entered into by any Member of the United Nations after the present Charter comes into force shall as soon as possible be registered with the Secretariat and published by it.

2. No party to any such treaty or international agreement which has not been registered in accordance with the provisions of paragraph 1 of this Article may invoke that treaty or agreement before any organ of the United Nations.

Article 103

In the event of a conflict between the obligations of the Members of the United Nations under the present Charter and their obligations under any other international agreement, their obligations under the present Charter shall prevail.

Article 104

The Organization shall enjoy in the territory of each of its Members such legal capacity as may be necessary for the exercise of its functions and the fulfillment of its purposes.

Article 105

1. The Organization shall enjoy in the territory of each of its Members such privileges and immunities as are necessary for the fulfillment of its purposes.

2. Representatives of the Members of the United Nations and officials of the Organization shall similarly enjoy such privileges and immunities as are necessary for the independent exercise of their functions in connection with the Organization.

3. The General Assembly may make recommendations with a view to determining the details of the application of paragraphs 1 and 2 of this Article or may propose conventions to the Members of the United Nations for this purpose.

CHAPTER XVII

TRANSITIONAL SECURITY ARRANGEMENTS

Article 106

Pending the coming into force of such special agreements referred to in Article 43 as in the opinion of the Security Council enable it to begin the exercise of its responsibilities under Article 42, the parties to the Four–Nation Declaration, signed at Moscow, October 30, 1943, and France, shall, in accordance with the provisions of paragraph 5 of that Declaration, consult with one another and as occasion requires with other Members of the United Nations with a view to such joint action on behalf of the Organization as may be necessary for the purpose of maintaining international peace and security.

Article 107

Nothing in the present Charter shall invalidate or preclude action, in relation to any state which during the Second World War has been an enemy of any signatory to the present Charter, taken or authorized as a result of that war by the Governments having responsibility for such action.

CHAPTER XVIII

AMENDMENTS

Article 108

Amendments to the present Charter shall come into force for all Members of the United Nations when they have been adopted by a vote of two thirds of the members of the General Assembly and ratified in accordance with their respective constitutional processes by two thirds of the Members of the United Nations, including all the permanent members of the Security Council.

*Article 109*c

1. A General Conference of the Members of the United Nations for the purpose of reviewing the present Charter may be held at a date and place to be fixed by a two-thirds vote of the members of the General Assembly and by a vote of any nine members of the Security Council. Each Member of the United Nations shall have one vote in the conference.

2. Any alteration of the present Charter recommended by a two-thirds vote of the conference shall take effect when ratified in accordance

c. Amended text of Article 109 that   came into force June 12, 1968.

with their respective constitutional processes by two thirds of the Members of the United Nations including all the permanent members of the Security Council.

3. If such a conference has not been held before the tenth annual session of the General Assembly following the coming into force of the present Charter, the proposal to call such a conference shall be placed on the agenda of that session of the General Assembly, and the conference shall be held if so decided by a majority vote of the members of the General Assembly and by a vote of any seven members of the Security Council.

Article 110

1. The present Charter shall be ratified by the signatory states in accordance with their respective constitutional processes.

2. The ratifications shall be deposited with the Government of the United States of America which shall notify all the signatory states of each deposit as well as the Secretary–General of the Organization when he has been appointed.

3. The present Charter shall come into force upon the deposit of ratifications by the Republic of China, France, the Union of Soviet Socialist Republics, the United Kingdom of Great Britain and Northern Ireland, and the united States of America, and by a majority of the other signatory states. A protocol of the ratifications deposited shall thereupon be drawn up by the Government of the United States of America, which shall communicate copies thereof to all the signatory states.

4. The states signatory to the present Charter which ratify it after it has come into force will become original Members of the United Nations on the date of the deposit of their respective ratifications.

Article 111

The present Charter, of which the Chinese, French, Russian, English, and Spanish texts are equally authentic, shall remain deposited in the archives of the Government of the United States of America. Duly certified copies thereof shall be transmitted by that Government to the Governments of the other signatory states.

IN FAITH WHEREOF the representatives of the Governments of the United Nations have signed the present Charter.

DONE at the city of San Francisco the sixth day of June, one thousand nine hundred and forty-five.

STATUTE OF THE INTERNATIONAL COURT OF JUSTICE

Article 1

THE INTERNATIONAL COURT OF JUSTICE established by the Charter of the United Nations as the principal judicial organ of the United Nations shall be constituted and shall function in accordance with the provisions of the present Statute.

CHAPTER I

ORGANIZATION OF THE COURT

Article 2

The Court shall be composed of a body of independent judges, elected regardless of their nationality from among persons of high moral character, who possess the qualifications required in their respective countries for appointment to the highest judicial offices, or are jurisconsults of recognized competence in international law.

Article 3

1.   The Court shall consist of fifteen members, no two of whom may be nationals of the same state.

2.   A person who for the purposes of membership in the Court could be regarded as a national of more than one state shall be deemed to be a national of the one in which he ordinarily exercises civil and political rights.

Article 4

1.   The members of the Court shall be elected by the General Assembly and by the Security Council from a list of persons nominated by the national groups in the Permanent Court of Arbitration, in accordance with the following provisions.

2.   In the case of Members of the United Nations not represented in the Permanent Court of Arbitration, candidates shall be nominated by national groups appointed for this purpose by their governments under the same conditions as those prescribed for members of the Permanent Court of Arbitration by Article 44 of the Convention of The Hague of 1907 for the pacific settlement of international disputes.

3.   The conditions under which a state which is a party to the present Statute but is not a Member of the United Nations may participate in electing the members of the Court shall, in the absence of a special agreement, be laid down by the General Assembly upon recommendation of the Security Council.

Article 5

1.   At least three months before the date of the election, the Secretary–General of the United Nations shall address a written request

to the members of the Permanent Court of Arbitration belonging to the states which are parties to the present Statute, and to the members of the national groups appointed under Article 4, paragraph 2, inviting them to undertake, within a given time, by national groups, the nomination of persons in a position to accept the duties of a member of the Court.

2. No group may nominate more than four persons, not more than two of whom shall be of their own nationality. In no case may the number of candidates nominated by a group be more than double the number of seats to be filled.

Article 6

Before making these nominations, each national group is recommended to consult its highest court of justice, its legal faculties and schools of law, and its national academics and national sections of international academies devoted to the study of law.

Article 7

1. The Secretary–General shall prepare a list in alphabetical order of all the persons thus nominated. Save as provided in Article 12, Paragraph 2, these shall be the only persons eligible.

2. The Secretary–General shall submit this list to the General Assembly and to the Security Council.

Article 8

The General Assembly and the Security Council shall proceed independently of one another to elect the members of the Court.

Article 9

At every election, the electors shall bear in mind not only that the persons to be elected should individually possess the qualifications required, but also that in the body as a whole the representation of the main forms of civilization and of the principal legal systems of the world should be assured.

Article 10

1. Those candidates who obtain an absolute majority of votes in the General Assembly and in the Security Council shall be considered as elected.

2. Any vote of the Security Council, whether for the election of judges or for the appointment of members of the conference envisaged in Article 12, shall be taken without any distinction between permanent and non-permanent members of the Security Council.

3. In the event of more than one national of the same state obtaining an absolute majority of the votes both of the General Assembly

and of the Security Council, the eldest of these only shall be considered as elected.

Article 11

If, after the first meeting held for the purpose of the election, one or more seats remain to be filled, a second and, if necessary, a third meeting shall take place.

Article 12

1. If, after the third meeting, one or more seats remain unfilled, a joint conference consisting of six members, three appointed by the General Assembly and three by the Security Council, may be formed at any time at the request of either the General Assembly or the Security Council, for the purpose of choosing by the vote of an absolute majority one name for each seat still vacant, to submit to the General Assembly and the Security Council for their respective acceptance.

2. If the joint conference is unanimously agreed upon any person who fulfils the required conditions, he may be included in its list, even though he was not included in the list of nominations referred to in Article 7.

3. If the joint conference is satisfied that it will not be successful in procuring an election, those members of the Court who have already been elected shall, within a period to be fixed by the Security Council, proceed to fill the vacant seats by selection from among those candidates who have obtained votes either in the General Assembly or in the Security Council.

4. In the event of an equality of votes among the judges, the eldest judge shall have a casting vote.

Article 13

1. The members of the Court shall be elected for nine years and may be re-elected; provided, however, that of the judges elected at the first election, the terms of five judges shall expire at the end of three years and the terms of five more judges shall expire at the end of six years.

2. The judges whose terms are to expire at the end of the above-mentioned initial periods of three and six years shall be chosen by lot to be drawn by the Secretary–General immediately after the first election has been completed.

3. The members of the Court shall continue to discharge their duties until their places have been filled. Though replaced, they shall finish any cases which they may have begun.

4. In the case of the resignation of a member of the Court, the resignation shall be addressed to the President of the Court for transmission to the Secretary–General. This last notification makes the place vacant.

Article 14

Vacancies shall be filled by the same method as that laid down for the first election, subject to the following provision: the Secretary–General shall, within one month of the occurrence of the vacancy, proceed to issue the invitations provided for in Article 5, and the date of the election shall be fixed by the Security Council.

Article 15

A member of the Court elected to replace a member whose term of office has not expired shall hold office for the remainder of his predecessor's term.

Article 16

1.   No member of the Court may exercise any political or administrative function, or engage in any other occupation of a professional nature.

2.   Any doubt on this point shall be settled by the decision of the Court.

Article 17

1.   No member of the Court may act as agent, counsel, or advocate in any case.

2.   No member may participate in the decision of any case in which he has previously taken part as agent, counsel, or advocate for one of the parties, or as a member of a national or international court, or of a commission of enquiry, or in any other capacity.

3.   Any doubt on this point shall be settled by the decision of the Court.

Article 18

1.   No member of the Court can be dismissed unless, in the unanimous opinion of the other members, he has ceased to fulfil the required conditions.

2.   Formal notification thereof shall be made to the Secretary–General by the Registrar.

3.   This notification makes the place vacant.

Article 19

The members of the Court, when engaged on the business of the Court, shall enjoy diplomatic privileges and immunities.

Article 20

Every member of the Court shall, before taking up his duties, make a solemn declaration in open court that he will exercise his powers impartially and conscientiously.

Article 21

1. The Court shall elect its President and Vice President for three years; they may be re-elected.

2. The Court shall appoint its Registrar and may provide for the appointment of such others as may be necessary.

Article 22

1. The seat of the Court shall be established at The Hague. This, however, shall not prevent the Court from sitting and exercising its functions elsewhere whenever the Court considers it desirable.

2. The President and the Registrar shall reside at the seat of the Court.

Article 23

1. The Court shall remain permanently in session, except during the judicial vacations, the dates and duration of which shall be fixed by the Court.

2. Members of the Court are entitled to periodic leave, the dates and duration of which shall be fixed by the Court, having in mind the distance between The Hague and the home of each judge.

3. Members of the Court shall be bound, unless they are on leave or prevented from attending by illness or other serious reasons duly explained to the President, to hold themselves permanently at the disposal of the Court.

Article 24

1. If, for some special reason, a member of the Court considers that he should not take part in the decision of a particular case, he shall so inform the President.

2. If the President considers that for some special reason one of the members of the Court should not sit in a particular case, he shall give him notice accordingly.

3. If in any such case the member of the Court and the President disagree, the matter shall be settled by the decision of the Court.

Article 25

1. The full Court shall sit except when it is expressly provided otherwise in the present Statute.

2. Subject to the condition that the number of judges available to constitute the Court is not thereby reduced below eleven, the Rules of the Court may provide for allowing one or more judges, according to circumstances and in rotation, to be dispensed from sitting.

3. A quorum of nine judges shall suffice to constitute the Court.

Article 26

1.   The Court may from time to time form one or more chambers, composed of three or more judges as the Court may determine, for dealing with particular categories of cases; for example, labor cases and cases relating to transit and communications.

2.   The Court may at any time form a chamber for dealing with a particular case. The number of judges to constitute such a chamber shall be determined by the Court with the approval of the parties.

3.   Cases shall be heard and determined by the chambers provided for in this Article if the parties so request.

Article 27

A judgment given by any of the chambers provided for in Articles 26 and 29 shall be considered as rendered by the Court.

Article 28

The chambers provided for in Articles 26 and 29 may, with the consent of the parties, sit and exercise their functions elsewhere than at The Hague.

Article 29

With a view to the speedy despatch of business, the Court shall form annually a chamber composed of five judges which, at the request of the parties, may hear and determine cases by summary procedure. In addition, two judges shall be selected for the purpose of replacing judges who find it impossible to sit.

Article 30

1.   The Court shall frame rules for carrying out its functions. In particular, it shall lay down rules of procedure.

2.   The Rules of the Court may provide for assessors to sit with the Court or with any of its chambers, without the right to vote.

Article 31

1.   Judges of the nationality of each of the parties shall retain their right to sit in the case before the Court.

2.   If the Court includes upon the Bench a judge of the nationality of one of the parties, any other party may choose a person to sit as judge. Such person shall be chosen preferably from among those persons who have been nominated as candidates as provided in Articles 4 and 5.

3.   If the Court includes upon the Bench no judge of the nationality of the parties, each of these parties may proceed to choose a judge as provided in paragraph 2 of this Article.

4.   The provisions of this Article shall apply to the case of Articles 26 and 29. In such cases, the President shall request one or, if necessary,

two of the members of the Court forming the chamber to give place to the members of the Court of the nationality of the parties concerned, and, failing such, or if they are unable to be present, to the judges specially chosen by the parties.

5. Should there be several parties in the same interest, they shall, for the purpose of the preceding provisions, be reckoned as one party only. Any doubt upon this point shall be settled by the decision of the Court.

6. Judges chosen as laid down in paragraphs 2, 3, and 4 of this Article shall fulfil the conditions required by Articles 2, 17 (paragraph 2), 20, and 24 of the present Statute. They shall take part in the decision on terms of complete equality with their colleagues.

Article 32

I. Each member of the Court shall receive an annual salary.

2. The President shall receive a special annual allowance.

3. The Vice–President shall receive a special allowance for every day on which he acts as President.

4. The judges chosen under Article 31, other than members of the Court, shall receive compensation for each day on which they exercise their functions.

5. These salaries, allowances, and compensation shall be fixed by the General Assembly. They may not be decreased during the term of office.

6. The salary of the Registrar shall be fixed by the General Assembly on the proposal of the Court.

7. Regulations made by the General Assembly shall fix the conditions under which retirement pensions may be given to members of the Court and to the Registrar, and the conditions under which members of the Court and the Registrar shall have their traveling expenses refunded.

8. The above salaries, allowances, and compensation shall be free of all taxation.

Article 33

The expenses of the Court shall be borne by the United Nations in such a manner as shall be decided by the General Assembly.

CHAPTER II

COMPETENCE OF THE COURT

Article 34

1. Only states may be parties in cases before the Court.

2. The Court, subject to and in conformity with its Rules, may request of public international organizations information relevant to

cases before it, and shall receive such information presented by such organizations on their own initiative.

3. Whenever the construction of the constituent instrument of a public international organization or of an international convention adopted thereunder is in question in a case before the Court, the Registrar shall so notify the public international organization concerned and shall communicate to it copies of all the written proceedings.

Article 35

1. The Court shall be open to the states parties to the present Statute.

2. The conditions under which the Court shall be open to other states shall, subject to the special provisions contained in treaties in force, be laid down by the Security Council, but in no case shall such conditions place the parties in a position of inequality before the Court.

3. When a state which is not a Member of the United Nations is a party to a case, the Court shall fix the amount which that party is to contribute towards the expenses of the Court. This provision shall not apply if such state is bearing a share of the expenses of the Court.

Article 36

1. The jurisdiction of the Court comprises all cases which the parties refer to it and all matters specially provided for in the Charter of the United Nations or in treaties and conventions in force.

2. The states parties to the present Statute may at any time declare that they recognize as compulsory *ipso facto* and without special agreement, in relation to any other state accepting the same obligation, the jurisdiction of the Court in all legal disputes concerning:

    a. the interpretation of a treaty;

    b. any question of international law;

    c. the existence of any fact which, if established, would constitute a breach of an international obligation;

    d. the nature or extent of the reparation to be made for the breach of an international obligation.

3. The declarations referred to above may be made unconditionally or on condition of reciprocity on the part of several or certain states, or for a certain time.

4. Such declarations shall be deposited with the Secretary–General of the United Nations, who shall transmit copies thereof to the parties to the Statute and to the Registrar of the Court.

5. Declarations made under Article 36 of the Statute of the Permanent Court of International Justice and which are still in force shall be deemed, as between the parties to the present Statute, to be acceptances of the compulsory jurisdiction of the International Court of Justice for

the period which they still have to run and in accordance with their terms.

6. In the event of a dispute as to whether the Court has jurisdiction, the matter shall be settled by the decision of the Court.

Article 37

Whenever a treaty or convention in force provides for reference of a matter to a tribunal to have been instituted by the League of Nations, or to the Permanent Court of International Justice, the matter shall, as between the parties to the present Statute, be referred to the International Court of Justice.

Article 38

1. The Court, whose function is to decide in accordance with international law such disputes as are submitted to it, shall apply:

　　a. international conventions, whether general or particular, establishing rules expressly recognized by the contesting states;

　　b. international custom, as evidence of a general practice accepted as law;

　　c. the general principles of law recognized by civilized nations;

　　d. subject to the provisions of Article 59, judicial decisions and the teachings of the most highly qualified publicists of the various nations, as subsidiary means for the determination of rules of law.

2. This provision shall not prejudice the power of the Court to decide a case *ex aequo et bono,* if the parties agree thereto.

CHAPTER III

PROCEDURE

Article 39

1. The official languages of the Court shall be French and English. If the parties agree that the case shall be conducted in French, the judgment shall be delivered in French. If the parties agree that the case shall be conducted in English, the judgment shall be delivered in English.

2. In the absence of an agreement as to which language shall be employed, each party may, in the pleadings, use the language which it prefers; the decision of the Court shall be given in French and English. In this case the Court shall at the same time determine which of the two texts shall be considered as authoritative.

3. The Court shall, at the request of any party, authorize a language other than French or English to be used by that party.

Article 40

1.   Cases are brought before the Court, as the case may be, either by the notification of the special agreement or by a written application addressed to the Registrar. In either case the subject of the dispute and the parties shall be indicated.

2.   The Registrar shall forthwith communicate the application to all concerned.

3.   He shall also notify the Members of the United Nations through the Secretary–General, and also any other states entitled to appear before the Court.

Article 41

1.   The Court shall have the power to indicate, if it considers that circumstances so require, any provisional measures which ought to be taken to preserve the respective rights of either party.

2.   Pending the final decision, notice of the measures suggested shall forthwith be given to the parties and to the Security Council.

Article 42

1.   The parties shall be represented by agents.

2.   They may have the assistance of counsel or advocates before the Court.

3.   The agents, counsel, and advocates of parties before the Court shall enjoy the privileges and immunities necessary to the independent exercise of their duties.

Article 43

1.   The procedure shall consist of two parts: written and oral.

2.   The written proceedings shall consist of the communication to the Court and to the parties of memorials, counter-memorials and, if necessary, replies; also all papers and documents in support.

3.   These communications shall be made through the Registrar, in the order and within the time fixed by the Court.

4.   A certified copy of every document produced by one party shall be communicated to the other party.

5.   The oral proceedings shall consist of the hearing by the Court of witnesses, experts, agents, counsel, and advocates.

Article 44

1.   For the service of all notices upon persons other than the agents, counsel, and advocates, the Court shall apply direct to the government of the state upon whose territory the notice has to be served.

2. The same provision shall apply whenever steps are to be taken to procure evidence on the spot.

Article 45

The hearing shall be under the control of the President or, if he is unable to preside, of the Vice President; if neither is able to preside, the senior judge present shall preside.

Article 46

The hearing in Court shall be public, unless the Court shall decide otherwise, or unless the parties demand that the public be not admitted.

Article 47

1. Minutes shall be made at each hearing and signed by the Registrar and the President.

2. These minutes alone shall be authentic.

Article 48

The Court shall make orders for the conduct of the case, shall decide the form and time in which each party must conclude its arguments, and make all arrangements connected with the taking of evidence.

Article 49

The Court may, even before the hearing begins, call upon the agents to produce any document or to supply any explanations. Formal note shall be taken of any refusal.

Article 50

The Court may, at any time, entrust any individual, body, bureau, commission, or other organization that it may select, with the task of carrying out an enquiry or giving an expert opinion.

Article 51

During the hearing any relevant questions are to be put to the witnesses and experts under the conditions laid down by the Court in the rules of procedure referred to in Article 30.

Article 52

After the Court has received the proofs and evidence within the time specified for the purpose, it may refuse to accept any further oral or written evidence that one party may desire to present unless the other side consents.

Article 53

1. Whenever one of the parties does not appear before the Court, or fails to defend its case, the other party may call upon the Court to decide in favor of its claim.

2. The Court must, before doing so, satisfy itself, not only that it has jurisdiction in accordance with Articles 36 and 37, but also that the claim is well founded in fact and law.

Article 54

1. When, subject to the control of the Court, the agents, counsel, and advocates have completed their presentation of the case, the President shall declare the hearing closed.

2. The Court shall withdraw to consider the judgment.

3. The deliberations of the Court shall take place in private and remain secret.

Article 55

1. All questions shall be decided by a majority of the judges present.

2. In the event of an equality of votes, the President or the judge who acts in his place shall have a casting vote.

Article 56

1. The judgment shall state the reasons on which it is based.

2. It shall contain the names of the judges who have taken part in the decision.

Article 57

If the judgment does not represent in whole or in part the unanimous opinion of the judges, any judge shall be entitled to deliver a separate opinion.

Article 58

The judgment shall be signed by the President and by the Registrar. It shall be read in open court, due notice having been given to the agents.

Article 59

The decision of the Court has no binding force except between the parties and in respect of that particular case.

Article 60

The judgment is final and without appeal. In the event of dispute as to the meaning or scope of the judgment, the Court shall construe it upon the request of any party.

Article 61

1. An application for revision of a judgment may be made only when it is based upon the discovery of some fact of such a nature as to be a decisive factor, which fact was, when the judgment was given,

unknown to the Court and also to the party claiming revision, always provided that such ignorance was not due to negligence.

2. The proceedings for revision shall be opened by a judgment of the Court expressly recording the existence of the new fact, recognizing that it has such a character as to lay the case open to revision, and declaring the application admissible on this ground.

3. The Court may require previous compliance with the terms of the judgment before it admits proceedings in revision.

4. The application for revision must be made at latest within six months of the discovery of the new fact.

5. No application for revision may be made after the lapse of ten years from the date of the judgment.

Article 62

1. Should a state consider that it has an interest of a legal nature which may be affected by the decision in the case, it may submit a request to the Court to be permitted to intervene.

2. It shall be for the Court to decide upon this request.

Article 63

1. Whenever the construction of a convention to which states other than those concerned in the case are parties is in question, the Registrar shall notify all such states forthwith.

2. Every state so notified has the right to intervene in the proceedings; but if it uses this right, the construction given by the judgment will be equally binding upon it.

Article 64

Unless otherwise decided by the Court, each party shall bear its own costs.

CHAPTER IV

ADVISORY OPINIONS

Article 65

1. The Court may give an advisory opinion on any legal question at the request of whatever body may be authorized by or in accordance with the Charter of the United Nations to make such a request.

2. Questions upon which the advisory opinion of the Court is asked shall be laid before the Court by means of a written request containing an exact statement of the question upon which an opinion is required, and accompanied by all documents likely to throw light upon the question.

Article 66

1. The Registrar shall forthwith give notice of the request for an advisory opinion to all states entitled to appear before the Court.

2. The Registrar shall also, by means of a special and direct communication, notify any state entitled to appear before the Court or international organization considered by the Court or, should it not be sitting, by the President, as likely to be able to furnish information on the question, that the Court will be prepared to receive, within a time limit to be fixed by the President, written statements, or to hear, at a public sitting to be held for the purpose, oral statements relating to the question.

3. Should any such state entitled to appear before the Court have failed to receive the special communication referred to in paragraph 2 of this Article, such state may express a desire to submit a written statement or to be heard; and the Court will decide.

4. States and organizations having presented written or oral statements or both shall be permitted to comment on the statements made by other states or organizations in the form, to the extent, and within the time limits which the Court, or, should it not be sitting, the President, shall decide in each particular case. Accordingly, the Registrar shall in due time communicate any such written statements to states and organizations having submitted similar statements.

Article 67

The Court shall deliver its advisory opinions in open court, notice having been given to the Secretary–General and to the representatives of Members of the United Nations, of other states and of international organizations immediately concerned.

Article 68

In the exercise of its advisory functions the Court shall further be guided by the provisions of the present Statute which apply in contentious cases to the extent to which it recognizes them to be applicable.

CHAPTER V

AMENDMENT

Article 69

Amendments to the present Statute shall be effected by the same procedure as is provided by the Charter of the United Nations for amendments to that Charter, subject however to any provisions which the General Assembly upon recommendation of the Security Council may adopt concerning the participation of states which are parties to the present Statute but are not Members of the United Nations.

Article 70

The Court shall have power to propose such amendments to the present Statute as it may deem necessary, through written communications to the Secretary–General, for consideration in conformity with the provisions of Article 69.

VIENNA CONVENTION ON THE LAW OF TREATIES

May 23, 1969, 1155 U.N.T.S. 331, 8 *International Legal Materials* 679 (1969).

PART I

INTRODUCTION

Article 1

Scope of the present Convention

The present Convention applies to treaties between States.

Article 2

Use of Terms

1. For the purposes of the present Convention:

(a) "treaty" means an international agreement concluded between States in written form and governed by international law, whether embodied in a single instrument or in two or more related instruments and whatever its particular designation;

(b) "ratification," "acceptance," "approval" and "accession" mean in each case the international act so named whereby a State establishes on the international plane its consent to be bound by a treaty;

(c) "full powers" means a document emanating from the competent authority of a State designating a person or persons to represent the State for negotiating, adopting or authenticating the text of a treaty, for expressing the consent of the State to be bound by a treaty, or for accomplishing any other act with respect to a treaty;

(d) "reservation" means a unilateral statement, however phrased or named, made by a State, when signing, ratifying, accepting, approving or acceding to a treaty, whereby it purports to exclude or to modify the legal effect of certain provisions of the treaty in their application to that State;

(e) "negotiating State" means a State which took part in the drawing up and adoption of the text of the treaty;

(f) "contracting State" means a State which has consented to be bound by the treaty, whether or not the treaty has entered into force;

(g) "party" means a State which has consented to be bound by the treaty and for which the treaty is in force;

(h) "third State" means a State not a party to the treaty;

(i) "international organization" means an intergovernmental organization.

2. The provisions of paragraph 1 regarding the use of terms in the present Convention are without prejudice to the use of those terms or to the meanings which may be given to them in the internal law of any State.

Article 3

International agreements not within the scope of the present Convention

The fact that the present Convention does not apply to international agreements concluded between States and other subjects of international law or between such other subjects of international law, or to international agreements not in written form, shall not affect:

(a) the legal force of such agreements;

(b) the application to them of any of the rules set forth in the present Convention to which they would be subject under international law independently of the Convention;

(c) the application of the Convention to the relations of States as between themselves under international agreements to which other subjects of international law are also parties.

Article 4

Non-retroactivity of the present Convention

Without prejudice to the application of any rules set forth in the present Convention to which treaties would be subject under international law independently of the Convention, the Convention applies only to treaties which are concluded by States after the entry into force of the present Convention with regard to such States.

Article 5

Treaties constituting international organizations and treaties adopted within an international organization

The present Convention applies to any treaty which is the constituent instrument of an international organization and to any treaty adopted within an international organization without prejudice to any relevant rules of the organization.

PART II

CONCLUSION AND ENTRY INTO FORCE OF TREATIES

SECTION 1: CONCLUSION OF TREATIES

Article 6

Capacity of States to conclude treaties

Every State possesses capacity to conclude treaties.

Article 7

Full powers

1. A person is considered as representing a State for the purpose of adopting or authenticating the text of a treaty or for the purpose of expressing the consent of the State to be bound by a treaty if:

(a) he produces appropriate full powers; or

(b) it appears from the practice of the States concerned or from other circumstances that their intention was to consider that person as representing the State for such purposes and to dispense with full powers.

2.   In virtue of their functions and without having to produce full powers, the following are considered as representing their State:

(a) Heads of State, Heads of Government and Ministers for Foreign Affairs, for the purpose of performing all acts relating to the conclusion of a treaty;

(b) heads of diplomatic missions, for the purpose of adopting the text of a treaty between the accrediting State and the State to which they are accredited;

(c) representatives accredited by States to an international conference or to an international organization or one of its organs, for the purpose of adopting the text of a treaty in that conference, organization or organ.

Article 8

Subsequent confirmation of an act performed without authorization

An act relating to the conclusion of a treaty performed by a person who cannot be considered under article 7 as authorized to represent a State for that purpose is without legal effect unless afterwards confirmed by that State.

Article 9

Adoption of the text

1.   The adoption of the text of a treaty takes place by the consent of all the States participating in its drawing up except as provided in paragraph 2.

2.   The adoption of the text of a treaty at an international conference takes place by the vote of two-thirds of the States present and voting, unless by the same majority they shall decide to apply a different rule.

Article 10

Authentication of the text

The text of a treaty is established as authentic and definitive:

(a) by such procedure as may be provided for in the text or agreed upon by the States participating in its drawing up; or

(b) failing such procedure, by the signature, signature *ad referendum* or initialing by the representatives of those States of the text of the treaty or of the Final Act of a conference incorporating the text.

Article 11

Means of expressing consent to be bound by a treaty

The consent of a State to be bound by a treaty may be expressed by signature, exchange of instruments constituting a treaty, ratification, acceptance, approval or accession, or by any other means if so agreed.

Article 12

Consent to be bound by a treaty expressed by signature

1. The consent of a State to be bound by a treaty is expressed by the signature of its representative when:

(a) the treaty provides that signature shall have that effect;

(b) it is otherwise established that the negotiating States were agreed that signature should have that effect; or

(c) the intention of the State to give that effect to the signature appears from the full powers of its representative or was expressed during the negotiation.

2. For the purposes of paragraph 1:

(a) the initialing of a text constitutes a signature of the treaty when it is established that the negotiating States so agreed;

(b) the signature *ad referendum* of a treaty by a representative, if confirmed by his State, constitutes a full signature of the treaty.

Article 13

*Consent to be bound by a treaty expressed by an exchange
of instruments constituting a treaty*

The consent of States to be bound by a treaty constituted by instruments exchanged between them is expressed by that exchange when:

(a) the instruments provide that their exchange shall have that effect; or

(b) it is otherwise established that those States were agreed that the exchange of instruments should have that effect.

Article 14

*Consent to be bound by a treaty expressed by
ratification, acceptance or approval*

1. The consent of a State to be bound by a treaty is expressed by ratification when:

(a) the treaty provides for such consent to be expressed by means of ratification;

(b) it is otherwise established that the negotiating States were agreed that ratification should be required;

(c) the representative of the State has signed the treaty subject to ratification; or

(d) the intention of the State to sign the treaty subject to ratification appears from the full powers of its representative or was expressed during the negotiation.

2. The consent of a State to be bound by a treaty is expressed by acceptance or approval under conditions similar to those which apply to ratification.

Article 15

Consent to be bound by a treaty expressed by accession

The consent of a State to be bound by a treaty is expressed by accession when:

(a) the treaty provides that such consent may be expressed by that State by means of accession;

(b) it is otherwise established that the negotiating States were agreed that such consent may be expressed by that State by means of accession; or

(c) all the parties have subsequently agreed that such consent may be expressed by that State by means of accession.

Article 16

Exchange or deposit of instruments of ratification,
acceptance, approval or accession

Unless the treaty otherwise provides, instruments of ratification, acceptance, approval or accession establish the consent of a State to be bound by a treaty upon:

(a) their exchange between the contracting States;

(b) their deposit with the depositary; or

(c) their notification to the contracting States or to the depositary, if so agreed.

Article 17

Consent to be bound by part of a treaty
and choice of differing provisions

1. Without prejudice to articles 19 to 23, the consent of a State to be bound by part of a treaty is effective only if the treaty so permits or the other contracting States so agree.

2. The consent of a State to be bound by a treaty which permits a choice between differing provisions is effective only if it is made clear to which of the provisions the consent relates.

Article 18

*Obligation not to defeat the object and purpose
of a treaty prior to its entry into force*

A State is obliged to refrain from acts which would defeat the object and purpose of a treaty when:

(a) it has signed the treaty or has exchanged instruments constituting the treaty subject to ratification, acceptance or approval, until it shall have made its intention clear not to become a party to the treaty; or

(b) it has expressed its consent to be bound by the treaty, pending the entry into force of the treaty and provided that such entry into force is not unduly delayed.

SECTION 2: RESERVATIONS

Article 19

Formulation of reservations

A State may, when signing, ratifying, accepting, approving or acceding to a treaty, formulate a reservation unless:

(a) the reservation is prohibited by the treaty;

(b) the treaty provides that only specified reservations, which do not include the reservation in question, may be made; or

(c) in cases not falling under sub-paragraphs (a) and (b), the reservation is incompatible with the object and purpose of the treaty.

Article 20

Acceptance of and objection to reservations

1. A reservation expressly authorized by a treaty does not require any subsequent acceptance by the other contracting States unless the treaty so provides.

2. When it appears from the limited number of the negotiating States and the object and purpose of a treaty that the application of the treaty in its entirety between all the parties is an essential condition of the consent of each one to be bound by the treaty, a reservation requires acceptance by all the parties.

3. When a treaty is a constituent instrument of an international organization and unless it otherwise provides, a reservation requires the acceptance of the competent organ of that organization.

4. In cases not falling under the preceding paragraphs and unless the treaty otherwise provides:

(a) acceptance by another contracting State of a reservation constitutes the reserving State a party to the treaty in relation to that other State if or when the treaty is in force for those States;

(b) an objection by another contracting State to a reservation does not preclude the entry into force of the treaty as between the objecting and reserving States unless a contrary intention is definitely expressed by the objecting State;

(c) an act expressing a State's consent to be bound by the treaty and containing a reservation is effective as soon as at least one other contracting State has accepted the reservation.

5. For the purposes of paragraphs 2 and 4 and unless the treaty otherwise provides, a reservation is considered to have been accepted by a State if it shall have raised no objection to the reservation by the end of a period of twelve months after it was notified of the reservation or by the date on which it expressed its consent to be bound by the treaty, whichever is later.

Article 21

Legal effects of reservations and of objections to reservations

1. A reservation established with regard to another party in accordance with articles 19, 20 and 23:

(a) modifies for the reserving State in its relations with that other party the provisions of the treaty to which the reservation relates to the extent of the reservation; and

(b) modifies those provisions to the same extent for that other party in its relations with the reserving State.

2. The reservation does not modify the provisions of the treaty for the other parties to the treaty *inter se*.

3. When a State objecting to a reservation has not opposed the entry into force of the treaty between itself and the reserving State, the provisions to which the reservation relates do not apply as between the two States to the extent of the reservation.

Article 22

Withdrawal of reservations and of objections to reservations

1. Unless the treaty otherwise provides, a reservation may be withdrawn at any time and the consent of a State which has accepted the reservation is not required for its withdrawal.

2. Unless the treaty otherwise provides, an objection to a reservation may be withdrawn at any time.

3. Unless the treaty otherwise provides, or it is otherwise agreed:

(a) the withdrawal of a reservation becomes operative in relation to another contracting State only when notice of it has been received by that State;

(b) the withdrawal of an objection to a reservation becomes operative only when notice of it has been received by the State which formulated the reservation.

Article 23

Procedure regarding reservations

1.   A reservation, an express acceptance of a reservation and an objection to a reservation must be formulated in writing and communicated to the contracting States and other States entitled to become parties to the treaty.

2.   If formulated when signing the treaty subject to ratification, acceptance or approval, a reservation must be formally confirmed by the reserving State when expressing its consent to be bound by the treaty. In such a case the reservation shall be considered as having been made on the date of its confirmation.

3.   An express acceptance of, or an objection to, a reservation made previously to confirmation of the reservation does not itself require confirmation.

4.   The withdrawal of a reservation or of an objection to a reservation must be formulated in writing.

SECTION 3: ENTRY INTO FORCE AND PROVISIONAL APPLICATION OF TREATIES

Article 24

Entry into force

1.   A treaty enters into force in such manner and upon such date as it may provide or as the negotiating States may agree.

2.   Failing any such provision or agreement, a treaty enters into force as soon as consent to be bound by the treaty has been established for all the negotiating States.

3.   When the consent of a State to be bound by a treaty is established on a date after the treaty has come into force, the treaty enters into force for that State on that date, unless the treaty otherwise provides.

4.   The provisions of a treaty regulating the authentication of its text, the establishment of the consent of States to be bound by the treaty, the manner or date of its entry into force, reservations, the functions of the depositary and other matters arising necessarily before the entry into force of the treaty apply from the time of the adoption of this text.

Article 25

Provisional application

1.   A treaty or a part of a treaty is applied provisionally pending its entry into force if:

(a) the treaty itself so provides; or

(b) the negotiating States have in some other manner so agreed.

2.   Unless the treaty otherwise provides or the negotiating States have otherwise agreed, the provisional application of a treaty or a part of

a treaty with respect to a State shall be terminated if that State notifies the other States between which the treaty is being applied provisionally of its intention not to become a party to the treaty.

PART III

OBSERVANCE, APPLICATION AND INTERPRETATION OF TREATIES

SECTION 1: OBSERVANCE OF TREATIES

Article 26

Pacta sunt servanda

Every treaty in force is binding upon the parties to it and must be performed by them in good faith.

Article 27

Internal law and observance of treaties

A party may not invoke the provisions of its internal law as justification for its failure to perform a treaty. This rule is without prejudice to Article 46.

SECTION 2: APPLICATION OF TREATIES

Article 28

Non-retroactivity of treaties

Unless a different intention appears from the treaty or is otherwise established, its provisions do not bind a party in relation to any act or fact which took place or any situation which ceased to exist before the date of the entry into force of the treaty with respect to that party.

Article 29

Territorial scope of treaties

Unless a different intention appears from the treaty or is otherwise established, a treaty is binding upon each party in respect of its entire territory.

Article 30

Application of successive treaties relating to the same subject-matter

1. Subject to Article 103 of the Charter of the United Nations, the rights and obligations of States parties to successive treaties relating to the same subject-matter shall be determined in accordance with the following paragraphs.

2. When a treaty specifies that it is subject to, or that is not to be considered as incompatible with, an earlier or later treaty, the provisions of that other treaty prevail.

3. When all the parties to the earlier treaty are parties also to the later treaty but the earlier treaty is not terminated or suspended in

operation under article 59, the earlier treaty applies only to the extent that its provisions are compatible with those of the later treaty.

4. When the parties to the later treaty do not include all the parties to the earlier one:

(a) as between States parties to both treaties the same rule applies as in paragraph 3;

(b) as between a State party to both treaties and a State party to only one of the treaties, the treaty to which both States are parties governs their mutual rights and obligations.

5. Paragraph 4 is without prejudice to article 41, or to any question of the termination or suspension of the operation of a treaty under article 60 or to any question of responsibility which may arise for a State from the conclusion or application of a treaty the provisions of which are incompatible with its obligations towards another State under another treaty.

SECTION 3: INTERPRETATION OF TREATIES

Article 31

General rule of interpretation

1. A treaty shall be interpreted in good faith in accordance with the ordinary meaning to be given to the terms of the treaty in their context and in the light of its object and purpose.

2. The context for the purpose of the interpretation of a treaty shall comprise, in addition to the text, including its preamble and annexes:

(a) any agreement relating to the treaty which was made between all the parties in connexion with the conclusion of the treaty;

(b) any instrument which was made by one or more parties in connexion with the conclusion of the treaty and accepted by the other parties as an instrument related to the treaty.

3. There shall be taken into account, together with the context:

(a) any subsequent agreement between the parties regarding the interpretation of the treaty or the application of its provisions;

(b) any subsequent practice in the application of the treaty which establishes the agreement of the parties regarding its interpretation;

(c) any relevant rules of international law applicable in the relations between the parties.

4. A special meaning shall be given to a term if it is established that the parties so intended.

Article 32

Supplementary means of interpretation

Recourse may be had to supplementary means of interpretation, including the preparatory work of the treaty and the circumstances of its conclusion, in order to confirm the meaning resulting from the application of article 31, or to determine the meaning when the interpretation according to article 31:

(a) leaves the meaning ambiguous or obscure; or

(b) leads to a result which is manifestly absurd or unreasonable.

Article 33

Interpretation of treaties authenticated in two or more languages

1. When a treaty has been authenticated in two or more languages, the text is equally authoritative in each language, unless the treaty provides or the parties agree that, in case of divergence, a particular text shall prevail.

2. A version of the treaty in a language other than one of those in which the text was authenticated shall be considered an authentic text only if the treaty so provides or the parties so agree.

3. The terms of the treaty are presumed to have the same meaning in each authentic text.

4. Except where a particular text prevails in accordance with paragraph 1, when a comparison of the authentic texts discloses a difference of meaning which the application of articles 31 and 32 does not remove, the meaning which best reconciles the texts, having regard to the object and purpose of the treaty, shall be adopted.

SECTION 4: TREATIES AND THIRD STATES

Article 34

General rule regarding third States

A treaty does not create either obligations or rights for a third State without its consent.

Article 35

Treaties providing for obligations for third States

An obligation arises for a third State from a provision of a treaty if the parties to the treaty intend the provision to be the means of establishing the obligation and the third State expressly accepts that obligation in writing.

Article 36

Treaties providing for rights for third States

1. A right arises for a third State from a provision of a treaty if the parties to the treaty intend the provision to accord that right either to the third State, or to a group of States to which it belongs, or to all States, and the third State assents thereto. Its assent shall be presumed so long as the contrary is not indicated, unless the treaty otherwise provides.

2. A State exercising a right in accordance with paragraph 1 shall comply with the conditions for its exercise provided for in the treaty or established in conformity with the treaty.

Article 37

Revocation or modification of obligations or rights of third States

1. When an obligation has arisen for a third State in conformity with article 35, the obligation may be revoked or modified only with the consent of the parties to the treaty and of the third State, unless it is established that they had otherwise agreed.

2. When a right has arisen for a third State in conformity with article 36, the right may not be revoked or modified by the parties if it is established that the right was intended not to be revocable or subject to modification without the consent of the third State.

Article 38

Rules in a treaty becoming binding on third States through international custom

Nothing in articles 34 to 37 precludes a rule set forth in the treaty from becoming binding upon a third State as a customary rule of international law, recognized as such.

PART IV

AMENDMENT AND MODIFICATION OF TREATIES

Article 39

General rule regarding the amendment of treaties

A treaty may be amended by agreement between the parties. The rules laid down in Part II apply to such an agreement except in so far as the treaty may otherwise provide.

Article 40

Amendment of multilateral treaties

1. Unless the treaty otherwise provides, the amendment of multilateral treaties shall be governed by the following paragraphs.

2. Any proposal to amend a multilateral treaty as between all the parties must be notified to all the contracting States, each one of which shall have the right to take part in:

(a) the decision as to the action to be taken in regard to such proposal;

(b) the negotiation and conclusion of any agreement for the amendment of the treaty.

3. Every State entitled to become a party to the treaty shall also be entitled to become a party to the treaty as amended.

4. The amending agreement does not bind any State already a party to the treaty which does not become a party to the amending agreement; article 30, paragraph 4(b), applies in relation to such State.

5. Any State which becomes a party to the treaty after the entry into force of the amending agreement shall, failing an expression of a different intention by that State:

(a) be considered as a party to the treaty as amended; and

(b) be considered as a party to the unamended treaty in relation to any party to the treaty not bound by the amending agreement.

Article 41

Agreements to modify multilateral treaties
between certain of the parties only

1. Two or more of the parties to a multilateral treaty may conclude an agreement to modify the treaty as between themselves alone if:

(a) the possibility of such a modification is provided for by the treaty; or

(b) the modification in question is not prohibited by the treaty and:

(i) does not affect the enjoyment by the parties of their rights under the treaty or the performance of their obligations;

(ii) does not relate to a provision, derogation from which is incompatible with the effective execution of the object and purpose of the treaty as a whole.

2. Unless in a case falling under paragraph 1(a) the treaty otherwise provides, the parties in question shall notify the other parties of their intention to conclude the agreement and of the modification to the treaty for which it provides.

PART V

INVALIDITY, TERMINATION AND SUSPENSION OF THE OPERATION OF TREATIES

SECTION 1: GENERAL PROVISIONS

Article 42

Validity and continuance in force of treaties

1. The validity of a treaty or of the consent of a State to be bound by a treaty may be impeached only through the application of the present Convention.

2. The termination of a treaty, its denunciation or the withdrawal of a party, may take place only as a result of the application of the provisions of the treaty or of the present Convention. The same rule applies to suspension of the operation of a treaty.

Article 43

Obligations imposed by international law independently of a treaty

The invalidity, termination or denunciation of a treaty, the withdrawal of a party from it, or the suspension of its operation, as a result of the application of the present Convention or of the provisions of the treaty, shall not in any way impair the duty of any State to fulfil any obligation embodied in the treaty to which it would be subject under international law independently of the treaty.

Article 44

Separability of treaty provisions

1. A right of a party, provided for in a treaty or arising under article 56, to denounce, withdraw from or suspend the operation of the treaty may be exercised only with respect to the whole treaty unless the treaty otherwise provides or the parties otherwise agree.

2. A ground for invalidating, terminating, withdrawing from or suspending the operation of a treaty recognized in the present Convention may be invoked only with respect to the whole treaty except as provided in the following paragraphs or in article 60.

3. If the ground relates solely to particular clauses, it may be invoked only with respect to those clauses where:

(a) the said clauses are separable from the remainder of the treaty with regard to their application;

(b) it appears from the treaty or is otherwise established that acceptance of those clauses was not an essential basis of the consent of the other party or parties to be bound by the treaty as a whole; and

(c) continued performance of the remainder of the treaty would not be unjust.

4. In cases falling under articles 49 and 50 the State entitled to invoke the fraud or corruption may do so with respect either to the whole treaty or, subject to paragraph 3, to the particular clauses alone.

5. In cases falling under articles 51, 52 and 53, no separation of the provisions of the treaty is permitted.

Article 45

Loss of a right to invoke a ground for invalidating, terminating, withdrawing from or suspending the operation of a treaty

A State may no longer invoke a ground for invalidating, terminating, withdrawing from or suspending the operation of a treaty under articles 46 to 50 or articles 60 and 62, if, after becoming aware of the facts:

(a) it shall have expressly agreed that the treaty is valid or remains in force or continues in operation, as the case may be; or

(b) it must by reason of its conduct be considered as having acquiesced in the validity of the treaty or in its maintenance in force or in operation, as the case may be.

SECTION 2: INVALIDITY OF TREATIES

Article 46

Provisions of internal law regarding competence to conclude treaties

1. A State may not invoke the fact that its consent to be bound by a treaty has been expressed in violation of a provision of its internal law regarding competence to conclude treaties as invalidating its consent unless that violation was manifest and concerned a rule of its internal law of fundamental importance.

2. A violation is manifest if it would be objectively evident to any State conducting itself in the matter in accordance with normal practice and in good faith.

Article 47

Specific restrictions on authority to express the consent of a State

If the authority of a representative to express the consent of a State to be bound by a particular treaty has been made subject to a specific restriction, his omission to observe that restriction may not be invoked as invalidating the consent expressed by him unless the restriction was notified to the other negotiating States prior to his expressing such consent.

Article 48

Error

1. A State may invoke an error in a treaty as invalidating its consent to be bound by the treaty if the error relates to a fact or situation which was assumed by that State to exist at the time when the treaty was concluded and formed an essential basis of its consent to be bound by the treaty.

2. Paragraph 1 shall not apply if the State in question contributed by its own conduct to the error or if the circumstances were such as to put that State on notice of a possible error.

3. An error relating only to the wording of the text of a treaty does not affect its validity; article 79 then applies.

Article 49

Fraud

If a State has been induced to conclude a treaty by the fraudulent conduct of another negotiating State, the State may invoke the fraud as invalidating its consent to be bound by the treaty.

Article 50

Corruption of a representative of a State

If the expression of a State's consent to be bound by a treaty has been procured through the corruption of its representative directly or indirectly by another negotiating State, the State may invoke such corruption as invalidating its consent to be bound by the treaty.

Article 51

Coercion of a representative of a State

The expression of a State's consent to be bound by a treaty which has been procured by the coercion of its representative through acts or threats directed against him shall be without any legal effect.

Article 52

Coercion of a State by the threat or use of force

A treaty is void if its conclusion has been procured by the threat or use of force in violation of the principles of international law embodied in the Charter of the United Nations.

Article 53

Treaties conflicting with a peremptory norm of general international law (jus cogens)

A treaty is void if, at the time of its conclusion, it conflicts with a peremptory norm of general international law. For the purposes of the present Convention, a peremptory norm of general international law is a norm accepted and recognized by the international community of States as a whole as a norm from which no derogation is permitted and which can be modified only by a subsequent norm of general international law having the same character.

SECTION 3: TERMINATION AND SUSPENSION OF THE OPERATION OF TREATIES

Article 54

Termination of or withdrawal from a treaty under its provisions or by consent of the parties

The termination of a treaty or the withdrawal of a party may take place:

(a) in conformity with the provisions of the treaty; or

(b) at any time by consent of all the parties after consultation with the other contracting States.

Article 55

Reduction of the parties to a multilateral treaty below the number necessary for its entry into force

Unless the treaty otherwise provides, a multilateral treaty does not terminate by reason only of the fact that the number of the parties falls below the number necessary for its entry into force.

Article 56

*Denunciation of or withdrawal from a treaty containing no provision
regarding termination, denunciation or withdrawal*

1. A treaty which contains no provision regarding its termination
and which does not provide for denunciation or withdrawal is not subject
to denunciation or withdrawal unless:

(a) it is established that the parties intended to admit the possibility
of denunciation or withdrawal; or

(b) a right of denunciation or withdrawal may be implied by the
nature of the treaty.

2. A party shall give not less than twelve months' notice of its
intention to denounce or withdraw from a treaty under paragraph 1.

Article 57

*Suspension of the operation of a treaty under its
provisions or by consent of the parties*

The operation of a treaty in regard to all the parties or to a
particular party may be suspended:

(a) in conformity with the provisions of the treaty; or

(b) at any time by consent of all the parties after consultation with
the other contracting States.

Article 58

*Suspension of the operation of a multilateral treaty
by agreement between certain of the parties only*

1. Two or more parties to a multilateral treaty may conclude an
agreement to suspend the operation of provisions of the treaty, temporarily and as between themselves alone, if:

(a) the possibility of such a suspension is provided for by the treaty;
or

(b) the suspension in question is not prohibited by the treaty and:

(i) does not affect the enjoyment by the other parties of their
rights under the treaty or the performance of their obligations;

(ii) is not incompatible with the object and purpose of the
treaty.

2. Unless in a case falling under paragraph 1(a) the treaty otherwise provides the parties in question shall notify the other parties of
their intention to conclude the agreement and of those provisions of the
treaty the operation of which they intend to suspend.

Article 59

*Termination or suspension of the operation of a treaty
implied by conclusion of a later treaty*

1. A treaty shall be considered as terminated if all the parties to it
conclude a later treaty relating to the same subject-matter and:

(a) it appears from the later treaty or is otherwise established that the parties intended that the matter should be governed by that treaty; or

(b) the provisions of the later treaty are so far incompatible with those of the earlier one that the two treaties are not capable of being applied at the same time.

2. The earlier treaty shall be considered as only suspended in operation if it appears from the later treaty or is otherwise established that such was the intention of the parties.

Article 60

Termination or suspension of the operation of
a treaty as a consequence of its breach

1. A material breach of a bilateral treaty by one of the parties entitles the other to invoke the breach as a ground for terminating the treaty or suspending its operation in whole or in part.

2. A material breach of a multilateral treaty by one of the parties entitles:

(a) the other parties by unanimous agreement to suspend the operation of the treaty in whole or in part or to terminate it either:

(i) in the relations between themselves and the defaulting State, or

(ii) as between all the parties;

(b) a party specially affected by the breach to invoke it as a ground for suspending the operation of the treaty in whole or in part in the relations between itself and the defaulting State;

(c) any party other than the defaulting State to invoke the breach as a ground for suspending the operation of the treaty in whole or in part with respect to itself if the treaty is of such a character that a material breach of its provisions by one party radically changes the position of every party with respect to the further performance of its obligations under the treaty.

3. A material breach of a treaty, for the purposes of this article, consists in:

(a) a repudiation of the treaty not sanctioned by the present Convention; or

(b) the violation of a provision essential to the accomplishment of the object or purpose of the treaty.

4. The foregoing paragraphs are without prejudice to any provision in the treaty applicable in the event of a breach.

5. Paragraphs 1 to 3 do not apply to provisions relating to the protection of the human person contained in treaties of a humanitarian character, in particular to provisions prohibiting any form of reprisals against persons protected by such treaties.

Article 61

Supervening impossibility of performance

1. A party may invoke the impossibility of performing a treaty as a ground for terminating or withdrawing from it if the impossibility results from the permanent disappearance or destruction of an object indispensable for the execution of the treaty. If the impossibility is temporary, it may be invoked only as a ground for suspending the operation of the treaty.

2. Impossibility of performance may not be invoked by a party as a ground for terminating, withdrawing from or suspending the operation of a treaty if the impossibility is the result of a breach by that party either of an obligation under the treaty or of any other international obligation owed to any other party to the treaty.

Article 62

Fundamental change of circumstances

1. A fundamental change of circumstances which has occurred with regard to those existing at the time of the conclusion of a treaty, and which was not foreseen by the parties, may not be invoked as a ground for terminating or withdrawing from the treaty unless:

(a) the existence of those circumstances constituted an essential basis of the consent of the parties to be bound by the treaty; and

(b) the effect of the change is radically to transform the extent of obligations still to be performed under the treaty.

2. A fundamental change of circumstances may not be invoked as a ground for terminating or withdrawing from a treaty:

(a) if the treaty establishes a boundary; or

(b) if the fundamental change is the result of a breach by the party invoking it either of an obligation under the treaty or of any other international obligation owed to any other party to the treaty.

3. If, under the foregoing paragraphs, a party may invoke a fundamental change of circumstances as a ground for terminating or withdrawing from a treaty it may also invoke the change as a ground for suspending the operation of the treaty.

Article 63

Severance of diplomatic or consular relations

The severance of diplomatic or consular relations between parties to a treaty does not affect the legal relations established between them by the treaty except in so far as the existence of diplomatic or consular relations is indispensable for the application of the treaty.

Article 64

*Emergence of a new peremptory norm of general
international law (jus cogens)*

If a new peremptory norm of general international law emerges, any existing treaty which is in conflict with that norm becomes void and terminates.

SECTION 4: PROCEDURE

Article 65

*Procedure to be followed with respect to invalidity, termination,
withdrawal from or suspension of the operation of a treaty*

1.   A party which, under the provisions of the present Convention, invokes either a defect in its consent to be bound by a treaty or a ground for impeaching the validity of a treaty, terminating it, withdrawing from it or suspending its operation, must notify the other parties of its claim. The notification shall indicate the measure proposed to be taken with respect to the treaty and the reasons therefor.

2.   If, after the expiry of a period which, except in cases of special urgency, shall not be less than three months after the receipt of the notification, no party has raised any objection, the party making the notification may carry out in the manner provided in article 67 the measure which it has proposed.

3.   If, however, objection has been raised by any other party, the parties shall seek a solution through the means indicated in Article 33 of the Charter of the United Nations.

4.   Nothing in the foregoing paragraphs shall affect the rights or obligations of the parties under any provisions in force binding the parties with regard to the settlement of disputes.

5.   Without prejudice to article 45, the fact that a State has not previously made the notification prescribed in paragraph 1 shall not prevent it from making such notification in answer to another party claiming performance of the treaty or alleging its violation.

Article 66

Procedures for judicial settlement, arbitration and conciliation

If, under paragraph 3 of article 65, no solution has been reached within a period of 12 months following the date on which the objection was raised, the following procedures shall be followed:

(a) any one of the parties to a dispute concerning the application or the interpretation of article 53 or 64 may, by a written application, submit it to the International Court of Justice for a decision unless the parties by common consent agree to submit the dispute to arbitration;

(b) any one of the parties to a dispute concerning the application or the interpretation of any of the other articles in Part V of the present Convention may set in motion the procedure specified in the Annex to the Convention by submitting a request to that effect to the Secretary–General of the United Nations.

Article 67

Instruments for declaring invalid, terminating, withdrawing from or suspending the operation of a treaty

1.   The notification provided for under article 65, paragraph 1 must be made in writing.

2.   Any act declaring invalid, terminating, withdrawing from or suspending the operation of a treaty pursuant to the provisions of the treaty or of paragraphs 2 or 3 of article 65 shall be carried out through an instrument communicated to the other parties. If the instrument is not signed by the Head of State, Head of Government or Minister for Foreign Affairs, the representative of the State communicating it may be called upon to produce full powers.

Article 68

Revocation of notifications and instruments provided for in articles 65 and 67

A notification or instrument provided for in articles 65 or 67 may be revoked at any time before it takes effect.

SECTION 5: CONSEQUENCES OF THE INVALIDITY, TERMINATION OR SUSPENSION OF THE OPERATION OF A TREATY

Article 69

Consequences of the invalidity of a treaty

1.   A treaty the invalidity of which is established under the present Convention is void. The provisions of a void treaty have no legal force.

2.   If acts have nevertheless been performed in reliance on such a treaty:

(a) each party may require any other party to establish as far as possible in their mutual relations the position that would have existed if the acts had not been performed;

(b) acts performed in good faith before the invalidity was invoked are not rendered unlawful by reason only of the invalidity of the treaty.

3.   In cases falling under articles 49, 50, 51 or 52, paragraph 2 does not apply with respect to the party to which the fraud, the act of corruption or the coercion is imputable.

4. In the case of the invalidity of a particular State's consent to be bound by a multilateral treaty, the foregoing rules apply in the relations between that State and the parties to the treaty.

Article 70

Consequences of the termination of a treaty

1. Unless the treaty otherwise provides or the parties otherwise agree, the termination of a treaty under its provisions or in accordance with the present Convention:

(a) releases the parties from any obligation further to perform the treaty;

(b) does not affect any right, obligation or legal situation of the parties created through the execution of the treaty prior to its termination.

2. If a State denounces or withdraws from a multilateral treaty, paragraph 1 applies in the relations between that State and each of the other parties to the treaty from the date when such denunciation or withdrawal takes effect.

Article 71

Consequences of the invalidity of a treaty which conflicts with a peremptory norm of general international law

1. In the case of a treaty which is void under article 53 the parties shall:

(a) eliminate as far as possible the consequences of any act performed in reliance on any provision which conflicts with the peremptory norm of general international law; and

(b) bring their mutual relations into conformity with the peremptory norm of general international law.

2. In the case of a treaty which becomes void and terminates under article 64, the termination of the treaty:

(a) releases the parties from any obligation further to perform the treaty;

(b) does not affect any right, obligation or legal situation of the parties created through the execution of the treaty prior to its termination; provided that those rights, obligations or situations may thereafter be maintained only to the extent that their maintenance is not in itself in conflict with the new peremptory norm of general international law.

Article 72

Consequences of the suspension of the operation of a treaty

1. Unless the treaty otherwise provides or the parties otherwise agree, the suspension of the operation of a treaty under its provisions or in accordance with the present Convention:

(a) releases the parties between which the operation of the treaty is suspended from the obligation to perform the treaty in their mutual relations during the period of the suspension;

(b) does not otherwise affect the legal relations between the parties established by the treaty.

2. During the period of the suspension the parties shall refrain from acts tending to obstruct the resumption of the operation of the treaty.

PART VI

MISCELLANEOUS PROVISIONS

Article 73

Cases of State succession, State responsibility and outbreak of hostilities

The provisions of the present Convention shall not prejudge any question that may arise in regard to a treaty from a succession of States or from the international responsibility of a State or from the outbreak of hostilities between States.

Article 74

Diplomatic and consular relations and the conclusion of treaties

The severance or absence of diplomatic or consular relations between two or more States does not prevent the conclusion of treaties between those States. The conclusion of a treaty does not in itself affect the situation in regard to diplomatic or consular relations.

Article 75

Case of an aggressor State

The provisions of the present Convention are without prejudice to any obligation in relation to a treaty which may arise for an aggressor State in consequence of measures taken in conformity with the Charter of the United Nations with reference to that State's aggression.

PART VII

DEPOSITARIES, NOTIFICATIONS, CORRECTIONS AND REGISTRATION

Article 76

Depositaries of treaties

1. The designation of the depositary of a treaty may be made by the negotiating States, either in the treaty itself or in some other manner. The depositary may be one or more States, an international organization or the chief administrative officer of the organization.

2. The functions of the depositary of a treaty are international in character and the depositary is under an obligation to act impartially in

their performance. In particular, the fact that a treaty has not entered into force between certain of the parties or that a difference has appeared between a State and a depositary with regard to the performance of the latter's functions shall not affect that obligation.

Article 77

Functions of depositaries

1.   The functions of a depositary, unless otherwise provided in the treaty or agreed by the contracting States, comprise in particular:

(a) keeping custody of the original text of the treaty and of any full powers delivered to the depositary;

(b) preparing certified copies of the original text and preparing any further text of the treaty in such additional languages as may be required by the treaty and transmitting them to the parties and to the States entitled to become parties to the treaty;

(c) receiving any signatures to the treaty and receiving and keeping custody of any instruments, notifications and communications relating to it;

(d) examining whether the signature or any instrument, notification or communication relating to the treaty is in due and proper form and, if need be, bringing the matter to the attention of the State in question;

(e) informing the parties and the States entitled to become parties to the treaty of acts, notifications and communications relating to the treaty;

(f) informing the States entitled to become parties to the treaty when the number of signatures or of instruments of ratification, acceptance, approval or accession required for the entry into force of the treaty has been received or deposited;

(g) registering the treaty with the Secretariat of the United Nations;

(h) performing the functions specified in other provisions of the present Convention.

2.   In the event of any difference appearing between a State and the depositary as to the performance of the latter's functions, the depositary shall bring the question to the attention of the signatory States and the contracting States or, where appropriate, of the competent organ of the international organization concerned.

Article 78

Notifications and communications

Except as the treaty or the present Convention otherwise provide, any notification or communication to be made by any State under the present Convention shall:

(a) if there is no depositary, be transmitted direct to the States for which it is intended, or if there is a depositary, to the latter;

(b) be considered as having been made by the State in question only upon its receipt by the State to which it was transmitted or, as the case may be, upon its receipt by the depositary;

(c) if transmitted to a depositary, be considered as received by the State for which it was intended only when the latter State has been informed by the depositary in accordance with article 77, paragraph l(e).

Article 79

Correction of errors in texts or in certified copies of treaties

1. Where, after the authentication of the text of a treaty, the signatory States and the contracting States are agreed that it contains an error, the error shall, unless they decide upon some other means of correction, be corrected:

(a) by having the appropriate correction made in the text and causing the correction to be initialled by duly authorized representatives;

(b) by executing or exchanging an instrument or instruments setting out the correction which it has been agreed to make; or

(c) by executing a corrected text of the whole treaty by the same procedure as in the case of the original text.

2. Where the treaty is one for which there is a depositary, the latter shall notify the signatory States and the contracting States of the error and of the proposal to correct it and shall specify an appropriate time-limit within which objection to the proposed correction may be raised. If, on the expiry of the time-limit:

(a) no objection has been raised, the depositary shall make and initial the correction in the text and shall execute a *procès-verbal* of the rectification of the text and communicate a copy of it to the parties and to the States entitled to become parties to the treaty;

(b) an objection has been raised, the depositary shall communicate the objection to the signatory States and to the contracting States.

3. The rules in paragraphs 1 and 2 apply also where the text has been authenticated in two or more languages and it appears that there is a lack of concordance which the signatory States and the contracting States agree should be corrected.

4. The corrected text replaces the defective text *ab initio*, unless the signatory States and the contracting States otherwise decide.

5. The correction of the text of a treaty that has been registered shall be notified to the Secretariat of the United Nations.

6. Where an error is discovered in a certified copy of a treaty, the depositary shall execute a *procès-verbal* specifying the rectification and

communicate a copy of it to the signatory States and to the contracting States.

Article 80

Registration and publication of treaties

1.   Treaties shall, after their entry into force, be transmitted to the Secretariat of the United Nations for registration or filing and recording, as the case may be, and for publication.

2.   The designation of a depositary shall constitute authorization for it to perform the acts specified in the preceding paragraph.

PART VIII

FINAL PROVISIONS

Article 81

Signature

The present Convention shall be open for signature by all States Members of the United Nations or of any of the specialized agencies or of the International Atomic Energy Agency or parties to the Statute of the International Court of Justice, and by any other State invited by the General Assembly of the United Nations to become a party to the Convention, as follows: until 30 November 1969, at the Federal Ministry for Foreign Affairs of the Republic of Austria, and subsequently, until 30 April 1970, at United Nations Headquarters, New York.

Article 82

Ratification

The present Convention is subject to ratification. The instruments of ratification shall be deposited with the Secretary–General of the United Nations.

Article 83

Accession

The present Convention shall remain open for accession by any State belonging to any of the categories mentioned in article 81. The instruments of accession shall be deposited with the Secretary–General of the United Nations.

Article 84

Entry into force

1.   The present Convention shall enter into force on the thirtieth day following the date of deposit of the thirty-fifth instrument of ratification or accession.

2.   For each State ratifying or acceding to the Convention after the deposit of the thirty-fifth instrument of ratification or accession, the

Convention shall enter into force on the thirtieth day after deposit by such State of its instrument of ratification or accession.

Article 85

Authentic texts

The original of the present Convention, of which the Chinese, English, French, Russian and Spanish texts are equally authentic, shall be deposited with the Secretary–General of the United Nations.

IN WITNESS WHEREOF the undersigned Plenipotentiaries, being duly authorized thereto by their respective Governments, have signed the present Convention.

DONE AT VIENNA, this twenty-third day of May, one thousand nine hundred and sixty-nine.

Annex

1. A list of conciliators consisting of qualified jurists shall be drawn up and maintained by the Secretary–General of the United Nations. To this end, every State which is a Member of the United Nations or a party to the present Convention shall be invited to nominate two conciliators, and the names of the persons so nominated shall constitute the list. The term of a conciliator, including that of any conciliator nominated to fill a casual vacancy, shall be five years and may be renewed. A conciliator whose term expires shall continue to fulfil any function for which he shall have been chosen under the following paragraph.

2. When a request has been made to the Secretary–General under article 66, the Secretary–General shall bring the dispute before a conciliation commission constituted as follows:

The State or States constituting one of the parties to the dispute shall appoint:

(a) one conciliator of the nationality of that State or of one of those States, who may or may not be chosen from the list referred to in paragraph 1; and

(b) one conciliator not of the nationality of that State or of any of those States, who shall be chosen from the list.

The State or States constituting the other party to the dispute shall appoint two conciliators in the same way. The four conciliators chosen by the parties shall be appointed within sixty days following the date on which the Secretary–General receives the request.

The four conciliators shall, within sixty days following the date of the last of their own appointments, appoint a fifth conciliator chosen from the list, who shall be chairman.

If the appointment of the chairman or of any of the other conciliators has not been made within the period prescribed above for such appointment, it shall be made by the Secretary–General within sixty days following the expiry of that period. The appointment of the chairman may be made by the Secretary–General either from the list or from the membership of the International Law Commission. Any of the periods within which appointments must be made may be extended by agreement between the parties to the dispute.

Any vacancy shall be filled in the manner prescribed for the initial appointment.

3.   The Conciliation Commission shall decide its own procedure. The Commission, with the consent of the parties to the dispute, may invite any party to the treaty to submit to it its views orally or in writing. Decisions and recommendations of the Commission shall be made by a majority vote of the five members.

4.   The Commission may draw the attention of the parties to the dispute to any measures which might facilitate an amicable settlement.

5.   The Commission shall hear the parties, examine the claims and objections, and make proposals to the parties with a view to reaching an amicable settlement of the dispute.

6.   The Commission shall report within twelve months of its constitution. Its report shall be deposited with the Secretary–General and transmitted to the parties to the dispute. The report of the Commission, including any conclusions stated therein regarding the facts or questions of law, shall not be binding upon the parties and it shall have no other character than that of recommendations submitted for the consideration of the parties in order to facilitate an amicable settlement of the dispute.

7.   The Secretary–General shall provide the Commission with such assistance and facilities as it may require. The expenses of the Commission shall be borne by the United Nations.

*

Index

References are to pages.

INTERVENTION—Cont'd
Humanitarian intervention 516, 521, 571, 573–574
Illegality of 514, 519–520, 524–525, 535–537
In civil wars and rebellions 519–520
To support self-determination 516–517, 521
United States, in Nicaragua 524–525, 535–537
World order and 521–523

IRAN
Diplomatic and Consular Staff Case 271–285
Hostages crisis 199–207, 271–286
Islamic revolution 271–285

IRAN-UNITED STATES CLAIMS TRIBUNAL, 201–202

IRAQ
Boundary with Kuwait 484, 489–490
Compensation for damages and environmental harm caused to Kuwait 484, 490, 548
Disarmament 548–549
Economic sanctions against 484, 540–541
Invasion of Kuwait 406, 483–485, 488–491, 538–549
Kurdish refugees 483–485, 490, 548
Oil export quotas 548
Security Council decisions concerning invasion of Kuwait 483–485, 488–491, 538–549
Security Council sanctions, expiration of 491, 548–549
Use of force against 539, 542–546

ISRAEL
Division of Palestine into independent Jewish and Arab states 476
Treaty interpretation 66–68

ITALY
ELSI Case 303–312
Invasion of Ethiopia 38, 462
Kellogg–Briand Pact 35–38

JAMAICA
Damian Thomas v. Jamaica 359–362
Denunciation of Optional Protocol to International Covenant on Civil and Political Rights 362–364
Record of compliance with International Covenant on Civil and Political Rights 359–362

JAPAN
Invasion of Manchuria 38, 462
Kellogg–Briand Pact 35–38
War crimes tribunal 398
War with Russia 243–244

JURISDICTION, 715–728
For jurisdiction of international courts and arbitral tribunals, see name of particular court or tribunal

JURISDICTION, 715–728—Cont'd
Adjudicatory 100–110, 210–220, 715, 720–722, 782
American Banana Co. v. United Fruit Co. 716–718
Balancing factors 744–749, 755–759
Blackmer v. United States 720–721
Effects (objective territorial) principle 100–110, 723–728, 744–762
Enforcement (executive) 715, 720–722
Foreign sovereign immunity and jurisdiction over foreign state defendants 779–806
Foreign state, definition of 788, 805–806
Forms of 715–728
Hartford Fire Insurance Co. v. California 750–759
Legislative 715, 719, 720–727, 744–762, 764–766, 817–822
Lifting the corporate veil 771, 816
Nationality principle 720–723
Over activities on high seas, by municipal courts 100–112, 238–240, 802
Over corporations 723–726, 728, 778
Party choice 728–744
Passive personality (nationality of victim) principle 100–110, 722, 789–791
Personal, and *forum non conveniens* 778
Protective principle 722–723
Resolving conflicts of jurisdiction 728–779
Schooner Exchange v. McFaddon 779–782
Territorial principle 194–195, 716–720, 722, 779–782
To adjudicate crimes 100–110, 210–220
Timberlane Co. v. Bank of America 744–748
United States v. Aluminum Co. of America 723–726

JUS COGENS
See also Sources of International Law
General principles of law, relationship to 138–139, 142
Individuals and 140, 142
International environmental law and 77, 80, 589
Invalidity of treaties that contradict 77, 80, 137–141
Natural law and 18, 142
Not listed in ICJ Statute 21
Obligations *erga omnes* and 147
Prohibition of the use of force 528, 536
Types of 137–142
Verdross, Alfred von and development of 137–141

JUS GENTIUM, 1

KUWAIT
Boundary with Iraq 484, 489–490
Compensation for damages and environmental harm caused by Iraq 484, 490, 548